CH00952145

The Editor

ALICE LEVINE is Professor of English at Hofstra University. She is co-editor with Jerome J. McGann of *Manuscripts of the Younger Romantics: A Facsimile of Manuscripts in the Pierpont Morgan Library. Poems in the Autograph of Lord Byron Once in the Possession of Countess Guiccioli: Volume I, Poems, 1807–1818; Volume II, Don Juan, Cantos I–V; Volume III, Poems, 1819–1822; Volume IV, Miscellaneous Poems*, and co-editor with Robert N. Keane of *Rereading Byron: Essays Selected From Hofstra University's Byron Bicentennial Conference*. She has also published several essays about Byron, including studies focusing on Byron and music.

A NORTON CRITICAL EDITION

BYRON'S POETRY AND PROSE

AUTHORITATIVE TEXTS
CRITICISM

Selected and Edited by

ALICE LEVINE
HOFSTRA UNIVERSITY

W • W • NORTON & COMPANY • *New York* • *London*

W. W. Norton & Company has been independent since its founding in 1923, when William Warder Norton and Mary D. Herter Norton first published lectures delivered at the People's Institute, the adult education division of New York City's Cooper Union. The firm soon expanded its program beyond the Institute, publishing books by celebrated academics from America and abroad. By mid-century, the two major pillars of Norton's publishing program—trade books and college texts—were firmly established. In the 1950s, the Norton family transferred control of the company to its employees, and today—with a staff of four hundred and a comparable number of trade, college, and professional titles published each year—W. W. Norton & Company stands as the largest and oldest publishing house owned wholly by its employees.

Manufacturing by LSC Communications, Crawfordsville.
Book design by Antonina Krass.
Composition by Westchester Book Group.
Production manager: Eric Pier-Hocking.

Library of Congress Cataloging-in-Publication Data

Byron, George Gordon Byron, Baron, 1788–1824.
[Selections. 2009]
Byron's poetry and prose : authoritative texts, criticism / selected and
edited By Alice Levine.—1st ed.
p. cm.—(A Norton critical edition)
Includes bibliographical references and index.
ISBN 978-0-393-92560-9 (pbk.)

I. Levine, Alice (Alice Judith)   II. Title.
PR4353.L48 2009
821'.7—dc22
2009012341

W. W. Norton & Company, Inc., 500 Fifth Avenue, New York, N.Y. 10110
www.wwnorton.com

W. W. Norton & Company Ltd., 15 Carlisle Street,
London W1D 3BS

3 4 5 6 7 8 9 0

Contents

Part Two: Years of Fame in Regency Society (1812–1816)

Part Three: Exile on Lake Geneva (April–October 1816)

Part Four: Final Pilgrimage—Italy and Greece (1816–1824)

CRITICISM

Introduction

Byron's Life in Poetry

From the day after the publication of the first two cantos of *Childe Harold's Pilgrimage*, when the twenty-four-year-old Lord Byron awoke and found himself famous,[1] he became the subject of the most intense interest, curiosity, gossip, adulation, and vilification. His poems were enormously popular during his lifetime, selling out in issues of thousands, and he remained a cultural force throughout the nineteenth century in England, Europe, and America. The remarkable events of his own life and his larger-than-life personality generated at least as much attention as his poetry. Born in London in 1788, George Gordon Byron was descended from Scottish lairds, the Gordons of Gight, on his mother's side, and the Buruns, contemporaries of William the Conqueror, on his father's, families known for their social irregularity and propensity for violence. A shy, sensitive boy with a congenitally deformed, or club, foot that would cause him to limp his entire life, Byron was raised by his mother, after his father (having already spent the fortune of his first wife) squandered her money and left them. At the impressionable age of ten, Byron succeeded to the peerage, with the attendant obsequies of servants, teachers, and companions. Then came a life in poetry—and out of it. In the short span of twenty-one years, from the time of his earliest poems in 1803 to his death at the age of thirty-six, Byron wrote thousands of pages of poetry and more than three thousand letters, yet few poets have led as eventful a life of social, political, and sexual engagement.

The arrangement of this Norton Critical Edition highlights the connection between Byron's extraordinary life and his poetry by its division into four units, each representing a period of Byron's life and work. Part One covers Byron's early years, beginning in 1803, at Harrow School and, after, at Trinity College, Cambridge, and in Southwell, England—the period of Byron's earliest friendships and loves; then, in 1809, came his first pilgrimage to the Peninsula (Spain and Portugal) and the Levant (Albania, Greece and Turkey), which culminated in the writing and publication, in March 1812, of the first two cantos of *Childe Harold*. Part Two encompasses the so-called "years of fame" in London (from 1812 to the spring of 1816), when Byron delivered his two impressive parliamentary speeches; wrote his immensely popular Eastern tales; became involved in a series of amorous adventures as well as an intense love affair with his half-sister, Augusta Leigh; and within one year's time married, became a father, was left by his wife, and in the wake of scandal departed England, never to

---

1. Byron's oft-quoted remark, "I awoke one morning and found myself famous" (*Life* 1:347).

return. Part Three is devoted to the summer and fall of 1816, when Byron resided at the Villa Diodati on Lake Geneva, Switzerland. During this period he befriended Mary and Percy Shelley (not yet married) and, under the combined influence of the Alpine scenery and his turbulent emotions over Augusta, his wife, and the separation scandal, wrote some of his most famous poems, including the third canto of *Childe Harold* and *Manfred*. Part Four covers the last period of Byron's life, starting from his arrival in Italy in October 1816. There his vitality was restored and his poetry given a new direction by life in Venice (including a period of outstanding debauchery), Italian literature, revolutionary activity, and his love for Teresa Guiccioli, the young wife of an old count. After writing his most admired works—the fourth and last canto of *Childe Harold, Don Juan*, and *The Vision of Judgment*—he departed for Greece in the summer of 1823 to assist in the war of independence from Turkey, and at the town of Misso-longhi the next spring, at the age of thirty-six, he died following convulsions and severe fever.

Byron himself recognized the contradictions that surfaced throughout his life and work and that emerged in his "changeable" personality, "being every thing by turns and nothing long . . . a strange mélange of good and evil."[2] In certain ways the quintessential Romantic, Byron nonetheless con-demned the "wrong revolutionary poetical system" (*BLJ* 5:265) of his con-temporaries, was an admirer of eighteenth-century Augustan poetry, especially Pope, and reached back to the self-consciously artful and witty verse style of earlier periods. The popular image of Byron as Europe's most famous brooding melancholiac contrasts with the equally popular images of Byron as Regency dandy and gentleman satirist, not to mention with the image of Byron as a man prone to corpulence and severe dieting. His image as the "mad, bad, and dangerous to know"[3] serial lover of women is offset by his bisexuality and the passionate love he felt for at least two young men. All of these images, moreover, fail to account for other dimensions of Byron's life and personality, such as his seriousness with respect to poetry, despite his frequent dismissals of "scribbling" ("who would write, who had anything better to do?" [*BLJ* 3:220]), and his tireless self-education. Hav-ing read the Old Testament by the time he was eight years old and know-ing much of Horace by heart, he remained throughout his life an avid reader of literature, history, and social philosophy, in English, Italian, and French. As he traveled, he immersed himself in different cultures and lan-guages. His vast reading and erudition are evident in the richly intertextual quality of his poetry and in the numerous linguistic, historical, and geograph-ical annotations he provided for his poems. In his personal and public life, his aristocratic vanity and self-indulgent excesses were counterbalanced by intellectual honesty, generosity, and courage—the last notably illustrated by his political engagements in Italy and Greece. Admitting constancy to only two sentiments, "a strong love of liberty, and a detestation of cant"[4] (con-ventional and hollow, insincere, or tendentious expressions of virtue, sen-timent, or piety), and claiming that he would rather "have a nod from an

---

2. *Lady Blessington's Conversations of Lord Byron*, ed. Ernest J. Lovell, p. 220.
3. Famous quotation by Lady Caroline Lamb (*Lady Morgan's Memoirs* [London, 1862], 2:200).
4. *Lady Blessington's Conversations*, p. 200.

American, than a snuff-box from an emperor" (*BLJ* 9:171), Byron became a figure of symbolic significance to the cause of democracy precisely because he fought "freedom's battle" (*The Giaour*, 123–25) as an "aristocratic rebel."[5] With merciless ridicule ("the only weapon the English climate cannot rust")[6] his satires humiliated many of the social and political elite of England (the more so because of Byron's fame and prestige), and for that and many heresies besides he was denied burial in Poets' Corner of Westminster Abbey. "The day will come," prophesied the Italian patriot Giuseppe Mazzini, "when Democracy will remember all that it owes to Byron."[7] Indeed, in 1969, England paid itself a belated honor by placing a plaque to Lord Byron in the Abbey.

It has become a cliché to say of Byron that his life was more poetic than any of his poems. That idea perhaps captures a truth about his life, but it does an immense injustice to his poetry. In addition to *Childe Harold's Pilgrimage*, Byron wrote nearly three hundred lyrics (including translations of classical and Italian poetry), nine tales, three historical and five speculative dramas, and eight satires, including his acclaimed masterpiece, *Don Juan*, left incomplete in its seventeenth canto at the time of his death. This enormous body of work records Byron's development as a poet, continual experimentation with poetic forms and meters, and impressive versification and narrative skill. While it has often been said that only with his discovery in 1817 of the *ottava rima* mock epic (the form in which he wrote *Beppo*, *Don Juan*, and *The Vision of Judgment*) did Byron come into his own and enter the ranks of the great poets, it was his emotionally expressive and emphatic poetic style, evident even in the early works, that captivated readers throughout the nineteenth century and merits appreciation today. In such popular works as *Childe Harold*, *The Giaour*, *Hebrew Melodies*, "Prometheus," *The Prisoner of Chillon*, *Manfred*, "To the Po," and "On This Day I Complete My Thirty-sixth Year," the special genius of the Romantic era's great comic poet was the voice he gave to sorrow, loss, desolation, decay, and death. "The day drags through though storms keep out the sun;/And thus the heart will break, yet brokenly live on" (*Childe Harold* III.287–88) is a typically Byronic thought. In his lyrics, love (or Byron) seems always to be bidding a tearful adieu, while the association of beauty or love with night or darkness is evoked in some of his most enduring lines, such as "She walks in beauty like the night" and "So we'll go no more a roving/ So late into the night."

Byron's imagery is characterized by sharp detail and, in contrast to the more concentrated imagery of Keats and Shelley, is essentially dramatic— as when he mourns his schooltime friend, the Duke of Dorset: "That heavy chill has frozen o'er the fountain of our tears, / And though the eye may sparkle still, 'tis where the ice appears" ("Stanzas for Music"); or when he imagines the dead and dying in "The Destruction of Sennacherib":

> And there lay the steed with his nostril all wide,
> But through it there roll'd not the breath of his pride;
> And the foam of his gasping lay white on the turf,
> And cold as the spray of the rock-beating surf.

5. Bertrand Russell, *A History of Western Philosophy*, p. 716.
6. *Lady Blessington's Conversations,*, p. 13.
7. As quoted in John Morley, *Fortnightly Review* (December, 1870); rpt. *Critical Miscellanies* (1871), p. 251.

The emotional impact of Byron's swift-moving verse, moreover, derives primarily from two qualities. First, the images (even if not the events) are grounded in recognizable life occurrences and human experiences; Byron kept a keen eye and ear on the external world and prided himself on factual precision, famously berating Wordsworth for inaccuracy in a poetic description of Greece.[8] Secondly, everything in Byron is at a heightened pitch—there is little in the way of moderation. Turn almost at random to one of his verses and you will find the stamp of what has been called his "strength," or "force," or "vehemence," which generates and is generated by tropes that are evocative, memorable, and uniquely Byronic:

> Eternal Spirit of the chainless mind,
> Brightest in dungeons, Liberty, thou art!
> For there the habitation is the heart,
> The heart which love of thee alone can bind.
> ("Sonnet on Chillon")

> What if thy deep and ample stream should be
> A mirror of my heart, where she may read
> The thousand thoughts I now betray to thee,
> Wild as thy wave and headlong as thy speed!
> ("To the Po")

A rapid succession of contrasting emotional extremes is the stylistic norm:

> Here the self-torturing sophist, wild Rousseau,
> The apostle of affliction, he who threw
> Enchantment over passion, and from woe
> Wrung overwhelming eloquence, first drew
> The breath which made him wretched; yet he knew
> How to make madness beautiful, and cast
> O'er erring deeds and thoughts a heavenly hue
> Of words, like sunbeams, dazzling as they past
> The eyes, which o'er them shed tears feelingly and fast.
> (*Childe Harold* III, stanza 77)

Byron deploys this same stylistic vehemence to scorn or berate—

> But France got drunk with blood to vomit crime,
> And fatal have her Saturnalia been
> To Freedom's cause, in every age and clime
> (*Childe Harold* IV.865–67)

or to humiliate his chosen enemies, such as the British foreign minister, Castlereagh:

> Cold-blooded, smooth-faced, placid miscreant!
> Dabbling its sleek young hands in Erin's gore,
> And thus for wider carnage taught to pant . . .

* * *

8. Letter to Leigh Hunt, October 30, 1815 (printed in this volume, p. 191).

> An orator of such set trash of phrase
> Ineffably—legitimately vile,
> That even its grossest flatterers dare not praise . . .
> (*Don Juan*, Dedication, 89–91, 97–99)

Thus, Byron raises the pitch of Wordsworth's famous definition of poetry as "the spontaneous overflow of powerful feelings,"[9] calling it, rather, "the lava of the imagination whose eruption prevents an earth-quake" (*BLJ* 3:179).

Yet Byron's poetry is dramatic not just with respect to diction and imagery, but in a wider sense, as the reader sees, or imagines, the man, Lord Byron, in the poems—almost like watching a character in a play. His most famous role is that of the "Byronic hero." Brooding and guilt-ridden, this "wandering outlaw of his own dark mind" (*Childe Harold* III.20) is also typically an outlaw in the literal sense, as well as a breaker of social, religious, and sexual taboos. Yet the Byronic hero is still a superior man, distinguished by his intensely and tragically passionate love, his intelligence, his courageous opposition to tyranny (in its various forms), and usually his birth as well:

> The common crowd but see the gloom
> Of wayward deeds—and fitting doom—
> The close observer can espy
> A noble soul, and lineage high.—
> (*The Giaour*, 866–69)

Then again, Byron is also recognizable as the detached, urbane, and witty narrator of *Don Juan*, a poem which, like *Childe Harold* and the body of Byron's poetry and letters taken as a whole, shuns philosophical consistency in favor of an existential method that embraces life's contradictions. In fact the contradictions so often observed in Byron's work and thought are simply the paradoxes and complexity of life and human nature dramatically portrayed: for "if a writer should be quite consistent / How could he possibly show things existent?" (*Don Juan* XV.695–96). Thus, love is "an unseen seraph" in *Childe Harold* (IV.1082) and yet "the very god of evil" in *Don Juan* (II.1639); the hours of young love "redeem Life's years of ill" (*Childe Harold* II.773), but, then again, "our young affections run to waste, / Or water but the desert . . ." (*Childe Harold* V.1072); and time may be the "Adorner of the ruin, comforter / And only healer when the heart hath bled" (*Childe Harold* IV.1163), while in another context time itself is the ruiner:

> Marriage from love, like vinegar from wine—
> A sad, sour sober beverage—by time
> Is sharpen'd from its high celestial flavour
> Down to a very homely household savor.
> (*Don Juan* III.37–40)

The narrator of *Don Juan* acknowledges being "Changeable . . . yet somehow '*Idem semper*'" (*Don Juan* XVII. 83), his "mobility" (XVI. 820) a sign of his engagement with life's varying experiences.

---

9. Wordsworth, Preface to the second edition of *Lyrical Ballads*.

Byron's life of travel provided him with an array of place-specific topics for his poems; however, the magnetic appeal to Byron's contemporaries of *Childe Harold*, the Eastern tales, and later *Don Juan* was not primarily due to their geographical or cultural descriptions. Rather, Byron's poetry of lands and customs is fundamentally the drama of Byron as exile—the drama of a man that unfolds the drama of a world. That world is Europe during the war-ravaged years that followed the French Revolution and after 1815, when (with the Congress of Vienna) the European monarchies were restored. This was a period when the hope of democracy, of "human nature seeming born again,"[1] was all but extinguished, and England was caught in a period of political reaction and imperialistic policies, betraying its liberal ideals through shameful intellectual evasions and hypocrisies. Lord Byron, the exile of that world, is not merely, like Wordsworth's poet, "a man speaking to men,"[2] but an empowered aristocrat who, for all his social standing, wealth, genius, and beauty, is unable to find happiness in such a world, or to right its wrongs. Byron bore across Europe "the pageant of *its* bleeding heart,"[3] thus living what Jerome McGann has called a "profoundly mythological life."[4] For exile in Byron's poems is not merely a literal or dramatic circumstance but is symbolic of a personal and societal alienation, a psychological and metaphysical condition. It became so central to Byron's identity and poetic program that we might say, echoing the terms Karl Marx used to characterize the recurrences of history, that exile occurred twice as a large thematic structure in Byron's works, the first time as tragedy in *Childe Harold* and the second time as farce in *Don Juan*.[5] In *Don Juan*, as in *Beppo* and *The Vision of Judgment*, Byron virtuosically adapted *ottava rima* as a vehicle for his unique purpose and style: a relentless facetiousness aimed at subverting the solemn cant of his age, in the manner of an English gentleman "rattl[ing] on exactly as I'd talk" (XV.151). Thus, he praises the pirate Lambro as:

> . . . the mildest manner'd man
> That ever scuttled ship or cut a throat:
> With such true breeding of a gentleman,
> You never could divine his real thought;
> No courtier could, and scarcely woman can
> Gird more deceit within a petticoat;
> Pity he loved adventurous life's variety,
> He was so great a loss to good society.
>
> (III, stanza 41)

Don Juan is considered, alongside *The Canterbury Tales*, to be one of the great comic poems in English. But its genre is complex, and in ridiculing self-delusion and the abuses of society its narrator acknowledges, "if I laugh at any mortal thing, / 'Tis that I may not weep" (IV.25–26).

---

1. Wordsworth, *The Prelude* (1850) 6.341.
2. Wordsworth's definition of the poet begins this way in Preface to the second edition of *Lyrical Ballads* (1800).
3. "What helps it now, that Byron bore, / With haughty scorn which mock'd the smart, / Through Europe to the Aetolian shore / The Pageant of his bleeding heart?" Matthew Arnold, "Stanzas from the Grand Chartreuse," lines 133–36.
4. *Byron* (Oxford Authors, 1986), p. xxii.
5. Karl Marx, *The Eighteenth Brumaire of Louis Napoleon* (1852).

Byron represents a dominant phase of romanticism, one that is both metaphysically and poetically the polar opposite of Wordsworthian romanticism. Wordsworth's God is "a motion and a spirit, that . . . rolls through all things"; memory and nature work together, benevolently, to persuade us that none of life's ills will "disturb / Our cheerful faith, that all which we behold / Is full of blessings" ("Tintern Abbey"). Byron's "Almighty" is an alien power that "glasses itself in tempests" (*Childe Harold* IV.1640), and memory takes the form of haunting recollections of bitterness or loss that have permanently alienated him from the beauty of the world. While to Wordsworth our disappointments are evidence that "our being's heart and home, / Is with infinitude . . . / And something evermore about to be" (*The Prelude*, 6.605–08), to Byron they signify our tragic dualism, that we are "half dust, half deity, alike unfit / To sink or soar" (*Manfred*, 1.2.301–02). Thus, for Byron, the years do not bring "the philosophic mind" ("Intimations" Ode) but loss, guilt, and the alternations of memory-obliterating sensation and "consciousness awaking to her woes" (*Childe Harold* I.941). Nor could the poetics of Wordsworth and Byron be more dissimilar for two poets of the same era. As one of the "Prophets of Nature" (*The Prelude*, 14.444), Wordsworth cultivated the style of the sincere, "overheard" poet, while Byron tended to address his readers (sometimes very particular readers) directly, and prophetic truth-telling is replaced by the contingent, potentially deceptive or manipulative, aspects of language. Very likely, from the effect that his earliest lyrics had on Southwell society and from his having learned the encoded style of the homoerotic love lyric ("that style in which more is meant than meets the Eye"),[6] Byron learned to write poems (and letters) susceptible of different readings depending upon context and the reader's point of view. Far from delivering universal "truths that wake, / To perish never" ("Intimations" Ode) Byron admits that in his poems "there is much which could not be appreciated / In any manner by the uninitiated" (*Don Juan* XIV. 175–76). This quality in fact relates to the special importance of knowing the historical and biographical contexts of Byron's poems and to his underestimation by the New Critics of the mid-twentieth century, who disparaged contextual approaches. "Wordsworthian" is an adjective mainly used by literary specialists to signify a unified philosophical outlook and the poetics that reflects it. "Byronic," on the other hand, is a commonly understood tag for a personality type remindful of the poet's various self-dramatizations, a personality and a poetry characterized by the contradictory elements of intense passion and aloofness, of moral transgressiveness and essential goodness, of *Weltschmerz* and wit.

In *Histoire de la littérature anglaise* (1863), Hippolyte Taine summarized the contributions of Wordsworth, Coleridge, Shelley, and Walter Scott in two sub-sections of one chapter but devoted an entire chapter to Byron, who "is so great and so English that from him alone we shall learn more truths of his country and of his age than from all the rest together."[7] Taine's observation does not gainsay the genius and importance of the other major poets of the period, but it highlights Byron's special significance during the

---

6. Charles Skinner Matthews, letter to Byron, June 22, 1809, printed in Louis Crompton, *Byron and Greek Love*, p. 128.
7. Translated by H. van Laun (London: Chatto and Windus, 1872), p. 271.

nineteenth century. Jane Baillie Welsh, upon hearing of Byron's death, wrote to her future husband, Thomas Carlyle: "My God, if they had said that the sun or the moon had gone out of the heavens, it could not have struck me with the idea of a more awful and dreary blank in the creation than the words, 'Byron is dead!'" Less publicized, until recently, was his equally important role in the emerging identity of the British homosexual writer, such as, notably, Oscar Wilde. His influence on the Continent is seen in the writing of Victor Hugo, Heinrich Heine, Mikhail Lermontov, and Aleksandr Pushkin, in the paintings of Eugène Delacroix, and in the music of Hector Berlioz, Robert Schumann, and Franz Liszt. If Byron's cultural conquest of Europe suggests a parallel with early-nineteenth-century Europe's other enlightened and exiled conquerer, Napoleon Bonaparte, the parallel was not lost on Byron, who dubbed himself "the grand Napoleon of the realms of rhyme" (*Don Juan* XI.440) and whose self-image was bound up with his conflicted admiration for the one European more famous than himself.

Byron, however, has not merely become a mythic embodiment of the nineteenth century. He has remained a recognizable presence in the modern era largely for his departure from the Romantic transcendental mode and his focus on the world and its events. The forward-looking insights of *Don Juan* are remarkable. It looks not to heaven but to science as "a thing to counterbalance human woes" (X.13). It observes that money, not monarchy, is the true despotism: "Who hold the balance of the world? Who reign / O'er congress, whether royalist or liberal? / . . . The shade of Buonaparte's noble daring?— / Jew Rothschild and his fellow Christian Baring" (referring to the great banking houses of Europe [XII, stanza 5]). *Don Juan*, further, raises issues of importance to feminism and gender studies: it persistently destabilizes gender stereotypes, while its various portrayals of how "man, to man so oft unjust, / Is always so to woman" (II. 1593–94) reflect Byron's awareness of the feminist debates of his day. Byron was one of the first multiculturalists, perceiving Europe as "a worn out portion of the globe" (*BLJ* 6.227). With great respect for accuracy and with considerable self-consciousness about the irony of the "orientalising" European poet, he appreciatively documented Muslim beliefs and practices in works like *The Giaour* and *Childe Harold*, intending, among other things, a retort to the ethnocentric prejudices that justified imperialistic policies. To Nietzsche, Byron, through his hero Manfred, signified a break with the traditional Christian world view in identifying damnation or salvation not as something external to the individual but within his own consciousness and acts. With the loss of traditional guideposts in the modern era, why and how to live become the central questions, as they are in Byron's major poems, and which he answered for the final time both in his life, by going to Greece to support the cause of freedom, and in the poem he wrote there, "On This Day I Complete My Thirty-sixth Year," in which he chooses "a soldier's grave." Byron shares with many modern and postmodern writers a postwar consciousness and sense of a moribund society. He anticipated James Joyce in taking as his materials the contemporary social, political, cultural, and linguistic landscape, at the center of which is situated his own perceiving consciousness—the product, exile, and conscience of his people. Like Joyce, Baudelaire, Beckett, and Nabokov (all of them writers of exile), Byron adopts a range of postmodern attitudes and rhetorical strategies: linguistic playfulness, sly narrative poses, intertextuality, artificiality, the absurd, and indeterminacy. "I leave the thing a problem, like all things" (XVII.97) is the inconclusive farewell gesture of *Don Juan*. Profoundly skeptical and conscious of his own (and his readers') linguistic manipulations and cultural entanglements ("I wish men to be free / As much from mobs as kings—from you as me" [IX. 199–200]), the poet of *Don Juan* offers the reader what the critic Helen Gardner called "the salutariness of being undeceived."[8] That's a somewhat sober pleasure for a comic poem, but, as Byron's poetry invites its readers, then as now, to consider, what is the alternative?

Selection and Arrangement of this Edition

In the preface to his *Selection from the Works of Lord Byron* (1866), Algernon Charles Swinburne observed that "no poet is so badly represented by a book of selections," that Byron "can only be judged or appreciated in the mass; the greatest of his works was the whole work taken together." The sheer quantity of Byron's occasional verse, the expansiveness of his narratives and dramas, the recurrence of themes and personae among many of his works, the central role of the digressions in *Childe Harold* and the *ottava rima* poems: these form a sprawling poetic journal, of which each part is fully understood only in relation to the poet's development over the course of his lifetime. In determining which poems to include in this edition, I was influenced by a poem's intrinsic merit, by its reflection of an important part of the poet's life or personality, or by its interest to the present generation of Byron scholars. Abridging *Don Juan* was painful; it should not be done, and I beg pardon of the poet, "pitying sore his mutilated case" (I.349), and of readers whose favorite passages are omitted; on the positive side, however, this Norton Critical Edition includes six cantos in their entirety and substantial selections of the rest of the poem.

Interest in the relationship between the events of Byron's life and his poetry has been a constant in Byron studies and is so now more than ever largely because of the biographical method of Jerome McGann's criticism and the many critics McGann has influenced. While a selected edition cannot show fully what John Murray expected his chronologically arranged edition of the complete poems and letters to show—that Byron's "compositions reflect constantly the incidents of his own career, the development of his sentiments, and the growth of his character"—the arrangement of the present Norton Critical Edition highlights the autobiographical context and the centrality of the letters and journals. Each of the four biographically defined units contains a selection of the poetry, in chronological order based on the date of composition, and of the letters and journals from the same period. A biographical headnote to each unit briefly summarizes the occurrences of the period that are relevant to the poems and letters included in that unit. The brilliant, chatty, gossipy, down-to-earth letters Byron wrote over the course of his lifetime provide a vivid glimpse of the man outside the poem during the time of its composition—an essential dimension to a full appreciation of the poem. Grouping these letters with

---

8. Helen Gardner, "Don Juan," in *The London Magazine*, July 1958), as quoted in Anne Barton, "Byron and the Mythology of Fact," (University of Nottingham, 1968; reprinted in this volume [see p. 823]).

the poems highlights the relevance of the life to the poetry and provides, within the parameters of a selected edition, units for studying Byron's poems in the context of his life.[9] Poems that were originally drafted as or as part of letters are included with the letters; having them in their original context conveys the seamless intertwining of Byron's living and writing, of his conversational prose style and his poetic voice.

With respect to the chronological arrangement of the poems, the placement of three poems requires clarification. *Childe Harold's Pilgrimage* is given as three separate units based on the separate times of composition and original publication dates: Cantos I and II in 1812, Canto III in 1816, and Canto IV in 1818. Byron ultimately regarded *Childe Harold* as a single poem, as it has typically been published since 1818; indeed, it does cohere as a unified, if irregular, work, despite the dissenting views of some critics. Still, critics and editors have presented valid reasons for printing and reading the poem as three separate works, or as two (cantos I–II and cantos III–IV). Presenting the poem as three units, moreover, highlights the poem's relation to Byron's biographical situation and development as a poet. *Manfred* was mostly drafted during the summer of 1816 in Switzerland and reflects, as do the other poems of this period, the influence of the Alpine setting and of the feelings that haunted Byron concerning Augusta, his estranged wife, and the recent domestic scandal. Therefore, although the third act was entirely revised after Byron went to Italy and the poem was not published until June 1817, *Manfred* is included in the third part of the book, which covers the period of its initial composition. *Don Juan*, though written and published in installments over the period 1818–1824, is, in contrast to *Childe Harold*, a poem that would lose more than it would gain from being broken up into its publication units. For one thing, *Don Juan* maintains a formal, thematic, and stylistic unity throughout, and its narrative subject is set in the past rather than in the poet's immediate geographical situation. Further, *Don Juan* was conceived *after* the essential biographical elements that inform it throughout: Byron's marriage and separation, and his involvements with English society, politics, and poetry. For these reasons, the selections from *Don Juan* are printed as a unit in Part Four of this Norton Critical Edition.

All of Byron's notes printed in *1832* for the poems or poetic excerpts in this edition are included among the footnotes, along with selected notes by Byron from other sources. Notes given in quotation marks are by Byron, unless otherwise attributed, to distinguish these notes from the editor's. Citations for Shakespeare correspond to *The Norton Shakespeare* (1997).

The criticism at the end of this volume is a very small selection of the wide array of critical responses to Byron from his own day to the present. In order to include as many recent scholars as possible, I have omitted the important generation of Byron scholars immediately preceding the present

9. A precedent for this organization is W. H. Auden's edition, *The Selected Poetry and Prose of Byron* (New American Library, 1966), which groups poems and letters together in biographical subdivisions. In the introduction to his edition, Auden explains: "If I had to introduce Byron to a student who knew nothing of his work, I would tell him: 'Before you attempt to read any of the poetry, read all of the prose, his letters and journals. Once you have read these, you will be able, when you come to the poems, to recognize immediately which are authentic and which are bogus.'" Whether or not one agrees with Auden or with the late Robert F. Gleckner (*Byron and the Ruins of Paradise*, xvi–xvii), who held that Byron posed as much in his letters as in his poems, one can hardly deny the helpfulness of the letters to an understanding of the biographical context of the poems.

one. This decision was based in part on the fact that the work of a number of those fine critics was included in the previous Byron Norton Critical Edition, on the desirability of including as many of today's scholars and recent theoretical approaches as possible, and on the fact that so much of the recent generation's scholarship has assimilated and built upon that of the former one. The Selected Bibliography and the recommended criticism given in the notes to individual poems include many of the valuable studies not represented among the critical essays in this volume.

A Biographical Register identifies the recipients of Byron's letters printed in this Norton Critical Edition, as well as many of the friends, associates, writers, and political figures to whom Byron's poetry or letters refer.

The Text of the Poems

Copy text and collations: The copy text for most of the poems in this Norton Critical Edition is *The Works of Lord Byron: With his Letters and Journals, and His Life, by Thomas Moore, Esq.*, edited by John Wright, 17 vols. (London: John Murray, 1832–34)(*1832*). This carefully prepared, important edition was the standard text for Byron's poems throughout the nineteenth century and even in the twentieth century was frequently preferred to the scholarly edition by E. H. Coleridge (1898–1904), which had been based on Murray's 1831 edition. In addition to printing many poems by Byron that had either not been published in his lifetime or had been published only in early, inconsistently prepared editions, *1832* standardized the printing of the poems, regularizing accidentals (e.g., spelling, capitalizations, apostrophes, and other punctuation), for the most part in accordance with Byron's explicit or implicit expectations. Byron's notes intended for publication with his poems were printed at the foot of the page and distinguished from the editor's notes.

Thanks to the fact that John Murray was a conservative and conscientious publisher, most of Byron's poetry has been reliably transmitted. At the same time, with the discovery of various manuscripts and corrected proofs, later editors have been able to correct the received texts, and some of the corrections are significant. For all poems I have compared the copy text (*1832*, with the exceptions described below) with the *Complete Poetical Works*, edited by Jerome J. McGann (Clarendon Press, 1980–93) (*CPW*). Where discrepancies between *1832* and *CPW* occur, I collated the editions of E. H. Coleridge (*C*) and of P. E. More (Riverside Press, 1905, based on and occasionally correcting *1832*) (*More*), and in some instances early editions or manuscripts. For the poems from *Hebrew Melodies*, I also compared the editions by T. L. Ashton and by Frederick Burwick and Paul Douglass. For *Don Juan*, whenever I found a discrepancy between *1832* and *CPW*, I consulted the *Don Juan Variorum Edition* (*DJV*) of Truman Guy Steffan and Willis W. Pratt (Texas, 1957, rev. 1971).

A few of the poems in this Norton Critical Edition are based on a text other than *1832*. In the case of *English Bards and Scotch Reviewers*, the wholesale elimination in *1832* of capitalized first letters of mid-line abstract nouns and of large and small capitals in proper names significantly altered the printing style and therefore visual effect of the text that appeared in Byron's lifetime; for this reason, the present text of *English*

Bards is based on C. The *1832* printing of *The Giaour* was also subject to excessive normalization (notably the routine conversion of Byron's numerous dashes to colons and commas); therefore, the seventh edition of *The Giaour*, the last edition for which Byron is known to have corrected proof, is the copy text for this poem. In the case of "To the Po," neither Murray nor Coleridge had access to the most reliable manuscript, Byron's fair copy, which is located in the Berg Collection of the New York Public Library and is the copy text for the present edition. Finally, the seventeenth canto fragment of *Don Juan* remained unpublished until *C*; I have used *More* as the base text for this poem.

Substantive corrections to the copy text: Where the collations have warranted a correction to the wording of the base text, the correction has been made and cited in the notes. All substantive discrepancies with *CPW* or with *1832* are noted.

Punctuation: The concept of authorized punctuation is elusive at best for a poet who relied on his editors for the punctuation of his poems— especially the matter of "stopping," or converting his habitual dashes to commas, semicolons, or periods—yet who made corrections to punctuation on proofs, and then, too, gave verbal instructions about punctuation, format, and other accidentals that his publisher might justifiably apply retroactively to earlier poems that he re-edited for later editions. Hence, for Byron's punctuation, no single type of primary source (e.g., manuscript, proof, early edition) may be automatically regarded as privileged.[1] As the carefully prepared work of Byron's lifelong publisher, *1832* is generally reliable with respect to punctuation, which comparison with early editions, other primary documents, and *CPW* confirms. In the present edition, where *CPW*, a manuscript, or early edition shows the punctuation of *1832* to be misleading or grammatically weaker than the earlier source, the *1832* punctuation is silently emended. On the same principle, I have restored many of Byron's expressive, if grammatically ambiguous, dashes and have eliminated unauthorized exclamation points. For *English Bards, The Giaour*, and "To the Po," errors or misleading punctuation in the copy texts (of the poems and notes) are silently corrected based on comparison with *1832* and *CPW*; for *Don Juan* XVII, corrections to punctuation have been made based on comparison with *CPW* and *DJV*.

Spelling and Apostrophes: The spelling of *1832* is adopted throughout with these exceptions: *Don Juan* XVII (not printed in *1832*); the spelling of Sathan in *The Vision of Judgment* (see the headnote to that poem); obvious careless or typographical errors, which are silently corrected. The use of the apostrophized form of the past tense and participle is inconsistent in Byron's manuscripts and between the manuscripts and the early editions. It is hard to object, either on grounds of readability or editorial responsibility, to the regularization of this printing convention in *1832*, the culmination of a process of regularizing this form over the course of Byron's lifetime, so that the apostrophe is consistently used to elide the unpronounced "e" of an "ed"-suffix when, and only when, it is not the silent "e" of the present tense form or otherwise required for the pronunciation (e.g., "thrill'd" but not "lov'd" or "depart'd"). In the present edition this

---

1. For a full discussion of the complexities of editing Byron's works, especially with respect to punctuation, see the editorial introductions in *CPW* 1 and *Cochran*.

practice is consistently applied, even to the poems for which *1832* is not the copy text.

Capitalization: With respect to mid-line, mid-sentence capitalizations, the manuscripts show considerable randomness and inconsistency, and this was clearly a matter for which Byron anticipated his editors' corrections. That said, for some poems *1832* tended rather liberally to convert capitals to lower case. In the present edition capitals are selectively restored based on comparison with holograph manuscripts (especially in the case of poems published posthumously from manuscript copies not by Byron), with early editions overseen by Byron, and with other relevant editions.

Titles and dates; stanza format and numbering; ligatures: With the exception of "To the Po. June 2nd 1819," which is the title on the holograph fair copy, the titles of the poems in this volume are taken from *1832*; the titles in *CPW*, if different, are noted. However, when the stanza divisions and numbering (or lack thereof) as given in *1832* contradict Byron's explicit intentions, the format has been silently corrected. For convenience, stanza numbers are always given in arabic, though they were mostly printed in roman in Byron's lifetime. When the date of a poem's composition is printed either as part of the title or at the end of the poem on the copy text, the present edition prints the date accordingly; otherwise, dates of composition and publication are given in the notes. Ligatures have been separated as is consistent with modern printing style.

Letters and Journals

The letters and journals in this Norton Critical Edition have been copied from *Byron's Letters and Journals*, edited by Leslie A. Marchand, 12 volumes (London: John Murray, 1973–82). As Marchand explains in his Editorial Note in volume one, many of the letters had been expurgated or in other ways bowdlerized by their recipients or later owners. While this was often done silently, Thomas Moore, who was the first to publish a collection of Byron's letters, indicated deletions with asterisks. In the present edition, for letters not printed in their entirety as they appear in Marchand's edition, omitted passages are indicated by plain dots.

Acknowledgments

Although only my name appears as editor of this Norton Critical Edition, preparing the texts of Byron's poems has been far from a lonely labor. Throughout, I have had for company and invaluable assistance the minds and work of Byron's most illustrious editors, from whose deservedly renowned editions I have derived the present one. Most of the poems have been based upon John Murray's monumental edition of 1832–34, *The Works of Lord Byron: With His Letters and Journals, and His Life, by Thomas Moore, Esq.*, 17 vols., with the poetry (vols. 7–17) edited by John Wright. Its conscientious preparation and consistent editorial procedures make this edition an excellent base text for the Norton Critical Edition. The nearly two centuries since the publication of this edition, however, have brought to light many textual authorities to which Murray did not have access, and in emending the Murray edition I have relied heavily upon the definitive edition to date of Byron's poetry: *Lord Byron: The Complete Poetical Works*, edited by Jerome J. McGann, 7 vols. (Clarendon Press, 1980–93). Scrupulously edited and based on a staggering array of early editions, manuscripts, and other authorized documents, McGann's edition contains a wealth of textual annotations and commentaries that were invaluable to me in preparing the texts and notes for the present edition.

Several other editions of Byron's poetry were important to my preparation of the texts and notes in this Norton Critical Edition: *The Works of Lord Byron. Poetry*, edited by E. H. Coleridge, 7 vols. (John Murray, 1899–1903); *The Poems of Byron*, edited by Paul Elmer More (Riverside, 1905); *Lord Byron: Selected Poems*, edited by Susan J. Wolfson and Peter J. Manning (Penguin, 1996); *Byron's Hebrew Melodies*, edited by Thomas L. Ashton (London, 1972); *A Selection of Hebrew Melodies, Ancient and Modern, by Isaac Nathan and Lord Byron*, edited by Frederick Burwick and Paul Douglass (University of Alabama, 1988); *Byron's Don Juan: A Variorum Edition*, edited by Truman Guy Steffan and Willis W. Pratt (University of Texas, 1957; rev. ed., 1971). Peter Cochran's online edition of Byron's poetry, begun in 1988 and accessible through the International Byron Society Web site, was particularly helpful for its fidelity to manuscripts, insights about transmission history, extensive notes on Byron's wide-ranging literary sources and allusions, and decipherment of numerous British colloquialisms.

I wish to express my respect and appreciation to the late Frank McConnell, editor of the previous Norton Critical Edition of Byron's poetry and prose; I have used or adapted many of his well-researched and succinct footnotes. Among the many excellent biographical and critical studies of Byron, the work of three scholars was especially useful to me in the preparation of the Introduction and the biographical headnotes: Leslie

A. Marchand's still unsurpassed three-volume *Byron: A Biography* (Knopf, 1957); the insightful biographical sketch by John D. Jump in his second chapter of *Byron* (Routledge Author Guides, 1972); Jerome McGann's penetrating contextual studies of Byron, particularly "Lord Byron and the Twin Opposites of Truth" (1989), "The Book of Byron and the Book of a World" (1985), and the Introduction to his one-volume Oxford World's Classics edition of Byron's poetry (2000).

I am very grateful to the John Murray Archive for its generous permission to reprint so large a selection from *Byron's Letters and Journals*, edited with devotion and unfailing scrupulousness by Leslie A. Marchand, 12 vols. (London: John Murray, 1974–94). For her gracious assistance in expediting the permission process, I would like to thank Mrs. Virginia Murray.

To two important scholars I owe an especially profound debt, not only for their supremely knowing advice concerning this Norton Critical Edition, but for their guidance, friendship, and faith in me throughout my academic career. I wish to express my deepest gratitude to Jerome J. McGann, the pre-eminent Byron scholar and my teacher and dissertation adviser at the University of Chicago. He introduced me to the pleasures (and pains) of editing Byron and has been a model and inspiration to me throughout my life as a teacher and scholar. To Donald H. Reiman, the leading textual scholar of English Romantic poetry whose unwaveringly high standards have made him the conscience for a generation of scholars, I wish to express my great appreciation for recommending me to W. W. Norton, thus allowing me the extraordinary experience and honor of editing Byron.

I recall with pleasure the many days I spent at the Carl H. Pforzheimer Collection of Shelley and His Circle at the New York Public Library and benefited from the helpful and knowledgeable assistance of Charles C. Carter, Daniel Dibbern, Doucet Devin Fischer, and Stephen S. Wagner. I especially appreciate Doucet's reading a draft of the introduction and the astute suggestions she made for it. For access to manuscripts, early editions, and other important texts, I would also like to thank the Berg Collection of the New York Public Library, the Collection of the Byron Society of America, Columbia University Library, the Henry E. Huntington Library, and the Pierpont Morgan Library. I am grateful to Hofstra University for supporting me through the years and granting me leave time for work on this edition.

Marsha M. Manns, co-founder with Leslie Marchand of the Byron Society of America and its indefatigable preserver and current chair of the board, has since my graduate school years continually encouraged and assisted my Byron research. I would like to thank her and the following colleagues and friends who provided me with information, inspiration, and conversation that contributed materially to this edition: James Chandler, Peter Cochran, Cheryl Giuliano, Peter Graham, J. Paul Hunter, W. Thomas MacCary, Julia Markus, Christine Philliou, Charles Robinson, Arthur Schwimmer, Andrew Stauffer, Jack G. Wasserman, Marjorie Weiss, Susan J. Wolfson, and the late Betty T. Bennett. I also wish to express my gratitude to my extremely helpful, highly skilled, and patient editors at W. W. Norton & Company, Brian Baker, Carol Bemis, Katharine Ings, and Marian Johnson, as well as to Assistant Editor Rivka Genesen and Norton's College Permissions Manager, Nancy Rodwan.

For permission to publish the criticism in the back of the book, as edited and/or revised for this edition, I thank the authors, original publishers, or other copyright holders as specified in the bibliographical note to each selection.

Finally, I wish to thank my daughter, Elena Weissman, for her meticulous formatting of Byron's letters and the bibliography, and my husband, Paul Weissman, for reading the manuscript, his tireless assistance with it, and his unfaltering sense of prose style (which is usually wasted on his legal briefs). I could not have completed this edition without their love and unflagging encouragement and support.

I dedicate this edition to my mother, Mollie Levine, and to the memory of my father, Milton Levine, who gave me their love and their love of literature.

Abbreviations

1832	*The Works of Lord Byron: With His Letters and Journals, And His Life, by Thomas Moore, Esq.* Edited by John Wright. 17 vols. London: John Murray, 1832–34.
BLJ	*Byron's Letters and Journals.* Edited by Leslie A. Marchand. 12 vols. London: John Murray, 1973–82.
C	*The Works of Lord Byron: A New, Revised and Enlarged Edition, with Illustrations. Poetry.* Edited by Ernest Hartley Coleridge. 7 vols. London: John Murray, 1898–1904.
Decline and Fall	*The History of the Decline and Fall of the Roman Empire.* By Edward Gibbon. Edited by H. H. Milman. 1845. 6 vols.
CPW	*Lord Byron: The Complete Poetical Works.* Edited by Jerome J. McGann. 7 vols. Oxford: Clarendon Press, 1980–93.
Cochran	Online edition of Byron's poems. Edited by Peter Cochran. International Byron Society website: www.internationalbyronsociety.org.
DJV	*Byron's Don Juan: A Variorum Edition.* 4 vols. Edited by Truman Guy Steffan and W. W. Pratt. Austin: University of Texas Press, 1957; rev. edn., 1971.
Fiery Dust	*Fiery Dust: Byron's Poetic Development.* By Jerome J. McGann. Chicago: University of Chicago Press, 1968.
Life	*Letters and Journals of Lord Byron: With Notices of his Life.* By Thomas Moore. 2 vols. London: John Murray, 1830.
LJ	*The Works of Lord Byron: A New, Revised and Enlarged Edition, with Illustrations. Letters and Journals.* Edited by Rowland E. Prothero. 6 vols. London: John Murray, 1898–1901.
Marchand	*Byron: A Biography.* By Leslie A. Marchand. 3 vols. New York: Alfred A. Knopf, 1957.
More	*The Complete Poetical Works of Lord Byron.* Edited by Paul Elmer More. Cambridge, MA: Riverside Press, Houghton Mifflin, 1905.
Nicholson	*Lord Byron: The Complete Miscellaneous Prose.* Edited by Andrew Nicholson. Oxford: Oxford University Press, 1991.

BYRON'S POETRY AND PROSE

Part One: Early Years and First Pilgrimage (1803–1812)

At the age of one, Byron had been taken by his mother to Aberdeen, Scotland, after his father had abandoned them. His formative years were influenced by mental and physical distress caused by his club foot and doctors' treatment of it, by his mother's volatile temperament, and by Presbyterian tutors and Calvinist nurses who introduced him to the idea of predestined evil, the Bible, and sex. When in 1798 he became the sixth Baron Byron of Rochdale (inheriting the title from his great-uncle), he and his mother returned to England, to reside at Newstead Abbey, the heavily mortgaged ancestral estate in Nottinghamshire. From 1801 to 1805 he attended Harrow School, during which period Newstead was leased to Lord Grey de Ruthven (with whom a sexual encounter seems to have occurred when Byron visited), and his mother made their home several miles away at Burgage Manor in Southwell. Here, when he was fifteen years old he fell in love with Mary Chaworth, a distant cousin who lived near Newstead at Annesley Hall; he began to correspond with his half-sister, Augusta (who married Colonel George Leigh in 1807); and he befriended his Southwell neighbors Elizabeth Pigot and her brother John. In October 1805, Byron entered Trinity College, Cambridge, where he formed close friendships with Francis Hodgson, Charles Skinner Matthews, Scrope Berdmore Davies, and especially John Cam Hobhouse, and fell passionately in love with the chorister John Edleston.

The following year Byron had his first collection of poems, *Fugitive Pieces*, printed by S. and J. Ridge and circulated privately among his friends. It included several ribald amatory poems that offended Southwell society, and a revised, "miraculously *chaste*" collection (*BLJ* 1:103), *Poems on Various Occasions*, was privately circulated a few months later. After he made further extensive changes to this collection, it was published as *Hours of Idleness* in June 1807 and then reissued as *Poems Original and Translated* (1808). Provoked by a derisive critique of *Hours of Idleness* by Henry Brougham that appeared anonymously in the *Edinburgh Review*, Byron published his boldly satiric *English Bards and Scotch Reviewers* (1809), which earned the critical respect denied to his earlier poems. In the summer of 1809, he sailed with Hobhouse to the Continent, where he met the Turkish despot Ali Pasha, swam the Hellespont, and wrote the first draft of *Childe Harold I–II*. He returned to England in July 1811, only to experience shock and grief over a rapid succession of deaths of close friends and loved ones, including his mother and Edleston, in whose memory he wrote the "Thyrza" poems. However, his return to England also saw the beginning of new friendships—notably with the poets Thomas Moore and Samuel Rogers—and the commencement of his relationship with the important publisher John Murray. Murray issued the first two cantos of *Childe Harold* on March 10, 1812—the day Byron awoke and found himself famous.

POETRY

A Fragment[1]

When, to their airy hall, my fathers' voice
Shall call my spirit, joyful in their choice;
When, poised upon the gale, my form shall ride,
Or, dark in mist, descend the mountain's side;
Oh! may my shade behold no sculptured urns   5
To mark the spot where earth to earth returns:
No lengthen'd scroll, no praise-encumber'd stone;
My epitaph shall be my name alone:
If *that* with honour fail to crown my clay,
Oh! may no other fame my deeds repay;   10
That, only *that*, shall single out the spot;
By that remember'd, or with that forgot.

                                             1803.

Fragment

Written Shortly After the Marriage of Miss Chaworth[1]

Hills of Annesley, bleak and barren,
    Where my thoughtless childhood stray'd,
How the northern tempests, warring,
    Howl above thy tufted shade!

Now no more, the hours beguiling,   5
    Former favourite haunts I see;
Now no more my Mary smiling,
    Makes ye seem a Heaven to me.

                                             1805.

The Cornelian[1]

1

No specious splendour of this stone
Endears it to my memory ever;

---

1. "A Fragment" was included in Byron's first, privately printed volume of poems, *Fugitive Pieces* (1806), and in his first publicly issued volume, *Hours of Idleness* (1807). In this poem, Byron attempts "to make the present a continuation of the heroic past" as he "confidently declares his kinship with his heroic forebears by employing an image of sublimity and grandeur . . . the mountains of Scotland" (*Fiery Dust*, p. 16). The poem reflects the influence of Ossian: a legendary third-century Gaelic warrior and bard whose poetry was reconstructed (if not actually written) by James Macpherson (1736–1796) and was widely popular in England and Europe during the later eighteenth and early nineteenth centuries.
1. When he was ten years old, Byron met the twelve-year-old Mary Ann Chaworth, a distant cousin who lived at Annesley Hall near Newstead, and by age sixteen he was distractedly in love with her. Grief-stricken upon hearing of her marriage to Jack Musters in 1805, he wrote these verses in imitation of Richard Gall's "Farewell to Ayrshire," then attributed to Robert Burns. They were first published in *Life* (1830).
1. Written in 1805 or 1806 in response to John Edleston's gift of a small heart-shaped cornelian, a semi-precious stone. At Cambridge, Byron grew passionately attached to the chorister Edleston,

With lustre *only once* it shone,
   But[2] blushes modest as the giver.

2

Some, who can sneer at friendship's ties,   5
   Have for my weakness oft reproved me,
Yet still the simple gift I prize,
   For I am sure the giver loved me.

3

He offer'd it with downcast look,
   As *fearful* that I might refuse it;   10
I told him when the gift I took,
   My *only fear* should be to lose it.

4

This pledge attentively I view'd,
   And *sparkling* as I held it near,
Methought one drop the stone bedew'd,   15
   And ever since *I've loved a tear.*

5

Still, to adorn his humble youth,
   Nor wealth nor birth their treasures yield;
But he who seeks the flowers of truth,
   Must quit the garden for the field.   20

6

'Tis not the plant uprear'd in sloth,
   Which beauty shows, and sheds perfume;
The flowers which yield the most of both
   In nature's wild luxuriance bloom.

7

Had Fortune aided nature's care,   25
   For once forgetting to be blind,
His would have been an ample share,
   If well proportion'd to his mind.

---

who was from a humble background and two years Byron's junior. (See letter to Elizabeth Pigot, July 5, 1807 [p. 101] and to Mrs. Margaret Pigot, October 28, 1811 [*BLJ* 2.119–20].) "The Cornelian" appeared only in the privately circulated *Fugitive Pieces* and *Poems on Various Occasions* (1807); Byron withdrew it for the publication of *Hours of Idleness*, having asked his Cambridge confidant Edward Noel Long to "keep the subject of my 'Cornelian' a Secret" (*BLJ* 1.110), and it remained unpublished until *1831.* Edleston died of consumption in May 1811 and is the subject of the "Thyrza" poems written later that year (see "To Thyrza," p. 98). On Byron's love for Edleston, see *Marchand* (1.107–108) and Crompton's *Byron and Greek Love.*
2. And (*1832*).

8

But had the Goddess clearly seen,
   His form had fix'd her fickle breast,   30
Her countless hoards would *his* have been,
   And none remain'd to give the rest.

Lachin Y Gair[1]

1

Away, ye gay landscapes! ye gardens of roses!
   In you let the minions of luxury rove;
Restore me the rocks where the snow-flake reposes,
   Though still they are sacred to freedom and love.
Yet, Caledonia! beloved are thy mountains,   5
   Round their white summits though elements war;
Though cataracts foam 'stead of smooth-flowing fountains,
   I sigh for the valley of dark Loch na Garr.

2

Ah! there my young footsteps in infancy wander'd;
   My cap was the bonnet, my cloak was the plaid;[2]   10
On chieftains long perish'd my memory ponder'd,
   As daily I strode through the pine-cover'd glade:
I sought not my home till the day's dying glory
   Gave place to the rays of the bright polar star;
For fancy was cheer'd by traditional story,   15
   Disclosed by the natives of dark Loch na Garr.

3

"Shades of the dead! have I not heard your voices
   Rise on the night-rolling breath of the gale?"
Surely the soul of the hero rejoices,
   And rides on the wind, o'er his own Highland vale.   20
Round Loch na Garr, while the stormy mist gathers,
   Winter presides in his cold icy car:
Clouds there encircle the forms of my Fathers;
   They dwell in the tempests of dark Loch na Garr.

---

1. Written early in 1807 and published the same year in *Hours of Idleness*. "Lachin y Gair, or, as it is pronounced in the Erse, Loch na Garr, towers proudly pre-eminent in the Northern Highlands, near Invercauld. One of our modern tourists mentions it as the highest mountain, perhaps, in Great Britain. Be this as it may, it is certainly one of the most sublime and picturesque amongst our 'Caledonian Alps.' Its appearance is of a dusky hue, but the summit is the seat of eternal snows. Near Lachin y Gair I spent some of the early part of my life, the recollection of which has given birth to the following stanzas." (Prefixed to the poem in *Hours of Idleness* and *Poems Original and Translated.*) The poem shows the influence of Ossian and is an imitation of Thomas Campbell's "Exile of Erin" (1801).
2. "This word is erroneously pronounced *plad*; the proper pronunciation (according to the Scotch) is shown by the orthography."

4

"Ill-starr'd,[3] though brave, did no visions foreboding   25
    Tell you that Fate had forsaken your cause?"
Ah! were you destined to die at Culloden,[4]
    Victory crown'd not your fall with applause:
Still were you happy in death's earthy slumber,
    You rest with your clan in the caves of Braemar;[5]   30
The Pibroch[6] resounds, to the piper's loud number,
    Your deeds on the echoes of dark Loch na Garr.

5

Years have roll'd on, Loch na Garr, since I left you,
    Years must elapse ere I tread you again:
Nature of verdure and flowers has bereft you,   35
    Yet still are you dearer than Albion's plain.
England! thy beauties are tame and domestic
    To one who has roved on the mountains afar:
Oh for the crags that are wild and majestic,
    The steep frowning glories of dark Loch na Garr!   40

I Would I Were a Careless Child[1]

1

I would I were a careless child,
    Still dwelling in my Highland cave,
Or roaming through the dusky wild,
    Or bounding o'er the dark blue wave;
The cumbrous pomp of Saxon[2] pride   5
    Accords not with the freeborn soul,
Which loves the mountain's craggy side,
    And seeks the rocks where billows roll.

2

Fortune! take back these cultured lands,
    Take back this name of splendid sound!   10

---

3. "I allude here to my maternal ancestors, 'the *Gordons*,' many of whom fought for the unfortunate Prince Charles, better known by the name of the Pretender. This branch was nearly allied by blood, as well as attachment, to the Stuarts. George, the second Earl of Huntley, married the Princess Annabella Stuart, daughter of James I, of Scotland. By her he left four sons: the third, Sir William Gordon, I have the honour to claim as one of my progenitors."
4. "Whether any perished in the Battle of Culloden, I am not certain; but, as many fell in the insurrection, I have used the name of the principal action, '*pars pro toto*.'"
5. "A tract of the Highlands so called. There is also a Castle of Braemar."
6. A kind of musical piece played on a bagpipe; in *Hours of Idleness*, Byron mistakenly annotated this as "the Bagpipe," for which he was ridiculed by Henry Brougham in his review (see p. 784).
1. Written in late 1807 or early 1808; published in *Poems Original and Translated* (1808) as "Stanzas" (the title in *CPW*). Stanzas 4–5 refer to Byron's carousing at Cambridge (see letter to Elizabeth Pigot, October 26, 1807, p. 103).
2. "Sassenach, or Saxon, a Gaelic word, signifying either Lowland or English."

I hate the touch of servile hands,
   I hate the slaves that cringe around.
Place me among the rocks I love,
   Which sound to Ocean's wildest roar;
I ask but this—again to rove   15
   Through scenes my youth hath known before.

3

Few are my years, and yet I feel
   The World was ne'er design'd for me:
Ah! why do dark'ning shades conceal
   The hour when man must cease to be?   20
Once I beheld a splendid dream,
   A visionary scene of bliss:
Truth!—wherefore did thy hated beam
   Awake me to a world like this?

4

I loved—but those I loved are gone;   25
   Had friends—my early friends are fled:
How cheerless feels the heart alone,
   When all its former hopes are dead!
Though gay companions o'er the bowl
   Dispel awhile the sense of ill,   30
Though Pleasure stirs the maddening soul,
   The heart—the heart is lonely still.

5

How dull! to hear the voice of those
   Whom Rank or Chance, whom Wealth or Power,
Have made, though neither friends nor foes,   35
   Associates of the festive hour.
Give me again a faithful few,
   In years and feelings still the same,
And I will fly the midnight crew,
   Where boist'rous Joy is but a name.   40

6

And Woman! lovely Woman, thou!
   My hope, my comforter, my all!
How cold must be my bosom now,
   When e'en thy smiles begin to pall,
Without a sigh would I resign   45
   This busy scene of splendid Woe,
To make that calm Contentment mine,
   Which Virtue knows, or seems to know.

7

Fain would I fly the haunts of men—
   I seek to shun, not hate mankind;   50
My breast requires the sullen glen,
   Whose gloom may suit a darken'd mind.
Oh! that to me the wings were given,
   Which bear the turtle to her nest!
Then would I cleave the vault of Heaven,   55
   To flee away, and be at rest.[3]

Lines Inscribed upon a Cup
Formed from a Skull[1]

1

Start not!—nor deem my spirit fled:
   In me behold the only skull,
From which, unlike a living head,
   Whatever flows is never dull.

2

I lived—I loved—I quaff'd like thee;   5
   I died—let earth my bones resign.
Fill up—thou canst not injure me;
   The worm hath fouler lips than thine.

3

Better to hold the sparkling grape
   Than nurse the earth-worm's slimy brood;   10
And circle in the goblet's shape
   The drink of Gods, than reptile's food.

4

Where once my wit perchance hath shone,
   In aid of others' let me shine;
And when, alas! our brains are gone,   15
   What nobler substitute than wine!

3. "'And I said, O that I had wings like a dove, for then would I fly away, and be at rest.'—Psalm lv.6. This verse also constitutes a part of the most beautiful anthem in our language."
1. Written in late November or early December 1808; first published in *Childe Harold's Pilgrimage, A Romaunt: And Other Poems* (1814). Years later Byron gave his friend Thomas Medwin the following account of this cup: "The gardener, in digging, discovered a skull that had probably belonged to some jolly friar or monk of the abbey, about the time it was dismonasteried. . . . Observing it to be of giant size, and in a perfect state of preservation, a strange fancy seized me of having it set and mounted as a drinking cup. I accordingly sent it to town, and it returned with a very high polish, and of a mottled colour like tortoiseshell" (Medwin's *Conversations* [1824], p. 87). The sentiment of the poem recalls the gravedigger scene from *Hamlet* (5.1).

5

Quaff while thou canst—another race,
When thou and thine like me are sped,
May rescue thee from earth's embrace,
And rhyme and revel with the dead.   20

6

Why not? since through life's little day
Our heads such sad effects produce;
Redeem'd from worms and wasting clay,
This chance is theirs to be of use.

Newstead Abbey, 1808.

FROM ENGLISH BARDS AND SCOTCH REVIEWERS   In the fall of
1807, Byron wrote a gently satiric work, "The British Bards." Through a series
of revisions and expansions, this poem became a sustained vituperation of
nearly three times that length against contemporary poets and critics. The cat-
alyst for the poem's transformation was the attack on Byron's first book of
poems, *Hours of Idleness*, by Henry Brougham, which appeared anonymously
in the *Edinburgh Review* in February 1808. *English Bards and Scotch Review-
ers* was first published anonymously in March 1809. Byron printed the second
edition under his name, adding a prose preface (omitted in the selections
below), and subsequent, expanded editions followed through 1810 and 1811,
while he was traveling on the Continent. By that time he had begun to regret
having written the poem, and he ordered a newly prepared, fifth edition sup-
pressed and all copies of the poem burned; his publisher, James Cawthorne,
however, released the fifth edition without Byron's authorization in 1816. As
Byron developed respectful and even friendly relationships with some of *En-
glish Bards'* more famous targets—Thomas Moore, Francis Jeffrey, "Monk"
Lewis, Lord Holland, and Walter Scott—he continually expressed his chagrin
over "that ferocious rhapsody" for "the wantonness or generality of many of its
attempted attacks" (*BLJ* 4:320, 286; see also *Don Juan* X, stanza 19), and in
1816, he expressed some his altered views in notes written onto a copy of the
poem (these notes appear in brackets). All the *same, English Bards*, showing the
influence of Horace, Juvenal, and Pope, among others, illustrates Byron's ear-
liest achievement in satire, the genre of his later, most admired poems—*Beppo*
(1817), *Don Juan* (1819–24), *The Vision of Judgment* (1821). The subject *En-
glish Bards* takes up, moreover, the decadence of contemporary poetry (citing
William Wordsworth, Samuel Taylor Coleridge, and Robert Southey as prime
offenders), is one that continued to preoccupy Byron, as shown by his return
to it ten years later in *Don Juan*.

From English Bards and Scotch Reviewers

A SATIRE[1]

"I had rather be a kitten, and cry mew!
Than one of these same metre ballad-mongers."
SHAKSPEARE [*I Henry IV*, 3.1.125–26]

"Such shameless bards we have; and yet 'tis true,
There are as mad, abandon'd critics too."
POPE [*Essay on Criticism*, 610–11]

STILL must I hear?[2]—shall hoarse FITZGERALD[3] bawl
His creaking couplets in a tavern hall,
And I not sing, lest, haply, Scotch Reviews
Should dub me scribbler, and denounce my Muse?[4]
Prepare for rhyme—I'll publish, right or wrong: 5
Fools are my theme, let Satire be my song.

Oh! Nature's noblest gift—my grey goose-quill!
Slave of my thoughts, obedient to my will,
Torn from thy parent bird to form a pen,
That mighty instrument of little men!   10
The pen! foredoom'd to aid the mental throes
Of brains that labour, big with Verse or Prose;
Though Nymphs forsake, and Critics may deride,
The Lover's solace, and the Author's pride.
What Wits! what Poets dost thou daily raise!   15
How frequent is thy use, how small thy praise!
Condemn'd at length to be forgotten quite,
With all the pages which 'twas thine to write.
But thou, at least, mine own especial pen!
Once laid aside, but now assumed again,   20
Our task complete, like Hamet's[5] shall be free;
Tho' spurn'd by others, yet beloved by me:
Then let us soar to-day; no common theme,
No Eastern vision, no distemper'd dream[6]
Inspires—our path, though full of thorns, is plain;   25
Smooth be the verse, and easy be the strain.

1. ["The *binding* of this volume is considerably too valuable for the contents. Nothing but the consideration of its being the property of another, prevents me from consigning this miserable record of misplaced anger and indiscriminate acrimony to the flames."—B.1816.]
2. "Imit[ation].—'Semper ego auditor tantum? nunquamne reponam, / Vexatus toties rauci Theseide Codri?' *Juv*[enal], Sat[ire]. I."
3. "Mr. Fitzgerald [William Thomas Fitzgerald (1759–1829)], facetiously termed by Cobbett the 'Small Beer Poet,' inflicts his annual tribute of verse on the Literary Fund: not content with writing, he spouts in person, after the company have imbibed a reasonable quantity of bad port, to enable them to sustain the operation." ["*'Hoarse Fitzgerald.'*— 'Right enough; but why notice such a mountebank.'—B.1816.]
4. A reference to the attack in the *Edinburgh Review* on Byron's first book of poems.
5. "Cid Hamet Benengeli promises repose to his pen in the last chapter of *Don Quixote*. Oh! that our voluminous gentry would follow the example of Cid Hamet Benengeli."
6. ["This must have been written in the spirit of prophecy."—B. 1816.] A reference to the fact that Byron would go on to write several Eastern tales in 1813 and 1814.

When Vice triumphant holds her sov'reign sway,
Obey'd by all who nought beside obey;
When Folly, frequent harbinger of crime,
Bedecks her cap with bells[7] of every Clime;   30
When Knaves and Fools combined o'er all prevail,
And weigh their Justice in a Golden Scale;
E'en then the boldest start from public sneers,
Afraid of Shame, unknown to other fears,
More darkly sin, by Satire kept in awe,   35
And shrink from Ridicule, though not from Law.

Such is the force of Wit! but not belong
To me the arrows of satiric song;
The royal vices of our age demand
A keener weapon, and a mightier hand.   40
Still there are follies, e'en for me to chase,
And yield at least amusement in the race:
Laugh when I laugh, I seek no other fame;
The cry is up, and scribblers are my game.
Speed, Pegasus![8]—ye strains of great and small,   45
Ode! Epic! Elegy!—have at you all!
I, too, can scrawl, and once upon a time
I pour'd along the town a flood of rhyme,
A schoolboy freak, unworthy praise or blame;
I printed—older children do the same.   50
'Tis pleasant, sure, to see one's name in print;
A Book's a Book, altho' there's nothing in't.
Not that a Title's sounding charm can save
Or scrawl or scribbler from an equal grave:
This LAMB must own, since his patrician name   55
Fail'd to preserve the spurious Farce from shame.[9]
No matter, GEORGE continues still to write,[1]
Tho' now the name is veil'd from public sight.
Moved by the great example, I pursue
The self-same road, but make my own review: 60
Not seek great JEFFREY'S[2] yet like him will be
Self-constituted Judge of Poesy.

＊   ＊   ＊

7. A cap with bells being the attire of a jester.
8. In classical mythology, the winged horse associated with poetic inspiration; see also line 145.
9. "This ingenuous youth is mentioned more particularly, with his production, in another place."
   George Lamb (1784–1834), who wrote farces; he was the son of Lady Melbourne (who became
   Byron's close friend and confidante in 1813) and brother-in-law of Lady Caroline Lamb, whose
   tempestuous affair with Byron became the subject of much of his correspondence with Lady Mel-
   bourne.
1. "In the Edinburgh Review." ["He's a very good fellow: and, except his mother and sister, the best
   of the set, to my mind."—B.1816.]
2. Francis Jeffrey (1773–1850), editor of the *Edinburgh Review*; Byron incorrectly believed Jeffrey
   was the author of Brougham's anonymous review of *Hours of Idleness*. Byron's notes to line 82,
   omitted in these selections, read: "Messrs. Jeffrey and Lamb are the alpha and omega, the first and
   last of the Edinburgh Review; the others are mentioned hereafter." ["Neither the heart nor the head
   of these gentlemen are at all what they are here represented.—at the time this was written (1808)
   I was personally unacquainted with either.—This was not just."—B. 1816.]

Time was, ere yet in these degenerate days
Ignoble themes obtain'd mistaken praise,
When Sense and Wit with Poesy allied,   105
No fabled Graces, flourish'd side by side,
From the same fount their inspiration drew,
And, rear'd by Taste, bloom'd fairer as they grew.
Then, in this happy Isle, a POPE'S[3] pure strain
Sought the rapt soul to charm, nor sought in vain;   110
A polish'd nation's praise aspired to claim,
And raised the people's, as the poet's fame.
Like him great DRYDEN pour'd the tide of song,
In stream less smooth, indeed, yet doubly strong.
Then CONGREVE'S scenes could cheer, or OTWAY'S melt—   115
For Nature then an English audience felt.
But why these names, or greater still, retrace,
When all to feebler Bards resign their place?
Yet to such times our lingering looks are cast,
When taste and reason with those times are past.   120
Now look around, and turn each trifling page,
Survey the precious works that please the age;
This truth at least let Satire's self allow,
No dearth of Bards can be complain'd of now.
The loaded Press beneath her labour groans,   125
And Printers' devils[4] shake their weary bones;
While SOUTHEY'S[5] Epics cram the creaking shelves,
And LITTLE'S Lyrics shine in hot-press'd twelves.[6]
Thus saith the Preacher: "Nought beneath the sun
Is new,"[7] yet still from change to change we run.   130
What varied wonders tempt us as they pass!
The Cow-pox, Tractors, Galvanism, and Gas[8]
In turns appear, to make the vulgar stare,
Till the swoln bubble bursts—and all is air!
Nor less new schools of Poetry arise,   135
Where dull pretenders grapple for the prize:
O'er Taste awhile these Pseudo-bards prevail;
Each country Book-club bows the knee to Baal,[9]
And, hurling lawful Genius from the throne,
Erects a shrine and idol of its own;   140
Some leaden calf—but whom it matters not,

3. Alexander Pope (1688–1744), and in lines 113–15 John Dryden (1631–1700), William Congreve (1670–1729), James Otway (1652–1685): poets Byron admired, whose poetic style he frequently contrasted favorably to that of his contemporaries.
4. Printers' apprentices, whose skin and clothes were blackened with ink stains.
5. Already a well-known poet when Byron wrote *English Bards*, Robert Southey (1774–1843) would become England's Poet Laureate in 1813. He was the object of Byron's animosity and derision throughout Byron's life (see "Dedication Stanzas" of *Don Juan* and *A Vision of Judgment*).
6. In book publishing, sheets of paper after printing were smoothed by pressing between cold or hot rollers; the duodecimo was an inexpensive book formed by folding sheets into twelve leaves. "Little" was a pseudonym of the Irish poet Thomas Moore (1779–1852), whom Byron later came to admire and who was to become one of Byron's closest friends.
7. "*Ecclesiastes, Cap I.*" "There is no new thing under the sun" (Eccles. 1.9).
8. Controversial or dubious medical innovations in Byron's day: cow pox—vaccination; tractors—a metallic cure-all prescribed by quacks; galvanism—therapeutic application of electricity to the body; gas—the exhilarating nitrous oxide ("laughing gas").
9. Canaanite deity; idol worship.

From soaring SOUTHEY, down to groveling STOTT.[1]
Behold! in various throngs the scribbling crew,
For notice eager, pass in long review:
Each spurs his jaded Pegasus apace,   145
And Rhyme and Blank maintain an equal race;
Sonnets on sonnets crowd, and ode on ode;
And Tales of Terror[2] jostle on the road;
Immeasurable measures move along,
For simpering Folly loves a varied song,   150
To strange, mysterious Dulness still the friend,
Admires the strain she cannot comprehend.
Thus Lays of Minstrels[3]—may they be the last!—
On half-strung harps whine mournful to the blast,
While mountain spirits prate to river sprites,   155
That dames may listen to the sound at nights;
And goblin brats of Gilpin Horner's brood
Decoy young Border-nobles through the wood,
And skip at every step, Lord knows how high,
And frighten foolish babes, the Lord knows why,   160
While high-born ladies in their magic cell,
Forbidding Knights to read who cannot spell,
Despatch a courier to a wizard's grave,
And fight with honest men to shield a knave.

Next view in state, proud prancing on his roan,   165
The golden-crested haughty Marmion,
Now forging scrolls, now foremost in the fight,
Not quite a Felon, yet but half a Knight,
The gibbet or the field prepared to grace;
A mighty mixture of the great and base.   170

---

1. "[Robert] Stott, better known in the 'Morning Post' by the name of Hafiz. This personage is at present the most profound explorer of the bathos. I remember, when the reigning family left Portugal, a special Ode of Master Stott's, beginning thus:—(*Stott loquitur quoad Hibernia.*)—'Princely offspring of Braganza, / Erin greets thee with a stanza,' &c. Also a Sonnet to Rats, well worthy of the subject, and a most thundering Ode, commencing as follows:—'Oh! for a Lay! loud as the surge / That lashes Lapland's sounding shore.' Lord have mercy on us! the 'Lay of the Last Minstrel' was nothing to this."
2. *Tales of Terror* (1801) by "Monk" Lewis (see note to line 265) and Walter Scott.
3. "See the 'Lay of the Last Minstrel,' *passim.* Never was any plan so incongruous and absurd as the groundwork of this production. The entrance of Thunder and Lightning, prologuising to Bayes' tragedy unfortunately takes away the merit of originality from the dialogue between Messieurs the Spirits of Flood and Fell in the first canto. Then we have the amiable William of Deloraine, 'a stark moss-trooper,' videlicet, a happy compound of poacher, sheep-stealer, and highwayman. The propriety of his magical lady's injunction not to read can only be equalled by his candid acknowledgment of his independence of the trammels of spelling, although, to use his own elegant phrase, ''twas his neck-verse at Harribee,' i.e. the gallows.—The biography of Gilpin Horner, and the marvellous pedestrian page, who travelled twice as fast as his master's horse, without the aid of seven-leagued boots, are *chefs-d'oeuvre* in the improvement of taste. For incident we have the invisible, but by no means sparing box on the ear bestowed on the page, and the entrance of a knight and charger into the castle, under the very natural disguise of a wain of hay. Marmion, the hero of the latter romance, is exactly what William of Deloraine would have been, had he been able to read and write. The poem was manufactured for Messrs Constable, Murray, and Miller, worshipful booksellers, in consideration of the receipt of a sum of money; and truly, considering the inspiration, it is a very creditable production. If Mr Scott will write for hire, let him do his best for his paymasters, but not disgrace his genius, which is undoubtedly great, by a repetition of black-letter ballad imitations." Byron's lifelong admiration for Walter Scott was soon to override these cavils. In a diary entry of 1813, Byron lauded Scott as "the Monarch of Parnassus, and the most *English* of Bards," and in 1821 Byron dedicated *Cain* to him.

And think'st thou, SCOTT! by vain conceit perchance,
On public taste to foist thy stale romance,
Though MURRAY with his MILLER may combine
To yield thy muse just half-a-crown per line?
No! when the sons of song descend to trade,   175
Their bays are sear, their former laurels fade,
Let such forego the poet's sacred name,
Who rack their brains for lucre, not for fame:
Still for stern Mammon[4] may they toil in vain!
And sadly gaze on Gold they cannot gain!   180
Such be their meed, such still the just reward
Of prostituted Muse and hireling bard!
For this we spurn Apollo's[5] venal son,
And bid a long "good night to Marmion."[6]

These are the themes that claim our plaudits now;   185
These are the Bards to whom the Muse must bow;
While MILTON, DRYDEN, POPE, alike forgot,
Resign their hallow'd Bays[7] to WALTER SCOTT.

The time has been, when yet the Muse was young,
When HOMER swept the lyre, and MARO[8] sung,   190
An Epic scarce ten centuries could claim,
While awe-struck nations hailed the magic name:
The work of each immortal Bard appears
The single wonder of a thousand years.[9]
Empires have moulder'd from the face of earth,   195
Tongues have expired with those who gave them birth,
Without the glory such a strain can give,
As even in ruin bids the language live.
Not so with us, though minor Bards, content,
On one great work a life of labour spent: 200
With eagle pinion soaring to the skies,
Behold the Ballad-monger SOUTHEY rise!
To him let CAMOËNS, MILTON, TASSO[1] yield,
Whose annual strains, like armies, take the field.
First in the ranks see Joan of Arc advance,   205
The scourge of England and the boast of France!
Though burnt by wicked BEDFORD for a witch,
Behold her statue placed in Glory's niche;

---

4. Material wealth (New Testament).
5. Apollo was the Greek god of music and poetry.
6. " 'Good Night to Marmion'—the pathetic and also prophetic exclamation of Henry Blount, Esq. on the death of honest Marmion." (*Marmion*, 6, stanza 28.)
7. Honorary garland or crown of bay leaves awarded for excellence, here signifying poetic fame.
8. Virgil (Publius Vergilius Maro, 70–19 B.C.E.), Rome's great epic poet.
9. "As the Odyssey is so closely connected with the story of the Iliad, they may almost be classed as one grand historical poem. In alluding to Milton and Tasso, we consider the 'Paradise Lost,' and 'Gierusalemme Liberata,' as their standard efforts; since neither the 'Jerusalem Conquered' of the Italian, nor the 'Paradise Regained' of the English bard, obtained a proportionate celebrity to their former poems. Query: Which of Mr. Southey's will survive?"
1. Torquato Tasso (1544–1595), Luis de Camoëns (1524–1580), John Milton (1608–1674): respectively, Italian, Portuguese, and English epic poets.

Her fetters burst, and just released from prison,
A virgin Phoenix from her ashes risen.   210
Next see tremendous Thalaba come on,[2]
Arabia's monstrous, wild, and wond'rous son;
Domdaniel's dread destroyer, who o'erthrew
More mad magicians than the world e'er knew.
Immortal Hero! all thy foes o'ercome,   215
For ever reign—the rival of Tom Thumb![3]
Since startled Metre fled before thy face,
Well wert thou doom'd the last of all thy race!
Well might triumphant Genii bear thee hence,
Illustrious conqueror of common sense!   220
Now, last and greatest, Madoc[4] spreads his sails,
Cacique[5] in Mexico, and Prince in Wales;
Tells us strange tales, as other travellers do,
More old than Mandeville's[6] and not so true.
Oh, SOUTHEY! SOUTHEY![7] cease thy varied song!   225
A bard may chaunt too often and too long:
As thou art strong in verse, in mercy, spare!
A fourth, alas! were more than we could bear.
But if, in spite of all the world can say,
Thou still wilt verseward plod thy weary way;   230
If still in Berkeley-Ballads most uncivil,
Thou wilt devote old women to the devil,[8]
The babe unborn thy dread intent may rue:
"God help thee," SOUTHEY,[9] and thy readers too.

    Next comes the dull disciple of thy school,   235
That mild apostate[1] from poetic rule,
The simple WORDSWORTH, framer of a lay
As soft as evening in his favourite May,[2]
Who warns his friend "to shake off toil and trouble,
And quit his books, for fear of growing double";[3]   240
Who, both by precept and example, shows

---

2. "'Thalaba,' Mr. Southey's second poem, is written in open defiance of precedent and poetry. Mr.
   S. wished to produce something novel and succeeded to a miracle. 'Joan of Arc,' was marvellous
   enough, but Thalaba was one of those poems 'which,' in the words of Porson, 'will be read when
   Homer and Virgil are forgotten, but—not till then.'"
3. The hero of *The Tragedy of Tragedies, or the Life and Death of Tom Thumb the Great* (1730), a farce
   by Henry Fielding.
4. The hero of Southey's poem *Madoc* (1805).
5. A native chief or prince of the aborigines in the West Indies.
6. Sir John Mandeville, presumed author of travel books written in the fourteenth century.
7. "We beg Mr. Southey's pardon: 'Madoc disdains the degrading title of epic.' See his preface. Why
   is epic degraded? and by whom? Certainly the late romaunts of Masters Cottle, Laureat Pye, Ogilvy,
   Hole, and gentle Mistress Cowley, have not exalted the epic muse; but, as Mr. Southey's poem 'dis-
   dains the appellation,' allow us to ask—has he substituted any thing better in its stead? or must he
   be content to rival Sir Richard Blackmore in the quantity as well as quality of his verse?"
8. "See, The Old Woman of Berkeley, a Ballad, by Mr. Southey, wherein an aged gentlewoman is car-
   ried away by Beelzebub, on a 'high trotting horse.'"
9. Echoes a parody of Southey's "Dactylics" in the *Anti-Jacobin*, "God help thee, silly one."
1. One who leaves a religious faith.
2. ["*Unjust*."—B.1816.]
3. "Lyrical Ballads [1800], p. 4—'The Tables Turned.' Stanza 1. 'Up, up my friend, and clear your
   looks; / Why all this toil and trouble? / Up, up, my friend, and quit your books, / Or surely you'll
   grow double.'"

That prose is verse, and verse is merely prose,[4]
Convincing all, by demonstration plain,
Poetic souls delight in prose insane;
And Christmas stories tortured into rhyme   245
Contain the essence of the true sublime.
Thus, when he tells the tale of Betty Foy,
The idiot mother of "an idiot Boy,"[5]
A moon-struck, silly lad, who lost his way,
And, like his bard, confounded night with day,[6]   250
So close on each pathetic part he dwells,
And each adventure so sublimely tells,
That all who view the "idiot in his glory"
Conceive the Bard the hero of the story.

Shall gentle COLERIDGE pass unnoticed here,   255
To turgid ode and tumid stanza dear?
Though themes of innocence amuse him best,
Yet still obscurity's a welcome guest.
If inspiration should her aid refuse
To him who takes a Pixy for a Muse,[7]   260
Yet none in lofty numbers can surpass
The bard who soars to elegize an ass:
So well the subject suits his noble mind,
He brays, the Laureate of the long-ear'd kind.

Oh! wonder-working LEWIS![8] Monk, or Bard,   265
Who fain would make Parnassus a church-yard!
Lo! wreaths of yew, not laurel,[9] bind thy brow,
Thy Muse a Sprite, Apollo's sexton thou!
Whether on ancient tombs thou tak'st thy stand,
By gibb'ring spectres hail'd, thy kindred band;   270
Or tracest chaste descriptions on thy page,
To please the females of our modest age;
All hail, M.P. ![1] from whose infernal brain
Thin sheeted phantoms glide, a grisly train;
At whose command "grim women" throng in crowds,   275
And kings of fire, of water, and of clouds,
With "small grey men,"—"wild yagers," and what-not,

---

4. Parodying Wordsworth's poetic theory as set forth in the Preface to the second edition of *Lyrical Ballads* (2nd. ed., 1800): e.g. ". . . there neither is, nor can be, any essential difference between the language of prose and metrical composition."
5. "The Idiot Boy," *Lyrical Ballads* (1798).
6. "Mr. W. in his preface labours hard to prove, that prose and verse are much the same; and certainly his precepts and practice are strictly conformable:—'And thus to Betty's questions he / Made answer, like a traveller bold. / The cock did crow, to-whoo, to-whoo, / And the sun did shine so cold,' &c. &c., p. 129."
7. "Coleridge's Poems, p. 11, 'Songs of the Pixies,' i.e. Devonshire Fairies; p. 42, we have, 'Lines to a young Lady:' and, p. 52, 'Lines to a young Ass.'"
8. Matthew Gregory ("Monk") Lewis (1775–1818), author of *The Monk* (1796), a gothic novel, and *Tales of Wonder* (1801), who later became a friend of Byron's.
9. *yew . . . laurel*: symbols, respectively, of sorrow or death (yew) and of distinctive achievement (laurel).
1. "'For every one knows little Matt's an M.P. '—See a poem to Mr. Lewis, in 'The Statesman,' supposed to be written by Mr. Jekyll." M.P.: Member of Parliament. Lewis frequently signed his works "M. G. Lewis, M.P." "All hail" echoes *Macbeth* 1.3.46–48.

To crown with honour thee and WALTER SCOTT:
Again, all hail! if tales like thine may please,
St. Luke alone can vanquish the disease:[2]   280
Even Satan's self with thee might dread to dwell,
And in thy skull discern a deeper hell.

*   *   *

Truth! rouse some genuine Bard, and guide his hand
To drive this pestilence from out the land.
Even I—least thinking of a thoughtless throng,
Just skill'd to know the right and choose the wrong,[3]   690
Freed at that age when Reason's shield is lost,
To fight my course through Passion's countless host,[4]
Whom every path of Pleasure's flow'ry way
Has lured in turn, and all have led astray—
E'en I must raise my voice, e'en I must feel   695
Such scenes, such men, destroy the public weal:
Altho' some kind, censorious friend will say,
"What art thou better, meddling fool,[5] than they?"
And every Brother Rake will smile to see
That miracle, a Moralist in me.   700
No matter—when some Bard in virtue strong,
GIFFORD[6] perchance, shall raise the chastening song,
Then sleep my pen for ever! and my voice
Be only heard to hail him and rejoice;
Rejoice, and yield my feeble praise, though I   705
May feel the lash that Virtue must apply.

*   *   *

Maid of Athens, Ere We Part[1]

Ζώη μοῦ, σάς ἀγαπῶ.[2]

1

Maid of Athens, ere we part,
Give, oh, give me back my heart!

2. Luke was a physician.
3. Ovid, *Metamorphoses*, 7.20–21.
4. ["Yes: and a precious chase they led me."—B.1816.]
5. ["*Fool* enough, certainly, then, and no wiser since."—B.1816.]
6. "[William] Gifford [1756–1826], author of the Baviad and Maeviad, the first satires of the day, and translator of Juvenal" (from Byron's note to line 818 of the poem). The *Baviad* and *Maeviad* were among Byron's models for *English Bards*.
1. Title in *CPW* (based on early editions): "Song [Ζώη μοῦ, σάς ἀγαπῶ] / Athens, 1810." Composed in Athens on February 9, 1810, and first published in *Childe Harold's Pilgrimage. A Romaunt* (1812), this poem was addressed to Teresa Macri, twelve-year-old daughter of Byron's landlady. On May 3, 1810, toward the end of a long letter to Henry Drury, Byron wrote: "I almost forgot to tell you that I am dying for love of three Greek Girls at Athens, sisters, two of whom have promised to accompany me to England, I lived in the same house, Teresa, Mariana, and Kattinka, are the names of these divinities all of them under 15" (*BLJ* 1:240).
2. "A Romaic expression of tenderness: If I translate it, I shall affront the gentlemen, as it may seem I supposed they could not; and if I do not I may affront the ladies. For fear of any misconstruction on the part of the latter I shall do so, begging pardon of the learned. It means, 'My Life, I love you!' which sounds very prettily in all languages. . . ." (Byron's note in the first edition.) The pronunciation is: zoë mou sas agapo.

Or, since that has left my breast,
Keep it now, and take the rest!
Hear my vow before I go,   5
Ζώη μοῦ, σάς ἀγαπῶ.

2

By those tresses unconfined,
Woo'd by each Aegean wind;
By those lids whose jetty fringe
Kiss thy soft cheeks' blooming tinge;   10
By those wild eyes like the roe,
Ζώη μοῦ, σάς ἀγαπῶ.

3

By that lip I long to taste;
By that zone-encircled waist;
By all the token-flowers[3] that tell   15
What words can never speak so well;
By Love's alternate joy and woe,
Ζώη μοῦ, σάς ἀγαπῶ.

4

Maid of Athens! I am gone:
Think of me, sweet! when alone.   20
Though I fly to Istambol,[4]
Athens holds my heart and soul:
Can I cease to love thee? No!
Ζώη μοῦ, σάς ἀγαπῶ.
                                          Athens, 1810.

Written after Swimming from Sestos to Abydos[1]

1

If, in the month of dark December,
Leander, who was nightly wont

---

3. "In the East (where ladies are not taught to write, lest they should scribble assignations) flowers, cinders, pebbles, &c. convey the sentiments of the parties by that universal deputy of Mercury— an old woman. A cinder says, 'I burn for thee;' a bunch of flowers tied with hair, 'Take me and fly;' but a pebble declares—what nothing else can."
4. "Constantinople."
1. Written on May 9, 1810, and first published in *Childe Harold's Pilgrimage, A Romaunt* (1812).
   "On the 3d of May, 1810, while the Salsette (Captain Bathurst) was lying in the Dardanelles, Lieutenant Ekenhead, of that frigate and the writer of these rhymes swam from the European shore to the Asiatic—by the by, from Abydos to Sestos would have been more correct. The whole distance, from the place whence we started to our landing on the other side, including the length we were carried by the current, was computed by those on board the frigate at upwards of four English miles; though the actual breadth is barely one. The rapidity of the current is such that no boat can row directly across, and it may, in some measure, be estimated from the circumstance of the whole distance being accomplished by one of the parties in an hour and five, and by the other in an hour and ten, minutes. The water was extremely cold, from the melting of the mountain snows. About

(What maid will not the tale remember?)
To cross thy stream, broad Hellespont!

2

If, when the wintry tempest roar'd,   5
He sped to Hero, nothing loth,
And thus of old thy current pour'd,
Fair Venus! how I pity both!

3

For *me*, degenerate modern wretch,
Though in the genial month of May,   10
My dripping limbs I faintly stretch,
And think I've done a feat to-day.

4

But since he cross'd the rapid tide,
According to the doubtful story,
To woo,—and—Lord knows what beside,   15
And swam for Love, as I for Glory;

5

'Twere hard to say who fared the best:
Sad mortals! thus the Gods still plague you!
He lost his labour, I my jest:
For he was drown'd, and I've the ague.   20

May 9, 1810.

---

three weeks before, in April, we had made an attempt; but, having ridden all the way from the Troad the same morning, and the water being of an icy chillness, we found it necessary to postpone the completion till the frigate anchored below the castles, when we swam the straits, as just stated; entering a considerable way above the European, and landing below the Asiatic, fort. Chevalier says that a young Jew swam the same distance for his mistress; and Oliver mentions its having been done by a Neapolitan; but our consul, Tarragona, remembered neither of these circumstances, and tried to dissuade us from the attempt. A number of the Salsette's crew were known to have accomplished a greater distance; and the only thing that surprised me was, that, as doubts had been entertained of the truth of Leander's story, no traveller had ever endeavoured to ascertain its practicability."

In Greek legend, Leander swam the Hellespont (Dardanelles) every night from Abydos to visit Hero, a priestess of Aphrodite in Sestos. One night he drowned in a storm, and Hero threw herself into the sea. Six days before writing this poem, Byron and a friend made the same swim (though in the reverse direction). Byron's pride in his prowess as a swimmer offset the humiliation he often felt since childhood due to his malformed right foot, which prevented him from participating in most other sports. Having boasted of swimming the Hellespont in seven separate letters written between May 3 and June 28, 1810, Byron wrote to his friend Francis Hodgson on July 4: "I shall begin by telling you, having only told it you twice before, that I swam from Sestos to Abydos. I do this that you may be impressed with proper respect for me, the performer; for I plume myself on this achievement more than I could possibly do on any kind of glory, political, poetical, or rhetorical." Byron further memorialized his natatory feat in *Don Juan* II, stanza 105 (p 449).

CHILDE HAROLD'S PILGRIMAGE   On July 2, 1809, with his friend John Cam Hobhouse, Byron left England for a tour of Portugal, Spain, Malta, Greece, Albania, and Turkey. When he returned in 1811, he brought with him two cantos of a long semiautobiographical poem that he had drafted in the fall of 1809 and spring of 1810 and that he called "Childe Burun's Pilgrimage," using an old form of the Byron family name. Robert Charles Dallas, a distant relative (eventually Byron's literary agent), urged him to publish the poem with the important bookseller John Murray. Even before returning to England Byron had begun the process of heavily revising the poem, which was published on March 10, 1812. The effect of Cantos I–II of *Childe Harold*, according to Thomas Moore, was "electric," the first edition of five hundred copies selling out in three days. Indeed, the ten editions of the poem that Murray published over the next three years, along with Byron's Eastern tales, led to Byron's enjoying an unprecedented celebrity in the literary and social world of England from 1812 to 1815. During his second and final exile from England, Byron wrote two additional cantos: Canto III, written in Switzerland in 1816, and Canto IV, written in Italy in 1817–18. Although Byron regarded *Childe Harold* as a single poetic unit, as Jerome McGann points out, "the work neither is nor was a unified composition," and it "can be read in three ways: as a single, integral poem, as two loosely related units (Cantos I–II and Cantos III–IV), or as three separate parts of one changing poetic project (Cantos I–II, Canto III, Canto IV)" (*CPW* 2.265).

Childe Harold originated as a sentimental travelogue poem, cast as (or parodying) a romance in the style of Edmund Spenser's *Faerie Queene* (1590, 1596), using Spenser's nine-line stanza and, intermittently, diction, and focusing on a young, questing hero. "Childe" was a medieval term for a young nobleman before taking his vows of knighthood. But readers quickly perceived that the doleful, wandering Harold was a thinly disguised alter ego of the poet— despite Byron's insistence that his "child of imagination" was intended only as a unifying device and an illustration of a "misdirected" soul that shows "that early perversion of mind and morals leads to satiety of past pleasures and disappointment in new ones . . ." (see the Preface and Addition to the Preface). The travelogue, moreover, provided the poet with a framework for expressing his sharp criticism of Europe's emerging political order: notably France's conflict with England; Napoleon's encroachment into Portugal and Spain and the subsequent Peninsular War; and the still feudal Ottoman empire in its dying stages, with the subjection to Turkey of Greece, the birthplace and symbol to Byron of civilization, freedom, and glory. This criticism is set against the poet's alternating responses to the world: on the one hand, his appreciation of nature and humankind, and; on the other, his acute awareness of human failures and history's perpetual disappointments.

Through a process of revision and accretions that continued throughout the publication of the first seven editions, *Childe Harold* I–II deepened into a serious personal poem and *Kunstlerroman*, or artist's biography. The deaths of his mother, John Edleston, and three close friends occurred while Byron was writing and revising the poem, and his deeply felt personal loss intensified and was intensified by his observation of history's recurrent wars and failures. Thus, like Goethe's best-selling novel *The Sorrows of Young Werther* (1774), *Childe Harold* captured the spirit of the age as a prime illustration of the literature of *Weltschmerz*—the world's sorrow experienced as a personal condition. "Pilgrimage," moreover, is ironic, secular, Romantic: the poet neither seeks nor discovers a shrine, and his only redemption is that of "Consciousness awaking to her woes" (I.941).

Besides the appeal of the mysteriously melancholy, deep-feeling yet aloof persona at the center of the poem, its immediate impact is traceable to the "Byronic" thought and style: the emotionally heightened rhetoric of loss

("Cold is the heart, fair Greece! that looks on thee, / Nor feels as lovers o'er the dust they loved" [II.127–28]); striking, dramatic descriptions—as of a bullfight in Cadiz ("Hark! heard you not the forest-monarch's roar? / Crashing the lance, he snuffs the spouting gore / Of man and steed, o'erthrown beneath his horn; / The throng'd arena shakes with shouts for more; / Yells the mad crowd o'er entrails freshly torn, / Nor shrinks the female eye, nor ev'n affects to mourn" [I.687–92]); topographical immediacy and intertextual echoes ("Ambracia's gulf behold, where once was lost / A world for woman . . ." [II.397–98, recalling Plutarch's, Shakespeare's, and Dryden's accounts of Antony's defeat at Actium as a result of following Cleopatra's ships]); classical prosody and Romantic rhetoric ("And must they fall? the young, the proud, the brave, / To swell one bloated Chief's unwholesome reign? / No step between submission and a grave? / The rise of rapine and the fall of Spain?" [I.549–52]).

Despite weaknesses, such as uneven verse quality and formal inconsistencies, *Childe Harold* I–II remains "one of the most important works in modern western literature" (*Fiery Dust*, 94). It provided the framework for the poetically more mature third and fourth cantos and the prototype of a range of literature depicting the man-of-sensibility as hero (or anti-hero) in an alienated (typically post-war) world—from Lermontov's *A Hero of Our Time* (1840) to Eliot's *The Waste Land* (1922), Salinger's *The Catcher in the Rye* (1951), and Kerouac's *On the Road* (1957). Yet the relation of the exile/pilgrim to the contemporary world in *Childe Harold* remains uniquely Byronic as an unfolding drama of engagement and alienation. The poet's acute awareness of history, political critique, and respectful observation of different countries and cultures disrupt the poem's Romantic interiority. These worldly preoccupations are evident not only in the body of the poem but in Byron's numerous, detailed, and sometimes lengthy notes, the cosmopolitan, at times sardonic, tone of which further destabilizes the poem's Romantic agenda. Finally, the relationship between the hero and poet-narrator (though weakly drawn in this poem) and the dominance of the narrator's commentaries and digressions represent Byron's earliest efforts in a form that he would eventually manage with unsurpassed virtuosity in his later masterwork, *Don Juan*.

Criticism: On *Childe Harold's Pilgrimage* I–IV, in addition to the critical commentaries and annotations in *C, CPW,* and *Cochran,* see: Blackstone, *Byron: A Survey;* Chalk, "*Childe Harold's Pilgrimage: a Romaunt* and the Influence of Local Attachment"; Curran, *Poetic Form and British Romanticism;* Gleckner, *Byron and the Ruins of Paradise;* Joseph, *Byron the Poet;* Martin, *Byron: A Poet Before His Public;* McGann, *Fiery Dust;* Ross, "Scott's Chivalric Pose: The Function of Metrical Romance in the Romantic Period." On Cantos I and II: In this Norton Critical Edition, see Jeffrey, Review of *Childe Harold's Pilgrimage* I–II (p. 785); McGann, "The Book of Byron and the Book of a World" (p. 828); Reiman, "Byron and the 'Other' " (p. 876); Lang, "Narcissus Jilted" (p. 972). See also: Borst, *Lord Byron's First Pilgrimage;* Cronin, "Mapping *Childe Harold* I and II"; Leask, "Byron and the Eastern Mediterranean: *Childe Harold* II and the 'polemic of Ottoman Greece'"; Marchand, *Byron: A Biography* (1.185–326); Martin, "Heroism and history: *Childe Harold* I and II and the Tales,"; St. Clair, *Lord Elgin and the Marbles* and *That Greece Might Still be Free;* Thomas, *Lord Byron's Iberian Pilgrimage.*

CHILDE HAROLD'S PILGRIMAGE

A ROMAUNT

L'univers est une espèce de livre, dont on n'a lu que la première page quand on n'a vu que son pays. J'en ai feuilleté un assez grand nombre, que j'ai trouvé également mauvaises. Cet examen ne m'a point été infructueux. Je haïssais ma patrie. Toutes les impertinences des peuples divers, parmi lesquels j'ai vécu, m'ont reconcilié avec elle. Quand je n'aurais tiré d'autre bénéfice de mes voyages que celui-là, je n'en regretterais ni les frais ni les fatigues.

LE COSMOPOLITE[1]

Preface to the First and Second Cantos

The following poem was written, for the most part, amidst the scenes which it attempts to describe. It was begun in Albania; and the parts relative to Spain and Portugal were composed from the author's observations in those countries. Thus much it may be necessary to state for the correctness of the descriptions. The scenes attempted to be sketched are in Spain, Portugal, Epirus, Acarnania, and Greece. There, for the present, the poem stops: its reception will determine whether the author may venture to conduct his readers to the capital of the East, through Ionia and Phrygia: these two cantos are merely experimental.

A fictitious character is introduced for the sake of giving some connection to the piece; which, however, makes no pretension to regularity. It has been suggested to me by friends, on whose opinions I set a high value, that in this fictitious character, 'Childe Harold,' I may incur the suspicion of having intended some real personage: this I beg leave, once for all, to disclaim—Harold is the child of imagination, for the purpose I have stated. In some very trivial particulars, and those merely local, there might be grounds for such a notion; but in the main points, I should hope, none whatever.

It is almost superfluous to mention that the appellation 'Childe,' as 'Childe Waters,' 'Childe Childers,' &c. is used as more consonant with the old structure of versification which I have adopted. The 'Good Night,' in the beginning of the first canto, was suggested by 'Lord Maxwell's Good Night,' in the Border Minstrelsy, edited by Mr Scott.[2]

With the different poems which have been published on Spanish subjects, there may be found some slight coincidence in the first part, which

1. "The universe is a sort of book, of which one has only read the first page when one has only seen one's country. I have perused a great number, which I have found equally bad. This study has not at all been unfruitful. I hated my country. All the foibles of the diverse people among whom I have lived have reconciled me with her. Should I not have reaped another benefit from my travels than that, I would regret neither the expense nor the effort." Fougeret de Monbron, *Le Cosmopolite, ou, le Citoyen du Monde* (London, 1753).
2. Walter Scott's *Minstrelsy of the Scottish Border* (1802). Other writers and works mentioned in the Preface and Addition to the Preface: James Beattie (Scottish scholar, 1735–1803), letter of September 22, 1766, in Forbes's *Life of Beattie* (1806) 1:89; Ludovico Ariosto (Italian poet, 1474–1533); James Thomson (Scottish poet, 1700–1748); Jean-Baptiste de la Curne de Sainte-Palaye (French scholar, 1697–1781), *Mémoires sur l'ancienne chevalrie* (Paris, 1781); Rolland d'Erceville, *Recherches . . . sur le Cours d'Amours* (Paris, 1787); Edmund Burke (British statesman and philosopher, 1729–1797), *Reflections on the Revolution in France* (1868), p. 89; Pierre Terrail, Chevalier de Bayard (c. 1474–1524), known widely as the knight "sans peur et sans reproche"; Joseph Banks, et al., *Hawkesworth's Voyages* (1773).

treats of the Peninsula, but it can only be casual; as, with the exception of a few concluding stanzas, the whole of this poem was written in the Levant.[3]

The stanza of Spenser, according to one of our most successful poets, admits of every variety. Dr Beattie makes the following observation:—'Not long ago I began a poem in the style and stanza of Spenser, in which I propose to give full scope to my inclination, and be either droll or pathetic, descriptive or sentimental, tender or satirical, as the humour strikes me; for, if I mistake not, the measure which I have adopted admits equally of all these kinds of composition.'—Strengthened in my opinion by such authority, and by the example of some in the highest order of Italian poets, I shall make no apology for attempts at similar variations in the following composition; satisfied that, if they are unsuccessful, their failure must be in the execution, rather than in the design sanctioned by the practice of Ariosto, Thomson, and Beattie.

London, February, 1812.

Addition to the Preface

I have now waited till almost all our periodical journals have distributed their usual portion of criticism. To the justice of the generality of their criticisms I have nothing to object: it would ill become me to quarrel with their very slight degree of censure, when, perhaps, if they had been less kind they had been more candid. Returning, therefore, to all and each my best thanks for their liberality, on one point alone shall I venture an observation. Amongst the many objections justly urged to the very indifferent character of the 'vagrant Childe' (whom, notwithstanding many hints to the contrary, I still maintain to be a fictitious personage), it has been stated, that, besides the anachronism, he is very *unknightly*, as the times of the Knights were times of Love, Honour, and so forth. Now, it so happens that the good old times, when 'l'amour du bon vieux temps, l'amour antique' flourished, were the most profligate of all possible centuries. Those who have any doubts on this subject may consult Sainte-Palaye, *passim*, and more particularly vol. ii. p.69. The vows of chivalry were no better kept than any other vows whatsoever; and the songs of the Troubadours were not more decent, and certainly were much less refined, than those of Ovid. The 'Cours d'amour, parlemens d'amour, ou de courtésie et de gentilesse' had much more of love than of courtesy or gentleness. See Roland on the same subject with Sainte-Palaye. Whatever other objection may be urged to that most unamiable personage Childe Harold, he was so far perfectly knightly in his attributes—'No waiter, but a knight templar.'[4] By the by, I fear that Sir Tristrem and Sir Lancelot were no better than they should be, although very poetical personages and true knights 'sans peur,' though not 'sans reproche.' If the story of the institution of the 'Garter' be not a fable, the knights of that order have for several centuries borne the badge of a Countess of Salisbury, of indifferent memory. So much for chivalry. Burke need

---

3. The lands bordering the eastern shores of the Mediterranean Sea, e.g., Albania, Greece, and Turkey.
4. *The Rovers, or the Double Arrangement* (*Poetry of the Anti-Jacobin* [1854], 199), by John Hookham Frere.

not have regretted that its days are over, though Marie-Antoinette was quite as chaste as most of those in whose honours lances were shivered, and knights unhorsed.

Before the days of Bayard, and down to those of Sir Joseph Banks (the most chaste and celebrated of ancient and modern times), few exceptions will be found to this statement; and I fear a little investigation will teach us not to regret these monstrous mummeries of the middle ages.

I now leave 'Childe Harold' to live his day, such as he is; it had been more agreeable, and certainly more easy, to have drawn an amiable character. It had been easy to varnish over his faults, to make him do more and express less, but he never was intended as an example, further than to show, that early perversion of mind and morals leads to satiety of past pleasures and disappointment in new ones, and that even the beauties of nature, and the stimulus of travel (except ambition, the most powerful of all excitements) are lost on a soul so constituted, or rather misdirected. Had I proceeded with the poem, this character would have deepened as he drew to the close; for the outline which I once meant to fill up for him was, with some exceptions, the sketch of a modern Timon, perhaps a poetical Zeluco.[5]

London, 1813.

To Ianthe[6]

Not in those climes where I have late been straying,
Though Beauty long hath there been matchless deem'd;
Not in those visions to the heart displaying
Forms which it sighs but to have only dream'd,
Hath aught like thee in truth or fancy seem'd: 5
Nor, having seen thee, shall I vainly seek
To paint those charms which varied as they beam'd—
To such as see thee not my words were weak;
To those who gaze on thee what language could they speak?

Ah! may'st thou ever be what now thou art,   10
Nor unbeseem the promise of thy spring,
As fair in form, as warm yet pure in heart,
Love's image upon earth without his wing,
And guileless beyond Hope's imagining!
And surely she who now so fondly rears   15
Thy youth, in thee, thus hourly brightening,
Beholds the rainbow of her future years,
Before whose heavenly hues all sorrow disappears.

5. *Timon*: a ruined nobleman turned misanthropic philosopher of Athens (fifth century B.C.E.) and subject of works by Pope and Shakespeare; cf. "I rest, a perfect Timon, not nineteen" ("Childish Recollections" [1806], variant, *CPW* 1.158). The eponymous villain-hero of a novel by John Moore (1789).
6. These stanzas were added in the seventh edition of the poem (1814). "*Ianthe*" ("flower of the Narcissus," Ovid, *Metamorphoses*) refers to Lady Charlotte Harley, the thirteen-year-old daughter of Lord and Lady Oxford; during 1812–14 Byron was romantically involved with Lady Oxford, referred to in lines 15–18.

Young Peri[7] of the West!—'tis well for me
My years already doubly number thine;   20
My loveless eye unmoved may gaze on thee,
And safely view thy ripening beauties shine;
Happy, I ne'er shall see them in decline;
Happier, that while all younger hearts shall bleed,
Mine shall escape the doom thine eyes assign   25
To those whose admiration shall succeed,
But mix'd with pangs to Love's even loveliest hours decreed.

Oh! let that eye, which, wild as the Gazelle's,
Now brightly bold or beautifully shy,
Wins as it wanders, dazzles where it dwells,   30
Glance o'er this page, nor to my verse deny
That smile for which my breast might vainly sigh,
Could I to thee be ever more than friend:
This much, dear maid, accord; nor question why
To one so young my strain I would commend,   35
But bid me with my wreath one matchless lily blend.

Such is thy name with this my verse entwined;
And long as kinder eyes a look shall cast
On Harold's page, Ianthe's here enshrined
Shall thus be first beheld, forgotten last: 40
My days once number'd, should this homage past
Attract thy fairy fingers near the lyre
Of him who hail'd thee, loveliest as thou wast,
Such is the most my memory may desire;
Though more than Hope can claim, could Friendship less
     require?   45

CANTO THE FIRST

1

Oh, thou! in Hellas[8] deem'd of heavenly birth,
Muse! form'd or fabled at the minstrel's will!
Since shamed full oft by later lyres on earth,
Mine dares not call thee from thy sacred hill:
Yet there I've wander'd by thy vaunted rill;   5
Yes! sigh'd o'er Delphi's long-deserted shrine,[9]
Where, save that feeble fountain, all is still;

---

7. In Persian mythology, a beautiful fairylike being descended from fallen angels.
8. Greece.
9. "The little village of Castri stands partly on the site of Delphi. Along the path of the mountain, from Chrysso, are the remains of sepulchres hewn in and from the rock. 'One,' said the guide, 'of a king who broke his neck hunting.' His majesty had certainly chosen the fittest spot for such an achievement. A little above Castri is a cave, supposed the Pythian, of immense depth; the upper part of it is paved, and now a cowhouse. On the other side of Castri stands a Greek monastery; some way above which is the cleft in the rock, with a range of caverns difficult of ascent, and apparently leading to the interior of the mountain; probably to the Corycian Cavern mentioned by Pausanias. From this part descend the fountain and the 'Dews of Castalie.'" Delphi is the site of the shrine and oracle of Apollo, Greek god of poetry.

Nor mote my shell awake the weary Nine[1]
To grace so plain a tale—this lowly lay of mine.

2

Whilome in Albion's[2] isle there dwelt a youth,   10
Who ne in virtue's ways did take delight;
But spent his days in riot most uncouth,
And vex'd with mirth the drowsy ear of Night.
Ah, me! in sooth he was a shameless wight,[3]
Sore given to revel and ungodly glee;   15
Few earthly things found favour in his sight
Save concubines and carnal companie,
And flaunting wassailers of high and low degree.

3

Childe Harold was he hight:[4]—but whence his name
And lineage long, it suits me not to say;   20
Suffice it, that perchance they were of fame,
And had been glorious in another day:
But one sad losel[5] soils a name for aye,
However mighty in the olden time;
Nor all that heralds rake from coffin'd clay,   25
Nor florid prose, nor honied lies of rhyme,
Can blazon evil deeds, or consecrate a crime.

4

Childe Harold bask'd him in the noontide sun,
Disporting there like any other fly;
Nor deem'd before his little day was done   30
One blast might chill him into misery.
But long ere scarce a third of his pass'd by,
Worse than adversity the Childe befell;
He felt the fulness of satiety:
Then loathed he in his native land to dwell,   35
Which seem'd to him more lone than Eremite's[6] sad cell.

5

For he through Sin's long labyrinth had run,
Nor made atonement when he did amiss,
Had sigh'd to many though he loved but one,
And that loved one, alas! could ne'er be his.   40

---

1. In Greek myth, the nine Muses were the inspiring goddesses of the various arts; *shell*: the lyre of
   the epic bard. *Mote*: might; Byron's use of Spenserian diction is generally abandoned after the
   opening thirteen stanzas.
2. England's; *Whilome*: once upon a time.
3. Person.
4. Called.
5. Scoundrel.
6. Hermit's.

Ah, happy she! to 'scape from him whose kiss
Had been pollution unto aught so chaste;
Who soon had left her charms for vulgar bliss,
And spoil'd her goodly lands to gild his waste,
Nor calm domestic peace had ever deign'd to taste.   45

6

And now Childe Harold was sore sick at heart,
And from his fellow bacchanals[7] would flee;
'Tis said, at times the sullen tear would start,
But Pride congeal'd the drop within his ee:
Apart he stalk'd in joyless reverie,   50
And from his native land resolved to go,
And visit scorching climes beyond the sea;
With pleasure drugg'd, he almost long'd for woe,
And e'en for change of scene would seek the shades below.

7

The Childe departed from his father's hall: 55
It was a vast and venerable pile;[8]
So old, it seemed only not to fall,
Yet strength was pillar'd in each massy aisle.
Monastic dome! condemn'd to uses vile!
Where Superstition once had made her den   60
Now Paphian girls[9] were known to sing and smile;
And monks might deem their time was come agen,
If ancient tales say true, nor wrong these holy men.

8

Yet oft-times in his maddest mirthful mood
Strange pangs would flash along Childe Harold's brow,   65
As if the memory of some deadly feud
Or disappointed passion lurk'd below:
But this none knew, nor haply cared to know;
For his was not that open, artless soul
That feels relief by bidding sorrow flow,   70
Nor sought he friend to counsel or condole,
Whate'er this grief mote be, which he could not control.

9

And none did love him—though to hall and bower
He gather'd revellers from far and near,

---

7. Worshipers of Bacchus, ancient Roman god of wine and revelry.
8. Cf. Newstead Abbey, Byron's ancestral estate.
9. I.e., concubines, prostitutes; the island Paphos was sacred to Aphrodite, goddess of beauty and love. In lines 60–63 Byron alludes to the long tradition of tales about secret licentiousness in monasteries, tales that were revived in Gothic novels of the Romantic period, particularly *The Monk* (1796) by Byron's friend Matthew G. Lewis. At Newstead, Byron would dress in friar's robes with his friends and play at being a dissolute monk.

He knew them flatt'rers of the festal hour;   75
The heartless parasites of present cheer.
Yea! none did love him—not his lemans[1] dear—
But pomp and power alone are woman's care,
And where these are light Eros finds a feere;[2]
Maidens, like moths, are ever caught by glare,   80
And Mammon wins his way where Seraphs[3] might despair.

10

Childe Harold had a mother—not forgot,
Though parting from that mother he did shun;
A sister whom he loved, but saw her not
Before his weary pilgrimage begun: 85
If friends he had, he bade adieu to none.
Yet deem not thence his breast a breast of steel:
Ye, who have known what 'tis to dote upon
A few dear objects, will in sadness feel
Such partings break the heart they fondly hope to heal.   90

11

His house, his home, his heritage, his lands,
The laughing dames in whom he did delight,
Whose large blue eyes, fair locks, and snowy hands
Might shake the saintship of an anchorite,[4]
And long had fed his youthful appetite;   95
His goblets brimm'd with every costly wine,
And all that mote to luxury invite,
Without a sigh he left, to cross the brine,
And traverse Paynim[5] shores, and pass Earth's central line.

12

The sails were fill'd, and fair the light winds blew,   100
As glad to waft him from his native home;
And fast the white rocks[6] faded from his view,
And soon were lost in circumambient foam:
And then, it may be, of his wish to roam
Repented he, but in his bosom slept   105
The silent thought, nor from his lips did come
One word of wail, whilst others sate and wept,
And to the reckless gales unmanly moaning kept.

---

1. Lovers.
2. Mate; *Eros*: Greek god of passionate love.
3. One of the nine orders of angels; *Mammon*: in medieval tradition, the demon of material wealth.
4. Religious hermit.
5. Medieval word for "pagan."
6. The famous white cliffs of Dover, in England's southeastern tip, traditionally the traveler's last sight of England.

13

But when the sun was sinking in the sea
He seized his harp, which he at times could string,   110
And strike, albeit with untaught melody,
When deem'd he no strange ear was listening:
And now his fingers o'er it he did fling,
And tuned his farewell in the dim twilight.
While flew the vessel on her snowy wing,   115
And fleeting shores receded from his sight,
Thus to the elements he pour'd his last 'Good Night.'

1

"Adieu, adieu! my native shore
      Fades o'er the waters blue;
The Night-winds sigh, the breakers roar,   120
      And shrieks the wild sea-mew.
Yon Sun that sets upon the sea
      We follow in his flight;
Farewell awhile to him and thee,
      My native Land—Good Night.   125

2

"A few short hours and He will rise
      To give the morrow birth;
And I shall hail the main and skies,
      But not my mother Earth.
Deserted is my own good hall,   130
      Its hearth is desolate;
Wild weeds are gathering on the wall;
      My dog howls at the gate.

3

"Come hither, hither, my little page![7]
      Why dost thou weep and wail?   135
Or dost thou dread the billows' rage,
      Or tremble at the gale?
But dash the tear-drop from thine eye;
      Our ship is swift and strong:
Our fleetest falcon scarce can fly   140
      More merrily along."

4

"Let winds be shrill, let waves roll high,
      I fear not wave nor wind;

---

7. Robert Rushton, son of a Newstead tenant, traveling with Byron, became homesick and returned home from Gibraltar.

Yet marvel not, Sir Childe, that I
    Am sorrowful in mind;   145
For I have from my father gone,
    A mother whom I love,
And have no friend, save these alone,
    But thee—and one above.

5

"My father bless'd me fervently,   150
    Yet did not much complain;
But sorely will my mother sigh
    Till I come back again."—
"Enough, enough, my little lad!
    Such tears become thine eye;   155
If I thy guileless bosom had,
    Mine own would not be dry.

6

"Come hither, hither, my staunch yeoman,
    Why dost thou look so pale?
Or dost thou dread a French foeman?   160
    Or shiver at the gale?"
"Deem'st thou I tremble for my life?
    Sir Childe, I'm not so weak;
But thinking on an absent wife
    Will blanch a faithful cheek.   165

7

"My spouse and boys dwell near thy hall,
    Along the bordering lake,
And when they on their father call,
    What answer shall she make?"
"Enough, enough, my yeoman good,   170
    Thy grief let none gainsay;
But I, who am of lighter mood,
    Will laugh to flee away.

8

"For who would trust the seeming sighs
    Of wife or paramour?   175
Fresh feres[8] will dry the bright blue eyes
    We late saw streaming o'er.
For pleasures past I do not grieve,
    Nor perils gathering near;
My greatest grief is that I leave   180
    No thing that claims a tear.

8. Companions; mates.

9

"And now I'm in the world alone,
    Upon the wide, wide sea:
But why should I for others groan,
    When none will sigh for me?   185
Perchance my dog will whine in vain,
    Till fed by stranger hands;
But long ere I come back again,
    He'd tear me where he stands.

10

"With thee, my bark, I'll swiftly go   190
    Athwart the foaming brine;
Nor care what land thou bear'st me to,
    So not again to mine.
Welcome, welcome, ye dark-blue waves!
    And when you fail my sight,   195
Welcome, ye deserts, and ye caves!
    My native Land—Good Night!"

14

On, on the vessel flies, the land is gone,
And winds are rude in Biscay's[9] sleepless bay.
Four days are sped, but with the fifth, anon,   200
New shores descried make every bosom gay;
And Cintra's[1] mountain greets them on their way,
And Tagus[2] dashing onward to the deep,
His fabled golden tribute bent to pay;
And soon on board the Lusian[3] pilots leap,   205
And steer 'twixt fertile shores where yet few rustics reap.

15

Oh, Christ! it is a goodly sight to see
What Heaven hath done for this delicious land!
What fruits of fragrance blush on every tree!
What goodly prospects o'er the hills expand!   210
But man would mar them with an impious hand:
And when the Almighty lifts his fiercest scourge
'Gainst those who most transgress his high command,

---

9. The Bay of Biscay is the traveler's entry into the waters of Spain and Portugal.
1. Cintra (or Sintra) is a Portuguese town near Lisbon, site of the infamous "Convention of Cintra" (1808), where England, after helping the Portuguese repel a French invasion, agreed to give the French Army safe conduct out of the country. Byron, like the other Romantics, felt that England's behavior was a betrayal of the nascent spirit of revolutionary nationalism (see stanzas 24–26)—for while the English would aid their satellite, Portugal, in resisting Napoleon's attempt to isolate England economically from the European Continent, they would not allow triumph to the point of real national independence from foreign policies.
2. Portugal's central river, which according to legend carried gold particles in its depths.
3. Portuguese, from "Lusitania," an ancient name for Portugal.

With treble vengeance will his hot shafts urge
Gaul's locust host,[4] and earth from fellest foemen purge.   215

16

What beauties doth Lisboa first unfold!
Her image floating on that noble tide,
Which poets vainly pave with sands of gold,
But now whereon a thousand keels did ride
Of mighty strength, since Albion was allied,   220
And to the Lusians did her aid afford:
A nation swoln with ignorance and pride,
Who lick yet loathe the hand that waves the sword
To save them from the wrath of Gaul's unsparing lord.[5]

17

But whoso entereth within this town,   225
That, sheening far, celestial seems to be,
Disconsolate will wander up and down,
'Mid many things unsightly to strange ee;
For hut and palace show like filthily:
The dingy denizens are rear'd in dirt;   230
Ne personage of high or mean degree
Doth care for cleanness of surtout or shirt,
Though shent with Egypt's plague, unkempt, unwash'd, unhurt.

18

Poor, paltry slaves! yet born 'midst noblest scenes—
Why, Nature, waste thy wonders on such men?   235
Lo! Cintra's glorious Eden intervenes
In variegated maze of mount and glen.
Ah, me! what hand can pencil guide, or pen,
To follow half on which the eye dilates
Through views more dazzling unto mortal ken   240
Than those whereof such things the bard relates,
Who to the awe-struck world unlock'd Elysium's[6] gates?

19

The horrid crags, by toppling convent crown'd,
The cork-trees hoar that clothe the shaggy steep,
The mountain-moss by scorching skies imbrown'd,   245
The sunken glen, whose sunless shrubs must weep,
The tender azure of the unruffled deep,
The orange tints that gild the greenest bough,
The torrents that from cliff to valley leap,

---

4. The French army, which had invaded Portugal.
5. Napoleon Bonaparte.
6. Elysium is the Paradise of Roman myth, described by Virgil (70–19 B.C.E.) in the sixth book of the
   Aeneid.

The vine on high, the willow branch below,   250
Mix'd in one mighty scene, with varied beauty glow.

20

Then slowly climb the many-winding way,
And frequent turn to linger as you go,
From loftier rocks new loveliness survey,
And rest ye at "Our Lady's house of woe,"[7]   255
Where frugal monks their little relics show,
And sundry legends to the stranger tell:
Here impious men have punish'd been, and lo!
Deep in yon cave Honorius long did dwell,
In hope to merit Heaven by making earth a Hell.   260

21

And here and there, as up the crags you spring,
Mark many rude-carved crosses near the path:
Yet deem not these devotion's offering—
These are memorials frail of murderous wrath:
For wheresoe'er the shrieking victim hath   265
Pour'd forth his blood beneath the assassin's knife,
Some hand erects a cross of mouldering lath;
And grove and glen with thousand such are rife
Throughout this purple land, where law secures not life.[8]

22

On sloping mounds, or in the vale beneath,   270
Are domes where whilome kings did make repair;
But now the wild flowers round them only breathe;
Yet ruin'd splendour still is lingering there.
And yonder towers the Prince's palace fair:
There thou too, Vathek![9] England's wealthiest son,   275

7. "The convent of 'Our Lady of Punishment,' *Nossa Señora de Pena*, on the summit of the rock. Below, at some distance, is the Cork Convent, where St. Honorius dug his den, over which is his epitaph. From the hills the sea adds to the beauty of the view.—[Since the publication of this poem, I have been informed of the misapprehension of the term *Nossa Señora de Pena*. It was owing to the want of the *tilde*, or mark over the *ñ* which alters the signification of the word: with it, *Peña* signifies a rock; without it, *Pena* has the sense I adopted. I do not think it necessary to alter the passage; as though the common acceptation affixed to it is 'Our Lady of the Rock,' I may well assume the other sense from the severities practised there.—*Note to 2d Edition*.]" Honorius was a sixteenth-century Capuchin monk who lived a life of total seclusion and self-denial in a cave near the convent.
8. "It is a well known fact, that in the year 1809, the assassinations in the streets of Lisbon and its vicinity were not confined by the Portuguese to their countrymen; but that Englishmen were daily butchered: and so far from redress being obtained, we were requested not to interfere if we perceived any compatriot defending himself against his allies. I was once stopped in the way to the theatre at eight o'clock in the evening, when the streets were not more empty than they generally are at that hour, opposite to an open shop, and in a carriage with a friend: had we not fortunately been armed, I have not the least doubt that we should have 'adorned a tale' instead of telling one. The crime of assassination is not confined to Portugal: in Sicily and Malta we are knocked on the head at a handsome average nightly, and not a Sicilian or Maltese is ever punished!"
9. William Beckford, author of *Vathek* (1786), one of the most famous and influential of Gothic novels. Much of Beckford's life was spent in a fantastic attempt to construct an architecture equivalent to his own romantic dreams, and his English home, Fonthill Abbey, is one of the most striking of eighteenth-century neo-Gothic buildings.

Once form'd thy Paradise, as not aware
When wanton Wealth her mightiest deeds hath done,
Meek Peace voluptuous lures was ever wont to shun.

23

Here didst thou dwell, here schemes of pleasure plan,
Beneath you mountain's ever beauteous brow: 280
But now, as if a thing unblest by Man,
Thy fairy dwelling is as lone as thou!
Here giant weeds a passage scarce allow
To halls deserted, portals gaping wide:
Fresh lessons to the thinking bosom, how   285
Vain are the pleasaunces on earth supplied,
Swept into wrecks anon by Time's ungentle tide!

24

Behold the hall where chiefs were late convened![1]
Oh! dome displeasing unto British eye!
With diadem hight foolscap, lo! a fiend,   290
A little fiend that scoffs incessantly,
There sits in parchment robe array'd, and by
His side is hung a seal and sable scroll,
Where blazon'd glare names known to chivalry,
And sundry signatures adorn the roll,   295
Whereat the Urchin points and laughs with all his soul.

25

Convention is the dwarfish demon styled
That foil'd the knights in Marialva's dome:
Of brains (if brains they had) he them beguiled,
And turn'd a nation's shallow joy to gloom.   300
Here Folly dash'd to earth the victor's plume,
And Policy regain'd what arms had lost:
For chiefs like ours in vain may laurels bloom!
Woe to the conqu'ring, not the conquer'd host,
Since baffled Triumph droops on Lusitania's coast!   305

26

And ever since that martial synod[2] met,
Britannia sickens, Cintra! at thy name;
And folks in office at the mention fret,
And fain would blush, if blush they could, for shame.
How will posterity the deed proclaim!   310
Will not our own and fellow-nations sneer,
To view these champions cheated of their fame,

---

1. "The Convention of Cintra was signed in the palace of the Marchese Marialva."
2. Assembly.

By foes in fight o'erthrown, yet victors here,
Where Scorn her finger points through many a coming year?

27

So deem'd the Childe, as o'er the mountains he   315
Did take his way in solitary guise:
Sweet was the scene, yet soon he thought to flee,
More restless than the swallow in the skies:
Though here awhile he learn'd to moralize,
For Meditation fix'd at times on him;   320
And conscious Reason whisper'd to despise
His early youth, misspent in maddest whim;
But as he gazed on truth his aching eyes grew dim.

28

To horse! to horse! he quits, for ever quits
A scene of peace, though soothing to his soul: 325
Again he rouses from his moping fits,
But seeks not now the harlot and the bowl.
Onward he flies, nor fix'd as yet the goal
Where he shall rest him on his pilgrimage;
And o'er him many changing scenes must roll   330
Ere toil his thirst for travel can assuage,
Or he shall calm his breast, or learn experience sage.

29

Yet Mafra[3] shall one moment claim delay,
Where dwelt of yore the Lusians' luckless queen;[4]
And church and court did mingle their array,   335
And mass and revel were alternate seen;
Lordlings and freres[5]—ill-sorted fry I ween!
But here the Babylonian whore[6] hath built
A dome, where flaunts she in such glorious sheen,
That men forget the blood which she hath spilt,   340
And bow the knee to Pomp that loves to varnish guilt.[7]

30

O'er vales that teem with fruits, romantic hills,
(Oh, that such hills upheld a freeborn race!)

3. A town just north of Lisbon.
4. Maria I of Portugal (1734–1816), who went mad after the death of her husband and one of her sons. From 1799 till her death she was queen in name only, with her son João acting as regent.
5. Monks.
6. The "whore of Babylon" in the book of Revelation was taken by many Protestants to represent the Catholic Church.
7. "The extent of Mafra is prodigious: it contains a palace, convent, and most superb church. The six organs are the most beautiful I ever beheld, in point of decoration: we did not hear them, but were told that their tones were correspondent to their splendour. Mafra is termed the Escurial of Portugal."

Whereon to gaze the eye with joyaunce fills,
Childe Harold wends through many a pleasant place.   345
Though sluggards deem it but a foolish chase,
And marvel men should quit their easy chair,
The toilsome way, and long, long league to trace,
Oh! there is sweetness in the mountain air,
And life, that bloated Ease can never hope to share.   350

31

More bleak to view the hills at length recede,
And, less luxuriant, smoother vales extend;
Immense horizon-bounded plains succeed!
Far as the eye discerns, withouten end,
Spain's realms appear whereon her shepherds tend   355
Flocks, whose rich fleece right well the trader knows—
Now must the pastor's arm his lambs defend:
For Spain is compass'd by unyielding foes,[8]
And all must shield their all, or share Subjection's woes.

32

Where Lusitania and her Sister meet,   360
Deem ye what bounds the rival realms divide?
Or ere the jealous queens of nations greet,
Doth Tayo[9] interpose his mighty tide?
Or dark Sierras rise in craggy pride?
Or fence of art, like China's vasty wall?—   365
Ne barrier wall, ne river deep and wide,
Ne horrid crags, nor mountains dark and tall,
Rise like the rocks that part Hispania's land from Gaul:

33

But these between a silver streamlet glides,
And scarce a name distinguisheth the brook,   370
Though rival kingdoms press its verdant sides.
Here leans the idle shepherd on his crook,
And vacant on the rippling waves doth look,
That peaceful still 'twixt bitterest foemen flow;
For proud each peasant as the noblest duke: 375
Well doth the Spanish hind the difference know
'Twixt him and Lusian slave, the lowest of the low.[1]

8. In 1808 Napoleon had forced Charles IV to abdicate the Spanish throne and had placed his own
   brother, Joseph, as king in Spain. The Spanish resented and violently resisted French occupation
   of their country throughout the Peninsular War (1808–14).
9. The Tagus River.
1. "As I found the Portuguese, so have I characterised them. That they are since improved, at least
   in courage, is evident. The late exploits of Lord Wellington have effaced the follies of Cintra. He
   has, indeed, done wonders: he has, perhaps, changed the character of a nation, reconciled rival
   superstitions, and baffled an enemy who never retreated before his predecessors.—1812." Byron
   had suppressed all but the first two sentences of this note; 1832 restored it from a manuscript.

34

But ere the mingling bounds have far been pass'd
Dark Guadiana[2] rolls his power along
In sullen billows, murmuring and vast,   380
So noted ancient roundelays among.
Whilome upon his banks did legions throng
Of Moor and Knight, in mailed splendour drest:
Here ceased the swift their race, here sunk the strong;[3]
The Paynim turban and the Christian crest   385
Mix'd on the bleeding stream,[4] by floating hosts oppress'd.

35

Oh, lovely Spain! renown'd, romantic land!
Where is that standard which Pelagio bore,
When Cava's traitor-sire first call'd the band
That dyed thy mountain streams with Gothic gore?[5]   390
Where are those bloody banners which of yore
Waved o'er thy sons, victorious to the gale,
And drove at last the spoilers to their shore?[6]
Red gleam'd the cross, and waned the crescent pale,
While Afric's echoes thrill'd with Moorish matrons' wail.   395

36

Teems not each ditty with the glorious tale?
Ah! such, alas! the hero's amplest fate!
When granite moulders and when records fail,
A peasant's plaint prolongs his dubious date.
Pride! bend thine eye from heaven to thine estate;   400
See how the Mighty shrink into a song!
Can Volume, Pillar, Pile preserve thee great?
Or must thou trust Tradition's simple tongue,
When Flattery sleeps with thee, and History does thee wrong?

37

Awake, ye sons of Spain! awake! advance![7]   405
Lo! Chivalry, your ancient goddess, cries,
But wields not, as of old, her thirsty lance,
Nor shakes her crimson plumage in the skies:

2. Spanish river flowing into Portugal.
3. Cf. Ecclesiastes 9.11: "The race is not to the swift, nor the battle to the strong. . . ."
4. Refers to the wars of liberation of the Spaniards ("Christian") from Moorish ("Paynim") occupation.
5. "Count Julian's daughter, the Helen of Spain. Pelagius preserved his independence in the fastnesses of the Asturias, and the descendants of his followers, after some centuries, completed their struggle by the conquest of Grenada." Count Julian of Ceuta (Cava) in 711 aided the Muslim invasion of Spain. This invasion was resisted heroically by the Christian king Pelagio (Pelayo), who ruled 718–37.
6. Ferdinand and Isabella expelled the Moors in 1492.
7. Stanzas 37–42 refer to a bloody battle between French and English troops fought at the town of Talavera de la Reina, near Madrid, on July 27–28, 1809.

Now on the smoke of blazing bolts she flies,
And speaks in thunder through yon engine's roar: 410
In every peal she calls—'Awake! arise!'
Say, is her voice more feeble than of yore,
When her war-song was heard on Andalusia's[8] shore?

38

Hark! heard you not those hoofs of dreadful note?
Sounds not the clang of conflict on the heath?   415
Saw ye not whom the reeking sabre smote;
Nor saved your brethren ere they sank beneath
Tyrants and tyrants' slaves?—the fires of death,
The bale-fires flash on high:—from rock to rock
Each volley tells that thousands cease to breathe;   420
Death rides upon the sulphury Siroc,[9]
Red Battle stamps his foot, and nations feel the shock.

39

Lo! where the Giant[1] on the mountain stands,
His blood-red tresses deep'ning in the sun,
With death-shot glowing in his fiery hands,   425
And eye that scorcheth all it glares upon;
Restless it rolls, now fix'd, and now anon
Flashing afar,—and at his iron feet
Destruction cowers, to mark what deeds are done;
For on this morn three potent nations meet,   430
To shed before his shrine the blood he deems most sweet.

40

By Heaven! it is a splendid sight to see
(For one who hath no friend, no brother there)
Their rival scarfs of mix'd embroidery,
Their various arms that glitter in the air!   435
What gallant war-hounds rouse them from their lair,
And gnash their fangs, loud yelling for the prey!
All join the chase, but few the triumph share;
The Grave shall bear the chiefest prize away,
And Havoc scarce for joy can number their array.   440

41

Three hosts combine to offer sacrifice;
Three tongues prefer strange orisons[2] on high;
Three gaudy standards flout the pale blue skies;
The shouts are France, Spain, Albion, Victory!

8. A region in southern Spain.
9. The Sirocco, the hot southern wind of the Mediterranean area.
1. Both a cannon and, figuratively, the gigantic power of Napoleonic France.
2. Prayers.

The foe, the victim, and the fond ally   445
That fights for all, but ever fights in vain,
Are met—as if at home they could not die—
To feed the crow on Talavera's[3] plain,
And fertilize the field that each pretends to gain.

42

There shall they rot—Ambition's honour'd fools!   450
Yes, Honour decks the turf that wraps their clay!
Vain Sophistry! in these behold the tools,
The broken tools, that tyrants cast away
By myriads, when they dare to pave their way
With human hearts—to what?—a dream alone.   455
Can despots compass aught that hails their sway?
Or call with truth one span of earth their own,
Save that wherein at last they crumble bone by bone?

43

Oh, Albuera,[4] glorious field of grief!
As o'er thy plain the Pilgrim[5] prick'd his steed,   460
Who could foresee thee, in a space so brief,
A scene where mingling foes should boast and bleed!
Peace to the perish'd! may the warrior's meed[6]
And tears of triumph their reward prolong!
Till others fall where other chieftains lead,   465
Thy name shall circle round the gaping throng,
And shine in worthless lays, the theme of transient song.

44

Enough of Battle's minions! let them play
Their game of lives, and barter breath for fame:
Fame that will scarce re-animate their clay,   470
Though thousands fall to deck some single name.
In sooth 'twere sad to thwart their noble aim
Who strike, blest hirelings! for their country's good,
And die, that living might have proved her shame;
Perish'd, perchance, in some domestic feud,   475
Or in a narrower sphere wild Rapine's path pursued.

45

Full swiftly Harold wends his lonely way
Where proud Sevilla triumphs unsubdued:
Yet is she free—the spoiler's wish'd-for prey!

---

3. See p. 38, n. 7.
4. A Spanish town where the British, Spanish, and Portuguese forces defeated the French army on May 16, 1811, all suffering severe losses.
5. Harold.
6. Reward.

Soon, soon shall Conquest's fiery foot intrude,   480
Blackening her lovely domes with traces rude.
Inevitable hour! 'Gainst fate to strive
Where Desolation plants her famish'd brood
Is vain, or Ilion, Tyre[7] might yet survive,
And Virtue vanquish all, and Murder cease to thrive.   485

46

But all unconscious of the coming doom,
The feast, the song, the revel here abounds;
Strange modes of merriment the hours consume,
Nor bleed these patriots with their country's wounds:
Nor here War's clarion, but Love's rebeck[8] sounds;   490
Here Folly still his votaries inthralls;
And young-eyed Lewdness walks her midnight rounds:
Girt with the silent crimes of Capitals,
Still to the last kind Vice clings to the tott'ring walls.

47

Not so the rustic—with his trembling mate   495
He lurks, nor casts his heavy eye afar,
Lest he should view his vineyard desolate,
Blasted below the dun hot breath of war.
No more beneath soft Eve's consenting star
Fandango[9] twirls his jocund castanet: 500
Ah, monarchs! could ye taste the mirth ye mar,
Not in the toils of Glory would ye fret;
The hoarse dull drum would sleep, and Man be happy yet!

48

How carols now the lusty muleteer?
Of love, romance, devotion is his lay,   505
As whilome he was wont the leagues to cheer,
His quick bells wildly jingling on the way?
No! as he speeds, he chants "Vivā el Rey!"[1]
And checks his song to execrate Godoy,
The royal wittol Charles, and curse the day   510

---

7. Ilion (Ilium, or Troy) and Tyre were splendid ancient cities whose falls have been the subject of
   moralizing reflections.
8. A Renaissance stringed musical instrument.
9. Lively Spanish dance, with dancer playing castanets.
1. "Vivā el Rey Fernando!' Long live King Ferdinand! is the chorus of most of the Spanish patriotic
   songs. They are chiefly in dispraise of the old King Charles, the Queen, and the Prince of Peace.
   I have heard many of them: some of the airs are beautiful. Don Manuel Godoy, the *Principe de la
   Paz*, of an ancient but decayed family, was born at Badajoz, on the frontiers of Portugal, and was
   originally in the ranks of the Spanish guards; till his person attracted the queen's eyes, and raised
   him to the dukedom of Alcudia, &c. &c. It is to this man that the Spaniards universally impute the
   ruin of their country." After Napoleon had replaced Charles IV with his brother, Joseph Bonaparte,
   Spanish resistance to French occupation centered around loyalty to the rightful, exiled king,
   Charles's son Ferdinand VII. It was Godoy, the Spanish diplomat and queen's lover, who first per-
   suaded Charles (the "wittol" or fool) to join in European resistance to the French Revolution in
   1793 and who in 1807–08 was instrumental in furthering French occupation of Spain.

When first Spain's queen beheld the black-eyed boy,
And gore-faced Treason sprung from her adulterate joy.

49

On yon long, level plain, at distance crown'd
With crags, whereon those Moorish turrets rest,
Wide scatter'd hoof-marks dint the wounded ground;   515
And, scathed by fire, the greensward's darken'd vest
Tells that the foe was Andalusia's guest:
Here was the camp, the watch-flame, and the host,
Here the bold peasant storm'd the dragon's nest;
Still does he mark it with triumphant boast,   520
And points to yonder cliffs, which oft were won and lost.

50

And whomsoe'er along the path you meet
Bears in his cap the badge of crimson hue,
Which tells you whom to shun and whom to greet:[2]
Woe to the man that walks in public view   525
Without of loyalty this token true:
Sharp is the knife, and sudden is the stroke;
And sorely would the Gallic[3] foeman rue,
If subtle poniards, wrapt beneath the cloke,
Could blunt the sabre's edge, or clear the cannon's smoke.   530

51

At every turn Morena's[4] dusky height
Sustains aloft the battery's iron load;
And, far as mortal eye can compass sight,
The mountain-howitzer, the broken road,
The bristling palisade, the fosse o'erflow'd,   535
The station'd bands, the never-vacant watch,
The magazine in rocky durance stow'd,
The holster'd steed beneath the shed of thatch,
The ball-piled pyramid,[5] the ever-blazing match,

52

Portend the deeds to come:—but he whose nod   540
Has tumbled feebler despots from their sway,
A moment pauseth ere he lifts the rod;
A little moment deigneth to delay:
Soon will his legions sweep through these their way;

2. "The red cockade, with 'Fernando VII,' in the centre." Refers to the restoration of Ferdinand VII
   in 1812.
3. French.
4. The mountain chain, chief bastion of the city of Seville's resistance to French siege.
5. "All who have seen a battery will recollect the pyramidal form in which shot and shells are piled.
   The Sierra Morena was fortified in every defile through which I passed in my way to Seville."

The West must own the Scourger[6] of the world.   545
Ah! Spain! how sad will be thy reckoning-day,
When soars Gaul's Vulture, with his wings unfurl'd,
And thou shalt view thy sons in crowds to Hades hurl'd.

53

And must they fall? the young, the proud, the brave,
To swell one bloated Chief's unwholesome reign?   550
No step between submission and a grave?
The rise of rapine and the fall of Spain?
And doth the Power that man adores ordain
Their doom, nor heed the suppliant's appeal?
Is all that desperate Valour acts in vain?   555
And Counsel sage, and patriotic Zeal,
The Veteran's skill, Youth's fire, and Manhood's heart of steel?

54

Is it for this the Spanish maid,[7] aroused,
Hangs on the willow her unstrung guitar,
And, all unsex'd, the anlace[8] hath espoused,   560
Sung the loud song, and dared the deed of war?
And she, whom once the semblance of a scar
Appall'd, an owlet's larum chill'd with dread,
Now views the column-scattering bay'net jar,
The falchion[9] flash, and o'er the yet warm dead   565
Stalks with Minerva's step where Mars[1] might quake to tread.

55

Ye who shall marvel when you hear her tale,
Oh! had you known her in her softer hour,
Mark'd her black eye that mocks her coal-black veil,
Heard her light, lively tones in Lady's bower,   570
Seen her long locks that foil the painter's power,
Her fairy form, with more than female grace,
Scarce would you deem that Saragoza's tower
Beheld her smile in Danger's Gorgon[2] face,
Thin the closed ranks, and lead in Glory's fearful chase.   575

56

Her lover sinks—she sheds no ill-timed tear;
Her chief is slain—she fills his fatal post;
Her fellows flee—she checks their base career;

6. Napoleon—"Gaul's Vulture" (line 547) and the "bloated Chief" (line 550).
7. Augustina, the "Maid of Saragoza." In 1808 in Saragoza (Saragossa), capital of the province of Aragon in Spain, the citizens, including the women, successfully held off an invading French army.
8. A long, tapering dagger.
9. A broad sword.
1. In Roman myth, Minerva was goddess of wisdom and Mars god of war.
2. In classical myth, a female monster whose gaze turned men to stone.

The foe retires—she heads the sallying host:
Who can appease like her a lover's ghost?   580
Who can avenge so well a leader's fall?
What maid retrieve when man's flush'd hope is lost?
Who hang so fiercely on the flying Gaul,
Foil'd by a woman's hand, before a batter'd wall?[3]

57

Yet are Spain's maids no race of Amazons,[4]   585
But form'd for all the witching arts of love:
Though thus in arms they emulate her sons,
And in the horrid phalanx dare to move,
'Tis but the tender fierceness of the dove,
Pecking the hand that hovers o'er her mate: 590
In softness as in firmness far above
Remoter females, famed for sickening prate;[5]
Her mind is nobler sure, her charms perchance as great.

58

The seal Love's dimpling finger hath impress'd
Denotes how soft that chin which bears his touch:[6]   595
Her lips, whose kisses pout to leave their nest,
Bid man be valiant ere he merit such:
Her glance how wildly beautiful! how much
Hath Phoebus[7] woo'd in vain to spoil her cheek,
Which glows yet smoother from his amorous clutch!   600
Who round the North for paler dames would seek?
How poor their forms appear! how languid, wan, and weak!

59

Match me, ye climes! which poets love to laud;
Match me, ye harams of the land! where now[8]
I strike my strain, far distant, to applaud   605
Beauties that ev'n a cynic must avow;
Match me those Houries,[9] whom ye scarce allow
To taste the gale lest Love should ride the wind,
With Spain's dark-glancing daughters—deign to know,

---

3. "Such were the exploits of the Maid of Saragoza, who by her valour elevated herself to the highest rank of heroines. When the author was at Seville she walked daily on the Prado, decorated with medals and orders, by command of the Junta."
4. The famous woman warriors of classical myth.
5. One of numerous unflattering references to English society women found in Byron's poetry and letters.
6. "'Sigilla in mento impressa Amoris digitulo / Vestigio demonstrant mollitudinem.'" AUL. GEL.
   Marks imprinted on the chin by the delicate finger of Love / Indicate softness in their traces; from *Papiapapae*, comedy by Marcus Terentius Varro (b. 116 B.C.E.); quoted by Aulus Gelius (b. ca. 135 C.E.) in *Noctes Atticae*. (Translation and Editor's note based on *Cochran*.)
7. Apollo, in his role as sun god; in the lines that follow Byron disparages the English aristocratic bias for fair-skinned women.
8. "This stanza was written in Turkey." (Byron's note on the fair copy continues, "with the greater part of the poem.")
9. A harem of angelic concubines promised in the Koran to the faithful after death.

There your wise Prophet's paradise we find,   610
His black-eyed maids of Heaven, angelically kind.

60

Oh, thou Parnassus![1] whom I now survey,
Not in the phrensy of a dreamer's eye,
Not in the fabled landscape of a lay,
But soaring snow-clad through thy native sky,   615
In the wild pomp of mountain majesty!
What marvel if I thus essay to sing?
The humblest of thy pilgrims passing by
Would gladly woo thine Echoes with his string,
Though from thy heights no more one Muse will wave
        her wing.   620

61

Oft have I dream'd of Thee! whose glorious name
Who knows not, knows not man's divinest lore:
And now I view thee, 'tis, alas! with shame
That I in feeblest accents must adore.
When I recount thy worshippers of yore   625
I tremble, and can only bend the knee;
Nor raise my voice, nor vainly dare to soar,
But gaze beneath thy cloudy canopy
In silent joy to think at last I look on Thee!

62

Happier in this than mightiest bards have been,   630
Whose fate to distant homes confined their lot,
Shall I unmoved behold the hallow'd scene,
Which others rave of, though they know it not?
Though here no more Apollo haunts his grot,
And thou, the Muses' seat, art now their grave,   635
Some gentle Spirit still pervades the spot,
Sighs in the gale, keeps silence in the cave,
And glides with glassy foot o'er yon melodious wave.

63

Of thee hereafter.—Ev'n amidst my strain
I turn'd aside to pay my homage here;   640
Forgot the land, the sons, the maids of Spain;
Her fate, to every freeborn bosom dear;
And hail'd thee, not perchance without a tear.
Now to my theme—but from thy holy haunt
Let me some remnant, some memorial bear;   645

---

1. "These stanzas [60–64] were written in Castri (Delphos), at the foot of Parnassus, now called
Λιακυρά (Liakura), Dec. 1809." Parnassus was the Greek mountain sacred to the Muses and to
the god of poetry, Apollo.

Yield me one leaf of Daphne's[2] deathless plant,
Nor let thy votary's hope be deem'd an idle vaunt.

64

But ne'er didst thou, fair Mount! when Greece was young,
See round thy giant base a brighter choir,
Nor e'er did Delphi, when her priestess sung   650
The Pythian[3] hymn with more than mortal fire,
Behold a train more fitting to inspire
The song of love than Andalusia's maids,
Nurst in the glowing lap of soft desire:
Ah! that to these were given such peaceful shades   655
As Greece can still bestow, though Glory fly her glades.

65

Fair is proud Seville; let her country boast
Her strength, her wealth, her site of ancient days;[4]
But Cadiz, rising on the distant coast,
Calls forth a sweeter, though ignoble praise.   660
Ah, Vice! how soft are thy voluptuous ways!
While boyish blood is mantling, who can 'scape
The fascination of thy magic gaze?
A Cherub-hydra[5] round us dost thou gape,
And mould to every taste thy dear delusive shape.   665

66

When Paphos[6] fell by time—accursed Time!
The Queen who conquers all must yield to thee—
The Pleasures fled, but sought as warm a clime;
And Venus, constant to her native sea,
To nought else constant, hither deign'd to flee;   670
And fix'd her shrine within these walls of white;
Though not to one dome circumscribeth she
Her worship, but, devoted to her rite,
A thousand altars rise, for ever blazing bright.

67

From morn till night, from night till startled Morn[7]   675
Peeps blushing on the revel's laughing crew,
The song is heard, the rosy garland worn;

2. Daphne, pursued by Apollo, was saved by being transformed into a laurel tree, an evergreen (Ovid, *Metamorphoses* 1).
3. From Pythios, an older name of Apollo's sacred grove, Delphi.
4. "Seville was the Hispalis of the Romans."
5. Cadiz, city of vice, is imagined by Byron as a combination of beautiful boy (cherub) and mythic, many-headed serpent.
6. Island sacred to Venus, Roman goddess of love, the "Queen" of the next line.
7. Echoes Milton, *Paradise Lost* I.742–43: ". . . from morn / To noon he fell, from noon to dewy eve."

Devices quaint, and frolics ever new,
Tread on each other's kibes.[8] A long adieu
He bids to sober joy that here sojourns: 680
Nought interrupts the riot, though in lieu
Of true devotion monkish incense burns,
And Love and Prayer unite, or rule the hour by turns.

68

The Sabbath comes, a day of blessed rest;
What hallows it upon this Christian shore?   685
Lo! it is sacred to a solemn feast;[9]
Hark! heard you not the forest-monarch's roar?
Crashing the lance, he snuffs the spouting gore
Of man and steed, o'erthrown beneath his horn;
The throng'd arena shakes with shouts for more;   690
Yells the mad crowd o'er entrails freshly torn,
Nor shrinks the female eye, nor ev'n affects to mourn.

69

The seventh day this; the jubilee of man.
London! right well thou know'st the day of prayer:
Then thy spruce citizen, wash'd artisan,   695
And smug apprentice gulp their weekly air:
Thy coach of hackney, whiskey,[1] one-horse chair,
And humblest gig through sundry suburbs whirl,
To Hampstead, Brentford, Harrow make repair;
Till the tired jade the wheel forgets to hurl,   700
Provoking envious gibe from each pedestrian churl.

70

Some o'er thy Thamis[2] row the ribbon'd fair,
Others along the safer turnpike fly;
Some Richmond-hill ascend, some scud to Ware,
And many to the steep of Highgate hie.   705
Ask ye, Boeotian shades! the reason why?[3]
'Tis to the worship of the solemn Horn,[4]
Grasp'd in the holy hand of Mystery,
In whose dread name both men and maids are sworn,
And consecrate the oath with draught, and dance till morn.   710

---

8. Boils or blisters on the feet; cf. *Hamlet* 5.1.129–30: "the toe of the peasant comes so near the heel of the courtier he galls his kibe."
9. Sarcastic, referring to a bullfight; in the next line, the "forest-monarch" is the bull in the ring.
1. A light carriage.
2. The river Thames in London, along with "Richmond-hill," "Ware," and "Highgate" (lines 704–05), a popular London scene of Sunday recreation.
3. "This was written at Thebes and consequently in the best situation for asking and answering such a question; not as the birthplace of Pindar, but as the capital of Boeotia, where the first riddle was propounded and solved."
   I.e., the riddle of the Sphinx, solved by Oedipus.
4. The reference is to a popular English drinking game in Byron's day, "swearing on the horns."

71

All have their fooleries—not alike are thine,
Fair Cadiz, rising o'er the dark blue sea!
Soon as the matin bell proclaimeth nine,
Thy saint adorers count the rosary:
Much is the VIRGIN teased to shrive them free   715
(Well do I ween the only virgin there)
From crimes as numerous as her beadsmen be;
Then to the crowded circus forth they fare:
Young, old, high, low, at once the same diversion share.

72

The lists are oped, the spacious area clear'd,   720
Thousands on thousands piled are seated round;
Long ere the first loud trumpet's note is heard,
Ne vacant space for lated wight is found:
Here dons, grandees, but chiefly dames abound,
Skill'd in the ogle of a roguish eye,   725
Yet ever well inclined to heal the wound;
None through their cold disdain are doom'd to die,
As moon-struck bards complain, by Love's sad archery.

73

Hush'd is the din of tongues—on gallant steeds,
With milk-white crest, gold spur, and light-poised lance, 730
Four cavaliers[5] prepare for venturous deeds,
And lowly bending to the lists advance;
Rich are their scarfs, their charges featly prance:
If in the dangerous game they shine to-day,
The crowd's loud shout and ladies' lovely glance,   735
Best prize of better acts, they bear away,
And all that kings or chiefs e'er gain their toils repay.

74

In costly sheen and gaudy cloak array'd,
But all afoot, the light-limb'd Matadore
Stands in the centre, eager to invade   740
The lord of lowing herds; but not before
The ground, with cautious tread, is traversed o'er,
Lest aught unseen should lurk to thwart his speed:
His arms a dart, he fights aloof, nor more
Can man achieve without the friendly steed—   745
Alas! too oft condemn'd for him to bear and bleed.

5. The picadors, who prepare the bull for the matador by taunting and enraging it from horseback.
Byron's precise description of the bullfight is perhaps the most famous passage in Canto I.

75

Thrice sounds the clarion; lo! the signal falls,
The den expands, and Expectation mute
Gapes round the silent circle's peopled walls.
Bounds with one lashing spring the mighty brute,   750
And, wildly staring, spurns, with sounding foot,
The sand, nor blindly rushes on his foe:
Here, there, he points his threatening front, to suit
His first attack, wide waving to and fro
His angry tail; red rolls his eye's dilated glow.   755

76

Sudden he stops; his eye is fix'd: away,
Away, thou heedless boy! prepare the spear:
Now is thy time, to perish, or display
The skill that yet may check his mad career.
With well-timed croupe[6] the nimble coursers veer;   760
On foams the bull, but not unscathed he goes;
Streams from his flank the crimson torrent clear:
He flies, he wheels, distracted with his throes;
Dart follows dart; lance, lance; loud bellowings speak his woes.

77

Again he comes; nor dart nor lance avail,   765
Nor the wild plunging of the tortured horse;
Though man and man's avenging arms assail,
Vain are his weapons, vainer is his force.
One gallant steed is stretch'd a mangled corse;
Another, hideous sight! unseam'd appears,   770
His gory chest unveils life's panting source;
Though death-struck, still his feeble frame he rears;
Staggering, but stemming all, his lord unharm'd he bears.

78

Foil'd, bleeding, breathless, furious to the last,
Full in the centre stands the bull at bay,   775
Mid wounds, and clinging darts, and lances brast,[7]
And foes disabled in the brutal fray:
And now the Matadores[8] around him play,
Shake the red cloak, and poise the ready brand:
Once more through all he bursts his thundering way—   780
Vain rage! the mantle quits the conynge[9] hand,
Wraps his fierce eye—'tis past—he sinks upon the sand!

---

6. Horse's hindquarters; Byron means *croupade*, a horse's high leap in which the hind legs are brought up under the belly.
7. Broken.
8. Byron conflates the cloak-waving *chulos* and the single matador who kills the bull.
9. Cunning.

79

Where his vast neck just mingles with the spine,
Sheathed in his form the deadly weapon lies.
He stops—he starts—disdaining to decline: 785
Slowly he falls, amidst triumphant cries,
Without a groan, without a struggle dies.
The decorated car appears—on high
The corse is piled—sweet sight for vulgar eyes—
Four steeds that spurn the rein, as swift as shy,   790
Hurl the dark bulk along, scarce seen in dashing by.

80

Such the ungentle sport that oft invites
The Spanish maid, and cheers the Spanish swain.
Nurtured in blood betimes, his heart delights
In vengeance, gloating on another's pain.   795
What private feuds the troubled village stain!
Though now one phalanx'd host should meet the foe,
Enough, alas! in humble homes remain,
To meditate 'gainst friends the secret blow,
For some slight cause of wrath, whence life's warm stream
        must flow.   800

81

But Jealousy has fled: his bars, his bolts,
His wither'd centinel, Duenna[1] sage!
And all whereat the generous soul revolts,
Which the stern dotard deem'd he could encage,
Have pass'd to darkness with the vanish'd age.   805
Who late so free as Spanish girls were seen
(Ere War uprose in his volcanic rage),
With braided tresses bounding o'er the green,
While on the gay dance shone Night's lover-loving Queen?

82

Oh! many a time, and oft, had Harold loved,   810
Or dream'd he loved, since Rapture is a dream;
But now his wayward bosom was unmoved,
For not yet had he drunk of Lethe's[2] stream;
And lately had he learn'd with truth to deem
Love has no gift so grateful as his wings: 815
How fair, how young, how soft soe'er he seem,
Full from the fount of Joy's delicious springs
Some bitter o'er the flowers its bubbling venom flings.[3]

1. An aged female escort for a Spanish lady of high birth, proverbial for sexual repression or prudery.
2. The river of forgetfulness in the classical underworld.
3. "'Medio de fonte leporum,'" &c.—Luc[retius, *De rerum natura* 4.1133–34]." ("From the heart of
    the fountain of delight rises a jet of bitterness that tortures us among the very flowers.")

83

Yet to the beauteous form he was not blind,
Though now it moved him as it moves the wise;   820
Not that Philosophy on such a mind
E'er deign'd to bend her chastely-awful eyes:
But Passion raves herself[4] to rest, or flies;
And Vice, that digs her own voluptuous tomb,
Had buried long his hopes, no more to rise: 825
Pleasure's pall'd victim! life-abhorring gloom
Wrote on his faded brow curst Cain's unresting doom.[5]

84

Still he beheld, nor mingled with the throng;
But view'd them not with misanthropic hate:
Fain would he now have join'd the dance, the song;   830
But who may smile that sinks beneath his fate?
Nought that he saw his sadness could abate:
Yet once he struggled 'gainst the demon's sway,
And as in Beauty's bower he pensive sate,
Pour'd forth this unpremeditated lay,   835
To charms as fair as those that soothed his happier day.

To Inez[6]

1

Nay, smile not at my sullen brow;
Alas! I cannot smile again:
Yet Heaven avert that ever thou
Shouldst weep, and haply weep in vain.   840

2

And dost thou ask, what secret woe
I bear, corroding joy and youth?
And wilt thou vainly seek to know
A pang, ev'n thou must fail to soothe?

3

It is not love, it is not hate,   845
Nor low Ambition's honours lost,
That bids me loathe my present state,
And fly from all I prized the most:

---

4. itself (1832, based on a transcript by Dallas).
5. The reference to Cain, who in Genesis 4 is condemned to wander the earth, marked forever as a sinner for the murder of his brother, Abel, is an important one. The figure of the exile, outcast, criminal, wanderer, and/or guilt-ridden individual recurs both in Byron's poetry (e.g., not only in his play *Cain* but in *Manfred, Prometheus*, the tales, and even perhaps in comic form in *Don Juan*) and in Romantic literature generally (e.g., Coleridge's *Rime of the Ancient Mariner* and Mary Shelley's *Frankenstein*).
6. These stanzas were probably addressed to Teresa Macri, one of the three daughters of Byron's landlady in Athens; then only twelve years old, she is also the subject of "Maid of Athens" (p. 18).

4

It is that weariness which springs
   From all I meet, or hear, or see: 850
To me no pleasure Beauty brings;
   Thine eyes have scarce a charm for me.

5

It is that settled, ceaseless gloom
   The fabled Hebrew wanderer[7] bore;
That will not look beyond the tomb,   855
   But cannot hope for rest before.

6

What Exile from himself can flee?
   To zones, though more and more remote,
Still, still pursues, where-e'er I be,
   The blight of life—the demon Thought.   860

7

Yet others rapt in pleasure seem,
   And taste of all that I forsake;
Oh! may they still of transport dream,
   And ne'er, at least like me, awake!

8

Through many a clime 'tis mine to go,   865
   With many a retrospection curst;
And all my solace is to know,
   Whate'er betides, I've known the worst.

9

What is that worst? Nay do not ask—
   In pity from the search forbear: 870
Smile on—nor venture to unmask
   Man's heart, and view the Hell that's there.

85

Adieu, fair Cadiz! yea, a long adieu!
Who may forget how well thy walls have stood?
When all were changing thou alone wert true,   875
First to be free and last to be subdued:
And if amidst a scene, a shock so rude,
Some native blood was seen thy streets to dye,

---

7. The "wandering Jew" of medieval legend, who, for cursing Christ at the crucifixion, was con-
demned to wander the earth for all time seeking the gift of death and peace. Compare "Cain's
unresting doom," line 827 and note.

A traitor only fell beneath the feud;[8]
Here all were noble, save Nobility;   880
None hugg'd a conqueror's chain, save fallen Chivalry!

86

Such be the sons of Spain, and strange her fate!
They fight for freedom who were never free,
A Kingless people for a nerveless state;
Her vassals combat when their chieftains flee,   885
True to the veriest slaves of Treachery:
Fond of a land which gave them nought but life,
Pride points the path that leads to Liberty;
Back to the struggle, baffled in the strife,
War, war is still the cry, 'War even to the knife!'[9]   890

87

Ye, who would more of Spain and Spaniards know,
Go, read whate'er is writ of bloodiest strife:
Whate'er keen Vengeance urged on foreign foe
Can act, is acting there against man's life:
From flashing scimitar to secret knife,   895
War mouldeth there each weapon to his need—
So may he guard the sister and the wife,
So may he make each curst oppressor bleed,
So may such foes deserve the most remorseless deed!

88

Flows there a tear of pity for the dead?   900
Look o'er the ravage of the reeking plain;
Look on the hands with female slaughter red;
Then to the dogs resign the unburied slain,
Then to the vulture let each corse remain;
Albeit unworthy of the prey-bird's maw,   905
Let their bleach'd bones, and blood's unbleaching stain,
Long mark the battle-field with hideous awe:
Thus only may our sons conceive the scenes we saw!

89

Nor yet, alas! the dreadful work is done;
Fresh legions pour adown the Pyrenees;   910
It deepens still, the work is scarce begun,
Nor mortal eye the distant end foresees.
Fall'n nations gaze on Spain; if freed, she frees
More than her fell Pizarros[1] once enchain'd:

8. "Alluding to the conduct and death of Solano, the governor of Cadiz, in May, 1809."
9. "'War to the knife.' Palafox's answer to the French general at the siege of Saragoza."
1. Francisco Pizarro, the sixteenth-century conqueror of Peru, led the Incas ("Quito's sons") into bondage; now Spain herself is in bondage while America (Columbia) is thriving, liberated from European rule.

Strange retribution! now Columbia's ease   915
Repairs the wrongs that Quito's sons sustain'd,
While o'er the parent clime prowls Murder unrestrain'd.

90

Not all the blood at Talavera[2] shed,
Not all the marvels of Barossa's fight,
Not Albuera lavish of the dead,   920
Have won for Spain her well asserted right.
When shall her Olive-Branch be free from blight?
When shall she breathe her from the blushing toil?
How many a doubtful day shall sink in night,
Ere the Frank robber turn him from his spoil,   925
And Freedom's stranger-tree grow native of the soil!

91

And thou, my friend![3]—since unavailing woe
Bursts from my heart, and mingles with the strain—
Had the sword laid thee with the mighty low,
Pride might forbid e'en Friendship to complain: 930
But thus unlaurel'd to descend in vain,
By all forgotten, save the lonely breast,
And mix unbleeding with the boasted slain,
While Glory crowns so many a meaner crest!
What hadst thou done to sink so peacefully to rest?   935

92

Oh, known the earliest, and esteem'd the most!
Dear to a heart where nought was left so dear!
Though to my hopeless days for ever lost,
In dreams deny me not to see thee here!
And Morn in secret shall renew the tear   940
Of Consciousness awaking to her woes,
And Fancy hover o'er thy bloodless bier,

---

2. Like Talavera and Albuera (stanzas 37–44), Barossa was the site of a battle (on March 5, 1811) in the Peninsular War with France.
3. "The Honourable John Wingfield, of the Guards, who died of a fever at Coimbra. I had known him ten years, the better half of his life, and the happiest part of mine. In the short space of one month, I have lost *her* who gave me being, and most of those who had made that being tolerable. To me the lines of Young are no fiction:—

> 'Insatiate archer: could not one suffice?
> Thy shaft flew thrice, and thrice my peace was slain,
> And thrice ere thrice yon moon had fill'd her horn.'

I should have ventured a verse to the memory of the late Charles Skinner Matthews, Fellow of Downing College, Cambridge, were he not too much above all praise of mine. His powers of mind, shown in the attainment of greater honours, against the ablest candidates, than those of any graduate on record at Cambridge, have sufficiently established his fame on the spot where it was acquired; while his softer qualities live in the recollection of friends who loved him too well to envy his superiority." Wingfield died in May 1811 and Matthews in August 1811. During the same summer and fall, while Byron was making his final corrections to Cantos I–II, he learned of the deaths of his mother and two other close friends, one of whom was his beloved Cambridge chorister, John Edelston, subject of *Childe Harold* II, stanzas 95–96, and the "Thyrza" lyrics (e.g., "To Thyrza" [p. 98]).

Till my frail frame return to whence it rose,
And mourn'd and mourner lie united in repose.

93

Here is one fytte[4] of Harold's pilgrimage: 945
Ye who of him may further seek to know,
Shall find some tidings in a future page,
If he that rhymeth now may scribble moe.
Is this too much? stern Critic! say not so:
Patience! and ye shall hear what he beheld   950
In other lands, where he was doom'd to go:
Lands that contain the monuments of Eld,
Ere Greece and Grecian arts by barbarous hands[5] were quell'd.

CANTO THE SECOND

1

Come, blue-eyed maid of heaven![1]—but thou, alas!
Didst never yet one mortal song inspire—
Goddess of Wisdom! here thy temple was,
And is, despite of war and wasting fire,[2]
And years, that bade thy worship to expire: 5
But worse than steel, and flame, and ages slow,
Is the dread sceptre and dominion dire
Of men who never felt the sacred glow
That thoughts of thee and thine on polish'd breasts bestow.

2

Ancient of days! august Athena![3] where,   10
Where are thy men of might? thy grand in soul?

---

4. Medieval word for "canto" or "section."
5. The Turks.
1. Athena (Homeric epithet).
2. "Part of the Acropolis was destroyed by the explosion of a magazine during the Venetian siege." In 1687, the Venetians bombarded the Turks.
3. "We can all feel, or imagine, the regret with which the ruins of cities once the capitals of empires, are beheld: the reflections suggested by such objects are too trite to require recapitulation. But never did the littleness of man, and the vanity of his very best virtues, of patriotism to exalt, and of valour to defend his country, appear more conspicuous than in the record of what Athens was, and the certainty of what she now is. This theatre of contention between mighty factions, of the struggles of orators, the exaltation and deposition of tyrants, the triumph and punishment of generals, is now become a scene of petty intrigue and perpetual disturbance, between the bickering agents of certain British nobility and gentry. The wild foxes, the owls and serpents in the ruins of Babylon,' were surely less degrading than such inhabitants. The Turks have the plea of conquest for their tyranny, and the Greeks have only suffered the fortune of war, incidental to the bravest; but how are the mighty fallen, when two painters contest the privilege of plundering the Parthenon, and triumph in turn, according to the tenor of each succeeding firman! Sylla could but punish, Philip subdue, and Xerxes burn Athens; but it remained for the paltry antiquarian, and his despicable agents, to render her contemptible as himself and his pursuits. The Parthenon, before its destruction in part, by fire during the Venetian siege, had been a temple, a church, and a mosque. In each point of view it is an object of regard: it changed its worshippers; but still it was a place of worship thrice sacred to devotion: its violation is a triple sacrilege. But—

> Man, proud man.
> Drest in a little brief authority,
> Plays such fantastic tricks before high heaven
> As make the angels weep.' "

Gone—glimmering through the dream of things that were:
First in the race that led to Glory's goal,
They won, and pass'd away—is this the whole
A schoolboy's tale, the wonder of an hour!   15
The warrior's weapon and the sophist's stole[4]
Are sought in vain, and o'er each mouldering tower,
Dim with the mist of years, gray flits the shade of power.

3

Son of the morning,[5] rise! approach you here!
Come—but molest not yon defenceless urn: 20
Look on this spot—a nation's sepulchre!
Abode of gods, whose shrines no longer burn.
Even gods must yield—religions take their turn:
'Twas Jove's—'tis Mahomet's—and other creeds
Will rise with other years, till man shall learn   25
Vainly his incense soars, his victim bleeds;
Poor child of Doubt and Death, whose hope is built on reeds.[6]

4

Bound to the earth, he lifts his eye to heaven—
Is't not enough, unhappy thing! to know
Thou art? Is this a boon so kindly given,   30
That being, thou would'st be again, and go,
Thou know'st not, reck'st not to what region, so
On earth no more, but mingled with the skies?
Still wilt thou dream on future joy and woe?
Regard and weigh yon dust before it flies: 35
That little urn saith more than thousand homilies.

5

Or burst the vanish'd Hero's lofty mound;
Far on the solitary shore he sleeps:[7]
He fell, and falling nations mourn'd around;
But now not one of saddening thousands weeps,   40
Nor warlike-worshipper his vigil keeps
Where demi-gods appear'd, as records tell.
Remove yon skull from out the scatter'd heaps:
Is that a temple[8] where a God may dwell?
Why ev'n the worm at last disdains her shatter'd cell!   45

---

4. Short cloak worn by the group of ancient Athenian philosophers known as Sophists.
5. I.e., man, or specifically here a person from the Levant, or lands on the Mediterranean Sea's eastern coast; also, epithet for Lucifer, the fallen angel of exalted aspirations, in Isaiah 14.12.
6. On the advice of his friend and literary agent, Robert Dallas, Byron withdrew a paragraph-length note criticizing religion; it is printed in Dallas, *Recollections*, pp. 171–72.
7. "It was not always the custom of the Greeks to burn their dead; the greater Ajax, in particular, was interred entire. Almost all the chiefs became gods after their decease; and he was indeed neglected, who had not annual games near his tomb, or festivals in honour of his memory by his countrymen, as Achilles, Brasidas, &c. and at last even Antinous, whose death was as heroic as his life was infamous."
8. The Parthenon, temple of Athena, on the Acropolis in Athens.

6

Look on its broken arch, its ruin'd wall,
Its chambers desolate, and portals foul:
Yes, this was once Ambition's airy hall,
The dome of Thought, the palace of the Soul:
Behold through each lack-lustre, eyeless hole,   50
The gay recess of Wisdom and of Wit
And Passion's host, that never brook'd control:
Can all saint, sage, or sophist ever writ,
People this lonely tower, this tenement refit?

7

Well didst thou speak, Athena's wisest son![9]   55
"All that we know is, nothing can be known."
Why should we shrink from what we cannot shun?
Each hath his pang, but feeble sufferers groan
With brain-born dreams of evil all their own.
Pursue what Chance or Fate proclaimeth best;   60
Peace waits us on the shores of Acheron:[1]
There no forced banquet claims the sated guest,
But Silence spreads the couch of ever welcome rest.

8

Yet if, as holiest men have deem'd, there be
A land of souls beyond that sable shore,   65
To shame the doctrine of the Sadducee[2]
And sophists, madly vain of dubious lore;
How sweet it were in concert to adore
With those who made our mortal labours light!
To hear each voice we fear'd to hear no more!   70
Behold each mighty shade reveal'd to sight,
The Bactrian, Samian[3] sage, and all who taught the right!

9

There, thou![4]—whose love and life together fled,
Have left me here to love and live in vain—
Twined with my heart, and can I deem thee dead,   75
When busy Memory flashes on my brain?
Well—I will dream that we may meet again,

9. Socrates.
1. In classical myth, a river in Hades, the underworld or land of the dead.
2. "The Sadducees did not believe in the Resurrection" (Byron's manuscript note). The Sadducees were a Jewish sect formed ca. 200 B.C.E., who upheld only the written law and not the oral tradition followed by the Pharisees.
3. Zoroaster of Bactria (in ancient Persia) and Pythagoras of Samos (in ancient Greece).
4. John Edleston, the choirboy at Cambridge whom Byron loved. Byron's deep feelings for Edleston upon learning of his death in 1811 are also the subject of stanzas 95 and 96, as well as "The Cornelian" (p. 4) and the "Thyrza" lyrics (see "To Thyrza" [p. 98]). Byron attempted to cover up the identity (and gender) of the subject of these stanzas and the Thyrza poems; however, the evidence that Edleston is the subject is fairly unassailable (see *Marchand* 1:107–08 and 295–99, and Crompton, pp. 175–79).

And woo the vision to my vacant breast:
If aught of young Remembrance then remain,
Be as it may Futurity's behest,   80
For me 'twere bliss enough to know thy spirit blest!

10

Here let me sit upon this massy stone,
The marble column's yet unshaken base;
Here, son of Saturn! was thy fav'rite throne:[5]
Mightiest of many such! Hence let me trace   85
The latent grandeur of thy dwelling-place.
It may not be: nor ev'n can Fancy's eye
Restore what Time hath labour'd to deface.
Yet these proud pillars claim no passing sigh;
Unmoved the Moslem[6] sits, the light Greek carols by.   90

11

But who, of all the plunderers of yon fane
On high, where Pallas[7] linger'd, loth to flee
The latest relic of her ancient reign;
The last, the worst, dull spoiler, who was he?
Blush, Caledonia![8] such thy son could be!   95
England! I joy no child he was of thine:
Thy free-born men should spare what once was free;
Yet they could violate each saddening shrine,
And bear these altars o'er the long-reluctant brine.[9]

12

But most the modern Pict's[1] ignoble boast,   100
To rive what Goth, and Turk, and Time hath spared:[2]
Cold as the crags upon his native coast,
His mind as barren and his heart as hard,
Is he whose head conceived, whose hand prepared,
Aught to displace Athena's poor remains: 105
Her sons too weak the sacred shrine to guard,
Yet felt some portion of their mother's pains,[3]
And never knew, till then, the weight of Despot's chains.

5. "The temple of Jupiter Olympius, of which sixteen columns, entirely of marble, yet survive: origi-
   nally there were one hundred and fifty. These columns, however, are by many supposed to have
   belonged to the Parthenon."
6. The Turkish occupiers.
7. Athena.
8. Poetic name of Scotland; the reference is to the earl of Elgin (1766–1841), a Scotsman, who col-
   lected sculptures from the Parthenon and other Athenian buildings and sold them to England,
   where they were placed in the British Museum in 1816. Byron's outrage at the plunder, as
   expressed in *Childe Harold* and "The Curse of Minerva" (1812), played a key role in altering the
   public's attitude toward England's possession of the "Elgin marbles." (See St. Clair, *Lord Elgin and
   the Marbles*.)
9. "The ship was wrecked in the Archipelago."
1. The Picts were early inhabitants of Scotland.
2. "See Appendix to this Canto [A], for a note too long to be placed here."
3. "I cannot resist availing myself of the permission of my friend Dr Clarke, whose name requires no
   comment with the public, but whose sanction will add tenfold weight to my testimony, to insert

13

What! shall it e'er be said by British tongue,
Albion was happy in Athena's tears?   110
Though in thy name the slaves her bosom wrung,
Tell not the deed to blushing Europe's ears;
The ocean queen, the free Britannia, bears
The last poor plunder from a bleeding land:
Yes, she, whose gen'rous aid her name endears,   115
Tore down those remnants with a harpy's hand,
Which envious Eld[4] forbore, and tyrants left to stand.

14

Where was thine Aegis,[5] Pallas! that appall'd
Stern Alaric and Havoc on their way?[6]
Where Peleus' son? whom Hell in vain enthrall'd,   120
His shade from Hades upon that dread day
Bursting to light in terrible array!
What! could not Pluto spare the chief once more,
To scare a second robber from his prey?
Idly he wander'd on the Stygian shore,[7]   125
Nor now preserved the walls he loved to shield before.

15

Cold is the heart, fair Greece! that looks on thee,
Nor feels as lovers o'er the dust they loved;
Dull is the eye that will not weep to see
Thy walls defaced, thy mouldering shrines removed   130
By British hands, which it had best behoved
To guard those relics ne'er to be restored.
Curst be the hour when from their isle they roved,
And once again thy hapless bosom gored,
And snatch'd thy shrinking Gods to northern climes abhorr'd!   135

16

But where is Harold? shall I then forget
To urge the gloomy wanderer o'er the wave?

---

the following extract from a very obliging letter of his to me, as a note to the above lines:—'When the last of the Metopes was taken from the Parthenon, and, in moving of it, a great part of the superstructure with one of the triglyphs was thrown down by the workmen whom Lord Elgin employed, the Disdar who beheld the mischief done to the building, took his pipe from his mouth, dropped a tear, and, in a supplicating tone of voice, said to Lusieri, Τέλος!—I was present.' The Disdar alluded to was the father of the present Disdar."
4. Age.
5. Shield.
6. "According to Zosimus, Minerva and Achilles frightened Alaric from the Acropolis; but others relate that the Gothic king was nearly as mischievous as the Scottish peer.—See CHANDLER." According to this account, the shade of "Peleus' son" (line 120), Achilles, rose from the underworld, Hades (line 121).
7. Refers to the River Styx in Hades; *Pluto*: ruler of the underworld in classical myth.

Little reck'd he of all that men regret;
No loved-one now in feign'd lament could rave;
No friend the parting hand extended gave,   140
Ere the cold stranger pass'd to other climes:
Hard is his heart whom charms may not enslave;
But Harold felt not as in other times,
And left without a sigh the land of war and crimes.[8]

17

He that has sail'd upon the dark blue sea   145
Has view'd at times, I ween, a full fair sight;
When the fresh breeze is fair as breeze may be
The white sail set, the gallant frigate tight;
Masts, spires, and strand retiring to the right,
The glorious main expanding o'er the bow,   150
The convoy spread like wild swans in their flight,
The dullest sailer wearing bravely now,
So gaily curl the waves before each dashing prow.

18

And oh, the little warlike world within!
The well-reeved guns, the netted canopy,[9]   155
The hoarse command, the busy humming din,
When, at a word, the tops are mann'd on high!
Hark, to the Boatswain's call, the cheering cry!
While through the seaman's hand the tackle glides;
Or schoolboy Midshipman that, standing by,   160
Strains his shrill pipe as good or ill betides,
And well the docile crew that skilful urchin guides.

19

White is the glassy deck, without a stain,
Where on the watch the staid Lieutenant walks:
Look on that part which sacred doth remain   165
For the lone chieftain, who majestic stalks,
Silent and fear'd by all—not oft he talks
With aught beneath him, if he would preserve
That strict restraint, which broken, ever balks
Conquest and Fame: but Britons rarely swerve   170
From law, however stern, which tends their strength to nerve.

20

Blow! swiftly blow, thou keel-compelling gale!
Till the broad sun withdraws his lessening ray;
Then must the pennant-bearer slacken sail,
That lagging barks may make their lazy way.   175

8. I.e., Spain, the subject (with Portugal) of Canto I.
9. "To prevent blocks or splinters from falling on deck during action."

Ah! grievance sore, and listless dull delay,
To waste on sluggish hulks the sweetest breeze!
What leagues are lost, before the dawn of day,
Thus loitering pensive on the willing seas,
The flapping sail haul'd down to halt for logs like these!   180

21

The moon is up; by Heaven, a lovely eve!
Long streams of light o'er dancing waves expand;
Now lads on shore may sigh, and maids believe:
Such be our fate when we return to land!
Meantime some rude Arion's[1] restless hand   185
Wakes the brisk harmony that sailors love;
A circle there of merry listeners stand,
Or to some well-known measure featly move,
Thoughtless, as if on shore they still were free to rove.

22

Through Calpe's[2] straits survey the steepy shore;   190
Europe and Afric on each other gaze!
Lands of the dark-eyed Maid and dusky Moor
Alike beheld beneath pale Hecate's blaze:[3]
Now softly on the Spanish shore she plays,
Disclosing rock, and slope, and forest brown,   195
Distinct, though darkening with her waning phase;
But Mauritania's[4] giant-shadows frown,
From mountain-cliff to coast descending sombre down.

23

'Tis night, when Meditation bids us feel
We once have loved, though love is at an end: 200
The heart, lone mourner of its baffled zeal,
Though friendless now, will dream it had a friend.
Who with the weight of years would wish to bend,
When Youth itself survives young Love and Joy?
Alas! when mingling souls forget to blend,   205
Death hath but little left him to destroy!
Ah! happy years! once more who would not be a boy?

24

Thus bending o'er the vessel's laving side,
To gaze on Dian's[5] wave-reflected sphere,

1. Arion was an ancient Greek poet mentioned in Herodotus's *Histories* 1.23.
2. Gibraltar's.
3. The moon, though Hecate is the ancient Greek goddess of the night and associated with the dark side of the moon. Lines 193–97 refer to the position of the moon when its light shines on Spain's coast but Africa's coast is in shadow.
4. Morocco's.
5. Diana was the Roman Artemis, goddess of the moon.

The soul forgets her schemes of Hope and Pride,   210
And flies unconscious o'er each backward year
None are so desolate but something dear,
Dearer than self, possesses or possess'd
A thought, and claims the homage of a tear;
A flashing pang! of which the weary breast   215
Would still, albeit in vain, the heavy heart divest.

25

To sit on rocks, to muse o'er flood and fell,
To slowly trace the forest's shady scene,
Where things that own not man's dominion dwell,
And mortal foot hath ne'er or rarely been;   220
To climb the trackless mountain all unseen,
With the wild flock that never needs a fold;
Alone o'er steeps and foaming falls to lean;
This is not solitude; 'tis but to hold
Converse with Nature's charms, and view her stores unroll'd.   225

26

But midst the crowd, the hum, the shock of men,
To hear, to see, to feel, and to possess,
And roam along, the world's tired denizen,
With none who bless us, none whom we can bless;
Minions of splendour shrinking from distress!   230
None that, with kindred consciousness endued,
If we were not, would seem to smile the less
Of all that flatter'd, follow'd, sought, and sued;
This is to be alone; this, this is solitude!

27

More blest the life of godly eremite,   235
Such as on lonely Athos may be seen,
Watching at eve upon the giant height,
Which looks o'er waves so blue, skies so serene,
That he who there at such an hour hath been
Will wistful linger on that hallow'd spot;   240
Then slowly tear him from the 'witching scene,
Sigh forth one wish that such had been his lot,
Then turn to hate a world he had almost forgot.

28

Pass we the long, unvarying course, the track
Oft trod, that never leaves a trace behind;   245
Pass we the calm, the gale, the change, the tacks,
And each well known caprice of wave and wind
Pass we the joys and sorrows sailors find,
Coop'd in their winged sea-girt citadel;

The foul, the fair, the contrary, the kind,   250
As breezes rise and fall and billows swell,
Till on some jocund morn—lo, land! and all is well

29

But not in silence pass Calypso's isles,[6]
The sister tenants of the middle deep;
There for the weary still a haven smiles,   255
Though the fair goddess long hath ceased to weep
And o'er her cliffs a fruitless watch to keep
For him who dared prefer a mortal bride:
Here, too, his boy[7] essay'd the dreadful leap
Stern Mentor urged from high to yonder tide;   260
While thus of both bereft, the nymph-queen doubly sigh'd.

30

Her reign is past, her gentle glories gone:
But trust not this; too easy youth, beware!
A mortal sovereign holds her dangerous throne,
And thou may'st find a new Calypso there.   265
Sweet Florence! could another ever share
This wayward, loveless heart, it would be thine:
But check'd by every tie, I may not dare
To cast a worthless offering at thy shrine,
Nor ask so dear a breast to feel one pang for mine.   270

31

Thus Harold deem'd, as on that lady's eye
He look'd, and met its beam without a thought,
Save Admiration glancing harmless by:
Love kept aloof, albeit not far remote,
Who knew his votary often lost and caught,   275
But knew him as his worshipper no more,
And ne'er again the boy his bosom sought:
Since now he vainly urged him to adore,
Well deem'd the little God his ancient sway was o'er.

32

Fair Florence found, in sooth with some amaze,   280
One who, 'twas said, still sigh'd to all he saw,
Withstand, unmoved, the lustre of her gaze,

6. "Goza is said to have been the island of Calypso." In *The Odyssey*, Calypso (the "fair goddess" and "nymph-queen") loved Odysseus, and despite his longing to return to his wife and home, she kept him on her island until ordered by the gods to release him. *Stanzas 29–30*: Actually, Ogygia, not Goza, is the island of Calypso, but Byron's connection of Goza and Malta ("sister tenants") allows the connection between Odysseus's bewitching nymph and Byron's "new Calypso," Mrs. Constance Spenser Smith ("Sweet Florence"), with whom he had an affair while at Malta.
7. Telemachus, Odysseus's son; in his search for his father, he is accompanied by Athena disguised as Odysseus's trusted friend, Mentor.

Which others hail'd with real or mimic awe,
Their hope, their doom, their punishment, their law;
All that gay Beauty from her bondsmen claims: 285
And much she marvell'd that a youth so raw
Nor felt, nor feign'd at least, the oft-told flames,
Which, though sometimes they frown, yet rarely anger dames.

33

Little knew she that seeming marble heart,
Now mask'd in silence or withheld by pride,   290
Was not unskilful in the spoiler's art,
And spread its snares licentious far and wide;
Nor from the base pursuit had turn'd aside,
As long as aught was worthy to pursue:
But Harold on such arts no more relied;   295
And had he doted on those eyes so blue,
Yet never would he join the lover's whining crew.

34

Not much he kens, I ween,[8] of woman's breast,
Who thinks that wanton thing is won by sighs;
What careth she for hearts when once possess'd?   300
Do proper homage to thine idol's eyes;
But not too humbly, or she will despise
Thee and thy suit, though told in moving tropes:
Disguise ev'n tenderness, if thou art wise;
Brisk Confidence still best with woman copes;   305
Pique her and soothe in turn, soon Passion crowns thy hopes.

35

'Tis an old lesson; Time approves it true,
And those who know it best, deplore it most;
When all is won that all desire to woo,
The paltry prize is hardly worth the cost: 310
Youth wasted, minds degraded, honour lost,
These are thy fruits, successful Passion! these!
If, kindly cruel, early Hope is crost,
Still to the last it rankles, a disease,
Not to be cured when Love itself forgets to please.   315

36

Away! nor let me loiter in my song,
For we have many a mountain-path to tread,
And many a varied shore to sail along,
By pensive Sadness, not by Fiction, led—
Climes, fair withal as ever mortal head   320

8. *kens . . . ween*: knows . . . suppose.

Imagined in its little schemes of thought;
Or e'er in new Utopias were ared,
To teach man what he might be, or he ought;
If that corrupted thing could ever such be taught.

37

Dear Nature is the kindest mother still,   325
Though alway changing, in her aspect mild;
From her bare bosom let me take my fill,
Her never-wean'd, though not her favour'd child.
Oh! she is fairest in her features wild,
Where nothing polish'd dares pollute her path: 330
To me by day or night she ever smiled,
Though I have mark'd her when none other hath,
And sought her more and more, and loved her best in wrath.

38

Land of Albania! where Iskander[9] rose,
Theme of the young, and beacon of the wise,   335
And he his namesake, whose oft-baffled foes
Shrunk from his deeds of chivalrous emprize:
Land of Albania![1] let me bend mine eyes
On thee, thou rugged nurse of savage men!
The cross descends, thy minarets arise,   340
And the pale crescent sparkles in the glen,
Through many a cypress grove within each city's ken.

39

Childe Harold sail'd, and pass'd the barren spot,
Where sad Penelope o'erlook'd the wave;[2]
And onward view'd the mount, not yet forgot,   345
The lover's refuge, and the Lesbian's grave.
Dark Sappho! could not verse immortal save
That breast imbued with such immortal fire?
Could she not live who life eternal gave?
If life eternal may await the lyre,   350
That only heaven to which Earth's children aspire.

40

'Twas on a Grecian autumn's gentle eve
Childe Harold hail'd Leucadia's cape afar;[3]
A spot he longed to see, nor cared to leave:
Oft did he mark the scenes of vanish'd war,   355

---

9. Alexander the Great (Turkish); "his namesake" (line 336) is Scandrberg, mentioned in *Decline and Fall*.
1. "See Appendix to this Canto, Note [B]."
2. "Ithaca." Penelope is the wife of Odysseus.
3. "Leucadia, now Santa Maura. From the promontory (the Lover's Leap) Sappho is said to have thrown herself."

Actium, Lepanto, fatal Trafalgar;[4]
Mark them unmoved, for he would not delight
(Born beneath some remote inglorious star)
In themes of bloody fray, or gallant fight,
But loathed the bravo's trade, and laughed at martial wight.   360

41

But when he saw the evening star above
Leucadia's far-projecting rock of woe,
And hail'd the last resort of fruitless love,
He felt, or deem'd he felt, no common glow:
And as the stately vessel glided slow   365
Beneath the shadow of that ancient mount,
He watch'd the billows' melancholy flow,
And, sunk albeit in thought as he was wont,
More placid seem'd his eye, and smooth his pallid front.

42

Morn dawns; and with it stern Albania's hills,   370
Dark Suli's rocks, and Pindus' inland peak,[5]
Robed half in mist, bedew'd with snowy rills,
Array'd in many a dun and purple streak,
Arise; and, as the clouds along them break,
Disclose the dwelling of the mountaineer: 375
Here roams the wolf, the eagle whets his beak,
Birds, beasts of prey, and wilder men appear,
And gathering storms around convulse the closing year.

43

Now Harold felt himself at length alone,
And bade to Christian tongues a long adieu;   380
Now he adventured on a shore unknown,
Which all admire, but many dread to view:
His breast was arm'd 'gainst fate, his wants were few;
Peril he sought not, but ne'er shrank to meet:
The scene was savage, but the scene was new;   385
This made the ceaseless toil of travel sweet,
Beat back keen winter's blast, and welcomed summer's heat.

44

Here the red cross, for still the cross is here,
Though sadly scoff'd at by the circumcised,

---

4. "Actium and Trafalgar need no further mention. The battle of Lepanto, equally bloody and considerable, but less known, was fought in the Gulf of Patras. Here the author of Don Quixote lost his left hand." The Battle of Lepanto, between the Holy League and the Ottoman fleet, took place in 1571. *Actium*: in northwest ancient Greece, site of the naval battle where Antony and Cleopatra were defeated by Octavian in 31 B.C.E.; *Trafalgar*: a cape in southwest Spain, site of British victory over French and Spanish fleets in 1805.
5. Mountainous regions in Albania.

Forgets that pride to pamper'd priesthood dear;   390
Churchman and votary alike despised.
Foul Superstition! howsoe'er disguised,
Idol, saint, virgin, prophet, crescent, cross,
For whatsoever symbol thou art prized,
Thou sacerdotal gain, but general loss!   395
Who from true worship's gold can separate the dross?

45

Ambracia's gulf behold, where once was lost
A world for woman,[6] lovely, harmless thing!
In yonder rippling bay, their naval host
Did many a Roman chief and Asian king[7]   400
To doubtful conflict, certain slaughter bring:
Look where the second Caesar's trophies rose:[8]
Now, like the hands that rear'd them, withering:
Imperial anarchs, doubling human woes!
GOD! was thy globe ordain'd for such to win and lose?   405

46

From the dark barriers of that rugged clime,
Ev'n to the centre of Illyria's[9] vales,
Childe Harold pass'd o'er many a mount sublime,
Through lands scarce noticed in historic tales;
Yet in famed Attica such lovely dales   410
Are rarely seen; nor can fair Tempe boast
A charm they know not; loved Parnassus fails,
Though classic ground and consecrated most,
To match some spots that lurk within this lowering coast.

47

He pass'd bleak Pindus, Acherusia's lake,[1]   415
And left the primal city of the land,
And onwards did his further journey take
To greet Albania's chief,[2] whose dread command
Is lawless law; for with a bloody hand
He sways a nation, turbulent and bold: 420

6. Cleopatra; a reference to Antony's retiring from the battle at Actium (in "Ambracia's gulf") to fol-
   low her, precipitating the surrender of his navy.
7. "It is said, that, on the day previous to the battle of Actium, Antony had thirteen kings at his levee."
8. "Nicopolis, whose ruins are most extensive, is at some distance from Actium, where the wall of the
   Hippodrome survives in a few fragments. These ruins are large masses of brickwork, the bricks of
   which are joined by interstices of mortar, as large as the bricks themselves, and equally durable."
   Octavian ("the second Caesar") built Nicopolis to commemorate his victory at Actium.
9. One of the areas in Greece made famous in classical literature, along with Attica (Athens), Tempe,
   and Mount Parnassus.
1. "According to Pouqueville, the lake of Yanina: but Pouqueville is always out."
2. "The celebrated Ali Pacha. Of this extraordinary man there is an incorrect account in Pouqueville's
   Travels." Byron describes his encounter with Ali Pacha in his letter to his mother, November 12,
   1809 (see p. 111). Cecil Lang discusses the significance to Byron of this encounter in "Narcissus
   Jilted: Byron, Don Juan and the Biographical Imperative" (see p. 972).

Yet here and there some daring mountain-band
Disdain his power, and from their rocky hold
Hurl their defiance far, nor yield, unless to gold.[3]

48

Monastic Zitza![4] from thy shady brow,
Thou small, but favour'd spot of holy ground!   425
Where'er we gaze, around, above, below,
What rainbow tints, what magic charms are found!
Rock, river, forest, mountain, all abound,
And bluest skies that harmonise the whole:
Beneath, the distant torrent's rushing sound   430
Tells where the volumed cataract doth roll
Between those hanging rocks, that shock yet please the soul.

49

Amidst the grove that crowns yon tufted hill,
Which, were it not for many a mountain nigh
Rising in lofty ranks, and loftier still,   435
Might well itself be deem'd of dignity,
The convent's white walls glisten fair on high:
Here dwells the caloyer,[5] nor rude is he,
Nor niggard of his cheer; the passer by
Is welcome still; nor heedless will he flee   440
From hence, if he delight kind Nature's sheen to see.

50

Here in the sultriest season let him rest,
Fresh is the green beneath those aged trees;
Here winds of gentlest wing will fan his breast,
From heaven itself he may inhale the breeze: 445
The plain is far beneath—oh! let him seize
Pure pleasure while he can; the scorching ray
Here pierceth not, impregnate with disease:
Then let his length the loitering pilgrim lay,
And gaze, untired, the morn, the noon, the eve away.   450

3. "Five thousand Suliotes, among the rocks and in the castle of Suli, withstood thirty thousand Alba-
nians for eighteen years; the castle at last was taken by bribery. In this contest there were several
acts performed not worthy of the better days of Greece." Suli: a region in northwestern Greece;
during the eighteenth century its inhabitants persistently fought the Turkish occupiers.
4. "The convent and village of Zitza are four hours' journey from Joannina or Yanina, the capital of
the Pachalick. In the valley the river Kalamas (once the Acheron) flows, and, not far from Zitza,
forms a fine cataract. The situation is perhaps the finest in Greece, though the approach to Del-
vinachi and parts of Acarnania and AEtolia may contest the palm. Delphi, Parnassus, and, in Attica,
even Cape Colonna and Port Raphti, are very inferior; as also every scene in Ionia, or the Troad: I
am almost inclined to add the approach to Constantinople; but, from the different features of the
last, a comparison can hardly be made."
5. "The Greek monks are so called."

51

Dusky and huge, enlarging on the sight,
Nature's volcanic amphitheatre,[6]
Chimaera's alps extend from left to right:
Beneath, a living valley seems to stir;
Flocks play, trees wave, streams flow, the mountain-fir   455
Nodding above; behold black Acheron![7]
Once consecrated to the sepulchre.
Pluto! if this be hell I look upon,
Close shamed Elysium's[8] gates, my shade shall seek for none.

52

Ne city's towers pollute the lovely view;   460
Unseen is Yanina,[9] though not remote,
Veil'd by the screen of hills: here men are few,
Scanty the hamlet, rare the lonely cot:
But peering down each precipice, the goat
Browseth; and, pensive o'er his scatter'd flock,   465
The little shepherd in his white capote[1]
Doth lean his boyish form along the rock,
Or in his cave awaits the tempest's short-lived shock.

53

Oh! where, Dodona![2] is thine aged grove,
Prophetic fount, and oracle divine?   470
What valley echo'd the response of Jove?
What trace remaineth of the Thunderer's shrine?
All, all forgotten—and shall man repine
That his frail bonds to fleeting life are broke?
Cease, fool! the fate of gods may well be thine: 475
Wouldst thou survive the marble or the oak?
When nations, tongues, and worlds must sink beneath the stroke!

54

Epirus'[3] bounds recede, and mountains fail;
Tired of up-gazing still, the wearied eye
Reposes gladly on as smooth a vale   480
As ever Spring yclad in grassy dye:
Ev'n on a plain no humble beauties lie,
Where some bold river breaks the long expanse,

6. "The Chimariot mountains appear to have been volcanic." By "Chimaera's Alps" (line 453) Byron probably meant the Ceraunian Mountains to the north of Jannina, not the Chimariot Mountains.
7. "Now called Kalamas."
8. In classical myth, Elysium was the abode of the blessed after death.
9. Ioannina, in northwest Greece.
1. "Albanese cloak." Usually hooded.
2. Located at the foot of Mount Tomaros (Mount Olytsika); the site, in classical myth, of the oracle of Jove (line 417), i.e., the Roman god Jupiter (or in Greek myth Zeus), father of the gods and god of thunder.
3. Ancient country of Greece in the region of present-day northwest Greece and southern Albania.

And woods along the banks are waving high,
  Whose shadows in the glassy waters dance,   485
Or with the moonbeam sleep in midnight's solemn trance.

55

The sun had sunk behind vast Tomerit,[4]
  And Laos wide and fierce came roaring by;[5]
The shades of wonted night were gathering yet,
  When, down the steep banks winding warily,   490
Childe Harold saw, like meteors in the sky,
  The glittering minarets of Tepalen,
Whose walls o'erlook the stream; and drawing nigh,
  He heard the busy hum of warrior-men
Swelling the breeze that sigh'd along the lengthening glen.   495

56

He pass'd the sacred Haram's silent tower,
  And underneath the wide o'erarching gate
Survey'd the dwelling of this chief of power,
  Where all around proclaim'd his high estate.
Amidst no common pomp the despot sate,   500
  While busy preparation shook the court,
Slaves, eunuchs, soldiers, guests, and santons[6] wait;
  Within, a palace, and without, a fort:
Here men of every clime appear to make resort.

57

Richly caparison'd, a ready row   505
  Of armed horse, and many a warlike store,
Circled the wide extending court below;
  Above, strange groups adorn'd the corridore:
And oft-times through the area's echoing door
  Some high-capp'd Tartar[7] spurr'd his steed away: 510
The Turk, the Greek, the Albanian, and the Moor,
  Here mingled in their many-hued array,
While the deep war-drum's sound announced the close of day.

58

The wild Albanian kirtled[8] to his knee,
  With shawl-girt head and ornamented gun,   515
And gold-embroider'd garments, fair to see:

---

4. "Anciently Mount Tomarus."
5. "The river Laos was full at the time the author passed it; and, immediately above Tepaleen, was to
   the eye as wide as the Thames at Westminster; at least in the opinion of the author and this fellow
   traveller. In the summer it must be much narrower. It certainly is the finest river in the Levant;
   neither Achelous, Alpheus, Acheron, Scamander, nor Cayster, approached it in breadth or beauty."
6. Muslim ascetics or dervishes.
7. A descendent of the Mongolian or Turkish tribes that in the Middle Ages overran Asia and eastern
   Europe.
8. Dressed in a tunic.

The crimson-scarfed men of Macedon;[9]
The Delhi[1] with his cap of terror on,
And crooked glaive; the lively, supple Greek;
And swarthy Nubia's mutilated son;[2]   520
The bearded Turk, that rarely deigns to speak,
Master of all around, too potent to be meek,

59

Are mix'd conspicuous: some recline in groups,
Scanning the motley scene that varies round;
There some grave Moslem to devotion stoops,   525
And some that smoke, and some that play, are found;
Here the Albanian proudly treads the ground;
Half whispering there the Greek is heard to prate;
Hark! from the mosque the nightly solemn sound,
The Muezzin's[3] call doth shake the minaret,   530
"There is no god but God!—to prayer—lo! God is great!"

60

Just at this season Ramazani's fast[4]
Through the long day its penance did maintain:
But when the lingering twilight hour was past,
Revel and feast assumed the rule again: 535
Now all was bustle, and the menial train
Prepared and spread the plenteous board within;
The vacant gallery now seem'd made in vain,
But from the chambers came the mingling din,
As page and slave anon were passing out and in.   540

61

Here woman's voice is never heard: apart,
And scarce permitted, guarded, veil'd, to move,
She yields to one her person and her heart,
Tamed to her cage, nor feels a wish to rove:
For, not unhappy in her master's love,   545
And joyful in a mother's gentlest cares,
Blest cares! all other feelings far above!
Herself more sweetly rears the babe she bears,
Who never quits the breast, no meaner passion shares.

62

In marble-paved pavilion, where a spring   550
Of living water from the centre rose,

9. Ancient country north of ancient Greece.
1. A fierce Turkish warrior.
2. Sudanese eunuch.
3. In the Muslim faith, the muezzin is the crier who from a minaret or tower summons the faithful
   to prayer five times a day.
4. The Muslim holy month, Ramadan, involving day-long fasts followed by nightly feasts.

Whose bubbling did a genial freshness fling,
And soft voluptuous couches breathed repose,
ALI[5] reclined, a man of war and woes:
Yet in his lineaments ye cannot trace,   555
While Gentleness her milder radiance throws
Along that aged venerable face,
The deeds that lurk beneath, and stain him with disgrace.

63

It is not that yon hoary lengthening beard
Ill suits the passions which belong to youth;   560
Love conquers age—so Hafiz[6] hath averr'd,
So sings the Teian,[7] and he sings in sooth—
But crimes that scorn the tender voice of Ruth,[8]
Beseeming all men ill, but most the man
In years, have mark'd him with a tiger's tooth;   565
Blood follows blood, and, through their mortal span,
In bloodier acts conclude those who with blood began.

64

'Mid many things most new to ear and eye
The pilgrim rested here his weary feet,
And gazed around on Moslem luxury,   570
Till quickly wearied with that spacious seat
Of Wealth and Wantonness, the choice retreat
Of sated Grandeur from the city's noise:
And were it humbler it in sooth were sweet;
But Peace abhorreth artificial joys,   575
And Pleasure, leagued with Pomp, the zest of both destroys.

65

Fierce are Albania's children, yet they lack
Not virtues, were those virtues more mature.
Where is the foe that ever saw their back?
Who can so well the toil of war endure?   580
Their native fastnesses not more secure
Than they in doubtful time of troublous need:
Their wrath how deadly! but their friendship sure,
When Gratitude or Valour bids them bleed,
Unshaken rushing on where'er their chief may lead.   585

66

Childe Harold saw them in their chieftain's tower
Thronging to war in splendour and success;

5. Ali Pacha, see note to line 418; the "chieftain" in line 586.
6. Fourteenth-century Persian poet.
7. Anacreon (sixth-century B.C.E.), poet from Teos in Ionia, noted for his love lyrics.
8. Book of Ruth (Hebrew Bible); Ruth, a young widow, shows love for and marries Boaz, an older man.

And after view'd them, when, within their power,
Himself awhile the victim of distress;
That saddening hour when bad men hotlier press: 590
But these did shelter him beneath their roof,
When less barbarians would have cheer'd him less,
And fellow-countrymen have stood aloof—⁹
In aught that tries the heart how few withstand the proof!

67

It chanced that adverse winds once drove his bark   595
Full on the coast of Suli's shaggy shore,
When all around was desolate and dark;
To land was perilous, to sojourn more;
Yet for a while the mariners forbore,
Dubious to trust where treachery might lurk: 600
At length they ventured forth, though doubting sore
That those who loathe alike the Frank and Turk
Might once again renew their ancient butcher-work.

68

Vain fear! the Suliotes stretch'd the welcome hand,
Led them o'er rocks and past the dangerous swamp,   605
Kinder than polish'd slaves though not so bland,
And piled the hearth, and wrung their garments damp,
And fill'd the bowl, and trimm'd the cheerful lamp,
And spread their fare; though homely, all they had:
Such conduct bears Philanthropy's rare stamp—   610
To rest the weary and to soothe the sad,
Doth lesson happier men, and shames at least the bad.

69

It came to pass, that when he did address
Himself to quit at length this mountain-land,
Combined marauders half-way barr'd egress,   615
And wasted far and near with glaive and brand;
And therefore did he take a trusty band
To traverse Acarnania's¹ forest wide.
In war well season'd, and with labours tann'd,
Till he did greet white Achelous' tide,   620
And from his further bank Aetolia's wolds espied.

70

Where lone Utraikey forms its circling cove,
And weary waves retire to gleam at rest,
How brown the foliage of the green hill's grove,

---

9. "Alluding to the wreckers of Cornwall."
1. Lines 618–22 mention several places in densely wooded regions of Albania where Byron traveled.

Nodding at midnight o'er the calm bay's breast,   625
As winds come lightly whispering from the west,
Kissing, not ruffling, the blue deep's serene:—
Here Harold was received a welcome guest;
Nor did he pass unmoved the gentle scene,
For many a joy could he from Night's soft presence glean.   630

71

On the smooth shore the night-fires brightly blazed,
The feast was done, the red wine circling fast,[2]
And he that unawares had there ygazed
With gaping wonderment had stared aghast;
For ere night's midmost, stillest hour was past,   635
The native revels of the troop began;
Each Palikar[3] his sabre from him cast,
And bounding hand in hand, man link'd to man,
Yelling their uncouth dirge, long daunced the kirtled clan.

72

Childe Harold at a little distance stood   640
And view'd, but not displeased, the revelrie,
Nor hated harmless mirth, however rude:
In sooth, it was no vulgar sight to see
Their barbarous, yet their not indecent, glee;
And, as the flames along their faces gleam'd,   645
Their gestures nimble, dark eyes flashing free,
The long wild locks that to their girdles stream'd,
While thus in concert they this lay half sang, half scream'd:—[4]

1

Tambourgi! Tambourgi![5] thy 'larum afar
Gives hope to the valiant, and promise of war;   650
All the sons of the mountains arise at the note,
Chimariot, Illyrian, and dark Suliote![6]

2

Oh! who is more brave than a dark Suliote,
In his snowy camese[7] and his shaggy capote?
To the wolf and the vulture he leaves his wild flock,   655
And descends to the plain like the stream from the rock.

---

2. "The Albanian Mussulmans do not abstain from wine, and, indeed, very few of the others."
3. "Palikar, shortened when addressed to a single person, from Παλικαρί, a general name for a sol-
   dier amongst the Greeks and Albanese who speak Romaic: it means, properly, 'a lad.' "
4. "For a specimen of the Albanian or Arnaout dialect of the Illyric, see Appendix to this Canto, Note
   [C]."
5. "Drummer."
6. "These stanzas are partly taken from different Albanese songs, as far as I was able to make them
   out by the exposition of the Albanese in Romaic and Italian."
7. Kilt.

3

Shall the sons of Chimari, who never forgive
The fault of a friend, bid an enemy live?
Let those guns so unerring such vengeance forego?
What mark is so fair as the breast of a foe?   660

4

Macedonia sends forth her invincible race;
For a time they abandon the cave and the chase:
But those scarfs of blood-red shall be redder, before
The sabre is sheathed and the battle is o'er.

5

Then the pirates of Parga[8] that dwell by the waves,   665
And teach the pale Franks what it is to be slaves,
Shall leave on the beach the long galley and oar,
And track to his covert the captive on shore.

6

I ask not the pleasures that riches supply,
My sabre shall win what the feeble must buy;   670
Shall win the young bride with her long flowing hair,
And many a maid from her mother shall tear.

7

I love the fair face of the maid in her youth,
Her caresses shall lull me, her music shall soothe;
Let her bring from the chamber her many-toned lyre,   675
And sing us a song on the fall of her sire.

8

Remember the moment when Previsa fell,[9]
The shrieks of the conquer'd, the conquerors' yell;
The roofs that we fired, and the plunder we shared,
The wealthy we slaughter'd, the lovely we spared.   680

9

I talk not of mercy, I talk not of fear;
He neither must know who would serve the Vizier:
Since the days of our prophet the Crescent ne'er saw
A chief ever glorious like Ali Pashaw.

---

8. A seaport.
9. "It was taken by storm from the French." I.e., Prevesa.

10

Dark Muchtar[1] his son to the Danube is sped,   685
Let the yellow-hair'd[2] Giaours[3] view his horse-tail[4] with dread;
When his Delhis[5] come dashing in blood o'er the banks,
How few shall escape from the Muscovite ranks!

11

Selictar![6] unsheathe then our chief's scimitār:
Tambourgi! thy 'larum gives promise of war.   690
Ye mountains, that see us descend to the shore,
Shall view us as victors, or view us no more!

73

Fair Greece! sad relic of departed worth![7]
Immortal, though no more; though fallen, great!
Who now shall lead thy scatter'd children forth,   695
And long accustom'd bondage uncreate?
Not such thy sons who whilome did await,
The hopeless warriors of a willing doom,
In bleak Thermopylae's[8] sepulchral strait—
Oh! who that gallant spirit shall resume,   700
Leap from Eurotas' banks, and call thee from the tomb?

74

Spirit of freedom! when on Phyle's brow[9]
Thou sat'st with Thrasybulus and his train,
Couldst thou forebode the dismal hour which now
Dims the green beauties of thine Attic plain?   705
Not thirty tyrants now enforce the chain,
But every carle[1] can lord it o'er thy land;
Nor rise thy sons, but idly rail in vain,
Trembling beneath the scourge of Turkish hand,
From birth till death enslaved; in word, in deed, unmann'd.   710

75

In all save form alone, how changed! and who
That marks the fire still sparkling in each eye,
Who but would deem their bosoms burn'd anew

1. Ali's oldest son, sent to oppose a Russian invasion across the Danube River in 1809.
2. "Yellow is the epithet given to the Russian"
3. "Infidel."
4. "The insignia of a Pacha"
5. "Horsemen, answering to our forlorn hope."
6. "Sword-bearer."
7. "Some thoughts on the present state of Greece will be found in Appendix to this Canto, Note [D]."
8. Where in 480 B.C.E. the Spartans in a heroic battle were defeated by the Persians. According to E. H. Coleridge, the meaning of lines 700–701 is: "When shall another Lysander spring from Laconia ('Eurotas' banks') and revive the heroism of the ancient Spartans" (C 2.150).
9. "Phyle, which commands a beautiful view of Athens, has still considerable remains: it was seized by Thrasybulus, previous to the expulsion of the Thirty." This seizure occurred in 403 B.C.E.
1. Obsolete form for churl or boorish person.

With thy unquenched beam, lost Liberty!
And many dream withal the hour is nigh   715
That gives them back their fathers' heritage:
For foreign arms and aid they fondly sigh,
Nor solely dare encounter hostile rage,
Or tear their name defiled from Slavery's mournful page.

76

Hereditary bondsmen! know ye not   720
Who would be free themselves must strike the blow?
By their right arms the conquest must be wrought?
Will Gaul or Muscovite redress ye? no!
True, they may lay your proud despoilers low,
But not for you will Freedom's altars flame.   725
Shades of the Helots![2] triumph o'er your foe!
Greece! change thy lords, thy state is still the same;
Thy glorious day is o'er, but not thine years of shame.

77

The city[3] won for Allah from the Giaour,
The Giaour from Othman's race again may wrest;   730
And the Serai's[4] impenetrable tower
Receive the fiery Frank, her former guest;[5]
Or Wahab's rebel brood who dared divest
The prophet's tomb[6] of all its pious spoil,
May wind their path of blood along the West;   735
But ne'er will freedom seek this fated soil,
But slave succeed to slave through years of endless toil.

78

Yet mark their mirth—ere lenten days begin,
That penance which their holy rites prepare
To shrive from man his weight of mortal sin,   740
By daily abstinence and nightly prayer;
But ere his sackcloth garb Repentance wear,
Some days of joyaunce are decreed to all,
To take of pleasaunce each his secret share,
In motley robe to dance at masking ball,   745
And join the mimic train of merry Carnival.

---

2. The serfs of ancient Laconia.
3. Constantinople ("Stamboul," in line 748, i.e., present-day Istanbul), built on the hills above the Bosporous Strait as the capital of the Byzantine Empire, fell to Ottoman rule ("Othman's race") in the fifteenth century. Byron was there from May 14 to July 14, 1810, during the Greek Orthodox Lent and the carnival that preceded it (described in stanzas 78–79).
4. Seraglio; harem or, in this sense, palace of the sultan.
5. "When taken by the Latins, and retained for several years."
6. "Mecca and Medina were taken some time ago by the Wahabees, a sect yearly increasing." Mohammed was buried in Medina.

79

And whose more rife with merriment than thine,
Oh Stamboul! once the empress of their reign?
Though turbans now pollute Sophia's shrine,[7]
And Greece her very altars eyes in vain: 750
(Alas! her woes will still pervade my strain!)
Gay were her minstrels once, for free her throng,
All felt the common joy they now must feign,
Nor oft I've seen such sight, nor heard such song,
As woo'd the eye, and thrill'd the Bosphorus along.   755

80

Loud was the lightsome tumult on the shore,
Oft Music changed, but never ceased her tone,
And timely echo'd back the measured oar,
And rippling waters made a pleasant moan:
The Queen of tides on high consenting shone,   760
And when a transient breeze swept o'er the wave,
'T was, as if darting from her heavenly throne,
A brighter glance her form reflected gave,
Till sparkling billows seem'd to light the banks they lave.

81

Glanced many a light caique[8] along the foam,   765
Danced on the shore the daughters of the land,
Ne thought had man or maid of rest or home,
While many a languid eye and thrilling hand
Exchanged the look few bosoms may withstand,
Or gently prest, return'd the pressure still: 770
Oh Love! young Love! bound in thy rosy band,
Let sage or cynic prattle as he will,
These hours, and only these, redeem Life's years of ill!

82

But, midst the throng in merry masquerade,
Lurk there no hearts that throb with secret pain,   775
Even through the closest searment[9] half betray?
To such the gentle murmurs of the main
Seem to re-echo all they mourn in vain;
To such the gladness of the gamesome crowd
Is source of wayward thought and stern disdain: 780
How do they loathe the laughter idly loud,
And long to change the robe of revel for the shroud!

---

7. Santa Sophia (or Hagia Sophia), a Christian church built in Constantinople during the Byzantine Empire, converted to a mosque after the Turkish invasion of 1453.
8. Pronounced kah-eek´; a long narrow rowboat typically used on the Bosphorus.
9. Cerement, cerecloth: wrapping for the dead, also bandages, the apparent meaning here, though the double entendre is suitable to the stanza as a whole and foreshadows "shroud" (line 782).

83

This must he feel, the true-born son of Greece,
If Greece one true-born patriot still can boast;
Not such as prate of war, but skulk in peace,   785
The bondsman's peace, who sighs for all he lost,
Yet with smooth smile his tyrant can accost,
And wield the slavish sickle, not the sword:
Ah! Greece! they love thee least who owe thee most;
Their birth, their blood, and that sublime record   790
Of hero sires, who shame thy now degenerate horde!

84

When riseth Lacedemon's[1] hardihood,
When Thebes Epaminondas[2] rears again,
When Athens' children are with hearts endued,
When Grecian mothers shall give birth to men,   795
Then may'st thou be restored; but not till then,
A thousand years scarce serve to form a state;
An hour may lay it in the dust: and when
Can man its shatter'd splendour renovate,
Recal its virtues back, and vanquish Time and Fate?   800

85

And yet how lovely in thine age of woe,
Land of lost gods and godlike men! art thou!
Thy vales of evergreen, thy hills of snow,[3]
Proclaim thee Nature's varied favourite now;
Thy fanes, thy temples to thy surface bow,   805
Commingling slowly with heroic earth,
Broke by the share of every rustic plough:
So perish monuments of mortal birth,
So perish all in turn, save well-recorded Worth;

86

Save where some solitary column mourns   810
Above its prostrate brethren of the cave;[4]
Save where Tritonia's[5] airy shrine adorns
Colonna's cliff,[6] and gleams along the wave;

---

1. Sparta's.
2. Theban general (418?–362 B.C.E.).
3. "On many of the mountains, particularly Kiakura, the snow never is entirely melted, notwithstanding the intense heat of the summer; but I never saw it lie on the plains, even in winter."
4. "Of Mount Pentelicus, from whence the marble was dug that constructed the public edifices of Athens. The modern name is Mount Mendeli. An immense cave, formed by the quarries, still remains, and will till the end of time."
5. Athena's.
6. "In all Attica, if we except Athens itself and Marathon, there is no scene more interesting than Cape Colonna. To the antiquary and artist, sixteen columns are an inexhaustible source of observation and design; to the philosopher, the supposed scene of some of Plato's conversations will not be unwelcome; and the traveller will be struck with the beauty of the prospect over 'Isles that crown the Aegean

Save o'er some warrior's half-forgotten grave,
Where the gray stones and unmolested grass   815
Ages, but not oblivion, feebly brave,
While strangers only not regardless pass,
Lingering like me, perchance, to gaze, and sigh "Alas!"

87

Yet are thy skies as blue, thy crags as wild;
Sweet are thy groves, and verdant are thy fields.   820
Thine olive ripe as when Minerva smiled,
And still his honied wealth Hymettus[7] yields;
There the blithe bee his fragrant fortress builds,
The freeborn wanderer of thy mountain-air;
Apollo still thy long, long summer gilds,   825
Still in his beam Mendeli's[8] marbles glare;
Art, Glory, Freedom fail, but Nature still is fair.

88

Where'er we tread 'tis haunted, holy ground;
No earth of thine is lost in vulgar mould,
But one vast realm of wonder spreads around,   830
And all the Muse's tales seem truly told,
Till the sense aches with gazing to behold
The scenes our earliest dreams have dwelt upon:
Each hill and dale, each deepening glen and wold
Defies the power which crush'd thy temples gone: 835
Age shakes Athena's tower, but spares gray Marathon.[9]

89

The sun, the soil, but not the slave, the same;
Unchanged in all except its foreign lord—

---

deep:' but, for an Englishman, Colonna has yet an additional interest, as the actual spot of Falconer's Shipwreck. Pallas and Plato are forgotten, in the recollection of Falconer and Campbell:—

'Here in the dead of night by Lonna's steep,
The seaman's cry was heard along the deep.'

This temple of Minerva may be seen at sea from a great distance. In two journeys which I made, and one voyage to Cape Colonna, the view from either side, by land, was less striking than the approach from the isles. In our second land excursion, we had a narrow escape from a party of Mainotes, concealed in the caverns beneath. We were told afterwards, by one of their prisoners, subsequently ransomed, that they were deterred from attacking us by the appearance of my two Albanians: conjecturing very sagaciously, but falsely, that we had a complete guard of these Arnaouts at hand, they remained stationary, and thus saved our party, which was too small to have opposed any effectual resistance. Colonna is no less a resort of painters than of pirates; there

'The hireling artist plants his paltry desk,
And makes degraded nature picturesque.'
(See Hodgson's Lady Jane Grey, &c)

But there Nature, with the aid of Art, has done that for herself. I was fortunate enough to engage a very superior German artist; and hope to renew my acquaintance with this and many other Levantine scenes, by the arrival of his performances."

7. A mountain near Athens.
8. See Byron's note to line 811.
9. A plain in southeast Greece where the Athenians ("Hellas' sword," line 841) defeated the Persians in 490 B.C.E.

Preserves alike its bounds and boundless fame
The Battle-field, where Persia's victim horde　　　　840
First bow'd beneath the brunt of Hellas' sword,
As on the morn to distant Glory dear,
When Marathon became a magic word;[1]
Which utter'd, to the hearer's eye appear
The camp, the host, the fight, the conqueror's career,　　　　845

90

The flying Mede,[2] his shaftless broken bow;
The fiery Greek, his red pursuing spear;
Mountains above, Earth's, Ocean's plain below;
Death in the front, Destruction in the rear!
Such was the scene—what now remaineth here?　　　　850
What sacred trophy marks the hallow'd ground,
Recording Freedom's smile and Asia's tear?
The rifled urn, the violated mound,
The dust thy courser's hoof, rude stranger! spurns around.

91

Yet to the remnants of thy splendour past　　　　855
Shall pilgrims, pensive, but unwearied, throng
Long shall the voyager, with th' Ionian blast,[3]
Hail the bright clime of battle and of song;
Long shall thine annals and immortal tongue
Fill with thy fame the youth of many a shore;　　　　860
Boast of the aged! lesson of the young!
Which sages venerate and bards adore,
As Pallas and the Muse unveil their awful lore.

92

The parted bosom clings to wonted home,
If aught that's kindred cheer the welcome hearth;　　　　865
He that is lonely, hither let him roam,
And gaze complacent on congenial earth.
Greece is no lightsome land of social mirth;
But he whom Sadness sootheth may abide,
And scarce regret the region of his birth,　　　　870
When wandering slow by Delphi's sacred side,
Or gazing o'er the plains where Greek and Persian died.

1. "'Siste Viator—heroa calcas!' was the epitaph on the famous Count Merci;—what then must be our feelings when standing on the tumulus of the two hundred (Greeks) who fell on Marathon? The principal barrow has recently been opened by Fauvel: few or no relics, as vases, &c. were found by the excavator. The plain of Marathon was offered to me for sale at the sum of sixteen thousand piastres, about nine hundred pounds! Alas!—'Expende—quot *libras* in duce summo—invenies!'— was the dust of Miltiades worth no more? It could scarcely have fetched less if sold by *weight*."
2. Persian.
3. The wind from the Ionian Sea, west of Greece.

93

Let such approach this consecrated land,
And pass in peace along the magic waste;
But spare its relics—let no busy hand   875
Deface the scenes, already how defaced!
Not for such purpose were these altars placed:
Revere the remnants nations once revered:
So may our country's name be undisgraced,
So may'st thou prosper where thy youth was rear'd,   880
By every honest joy of love and life endear'd!

94

For thee, who thus in too protracted song
Hast soothed thine idlesse with inglorious lays,
Soon shall thy voice be lost amid the throng
Of louder minstrels in these later days: 885
To such resign the strife for fading bays—
Ill may such contest now the spirit move
Which heeds nor keen reproach nor partial praise;
Since cold each kinder heart that might approve,
And none are left to please when none are left to love.   890

95

Thou too art gone, thou loved and lovely one![4]
Whom youth and youth's affections bound to me;
Who did for me what none beside have done,
Nor shrank from one albeit unworthy thee.
What is my being? thou hast ceased to be!   895
Nor staid to welcome here thy wanderer home,
Who mourns o'er hours which we no more shall see—
Would they had never been, or were to come!
Would he had ne'er return'd to find fresh cause to roam!

96

Oh! ever loving, lovely, and beloved!   900
How selfish Sorrow ponders on the past,
And clings to thoughts now better far removed!
But Time shall tear thy shadow from me last.
All thou couldst have of mine, stern Death! thou hast;
The parent, friend, and now the more than friend: 905
Ne'er yet for one thine arrows flew so fast,
And grief with grief continuing still to blend,
Hath snatch'd the little joy that life had yet to lend.

4. Edleston; see note to line 73.

97

Then must I plunge again into the crowd,
And follow all that Peace disdains to seek?   910
Where Revel calls, and Laughter, vainly loud,
False to the heart, distorts the hollow cheek,
To leave the flagging spirit doubly weak;
Still o'er the features, which perforce they cheer,
To feign the pleasure or conceal the pique,   915
Smiles form the channel of a future tear,
Or raise the writhing lip with ill-dissembled sneer.

98

What is the worst of woes that wait on age?
What stamps the wrinkle deeper on the brow?
To view each loved one blotted from life's page,   920
And be alone on earth, as I am now.
Before the Chastener humbly let me bow:
O'er hearts divided and o'er hopes destroy'd,
Roll on, vain days! full reckless may ye flow,
Since Time hath reft whate'er my soul enjoy'd,   925
And with the ills of Eld mine earlier years alloy'd.

Appendix to Canto the Second

Note [A]

"To rive what Goth, and Turk, and Time hath spared."
STANZA [12] LINE 2.

At this moment (January 3, 1810), besides what has been already deposited in London, an Hydriot vessel is in the Pyraeus to receive every portable relic. Thus, as I heard a young Greek observe, in common with many of his countrymen—for, lost as they are, they yet feel on this occasion—thus may Lord Elgin boast of having ruined Athens. An Italian painter of the first eminence, named Lusieri, is the agent of devastation; and like the Greek *finder* of Verres in Sicily, who followed the same profession, he has proved the able instrument of plunder. Between this artist and the French Consul Fauvel, who wishes to rescue the remains for his own government, there is now a violent dispute concerning a car employed in their conveyance, the wheel of which—I wish they were both broken upon it—has been locked up by the Consul, and Lusieri has laid his complaint before the Waywode. Lord Elgin has been extremely happy in his choice of Signor Lusieri. During a residence of ten years in Athens, he never had the curiosity to proceed as far as Sunium (now Caplonna), till he accompanied us in our second excursion. However, his works, as far as they go, are most beautiful: but they are almost all unfinished. While he and his patrons confine themselves to tasting medals, appreciating cameos, sketching columns, and cheapening gems, their little absurdities are as harmless as insect or fox-hunting, maiden speechifying, barouche-driving, or any such pastime; but when they carry away three or four shiploads of the most valuable and massy relics that time and barbarism have left to the most injured and most celebrated of cities; when they destroy, in a vain attempt to tear down, those works which have been the admiration of ages, I know no motive which can excuse, no name which can designate, the perpetrators of this dastardly devastation. It was not the least of the crimes laid to the charge of Verres, that he had plundered Sicily, in the manner since imitated at Athens. The most unblushing impudence could hardly go farther than to affix the name of its plunderer to the walls of the Acropolis; while the wanton and useless deface-ment of the whole range of the basso-relievos, in one compartment of the tem-ple, will never permit that name to be pronounced by an observer without execration.

On this occasion I speak impartially: I am not a collector or admirer of col-lections, consequently no rival; but I have some early prepossession in favour of Greece, and do not think the honour of England advanced by plunder, whether of India or Attica.

Another noble Lord has done better, because he has done less: but some oth-ers, more or less noble, yet 'all honourable men,' have done *best*, because, after a deal of excavation and execration, bribery to the Waywode, mining and coun-termining, they have done nothing at all. We had such ink-shed, and wine-shed, which almost ended in bloodshed! Lord E.'s 'prig'—see Jonathan Wild for the definition of 'priggism'—quarrelled with another, *Gropius** by name (a very good name too for his business), and muttered something about satisfaction, in a verbal answer to a note of the poor Prussian: this was stated at table to Gropius, who laughed, but could eat no dinner afterwards. The rivals were not reconciled when I left Greece. I have reason to remember their squabble, for they wanted to make me their arbitrator.

Note [B]

> *"Land of Albania! let me bend mine eyes*
> *On thee, thou rugged nurse of savage men!"*
> STANZA [37]. LINES 5 and 6.

Albania comprises part of Macedonia, Illyria, Chaonia, and Epirus. Iskander is the Turkish word for Alexander; and the celebrated Scanderbeg (Lord Alexan-der) is alluded to in the third and fourth lines of the thirty-eighth stanza. I do not know whether I am correct in making Scanderbeg the countryman of Alexander, who was born at Pella in Macedon, but Mr. Gibbon terms him so, and adds Pyrrhus to the list, in speaking of his exploits.

Of Albania Gibbon remarks, that a country "within sight of Italy is less known than the interior of America." Circumstances, of little consequence to mention, led Mr. Hobhouse and myself into that country before we visited any other part of the Ottoman dominions; and with the exception of Major Leake, then offi-cially resident at Joannina, no other Englishmen have ever advanced beyond the capital into the interior, as that gentleman very lately assured me. Ali Pacha was at that time (October, 1809) carrying on war against Ibrahim Pacha, whom he had driven to Berat, a strong fortress which he was then besieging: on our arrival at Joannina we were invited to Tepaleni, his highness's birthplace, and favourite Serai, only one day's distance from Berat; at this juncture the Vizier

---

* This Sr Gropius was employed by a noble Lord for the sole purpose of sketching, in which he excels; but I am sorry to say, that he has, through the abused sanction of that most respectable name, been treading at humble distance in the steps of Sr Lusieri.—A shipful of his trophies was detained, and I believe confiscated, at Constantinople, in 1810. I am most happy to be now enabled to state, that 'this was not in his bond;' that he was employed solely as a painter, and that his noble patron dis-avows all connection with him, except as an artist. If the error in the first and second edition of this poem has given the noble Lord a moment's pain, I am very sorry for it: Sr Gropius has assumed for years the name of his agent; and though I cannot much condemn myself for sharing in the mistake of so many, I am happy in being one of the first to be undeceived. Indeed, I have as much pleasure in contradicting this as I felt regret in stating it.—*Note to third edition.*

had made it his headquarters. After some stay in the capital, we accordingly fol-
lowed; but though furnished with every accommodation, and escorted by one
of the Vizier's secretaries, we were nine days (on account of the rains) in accom-
plishing a journey which, on our return, barely occupied four. On our route we
passed two cities, Argyrocastro and Libochabo, apparently little inferior to Yan-
ina in size; and no pencil or pen can ever do justice to the scenery in the vicin-
ity of Zitza and Delvinachi, the frontier village of Epirus and Albania Proper.

On Albania and its inhabitants I am unwilling to descant, because this will
be done so much better by my fellow-traveller, in a work which may probably
precede this in publication, that I as little wish to follow as I would to antici-
pate him. But some few observations are necessary to the text. The Arnaouts,
or Albanese, struck me forcibly by their resemblance to the Highlanders of
Scotland, in dress, figure, and manner of living. Their very mountains seemed
Caledonian, with a kinder climate. The kilt, though white; the spare, active
form; their dialect, Celtic in its sound, and their hardy habits, all carried me
back to Morven. No nation are so detested and dreaded by their neighbours as
the Albanese; the Greeks hardly regard them as Christians, or the Turks as
Moslems; and in fact they are a mixture of both, and sometimes neither. Their
habits are predatory—all are armed; and the red-shawled Arnaouts, the Mon-
tenegrins, Chimariots, and Gegdes, are treacherous; the others differ somewhat
in garb, and essentially in character. As far as my own experience goes, I can
speak favourably. I was attended by two, an Infidel and a Mussulman, to Con-
stantinople and every other part of Turkey which came within my observation;
and more faithful in peril, or indefatigable in service, are rarely to be found. The
Infidel was named Basilius, the Moslem, Dervish Tahiri; the former a man of
middle age, and the latter about my own. Basili was strictly charged by Ali Pacha
in person to attend us; and Dervish was one of fifty who accompanied us
through the forests of Acarnania to the banks of Achelous, and onward to Mes-
salonghi in Aetolia. There I took him into my own service, and never had occa-
sion to repent it till the moment of my departure.

When in 1810, after the departure of my friend Mr Hobhouse for England,
I was seized with a severe fever in the Morea, these men saved my life by fright-
ening away my physician, whose throat they threatened to cut if I was not cured
within a given time. To this consolatory assurance of posthumous retribution,
and a resolute refusal of Dr Romanelli's prescriptions, I attributed my recovery.
I had left my last remaining English servant at Athens; my dragoman was as ill
as myself, and my poor Arnaouts nursed me with an attention which would have
done honour to civilisation. They had a variety of adventures; for the Moslem,
Dervish, being a remarkably handsome man, was always squabbling with the
husbands of Athens; insomuch that four of the principal Turks paid me a visit
of remonstrance at the Convent, on the subject of his having taken a woman
from the bath—whom he had lawfully bought however—a thing quite contrary
to etiquette. Basili also was extremely gallant amongst his own persuasion, and
had the greatest veneration for the church, mixed with the highest contempt of
churchmen, whom he cuffed upon occasion in a most heterodox manner. Yet
he never passed a church without crossing himself; and I remember the risk he
ran in entering St Sophia, in Stambol, because it had once been a place of his
worship. On remonstrating with him on his inconsistent proceedings, he invari-
ably answered, 'Our church is holy, our priests are thieves;' and then he crossed
himself as usual, and boxed the ears of the first 'papas' who refused to assist in
any required operation, as was always found to be necessary where a priest had
any influence with the Cogia Bashi of his village. Indeed, a more abandoned
race of miscreants cannot exist than the lower orders of the Greek clergy.

When preparations were made for my return, my Albanians were summoned
to receive their pay. Basili took his with an awkward show of regret at my
intended departure, and marched away to his quarters with his bag of piastres.

I sent for Dervish, but for some time he was not to be found; at last he entered, just as Signor Logotheti, father to the ci-devant Anglo consul of Athens, and some other of my Greek acquaintances, paid me a visit. Dervish took the money, but on a sudden dashed it to the ground; and clasping his hands, which he raised to his forehead, rushed out of the room weeping bitterly. From that moment to the hour of my embarkation, he continued his lamentations, and all our efforts to console him only produced this answer, 'Μά φεινει,' 'He leaves me.' Signor Logotheti, who never wept before for any thing less than the loss of a para (about the fourth of a farthing), melted; the padre of the convent, my attendants, my visiters—and I verily believe that even Sterne's 'foolish fat scullion' would have left her 'fish-kettle,' to sympathise with the unaffected and unexpected sorrow of this barbarian.

For my own part, when I remembered that, a short time before my departure from England, a noble and most intimate associate had excused himself from taking leave of me because he had to attend a relation 'to a milliner's,' I felt no less surprised than humiliated by the present occurrence and the past recollection. That Dervish would leave me with some regret was to be expected: when master and man have been scrambling over the mountains of a dozen provinces together, they are unwilling to separate; but his present feelings, contrasted with his native ferocity, improved my opinion of the human heart. I believe this almost feudal fidelity is frequent amongst them. One day, on our journey over Parnassus, an Englishman in my service gave him a push in some dispute about the baggage, which he unluckily mistook for a blow; he spoke not, but sat down leaning his head upon his hands. Foreseeing the consequences, we endeavoured to explain away the affront, which produced the following answer:—'I *have been* a robber; I *am* a soldier; no captain ever struck me; *you* are my master, I have eaten your bread, but by *that* bread! (an usual oath) had it been otherwise, I would have stabbed the dog your servant, and gone to the mountains.' So the affair ended, but from that day forward, he never thoroughly forgave the thoughtless fellow who insulted him. Dervish excelled in the dance of his country, conjectured to be a remnant of the ancient Pyrrhic: be that as it may, it is manly, and requires wonderful agility. It is very distinct from the stupid Romaika, the dull round-about of the Greeks, of which our Athenian party had so many specimens.

The Albanians in general (I do not mean the cultivators of the earth in the provinces, who have also that appellation, but the mountaineers) have a fine cast of countenance; and the most beautiful women I ever beheld, in stature and in features, we saw *levelling* the *road* broken down by the torrents between Delvinachi and Libochabo. Their manner of walking is truly theatrical; but this strut is probably the effect of the capote, or cloak, depending from one shoulder. Their long hair reminds you of the Spartans, and their courage in desultory warfare is unquestionable. Though they have some cavalry amongst the Gegdes, I never saw a good Arnaout horseman; my own preferred the English saddles, which, however, they could never keep. But on foot they are not to be subdued by fatigue.

Note [C]

"While thus in concert," &c.

STANZA [72]. LINE LAST.

As a specimen of the Albanian or Arnaout dialect of the Illyric, I here insert two of their most popular choral songs, which are generally chanted in dancing by men or women indiscriminately. The first words are merely a kind of chorus without meaning, like some in our own and all other languages.

1.

Bo, Bo, Bo, Bo, Bo, Bo,
Naciarura, popuso.

1.

Lo, Lo, I come, I come; be
thou silent.

2.

Naciarura na civin
Ha pen derini ti hin.

2.

I come I run; open the door
that I may enter.

3.

Ha pe uderi escrotini
Ti vin ti mar servetini.

3.

Open the door by halves, that I
may take my turban.

4.

Caliriote me surme
Ea ha pe pse dua tive.

4.

Caliriotes* with the dark eyes,
open the gate, that I may enter.

5.

Buo, Bo, Bo, Bo, Bo,
Gi egem spirta esimiro.

5.

Lo, Lo, I hear thee, my soul.

6.

Caliriote vu le funde
Ede vete tunde tunde.

6.

An Arnaout girl, in costly garb,
walks with graceful pride.

7.

Caliriote me surme
Ti mi put e poi mi le.

7.

Caliriot maid of the dark eyes,
give me a kiss.

8.

Se ti puta citi mora
Si mi ri ni veti udo gia.

8.

If I have kissed thee, what hast
thou gained? My soul is con-
sumed with fire.

9.

Va le ni il che cadale
Celo more, more celo.

9.

Dance lightly, more gently, and
gently still.

10.

Plu hari ti tirete
Ply huron cia pra seti.

10.

Make not so much dust to de-
stroy your embroidered hose.

The last stanza would puzzle a commentator: the men have certainly buskins of the most beautiful texture, but the ladies (to whom the above is supposed to be addressed) have nothing under their little yellow boots and slippers but a well-turned and sometimes very white ankle. The Arnaout girls are much handsomer than the Greeks, and their dress is far more picturesque. They preserve their shape much longer also, from being always in the open air. It is to be observed, that the Aranout is not a *written* language: the words of this song, therefore, as well as the one which follows, are spelt according to their pronunciation. They are copied by one who speaks and understands the dialect perfectly, and who is a native of Athens.

1.

Ndi sefda tinde ulavossa
Vettimi upri vi lofsa.

1.

I am wounded by thy love, and
have loved but to scorch myself.

---

* The Albanese, particularly the women, are frequently termed "Caliriotes;" for what reason I enquired in vain.

2.

Ah vaisisso mi privi lofse
Si mi rini mi la vosse.

2.

Thou hast consumed me! Ah,
maid! thou hast struck me to
the heart.

3.

Uti tasa roba stua
Sitti eve tulati dua.

3.

I have said I wish no dowry, but
thine eyes and eye lashes.

4.

Roba stinori ssidua
Qu mi sini vetti dua.

4.

The accursed dowry I want not,
but thee only.

5.

Qurmini dua civileni
Roba ti siarmi tildi eni.

5.

Give me thy charms, and let the
portion feed the flames.

6.

Utara pisa vaisisso me simi rin
ti hapti
Eti mi bire a piste si gui dendroi
tiltati.

6.

I have loved thee, maid, with
a sincere soul, but thou hast
left me like a withered tree.

7.

Udi vura udorini udiri cicova
cilti mora
Udorini talti hollna u ede
caimoni mora.

7.

If I have placed my hand on
thy bosom, what have I gained?
my hand is with drawn, but
retains the flame.

I believe the two last stanzas, as they are in a different measure, ought to belong to another ballad. An idea something similar to the thought in the last lines was expressed by Socrates, whose arm having come in contact with one of his "ὑποζολπιοι," Critobulus or Cleobulus, the philososopher complained of a shooting pain as far as his shoulder for some days after, and therefore very properly resolved to teach his disciples in future without touching them.

Note [D]. See p. [76].

"Fair Greece! sad relic of departed worth!
Immortal, though no more; though fallen, great!"
STANZA [73]. LINES 1 AND 2.

1

Before I say any thing about a city of which every body, traveller or not, has thought it necessary to say something, I will request Miss Owenson, when she next borrows an Athenian heroine for her four volumes, to have the goodness to marry her to somebody more of a gentleman than a "Disdar Aga" (who by the by is not an Aga), the most impolite of petty officers, the greatest patron of larceny Athens ever saw (except Lord E.), and the unworthy occupant of the Acropolis, on a handsome annual stipend of 150 piastres (eight pounds sterling), out of which he has only to pay his garrison, the most ill-regulated corps in the ill-regulated Ottoman Empire. I speak it tenderly, seeing I was once the cause of the husband of "Ida of Athens" nearly suffering the bastinado; and because the said "Disdar" is a turbulent husband, and beats his wife; so that I exhort and beseech Miss Owenson to sue for a separate maintenance in behalf of "Ida." Having premised thus much, on a matter of such import to the readers of romances, I may now leave Ida, to mention her birthplace.

Setting aside the magic of the name, and all those associations which it would be pedantic and superfluous to recapitulate, the very situation of Athens would render it the favourite of all who have eyes for art or nature. The climate, to me at least, appeared a perpetual spring; during eight months I never passed a day without being as many hours on horse-back: rain is extremely rare, snow never lies in the plains, and a cloudy day is an agreeable rarity. In Spain, Portugal, and every part of the East which I visited, except Ionia and Attica, I perceived no such superiority of climate to our own; and at Constantinople, where I passed May, June, and part of July (1810), you might "damn the climate, and complain of spleen," five days out of seven.

The air of the Morea is heavy and unwholesome, but the moment you pass the isthmus in the direction of Megara the change is strikingly perceptible. But I fear Hesiod will still be found correct in his description of a Boeotian winter.

We found at Livadia an "esprit fort" in a Greek bishop, of all free-thinkers! This worthy hypocrite rallied his own religion with great intrepidity (but not before his flock), and talked of a mass as a "coglioneria." It was impossible to think better of him for this; but, for a Boeotian, he was brisk with all his absurdity. This phenomenon (with the exception indeed of Thebes, the remains of Chaeronea, the plain of Platea, Orchomenus, Livadia, and its nominal cave of Trophonius) was the only remarkable thing we saw before we passed Mount Cithaeron.

The fountain of Dirce turns a mill: at least my companion (who, resolving to be at once cleanly and classical, bathed in it) pronounced it to be the fountain of Dirce, and any body who thinks it worth while may contradict him. At Castri we drank of half a dozen streamlets, some not of the purest, before we decided to our satisfaction which was the true Castalian, and even that had a villanous twang, probably from the snow, though it did nor throw us into an epic fever, like poor Dr. Chandler.

From Fort Phyle, of which large remains still exist, the Plain of Athens, Pentelicus, Hymettus, the Aegean, and the Acropolis, burst upon the eye at once; in my opinion, a more glorious prospect than even Cintra or Istambol. Not the view from the Troad, with Ida, the Hellespont, and the more distant Mount Athos, can equal it, though so superior in extent.

I heard much of the beauty of Arcadia, but excepting the view from the monastery of Megaspelion (which is inferior to Zitza in a command of country) and the descent from the mountains on the way from Tripolitza to Argos, Arcadia has little to recommend it beyond the name.

"Sternitur, et *dulces* moriens reminiscitur Argos."

Virgil could have put this into the mouth of none but an Argive, and (with reverence be it spoken) it does not deserve the epithet. And if the Polynices of Statius, "In mediis audit duo litora campis," did actually hear both shores in crossing the isthmus of Corinth, he had better ears than have ever been worn in such a journey since.

"Athens," says a celebrated topographer, "is still the most polished city of Greece." Perhaps it may of *Greece*, but not of the *Greeks*; for Joannina in Epirus is universally allowed, amongst themselves, to be superior in the wealth, refinement, learning, and dialect of its inhabitants. The Athenians are remarkable for their cunning; and the lower orders are not improperly characterised in that proverb, which classes them with "the Jews of Salonica, and the Turks of the Negropont."

Among the various foreigners resident in Athens, French, Italians, Germans, Ragusans, &c., there was never a difference of opinion in their estimate of the Greek character, though on all other topics they disputed with great acrimony.

M. Fauvel, the French consul, who has passed thirty years principally at Athens, and to whose talents as an artist, and manners as a gentleman, none who have known him can refuse their testimony, has frequently declared in my hearing, that the Greeks do not deserve to be emancipated; reasoning on the grounds of their "national and individual depravity!" while he forgot that such depravity is to be attributed to causes which can only be removed by the measure he reprobates.

M. Roque, a French merchant of respectability long settled in Athens, asserted with the most amusing gravity, "Sir, they are the same *canaille* that existed *in the days of Themistocles!*" an alarming remark to the "Laudator temporis acti." The ancients banished Themistocles; the moderns cheat Monsieur Roque: thus great men have ever been treated!

In short, all the Franks who are fixtures, and most of the Englishmen, Germans, Danes, &c. of passage, came over by degrees to their opinion, on much the same grounds that a Turk in England would condemn the nation by wholesale, because he was wronged by his lacquey, and overcharged by his washerwoman.

Certainly it was not a little staggering when the Sieurs Fauvel and Lusieri, the two greatest demagogues of the day, who divide between them the power of Pericles and the popularity of Cleon, and puzzle the poor Waywode with perpetual differences, agreed in the utter condemnation, "nulla virtute redemptum," of the Greeks in general, and of the Athenians in particular.

For my own humble opinion, I am loth to hazard it, knowing as I do, that there be now in MS. no less than five tours of the first magnitude and of the most threatening aspect, all in typographical array, by persons of wit, and honour, and regular common-place books: but, if I may say this without offence, it seems to me rather hard to declare so positively and pertinaciously, as almost every body has declared, that the Greeks, because they are very bad, will never be better.

Eton and Sonnini have led us astray by their panegyrics and projects; but, on the other hand, De Pauw and Thornton have debased the Greeks beyond their demerits.

The Greeks will never be independent; they will never be sovereigns as heretofore, and God forbid they ever should! but they may be subjects without being slaves. Our colonies are not independent, but they are free and industrious, and such may Greece be hereafter.

At present, like the Catholics of Ireland and the Jews throughout the world, and such other cudgelled and heterodox people, they suffer all the moral and physical ills that can afflict humanity. Their life is a struggle against truth; they are vicious in their own defence. They are so unused to kindness, that when they occasionally meet with it they look upon it with suspicion, as a dog often beaten snaps at your fingers if you attempt to caress him. "They are ungrateful, notoriously, abominably ungrateful!"—this is the general cry. Now, in the name of Nemesis! for what are they to be grateful? Where is the human being that ever conferred a benefit on Greek or Greeks? They are to be grateful to the Turks for their fetters, and to the Franks for their broken promises and lying counsels. They are to be grateful to the artist who engraves their ruins, and to the antiquary who carries them away; to the traveller whose janissary flogs them, and to the scribbler whose journal abuses them! This is the amount of their obligations to foreigners.

II.

Franciscan Convent, Athens, January 23, 1811.

Amongst the remnants of the harbarous policy of the earlier ages, are the traces of bondage which yet exist in different countries; whose inhabitants, however divided in religion and manners, almost all agree in oppression.

The English have at last compassionated their negroes, and under a less bigoted government, may probably one day release their Catholic brethren: but the interposition of foreigners alone can emancipate the Greeks, who, otherwise, appear to have as small a chance of redemption from the Turks, as the Jews have from mankind in general.

Of the ancient Greeks we know more than enough; at least the younger men of Europe devote much of their time to the study of the Greek writers and history, which would be more usefully spent in mastering their own. Of the moderns, we are perhaps more neglectful than they deserve; and while every man of any pretensions to learning is tiring out his youth, and often his age, in the study of the language and of the harangues of the Athenian demagogues in favour of freedom, the real or supposed descendants of these sturdy republicans are left to the actual tyranny of their masters, although a very slight effort is required to strike off their chains.

To talk, as the Greeks themselves do, of their rising again to their pristine superiority, would be ridiculous; as the rest of the world must resume its barbarism, after reasserting the sovereignty of Greece: but there seems to be no very great obstacle, except in the apathy of the Franks, to their becoming an useful dependency, or even a free state with a proper guarantee;—under correction, however, be it spoken, for many and well-informed men doubt the practicability even of this.

The Greeks have never lost their hope, though they are now more divided in opinion on the subject of their probable deliverers. Religion recommends the Russians; but they have twice been deceived and abandoned by that power, and the dreadful lesson they received after the Muscovite desertion in the Morea has never been forgotten. The French they dislike; although the subjugation of the rest of Europe will, probably, be attended by the deliverance of continental Greece. The islanders look to the English for succour, as they have very lately possessed themselves of the Ionian republic, Corfu excepted. But whoever appear with arms in their hands will be welcome; and when that day arrives, Heaven have mercy on the Ottomans, they cannot expect it from the Giaours.

But instead of considering what they have been, and speculating on what they may be, let us look at them as they are.

And here it is impossible to reconcile the contrariety of opinions: some, particularly the merchants, decrying the Greeks in the strongest language; others, generally travellers, turning periods in their eulogy, and publishing very curious speculations grafted on their former state, which can have no more effect on their present lot, than the existence of the Incas on the future fortunes of Peru.

One very ingenious person terms them the "natural allies of Englishmen;" another no less ingenious, will not allow them to be the allies of anybody, and denies their very descent from the ancients; a third, more ingenious than either, builds a Greek empire on a Russian foundation, and realises (on paper) all the chimeras of Catharine II. As to the question of their descent, what can it import whether the Mainotes are the lineal Laconians or not? or the present Athenians as indigenous as the bees of Hymettus, or as the grasshoppers, to which they once likened themselves; What Englishman cares if he be of a Danish, Saxon, Norman, or Trojan blood? or who, except a Welshman, is afflicted with a desire of being descended from Caractacus?

The poor Greeks do not so much abound in the good things of this world, as to render even their claims to antiquity an object of envy; it is very cruel, then, in Mr. Thornton to disturb them in the possession of all that time has left them; viz. their pedigree, of which they are the more tenacious, as it is all they can call their own. It would be worth while to publish together, and compare, the works of Messrs. Thornton and De Pauw, Eton and Sonnini; paradox on one side, and prejudice on the other. Mr. Thornton conceives himself to have claims to public confidence from a fourteen years' residence at Pera; perhaps he may on the subject of the Turks, but this can give him no more insight into the real state of Greece and her inhabitants, than as many years spent in Wapping into that of the Western Highlands.

The Greeks of Constantinople live in Fanal; and if Mr. Thornton did not oftener cross the Golden Horn than his brother merchants are accustomed to do, I should place no great reliance on his information. I actually heard one of these gentlemen boast of their little general intercourse with the city, and assert of himself, with an air of triumph, that he had been but four times at Constantinople in as many years.

As to Mr. Thornton's voyages in the Black Sea with Greek vessels, they gave him the same idea of Greece as a cruise to Berwick in a Scotch smack would of Johnny Grot's house. Upon what grounds then does he arrogate the right of condemning by wholesale a body of men, of whom he can know little? It is rather a curious circumstance that Mr. Thornton, who so lavishly dispraises Pouqueville on every occasion of mentioning the Turks, has yet recourse to him as authority on the Greeks, and terms him an impartial observer. Now, Dr. Pouqueville is as little entitled to that appellation, as Mr. Thornton to confer it on him.

The fact is, we are deplorably in want of information on the subject of the Greeks, and in particular their literature; nor is there any probability of our being better acquainted, till our intercourse becomes more intimate, or their independence confirmed: the relations of passing travellers are as little to be depended on as the invectives of angry factors; but till something more can be attained, we must be content with the little to be acquired from similar sources.*

However defective these may be, they are preferablé to the paradoxes of men who have read superficially of the ancients, and seen nothing of the moderns, such as De Pauw; who, when he asserts that the British breed of horses is ruined by Newmarket, and that the Spartans were cowards in the field, betrays an equal knowledge of English horses and Spartan men. His "philosophical observations" have a much better claim to the title of "poetical." It could not be expected that he who so liberally condemns some of the most celebrated institutions of the ancient, should have mercy on the modern Greeks; and it fortunately happens, that the absurdity of his hypothesis on their forefathers refutes his sentence on themselves.

Let us trust, then, that, in spite of the prophecies of De Pauw, and the doubts of Mr. Thornton, there is a reasonable hope of the redemption of a race of men, who, whatever may be the errors of their religion and policy, have been amply punished by three centuries and a half of captivity.

---

* A word, *en passant*, with Mr. Thornton and Dr. Pouqueville, who have been guilty between them of sadly clipping the Sultan's Turkish.

Dr. Pouqueville tells a long story of a Moslem who swallowed corrosive sublimate in such quantities that he acquired the name of "*Suleyman Yeyen*," i. e. quoth the Doctor, "*Suleyman, the eater of corrosive sublimate.*" "Aha," thinks Mr. Thornton, (angry with the Doctor for the fiftieth time), "have I caught you?"—Then, in a note twice the thickness of the Doctor's anecdote, he questions the Doctor's proficiency in the Turkish tongue, and his veracity in his own.—"For," observes Mr. Thornton (after inflicting on us the tough participle of a Turkish verb), "it means nothing more than *Suleyman the eater,*" and quite cashiers the supplementary "*sublimate.*" Now both are right, and both are wrong. If Mr. Thornton, when he next resides, "fourteen years in the factory," will consult his Turkish dictionary, or ask any of his Stamboline acquaintance, he will discover that "*Suleyma'n yeyen,*" put together discreetly, mean the "*Swallower of sublimate,*" without any "*Suleyman*" in the case: "*Suleyma*" signifying "*corrosive sublimate,*" and not being a proper name on this occasion, although it be an orthodox name enough with the addition of *n.* After Mr. Thornton's frequent hints of profound Orientalism, he might have found this out before he sang such paeans over Dr. Pouqueville.

After this, I think "Travellers *versus* Factors" shall be our motto, though the above Mr. Thornton has condemned "hoc genus omne," for mistake and misrepresentation. "Ne Sutor ultra crepidam," "No merchant beyond his bales." N. B. For the benefit of Mr. Thornton, "Sutor" is not a proper name.

III.

Athens, Franciscan Convent, March 17. 1811

"I must have some talk with this learned Theban."

Some time after my return from Contantinople to this city I received the thirty-first number of the Edinburgh Review as a great favour, and certainly at this distance an acceptable one, from the captain of an English frigate off Salamis. In that number, Art. 3. containing the review of a French translation of Strabo, there are introduced some remarks on the modern Greeks and their literature, with a short account of Coray, a co-translator in the French version. On those remarks I mean to ground a few observations; and the spot where I now write will, I hope, be sufficient excuse for introducing them in a work in some degree connected with the subject. Coray, the most celebrated of living Greeks, at least among the Franks, was born at Scio (in the Review, Smyrna is stated, I have reason to think, incorrectly), and besides the translation of Beccaria and other works mentioned by the Reviewer, has published a lexicon in Romaic and French, if I may trust the assurance of some Danish travellers lately arrived from Paris; but the latest we have seen here in French and Greek is that of Gregory Zolikogloou.* Coray has recently been involved in an unpleasant controversy with M. Gail,† a Parisian commentator and editor of some translations from the Greek poets, in consequence of the Institute having awarded him the prize for his version of Hippocrates "Περὶ ὑδάτων," &c. to the disparagement, and consequently displeasure, of the said Gail. To his exertions, literary and patriotic, great praise is undoubtedly due, but a part of that praise ought not to be withheld from the two brothers Zosimado (merchants settled in Leghorn), who sent him to Paris, and maintained him, for the express purpose of elucidating the ancient, and adding to the modern, researches of his countrymen. Coray, however, is not considered by his countrymen equal to some who lived in the two last centuries; more particularly Dorotheus of Mitylene, whose Hellenic writings are so much esteemed by the Greeks, that Meletius terms him "Μετὰ τὸν Θουκυδίδην καὶ Ξενοφῶντα ἄριστος Ἑλλήνων." (P. 224. Ecclesiastical History, vol. iv.)

Panagiotes Kodrikas, the translator of Fontenelle, and Kamarases, who translated Ocellus Lucanus on the Universe into French, Christodoulus, and more particularly Psalida, whom I have conversed with in Joannina, are also in high repute among their literati. The last mentioned has published in Romaic and Latin a work on "True Happiness," dedicated to Catherine II. But Polyzois, who is stated by the Reviewer to be the only modern except Coray who has distinguished himself by a knowledge of Hellenic, if he be the Polyzois Lampanitziotes of Yanina, who has published a number of editions in Romaic, was neither more nor less than an itinerant vender of books; with the contents of which he had no concern beyond his name on the title page, placed there to secure his property in the publication; and he was, moreover, a man utterly destitute of scholastic acquirements. As the name, however, is not uncommon, some other Polyzois may have edited the Epistles of Aristaenetus.

It is to be regretted that the system of continental blockade has closed the few channels through which the Greeks received their publications, particularly Venice and Trieste. Even the common grammars for children are become

---

* I have in my possession an excellent lexicon "τριγλωσσον," which I received in exchange from S. G—, Esq. for a small gem: my antiquarian friends have never forgotten it, or forgiven me.
† In Gail's pamphlet against Coray, he talks of "throwing the insolent Hellenist out of the windows." On this a French critic exclaims, "Ah, my God! throw an Hellenist out of the window! what sacrilege!" It certainly would be a serious business for those authors who dwell in the attics: but I have quoted the passage merely to prove the similarity of style among the controversialists of all polished countries; London or Edinburgh could hardly parallel this Parisian ebullition.

too dear for the lower orders. Amongst their original works the Geography of Meletius, Archbishop of Athens, and a multitude of theological quartos and poetical pamphlets, are to be met with; their grammars and lexicons of two, three, and four languages are numerous and excellent. Their poetry is in rhyme.

The most singular piece I have lately seen is a satire in dialogue between a Russian, English, and French traveller, and the Waywode of Wallachia (or Blackbey, as they term him), an archbishop, a merchant, and Cogia Bachi (or primate), in succession; to all of whom under the Turks the writer attributes their present degeneracy. Their songs are sometimes pretty and pathetic; their tune, generally unpleasing to the ear of a Frank; the best is the famous "Δεῦτε παῖδες τῶν Ἑλλήνων" by the unfortunate Riga. But from a catalogue of more than sixty authors, now before me, only fifteen can be found who have touched on any theme except theology.

I am intrusted with a commission by a Greek of Athens named Marmarotouri to make arrangements, if possible, for printing in London a translation of Barthelemi's Anacharsis in Romaic, as he has no other opportunity, unless he despatches the MS. to Vienna by the Black Sea and Danube.

The Reviewer mentions a school established at Hecatonesi, and suppressed at the instigation of Sebastiani: he means Cidonies, or, in Turkish, Haivali; a town on the continent, where that institution for a hundred students and three professors still exists. It is true that this establishment was disturbed by the Porte, under the ridiculous pretext that the Greeks were constructing a fortress instead of a college: but on investigation, and the payment of some purses to the Divan, it has been permitted to continue. The principal professor, named Ueniamin (i. e. Benjamin), is stated to be a man of talent, but a freethinker. He was born in Lesbos, studied in Italy, and is master of Hellenic, Latin, and some Frank languages; besides a smattering of the sciences.

Though it is not my intention to enter farther on this topic than may allude to the article in question, I cannot but observe that the Reviewer's lamentation over the fall of the Greeks appears singular, when he closes it with these words: "*The change is to be attributed to their misfortunes rather than to any 'physical degradation.'*" It may be true that the Greeks are not physically degenerated, and that Constantinople contained on the day when it changed masters as many men of six feet and upwards as in the hour of prosperity; but ancient history and modern politics instruct us that something more than physical perfection is necessary to preserve a state in vigour and independence; and the Greeks, in particular, are a melancholy example of the near connection between moral degradation and national decay.

The Reviewer mentions a plan "*we believe*" by Potemkin for the purification of the Romaic; and I have endeavoured in vain to procure any tidings or traces of its existence. There was an academy in St. Petersburg for the Greeks; but it was suppressed by Paul, and has not been revived by his successor.

There is a slip of the pen, and it can only be a slip of the pen, in p. 58. No. 31. of the Edinburgh Review, where these words occur:—"We are told that when the capital of the East yielded to *Solyman*"—It may be presumed that this last word will, in a future edition, be altered to Mahomet II.* The "ladies of Constantinople," it seems, at that period spoke a dialect, "which would not have

---

* In a former number of the Edinburgh Review, 1808, it is observed: "Lord Byron passed some of his early years in Scotland, where he might have learned that *pibroch* does not mean a *bagpipe*, any more than *duet* means a *fiddle*." Query,—Was it in Scotland that the young gentlemen of the Edinburgh Review *learned* that *Solyman* means *Mahomet II*, any more than *criticism* means *infallibility?*—but thus it is,

"Caedimus inque vicem praebemus crura sagittis."

The mistake seemed so completely a lapse of the pen (from the great *similarity* of the two words, and the *total absence of error* from the former pages of the literary leviathan) that I should have passed it over as in the text, had I not perceived in the Edinburgh Review much facetious exultation

disgraced the lips of an Athenian." I do not know how that might be, but am sorry to say the ladies in general, and the Athenians in particular, are much altered; being far from choice either in their dialect or expressions, as the whole Attic race are barbarous to a proverb:—

"Ω Αθηνα προτη χωρα
Τι γαιδαρονς τρεφεις τωρα."

In Gibbon, vol. x. p. 161, is the following sentence:—
"The vulgar dialect of the city was gross and barbarous, though the compositions of the church and palace sometimes affected to copy the purity of the Attic models." Whatever may be asserted on the subject, it is difficult to conceive that the "ladies of Constantinople," in the reign of the last Cæsar, spoke a purer dialect than Anna Comnena wrote three centuries before: and those royal pages are not esteemed the best models of composition, although the princess γλωτταν ειχεν ΑΚΡΙΒΩΣ Αττικιςουσαν. In the Fanal, and in Yanina, the best Greek is spoken: in the latter there is a flourishing school under the direction of Psalida.

There is now in Athens a pupil of Psalida's, who is making a tour of observation through Greece: he is intelligent, and better educated than a fellow-commoner of most colleges. I mention this as a proof that the spirit of inquiry is not dormant among the Greeks.

The Reviewer mentions Mr. Wright, the author of the beautiful poem "Horae Ionicae," as qualified to give details of these nominal Romans and degenerate Greeks; and also of their language: but Mr. Wright, though a good poet and an able man, has made a mistake where he states the Albanian dialect of the Romaic to approximate nearest to the Hellenic: for the Albanians speak a Romaic as notoriously corrupt as the Scotch of Aberdeenshire, or the Italian of Naples. Yanina, (where, next to the Fanal, the Greek is purest,) although the capital of Ali Pacha's dominions, is not in Albania but Epirus; and beyond Delvinachi in Albania Proper up to Argyrocastro and Tepaleen (beyond which I did not advance) they speak worse Greek than even the Athenians. I was attended for a year and a half by two of these singular mountaineers, whose mother tongue is Illyric, and I never heard them or their countrymen (whom I have seen, not only at home, but to the amount of twenty thousand in the army of Vely Pacha) praised for their Greek, but often laughed at for their provincial barbarisms.

I have in my possession about twenty-five letters, amongst which some from the Bey of Corinth, written to me by Notaras, the Cogia Bachi, and others by the dragoman of the Caimacam of the Morea (which last governs in Vely Pacha's absence) are said to be favourable specimens of their epistolary style. I also received some at Constantinople from private persons, written in a most hyperbolical style, but in the true antique character.

The Reviewer proceeds, after some remarks on the tongue in its past and present state, to a paradox (page 59.) on the great mischief the knowledge of his own language has done to Coray, who, it seems, is less likely to understand the ancient Greek, because he is perfect master of the modern! This observation follows a paragraph, recommending, in explicit terms, the study of the Romaic, as "a powerful auxiliary," not only to the traveller and foreign merchant, but also to the classical scholar; in short, to every body except the only person who can be thoroughly acquainted with its uses; and by a parity of reasoning, our old language is conjectured to be probably more attainable by "foreigners"

---

on all such detections, particularly a recent one, where words and syllables are subjects of disquisition and transposition; and the above-mentioned parallel passage in my own case irresistibly propelled me to hint how much easier it is to be critical than correct. The *gentlemen*, having enjoyed many a *triumph* on such victories, will hardly begrudge me a slight *ovation* for the present.

than by ourselves! Now, I am inclined to think, that a Dutch Tyro in our tongue (albeit himself of Saxon blood) would be sadly perplexed with "Sir Tristrem," or any other given "Authinleck MS." with or without a grammar or glossary; and to most apprehensions it seems evident, that none but a native can acquire a competent, far less complete, knowledge of our obsolete idioms. We may give the critic credit for his ingenuity, but no more believe him than we do Smollett's Lismahago, who maintains that the purest English is spoken in Edinburgh. That Coray may err is very possible; but if he does, the fault is in the man rather than in his mother tongue, which is, as it ought to be, of the greatest aid to the native student.—Here the Reviewer proceeds to business on Strabo's translators, and here I close my remarks.

Sir W. Drummond, Mr. Hamilton, Lord Aberdeen, Dr. Clarke, Captain Leake, Mr. Gell, Mr. Walpole, and many others now in England, have all the requisites to furnish details of this fallen people. The few observations I have offered I should have left where I made them, had not the article is question, and above all the spot where I read it, induced me to advert to those pages, which the advantage of my present situation enabled me to clear, or at least to make the attempt.

I have endeavoured to wave the personal feelings, which rise in despite of me in touching upon any part of the Edinburgh Review; not from a wish to conciliate the favour of its writers, or to cancel the remembrance of a syllable I have formerly published, but simply from a sense of the impropriety of mixing up private resentments with a disquisition of the present kind, and more particularly at this distance of time and place.

ADDITIONAL NOTE,

ON THE TURKS.

The difficulties of travelling in Turkey have been much exaggerated, or rather have considerably diminished of late years. The Mussulmans have been beaten into a kind of sullen civility, very comfortable to voyagers.

It is hazardous to say much on the subject of Turks and Turkey; since it is possible to live amongst them twenty years without acquiring information, at least from themselves. As far as my own slight experience carried me, I have no complaint to make; but am indebted for many civilities (I might almost say for friendship), and much hospitality, to Ali Pacha, his son Veli Pacha of the Morea, and several others of high rank in the provinces. Suleyman Aga, late Governor of Athens, and now of Thebes, was a *bon vivant*, and as social a being as ever sat cross-legged at a tray or a table. During the carnival, when our English party were masquerading, both himself and his successor were more happy to "receive masks" than any dowager in Grosvenor-square.

On one occasion of his supping at the convent, his friend and visiter, the Cadi of Thebes, was carried from table perfectly qualified for any club in Christendom; while the worthy Waywode himself triumphed in his fall.

In all money transactions with the Moslems, I ever found the strictest honour, the highest disinterestedness. In transacting business with them, there are none of those dirty peculations, under the name of interest, difference of exchange, commission, &c. &c. uniformly found in applying to a Greek consul to cash bills, even on the first houses in Pera.

With regard to presents, an established custom in the East, you will rarely find yourself a loser; as one worth acceptance is generally returned by another of similar value—a horse, or a shawl.

In the capital and at court the citizens and courtiers are formed in the same school with those of Christianity; but there does not exist a more honourable, friendly, and high-spirited character than the true Turkish provincial Aga, or Moslem country gentleman. It is not meant here to designate the governors of towns, but those Agas who, by a kind of feudal tenure, possess lands and houses, of more or less extent, in Greece and Asia Minor.

The lower orders are in as tolerable discipline as the rabble in countries with greater pretensions to civilisation. A Moslem, in walking the streets of our country-towns, would be more incommoded in England than a Frank in a similar situation in Turkey. Regimentals are the best travelling dress.

The best accounts of the religion and different sects of Islamism, may be found in D'Ohsson's French; of their manners, &c. perhaps in Thornton's English. The Ottomans, with all their defects, are not a people to be despised. Equal, at least, to the Spaniards, they are superior to the Portuguese. If it be difficult to pronounce what they are, we can at least say what they are *not*: they are *not* treacherous, they are *not* cowardly, they do *not* burn heretics, they are *not* assassins, nor has an enemy advanced to *their* capital. They are faithful to their sultan till he becomes unfit to govern, and devout to their God without an inquisition. Were they driven from St. Sophia to-morrow, and the French or Russians enthroned in their stead, it would become a question whether Europe would gain by the exchange? England would certainly be the loser.

With regard to that ignorance of which they are so generally, and sometimes justly accused, it may be doubted, always excepting France and England, in what useful points of knowledge they are excelled by other nations. Is it in the common arts of life? In their manufactures? Is a Turkish sabre inferior to a Toledo? or is a Turk worse clothed or lodged, or fed and taught, than a Spaniard? Are their Pachas worse educated than a Grandee? or an Effendi than a Knight of St. Jago? I think not.

I remember Mahmout, the grandson of Ali Pacha, asking whether my fellow-traveller and myself were in the upper or lower House of Parliament. Now, this question from a boy of ten years old proved that his education had not been neglected. It may be doubted if an English boy at that age knows the difference of the Divan from a College of Dervises; but I am very sure a Spaniard does not. How little Mahmout, surrounded, as he had been, entirely by his Turkish tutors, had learned that there was such a thing as a Parliament, it were useless to conjecture, unless we suppose that his instructors did not confine his studies to the Koran.

In all the mosques there are schools established, which are very regularly attended; and the poor are taught without the church of Turkey being put into peril. I believe the system is not yet printed (though there is such a thing as a Turkish press, and books printed on the late military institution of the Nizam Gedidd); nor have I heard whether the Mufti and the Mollas have subscribed, or the Caimacam and the Tefterdar taken the alarm, for fear the ingenuous youth of the turban should be taught not to "pray to God their way." The Greeks also—a kind of Eastern Irish papists—have a college of their own at Maynooth—no, at Haivali; where the heterodox receive much the same kind of countenance from the Ottoman as the Catholic college from the English legislature. Who shall then affirm, that the Turks are ignorant bigots, when they thus evince the exact proportion of Christian charity which is tolerated in the most prosperous and orthodox of all possible kingdoms? But though they allow all this, they will not suffer the Greeks to participate in their privileges: no, let them fight their battles, and pay their haratch (taxes), be drubbed in this world, and damned in the next. And shall we then emancipate our Irish Helots? Mahomet forbid! We should then be bad Mussulmans, and worse Christians: at present we unite the best of both—jesuitical faith, and something not much inferior to Turkish toleration.[1]

---

1. An additional lengthy appendix ("Remarks on the Romaic or Modern Greek Language, with Specimens and Translations"), printed in the early editions of *Childe Harold*, further reveals Byron's scholarly industriousness.

To Thyrza[1]

Without a stone to mark the spot,
   And say, what Truth might well have said,
By all, save one, perchance forgot,
   Ah, wherefore art thou lowly laid?
By many a shore and many a sea   5
   Divided, yet beloved in vain;
The past, the future fled to thee
   To bid us meet—no—ne'er again!
Could this have been—a word, a look
   That softly said, "We part in peace,"   10
Had taught my bosom how to brook,
   With fainter sighs, thy soul's release.
And didst thou not, since Death for thee
   Prepared a light and pangless dart,
Once long for him thou ne'er shalt see,   15
   Who held, and holds thee in his heart?
Oh! who like him had watch'd thee here?
   Or sadly mark'd thy glazing eye,
In that dread hour ere death appear,
   When silent Sorrow fears to sigh,   20
Till all was past? But when no more
   'Twas thine to reck of human woe,
Affection's heart-drops, gushing o'er,
   Had flow'd as fast—as now they flow.
Shall they not flow, when many a day   25
   In these, to me, deserted towers,[2]
Ere call'd but for a time away,
   Affection's mingling tears were ours?
Ours too the glance none saw beside;
   The smile none else might understand; 30
The whisper'd thought of hearts allied,
   The pressure of the thrilling hand;
The kiss, so guiltless and refined
   That Love each warmer wish forebore;
Those eyes proclaim'd so pure a mind,   35
   Even passion blush'd to plead for more.
The tone, that taught me to rejoice,
   When prone, unlike thee, to repine;
The song, celestial from thy voice,
   But sweet to me from none but thine;   40

1. Byron wrote this poem on October 11, 1811, upon learning of the death of John Edleston, a choir-boy at Cambridge whom Byron loved. It was first published in *Childe Harold's Pilgrimage, A Romaunt* (1812). This poem is one of several addressed to Edelston as "Thyrza," whose identity and especially whose gender Byron and his nineteenth-century commentators intentionally obscured and who is also the subject of *Childe Harold* II, stanzas 9 and 95–96. Byron said that the name "Thyrza" was taken from Abel's wife's name in a play by Solomon Gessner called *The Death of Abel* (1758). As likely a source is *The Greek Anthology* (C 3:32n). *Criticism:* Crompton, *Byron and Greek Love.*
2. Newstead Abbey, Byron's ancestral home.

The pledge we wore—I wear it still,[3]
    But where is thine?—Ah, where art thou?
Oft have I borne the weight of ill,
    But never bent beneath till now!
Well hast thou left in life's best bloom   45
    The cup of woe for me to drain.
If rest alone be in the tomb,
    I would not wish thee here again;
But if in worlds more blest than this
    Thy virtues seek a fitter sphere,   50
Impart some portion of thy bliss,
    To wean me from mine anguish here.
Teach me—too early taught by thee!
    To bear, forgiving and forgiven:
On earth thy love was such to me;   55
    It fain would form my hope in heaven!

October 11, 1811.

LETTERS AND JOURNAL

To Mrs. Catherine Gordon Byron

[Harrow-on-the-Hill, May 1–10, 1804?]

My Dear Mother—I received your letter and was very Glad to hear that you are well, I am very comfortable here as far as relates to my Comrades, but, I have got into two or three scrapes with Drury[1] and the other Masters, which are not very convenient, the other day as he was reprimanding me, (perhaps very properly) for my misdeeds he uttered the following words, "it is not probable that from your age and situation in the School your Friends will permit you to remain longer than Summer, but because you are about to leave Harrow, it is no reason you are to make the house a scene of riot and Confusion." this and much more said the Doctor, and I am informed From creditable authority that Dr. Drury, Mr. Evans and Mark Drury said I was a *Blackguard,* that Mark Drury said so I *know,* but I am inclined to doubt the authenticity of the report as to the rest, perhaps it is true perhaps not, but thank God they may call me a Blackguard, but they can never make me one, if Dr. Drury can bring one boy or any one else to say that I have committed a dishonourable action, and to prove it, I am content, but otherwise I am stigmatized without a cause, and I disdain and despise the malicious efforts of him and his Brother. His Brother Mark not Henry Drury[2] (whom I will do the Justice to say has never since last year interfered with me) is continually reproaching me with the narrowness of

---

3. A small cornelian heart given by Edleston to Byron in 1805 or 1806 and the subject of his poem "The Cornelian" (p. 4). Byron did not actually have the "pledge" in his possession at the time of Edleston's death (see letter to Mrs. Margaret Pigot, October 28, 1811 [*BLJ* 2:119–20]).
1. Dr. Joseph Drury, the Headmaster.
2. Dr. Drury's son Henry was Byron's first tutor at Harrow and his friend.

my fortune, to what end I know not[;] his intentions may be Good, but his manner is disagreeable, I see no reason why I am to be reproached with it. I have as much money, as many Clothes, and in every respect of appearance am equal if not superior to most of my schoolfellows, and if my fortune is narrow, it is my misfortune not my fault. But however the way to *riches* to *Greatness* lies before me, I can, I will cut myself a path through the world or perish in the attempt. others have begun life with nothing and ended Greatly. And shall I who have a competent if not a large fortune, remain idle, No, I will carve myself the passage to Grandeur, but never with Dishonour. These Madam are my intentions, but why this upstart Son of a Button maker is to reproach me about an estate which however, is far superior to his own, I know not, but that he should call me a Blackguard, is far worse, on account of the former I can blame only Hanson (and that officious Friend Lord Grey de Ruthyn,[3] whom I shall ever consider my most inveterate enemy), it is a mere trifle, but the latter I cannot bear, I have not deserved it, and I will not be insulted with impunity. Mr. Mark Drury rides out with his Son, sees me at a distance on a poney which I hired to go to the bathing place which is too far for me to walk, he calls out, tells his son I am a Blackguard, This son, who is no friend of mine comes home relates the story to his companions, possibly with a few exaggerations, but however the Greatest part was true, and I am to be considered as such a person by my comrades, it shall not be, I will say no more, I only hope you will take this into your consideration and remove me at Summer from a place where I am goaded with insults by those from whom I little deserved it.

I remain your affectionate Son,
BYRON

To Augusta Byron

Trin. Coll. Novr. 6th, 1805

My Dear Augusta—As might be supposed I like a College Life extremely, especially as I have escaped the Trammels or rather *Fetters* of my domestic Tyrant Mrs Byron, who continued to plague me during my visit in July and September. I am now most pleasantly situated in *Super*excellent Rooms, flanked on one side by my Tutor, on the other by an old Fellow, both of whom are rather checks upon my *vivacity*. I am allowed 500 a year, a Servant and Horse, so Feel as independent as a German Prince who coins his own Cash, or a Cherokee Chief who coins no Cash at all, but enjoys what is more precious, Liberty. I talk in raptures of that *Goddess* because my amiable Mama was so despotic. I am afraid the Specimens I have lately given her, of my Spirit, and determination to submit to no more unreasonable commands, (or the insults which follow a refusal to obey her implicitly whether right or wrong,) have given high offence, as I had a most *fiery* Letter from the *Court* at *Southwell* on Tuesday, because I would not turn off my Servant, (whom I had not the least reason to distrust, and who had an

---

3. In 1803, twenty-three-year-old Baron Gray de Ruthyn leased Byron's ancestral mansion, Newstead Abbey, for the period until Byron would come of age; he invited Byron to stay there with him in November of that year, when he seems to have offended the poet by his sexual advances. *Hanson*: John Hanson, Byron's solicitor, business agent (who managed the Newstead and Rochdale estates), and friend.

excellent Character from his last Master) at her suggestion from some caprice she had taken into her head.[1] I sent back to the Epistle which was couched in *elegant* terms a severe answer, which so nettled her Ladyship, that after reading it she returned it in a Cover without *deigning* a Syllable in return. The Letter and my answer you shall behold when you next see me, that you may judge of the Comparative merits of Each. I shall let her go on in the *Heroics*, till she cools, without taking the least notice. Her Behaviour to me for the last two Years neither merits my respect, nor deserves my affection. I am comfortable here, and having one of the best allowances in College, go on Gaily, but not extravagantly. I need scarcely inform you that I am not the least obliged to Mrs. B for it, as it comes off of my property, and She refused to fit out a single thing for me from her own pocket, my Furniture is paid for & she has moreover a handsome addition made to her own income, which I do not in the least regret, as I would wish her to be happy, but by *no means* to live with me in *person*. The sweets of her society I have already drunk to the last dregs, I hope we shall meet on more affectionate Terms, or meet no more. But why do I say? *meet*, her temper precludes every idea of happiness, and therefore in future I shall avoid her *hospitable* mansion, though she has the folly to suppose She is to be Mistress of my house when I come of [age]. I must apologize to you for the [dullness?] Of this letter, but to tell you the [truth the effects?] of last nights Claret have no[t gone?] out of my head, as I supped with a large party. I suppose that Fool Hanson in his *vulgar Idiom*, by the word Jolly did not mean Fat, but High Spirits, for so far from increasing I have lost one pound in a fortnight as I find by being regularly weighed. Adieu, Dearest Augusta.

[Signature cut out]

To Elizabeth Bridget Pigot

Trin. Coll. Camb. July 5th. 1807
My dear *Eliza*,—Since my last letter I have determined to reside *another year* at *Granta*[1] as my Rooms &c. &c. are finished in *great Style*, several old friends *come up* again, & many *new* acquaintances made, consequently my Inclination leads me *forward*, & I shall return to College in October if still *alive*. My life here has been one continued *routine* of Dissipation, out at different places every day, engaged to more *dinners* &c. &c. than my *stay* would permit me to *fulfil*, at this moment I write with a *bottle* of *Claret* in my *Head*, & *tears* in my *eyes*, for I have just parted from "my *Corneilan*"[2] who spent the evening with me; as it was our last Interview, I postponed my engagements to devote the hours of the *Sabbath* to friendship, Edleston & I have separated for the present, & my mind is a *Chaos* of *hope* & *Sorrow*.— Tomorrow I set out for London, you will address your answer to "*Gordon's Hotel*" *Albemarle Street*, where I *sojourn*, during my visit to the *Metropolis*.—I rejoice to hear you are interested in my "protegè", he has been my *almost constant* associate since October 1805, when I entered Trinity

1. Byron's mother was right: the servant (Francis Boyce) was found to be stealing from his master.
1. I.e., Cambridge (Granta is an earlier name of the River Cam).
2. The chorister John Edleston; see "The Cornelian" and note (p. 4).

College; his *voice* first attracted my notice, his *countenance* fixed it, & his *manners* attached me to him forever, he departs for a *mercantile house* in *Town*, in October, & we shall probably not meet, till the expiration of my minority, when I shall leave to his *decision*, either *entering* as a *Partner* through my Interest, or residing with me altogether. Of course he *would* in his present *frame* of mind prefer the *latter*, but he may alter his opinion previous to that period, however he shall have his choice, I certainly *love* him more than any human being, & neither *time* or Distance have had the least effect on my (in general) changeable Disposition.—In short, We shall put *Lady E. Butler*, & Miss *Ponsonby*[3] to the *Blush*, *Pylades* & *Orestes* out of countenance, & want nothing but a *Catastrophe* like *Nisus* & *Euryalus*, to give *Jonathan* & *David* the *"go by"*.—He certainly is perhaps more *attached* to *me*, than even I am in *return*, during the whole of my residence at *Cambridge*, we met every day summer & Winter, without passing *one tiresome moment*, & separated *each time* with increasing Reluctance. I hope you will *one day* see *us* together, he is the only *being* I esteem, though I *like many*.— The Marquis of *Tavistock* was down the other day, I supped with him at his *Tutor's*, entirely a *whig party*, the opposition *muster* very *strong* here, & Lord Hartington, the Duke of Leinster, &c. &c. are to join us in October, so every thing will be *splendid*.—The *Music* is all over at present, met with another *"accidency"*, upset a *Butter Boat* in the *lap* of a *lady*, looked very *blue*, *spectators* grinned, *"curse em"* apropos, sorry to say, been *drunk* every day, & not quite *sober yet*, however touch no meat, nothing but fish, soup & vegetables, consequently does me no harm, sad dogs all the *Cantabs*,[4] mem, *we* *mean* to reform next January.—This place is a *Monotony* of *endless variety*, *like it*, hate Southwell, full of old maids, how is Anne Becher? wants a husband, *men scarce*, wont *bite*, mem—tell Anne to fish more cautiously or the *Gudgeons* will be off; catch nothing but *Roach* & *Dace*.—Write soon, has Ridge[5] sold well? or do the Ancients demur? what Ladies have bought? all disappointed I dare say nothing *indecent* in the present publication, ⟨sorry for it⟩ *bad* Mary's the Image of Anne Houson,[6] thought it was her, all in the wrong, the Lady stared, so did I, I blushed, so did *not* the Lady, sad thing, wish women, had *more modesty*.—Talking of women brings my *terrier Fanny* into my head[;] how is she? very well I thank you.—Got a Headach, must go to bed, up early in the morning to travel, my "protegé" breakfasts with me, parting spoils my appetite, excepting from Southwell, mem—*I hate Southwell*,

yours ever
BYRON

---

3. Two aristocratic women who dressed as men and, since 1779, had been living together. The sentence continues to mention significant male friendships of classical literature and of the Bible.
4. Cantabrigian: a student of Cambridge.
5. John Ridge printed Byron's first publicly issued poems, *Hours of Idleness*, in the last week of June 1807.
6. A Southwell girl to whom Byron had addressed some early poems. *Mary's*: St. Mary's the Great, the church at Cambridge University.

To Elizabeth Bridget Pigot

Trinity College Cambridge
October 26th, 1807

My dear Elizabeth,—Fatigued with sitting up till four in the morning for these last two days at Hazard,[1] I take up my pen to enquire how your Highness, & the rest of my female acquaintance at the seat of Archiepiscopal Grandeur *Southwell,* go on.—I know I deserve a scolding for my negligence in not writing more frequently, but racing up & down the Country for these last three months, how was it possible to fulfil the Duties of a Correspondent?—Fixed at last for 6 weeks, I write, as *thin* as ever (not having gained an ounce since my Reduction)[2] & rather in better humour, for after all, *Southwell* was a detestable residence; thank St. Dominic I have done with it, I have been twice within 8 miles of it, but could not prevail on myself to *suffocate* in its heavy atmosphere.—This place is wretched enough, a villainous Chaos of Dice and Drunkenness, nothing but Hazard and Burgundy, Hunting, Mathematics and Newmarket, Riot and Racing, yet it is a Paradise compared with the eternal dullness of Southwell, oh! the misery of doing nothing, but make *Love, enemies,* and *Verses.*—Next January (but this is *entre nous* only, and pray let it be so, or my maternal persecutor will be throwing her Tomahawk at any of my curious projects) I am going to *Sea* for four of [or?] five months, with my Cousin Capt. Bettesworth, who commands the Tartar the finest frigate in the navy.[3] I have seen most scenes, and wish to look at a naval life.—We are going probably to the Mediterranean, or to the West Indies, or to the Devil, and if there is a possibility of taking me to the Latter, Bettesworth will do it, for he has received four and twenty wounds in different places, and at this moment possesses a Letter from the late Ld. Nelson,[4] stating Bettesworth as the only officer of the navy who had more wounds than himself.— — —I have got a new friend, the finest in the world, a *tame Bear,* when I brought him here, they asked me what I meant to do with him, and my reply was "he should *sit* for a *Fellowship.*"—Sherard[5] will explain the meaning of the sentence if it is ambiguous.—This answer delighted them not,—we have eternal parties here, and this evening a large assortment of *Jockies,* Gamblers, *Boxers, Authors, parsons,* and *poets,* sup with me.—A precious Mixture, but they go on well together, and for me, I am a *spice* of every thing except a Jockey, by the bye, I was dismounted again the other day.— —Thank your Brother in my name, for his Treatise. I have written 214 pages of a novel, one poem of 380 Lines, to be published (without my name) in a few weeks, with notes, 560 Lines of Bosworth Field, and 250 Lines of another poem in rhyme, besides half a dozen smaller pieces, the poem to be published is a Satire, apropos, I have been praised to the Skies in the Critical Review, and

---

1. Gamblers' game played with dice.
2. Troubled by a weight problem throughout most of his life, Byron undertook severe diets from time to time, and his weight fluctuated considerably.
3. Bettesworth was killed in 1808 while in command of the *Tartar.*
4. Viscount Horatio Nelson (1758–1805), heroic and victorious British admiral during the Napoleonic Wars.
5. Probably a cousin of the Pigots.

abused equally in another publication,[6] so much the Better, they tell me, for the sale of the Book, it keeps up controversy, and prevents it from being forgotten, besides the first men of all ages have had their share, nor do the humblest escape, so I bear it like a philosopher, it is odd enough the two opposite Critiques came out on the same day, and out of five pages of abuse, [my?] Censor only quotes *two lines*, from different poems, in support of his opinion, now the proper way to *cut* up, is to quote long passages, and make them appear absurd, because simple allegation is no proof.—on the other hand, there are seven pages of praise, and more than *my modesty* will allow, said on the subject.—Adieu yours truly

BYRON

P.S—Write, Write, Write!!!

To Robert Charles Dallas

Dorant's [Hotel]. Albemarle St.

January 21st. 1808

Sir,—Whenever Leisure and Inclination permit me the pleasure of a visit, I shall feel truly gratified in a personal acquaintance with one, whose mind has been long known to me in his Writings.—You are so far correct in your conjecture, that I am a member of the University of Cambridge, where I shall take my degree of A. M. this term, but were Reasoning, Eloquence or Virtue the objects of my search, Granta[1] is not their metropolis, nor is the place of her Situation an "El Dorado" far less an Utopia, the Intellects of her children are as stagnant as her Cam, and their pursuits limited to the Church,—not of Christ, but of the nearest Benefice.—As to my reading, I believe I may aver without hyperbole, it has been tolerably extensive in the historical department, so that few nations exist or have existed with whose records I am not in some degree acquainted from Herodotus down to Gibbon.—Of the Classics I know about as much as most Schoolboys after a Discipline of thirteen years, of the *Law* of the *Land* as much as enables me to keep "within the Statute" (to use the Poacher's vocabulary) I did study "the Spirit of Laws" and the Law of Nations,[2] but when I saw the Latter violated every month, I gave up my attempts at so useless an accomplishment.—Of Geography—I have seen more land on maps than I should wish to traverse on foot, of Mathematics enough to give me the headache without clearing the part affected, of Philosophy Astronomy and Metaphysicks, more than I can comprehend, and of Common Sense, so little, that I mean to leave a Byronian prize at each of our "Alma Matres" for the first Discovery, though I rather fear that of the Longitude will precede it.—I once thought myself a Philosopher and talked nonsense with great Decorum, I defied pain and preached up equanimity, for some time this did very well, for no one was in *pain* for me but my Friends, and none

---

6. The *Edinburgh Review*, which printed Henry Brougham's harsh critique of *Hours of Idleness*; excerpts from Brougham's review are on pp. 784–85. *One poem of 380 Lines*: "British Bards," the early, much shorter version of what became *English Bards and Scotch Reviewers*, published in 1809.

1. Cambridge.

2. *The Spirit of Laws* (1748) by Montesquieu and *The Law of Nations* (1758) by Emerich de Vattel.

lost their patience but my hearers, at last a fall from my horse convinced
me, bodily suffering was an Evil, and the worst of an argument overset my
maxims and my temper at the same moment, so I quitted Zeno for Aristip-
pus, and conceive that Pleasure constitutes the "το Καλov."³—In Moral-
ity I prefer Confucius to the ten Commandments, and Socrates to St. Paul
(though the two latter agree in their opinion of marriage) in Religion, I
favour the Catholic Emancipation but do not acknowledge the Pope, and I
have refused to take the Sacrament because I do not think eating Bread or
drinking wine from the hand of an earthly vicar, will make me an Inheritor
of Heaven.—I hold virtue in general, or the virtues severally, to be only in
the Disposition, each *a feeling* not a principle.—I believe Truth the prime
attribute of the Deity, and Death an eternal Sleep, at least of the Body.—You
have here a brief compendium of the Sentiments of the *wicked* George Ld.
B.—and till I get a new suit you will perceive I am badly cloathed. I remain

yours very truly
BYRON

To Charles Skinner Matthews

Falmouth June 22 [*1809*]

My dear Mathieu,—I take up the pen which our friend has for a moment
laid down merely to express a vain wish that you were with us in this delec-
table region, as I do not think Georgia itself can emulate in capabilities or
incitements to the "Plen. and optabil.—Coit."¹ the port of Falmouth &
parts adjacent.— —We are surrounded by Hyacinths² & other flowers of
the most fragrant [na]ture, & I have some intention of culling a handsome
Bouquet to compare with the exotics we expect to meet in Asia.—One speci-
men I shall certainly carry off, but of this hereafter.—Adieu Mathieu!— —

To Francis Hodgson

*Falmouth Roads—June 30th 1809*¹

1

Huzza! Hodgson, we are going,
Our embargo's off at last
Favourable Breezes blowing
Bend the canvass oer the mast,

3. The Beautiful.
1. A reference to "Coitum plenum et optabilem" ("full and to-be-wished-for intercourse") from Petro-
nius's *Satyricon* (Latin novel, c. first century C.E.), para. 86, sec. 4; *our friend*: Hobhouse.
2. Hyacinth was a youth beloved by Apollo, and the name is associated with young male beauty.
Matthews was one of the close circle of Byron's friends at Cambridge who were open among one
another about their otherwise covert homosexual relationships. Given the harsh social and legal
punishments for homosexuality at this time, they communicated via a coded language, of which
this letter is an instance. For the fullest discussion to date of this subject and of Byron's bisexual-
ity, see Crompton, *Byron and Greek Love*.
1. The ebullience of this verse epistle, written two days before Byron set sail for Lisbon, shows a
different side to Byron's moods during this journey from the one recorded in *Childe Harold* I–II.
It was first published in *Life*.

From aloft the signal's streaming
Hark! the farewell gun is fired,
Women screeching, Tars[2] blaspheming,
Tells us that our time's expired
Here's a rascal
Come to task all
Prying from the custom house,
Trunks unpacking
Cases cracking
Not a corner for a mouse
Scapes unsearched amid the racket
Ere we sail on board the Packet.[3]—

2

Now our boatmen quit their mooring
And all hands must ply the oar;
Baggage from the quay is lowering,
We're impatient—push from shore—
"Have a care! that Case holds liquor
"Stop the boat—I'm sick—oh Lord!
"Sick Maam! damme, you'll be sicker
Ere you've been an hour on board
Thus are screaming
Men & women
Gemmen, Ladies, servants, Jacks,
Here entangling
All are wrangling
Stuck together close as wax,
Such the genial noise & racket
Ere we reach the Lisbon Packet,

3

Now we've reached her, lo! the Captain
Gallant Kidd[4] commands the crew
Passengers *now* their berths are clapt in
Some to grumble, some to spew,
Heyday! call you that a Cabin?
Why tis hardly three feet square
Not enough to stow Queen Mab[5] in,
Who the deuce can harbour there?
Who Sir? plenty
Nobles twenty
Did at once my vessel fill
Did they—Jesus!
How you squeeze us
Would to God, they did so still,

2. Informal word for sailors.
3. A boat that carries passengers, mail, or goods.
4. The piratical Captain William Kidd (1645–1701).
5. A legendary fairy referred to in *Romeo and Juliet* 1.4.53–94.

Then I'd scape the heat & racket
Of the good ship, Lisbon Packet.

———————

Note + Erratum—
 For *"gallant"* read *"gallows."*—

4

Fletcher, Murray, Bob,[6] where are you?
  Stretched along the deck like logs
Bear a hand—you jolly tar you!
  Here's a rope's end for the dogs,
Hobhouse muttering fearful curses
  As the hatchway down he rolls
Now his breakfast, now his verses
  Vomits forth & damns our souls,
    Here's a stanza
    On Braganza
Help!—a couplet—no, a cup
    Of warm water,
    What's the matter?
Zounds! my liver's coming up,
I shall not survive the racket
Of this brutal Lisbon Packet.—

5

Now at length we're off for Turkey,
  Lord knows when we shall come back,
Breezes foul, & tempests murkey,
  May unship us in a crack,
But since life at most a jest is
  As Philosophers allow
Still to laugh by far the best is,
  Then laugh on—as I do now,
    Laugh at all things
    Great & small things,
    Sick or well, at sea or shore,
    While we're quaffing
    Let's have laughing
Who the Devil cares for more?
Save good wine, & who would lack it?
Even on board the Lisbon Packet.

                                      BYRON

———————

6. In addition to his close friend, John Cam Hobhouse, traveling with Byron were three Newstead
   residents: William Fletcher, Byron's servant; Joe Murray, an old servant of the previous Lord Byron;
   Robert Rushton, son of a Newstead tenant, befriended by Byron and taken along as his page.

To Francis Hodgson

Lisbon, July 16th, 1809

Thus far have we pursued our route, and seen all sorts of marvellous sights, palaces, convents, & c.—which, being to be heard in my friend Hobhouse's forthcoming Book of Travels, I shall not anticipate by smuggling any account whatsoever to you in a private and clandestine manner. I must just observe that the village of Cintra[1] in Estramadura is the most beautiful, perhaps in the world.* * *

I am very happy here, because I loves oranges, and talk bad Latin to the monks, who understand it, as it is like their own,—and I goes into society (with my pocket-pistols),[2] and I swims in the Tagus all across at once, and I rides on an ass or a mule, and swears Portuguese, and have got a diarrhoea and bites from the mosquitoes. But what of that? Comfort must not be expected by folks that go a pleasuring.* * *

When the Portuguese are pertinacious, I say, "Carracho!"—the great oath of the grandees, that very well supplies the place of "Damme,"—and, when dissatisfied with my neighbor, I pronounce him "Ambra di merdo." With these two phrases, and a third, "Avra Bouro," which signifieth "Get an ass," I am universally understood to be a person of degree and a master of languages. How merrily we lives that travellers be!—if we had food and raiment. But, in sober sadness, any thing is better than England, and I am infinitely amused with my pilgrimage as far as it has gone.

To-morrow we start to ride post near 400 miles as far as Gibraltar, where we embark for Melita [Malta?] and Byzantium. A letter to Malta will find me, or to be forwarded, if I am absent. Pray embrace the Drury and Dwyer and all the Ephesians[3] you encounter. I am writing with Butler's donative pencil,[4] which makes my bad hand worse. Excuse illegibility.* * *

Hodgson! send me the news, and the deaths and defeats and capital crimes and the misfortunes of one's friends; and let us hear of literary matters, and the controversies and the criticisms. All this will be pleasant— "Suave mari magno," & c.[5] Talking of that, I have been seasick, and sick of the sea. Adieu. Yours faithfully, & c.

To Mrs. Catherine Gordon Byron

Gibraltar
August 11th, 1809

Dear Mother,—I have been so much occupied since my departure from England that till I could address you a little at length, I have forborn writing altogether.—As I have now passed through Portugal & a considerable

---

1. See *Childe Harold* I, stanza 18 (p. 33).
2. In a note to *Childe Harold* I. 269, Byron recounts his own experience of Lisbon's street crime.
3. Elizabethan slang for good fellows or companions; Henry Drury, see p. 99, note 2; Dwyer is unidentified.
4. A gold pen that had been a gift of Dr. George Butler, the Harrow headmaster.
5. The passage referred to is from Lucretius, *De Rerum Natura* (2.1): "Pleasant it is, when over a great sea the winds trouble the waters, to gaze from shore upon another's great tribulation; not because any man's troubles are a delectable joy, but because to perceive you are free of them yourself is pleasant."

part of Spain, & have leisure at this place I shall endeavour to give you a
short detail of my movements.—We sailed from Falmouth on the 2d. of
July, reached Lisbon after a very favourable passage of four days and a half,
and took up our abode for a time in that city.—It has been often described
without being worthy of description, for, except the view from the Tagus
which is beautiful, and some fine churches & convents it contains little but
filthy streets & more filthy inhabitants.—To make amends for this the vil-
lage of Cintra about fifteen miles from the capitol is perhaps in every
respect the most delightful in Europe, it contains beauties of every descrip-
tion natural & artificial, Palaces and gardens rising in the midst of rocks,
cataracts, and precipices, convents on stupendous heights a distant view of
the sea and the Tagus, and besides (though that is a secondary considera-
tion) is remarkable as the scene of Sir H[ew] D[alrymple]'s convention.[1]—
It unites in itself all the wildness of the Western Highlands with the verdure
of the South of France. Near this place about 10 miles to the right is the
palace of Mafra[2] the boast of Portugal, as it might be of any country, in
point of magnificence without elegance, there is a convent annexed, the
monks who possess large revenues are courteous enough, & understand
Latin, so that we had a long conversation, they have a large Library & asked
[me?] if the *English* had *any books* in their country.——I sent my baggage
& part of the servants by sea to Gibraltar, and travelled on horseback from
Aldea Gallega (the first stage from Lisbon which is only accessible by
water) to Seville (one of the most famous cities in Spain where the Gov-
ernment called the Junta is now held) the distance to Seville is nearly four
hundred miles & to Cadiz about 90 further towards the Coast.—I had
orders from the Government & every possible accommodation on the road,
as an English nobleman in an English uniform is a very respectable per-
sonage in Spain at present. The horses are remarkably good, and the roads
(I assure you upon my honour for you will hardly believe it) very far supe-
rior to the best British roads, without the smallest toll or turnpike, you will
suppose this when I rode post to Seville in four days, through this parch-
ing country in the midst of summer, without fatigue or annoyance.—Seville
is a beautiful town, though the streets are narrow they are clean, we lodged
in the house of two Spanish unmarried ladies, who possess *six* houses in
Seville, and gave me a curious specimen of Spanish manners.—They are
women of character, and the eldest a fine woman, the youngest pretty but
not so good a figure as Donna Josepha, the freedom of women which is gen-
eral here astonished me not a little, and in the course of further observa-
tion I find that reserve is not the characteristic of the Spanish belles, who
are in general very handsome, with large black eyes, and very fine forms.—
The eldest honoured your *unworthy* son with very particular attention,
embracing him with great tenderness at parting (I was there but 3 days) after
cutting off a lock of his hair, & presenting him with one of her own about
three feet in length, which I send, and beg you will retain till my return.—
Her last words were "Adio tu hermoso! me gusto mucho" "Adieu, you pretty
fellow you please me much."—She offered a share of her apartment which

---

1. The Convention of Cintra (August 30, 1808), negotiated with the French commander by Sir Hew
   Dalrymple, allowed the French to withdraw from Portugal with their arms, thus avoiding uncon-
   ditional surrender. Byron criticizes the Convention in *Childe Harold* I, stanzas 24–26 (p. 35).
2. The huge monastery completed in 1730.

my *virtue* induced me to decline, she laughed and said I had some English "Amante," (lover) and added that she was going to be married to an officer in the Spanish army.—I left Seville and rode on to Cadiz! through a beautiful country, at Xeres where the Sherry we drink is made I met a great merchant a Mr. Gordon of Scotland, who was extremely polite and favoured me with the Inspection of his vaults & cellars, so that I quaffed at the Fountain head.—Cadiz, sweet Cadiz! is the most delightful town I ever beheld, very different from our English cities in every respect except cleanliness (and it is as clean as London) but still beautiful and full of the finest women in Spain, the Cadiz belles being the Lancashire witches of their land.—Just as I was introduced and began to like the grandees I was forced to leave it for this cursed place, but before I return to England I will visit it again.— The night before I left it, I sat in the box at the opera with Admiral Cordova's family, he is the commander whom Ld. St. Vincent defeated in 1797, and has an aged wife and a fine daughter.— — —Signorita Cordova the girl is very pretty in the Spanish style, in my opinion by no means inferior to the English in charms, and certainly superior in fascination.—Long black hair, dark languishing eyes, *clear* olive complexions, and forms more graceful in motion than can be conceived by an Englishman used to the drowsy listless air of his countrywomen, added to the most becoming dress & at the same time the most decent in the world, render a Spanish beauty irresistible. I beg leave to observe that Intrigue here is the business of life, when a woman marries she throws off all restraint, but I believe their conduct is chaste enough before.—If you make a proposal which in England would bring a box on the ear from the meekest of virgins, to a Spanish girl, she thanks you for the honour you intend her, and replies "wait till I am married, & I shall be too happy."—This is literally & strictly true.—Miss C[ordova] & her little brother understood a little French, and after regretting my ignorance of the Spanish she proposed to become my preceptress in that language; I could only reply by a low bow, and express my regret that I quitted Cadiz too soon to permit me to make the progress which would doubtless attend my studies under so charming a directress; I was standing at the back of the box which resembles our opera boxes (the theatre is large and finely decorated, the music admirable) in the manner which Englishmen generally adopt for fear of incommoding the ladies in front, when this fair Spaniard dispossessed an old women (an aunt or a duenna) of her chair, and commanded me to be seated next herself, at a tolerable distance from her mamma.—At the close of the performance I withdrew and was lounging with a party of men in the passage, when "en passant" the Lady turned round and called me, & I had the honour of attending her to the Admiral's mansion.—I have an invitation on my return to Cadiz which I shall accept, if I repass through the country on my way from Asia.—I have met Sir John Carr Knight errant at Seville & Cadiz, he is a pleasant man.— I like the Spaniards much, you have heard of the battle near Madrid,[3] & in England they will call it a victory, a pretty victory! two hundred officers and 5000 men killed all English, and the French in as great force as ever.—I should have joined the army but we have no time to lose before we get up the Mediterranean & Archipelago,—I am going over to Africa tomorrow, it is only six miles from this Fortress.—My next stage is Cagliari in Sardinia

3. The battle of Talavera, July 27–28, 1809. See *Childe Harold* I, stanzas 37–42 (pp. 38–40).

where I shall be presented to his S[ardinian] Majesty, I have a most superb uniform as a court dress, indispensable in travelling.—

. . .

BYRON

P.S.—So Ld. Grey[4] is married to a rustic, well done! if I wed I will bring you home a sultana with half a score cities for a dowry, and reconcile you to an Ottoman daughter in law with a bushel of pearls not larger than ostrich eggs or smaller than Walnuts.— —

To Mrs. Catherine Gordon Byron

Prevesa. Nov. 12th. 1809

My dear Mother,—I have now been some time in Turkey: this place is on the coast but I have traversed the interior of the province of Albania on a visit to the Pacha.[1]—I left Malta in the Spider a brig of war on the 21st. of Septr. & arrived in eight days at Prevesa.—I thence have been about 150 miles as far as Tepaleen his highness's country palace where I staid three days.—The name of the Pacha is Ali, & he is considered a man of the first abilities, he governs the whole of Albania (the ancient Illyricum) Epirus, & part of Macedonia, his Son *Velly* Pacha to whom he has given me letters governs the Morea[2] & he has great influence in Egypt, in short he is one of the most powerful men in the Ottoman empire.—When I reached Yanina the capital after a journey of three days over the mountains through a country of the most picturesque beauty, I found that Ali Pacha was with his army in Illyricum besieging Ibraham Pacha in the castle of Berat.—He had heard that an Englishman of rank was in his dominions & had left orders in Yanina with the Commandant to provide a house & supply me with every kind of necessary, *gratis*, & though I have been allowed to make presents to the slaves &c. I have not been permitted to pay for single article of household consumption.—I rode out on the viziers[3] horses & saw the palaces of himself & grandsons, they are splendid but too much ornamented with silk & gold.—I then went over the mountains through Zitza a village with a Greek monastery (where I slept on my return) in the most beautiful Situation (always excepting Cintra in Portugal) I ever beheld.[4]—In nine days I reached Tepaleen, our Journey was much prolonged by the torrents that had fallen from the mountains & intersected the roads. I shall never forget the singular scene on entering Tepaleen at five in the afternoon as the Sun was going down, it brought to my recollection (with some change of *dress* however) Scott's description of Branksome Castle in his lay,[5] & the feudal system.—The Albanians in their dresses (the most magnificent in the world, consisting of a long *white kilt*, gold worked cloak, crimson velvet

---

4. See p. 100, n. 4.
1. "Pacha" (Byron's spelling of Pasha), a title of high rank in Turkish domains. Ali Pasha (1741–1822), of Tepelene in Albania, had driven out the fierce Suliotes and became the despotic ruler of the Epirus, a part of Albania and the adjacent area in the northwest of Greece.
2. Peloponnesus.
3. A high official in certain Muslim countries.
4. Zitza and Cintra are, respectively, the focus of *Childe Harold* II, stanzas 48–52 (pp. 68–69), and I, stanzas 18–26 (pp. 33–36).
5. *The Lay of the Last Minstrel* (1805).

gold laced jacket & waistcoat, silver mounted pistols & daggers,) the Tartars with their high caps, the Turks in their vast pelises & turbans, the soldiers & black slaves with the horses, the former stretched in groupes in an immense open gallery in front of the palace, the latter placed in a kind of cloister below it, two hundred steeds ready caparisoned to move in a moment, couriers entering or passing out with dispatches, the kettle drums beating, boys calling the hour from the minaret of the mosque, altogether, with the singular appearance of the building itself, formed a new & delightful spectacle to a stranger.—I was conducted to a very handsome apartment & my health enquired after by the vizier's secretary "a la mode de Turque."—The next day I was introduced to Ali Pacha, I was dressed in a full suit of Staff uniform with a very magnificent sabre &c.— —The Vizier received me in a large room paved with marble, a fountain was playing in the centre, the apartment was surrounded by scarlet Ottomans, he received me *standing*, a wonderful compliment from a Mussulman, & made me sit down on his right hand.—I have a Greek interpreter for general use, but a Physician of Ali's named [Seculario?] who understands Latin acted for me on this occasion.—His first question was why at so early an age I left my country? (the Turks have no idea of travelling for amusement) he then said the English Minister Capt. Leake had told him I was of a great family, & desired his respects to my mother, which I now in the name of Ali Pacha present to you. He said he was certain I was a man of birth because I had small ears, curling hair, & little white hands, and expressed himself pleased with my appearance & garb.—He told me to consider him as a father whilst I was in Turkey, & said he looked on me as his son.—Indeed he treated me like a child, sending me almonds & sugared sherbet, fruit & sweetmeats 20 times a day.—He begged me to visit him often, and at night when he was more at leisure—I then after coffee & pipes retired for the first time. I saw him thrice afterwards.—It is singular that the Turks who have no heriditary dignities & few great families except the Sultan's pay so much respect to birth, for I found my pedigree more regarded than even my title.—His Highness is 60 years old, very fat & not tall, but with a fine face, light blue eyes & a white beard, his manner is very kind & at the same time he possesses that dignity which I find universal amongst the Turks.— —He has the appearance of any thing but his real character, for he is a remorseless tyrant, guilty of the most horrible cruelties,[6] very brave & so good a general, that they call him the Mahometan Buonaparte.—Napoleon has twice offered to make him King of Epirus, but he prefers the English interest & abhors the French as he himself told me, he is of so much consequence that he is much courted by both, the Albanians being the most warlike subjects of the Sultan, though Ali is only nominally dependent on the Porte. He has been a mighty warrior, but is as barbarous as he is successful, roasting rebels &c. &c.—Bonaparte sent him a snuffbox with his picture[;] he said the snuffbox was very well, but the picture he could excuse, as he neither liked *it* nor the *original*.—His ideas of judging of a man's birth from ears, hands &c. were curious enough.—To me he was indeed a father, giving me letters, guards, & every possible accommodation.—Our next conversations were of war & travelling, politics & England.—He called my

---

6. Ali Pasha was a model for Haidee's father, the pirate Lambro, in *Don Juan*, "the mildest manner'd man / That ever scuttled ship or cut a throat" (III.321–22).

Albanian soldier who attends me, and told him to protect me at all hazards.—His name is Viscillie & like all the Albanians he is brave, rigidly honest, & faithful, but they are cruel though not treacherous, & have several vices, but no meannesses.—They are perhaps the most beautiful race in point of countenance in the world, their women are sometimes handsome also, but they are treated like slaves, *beaten* & in short complete beasts of burthen, they plough, dig & sow, I found them carrying wood & actually repairing the highways, the men are all soldiers, & war & the chase their sole occupations, the women are the labourers, which after all is no great hardship in so delightful a climate, yesterday the 11th. Nov. I bathed in the sea, today It is so hot that I am writing in a shady room of the English Consul's with three doors wide open no fire or even *fireplace* in the house except for culinary purposes.—The Albanians [11 lines crossed out] Today I saw the remains of the town of *Actium* near which Anthony lost the world in a small bay where two frigates could hardly manouvre, a broken wall is the sole remnant.—On another part of the gulph stand the ruins of Nicopolis built by Augustus in honour of his victory.— — — Last night I was at a Greek marriage, but this & 1000 things more I have neither time or *space* to describe.—I am going tomorrow with a guard of fifty men to Patras in the Morea, & thence to Athens where I shall winter.—Two days ago I was nearly lost in a Turkish ship of war owing to the ignorance of the captain & crew though the storm was not violent.—Fletcher yelled after his wife, the Greeks called on all the Saints, the Mussulmen on Alla, the Captain burst into tears & ran below deck telling us to call on God, the sails were split, the mainyard shivered, the wind blowing fresh, the night setting in, & all our chance was to make Corfu which is in possession of the French, or (as Fletcher *pathetically* termed it) "a *watery* grave."—I did what I could to console Fletcher but finding him incorrigible wrapped myself up in my Albanian capote (an immense cloak) & lay down on deck to wait the worst, I have learnt to philosophize on my travels, & if I had not, complaint was useless.—Luckily the wind abated & only drove us on the coast of Suli on the main land where we landed & proceeded by the help of the natives to Prevesa again; but I shall not trust Turkish Sailors in future, though the Pacha had ordered one of his own galleots[7] to take me to Patras, I am therefore going as far as Missolonghi by land & there have only to cross a small gulph to get to Patras.—Fletcher's next epistle will be full of marvels, we were one night lost for *nine* hours in the mountains in a *thunder* storm, & since nearly wrecked, in both cases Fletcher was sorely bewildered, from apprehensions of famine & banditti in the first, & drowning in the second instance.—His eyes were a little hurt by the lightning or crying (I dont know which) but are now recovered.—When you write address to me at Mr. *Strané's* English Consul, Patras, Morea.— — — I could tell you I know not how many incidents that I think would amuse you, but they crowd on my mind as much as would swell my paper, & I can neither arrange them in the one, or put them down on the other, except in the greatest confusion & in my usual horrible hand.—I like the Albanians much, they are not all Turks, some tribes are Christians, but their religion makes little difference in their manner or conduct; they are esteemed the best troops in the Turkish service.—I lived on my route two days at once, & three days again in a

---

7. Small sailing vessels.

Barrack at Salora, & never found soldiers so tolerable, though I have been in the garrisons of Gibraltar & Malta & seen Spanish, French, Sicilian & British troops in abundance, I have had nothing stolen, & was always welcome to their provision & milk.—Not a week ago, an Albanian chief (every village has its chief who is called Primate) after helping us out of the Turkish Galley in her distress, feeding us & lodging my suite consisting of Fletcher, a Greek, Two Albanians, a Greek Priest and my companion Mr. Hobhouse, refused any compensation but a written paper stating that I was well received, & when I pressed him to accept a few sequins, "no, he replied, I wish you to love me, not to pay me." These were his words.—It is astonishing how far money goes in this country, while I was in the capital, I had nothing to pay by the vizier's order, but since, though I have generally had sixteen horses & generally 6 or 7 men, the expence has not been *half* as much as staying only 3 weeks in Malta, though Sir A. Ball the governor gave me a house for nothing, & I had only *one servant*.—By the bye I expect Hanson[8] to remit regularly, for I am not about to stay in this province for ever, let him write to me at Mr. Strané's, English Consul, Patras.——The fact is, the fertility of the plains are wonderful, & specie is scarce, which makes this remarkable cheapness.—I am now going to Athens to study modern Greek which differs much from the ancient though radically similar.—I have no desire to return to England, nor shall I unless compelled by absolute want & Hanson's neglect, but I shall not enter Asia for a year or two as I have much to see in Greece & I may perhaps cross into Africa at least the Aegyptian part.—Fletcher like all Englishmen is very much dissatisfied, though a little reconciled to the Turks by a present of 80 piastres from the vizier, which if you consider every thing & the value of specie here is nearly worth ten guineas English.—He has suffered nothing but from *cold*, heat, & vermin which those who lie in cottages & cross mountains in a wild country must undergo, & of which I have equally partaken with himself, but he is not valiant, & is afraid of robbers & tempests.—I have no one to be remembered to in England, & wish to hear nothing from it but that you are well, & a letter or two on business from Hanson, whom you may tell to write.— —I will write when I can, & beg you to believe me,

yr affect. Son
BYRON

P.S.—I have some very "magnifique" Albanian dresses the only expensive articles in this country they cost 50 guineas each & have so much gold they would cost in England two hundred.[9]—I have been introduced to Hussein Bey, & Mahmout Pacha both little boys grandchildren of Ali at Yanina. They are totally unlike our lads, have painted complexions like rouged dowagers, large black eyes & features perfectly regular. They are the prettiest little animals I ever saw, & are broken into the court ceremonies already, the Turkish salute is a slight inclination of the head with the hand on the breast, intimates always kiss, Mahmout is ten years old & hopes to see me again, we are friends without understanding each other, like many other

---

8. See, p. 100, n. 3.
9. Byron wore one of these dresses in the well-known portrait by Thomas Phillips; he eventually gave it to a female friend for a masquerade.

folks, though from a different cause;—he has given me a letter to his father in the Morea, to whom I have also letters from Ali *Pacha*.—

To John Cam Hobhouse[1]

Patras. July 29th. 1810

. . . At Vostitza I found my dearly-beloved Eustathius[2]—ready to follow me not only to England, but to Terra Incognita, if so be my compass pointed that way.—This was four days ago, at present affairs are a little changed.— The next morning I found the dear soul upon horseback clothed very sprucely in Greek Garments, with those ambrosial curls hanging down his amiable back, and to my utter astonishment and the great abomination of Fletcher, a *parasol* in his hand to save his complexion from the heat.— However in spite of the *Parasol* on we travelled very much enamoured, as it should seem, till we got to Patras, where Strané[3] received us into his new house where I now scribble.—Next day he went to visit some accursed cousin and the day after we had a grand quarrel, Strané said I spoilt him, I said nothing, the child was as froward as an unbroken colt, and Strainé's Janizary said I must not be surprised, for he was too *true* a *Greek* not to be disagreeable.—I think I never in my life took so much pains to please any one, or succeeded so ill, I particularly *avoided* every thing which *could possibly give* the *least offence* in any *manner*, somebody says that those who try to please will please, this I know not; but I am sure that no one likes to fail in the attempt.—At present he goes back to his father, though he is now become more tractable.—Our *parting* was vastly pathetic, as many kisses as would have sufficed for a boarding school, and embraces enough to have ruined the character of a county in England, besides tears (not on *my* part) and expressions of "Tenerezza" to a vast amount.—All this and the warmth of the weather has quite overcome me. Tomorrow I will continue, at present "to bed, "to bed, "to bed".—The youth insists on seeing me tomorrow, the issue of which interview you shall hear.—I wish you a pleasant sleep.—

Sheet second. July 30th, 1810—
I hope you have slept well, I have only dosed, for this last six days I have slept little and eaten less, the heat has burnt me brown, and as for Fletcher he is a walking Cinder.—My new Greek acquaintance has called thrice, and we improve vastly, in good truth, so it ought to be, for I have quite exhausted my poor powers of pleasing, which God knows are little enough, Lord help me!—We are to go on to Tripolitza and Athens together, I do not know what has put him into such good humour unless it is some Sal Volatile.[4] I administered for his headach and a green shade instead of that effeminate parasol, but so it is, we have *redintegrated* (a new *word* for you) our affections at a great rate.—Now is not all this very ridiculous? pray tell Matthews it would do his heart good to see me travelling with my Tartar, Albanians, Buffo, Fletcher and this amiable παιδη[5] prancing by my side.— . . .

1. Hobhouse had returned to England on July 17.
2. Eustathius Georgiou, a young boy whom Byron and Hobhouse had met during their visit to Vostitza the previous December.
3. British Vice-Consul at Patras.
4. Smelling-salt.
5. Boy.

Journal

["Four or Five Reasons in Favour of a Change"]

B. Malta, May 22d. 1811

1st At twenty three the best of life is over and its bitters double. 2ndly I have seen mankind in various Countries and find them equally despicable, if anything the Balance is rather in favour of the Turks. 3dly I am sick at heart.

"Me jam nec *faemina* . . .
Nec *Spes animi credula mutui*
Nec *certare* juvat *Mero*.[1]

4thly A man who is lame of one leg is in a state of bodily inferiority which increases with years and must render his old age more peevish & intolerable. Besides in another existence I expect to have *two* if not *four* legs by way of compensation.

5thly I grow selfish & misanthropical, something like the "jolly Miller" "I care for nobody no not I and Nobody cares for me."

6thly My affairs at home and abroad are gloomy enough.

7thly I have outlived all my appetites and most of my vanities aye even the vanity of authorship.

To Francis Hodgson

Newstead Abbey, September 3, 1811

My dear Hodgson,—I will have nothing to do with your immortality; we are miserable enough in this life, without the absurdity of speculating upon another. If men are to live, why die at all? and if they die, why disturb the sweet and sound sleep that "knows no waking"? "Post mortem nihil est, ipsaque Mors nihil . . . quaeris quo jaceas post obitum loco? Quo *non* Nata jacent".[1]

As to revealed religion, Christ came to save men; but a good Pagan will go to heaven, and a bad Nazarene to hell; "Argal" (I argue like the gravedigger)[2] why are not all men Christians? or why are any? If mankind may be saved who never heard or dreamt, at Timbuctoo, Otaheite,[3] Terra Incognita, &c., of Galilee and its Prophet, Christianity is of no avail, if they cannot be saved without, why are not all orthodox? It is a little hard to send a man preaching to Judæa, and leave the rest of the world—Negers and what not—*dark* as their complexions, without a ray of light for so many years to lead them on high; and who will believe that God will damn men for not knowing what they were never taught? I hope I am sincere; I was so at least

---

1. Byron quotes from memory and inexactly a passage from the first ode of book four by Horace: "These days I take no joy / In the naive hope of mutual love with woman or boy, / Or drinking bouts with men, / Or garlanding my temples with fresh flowers" (trans. James Michie [Orion Press, 1963]).
1. Seneca, *Troades*, 397ff. "There is nothing after death, and death itself is nothing. You seek the place where one lies after death? Where those unborn lie."
2. *Hamlet* 5.1.12.
3. Unexplored earthly regions; *Otaheite*: Tahiti.

on a bed of sickness in a far distant country, when I had neither friend, nor comforter, nor hope, to sustain me. I looked to death as a relief from pain, without a wish for an after-life, but a confidence that the God who punishes in this existence had left that last asylum for the weary.

'Ον ὁ θεὸς ἀγαπάει ἀποθνῄσκει νέος.[4]

I am no Platonist, I am nothing at all; but I would sooner be a Paulician, Manichean, Spinozist, Gentile, Pyrrhonian, Zoroastrian,[5] than one of the seventy-two villainous sects who are tearing each other to pieces for the love of the Lord and hatred of each other. Talk of Galileeism? Show me the effects—are you better, wiser, kinder by your precepts? I will bring you ten Mussulmans shall shame you in all good-will towards men, prayer to God, and duty to their neighbours. And is there a Talapoin, or a Bonze,[6] who is not superior to a fox-hunting curate? But I will say no more on this endless theme; let me live, well if possible, and die without pain. The rest is with God, who assuredly, had He *come* or *sent*, would have made Himself manifest to nations, and intelligible to all.[7]

I shall rejoice to see you. My present intention is to accept Scrope Davies's invitation; and then, if you accept mine, we shall meet *here* and *there*. Did you know poor Matthews? I shall miss him much at Cambridge.

To Francis Hodgson

8, *St. James's Street, February 16, 1812*

Dear Hodgson,—I send you a proof. Last week I was very ill and confined to bed with stone in the kidney, but I am now quite recovered. The women are gone to their relatives, after many attempts to explain what was already too clear. If the stone had got into my heart instead of my kidneys, it would have been all the better. However, I have quite recovered *that* also, and only wonder at my folly in excepting my own strumpets from the general corruption,—albeit a two months' weakness is better than ten years. I have one request to make, which is, never to mention a woman again in any letter to me, or even allude to the existence of the sex. I won't even read a word of the feminine gender;—it must all be *propria quae maribus*.[1]

In the spring of 1813 I shall leave England for ever. Every thing in my affairs tends to this, and my inclinations and health do not discourage it. Neither my habits nor constitution are improved by your customs or your climate. I shall find employment in making myself a good Oriental scholar.

---

4. Whom the gods love die young.
5. Various heretical or non-Christian sects; "Gentile" in this context means heathen or pagan.
6. *Talapoin . . . Bonze*: Buddhist monks of Indo-Chinese countries.
7. Byron's views on religion in general and Christianity in particular were inconsistent and ranged from skeptical to respectful. Hodgson, who was soon to enter the ministry, provoked Byron's irreverence, as in this letter and the one he wrote to Hodgson ten days later, in which he opined: "the basis of your religion is *injustice*; the *Son of God*, the *pure*, the *immaculate*, the *innocent*, is sacrificed for the *guilty*. This proves *His* heroism; but no more does away with man's guilt than a schoolboy's volunteering to be flogged for another would exculpate the dunce from negligence, or preserve him from the rod. . . . As to miracles, I agree with Hume that it is more probable men should *lie* or be *deceived*, than that things out of the course of nature should so happen" (*BLJ* 2.97). *David Hume*: Scottish philosopher (1711–1776), whose works include *An Enquiry concerning Human Understanding* (including "Of Miracles") (1748) and *Dialogues concerning Natural Religion* (1779).
1. Only what is appropriate for men.

I shall retain a mansion in one of the fairest islands, and retrace, at intervals, the most interesting portions of the East. In the mean time, I am adjusting my concerns, which will (when arranged) leave me with wealth sufficient even for home, but enough for a principality in Turkey. At present they are involved, but I hope, by taking some necessary but unpleasant steps, to clear every thing. Hobhouse is expected daily in London: we shall be very glad to see him; and, perhaps, you will come up and "drink deep ere he depart,"[2] if not, "Mahomet must come to the mountain;"—but Cambridge will bring sad recollections to him, and worse to me, though for very different reasons. I believe the only human being, that ever loved me in truth and entirely, was of, or belonging to, Cambridge, and, in that, no change can now take place.[3] There is one consolation in death—where he sets his seal, the impression can neither be melted nor broken, but endureth for ever.

Yours always,
B.

P.S.—I almost rejoice when one I love dies young, for I could never bear to see them old or altered.

---

2. "We'll teach you to drink deep ere you depart" (echoing *Hamlet* 1.2.17).
3. Byron refers to John Edleston; see *Childe Harold* II, stanzas 9, 95, and 96 (pp. 57, 82), "The Cornelian" (p. 4), and "To Thyrza" (p. 98).

Part Two: Years of Fame
in Regency Society (1812–1816)

Byron delivered his maiden speech in the House of Lords on February 27, 1812, two weeks before he would achieve instant fame with the publication of the first two cantos of *Childe Harold's Pilgrimage*. In the speech he vigorously argued against the death penalty for "framebreakers," factory workers whose jobs were being replaced by machines and who protested by destroying them. Welcomed into the coterie of aristocratic Whigs who opposed the reactionary policies of the Tory government, Byron was a frequent guest at Holland House, the home of party leader Lord Holland and a salon for Whig society. However, Byron soon discovered his disinclination for speech-making, and after another address to the House (this one in support of Catholic Emancipation, extending to Catholics the right to vote and hold public office), his parliamentary career waned. Nonetheless, his opposition to the political status quo and passion for reform would continue to be central to his poetry, even to those poems which did not immediately appear to concern contemporary British politics, such as the Eastern tales he produced between 1813 and 1814. These immensely popular poems—*The Giaour, The Bride of Abydos, The Corsair*, and *Lara*—with their passionate and tormented Byronic heroes, fueled his ever-increasing celebrity, described by the Duchess of Devonshire in a letter written to her son in America shortly after the publication of *Childe Harold I–II*:

> The subject of conversation, of curiosity, of enthusiasm almost, one might say, of the moment is not Spain or Portugal, Warriors or Patriots, but Lord Byron! . . . [*Childe Harold's Pilgrimage*] is on every table, and himself courted, visited, flattered and praised whenever he appears. He has a pale, sickly, but handsome countenance, a bad figure, animated and amusing conversation, and, in short, he is really the only topic almost of conversation—the men jealous of him, the women of each other.

Byron became something of a Regency dandy—one of the fashionable gentlemen of the period during which, because of the insanity of King George III, his son (the future King George IV) ruled as Prince Regent. From the fall of 1812 through the fall of 1814 he was involved in a number of amorous relationships that became the subject of gossip then and of biographies ever since. Foremost among these for sheer tempestuousness and indiscretion was his affair with Lady Caroline Lamb, whose husband, William Lamb, was a son of Lady Melbourne, one of Byron's dearest friends and his closest confidante during these years. Partly to extricate himself from dissipation and scandal, to regularize his existence, and to alleviate severe financial distress, he proposed marriage to Anne Isabella (Annabella) Milbanke, a thoughtful, intellectual, wealthy young woman whose poetry Caroline Lamb, her cousin, had brought to Byron's attention. Annabella Milbanke turned down Byron's first proposal, and in early 1813 he became the lover of Lady Oxford, a worldly, mature mother of six, and shortly after that, of his half-sister, Augusta Leigh. The relationship with Augusta was undoubtedly one of the most complex of Byron's lifetime and seems to have run the emotional gamut from childlike playfulness to deep friendship, passion, and guilt. (Some of the poetry Byron wrote to or about Augusta after he left England is found in Part Three of the present Norton Critical Edition.)

After an unconsummated flirtation with Lady Frances Wedderburn Webster, the young neglected wife of a close friend (and the secret subject of "When We Two Parted"), Byron proposed a second time to Annabella. This time, with a view to reforming him, she accepted, and they were married on January 2, 1815. The marriage lasted one year. Even the birth of a daughter, Augusta Ada, could not save it from falling victim to their essential incompatibility, not to mention Byron's extreme mood swings, emotional outbursts, heavy drinking, relationship with Augusta, and perhaps unconventional (and then illegal) sexual practices. Byron, nonetheless, was as disappointed, astonished, and outraged by Annabella's insistence on a formal separation (divorce) as he had been by Napoleon's disgraceful exile at Elba the previous April and final defeat at Waterloo on June 18, 1815, a triumph for the Tories. During this difficult period Byron remained socially engaged through his role on the management board of Drury Lane Theatre and his friendship with two men who stood at the opposite poles of the political spectrum: Leigh Hunt, recently released from prison for seditious libel, and Walter Scott, whom Byron greatly admired despite Scott's political conservatism. However, the scandal generated by his wife's supporters eventually led to mounting embarrassment, and a humiliating incident at a party given by Lady Jersey, where he was "cut" by his former acquaintances, prompted his decision to leave England. His close friend Hobhouse saw him off at Dover on April 25, 1816. Lord Byron would never see England, or his daughter, again.

POETRY

An Ode to the Framers of the Frame Bill[1]

Oh well done Lord E[ldo]n! and better Lord R[yde]r![2]
Britannia must prosper with councils like yours;
Hawkesbury, Harrowby,[3] help you to guide her,
Whose remedy only must *kill* ere it cures:
Those villains, the Weavers, are all grown refractory,   5
Asking some succour for Charity's sake—
So hang them in clusters round each Manufactory,
That will at once put an end to *mistake*.[4]

---

1. Written on March 1, 1812, and published the next day in the *Morning Chronicle*. The Tories, led by Lord Liverpool, introduced a bill in the House of Lords seeking the death penalty for frame breaking (see Part Two headnote). The Whigs opposed the measure, and on February 27, Byron delivered his maiden speech in the House opposing the bill, eloquently evoking the desperate plight of the workers (printed in *Nicholson*); see also letter to Lord Holland (p. 169). The frame breakers became the subject of another of Byron's poems, "Song for the Luddites" (1816; *CPW* 4:48). Criticism: Kelsall, "Byron's Politics" (p. 855), and Mole, "Byron's 'Ode to the Framers of the Frame Bill': The Embarrassment of Industrial Culture."
2. Lord Eldon and Lord Ryder were, respectively, the Tory Lord Chancellor and Home Secretary.
3. Baron Hawkesbury was Lord Liverpool; Baron Harrowby was the father of Lord Eldon.
4. "Mistake" was Lord Eldon's characterization of the riots.

The rascals, perhaps, may betake them to robbing,
The dogs to be sure have got nothing to eat—   10
So if we can hang them for breaking a bobbin,
'Twill save all the Government's money and meat:
Men are more easily made than machinery—
Stockings fetch better prices than lives—
Gibbets on Sherwood[5] will *heighten* the scenery,   15
Showing how Commerce, *how* Liberty thrives!

Justice is now in pursuit of the wretches,
Grenadiers, Volunteers, Bow-street Police,
Twenty-two Regiments, a score of Jack Ketches,[6]
Three of the Quorum[7] and two of the Peace;   20
Some Lords, to be sure, would have summoned the Judges,
To take their opinion, but that they ne'er shall,
For LIVERPOOL such a concession begrudges,
So now they're condemned by *no Judges* at all.

Some folks for certain have thought it was shocking,   25
When Famine appeals, and when Poverty groans,
That life should be valued at less than a stocking,
And breaking of frames lead to breaking of bones.
If it should prove so, I trust, by this token,
(And who will refuse to partake in the hope?)   30
That the frames of the fools may be first to be *broken*,
Who, when asked for a *remedy*, sent down a *rope*.

THE GIAOUR   After beginning *The Giaour* in late 1812, Byron continued
to expand "this snake of a poem—which has been lengthening its rattles every
month" (*BLJ* 3:100). From an initial version of 344 lines, it evolved to the 684
lines of the first edition, published in June 1813, and reached its total of 1,334
lines in the seventh edition, published in December.
    The first of Byron's enormously popular Eastern tales, *The Giaour* tells the
story of a young Venetian in Turkish-ruled Athens. He—the "Giaour" (pro-
nounced with a soft "g" and rhyming with "power," and meaning an infidel to
the Muslim faith)—and Leila, the favorite wife of a Turkish emir named Has-
san, became lovers, and as a traditional Turkish punishment for adultery, Has-
san has Leila sewn into a sack and thrown into the sea, resulting in the Giaour's
revenge upon Hassan. Much of the poem's interest lies in the shifting symbolic
relations of the Giaour, Leila, Hassan. From his physical description when he
is introduced, the Giaour is instantly recognizable as a Byronic hero (see Intro-
duction, p. xv): "Though young and pale, that sallow front / Is scathed by fiery
passion's brunt" (194–95). Leila, like her people, the Circassians (from the
Caucasus in southwest Russia), and like Greece (foregrounded as the poem's
subject in the opening 167 lines), is identified with beauty and is enslaved to
the powerful Turk, Hassan. Her adultery, on one level, signifies "the controlless

5. Gallows built on the trees of Sherwood Forest, in Nottingham, where the riots broke out; this was
    Byron's county seat, the location of his ancestral home, Newstead Abbey.
6. Jack Ketch was a name for an official executioner.
7. Three Justices of the Quorum, necessary to constitute a bench.

core of human hearts" (*Don Juan* I. 924–25), a nature-affirming and political formulation of love that is a recurrent theme in Byron's works. On another level, while in the story the Giaour and Hassan are enemies, symbolically they are linked through the theme of (male) power, particularly as it relates to the possession of a beautiful woman; as the Giaour acknowledges after killing Hassan for enacting the barbarous punishment for adultery on Leila: "Yet did he but what I had done / Had she been false to more than one" (1062–63). But the poem contains a political allegory as well, and even that reading is double-edged. The fact that Leila's rebellion against her Turkish master takes the form of love for a European suggests the plight of Greece under Turkish rule. At least it suggests a European's view of that plight, for, at the same time, the Turkish conqueror signifies Europe's, and particularly Britain's, self-serving, imperialistic policies, shamefully illustrated by Lord Elgin's recent appropriation of the Parthenon marbles, the subject of Byron's *Curse of Minerva* (1811). (See also *Childe Harold* II, stanzas 73–93, written in Greece during the same period that Byron was finding material for *The Giaour*). This interpretation of *The Giaour* is reinforced by the poem's Advertisement and by Byron's numerous notes that, either in their content or in their urbane or self-consciously scholarly tone, ironically offset the Romantic tale.

The fragmented, nonchronological narrative, using multiple and not clearly identifiable speakers, is hard to follow. In fact, the disjointed quality of the poem, conceived as a something of an experiment in narrative form, was compounded by Byron's continuing to insert new passages as he prepared the first seven editions. (Critical opinion of the poem has ranged from charges of haste and sloppiness to admiration at the imaginative narrative conception, which foreshadows the *Rashomon*-like approach of many modern lyrical narratives.) The following is an outline of the poem: It begins with a meditation on Greece by the poet (whom the reader may identify as Byron), in which the natural beauty and past glory of ancient Greece are contrasted with its present decay under Turkish rule. "A mournful tale" is introduced, whose narrator (according to the note to line 1334) is "one of the coffee-house story-tellers who abound in the Levant, and sing or recite their narratives." Consistent with ballad style, the storyteller-narrator assumes the voice of other character-narrators, who report events from their point of view; a fisherman and other narrators with a strong Turkish bias emerge from and merge with the storyteller's narrative. As the ballad's "translator" (according to the same note), the poet inserts his meditations on the events and emotions described in the storyteller's tale. Additional speakers include a monk and the Giaour himself, whose confession to a friar forms the final section of the poem and recounts the entire story from the Giaour's point of view.

Sources: The story had some basis in an actual incident involving a young woman in Athens whom Byron rescued from Leila's fate, though he repeatedly denied that they had been lovers; see Byron's note for line 1334, his journal entry of December 5, 1813 (*BLJ* 3:230), *CPW* 3:422–24, and *Marchand*, 1:257–58. In addition to his own travels in and first-hand familiarity with the culture of the Near East, Byron's sources for *The Giaour* (and its numerous annotations) include Barthélemy d'Herbelot's *Bibliothèque Orientale* (1697), William Beckford's *Vathek* (1786), and the Koran in George Sale's translation (1734). His model and inspiration for the fragmented narrative form was *The Voyage of Columbus* (1812) by Samuel Rogers, to whom Byron dedicated *The Giaour*.

Criticism: In this volume, see: Butler, "The Orientalism of Byron's *Giaour*" (p. 882); Franklin, "'A Soulless Toy for Tyrant's Lust?': The Heroine as Passive Victim" (p. 891); McGann, "The Book of Byron and the Book of a World" (p. 828). See also: Gleckner, *Byron and the Ruins of Paradise*; Levinson, *The Romantic Fragment Poem*; Manning, *Byron and His Fictions*; McGann, *Fiery*

Dust: Sharafuddin, "Byron's 'Turkish Tales' and Realistic Orientalism"; Sundell, "The Development of the Giaour"; Watkins, *Social Relations in Byron's Eastern Tales*. For a detailed discussion and chart of the poem's accretions through the first seven editions, see *CPW* 3: 406–14.

THE GIAOUR

A FRAGMENT OF A TURKISH TALE

> One fatal remembrance—one sorrow that throws
> Its bleak shade alike o'er our joys and our woes—
> To which Life nothing darker nor brighter can bring,
> For which joy hath no balm—and affliction no sting.
> [Thomas] Moore [*Irish Melodies*]

To SAMUEL ROGERS, ESQ.
As a slight but most sincere token of admiration of his genius, respect for his character, and gratitude for his friendship, this production is inscribed by his obliged and affectionate servant,

BYRON
London, May, 1813

Advertisement

The tale which these disjointed fragments present is founded upon circumstances now less common in the East than formerly; either because the ladies are more circumspect than in the "olden time," or because the Christians have better fortune, or less enterprise. The story, when entire, contained the adventures of a female slave, who was thrown, in the Mussulman manner, into the sea for infidelity, and avenged by a young Venetian, her lover, at the time the Seven Islands were possessed by the Republic of Venice, and soon after the Arnauts[1] were beaten back from the Morea, which they had ravaged for some time subsequent to the Russian invasion. The desertion of the Mainotes,[2] on being refused the plunder of Misitra, led to the abandonment of that enterprise, and to the desolation of the Morea, during which the cruelty exercised on all sides was unparalleled even in the annals of the faithful.[3]

> No breath of air to break the wave
> That rolls below the Athenian's grave,
> That tomb[4] which, gleaming o'er the cliff,
> First greets the homeward-veering skiff,

---

1. Albanians. Albania, in the western Balkan peninsula, was also under Turkish domination in the early nineteenth century.
2. Inhabitants of Peloponnesus (Morea), the southern section of Greece around Sparta. Anticipating the general Greek revolution against the Turks by fifty years, the Mainotes had begun a bloody and ruthless campaign against their Turkish overlords in 1770, and by 1779 they had established their territory as a virtually independent state.
3. The historical background Byron gives situates the story shortly after 1779 (see *CPW* 1:415).
4. "The tomb above the rocks on the promontory, by some supposed the sepulchre of Themistocles." Themistocles was the fifth century B.C.E. leader of Athens during the Persian wars; in line 5 he is said to have saved his native land in vain since, in the early nineteenth century, Greece was under the hegemony of the Ottoman Empire.

High o'er the land he saved in vain—   5
When shall such hero live again?

          *   *   *   *   *   *   * *5

Fair clime! where every season smiles
Benignant o'er those blessed isles,
Which, seen from far Colonna's height,[6]
Make glad the heart that hails the sight.   10
And lend to loneliness delight.
There mildly dimpling—Ocean's cheek
Reflects the tints of many a peak
Caught by the laughing tides that lave
These Edens of the eastern wave;   15
And if at times a transient breeze
Break the blue crystal of the seas,
Or sweep one blossom from the trees,
How welcome is each gentle air,
That wakes and wafts the odours there!   20
For there—the Rose o'er crag or vale,
Sultana of the Nightingale,[7]
    The maid for whom his melody—
    His thousand songs are heard on high,
Blooms blushing to her lover's tale;   25
His queen, the garden queen, his Rose,
Unbent by winds, unchill'd by snows,
Far from the winters of the west,
By every breeze and season blest,
Returns the sweets by nature given   30
In softest incense back to heaven;
And grateful yields that smiling sky
Her fairest hue and fragrant sigh.
And many a summer flower is there,
And many a shade that love might share,   35
And many a grotto, meant for rest,
That holds the pirate for a guest;
Whose bark in sheltering cove below
Lurks for the passing peaceful prow,
Till the gay mariner's guitar[8]   40
Is heard, and seen the evening star;
Then stealing with the muffled oar,
Far shaded by the rocky shore,
Rush the night-prowlers on the prey,

---

5. The asterisks throughout *The Giaour* are Byron's and indicate breaks in the story, not deleted text.
6. Colonna (present-day Cape Sunium) was an ancient city at the southern-most tip of Greece. The poet gazes at the Greek isles (the "Edens of the eastern wave," line 15) from this promontory.
7. "The attachment of the nightingale to the rose is a well-known Persian fable—if I mistake not, the 'bulbul of a thousand tales' is one of his appellations." *Sultana*: queen or mistress.
8. "The guitar is the constant amusement of the Greek sailor by night; with a steady fair wind, and during a calm, it is accompanied always by the voice, and often by dancing."

And turn to groans his roundelay.[9]   45
Strange—that where Nature loved to trace,
As if for Gods, a dwelling-place,
And every charm and grace hath mix'd
Within the paradise she fix'd—
There man, enamour'd of distress,   50
Should mar it into wilderness,[1]
And trample, brute-like, o'er each flower
That tasks not one laborious hour;
Nor claims the culture of his hand
To bloom along the fairy land,   55
But springs as to preclude his care,
And sweetly woos him—but to spare!
Strange—that where all is peace beside
There passion riots in her pride,
And lust and rapine wildly reign,   60
To darken o'er the fair domain.
It is as though the fiends prevail'd
Against the seraphs they assail'd,
And, fix'd on heavenly thrones, should dwell
The freed inheritors of hell—   65
So soft the scene, so form'd for joy,
So curst the tyrants that destroy!

    He who hath bent him o'er the dead,
Ere the first day of death is fled,
The first dark day of nothingness,   70
The last of danger and distress,
(Before Decay's effacing fingers
Have swept the lines where beauty lingers,)
And mark'd the mild angelic air—
The rapture of repose that's there—   75
The fix'd yet tender traits that streak
The languor of the placid cheek,
And—but for that sad shrouded eye,
    That fires not—wins not—weeps not—now—
    And but for that chill changeless brow,   80
Where cold Obstruction's apathy[2]
    Appals the gazing mourner's heart,
    As if to him it could impart
    The doom he dreads, yet dwells upon—
Yes—but for these and these alone,   85
    Some moments—aye—one treacherous hour,
He still might doubt the tyrant's power,
So fair—so calm—so softly seal'd

---

9. Song, ballad.
1. Cf. *Childe Harold* I, stanza 15 (pp. 32–33).
2. "'Ay, but to die and go we know not where, / To lye in cold obstruction?' *Measure for Measure* [3.1.118–19]."

The first—last look—by death reveal'd![3]
Such is the aspect of this shore—   90
'Tis Greece—but living Greece no more!
So coldly sweet, so deadly fair,
We start—for soul is wanting there.
Hers is the loveliness in death,
That parts not quite with parting breath;   95
But beauty with that fearful bloom,
That hue which haunts it to the tomb—
Expression's last receding ray,
A gilded halo hovering round decay,
The farewell beam of Feeling past away!   100
Spark of that flame—perchance of heavenly birth—
Which gleams—but warms no more its cherish'd earth!

Clime of the unforgotten brave!—
Whose land from plain to mountain-cave
Was Freedom's home or Glory's grave—   105
Shrine of the mighty! can it be,
That this is all remains of thee?
Approach, thou craven crouching slave—
Say, is not this Thermopylae?[4]
These waters blue that round you lave   110
Oh servile offspring of the free—
Pronounce what sea, what shore is this?
The gulf, the rock of Salamis![5]
These scenes—their story not unknown—
Arise, and make again your own;   115
Snatch from the ashes of your sires
The embers of their former fires,
And he who in the strife expires
Will add to theirs a name of fear,
That Tyranny shall quake to hear,   120
And leave his sons a hope, a fame,
They too will rather die than shame;
For Freedom's battle once begun,
Bequeath'd by bleeding Sire to Son,
Though baffled oft is ever won.   125
Bear witness, Greece, thy living page,
Attest it many a deathless age!
While kings in dusty darkness hid,
Have left a nameless pyramid,
Thy heroes, though the general doom   130

---

3. "I trust that few of my readers have ever had an opportunity of witnessing what is here attempted
   in description, but those who have will probably retain a painful remembrance of that singular
   beauty which pervades, with few exceptions, the features of the dead, a few hours, and but for a
   few hours, after 'the spirit is not there.' It is to be remarked in cases of violent death by gun-shot
   wounds, the expression is always that of languor, whatever the natural energy of the sufferer's char-
   acter: but in death from a stab the countenance preserves its traits of feeling or ferocity, and the
   mind its bias, to the last."
4. Scene of the heroic resistance by Spartan soldiers to a Persian invasion, 480 B.C.E.
5. Scene of the Greeks' defeat of the Persian fleet, 480 B.C.E.

Hath swept the column from their tomb,
A mightier monument command,
The mountains of their native land!
There points thy Muse to stranger's eye,
The graves of those that cannot die!   135
'Twere long to tell, and sad to trace,
Each step from splendour to disgrace;
Enough—no foreign foe could quell
Thy soul, till from itself it fell;
Yes! Self-abasement paved the way   140
To villain-bonds and despot-sway.

What can he tell who treads thy shore?
   No legend of thine olden time,
No theme on which the muse might soar,
High as thine own in days of yore,   145
   When man was worthy of thy clime.
The hearts within thy valleys bred,
The fiery souls that might have led
   Thy sons to deeds sublime,
Now crawl from cradle to the grave,   150
Slaves—nay, the bondsmen of a slave,[6]
   And callous, save to crime;
Stain'd with each evil that pollutes
Mankind, where least above the brutes;
Without even savage virtue blest,   155
Without one free or valiant breast.
Still to the neighbouring ports they waft
Proverbial wiles, and ancient craft,
In this the subtle Greek is found,
For this, and this alone, renown'd.   160
In vain might Liberty invoke
The spirit to its bondage broke,
Or raise the neck that courts the yoke:
No more her sorrows I bewail,
Yet this will be a mournful tale,   165
And they who listen may believe,
Who heard it first had cause to grieve.

          *   *   *   *   *   *   *   *

   Far, dark, along the blue sea glancing,[7]
The shadows of the rocks advancing
Start on the fisher's eye like boat   170
Of island-pirate or Mainote;[8]
And fearful for his light caique

---

6. "Athens is the property of the Kislar Aga (the slave of the seraglio and guardian of the women), who appoints the Waywode. A pander and eunuch—these are not polite yet true appellations—now *governs* the governor of Athens."
7. The narrative of the coffee-house storyteller (see headnote) begins here.
8. The anonymous Turkish fisherman is quite right to be frightened at the possibility of meeting one of the fierce and nationalistic Mainotes.

He shuns the near but doubtful creek,
Though worn and weary with his toil,
And cumber'd with his scaly spoil,   175
Slowly, yet strongly, plies the oar,
Till Port Leone's[9] safer shore
Receives him by the lovely light
That best becomes an Eastern night.

*   *   *   *   *   *   *   *

Who thundering comes on blackest steed[1]   180
With slacken'd bit and hoof of speed?
Beneath the clattering iron's sound
The cavern'd echoes wake around
In lash for lash, and bound for bound;
The foam that streaks the courser's side   185
Seems gather'd from the ocean-tide:
Though weary waves are sunk to rest,
There's none within his rider's breast,
And though to-morrow's tempest lower,
'Tis calmer than thy heart, young Giaour![2]   190
I know thee not, I loathe thy race,
But in thy lineaments I trace
What time shall strengthen, not efface;
Though young and pale, that sallow front
Is scathed by fiery passion's brunt,   195
Though bent on earth thine evil eye
As meteor like thou glidest by,
Right well I view and deem thee one
Whom Othman's sons[3] should slay or shun.

On—on he hasten'd—and he drew   200
My gaze of wonder as he flew:
Though like a demon of the night
He pass'd and vanished from my sight,
His aspect and his air impress'd
A troubled memory on my breast;   205
And long upon my startled ear
Rung his dark courser's hoofs of fear.
He spurs his steed—he nears the steep,
That jutting shadows o'er the deep—
He winds around—he hurries by—   210
The rock relieves him from mine eye—
For well I ween unwelcome he
Whose glance is fix'd on those that flee;
And not a star but shines too bright

9. Ancient name of the port of Athens (Piraeus).
1. The narrating voice is that of the Turkish fisherman who has just put his boat to shore at Port Leone; he witnesses the Giaour's flight along the seashore as he pursues Hassan.
2. "Infidel."
3. Turks, after the name of the thirteenth-century founder of the Turkish (Ottoman) Empire.

On him who takes such timeless flight.   215
He wound along—but ere he pass'd
One glance he snatch'd—as if his last—
A moment check'd his wheeling steed—
A moment breathed him from his speed—
A moment on his stirrup stood—   220
Why looks he o'er the olive wood?—
The crescent glimmers on the hill,
The Mosque's high lamps are quivering still;
Though too remote for sound to wake
In echoes of the far tophaike,[4]   225
The flashes of each joyous peal
Are seen to prove the Moslem's zeal.
To-night—set Rhamazani's[5] sun—
To-night—the Bairam feast's begun—
To-night—but who and what art thou   230
Of foreign garb and fearful brow?
And what are these to thine or thee,
That thou should'st either pause or flee?
He stood—some dread was on his face—
Soon Hatred settled in its place—   235
It rose not with the reddening flush
Of transient Anger's darkening blush,
But pale as marble o'er the tomb,
Whose ghastly whiteness aids its gloom.
His brow was bent—his eye was glazed—   240
He raised his arm, and fiercely raised;
And sternly shook his hand on high,
As doubting to return or fly;—
Impatient of his flight delay'd
Here loud his raven charger neigh'd—   245
Down glanced that hand, and grasp'd his blade—
That sound had burst his waking dream,
As Slumber starts at owlet's scream.—
The spur hath lanced his courser's sides—
Away—away—for life he rides—   250
Swift as the hurl'd on high jerreed,[6]
Springs to the touch his startled steed;
The rock is doubled—and the shore
Shakes with the clattering tramp no more—
The crag is won—no more is seen   255
His Christian crest and haughty mien.—
'Twas but an instant—he restrain'd

---

4. "'Tophaike,' musket.—The Bairam is announced by the cannon at sunset; the illumination of the Mosques, and the firing of all kinds of small arms, loaded with *ball*, proclaim it during the night."
5. Ramadan, the Muslim month of daily expiation and fasting; the day's abstinence is succeeded by a nightly feast, "Bairam."
6. "Jerreed, or Djerrid, a blunted Turkish javelin, which is darted from horseback with great force and precision. It is a favourite exercise of the Mussulmans; but I know not if it can be called a *manly* one, since the most expert in the art are the Black Eunuchs of Constantinople.—I think, next to these, a Mamlouk at Smyrna was the most skilful that came within my observation." *Mamlouk*: a slave warrior.

That fiery barb[7] so sternly rein'd—
'Twas but a moment that he stood,
Then sped as if by death pursued;   260
But in that instant, o'er his soul
Winters of Memory seem'd to roll,
And gather in that drop of time
A life of pain, an age of crime.
O'er him who loves, or hates, or fears,   265
Such moment pours the grief of years—
What felt *he* then—at once opprest
By all that most distracts the breast?
That pause—which ponder'd o'er his fate,
Oh, who its dreary length shall date!   270
Though in Time's record nearly nought,
It was Eternity to Thought!
For infinite as boundless space
The thought that Conscience must embrace,
Which in itself can comprehend   275
Woe without name—or hope—or end.—

    The hour is past, the Giaour is gone,
And did he fly or fall alone?
Woe to that hour he came or went!
The curse for Hassan's sin was sent   280
To turn a palace to a tomb;
He came, he went, like the Simoom,[8]
That harbinger of fate and gloom,
Beneath whose widely-wasting breath
The very cypress droops to death—   285
Dark tree—still sad, when others' grief is fled,
The only constant mourner o'er the dead!

    The steed is vanished from the stall,[9]
No serf is seen in Hassan's hall;
The lonely Spider's thin grey pall   290
Waves slowly widening o'er the wall;
The Bat builds in his Haram bower;
And in the fortress of his power
The Owl usurps the beacon-tower;
The wild-dog howls o'er the fountain's brim,   295
With baffled thirst, and famine, grim,
For the stream has shrunk from its marble bed,
Where the weeds and the desolate dust are spread.
'Twas sweet of yore to see it play
And chase the sultriness of day—   300
As springing high the silver dew

---

7. The Giaour's steed, a Barbary or Arabian stallion.
8. "The blast of the desert, fatal to every thing living, and often alluded to in eastern poetry."
9. In this passage (lines 288–351), the storyteller jumps ahead in time to the desolation of Hassan's palace after he has been killed by the Giaour.

In whirls fantastically flew,
And flung luxurious coolness round
The air, and verdure o'er the ground.—
'Twas sweet, when cloudless stars were bright,   305
To view the wave of watery light,
And hear its melody by night.—
And oft had Hassan's Childhood play'd
Around the verge of that cascade;
And oft upon his mother's breast   310
That sound had harmonized his rest;
And oft had Hassan's Youth along
Its bank been soothed by Beauty's song;
And softer seem'd each melting tone
Of Music mingled with its own.—   315
But ne'er shall Hassan's Age repose
Along the brink at Twilight's close—
The stream that fill'd that font is fled—
The blood that warm'd his heart is shed!—
And here no more shall human voice   320
Be heard to rage—regret—rejoice—
The last sad note that swell'd the gale
Was woman's wildest funeral wail—
That quench'd in silence—all is still,
But the lattice that flaps when the wind is shrill—   325
Though raves the gust, and floods the rain,
No hand shall close its clasp again.
On desert sands 'twere joy to scan
The rudest steps of fellow man,
So here the very voice of Grief   330
Might wake an Echo like relief—
At least 'twould say, "All are not gone;
There lingers Life, though but in one"—
For many a gilded chamber's there,
Which Solitude might well forbear;   335
Within that dome as yet Decay
Hath slowly worked her cankering way—
But Gloom is gather'd o'er the gate,
Nor there the Fakir's[1] self will wait;
Nor there will wandering Dervise stay,   340
For Bounty cheers not his delay;
Nor there will weary stranger halt
To bless the sacred "bread and salt."[2]
Alike must Wealth and Poverty
Pass heedless and unheeded by,   345
For Courtesy and Pity died
With Hassan on the mountain side.—
His roof—that refuge unto men—

---

1. An Arabic word for a Muslim ascetic or mendicant monk, some of whom perform feats of endurance or apparent magic; in Turkish, a "Dervise," or dervish, who are known for ecstatic observances.
2. "To partake of food—to break bread and salt with your host—ensures the safety of the guest, even though an enemy; his person from that moment is sacred."

Is Desolation's hungry den.—
The guest flies the hall, and the vassal from labour,   350
Since his turban was cleft by the infidel's sabre![3]

*   *   *   *   *   *   *   *

I hear the sound of coming feet,[4]
But not a voice mine ear to greet—
More near—each turban I can scan,
And silver-sheathed ataghan;[5]   355
The foremost of the band is seen
An Emir[6] by his garb of green:
"Ho! who art thou?"—"This low salam[7]
Replies of Moslem faith I am.
The burthen ye so gently bear,   360
Seems one that claims your utmost care,
And, doubtless, holds some precious freight,
My humble bark would gladly wait."

"Thou speakest sooth,[8] thy skiff unmoor,
And waft us from the silent shore;   365
Nay, leave the sail still furl'd, and ply
The nearest oar that's scatter'd by,
And midway to those rocks where sleep
The channel'd waters dark and deep.—
Rest from your task—so—bravely done,   370
Our course has been right swiftly run,
Yet 'tis the longest voyage, I trow,
That one of"— *   *   *   *

*   *   *   *   *   *   *   *

Sullen it plunged, and slowly sank,
The calm wave rippled to the bank;   375
I watch'd it as it sank, methought
Some motion from the current caught
Bestirr'd it more,—'twas but the beam
That checker'd o'er the living stream—
I gaz'd, till vanishing from view,   380

3. "I need hardly observe, that Charity and Hospitality are the first duties enjoined by Mahomet; and
   to say truth, very generally practised by his disciples. The first praise that can be bestowed on a
   chief, is a panegyric on his bounty; the next, on his valour."
4. The narrative becomes a dialogue between an anonymous boatman and Hassan; the boatman may
   be the same fisherman who saw the Giaour speed by in the earlier passage, though the present pas-
   sage is a flashback to Hassan's drowning of Leila, which in the story precedes the fisherman's sight-
   ing of the tormented, vengeful Giaour.
5. "The ataghan, a long dagger worn with pistols in the belt, in a metal scabbard, generally of silver;
   and, among the wealthier, gilt, or of gold."
6. "Green is the privileged colour of the prophet's numèrous pretended descendants; with them, as
   here, faith (the family inheritance) is supposed to supersede the necessity of good works; they are
   the worst of a very indifferent brood."
7. "'Salam aleikoum! aleikoum salam!' peace be with you; be with you peace—the salutation reserved
   for the faithful;—to a Christian, 'Urlarula,' a good journey; or 'saban hiresem, saban serula'; good
   morn, good even; and sometimes, 'may your end be happy'; are the usual salutes."
8. Truth.

Like lessening pebble it withdrew;
Still less and less, a speck of white
That gemm'd the tide, then mock'd the sight;
And all its hidden secrets sleep,
Known but to Genii[9] of the deep,   385
Which, trembling in their coral caves,
They dare not whisper to the waves.

      *   *   *   *   *   *   *   *

   As rising on its purple wing[1]
The insect-queen[2] of eastern spring,
O'er emerald meadows of Kashmeer   390
Invites the young pursuer near,
And leads him on from flower to flower
A weary chase and wasted hour,
Then leaves him, as it soars on high
With panting heart and tearful eye: 395
So Beauty lures the full-grown child
With hue as bright, and wing as wild;
A chase of idle hopes and fears,
Begun in folly, closed in tears.
If won, to equal ills betrayed,   400
Woe waits the insect and the maid,
A life of pain, the loss of peace,
From infant's play, or man's caprice:
The lovely toy so fiercely sought
Has lost its charm by being caught,   405
For every touch that woo'd its stay
Has brush'd the brightest hues away
Till charm, and hue, and beauty gone,
'Tis left to fly or fall alone.
With wounded wing, or bleeding breast,   410
Ah! where shall either victim rest?
Can this with faded pinion soar
From rose to tulip as before?
Or Beauty, blighted in an hour,
Find joy within her broken bower?   415
No: gayer insects fluttering by
Ne'er droop the wing o'er those that die,
And lovelier things have mercy shown
To every failing but their own,
And every woe a tear can claim   420
Except an erring sister's shame.

      *   *   *   *   *   *   *   *

---

9. Nature spirits of Arabian folklore.
1. The two segments beginning here are the poet's meditations prompted by the story.
2. "The blue-winged butterfly of Kashmeer, the most rare and beautiful of the species."

The Mind, that broods o'er guilty woes,
  Is like the Scorpion[3] girt by fire,
In circle narrowing as it glows,
The flames around their captive close,   425
Till inly search'd by thousand throes,
  And maddening in her ire,
One sad and sole relief she knows,
The sting she nourish'd for her foes,
Whose venom never yet was vain,   430
Gives but one pang, and cures all pain,
And darts into her desperate brain.—
So do the dark in soul expire,
Or live like Scorpion girt by fire;
So writhes the mind Remorse hath riven,   435
Unfit for earth, undoom'd for heaven,
Darkness above, despair beneath,
Around it flame, within it death!—

          *   *   *   *   *   *   *   *

Black Hassan from the Haram flies,[4]
Nor bends on woman's form his eyes,   440
The unwonted chase each hour employs,
Yet shares he not the hunter's joys.
Not thus was Hassan wont to fly
When Leila dwelt in his Serai.[5]
Doth Leila there no longer dwell?   445
That tale can only Hassan tell:
Strange rumours in our city say
Upon that eve she fled away
When Rhamazan's[6] last sun was set,
And flashing from each minaret   450
Millions of lamps proclaim'd the feast
Of Bairam through the boundless East.
'Twas then she went as to the bath,
Which Hassan vainly search'd in wrath,
But[7] she was flown her master's rage   455
In likeness of a Georgian page,[8]

---

3. "Alluding to the dubious suicide of the scorpion, so placed for experiment by gentle philosophers. Some maintain that the position of the sting, when turned towards the head, is merely a convulsive movement; but others have actually brought in the verdict 'Felo de se.' The scorpions are surely interested in a speedy decision of the question; as, if once fairly established as insect Catos, they will probably be allowed to live as long as they think proper, without being martyred for the sake of an hypothesis."
4. The storyteller resumes his narrative here with the details of Hassan's discovery of Leila's infidelity, a description of Leila's beauty, Hassan's pursuit of the Giaour into the mountainside, and the massacring of Hassan and his vassals by the Giaour and a band of Arnauts.
5. Seraglio, the apartments in which a Sultan's harem lived.
6. "The cannon at sunset close the Rhamazan; see note [above, line 225]."
7. For (1832).
8. A Georgian is a native of the southern Caucasus. Leila's disguising herself as a page to escape her husband and meet her lover was likely suggested by the behavior of Byron's headstrong lover Lady Caroline Lamb.

And far beyond the Moslem's power
Had wrong'd him with the faithless Giaour.
Somewhat of this had Hassan deem'd,
But still so fond, so fair she seem'd,   460
Too well he trusted to the slave
Whose treachery deserv'd a grave:
And on that eve had gone to mosque,
And thence to feast in his kiosk.⁹
Such is the tale his Nubians¹ tell,   465
Who did not watch their charge too well;
But others say, that on that night,
By pale Phingari's² trembling light,
The Giaour upon his jet black steed
Was seen—but seen alone to speed   470
With bloody spur along the shore,
Nor maid nor page behind him bore.

      ✳ ✳ ✳ ✳ ✳ ✳ ✳ ✳

Her eye's dark charm 'twere vain to tell,
But gaze on that of the Gazelle,
It will assist thy fancy well,   475
As large, as languishingly dark,
But Soul beam'd forth in every spark
That darted from beneath the lid,
Bright as the jewel of Giamschid.³
Yea, *Soul*, and should our prophet⁴ say   480
That form was nought but breathing clay,
By Alla! I would answer nay;
Though on Al-Sirat's⁵ arch I stood,
Which totters o'er the fiery flood,
With Paradise within my view,   485
And all his Houris⁶ beckoning through.
Oh! who young Leila's glance could read
And keep that portion of his creed
Which saith that woman is but dust,

9. An open pavilion or summerhouse.
1. Black slaves from the area of the Sudan, often used as harem eunuchs.
2. "Phingari, the moon."
3. "The celebrated fabulous ruby of Sultan Giamschid, the embellisher of Istakhar; from its splendour, named Schebgerag, 'the torch of night'; also 'the cup of the sun,' &c.—In the first editions, 'Giamschid' was written as a word of three syllables; so D'Herbelot has it; but I am told Richardson reduces it to a dissylable, and writes 'Jamshid.' I have left in the text the orthography of the one with the pronunciation of the other." *D'Herbelot*: see headnote; John Richardson's *Dictionary of Persian, Arabic, and English* (1777).
4. Mohammed.
5. "Al-Sirat, the bridge of breadth less than the thread of a famished spider, and sharper than the edge of a sword, over which the Mussulmans must *skate* into Paradise, to which it is the only entrance; but this is not the worst, the river beneath being hell itself, into which, as may be expected, the unskilful and tender of foot contrive to tumble with a 'facilis descensus Averni' [Virgil, *Aeneid* 6.26], not very pleasing in prospect to the next passenger. There is a shorter cut downwards for the Jews and Christians."
6. The beautiful virgins provided in Paradise for faithful Muslims. The word derives from the Arabic for a "gazelle-eyed" female, i.e., black-eyed like the gazelle (cf. line 474).

A soulless toy for tyrant's lust?[7]   490
On her might Muftis[8] gaze, and own
That through her eye the Immortal shone—
On her fair cheek's unfading hue,
The young pomegranate's[9] blossoms strew
Their bloom in blushes ever new—   495
Her hair in hyacinthine[1] flow
When left to roll its folds below,
As midst her handmaids in the hall
She stood superior to them all,
Hath swept the marble where her feet   500
Gleam'd whiter than the mountain sleet
Ere from the cloud that gave it birth,
It fell, and caught one stain of earth.
The cygnet nobly walks the water—
So moved on earth Circassia's daughter[2]—   505
The loveliest bird of Franguestan![3]
As rears her crest the ruffled Swan,
    And spurns the wave with wings of pride,
When pass the steps of stranger man
    Along the banks that bound her tide;   510
Thus rose fair Leila's whiter neck:—
Thus arm'd with beauty would she check
Intrusion's glance, till Folly's gaze
Shrunk from the charms it meant to praise.
Thus high and graceful was her gait;   515
Her heart as tender to her mate—
Her mate—stern Hassan, who was he?
Alas! that name was not for thee!

            *   *   *   *   *   *   *   *

Stern Hassan hath a journey ta'en
With twenty vassals in his train,   520
Each arm'd as best becomes a man
With arquebuss[4] and ataghan;
The chief before, as deck'd for war,
Bears in his belt the scimitar
Stain'd with the best of Arnaut[5] blood,   525
When in the pass the rebels stood,

7. "A vulgar error; the Koran allots at least a third of Paradise to well-behaved women; but by far the greater number of Mussulmans interpret the text their own way, and exclude their moieties from heaven. Being enemies to Platonics, they cannot discern 'any fitness of things' in the souls of the other sex, conceiving them to be superseded by the Houris."
8. Deputies to the Sultan's adviser in applying Muslim law.
9. "An oriental simile, which may, perhaps, though fairly stolen, be deemed 'plus Arabe qu'en Arabie.'"
1. "Hyacinthine, in Arabic 'Sunbul'; as common a thought in the eastern poets as it was among the Greeks."
2. Calling Leila, a native of the northern Caucasus, "Circassia's daughter" emphasizes her situation as a conquest of the Turkish Empire—a deliberate parallel to the situation of enslaved Greece, with reference to which Byron begins *The Giaour*.
3. "'Franguestan,' Circassia."
4. Turkish long rifle.
5. See Advertisement and note 1, p. 123.

And few return'd to tell the tale
Of what befell in Parne's vale.[6]
The pistols which his girdle bore
Were those that once a pasha[7] wore,   530
Which still, though gemm'd and boss'd with gold,
Even robbers tremble to behold.—
'Tis said he goes to woo a bride
More true than her who left his side;
The faithless slave that broke her bower,   535
And, worse than faithless, for a Giaour!—

   ✳   ✳   ✳   ✳   ✳   ✳   ✳   ✳

The sun's last rays are on the hill,
And sparkle in the fountain rill,
Whose welcome waters, cool and clear,
Draw blessings from the mountaineer;   540
Here may the loitering merchant Greek
Find that repose 'twere vain to seek
In cities lodged too near his lord,
And trembling for his secret hoard—
Here may he rest where none can see,   545
In crowds a slave, in deserts free;
And with forbidden wine[8] may stain
The bowl a Moslem must not drain.—

   ✳   ✳   ✳   ✳   ✳   ✳   ✳   ✳

The foremost Tartar's[9] in the gap,
Conspicuous by his yellow cap;   550
The rest in lengthening line the while
Wind slowly through the long defile;
Above, the mountain rears a peak,
Where vultures whet the thirsty beak,
And their's may be a feast to-night,   555
Shall tempt them down ere morrow's light.
Beneath, a river's wintry stream
Has shrunk before the summer beam,
And left a channel bleak and bare,
Save shrubs that spring to perish there.   560
Each side the midway path there lay
Small broken crags of granite gray,
By time or mountain lightning riven,
From summits clad in mists of heaven;
For where is he that hath beheld   565
The peak of Liakura[1] unveil'd?

6. The valley of Mount Parnes (Parnassus), northwest of Athens.
7. In Turkish dominions, an honorary term added to the name of a man of high rank.
8. The Koran forbids the drinking of alcoholic beverages.
9. Member of a Turkic group in Russia, famous for their ferocity.
1. Mount Parnassus.

✳   ✳   ✳   ✳   ✳   ✳   ✳   ✳

They reach the grove of pine at last:
"Bismillah![2] now the peril's past;
For yonder view the opening plain,
And there we'll prick our steeds amain":   570
The Chiaus[3] spake, and as he said,
A bullet whistled o'er his head;
The foremost Tartar bites the ground!
 Scarce had they time to check the rein
Swift from their steeds the riders bound,   575
 But three shall never mount again,
Unseen the foes that gave the wound,
 The dying ask revenge in vain.
With steel unsheath'd, and carbine bent,
Some o'er their courser's harness leant,   580
 Half shelter'd by the steed,
Some fly behind the nearest rock,
And there await the coming shock,
 Nor tamely stand to bleed
Beneath the shaft of foes unseen,   585
Who dare not quit their craggy screen.
Stern Hassan only from his horse
Disdains to light, and keeps his course,
Till fiery flashes in the van
Proclaim too sure the robber-clan   590
Have well secured the only way
Could now avail the promised prey;
Then curl'd his very beard[4] with ire,
And glared his eye with fiercer fire.
"Though far and near the bullets hiss,   595
I've scaped a bloodier hour than this."
And now the foe their covert quit,
And call his vassals to submit;
But Hassan's frown and furious word
Are dreaded more than hostile sword,   600
Nor of his little band a man
Resign'd carbine or ataghan—
Nor raised the craven cry, Amaun![5]
In fuller sight, more near and near,
The lately ambush'd foes appear,   605
And issuing from the grove advance
Some who on battle charger prance.—
Who leads them on with foreign brand,

2. "Bismillah—'In the name of God'; the commencement of all the chapters the Koran but one, and of prayer and thanksgiving."
3. A Turkish messenger.
4. "A phenomenon not uncommon with an angry Mussulman. In 1809, the Capitan Pacha's whiskers at a diplomatic audience were no less lively with indignation than a tiger cat's, to the horror of all the dragomans; the portentous mustachios twisted, they stood erect of their own accord, and were expected every moment to change their colour, but at last condescended to subside, which, probably, saved more heads than they contained hairs."
5. " 'Amaun,' quarter, pardon." [Arabic word.]

Far flashing in his red right hand?
" 'Tis he—'tis he—I know him now,   610
I know him by his pallid brow;
I know him by the evil eye[6]
That aids his envious treachery;
I know him by his jet-black barb,
Though now array'd in Arnaut garb,   615
Apostate from his own vile faith,
It shall not save him from the death;
'Tis he, well met in any hour,
Lost Leila's love—accursed Giaour!"

   As rolls the river into ocean,   620
In sable torrent wildly streaming;
   As the sea-tide's opposing motion
In azure column proudly gleaming,
Beats back the current many a rood,
In curling foam and mingling flood;   625
While eddying whirl, and breaking wave,
Roused by the blast of winter, rave;
Through sparkling spray in thundering clash,
The lightnings of the waters flash
In aweful whiteness o'er the shore,   630
That shines and shakes beneath the roar;
Thus—as the stream and ocean greet,
With waves that madden as they meet—
Thus join the bands whom mutual wrong,
And fate and fury drive along.   635
The bickering sabres' shivering jar;
   And pealing wide—or ringing near
   Its echoes on the throbbing ear,
The deathshot hissing from afar—
The shock—the shout—the groan of war—   640
   Reverberate along that vale,
   More suited to the shepherd's tale:
Though few the numbers—their's the strife,
That neither spares nor speaks for life!
Ah! fondly youthful hearts can press,   645
To seize and share the dear caress;
But Love itself could never pant
For all that Beauty sighs to grant
With half the fervour Hate bestows
Upon the last embrace of foes,   650
When grappling in the fight they fold
Those arms that ne'er shall lose their hold;
Friends meet to part—Love laughs at faith;—
True foes, once met, are join'd till death!

     *   *   *   *   *   *   *   *

6. "The 'evil eye,' a common superstition in the Levant, and of which the imaginary effects are yet
very singular on those who conceive themselves affected."

With sabre shiver'd to the hilt,   655
Yet dripping with the blood he spilt;
Yet strain'd within the sever'd hand
Which quivers round that faithless brand;
His turban far behind him roll'd,
And cleft in twain its firmest fold;   660
His flowing robe by falchion[7] torn,
And crimson as those clouds of morn
That streak'd with dusky red, portend
The day shall have a stormy end;
A stain on every bush that bore   665
A fragment of his palampore,[8]
His breast with wounds unnumber'd riven,
His back to earth, his face to heaven,
Fall'n Hassan lies—his unclosed eye
Yet lowering on his enemy,   670
As if the hour that seal'd his fate,
Surviving left his quenchless hate;
And o'er him bends that foe with brow
As dark as his that bled below.—

                  *   *   *   *   *   *   *   *

"Yes, Leila sleeps beneath the wave,[9]   675
But his shall be a redder grave;
Her spirit pointed well the steel
Which taught that felon heart to feel.
He call'd the Prophet, but his power
Was vain against the vengeful Giaour: 680
He call'd on Alla—but the word
Arose unheeded or unheard.
Thou Paynim[1] fool!—could Leila's prayer
Be pass'd, and thine accorded there?
I watch'd my time, I leagued with these,   685
The traitor in his turn to seize;
My wrath is wreak'd, the deed is done,
And now I go—but go alone."

                  *   *   *   *   *   *   *   *
                  *   *   *   *   *   *   *   *

The browsing camels' bells are tinkling[2]—
His Mother look'd from her lattice high,   690
    She saw the dews of eve besprinkling
The pasture green beneath her eye,

---

7. A broad, curved sword.
8. "The flowered shawls generally worn by persons of rank."
9. In this short passage, the Giaour himself speaks for the first time in the poem.
1. Pagan.
2. Lines 689–722 describe the anticipation of Hassan's mother for her son's return (recalling Judges
   5.28–30) followed by the arrival of a Tartar bringing the news of his death.

She saw the planets faintly twinkling,
" 'Tis twilight—sure his train is nigh."—
She could not rest in the garden-bower,   695
But gazed through the grate of his steepest tower—
"Why comes he not? his steeds are fleet,
Nor shrink they from the summer heat;
Why sends not the Bridegroom his promised gift:
Is his heart more cold, or his barb less swift?   700
Oh, false reproach! yon Tartar now
Has gain'd our nearest mountain's brow,
And warily the steep descends,
And now within the valley bends;
And he bears the gift at his saddle bow—   705
How could I deem his courser slow?
Right well my largess shall repay
His welcome speed, and weary way."—
The Tartar lighted at the gate,
But scarce upheld his fainting weight;   710
His swarthy visage spake distress,
But this might be from weariness;
His garb with sanguine spots was dyed,
But these might be from his courser's side;—
He drew the token from his vest—   715
Angel of Death! 'tis Hassan's cloven crest!
His calpac³ rent—his caftan red—
"Lady, a fearful bride thy Son hath wed—
Me, not from mercy, did they spare,
But this empurpled pledge to bear.   720
Peace to the brave! whose blood is spilt—
Woe to the Giaour! for his the guilt."

                    *   *   *   *   *   *   *   *

A turban⁴ carved in coarsest stone,⁵
A pillar with rank weeds o'ergrown,
Whereon can now be scarcely read   725
The Koran verse that mourns the dead,
Point out the spot where Hassan fell
A victim in that lonely dell.
There sleeps as true an Osmanlie⁶
As e'er at Mecca⁷ bent the knee;   730
As ever scorn'd forbidden wine,
Or pray'd with face towards the shrine,
In orisons resumed anew

---

3. "The 'Calpac' is the solid cap or centre part of the head-dress; the shawl is wound round it, and forms the turban."
4. "The turban—pillar—and inscriptive verse, decorate the tombs of the Osmanlies, whether in the cemetery or the wilderness. In the mountains you frequently pass similar mementos; and on enquiry you are informed that they record some victim of rebellion, plunder, or revenge."
5. In lines 723–86 a Turk contrasts the fates of Hassan and the Giaour.
6. Turk.
7. The sacred city of Islam, site of its holy mosque.

At solemn sound of "Alla Hu!"[8]
Yet died he by a stranger's hand,   735
And stranger in his native land—
Yet died he as in arms he stood,
And unavenged, at least in blood.
But him the maids of Paradise
    Impatient to their halls invite,   740
And the dark Heaven of Houris' eyes
    On him shall glance for ever bright;
They come—their kerchiefs green they wave,[9]
And welcome with a kiss the brave!
Who falls in battle 'gainst a Giaour,   745
Is worthiest an immortal bower.

                *   *   *   *   *   *   *   *

But thou, false Infidel! shalt writhe
Beneath avenging Monkir's[1] scythe;
And from its torment 'scape alone
To wander round lost Eblis'[2] throne;   750
And fire unquench'd, unquenchable—
Around—within—thy heart shall dwell;
Nor ear can hear, nor tongue can tell
The tortures of that inward hell!—
But first, on earth as Vampire[3] sent,   755
Thy corse shall from its tomb be rent;
Then ghastly haunt thy native place,
And suck the blood of all thy race;
There from thy daughter, sister, wife,
At midnight drain the stream of life;   760
Yet loathe the banquet which perforce
Must feed thy livid living corse;

8. "'Alla Hu!' the concluding words of the Muezzin's call to prayer from the highest gallery on the exterior of the Minaret. On a still evening, when the Muezzin has a fine voice (which they frequently have), the effect is solemn and beautiful beyond all the bells in Christendom."
9. "The following is part of a battle song of the Turks:—'I see—I see a dark-eyed girl of Paradise, and she waves a handkerchief, a kerchief of green; and cries aloud, "Come, kiss me, for I love thee,"' &c."
1. "Monkir and Nekir are the inquisitors of the dead, before whom the corpse undergoes a slight noviciate and preparatory training for damnation. If the answers are none of the clearest, he is hauled up with a scythe and thumped down with a red hot mace till properly seasoned, with a variety of subsidiary probations. The office of these angels is no sinecure; there are but two; and the number of orthodox deceased being in a small proportion to the remainder, their hands are always full. See *Relig. Ceremon.* and Sale's *Koran.*"
2. "Eblis, the Oriental Prince of Darkness."
3. "The Vampire superstition is still general in the Levant. Honest Tournefort tells a long story, which Mr. Southey, in the notes on *Thalaba,* quotes, about these 'Vroucolochas,' as he calls them. The Romaic term is 'Vardoulacha.' I recollect a whole family being terrified by the scream of a child, which they imagined must proceed from such a visitation. The Greeks never mention the word without horror. I find that 'Broucolokas' is an old legitimate Hellenic appellation—at least is so applied to Arsenius, who, according to the Greeks, was after his death animated by the Devil.— The moderns, however, use the word I mention."
   Byron's reference to the "Vampire" is among the earliest uses of the word in English literature, and the popularity of *The Giaour* contributed significantly to its familiarity and subsequent literary uses. Byron's continued interest in the subject resulted in a tale that he began during the summer of 1816; it was completed by his doctor, John Polidori, who entitled it "The Vampire" and published it under Byron's name.

Thy victims ere they yet expire
Shall know the daemon for their sire,
As cursing thee, thou cursing them,   765
Thy flowers are wither'd on the stem.
But one that for thy crime must fall—
The youngest—most beloved of all,
Shall bless thee with a *father's* name—
That word shall wrap thy heart in flame!   770
Yet must thou end thy task, and mark
Her cheek's last tinge, her eye's last spark,
And the last glassy glance must view
Which freezes o'er its lifeless blue;
Then with unhallow'd hand shalt tear   775
The tresses of her yellow hair,
Of which in life a lock when shorn
Affection's fondest pledge was worn;
But now is borne away by thee,
Memorial of thine agony!   780
Wet with thine own best blood shall drip,[4]
Thy gnashing tooth and haggard lip;
Then stalking to thy sullen grave—
Go—and with Gouls and Afrits[5] rave;
Till these in horror shrink away   785
From spectre more accursed than they!

            *   *   *   *   *   *   *   *

"How name ye yon lone Caloyer?[6]
His features I have scann'd before
In mine own land—'tis many a year,
Since, dashing by the lonely shore,   790
I saw him urge as fleet a steed
As ever served a horseman's need.
But once I saw that face—yet then
It was so mark'd with inward pain
I could not pass it by again;   795
It breathes the same dark spirit now,
As death were stamped upon his brow."

"'Tis twice three years at summer tide
Since first among our freres he came;
And here it soothes him to abide   800
For some dark deed he will not name.
But never at our vesper[7] prayer,

---

4. "The freshness of the face, and the wetness of the lip with blood, are the never-failing signs of a Vampire. The stories told in Hungary and Greece of these foul feeders are singular, and some of the most *incredibly* attested."
5. Muslim demons.
6. The speaker is the same fisherman who had previously caught sight of the Giaour in pursuit of Hassan. He converses with a monk in the community where the Giaour has become a "caloyer," or religious recluse, for the past six years.
7. The evening prayer.

Nor e'er before confession chair
Kneels he, nor recks[8] he when arise
Incense or anthem to the skies,   805
But broods within his cell alone,
His faith and race alike unknown.
The sea from Paynim land he crost,
And here ascended from the coast,
Yet seems he not of Othman race,   810
But only Christian in his face:
I'd judge him some stray renegade,
Repentant of the change he made,
Save that he shuns our holy shrine,
Nor tastes the sacred bread and wine.   815
Great largess to these walls he brought,
And thus our abbot's favour bought;
But were I Prior,[9] not a day
Should brook such stranger's further stay,
Or pent within our penance cell   820
Should doom him there for aye to dwell.
Much in his visions mutters he
Of maiden 'whelmed beneath the sea;
Of sabres clashing—foemen flying,
Wrongs avenged—and Moslem dying.   825
On cliff he hath been known to stand,
And rave as to some bloody hand
Fresh sever'd from its parent limb,
Invisible to all but him,
Which beckons onward to his grave,   830
And lures to leap into the wave."

               * * * * * * * *
               * * * * * * * *

Dark and unearthly is the scowl[1]
That glares beneath his dusky cowl[2]—
The flash of that dilating eye
Reveals too much of times gone by—   835
Though varying—indistinct its hue,
Oft will his glance the gazer rue—
For in it lurks that nameless spell
Which speaks—itself unspeakable—
A spirit yet unquell'd and high   840
That claims and keeps ascendancy,
And like the bird whose pinions quake[3]—

8. Heeds.
9. An officer in a monastery just below an abbot.
1. The storyteller resumes his narration.
2. Monk's hood. The Giaour, though a lay resident in the monastery, could nevertheless dress in
   monastic habit.
3. Byron alludes to the legend that snakes can mesmerize birds. Cf. the reference to the Giaour as
   "Gorgon" at line 896.

But cannot fly the gazing snake—
Will others quail beneath his look,
Nor 'scape the glance they scarce can brook.   845
From him the half-affrighted Friar
When met alone would fain retire—
As if that eye and bitter smile
Transferr'd to others fear and guile—
Not oft to smile descendeth he,   850
And when he doth 'tis sad to see
That he but mocks at Misery.
How that pale lip will curl and quiver!
Then fix once more as if for ever—
As if his sorrow or disdain   855
Forbade him e'er to smile again.—
Well were it so—such ghastly mirth
From joyaunce ne'er deriv'd its birth.—
But sadder still it were to trace
What once were feelings in that face—   860
Time hath not yet the features fix'd,
But brighter traits with evil mix'd—
And there are hues not always faded,
Which speak a mind not all degraded
Even by the crimes through which it waded—   865
The common crowd but see the gloom
Of wayward deeds—and fitting doom—
The close observer can espy
A noble soul, and lineage high.—
Alas! though both bestow'd in vain,   870
Which Grief could change—and Guilt could stain—
It was no vulgar tenement
To which such lofty gifts were lent,
And still with little less than dread
On such the sight is riveted.—   875
The roofless cot decayed and rent,
    Will scarce delay the passer by—
The tower by war or tempest bent,
While yet may frown one battlement,
    Demands and daunts the stranger's eye—   880
Each ivied arch—and pillar lone,
Pleads haughtily for glories gone!

"His floating robe around him folding,[4]
    Slow sweeps he through the column'd aisle—
With dread beheld—with gloom beholding   885
    The rites that sanctify the pile.
But when the anthem shakes the choir,
And kneel the monks—his steps retire—
By yonder lone and wavering torch

---

4. The speaker is again a monk of the abbey, puzzled and frightened at the Giaour's presence.

His aspect glares within the porch;[5]   890
There will he pause till all is done—
And hear the prayer—but utter none.
See—by the half-illumined wall
His hood fly back—his dark hair fall—
That pale brow wildly wreathing round,   895
As if the Gorgon[6] there had bound
The sablest of the serpent-braid
That o'er her fearful forehead stray'd.
For he declines the convent oath,
And leaves those locks unhallow'd[7] growth—   900
But wears our garb in all beside;
And—not from piety but pride
Gives wealth to walls that never heard
Of his one holy vow nor word.—
Lo!—mark ye—as the harmony   905
Peals louder praises to the sky—
That livid cheek—that stony air
Of mix'd defiance and despair!
Saint Francis! keep him from the shrine!
Else may we dread the wrath divine   910
Made manifest by awful sign.—
If ever evil angel bore
The form of mortal, such he wore—
By all my hope of sins forgiven
Such looks are not of earth nor heaven!"   915

To love the softest hearts are prone,[8]
But such can ne'er be all his own;
Too timid in his woes to share,
Too meek to meet, or brave despair;
And sterner hearts alone may feel   920
The wound that time can never heal.
The rugged metal of the mine
Must burn before its surface shine,
But plunged within the furnace-flame,
It bends and melts—though still the same;   925
Then temper'd to thy want, or will,
'Twill serve thee to defend or kill;
A breast-plate for thine hour of need,
Or blade to bid thy foeman bleed;
But if a dagger's form it bear,   930
Let those who shape its edge, beware!
Thus passion's fire, and woman's art,
Can turn and tame the sterner heart;
From these its form and tone are ta'en,

---

5. That is, during holy services the Giaour retires to the central enclosed patio area of the monastery.
6. A monster in Greek mythology whose gaze could turn a man to stone.
7. A true monk would have undergone a ritual shaving of the head (tonsure) to signal his entry into monastic discipline.
8. Lines 916–70 give the poet's reflections.

And what they make it, must remain,   935
But break—before it bend again.

        *   *   *   *   *   *   *   *

        *   *   *   *   *   *   *   *

If solitude succeed to grief,
Release from pain is slight relief;
The vacant bosom's wilderness
Might thank the pang that made it less.   940
We loathe what none are left to share—
Even bliss—'twere woe alone to bear;
The heart once left thus desolate
Must fly at last for ease—to hate.
It is as if the dead could feel   945
The icy worm around them steal,
And shudder, as the reptiles creep
To revel o'er their rotting sleep
Without the power to scare away
The cold consumers of their clay!   950
It is as if the desert-bird,[9]
   Whose beak unlocks her bosom's stream
   To still her famish'd nestlings' scream,
Nor mourns a life to them transferr'd,
Should rend her rash devoted breast,   955
And find them flown her empty nest.
The keenest pangs the wretched find
   Are rapture to the dreary void—
The leafless desert of the mind—
   The waste of feelings unemploy'd—   960
Who would be doom'd to gaze upon
A sky without a cloud or sun?
Less hideous far the tempest's roar,
Than ne'er to brave the billows more—
Thrown, when the war of winds is o'er,   965
A lonely wreck on fortune's shore,
'Mid sullen calm, and silent bay,
Unseen to drop by dull decay;—
Better to sink beneath the shock
Than moulder piecemeal on the rock!   970

        *   *   *   *   *   *   *   *

"Father! thy days have pass'd in peace,[1]
'Mid counted beads, and countless prayer;
To bid the sins of others cease,

---

9. "The pelican is, I believe, the bird so libelled, by the imputation of feeding her chickens with her blood."
1. At this point, the Giaour himself speaks again. His "confession" is a new version of the story as we have already pieced it together from its multiple narrators, now told from within the Giaour's consciousness.

Thyself without a crime or care,
Save transient ills that all must bear,   975
Has been thy lot, from youth to age,
And thou wilt bless thee from the rage
Of passions fierce and uncontroll'd,
Such as thy penitents unfold,
Whose secret sins and sorrows rest   980
Within thy pure and pitying breast.
My days, though few, have pass'd below
In much of joy, but more of woe;
Yet still in hours of love or strife,
I've 'scaped the weariness of life;   985
Now leagued with friends, now girt by foes,
I loathed the languor of repose;
Now nothing left to love or hate,
No more with hope or pride elate;
I'd rather be the thing that crawls   990
Most noxious o'er a dungeon's walls,
Than pass my dull, unvarying days,
Condemn'd to meditate and gaze—
Yet, lurks a wish within my breast
For rest—but not to feel 'tis rest—   995
Soon shall my fate that wish fulfil;
And I shall sleep without the dream
Of what I was, and would be still,
Dark as to thee my deeds may seem—
My memory now is but the tomb   1000
Of joys long dead—my hope—their doom—
Though better to have died with those
Than bear a life of lingering woes—
My spirit shrunk not to sustain
The searching throes of ceaseless pain;   1005
Nor sought the self-accorded grave
Of ancient fool, and modern knave:
Yet death I have not fear'd to meet,
And in the field it had been sweet
Had danger woo'd me on to move   1010
The slave of glory, not of love.
I've braved it—not for honour's boast;
I smile at laurels won or lost.—
To such let others carve their way,
For high renown, or hireling pay;   1015
But place again before my eyes
Aught that I deem a worthy prize—
The maid I love—the man I hate—
And I will hunt the steps of fate,
(To save or slay—as these require)   1020
Through rending steel, and rolling fire;
Nor need'st thou doubt this speech from one
Who would but do—what he *hath* done.
Death is but what the haughty brave—

The weak must bear—the wretch must crave—   1025
Then let Life go to him who gave:
I have not quail'd to danger's brow—
When high and happy—need I *now*?

        *   *   *   *   *   *   *   *

"I loved her, friar! nay, adored—
    But these are words that all can use—   1030
I proved it more in deed than word—
    There's blood upon that dinted sword—
    A stain its steel can never lose:
'Twas shed for her, who died for me,
    It warm'd the heart of one abhorr'd: 1035
Nay, start not—no—nor bend thy knee,
    Nor midst my sins such act record;
Thou wilt absolve me from the deed,
For he was hostile to thy creed!
The very name of Nazarene[2]   1040
Was wormwood[3] to his Paynim spleen.
Ungrateful fool! since but for brands,
Well wielded in some hardy hands,
And wounds by Galileans[4] given,
The surest pass to Turkish heav'n,   1045
For him his Houris still might wait
Impatient at the prophet's gate.
I loved her—love will find its way
Through paths where wolves would fear to prey,
And if it dares enough, 'twere hard   1050
If passion met not some reward—
No matter how—or where—or why,
I did not vainly seek—nor sigh:
Yet sometimes with remorse in vain
I wish she had not loved again.   1055
She died—I dare not tell thee how,
But look—'tis written on my brow!
There read of Cain[5] the curse and crime,
In characters unworn by time:
Still, ere thou dost condemn me—pause—   1060
Not mine the act, though I the cause;
Yet did he but what I had done
Had she been false to more than one;
Faithless to him—he gave the blow,
But true to me—I laid him low;   1065
Howe'er deserved her doom might be,

2. Christian, from Jesus's home, Nazareth.
3. Plant with an extremely bitter taste.
4. Christians.
5. The Giaour condemns himself for Leila's death in terms of the story of Cain (Genesis 4), which
    was of great importance for Byron's imagination (cf. *Childe Harold* I. 826–27 [p. 51], *Manfred*
    1.1.249 [p. 255], and Byron's drama *Cain, A Mystery*).

Her treachery was truth to me;
To me she gave her heart, that all
Which tyranny can ne'er enthrall;
And I, alas! too late to save,   1070
Yet all I then could give—I gave—
'Twas some relief—our foe a grave.
His death sits lightly; but her fate
Has made me—what thou well may'st hate.
His doom was seal'd—he knew it well,   1075
Warn'd by the voice of stern Taheer,[6]
Deep in whose darkly boding ear[7]
The deathshot peal'd of murder near—
As filed the troop to where they fell!
He died too in the battle broil—   1080
A time that heeds nor pain nor toil—
One cry to Mahomet for aid,
One prayer to Alla—all he made:
He knew and cross'd me in the fray—
I gazed upon him where he lay,   1085
And watched his spirit ebb away;
Though pierced like Pard[8] by hunters' steel,
He felt not half that now I feel.
I search'd, but vainly search'd to find,
The workings of a wounded mind;   1090
Each feature of that sullen corse
Betrayed his rage, but no remorse.

6. Hassan's soothsayer.
7. "This superstition of a second hearing (for I never met with downright second-sight in the East) fell once under my own observation. On my third journey to Cape Colonna, early in 1811, as we passed through the defile that leads from the hamlet between Keratia and Colonna, I observed Dervish Tahiri riding rather out of the path, and leaning his head upon his hand, as if in pain. I rode up and enquired. 'We are in peril,' he answered. 'What peril? we are not now in Albania, nor in the passes to Ephesus, Messalunghi, or Lepanto; there are plenty of us, well armed, and the Choriates have not courage to be thieves.'—True, Affendi, but nevertheless the shot is ringing in my ears.'—'The shot! not a tophaike has been fired this morning.'—'I hear it notwithstanding—Bom—Bom—as plainly as I hear your voice.'—'Psha!'—'As you please, Affendi; if it is written, so will it be.'—I left this quick-eared predestinarian, and rode up to Basili, his Christian compatriot, whose ears, though not at all prophetic, by no means relished the intelligence. We all arrived at Colonna, remained some hours, and returned leisurely, saying a variety of brilliant things, in more languages than spoiled the building of Babel, upon the mistaken seer. Romaic, Arnaout, Turkish, Italian, and English were all exercised, in various conceits, upon the unfortunate Mussulman. While we were contemplating the beautiful prospect, Dervish was occupied about the columns. I thought he was deranged into an antiquarian, and asked him if he had become a 'Palao-castro' man: 'No,' said he, 'but these pillars will be useful in making a stand'; and added other remarks, which at least evinced his own belief in his troublesome faculty of *forehearing*. On our return to Athens we heard from Leoné (a prisoner set ashore some days after) of the intended attack of the Mainotes, mentioned, with the cause of its not taking place, in the notes to Childe Harold, Canto 2d. I was at some pains to question the man, and he described the dresses, arms, and marks of the horses of our party so accurately, that with other circumstances, we could not doubt of *his* having been in 'villanous company,' and ourselves in a bad neighbourhood. Dervish became a soothsayer for life, and I dare say is now hearing more musketry than ever will be fired, to the great refreshment of the Arnaouts of Berat, and his native mountains.—I shall mention one trait more of this singular race. In March, 1811, a remarkably stout and active Arnaout came (I believe the fiftieth on the same errand) to offer himself as an attendant, which was declined: 'Well, Affendi,' quoth he, 'may you live!—you would have found me useful. I shall leave the town for the hills tomorrow, in the winter I return, perhaps you will then receive me.'—Dervish, who was present, remarked as a thing of course, and of no consequence, 'in the mean time he will join the Klephtes' (robbers), which was true to the letter. If not cut off, they come down in the winter, and pass it unmolested in some town, where they are often as well known as their exploits."
8. Leopard.

Oh, what had Vengeance given to trace
Despair upon his dying face!
The late repentance of that hour,   1095
When Penitence hath lost her power
To tear one terror from the grave—
And will not soothe, and can not save!

                 *   *   *   *   *   *   *   *

"The cold in clime are cold in blood,
Their love can scarce deserve the name;   1100
But mine was like the lava flood
That boils in Aetna's[9] breast of flame.
I cannot prate in puling strain
Of ladye-love, and beauty's chain;
If changing cheek, and scorching vein—   1105
Lips taught to writhe, but not complain—
If bursting heart, and madd'ning brain—
And daring deed, and vengeful steel—
And all that I have felt—and feel—
Betoken love—that love was mine,   1110
And shown by many a bitter sign.
'Tis true, I could not whine nor sigh,
I knew but to obtain or die.
I die—but first I have possess'd,
And come what may, I *have been* blest;   1115
Shall I the doom I sought upbraid?
No—reft of all—yet undismay'd
But for the thought of Leila slain,
Give me the pleasure with the pain,
So would I live and love again.   1120
I grieve, but not, my holy guide!
For him who dies, but her who died;
She sleeps beneath the wandering wave—
Ah! had she but an earthly grave,
This breaking heart and throbbing head   1125
Should seek and share her narrow bed.
She was a form of life and light—
That seen—became a part of sight,
And rose—where'er I turned mine eye—
The Morning-star of Memory!   1130

"Yes, Love indeed is light from heaven—
   A spark of that immortal fire
With angels shared—by Alla given,
   To lift from earth our low desire.
Devotion wafts the mind above,   1135
But Heaven itself descends in love—

9. An active volcano in East Sicily.

A feeling from the Godhead caught,
To wean from self each sordid thought—
A Ray of him who form'd the whole—
A Glory circling round the soul!   1140
I grant *my* love imperfect—all
That mortals by the name miscall—
Then deem it evil—what thou wilt—
But say, oh say, *hers* was not guilt!
She was my life's unerring light—   1145
That quench'd—what beam shall break my night?
Oh! would it shone to lead me still,
Although to death or deadliest ill!—
Why marvel ye, if they who lose
    This present joy, this future hope,   1150
    No more with sorrow meekly cope—
In phrensy then their fate accuse—
In madness do those fearful deeds
    That seem to add but guilt to woe?
Alas! the breast that inly bleeds   1155
    Hath nought to dread from outward blow—
Who falls from all he knows of bliss,
Cares little into what abyss.—
Fierce as the gloomy vulture's now
    To thee, old man, my deeds appear—   1160
I read abhorrence on thy brow,
    And this too was I born to bear!
'Tis true, that, like that bird of prey,
With havock have I mark'd my way—
But this was taught me by the dove[1]—   1165
To die—and know no second love.
This lesson yet hath man to learn,
Taught by the thing he dares to spurn—
The bird that sings within the brake,
The swan that swims upon the lake,   1170
One mate, and one alone, will take.
And let the fool still prone to range,
And sneer on all who cannot change—
Partake his jest with boasting boys,
I envy not his varied joys—   1175
But deem such feeble, heartless man,
Less than yon solitary swan—
Far—far beneath the shallow maid
He left believing and betray'd.
Such shame at least was never mine—   1180
Leila—each thought was only thine!—
My good, my guilt, my weal, my woe,
My hope on high—my all below.
Earth holds no other like to thee,

1. According to legend, the dove is monogamous and dies of grief when its mate dies.

Or if it doth, in vain for me—   1185
For worlds I dare not view the dame
Resembling thee, yet not the same.
The very crimes that mar my youth,
This bed of death—attest my truth—
'Tis all too late—thou wert—thou art   1190
The cherish'd madness of my heart!

"And she was lost—and yet I breathed,
    But not the breath of human life—
A serpent round my heart was wreathed,
    And stung my every thought to strife.—   1195
Alike all time—abhorr'd all place,
Shuddering I shrunk from Nature's face,
Where every hue that charm'd before
The blackness of my bosom wore:—
The rest—thou dost already know,   1200
And all my sins and half my woe—
But talk no more of penitence,
Thou see'st I soon shall part from hence—
And if thy holy tale were true—
The deed that's done canst *thou* undo?   1205
Think me not thankless—but this grief
Looks not to priesthood for relief.[2]
My soul's estate in secret guess—
But wouldst thou pity more—say less—
When thou canst bid my Leila live,   1210
Then will I sue thee to forgive;
Then plead my cause in that high place
Where purchased masses proffer grace—
Go—when the hunter's hand hath wrung
From forest-cave her shrieking young,   1215
And calm the lonely lioness—
But soothe not—mock not *my* distress!

"In earlier days, and calmer hours,
    When heart with heart delights to blend,
Where bloom my native valley's bowers—   1220
    I had—Ah! have I now?—a friend!—
To him this pledge I charge thee send—
    Memorial of a youthful vow;
I would remind him of my end,—
    Though souls absorb'd like mine allow   1225
Brief thought to distant friendship's claim,
Yet dear to him my blighted name.

---

2. "The monk's sermon is omitted. It seems to have had so little effect upon the patient, that it could
have no hopes from the reader. It may be sufficient to say, that it was of a customary length (as may
be perceived from the interruptions and uneasiness of the penitent), and was delivered in the usual
tone of all orthodox preachers." In fact, the act of confession is nearly undone by the Giaour's lack
of penitence and respect for priestly authority. Cf. *Manfred* 3.1.52–78 (pp. 274–75).

'Tis strange—he prophesied my doom,
   And I have smiled—(I then could smile—)
When Prudence would his voice assume,   1230
   And warn—I reck'd not what—the while—
But now remembrance whispers o'er
Those accents scarcely mark'd before.
Say—that his bodings came to pass,
   And he will start to hear their truth,   1235
   And wish his words had not been sooth:
Tell him—unheeding as I was—
   Through many a busy bitter scene
   Of all our golden youth had been—
In pain, my faultering tongue had tried   1240
To bless his memory ere I died;
But heaven in wrath would turn away,
If Guilt should for the guiltless pray.
I do not ask him not to blame—
Too gentle he to wound my name;   1245
And what have I to do with fame?
I do not ask him not to mourn,
Such cold request might sound like scorn;
And what than friendship's manly tear
May better grace a brother's bier?   1250
But bear this ring—his own of old—
And tell him—what thou dost behold!
The wither'd frame, the ruin'd mind,
The wrack by passion left behind—
A shrivell'd scroll, a scatter'd leaf,   1255
Sear'd by the autumn blast of grief!

         ❊   ❊   ❊   ❊   ❊   ❊   ❊   ❊

"Tell me no more of fancy's gleam,
No, father, no, 'twas not a dream;
Alas! the dreamer first must sleep,
I only watch'd, and wish'd to weep;   1260
But could not, for my burning brow
Throbb'd to the very brain as now.
I wish'd but for a single tear,
As something welcome, new, and dear;
I wish'd it then—I wish it still,   1265
Despair is stronger than my will.
Waste not thine orison—despair
Is mightier than thy pious prayer;
I would not, if I might, be blest;
I want no paradise—but rest.   1270
'Twas then, I tell thee, father! then
I saw her—yes—she lived again;
And shining in her white symar,[3]

---

3. "'Symar,' a shroud."

As through yon pale gray cloud—the star
Which now I gaze on, as on her   1275
Who look'd and looks far lovelier;
Dimly I view its trembling spark—
To-morrow's night shall be more dark—
And I—before its rays appear,
That lifeless thing the living fear.   1280
I wander, father! for my soul
Is fleeting towards the final goal;
I saw her, friar! and I rose,
Forgetful of our former woes;
And rushing from my couch, I dart,   1285
And clasp her to my desperate heart;
I clasp—what is it that I clasp?
No breathing form within my grasp,
No heart that beats reply to mine,
Yet, Leila! yet the form is thine!   1290
And art thou, dearest, changed so much,
As meet my eye, yet mock my touch?
Ah! were thy beauties e'er so cold,
I care not—so my arms enfold
The all they ever wish'd to hold.   1295
Alas! around a shadow prest,
They shrink upon my lonely breast;
Yet still—'tis there—in silence stands,
And beckons with beseeching hands!
With braided hair, and bright-black eye—   1300
I knew 'twas false—she could not die!
But he is dead—within the dell
I saw him buried where he fell;
He comes not—for he cannot break
From earth—why then art thou awake?   1305
They told me, wild waves roll'd above
The face I view, the form I love;
They told me—'twas a hideous tale!
I'd tell it—but my tongue would fail—
If true—and from thine ocean-cave   1310
Thou com'st to claim a calmer grave;
Oh! pass thy dewy fingers o'er
This brow that then will burn no more;
Or place them on my hopeless heart—
But, shape or shade!—whate'er thou art,   1315
In mercy, ne'er again depart—
Or farther with thee bear my soul
Than winds can waft—or waters roll!—

＊   ＊   ＊   ＊   ＊   ＊   ＊   ＊

"Such is my name, and such my tale,
    Confessor—to thy secret ear,   1320
I breathe the sorrows I bewail,

And thank thee for the generous tear
This glazing eye could never shed.
Then lay me with the humblest dead,
And save the cross above my head,   1325
Be neither name nor emblem spread—
By prying stranger to be read,
Or stay the passing pilgrim's tread."
He pass'd—nor of his name and race
Hath left a token or a trace,   1330
Save what the father must not say
Who shrived him on his dying day;[4]
This broken tale was all we knew
Of her he loved, or him he slew.[5]

Ode to Napoleon Buonaparte[1]

"Expende Annibalem:—quot libras in duce summo Invenies!"
                                           JUVENAL, *Sat.* X.[2]

"The Emperor Nepos was acknowledged by the Senate, by the Italians, and
by the Provincials of Gaul; his moral virtues, and military talents, were
loudly celebrated; and those who derived any private benefit from his gov-
ernment announced in prophetic strains the restoration of public felicity.

  ✳   ✳   ✳   ✳   ✳   ✳   ✳   ✳

  ✳   ✳   ✳   ✳   ✳   ✳   ✳   ✳

By this shameful abdication, he protracted his life a few years, in a very
ambiguous state, between an Emperor and an Exile, till—"
                          GIBBON's *Decline and Fall*, vol. vi. p. 220.

1

'Tis done—but yesterday a King!
And arm'd with Kings to strive—

4. According to the ritual of confession, the friar is bound to absolute confidentiality.
5. "The circumstance to which the above story relates was not very uncommon in Turkey. A few years
   ago the wife of Muchtar Pacha complained to his father of his son's supposed infidelity; he asked
   with whom, and she had the barbarity to give in a list of the twelve handsomest women in Yanina.
   They were seized, fastened up in sacks, and drowned in the lake the same night! One of the guards
   who was present informed me, that not one of the victims uttered a cry, or showed a symptom of
   terror at so sudden a 'wrench from all we know, from all we love.' The fate of Phrosine, the fairest
   of this sacrifice, is the subject of many a Romaic and Arnaout ditty. The story in the text is one told
   of a young Venetian many years ago, and now nearly forgotten. I heard it by accident recited by
   one of the coffee-house story-tellers who abound in the Levant, and sing or recite their narratives.
   The additions and interpolations by the translator will be easily distinguished from the rest, by the
   want of Eastern imagery; and I regret that my memory has retained so few fragments of the origi-
   nal. For the contents of some of the notes I am indebted partly to D'Herbelot, and partly to that
   most Eastern, and, as Mr Weber justly entitles it, 'sublime tale,' the 'Caliph Vathek.' I do not know
   from what source the author of that singular volume may have drawn his materials; some of his
   incidents are to be found in the 'Bibliothèque Orientale'; but for correctness of costume, beauty
   of description, and power of imagination, it far surpasses all European imitations; and bears such
   marks of originality, that those who have visited the East will find some difficulty in believing it to
   be more than a translation. As an Eastern tale, even Rasselas must bow before it; his 'Happy Val-
   ley' will not bear a comparison with the 'Hall of Eblis.'" Byron's note refers to Samuel Johnson's
   Rasselas (1759) and William Beckford's *Vathek* (1786).
1. After the dazzling popular success of *The Corsair*, Byron decided to abandon poetry. However, he
   found Napoleon's first defeat in March 1814 and his acceptance of exile on Elba (rather than, to
   Byron's thinking, honorable suicide) a "*physically* irresistible" occasion for verse (*BLJ* 4:102; see also

And now thou art a nameless thing:
   So abject—yet alive!
Is this the man of thousand thrones,   5
Who strew'd our earth with hostile bones,
   And can he thus survive?
Since he, miscall'd the Morning Star,
Nor man nor fiend hath fallen so far.[3]

2

Ill-minded man! why scourge thy kind   10
   Who bow'd so low the knee?
By gazing on thyself grown blind,
   Thou taught'st the rest to see.
With might unquestion'd,—power to save,—
Thine only gift hath been the grave   15
   To those that worshipp'd thee;
Nor till thy fall could mortals guess
Ambition's less than littleness!

3

Thanks for that lesson—it will teach
   To after-warriors more   20
Than high Philosophy can preach,
   And vainly preach'd before.
That spell upon the minds of men
Breaks never to unite again,
   That led them to adore   25
Those Pagod[4] things of sabre-sway,
With fronts of brass, and feet of clay.

4

The triumph, and the vanity,
   The rapture of the strife[5]—

Journal entries of November 17, 1813, and February 18, April 8, and April 9, 1814 [pp. 180, 184–85]). For Byron it was "impossible not to be dazzled and overwhelmed by [Napoleon's] character and career" (*BLJ* 4:284). Aware that admiration for England's (and much of Europe's) enemy would jeopardize his reputation and provoke a backlash, he assured Murray when he sent him the Ode on April 10 that "it contains nothing in *his* favour—& no allusion whatever to our own Government or the Bourbons" (*BLJ* 4:94). However, he expressed his thoughts more frankly to Annabella Milbanke: "Buonaparte has fallen—I regret it—& the restoration of the despicable Bourbons—the triumph of tameness over talent—and the utter wreck of a mind which I thought superior even to Fortune—it has utterly confounded and baffled me . . ." (*BLJ* 4:101). Byron's interest in Napoleon was not merely political; Byron related personally to Napoleon's "character and career," as is evident in *Childe Harold* III, stanzas 36–45 (pp. 205–08), and *Don Juan* XI, stanzas 55–56 (p. 593). In 1938, the Austrian American composer Arnold Schoenberg composed a chamber music setting of the poem as a statement against Hitler.
    Criticism: Bainbridge, *Napoleon and English Romanticism*; Clubbe, "Byron and Napoleon 1814–1816"; Giuliano, *Manuscripts of the Younger Romantics*, vol. 11; Hogg, "Byron's Vacillating Attitude Towards Napoleon."
2. Produce the urn that Hannibal contains, / And weigh the mighty dust which yet remains; / *And is this all!* (William Gifford's *Translation of Juvenal* [1817], Tenth Satire, lines 147–48.)
3. Lucifer (Isaiah 14.12).
4. An idol.
5. " 'Certaminis *gaudia*'—the expression of Attila in his harangue to his army, previous to the battle of Chalons, given in Cassiodorus."

The earthquake voice of Victory,   30
  To thee the breath of life;
The sword, the sceptre, and that sway
Which man seem'd made but to obey,
  Wherewith renown was rife—
All quell'd!—Dark Spirit! what must be   35
The madness of thy memory!

5

The Desolator desolate!
  The Victor overthrown!
The Arbiter of others' fate
  A Suppliant for his own!   40
Is it some yet imperial hope
That with such change can calmly cope?
  Or dread of death alone?
To die a prince—or live a slave—
Thy choice is most ignobly brave!   45

6

He who of old would rend the oak,[6]
  Dream'd not of the rebound;
Chain'd by the trunk he vainly broke—
  Alone—how look'd he round?
Thou in the sternness of thy strength   50
An equal deed hast done at length,
  And darker fate hast found:
He fell, the forest-prowlers' prey;
But thou must eat thy heart away!

7

The Roman,[7] when his burning heart   55
  Was slaked with blood of Rome,
Threw down the dagger—dared depart,
  In savage grandeur, home.—
He dared depart in utter scorn
Of men that such a yoke had borne,   60
  Yet left him such a doom!
His only glory was that hour
Of self-upheld abandon'd power.

8

The Spaniard,[8] when the lust of sway
  Had lost its quickening spell,   65

---

6. Milo, famous Athenian athlete; Byron refers to his bizarre death by having his hands wedged in the trunk of a tree.
7. Lucius Sulla, dictator who resigned in 79 B.C.E.
8. Charles I, king of Spain from 1516 and, as Charles V, Holy Roman Emperor from 1519, until his abdication in 1556.

Cast crowns for rosaries away,
  An empire for a cell;
A strict accountant of his beads,
A subtle disputant on creeds,
  His dotage trifled well: 70
Yet better had he neither known
A bigot's shrine, nor despot's throne.

9

But thou—from thy reluctant hand
  The thunderbolt is wrung—
Too late thou leav'st the high command   75
  To which thy weakness clung;
All Evil Spirit as thou art,
It is enough to grieve the heart
  To see thine own unstrung;
To think that God's fair world hath been   80
The footstool of a thing so mean;

10

And Earth hath spilt her blood for him,
  Who thus can hoard his own!
And Monarchs bow'd the trembling limb,
  And thank'd him for a throne!   85
Fair Freedom! we may hold thee dear,
When thus thy mightiest foes their fear
  In humblest guise have shown.
Oh! ne'er may tyrant leave behind
A brighter name to lure mankind!   90

11

Thine evil deeds are writ in gore,
  Nor written thus in vain—
Thy triumphs tell of fame no more,
  Or deepen every stain:
If thou hadst died as honour dies,   95
Some new Napoleon might arise,
  To shame the world again—
But who would soar the solar height,
To set in such a starless night?

12

Weigh'd in the balance, hero dust   100
  Is vile as vulgar clay;
Thy scales, Mortality! are just
  To all that pass away:
But yet methought the living great
Some higher sparks should animate,   105
  To dazzle and dismay:

Nor deem'd Contempt could thus make mirth
Of these, the Conquerors of the earth.

13

And she, proud Austria's mournful flower,[9]
   Thy still imperial bride;   110
How bears her breast the torturing hour?
   Still clings she to thy side?
Must she too bend, must she too share
Thy late repentance, long despair,
   Thou throneless Homicide?   115
If still she loves thee, hoard that gem,
'Tis worth thy vanish'd diadem!

14

Then haste thee to thy sullen Isle,
   And gaze upon the sea;
That element may meet thy smile—   120
   It ne'er was ruled by thee!
Or trace with thine all idle hand
In loitering mood upon the sand
   That Earth is now as free!
That Corinth's pedagogue[1] hath now   125
Transferr'd his by-word to thy brow.

15

Thou Timour![2] in his captive's cage
   What thoughts will there be thine,
While brooding in thy prison'd rage?
   But one—'The world *was* mine';   130
Unless, like he of Babylon,[3]
All sense is with thy sceptre gone,
   Life will not long confine
That spirit pour'd so widely forth—
So long obey'd—so little worth!   135

16

Or like the thief of fire from heaven,[4]
   Wilt thou withstand the shock?
And share with him, the unforgiven,
   His vulture and his rock!

9. The Austrian princess Marie Louise, second wife of Napoleon.
1. Dionysius the Younger, tyrant of Syracuse who was twice banished and who retired to Corinth in 344 B.C.E., where he is said to have opened a school for boys.
2. Tamerlane, who in 1402 confined the conquered Sultan of Turkey, Bajazet I, to a cage to prevent his escape.
3. Nebuchadnezzar, biblical king of Babylon; Daniel 4.23–33 tells of his madness during the time of his successor.
4. Prometheus.

Foredoom'd by God—by man accurst,   140
And that last act, though not thy worst,
The very Fiend's arch mock;[5]
He in his fall preserved his pride,
And, if a mortal, had as proudly died!

17[6]

There was a day—there was an hour,   145
    While earth was Gaul's—Gaul thine—
When that immeasurable power
    Unsated to resign
Had been an act of purer fame
Than gathers round Marengo's name[7]   150
    And gilded thy decline,
Through the long twilight of all time,
Despite some passing clouds of crime.

18

But thou forsooth must be a king,
    And don the purple vest,—   155
As if that foolish robe could wring
    Remembrance from thy breast.
Where is that faded garment? where
The gewgaws thou wert fond to wear,
    The star—the string—the crest?   160
Vain froward child of empire! say,
Are all thy playthings snatch'd away?

19

Where may the wearied eye repose
    When gazing on the Great;
Where neither guilty glory glows,   165
    Nor despicable state?
Yes—one—the first—the last—the best—
The Cincinnatus[8] of the West,
    Whom envy dared not hate,
Bequeath'd the name of Washington,   170
To make man blush there was but one!

---

5. "'The fiend's arch mock. / To lip a wanton, and suppose her chaste.'—Shakespeare." See *Othello*
   4.1.69–70. Napoleon was rumored to have had a casual affair just before leaving for Elba.
6. Byron wrote stanzas 17–19 at the request of his publisher, John Murray, in order to avoid a stamp
   tax on publications of less than a single sheet. Murray did not add them to the poem, however,
   following Byron's explicit instructions (*BLJ* 4:103–04, 107). They were first printed in *Life*, were
   printed as "Additional Stanzas" in Murray's 1831 edition of the collected poetry, and were incor-
   porated into the poem in 1832 and in most editions since then. In *CPW*, McGann removes them
   from the poem, printing them as "Additional Stanzas" (3:265–66).
7. Napoleon defeated the Austrians at Marengo in northern Italy in 1800.
8. Roman patriot (fifth century B.C.E.).

FROM HEBREW MELODIES   The following four poems belong to this collection of lyrics, originally published with music by the Jewish composer Isaac Nathan (1792–1864) as *A Selection of Hebrew Melodies, Ancient and Modern*. In 1814, at the suggestion of his friend and banker Douglas Kinnaird, Byron agreed to give Nathan a number of lyrics to be set to his arrangements of ancient liturgical airs. (See Byron's letter to Annabella Millbanke, October 20, 1814 [p. 189].) Many, but not all, of the poems deal with Old Testament themes; some of the poems, in fact, were written before the project with Nathan began. Twenty-four of the thirty poems that Nathan published with music between 1815 and 1829 were also published by John Murray in 1815 as *Hebrew Melodies*. For the complex composition and publication history of *Hebrew Melodies*, see: CPW 3:465–67; Ashton, *Byron's Hebrew Melodies*; Burwick and Douglass, eds., *A Selection of Hebrew Melodies*.

She Walks in Beauty[1]

1

She walks in beauty, like the night
  Of cloudless climes and starry skies;
And all that's best of dark and bright
  Meet in her aspect and her eyes:
Thus mellow'd to that tender light   5
  Which heaven to gaudy day denies.

2

One shade the more, one ray the less,
  Had half impair'd the nameless grace
Which waves in every raven tress,
  Or softly lightens o'er her face;   10
Where thoughts serenely sweet express
  How pure, how dear their dwelling-place.

3

And on that cheek, and o'er that brow,
  So soft, so calm, yet eloquent,
The smiles that win, the tints that glow,   15
  But tell of days in goodness spent,
A mind at peace with all below,
  A heart whose love is innocent!

---

1. On June 11, 1814, Byron attended a party where he saw his cousin's wife, Anne Horton Wilmot, who was dressed in mourning, with dark spangles on her dress. Struck by her beauty, Byron returned home and drafted this poem (see *BLJ* 4:124, n. 1).

Sun of the Sleepless[1]

Sun of the sleepless! melancholy star!
Whose tearful beam glows tremulously far,
That show'st the darkness thou canst not dispel,
How like art thou to joy remember'd well!
So gleams the past, the light of other days,   5
Which shines, but warms not with its powerless rays;
A night-beam Sorrow watcheth to behold,
Distinct, but distant—clear—but, oh how cold!

The Destruction of Sennacherib[1]

1

The Assyrian came down like the wolf on the fold,
And his cohorts were gleaming in purple and gold;
And the sheen of their spears was like stars on the sea,
When the blue wave rolls nightly on deep Galilee.

2

Like the leaves of the forest when Summer is green,   5
That host with their banners at sunset were seen:
Like the leaves of the forest when Autumn hath blown,
That host on the morrow lay wither'd and strown.

3

For the Angel of Death spread his wings on the blast,
And breathed in the face of the foe as he pass'd;   10
And the eyes of the sleepers wax'd deadly and chill,
And their hearts but once heaved, and for ever grew still!

4

And there lay the steed with his nostril all wide,
But through it there roll'd not the breath of his pride:
And the foam of his gasping lay white on the turf,   15
And cold as the spray of the rock-beating surf.

---

1. Composed on September 8, 1814, as part of an unfinished poem, this lyric to the moon has been praised as one of Byron's finest, and, after Nathan, was set to music by many composers, including Robert Schumann, Felix Mendelssohn, and Hugo Wolf. The poem recalls the famous line from the Paolo and Francesca episode in Canto 5 of Dante's *Inferno*: "There is no greater sorrow than to recall happy times in misery." For Byron's translation of this episode, see "Francesca of Rimini" (p. 683).

1. Drafted on February 19, 1815. Sennacherib, King of Assyria (705–681 B.C.E.), launched an attack against Judah under the reign of King Hezekiah, only to have the entire encamped army smitten by the Lord during the night (2 Kings 19 and Isaiah 37). For Byron's later association of this biblical episode with contemporary politics in Italy, see his letter of September 7, 1820 (*BLJ* 7:172).
   Textual Note: The name of the Assyrian king in the poem's title is given as "Semnacherib" in *CPW*, based on a likely error in the manuscript and early editions.

5

And there lay the rider distorted and pale,
With the dew on his brow, and the rust on his mail;
And the tents were all silent, the banners alone,
The lances unlifted, the trumpet unblown.   20

6

And the widows of Ashur[2] are loud in their wail,
And the idols are broke in the temple of Baal;[3]
And the might of the Gentile,[4] unsmote by the sword,
Hath melted like snow in the glance of the Lord!

Stanzas for Music[1]

"Felix qui potuit rerum cognoscere causas."
Virgil.

1

They say that Hope is happiness—
    But genuine Love must prize the past,
And Memory wakes the thoughts that bless:
    They rose the first—they set the last.

2

And all that Memory loves the most   5
    Was once our only Hope to be,
And all that Hope adored and lost
    Hath melted into Memory.

3

Alas! it is delusion all—
    The future cheats us from afar: 10
Nor can we be what we recall,
    Nor dare we think on what we are.

---

2. Assyria.
3. Deity worshiped by the Assyrians.
4. Non-Hebrews, i.e., Sennacherib, or the Assyrians.
1. Probably written in late 1814; first published with Nathan's musical arrangement in *A Selection of Hebrew Melodies*, rev. ed., 1827–29. Its first appearance in a Murray edition of Byron's poems is 1832, where the title "Stanzas for Music" was supplied. The epigraph from Virgil's *Georgics* (2.490), omitted in *1832*, translates as follows: "Happy he is who has been able to gain knowledge of the causes of things." When his friend Douglas Kinnaird derided the poem after reading the first draft, Byron burned it, but he later gave Nathan another copy. It is the only lyric of the thirty *Hebrew Melodies* composed and published by Nathan that Swinburne included in his edition of Byron's poems.

Stanzas for Music[1]

O Lachrymarum fons, tenero sacros
Ducentium ortus ex animo: quater
Felix! in imo qui scatentem
Pectore te, pia Nympha, sensit.
GRAY's *Poemata*[2]

1

There's not a joy the world can give like that it takes away,
When the glow of early thought declines in feeling's dull decay;
'Tis not on youth's smooth cheek the blush alone, which fades so fast,
But the tender bloom of heart is gone, ere youth itself be past.

2

Then the few whose spirits float above the wreck of happiness   5
Are driven o'er the shoals of guilt or ocean of excess:
The magnet of their course is gone, or only points in vain
The shore to which their shiver'd sail shall never stretch again.

3

Then the mortal coldness of the soul like death itself comes down;
It cannot feel for others' woes, it dare not dream its own;   10
That heavy chill has frozen o'er the fountain of our tears,
And though the eye may sparkle still, 'tis where the ice appears.

4

Though wit may flash from fluent lips, and mirth distract the breast,
Through midnight hours that yield no more their former hope of rest;
'Tis but as ivy-leaves around the ruin'd turret wreath,   15
All green and wildly fresh without, but worn and grey beneath.

5

Oh could I feel as I have felt,—or be what I have been,
Or weep as I could once have wept, o'er many a vanish'd scene;
As springs in deserts found seem sweet, all brackish though they be,
So midst the wither'd waste of life, those tears would flow to me.   20

1815.

---

1. Byron wrote this poem in mid February 1815 upon learning of the death of the Duke of Dorset, one of his close friends from his Harrow school days. He sent the lyric to Moore in a letter of March 2, 1815, quipping, "I feel merry enough to send you a sad song" (*BLJ* 4:277). It was first published in 1815 in sheet music, for voice and piano accompaniment by Sir John Stevenson, and printed in revised form in *Poems* (1816). A year after writing the poem and now connecting the emotions described in the poem to his recent marriage separation, Byron referred to the poem in another letter to Moore "as being the truest, though the most melancholy, I ever wrote" and "a little prophetic" (*BLJ* 5:45).
2. "O fount of tears, that draw their sacred sources from the tender mind; four times happy is he who has felt you, holy Nymph, gushing forth from the depth of his heart" (trans. George E. Haggerty). The English poet Thomas Gray (1716–1771) wrote this stanza to Richard West, a boy at Eton College who inspired some of Gray's most moving poetry.

When We Two Parted[1]

1

When we two parted
  In silence and tears,
Half broken-hearted
  To sever for years,
Pale grew thy cheek and cold,   5
  Colder thy kiss;
Truly that hour foretold
  Sorrow to this.

2

The dew of the morning
  Sunk chill on my brow—   10
It felt like the warning
  Of what I feel now.
Thy vows are all broken,
  And light is thy fame;
I hear thy name spoken,   15
  And share in its shame.

3

They name thee before me,
  A knell to mine ear;
A shudder comes o'er me—
  Why wert thou so dear?   20
They know not I knew thee,
  Who knew thee too well:—
Long, long shall I rue thee,
  Too deeply to tell.

4

In secret we met—   25
  In silence I grieve,
That thy heart could forget,
  Thy spirit deceive.
If I should meet thee
  After long years,   30
How should I greet thee?—
  With silence and tears.

1. Written in 1815 and published that year in sheet-music form with music by Isaac Nathan, composer of *Hebrew Melodies* (see p. 162). Most nineteenth- and early twentieth-century editions assign 1808 as the date of composition, which is the date Byron gave the poem when it was published in *Poems* (1816). By the false date Byron obscured the poem's subject, Lady Frances Wedderburn Webster, a friend's wife with whom he had had a brief, unconsummated affair in 1813 and whose subsequent scandalous affair with the Duke of Wellington prompted the writing of this poem. For two versions of a stanza removed from the poem's MS, see *CPW* 3:320 and 475. Criticism: McGann, "Byron and the Truth in Masquerade."

Stanzas for Music[1]

There be none of Beauty's daughters
With a magic like thee;
And like music on the waters
Is thy sweet voice to me:
When, as if its sound were causing   5
The charmed ocean's pausing,
The waves lie still and gleaming,
And the lulled winds seem dreaming.

And the midnight moon is weaving
Her bright chain o'er the deep;   10
Whose breast is gently heaving,
As an infant's asleep:
So the spirit bows before thee,
To listen and adore thee;
With a full but soft emotion,   15
Like the swell of Summer's ocean.

Fare Thee Well![1]

"Alas! they had been friends in Youth;
But whispering tongues can poison truth;
And constancy lives in realms above;
And Life is thorny; and youth is vain:
And to be wroth with one we love,
Doth work like madness in the brain;

          * * * * * * * *

But never either found another
To free the hollow heart from paining—
They stood aloof, the scars remaining,

1. Murray received this poem from Byron in March 1816; it was first published in *Poems* (1816). In writing the poem, Byron most likely was thinking of Claire Clairmont, Mary Shelley's stepsister, who pursued a relationship with Byron and who had a beautiful singing voice. She eventually bore their child, Allegra. Marchand conjectures that the poem may have been written earlier and refer to John Edleston, the Cambridge chorister whom Byron loved (see p. 98, n. 1, and *Marchand* 1:313n). McGann, however, considers the dating "unmistakable" and the association with Claire Clairmont "quite persuasive" (*CPW* 3:493).
1. Byron wrote this poem on March 18, 1816, the day after he and his wife signed their separation agreement. He sent it to her along with a note aimed, unsuccessfully, at softening her towards a reconciliation (see letter of February 8, 1816 [p. 193], as well as *BLJ* 5:51–52 and 7:199). Although the poem was first printed for private circulation, an unauthorized reprinting appeared in the April 14 issue of the *Champion*, a Tory paper. The first authorized printing was in *Poems* (1816), where the epigraph from *Christabel* was added. Fueled by the poem's various reprintings alongside Byron's poems on Napoleon, a public attack on Byron, who was an outspoken critic of the Tories and of the morals of the Prince Regent, was motivated as much by politics as by moral outrage at his domestic circumstances. For Wordsworth's vitriolic response to the poem, see p. 782. Criticism: Elledge, "Talented Equivocation: Byron's 'Fare thee well!' "; Erdman, " 'Fare thee well!'—Byron's Last Days in England"; McGann, "Byron and the Truth in Masquerade."
   Textual Note: In 1832, the poem was separated into unnumbered quatrains, as it appears in the numerous editions based on *1832*; Byron's latest corrected proof, however, gives the poem as continuous verses.

Like cliffs, which had been rent asunder;
  A dreary sea now flows between,
But neither heat, nor frost, nor thunder
  Shall wholly do away, I ween,
The marks of that which once hath been."
           COLERIDGE's *Christabel*.[2]

Fare thee well! and if for ever—
  Still for ever, fare *thee well*—
Even though unforgiving, never
  'Gainst thee shall my heart rebel.
Would that breast were bared before thee   5
  Where thy head so oft hath lain,
While that placid sleep came o'er thee
  Which thou ne'er canst know again:
Would that breast by thee glanced over,
  Every inmost thought could show!   10
Then thou would'st at last discover
  'Twas not well to spurn it so.
Though the world for this commend thee—
  Though it smile upon the blow,
Even its praises must offend thee,   15
  Founded on another's woe:
Though my many faults defaced me,
  Could no other arm be found
Than the one which once embraced me,
  To inflict a cureless wound?   20
Yet—oh, yet—thyself deceive not—
  Love may sink by slow decay,
But by sudden wrench, believe not
  Hearts can thus be torn away:
Still thine own its life retaineth—   25
  Still must mine—though bleeding—beat,
And the undying thought which paineth
  Is—that we no more may meet.
These are words of deeper sorrow
  Than the wail above the dead;   30
Both shall live—but every morrow
  Wake us from a widow'd bed.
And when thou wouldst solace gather—
  When our child's first accents flow—
Wilt thou teach her to say—"Father!"   35
  Though his care she must forego?
When her little hands shall press thee—
  When her lip to thine is press'd—
Think of him whose prayer shall bless thee—
  Think of him thy love had bless'd.   40

2. Composed 1797–1801, published 1816; lines 408–13, 419–26. Byron had heard *Christabel* recited in 1811; he expressed his admiration of it in a letter to Coleridge dated October 18, 1815 (p. 191).

Should her lineaments resemble
Those thou never more may'st see—
Then thy heart will softly tremble
With a pulse yet true to me.
All my faults—perchance thou knowest—   45
All my madness—none can know;
All my hopes—where'er thou goest—
Wither—yet with *thee* they go.
Every feeling hath been shaken;
Pride—which not a world could bow—   50
Bows to thee—by thee forsaken,
Even my soul forsakes me now.
But 'tis done—all words are idle—
Words from me are vainer still;
But the thoughts we cannot bridle   55
Force their way without the will.
Fare thee well!—thus disunited—
Torn from every nearer tie—
Sear'd in heart—and lone—and blighted—
More than this I scarce can die.   60

LETTERS AND JOURNAL

To Lord Holland

8 St. James's Street February 25th. 1812
My Lord,—With my best thanks I have the honour to return the Notts
letter to your Lordship.—I have read it with attention, but do not think I
shall venture to avail myself of it's contents, as my view of the question dif-
fers in some measure from Mr. Coldham's.—I hope I do not wrong him, but
his objections to ye. bill[1] appear to me to be founded on certain apprehen-
sions that he & his coadjutors might be mistaken for the *"original advisers"*
(to quote him) of the measure.— —For my own part, I consider the man-
ufacturers as a much injured body of men sacrificed to ye. views of certain
individuals who have enriched themselves by those practices which have
deprived the frame workers of employment.—For instance;—by the adop-
tion of a certain kind of frame 1 man performs ye. work of 7—6 are thus
thrown out of business.—But it is to be observed that ye. work thus done
is far inferior in quality, hardly marketable at home, & hurried over with a
view to exportation.—Surely, my Lord, however we may rejoice in any
improvement in ye. arts which may be beneficial to mankind; we must not
allow mankind to be sacrificed to improvements in Mechanism. The main-
tenance & well doing of ye. industrious poor is an object of greater conse-
quence to ye. community than ye. enrichment of a few monopolists by any

---

1. The bill introduced by the Tories to make frame-breaking—the destruction of weaving frames by
the factory workers ("manufacturers") whom they displaced—a capital offense. See "Ode to the
Framers of the Frame Bill" (p. 120).

improvement in ye. implements of trade, which deprives ye workman of his bread, & renders ye. labourer "unworthy of his hire."—My own motive for opposing ye. bill is founded on it's palpable injustice, & it's certain inefficacy.— —I have seen the state of these miserable men, & it is a disgrace to a civilized country.—Their excesses may be condemned, but cannot be subject of wonder.—The effect of ye. present bill would be to drive them into actual rebellion.—The few words I shall venture to offer on Thursday will be founded upon these opinions formed from my own observations on ye. spot.—By previous enquiry I am convinced these men would have been restored to employment & ye. county to tranquillity.—It is perhaps not yet too late & is surely worth the trial. It can never be too late to employ force in such circumstances.— —I believe your Lordship does not coincide with me entirely on this subject, & most cheerfully & sincerely shall I submit to your superior judgment & experience, & take some other line of argument against ye. bill, or be silent altogether, should you deem it more adviseable.— —Condemning, as every one must condemn the conduct of these wretches, I believe in ye. existence of grievances which call rather for pity than punishment.— —I have ye honour to be with great respect, my Lord, yr. Lordship's

> most obedt. & obliged Servt.
> BYRON

P.S.—I am a little apprehensive that your Lordship will think me too lenient towards these men, & *half a framebreaker myself.*

To Lady Caroline Lamb

May 1st. 1812

My dear Lady Caroline,[1]—I have read over the few poems of Miss Milbank with attention.—They display fancy, feeling, & a little practice would very soon induce facility of expression.—Though I have an abhorrence of Blank verse, I like the lines on Dermody[2] so much that I wish they were in rhyme.—The lines in the cave at Seaham[3] have a turn of thought which I cannot sufficiently commend & here I am at least candid as my own opinions differ upon such subjects.—The first stanza is very good indeed, & the others with a few slight alterations might be rendered equally excellent.— The last are smooth & pretty.—But these are all, has she no others?— — She certainly is a very extraordinary girl, who would imagine so much strength & variety of thought under that placid countenance?— —It is not necessary for Miss M. to be an authoress, indeed I do not think publishing at all creditable either to men or women, and (though you will not believe me) very often feel ashamed of it myself, but I have no hesitation in saying that she has talents, which were it proper or requisite to indulge, would have led to distinction.—A friend of mine (fifty years old & an author but

---

1. Wife of William Lamb, she and Byron were having a tempestuous (and on her part obsessive) love affair. Byron's future wife, Anne Isabella Milbanke, was William Lamb's cousin.
2. Thomas Dermody, Irish poet (1775–1802).
3. Location of the Milbanke home, near Durham.

not *Rogers*)[4] has just been here, as there is no name to the M.S.S. I shewed them to him, & he was much more enthusiastic in his praises than I have been.—He thinks them beautiful; I shall content myself with observing that they are better much better than anything of Miss M's protegee Blacket.[5] You will say as much of this to Miss M. as you think proper.—I say all this very sincerely, I have no desire to be better acquainted with Miss Milbank, she is too good for a fallen spirit to know or wish to know, & I should like her more if she were less perfect.—

Believe me yrs. ever most truly
B.

To Walter Scott

St. James's Street July sixth 1812

Sir,—I have just been honoured with your letter.—I feel sorry that you should have thought it worth while to notice the "evil works of my nonage"[1] as the thing is suppressed *voluntarily* & your explanation is too kind not to give me pain.—The satire was written when I was very young & very angry, & fully bent on displaying my wrath & my wit, & now I am haunted by the ghosts of my wholesale Assertions.—I cannot sufficiently thank you for your praise and now wa[i]ving myself let me talk to you of the Prince R[egen]t's.[2] He ordered me to be presented to him at a ball, & after some sayings peculiarly pleasing from royal lips, as to my own attempts; he talked to me of you & your immortalities; he preferred you to every bard past & present, & asked which of your works pleased me most, it was a difficult question—I answered, I thought the "Lay" he said his own opinion was nearly similar; in speaking of the others I told him that I thought you more particularly the poet of *Princes*, as *they* never appeared more fascinating than in Marmion & the Lady of the Lake, he was pleased to coincide & to dwell on the description of your James's no less royal than poetical.—He spoke alternately of Homer & yourself & seemed well acquainted with both, so that (with the exception of the Turks[3] & your humble servant) you were in very good company.—I defy Murray to have exaggerated his R[oyal] H[ighness]'s opinion of your powers, nor can I pretend to enumerate all he said on the subject, but it may give you pleasure to hear that it was conveyed in language which would only suffer by my attempting to transcribe it, & with a tone & taste which gave me a very high idea of his abilities & accomplishments, which I had hitherto considered as confined to *manners*, certainly superior to those of any living *gentleman.—* —This interview was accidental;—I never went to the levee, for having seen the courts of Mussulman & Catholic sovereigns, my curiosity was sufficiently allayed, & my politics being as perverse as my rhymes, I had in fact "no business there."—To be thus praised by your Sovereign must be gratifying to you, & if the

4. Byron may mean Robert Dallas.
5. Joseph Blackett, English cobbler-poet (1786–1810).
1. Period of minority, immaturity; the reference is to *English Bards and Scotch Reviewers.*
2. George, Prince of Wales, Prince Regent 1811–20, after which King George IV.
3. The Turkish Ambassador and his associates were present at the ball.

gratification is not allayed by the communication being made through me, the bearer of it will consider himself very fortunately & sincerely

yr obliged & obedt. Servt.
BYRON

P.S.—Excuse this scrawl scratched in a great hurry & just after a journey.—

To Lady Melbourne

Septr. 25th. 1812

My dear Ly. M.—It would answer no purpose to write a syllable on any subject whatever & neither accelerate nor retard what we wish to prevent, she[1] must be left to Chance: conjugal affection and the Kilkenny Theatricals are equally in your favour—for my part it is an accursed business *towards* nor *from* which I shall not move a single step; if she throws herself upon me "cosi finiva"[2] if not, the sooner it is over the better—from this moment I have done with it, only before she returns allow me to know that I may act accordingly; but there will be nothing to fear before that time, as if a woman & a selfish woman also, would not fill up the vacancy with the first comer?—As to Annabella she requires time & all the cardinal virtues, & in the interim I am a little verging towards one who demands neither, & saves me besides the trouble of marrying by being married already.— —She besides does not speak English, & to me nothing but Italian, a great point, for from certain coincidences the very sound of that language is Music to me, & she has black eyes & *not* a very white skin, & reminds me of many in the Archipelago I wished to forget, & makes me forget what I ought to remember, all which are against me.—I only wish she did not swallow so much supper, chicken wings—sweetbreads,—custards—peaches & *Port* wine—a woman should never be seen eating or drinking, unless it be *lobster sallad* & *Champagne*, the only truly feminine & becoming viands.—I recollect imploring one Lady not to eat more than a fowl at a sitting without effect, & have never yet made a single proselyte to Pythagoras.[3]—Now a word to yourself—a much more pleasing topic than any of the preceding.—I have no very high opinion of your sex, but when I do see a woman superior not only to all her own but to most of ours I worship her in proportion as I despise the rest.—And when I know that men of the first judgment & the most distinguished abilities have entertained & do entertain an opinion which my own humble observation without any great effort of discernment has enabled me to confirm on the same subject, you will not blame me for following the example of my elders & betters & admiring you certainly as much as you ever were admired.—My only regret is that the very awkward circumstances in which we are placed prevents & will prevent the improvement of an acquaintance which I now almost regret having made—but recollect whatever happens that the loss of it must give

---

1. Lady Caroline Lamb (see p. 170, n. 1) was Lady Melbourne's daughter-in-law.
2. Thus it ends (Italian).
3. Greek philosopher (sixth century B.C.E.), advocated strict dietary practices in order to purify the soul.

me more pain than even the *precious* [*previous?*] *acquisition* (& this is saying *much*) which will occasion that loss. Ld. Jersey has reinvited me to M[iddleton] for the 4 Octr. & I will be there if possible, in the mean time whatever step you take to break off this affair has my full concurrence—but *what* you wished me to write would be a little too indifferent; and *that* now would be an insult, & I am much more unwilling to hurt her feelings now than ever, (not from the mere apprehension of a disclosure in her wrath) but I have always felt that one who has given up much, has a claim upon *me* (at least—whatever she deserve from others) for every respect that she may not feel her own degradation, & this is the reason that I have not written at all lately, lest some expression might be misconstrued by her.— When the Lady herself begins the quarrel & adopts a new "Cortejo"[4] then my Conscience is comforted.—She has not written to me for some days, which is either a very bad or very good omen.—

yrs. ever

I observe that C[aroline] in her late epistles, lays peculiar stress upon her powers of attraction, upon W[illiam]'s attachment &c. & by way of enhancing the extreme value of her regards, tells me, that she "could make any one in love with her" an amiable accomplishment—but unfortunately a little too general to be valuable, for was there ever yet a woman, not absolutely disgusting, who could not say or do the same thing? any woman can *make* a man in *love* with her, show me her who can *keep* him so?—*You* perhaps *can* show me such a woman but I have not seen her for these—*three weeks.*—

To Lady Caroline Lamb

4 Bennet Street April 29th. 1813

If you still persist in your intention of meeting me in opposition to the wishes of your own friends & of mine—it must even be so—I regret it & acquiesce with reluctance.— — —I am not ignorant of the very extraordinary language you have held not only to me but others—& your avowal of your determination to obtain what you are pleased to call "revenge"—nor have I now to learn that an incensed woman is a dangerous enemy.— Undoubtedly those against whom we can make no defence—whatever they say or do—must be formidable—your words & actions have lately been tolerably portentous—& might justify me in avoiding the demanded interview—more especially as I believe you fully capable of performing all your menaces—but as I once hazarded every thing *for* you—I will not shrink *from* you—perhaps I deserve punishment—if so—you are quite as proper a person to inflict it as any other. You say you will "*ruin me*"—I thank you—but I have done that for myself already—you say you will "destroy me" perhaps you will only save me the trouble.—It is useless to reason with you—to repeat what you already know—that I have in reality saved you from utter & impending destruction.—Every one who knows you—knows

4. Lover of a married woman (Spanish).

this also—but they do not know as yet what you may & will tell them as I now tell you—that it is in a great measure owing to this persecution—to the accursed things you have said—to the extravagances you have committed—that I again adopt the resolution of quitting this country—In your assertions—you have either *belied* or *betrayed* me—take your choice—in your actions—you have hurt only yourself—but is that nothing to one who wished you well?— —I have only one request to make—which is not to attempt to see Ly. O[xford][1]—on her you have no claim.—You will settle—as you please—the arrangement of this conference—I do not leave England till June—but the sooner it is over the better—I once wished for your own sake Ly. M[elbourne] to be present—but if you are to fulfil any of your threats in word or deed—we had better be alone—

yrs. ever

To John Murray

August 26th. 1813

Dear Sir—I have looked over & corrected one proof[1] but not so carefully (God knows if you can read it through but I can't) as to preclude your eye from discovering some omission of mine or commission of ye. Printer.—If you have patience look it over—do you know any body who can *stop*—I mean *point*—commas & so forth—for I am I fear a sad hand at your punctuation. I have but with some difficulty *not* added any more to this snake of a poem—which has been lengthening its rattles every month—it is now fearfully long—being more than a Canto & a half of C[hilde] H[arold]—which contains but 882 lines per book—with all late additions inclusive.— — —The last lines Hodgson likes—& it is not often he does—& when he don't—he tells me with great energy—& then I fret & alter—I have thrown them in to soften the ferocity of our Infidel—& for a dying man have given him a good deal to say for himself—Do you think you shall get hold of the *female* M.S. you spoke of today—if so—you will let me have a glimpse—but don't tell our *master* (not W's) or we shall be buffeted.—I was quite sorry to hear you say you staid in town on my account—& I hope sincerely you did not mean so superfluous a piece of politeness.— — —Our 6 critiques!—they would have made half a quarterly by themselves—but this is the age of Criticism.—

Ever yrs.
B

To Lady Melbourne

Septr. 5th. 1813

Dear Lady Melbourne—I return you the plan of A[nnabella]'s spouse elect[1] of which I shall say nothing because I do not understand it—though

---

1. Lady Jane Oxford, with whom Byron was having an affair.
1. Of *The Giaour.*
1. Annabella Milbanke had sent Lady Melbourne, her aunt, a statement about her requirements in a husband.

I dare say it is exactly what it ought to be.—Neither do I know why I am writing this note as I mean to call on you—unless it be to try your "new patent pens" which delight me infinitely with their colours—I have pitched upon a yellow one to begin with—Very likely you will be out—& I must return you the annexed epistles—I would rather have seen your answer— she seems to have been spoiled—not as children usually are—but systematically Clarissa Harlowed into an awkward kind of correctness—with a dependence upon her own infallibility which will or may lead her into some egregious blunder—I don't mean the usual error of young gentlewomen— but she will find exactly what she wants—& then discover that it is much more dignified than entertaining.—[two pages torn away] . . . in town—. . . .

To Annabella Milbanke

Septr 6th 1813

Agreed—I will write to you occasionally & you shall answer at your leisure & discretion.—You must have deemed me very vain & selfish to imagine that your candour could offend—I see nothing that "could hurt my feelings" in your correspondence—you told me you declined me as a lover but wished to retain me as a friend—now as one may meet with a good deal of what is called love in this best of all possible worlds—& very rarely with friendship I could not find fault—upon calculation at least.—I am afraid my first letter was written during some of those moments which have induced your belief in my *general despondency*—now in common I believe with most of mankind—I have in the course of a very useless & ill regulated life encountered events which have left a deep *impression*—perhaps something at the time recalled *this* so forcibly as to make it apparent in my answer—but I am not conscious of any habitual or at least long continued pressure on my spirits.—On the contrary—with the exception of an occasional spasm—I look upon myself as a very facetious personage—& may safely appeal to most of my acquaintance (Ly. M.[1] for instance) in proof of my assertion.—Nobody laughs more—& though your friend Joanna Baillie[2] says somewhere that "Laughter is the *child* of Misery" yet I don't believe her—(unless indeed in a hysteric)—though I think it is sometimes the *Parent.*—Nothing would do me more honour than the acquaintance of that Lady—who does not possess a more enthusiastic admirer than myself—she is our only dramatist since Otway & Southerne—I don't except Home[3]— With all my presumed prejudice against your sex or rather the perversion of manners & principle in many which you admit in some circles—I think the worst woman that ever existed would have made a *man* of very passable reputation—they are all better than us—& their faults such as they are must originate with ourselves.—Your sweeping sentence "in the circles where we have met" amuses me much when I recollect some of those who constituted that society—after all bad as it is it has it's agremens.—The great object of life is Sensation—to feel that we exist—even though in

---

1. Lady Melbourne.
2. Scottish dramatist and poet (1762–1851).
3. John Home (1722–1808); Thomas Otway (1652–1685); Thomas Southerne (1659–1746).

pain—it is this "craving void" which drives us to Gaming—to Battle—to Travel—to intemperate but keenly felt pursuits of every description whose principal attraction is the agitation inseparable from their accomplishment.— —

. . .

ever yrs.

B

To Lady Melbourne

Aston Hall Rotherham—Septr. 21st. 1813

My dear Ly. M[elbourn]e—My stay at Cambridge was very short—but feeling feverish & restless in town I flew off & here I am on a visit to my friend Webster[1] now married—& (according to ye. Duke of Buckingham's curse—) "settled in ye. country."—His bride Lady Frances is a pretty pleasing woman—but in delicate health & I fear going—if not gone—into a decline—Stanhope & his wife—pretty & pleasant too but not at all consumptive—left us today—leaving only ye. family—another single gentleman & your slave.—The sister Ly. Catherine is here too—& looks very pale from a *cross* in her love for Lord Bury (Ld. Alb[emarl]e's son) in short we are a society of happy wives & unfortunate maidens.—The place is very well & quiet & the children only scream in a low voice—so that I am not much disturbed & shall stay a few days in tolerable repose.—W[ebster] don't want sense nor good nature but both are occasionally obscured by his suspicions & absurdities of all descriptions—he is passionately fond of having his wife admired—& at the same time jealous to jaundice of every thing & every body—I have hit upon the medium of praising her to him perpetually behind her back—& never looking at her before his face—as for her I believe she is disposed to be very faithful—& I don't think any one now here is inclined to put her to the test.—W[ebster] himself is with all his jealousy & admiration a little tired—he has been lately at Newstead—& wants to go again—I suspected this sudden penchant & soon discovered that a foolish nymph of the Abbey—about whom fortunately I care not—was the attraction—now if I wanted to make mischief—I could extract much good perplexity from a proper management of such events—but I am grown so good or so indolent—that I shall not avail myself of so pleasant an opportunity of tormenting mine host—though he deserves it for poaching.—I believe he has hitherto been unsuccessful—or rather it is too astonishing to be believed.—He proposed to me with great gravity to carry him over there—& I replied with equal candour that *he* might set out when he pleased but that I should remain here to take care of his household in the interim—a proposition which I thought very much to the purpose—but which did not seem at all to his satisfaction—by way of opiate he preached me a sermon on his wife's good qualities concluding by an assertion that in all moral & mortal qualities she was very like "*Christ*!!!["] I think the virgin Mary would have been a more appropriate typification—but it was the first comparison of the kind I ever heard & made me laugh till he was angry—

---

1. James Wedderburn Webster, with whose wife Byron became romantically involved, though the affair was unconsummated. See letter to Lady Melbourne, Oct. 8, 1813 (p. 177).

& then I got out of humour too—which pacified him & shortened his panegyric—Ld. Petersham[2] is coming here in a day or two—who will certainly flirt furiously with Ly. F[rances]—& I shall have some comic Iagoism with our little Othello—I should have no chance with his Desdemona myself—but a more lively & better dressed & formed personage might in an innocent way—for I really believe the girl is a very good well disposed wife & will do very well if she lives & he himself don't tease her into some dislike of her lawful owner.— —I passed through Hatfield the night of your *ball*—suppose we had jostled at a turnpike!!—At Bugden I blundered on a Bishop—the Bishop put me in mind of ye Government—the Government of the Governed—& the governed of their *indifference* towards their governors which you must have remarked as to all *parties*—these reflections expectorated as follows—you know I *never* send you my scribblings & when you read these you will wish I never may.—

Tis said—*Indifference* marks the present time
Then hear the reason—though 'tis told in rhyme—
A King who *can't*—a Prince of Wales who *don't*—
Patriots who *shan't*—Ministers who *won't*—
What matters who are *in* or *out* of place
The *Mad*—the *Bad*—the *Useless*—or the *Base?*[3]

you may read the 2d. couplet *so* if you like—

"A King who *cannot*—& a Prince who don't—
Patriots who *would not*—ministers who won't—"

I am asked to stay for the Doncaster races but I am not in plight—& am a miserable beau at the best of times—so I shall even return to town or elsewhere—and in the mean time ever am

yrs. dear Ly. M[elbourn]e
B

P.S.—If you write address to B[enne]t Street, were I once gone—I should not wish my letters to travel *here* after me for fear of *accidents.*— —
— —There is a delightful epitaph on Voltaire in Grimm[4]—I read it coming down—the French I should probably misspell so take it only in bad English—"Here lies the spoilt child of the/a world which he spoiled."—It is good short & true.— — —

To Lady Melbourne

Octr. 8th. 1813

My dear Ly. M[elbourn]e— . . . — — — — —In these last few days I have had a good deal of conversation with an amiable persion—whom (as

2. The same Lord Stanhope referred to earlier in the letter.
3. First published in a collected edition of the poems in *CPW* 1:91 (1980), entitled "[Politics in 1813. To Lady Melbourne]."
4. Voltaire (François Marie Arouet, 1694–1778), French Enlightenment philosopher and author; Baron de Grimm's *Correspondance Littéraire, Philosophique et Critique*, reviewed in the *Edinburgh Review*, July 1813.

we deal in *letters*—& initials only) we will denominate *Ph.* [Frances][1]—well—these things are dull in detail—take it once—I have made love—& if I am to believe mere *words* (for there we have hitherto stopped) it is returned.—I must tell you the place of declaration however—a billiard room!—I did not as C[aroline] says "kneel in the middle of the room" but like Corporal Trim to the Nun—"I made a speech"[2]—which as you might not listen to it with the same patience—I shall not transcribe.—We were before on very amiable terms—& I remembered being asked an odd question—"how a woman who liked a man could inform him of it—when he did not perceive it"—I also observed that we went on with our game (of billiards) without *counting* the *hazards*—& supposed that—as mine certainly were not—the thoughts of the other party also were not exactly occupied by what was our ostensible pursuit.—Not quite though pretty well satisfied with my progress—I took a very imprudent step—with pen & paper—in tender & tolerably turned *prose* periods (no *poetry* even when in earnest) here were risks certainly—first how to convey—then how it would be received—it was received however & deposited not very far from the heart which I wished it to reach—when who should enter the room but the person who ought at that moment to have been in the Red sea if Satan had any civility—but *she* kept her countenance & the paper—& I my composure as well as I could.—It was a risk—& *all* had been lost by failure—but then recollect—how much more I had to gain by the reception—if not declined—& how much one always hazards to obtain anything worth having.—My billet prospered—it did more—it even (I am this moment interrupted by the *Marito*—& write this before him—he has brought me a political pamphlet in M.S. to decypher & applaud—I shall content myself with the last—Oh—he is gone again)—my billet produced an *answer*—a very unequivocal one too—but a little too much about virtue—& indulgence of attachment in some sort of etherial process in which the soul is principally concerned—which I don't very well understand—being a bad metaphysician—but one generally *ends* & *begins* with Platonism—& as my proselyte is only twenty—there is time enough to materialize—I hope nevertheless this spiritual system won't last long—& at any rate must make the experiment.—I remember my last case was the reverse—as Major O'Flaherty recommends "we fought first & explained afterwards."—This is the present state of things—much mutual profession—a good deal of melancholy—which I am sorry to say was remarked by "the Moor" & as much love as could well be made considering the time place & circumstances.— —I need not say that the folly & petulance of—[Webster] have tended to all this—if a man is not contented with a pretty woman & not only runs after any little country girl he meets with but absolutely boasts of it—he must not be surprised if others admire that which he knows not how to value—besides he literally provoked & goaded me into it—by something not unlike bullying—*indirect* to be sure—but tolerably obvious—"he *would* do this—& he would do that—if any man["] &c. &c.—& *he* thought that

1. Lady Frances Webster, the wife of Byron's Cambridge friend James Wedderburn Webster, to whom he became romantically attached while a guest at the Websters' home, but whom he ultimately "spared" (*BLJ* 3:146). The incident in this letter describes—in which a game of billiards serves as a backdrop to an assignation—is humorously recalled in *Don Juan* 15, stanza 100. Lady Frances is the subject of "When We Two Parted," (p. 166).
2. Laurence Sterne, *Tristram Shandy* (Book 8, Chap. 22).

every woman "was *his* lawful prize nevertheless["]—Oons! who is this strange monopolist?—it is odd enough but on other subjects he is like other people but on this he seems infatuated—if he had been rational—& not prated of his pursuits—I should have gone on very well—as I did at Middleton—even now I shan't quarrel with him—if I can help it—but one or two of his speeches has blackened the blood about my heart—& curdled the milk of kindness—if put to the proof—I shall behave like other people I presume.— I have heard from A[nnabella]—but her letter to me is *melancholy*—about her old friend Miss M[ontgomer]y's departure &c.—&c.—I wonder who will have her at last—her letter to you is *gay*—you say—that to me must have been written at the same time—the little demure Nonjuror!— — —I wrote to C[aroline] the other day—for I was afraid she might repeat the last year's epistle—& make it *circular* among my friends.— — —Good evening—I am now going to *billiards.*—

P.S. 6 o'clock—This business is growing serious—& I think *Platonism* in some peril—There has been very nearly a scene—almost an *hysteric* & really without cause for I was conducting myself with (to me) very irksome decorum—her *expressions* astonish me—so young & cold as she appeared—but these professions must end as usual—& *would*—I think— *now*—had "l'occasion" been *not* wanting—had any one come in during the *tears* & consequent consolation all had been spoiled—we must be more cautious or less larmoyante.— — —

P.S. second—10 o'clock—I write to you just escaped from Claret & vociferation—on G–d knows what paper—my Landlord[3] is a rare gentleman—he has just proposed to me a bet "that *he* for a certain sum wins any given *woman*—against any given *homme* including *all friends* present["]—which I declined with becoming deference to him & the rest of the company—is not this at this moment a perfect comedy?—I forgot to mention that on his entrance yesterday during the letter scene—it reminded me so much of an awkward passage in "the Way to keep him"[4] between Lovemore—Sir Bashful—& my Lady—that embarrassing as it was I could hardly help laughing—I hear his voice in the passage—he wants me to go to a ball at Sheffield—& is talking to me as I write—Good Night. I am in the act of praising his pamphlet.—I don't half like your story of *Corinne*—some day I will tell you why—If I can—but at present—Good Night.

To Annabella Milbanke

Novr. 29th. 1813
. . . I by no means rank poetry or poets high in the scale of intellect—this may look like Affectation—but it is my real opinion—it is the lava of the imagination whose eruption prevents an earth-quake—they say Poets never or rarely go *mad*—Cowper & Collins[1] are instances to the contrary—(but

---

3. I.e., Webster.
4. Title of an eighteenth-century comedy by Arthur Murphy.
1. William Cowper (1731–1800); William Collins (1721–1759).

Cowper was no poet)—it is however to be remarked that they rarely do—
but are generally so near it—that I cannot help thinking rhyme is so far use-
ful in anticipating & preventing the disorder.—I prefer the talents of
action—of war—or the Senate—or even of Science—to all the speculations
of these mere dreamers of another existence (I don't mean *religiously* but
fancifully) and spectators of this.— —Apathy—disgust—& perhaps inca-
pacity have rendered me now a mere spectator—but I have occasionally
mixed in the active & tumultuous departments of existence—& on these
alone my *recollection* rests with any satisfaction—though not the *best* parts
of it.— . . .

ever yrs. most truly

B

Journal, November 16, 1813–April 10, 1814[1]

Nov. 16th

. . . . Read Burns to-day. What would he have been, if a patrician? We
should have had more polish—less force—just as much verse, but no
immortality—a divorce and a duel or two, the which had he survived, as his
potations must have been less spirituous. . . .

Nov. 17th

. . . . What strange tidings from the Anakim[2] of anarchy—Buonaparte! Ever
since I defended my bust of him at Harrow against the rascally time-
servers, when the war broke out in 1803, he has been a "Héros de Roman"
of mine—on the continent; I don't want him here. But I don't like those
same flights—leaving of armies, &c. &c. I am sure when I fought for his
bust at school, I did not think he would run away from himself. But I
should not wonder if he banged them yet. To be beat by men would be
something; but by three stupid, legitimate-old-dynasty boobies of regular-
bred sovereigns—O-hone-a-rie!—O-hone-a-rie! It must be, as Cobbett[3]
says, his marriage with the thick-lipped and thick-headed *Autrichienne*[4]
brood. He had better have kept to her who was kept by Barras.[5] I never
knew any good come of your young wife, and legal espousals, to any but
your "sober-blooded boy" who "eats fish" and drinketh "no sack."[6] Had he
not the whole opera? all Paris? all France? But a mistress is just as
perplexing—that is, *one*—two or more are manageable by division. . . .

✻   ✻   ✻

Wednesday, 24th

. . . . To Lady Melbourne I write with most pleasure—and her answers, so
sensible, so *tactique*—I never met with half her talent. If she had been a
few years younger, what a fool she would have made of me, had she thought
it worth her while,—and I should have lost a valuable and most agreeable

---

1. Byron began keeping a journal on November 14, 1813. The final entry is dated April 19, 1814.
2. Race of Giants in the Hebrew Bible.
3. William Cobbett (1763?–1835), British journalist and reformer.
4. In 1810 Napoleon married Marie Louise of Austria.
5. I.e., Josephine.
6. Cf. 2 *Henry IV* 4.2.79–83.

friend. Mem. a mistress never is nor can be a friend. While you agree, you are lovers; and, when it is over, any thing but friends.

I have not answered W. Scott's last letter,—but I will. I regret to hear from others, that he has lately been unfortunate in pecuniary involvements. He is undoubtedly the Monarch of Parnassus, and the most *English* of bards. I should place Rogers next in the living list—(I value him more as the last of the *best* school)—Moore and Campbell both *third*—Southey and Wordsworth and Coleridge—the rest ὁι πολλοι[1]—thus:—

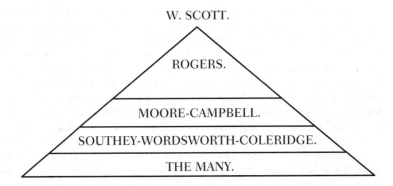

There is a triangular "Gradus ad Parnassum!"[2]—the names are too numerous for the base of the triangle. Poor Thurlow has gone wild about the poetry of Queen Bess's reign—*c'est dommage*. I have ranked the names upon my triangle more upon what I believe popular opinion, than any decided opinion of my own. For, to me, some of M[oor]e's last *Erin* sparks—"As a beam o'er the face of the waters"—"When he who adores thee"—"Oh blame not"—and "Oh breath not his name"—are worth all the Epics that ever were composed. . . .

Thursday, 26th November

. . . . I have been thinking lately a good deal of Mary Duff.[1] How very odd that I should have been so utterly, devotedly fond of that girl, at an age when I could neither feel passion, nor know the meaning of the word. And the effect! My mother used always to rally me about this childish amour; and, at last, many years after, when I was sixteen, she told me one day, "Oh, Byron, I have had a letter from Edinburgh, from Miss Abercromby, and your old sweetheart Mary Duff is married to a Mr. Coe." And what was my answer? I really cannot explain or account for my feelings at that moment; but they nearly threw me into convulsions, and alarmed my mother so much, that after I grew better, she generally avoided the subject—to *me*— and contented herself with telling it to all her acquaintance. Now, what could this be? I had never seen her since her mother's faux pas at Aberdeen had been the cause of her removal to her grandmother's at Banff; we were both the merest children. I had and have been attached fifty times since

---

1. *Hoi polloi*: the many (Greek).
2. Literally, "a step to Parnassus," title of a text for teaching the basics of Latin poetry.
1. A distant cousin of Byron's whom he met in Scotland very likely in the summer of 1795, when he was seven years old.

that period; yet I recollect all we said to each other, all our caresses, her features, my restlessness, sleeplessness, my tormenting my mother's maid to write for me to her, which she at last did, to quiet me. Poor Nancy thought I was wild, and, as I could not write for myself, became my secretary. I remember, too, our walks, and the happiness of sitting by Mary, in the children's apartment, at their house not far from Plainstones at Aberdeen, while her lesser sister Helen played with the doll, and we sat gravely making love, in our way. How the deuce did all this occur so early? where could it originate? I certainly had no sexual ideas for years afterwards; and yet my misery, my love for that girl were so violent, that I sometimes doubt if I have ever been really attached since. Be that as it may, hearing of her marriage several years after was like a thunder-stroke—it nearly choked me—to the horror of my mother and the astonishment and almost incredulity of every body. And it is a phenomenon in my existence (for I was not eight years old) which has puzzled, and will puzzle me to the latest hour of it; and lately, I know not why, the *recollection* (*not* the attachment) has recurred as forcibly as ever. I wonder if she can have the least remembrance of it or me? or remember her pitying sister Helen for not having an admirer too? How very pretty is the perfect image of her in my memory—her brown, dark hair, and hazel eyes; her very dress! I should be quite grieved to see *her now*; the reality, however beautiful, would destroy, or at least confuse, the features of the lovely Peri which then existed in her, and still lives in my imagination, at the distance of more than sixteen years. I am now twenty-five and odd months. . . .

Sunday, 28th. Monday, 29th. Tuesday, 30th.

. . . . To-day (Tuesday) a very pretty billet from M. la Baronne de Staël Holstein.[1] She is pleased to be much pleased with my mention of her and her last work in my notes. I spoke as I thought. Her works are my delight, and so is she herself, for—half an hour. I don't like her politics—at least, her *having changed* them; had she been *qualis ab incepto*,[2] it were nothing. But she is a woman by herself, and has done more than all the rest of them together, intellectually;—she ought to have been a man. She *flatters* me very prettily in her note;—but I *know* it. The reason that adulation is not displeasing is, that, though untrue, it shows one to be of consequence enough, in one way or other, to induce people to lie, to make us their friend:—that is their concern.

. . . . Yesterday, a very pretty letter from Annabella, which I answered. What an odd situation and friendship is ours!—without one spark of love on either side, and produced by circumstances which in general lead to coldness on one side, and aversion on the other. She is a very superior woman, and very little spoiled, which is strange in an heiress—a girl of twenty—a peeress that is to be, in her own right—an only child, and a *savante*, who has always had her own way. She is a poetess—a mathematician—a metaphysician, and yet, withal, very kind, generous, and gentle, with very little pretension. Any other head would be turned with half her acquisitions, and a tenth of her advantages. . . .

---

1. Madame Germaine de Staël (1766–1817), French-Swiss woman of letters (see Biographical Register).
2. The same as from the beginning (Horace, *Ars Poetica*, 127).

Sunday, December 5th.

Dallas's nephew (son to the American Attorney-general) is arrived in this country, and tells Dallas that my rhymes are very popular in the United States. These are the first tidings that have ever sounded like *Fame* to my ears—to be redde on the banks of the Ohio! The greatest pleasure I ever derived, of this kind, was from an extract, in Cooke the actor's life, from his journal, stating that in the reading-room of Albany, near Washington, he perused English Bards and Scotch Reviewers. To be popular in a rising and far country has a kind of *posthumous feel,* very different from the ephemeral *éclât* and fête-ing, buzzing and party-ing compliments of the well-dressed multitude. I can safely say that, during my *reign* in the spring of 1812, I regretted nothing but its duration of six weeks instead of a fortnight, and was heartily glad to resign. . . .

December 17, 18.

. . . . Redde some Italian, and wrote two Sonnets on * * * [1] I never wrote but one sonnet before, and that was not in earnest, and many years ago, as an exercise—and I will never write another. They are the most puling, petrifying, stupidly platonic compositions. I detest the Petrarch so much, that I would not be the man even to have obtained his Laura, which the metaphysical, whining dotard never could.

January 16, 1814.

. . . . I am getting rather into admiration of [Lady Juliana Annesley?] the youngest sister of [Lady F. Webster]. A wife would be my salvation. I am sure the wives of my acquaintances have hitherto done me little good. [Juliana?] is beautiful, but very young, and, I think, a fool. But I have not seen enough to judge; besides, I hate an *esprit* in petticoats. That she won't love me is very probable, nor shall I love her. But, on my system, and the modern system in general, that don't signify. The business (if it came to business) would probably be arranged between papa and me. She would have her own way; I am good-humoured to women, and docile; and, if I did not fall in love with her, which I should try to prevent, we should be a very comfortable couple. As to conduct, *that* she must look to. * * * * * * * But *if* I love, I shall be jealous;—and for that reason I will not be in love. Though, after all, I doubt my temper, and fear I should not be so patient as becomes the *bienséance*[1] of a married man in my station. * * * * Divorce ruins the poor *femme,* and damages are a paltry compensation. I do fear my temper would lead me into some oriental tricks of vengeance, or, at any rate, into a summary appeal to the court of twelve paces. So "I'll none on't," but e'en remain single and solitary;—though I should like to have somebody now and then to yawn with one.

W[ard], and, after him, * * *, has stolen one of my buffooneries about Mde. de Staël's Metaphysics and the Fog, and passed it, by speech and letter, as their own. As Gibbet says, "they are the most of a gentleman of any on the road."[2] W. is in sad enmity with the Whigs about this Review of Fox[3]

---

1. Lady Frances Webster ("To Genevra").
1. Decorum (French).
2. George Farquhar, *The Beaux' Stratagem* (1707), 4.3.
3. Charles James Fox (1749–1806), Member of Parliament, outstanding Whig proponent of liberal reform.

(if he *did* review him);—all the epigrammatists and essayists are at him. I hate *odds*, and wish he may beat them. As for me, by the blessing of indifference, I have simplified my politics into an utter detestation of all existing governments; and, as it is the shortest and most agreeable and summary feeling imaginable, the first moment of an universal republic would convert me into an advocate for single and uncontradicted despotism. The fact is, riches are power, and poverty is slavery all over the earth, and one sort of establishment is no better, nor worse, for a *people* than another. I shall adhere to my party, because it would not be honourable to act otherwise; but, as to *opinions*, I don't think politics *worth* an *opinion*. *Conduct* is another thing:—if you begin with a party, go one with them. I have no consistency, except in politics; and *that* probably arises from my indifference on the subject altogether.

> *Feb. 18. Midnight*

Napoleon!—this week will decide his fate. All seems against him; but I believe and hope he will win—at least, beat back the Invaders. What right have we to prescribe sovereigns to France? Oh for a Republic! "Brutus, thou sleepest."[1] Hobhouse abounds in continental anecdotes of this extraordinary man; all in favour of his intellect and courage, but against his *bonhommie*. No wonder;—how should he, who knows mankind well, do other than despise and abhor them?

The greater the equality, the more impartially evil is distributed, and becomes lighter by the division among so many—therefore, a Republic!

> *Sunday, February 27th.*

Here I am, alone, instead of dining at Lord H.'s, where I was asked,—but not inclined to go any where. Hobhouse says I am growing a *loup garou*,—a solitary hobgoblin. True;—"I am myself alone."[1] The last week has passed in reading—seeing plays—now and then, visitors—sometimes yawning and sometimes sighing, but no writing,—save of letters. If I could always read, I should never feel the want of society. Do I regret it?—um!—"Man delights not me,"[2] and only one woman—at a time.

There is something to me very softening in the presence of a woman,—some strange influence, even if one is not in love with them,—which I cannot at all account for, having no very high opinion of the sex. But yet,—I always feel in better humour with myself and every thing else, if there is a woman within ken. Even Mrs. Mule, my firelighter,—the most ancient and withered of her kind,—and (except to myself) not the best-tempered—always makes me laugh,—no difficult task when I am "i' the vein."[3]

Heigho! I would I were in mine island!—I am not well; and yet I look in good health. At times, I fear, "I am not in my perfect mind;"[4]—and yet my heart and head have stood many a crash, and what should ail them now? They prey upon themselves, and I am sick—sick—"prithee, undo this button—why should a cat, a rat, a dog have life—and *thou* no life at all?"[5]

---

1. *Julius Caesar* 2.1.46.
1. *Richard Duke of York* [3 *Henry VI*] 5.6.84.
2. *Hamlet* 2.2.298.
3. *Richard III* 4.2.121.
4. *King Lear* 4.6.56.
5. *King Lear* 5.3.281–82.

Six-and-twenty years, as they call them,—why, I might and should have been a Pasha by this time. "I 'gin to be a-weary of the sun."[6]

Buonaparte is not yet beaten; but has rebutted Blucher, and repiqued S[ch]wartzenburg. This it is to have a head. If he again wins, "vae victis!"[7]

April 8th.

Out of town six days. On my return, found my poor little pagod, Napoleon, pushed off his pedestal;—the thieves are in Paris. It is his own fault. Like Milo,[1] he would rend the oak; but it closed again, wedged his hands, and now the beasts—lion, bear, down to the dirtiest jackall—may all tear him. That Muscovite winter *wedged* his arms;—ever since, he has fought with his feet and teeth. The last may still leave their marks; and "I guess now" (as the Yankees say) that he will yet play them a pass. He is in their rear—between them and their homes. Query—will they ever reach them?

Saturday, April 9th, 1814.

I mark this day!

Napoleon Buonaparte has abdicated the throne of the world. "Excellent well." Methinks Sylla did better; for he revenged and resigned in the height of his sway, red with the slaughter of his foes—the finest instance of glorious contempt of the rascals upon record. Dioclesian[1] did well too—Amurath[2] not amis, had he become aught except a dervise—Charles the Fifth but so so—but Napoleon, worst of all. What! wait till they were in his capital, and then talk of his readiness to give up what is already gone!! "What whining monk art thou—what holy cheat?"[3] 'Sdeath!—Dionysius at Corinth was yet a king to this. The "Isle of Elba" to retire to!—Well—if it had been Caprea,[4] I should have marvelled less. "I see men's minds are but a parcel of their fortunes."[5] I am utterly bewildered and confounded.

I don't know—but I think I, even *I* (an insect compared with this creature), have set my life on casts not a millionth part of this man's. But, after all, a crown may be not worth dying for. Yet to outlive *Lodi*[6] for this!!! Oh that Juvenal or Johnson could rise from the dead! "Expende—quot libras in duce summo invenies?" I knew they were light in the balance of mortality; but I thought their living dust weighed more *carats*. Alas! this imperial diamond hath a flaw in it, and is now hardly fit to stick in a glazier's pencil:—the pen of the historian won't rate it worth a ducat.

Psha! "something too much of this."[7] But I won't give him up even now; though all his admirers have, "like the Thanes, fallen from him."[8]

---

6. *Macbeth* 5.5.47.
7. Woe to the vanquished! (Latin). Spoken by Brennus, chief of the Gauls, 390 B.C.E., and quoted by Livy (59 B.C.E.–17 C.E.) in *Ab Urbe condita*, 5:48.9.
1. For historical and literary references in the April 8–9 journal entries, see notes to "Ode to Napoleon Buonaparte" (p. 156).
2. Murad, late-sixteenth-century Ottoman Sultan, famous for his large harem; *Dioclesian*: Diocletian, Roman emperor (284–305).
3. Thomas Otway, *Venice Preserved* (1682), 4.2.
4. Capri.
5. *Antony and Cleopatra* 3.13.30–31: "I see men's judgements are / A parcel of their fortunes . . ."
6. In Italy, where Napoleon defeated the Austrians in 1796.
7. *Hamlet* 3.2.67.
8. Alluding to *Macbeth* 5.3.

April 10th.

I do not know that I am happiest when alone; but this I am sure of, that I never am long in the society even of *her* I love, (God knows too well, and the Devil probably too,) without a yearning for the company of my lamp and my utterly confused and tumbled-over library. Even in the day, I send away my carriage oftener than I use or abuse it. *Per esempio,*—I have not stirred out of these rooms for these four days past: but I have sparred for exercise (windows open) with Jackson an hour daily, to attenuate and keep up the ethereal part of me. The more violent the fatigue, the better my spirits for the rest of the day; and then, my evenings have that calm nothingness of languor, which I most delight in. To-day I have boxed one hour—written an ode to Napoleon Buonaparte—copied it—eaten six biscuits—drunk four bottles of soda water—redde away the rest of my time—besides giving poor * * a world of advice about this mistress of his, who is plaguing him into a phthisic and intolerable tediousness. I am a pretty fellow truly to lecture about "the sect." No matter, my counsels are all thrown away.

To James Hogg[1]

Albany, March 24, [1814]

. . .

You are mistaken, my good fellow, in thinking that I (or, indeed, that any living verse-writer—for we shall sink *poets*) can write as well as Milton. Milton's Paradise Lost is, as a whole, a heavy concern; but the two first books of it are the very finest poetry that has ever been produced in this world— at least since the flood—for I make little doubt Abel was a fine pastoral poet, and Cain a fine bloody poet, and so forth; but we, now-a-days, even we, (you and *I*, i.e.) know no more of their poetry than the *brutum vulgus*— I beg pardon, the swinish multitude, do of Wordsworth and Pye.[2] Poetry must always exist, like drink, where there is a demand for it. And Cain's may have been the brandy of the Antedeluvians, and Abel's the small [?] still.

Shakespeare's name, you may depend on it, stands absurdly too high and will go down. He had no invention as to stories, none whatever. He took all his plots from old novels, and threw their stories into a dramatic shape, at as little expense of thought as you or I could turn his plays back again into prose tales. That he threw over whatever he did write some flashes of genius, nobody can deny: but this was all. Suppose any one to have the *dramatic* handling for the first time of such ready-made stories as Lear, Macbeth, &c. and he would be a sad fellow, indeed, if he did not make something very grand of them. [As] for his historical plays, properly historical, I mean, they were mere redressings of former plays on the same subjects, and in twenty cases out of twenty-one, the finest, the very finest things, are taken all but *verbatim* out of the old affairs. You think, no doubt, that *A horse, a horse, my kingdom for a horse*! is Shakespeare's. Not a syllable of it. You will find it all in the old nameless dramatist. Could not one take up Tom Jones and improve it, without being a greater genius than

---

1. Scottish poet and novelist (1770–1835) known as the "Ettrick Shepherd."
2. Henry James Pye (1745–1813) became poet laureate in 1790 but was frequently ridiculed by his contemporaries.

Fielding? I, for my part, think Shakespeare's plays might be improved, and the public seem, and have seemed for to think so too, for not one of his is or ever has been acted as he wrote it; and what the pit applauded three hundred years past, is five times out of ten not Shakespeare's, but Cibber's.[3]

Stick you to Walter Scott, my good friend, and do not talk any more stuff about his not being willing to give you real advice, if you really will ask for real advice. You love Southey, forsooth—I am sure Southey loves nobody but himself, however. I hate these talkers one and all, body and soul. They are a set of the most despicable impostors—that is my opinion of them. They know nothing of the world; and what is poetry, but the reflection of the world? What sympathy have this people with the spirit of this stirring age? They are no more able to understand the least of it, than your *lass*— nay, I beg her pardon, *she* may very probably have intense sympathy with both its spirit, (I mean the whisky,) and its body (I mean the bard.) They are mere old wives. Look at their beastly vulgarity, when they wish to be homely; and their exquisite stuff, when they clap on sail, and aim at fancy. Coleridge is the best of the trio—but bad is the best. Southey should have been a parish-clerk, and Wordsworth a man-midwife—both in darkness. I doubt if either of them ever got drunk, and I am of the old creed of Homer the wine-bibber. Indeed I think you and Burns have derived a great advantage from this, that being poets, and drinkers of wine, you have had a new potation to rely upon. Your whisky has made you original. I have always thought it a fine liquor. I back you against beer at all events, gill to gallon. . . .

Dear sir, believe me sincerely yours,
BYRON

To Lady Melbourne

June 26th. 1814

My dear Ly. M[elbourn]e.—(⟨I have⟩ to continue the conversation which Ld. C[owpe]r has broken off by falling asleep—& his wife by keeping awake—) I know nothing of C[aroline]'s[1] last night adventures; to prove it there is her letter—which I have not read through—nor answered—nor written these two months—& then only by *desire* to keep her quiet.— — — You talked to me—about keeping her out—it is impossible—she comes at all times—at any time—& the moment the door is open in she walks—I can't throw her out of the window—as to getting rid of her—that is rational—& probable—but *I* will not receive her.—The Bessboroughs may take her if they please—or any steps they please—I have no hesitation in saying—that I have made up my mind as to the alternative—and would

3. Colley Cibber (1671–1757), actor, playwright, reviser of Shakespeare's plays, and eventually poet laureate, was frequently attacked by other writers, such as Pope, who made him the hero of the *Dunciad*. Byron opposed the Romantic writers' "bardolatry," believing that Shakespeare is "the *worst* of models—though the most extraordinary of writers" (*BLJ* 8:152). But the degree of Byron's appreciation of Shakespeare is easily measured by the frequency of allusions and quotations from the plays in the letters, journals, and poetry. In fact, in his own lifetime he was chagrined by accusations of borrowing from Shakespeare (see Hunt, *Lord Byron and Some of His Contemporaries* 1:76–77). (The relationship between the two poets is the subject of Knight, *Byron and Shakespeare*, and Barton, "Byron and Shakespeare."
1. Lady Caroline Lamb (see p. 170, n. 1, and p. 173).

sooner—much sooner be with the dead in purgatory—than with her—
Caroline (I put the name at length as I am not jesting) upon earth.— —She
may hunt me down—it is in the power of any mad or bad woman to do so
by any man—but *snare* me she shall not—torment me she may—how am I
to bar myself from her!—I am already almost a prisoner—she has no
shame—no feeling—no one estimable or redeemable quality.—These are
strong words—but I know what I am writing—they avail nothing but to
convince you of my own determination—my first object in such a dilemma
would be to take ⟨Augusta?⟩ with me—that might fail—so much the
better—but even if it did—I would lose an hundred souls rather than be
bound to C[aroline]—if there is one human being whom I do utterly *detest*
& *abhor*—it is she—& all things considered—I feel to myself justified in so
doing—she has been an adder in my path ever since my return to this
country—she has often belied—& sometimes betrayed me—she has
crossed me every where—she has watched—& worried & *guessed*—& been
a curse to me & mine.— —You may shew *her* this if you please—or to any-
one you please—if these were the last words I were to write upon earth—
I would not revoke one letter—except to make it more legible.—

ever yours most sincerely
BYRON

To Thomas Moore

Newstead Abbey, Septr. 20th, 1814

Here's to her who long
Hath waked the poet's sigh!
The girl who gave to song
What gold could never buy.

My dear Moore, I am going to be married—that is, I am accepted, and
one usually hopes the rest will follow. My mother of the Gracchi[1] (that *are*
to be) *you* think too strait-laced for me, although the paragon of only chil-
dren, and invested with "golden opinions of all sorts of men,"[2] and full of
"most blest conditions,"[3] as Desdemona herself. Miss Milbanke is the lady,
and I have her father's invitation to proceed there in my elect capacity,—
which, however, I cannot do till I have settled some business in London,
and got a blue coat.

She is said to be an heiress, but of that I really know nothing certainly,
and shall not inquire. But I do know, that she has talents and excellent
qualities, and you will not deny her judgment, after having refused six suit-
ors and taken me.

Now, if you have any thing to say against this, pray do; my mind's made
up, positively fixed, determined, and therefore I will listen to reason,
because now it can do no harm. Things may occur to break it off, but I will
hope not. In the mean time, I tell you (a *secret*, by the by,—at least, till I
know she wishes it to be public) that I have proposed and am accepted. You

1. Two brothers who were Roman statesmen, second century B.C.E.
2. Cf. *Macbeth* 1.7.33.
3. *Othello* 2.1.241–42.

need not be in a hurry to wish me joy, for one mayn't be married for months. I am going to town to-morrow; but expect to be here, on my way there, within a fortnight. If this had not happened, I should have gone to Italy. In my way down, perhaps, you will meet me at Nottingham, and come over with me here. I need not say that nothing will give me greater pleasure. I must, of course, reform thoroughly; and, seriously, if I can contribute to her happiness, I shall secure my own. She is so good a person, that—that—in short, I wish I was a better.

Ever, &c.

To Annabella Milbanke

Octr. 20th. 1814

I have been so much amused with your "extracts" though I had no idea what evil spirit I then appeared in your eyes—you were quite right however as far as *appearances*—but that was not my natural character—I was just returned from a far country where everything was different—& felt bewildered & not very happy in my own which I had left without regret & returned to without interest—I found myself I did not very well know why—an object of curiosity which I never wished to excite—and about a poem which I had no conception was to make such a fuss—my mind & my feelings were moreover occupied with considerations which had nothing in common with the circle where I was whirling—so that no wonder I was repulsive & cold—I never could conquer my disposition to be both in a crowd from which I was always wishing myself away.— — —Those who know me most intimately can tell you that I am if anything too *childish* with a greater turn for the ridiculous than anything serious—and—I could hope—not very illnatured *off the stage*—and if angry never *loud*—I can't say much for these qualifications—but I have such a regard for yours—that I am sure we shall be a very happy couple—I wish you had a greater passion for governing—for I don't shine in conducting myself—and am very docile with a gentle guide.—One of Augusta's friends writes to her & says she is so afraid—now I am to be married "that I shall become a good sort of man" an awful anticipation!—the P[rince] R[egent] has been at Brocket & talked on the subject to Ly. M[elbourne] by no means ill-naturedly—as is his usual way—& might be excuseable enough as far as *I* am concerned—among other things he said "between her prose & his poetry what may we not expect"—as if—we were to do nothing else but make books—I am sure the employments the Morning Post found out for us would be much more useful & quite as entertaining—particularly the care of the poultry &c. &c.— — — —I am only waiting for Mr. Hanson's return to set him off—& follow myself.—if—Dearest— —these men of parchment can *settle* us—or put us in the way of being settled within a reasonable time—you will not long defer taking a name to which you will do more honour than has been conferred upon it since it's first inscription in "Domesday Boke" with the signature of my Progenitors Erneis & *Ralph*—so you see your papa—& the papa of all my papas were synonimous.—ever my Love

yr. own

B

P.S.—Oh—I must tell you one of my present avocations.—D[ougla]s Kinnaird (a friend of mine brother to Lord Kd) applied to me to write words for a musical composer who is going to publish the *real old undisputed Hebrew melodies* which are beautiful & to which David & the prophets actually sang the "songs of Zion"—& I have done nine or ten—on the sacred model—partly from Job &c. & partly my own imagination—but I hope a little better than Sternhold & Hopkins[1]—it is odd enough that this should fall to my lot—who have been abused as "an infidel"—Augusta says "they will call me a *Jew* next."

To Lady Melbourne

Novr. 13th. 1814

My dear Lady Mel[bourn]e.—I delivered your letters—but have only mentioned ye receipt of your *last* to myself.— — — —Do you know I have great doubts—if this will be a marriage now.—her disposition is the very reverse of *our* imaginings—she is overrun with fine feelings—scruples about herself & *her* disposition (I suppose in fact she means mine) and to crown all is taken ill once every 3 days with I know not what—but the day before and the day after she seems well—looks & eats well & is cheerful & confiding & in short like any other person in good health & spirits.—A few days ago she made one *scene*—not altogether out of C[aroline]'s style—it was too long & too trifling in fact for me to transcribe—but it did me no good— —in the article of conversation however she has improved with a vengeance—but I don't much admire these same agitations upon slight occasions.—I don't know—but I think it by no means impossible you will see me in town soon—I can only interpret these things one way—& merely wait to be certain to make my obeisances and "exit singly." I hear of nothing but "feeling" from morning till night—except from Sir Ralph with whom I go on to admiration—Ly. M[ilbanke] too is pretty well—but I am never sure of A[nnabella]—for a moment—the least word—and you know I rattle on through thick & thin (always however avoiding anything I think can offend her favourite notions) if only to prevent me from yawning—the least word—or alteration of tone—has some inference drawn from it— sometimes we are too much alike—& then again too unlike—this comes of *system*—& squaring her notions to the Devil knows what—for my part I have lately had recourse to the eloquence of *action* (which Demosthenes[1] calls the first part of oratory) & find it succeeds very well & makes her very quiet which gives me some hopes of the efficacy of the "calming process" so renowned in "*our* philosophy."—In fact and entre nous it is really amusing—she is like a child in that respect—and quite *caressable* into kindness and good humour—though I don't think her temper *bad* at any time— but very *self*-tormenting—and anxious—and romantic.— — — — —In short—it is impossible to foresee how this will end *now*—anymore than 2 years ago—if there is a break—it shall be *her* doing not mine.—

ever yrs. most truly

B

---

1. In 1547, Thomas Sternhold and John Hopkins had published a collection of the Psalms in metrical verse; musical composer: Isaac Nathan.
1. Considered the greatest of Greek orators (384–322 B.C.E.).

To Samuel Taylor Coleridge

13—Terrace Piccadilly—Oct. 18th. 1815

Dear Sir—Your letter I have just received.—I will willingly do whatever you direct about the volumes in question—the sooner the better—it shall not be for want of endeavour on my part—as a Negociator with the "Trade" (to talk technically) that you are not enabled to do yourself justice.—Last Spring I saw W[alte]r Scott—he repeated to me a considerable portion of an unpublished poem of yours[1]—the wildest & finest I ever heard in that kind of composition—the title he did not mention—but I think the heroine's name was Geraldine—at all events—the "toothless mastiff bitch"—& the "witch Lady"—the descriptions of the hall—the lamp suspended from the image—& more particularly of the *Girl* herself as she went forth in the evening—all took a hold on my imagination which I never shall wish to shake off.—I mention this—not for the sake of boring you with compliments—but as a prelude to the hope that this poem is or is to be in the volumes you are now about to publish.—I do not know that even "Love" or the "Ancient Mariner" are so impressive—& to me there are few things in our tongue beyond these two productions.— —W[alte]r Scott is a staunch & sturdy admirer of yours—& with a just appreciation of your capacity—deplored to me the want of inclination & exertion which prevented you from giving full scope to your mind.—I will answer your question as to the "Beggar's [Bush?]"[2]—tomorrow—or next day—I shall see Rae & Dibdin (the acting M[anage]rs) tonight for that purpose.—Oh—your tragedy—I do not wish to hurry you—but I am indeed very anxious to have it under consideration—it is a field in which there are none living to contend against you & in which I should take a pride & pleasure in seeing you compared with the dead—I say this *not* disinterestly but as a *Committee* man—we have nothing even tolerable—except a tragedy of Sotheby's—which shall not interfere with yours—when ready—you can have no idea what trash there is in the four hundred *fallow* dramas now lying on the shelves of D[rury] L[ane]. I never thought so highly of good writers as lately—since I have had an opportunity of comparing them with the bad.—

ever yrs. truly
BYRON

To Leigh Hunt

13 Terrace Piccadilly Septr.—Octr. 30th. 1815

My dear Hunt—Many thanks for your books of which you already know my opinion.—Their external splendour should not disturb you as inappropriate—they have still more within than without.— —I take leave to differ from you on Wordsworth as freely as I once agreed with you—at that time I gave him credit for promise which is unfulfilled—I still think his capacity warrants all you say of *it* only—but that his performances since

1. *Christabel.*
2. Referring to a never-completed tragedy Coleridge was writing, which he hoped to submit to the Drury Lane Theatre committee, of which Byron was a member.

"Lyrical Ballads"—are miserably inadequate to the ability which lurks within him:—there is undoubtedly much natural talent spilt over "the Excursion" but it is rain upon rocks where it stands & stagnates—or rain upon sands where it falls without fertilizing—who can understand him?—let those who do make him intelligible.—Jacob Behman—Swedenborg—& Joanna Southcote[1] are mere types of this Arch-Apostle of mystery & mysticism—but I have done:—no I have not done—for I have two petty & perhaps unworthy objections in small matters to make to him—which with his pretension to accurate observation & fury against Pope's false translation of the "Moonlight scene in Homer"[2] I wonder he should have fallen into—these be they.—He says of Greece in the body of his book—that it is a land of

"*rivers—fertile* plains—& *sounding* shores
Under a cope of *variegated* sky"[3]

The rivers are dry half the year—the plains are barren—and the shores *still* & *tideless* as the Mediterranean can make them—the Sky is anything but variegated—being for months & months—but "darkly—deeply—beautifully blue."—The next is in his notes—where he talks of our "Monuments crowded together in the busy &c. of a large town"—as compared with the "still seclusion of a Turkish cemetery in some *remote* place"—this is pure stuff—for *one* monument in our Churchyards—there are *ten* in the Turkish—& so crowded that you cannot walk between them—they are always close to the walks of the towns—that is—merely divided by a path or road—and as to "*remote* places"—men never take the trouble in a barbarous country to carry their dead very far—they must have lived near to where they are buried—there are no cemeteries in "remote places"—except such as have the cypress & the tombstone still left when the olive & the habitation of the living have perished.— —These things I was struck with as coming peculiarly in my own way—and in both of these he is wrong—yet I should have noticed neither but for his attack on Pope for a like blunder—and a peevish affectation about him of despising a popularity which he will never obtain.—I write in great haste—& I doubt—*not* much to the purpose—but you have it hot & hot—just as it comes—& so let it go.— —By the way—both he & you go too far against Pope's "so when the Moon &c." it is no translation I know—but it is not such *false* description as asserted—I have read it on the spot—there is a burst—and a lightness—and a glow—about the night in the Troad—which makes the "planets vivid"—& the "pole glowing" the moon is—at least the sky is clearness itself—and I know no more appropriate expression for the expansion of such a heaven—over the scene—the plain—the sea—the sky—Ida—the Hellespont—Simois—Scamander—and the isles—than that of a "flood of Glory."— —I am getting horribly lengthy—& must stop— . . .

ever yrs very truly & affectly.
BYRON

.   .   .

---

1. The mystics Joanna Southcott (1750–1814), Jakob Boehme (1575–1624), and Emanuel Swedenborg (1688–1772).
2. *The Iliad* 8.
3. *The Excursion* 4 (first ed., 1814).

To Lady Byron

February 8th. 1816

All I can say seems useless—and all I could say—might be no less unavailing—yet I still cling to the wreck of my hopes—before they sink forever.— —Were you then *never* happy with me?—did you never at any time or times express yourself so?—have no marks of affection—of the warmest & most reciprocal attachment passed between us?—or did in fact hardly a day go down without some such on one side and generally on both?—do not mistake me—[two lines crossed out] I have not denied my state of mind—but you know it's causes—& were those deviations from calmness never followed by acknowledgement & repentance?—was not the last which occurred more particularly so?—& had I not—had we not—the days before & on the day when we parted—every reason to believe that we loved each other—that we were to meet again—were not your letters kind?—had I not acknowledged to you all my faults & follies—& assured you that some had not—& would not be repeated?—I do not require these questions to be answered to me—but to your own heart.— —The day before I received your father's letter—I had fixed a day for rejoining you— if I did not write lately—Augusta did—and as you had been my proxy in correspondence with her—so did I imagine—she might be the same for me to you.—Upon your letter to me—this day—I surely may remark—that it's expressions imply a treatment which I am incapable of inflicting—& you of imputing to me—if aware of their latitude—& the extent of the inferences to be drawn from them.—This is not just— —but I have no reproaches— nor the wish to find cause for them.— —Will you see me?—when & where you please—in whose presence you please:—the interview shall pledge you to nothing—& I will say & do nothing to agitate either—it is torture to correspond thus—& there are things to be settled & said which cannot be written.— —You say "it is my disposition to deem what I *have worthless*"— did I deem *you* so?—did I ever so express myself to you—or of you—to others?— —You are much changed within these twenty days or you would never have thus poisoned your own better feelings—and trampled upon mine.— —

ever yrs. most truly & affectionately
B

Part Three: Exile on Lake Geneva (April–October 1816)

Self-exiled from England in the wake of scandal over his marital separation, Byron sailed for Belgium at the end of April 1816, beginning the third canto of *Childe Harold's Pilgrimage* while at sea. He disembarked at Ostend where, as Dr. John Polidori, his personal physician traveling with him, recorded in his diary, as soon as he reached his room at the inn he "fell like a thunderbolt upon the chambermaid." He then traveled through Belgium, visiting the field of Waterloo, site of Napoleon's final defeat the previous June. His thoughts there about the French emperor's self-determined rise and fall—a projection of Byron's own self-imagining—are recorded in *Childe Harold* III. After traveling through Germany along the Rhine, he arrived at Lake Geneva on May 24, and only a few days later began his important friendship with Percy Shelley, who, though married, had eloped to Switzerland with Mary Godwin. Her stepsister, Claire Clairmont, had accompanied them with the intention, quickly realized, of resuming the affair with Byron that she had initiated a few weeks before in London. Byron moved into the Villa Diodati on Lake Geneva, where he spent many evenings in the company of Shelley, Mary, Claire, and Polidori. This was the memorable rainy June that gave rise to the famous ghost-story writing contest which resulted in Mary Shelley's *Frankenstein* (as well as Byron's Gothic fragment, completed by Polidori and published in 1819 as *The Vampyre,* under Byron's name). Byron and Shelley toured the Lake Geneva area, visiting the Château de Chillon, and under Shelley's influence Byron read Wordsworth more sympathetically than at any other time of his life. Byron became a frequent guest of the great French writer and intellectual Madame de Staël, whose home at Coppet on Lake Geneva was a salon for celebrated writers and artists. In late August, Byron's close friend John Cam Hobhouse arrived in Switzerland, and with him Byron toured the Alps, keeping a journal for his half-sister, Augusta Leigh. Inspired by the majestic Alpine scenery, still deeply disturbed by the separation and his wife's treatment of him, and haunted by his love for Augusta, Byron wrote a draft of the first two acts of *Manfred.* Although the final act of the drama would not be completed until May 1817, seven months after Byron left Swizterland for Italy, *Manfred* is included in Part Three of this Norton Critical Edition as it is informed not only by the Alpine atmosphere but by the preoccupations of the poet during the summer and early fall of 1816, when he was (as he recounted to Thomas Moore in a letter of January 28, 1817) "half mad . . . between metaphysics, mountains, lakes, love unextinguishable, thoughts unutterable, and the nightmare of my own delinquencies."

POETRY

Childe Harold's Pilgrimage

CANTO THE THIRD[1]

"A fin que cette application vous forçât de penser à autre chose; il n'y a en vérité de remède que celui-là et le temps."—*Lettre du Roi de Prusse à D'Alembert, Sept.* 7, 1776.[2]

1

Is thy face like thy mother's, my fair child!
ADA![3] sole daughter of my house and heart?
When last I saw thy young blue eyes they smiled,
And when we parted,—not as now we part,
But with a hope.—[4]   5
                    Awaking with a start,
The waters heave around me; and on high
The winds lift up their voices: I depart,
Whither I know not; but the hour's gone by,
When Albion's lessening shores could grieve or glad mine eye.[5]

2

Once more upon the waters! yet once more!   10
And the waves bound beneath me as a steed
That knows his rider. Welcome, to their roar!
Swift be their guidance, wheresoe'er it lead!
Though the strain'd mast should quiver as a reed,
And the rent canvass fluttering strew the gale,   15

---

1. Byron began the third canto of *Childe Harold* on April 25, 1816, while still on the sea voyage from England; it was published on November 18, 1816. Canto III not only reflects Byron's maturing poetic skill in comparison to the first two cantos, but it departs from those cantos in significant ways. For one thing, Byron's recurrent attempts in Cantos I–II to distinguish Harold from the narrator are all but abandoned in the third canto, as the fictional pilgrim merges with and is finally subsumed by the narrating poet. Further, the "more intense sensibility" and "deeper and more matured reflections" for which Jeffrey praised Canto III in the *Edinburgh Review* (see pp. 787ff.) are owing not merely to a change from the earlier cantos' sunlit Mediterranean topography to the castled crags of the Rhine valley and "cold sublimity" (line 594) of the Alps. Nor should the often-observed Wordsworthian influence be overstated; as Byron told Medwin, "while in Switzerland, Shelley would dose me on Wordsworth physic even to nausea" [*Conversations of Lord Byron*, p. 194]. The canto was written during the most emotionally turbulent period of Byron's life (the aftermath of his marital separation, scandal, departure from England, and separation from his sister and his daughter), and its force and unity derive from the poet's psychological state at this time. Whether describing recent or ancient historic events (such as the battles of Waterloo or Marathon), admiring world-historical individuals (most prominently Napoleon and Rousseau) for their Promethean character and fate, or identifying with the thunderstorm's "fierce and far delight" (line 871), Byron projects onto the external world his recent personal losses, struggles, and desires.
    Criticism: In addition to works listed in the headnote to *Childe Harold* I–II and Manning, "The Sublime Self and the Single Voice" (p. 898), see: Emerson, "Byron's 'One Word'"; Hodgson, "The Structures of *Childe Harold* III; Lovell, *The Record of a Quest*; Newey, "Authoring the Self: *Childe Harold* III and IV"; Rawes, "1816–17: *Childe Harold* III and *Manfred*."; Rutherford, *Byron: A Critical Study.*
2. "In the end this effort forces you to think of something else; there is truly only that remedy and time."
3. Augusta Ada Byron, born to Lord and Lady Byron on December 10, 1815; Byron never saw her again after Lady Byron left him in January 1816.
4. Byron's hope for a reconciliation with his estranged wife, a hope that was never to be realized.
5. On April 25, 1816, Byron sailed from England ("Albion") never to return.

Still must I on; for I am as a weed,
Flung from the rock, on Ocean's foam, to sail
Where'er the surge may sweep, or[6] tempest's breath
    prevail.

3

In my youth's summer I did sing of One,[7]
The wandering outlaw of his own dark mind;   20
Again I seize the theme, then but begun,
And bear it with me, as the rushing wind
Bears the cloud onwards: in that Tale I find
The furrows of long thought, and dried-up tears,
Which, ebbing, leave a sterile track behind,   25
O'er which all heavily the journeying years
Plod the last sands of life,—where not a flower appears.

4

Since my young days of passion—joy, or pain,
Perchance my heart and harp have lost a string,
And both may jar: it may be, that in vain   30
I would essay as I have sung to sing.
Yet, though a dreary strain, to this I cling;
So that it wean me from the weary dream
Of selfish grief or gladness—so it fling
Forgetfulness around me—it shall seem   35
To me, though to none else, a not ungrateful theme.

5

He, who grown aged in this world of woe,
In deeds, not years, piercing the depths of life,
So that no wonder waits him; nor below
Can love, or sorrow, fame, ambition, strife,   40
Cut to his heart again with the keen knife
Of silent, sharp endurance: he can tell
Why thought seeks refuge in lone caves, yet rife
With airy images, and shapes which dwell
Still unimpair'd, though old, in the soul's haunted cell.   45

6

'Tis to create, and in creating live
A being more intense, that we endow
With form our fancy, gaining as we give
The life we image, even as I do now.
What am I? Nothing: but not so art thou,[8]   50

---

6. the (*1832*).
7. Harold.
8. Harold.

Soul of my thought! with whom I traverse earth,
Invisible but gazing, as I glow
Mix'd with thy spirit, blended with thy birth,
And feeling still with thee in my crush'd feelings' dearth.

7

Yet must I think less wildly:—I *have* thought   55
Too long and darkly, till my brain became,
In its own eddy boiling and o'erwrought,
A whirling gulf of phantasy and flame:
And thus, untaught in youth my heart to tame,
My springs of life were poison'd. 'Tis too late!   60
Yet am I changed; though still enough the same
In strength to bear what time can not abate,
And feed on bitter fruits without accusing Fate.

8

Something too much of this:—but now 'tis past,
And the spell closes with its silent seal.   65
Long absent HAROLD re-appears at last;
He of the breast which fain no more would feel,
Wrung with the wounds which kill not, but ne'er heal;
Yet Time, who changes all, had alter'd him
In soul and aspect as in age: years steal   70
Fire from the mind as vigour from the limb;
And life's enchanted cup but sparkles near the brim.

9

His had been quaff'd too quickly, and he found
The dregs were wormwood;[9] but he fill'd again,
And from a purer fount, on holier ground,[1]   75
And deem'd its spring perpetual; but in vain!
Still round him clung invisibly a chain
Which gall'd for ever, fettering though unseen,
And heavy though it clank'd not; worn with pain,
Which pined although it spoke not, and grew keen,   80
Entering with every step he took through many a scene.

10

Secure in guarded coldness, he had mix'd
Again in fancied safety with his kind,
And deem'd his spirit now so firmly fix'd
And sheathed with an invulnerable mind,   85
That, if no joy, no sorrow lurk'd behind;
And he, as one, might 'midst the many stand
Unheeded, searching through the crowd to find

9. A bitter herb, regarded in folklore as causing madness.
1. Greece, where the first two cantos of *Childe Harold* were written.

Fit speculation; such as in strange land
He found in wonder-works of God and Nature's hand.   90

11

But who can view the ripen'd rose, nor seek
To wear it? who can curiously behold
The smoothness and the sheen of beauty's cheek,
Nor feel the heart can never all grow old?
Who can contemplate Fame through clouds unfold   95
The star which rises o'er her steep, nor climb?
Harold, once more within the vortex, roll'd
On with the giddy circle, chasing Time,
Yet with a nobler aim than in his youth's fond² prime.

12

But soon he knew himself the most unfit   100
Of men to herd with Man; with whom he held
Little in common; untaught to submit
His thoughts to others, though his soul was quell'd
In youth by his own thoughts; still uncompell'd,
He would not yield dominion of his mind   105
To spirits against whom his own rebell'd;
Proud though in desolation; which could find
A life within itself, to breathe without mankind.

13

Where rose the mountains, there to him were friends;
Where roll'd the ocean, thereon was his home;   110
Where a blue sky, and glowing clime, extends,
He had the passion and the power to roam;
The desert, forest, cavern, breaker's foam,
Were unto him companionship; they spake
A mutual language, clearer than the tome   115
Of his land's tongue, which he would oft forsake,
For Nature's pages glass'd by sunbeams on the lake.

14

Like the Chaldean,³ he could watch the stars,
Till he had peopled them with beings bright
As their own beams; and earth, and earth-born jars,   120
And human frailties, were forgotten quite:
Could he have kept his spirit to that flight
He had been happy; but this clay will sink
Its spark immortal, envying it the light
To which it mounts, as if to break the link   125
That keeps us from yon heaven which woos us to its brink.

---

2. Foolishly credulous.
3. Babylonian astronomers and seers.

15

But in Man's dwellings he became a thing
Restless and worn, and stern and wearisome,
Droop'd as a wild-born falcon with clipt wing,
To whom the boundless air alone were home: 130
Then came his fit again, which to o'ercome,
As eagerly the barr'd-up bird will beat
His breast and beak against his wiry dome
Till the blood tinge his plumage, so the heat
Of his impeded soul would through his bosom eat.   135

16

Self-exiled Harold wanders forth again,
With nought of hope left, but with less of gloom;
The very knowledge that he lived in vain,
That all was over on this side the tomb,
Had made Despair a smilingness assume,   140
Which, though 'twere wild,—as on the plunder'd wreck
When mariners would madly meet their doom
With draughts intemperate on the sinking deck,—
Did yet inspire a cheer, which he forebore to check.

17

Stop!—for thy tread is on an Empire's dust!⁴   145
An Earthquake's spoil is sepulchred below!
Is the spot mark'd with no colossal bust?
Nor column trophied for triumphal show?
None; but the moral's truth tells simpler so,
As the ground was before, thus let it be;—   150
How that red rain hath made the harvest grow!
And is this all the world has gain'd by thee,
Thou first and last of fields! king-making Victory?⁵

18

And Harold stands upon this place of skulls,
The grave of France, the deadly Waterloo;   155
How in an hour the power which gave annuls
Its gifts, transferring fame as fleeting too!
In "pride of place"⁶ here last the eagle flew,
Then tore with bloody talon the rent plain,
Pierced by the shaft of banded nations through;   160

---

4. Waterloo, the site in Belgium where on June 18, 1815, the allied English and European armies, led by the Duke of Wellington, met and routed the French army. It was the final defeat for Napoleon, emperor of France (1804–15), and for his dream of a united Europe under his control.
5. An ironic, contemptuous reference to the monarch-restoring Congress of Vienna; Napoleon's defeat resulted not only in restoring the Bourbons to the throne of France but in strengthening the power and confidence of monarchies throughout Europe.
6. "'Pride of place' is a term of falconry, and means the highest pitch of flight. See *Macbeth*, &c. [2.4.12] 'An eagle towering in his pride of place,' [2.4.12] &c."

Ambition's life and labours all were vain;
He wears the shatter'd links of the world's broken chain.[7]

19

Fit retribution! Gaul[8] may champ the bit
And foam in fetters;—but is Earth more free?
Did nations combat to make *One* submit;   165
Or league to teach all kings true sovereignty?
What! shall reviving Thraldom again be
The patch'd-up idol of enlighten'd days?
Shall we, who struck the Lion down, shall we
Pay the Wolf homage? proffering lowly gaze   170
And servile knees to thrones? No; *prove*[9] before ye praise!

20

If not, o'er one fallen despot boast no more!
In vain fair cheeks were furrow'd with hot tears
For Europe's flowers long rooted up before
The trampler of her vineyards; in vain years   175
Of death, depopulation, bondage, fears,
Have all been borne, and broken by the accord
Of roused-up millions: all that most endears
Glory, is when the myrtle wreathes a sword
Such as Harmodius[1] drew on Athens' tyrant lord.   180

21

There was a sound of revelry by night,
And Belgium's capital had gather'd then
Her Beauty and her Chivalry, and bright
The lamps shone o'er fair women and brave men;
A thousand hearts beat happily; and when   185
Music arose with its voluptuous swell,
Soft eyes look'd love to eyes which spake again,
And all went merry as a marriage-bell;[2]
But hush! hark! a deep sound strikes like a rising knell!

22

Did ye not hear it?—No; 'twas but the wind,   190
Or the car rattling o'er the stony street;

---

7. Reference to Napoleon's final imprisonment on the island of St. Helena.
8. France.
9. Demonstrate or test the value of something.
1. "See the famous song on Harmodius and Aristogiton. The best English translation is in Bland's Anthology, by Mr (Now Sir Thomas) Denham,—'With myrtle my sword will I wreathe,' &c." Byron refers to sixth-century B.C.E. Athenian patriots who attempted to assassinate the tyrants Hipparchus and Hippias (only Hipparchus was killed). Myrtle thereafter became symbolically associated with upholders of liberty.
2. "On the night previous to the action, it is said that a ball was given at Brussels." The Duchess of Richmond gave a lavish ball on June 15, 1815, actually the eve of the battle of Quatre-bras, three days prior to the battle of Waterloo.

On with the dance! let joy be unconfined;
No sleep till morn, when Youth and Pleasure meet
To chase the glowing Hours with flying feet—
But, hark!—that heavy sound breaks in once more,   195
As if the clouds its echo would repeat;
And nearer, clearer, deadlier than before!
Arm! Arm! and out[3]—it is—the cannon's opening roar!

23

Within a window'd niche of that high hall
Sate Brunswick's fated chieftain;[4] he did hear   200
That sound the first amidst the festival,
And caught its tone with Death's prophetic ear;
And when they smiled because he deem'd it near,
His heart more truly knew that peal too well
Which stretch'd his father on a bloody bier,   205
And roused the vengeance blood alone could quell:
He rush'd into the field, and, foremost fighting, fell.

24

Ah! then and there was hurrying to and fro,
And gathering tears, and tremblings of distress,
And cheeks all pale, which but an hour ago   210
Blush'd at the praise of their own loveliness;
And there were sudden partings, such as press
The life from out young hearts, and choking sighs
Which ne'er might be repeated; who could guess
If ever more should meet those mutual eyes,   215
Since upon nights[5] so sweet such awful morn could rise?

25

And there was mounting in hot haste: the steed,
The mustering squadron, and the clattering car,
Went pouring forward in[6] impetuous speed,
And swiftly forming in the ranks of war;   220
And the deep thunder peal on peal afar;
And near, the beat of the alarming drum
Roused up the soldier ere the morning star;
While throng'd the citizens with terror dumb,
Or whispering, with white lips—"The foe! They come! they
          come!"   225

3. *and out*: it is (*1832*).
4. Frederick William, Duke of Brunswick (1771–1815) and nephew of George III, fell at Quatre-bras;
   his father (line 205), Charles William Ferdinand, a passionate opponent of Napoleon, had died in
   1806 at the battle of Auerstädt.
5. night (*1832*).
6. with (*1832*).

26

And wild and high the "Cameron's gathering"[7] rose!
The war-note of Lochiel, which Albyn's hills
Have heard, and heard, too, have her Saxon foes:—
How in the noon of night that pibroch[8] thrills,
Savage and shrill! But with the breath which fills   230
Their mountain-pipe, so fill the mountaineers
With the fierce native daring which instils
The stirring memory of a thousand years,
And Evan's, Donald's[9] fame rings in each clansman's ears!

27

And Ardennes[1] waves above them her green leaves,   235
Dewy with nature's tear-drops, as they pass,
Grieving, if aught inanimate e'er grieves,
Over the unreturning brave,—alas!
Ere evening to be trodden like the grass
Which now beneath them, but above shall grow   240
In its next verdure, when this fiery mass
Of living valour, rolling on the foe
And burning with high hope, shall moulder cold and low.

28

Last noon beheld them full of lusty life,
Last eve in Beauty's circle proudly gay,   245
The midnight brought the signal-sound of strife,
The morn the marshalling in arms,—the day
Battle's magnificently-stern array!
The thunder-clouds close o'er it, which when rent
The earth is cover'd thick with other clay,   250
Which her own clay shall cover, heap'd and pent,
Rider and horse,—friend, foe,—in one red burial blent!

29

Their praise is hymn'd by loftier harps than mine;
Yet one[2] I would select from that proud throng,
Partly because they blend me with his line,   255

---

7. The battle song of the Camerons, a Scottish clan; in the next line *Lochiel* is the title of the clan's chief, and *Albyn* refers to Scotland.
8. Pronounced pee'-brahk; musical piece for bagpipe, usually martial in character.
9. "Sir Evan Cameron, and his descendant Donald, the 'gentle Lochiel' of the 'forty-five.'" Sir Evan Cameron resisted Cromwell and fought for James II in 1689; in 1745 his grandson Donald Cameron fought to restore the Stuarts.
1. "The wood of Soignies is supposed to be a remnant of the forest of Ardennes, famous in Boiardo's *Orlando*, and immortal in Shakespeare's 'As You Like It.' It is also celebrated in Tacitus as being the spot of successful defence by the Germans against the Roman encroachments. I have ventured to adopt the name connected with nobler associations than those of mere slaughter." Byron refers to the woods near Brussels and Waterloo. (For corrections to Byron's explanatory note, see *CPW* 2:302.)
2. Frederick Howard, son of the Earl of Carlisle, whom Byron had satirized in *English Bards and Scotch Reviewers*.

And partly that I did his sire some wrong,
And partly that bright names will hallow song;
And his was of the bravest, and when shower'd
The death-bolts deadliest the thinn'd files along,
Even where the thickest of war's tempest lower'd,   260
They reach'd no nobler breast than thine, young, gallant
    Howard!

30

There have been tears and breaking hearts for thee,
And mine were nothing, had I such to give;
But when I stood beneath the fresh green tree,
Which living waves where thou didst cease to live,   265
And saw around me the wide field revive
With fruits and fertile promise, and the Spring
Come forth her work of gladness to contrive,
With all her reckless birds upon the wing,
I turn'd from all she brought to those she could not bring.[3]   270

31

I turn'd to thee, to thousands, of whom each
And one as all a ghastly gap did make
In his own kind and kindred, whom to teach
Forgetfulness were mercy for their sake;
The Archangel's trump[4] not Glory's, must awake   275
Those whom they thirst for; though the sound of Fame
May for a moment soothe, it cannot slake
The fever of vain longing, and the name
So honour'd but assumes a stronger, bitterer claim.

32

They mourn, but smile at length; and, smiling, mourn: 280
The tree will wither long before it fall;
The hull drives on, though mast and sail be torn;
The roof-tree sinks, but moulders on the hall
In massy hoariness; the ruin'd wall

3. "My guide from Mont St Jean over the field seemed intelligent and accurate. The place where Major Howard fell was not far from two tall and solitary trees (there was a third cut down, or shivered in the battle), which stand a few yards from each other at a pathway's side. Beneath these he died and was buried. The body has since been removed to England. A small hollow for the present marks where it lay, but will probably soon be effaced; the plough has been upon it, and the grain is,—After pointing out the different spots where Picton and other gallant men had perished; the guide said, 'Here Major Howard lay: I was near him when wounded.' I told him my relationship, and he seemed then still more anxious to point out the particular spot and circumstances. The place is one of the most marked in the field, from the peculiarity of the two trees above mentioned. I went on horseback twice over the field, comparing it with my recollection of similar scenes. As a plain, Waterloo seems marked out for the scene of some great action, though this may be mere imagination: I have viewed with attention those of Platea, Troy, Mantinea, Leuctra, Chaeronea, and Marathon; and the field around Mont St Jean and Hougoumont appears to want little but a better cause, and that undefinable but impressive halo which the lapse of ages throws around a celebrated spot, to vie in interest with any or all of these, except, perhaps, the last mentioned."
4. In the Book of Revelation, the trumpet that the Archangel shall sound at the end of the world to signal the resurrection of the dead.

Stands when its wind-worn battlements are gone;   285
The bars survive the captive they enthral;
The day drags through though storms keep out the sun;
And thus the heart will break, yet brokenly live on:

33

Even as a broken mirror, which the glass
In every fragment multiplies; and makes   290
A thousand images of one that was,
The same, and still the more, the more it breaks;
And thus the heart will do which not forsakes,
Living in shatter'd guise, and still, and cold,
And bloodless, with its sleepless sorrow aches,   295
Yet withers on till all without is old,
Showing no visible sign, for such things are untold.

34

There is a very life in our despair,
Vitality of poison,—a quick root
Which feeds these deadly branches; for it were   300
As nothing did we die; but Life will suit
Itself to Sorrow's most detested fruit,
Like to the apples[5] on the Dead Sea's shore,
All ashes to the taste: Did man compute
Existence by enjoyment, and count o'er   305
Such hours 'gainst years of life,—say, would he name
     threescore?

35

The Psalmist[6] number'd out the years of man:
They are enough; and if thy tale be *true*,
Thou, who didst grudge him even that fleeting span,
More than enough, thou fatal Waterloo!   310
Millions of tongues record thee, and anew
Their children's lips shall echo them, and say—
"Here, where the sword united nations drew,
Our countrymen were warring on that day!"
And this is much, and all which will not pass away.   315

36

There sunk the greatest, nor the worst of men,[7]
Whose spirit antithetically mixt
One moment of the mightiest, and again
On little objects with like firmness fixt,

---

5. "The (fabled) apples on the brink of the lake Asphaltes were said to be fair without, and, within, ashes. *Vide* Tacitus, *Histor. lib.* v. 7."
6. King David, traditionally regarded as author of the Psalms.
7. Napoleon Bonaparte (1769–1821), French emperor 1804–15.

Extreme in all things! hadst thou been betwixt,   320
Thy throne had still been thine, or never been;
For daring made thy rise as fall: thou seek'st
Even now to re-assume the imperial mien,
And shake again the world, the Thunderer of the scene!

37

Conqueror and captive of the earth art thou!   325
She trembles at thee still, and thy wild name
Was ne'er more bruited in men's minds than now
That thou art nothing, save the jest of Fame,
Who woo'd thee once, thy vassal, and became
The flatterer of thy fierceness, till thou wert   330
A god unto thyself; nor less the same
To the astounded kingdoms all inert,
Who deem'd thee for a time whate'er thou didst assert.

38

Oh, more or less than man—in high or low,
Battling with nations, flying from the field;   335
Now making monarchs' necks thy footstool, now
More than thy meanest soldier taught to yield;
An empire thou couldst crush, command, rebuild,
But govern not thy pettiest passion, nor,
However deeply in men's spirits skill'd,   340
Look through thine own, nor curb the lust of war,
Nor learn that tempted Fate will leave the loftiest star.

39

Yet well thy soul hath brook'd the turning tide
With that untaught innate philosophy,
Which, be it wisdom, coldness, or deep pride,   345
Is gall and wormwood to an enemy.
When the whole host of hatred stood hard by,
To watch and mock thee shrinking, thou hast smiled
With a sedate and all-enduring eye;—
When Fortune fled her spoil'd and favourite child,   350
He stood unbow'd beneath the ills upon him piled.

40

Sager than in thy fortunes; for in them
Ambition steel'd thee on too far to show
That just habitual scorn which could contemn
Men and their thoughts; 'twas wise to feel, not so   355
To wear it ever on thy lip and brow,
And spurn the instruments thou wert to use
Till they were turn'd unto thine overthrow;
'Tis but a worthless world to win or lose;
So hath it proved to thee, and all such lot who choose.   360

41

If, like a tower upon a headlong rock,
Thou hadst been made to stand or fall alone,
Such scorn of man had help'd to brave the shock;
But men's thoughts were the steps which paved thy
        throne,
Their admiration thy best weapon shone;   365
The part of Philip's son[8] was thine, not then
(Unless aside thy purple had been thrown)
Like stern Diogenes to mock at men;
For sceptred cynics earth were far too wide a den.[9]

42

But quiet to quick bosoms is a hell,   370
And *there* hath been thy bane; there is a fire
And motion of the soul which will not dwell
In its own narrow being, but aspire
Beyond the fitting medium of desire;
And, but once kindled, quenchless evermore,   375
Preys upon high adventure, nor can tire
Of aught but rest; a fever at the core,
Fatal to him who bears, to all who ever bore.

43

This makes the madmen who have made men mad
By their contagion; Conquerors and Kings,   380
Founders of sects and systems, to whom add
Sophists, Bards, Statesmen, all unquiet things
Which stir too strongly the soul's secret springs,
And are themselves the fools to those they fool;
Envied, yet how unenviable! what stings   385
Are theirs! One breast laid open were a school
Which would unteach mankind the lust to shine or rule:

44

Their breath is agitation, and their life
A storm whereon they ride, to sink at last,
And yet so nursed and bigoted to strife,   390
That should their days, surviving perils past,
Melt to calm twilight, they feel overcast

8. Alexander the Great (356–323 B.C.E.), conqueror of the ancient world. He is reported to have said
   that if he had not been king (i.e., wearer of the "purple"), he would have wished to be the philos-
   opher Diogenes (d. 323 B.C.E.), one of the Cynics, who claimed distrust of all human pretensions
   to honesty or virtue.
9. "The great error of Napoleon, 'if we have writ our annals true,' was a continued obtrusion on man-
   kind of his want of all community of feeling for, or with them; perhaps more offensive to human
   vanity than the active cruelty of more trembling and suspicious tyranny. Such were his speeches
   to public assemblies as well as individuals; and the single expression which he is said to have used
   on returning to Paris after the Russian winter had destroyed his army, rubbing his hands over a fire,
   'This is pleasanter than Moscow,' would probably alienate more favour from his cause than the
   destruction and reverses which led to the remark."

With sorrow and supineness, and so die;
Even as a flame unfed, which runs to waste
With its own flickering, or a sword laid by,   395
Which eats into itself, and rusts ingloriously.

45

He who ascends to mountain-tops, shall find
The loftiest peaks most wrapt in clouds and snow;
He who surpasses or subdues mankind,
Must look down on the hate of those below.   400
Though high *above* the sun of glory glow,
And far *beneath* the earth and ocean spread,
Round him are icy rocks, and loudly blow
Contending tempests on his naked head,
And thus reward the toils which to those summits led.   405

46

Away with these! true Wisdom's world will be
Within its own creation, or in thine,
Maternal Nature! for who teems like thee,
Thus on the banks of thy majestic Rhine?
There Harold gazes on a work divine,   410
A blending of all beauties; streams and dells,
Fruit, foliage, crag, wood, cornfield, mountain, vine,
And chiefless castles breathing stern farewells
From gray but leafy walls, where Ruin greenly dwells.

47

And there they stand, as stands a lofty mind,   415
Worn, but unstooping to the baser crowd,
All tenantless, save to the crannying wind,
Or holding dark communion with the cloud.
There was a day when they were young and proud,
Banners on high, and battles pass'd below;   420
But they who fought are in a bloody shroud,
And those which waved are shredless dust ere now,
And the bleak battlements shall bear no future blow.

48

Beneath these battlements, within those walls,
Power dwelt amidst her passions; in proud state   425
Each robber chief upheld his armed halls,
Doing his evil will, nor less elate
Than mightier heroes of a longer date.
What want these outlaws[1] conquerors should have

---

1. "'What wants that knave that a king should have?' was King James's question on meeting Johnny Armstrong and his followers in full accoutrements.—See the Ballad." In 1532 Armstrong, Laird of Gilnockie, surrendered to James V in such splendid attire that the king had him hanged for insolence; see *Minstrelsy of the Scottish Border* (1810).

But History's purchased page to call them great?   430
A wider space, an ornamented grave?
Their hopes were not less warm, their souls were full as
     brave.

49

In their baronial feuds and single fields,
What deeds of prowess unrecorded died!
And Love, which lent a blazon to their shields,   435
With emblems well devised by amorous pride,
Through all the mail of iron hearts would glide;
But still their flame was fierceness, and drew on
Keen contest and destruction near allied,
And many a tower for some fair mischief won,   440
Saw the discolour'd Rhine beneath its ruin run.

50

But Thou, exulting and abounding river!
Making thy waves a blessing as they flow
Through banks whose beauty would endure for ever
Could man but leave thy bright creation so,   445
Nor its fair promise from the surface mow
With the sharp scythe of conflict,—then to see
Thy valley of sweet waters, were to know
Earth paved like Heaven; and to seem such to me,
Even now what wants thy stream?—that it should Lethe[2] be.   450

51

A thousand battles have assail'd thy banks,
But these and half their fame have pass'd away,
And Slaughter heap'd on high his weltering ranks;
Their very graves are gone, and what are they?
Thy tide wash'd down the blood of yesterday,   455
And all was stainless, and on thy clear stream
Glass'd with its dancing light the sunny ray;
But o'er the blacken'd memory's blighting dream
Thy waves would vainly roll, all sweeping as they seem.

52

Thus Harold inly said, and pass'd along,   460
Yet not insensibly to all which here
Awoke the jocund birds to early song
In glens which might have made even exile dear:
Though on his brow were graven lines austere,
And tranquil sternness which had ta'en the place   465
Of feelings fierier far but less severe,

---

2. The river of forgetfulness in the classical underworld.

Joy was not always absent from his face,
But o'er it in such scenes would steal with transient trace.

53

Nor was all love shut from him, though his days
Of passion had consumed themselves to dust.   470
It is in vain that we would coldly gaze
On such as smile upon us; the heart must
Leap kindly back to kindness, though disgust
Hath wean'd it from all worldlings: thus he felt,
For there was soft remembrance, and sweet trust   475
In one fond breast,[3] to which his own would melt,
And in its tenderer hour on that his bosom dwelt.

54

And he had learn'd to love,—I know not why,
For this in such as him seems strange of mood,—
The helpless looks of blooming infancy,   480
Even in its earliest nurture; what subdued,
To change like this, a mind so far imbued
With scorn of man, it little boots to know;
But thus it was; and though in solitude
Small power the nipp'd affections have to grow,   485
In him this glow'd when all beside had ceased to glow.

55

And there was one soft breast, as hath been said,
Which unto his was bound by stronger ties
Than the church links withal; and, though unwed,
That love was pure, and, far above disguise,   490
Had stood the test of mortal enmities
Still undivided, and cemented more
By peril, dreaded most in female eyes;
But this was firm, and from a foreign shore
Well to that heart might his these absent greetings pour! 495

1

The castled crag of Drachenfels[4]
Frowns o'er the wide and winding Rhine,
Whose breast of waters broadly swells
Between the banks which bear the vine,

3. Augusta Leigh, Byron's half-sister.
4. "The castle of Drachenfels stands on the highest summit of 'the Seven Mountains,' over the Rhine banks: it is in ruins, and connected with some singular traditions: it is the first in view on the road from Bonn, but on the opposite side of the river; on this bank, nearly facing it, are the remains of another, called the Jew's Castle, and a large cross commemorative of the murder of a chief by his brother. The number of castles and cities along the course of the Rhine on both sides is very great, and their situations remarkably beautiful." Byron sent his first draft of the Drachenfels lyric to his sister in England; it bears the headnote: "May 11th 1816. Written on the banks of the Rhine to my dearest Augusta with some flowers."

And hills all rich with blossom'd trees,   500
And fields which promise corn and wine,
And scatter'd cities crowning these,
Whose far white walls along them shine,
Have strew'd a scene, which I should see
With double joy wert *thou* with me.   505

2

And peasant girls, with deep blue eyes,
And hands which offer early flowers,
Walk smiling o'er this paradise;
Above, the frequent feudal towers
Through green leaves lift their walls of gray;   510
And many a rock which steeply lowers,
And noble arch in proud decay,
Look o'er this vale of vintage-bowers;
But one thing want these banks of Rhine,—
Thy gentle hand to clasp in mine!   515

3

I send the lilies given to me;
Though long before thy hand they touch,
I know that they must wither'd be,
But yet reject them not as such;
For I have cherish'd them as dear,   520
Because they yet may meet thine eye,
And guide thy soul to mine even here,
When thou behold'st them drooping nigh,
And know'st them gather'd by the Rhine,
And offer'd from my heart to thine!   525

4

The river nobly foams and flows,
The charm of this enchanted ground,
And all its thousand turns disclose
Some fresher beauty varying round:
The haughtiest breast its wish might bound   530
Through life to dwell delighted here;
Nor could on earth a spot be found
To nature and to me so dear,
Could thy dear eyes in following mine
Still sweeten more these banks of Rhine!   535

56

By Coblentz,[5] on a rise of gentle ground,
There is a small and simple pyramid,
Crowning the summit of the verdant mound;

5. German city on the Rhine.

Beneath its base are heroes' ashes hid,
Our enemy's—but let not that forbid   540
Honour to Marceau![6] o'er whose early tomb
Tears, big tears, gush'd from the rough soldier's lid,
Lamenting and yet envying such a doom,
Falling for France, whose rights he battled to resume.

57

Brief, brave, and glorious was his young career,—   545
His mourners were two hosts, his friends and foes;
And fitly may the stranger lingering here
Pray for his gallant spirit's bright repose;
For he was Freedom's champion, one of those,
The few in number, who had not o'erstept   550
The charter to chastise which she bestows
On such as wield her weapons; he had kept
The whiteness of his soul, and thus men o'er him wept.[7]

58

Here Ehrenbreitstein,[8] with her shatter'd wall
Black with the miner's blast, upon her height   555
Yet shows of what she was, when shell and ball
Rebounding idly on her strength did light:
A tower of victory! from whence the flight
Of baffled foes was watch'd along the plain;
But Peace destroy'd what War could never blight,   560
And laid those proud roofs bare to Summer's rain—
On which the iron shower for years had pour'd in vain.

59

Adieu to thee, fair Rhine! How long delighted
The stranger fain would linger on his way!
Thine is a scene alike where souls united   565

6. French general who was killed in 1796 in a battle against the army of Archduke Charles of Austria; see Byron's note, below.
7. "The monument of the young and lamented General Marceau (killed by a rifle-ball at Alterkirchen, on the last day of the fourth year of the French republic) still remains as described. The inscriptions on his monument are rather too long, and not required: his name was enough; France adored, and her enemies admired; both wept over him. His funeral was attended by the generals and detachments from both armies. In the same grave General Hoche is interred, a gallant man also in every sense of the word; but though he distinguished himself greatly in battle, he had not the good fortune to die there: his death was attended by suspicions of poison. A separate monument (not over his body, which is buried by Marceau's) is raised for him near Andernach, opposite to which one of his most memorable exploits was performed, in throwing a bridge to an island on the Rhine. The shape and style are different from that of Marceau's, and the inscription more simple and pleasing:—'The Army of the Sambre and Meuse to its Commander-in-Chief Hoche.' This is all, and as it should be. Hoche was esteemed among the first of France's earlier generals, before Buonaparte monopolised her triumphs. He was the destined commander of the invading army of Ireland."
8. "Ehrenbreitstein, i.e. 'the broad stone of honour,' one of the strongest fortresses in Europe, was dismantled and blown up by the French at the truce of Leoben. It had been, and could only be, reduced by famine or treachery. It yielded to the former, aided by surprise. After having seen the fortifications of Gibraltar and Malta, it did not much strike by comparison; but the situation is commanding. General Marceau besieged it in vain for some time, and I slept in a room where I was shown a window at which he is said to have been standing observing the progress of the siege by moonlight, when a ball struck immediately below it."

Or lonely Contemplation thus might stray;
And could the ceaseless vultures cease to prey
On self-condemning bosoms, it were here,
Where Nature, nor too sombre nor too gay,
Wild but not rude, awful yet not austere,   570
Is to the mellow Earth as Autumn to the year.

60

Adieu to thee again! a vain adieu!
There can be no farewell to scene like thine;
The mind is colour'd by thy every hue;
And if reluctantly the eyes resign   575
Their cherish'd gaze upon thee, lovely Rhine!
'Tis with the thankful glance of parting praise;
More mighty spots may rise—more glaring shine,
But none unite in one attaching maze
The brilliant, fair, and soft,—the glories of old days,   580

61

The negligently grand, the fruitful bloom
Of coming ripeness, the white city's sheen,
The rolling stream, the precipice's gloom,
The forest's growth, and Gothic walls between,
The wild rocks shaped as they had turrets been   585
In mockery of man's art; and these withal
A race of faces happy as the scene,
Whose fertile bounties here extend to all,
Still springing o'er thy banks, though Empires near them
    fall.

62

But these recede. Above me are the Alps,   590
The palaces of Nature, whose vast walls
Have pinnacled in clouds their snowy scalps,
And throned Eternity in icy halls
Of cold sublimity, where forms and falls
The avalanche—the thunderbolt of snow!   595
All that expands the spirit, yet appals,
Gather around these summits, as to show
How Earth may pierce to Heaven, yet leave vain man
    below.

63

But ere these matchless heights I dare to scan,
There is a spot should not be pass'd in vain,—   600
Morat!⁹ the proud, the patriot field! where man

9. Site where in 1476 Swiss patriots defeated a much larger invading army from Burgundy; the Burgundian dead were left unburied and a pile of their bones remained at the scene in 1816 (see Byron's note to line 607).

May gaze on ghastly trophies of the slain,
Nor blush for those who conquer'd on that plain;
Here Burgundy bequeath'd his tombless host,
A bony heap, through ages to remain,   605
Themselves their monument;—the Stygian[1] coast
Unsepulchred they roam'd, and shriek'd each wandering
     ghost.[2]

64

While Waterloo with Cannae's carnage vies,
Morat and Marathon twin names shall stand;[4]
They were true Glory's stainless victories,   610
Won by the unambitious heart and hand
Of a proud, brotherly, and civic band,
All unbought champions in no princely cause
Of vice-entail'd Corruption; they no land
Doom'd to bewail the blasphemy of laws   615
Making kings' rights divine, by some Draconic[4] clause.

65

By a lone wall a lonelier column rears
A gray and grief-worn aspect of old days;
'Tis the last remnant of the wreck of years,
And looks as with the wild-bewilder'd gaze   620
Of one to stone converted by amaze,
Yet still with consciousness; and there it stands
Making a marvel that it not decays,
When the coeval[5] pride of human hands,
Levell'd Aventicum,[6] hath strew'd her subject lands.   625

66

And there—oh! sweet and sacred be the name!—
Julia—the daughter, the devoted—gave
Her youth to Heaven; her heart, beneath a claim

---

1. Referring to the River Styx in the classical underworld.
2. "The chapel is destroyed, and the pyramid of bones diminished to a small number by the Burgundian legion in the service of France; who anxiously effaced this record of their ancestors' less successful invasions. A few still remain, notwithstanding the pains taken by the Burgundians for ages (all who passed that way removing a bone to their own country), and the less justifiable larcenies of the Swiss postilions, who carried them off to sell for knife-handles; a purpose for which the whiteness imbibed by the bleaching of years had rendered them in great request. Of these relics I ventured to bring away as much as may have made a quarter of a hero, for which the sole excuse is, that if I had not, the next passer by might have perverted them to worse uses than the careful preservation which I intend for them."
3. Cannae was the site of a bloody battle between Rome and Carthage (216 B.C.E.); like Waterloo, it was a battle for power. Marathon refers to the famous battle in 490 B.C.E., in which the Greeks defeated a much larger invading army from Persia; like Morat, it was battle in which men fought for their liberty.
4. Draco (seventh century B.C.E.), an Athenian statesman, was notorious for the harshness of his penal code.
5. Of the same time of origin.
6. "Aventicum, near Morat, was the Roman capital of Helvetia, where Avenches now stands." I.e., the column at which Byron gazes has survived the Roman capital of Switzerland.

Nearest to Heaven's, broke o'er a father's grave.
Justice is sworn 'gainst tears, and hers would crave   630
The life she lived in; but the judge was just,
And then she died on him she could not save.
Their tomb was simple, and without a bust,
And held within their urn one mind, one heart, one dust.[7]

67

But these are deeds which should not pass away,   635
And names that must not wither, though the earth
Forgets her empires with a just decay,
The enslavers and the enslaved, their death and birth;
The high, the mountain-majesty of worth
Should be, and shall, survivor of its woe,   640
And from its immortality look forth
In the sun's face, like yonder Alpine snow,[8]
Imperishably pure beyond all things below.

68

Lake Leman[9] woos me with its crystal face,
The mirror where the stars and mountains view   645
The stillness of their aspect in each trace
Its clear depth yields of their far height and hue:
There is too much of man here, to look through
With a fit mind the might which I behold;
But soon in me shall Loneliness renew   650
Thoughts hid, but not less cherish'd than of old,
Ere mingling with the herd had penn'd me in their fold.

69

To fly from, need not be to hate, mankind:
All are not fit with them to stir and toil,
Nor is it discontent to keep the mind   655
Deep in its fountain, lest it overboil
In the hot throng, where we become the spoil
Of our infection, till too late and long
We may deplore and struggle with the coil,[1]

7. "Julia Alpinula, a young Aventian priestess, died soon after a vain endeavour to save her father, con-
demned to death as a traitor by Aulus Caecina. Her epitaph was discovered many years ago;—it is
thus:—'Julia Alpinula: Hic jaceo. Infelicis patris infelix proles. Deae Aventiae Sacerdos. Exorare
patris necem non potui: Male mori in fatis ille erat. Vixi annos XXIII.'—I know of no human com-
position so affecting as this, nor a history of deeper interest. These are the names and actions which
ought not to perish, and to which we turn with a true and healthy tenderness, from the wretched
and glittering detail of a confused mass of conquests and battles, with which the mind is roused
for a time to a false and feverish sympathy, from whence it recurs at length with all the nausea con-
sequent on such intoxication."
8. "This is written in the eye of Mont Blanc (June 3d, 1816), which even at this distance dazzles
mine.—(July 20th.) I this day observed for some time the distinct reflection of Mont Blanc and
Mont Argentière in the calm of the lake, which I was crossing in my boat; the distance of these
mountains from their mirror is sixty miles."
9. Lake Geneva.
1. The mortal body; e.g., "this mortal coil," *Hamlet* 3.1.69.

In wretched interchange of wrong for wrong   660
Midst a contentious world, striving where none are strong.

70

There, in a moment, we may plunge our years
In fatal penitence, and in the blight
Of our own soul turn all our blood to tears,
And colour things to come with hues of Night;   665
The race of life becomes a hopeless flight
To those that walk in darkness: on the sea,
The boldest steer but where their ports invite,
But there are wanderers o'er Eternity
Whose bark drives on and on, and anchor'd ne'er shall be.   670

71

Is it not better, then, to be alone,
And love Earth only for its earthly sake?
By the blue rushing of the arrowy Rhone,[2]
Or the pure bosom of its nursing lake,
Which feeds it as a mother who doth make   675
A fair but froward infant her own care,
Kissing its cries away as these awake;—
Is it not better thus our lives to wear,
Than join the crushing crowd, doom'd to inflict or bear?

72

I live not in myself, but I become   680
Portion of that around me; and to me
High mountains are a feeling, but the hum
Of human cities torture: I can see
Nothing to loathe in nature, save to be
A link reluctant in a fleshly chain,   685
Class'd among creatures, when the soul can flee,
And with the sky, the peak, the heaving plain
Of ocean, or the stars, mingle, and not in vain.

73

And thus I am absorb'd, and this is life:
I look upon the peopled desert past,   690
As on a place of agony and strife,
Where, for some sin, to sorrow I was cast,
To act and suffer, but remount at last
With a fresh pinion; which I feel to spring,
Though young, yet waxing vigorous, as the blast   695
Which it would cope with, on delighted wing,
Spurning the clay-cold bonds which round our being cling.

2. "The colour of the Rhone at Geneva is blue, to a depth of tint which I have never seen equalled in water, salt or fresh, except in the Mediterranean and Archipelago."

74

And when, at length, the mind shall be all free
From what it hates in this degraded form,
Reft of its carnal life, save what shall be   700
Existent happier in the fly and worm,—
When elements to elements conform,
And dust is as it should be, shall I not
Feel all I see, less dazzling, but more warm?
The bodiless thought? the Spirit of each spot?   705
Of which, even now, I share at times the immortal lot?

75

Are not the mountains, waves, and skies, a part
Of me and of my soul, as I of them?
Is not the love of these deep in my heart
With a pure passion? should I not contemn   710
All objects, if compared with these? and stem
A tide of suffering, rather than forego
Such feelings for the hard and worldly phlegm
Of those whose eyes are only turn'd below,
Gazing upon the ground, with thoughts which dare not
    glow?   715

76

But this is not my theme; and I return
To that which is immediate, and require
Those who find contemplation in the urn,
To look on One,[3] whose dust was once all fire,
A native of the land where I respire   720
The clear air for a while—a passing guest,
Where he became a being,—whose desire
Was to be glorious; 'twas a foolish quest,
The which to gain and keep, he sacrificed all rest.

77

Here the self-torturing sophist, wild Rousseau,   725
The apostle of affliction, he who threw
Enchantment over passion, and from woe
Wrung overwhelming eloquence, first drew
The breath which made him wretched; yet he knew
How to make madness beautiful, and cast   730
O'er erring deeds and thoughts a heavenly hue
Of words, like sunbeams, dazzling as they past
The eyes, which o'er them shed tears feelingly and fast.[4]

3. Jean-Jacques Rousseau (1712–1778), French philosopher and novelist, born in Geneva; he was one of the first and most influential Romantic thinkers.
4. Lines 730–33, like stanza 79, refer to Rousseau's *Julie, ou la Nouvelle Héloïse* (1761), which portrays the illicit love between its passionate heroine and her tutor.

78

His love was passion's essence—as a tree
On fire by lightning; with ethereal flame   735
Kindled he was, and blasted; for to be
Thus, and enamour'd, were in him the same.
But his was not the love of living dame,
Nor of the dead who rise upon our dreams,
But of ideal beauty, which became   740
In him existence, and o'erflowing teems
Along his burning page, distemper'd though it seems.

79

This breathed itself to life in Julie, this
Invested her with all that's wild and sweet;
This hallow'd, too, the memorable kiss[5]   745
Which every morn his fever'd lip would greet,
From hers, who but with friendship his would meet;
But to that gentle touch, through brain and breast
Flash'd the thrill'd spirit's love-devouring heat;
In that absorbing sigh perchance more blest   750
Than vulgar minds may be with all they seek possest.

80

His life was one long war with self-sought foes,
Or friends by him self-banish'd;[6] for his mind
Had grown Suspicion's sanctuary, and chose,
For its own cruel sacrifice, the kind,   755
'Gainst whom he raged with fury strange and blind.
But he was phrensied,—wherefore, who may know?
Since cause might be which skill could never find;
But he was phrensied by disease or woe,
To that worst pitch of all, which wears a reasoning show.   760

81

For then he was inspired, and from him came,
As from the Pythian's mystic cave of yore,
Those oracles which set the world in flame,[7]
Nor ceased to burn till kingdoms were no more:
Did he not this for France? which lay before   765

---

5. "This refers to the account in his 'Confessions' of his passion for the Comtesse d'Houdetot (the mistress of St Lambert), and his long walk every morning, for the sake of the single kiss which was the common salutation of French acquaintance. Rousseau's description of his feelings on this occasion may be considered as the most passionate, yet not impure, description and expression of love that ever kindled into words; which, after all, must be felt, from their very force, to be inadequate to the delineation: a painting can give no sufficient idea of the ocean."
6. These include the philosophers Diderot, Voltaire, and Hume.
7. Rousseau's writings have been regarded as inspiring the French Revolution; thus, Byron likens them to the oracles of Apollo, heard at the god's shrine at Delphi (formerly Pythios), according to ancient belief.

Bow'd to the inborn tyranny of years?
Broken and trembling to the yoke she bore,
Till by the voice of him and his compeers
Roused up to too much wrath, which follows o'ergrown
    fears?

82

They made themselves a fearful monument! 770
The wreck of old opinions—things which grew,
Breathed from the birth of time: the veil they rent,
And what behind it lay, all earth shall view.
But good with ill they also overthrew,
Leaving but ruins, wherewith to rebuild 775
Upon the same foundation, and renew
Dungeons and thrones, which the same hour refill'd,
As heretofore, because ambition was self-will'd.

83

But this will not endure, nor be endured!
Mankind have felt their strength, and made it felt. 780
They might have used it better, but, allured
By their new vigour, sternly have they dealt
On one another; pity ceased to melt
With her once natural charities. But they,
Who in oppression's darkness caved had dwelt, 785
They were not eagles, nourish'd with the day;
What marvel then, at times, if they mistook their prey?

84

What deep wounds ever closed without a scar?
The heart's bleed longest, and but heal to wear
That which disfigures it; and they who war 790
With their own hopes, and have been vanquish'd, bear
Silence, but not submission: in his lair
Fix'd Passion holds his breath, until the hour
Which shall atone for years; none need despair:
It came, it cometh, and will come,—the power 795
To punish or forgive—in *one* we shall be slower.

85

Clear, placid Leman! thy contrasted lake,
With the wild world I dwelt in, is a thing
Which warns me, with its stillness, to forsake
Earth's troubled waters for a purer spring. 800
This quiet sail is as a noiseless wing
To waft me from distraction; once I loved
Torn ocean's roar, but thy soft murmuring
Sounds sweet as if a Sister's voice reproved,
That I with stern delights should e'er have been so moved. 805

86

It is the hush of night, and all between
Thy margin and the mountains, dusk, yet clear,
Mellow'd and mingling, yet distinctly seen,
Save darken'd Jura,[8] whose capt heights appear
Precipitously steep; and drawing near,   810
There breathes a living fragrance from the shore,
Of flowers yet fresh with childhood; on the ear
Drops the light drip of the suspended oar,
Or chirps the grasshopper one good-night carol more;

87

He is an evening reveller, who makes   815
His life an infancy, and sings his fill;
At intervals, some bird from out the brakes
Starts into voice a moment, then is still.
There seems a floating whisper on the hill,
But that is fancy, for the starlight dews   820
All silently their tears of love instil,
Weeping themselves away, till they infuse
Deep into Nature's breast the spirit of her hues.

88

Ye stars! which are the poetry of heaven!
If in your bright leaves we would read the fate   825
Of men and empires,—'tis to be forgiven,
That in our aspirations to be great,
Our destinies o'erleap their mortal state,
And claim a kindred with you; for ye are
A beauty and a mystery, and create   830
In us such love and reverence from afar,
That fortune, fame, power, life, have named themselves a
    star.

89

All heaven and earth are still—though not in sleep,
But breathless, as we grow when feeling most;
And silent, as we stand in thoughts too deep:—   835
All heaven and earth are still: From the high host
Of stars, to the lull'd lake and mountain-coast,
All is concenter'd in a life intense,
Where not a beam, nor air, nor leaf is lost,
But hath a part of being, and a sense   840
Of that which is of all Creator and defence.

---

8. The mountain range between Switzerland and France.

90

Then stirs the feeling infinite, so felt
In solitude, where we are *least* alone;
A truth, which through our being then doth melt
And purifies from self: it is a tone,   845
The soul and source of music, which makes known
Eternal harmony, and sheds a charm,
Like to the fabled Cytherea's zone,[9]
Binding all things with beauty;—'twould disarm
The spectre Death, had he substantial power to harm.   850

91

Not vainly did the early Persian[1] make
His altar the high places and the peak
Of earth-o'ergazing mountains,[2] and thus take
A fit and unwall'd temple, there to seek
The Spirit, in whose honour shrines are weak,   855
Uprear'd of human hands. Come, and compare
Columns and idol-dwellings, Goth or Greek,
With Nature's realms of worship, earth and air,
Nor fix on fond abodes to circumscribe thy prayer!

92

Thy sky is changed!—and such a change! Oh night,   860
And storm, and darkness, ye are wondrous strong,
Yet lovely in your strength, as is the light

9. The belt of Aphrodite (Cytherea), goddess of love, which endowed its wearer with the power of instilling love in others.
1. This reference is perhaps taken from Herodotus 1.131 or suggested by Wordsworth, *The Excursion* 4.670 *ff.*
2. "It is to be recollected, that the most beautiful and impressive doctrines of the divine Founder of Christianity were delivered, not in the *Temple*, but on the *Mount*. To wave the question of devotion, and turn to human eloquence,—the most effectual and splendid specimens were not pronounced within walls. Demosthenes addressed the public and popular assemblies. Cicero spoke in the forum. That this added to their effect on the mind of both orator and hearers, may be conceived from the difference between what we read of the emotions then and there produced, and those we ourselves experience in the perusal in the closet. It is one thing to read the Iliad at Sigaeum and on the tumuli, or by the springs with Mount Ida above, and the plain and rivers and Archipelago around you; and another to trim your taper over it in a snug library—*this* I know. Were the early and rapid progress of what is called Methodism to be attributed to any cause beyond the enthusiasm excited by its vehement faith and doctrines (the truth or error of which I presume neither to canvass nor question), I should venture to ascribe it to the practice of preaching in the *fields*, and the unstudied and extemporaneous effusions of its teachers.—The Mussulmans, whose erroneous devotion (at least in the lower orders) is most sincere, and therefore impressive, are accustomed to repeat their prescribed orisons and prayers, wherever they may be, at the stated hours—of course, frequently in the open air, kneeling upon a light mat (which they carry for the purpose of a bed or cushion as required): the ceremony lasts some minutes, during which they are totally absorbed, and only living in their supplication: nothing can disturb them. On me the simple and entire sincerity of these men, and the spirit which appeared to be within and upon them, made a far greater impression than any general rite which was ever performed in places of worship, of which I have seen those of almost every persuasion under the sun; including most of our own sectaries, and the Greek, the Catholic, the Armenian, the Lutheran, the Jewish, and the Mahometan. Many of the negroes, of whom there are numbers in the Turkish empire, are idolaters, and have free exercise of their belief and its rites: some of these I had a distant view of at Patras; and, from what I could make out of them, they appeared to be of a truly Pagan description, and not very agreeable to a spectator."

Of a dark eye in woman! Far along,
From peak to peak, the rattling crags among
Leaps the live thunder! Not from one lone cloud,   865
But every mountain now hath found a tongue,
And Jura answers, through her misty shroud,
Back to the joyous Alps, who call to her aloud!

93

And this is in the night:—Most glorious night!
Thou wert not sent for slumber! let me be   870
A sharer in thy fierce and far delight,—
A portion of the tempest and of thee![3]
How the lit lake shines, a phosphoric sea,
And the big rain comes dancing to the earth!
And now again 'tis black,—and now, the glee   875
Of the loud hills shakes with its mountain-mirth,
As if they did rejoice o'er a young earthquake's birth.

94

Now, where the swift Rhone cleaves his way between
Heights which appear as lovers who have parted[4]
In hate, whose mining depths so intervene,   880
That they can meet no more, though broken-hearted:
Though in their souls, which thus each other thwarted,
Love was the very root of the fond rage
Which blighted their life's bloom, and then departed—
Itself expired, but leaving them an age   885
Of years all winters,—war within themselves to wage.

95

Now, where the quick Rhone thus hath cleft his way,
The mightiest of the storms hath ta'en his stand:
For here, not one, but many, make their play,
And fling their thunder-bolts from hand to hand,   890
Flashing and cast around: of all the band,
The brightest through these parted hills hath fork'd
His lightnings,—as if he did understand,
That in such gaps as desolation work'd,
There the hot shaft should blast whatever therein lurk'd.   895

96

Sky, mountains, river, winds, lake, lightnings! ye!
With night, and clouds, and thunder, and a soul

---

3. "The thunder-storm to which these lines refer occurred on the 13th of June, 1816, at midnight. I have seen, among the Acrocerauniam mountains of Chimari, several more terrible, but none more beautiful."
4. Cf. Coleridge, "They stood aloof, the scars remaining, / Like cliffs which had been rent asunder" (*Christabel* 2.421–22). These lines are from the same section in *Christabel* from which Byron took the epigraph for "Fare Thee Well!"

To make these felt and feeling, well may be
Things that have made me watchful; the far roll
Of your departing voices, is the knoll[5]   900
Of what in me is sleepless,—if I rest.
But where of ye, oh tempests! is the goal?
Are ye like those within the human breast?
Or do ye find, at length, like eagles, some high nest?

97

Could I embody and unbosom now   905
That which is most within me,—could I wreak
My thoughts upon expression, and thus throw
Soul, heart, mind, passions, feelings, strong or weak,
All that I would have sought, and all I seek,
Bear, know, feel, and yet breathe—into *one* word,   910
And that one word were Lightning, I would speak;
But as it is, I live and die unheard,
With a most voiceless thought, sheathing it as a sword.

98

The morn is up again, the dewy morn,
With breath all incense, and with cheek all bloom,   915
Laughing the clouds away with playful scorn,
And living as if earth contain'd no tomb,—
And glowing into day: we may resume
The march of our existence: and thus I,
Still on thy shores, fair Leman! may find room   920
And food for meditation, nor pass by
Much, that may give us pause, if ponder'd fittingly.

99

Clarens! sweet Clarens,[6] birthplace of deep Love!
Thine air is the young breath of passionate thought;
Thy trees take root in Love; the snows above   925
The very Glaciers have his colours caught,
And sunset into rose-hues sees them wrought
By rays which sleep there lovingly: the rocks,
The permanent crags, tell here of Love, who sought
In them a refuge from the worldly shocks,   930
Which stir and sting the soul with hope that woos, then
    mocks.

100

Clarens! by heavenly feet thy paths are trod,—
Undying Love's, who here ascends a throne
To which the steps are mountains; where the god

---

5. Archaic form of "knell": the tolling sound of a bell.
6. Village on Lake Geneva, described in Rousseau's *Julie*.

Is a pervading life and light,—so shown   935
Not on those summits solely, nor alone
In the still cave and forest; o'er the flower
His eye is sparkling, and his breath hath blown,
His soft and summer breath, whose tender power
Passes the strength of storms in their most desolate hour.[7]   940

101

All things are here of *him*; from the black pines,
Which are his shade on high, and the loud roar
Of torrents, where he listeneth, to the vines
Which slope his green path downward to the shore,
Where the bow'd waters meet him, and adore,   945
Kissing his feet with murmurs; and the wood,
The covert of old trees, with trunks all hoar,
But light leaves, young as joy, stands where it stood,
Offering to him, and his, a populous solitude,—

102

A populous solitude of bees and birds,   950
And fairy-form'd and many-colour'd things,

---

7. "Rousseau's Héloïse, Lettre 17, Part IV., note. 'Ces montagnes sont si hautes qu'une demi-heure
après le soleil couche, leurs sommets sont éclairés de ses rayons; dont le rouge forme sur ces cimes
blanches *une belle couleur de rose*, qu'on aperçoit de fort loin.'—This applies more particularly to
the heights over Meillerie.—'J'allai à Vevay loger à la Clef, et pendant deux jours que j'y restai sans
voir personne, je pris pour cette ville un amour qui m'a suivi dans tous mes voyages, et qui m'y a
fait établir enfin les héros de mon roman. Je dirois volontiers à ceux qui ont du goût et qui sont
sensibles: Allez à Vevay—visitez le pays, examinez les sites, promenez-vous sur le lac, et dites si la
Nature n'a pas fait ce beau pays pour une Julie, pour une Claire, et pour un St Preux; mais ne les
y cherchez pas.'—*Les Confessions*, livre iv. p. 306, Lyon, ed. 1796.—In July, 1816, I made a voyage
round the Lake of Geneva; and, as far as my own observations have led me in a not uninterested
nor inattentive survey of all the scenes most celebrated by Rousseau in his 'Héloïse,' I can safely
say, that in this there is no exaggeration. It would be difficult to see Clarens (with the scenes around
it, Vevay, Chillon, Bôveret, St Gingo, Meillerie, Eivan, and the entrances of the Rhone) without
being forcibly struck with its peculiar adaptation to the persons and events with which it has been
peopled. But this is not all; the feeling with which all around Clarens, and the opposite rocks of
Meillerie, is invested, is of a still higher and more comprehensive order than the mere sympathy
with individual passion; it is a sense of the existence of love in its most extended and sublime capac-
ity, and of our own participation of its good and of its glory: it is the great principle of the universe,
which is there more condensed, but not less manifested; and of which, though knowing ourselves
a part, we lose our individuality, and mingle in the beauty of the whole.—If Rousseau had never
written, nor lived, the same associations would not less have belonged to such scenes. He has
added to the interest of his works by their adoption; he has shown his sense of their beauty by the
selection; but they have done that for him which no human being could do for them.—I had the
fortune (good or evil as it might be) to sail from Meillerie (where we landed for some time) to St
Gingo during a lake storm, which added to the magnificence of all around, although occasionally
accompanied by danger to the boat, which was small and overloaded. It was over this very part of
the lake that Rousseau has driven the boat of St Preux and Madame Wolmar to Meillerie for shel-
ter during a tempest. On gaining the shore at St Gingo, I found that the wind had been sufficiently
strong to blow down some fine old chestnut trees on the lower part of the mountains. On the oppo-
site height of Clarens is a château. The hills are covered with vineyards, and interspersed with some
small but beautiful woods; one of these was named the 'Bosquet de Julie;' and it is remarkable that,
though long ago cut down by the brutal selfishness of the monks of St Bernard (to whom the land
appertained), that the ground might be enclosed into a vineyard for the miserable drones of an exe-
crable superstition, the inhabitants of Clarens still point out the spot where its trees stood, calling
it by the name which consecrated and survived them. Rousseau has not been particularly fortu-
nate in the preservation of the 'local habitations' he has given to 'airy nothings.' The Prior of Great
St Bernard has cut down some of his woods for the sake of a few casks of wine, and Buonaparte
has levelled part of the rocks of Meillerie in improving the road to the Simplon. The road is an
excellent one; but I cannot quite agree with a remark which I heard made, that 'La route vaut mieux
que les souvenirs.'"

Who worship him with notes more sweet than words,
And innocently open their glad wings,
Fearless and full of life: the gush of springs,
And fall of lofty fountains, and the bend   955
Of stirring branches, and the bud which brings
The swiftest thought of beauty, here extend,
Mingling, and made by Love, unto one mighty end.

103

He who hath loved not, here would learn that lore,
And make his heart a spirit; he who knows   960
That tender mystery, will love the more,
For this is Love's recess, where vain men's woes,
And the world's waste, have driven him far from those,
For 'tis his nature to advance or die;
He stands not still, but or decays, or grows   965
Into a boundless blessing, which may vie
With the immortal lights, in its eternity!

104

'Twas not for fiction chose Rousseau this spot,
Peopling it with affections; but he found
It was the scene which passion must allot   970
To the mind's purified beings; 'twas the ground
Where early Love his Psyche's[8] zone unbound,
And hallow'd it with loveliness: 'tis lone,
And wonderful, and deep, and hath a sound,
And sense, and sight of sweetness; here the Rhone   975
Hath spread himself a couch, the Alps have rear'd a throne.

105

Lausanne! and Ferney! ye have been the abodes
Of names which unto you bequeath'd a name;[9]
Mortals, who sought and found, by dangerous roads,
A path to perpetuity of fame: 980
They were gigantic minds, and their steep aim
Was, Titan-like, on daring doubts to pile
Thoughts which should call down thunder, and the flame
Of Heaven, again assail'd, if Heaven the while
On man and man's research could deign do more than smile.   985

---

8. Greek name for the soul. In the myth of Cupid and Psyche (Love and the Soul), the young girl Psyche was loved by Cupid, god of love, who "unbound" her "zone," or undressed her, discovering her naked beauty.
9. "Voltaire and Gibbon." *Lausanne*: the Swiss home of the English historian Edward Gibbon (1737–1794), author of *The Decline and Fall of the Roman Empire* (1776–1788), one of the most influential historical works of modern times. *Ferney*: the home of the French philosopher François Marie Arouet (Voltaire) (1694–1778), a leading figure of the Enlightenment and author of the satirical masterpiece *Candide* (1759).

106

The one[1] was fire and fickleness, a child,
Most mutable in wishes, but in mind,
A wit as various,—gay, grave, sage, or wild,—
Historian, bard, philosopher, combined;
He multiplied himself among mankind,   990
The Proteus[2] of their talents: But his own
Breathed most in ridicule,—which, as the wind,
Blew where it listed, laying all things prone,—
Now to o'erthrow a fool, and now to shake a throne.

107

The other,[3] deep and slow, exhausting thought,   995
And hiving wisdom with each studious year,
In meditation dwelt, with learning wrought,
And shaped his weapon with an edge severe,
Sapping a solemn creed with solemn sneer;[4]
The lord of irony,—that master-spell,   1000
Which stung his foes to wrath, which grew from fear,
And doom'd him to the zealot's ready Hell,
Which answers to all doubts so eloquently well.

108

Yet, peace be with their ashes,—for by them,
If merited, the penalty is paid;   1005
It is not ours to judge,—far less condemn;
The hour must come when such things shall be made
Known unto all,—or hope and dread allay'd
By slumber, on one pillow,—in the dust,
Which, thus much we are sure, must lie decay'd;   1010
And when it shall revive, as is our trust,
'Twill be to be forgiven, or suffer what is just.

109

But let me quit man's works, again to read
His Maker's, spread around me, and suspend
This page, which from my reveries I feed,   1015
Until it seems prolonging without end.
The clouds above me to the white Alps tend,
And I must pierce them, and survey whate'er
May be permitted, as my steps I bend
To their most great and growing region, where   1020
The earth to her embrace compels the powers of air.

1. Voltaire.
2. The old man of the sea in Greek mythology, capable of changing his shape at will, referring here
   to the multifaceted genius of Voltaire.
3. Gibbon.
4. Like Voltaire, Gibbon held Christianity in contempt as a relic of superstition.

110

Italia! too, Italia! looking on thee,
Full flashes on the soul the light of ages,
Since the fierce Carthaginian[5] almost won thee,
To the last halo of the chiefs and sages   1025
Who glorify thy consecrated pages;
Thou wert the throne and grave of empires; still,
The fount at which the panting mind assuages
Her thirst of knowledge, quaffing there her fill,
Flows from the eternal source of Rome's imperial hill.   1030

111

Thus far have I proceeded in a theme
Renew'd with no kind auspices:—to feel
We are not what we have been, and to deem
We are not what we should be,—and to steel
The heart against itself; and to conceal,   1035
With a proud caution, love, or hate, or aught,—
Passion or feeling, purpose, grief, or zeal,—
Which is the tyrant spirit of our thought,
Is a stern task of soul:—No matter,—it is taught.

112

And for these words, thus woven into song,   1040
It may be that they are a harmless wile,—
The colouring of the scenes which fleet along,
Which I would seize, in passing, to beguile
My breast, or that of others, for a while.
Fame is the thirst of youth,—but I am not   1045
So young as to regard men's frown or smile,
As loss or guerdon[6] of a glorious lot;
I stood and stand alone,—remember'd or forgot.

113

I have not loved the world, nor the world me;
I have not flatter'd its rank breath, nor bow'd   1050
To its idolatries a patient knee,—
Nor coin'd my cheek to smiles,—nor cried aloud
In worship of an echo; in the crowd
They could not deem me one of such; I stood
Among them, but not of them; in a shroud   1055
Of thoughts which were not their thoughts, and still
        could,
Had I not filed[7] my mind, which thus itself subdued.

---

5. Hannibal (247–183 B.C.E.), Rome's most dangerous adversary in the Punic Wars with Carthage.
6. Reward.
7. "—'If it be thus, / For Banquo's issue have I *filed* my mind.'—*Macbeth* [3.1.65–66]." *filed*: defiled.

114

I have not loved the world, nor the world me,—
But let us part fair foes; I do believe,
Though I have found them not, that there may be   1060
Words which are things,—hopes which will not deceive,
And virtues which are merciful, nor weave
Snares for the failing: I would also deem
O'er others' griefs that some sincerely grieve;[8]
That two, or one, are almost what they seem,   1065
That goodness is no name, and happiness no dream.

115

My daughter! with thy name this song begun—
My daughter! with thy name thus much shall end—
I see thee not,—I hear thee not,—but none
Can be so wrapt in thee; thou art the friend   1070
To whom the shadows of far years extend:
Albeit my brow thou never should'st behold,
My voice shall with thy future visions blend,
And reach into thy heart,—when mine is cold,—
A token and a tone, even from thy father's mould.   1075

116

To aid thy mind's development,—to watch
Thy dawn of little joys,—to sit and see
Almost thy very growth,—to view thee catch
Knowledge of objects,—wonders yet to thee!
To hold thee lightly on a gentle knee,   1080
And print on thy soft cheek a parent's kiss,—
This, it should seem, was not reserved for me;
Yet this was in my nature:—as it is,
I know not what is there, yet something like to this.

117

Yet, though dull Hate as duty should be taught,   1085
I know that thou wilt love me; though my name
Should be shut from thee, as a spell still fraught
With desolation,—and a broken claim:
Though the grave closed between us,—'twere the same,
I know that thou wilt love me; though to drain   1090
My blood from out thy being were an aim,
And an attainment,—all would be in vain,—
Still thou would'st love me, still that more than life retain.

---

8. "It is said by Rochefoucault, that 'there is always something in the misfortunes of men's best friends not displeasing to them.'" In *Réflections ou Maximes Morales* (1665).

118

The child of love,—though born in bitterness
And nurtured in convulsion,—of thy sire   1095
These were the elements,—and thine no less.
As yet such are around thee,—but thy fire
Shall be more temper'd, and thy hope far higher.
Sweet be thy cradled slumbers! O'er the sea,
And from the mountains where I now respire,   1100
Fain would I waft such blessing upon thee,
As, with a sigh, I deem thou might'st have been to me!

THE PRISONER OF CHILLON

A FABLE[1]

Sonnet on Chillon

Eternal Spirit of the chainless Mind!
Brightest in dungeons, Liberty! thou art,
For there thy habitation is the heart—
The heart which love of thee alone can bind;
And when thy sons to fetters are consign'd—   5

---

1. Written in Switzerland during the summer of 1816, after Byron and Shelley had visited the Castle of Chillon, and published by John Murray in *The Prisoner of Chillon and Other Poems* on December 5. The poem is a dramatic monologue spoken by François Bonivard (1493–1570), a Genevese priest and patriot who had been imprisoned in the Castle's dungeon for six years by Duke Charles III of Savoy. Especially in the prefatory sonnet, written after he completed the tale, Byron casts Bonivard as a martyr to the cause of political liberty, though some historians' accounts of Bonivard modify Byron's idealized view of him. The poem forcefully and with considerable psychological realism depicts the experience of confinement and isolation. As in "Prometheus," the characteristic Byronic romanticism of *The Prisoner of Chillon* lies in the tragic triumph of the striving hero's humanity opposing the reactionary forces of power.
  Criticism: Manning, "The Sublime Self and the Single Voice (p. 898); see also: Amstel, "The True Story of the Prisoner of Chillon"; McGann, *Fiery Dust*; Rutherford, *Byron: A Critical Study*; Stafford, *The Last of the Race: the Growth of a Myth from Milton to Darwin*.
  Byron's note: "When this poem was composed, I was not sufficiently aware of the history of Bonnivard, or I should have endeavoured to dignify the subject by an attempt to celebrate his courage and his virtues. With some account of his life I have been furnished, by the kindness of a citizen of that republic, which is still proud of the memory of a man worthy of the best age of ancient freedom:—
  'François de Bonnivard, fils de Louis de Bonnivard, originaire de Seyssel et Seigneur de Lunes, naquit en 1496. Il fit ses études à Turin: en 1510 Jean Aimé de Bonnivard, son oncle, lui résigna le Prieuré de St. Victor, qui aboutissoit aux murs de Genève, et qui formoit un bénéfice considérable.
  'Ce grand homme—(Bonnivard mérite ce titre par la force de son âme, la droiture de son coeur, la noblesse de ses intentions, la sagesse de ses conseils, le courage de ses démarches, l'étendue de ses connaissances et la vivacité de son esprit),—ce grand homme, qui excitera l'admiration de tous ceux qu'une vertu héroïque peut encore émouvoir, inspirera encore la plus vive reconnaissance dans les coeurs des Génévois qui aiment Genève. Bonnivard en fut toujours un des plus fermes appuis: pour assurer la liberté de notre République, il ne craignit pas de perdre souvent la sienne; il oublia son repos; il méprisa ses richesses; il ne négligea rien pour affermir le bonheur d'une patrie qu'il honora de son choix: dès ce moment il la chérit comme le plus zélé de ses citoyens; il la servit avec l'intrépidité d'un héros, et il écrivit son Histoire avec la naïveté d'un philosophe et la chaleur d'un patriote.
  'Il dit dans le commencement de son Histoire de Genève, que, *dès qu'il eut commencé de lire l'histoire des nations, il se sentit entrainé par son goût pour les Républiques, dont il épousa toujours les intérêts*: c'est ce goût pour la liberté qui lui fit sans doute adopter Genève pour sa patrie.

To fetters, and the damp vault's dayless gloom,
Their country conquers with their martyrdom,
And Freedom's fame finds wings on every wind.
Chillon! thy prison is a holy place,
And thy sad floor an altar—for 'twas trod,   10
Until his very steps have left a trace
Worn, as if thy cold pavement were a sod,
By Bonnivard!—May none those marks efface!
For they appeal from tyranny to God.

1

My hair is grey, but not with years,
       Nor grew it white
       In a single night,[2]
As men's have grown from sudden fears:
My limbs are bow'd, though not with toil,   5
       But rusted with a vile repose,
For they have been a dungeon's spoil,
And mine has been the fate of those
To whom the goodly earth and air
Are bann'd, and barr'd—forbidden fare;   10
But this was for my father's faith
I suffer'd chains and courted death;
That father perish'd at the stake

'Bonnivard, encore jeune, s'annonça hautement comme le défenseur de Genève contre le Duc de Savoye et l'Evéque.

'En 1519, Bonnivard devient le martyr de sa patrie: Le Duc de Savoye étant entré dans Genève avec cinq cent hommes, Bonnivard craint le ressentiment du Duc; il voulut se retirer à Fribourg pour en éviter les suites; mais il fut trahi par deux hommes qui l'accompagnoient, et conduit par ordre du Prince à Grolée, où il resta prisonnier pendant deux ans. Bonnivard étoit malheureux dans ses voyages: comme ses malheurs n'avoient point ralenti son zèle pour Genève, il étoit toujours un ennemi redoutable pour ceux qui la menaçoient, et par conséquent il devoit être exposé à leurs coups. Il fut recontré en 1530 sur le Jura par des voleurs, qui le dépouillèrent, et qui le mirent encore entre les mains du Duc de Savoye: ce Prince le fit enfermer dans le Château de Chillon, où il resta sans être interrogé jusques en 1536; il fut alors delivré par les Bernois, qui s'emparèrent du Pays de Vaud.

'Bonnivard, en sortant de sa captivité, eut le plaisir de trouver Genève libre et réformée: la République s'empressa de lui témoigner sa reconnaissance, et de le dédommager des maux qu'il avoit soufferts; elle le reçut Bourgeois de la ville au mois de Juin, 1536; elle lui donna la maison habitée autrefois par le Vicaire-Général, et elle lui assigna une pension de deux cent écus d'or tant qu'il séjourneroit à Genève. Il fut admis dans le Conseil de Deux-Cent en 1537.

'Bonnivard n'a pas fini d'être utile: après avoir travaillé à rendre Genève libre, il réussit à la rendre tolérante. Bonnivard engagea le Conseil à accorder aux Ecclésiastiques et aux paysans un tems suffisant pour examiner les propositions qu'on leur faisoit; il réussit par sa douceur: on prêche toujours le Christianisme avec succès quand on le prêche avec charité.

'Bonnivard fut savant: ses manuscrits, qui sont dans la Bibliothèque publique, prouvent qu'il avoit bien lu les auteurs classiques Latins, et qu'il avoit approfondi la théologie et l'histoire. Ce grand homme aimoit les sciences, et il croyoit qu'elles pouvoient faire la gloire de Genève; aussi il ne négligea rien pour les fixer dans cette ville naissante; en 1551 il donna sa bibliothèque au public; elle fut le commencement de notre bibliothèque publique; et ces livres sont en partie les rares et belles éditions du quinzième siècle qu'on voit dans notre collection. Enfin, pendant la même année, ce bon patriote institua la République son héritière, à condition qu'elle employeroit ses biens à entretenir le collège dont on projettoit la fondation.

'Il paroit que Bonnivard mourut en 1570; mais on ne peut l'assurer, parcequ'il y a une lacune dans le Nécrologe depuis le mois de Juillet, 1570, jusques en 1571.' "

2. "Ludovico Sforza, and others.—The same is asserted of Marie Antoinette's, the wife of Louis the Sixteenth, though not in quite so short a period. Grief is said to have the same effect: to such, and not to fear, this change in *hers* was to be attributed."

For tenets he would not forsake;
And for the same his lineal race   15
In darkness found a dwelling-place;
We were seven—who now are one,
   Six in youth, and one in age,[3]
Finish'd as they had begun,
   Proud of Persecution's rage;   20
One in fire, and two in field,
Their belief with blood have seal'd:
Dying as their father died,
For the God their foes denied;—
Three were in a dungeon cast,   25
Of whom this wreck is left the last.

2

There are seven pillars of Gothic mould,
In Chillon's dungeons deep and old,
There are seven columns, massy and grey,
Dim with a dull imprison'd ray,   30
A sunbeam which hath lost its way,
And through the crevice and the cleft
Of the thick wall is fallen and left;
Creeping o'er the floor so damp,
Like a marsh's meteor lamp: 35
And in each pillar there is a ring,
   And in each ring there is a chain;
That iron is a cankering thing,
   For in these limbs its teeth remain,
With marks that will not wear away,   40
Till I have done with this new day,
Which now is painful to these eyes,
Which have not seen the sun so rise
For years—I cannot count them o'er,
I lost their long and heavy score   45
When my last brother droop'd and died,
And I lay living by his side.

3

They chain'd us each to a column stone,
And we were three—yet, each alone;
We could not move a single pace,   50
We could not see each other's face,
But with that pale and livid light
That made us strangers in our sight:
And thus together—yet apart,
Fetter'd in hand, but pined in heart;   55
'Twas still some solace, in the dearth

---

3. The historical Bonivard had only two brothers, neither of whom (contrary to Byron's tale) seems to have shared his imprisonment.

Of the pure elements of earth,
To hearken to each other's speech,
And each turn comforter to each
With some new hope or legend old,   60
Or song heroically bold;
But even these at length grew cold.
Our voices took a dreary tone,
An echo of the dungeon stone,
    A grating sound—not full and free   65
    As they of yore were wont to be:
    It might be fancy—but to me
They never sounded like our own.

4

I was the eldest of the three,
    And to uphold and cheer the rest   70
    I ought to do—and did my best—
And each did well in his degree.
    The youngest, whom my father loved,
Because our mother's brow was given
To him—with eyes as blue as heaven,   75
    For him my soul was sorely moved:
And truly might it be distress'd
To see such bird in such a nest;
For he was beautiful as day—
    (When day was beautiful to me   80
    As to young eagles, being free)—
    A polar day, which will not see
A sunset till its summer's gone,
    Its sleepless summer of long light,
The snow-clad offspring of the sun: 85
    And thus he was as pure and bright,
And in his natural spirit gay,
With tears for nought but others' ills,
And then they flow'd like mountain rills,
Unless he could assuage the woe   90
Which he abhorr'd to view below.

5

The other was as pure of mind,
But form'd to combat with his kind;
Strong in his frame, and of a mood
Which 'gainst the world in war had stood,   95
And perish'd in the foremost rank
    With joy:—but not in chains to pine:
His spirit wither'd with their clank,
    I saw it silently decline—
    And so perchance in sooth did mine: 100
But yet I forced it on to cheer
Those relics of a home so dear.

He was a hunter of the hills,
  Had follow'd there the deer and wolf;
  To him this dungeon was a gulf,   105
And fetter'd feet the worst of ills.

6

Lake Leman[4] lies by Chillon's walls:
A thousand feet in depth below
Its massy waters meet and flow;
Thus much the fathom-line was sent   110
From Chillon's snow-white battlement,[5]
  Which round about the wave inthrals:
  A double dungeon wall and wave
Have made—and like a living grave.
Below the surface of the lake[6]   115
The dark vault lies wherein we lay,
We heard it ripple night and day;
  Sounding o'er our heads it knock'd;
And I have felt the winter's spray
Wash through the bars when winds were high   120
And wanton in the happy sky;
  And then the very rock hath rock'd,
  And I have felt it shake, unshock'd,
Because I could have smiled to see
The death that would have set me free.   125

7

I said my nearer brother pined,
I said his mighty heart declined,
He loathed and put away his food;
It was not that 'twas coarse and rude,
For we were used to hunter's fare,   130
And for the like had little care:
The milk drawn from the mountain goat
Was changed for water from the moat,
Our bread was such as captive's tears
Have moisten'd many a thousand years,   135
Since man first pent his fellow men

4. Lake Geneva.
5. "The Château de Chillon is situated between Clarens and Villeneuve, which last is at one extremity of the Lake of Geneva. On its left are the entrances of the Rhone, and opposite are the heights of Meillerie and the range of Alps above Boveret and St. Gingo. Near it, on a hill behind, is a torrent: below it, washing its walls, the lake has been fathomed to the depth of 800 feet, French measure: within it are a range of dungeons, in which the early reformers, and subsequently prisoners of state, were confined. Across one of the vaults is a beam black with age, on which we were informed that the condemned were formerly executed. In the cells are seven pillars, or, rather, eight, one being half merged in the wall; in some of these are rings for the fetters and the fettered: in the pavement the steps of Bonnivard have left their traces. He was confined here several years. It is by this castle that Rousseau has fixed the catastrophe of his Héloïse, in the rescue of one of her children by Julie from the water; the shock of which, and the illness produced by the immersion, is the cause of her death. The château is large, and seen along the lake for a great distance. The walls are white."
6. The vault was not, in fact, "below the surface of the lake."

Like brutes within an iron den;
But what were these to us or him?
These wasted not his heart or limb;
My brother's soul was of that mould   140
Which in a palace had grown cold,
Had his free breathing been denied
The range of the steep mountain's side;
But why delay the truth?—he died.
I saw, and could not hold his head,   145
Nor reach his dying hand—nor dead,—
Though hard I strove, but strove in vain,
To rend and gnash my bonds in twain.
He died—and they unlock'd his chain,
And scoop'd for him a shallow grave   150
Even from the cold earth of our cave.
I begg'd them, as a boon, to lay
His corse in dust whereon the day
Might shine—it was a foolish thought,
But then within my brain it wrought,   155
That even in death his freeborn breast
In such a dungeon could not rest.
I might have spared my idle prayer—
They coldly laugh'd—and laid him there:
The flat and turfless earth above   160
The being we so much did love;
His empty chain above it leant,
Such murder's fitting monument!

8

But he, the favourite and the flower,
Most cherish'd since his natal hour,   165
His mother's image in fair face,
The infant love of all his race,
His martyr'd father's dearest thought,
My latest care, for whom I sought
To hoard my life, that his might be   170
Less wretched now, and one day free;
He, too, who yet had held untired
A spirit natural or inspired—
He, too, was struck, and day by day
Was wither'd on the stalk away.   175
Oh, God! it is a fearful thing
To see the human soul take wing
In any shape, in any mood:—
I've seen it rushing forth in blood,
I've seen it on the breaking ocean   180
Strive with a swoln convulsive motion,
I've seen the sick and ghastly bed
Of Sin delirious with its dread:
But these were horrors—this was woe

Unmix'd with such—but sure and slow: 185
He faded, and so calm and meek,
So softly worn, so sweetly weak,
So tearless, yet so tender—kind,
And grieved for those he left behind;
With all the while a cheek whose bloom   190
Was as a mockery of the tomb,
Whose tints as gently sunk away
As a departing rainbow's ray—
An eye of most transparent light,
That almost made the dungeon bright,   195
And not a word of murmur—not
A groan o'er his untimely lot,—
A little talk of better days,
A little hope my own to raise,
For I was sunk in silence—lost   200
In this last loss, of all the most;
And then the sighs he would suppress
Of fainting nature's feebleness,
More slowly drawn, grew less and less:
I listen'd, but I could not hear—   205
I call'd, for I was wild with fear;
I knew 'twas hopeless, but my dread
Would not be thus admonished;
I call'd, and thought I heard a sound—
I burst my chain with one strong bound,   210
And rush'd to him:—I found him not,
I only stirr'd in this black spot,
I only lived—*I* only drew
The accursed breath of dungeon-dew;
The last—the sole—the dearest link   215
Between me and the eternal brink,
Which bound me to my failing race,
Was broken in this fatal place.
One on the earth, and one beneath—
My brothers—both had ceased to breathe: 220
I took that hand which lay so still,
Alas! my own was full as chill;
I had not strength to stir, or strive,
But felt that I was still alive—
A frantic feeling, when we know   225
That what we love shall ne'er be so.
   I know not why
   I could not die,[7]
I had no earthly hope—but faith,
And that forbade a selfish death.   230

---

7. Cf. Coleridge's *Rime of the Ancient Mariner*, Part 4, line 262: "And yet I could not die." Byron greatly admired Coleridge's poem, and various passages in *Prisoner* (e.g., 13.351–65 and 14.381–88) recall the imagery and language of Part 4 of the *Rime*, in which the Mariner's spell of desolation is described and then lifted.

9

What next befell me then and there
   I know not well—I never knew—
First came the loss of light, and air,
   And then of darkness too:
I had no thought, no feeling—none—   235
Among the stones I stood a stone,
And was, scarce conscious what I wist,
As shrubless crags within the mist;
For all was blank, and bleak, and grey,
It was not night—it was not day,   240
It was not even the dungeon-light,
So hateful to my heavy sight,
But vacancy absorbing space,
And fixedness—without a place;
There were no stars—no earth—no time—   245
No check—no change—no good—no crime—
But silence, and a stirless breath
Which neither was of life nor death;
A sea of stagnant idleness,
Blind, boundless, mute, and motionless!   250

10

A light broke in upon my brain,—
   It was the carol of a bird;
It ceased, and then it came again,
   The sweetest song ear ever heard,
And mine was thankful till my eyes   255
Ran over with the glad surprise,
And they that moment could not see
I was the mate of misery;
But then by dull degrees came back
My senses to their wonted track,   260
I saw the dungeon walls and floor
Close slowly round me as before,
I saw the glimmer of the sun
Creeping as it before had done,
But through the crevice where it came   265
That bird was perch'd, as fond and tame,
   And tamer than upon the tree;
A lovely bird, with azure wings,
And song that said a thousand things,
   And seem'd to say them all for me!   270
I never saw its like before,
I ne'er shall see its likeness more:
It seem'd like me to want a mate,
But was not half so desolate,
And it was come to love me when   275
None lived to love me so again,

And cheering from my dungeon's brink,
Had brought me back to feel and think.
I know not if it late were free,
   Or broke its cage to perch on mine,   280
But knowing well captivity,
   Sweet bird! I could not wish for thine!
Or if it were, in winged guise,
A visitant from Paradise;
For—Heaven forgive that thought! the while   285
Which made me both to weep and smile;
I sometimes deem'd that it might be
My brother's soul come down to me;
But then at last away it flew,
And then 'twas mortal—well I knew,   290
For he would never thus have flown,
And left me twice so doubly lone,—
Lone—as the corse within its shroud,
Lone—as a solitary cloud,
   A single cloud on a sunny day,   295
While all the rest of heaven is clear,
A frown upon the atmosphere,
That hath no business to appear
   When skies are blue, and earth is gay.

11

A kind of change came in my fate,   300
My keepers grew compassionate;
I know not what had made them so,
They were inured to sights of woe,
But so it was:—my broken chain
With links unfasten'd did remain,   305
And it was liberty to stride
Along my cell from side to side,
And up and down, and then athwart,
And tread it over every part;
And round the pillars one by one,   310
Returning where my walk begun,
Avoiding only, as I trod,
My brothers' graves without a sod;
For if I thought with heedless tread
My step profaned their lowly bed,   315
My breath came gaspingly and thick,
And my crush'd heart fell blind and sick.

12

I made a footing in the wall,
   It was not therefrom to escape,
For I had buried one and all   320
   Who loved me in a human shape;

And the whole earth would henceforth be
A wider prison unto me:
No child—no sire—no kin had I,
No partner in my misery;   325
I thought of this, and I was glad,
For thought of them had made me mad;
But I was curious to ascend
To my barr'd windows, and to bend
Once more, upon the mountains high,   330
The quiet of a loving eye.

13

I saw them—and they were the same,
They were not changed like me in frame;
I saw their thousand years of snow
On high—their wide long lake below,   335
And the blue Rhone in fullest flow;
I heard the torrents leap and gush
O'er channell'd rock and broken bush;
I saw the white-wall'd distant town,[9]
And whiter sails go skimming down;   340
And then there was a little isle,[1]
Which in my very face did smile,
       The only one in view;
A small green isle, it seem'd no more,
Scarce broader than my dungeon floor,   345
But in it there were three tall trees,
And o'er it blew the mountain breeze,
And by it there were waters flowing,
And on it there were young flowers growing,
       Of gentle breath and hue.   350
The fish swam by the castle wall,
And they seem'd joyous each and all;
The eagle rode the rising blast,
Methought he never flew so fast
As then to me he seem'd to fly,   355
And then new tears came in my eye,
And I felt troubled—and would fain
I had not left my recent chain;
And when I did descend again,
The darkness of my dim abode   360
Fell on me as a heavy load;
It was as is a new-dug grave,
Closing o'er one we sought to save,—

---

9. "Between the entrances of the Rhone and Villeneuve, not far from Chillon, is a very small island;
the only one I could perceive, in my voyage round and over the lake, within its circumference. It
contains a few trees (I think not above three), and from its singleness and diminutive size has a
peculiar effect upon the view."
1. Villeneuve, according to Byron's notes; McGann suggests "the white-walled distant town" is, rather,
St. Gingolph or Meillerie (*CPW* 4:453).

And yet my glance, too much oppress'd,
Had almost need of such a rest.   365

14

It might be months, or years, or days,
    I kept no count—I took no note,
I had no hope my eyes to raise,
    And clear them of their dreary mote;
At last men came to set me free,[2]   370
    I ask'd not why, and reck'd not where,
It was at length the same to me,
Fetter'd or fetterless to be,
    I learn'd to love despair.
And thus when they appear'd at last,   375
And all my bonds aside were cast,
These heavy walls to me had grown
A hermitage—and all my own!
And half I felt as they were come
To tear me from a second home: 380
With spiders I had friendship made,
And watch'd them in their sullen trade,
Had seen the mice by moonlight play,
And why should I feel less than they?
We were all inmates of one place,   385
And I, the monarch of each race,
Had power to kill—yet, strange to tell!
In quiet we had learn'd to dwell—[3]
My very chains and I grew friends,
So much a long communion tends   390
To make us what we are:—even I
Regain'd my freedom with a sigh.

Prometheus[1]

1

Titan! to whose immortal eyes
    The sufferings of mortality,
    Seen in their sad reality,
Were not as things that gods despise;

2. Bonivard was liberated by the Bernese in 1536.
3. After line 388, CPW restores the following two lines from the poem's manuscripts: "Nor slew I of
    my subjects one, / What Sovereign hath so little done?" These lines were dropped in the first edi-
    tion without Byron's authorization and undoubtedly because of the political conservatism of Gif-
    ford, the poem's editor. Byron, however (though without having seen the printed poem), seems to
    have accepted that "a line or so" was excised by Gifford (BLJ 5:169).
1. Written in July or early August 1816 and published on December 5 in The Prisoner of Chillon and
    Other Poems. Prometheus, greatest of the Titans of classical mythology, first gave man the gift of
    fire, stealing it from the Olympian gods. To punish him and to coerce from him the secret of the
    gods' eventual defeat, which Prometheus (whose name means "forethought") knew, Zeus ("the Thun-
    derer" [line 26]) chained him to a mountain in the Caucasus where, every day, a vulture tore his
    flesh and feasted on his liver, which grew back during the night. He never capitulated and was even-
    tually liberated by Hercules. Prometheus, who since ancient Greece has symbolized the great rebel

What was thy pity's recompense?   5
A silent suffering, and intense;
The rock, the vulture, and the chain,
All that the proud can feel of pain,
The agony they do not show,
The suffocating sense of woe,   10
    Which speaks but in its loneliness,
And then is jealous lest the sky
Should have a listener, nor will sigh
Until its voice is echoless.

2

Titan! to thee the strife was given   15
    Between the suffering and the will,
    Which torture where they cannot kill;
And the inexorable Heaven,
And the deaf tyranny of Fate,
The ruling principle of Hate,   20
Which for its pleasure doth create
The things it may annihilate,
Refused thee even the boon to die:
The wretched gift eternity
Was thine—and thou hast borne it well.   25
All that the Thunderer wrung from thee
Was but the menace which flung back
On him the torments of thy rack;
The fate thou didst so well foresee,
But would not to appease him tell;   30
And in thy Silence was his Sentence,
And in his Soul a vain repentance,
And evil dread so ill dissembled,
That in his hand the lightnings trembled.

3

Thy Godlike crime was to be kind,   35
    To render with thy precepts less
    The sum of human wretchedness,
And strengthen Man with his own mind;
And baffled as thou wert from high,
Still in thy patient energy,   40

---

against injustice and implacable power, became for the Romantics the archetype of the visionary, revolutionary mind, "the type of the highest perfection of moral and intellectual nature, impelled by the purest and the truest motives to the best and noblest ends" (Shelley, Preface to *Prometheus Unbound*). The Prometheus myth held a central interest for Byron, as he acknowledged to Murray: "Of the Prometheus of Aeschylus I was passionately fond as a boy—(it was one of the Greek plays we read thrice a year at Harrow) . . . [it] has always been so much in my head—that I can easily conceive its influence over all or anything that I have written" (BLJ 5:268; see also *Childe Harold* IV, stanza 163 (p. 342), "The Prophecy of Dante" 4. 10–19, and "From the Prometheus Vinctus of Aeschylus"). For a feminist reevaluation of this tragic overreacher, see *Frankenstein: or the Modern Prometheus*, begun by Mary Shelley during the same summer of 1816, when she and Percy Shelley were regular visitors of Byron's at the Villa Diodati.
    Criticism: Clubbe, "The New Prometheus of New Men"; Goslee, "Pure Stream from a Troubled Source: Byron, Schlegel, and 'Prometheus.' "

In the endurance, and repulse
　Of thine impenetrable Spirit,
Which Earth and Heaven could not convulse,
　A mighty lesson we inherit:
Thou art a symbol and a sign   45
　To Mortals of their fate and force;
Like thee, Man is in part divine,
　A troubled stream from a pure source;
And Man in portions can foresee
His own funereal destiny;   50
His wretchedness, and his resistance,
And his sad unallied existence:
To which his Spirit may oppose
Itself—an² equal to all woes,
　And a firm will, and a deep sense,   55
Which even in torture can descry
　Its own concenter'd recompense,
Triumphant where it dares defy,
And making Death a Victory.

　　　　　　　　　　Diodati, July, 1816.

Epistle to Augusta¹

1

My Sister—my sweet Sister—if a name
　Dearer and purer were—it should be thine.
Mountains and seas divide us—but I claim
　No tears—but tenderness to answer mine:
Go where I will, to me thou art the same—   5
　A loved regret which I would not resign.
There yet are two things in my destiny,—
　A world to roam through—and a home with thee.

2

The first were nothing—had I still the last,
　It were the haven of my happiness—   10

---

2. and (1832).
1. Having left England in self-imposed exile in April 1816 amid the scandal surrounding his marital
　separation and rumors of his affair with his half-sister, Augusta Leigh, Byron wrote the "Epistle to
　Augusta" that summer. However, he told his publisher not to publish the poem without Augusta's
　approval, which she withheld, and so it was not published until 1830 in Moore's *Life*. "Epistle to
　Augusta" is the first of Byron's poems in the *ottava rima* stanza, typically associated with his comic
　masterpieces, *Beppo*, *Don Juan*, and *The Vision of Judgment*.
　　Textual Note: Life was the basis for *1832* and all subsequent printings of the poem prior to *CPW*,
　which is based on Byron's draft manuscript (*CPW* 4:35–40, 458). For the Norton Critical Edition,
　1832 has been compared with the manuscript, *CPW*, and *More*. Wording from the manuscript has
　been restored, and variants in *1832* or *CPW* are given in footnotes.

But other claims and other ties thou hast—
And mine is not the wish to make them less.
A strange doom was thy father's son's[2] and past
Recalling—as it lies beyond redress;
Reversed for him our grandsire's[3] fate of yore,—   15
He had no rest at sea—nor I on shore.

3

If my inheritance of storms hath been
In other elements—and on the rocks
Of perils overlook'd or unforeseen
I have sustain'd my share of worldly shocks,   20
The fault was mine—nor do I seek to screen
My errors with defensive paradox;
I have been cunning in mine overthrow,
The careful pilot of my proper woe.

4

Mine were my faults—and mine be their reward.   25
My whole life was a contest—since the day
That gave me being gave me that which marr'd
The gift—a fate or will that walk'd astray;[4]
And I at times have found the struggle hard—
And thought of shaking off my bonds of clay—   30
But now I fain would for a time survive
If but to see what next can well arrive.

5

Kingdoms and empires in my little day
I have outlived, and yet I am not old;
And when I look on this, the petty spray   35
Of my own years of trouble, which have roll'd
Like a wild bay of breakers, melts away:
Something—I know not what—does still uphold
A spirit of slight patience;—not in vain,
Even for its own sake, do we purchase pain.   40

6

Perhaps—the workings of defiance stir
Within me,—or perhaps a cold despair—

---

2. I.e., Byron's; Byron and Augusta were children of the same father by different wives; *was*: is (1832).
3. "Admiral Byron was remarkable for never making a voyage without a tempest. He was known to the sailors by the facetious name of 'Foul-weather Jack.' . . .

> 'But, though it were tempest-toss'd,
> Still his bark could not be lost.'

He returned safely from the wreck of the Wager (in Anson's Voyage), and subsequently circumnavigated the world, many years after, as commander of a similar expedition."
4. Literally, as Byron related the deformity of his foot, which gave him a limping gait and caused him intense embarrassment, to his sense of predestined damnation.

Brought on when ills habitually recur,—
   Perhaps a kinder clime—or purer air
(For to all such[5] may change of soul refer—   45
   And with light armour we may learn to bear)
Have taught me a strange quiet, which was not
The chief companion of a calmer lot.

7

I feel almost at times as I have felt
   In happy childhood; trees and flowers and brooks,   50
Which do remember me of where I dwelt
   Ere my young mind was sacrificed to books,
Come as of yore upon me—and can melt
   My heart with recognition of their looks—
And even at moments I could think I see   55
Some living things[6] to love—but none like thee.

8

Here are the Alpine landscapes—which create
   A fund for contemplation;—to admire
Is a brief feeling of a trivial date—
   But something worthier do such scenes inspire: 60
Here to be lonely is not desolate—
   For much I view which I could most desire—
And above all a lake I can behold—
Lovelier—not dearer—than our own of old.[7]

9

Oh that thou wert but with me!—but I grow   65
   The fool of my own wishes—and forget
The solitude which I have vaunted so
   Has lost its praise in this but one regret;
There may be others which I less may show;—
   I am not of the plaintive mood—and yet   70
I feel an ebb in my philosophy,
And the tide rising in my alter'd eye.

10

I did remind thee of our own dear lake,
   By the old Hall which may be mine no more.
Leman's is fair—but think not I forsake   75
   The sweet remembrance of a dearer shore:
Sad havoc Time must with my memory make
   Ere that or thou can fade these eyes before—

---

5. *to all such*: even to this (*1832*).
6. thing (*1832*).
7. Byron's view of Lake Geneva, also called Lake Leman (line 75), reminds him of the lake at Newstead Abbey.

Though like all things which I have loved—they are
Resign'd for ever—or divided far.— — —   80

11

The world is all before me—I but ask
   Of Nature that with which she will comply—
It is but in her summer's sun to bask—
   To mingle in[8] the quiet of her sky—
To see her gentle face without a mask   85
   And never gaze on it with apathy.
She was my early friend—and now shall be
My Sister—till I look again on thee.

12

I can reduce all feelings but this one
   And that I would not—for at length I see   90
Such scenes as those wherein my life begun,
   The earliest—were[9] the only paths for me.
Had I but sooner known[1] the crowd to shun
   I had been better than I now can be;
The passions which have torn me would have slept—   95
I had not suffer'd—and thou hadst not wept.

13

With false ambition what had I to do?
   Little with love, and least of all with fame;
And yet they came unsought and with me grew,
   And made me all which they can make—a Name.   100
Yet this was not the end I did pursue—
   Surely I once beheld a nobler aim.
But all is over—I am one the more
To baffled millions which have gone before.

14

And for the future—this world's future may   105
   From me demand but little of[2] my care;
I have outlived myself by many a day,
   Having survived so many things that were;
My years have been no slumber—but the prey
   Of ceaseless vigils; for I had the share   110
Of life which might have fill'd a century,
Before its fourth in time had pass'd me by.

8. with (1832).
9. even (1832).
1. learnt (1832).
2. from (CPW).

15

And for the remnants³ which may be to come
 I am content—and for the past I feel
Not thankless,—for within the crowded sum   115
 Of struggles, happiness at times would steal;
And for the present—I would not benumb
 My feelings farther.—Nor shall I conceal
That with all this I still can look around
And worship Nature with a thought profound.   120

16

For thee—my own sweet Sister!—in thy heart
 I know myself secure—as thou in mine;
We were and are—I am—even as thou art—
 Beings who ne'er each other can resign;
It is the same, together or apart—   125
 From life's commencement to its slow decline—
We are entwined;—let death come slow or fast—
The tie which bound the first endures the last.

Darkness¹

I had a dream, which was not all a dream.
The bright sun was extinguish'd, and the stars
Did wander darkling in the eternal space,
Rayless, and pathless, and the icy earth
Swung blind and blackening in the moonless air;   5
Morn came and went—and came, and brought no day,
And men forgot their passions in the dread
Of this their desolation; and all hearts
Were chill'd into a selfish prayer for light:
And they did live by watchfires—and the thrones,   10
The palaces of crowned kings—the huts,
The habitations of all things which dwell,
Were burnt for beacons; cities were consumed,
And men were gather'd round their blazing homes
To look once more into each other's face;   15
Happy were those who dwelt within the eye
Of the volcanos, and their mountain-torch:
A fearful hope was all the world contain'd;
Forests were set on fire—but hour by hour
They fell and faded—and the crackling trunks   20
Extinguish'd with a crash—and all was black.

---

3. remnant (1832).
1. Written in the summer of 1816 and published on December 5 in *The Prisoner of Chillon and Other Poems*. "Darkness" was probably inspired by *The Last Man* (1806), a translation of a French novel by Cousin de Grainville, though its theme, the end of human life on earth, is one that caught the imagination of many Romantic and later-nineteenth-century writers. On the poem's sources and echoes, see *CPW* 4:459–60 and R. J. Dingley, "'I had a dream.'"

The brows of men by the despairing light
Wore an unearthly aspect, as by fits
The flashes fell upon them; some lay down
And hid their eyes and wept; and some did rest   25
Their chins upon their clenched hands, and smiled;
And others hurried to and fro, and fed
Their funeral piles with fuel, and look'd up
With mad disquietude on the dull sky,
The pall of a past world; and then again   30
With curses cast them down upon the dust,
And gnash'd their teeth and howl'd: the wild birds shriek'd,
And, terrified, did flutter on the ground,
And flap their useless wings; the wildest brutes
Came tame and tremulous; and vipers crawl'd   35
And twined themselves among the multitude,
Hissing, but stingless—they were slain for food:
And War, which for a moment was no more,
Did glut himself again;—a meal was bought
With blood, and each sate sullenly apart   40
Gorging himself in gloom: no love was left;
All earth was but one thought—and that was death,
Immediate and inglorious; and the pang
Of famine fed upon all entrails—men
Died, and their bones were tombless as their flesh;   45
The meagre by the meagre were devour'd,
Even dogs assail'd their masters, all save one,
And he was faithful to a corse, and kept
The birds and beasts and famish'd men at bay,
Till hunger clung² them, or the dropping dead   50
Lured their lank jaws; himself sought out no food,
But with a piteous and perpetual moan,
And a quick desolate cry, licking the hand
Which answer'd not with a caress—he died.
The crowd was famish'd by degrees; but two   55
Of an enormous city did survive,
And they were enemies; they met beside
The dying embers of an altar-place
Where had been heap'd a mass of holy things
For an unholy usage; they raked up,   60
And shivering scraped with their cold skeleton hands
The feeble ashes, and their feeble breath
Blew for a little life, and made a flame
Which was a mockery; then they lifted up
Their eyes as it grew lighter, and beheld   65
Each other's aspects—saw, and shriek'd, and died—
Even of their mutual hideousness they died,
Unknowing who he was upon whose brow
Famine had written Fiend. The world was void,
The populous and the powerful—was a lump,   70

---

2. Shriveled (obsolete usage but echoing Shakespeare, "Till famine cling thee" [*Macbeth* 5.5.38]).

Seasonless, herbless, treeless, manless, lifeless—
A lump of death—a chaos of hard clay.
The rivers, lakes, and ocean all stood still,
And nothing stirr'd within their silent depths;
Ships sailorless lay rotting on the sea,   75
And their masts fell down piecemeal; as they dropp'd
They slept on the abyss without a surge—
The waves were dead; the tides were in their grave,
The moon, their mistress, had expired before;
The winds were wither'd in the stagnant air,   80
And the clouds perish'd; Darkness had no need
Of aid from them—She was the Universe.

Diodati, July, 1816

MANFRED   Byron began *Manfred* in Switzerland in August 1816, finished
a first version in Venice in early 1817, and revised the play that spring. The orig-
inal version included two passages (a part of the Incantation in 1.1 and a lyric,
"Ashtaroth's Song") that were written years before, probably in late 1813, when
Byron first encountered Goethe's *Faust* and contemplated writing a "Witch
drama" (*CPW* 4:462). In 1816, inspired by bitter feelings about his wife, Byron
added stanzas five and six to the Incantation, which was published as a sepa-
rate poem in *The Prisoner of Chillon and Other Poems* (December 5, 1816).
Criticism of the original third act by Byron's editor, William Gifford, prompted
Byron to acknowledge that it was "d—d bad" and to revise it (*BLJ* 5:211). (For
the original version of the third act, see *CPW* 4: 467–71 or *Cochran*.) *Manfred*
was published on June 16, 1817.
    Manfred gives dramatic form to the personality, psychology, and moral and
metaphysical speculations of the Byronic hero. The familiar Byronic theme of
loss—of lost love, in particular—informs Manfred's tormented brooding over
the woman he has loved and says he has destroyed, Astarte. That their rela-
tionship was incestuous seems bound up with the cause of her death, and
though the way in which she died is never identified, it provides the mysterious
core of Manfred's guilt, alienation, and suicidal leanings.
    Manfred was begun during the same summer that Mary Godwin, who with
Percy Shelley was a frequent visitor of Byron's at the Villa Diodati on Lake
Geneva, began *Frankenstein*, and both works reflect some of the same influ-
ences: the grandly beautiful if forbidding Alpine scenery; Gothic literature, with
its theme of secret sin; the writers' personal guilt, turbulent emotions, and expe-
rience of ostracism, deriving from illicit romantic entanglements—i.e., Mary's
elopement with the then-married Percy Shelley and Byron's incestuous rela-
tionship with his half-sister, Augusta Leigh. That summer, Byron's friend, the
Gothic novelist, Matthew "Monk" Lewis had translated parts of Goethe's *Faust*
for him. Byron acknowledged the influence of *Faust* on *Manfred*, but that influ-
ence is chiefly apparent in Manfred's opening speech, which presents the pro-
tagonist as a philosopher and scientist who rues the ineffectuality of "the
wisdom of the world" (1.1.14) and turns to the supernatural. Yet Goethe was
only among the first to recognize that *Faust* was "completely formed anew" in
Manfred (*LJ* 5:506). For one thing, while Faust embraces first the devil and
then the redemption of Christianity, Manfred remains starkly self-reliant,
rejecting the power of any supernatural being, demonic or divine, over the indi-
vidual mind. This difference between the two works undoubtedly underlies the
emphatic preference expressed by the German existentialist philosopher
Friedrich Nietzsche for Byron's poem: "I must be profoundly related to Byron's

Manfred: all these abysses I found in myself . . . . I have no word, only a glance, for those who dare to pronounce the word 'Faust' in the presence of Manfred" (*Ecce Homo* [written 1888], translated by Walter Kaufmann [Vintage, 1969], p. 245). In fact, *Manfred* reflects the influence of various literary works and is filled with Shakespearean and biblical echoes (see *CPW* 4:465–67, *Cochran*, and Looper, *Byron and the Bible*).

Byron, however, when asked about the poem's origins, referred to the Alpine Journal he kept for Augusta (see pp. 286–91) and averred that "the *Staubach* & the *Jungfrau*—and something else—much more than Faustus" was the source of the drama (*BLJ* 7:113). This "something else" was his memories of Augusta and his bitter feelings over his separation from his wife—the autobiographical references in the poem that, when it was read in England, refueled the social scandal that had led to Byron's departure from England earlier that year. Thus, in *Manfred*, the moral myth of the flawed overreacher is transformed into something of a Romantic loco-descriptive lyric meditation and personal *cri de coeur*—a sort of anti-"Intimations Ode," in which our past years bring a perpetual curse. At the same time, Byron's clear sense of the poem's readers (the readers in England who would be aware of the poem's autobiographical references) undermines the "overheard" sincere Romantic style and superimposes on it what McGann identifies as the "equivocal style" ("Lord Byron and the Truth in Masquerade," p. 15) that bespeaks the "shut soul's hypocrisy" (1.1.245).

Although Byron had sat on the board of London's Drury Lane Theatre (with its capacity for spectacular scenery), *Manfred*, like all the other plays Byron wrote (*Marino Faliero* in 1820; *Cain, Sardanapalus, The Two Foscari and Heaven and Earth* in 1821; *Werner* and *The Deformed Transformed* in 1822), was not intended to be staged but, rather, as a closet drama. Perhaps unsurprisingly, then, nineteenth-century stagings resulted in certain bowdlerizations—so that at Covent Garden (1834) Astarte saved Manfred from the demons, and at Sadlers Wells (1863) Manfred was crushed by an avalanche. Of Byron's works, *Manfred* was one of the most widely translated and read throughout Europe during the nineteenth century. Symphonic interpretations of the play were composed by Robert Schumann (*Manfred Overture and Incidental Music*, 1862) and by Peter Ilych Tchaikovsky (*Manfred Symphony*, 1886). The excessive angst and morbid sensitivity of Byron's hero, moreover, proved irresistible to the great Victorian parodists Gilbert and Sullivan; in *Patience* (1881), among the numerous historical and fictional personalities who, taken together, comprise the character of the English army's Heavy Dragoon is a "little of Manfred (but not very much of him)."

Criticism: In this volume, see Manning, "The Sublime Self and the Single Voice" (p. 898) and Richardson, "Byron and the Theatre" (p. 920). See also: Butler, *Byron and Goethe*; Chew: *The Dramas of Lord Byron: A Critical Study*; Elledge, *Byron and the Dynamics of Metaphor*; Lovelace, *Astarte*; Martin, *Byron: A Poet Before His Public*; McGann, *Byron and Wordsworth* and "Lord Byron and the Truth in Masquerade"; Sperry, "Byron and the Meaning of Manfred"; Thorslev, *The Byronic Hero*.

MANFRED

A DRAMATIC POEM

> There are more things in heaven and earth, Horatio,
> Than are dreamt of in your philosophy.
> [Shakespeare, *Hamlet*, 1.5.168–69]

Dramatis Personae

Manfred
Chamois Hunter
Abbot of St. Maurice
Manuel
Herman

Witch of the Alps
Arimanes
Nemesis
The Destinies
Spirits, &c.

The Scene of the Drama is amongst the Higher Alps—partly in the Castle of Manfred, and partly in the Mountains.

Act 1

SCENE 1

MANFRED[1] *alone.—Scene, a Gothic Gallery.—Time, Midnight.*

MAN.   The lamp must be replenish'd, but even then
It will not burn so long as I must watch:
My slumbers—if I slumber—are not sleep,
But a continuance of enduring thought,
Which then I can resist not: in my heart   5
There is a vigil, and these eyes but close
To look within; and yet I live, and bear
The aspect and the form of breathing men.
But grief should be the instructor of the wise;
Sorrow is knowledge:[2] they who know the most   10
Must mourn the deepest o'er the fatal truth,
The Tree of Knowledge is not that of Life.[3]
Philosophy and science, and the springs[4]
Of wonder, and the wisdom of the world,

---

1. The name may come from Dante's *Purgatorio* (3.121–24), Horace Walpole's *The Castle of Otranto* (1764), and *Bertram, or the Castle of St. Aldobrand*, by Charles Maturin (1782–1824), a play that Byron admired and recommended for Drury Lane, where it was performed in May 1816.
2. Cf. Ecclesiastes 1.18: "For in much wisdom is much grief: and he that increaseth knowledge increaseth sorrow."
3. Cf. Genesis 2–3. After Adam and Eve ate from the forbidden tree of knowledge of good and evil, the Lord barred their way to the tree of life.
4. Lines 13–19 echo Goethe's *Faust*, as well as Christopher Marlowe's *Tragedy of Dr. Faustus* (1604).

I have essay'd, and in my mind there is   15
A power to make these subject to itself—
But they avail not: I have done men good,
And I have met with good even among men—
But this avail'd not: I have had my foes,
And none have baffled, many fallen before me—   20
But this avail'd not:—Good, or evil, life,
Powers, passions, all I see in other beings,
Have been to me as rain unto the sands,
Since that all-nameless hour. I have no dread,
And feel the curse to have no natural fear,   25
Nor fluttering throb, that beats with hopes or wishes,
Or lurking love of something on the earth.—
Now to my task.—
                          Mysterious Agency!
Ye spirits of the unbounded Universe!
Whom I have sought in darkness and in light—   30
Ye, who do compass earth about, and dwell
In subtler essence—ye, to whom the tops
Of mountains inaccessible are haunts,
And earth's and ocean's caves familiar things—
I call upon ye by the written charm   35
Which gives me power upon you—Rise! appear!
                          [*A pause.*]
They come not yet.—Now by the voice of him
Who is the first among you⁵—by this sign,
Which makes you tremble—by the claims of him
Who is undying,—Rise! appear!—Appear!   40
                          [*A pause.*]
If it be so.—Spirits of earth and air,
Ye shall not thus elude me: by a power,
Deeper than all yet urged, a tyrant-spell,
Which had its birthplace in a star condemn'd,
The burning wreck of a demolish'd world,   45
A wandering hell in the eternal space;
By the strong curse which is upon my soul,
The thought which is within me and around me,
I do compel ye to my will.—Appear!
     [*A star is seen at the darker end of the gallery: it is stationary; and a
     voice is heard singing.*]

FIRST SPIRIT.
     Mortal! to thy bidding bow'd,   50
     From my mansion in the cloud,
     Which the breath of twilight builds,
     And the summer's sunset gilds
     With the azure and vermilion,

5. In 2.4 the Spirits identify Arimanes as their master; the reference here, though, could signify God
or some Satanic power—or even Manfred himself—and its ambiguity is consistent with the effect
of mystery throughout the play.

Which is mix'd for my pavilion;   55
Though thy quest may be forbidden,
On a star-beam I have ridden;
To thine adjuration bow'd,
Mortal—be thy wish avow'd!

Voice of the SECOND SPIRIT.

Mont Blanc[6] is the monarch of mountains;   60
     They crown'd him long ago
On a throne of rocks, in a robe of clouds,
     With a diadem of snow.
Around his waist are forests braced,
     The Avalanche in his hand;   65
But ere it fall, that thundering ball
     Must pause for my command.
The Glacier's cold and restless mass
     Moves onward day by day;
But I am he who bids it pass,   70
     Or with its ice delay.
I am the spirit of the place,
     Could make the mountain bow
And quiver to his cavern'd base—
     And what with me wouldst *Thou?*   75

Voice of the THIRD SPIRIT.

In the blue depth of the waters,
     Where the wave hath no strife,
Where the wind is a stranger,
     And the sea-snake hath life,
Where the Mermaid is decking   80
     Her green hair with shells;
Like the storm on the surface
     Came the sound of thy spells;
O'er my calm Hall of Coral
     The deep echo roll'd—   85
To the Spirit of Ocean
     Thy wishes unfold!

FOURTH SPIRIT.

Where the slumbering earthquake
     Lies pillow'd on fire,
And the lakes of bitumen[7]   90
     Rise boilingly higher;
Where the roots of the Andes
     Strike deep in the earth,

---

6. On the border between France and Italy, the highest of the Alps mountains and a crucial scene for Romantic poetry. Percy Shelley's "Mont Blanc" (1816), Mary Shelley's *Frankenstein* (1818), and *Manfred* all utilize this impressive, glacier-capped peak in their contemplation of human striving against an alien, impassive cosmos.
7. Volcanic rock, here in its molten form.

As their summits to heaven
   Shoot soaringly forth;   95
I have quitted my birthplace,
   Thy bidding to bide—
Thy spell hath subdued me,
   Thy will be my guide!

FIFTH SPIRIT.

I am the Rider of the wind,   100
   The Stirrer of the storm;
The hurricane I left behind
   Is yet with lightning warm;
To speed to thee, o'er shore and sea
   I swept upon the blast: 105
The fleet I met sail'd well, and yet
   'Twill sink ere night be past.

SIXTH SPIRIT.

My dwelling is the shadow of the night,
Why doth thy magic torture me with light?

SEVENTH SPIRIT.

The star which rules thy destiny   110
Was ruled, ere earth began, by me:
It was a world as fresh and fair
As e'er revolved round sun in air;
Its course was free and regular,
Space bosom'd not a lovelier star.   115
The hour arrived—and it became
A wandering mass of shapeless flame,
A pathless comet, and a curse,
The menace of the universe;
Still rolling on with innate force,   120
Without a sphere, without a course,
A bright deformity on high,
The monster of the upper sky!
And thou! beneath its influence born—
Thou worm! whom I obey and scorn—   125
Forced by a power (which is not thine,
And lent thee but to make thee mine)
For this brief moment to descend,
Where these weak spirits round thee bend
And parley with a thing like thee—   130
What wouldst thou, Child of Clay! with me?

The SEVEN SPIRITS.

Earth, ocean, air, night, mountains, winds, thy star,
   Are at thy beck and bidding, Child of Clay!
Before thee at thy quest their spirits are—
   What wouldst thou with us, son of mortals—say?   135

MAN. Forgetfulness—
FIRST SPIRIT. Of what—of whom—and why?
MAN. Of that which is within me; read it there—
    Ye know it, and I cannot utter it.
SPIRIT. We can but give thee that which we possess:
    Ask of us subjects, sovereignty, the power   140
    O'er earth, the whole, or portion, or a sign
    Which shall control the elements, whereof
    We are the dominators, each and all,
    These shall be thine.
MAN. Oblivion, self-oblivion—
    Can ye not wring from out the hidden realms   145
    Ye offer so profusely what I ask?
SPIRIT. It is not in our essence, in our skill;
    But—thou mayst die.
MAN. Will death bestow it on me?
SPIRIT. We are immortal, and do not forget;
    We are eternal; and to us the past   150
    Is, as the future, present. Art thou answer'd?
MAN. Ye mock me—but the power which
      brought ye here
    Hath made you mine. Slaves, scoff not at my will!
    The mind, the spirit, the Promethean[8] spark,
    The lightning of my being, is as bright,   155
    Pervading, and far darting as your own,
    And shall not yield to yours, though coop'd in clay!
    Answer, or I will teach you what I am.
SPIRIT. We answer as we answer'd; our reply
    Is even in thine own words.
MAN. Why say ye so?   160
SPIRIT. If, as thou say'st, thine essence be as ours,
    We have replied in telling thee, the thing
    Mortals call death hath nought to do with us.
MAN. I then have call'd ye from your realms in vain;
    Ye cannot, or ye will not, aid me.
SPIRIT. Say;   165
    What we possess we offer; it is thine:
    Bethink ere thou dismiss us, ask again—
    Kingdom, and sway, and strength, and length of days——
MAN. Accursed! what have I to do with days?
    They are too long already.—Hence—begone!   170
SPIRIT. Yet pause: being here, our will would do thee service;
    Bethink thee, is there then no other gift
    Which we can make not worthless in thine eyes?
MAN. No, none: yet stay—one moment, ere we part—
    I would behold ye face to face. I hear   175
    Your voices, sweet and melancholy sounds,
    As music on the waters;[9] and I see

8. Divine or life-giving (cf. *Othello* 5.2.12); see note to "Prometheus" (p. 239).
9. Cf. "Stanzas to Music," lines 3–4 (p. 167).

The steady aspect of a clear large star;
But nothing more. Approach me as ye are,
Or one, or all, in your accustom'd forms.   180
SPIRIT.   We have no forms, beyond the elements
Of which we are the mind and principle:
But choose a form—in that we will appear.
MAN.   I have no choice; there is no form on earth
Hideous or beautiful to me. Let him,   185
Who is most powerful of ye, take such aspect
As unto him may seem most fitting—Come!
SEVENTH SPIRIT. (*Appearing in the shape of a beautiful female figure.*)[1]
                                              Behold!
MAN.   Oh God! if it be thus, and *thou*
Art not a madness and a mockery,
I yet might be most happy. I will clasp thee,   190
And we again will be——   [*The figure vanishes.*]
                    My heart is crush'd!
                              [MANFRED *falls senseless.*]

    (*A Voice is heard in the Incantation which follows.*)[2]

              When the moon is on the wave,
                And the glow-worm in the grass,
              And the meteor on the grave,
                And the wisp on the morass;   195
              When the falling stars are shooting,
              And the answer'd owls are hooting,
              And the silent leaves are still
              In the shadow of the hill,
              Shall my soul be upon thine,   200
              With a power and with a sign.

              Though thy slumber may be deep,
              Yet thy spirit shall not sleep;
              There are shades which will not vanish,
              There are thoughts thou canst not banish;   205
              By a power to thee unknown,
              Thou canst never be alone;
              Thou art wrapt as with a shroud,
              Thou art gather'd in a cloud;
              And for ever shalt thou dwell   210
              In the spirit of this spell.

              Though thou seest me not pass by,
              Thou shalt feel me with thine eye
              As a thing that, though unseen,
              Must be near thee, and hath been;   215
              And when in that secret dread
              Thou hast turn'd around thy head,

---

1. Astarte, the object of Manfred's love and guilt; Manfred describes her and their relationship in 2.2.104–21, and he conjures her presence in 2.4.82–156.
2. The Incantation (lines 192–261) was first published in 1816 (see headnote).

Thou shalt marvel I am not
As thy shadow on the spot,
And the power which thou dost feel   220
Shall be what thou must conceal.

And a magic voice and verse
Hath baptized thee with a curse;
And a spirit of the air
Hath begirt thee with a snare;   225
In the wind there is a voice
Shall forbid thee to rejoice;
And to thee shall Night deny
All the quiet of her sky;
And the day shall have a sun,   230
Which shall make thee wish it done.

From thy false tears I did distil[3]
An essence which hath strength to kill;
From thy own heart I then did wring
The black blood in its blackest spring;   235
From thy own smile I snatch'd the snake,
For there it coil'd as in a brake;
From thy own lip I drew the charm
Which gave all these their chiefest harm;
In proving every poison known,   240
I found the strongest was thine own.

By thy cold breast and serpent smile,
By thy unfathom'd gulfs of guile,
By that most seeming virtuous eye,[4]
By thy shut soul's hypocrisy;   245
By the perfection of thine art
Which pass'd for human thine own heart;
By thy delight in others' pain,
And by thy brotherhood of Cain,
I call upon thee! and compel   250
Thyself to be thy proper Hell![5]

And on thy head I pour the vial
Which doth devote thee to this trial;
Nor to slumber, nor to die,
Shall be in thy destiny;   255
Though thy death shall still seem near
To thy wish, but as a fear;
Lo! the spell now works around thee,
And the clankless chain hath bound thee;

3. Lines 232–51, added to an earlier version of the Incantation, were written with Lady Byron in mind. Of interest is the fact that the bitter charges Byron directed toward his wife are in the context of the play directed at Manfred, Byron's alter ego.
4. Cf. "most seeming-virtuous queen" (*Hamlet* 1.5.46).
5. Cf. *Paradise Lost* 4.75: "Which way I fly is Hell; myself am Hell"; also cf. *Childe Harold* I, "To Inez," stanza 6 (p. 52).

O'er thy heart and brain together   260
Hath the word been pass'd—now wither!

SCENE 2

The Mountain of the Jungfrau.[1]*—Time, Morning.—*
MANFRED *alone upon the Cliffs.*

MAN.   The spirits I have raised abandon me—
The spells which I have studied baffle me—
The remedy I reck'd of tortured me;
I lean no more on super-human aid,
It hath no power upon the past, and for   5
The future, till the past be gulf'd in darkness,
It is not of my search.—My mother Earth!
And thou fresh breaking Day, and you, ye Mountains,
Why are ye beautiful? I cannot love ye.
And thou, the bright eye of the universe,   10
That openest over all, and unto all
Art a delight—thou shin'st not on my heart.
And you, ye crags, upon whose extreme edge
I stand, and on the torrent's brink beneath
Behold the tall pines dwindled as to shrubs   15
In dizziness of distance; when a leap,
A stir, a motion, even a breath, would bring
My breast upon its rocky bosom's bed
To rest for ever—wherefore do I pause?[2]
I feel the impulse—yet I do not plunge;   20
I see the peril—yet do not recede;
And my brain reels—and yet my foot is firm:
There is a power upon me which withholds,
And makes it my fatality to live;
If it be life to wear within myself   25
This barrenness of spirit, and to be
My own soul's sepulchre, for I have ceased
To justify my deeds unto myself—
The last infirmity of evil. Ay,
Thou winged and cloud-cleaving minister,   30
                                    [*An eagle passes.*]
Whose happy flight is highest into heaven,
Well may'st thou swoop so near me—I should be
Thy prey, and gorge thine eaglets; thou art gone
Where the eye cannot follow thee; but thine
Yet pierces downward, onward, or above,   35
With a pervading vision.—Beautiful!
How beautiful is all this visible world![3]
How glorious in its action and itself!

---

1. One of the tallest of the Swiss Alps.
2. Manfred's contemplation of suicide, lines 19–26, recalls the "To be or not to be" soliloquy in *Hamlet* (3.1.58*ff.*).
3. Lines 37–47 recall *Hamlet* 2.2.289–298.

But we, who name ourselves its sovereigns, we,
Half dust, half deity, alike unfit   40
To sink or soar, with our mix'd essence make
A conflict of its elements, and breathe
The breath of degradation and of pride,
Contending with low wants and lofty will,
Till our mortality predominates,   45
And men are—what they name not to themselves,
And trust not to each other. Hark! the note,
        [*The Shepherd's pipe in the distance is heard.*]
The natural music of the mountain reed—
For here the patriarchal days are not
A pastoral fable—pipes in the liberal air,   50
Mix'd with the sweet bells of the sauntering herd;
My soul would drink those echoes.—Oh, that I were
The viewless spirit of a lovely sound,
A living voice, a breathing harmony,
A bodiless enjoyment—born and dying   55
With the blest tone which made me!

        Enter from below a CHAMOIS[4] HUNTER.
CHAMOIS HUNTER.   Even so
This way the chamois leapt: her nimble feet
Have baffled me; my gains to-day will scarce
Repay my break-neck travail.—What is here?
Who seems not of my trade, and yet hath reach'd   60
A height which none even of our mountaineers,
Save our best hunters, may attain: his garb
Is goodly, his mien manly, and his air
Proud as a free-born peasant's, at this distance.—
I will approach him nearer.
MAN. (*not perceiving the other*).   To be thus—   65
Grey-hair'd with anguish, like these blasted pines,
Wrecks of a single winter, barkless, branchless,
A blighted trunk upon a cursed root,
Which but supplies a feeling to decay—
And to be thus, eternally but thus,   70
Having been otherwise! Now furrow'd o'er
With wrinkles, plough'd by moments, not by years
And hours—all tortured into ages—hours
Which I outlive!—Ye toppling crags of ice!
Ye avalanches, whom a breath draws down   75
In mountainous o'erwhelming, come and crush me—
I hear ye momently above, beneath,
Crash with a frequent conflict; but ye pass,
And only fall on things that still would live;
On the young flourishing forest, or the hut   80
And hamlet of the harmless villager.

4. Mountain antelope (pronounced "shammy").

C. HUN.   The mists begin to rise from up the valley;
 I'll warn him to descend, or he may chance
 To lose at once his way and life together.
MAN.   The mists boil up around the glaciers; clouds   85
 Rise curling fast beneath me, white and sulphury,
 Like foam from the roused ocean of deep Hell,
 Whose every wave breaks on a living shore,
 Heap'd with the damn'd like pebbles.—I am giddy.
C. HUN.   I must approach him cautiously; if near,   90
 A sudden step will startle him, and he
 Seems tottering already.
MAN.   Mountains have fallen,
 Leaving a gap in the clouds, and with the shock
 Rocking their Alpine brethren; filling up
 The ripe green valleys with destruction's splinters; 95
 Damming the rivers with a sudden dash,
 Which crush'd the waters into mist, and made
 Their fountains find another channel—thus,
 Thus, in its old age, did Mount Rosenberg[5]—
 Why stood I not beneath it?
C. HUN.   Friend! have a care,   100
 Your next step may be fatal!—for the love
 Of him who made you, stand not on that brink!
MAN. (*not hearing him*).   Such would have been for me a fitting
  tomb;
 My bones had then been quiet in their depth;
 They had not then been strewn upon the rocks   105
 For the wind's pastime—as thus—thus they shall be—
 In this one plunge.—Farewell, ye opening heavens!
 Look not upon me thus reproachfully—
 Ye were not meant for me—Earth! take these atoms!
  [As MANFRED *is in act to spring from the cliff, the* CHAMOIS
  HUNTER *seizes and retains him with a sudden grasp.*]
C. HUN.   Hold, madman!—though aweary of thy life, 110
 Stain not our pure vales with thy guilty blood—
 Away with me——I will not quit my hold.
MAN.   I am most sick at heart—nay, grasp me not—
 I am all feebleness—the mountains whirl
 Spinning around me——I grow blind——What art thou? 115
C. HUN.   I'll answer that anon.—Away with me——
 The clouds grow thicker——there—now lean on me—
 Place your foot here—here, take this staff, and cling
 A moment to that shrub—now give me your hand,
 And hold fast by my girdle—softly—well—   120
 The Chalet will be gain'd within an hour—
 Come on, we'll quickly find a surer footing,
 And something like a pathway, which the torrent

---

5. On September 2, 1806, Mount Rossberg was the scene of a massive avalanche that killed several
hundred people in the villages below it.

Hath wash'd since winter.—Come, 'tis bravely done—
You should have been a hunter.—Follow me.   125
[*As they descend the rocks with difficulty, the scene closes.*]

Act 2

SCENE 1

A Cottage amongst the Bernese Alps.

MANFRED *and the* CHAMOIS HUNTER.

C. HUN. No, no—yet pause—thou must not yet go forth:
Thy mind and body are alike unfit
To trust each other, for some hours, at least;
When thou art better, I will be thy guide—
But whither?
MAN.   It imports not: I do know   5
My route full well, and need no further guidance.
C. HUN. Thy garb and gait bespeak thee of high lineage—
One of the many chiefs, whose castled crags
Look o'er the lower valleys[1]—which of these
May call thee lord? I only know their portals;   10
My way of life leads me but rarely down
To bask by the huge hearths of those old halls,
Carousing with the vassals; but the paths,
Which step from out our mountains to their doors,
I know from childhood—which of these is thine?   15
MAN. No matter.
C. HUN.   Well, sir, pardon me the question,
And be of better cheer. Come, taste my wine;
'Tis of an ancient vintage; many a day
'T has thawed my veins among our glaciers, now
Let it do thus for thine—Come, pledge me fairly.   20
MAN. Away, away! there's blood upon the brim!
Will it then never—never sink in the earth?
C. HUN. What dost thou mean? thy senses wander from thee.
MAN. I say 'tis blood—my blood! the pure warm stream
Which ran in the veins of my fathers, and in ours   25
When we were in our youth, and had one heart,
And loved each other as we should not love,[2]
And this was shed: but still it rises up,
Colouring the clouds, that shut me out from heaven,
Where thou[3] art not—and I shall never be.   30
C. HUN. Man of strange words, and some half-maddening sin,
Which makes thee people vacancy, whate'er
Thy dread and sufferance be, there's comfort yet—
The aid of holy men, and heavenly patience——

---

1. Cf. *Childe Harold* III, stanzas 48–49 (pp. 208–11) and "The Castled Crag of Drachenfels."
2. The reference of this passage to Byron's relationship with his half-sister, Augusta, was scandalously obvious to his wife, friends, and social circle, if not to the contemporary public at large.
3. Referring to Astarte, not to the chamois hunter.

MAN.   Patience and patience! Hence—that word was made   35
  For brutes of burthen, not for birds of prey;
  Preach it to mortals of a dust like thine,—
  I am not of thine order.
C. HUN.   Thanks to heaven!
  I would not be of thine for the free fame
  Of William Tell;[4] but whatsoe'er thine ill,   40
  It must be borne, and these wild starts are useless.
MAN.   Do I not bear it?—Look on me—I live.
C. HUN.   This is convulsion, and no healthful life.
MAN.   I tell thee, man! I have lived many years,
  Many long years, but they are nothing now   45
  To those which I must number: ages—ages—
  Space and eternity—and consciousness,
  With the fierce thirst of death—and still unslaked!
C. HUN.   Why, on thy brow the seal of middle age
  Hath scarce been set; I am thine elder far.   50
MAN.   Think'st thou existence doth depend on time?
  It doth; but actions are our epochs:[5] mine
  Have made my days and nights imperishable,
  Endless, and all alike, as sands on the shore,
  Innumerable atoms, and one desert,   55
  Barren and cold, on which the wild waves break,
  But nothing rests, save carcasses and wrecks,
  Rocks, and the salt-surf weeds of bitterness.
C. HUN.   Alas! he's mad—but yet I must not leave him.
MAN.   I would I were—for then the things I see   60
  Would be but a distemper'd dream.
C. HUN.   What is it
  That thou dost see, or think thou look'st upon?
MAN.   Myself, and thee—a peasant of the Alps—
  Thy humble virtues, hospitable home,
  And spirit patient, pious, proud, and free;   65
  Thy self-respect, grafted on innocent thoughts;
  Thy days of health, and nights of sleep; thy toils,
  By danger dignified, yet guiltless; hopes
  Of cheerful old age and a quiet grave,
  With cross and garland over its green turf,   70
  And thy grandchildren's love for epitaph;
  This do I see—and then I look within—
  It matters not—my soul was scorch'd already!
C. HUN.   And would'st thou then exchange thy lot for mine?
MAN.   No, friend! I would not wrong thee, nor exchange   75
  My lot with living being: I can bear—
  However wretchedly, 'tis still to bear—
  In life what others could not brook to dream,
  But perish in their slumber.
C. HUN.   And with this—

---

4. The legendary Swiss patriot, forced by the Austrian governor to shoot an apple off his son's head.
5. Compare *Childe Harold* III, stanza 5 (p. 197).

This cautious feeling for another's pain,   80
Canst thou be black with evil?—say not so.
Can one of gentle thoughts have wreak'd revenge
Upon his enemies?
MAN.   Oh! no, no, no!
My injuries came down on those who loved me—
On those whom I best loved: I never quell'd   85
An enemy, save in my just defence—
My wrongs were all on those I should have cherished[6]
But my embrace was fatal.
C. HUN.   Heaven give thee rest!
And penitence restore thee to thyself;
My prayers shall be for thee.
MAN.   I need them not,   90
But can endure thy pity. I depart—
'Tis time—farewell!—Here's gold, and thanks for thee—
No words—it is thy due.—Follow me not—
I know my path—the mountain peril's past:
And once again, I charge thee, follow not!   95
                    [*Exit* MANFRED.]

SCENE 2

A lower Valley in the Alps.—A Cataract.

Enter MANFRED.
It is not noon—the sunbow's rays[1] still arch
The torrent with the many hues of heaven,
And roll the sheeted silver's waving column
O'er the crag's headlong perpendicular,
And fling its lines of foaming light along,   5
And to and fro, like the pale courser's tail,
The Giant steed, to be bestrode by Death,
As told in the Apocalypse.[2] No eyes
But mine now drink this sight of loveliness;
I should be sole in this sweet solitude,   10
And with the Spirit of the place divide
The homage of these waters.—I will call her.
        [MANFRED *takes some of the water into the palm of his hand, and flings*
        it into the air, muttering the adjuration. After a pause, the WITCH OF
        THE ALPS *rises beneath the arch of the sunbow of the torrent.*]
Beautiful Spirit! with thy hair of light,
And dazzling eyes of glory, in whose form
The charms of Earth's least mortal daughters grow   15
To an unearthly stature, in an essence
Of purer elements; while the hues of youth,—
Carnation'd like a sleeping infant's cheek,

---

6. One of three lines (along with 2.2.168 and 2.4.166) that are in the original draft but that Byron omitted from the fair copy apparently due to an eye skip; as a result, these lines were omitted in 1832 and all printed editions prior to *CPW.*
1. "This iris is formed by the rays of the sun over the lower part of the Alpine torrents: it is exactly like a rainbow come down to pay a visit, and so close that you may walk into it: this effect lasts until noon."
2. Revelation 6.8.

Rock'd by the beating of her mother's heart,
Or the rose tints, which summer's twilight leaves   20
Upon the lofty glacier's virgin snow,
The blush of earth embracing with her heaven,—
Tinge thy celestial aspect, and make tame
The beauties of the sunbow which bends o'er thee.
Beautiful Spirit! in thy calm clear brow,   25
Wherein is glass'd serenity of soul,
Which of itself shows immortality,
I read that thou wilt pardon to a Son
Of Earth, whom the abstruser powers permit
At times to commune with them—if that he   30
Avail him of his spells—to call thee thus,
And gaze on thee a moment.
WITCH.   Son of Earth!
I know thee, and the powers which give thee power;
I know thee for a man of many thoughts,
And deeds of good and ill, extreme in both,   35
Fatal and fated in thy sufferings.
I have expected this—what would'st thou with me?
MAN.   To look upon thy beauty—nothing further.
The face of the earth hath madden'd me, and I
Take refuge in her mysteries, and pierce   40
To the abodes of those who govern her—
But they can nothing aid me. I have sought
From them what they could not bestow, and now
I search no further.
WITCH.   What could be the quest
Which is not in the power of the most powerful,   45
The rulers of the invisible?[3]
MAN.   A boon;
But why should I repeat it? 'twere in vain.
WITCH.   I know not that; let thy lips utter it.
MAN.   Well, though it torture me, 'tis but the same;
My pang shall find a voice. From my youth upwards   50
My spirit walk'd not with the souls of men,
Nor look'd upon the earth with human eyes;
The thirst of their ambition was not mine,
The aim of their existence was not mine;
My joys, my griefs, my passions, and my powers,   55
Made me a stranger; though I wore the form,
I had no sympathy with breathing flesh,
Nor midst the creatures of clay that girded me
Was there but one who——but of her anon.
I said, with men, and with the thoughts of men,   60
I held but slight communion; but instead,
My joy was in the Wilderness, to breathe
The difficult air of the iced mountain's top,
Where the birds dare not build, nor insect's wing

---

3. The Seven Spirits in 1.1.

Flit o'er the herbless granite; or to plunge   65
Into the torrent, and to roll along
On the swift whirl of the new breaking wave
Of river-stream, or ocean, in their flow.
In these my early strength exulted;[4] or
To follow through the night the moving moon,   70
The stars and their development; or catch
The dazzling lightnings till my eyes grew dim;
Or to look, list'ning, on the scatter'd leaves,
While Autumn winds were at their evening song.
These were my pastimes, and to be alone;   75
For if the beings, of whom I was one,—
Hating to be so,—cross'd me in my path,
I felt myself degraded back to them,
And was all clay again. And then I dived,
In my lone wanderings, to the caves of death,   80
Searching its cause in its effect; and drew
From wither'd bones, and skulls, and heap'd up dust,
Conclusions most forbidden. Then I pass'd
The nights of years in sciences untaught,
Save in the old time; and with time and toil,   85
And terrible ordeal, and such penance
As in itself hath power upon the air,
And spirits that do compass air and earth,
Space, and the peopled infinite, I made
Mine eyes familiar with Eternity,   90
Such as, before me, did the Magi, and
He who from out their fountain dwellings raised
Eros and Anteros,[5] at Gadara,
As I do thee;—and with my knowledge grew
The thirst of knowledge, and the power and joy   95
Of this most bright intelligence, until——
WITCH.   Proceed.
MAN.   Oh! I but thus prolong'd my words,
Boasting these idle attributes, because
As I approach the core of my heart's grief—
But to my task. I have not named to thee   100
Father or mother, mistress, friend, or being,
With whom I wore the chain of human ties;
If I had such, they seem'd not such to me—
Yet there was one——
WITCH.   Spare not thyself—proceed.
MAN.   She was like me in lineaments—her eyes,   105
Her hair, her features, all, to the very tone
Even of her voice, they said were like to mine;
But soften'd all, and temper'd into beauty;

---

4. A clear autobiographical reference, given Byron's pride in his swimming ability.
5. "The philosopher Jamblicus. The story of the raising of Eros and Anteros may be found in his life
by Eunapius. It is well told." The fourth-century Neoplatonic philosopher Iamblichus was sup-
posed to have summoned the deities Eros and Anteros from a spring in Gadara, Syria; Eros is the
god of love; Anteros, or "anti-love," is the avenging deity of disappointed or betrayed love.

She had the same lone thoughts and wanderings,
The quest of hidden knowledge, and a mind   110
To comprehend the universe: nor these
Alone, but with them gentler powers than mine,
Pity, and smiles, and tears—which I had not;
And tenderness—but that I had for her;
Humility—and that I never had.   115
Her faults were mine—her virtues were her own—
I loved her, and destroy'd her!
WITCH.   With thy hand?
MAN.   Not with my hand, but heart—which broke her heart—
It gazed on mine, and wither'd. I have shed
Blood, but not hers—and yet her blood was shed—   120
I saw—and could not stanch it.
WITCH.   And for this—
A being of the race thou dost despise,
The order which thine own would rise above,
Mingling with us and ours, thou dost forego
The gifts of our great knowledge, and shrink'st back   125
To recreant mortality——Away!
MAN.   Daughter of Air! I tell thee, since that hour—
But words are breath—look on me in my sleep,
Or watch my watchings—Come and sit by me!
My solitude is solitude no more,   130
But peopled with the Furies;—I have gnash'd
My teeth in darkness till returning morn,
Then cursed myself till sunset;—I have pray'd
For madness as a blessing—'tis denied me.
I have affronted death—but in the war   135
Of elements the waters shrunk from me,
And fatal things pass'd harmless—the cold hand
Of an all-pitiless demon held me back,
Back by a single hair, which would not break.
In fantasy, imagination, all   140
The affluence of my soul—which one day was
A Croesus[6] in creation—I plunged deep,
But, like an ebbing wave, it dash'd me back
Into the gulf of my unfathom'd thought.
I plunged amidst mankind—Forgetfulness   145
I sought in all, save where 'tis to be found,
And that I have to learn—my sciences,
My long pursued and super-human art,
Is mortal here—I dwell in my despair—
And live—and live for ever.[7]
WITCH.   It may be   150

6. King of Lydia, 560–546 B.C.E., noted for his great wealth.
7. The theme of unrelenting guilt alludes to the legend of Ahusuerus, the Wandering Jew, a familiar
figure in Gothic and Romantic literature. Ahusueras was said to have cursed Christ at the Cruci-
fixion, for which he was condemned to wander the earth, guilt-ridden, till the Second Coming.
Other literary echoes and parallels include Cain (Genesis 4), already connected to Manfred in the
"Incantation"; Satan in *Paradise Lost* (whose internalization of Hell is also echoed in *Manfred*
[1.1.251]), and perhaps Adam ("why do I overlive?" [10.773]); and Coleridge's Ancient Mariner.

That I can aid thee.
MAN.   To do this thy power
Must wake the dead, or lay me low with them.
Do so—in any shape—in any hour—
With any torture—so it be the last.
WITCH.   That is not in my province; but if thou   155
Wilt swear obedience to my will, and do
My bidding, it may help thee to thy wishes.
MAN.   I will not swear—Obey! and whom? the spirits
Whose presence I command, and be the slave
Of those who served me—Never!
WITCH.   Is this all?   160
Hast thou no gentler answer?—Yet bethink thee,
And pause ere thou rejectest.
MAN.   I have said it.
WITCH.   Enough!—I may retire then—say!
MAN.   Retire!
                [*The* WITCH *disappears.*]
MAN. (*alone*).   We are the fools of time and terror: Days
Steal on us and steal from us; yet we live,   165
Loathing our life, and dreading still to die.
In all the days of this detested yoke—
This heaving burthen, this accursed breath,[8]
This vital weight upon the struggling heart,
Which sinks with sorrow, or beats quick with pain,   170
Or joy that ends in agony or faintness—
In all the days of past and future, for
In life there is no present, we can number
How few—how less than few—wherein the soul
Forbears to pant for death, and yet draws back   175
As from a stream in winter, though the chill
Be but a moment's. I have one resource
Still in my science—I can call the dead,
And ask them what it is we dread to be:
The sternest answer can but be the Grave,   180
And that is nothing—if they answer not—
The buried Prophet[9] answered to the Hag
Of Endor; and the Spartan Monarch[1] drew
From the Byzantine maid's unsleeping spirit
An answer and his destiny—he slew   185
That which he loved, unknowing what he slew,
And died unpardon'd—though he call'd in aid
The Phyxian Jove, and in Phigalia roused
The Arcadian Evocators to compel
The indignant shadow to depose her wrath,   190

---

8. Restored line based on the draft manuscript (see p. 261, n. 6).
9. King Saul ordered the Witch of Endor to raise the spirit of the prophet Samuel, who foretold Saul's death (1 Samuel 28).
1. Pausanias (king of Sparta) was deceived into killing his bride, Cleonice, on their wedding night. Overcome with remorse and haunted by Cleonice's ghost, Pausanias had the priests of Zeus in Phigalia ("Arcadian Evocators") raise Cleonice, who prophesied that the king's troubles would soon be over. This was an ambiguous prophecy of Pausanias's impending death.

Or fix her term of vengeance—she replied
In words of dubious import, but fulfill'd.[2]
If I had never lived, that which I love
Had still been living; had I never loved,
That which I love would still be beautiful—   195
Happy and giving happiness. What is she?
What is she now?—a sufferer for my sins—
A thing I dare not think upon—or nothing.
Within few hours I shall not call in vain—
Yet in this hour I dread the thing I dare: 200
Until this hour I never shrunk to gaze
On spirit, good or evil—now I tremble,
And feel a strange cold thaw upon my heart.
But I can act even what I most abhor,
And champion human fears.—The night approaches.   205
[Exit.]

SCENE 3

The Summit of the Jungfrau Mountain.

Enter FIRST DESTINY.
The moon is rising broad, and round, and bright;
And here on snows, where never human foot
Of common mortal trod, we nightly tread,
And leave no traces; o'er the savage sea,
The glassy ocean of the mountain ice,   5
We skim its rugged breakers, which put on
The aspect of a tumbling tempest's foam,
Frozen in a moment—a dead whirlpool's image.
And this most steep fantastic pinnacle,
The fretwork of some earthquake—where the clouds   10
Pause to repose themselves in passing by—
Is sacred to our revels, or our vigils;
Here do I wait my sisters, on our way
To the Hall of Arimanes, for to-night
Is our great festival—'tis strange they come not.   15

A Voice without, singing.
The Captive Usurper,[1]
    Hurl'd down from the throne,
Lay buried in torpor,
    Forgotten and lone;
I broke through his slumbers,   20
    I shiver'd his chain,
I leagued him with numbers—
    He's Tyrant again!

2. "The story of Pausanias, king of Sparta (who commanded the Greeks at the battle of Platea, and afterwards perished for an attempt to betray the Lacedaemonians), and Cleonice, is told in Plutarch's life of Cimon; and in the Laconics of Pausanias the sophist, in his description of Greece."
1. Napoleon; a prophecy that he will return from his exile on St. Helena as he had from Elba.

With the blood of a million he'll answer my care,
With a nation's destruction—his flight and despair.   25

Second Voice, without.
The ship sail'd on, the ship sail'd fast,
But I left not a sail, and I left not a mast;
There is not a plank of the hull or the deck,
And there is not a wretch to lament o'er his wreck;
Save one, whom I held, as he swam, by the hair,[2]   30
And he was a subject well worthy my care;
A traitor on land, and a pirate at sea—
But I saved him to wreak further havoc for me!

FIRST DESTINY, *answering.*
The city lies sleeping;
The morn, to deplore it,   35
May dawn on it weeping:
Sullenly, slowly,
The black plague flew o'er it—
Thousands lie lowly;
Tens of thousands shall perish—   40
The living shall fly from
The sick they should cherish;
But nothing can vanquish
The touch that they die from.
Sorrow and anguish,   45
And evil and dread,
Envelope a nation—
The blest are the dead,
Who see not the sight
Of their own desolation—   50
This work of a night—
This wreck of a realm—this deed of my doing—
For ages I've done, and shall still be renewing!

Enter the SECOND *and* THIRD DESTINIES.

The Three.
Our hands contain the hearts of men,
Our footsteps are their graves;   55
We only give to take again
The spirits of our slaves!

FIRST DES.   Welcome!—Where's Nemesis?[3]
SECOND DES.   At some great work;

---

2. Possibly a reference to Thomas Cochrane, tenth Earl of Dundonald (1775–1860), an admiral imprisoned for his exposure of Admiralty corruption. The Destinies, thus, favor those who disrupt monarchy.
3. In classical mythology, the goddess of divine retribution or punishment; here, the servant of Arimanes.

But what I know not, for my hands were full.
THIRD DES.   Behold she cometh.

Enter NEMESIS.

FIRST DES.   Say, where hast thou been?   60
My sisters and thyself are slow to-night.
NEM.   I was detain'd repairing shatter'd thrones,[4]
Marrying fools, restoring dynasties,
Avenging men upon their enemies,
And making them repent their own revenge;   65
Goading the wise to madness; from the dull
Shaping out oracles to rule the world
Afresh, for they were waxing out of date,
And mortals dared to ponder for themselves,
To weigh kings in the balance, and to speak   70
Of freedom, the forbidden fruit.—Away!
We have outstay'd the hour—mount we our clouds!
                              [*Exeunt.*]

SCENE 4

The Hall of Arimanes[1]—*Arimanes on his Throne, a Globe*
of Fire, surrounded by the Spirits.

Hymn of the SPIRITS.
Hail to our Master!—Prince of Earth and Air!
   Who walks the clouds and waters—in his hand
The sceptre of the elements, which tear
   Themselves to chaos at his high command!
He breatheth—and a tempest shakes the sea;   5
   He speaketh—and the clouds reply in thunder;
He gazeth—from his glance the sunbeams flee;
   He moveth—earthquakes rend the world asunder.
Beneath his footsteps the volcanoes rise;
   His shadow is the Pestilence; his path   10
The comets herald through the crackling skies;
   And planets turn to ashes at his wrath.
To him War offers daily sacrifice;
   To him Death pays his tribute; Life is his,
With all its infinite of agonies—   15
   And his the spirit of whatever is!

Enter the DESTINIES *and* NEMESIS.
FIRST DES.   Glory to Arimanes! on the earth
His power increaseth—both my sisters did
His bidding, nor did I neglect my duty!

---

4. The restoration of the monarchies after the fall of Napoleon; working through the Congress of Vienna ("repairing shatter'd thrones"), Nemesis is not intending to do a good deed, as the rest of the speech makes clear.
1. The Prince of the Powers of the Air; his name derives from the Persian Ahriman, the principle of evil and death in Zoroastrianism.

SECOND DES.   Glory to Arimanes! we who bow   20
  The necks of men, bow down before his throne!
THIRD DES.   Glory to Arimanes! we await
  His nod!
NEM.   Sovereign of Sovereigns! we are thine,
  And all that liveth, more or less, is ours,
  And most things wholly so; still to increase   25
  Our power, increasing thine, demands our care,
  And we are vigilant—Thy late commands
  Have been fulfill'd to the utmost.

Enter MANFRED.

A SPIRIT.   What is here?
  A mortal!—Thou most rash and fatal wretch,
  Bow down and worship!
SECOND SPIRIT.   I do know the man—   30
  A Magian[2] of great power, and fearful skill!
THIRD SPIRIT.   Bow down and worship, slave!—
                        What, know'st thou not
  Thine and our Sovereign?—Tremble, and obey!
  ALL THE SPIRITS.   Prostrate thyself, and thy condemned clay,
  Child of the Earth! or dread the worst.
MAN.   I know it;   35
  And yet ye see I kneel not.
  FOURTH SPIRIT.   'Twill be taught thee.
MAN.   'Tis taught already;—many a night on the earth,
  On the bare ground, have I bow'd down my face,
  And strew'd my head with ashes; I have known
  The fulness of humiliation, for   40
  I sunk before my vain despair, and knelt
  To my own desolation.
FIFTH SPIRIT.   Dost thou dare
  Refuse to Arimanes on his throne
  What the whole earth accords, beholding not
  The terror of his Glory?—Crouch! I say.   45
MAN.   Bid *him* bow down to that which is above him,
  The overruling Infinite—the Maker
  Who made him not for worship—let him kneel,
  And we will kneel together.
THE SPIRITS.   Crush the worm!
  Tear him in pieces!—
FIRST DES.   Hence! Avaunt!—he's mine.   50
  Prince of the Powers invisible! This man
  Is of no common order, as his port
  And presence here denote; his sufferings
  Have been of an immortal nature, like
  Our own; his knowledge, and his powers and will,   55
  As far as is compatible with clay,
  Which clogs the ethereal essence, have been such

---

2. Magician, sorcerer.

As clay hath seldom borne; his aspirations
Have been beyond the dwellers of the earth,
And they have only taught him what we know—   60
That knowledge is not happiness, and science
But an exchange of ignorance for that
Which is another kind of ignorance.[3]
This is not all—the passions, attributes
Of earth and heaven, from which no power, nor being,   65
Nor breath from the worm upwards is exempt,
Have pierced his heart; and in their consequence
Made him a thing, which I, who pity not,
Yet pardon those who pity. He is mine,
And thine, it may be—be it so, or not,   70
No other Spirit in this region hath
A soul like his—or power upon his soul.
NEM.   What doth he here then?
FIRST DES.   Let him answer that.
MAN.   Ye know what I have known; and without power
I could not be amongst ye: but there are   75
Powers deeper still beyond—I come in quest
Of such, to answer unto what I seek.
NEM.   What would'st thou?
MAN.   Thou canst not reply to me.
Call up the dead—my question is for them.
NEM.   Great Arimanes, doth thy will avouch   80
The wishes of this mortal?
ARI.   Yea.
NEM.   Whom would'st thou
Uncharnel?
MAN.   One without a tomb—call up Astarte.[4]

NEMESIS.
Shadow! or Spirit!
Whatever thou art,
Which still doth inherit   85
The whole or a part
Of the form of thy birth,
Of the mould of thy clay,
Which return'd to the earth,
Re-appear to the day!   90
Bear what thou borest,
The heart and the form,
And the aspect thou worest

---

3. Cf. *Faust* 1.360–64; also, the reference to Socrates in *Childe Harold* II.55–56: "Well didst thou speak, Athena's wisest son! / 'All that we know is, nothing can be known.'"
4. The Phoenician goddess of love and beauty. The name of this pagan deity (alternatively Astoreth and Ashtaroth) occurs in Judges 2.13, 2 Kings 23.13, and *Paradise Lost* 1.421, 437–46. In the sixty-seventh of Montesquieu's *Lettres Persanes* (1721), Astarte is the sister in a tale of sibling incest. See also Shelley's *Alastor* (1816), 129–39 and 149*ff*. In the Middle Ages, Ashtaroth became a devil, and Byron's original, discarded third act of *Manfred* has the figure of Ashtaroth as an abbot-taunting demon.

Redeem from the worm.
Appear!—Appear!—Appear!   95
Who sent thee there requires thee here!
[*The Phantom of* ASTARTE *rises and stands in the midst.*]
MAN.   Can this be death? there's bloom upon her cheek;
But now I see it is no living hue,
But a strange hectic—like the unnatural red
Which Autumn plants upon the perish'd leaf.[5]   100
It is the same! Oh, God! that I should dread
To look upon the same—Astarte!—No,
I cannot speak to her—but bid her speak—
Forgive me or condemn me.

NEMESIS.
By the power which hath broken   105
The grave which enthrall'd thee,
Speak to him who hath spoken,
Or those who have call'd thee!

MAN.   She is silent,
And in that silence I am more than answer'd.   110
NEM.   My power extends no further. Prince of air!
It rests with thee alone—command her voice.
ARI.   Spirit—obey this sceptre!
NEM.   Silent still!
She is not of our order, but belongs
To the other powers. Mortal! thy quest is vain,   115
And we are baffled also.
MAN.   Hear me, hear me—
Astarte! my beloved! speak to me:
I have so much endured—so much endure—
Look on me! the grave hath not changed thee more
Than I am changed for thee. Thou lovedst me   120
Too much, as I loved thee: we were not made
To torture thus each other, though it were
The deadliest sin to love as we have loved.
Say that thou loath'st me not—that I do bear
This punishment for both—that thou wilt be   125
One of the blessed—and that I shall die;
For hitherto all hateful things conspire
To bind me in existence—in a life
Which makes me shrink from immortality—
A future like the past. I cannot rest.   130
I know not what I ask, nor what I seek:
I feel but what thou art—and what I am;
And I would hear yet once before I perish
The voice which was my music—Speak to me!
For I have call'd on thee in the still night,   135
Startled the slumbering birds from the hush'd boughs,

5. Compare Shelley's "Ode to the West Wind," lines 1–5.

And woke the mountain wolves, and made the caves
Acquainted with thy vainly echoed name,
Which answer'd me—many things answer'd me—
Spirits and men—but thou wert silent all.   140
Yet speak to me! I have outwatch'd the stars,
And gazed o'er heaven in vain in search of thee.
Speak to me! I have wander'd o'er the earth,
And never found thy likeness—Speak to me!
Look on the fiends around—they feel for me: 145
I fear them not, and feel for thee alone—
Speak to me! though it be in wrath;—but say—
I reck not what—but let me hear thee once—
This once—once more!

PHANTOM OF ASTARTE.   Manfred!

MAN.   Say on, say on—
I live but in the sound—it is thy voice!   150

PHAN.   Manfred! To-morrow ends thine earthly ills.[6]
Farewell!

MAN.   Yet one word more—am I forgiven?

PHAN.   Farewell!

MAN.   Say, shall we meet again?

PHAN.   Farewell!

MAN.   One word for mercy! Say, thou lovest me.

PHAN.   Manfred!

            [*The Spirit of* ASTARTE *disappears.*]

NEM.   She's gone, and will not be recall'd;   155
Her words will be fulfill'd. Return to the earth.

A SPIRIT.   He is convulsed—This is to be a mortal
And seek the things beyond mortality.

ANOTHER SPIRIT.   Yet, see, he mastereth himself, and makes
His torture tributary to his will.   160
Had he been one of us, he would have made
An awful spirit.

NEM.   Hast thou further question
Of our great sovereign, or his worshippers?

MAN.   None.

NEM.   Then for a time farewell.

MAN.   We meet then—
Where? On the earth?

NEM.   That will be seen hereafter.[7]   165

MAN.   Even as thou wilt: and for the grace accorded
I now depart a debtor. Fare ye well!

                              [*Exit* MANFRED]
                    (*Scene closes.*)

---

6. Thus, Astarte's prophecy of the end to Manfred's earthly ills, i.e., his death, echoes those of the
   ghosts of Samuel and Cleonice that Manfred refers to in 2.2.178–92.
7. Restored line based on the draft manuscript (see p. 261, n. 6).

Act 3[1]

scene 1

A Hall in the Castle of Manfred.

Manfred *and* Herman.

man.   What is the hour?
her.   It wants but one till sunset,
And promises a lovely twilight.
man.   Say,
Are all things so disposed of in the tower
As I directed?
her.   All, my lord, are ready:
Here is the key and casket.
man.   It is well: 5
Thou may'st retire.   [*Exit* Herman.]
man. (*alone*).   There is a calm upon me—
Inexplicable stillness! which till now
Did not belong to what I knew of life.
If that I did not know philosophy
To be of all our vanities the motliest,   10
The merest word that ever fool'd the ear
From out the schoolman's jargon, I should deem
The golden secret, the sought "Kalon,"[2] found,
And seated in my soul. It will not last,
But it is well to have known it, though but once: 15
It hath enlarged my thoughts with a new sense,
And I within my tablets would note down
That there is such a feeling. Who is there?

Re-enter Herman.

her.   My lord, the abbot of St. Maurice craves
To greet your presence.

Enter the Abbot of St. Maurice.[3]

abbot.   Peace be with Count Manfred!   20
man.   Thanks, holy father! welcome to these walls;
Thy presence honours them, and blesseth those
Who dwell within them.
abbot.   Would it were so, Count!—
But I would fain confer with thee alone.
man.   Herman, retire.—What would my reverend guest?   25
                    [*Exit* Herman.]
abbot.   Thus, without prelude:—Age and zeal, my office,
And good intent, must plead my privilege;
Our near, though not acquainted neighbourhood,

---

1. On Byron's revision of Act 3 see headnote. For the original third act see *CPW* 4:467–71 or *Cochran.*
2. The beautiful, as understood in Platonic philosophy, i.e., the highest good.
3. St. Maurice is located in the Rhone valley, southeast of Chillon; the Augustinian priory there is the earliest Christian site in Switzerland.

May also be my herald. Rumours strange,
And of unholy nature, are abroad,   30
And busy with thy name; a noble name
For centuries: may he who bears it now
Transmit it unimpair'd!
MAN.   Proceed,—I listen.
ABBOT.   'Tis said thou holdest converse with the things
Which are forbidden to the search of man;   35
That with the dwellers of the dark abodes,
The many evil and unheavenly spirits
Which walk the valley of the shade of death,
Thou communest. I know that with mankind,
Thy fellows in creation, thou dost rarely   40
Exchange thy thoughts, and that thy solitude
Is as an anchorite's,[4] were it but holy.
MAN.   And what are they who do avouch these things?
ABBOT.   My pious brethren—the scared peasantry—
Even thy own vassals—who do look on thee   45
With most unquiet eyes. Thy life's in peril.
MAN.   Take it.
ABBOT.   I come to save, and not destroy—
I would not pry into thy secret soul;
But if these things be sooth, there still is time
For penitence and pity: reconcile thee   50
With the true church, and through the church to heaven.
MAN.   I hear thee. This is my reply: whate'er
I may have been, or am, doth rest between
Heaven and myself.—I shall not choose a mortal
To be my mediator. Have I sinn'd   55
Against your ordinances? prove and punish!
ABBOT.   My son! I did not speak of punishment,
But penitence and pardon;—with thyself
The choice of such remains—and for the last,
Our institutions and our strong belief   60
Have given me power to smooth the path from sin
To higher hope and better thoughts; the first
I leave to heaven,—"Vengeance is mine alone!"[5]
So saith the Lord, and with all humbleness
His servant echoes back the awful word.   65
MAN.   Old man! there is no power in holy men,
Nor charm in prayer—nor purifying form
Of penitence—nor outward look—nor fast—
Nor agony—nor, greater than all these,
The innate tortures of that deep despair,   70
Which is remorse without the fear of hell,
But all in all sufficient to itself
Would make a hell of heaven—can exorcise
From out the unbounded spirit the quick sense

4. Hermit's.
5. Cf. Romans 12.19 and Deuteronomy 32.35.

Of its own sins, wrongs, sufferance, and revenge   75
Upon itself; there is no future pang
Can deal that justice on the self-condemn'd
He deals on his own soul.
ABBOT.   All this is well;
For this will pass away, and be succeeded
By an auspicious hope, which shall look up   80
With calm assurance to that blessed place,
Which all who seek may win, whatever be
Their earthly errors, so they be atoned:
And the commencement of atonement is
The sense of its necessity.—Say on—   85
And all our church can teach thee shall be taught;
And all we can absolve thee shall be pardon'd.
MAN.   When Rome's sixth emperor[6] was near his last,
The victim of a self-inflicted wound,
To shun the torments of a public death   90
From senates once his slaves, a certain soldier,
With show of loyal pity, would have stanch'd
The gushing throat with his officious robe;
The dying Roman thrust him back, and said—
Some empire still in his expiring glance—   95
"It is too late—is this fidelity?"
ABBOT.   And what of this?
MAN.   I answer with the Roman—
"It is too late!"
ABBOT.   It never can be so,
To reconcile thyself with thy own soul,
And thy own soul with heaven. Hast thou no hope?   100
'Tis strange—even those who do despair above,
Yet shape themselves some fantasy on earth,
To which frail twig they cling, like drowning men.
MAN.   Ay—father! I have had those earthly visions
And noble aspirations in my youth,   105
To make my own the mind of other men,
The enlightener of nations; and to rise
I knew not whither—it might be to fall;
But fall, even as the mountain-cataract,
Which having leapt from its more dazzling height,   110
Even in the foaming strength of its abyss
(Which casts up misty columns that become
Clouds raining from the re-ascended skies),
Lies low but mighty still.—But this is past,
My thoughts mistook themselves.
ABBOT.   And wherefore so?   115
MAN.   I could not tame my nature down; for he
Must serve who fain would sway—and soothe—and sue—
And watch all time—and pry into all place—

---

6. The reference is to Nero, Rome's fifth emperor, whose suicide is described in *Lives of the Caesars*
6, chap. 49 by Suetonius (ca. C.E. 69–140).

And be a living lie—who would become
A mighty thing amongst the mean, and such   120
The mass are; I disdain'd to mingle with
A herd, though to be leader—and of wolves.
The lion is alone, and so am I.
ABBOT.   And why not live and act with other men?
MAN.   Because my nature was averse from life;   125
   And yet not cruel; for I would not make,
   But find a desolation:—like the wind,
   The red-hot breath of the most lone Simoom,[7]
   Which dwells but in the desert, and sweeps o'er
   The barren sands which bear no shrubs to blast,   130
   And revels o'er their wild and arid waves,
   And seeketh not, so that it is not sought,
   But being met is deadly; such hath been
   The course of my existence; but there came
   Things in my path which are no more.
ABBOT.   Alas!   135
   I 'gin to fear that thou art past all aid
   From me and from my calling; yet so young,
   I still would——
MAN.   Look on me! there is an order
   Of mortals on the earth, who do become
   Old in their youth, and die ere middle age,   140
   Without the violence of warlike death;
   Some perishing of pleasure—some of study—
   Some worn with toil—some of mere weariness—
   Some of disease—and some insanity—
   And some of wither'd, or of broken hearts;   145
   For this last is a malady which slays
   More than are number'd in the lists of Fate,
   Taking all shapes, and bearing many names.
   Look upon me! for even of all these things
   Have I partaken; and of all these things,   150
   One were enough; then wonder not that I
   Am what I am, but that I ever was,
   Or having been, that I am still on earth.
ABBOT.   Yet, hear me still——
MAN.   Old man! I do respect
   Thine order, and revere thine years; I deem   155
   Thy purpose pious, but it is in vain:
   Think me not churlish; I would spare thyself,
   Far more than me, in shunning at this time
   All further colloquy—and so—farewell.
                     [*Exit* MANFRED.]
ABBOT.   This should have been a noble creature: he   160
   Hath all the energy which would have made
   A goodly frame of glorious elements,
   Had they been wisely mingled; as it is,

---

7. The hot wind of the desert; cf. *The Giaour*, lines 282–85 and note (p. 130).

It is an awful chaos—light and darkness—
And mind and dust—and passions and pure thoughts   165
Mix'd, and contending without end or order,
All dormant or destructive: he will perish,
And yet he must not; I will try once more,
For such are worth redemption; and my duty
Is to dare all things for a righteous end.   170
I'll follow him—but cautiously, though surely.
                                        [*Exit* Abbot.]

SCENE 2

Another Chamber.

Manfred *and* Herman.

HER.   My lord, you bade me wait on you at sunset:
He sinks behind the mountain.
MAN.   Doth he so?
I will look on him.
        [Manfred *advances to the Window of the Hall.*]
                    Glorious Orb! the idol[1]
Of early nature, and the vigorous race
Of undiseased mankind, the giant sons[2]   5
Of the embrace of angels, with a sex
More beautiful than they, which did draw down
The erring spirits who can ne'er return.—
Most glorious orb! that wert a worship, ere
The mystery of thy making was reveal'd!   10
Thou earliest minister of the Almighty,
Which gladden'd, on their mountain tops, the hearts
Of the Chaldean[3] shepherds, till they pour'd
Themselves in orisons! Thou material God!
And representative of the Unknown—   15
Who chose thee for his shadow! Thou chief star!
Centre of many stars! which mak'st our earth
Endurable, and temperest the hues
And hearts of all who walk within thy rays!
Sire of the seasons! Monarch of the climes,   20
And those who dwell in them! for near or far,
Our inborn spirits have a tint of thee,
Even as our outward aspects;—thou dost rise,
And shine, and set in glory. Fare thee well!
I ne'er shall see thee more. As my first glance   25

1. Of the following lines Byron wrote to John Murray, July 9, 1817: "Pray was Manfred's speech to *the Sun* still retained in Act 3rd?—I hope so—it was one of the best in the thing—& better than the Colosseum" (*BLJ* 5:249). Byron refers to the Coliseum passage in 3.4.8–41.
2. "'And it came to pass, that the *Sons of God* saw the daughters of men, that they were fair,' &c.— 'There were giants in the earth in those days; and also after that, when the *Sons of God* came in unto the daughters of men, and they bare children to them, the same became mighty men which were of old, men of renown.'—*Genesis*, ch. vi, verses 2 and 4."
3. Of the people and region in Mesopotamia where the worship of the Hebrew God began (Genesis 11.31).

Of love and wonder was for thee, then take
My latest look: thou wilt not beam on one
To whom the gifts of life and warmth have been
Of a more fatal nature. He is gone:
I follow.   30

[Exit MANFRED.]

SCENE 3

The Mountains—The Castle of Manfred at some distance—
A Terrace before a Tower.—Time, Twilight.

HERMAN, MANUEL, and other Dependants of MANFRED.

HER.   'Tis strange enough; night after night, for years,
He hath pursued long vigils in this tower,
Without a witness. I have been within it,—
So have we all been oft-times; but from it,
Or its contents, it were impossible   5
To draw conclusions absolute, of aught
His studies tend to. To be sure, there is
One chamber where none enter: I would give
The fee of what I have to come these three years,
To pore upon its mysteries.
MANUEL.   'Twere dangerous;   10
Content thyself with what thou know'st already.
HER.   Ah! Manuel! thou art elderly and wise,
And couldst say much; thou hast dwelt within the castle—
How many years is't?
MANUEL.   Ere Count Manfred's birth,
I served his father, whom he nought resembles.   15
HER.   There be more sons in like predicament.
But wherein do they differ?
MANUEL.   I speak not
Of features or of form, but mind and habits;
Count Sigismund[1] was proud,—but gay and free,—
A warrior and a reveller; he dwelt not   20
With books and solitude, nor made the night
A gloomy vigil, but a festal time,
Merrier than day; he did not walk the rocks
And forests like a wolf, nor turn aside
From men and their delights.
HER.   Beshrew the hour,   25
But those were jocund times! I would that such
Would visit the old walls again; they look
As if they had forgotten them.
MANUEL.   These walls
Must change their chieftain first. Oh! I have seen
Some strange things in them, Herman.

---

1. Byron may have taken the name of Manfred's father from a Duke of Burgundy who, in 515, endowed the priory of St. Maurice.

HER.   Come, be friendly;   30
Relate me some to while away our watch:
I've heard thee darkly speak of an event
Which happen'd hereabouts, by this same tower.
MANUEL.   That was a night indeed! I do remember
'Twas twilight, as it may be now, and such   35
Another evening;—yon red cloud, which rests
On Eigher's[2] pinnacle, so rested then,—
So like that it might be the same; the wind
Was faint and gusty, and the mountain snows
Began to glitter with the climbing moon;   40
Count Manfred was, as now, within his tower,—
How occupied, we knew not, but with him
The sole companion of his wanderings
And watchings—her, whom of all earthly things
That lived, the only thing he seem'd to love,—   45
As he, indeed, by blood was bound to do,
The lady Astarte, his——
                         Hush! who comes here?
Enter the ABBOT.
ABBOT.   Where is your master?
HER.   Yonder, in the tower.
ABBOT.   I must speak with him.
MANUEL.   'Tis impossible;
He is most private, and must not be thus   50
Intruded on.
ABBOT.   Upon myself I take
The forfeit of my fault, if fault there be—
But I must see him.
HER.   Thou hast seen him once
This eve already.
ABBOT.   Sirrah![3] I command thee,
Knock, and apprize the Count of my approach.   55
HER.   We dare not.
ABBOT.   Then it seems I must be herald
Of my own purpose.
MANUEL.   Reverend father, stop—
I pray you pause.
ABBOT.   Why so?
MANUEL.   But step this way,
And I will tell you further.
                              [*Exeunt.*]

---

2. The Grosse Eiger, a mountain in the Swiss Alps east of the Jungfrau.
3. "Herman" in all editions prior to *CPW*, an unauthorized alteration.

SCENE 4

Interior of the Tower.

MANFRED *alone.*

The stars are forth, the moon above the tops
Of the snow-shining mountains.—Beautiful!
I linger yet with Nature, for the night
Hath been to me a more familiar face
Than that of man; and in her starry shade   5
Of dim and solitary loveliness,
I learn'd the language of another world.
I do remember me, that in my youth,
When I was wandering,—upon such a night
I stood within the Coliseum's wall,[1]   10
Midst the chief relics of almighty Rome;
The trees which grew along the broken arches
Waved dark in the blue midnight, and the stars
Shone through the rents of ruin; from afar
The watchdog bay'd beyond the Tiber;[2] and   15
More near from out the Caesars' palace came
The owl's long cry, and, interruptedly,
Of distant sentinels the fitful song
Begun and died upon the gentle wind.
Some cypresses beyond the time-worn breach   20
Appear'd to skirt the horizon, yet they stood
Within a bowshot—where the Caesars dwelt,
And dwell the tuneless birds of night amidst
A grove which springs through levell'd battlements
And twines its roots with the imperial hearths.   25
Ivy usurps the laurel's place of growth;—
But the gladiators' bloody Circus stands,
A noble wreck in ruinous perfection!
While Caesar's chambers, and the Augustan halls,
Grovel on earth in indistinct decay.—   30
And thou didst shine, thou rolling moon, upon
All this, and cast a wide and tender light,
Which soften'd down the hoar austerity
Of rugged desolation, and fill'd up,
As 'twere anew, the gaps of centuries;   35
Leaving that beautiful which still was so,
And making that which was not, till the place
Became religion, and the heart ran o'er
With silent worship of the great of old!—
The dead, but sceptred sovereigns, who still rule   40
Our spirits from their urns.—
                                   'Twas such a night!
'Tis strange that I recall it at this time;

---

1. Cf. this passage on the Colosseum with *Childe Harold* IV, stanzas 128–31 and 139–47 (pp. 333, 336–38).
2. The river of Rome.

But I have found our thoughts take wildest flight
Even at the moment when they should array
Themselves in pensive order.
   Enter the ABBOT.
ABBOT.   My good lord!   45
I crave a second grace for this approach;
But yet let not my humble zeal offend
By its abruptness—all it hath of ill
Recoils on me; its good in the effect
May light upon your head—could I say *heart*— 50
Could I touch *that*, with words or prayers, I should
Recall a noble spirit which hath wander'd
But is not yet all lost.
MAN.   Thou know'st me not;
My days are number'd, and my deeds recorded:
Retire, or 'twill be dangerous—Away!   55
ABBOT. Thou dost not mean to menace me?
MAN.   Not I;
I simply tell thee peril is at hand,
And would preserve thee.
ABBOT.   What dost thou mean?
MAN.   Look there!
What dost thou see?
ABBOT.   Nothing.
MAN.   Look there, I say,
And steadfastly;—now tell me what thou seest? 60
ABBOT. That which should shake me,—but I fear it not—
I see a dusk and awful figure rise
Like an infernal god from out the earth;
His face wrapt in a mantle, and his form
Robed as with angry clouds: he stands between 65
Thyself and me—but I do fear him not.
MAN. Thou hast no cause—he shall not harm thee—but
His sight may shock thine old limbs into palsy.
I say to thee—Retire!
ABBOT.   And I reply—
Never—till I have battled with this fiend:— 70
What doth he here?
MAN.   Why—ay—what doth he here?
I did not send for him,—he is unbidden.
ABBOT. Alas! lost mortal! what with guests like these
Hast thou to do? I tremble for thy sake:
Why doth he gaze on thee, and thou on him? 75
Ah! he unveils his aspect: on his brow
The thunder-scars are graven; from his eye
Glares forth the immortality of hell—
Avaunt!——
MAN. Pronounce—what is thy mission?
SPIRIT.   Come!
ABBOT. What art thou, unknown being? answer!—speak! 80

SPIRIT. The genius[3] of this mortal.—Come! 'tis time.
MAN. I am prepared for all things, but deny
    The power which summons me. Who sent thee here?
SPIRIT. Thou'lt know anon—Come! come!
MAN.   I have commanded
    Things of an essence greater far than thine,   85
    And striven with thy masters. Get thee hence!
SPIRIT. Mortal! thine hour is come—Away! I say.
MAN. I knew, and know my hour is come, but not
    To render up my soul to such as thee:
    Away! I'll die as I have lived—alone.   90
SPIRIT. Then I must summon up my brethren.—Rise!
                    [*Other Spirits rise up.*]
ABBOT. Avaunt! ye evil ones!—Avaunt! I say,—
    Ye have no power where piety hath power,
    And I do charge ye in the name——
SPIRIT.   Old man!
    We know ourselves, our mission, and thine order;   95
    Waste not thy holy words on idle uses,
    It were in vain: this man is forfeited.
    Once more I summon him—Away! away!
MAN. I do defy ye,—though I feel my soul
    Is ebbing from me, yet I do defy ye;   100
    Nor will I hence, while I have earthly breath
    To breathe my scorn upon ye—earthly strength
    To wrestle, though with spirits; what ye take
    Shall be ta'en limb by limb.
SPIRIT.   Reluctant mortal!
    Is this the Magian who would so pervade   105
    The world invisible, and make himself
    Almost our equal?—Can it be that thou
    Art thus in love with life? the very life
    Which made thee wretched!
MAN.   Thou false fiend, thou liest!
    My life is in its last hour,—*that* I know,   110
    Nor would redeem a moment of that hour;
    I do not combat against death, but thee
    And thy surrounding angels; my past power
    Was purchased by no compact with thy crew,
    But by superior science—penance—daring—   115
    And length of watching—strength of mind—and skill
    In knowledge of our fathers—when the earth
    Saw men and spirits walking side by side,
    And gave ye no supremacy: I stand
    Upon my strength—I do defy—deny—   120
    Spurn back, and scorn ye!—
SPIRIT.   But thy many crimes
    Have made thee——

---

3. Guiding spirit.

MAN.   What are they to such as thee?
Must crimes be punish'd but by other crimes,
And greater criminals?—Back to thy hell!
Thou hast no power upon me, *that* I feel;   125
Thou never shalt possess me, *that* I know:
What I have done is done; I bear within
A torture which could nothing gain from thine:
The mind which is immortal makes itself
Requital for its good or evil thoughts—   130
Is its own origin of ill and end—[4]
And its own place and time—its innate sense,
When stripp'd of this mortality, derives
No colour from the fleeting things without,
But is absorb'd in sufferance or in joy,   135
Born from the knowledge of its own desert.
Thou didst not tempt me, and thou couldst not tempt me;
I have not been thy dupe, nor am thy prey—
But was my own destroyer, and will be
My own hereafter.[5]—Back, ye baffled fiends!   140
The hand of death is on me—but not yours!
       [*The Demons disappear.*]
ABBOT.   Alas! how pale thou art—thy lips are white—
And thy breast heaves—and in thy gasping throat
The accents rattle—Give thy prayers to heaven—
Pray—albeit but in thought,—but die not thus.   145
MAN.   'Tis over—my dull eyes can fix thee not;
But all things swim around me, and the earth
Heaves as it were beneath me. Fare thee well—
Give me thy hand.
ABBOT.   Cold—cold—even to the heart—
But yet one prayer—Alas! how fares it with thee?   150
MAN.   Old man! 'tis not so difficult to die.[6]
       [MANFRED *expires.*]
ABBOT.   He's gone—his soul hath ta'en its earthless flight—
Whither? I dread to think—but he is gone.

LETTERS AND JOURNAL

To John Murray

Diodati.—August 28th. 1816
Dear Sir—The Manuscript (containing the third Canto of Childe
Harold—the Castle of Chillon &c. &c.) is consigned to the care of my
friend Mr. Shelley—who will deliver this letter along with it.—Mr. Gifford

4. Cf. *Paradise Lost* 1.254–55.
5. Cf. "Epistle to Augusta," lines 23–24 (p. 242).
6. At the urging of William Gifford, the poem's editor, John Murray omitted this line from the first
   edition. Enraged, Byron wrote to Murray: "You have destroyed the whole effect & moral of the
   poem by omitting the last line of Manfred's speaking" (*BLJ* 5:257).

will perhaps be kind enough to read it over;—I know not well to whom to consign the correction of the proofs—nor indeed who would be good natured enough to overlook it in its progress—as I feel very anxious that it should be published with as few errata as possible.— —Perhaps—my friend Mr. Moore (if in town) would do this.— —If not—Mr. S[helley] will take it upon himself,—and in any case—he is authorized to act for me in treating with you &c. &c. on this subject.[1]— —You talked of a letter— which was to be sent by you to me—but I have received none—before—or since—one by Mr. Browne.—As that Gentleman returned by Brussels— which is the longest route—I declined troubling him with the care of this packet.— —Believe me very truly yours.

BYRON

P.S.—There is in the volume—an epistle to Mrs. Leigh—on which I should wish her to have her opinion consulted—before the publication— if she objects—of course—*omit* it.[2]— —I have been very glad to hear you are well—& well-doing—and that you stopped Master Cawthorne in his foolish attempts to republish the E[nglish] B[ards] & S[cotch] R[eviewers].—I wish you all good things.— —

To Augusta Leigh

[Diodati—Geneva Sept. 8th. 1816]

My dearest Augusta—By two opportunities of private conveyance—I have sent answers to your letter delivered by Mr. H[obhouse].— — S[crope][1] is on his return to England—& may probably arrive before this.— He is charged with a few packets of seals—necklaces—balls &c.—& I know not what—formed of Chrystals—Agates—and other stones—*all of* & *from Mont Blanc* bought & brought by me on & from the spot—expressly for you to divide among yourself and the children—including also your niece Ada,[2] for whom I selected a ball (of Granite—a soft substance by the way—but the only one there) wherewithall to roll & play—when she is old enough— and mischievous enough—and moreover a Chrystal necklace—and any- thing else you may like to add for her—the Love!— —The rest are for you—& the Nursery—but particularly Georgiana[3]—who has sent me a very nice letter.—I hope Scrope will carry them all safely—as he promised— — There are seals & all kinds of fooleries—pray—like them—for they come from a very curious place (nothing like it hardly in all I ever saw)—to say nothing of the giver.— —And so—Lady B[yron] has been "kind to you" you tell me—"very kind"—umph—it is as well she should be kind to some of us—and I am glad she has the heart & the discernment to be still *your* friend—you was ever so to her.—I heard the other day—that she was very

---

1. Byron's ambiguity about who should edit *Childe Harold* III and *The Prisoner of Chillon* had seri- ous consequences for printed editions of these poems. More partial to William Gifford's conser- vative politics than to Shelley's radicalism, Murray eventually persuaded Byron to accept the former as editor, which resulted in the deletion of some of Byron's more radical notes to *Childe Harold* III, as well as various other textual changes that annoyed Byron (see previous note and *BLJ* 5:154 and 169).
2. Augusta Leigh did object to the publication of "Epistle to Augusta," and it was omitted from *The Prisoner of Chillon and Other Poems*.
1. Scrope Davies, one of Byron's Cambridge friends.
2. Byron and Annabella's nine-month-old daughter.
3. Byron's niece, Augusta's eldest child.

unwell—I was shocked enough—and sorry enough—God knows—but never mind;—H[obhouse] tells me however that she is *not* ill—that she *had* been indisposed—but is better & well to do.—this is a relief.— —As for me I am in good health—& fair—though very unequal—spirits—but for all that—she—or rather—the Separation—has broken my heart—I feel as if an Elephant had trodden on it—I am convinced I shall never get over it— but I try.— —I had enough before I ever knew her and more than enough— but time & agitation had done something for me; but this last wreck has affected me very differently,—if it were *acutely*—it would not signify—but it is not that,—I breathe lead.— —While the storm lasted & you were all pressing & comforting me with condemnation in Piccadilly—it was bad enough—& violent enough—but it is worse now.—I have neither strength nor spirits—nor inclination to carry me through anything which will clear my brain or lighten my heart.—I mean to cross the Alps at the end of this month—and go—God knows where—by Dalmatia—up to the Arnauts again—if nothing better can be done;—I have still a world before me— this—or the next.— —H[obhouse] has told me all the strange stories in circulation of me & mine;—*not* true,—I have been in some danger on the lake—(near Meillerie) but nothing to speak of; and as to all these "mistresses"—Lord help me—I have had but one.[4]—Now—don't scold—but what could I do?—a foolish girl—in spite of all I could say or do—would come after me—or rather went before me—for I found her here—and I have had all the plague possible to persuade her to go back again—but at last she went.—Now—dearest—I do most truly tell thee—that I could not help this—that I did all I could to prevent it—& have at last put an end to it.—I am not in love—nor have any love left for any,—but I could not exactly play the Stoic[5] with a woman—who had scrambled eight hundred miles to unphilosophize me—besides I had been regaled of late with so many "two courses and a *desert*" (Alas!) of aversion—that I was fain to take a little love (if pressed particularly) by way of novelty.— —And now you know all that I know of that matter—& it is over. Pray—write—I have heard nothing since your last—at least a month or five weeks ago.— —I go out very little—except into the *air*—and on journeys—and on the water—and to Coppet—where Me. de Stael[6] has been particularly kind & friendly towards me—& (I hear) fought battles without number in my very indifferent cause.—It has (they say) made quite as much noise on this as the other side of "La Manche"[7]—Heaven knows why—but I seem destined to set people by the ears.— —Don't hate me—but believe me ever

yrs. most affectly.
B

---

4. Claire Clairmont, Mary Shelley's stepsister, who bore a daughter of Byron's, Allegra, on January 12, 1817.
5. Referring to the ancient Greek philosophy that men should forego pleasures and withstand suffering.
6. Germaine de Staël (1766–1817), French-Swiss writer whose Paris salon and, later (when Byron knew her), estate at Coppet on Lake Geneva attracted famous political figures, artists, writers, and intellectuals.
7. French name for the English Channel.

From Alpine Journal

Clarens. Septr. 18th. 1816

Yesterday September 17th. 1816—I set out (with H[obhouse]) on an excursion of some days to the Mountains.—I shall keep a short journal of each day's progress for my Sister Augusta—

Sept. 17th.—

Rose at 5.—left Diodati about seven—in one of the country carriages—(a Charaban)—our servants on horseback—weather very fine—the Lake calm and clear—Mont Blanc—and the Aiguille of Argentière both very distinct— the borders of the Lake beautiful—reached Lausanne before Sunset— stopped & slept at Ouchy.—H[obhouse] went to dine with a Mr. Okeden—I remained at our Caravansera (though invited to the house of H's friend—too lazy or tired—or something else to go) and wrote a letter to Augusta—Went to bed at nine—sheets damp—swore and stripped them off & flung them—Heaven knows where—wrapt myself up in the blankets— and slept like a Child of a month's existence—till 5 o Clock of

Septr. 18th.

... —Walked down to the Lake side—servants—Carriage—saddle horses—all set off and left us plantés la by some mistake—and we walked on after them towards Clarens—H[obhouse] ran on before and overtook them at last—arrived the second time (1st time was by water) at Clarens beautiful Clarens!—went to Chillon through Scenery worthy of I know not whom—went over the Castle of Chillon again—on our return met an English party in a carriage—a lady in it fast asleep!—fast asleep in the most anti-narcotic spot in the world—excellent—I remember at Chamouni—in the very eyes of Mont Blanc—hearing another woman—English also— exclaim to her party—"did you ever see any thing more *rural*"—as if it was Highgate or Hampstead—or Brompton—or Hayes[1]—"*Rural*" quotha!— Rocks—pines—torrents—Glaciers—Clouds—and Summits of eternal snow far above them—and "*Rural*!" I did not know the thus exclaiming fair one—but she was a—very good kind of a woman.— —After a slight & short dinner—we visited the Chateau de Clarens—an English woman has rented it recently—(it was not let when I saw it first) the roses are gone with their Summer—the family out—but the servants desired us to walk over the interior—saw on the table of the saloon—Blair's sermons—and somebody else's (I forgot who's—) sermons—and a set of noisy children—saw all worth seeing and then descended to the "Bosquet de Julie" &c. &c.—our Guide full of *Rousseau*—whom he is eternally confounding with *St. Preux*—and mixing the man and the book—on the steps of a cottage in the village—I saw a young *paysanne*—beautiful as Julie herself—went again as far as Chillon to revisit the little torrent from the hill behind it—Sunset— reflected in the lake—have to get up at 5 tomorrow to cross the mountains on horseback—carriage to be sent round—lodged at my old Cottage— hospitable & comfortable—tired with a longish ride—on the Colt—and the subsequent jolting of the Charaban—and my scramble in the hot sun— shall go to bed—thinking of you dearest Augusta.— —Mem.—The Corpo-

1. Towns and suburbs in England.

ral who showed the wonders of Chillon was as drunk as Blucher[2]—and (to
my mind) as great a man.—He was *deaf* also—and thinking every one else
so—roared out the legends of the Castle so fearfully that H[obhouse] got
out of humour—however we saw all things from the Gallows to the Dun-
geon (the *Potence* & the *Cachets*) and returned to Clarens with more free-
dom than belonged to the 15th. Century.— —At Clarens—the only book
(except the Bible) a translation of "*Cecilia*" (Miss Burney's *Cecilia*) and the
owner of the Cottage had also called her dog (a fat Pug *ten* years old—and
hideous as *Tip*)[3] after Cecilia's (or rather Delville's) dog—Fidde—

Septr. 19th.

Rose at 5—ordered the carriage round.—Crossed the mountains to Mont-
bovon on horseback—and on Mules—and by dint of scrambling on foot
also,—the whole route beautiful as a *Dream* and now to me almost as
indistinct,—I am so tired—for though healthy I have not the strength I pos-
sessed but a few years ago.—At Mont Davant we breakfasted—afterwards
on a steep ascent—dismounted—tumbled down & cut a finger open—the
baggage also got loose and fell down a ravine, till stopped by a large tree—
swore—recovered baggage—horse tired & dropping—mounted Mule—at
the approach of the summit of Dent Jamant—dismounted again with H. &
all the party.—Arrived at a lake in the very nipple of the bosom of the
Mountain.—left our quadrupeds with a Shepherd—& ascended further—
came to some snow in patches—upon which my forehead's perspiration fell
like rain making the same dints as in a sieve—the chill of the wind & the
snow turned me giddy—but I scrambled on & upwards—H. went to the
highest *pinnacle*—I did not—but paused within a few yards (at an opening
of the Cliff)—in coming down the Guide tumbled three times—I fell a
laughing & tumbled too—the descent luckily soft though steep & slippery—
H. also fell—but nobody hurt. The whole of the Mountain superb—the
shepherd on a very steep & high cliff playing upon his *pipe*—very different
from Arcadia—(where I saw the pastors with a long Musquet instead of a
Crook—and pistols in their Girdles)—our Swiss Shepherd's pipe was
sweet—& his time agreeable—saw a cow strayed—told that they often break
their necks on & over the crags—descended to Montbovon—pretty scraggy
village with a wild river—and a wooden bridge.—H. went to fish—caught
one—our carriage not come—our horses—mules &c. knocked up—
ourselves fatigued—(but so much the better—I shall sleep). The view from
the highest point of today's journey comprized on one side the greatest part
of Lake Leman—on the other—the valleys & mountains of the Canton
Fribourg—and an immense plain with the Lakes of Neufchatel & Morat—
and all which the borders of these and of the Lake of Geneva inherit—we
had both sides of the Jura before us in one point of view, with Alps in
plenty.—In passing a ravine—the Guide recommended strenuously a quick-
ening of pace—as the stones fall with great rapidity & occasional damage—
the advice is excellent—but like most good advice impracticable—the road
being so rough in this precise point—that neither mules nor mankind—nor
horses—can make any violent progress.—Passed without any fractures or
menace thereof.—The music of the Cows' bells (for their wealth like the

2. Prussian Field Marshal Blücher (1742–1819).
3. Augusta's dog.

Patriarchs is cattle) in the pastures (which reach to a height far above any mountains in Britain—) and the Shepherds' shouting to us from crag to crag & playing on their reeds where the steeps appeared almost inaccessible, with the surrounding scenery—realized all that I have ever heard or imagined of a pastoral existence—much more so than Greece or Asia Minor—for there we are a little too much of the sabre & musquet order—and if there is a Crook in one hand, you are sure to see a gun in the other—but this was pure and unmixed—solitary—savage and patriarchal—the effect I cannot describe—as we went they played the "Ranz des Vaches"[4] and other airs by way of farewell.—I have lately repeopled my mind with Nature.

. . .

Septr. 22d.

Left Thoun in a boat which carried us the length of the lake in three hours—the lake small—but the banks fine—rocks down to the water's edge.—Landed at Neuhause—passed Interlachen—entered upon a range of scenes beyond all description—or previous conception.—Passed a rock—inscription—2 brothers—one murdered the other—just the place fit for it.—After a variety of windings came to an enormous rock—Girl with fruit—very pretty—blue eyes—good teeth—very fair—long but good features—reminded me of Fy.[5] bought some of her pears—and patted her upon the cheek—the expression of her face very mild—but good—and not at all coquettish.—Arrived at the foot of the Mountain (the Yung-frau—i.e. the Maiden) Glaciers—torrents—one of these torrents *nine hundred feet* in height of visible descent—lodge at the Curate's—set out to see the Valley— heard an Avalanche fall—like thunder—saw Glacier—enormous—Storm came on—thunder—lightning—hail—all in perfection—and beautiful—I was on horseback—Guide wanted to carry my cane—I was going to give it him when I recollected that it was a Swordstick and I thought that the light-ning might be attracted towards him—kept it myself—a good deal encum-bered with it & my cloak—as it was too heavy for a whip—and the horse was stupid—& stood still every other peal. Got in—not very wet—the Cloak being staunch—H. wet through—H. took refuge in cottage—sent man— umbrella—& cloak (from the Curate's when I arrived—) after him.—Swiss Curate's house—very good indeed—much better than most English Vicarages—it is immediately opposite the torrent I spoke of—the torrent is in shape curving over the rock—like the *tail* of a white horse streaming in the wind—such as it might be conceived would be that of the "*pale* horse" on which *Death* is mounted in the Apocalypse.[6]—It is neither mist nor water but a something between both—it's immense height (nine hundred feet) gives it a wave—a curve—a spreading here—a condensation there— wonderful—& indescribable.—I think upon the whole—that this day has been better than any of this present excursion.—

Septr. 23d.

Before ascending the mountain[7]—went to the torrent (7 in the morning) again—the Sun upon it forming a *rainbow* of the lower part of all colours—

4. A typical Alpine herdsman's melody used in calling the cattle.
5. Frances (Fanny) Webster.
6. Revelation 6.
7. The Jungfrau, one of the highest mountains in the Swiss Alps.

but principally purple and gold—the bow moving as you move—I never saw anything like this—it is only in the Sunshine.— —Ascended the Wengren [sic][8] Mountain.— —at noon reached a valley near the summit—left the horses—took off my coat & went to the summit—7000 feet (English feet) above the level of the *sea*—and about 5000 above the valley we left in the morning—on one side our view comprized the *Yung frau* with all her glaciers—then the *Dent d'Argent*—shining like truth—then the *little Giant* (the Kleiner EIgher) & the great Giant (the Grosser EIgher) and last not least—the Wetterhorn.—The height of the Yung frau is 13000 feet above the sea—and 11000 above the valley—she is the highest of this range,—heard the Avalanches falling every five minutes nearly—as if God was pelting the Devil down from Heaven with snow balls—from where we stood on the *Wengren* [sic] Alp—we had all these in view on one side—on the other the clouds rose from the opposite valley curling up perpendicular precipices—like the foam of the Ocean of Hell during a Springtide—it was white & sulphery—and immeasurably deep in appearance—the side we ascended was (of course) not of so precipitous a nature—but on arriving at the summit we looked down the other side upon a boiling sea of cloud—dashing against the crags on which we stood (these crags on one side quite perpendicular);—staid a quarter of an hour—began to descend—quite clear from cloud on that side of the mountain—in passing the masses of snow—I made a snowball & pelted H. with it—got down to our horses again—eat something—remounted—heard the Avalanches still—came to a morass—H. dismounted—H. got well over—I tried to pass my horse over—the horse sunk up [to] the chin—& of course he & I were in the mud together—bemired all over—but not hurt—laughed & rode on.—Arrived at the Grindenwald—dined—mounted again & rode to the higher Glacier—twilight—but distinct—very fine Glacier—like a *frozen hurricane*—Starlight—beautiful—but a devil of a path—never mind—got safe in—a little lightning—but the whole of the day as fine in point of weather—as the day on which Paradise was made.—Passed *whole woods of withered pines*—*all withered*—trunks stripped & barkless—branches lifeless—done by a single winter—their appearance reminded me of me & my family.—

Septr. 24th.

Set out at seven—up at five—passed the black Glacier—the Mountain Wetterhorn on the right—crossed the Scheideck mountain—came to the Rose Glacier—said to be the largest & finest in Switzerland.—*I* think the Bossons Glacier at Chamouni—as fine—H. does not—came to the Reichenback waterfall—two hundred feet high—halted to rest the horses—arrived in the valley of Oberhasli—rain came on—drenched a little—only 4 hours rain however in 8 days—came to Lake of Brientz—then to town of Brientz—changed—H. hurt his head against door.—In the evening four Swiss Peasant Girls of Oberhasli came & sang the airs of their country—two of the voices beautiful—the tunes also—they sing too that *Tyrolese*[9] *air* & song which you love—Augusta—because I love it—& I love because you love it—they are still singing—Dearest—you do not know how I should have liked this—were you with me—the airs are so wild & original

8. I.e., Wengen.
9. Tyrol is an Alpine province in western Austria.

& at the same time of great sweetness.— —The singing is over—but below stairs I hear the notes of a Fiddle which bode no good to my nights rest.— The Lord help us!—I shall go down & see the dancing.—

Septr. 25th.

The whole town of Brientz were apparently gathered together in the rooms below—pretty music—& excellent Waltzing—none but peasants—the dancing much better than in England—the English can't Waltz—never could—nor ever will.—One man with his pipe in his mouth—but danced as well as the others—some other dances in pairs—and in fours—and very good.— —I went to bed but the revelry continued below late & early.— Brientz but a village.— —Rose early.—Embarked on the Lake of Brientz.— Rowed by women in a long boat—one very young & very pretty—seated myself by her—& began to row also—presently we put to shore & another woman jumped in—it seems it is the custom here for the boats to be *manned by women*—for of five men & three women in our bark—all the women took an oar—and but one man.— —Got to Interlachen in three hours—pretty Lake—not so large as that of Thoun.—Dined at Interlachen—Girl gave me some flowers—& made me a speech in German—of which I know nothing—I do not know whether the speech was pretty but as the woman was—I hope so.—Saw another—very pretty too—and *tall* which I prefer—I hate short women—for more reasons than one.[1]—Reembarked on the Lake of Thoun—fell asleep part of the way— sent our horses round—found people on the shore blowing up a rock with gunpowder—they blew it up near our boat—only telling us a minute before—mere stupidity—but they might have broke our noddles.—Got to Thoun in the Evening—the weather has been tolerable the whole day—but as the wild part of our tour is finished, it don't matter to us—in all the desirable part—we have been most lucky in warmth & clearness of Atmosphere—for which "Praise we the Lord."— —

Septr. 26th.

Being out of the mountains my journal must be as flat as my journey.— — From Thoun to Bern good road—hedges—villages—industry— prosperity—and all sorts of tokens of insipid civilization.— —From Bern to Fribourg.—Different Canton—Catholics—passed a field of Battle—Swiss beat the French—in one of the late wars against the French Republic.— Bought a dog—a very ugly dog—but "*tres mechant*". this was his great recommendation in the owner's eyes & mine—for I mean him to watch the carriage—he hath no tail—& is called "Mutz"—which signifies "*Short-tail*"—he is apparently of the Shepherd dog genus!—The greater part of this tour has been on horseback—on foot—and on mule;—the Filly (which is one of two young horses I bought of the Baron de Vincy) carried me very well—she is young and as quiet as anything of her sex can be—very goodtempered—and perpetually neighing—when she wants any thing— which is every five minutes—I have called her *Biche*—because her manners are not unlike a little dog's—but she is a very tame—pretty childish quadruped.—

---

1. A reference to his wife; cf. "Her stature tall—I hate a dumpy woman" (*Don Juan* I.488).

Septr. 28th. [27th.]

Saw the tree planted in honour of the battle of Morat—340 years old—a good deal decayed.—Left Fribourg—but first saw the Cathedral—high tower—overtook the baggage of the Nuns of La Trappe who are removing to Normandy from their late abode in the Canton of Fribourg—afterwards a coach with a quantity of Nuns in it—Nuns old—proceeded along the banks of the Lake of Neufchatel—very pleasing & soft—but not so mountainous—at least the Jura not appearing so—after the Bernese Alps— reached Yverdun in the dusk—a long line of large trees on the border of the lake—fine & sombre—the Auberge nearly full—with a German Princess & suite—got rooms—we hope to reach Diodati the day after tomorrow—and I wish for a letter from you my own dearest Sis—May your sleep be soft and your dreams of me.—I am going to bed—good night.—

Septr. 29th. [28th.]

Passed through a fine & flourishing country—but not mountainous—in the evening reached Aubonne (the entrance & bridge something like that of Durham) which commands by far the fairest view of the Lake of Geneva— twilight—the Moon on the Lake—a grove on the height—and of very noble trees.—Here Tavernier (the Eastern traveller) bought (or built) the Chateau because the site resembled and equalled that of *Erivan* (a frontier city of Persia) here he finished his voyages—and I this little excursion—for I am within a few hours of Diodati—& have little more to see—& no more to say.—In the weather for this tour (of 13 days) I have been very fortunate—fortunate in a companion (Mr. H[obhous]e) fortunate in our prospects—and exempt from even the little petty accidents & delays which often render journeys in a less wild country—disappointing.—I was disposed to be pleased—I am a lover of Nature—and an Admirer of Beauty— I can bear fatigue—& welcome privation—and have seen some of the noblest views in the world.—But in all this—the recollections of bitterness—& more especially of recent & more home desolation—which must accompany me through life—have preyed upon me here—and neither the music of the Shepherd—the crashing of the Avalanche—nor the torrent—the mountain—the Glacier—the Forest—nor the Cloud—have for one moment—lightened the weight upon my heart—nor enabled me to lose my own wretched identity in the majesty & the power and the Glory— around—above—& beneath me.—I am past reproaches—and there is a time for all things—I am past the wish of vengeance—and I know of none like for what I have suffered—but the hour will come—when what I feel must be felt—& the— —but enough.— —To you—dearest Augusta—I send—and *for* you—I have kept this record of what I have seen & felt.— Love me as you are beloved by me.— —

Part Four: Final Pilgrimage—Italy and Greece (1816–1824)

"Venice," Byron wrote to Thomas Moore on November 17, 1816, "has always been (next to the East), the greenest island of my imagination." That Byron chose to live a significant portion of the last eight years of his life in Venice and Greece seems, retrospectively, like the fulfillment of a fate—both for Byron and for western culture. The romantic aura cast by these sites of natural beauty and faded glory on the imagination of two centuries of writers, artists, and travelers is largely traceable to Byron's life in Venice, his death in Greece, and the poetry and letters he wrote at and about both places during the final years of his life. In early October 1816, he had left Switzerland with Hobhouse, and, after a few weeks in Milan, arrived at Venice, where he would live for the next three years. The unique beauty of the city's natural setting (with "her tiara of proud towers" arising from the sea [*Childe Harold* IV.11]), along with its seductive combination of vitality and decadence, provided a welcome contrast to the "tight little island" of England (*BLJ* 5:136), with its more calculating industriousness and moral hypocrisies. At Venice, Byron immediately fell in love with Marianna Segati, the wife of his landlord. During the spring of 1817, he traveled to Rome, stopping along the way at Padua, Ferrara, Bologna, and Florence. At Rome, he finished *Manfred* and began recording his impressions of Italy for what would be the fourth and final canto of *Childe Harold's Pilgrimage*. After returning to Venice via the town of La Mira along the Brenta River, where he spent summer months, he fell in love again, this time with a baker's wife, the volatile Margarita Cogni. In the fall, the English and Italian mock epic poetry Byron had been reading, combined with his familiarity with Venetian customs and mores (especially marital and extramarital relations Italian style), inspired the writing of *Beppo*: an "experiment" in *ottava rima* that prepared for his major works in the same meter and manner—*Don Juan*, begun in the summer of 1818, and *The Vision of Judgment*, written in the fall of 1821.

Having leased the Palazzo Mocenigo on the Grand Canal, Byron headed a grand household that included more than a dozen servants and an impressive menagerie of animals. In addition to his exceptional poetic productivity during this period, Byron's daily life in Venice included the study of the Armenian language at a nearby Armenian monastery, evenings at *conversazioni*, the theater, or the opera, prodigious swimming feats in the Adriatic and the Grand Canal, and regular rides on his horses at Lido beach. (The arrival of Byron's horses at Venice caused quite a stir; as Henry Matthews, the brother of Charles Skinner Matthews, recorded: "There are only eight horses in Venice: four are of brass, over the gate of the cathedral; and the other four are alive in Lord Byron's stable" [*The Diary of an Invalid* (1820), p. 281].) Despite these wholesome activities, however, Byron grew fat and dissipated enjoying a life of remarkable sensual indulgence, particularly during the Carnival seasons of 1818 and 1819. The extent of his debauchery appalled Shelley when he visited in 1818; as Shelley reported to Thomas Love Peacock: "L[ord] B[yron] is familiar with the lowest sort of . . . women, the people his gondolieri pick up in the streets.

He allows fathers and mothers to bargain with him for their daughters. . . . He associates with wretches who seem almost to have lost the gait and physiognomy of man, and who do not scruple to avow practices which are not only not named but I believe seldom even conceived in England" (letter to Peacock, December [17 or 18], 1818).

Byron completed the first two cantos of *Don Juan* in 1819, during the same time that he began writing his memoirs, which he gave to Thomas Moore, intending them for posthumous publication (an intention thwarted through the determination of John Murray, John Cam Hobhouse, and Lady Byron to have them burned shortly after Byron's death). In the spring of 1819, he fell in love with Teresa Guiccioli, the twenty-one-year-old wife of a count from Ravenna three times her age. Teresa was aristocratic, lively, intelligent, and from a family of liberal patriots, and Byron became her *cavalier servente*, the quasi-accepted lover of a married woman, adept at an array of formalities: "I double a shawl with considerable alacrity—but have not yet arrived at the perfection of putting it on the right way—and I hand in and out, and know my post in a Conversazione—and theatre" (p. 758). Thus having exchanged promiscuity for "the strictest adultery" (p. 752), Byron followed Teresa to Ravenna, to Bologna, to La Mira, and back to Ravenna, where in 1820 he moved into the upper floor of the Guiccioli palace and settled into a comfortable daily routine—riding, spending evenings with Teresa, and writing into the early morning hours. Eventually, Teresa obtained a separation from the Count. Byron, meanwhile, became increasingly involved with the Carbonari, the secret revolutionary society to which Ruggero and Pietro Gamba, Teresa's father and brother, belonged. The failure of the Carbonari uprising against the Austrians led to the family's seeking political asylum in Tuscany, and in October 1821, Byron moved to Pisa, where he enjoyed the company of the Gambas and of Mary and Percy Shelley (who had moved there the previous year). In April 1822, Byron resumed work on Canto VI of *Don Juan*, which he had left off writing nearly a year before at the insistence of Teresa, who considered the poem immoral but who finally lifted her ban. Not that Byron's pen was idle when he was not writing *Don Juan*: the works he wrote in 1820 and 1821, besides *The Vision of Judgment*, include *Marino Faliero, Sardanapalus, The Two Foscari, Cain,* and *Heaven and Earth.* The period of relative contentment in Pisa was broken in April 1822 by the death of Allegra, Byron's five-year-old daughter with Claire Clairmont, whom he had sent to a convent for her upbringing. Another tragic death would soon follow: on July 8, shortly after the arrival of Leigh Hunt, with whom Byron and Shelley discussed plans for a periodical to be called *The Liberal,* Shelley drowned in the Bay of Spezia while sailing his newly built "Don Juan." Byron's interest in *The Liberal* waned, though four issues were printed, the first of which published *The Vision of Judgment*—landing its publisher, John Hunt, Leigh Hunt's brother, a conviction for seditious libel. It was also John Hunt to whom Byron turned for the publication of *Don Juan* beginning with Canto VI, after increasing difficulties with the cautious John Murray over the printing of his indecorous, heterodox, and potentially libelous verse led Byron to break with his former publisher.

With news of the Greek War of Independence and feeling that "a man should not consume his life at the side and on the bosom—of a woman" (p. 752)—and even with a presentiment of his own death in Greece—Byron accepted an invitation to go to Greece as a member of the London Greek Committee. After a stay at the port of Genoa, where he enjoyed the friendship of Lady Blessington, who was visiting from England with her husband and who recorded their lively conversations, he departed for Greece on the brig Hercules on July 13, in the company of Pietro Gamba and E. J. Trelawny, one of his and Shelley's friends at Pisa. He passed a few months on the island of Cephalonia before making the voyage to Missolonghi on the mainland, where he arrived on January 3, 1824, having narrowly escaped both shipwreck and Turkish capture. What he did not escape was perhaps his only experience since adolescence of unrequited love. He became deeply attached to Loukas Chalandritsanos, who was fifteen years old when Byron rescued his family of war refugees. Byron made him his page, saw to his family's financial support, and gave poetic form to his passionate feelings in "On This Day I Complete My Thirty-Sixth Year." Troubled by quarreling Greek factions and extremists (even at one point arranging the return of Turkish captives), he supported the moderate leader, Mavrocordatos, and helped form an artillery corps of Greek Suliotes. In February, however, Byron suffered severe convulsions, and in April fell seriously ill with a high fever. Further weakened by "bleeding," the only treatment known to his doctors, he died on April 19. Ironically, nothing he could have done in his life could have been as effective as the news of his death in uniting Greece and in gaining for its cause sympathy and support throughout Europe.

POETRY

CHILDE HAROLD'S PILGRIMAGE

CANTO THE FOURTH[1]

Visto ho Toscana, Lombardia, Romagna,
Quel Monte che divide, e quel che serra
Italia, e un mare e l' altro, che la bagna.

Ariosto, Satira iii.

Venice, January 2, 1818.

TO JOHN HOBHOUSE, ESQ. A.M. F.R.S. &c. &c. &c.

MY DEAR HOBHOUSE,

After an interval of eight years between the composition of the first and last cantos of Childe Harold, the conclusion of the poem is about to be submitted to the public. In parting with so old a friend, it is not extraordinary

---

1. In April 1817, Byron took a short trip from Venice to Rome, where he joined his friend and former travel companion, John Cam Hobhouse, stopping along the way at Padua, Ferrara, Bologna, and Florence. After returning to Venice in June and settling in at his summer home at nearby La Mira, he began the fourth canto of *Childe Harold.* The extensive historical annotations written by Hobhouse and published with the poem in April 1818, are omitted from the present edition due to space limitations; for these notes see *CPW* 2:218–64.

   In the fourth canto, as Byron observes in the prefatory dedication letter to Hobhouse, "there will be found less of the pilgrim than in any of the preceding, and that little slightly, if at all, separated from the author speaking in his own person." This final merging of hero and poet-narrator merely acknowledges their implicit identity in the preceding cantos (understood by Byron's readers), while the canto's setting in post-Napoleonic, pre-Risorgimento Italy allows for a culmination of themes introduced throughout *Childe Harold*: the grandeur of past civilizations set against a backdrop of natural beauty—with Venice as the starting point and paradigm; present-day ruins as ironic reminders of past vitality and glory; the descent from freedom and power to political submission to foreign rulers; the human scope for violence and revenge, on the one hand, and, on the other, redemptive sympathy and love (generally signified by female figures, historical and mythological). The special focus of the Italian canto is on art—on the echoes of Tasso, Petrarch, Shakespeare, and "things to greet the heart and eyes" (line 541). Italy, thus, with its "fatal gift of beauty" (line 371) objectifies the condition of the poet, who is "a ruin amidst ruins" (line 219), yet through his art "essentially immortal" (line 38). Like Canto III, Canto IV is informed by Byron's bitterness over his marital separation and the ensuing scandal and ostracism that prompted his self-exile from England. However, opposing the personal and historical arcs of desire and disappointment traceable throughout the four cantos of *Childe Harold* is the persistent beauty of Italy which inspires the

that I should recur to one still older and better,—to one who has beheld the birth and death of the other, and to whom I am far more indebted for the social advantages of an enlightened friendship, than—though not ungrateful—I can, or could be, to Childe Harold, for any public favour reflected through the poem on the poet,—to one, whom I have known long, and accompanied far, whom I have found wakeful over my sickness and kind in my sorrow, glad in my prosperity and firm in my adversity, true in counsel and trusty in peril,—to a friend often tried and never found wanting;—to yourself.

In so doing, I recur from fiction to truth; and in dedicating to you in its complete, or at least concluded state, a poetical work which is the longest, the most thoughtful and comprehensive of my compositions, I wish to do honour to myself by the record of many years' intimacy with a man of learning, of talent, of steadiness, and of honour. It is not for minds like ours to give or to receive flattery; yet the praises of sincerity have ever been permitted to the voices of friendship; and it is not for you, nor even for others, but to relieve a heart which has not elsewhere, or lately, been so much accustomed to the encounter of good-will as to withstand the shock firmly, that I thus attempt to commemorate your good qualities, or rather the advantages which I have derived from their exertion. Even the recurrence of the date of this letter, the anniversary of the most unfortunate day of my past existence, but which cannot poison my future while I retain the resource of your friendship, and of my own faculties, will henceforth have a more agreeable recollection for both, inasmuch as it will remind us of this my attempt to thank you for an indefatigable regard, such as few men have experienced, and no one could experience, without thinking better of his species and of himself.

It has been our fortune to traverse together, at various periods, the countries of chivalry, history, and fable—Spain, Greece, Asia Minor, and Italy; and what Athens and Constantinople were to us a few years ago, Venice and Rome have been more recently. The poem also, or the pilgrim, or both, have accompanied me from first to last; and perhaps it may be a pardonable vanity which induces me to reflect with complacency on a composition which in some degree connects me with the spot where it was produced, and the objects it would fain describe; and however unworthy it may be deemed of those magical and memorable abodes, however short it may fall of our distant conceptions and immediate impressions, yet as a mark of respect for what is venerable, and of feeling for what is glorious, it has been to me a source of pleasure in the production, and I part with it with a kind of regret, which I hardly suspected that events could have left me for imaginary objects.

With regard to the conduct of the last canto, there will be found less of the pilgrim than in any of the preceding, and that little slightly, if at all, separated from the author speaking in his own person. The fact is, that I had become weary of drawing a line which every one seemed determined not to

---

suffering poet to affirm that "there is that within me which shall tire / Torture and Time, and breathe when I expire" (lines 1228–29). The poem ends at the ocean, which, fittingly for a pilgrimage, reveals a transcendent power that is "boundless, endless, and sublime" (line 1643).
    Criticism: In addition to works listed in the headnote to *Childe Harold* I–II and Christensen, "The Shaping Spirit of Ruin: *Childe Harold* IV" (p. 926), see: Bone, "*Childe Harold's Pilgrimage* IV, *Don Juan* and *Beppo*," in Bone, ed., *The Cambridge Companion to Byron*; Blackstone, *Byron: A Survey*; Newey, "Authoring the Self: *Childe Harold* III and IV."

perceive: like the Chinese in Goldsmith's 'Citizen of the World,' whom nobody would believe to be a Chinese, it was in vain that I asserted, and imagined that I had drawn, a distinction between the author and the pilgrim; and the very anxiety to preserve this difference, and disappointment at finding it unavailing, so far crushed my efforts in the composition, that I determined to abandon it altogether—and have done so. The opinions which have been, or may be, formed on that subject, are *now* a matter of indifference; the work is to depend on itself, and not on the writer; and the author, who has no resources in his own mind beyond the reputation, transient or permanent, which is to arise from his literary efforts, deserves the fate of authors.[2]

In the course of the following canto it was my intention, either in the text or in the notes, to have touched upon the present state of Italian literature, and perhaps of manners. But the text, within these limits I proposed, I soon found hardly sufficient for the labyrinth of external objects, and the consequent reflections; and for the whole of the notes, excepting a few of the shortest, I am indebted to yourself, and these were necessarily limited to the elucidation of the text.

It is also a delicate, and no very grateful task, to dissert upon the literature and manners of a nation so dissimilar; and requires an attention and impartiality which would induce us—though perhaps no inattentive observers, nor ignorant of the language or customs of the people amongst whom we have recently abode—to distrust, or at least defer our judgment, and more narrowly examine our information. The state of literary, as well as political party, appears to run, or to *have* run, so high, that for a stranger to steer impartially between them is next to impossible. It may be enough, then, at least for my purpose, to quote from their own beautiful language—
'Mi pare che in un paese tutto poetico, che vante la lingua la più nobile ed insieme la più dolce, tutte tutte le vie diverse si possono tentare, e che sinche la patria di Alfieri e di Monti non ha perduto l'antico valore, in tutte essa dovrebbe essere la prima.' Italy has great names still—Canova, Monti, Ugo Foscolo, Pindemonte, Visconti, Morelli, Cicognara, Albrizzi, Mezzophanti, Mai, Mustoxidi, Aglietti, and Vacca, will secure to the present generation an honourable place in most of the departments of Art, Science, and Belles Lettres; and in some the very highest—Europe—the World—has but one Canova.

It has been somewhere said by Alfieri, that 'La pianta uomo nasce più robusta in Italia che in qualunque altra terra—e che gli stessi atroci delitti che vi si commettono ne sono una prova.' Without subscribing to the latter part of his proposition, a dangerous doctrine, the truth of which may be disputed on better grounds, namely, that the Italians are in no respect more ferocious than their neighbours, that man must be wilfully blind, or ignorantly heedless, who is not struck with the extraordinary capacity of this people, or, if such a word be admissible, their *capabilities*, the facility of their acquisitions, the rapidity of their conceptions, the fire of their genius, their sense of beauty, and, amidst all the disadvantages of repeated revolutions, the desolation of battles, and the despair of ages, their still unquenched 'longing after immortality,'—the immortality of independence.

---

2. In the manuscript, Byron continues this paragraph with a discusson of the conflict between Classic and Romantic poetry (see *CPW* 2: 122n).

And when we ourselves, in riding round the walls of Rome, heard the simple lament of the labourers' chorus, 'Roma! Roma! Roma! Roma non è più come era prima,' it was difficult not to contrast this melancholy dirge with the bacchanal roar of the songs of exultation still yelled from the London taverns, over the carnage of Mont St Jean, and the betrayal of Genoa, of Italy, of France, and of the world, by men whose conduct you yourself have exposed in a work worthy of the better days of our history. For me,—

'Non movero mai corda
Ove la turba di sue ciance assorda.'

What Italy has gained by the late transfer of nations, it were useless for Englishmen to enquire, till it becomes ascertained that England has acquired something more than a permanent army and a suspended Habeas Corpus; it is enough for them to look at home. For what they have done abroad, and especially in the South, 'Verily they *will have* their reward,' and at no very distant period.

Wishing you, my dear Hobhouse, a safe and agreeable return to that country whose real welfare can be dearer to none than to yourself, I dedicate to you this poem in its completed state; and repeat once more how truly I am ever,

                              Your obliged
                                        And affectionate friend,
                                                            BYRON.

1

I stood in Venice, on the Bridge of Sighs;[1]
A palace and a prison on each hand:
I saw from out the wave her structures rise
As from the stroke of the enchanter's wand:
A thousand years their cloudy wings expand   5
Around me, and a dying Glory smiles
O'er the far times, when many a subject land
Look'd to the winged Lion's[2] marble piles,
Where Venice sate in state, throned on her hundred isles!

2

She looks a sea Cybele, fresh from ocean,[3]   10
Rising with her tiara of proud towers
At airy distance, with majestic motion,
A ruler of the waters and their powers:
And such she was;—her daughters had their dowers

1. "The 'Bridge of Sighs' (il Ponte dei Sospiri) divides the Doge's Palace from the state prison.—It is roofed and *divided* by a wall into two passages.—By the one—the prisoner was conveyed to judgment—by the other he returned to death, being generally strangled in an adjoining chamber"—from a manuscript note by Byron.
2. The emblem of St. Mark the Evangelist, patron saint of Venice.
3. "Sabellicus [Marcus Sabellicus, 1436–1506], describing the appearance of Venice, has made use of the above image, which would not be poetical were it not true.—'Quo fit ut qui superne urbem contempletur, turritam telluris imaginem medio Oceano figuratam se putet inspicere.'" *Cybele*: in Greek mythology, the mother of the gods, represented as wearing a crown of towers.

From spoils of nations, and the exhaustless East   15
Pour'd in her lap all gems in sparkling showers.[4]
In purple was she robed, and of her feast
Monarchs partook, and deem'd their dignity increased.

3

In Venice Tasso's echoes are no more,[5]
And silent rows the songless gondolier;   20
Her palaces are crumbling to the shore,
And music meets not always now the ear:
Those days are gone—but Beauty still is here.
States fall, arts fade—but Nature doth not die,
Nor yet forget how Venice once was dear,   25
The pleasant place of all festivity,
The revel of the earth, the masque[6] of Italy!

4

But unto us she hath a spell beyond
Her name in story, and her long array
Of mighty shadows, whose dim forms despond   30
Above the dogeless[7] city's vanish'd sway;
Ours is a trophy which will not decay
With the Rialto;[8] Shylock and the Moor,
And Pierre, can not be swept or worn away—
The keystones of the arch! though all were o'er,   35
For us repeopled were the solitary shore.

5

The beings of the mind are not of clay;
Essentially immortal, they create
And multiply in us a brighter ray
And more beloved existence: that which Fate   40
Prohibits to dull life, in this our state
Of mortal bondage, by these spirits supplied
First exiles, then replaces what we hate;
Watering the heart whose early flowers have died,
And with a fresher growth replenishing the void.   45

6

Such is the refuge of our youth and age,
The first from Hope, the last from Vacancy;

4. In the early fifteenth century, Venice was the leading European sea power, enriched by Asian goods.
5. Torquato Tasso (1544–1595), Venetian poet and author of the Renaissance epic *Jerusalem Delivered*; Venetian gondoliers once routinely sang alternate stanzas of Tasso's epic to each other as their boats passed.
6. A ceremonial court entertainment common during the early seventeenth century.
7. The last doge (ruler) of Venice was deposed by Napoleon in 1797; in 1817 Venice was under Austrian rule.
8. The famed marble bridge spanning the Grand Canal, the city's early center of business; Shylock, the Moor, and Pierre are central characters in, respectively, Shakespeare's *The Merchant of Venice* and *Othello* and Thomas Otway's play *Venice Preserved* (1682).

And this worn feeling peoples many a page,
And, may be, that which grows beneath mine eye:
Yet there are things whose strong reality   50
Outshines our fairy-land; in shape and hues
More beautiful than our fantastic sky,
And the strange constellations which the Muse[9]
O'er her wild universe is skilful to diffuse:

7

I saw or dream'd of such,—but let them go,—   55
They came like truth, and disappear'd like dreams;
And whatsoe'er they were—are now but so:
I could replace them if I would; still teems
My mind with many a form which aptly seems
Such as I sought for, and at moments found;   60
Let these too go—for waking Reason deems
Such over-weening phantasies unsound,
And other voices speak, and other sights surround.

8

I've taught me other tongues—and in strange eyes
Have made me not a stranger; to the mind   65
Which is itself, no changes bring surprise;
Nor is it harsh to make, nor hard to find
A country with—ay, or without mankind;
Yet was I born where men are proud to be,
Not without cause; and should I leave behind   70
The inviolate island of the sage and free,
And seek me out a home by a remoter sea,

9

Perhaps I loved it well; and should I lay
My ashes in a soil which is not mine,
My spirit shall resume it—if we may   75
Unbodied choose a sanctuary. I twine
My hopes of being remember'd in my line
With my land's language: if too fond and far
These aspirations in their scope incline,—
If my fame should be, as my fortunes are,   80
Of hasty growth and blight, and dull Oblivion bar

10

My name from out the temple where the dead
Are honour'd by the nations—let it be—
And light the laurels on a loftier head!

---

9. In classical myth and epic, one of the nine daughters of Zeus and Mnemosyne (Memory) who
   inspires the poet.

And be the Spartan's epitaph on me—   85
"Sparta hath many a worthier son than he."[1]
Meantime I seek no sympathies, nor need;
The thorns which I have reap'd are of the tree
I planted,—they have torn me,—and I bleed:
I should have known what fruit would spring from such a seed.   90

11

The spouseless Adriatic mourns her lord;
And, annual marriage now no more renew'd,
The Bucentaur[2] lies rotting unrestored,
Neglected garment of her widowhood!
St. Mark yet sees his lion where he stood[3]   95
Stand, but in mockery of his wither'd power,
Over the proud Place where an Emperor sued,[4]
And monarchs gazed and envied in the hour
When Venice was a queen with an unequall'd dower.

12

The Suabian sued, and now the Austrian reigns[5]—   100
An Emperor tramples where an Emperor knelt;
Kingdoms are shrunk to provinces, and chains
Clank over sceptred cities; nations melt
From power's high pinnacle, when they have felt
The sunshine for a while, and downward go   105
Like lauwine[6] loosen'd from the mountain's belt;
Oh for one hour of blind old Dandolo![7]
Th' octogenarian chief, Byzantium's conquering foe.

13

Before St. Mark still glow his steeds of brass,[8]
Their gilded collars glittering in the sun;   110
But is not Doria's menace come to pass?[9]
Are they *not bridled?*—Venice, lost and won,

1. "The answer of the mother of Brasidas, the Lacedaemonian general, to the strangers who praised the memory of her son." Brasidas died 422 B.C.E., in the first decade of the Peloponnesian War.
2. The state barge in which, on Ascension Day, the doge of Venice would drop a ring into the Adriatic, symbolically marrying the city to the sea; the vessel was destroyed by the French in 1797, and Byron viewed its broken remains.
3. The statue of the winged lion that stands atop a column next to the Doge's Palace in St. Mark's Square.
4. Lines 97–101 refer to the humiliating submission of Frederic Barbarossa, Duke of Suabia, to the Pope in 1177.
5. The Austrian emperor is Francis I (1804–1835).
6. Pronounced lo´-win; avalanche.
7. Enrico Dandolo, doge 1192–1205, considered founder of the Venetian Empire; he commanded the fleet in the capture of Constantinople ("Byzantium," line 108) in 1204, where according to legend he was blinded by the Byzantine emperor. Line 107 echoes Walter Scott, "Oh, for one hour of Dundee!" (*Tales of a Grandfather* [1830], series III, chap. 10).
8. The original four brass horses that stood before the basilica of the Doge's Palace had been looted from Constantinople in 1204 during the Fourth Crusade; taken from Venice by Napoleon in 1797, they were restored to Venice in 1815.
9. A threat to bridle the horses of St. Mark was attributed to a Genovese admiral, Pietro Doria (1330–1404).

Her thirteen hundred years of freedom done,
Sinks, like a sea-weed, into whence she rose!
Better be whelm'd beneath the waves, and shun,   115
Even in destruction's depth, her foreign foes,
From whom submission wrings an infamous repose.

14

In youth she was all glory,—a new Tyre,[1]—
Her very by-word sprung from victory,
The "Planter of the Lion,"[2] which through fire   120
And blood she bore o'er subject earth and sea;
Though making many slaves, herself still free,
And Europe's bulwark 'gainst the Ottomite;[3]
Witness Troy's rival, Candia![4] Vouch it, ye
Immortal waves that saw Lepanto's[5] Fight!   125
For ye are names no time nor tyranny can blight.

15

Statues of glass—all shiver'd—the long file
Of her dead Doges are declined to dust;
But where they dwelt, the vast and sumptuous pile
Bespeaks the pageant of their splendid trust;   130
Their sceptre broken, and their sword in rust,
Have yielded to the stranger: empty halls,
Thin streets, and foreign aspects, such as must
Too oft remind her who and what enthrals,
Have flung a desolate cloud o'er Venice' lovely walls.   135

16

When Athens' armies fell at Syracuse,
And fetter'd thousands bore the yoke of war,
Redemption rose up in the Attic Muse,[6]
Her voice their only ransom from afar:
See! as they chant the tragic hymn, the car   140
Of the o'ermaster'd victor stops, the reins
Fall from his hands—his idle scimitar[7]
Starts from its belt—he rends his captive's chains,
And bids him thank the bard for freedom and his strains.

---

1. Ancient seaport in Phoenicia, one of the great cities of antiquity.
2. "That is, the Lion of St. Mark, the standard of the republic, which is the origin of the word Pantaloon—Piantaleone, Pantaleon, Pantaloon."
3. People of the Turkish Empire. "Shakespeare is my authority for the word Ottomite for Ottoman" (Byron's manuscript note; see *Othello* 2.3.154.)
4. Capital of Crete, vital part of the Venetian Empire before 1669; it fell to the Turks, as Troy to Greece, after a bombardment lasting many years.
5. Battle of Lepanto, October 7, 1571, ended Turkish naval supremacy in the Mediterranean.
6. "The story is told in Plutarch's Life of Nicias." Syracuse defeated Athens in 414 B.C.E.
7. Curved sword of Asian origin.

17

Thus, Venice, if no stronger claim were thine,   145
Were all thy proud historic deeds forgot,
Thy choral memory of the Bard divine,
Thy love of Tasso, should have cut the knot[8]
Which ties thee to thy tyrants; and thy lot
Is shameful to the nations,—most of all,   150
Albion! to thee: the Ocean queen should not
Abandon Ocean's children; in the fall
Of Venice think of thine, despite thy watery wall.

18

I loved her from my boyhood—she to me
Was as a fairy city of the heart,   155
Rising like water-columns from the sea,
Of joy the sojourn, and of wealth the mart;
And Otway, Radcliffe, Schiller, Shakspeare's art,[9]
Had stamp'd her image in me, and even so,
Although I found her thus, we did not part,   160
Perchance even dearer in her day of woe,
Than when she was a boast, a marvel, and a show.

19

I can repeople with the past—and of
The present there is still for eye and thought,
And meditation chasten'd down, enough;   165
And more, it may be, than I hoped or sought;
And of the happiest moments which were wrought
Within the web of my existence, some
From thee, fair Venice! have their colours caught:
There are some feelings Time cannot benumb,   170
Nor Torture shake, or mine would now be cold and dumb.

20

But from their nature will the tannen grow[1]
Loftiest on loftiest and least shelter'd rocks,
Rooted in barrenness, where nought below
Of soil supports them 'gainst the Alpine shocks   175
Of eddying storms; yet springs the trunk, and mocks
The howling tempest, till its height and frame
Are worthy of the mountains from whose blocks
Of bleak, gray granite into life it came,
And grew a giant tree;—the mind may grow the same.   180

8. The Treaty of Paris (1814) returned Venice to Austrian rule; Castlereagh was the delegate from England ("Albion," line 151). *Tasso*: see p. 299, n. 5.
9. "Venice Preserved; Mysteries of Udolpho; the Ghost-Seer, or Armenian; the Merchant of Venice; Othello." *Radcliffe*: Ann Radcliffe (1764–1823), English author of Gothic novels. *Schiller*: Friedrich von Schiller (1759–1805), German poet, playwright, philosopher and historian.
1. "*Tannen* is the plural of *tanne*, a species of fir peculiar to the Alps, which only thrives in very rocky parts, where scarcely soil sufficient for its nourishment can be found. On these spots it grows to a greater height than any other mountain tree."

21

Existence may be borne, and the deep root
Of life and sufferance make its firm abode
In bare and desolated bosoms: mute
The camel labours with the heaviest load,
And the wolf dies in silence,—not bestow'd   185
In vain should such example be; if they,
Things of ignoble or of savage mood,
Endure and shrink not, we of nobler clay
May temper it to bear,—it is but for a day.

22

All suffering doth destroy, or is destroy'd,   190
Even by the sufferer; and, in each event,
Ends:—Some, with hope replenish'd and rebuoy'd,
Return to whence they came—with like intent,
And weave their web again; some, bow'd and bent,
Wax gray and ghastly, withering ere their time,   195
And perish with the reed on which they leant;
Some seek devotion, toil, war, good or crime,
According as their souls were form'd to sink or climb:

23

But ever and anon of griefs subdued
There comes a token like a scorpion's sting,   200
Scarce seen, but with fresh bitterness imbued;
And slight withal may be the things which bring
Back on the heart the weight which it would fling
Aside for ever: it may be a sound—
A tone of music—summer's eve—or spring—   205
A flower—the wind—the ocean—which shall wound,
Striking the electric chain wherewith we are darkly bound;

24

And how and why we know not, nor can trace
Home to its cloud this lightning of the mind,
But feel the shock renew'd, nor can efface   210
The blight and blackening which it leaves behind,
Which out of things familiar, undesign'd,
When least we deem of such, calls up to view
The spectres whom no exorcism can bind,
The cold—the changed—perchance the dead—anew,   215
The mourn'd, the loved, the lost—too many!—yet how few!

25

But my soul wanders; I demand it back
To meditate amongst decay, and stand
A ruin amidst ruins; there to track

Fall'n states and buried greatness, o'er a land   220
Which *was* the mightiest in its old command,
And *is* the loveliest, and must ever be
The master-mould of Nature's heavenly hand,
Wherein were cast the heroic and the free,
The beautiful, the brave—the lords of earth and sea,   225

26

The commonwealth of kings, the men of Rome!
And even since, and now, fair Italy!
Thou art the garden of the world, the home
Of all Art yields, and Nature can decree;
Even in thy desert, what is like to thee?   230
Thy very weeds are beautiful, thy waste
More rich than other climes' fertility;
Thy wreck a glory, and thy ruin graced
With an immaculate charm which cannot be defaced.

27

The moon is up, and yet it is not night—   235
Sunset divides the sky with her—a sea
Of glory streams along the Alpine height
Of blue Friuli's mountains;[2] Heaven is free
From clouds, but of all colours seems to be
Melted to one vast Iris of the West,   240
Where the Day joins the past Eternity;
While, on the other hand, meek Dian's crest
Floats through the azure air—an island of the blest![3]

28

A single star is at her side, and reigns
With her o'er half the lovely heaven; but still   245
Yon sunny sea heaves brightly, and remains
Roll'd o'er the peak of the far Rhaetian hill,[4]
As Day and Night contending were, until
Nature reclaim'd her order:—gently flows
The deep-dyed Brenta, where their hues instil   250
The odorous purple of a new-born rose,
Which streams upon her stream, and glass'd within it glows,

29

Fill'd with the face of heaven, which, from afar,
Comes down upon the waters; all its hues,

2. The Friulian Alps are northeast of Venice.
3. "The above description may seem fantastical or exaggerated to those who have never seen an Oriental or an Italian sky, yet it is but a literal and hardly sufficient delineation of an August evening (the eighteenth), as contemplated in one of many rides along the banks of the Brenta, near La Mira."
4. The Rhaetian Alps are northwest of Venice.

From the rich sunset to the rising star,   255
Their magical variety diffuse:
And now they change; a paler shadow strews
Its mantle o'er the mountains; parting day
Dies like the dolphin, whom each pang imbues
With a new colour as it gasps away,   260
The last still loveliest, till—'tis gone—and all is gray.

30

There is a tomb in Arqua;[5]—rear'd in air,
Pillar'd in their sarcophagus, repose
The bones of Laura's lover: here repair
Many familiar with his well-sung woes,   265
The pilgrims of his genius. He arose
To raise a language, and his land reclaim
From the dull yoke of her barbaric foes:
Watering the tree which bears his lady's name
With his melodious tears, he gave himself to fame.   270

31

They keep his dust in Arqua, where he died;
The mountain-village where his latter days
Went down the vale of years; and 'tis their pride—
An honest pride—and let it be their praise,
To offer to the passing stranger's gaze   275
His mansion and his sepulchre; both plain
And venerably simple, such as raise
A feeling more accordant with his strain
Than if a pyramid form'd his monumental fane.

32

And the soft quiet hamlet where he dwelt   280
Is one of that complexion which seems made
For those who their mortality have felt,
And sought a refuge from their hopes decay'd
In the deep umbrage of a green hill's shade,
Which shows a distant prospect far away   285
Of busy cities,[6] now in vain display'd,
For they can lure no further; and the ray
Of a bright sun can make sufficient holiday.

33

Developing the mountains, leaves, and flowers,
And shining in the brawling brook, where-by,   290

5. The tomb of Petrarch (Francesco Petrarca, 1304–1374), Italian humanist and poet, lies in this vil-
   lage in the Euganean hills in northeast Italy. Petrarch's poetry, especially his sonnets to Laura, con-
   tributed significantly to the Italian language and literary tradition; "Laura's lover" (line 264) is
   meant in the ideal sense as the identity of Laura or whether or not she knew of Petrarch's existence
   is not definitively known.
6. Venice and Padua.

Clear as its current, glide the sauntering hours
With a calm languor, which, though to the eye
Idlesse it seem, hath its morality.
  If from society we learn to live,
'Tis solitude should teach us how to die;   295
It hath no flatterers; vanity can give
No hollow aid; alone—man with his God must strive:

34

Or, it may be, with demons, who impair[7]
The strength of better thoughts, and seek their prey
In melancholy bosoms, such as were   300
Of moody texture from their earliest day,
And loved to dwell in darkness and dismay,
  Deeming themselves predestined to a doom
Which is not of the pangs that pass away;
Making the sun like blood, the earth a tomb,   305
The tomb a hell, and hell itself a murkier gloom.

35

Ferrara![8] in thy wide and grass-grown streets,
Whose symmetry was not for solitude,
There seems as 'twere a curse upon the seats
Of former sovereigns, and the antique brood   310
Of Este, which for many an age made good
Its strength within thy walls, and was of yore
  Patron or tyrant, as the changing mood
Of petty power impell'd, of those who wore
The wreath which Dante's[9] brow alone had worn before.   315

36

And Tasso is their glory and their shame.
Hark to his strain! and then survey his cell!
And see how dearly earn'd Torquato's fame,
And where Alfonso bade his poet dwell:
The miserable despot could not quell   320
The insulted mind he sought to quench, and blend
  With the surrounding maniacs, in the hell
Where he had plunged it. Glory without end
Scatter'd the clouds away—and on that name attend

---

7. "The struggle is to the full as likely to be with demons as with our better thoughts. Satan chose the wilderness for the temptation of our Saviour. And our unsullied John Locke preferred the presence of a child to complete solitude."
8. Home of Torquato Tasso (see p. 299, n. 5) and seat of the House of Este. Stanzas 35–39 allude to the legend of Tasso's persecution and imprisonment by Alphonso II, Marquess of Este, a tragic subject to which Byron was personally drawn and which is the basis for his narrative poem *The Lament of Tasso* (1817).
9. Dante Alighieri (1265–1321), author of the *Divine Comedy*.

37

The tears and praises of all time; while thine   325
Would rot in its oblivion—in the sink
Of worthless dust, which from thy boasted line
Is shaken into nothing; but the link
Thou formest in his fortunes bids us think
Of thy poor malice, naming thee with scorn—   330
Alfonso! how thy ducal pageants shrink
From thee! if in another station born,
Scarce fit to be the slave of him thou mad'st to mourn:

38

Thou! form'd to eat, and be despised, and die,
Even as the beasts that perish, save that thou   335
Hadst a more splendid trough and wider sty:
He! with a glory round his furrow'd brow,
Which emanated then, and dazzles now,
In face of all his foes, the Cruscan[1] quire,
And Boileau, whose rash envy could allow   340
No strain which shamed his country's creaking lyre,
That whetstone of the teeth—monotony in wire!

39

Peace to Torquato's injured shade! 'twas his
In life and death to be the mark where Wrong
Aim'd with her poison'd arrows, but to miss.   345
Oh, victor unsurpass'd in modern song!
Each year brings forth its millions; but how long
The tide of generations shall roll on,
And not the whole combined and countless throng
Compose a mind like thine? though all in one   350
Condensed their scatter'd rays, they would not form a sun.

40

Great as thou art, yet parallel'd by those,
Thy countrymen, before thee born to shine,
The Bards[2] of Hell and Chivalry: first rose
The Tuscan father's comedy divine;   355
Then, not unequal to the Florentine,
The southern Scott the minstrel who call'd forth
A new creation with his magic line,
And, like the Ariosto of the North,
Sang ladye-love and war, romance and knightly worth.   360

---

1. The Accademia della Crusca, founded in 1542 in Florence, criticized Tasso's poetry, as did the
   French critic and poet, Nicolas Boileau-Despréaux (1636–1711).
2. Dante and the poet Ludovico Ariosto (1474–1533), author of the epic *Orlando Furioso* (1532); in
   lines 357–60 Byron compares Ariosto with the Scottish novelist and poet Sir Walter Scott
   (1771–1832).

41

The lightning rent from Ariosto's bust[3]
The iron crown of laurel's mimic'd leaves;
Nor was the ominous element unjust,
For the true laurel-wreath which Glory weaves
Is of the tree no bolt of thunder cleaves,   365
And the false semblance but disgraced his brow;
Yet still, if fondly Superstition grieves,
Know, that the lightning sanctifies below
Whate'er it strikes;—yon head is doubly sacred now.

42

Italia! oh Italia! thou who hast   370
The fatal gift of beauty, which became
A funeral dower of present woes and past,
On thy sweet brow is sorrow plough'd by shame,
And annals graved in characters of flame.
Oh, God! that thou wert in thy nakedness   375
Less lovely or more powerful, and couldst claim
Thy right, and awe the robbers back, who press
To shed thy blood, and drink the tears of thy distress;

43

Then might'st thou more appal; or, less desired,
Be homely and be peaceful, undeplored   380
For thy destructive charms; then, still untired,
Would not be seen the armed torrents pour'd
Down the deep Alps; nor would the hostile horde
Of many-nation'd spoilers from the Po[4]
Quaff blood and water; nor the stranger's sword   385
Be thy sad weapon of defence, and so,
Victor or vanquish'd, thou the slave of friend or foe.[5]

44

Wandering in youth, I traced the path of him,[6]
The Roman friend of Rome's least-mortal mind,
The friend of Tully: as my bark did skim   390

3. Ariosto's tomb was supposed to have been struck by lightning; the rest of the stanza refers to superstitions about lightning.
4. River in northern Italy.
5. "The two stanzas xlii. and xliii. are, with the exception of a line or two, a translation of the famous sonnet of Filicaja:—'Italia, Italia, O tu cui feo la sorte!'"
6. "The celebrated letter of Servius Sulpicius to Cicero, on the death of his daughter, describes as it then was, and now is, a path which I often traced in Greece, both by sea and land, in different journeys and voyages. 'On my return from Asia, as I was sailing from Aegina towards Megara, I began to contemplate the prospect of the countries around me: Aegina was behind, Megara before me; Piraeus on the right, Corinth on the left: all which towns, once famous and flourishing, now lie overturned and buried in their ruins. Alas! how do we poor mortals fret and vex ourselves if any of our friends happen to die or be killed, whose life is yet so short, when the carcasses of so many noble cities lie here exposed before me in one view.'—See Middleton's Cicero, vol. ii, p. 371." Servius Sulpicius was a friend of Rome's greatest orator, Marcus Tullius Cicero (Tully, 106–43 B.C.E.)

The bright blue waters with a fanning wind,
Came Megara before me, and behind
Aegina lay, Piraeus on the right,
And Corinth on the left; I lay reclined
Along the prow, and saw all these unite   395
In ruin, even as he had seen the desolate sight;

45

For Time hath not rebuilt them, but uprear'd
Barbaric dwellings on their shatter'd site,
Which only make more mourn'd and more endear'd
The few last rays of their far-scatter'd light,   400
And the crush'd relics of their vanish'd might.
The Roman saw these tombs in his own age,
These sepulchres of cities, which excite
Sad wonder, and his yet surviving page
The moral lesson bears, drawn from such pilgrimage.   405

46

That page is now before me, and on mine
His country's ruin added to the mass
Of perish'd states he mourn'd in their decline,
And I in desolation: all that *was*
Of then destruction *is*; and now, alas!   410
Rome—Rome imperial, bows her to the storm,
In the same dust and blackness, and we pass
The skeleton of her Titanic form,[7]
Wrecks of another world, whose ashes still are warm.

47

Yet, Italy! through every other land   415
Thy wrongs[8] should ring, and shall, from side to side.
Mother of Arts! as once of arms; thy hand
Was then our guardian, and is still our guide;
Parent of our Religion! whom the wide
Nations have knelt to for the keys of heaven!   420
Europe, repentant of her parricide,
Shall yet redeem thee, and, all backward driven,
Roll the barbarian tide, and sue to be forgiven.

48

But Arno[9] wins us to the fair white walls,
Where the Etrurian Athens claims and keeps   425

---

7. "It is Poggio, who, looking from the Capitoline hill upon ruined Rome, breaks forth into the excla-
   mation, 'Ut nunc omni decore nudata, prostrata jacet, instar gigantei cadaveris corrupti atque
   undique exesi.'" Poggio Bracciolini (1380–1452), Italian humanist. *Titanic*: huge—from the
   mythical Titans, the deities whose reign preceded the Olympians.
8. I.e., wrongs done to Italy.
9. River in Florence, "the Etrurian Athens" (line 425), i.e., as rich in arts and quality of life as ancient
   Athens. Etruria is the ancient name of the region surrounding Florence, modern Tuscany.

A softer feeling for her fairy halls.
Girt by her theatre of hills, she reaps
Her corn, and wine, and oil, and Plenty leaps
To laughing life, with her redundant horn.
Along the banks where smiling Arno sweeps   430
Was modern Luxury of Commerce born,
And buried Learning rose, redeem'd to a new morn.

49

There, too, the Goddess loves in stone,[1] and fills
The air around with beauty; we inhale
The ambrosial aspect, which, beheld, instils   435
Part of its immortality; the veil
Of heaven is half undrawn; within the pale
We stand, and in that form and face behold
What mind can make, when Nature's self would fail;
And to the fond idolaters of old   440
Envy the innate flash which such a soul could mould:

50

We gaze and turn away, and know not where,
Dazzled and drunk with beauty, till the heart
Reels with its fulness; there—for ever there—
Chain'd to the chariot of triumphal Art,   445
We stand as captives, and would not depart.
Away!—there need no words, nor terms precise,
The paltry jargon of the marble mart,
Where Pedantry gulls Folly—we have eyes:
Blood—pulse—and breast, confirm the Dardan Shepherd's prize.[2] 450

51

Appear'dst thou not to Paris in this guise?
Or to more deeply blest Anchises?[3] or,
In all thy perfect goddess-ship, when lies
Before thee thy own vanquish'd Lord of War?[4]
And gazing in thy face as toward a star,   455
Laid on thy lap, his eyes to thee upturn,
Feeding on thy sweet cheek![5] while thy lips are
With lava kisses melting while they burn,
Shower'd on his eyelids, brow, and mouth, as from an urn!

---

1. The Venus of Medici, in the Uffizi Gallery.
2. In Greek legend, Paris (the Dardan shepherd) awarded the prize for beauty to Aphrodite—Venus, in the Roman nomenclature.
3. Father of Venus's son Aeneas.
4. Mars, lover of Venus.
5. "Ὀφθαλμοὺς ἑστιᾶν.
   'Atque oculos pascat uterque suos.'—OVID. Amor. lib. ii."

52

Glowing, and circumfused in speechless love,   460
Their full divinity inadequate
That feeling to express, or to improve,
The gods become as mortals, and man's fate
Has moments like their brightest; but the weight
Of earth recoils upon us;—let it go!   465
We can recal such visions, and create,
From what has been, or might be, things which grow
Into thy statue's form, and look like gods below.

53

I leave to learned fingers, and wise hands,
The artist and his ape, to teach and tell   470
How well his connoisseurship understands
The graceful bend, and the voluptuous swell:
Let these describe the undescribable:
I would not their vile breath should crisp the stream
Wherein that image shall for ever dwell;   475
The unruffled mirror of the loveliest dream
That ever left the sky on the deep soul to beam.

54

In Santa Croce's[6] holy precints lie[7]
Ashes which make it holier, dust which is

6. The basilica of this large Franciscan church in Florence contains the tombs of some of the city's most illustrious individuals, as those named in this stanza: the painter and sculptor Michelangelo (1475–1564), the poet Vittorio, Count Alfieri (1749–1803), the astronomer Galileo Galilei (1564–1642), and the writer and statesman Niccolo Machiavelli (1469–1527).
7. "This name will recall the memory, not only of those whose tombs have raised the Santa Croce into the centre of pilgrimage, the Mecca of Italy, but of her whose eloquence was poured over the illustrious ashes, and whose voice is now as mute as those she sung. CORINNA is no more, and with her should expire the fear, the flattery, and the envy, which threw too dazzling or too dark a cloud round the march of genius, and forbad the steady gaze of disinterested criticism. We have her picture embellished or distorted, as friendship or detraction has held the pencil: the impartial portrait was hardly to be expected from a contemporary. The immediate voice of her survivors will, it is probable, be far from affording a just estimate of her singular capacity. The gallantry, the love of wonder, and the hope of associated fame, which blunted the edge of censure, must cease to exist.—The dead have no sex; they can surprise by no new miracles; they can confer no privilege: Corinna has ceased to be a woman—she is only an author: and it may be foreseen that many will repay themselves for former complaisance, by a severity to which the extravagance of previous praises may perhaps give the colour of truth. The latest posterity, for to the latest posterity they will surely descend, will have to pronounce upon her various productions; and the longer the vista through which they are seen, the more accurately minute will be the object, the more certain the justice, of the decision. She will enter into that existence in which the great writers of all ages and nations are, as it were, associated in a world of their own, and, from that superior sphere, shed their eternal influence for the control and consolation of mankind. But the individual will gradually disappear as the author is more distinctly seen: some one, therefore, of all those whom the charms of involuntary wit, and of easy hospitality, attracted within the friendly circles of Coppet, should rescue from oblivion those virtues which, although they are said to love the shade, are, in fact, more frequently chilled than excited by the domestic cares of private life. Some one should be found to portray the unaffected graces with which she adorned those dearer relationships, the performance of whose duties is rather discovered amongst the interior secrets, than seen in the outward management, of family intercourse; and which, indeed, it requires the delicacy of genuine affection to qualify for the eye of an indifferent spectator. Some one should be found, not to celebrate, but to describe, the amiable mistress of an open mansion, the centre of a society, ever varied, and always pleased, the creator of which, divested of the ambition and the arts of public rivalry, shone forth only to give fresh animation to those around her. The mother tenderly affectionate and tenderly beloved, the

Even in itself an immortality,   480
Though there were nothing save the past, and this,
The particle of those sublimities
Which have relapsed to chaos:—here repose
Angelo's, Alfieri's bones, and his,
The starry Galileo, with his woes;   485
Here Machiavelli's earth return'd to whence it rose.

55

These are four minds, which, like the elements,
Might furnish forth creation:—Italy!
Time, which hath wrong'd thee with ten thousand rents
Of thine imperial garment, shall deny,   490
And hath denied, to every other sky,
Spirits which soar from ruin:—thy decay
Is still impregnate with divinity,
Which gilds it with revivifying ray;
Such as the great of yore, Canova[8] is to-day.   495

56

But where repose the all Etruscan[9] three—
Dante, and Petrarch, and, scarce less than they,
The Bard of Prose,[1] creative spirit! he
Of the Hundred Tales of love—where did they lay
Their bones, distinguish'd from our common clay   500
In death as life? Are they resolved to dust,
And have their country's marbles nought to say?
Could not her quarries furnish forth one bust?
Did they not to her breast their filial earth intrust?

57

Ungrateful Florence! Dante sleeps afar,[2]   505
Like Scipio, buried by the upbraiding shore;
Thy factions, in their worse than civil war,
Proscribed the bard whose name for evermore
Their children's children would in vain adore
With the remorse of ages; and the crown   510

---

friend unboundedly generous, but still esteemed, the charitable patroness of all distress, cannot be forgotten by those whom she cherished, and protected, and fed. Her loss will be mourned the most where she was known the best; and, to the sorrows of very many friends, and more dependants, may be offered the disinterested regret of a stranger, who, amidst the sublimer scenes of the Leman lake, received his chief satisfaction from contemplating the engaging qualities of the incomparable Corinna." Madame de Staël, the celebrated social critic and writer, died in July 1817. Byron had enjoyed her company and illustrious coterie while they were both living at Lake Geneva. In his note, he refers to her as Corinna, the heroine of one of her novels.
8. Antonio Canova (1757–1822), sculptor.
9. Tuscan, Florentine.
1. Giovanni Boccaccio (1313–1375), author of Decameron ("the Hundred Tales of love," line 499).
2. Echoing the epitaph of Scipio Africanus ("Ingrata patria"), Rome's military hero exiled from Rome for political reasons as Dante was exiled from Florence. Given his own recent experience in England—the scandal of his marriage separation prompting his expatriation—Byron identified with the illustrious exiles of stanzas 56–59 as victims of their own people's ingratitude.

Which Petrarch's laureate brow supremely wore,
Upon a far and foreign soil had grown,[3]
His life, his fame, his grave, though rifled—not thine own.

58

Boccaccio to his parent earth bequeath'd[4]
His dust,—and lies it not her Great among,   515
With many a sweet and solemn requiem breathed
O'er him who form'd the Tuscan's siren tongue?
That music in itself, whose sounds are song,
The poetry of speech? No;—even his tomb
Uptorn, must bear the hyaena bigot's wrong,   520
No more amidst the meaner dead find room,
Nor claim a passing sigh, because it told for *whom!*

59

And Santa Croce wants their mighty dust;
Yet for this want more noted, as of yore
The Caesar's pageant, shorn of Brutus' bust,[5]   525
Did but of Rome's best Son remind her more:
Happier Ravenna! on thy hoary shore,
Fortress of falling empire! honour'd sleeps
The immortal exile;—Arqua,[6] too, her store
Of tuneful relics proudly claims and keeps,   530
While Florence vainly begs her banish'd dead and weeps.

60

What is her pyramid of precious stones?[7]
Of porphyry, jasper, agate, and all hues
Of gem and marble, to encrust the bones
Of merchant-dukes? the momentary dews   535
Which, sparkling to the twilight stars, infuse
Freshness in the green turf that wraps the dead,
Whose names are mausoleums of the Muse,
Are gently prest with far more reverent tread
Than ever paced the slab which paves the princely head.   540

61

There be more things to greet the heart and eyes
In Arno's dome of Art's most princely shrine,[8]

---

3. Offers of the laurel wreath for poetic achievement came to Petrarch from Rome and Paris.
4. The town of Certaldo. The tomb of Boccaccio, a church satirist, was removed from the central part of the church by orders of the ecclesiastical authorities ("hyaena bigot," line 520).
5. Marcus Junius Brutus (85?–42 B.C.E.), Roman military hero involved in the plot to kill Julius Caesar; his bust was therefore barred at the pageant decreed by Tiberius Caesar. During the Gallic and Civil wars, Brutus (the "immortal exile," line 529) had led military victories from Ravenna, then a seaport and key city of the empire.
6. See p. 306, n. 5.
7. The Medici chapel.
8. The Uffizi or Pitti Palace; see *BLJ* 5.218.

Where Sculpture with her rainbow sister vies;
There be more marvels yet—but not for mine;
For I have been accustom'd to entwine   545
My thoughts with Nature rather in the fields,
Than Art in galleries: though a work divine
Calls for my spirit's homage, yet it yields
Less than it feels, because the weapon which it wields

62

Is of another temper, and I roam   550
By Thrasimene's lake,⁹ in the defiles
Fatal to Roman rashness, more at home;
For there the Carthaginian's warlike wiles
Come back before me, as his skill beguiles
The host between the mountains and the shore,   555
Where Courage falls in her despairing files,
And torrents, swoll'n to rivers with their gore,
Reek through the sultry plain, with legions scatter'd o'er,

63

Like to a forest fell'd by mountain winds;
And such the storm of battle on this day,   560
And such the frenzy, whose convulsion blinds
To all save carnage, that, beneath the fray,
An earthquake reel'd unheededly away!
None felt stern Nature rocking at his feet,
And yawning forth a grave for those who lay   565
Upon their bucklers¹ for a winding sheet;
Such is the absorbing hate when warring nations meet!

64

The Earth to them was as a rolling bark
Which bore them to Eternity; they saw
The Ocean round, but had no time to mark   570
The motions of their vessel; Nature's law,
In them suspended, reck'd not of the awe
Which reigns when mountains tremble, and the birds
Plunge in the clouds for refuge and withdraw
From their down-toppling nests; and bellowing herds   575
Stumble o'er heaving plains, and man's dread hath no words.

65

Far other scene is Thrasimene now;
Her lake a sheet of silver, and her plain
Rent by no ravage save the gentle plough;

9. Where Hannibal (the Carthaginian in line 533) defeated the Romans in 217 B.C.E.
1. Shields, which serve as a burial cover ("winding sheet").

Her aged trees rise thick as once the slain   580
Lay where their roots are; but a brook hath ta'en—
A little rill of scanty stream and bed—
A name of blood from that day's sanguine rain;
And Sanguinetto[2] tells ye where the dead
Made the earth wet, and turn'd the unwilling waters red.   585

66

But thou, Clitumnus! in thy sweetest wave
Of the most living crystal that was e'er
The haunt of river nymph, to gaze and lave
Her limbs where nothing hid them, thou dost rear
Thy grassy banks whereon the milk-white steer   590
Grazes; the purest god of gentle waters!
And most serene of aspect, and most clear;
Surely that stream was unprofaned by slaughters—
A mirror and a bath for Beauty's youngest daughters!

67

And on thy happy shore a Temple still,   595
Of small and delicate proportion, keeps,
Upon a mild declivity of hill,
Its memory of thee; beneath it sweeps
Thy current's calmness; oft from out it leaps
The finny darter with the glittering scales,   600
Who dwells and revels in thy glassy deeps;
While, chance, some scatter'd water-lily sails
Down where the shallower wave still tells its bubbling tales.

68

Pass not unblest the Genius of the place!
If through the air a zephyr[3] more serene   605
Win to the brow, 'tis his; and if ye trace
Along his margin a more eloquent green,
If on the heart the freshness of the scene
Sprinkle its coolness, and from the dry dust
Of weary life a moment lave it clean   610
With Nature's baptism,—'tis to him ye must
Pay orisons for this suspension of disgust.[4]

69

The roar of waters!—from the headlong height
Velino cleaves the wave-worn precipice;
The fall of waters! rapid as the light   615

---

2. Literally "little bloody one": name of the brook mentioned in line 581; contrasted with the river
   Clitumnus (line 586) in central Italy.
3. Gentle breeze.
4. Literally the inability to enjoy taste, i.e., to feel pleasure in nature or life; *orisons*: prayers.

The flashing mass foams shaking the abyss;
The hell of waters! where they howl and hiss,
And boil in endless torture; while the sweat
Of their great agony, wrung out from this
Their Phlegethon,[5] curls round the rocks of jet   620
That gird the gulf around, in pitiless horror set,

70

And mounts in spray the skies, and thence again
Returns in an unceasing shower, which round,
With its unemptied cloud of gentle rain,
Is an eternal April to the ground,   625
Making it all one emerald:—how profound
The gulf! and how the giant element
From rock to rock leaps with delirious bound,
Crushing the cliffs, which, downward worn and rent
With his fierce footsteps, yield in chasms a fearful vent   630

71

To the broad column which rolls on, and shows
More like the fountain of an infant sea
Torn from the womb of mountains by the throes
Of a new world, than only thus to be
Parent of rivers, which flow gushingly,   635
With many windings, through the vale:—Look back!
Lo! where it comes like an eternity,
As if to sweep down all things in its track,
Charming the eye with dread,—a matchless cataract,[6]

72

Horribly beautiful! but on the verge,   640
From side to side, beneath the glittering morn,
An Iris sits, amidst the infernal surge,[7]
Like Hope upon a death-bed, and, unworn
Its steady dyes, while all around is torn
By the distracted waters, bears serene   645

---

5. In classical myth, a river of fire in Hades.
6. "I saw the 'Cascata del marmore' of Terni twice, at different periods; once from the summit of the precipice, and again from the valley below. The lower view is far to be preferred, if the traveller has time for one only; but in any point of view, either from above or below, it is worth all the cascades and torrents of Switzerland put together: the Staubach, Reichenbach, Pisse Vache, fall of Arpenaz, &c. are rills in comparative appearance. Of the fall of Schaffhausen I cannot speak, not yet having seen it."
7. "Of the time, place, and qualities of this kind of iris, the reader will see a short account in a note to *Manfred*. The fall looks so much like 'the hell of waters,' that Addison thought the descent alluded to by the gulf in which Alecto plunged into the infernal regions. It is singular enough, that two of the finest cascades in Europe should be artificial—this of the Velino, and the one at Tivoli. The traveller is strongly recommended to trace the Velino, at least as high as the little lake, called *Pie' di Lup*. The Reatine territory was the Italian Tempe (Cicer. Epist. ad Attic. xv. lib. iv.), and the ancient naturalist (Plin. Hist. Nat. lib. ii. cap. lxii), amongst other beautiful varieties, remarked the daily rainbows of the lake Velinus. A scholar of great name has devoted a treatise to this district alone. Ald. Manut de Reatina Urbe Agroque, ap. Sallengre, Thesaur. tom. i. p. 773."

Its brilliant hues with all their beams unshorn:
Resembling, 'mid the torture of the scene,
Love watching Madness with unalterable mien.

73

Once more upon the woody Apennine,[8]
The infant Alps, which—had I not before   650
Gazed on their mightier parents, where the pine
Sits on more shaggy summits, and where roar
The thundering lauwine[9]—might be worshipp'd more;
But I have seen the soaring Jungfrau[1] rear
Her never-trodden snow, and seen the hoar   655
Glaciers of bleak Mont Blanc both far and near,
And in Chimari heard the thunder-hills of fear,

74

Th' Acroceraunian mountains[2] of old name;
And on Parnassus seen the eagles fly
Like spirits of the spot, as 'twere for fame,   660
For still they soar'd unutterably high:
I've look'd on Ida with a Trojan's eye;
Athos, Olympus, Aetna, Atlas, made
These hills seem things of lesser dignity,
All, save the lone Soracte's[3] heights display'd   665
Not *now* in snow, which asks the lyric Roman's[4] aid.

75

For our remembrance, and from out the plain
Heaves like a long-swept wave about to break,
And on the curl hangs pausing: not in vain
May he, who will, his recollections rake   670
And quote in classic raptures, and awake
The hills with Latian[5] echoes; I abhorr'd
Too much, to conquer for the poet's sake,
The drill'd dull lesson, forced down word by word[6]
In my repugnant youth, with pleasure to record   675

---

8. A mountain range extending the entire length of Italy.
9. "In the greater part of Switzerland, the avalanches are known by the name of lauwine."
1. Among the tallest peaks in the Alps; Mont Blanc (line 656) is the tallest; Chimari (line 657) refers to the volcanic Chimaera, or Chimariot, mountains (see also *Childe Harold* II. 453 [p. 69]).
2. In western Greece. This stanza mentions some of the tallest peaks in Greece, including Parnassus (line 659), in classical myth the dwelling of Apollo and the Muses and therefore the home of poetry, and Ida (line 662), highest summit of Crete and birthplace of Zeus, which Byron had viewed from Troy in 1810; see *Childe Harold* I, stanzas 60–64 (pp. 45–46).
3. Now Santo Oreste, mountain north of Rome.
4. Horace, Roman poet (65 B.C.E.–8 B.C.E.).
5. Latin.
6. "These stanzas may probably remind the reader of Ensign Northerton's remarks, 'D—n Homo,' &c.; but the reasons for our dislike are not exactly the same. I wish to express, that we become tired of the task before we can comprehend the beauty; that we learn by rote before we can get by heart; that the freshness is worn away, and the future pleasure and advantage deadened and destroyed, by the didactic anticipation, at an age when we can neither feel nor understand the power of compositions which it requires an acquaintance with life, as well as Latin and Greek, to relish, or to

76

Aught that recalls the daily drug which turn'd
My sickening memory; and, though Time hath taught
My mind to meditate what then it learn'd,
Yet such the fix'd inveteracy wrought
By the impatience of my early thought,   680
That, with the freshness wearing out before
My mind could relish what it might have sought,
If free to choose, I cannot now restore
Its health; but what it then detested, still abhor.

77

Then farewell, Horace; whom I hated so,   685
Not for thy faults, but mine; it is a curse
To understand, not feel thy lyric flow,
To comprehend, but never love thy verse,
Although no deeper Moralist rehearse
Our little life, nor Bard prescribe his art,   690
Nor livelier Satirist the conscience pierce,
Awakening without wounding the touch'd heart,
Yet fare thee well—upon Soracte's ridge we part.

78

Oh Rome! my country! city of the soul!
The orphans of the heart must turn to thee,   695
Lone mother of dead empires! and control
In their shut breasts their petty misery.
What are our woes and sufferance? Come and see
The cypress,[7] hear the owl, and plod your way
O'er steps of broken thrones and temples, Ye!   700
Whose agonies are evils of a day—
A world is at our feet as fragile as our clay.

79

The Niobe[8] of nations! there she stands,
Childless and crownless, in her voiceless woe;

reason upon. For the same reason, we never can be aware of the fulness of some of the finest passages of Shakespeare ('To be, or not to be,' for instance), from the habit of having them hammered into us at eight years old, as an exercise, not of mind, but of memory: so that when we are old enough to enjoy them, the taste is gone, and the appetite palled. In some parts of the continent, young persons are taught from more common authors, and do not read the best classics till their maturity. I certainly do not speak on this point from any pique or aversion towards the place of my education. I was not a slow, though an idle boy; and I believe no one could, or can be, more attached to Harrow than I have always been, and with reason;—a part of the time passed there was the happiest of my life; and my preceptor, the Rev. Dr Joseph Drury, was the best and worthiest friend I ever possessed, whose warnings I have remembered but too well, though too late, when I have erred,—and whose counsels I have but followed when I have done well or wisely. If ever this imperfect record of my feelings towards him should reach his eyes, let it remind him of one who never thinks of him but with gratitude and veneration—of one who would more gladly boast of having been his pupil, if, by more closely following his injunctions, he could reflect any honour upon his instructor."
7. Cypress tree and owl are traditional symbols of death.
8. Apollo slew Niobe's twelve children, and she was turned into a rock that wept continually (Ovid, *Metamorphosis* 6).

An empty urn within her wither'd hands,   705
Whose holy dust was scatter'd long ago;
The Scipios[9] tomb contains no ashes now;
The very sepulchres lie tenantless
Of their heroic dwellers: dost thou flow,
Old Tiber![1] through a marble wilderness?   710
Rise, with thy yellow waves, and mantle her distress.

80

The Goth,[2] the Christian, Time, War, Flood, and Fire,
Have dealt upon the seven-hill'd city's pride;
She saw her glories star by star expire,
And up the steep barbarian monarchs ride,   715
Where the car climb'd the capitol; far and wide
Temple and tower went down, nor left a site:—
Chaos of ruins! who shall trace the void,
O'er the dim fragments cast a lunar light,
And say, "here was, or is," where all is doubly night?   720

81

The double night of ages, and of her,
Night's daughter, Ignorance, hath wrapt and wrap
All round us; we but feel our way to err:
The ocean hath his chart, the stars their map,
And Knowledge spreads them on her ample lap;   725
But Rome is as the desert, where we steer
Stumbling o'er recollections; now we clap
Our hands, and cry "Eureka!"[3] it is clear—
When but some false mirage of ruin rises near.

82

Alas! the lofty city! and alas!   730
The trebly hundred triumphs![4] and the day
When Brutus made the dagger's edge surpass
The conqueror's sword in bearing fame away!
Alas, for Tully's voice, and Virgil's[5] lay,
And Livy's pictured page!—but these shall be   735
Her resurrection; all beside—decay.
Alas, for Earth, for never shall we see
That brightness in her eye she bore when Rome was free!

---

9. Ancient Roman family, including triumphant generals during the Punic Wars (264–146 B.C.E.).
1. River in Rome.
2. Teutonic ("barbarian," line 715) invaders of Rome during the third to fifth centuries.
3. Exclamation of discovery, from the Greek "I have found it!"
4. "Orosius gives 320 for the number of triumphs. He is followed by Panvinius; and Panvinius by Mr. Gibbon and the modern writers."
5. Publius Virgilius Maro, Roman poet (70–19 B.C.E.), author of *The Aeneid; Brutus:* see p. 314, n. 5; *Tully:* see p. 309, n. 6. *Livy:* Roman historian (59 B.C.E.–C.E. 17).

83

Oh thou, whose chariot roll'd on Fortune's wheel,
Triumphant Sylla!⁶ Thou, who didst subdue   740
Thy country's foes ere thou wouldst pause to feel
The wrath of thy own wrongs, or reap the due
Of hoarded vengeance till thine eagles flew
O'er prostrate Asia;—thou, who with thy frown
Annihilated senates—Roman, too,   745
With all thy vices, for thou didst lay down
With an atoning smile a more than earthly crown—

84

The dictatorial wreath,⁷—couldst thou divine
To what would one day dwindle that which made
Thee more than mortal? and that so supine⁸   750
By aught than Romans Rome should thus be laid?
She who was named Eternal, and array'd
Her warriors but to conquer—she who veil'd
Earth with her haughty shadow, and display'd,
Until the o'er-canopied horizon fail'd,   755
Her rushing wings—Oh! she who was Almighty hail'd!

85

Sylla was first of victors; but our own
The sagest of usurpers, Cromwell,⁹ he
Too swept off senates while he hew'd the throne
Down to a block—immortal rebel! See   760
What crimes it costs to be a moment free
And famous through all ages! but beneath
His fate the moral lurks of destiny;
His day of double victory and death
Beheld him win two realms, and, happier, yield his breath.¹   765

---

6. I.e., Sulla, Lucius Cornelius (138–78 B.C.E.), Roman general, "first of victors" (line 757); he defeated Mithridates, king of Pontus ("prostrate Asia," line 744).
7. "Certainly, were it not for these two traits in the life of Sylla, alluded to in this stanza, we should regard him as a monster unredeemed by any admirable quality. The *atonement* of his voluntary resignation of empire may perhaps be accepted by us, as it seems to have satisfied the Romans, who if they had not respected must have destroyed him. There could be no mean, no division of opinion; they must have all thought, like Eucrates, that what had appeared ambition was a love of glory, and that what had been mistaken for pride was a real grandeur of the soul.—('Seigneur, vous changez toutes mes idées, de la façon dont je vous vois agir. Je croyois que vous aviez de l'ambition, mais aucun haute; mais je ne soupçonnois pas qu'elle fût grande.'—*Dialogue de Sylla et d'Eucrate.*) *Considérations . . . de la Grandeur des Romains, etc.*, Paris, 1795, ii. 219. By Charles de Secondat, Baron de Montesquieu."
8. Defeated, lowered; literally, lying on the back.
9. Oliver Cromwell (1599–1658), Lord Protector of England, dissolved Parliament and subdued Ireland and Scotland ("two realms," line 765).
1. "On the 3rd of September Cromwell gained the victory of Dunbar: a year afterwards he obtained 'his crowning mercy' of Worcester; and a few years after, on the same day, which he had ever esteemed the most fortunate for him, died."

86

The third of the same moon whose former course
Had all but crown'd him, on the selfsame day
Deposed him gently from his throne of force,
And laid him with the earth's preceding clay.
And show'd not Fortune thus how fame and sway,   770
And all we deem delightful, and consume
Our souls to compass through each arduous way,
Are in her eyes less happy than the tomb?
Were they but so in man's, how different were his doom!

87

And thou, dread statue![2] yet existent in   775
The austerest form of naked majesty,
Thou who beheldest, 'mid the assassins' din,
At thy bathed base the bloody Caesar lie,
Folding his robe in dying dignity,
An offering to thine altar from the queen   780
Of gods and men, great Nemesis![3] did he die,
And thou, too, perish, Pompey? have ye been
Victors of countless kings, or puppets of a scene?

88

And thou, the thunder-stricken nurse of Rome!
She-wolf![4] whose brazen-imaged dugs impart   785
The milk of conquest yet within the dome
Where, as a monument of antique art,
Thou standest:—Mother of the mighty heart,
Which the great founder suck'd from thy wild teat,
Scorch'd by the Roman Jove's etherial dart,   790
And thy limbs black with lightning—dost thou yet
Guard thine immortal cubs, nor thy fond charge forget?

89

Thou dost;—but all thy foster-babes are dead—
The men of iron; and the world hath rear'd
Cities from out their sepulchres: men bled   795
In imitation of the things they fear'd,
And fought and conquer'd, and the same course steer'd,
At apish distance; but as yet none have,
Nor could, the same supremacy have near'd,
Save one vain man,[5] who is not in the grave,   800
But, vanquish'd by himself, to his own slaves a slave—

---

2. Of the Roman general Pompey (106–48 B.C.E.), Caesar's rival; Byron refers to a statue in the
Palazzo Spada, which is not the same statue of Pompey before which Caesar was killed.
3. Mythological goddess of retribution; see also line 1181 and *Manfred* 2.3.62–71 (p. 268). "She is
my particular belief and acquaintance," Byron wrote on the proof.
4. According to legend, a she-wolf suckled Rome's founders, Romulus and Remus.
5. Napoleon, in exile on St. Helena. Compare stanzas 89–92 to *Ode to Napoleon Buonaparte* (p. 156).

90

The fool of false dominion—and a kind
Of bastard Caesar, following him of old
With steps unequal; for the Roman's mind
Was modell'd in a less terrestrial mould,[6]   805
With passions fiercer, yet a judgment cold,
And an immortal instinct which redeem'd
The frailties of a heart so soft, yet bold,
Alcides[7] with the distaff now he seem'd
At Cleopatra's[8] feet,—and now himself he beam'd.   810

91

And came—and saw—and conquer'd![9] But the man
Who would have tamed his eagles down to flee,
Like a train'd falcon, in the Gallic[1] yan,
Which he, in sooth, long led to victory,
With a deaf heart which never seem'd to be   815
A listener to itself, was strangely framed;
With but one weakest weakness—vanity,
Coquettish in ambition—still he aim'd—
At what? can he avouch—or answer what he claim'd?

92

And would be all or nothing—nor could wait   820
For the sure grave to level him; few years
Had fix'd him with the Caesars in his fate,
On whom we tread: For *this* the conqueror rears
The arch of triumph! and for this the tears
And blood of earth flow on as they have flow'd,   825
An universal deluge, which appears
Without an ark for wretched man's abode,
And ebbs but to reflow!—Renew thy rainbow, God!

93

What from this barren being do we reap?
Our senses narrow, and our reason frail,   830
Life short, and truth a gem which loves the deep,
And all things weigh'd in custom's falsest scale;
Opinion an omnipotence,[2]—whose veil
Mantles the earth with darkness, until right

---

6. Perhaps referring to Napoleon's lack of religion, in contrast to Caesar's "immortal instinct" (line 807).
7. Hercules, a son of Zeus; noted for his strength, he turned his club into a distaff (used by women in spinning).
8. Queen of Egypt (51–30 B.C.E.) loved by Julius Caesar.
9. Caesar's oft-quoted boast, "*Veni, Vidi, Vici.*"
1. French.
2. *Opinion an omnipotence*: an idea from William Godwin's *Enquiry Concerning Political Justice* (1793), 1.10.

And wrong are accidents, and men grow pale   835
Lest their own judgments should become too bright,
And their free thoughts be crimes, and earth have too much light.

94

And thus they plod in sluggish misery,
Rotting from sire to son, and age to age,
Proud of their trampled nature, and so die,   840
Bequeathing their hereditary rage
To the new race of inborn slaves, who wage
War for their chains, and rather than be free,
Bleed gladiator-like,[3] and still engage
Within the same arena where they see   845
Their fellows fall before, like leaves of the same tree.

95

I speak not of men's creeds—they rest between
Man and his Maker—but of things allow'd,
Averr'd, and known,—and daily, hourly seen—
The yoke that is upon us doubly bow'd,   850
And the intent of tyranny avow'd,
The edict of Earth's rulers, who are grown
The apes of him who humbled once the proud,
And shook them from their slumbers on the throne;
Too glorious, were this all his mighty arm had done.   855

96

Can tyrants but by tyrants conquer'd be,
And Freedom find no champion and no child
Such as Columbia[4] saw arise when she
Sprung forth a Pallas, arm'd and undefiled?
Or must such minds be nourish'd in the wild,   860
Deep in the unpruned forest, 'midst the roar
Of cataracts, where nursing Nature smiled
On infant Washington? Has Earth no more
Such seeds within her breast, or Europe no such shore?

97

But France got drunk with blood to vomit crime,[5]   865
And fatal have her Saturnalia been
To Freedom's cause, in every age and clime;
Because the deadly days which we have seen,
And vile Ambition, that built up between
Man and his hopes an adamantine wall,   870

---

3. See below, stanzas 140–42.
4. America, compared in the next line to Pallas Athena, Greek goddess of battle, justice, and wisdom, who sprang full-grown from the brow of Zeus.
5. The Reign of Terror described as orgies ("Saturnalia") of blood-spilling.

And the base pageant[6] last upon the scene,
Are grown the pretext for the eternal thrall
Which nips life's tree, and dooms man's worst—his second fall.

98

Yet, Freedom! yet thy banner, torn, but flying,
Streams like the thunder-storm *against* the wind;   875
Thy trumpet voice, though broken now and dying,
The loudest still the tempest leaves behind;
Thy tree hath lost its blossoms, and the rind,
Chopp'd by the axe, looks rough and little worth,
But the sap lasts, and still the seed we find   880
Sown deep, even in the bosom of the North;
So shall a better spring less bitter fruit bring forth.

99

There is a stern round tower of other days,[7]
Firm as a fortress, with its fence of stone,
Such as an army's baffled strength delays,   885
Standing with half its battlements alone,
And with two thousand years of ivy grown,
The garland of eternity, where wave
The green leaves over all by time o'erthrown;—
What was this tower of strength? within its cave   890
What treasure lay so lock'd, so hid?—A woman's grave.

100

But who was she, the lady of the dead,
Tomb'd in a palace? Was she chaste and fair?
Worthy a king's—or more—a Roman's bed?
What race of chiefs and heroes did she bear?   895
What daughter of her beauties was the heir?
How lived—how loved—how died she? Was she not
So honour'd—and conspicuously there,
Where meaner relics must not dare to rot,
Placed to commemorate a more than mortal lot?   900

101

Was she as those who love their lords, or they
Who love the lords of others? such have been
Even in the olden time, Rome's annals say.
Was she a matron of Cornelia's[8] mien,

---

6. The Congress of Vienna (September 1815), which restored the monarchies after Napoleon's defeat.
7. "Alluding to the tomb of Cecilia Metella, called Capo di Bove." Cecilia Metella (stanzas 99–104) lived during the first century, but nothing is known about this "lady of the dead" (line 892).
8. Daughter of Scipio Africanus; as a widow, she devoted herself to instilling civic duty in her sons, the Gracchi; her renown as a model Roman matron contrasts with that of Cleopatra (lines 905–906).

Or the light air of Egypt's graceful queen,   905
Profuse of joy—or 'gainst it did she war,
Inveterate in virtue? Did she lean
To the soft side of the heart, or wisely bar
Love from amongst her griefs?—for such the affections are.

102

Perchance she died in youth: it may be, bow'd   910
With woes far heavier than the ponderous tomb
That weigh'd upon her gentle dust, a cloud
Might gather o'er her beauty, and a gloom
In her dark eye, prophetic of the doom
Heaven gives its favourites—early death,[9] yet shed   915
A sunset charm around her, and illume
With hectic[1] light, the Hesperus of the dead,
Of her consuming cheek the autumnal leaf-like red.

103

Perchance she died in age—surviving all,
Charms, kindred, children—with the silver gray   920
On her long tresses, which might yet recal,
It may be, still a something of the day
When they were braided, and her proud array
And lovely form were envied, praised, and eyed
By Rome—but whither would Conjecture stray?   925
Thus much alone we know—Metella died,
The wealthiest Roman's wife: Behold his love or pride!

104

I know not why—but standing thus by thee
It seems as if I had thine inmate known,
Thou tomb! and other days come back on me   930
With recollected music, though the tone
Is changed and solemn, like the cloudy groan
Of dying thunder on the distant wind;
Yet could I seat me by this ivied stone
Till I had bodied forth the heated mind   935
Forms from the floating wreck which Ruin leaves behind;

105

And from the planks, far shatter'd o'er the rocks,
Built me a little bark of hope, once more
To battle with the ocean and the shocks
Of the loud breakers, and the ceaseless roar   940

9. Echoes "Whom the gods love dies young" (Menander, c. 342–291 B.C.E.); cf. *Don Juan* 4.89.
1. The evening star; *hectic*: reddish, as flushed with fever; cf. Shelley's "Ode to the West Wind" (1819), line 4.

Which rushes on the solitary shore
Where all lies founder'd that was ever dear:
But could I gather from the wave-worn store
Enough for my rude boat, where should I steer?
There woos no home, nor hope, nor life, save what is here.   945

106

Then let the winds howl on! their harmony
Shall henceforth be my music, and the night
The sound shall temper with the owlets' cry,
As I now hear them, in the fading light
Dim o'er the bird of darkness' native site,   950
Answering each other on the Palatine,[2]
With their large eyes, all glistening gray and bright,
And sailing pinions.—Upon such a shrine
What are our petty griefs?—let me not number mine.

107

Cypress and ivy, weed and wallflower grown   955
Matted and mass'd together, hillocks heap'd
On what were chambers, arch crush'd, column strown
In fragments, choked up vaults, and frescos steep'd
In subterranean damps, where the owl peep'd,
Deeming it midnight:—Temples, baths, or halls?   960
Pronounce who can; for all that Learning reap'd
From her research hath been, that these are walls—
Behold the Imperial Mount! 'tis thus the mighty falls.[3]

108

There is the moral of all human tales;[4]
'Tis but the same rehearsal of the past,   965
First Freedom, and then Glory—when that fails,
Wealth, vice, corruption,—barbarism at last.
And History, with all her volumes vast,
Hath but *one* page,—'tis better written here,
Where gorgeous Tyranny hath thus amass'd   970

---

2. The hill in Rome that formed the original center of city life and on which the imperial palace was built.
3. "The Palatine is one mass of ruins, particularly on the side towards the Circus Maximus. The very soil is formed of crumbled brickwork. Nothing has been told, nothing can be told, to satisfy the belief of any but a Roman antiquary."
4. "The author of the Life of Cicero, speaking of the opinion entertained of Britain by that orator and his cotemporary Romans, has the following eloquent passage:—'From their railleries of this kind, on the barbarity and misery of our island, one cannot help reflecting on the surprising fate and revolutions of kingdoms; how Rome, once the mistress of the world, the seat of arts, empire, and glory, now lies sunk in sloth, ignorance, and poverty, enslaved to the most cruel as well as to the most contemptible of tyrants, superstition and religious imposture: while this remote country, anciently the jest and contempt of the polite Romans, is become the happy seat of liberty, plenty, and letters; flourishing in all the arts and refinements of civil life; yet running perhaps the same course which Rome itself had run before it, from virtuous industry to wealth; from wealth to luxury; from luxury to an impatience of discipline, and corruption of morals: till, by a total degeneracy and loss of virtue, being grown ripe for destruction, it fall a prey at last to some hardy oppressor, and, with the loss of liberty, losing every thing that is valuable, sinks gradually again into its original barbarism.'"

All treasures, all delights, that eye or ear,
Heart, soul could seek, tongue ask—Away with words! draw near,

109

Admire, exult—despise—laugh, weep,—for here
There is such matter for all feeling:—Man!
Thou pendulum betwixt a smile and tear,   975
Ages and realms are crowded in this span,
This mountain, whose obliterated plan
The pyramid of empires pinnacled,
Of Glory's gewgaws[5] shining in the van
Till the sun's rays with added flame were fill'd!   980
Where are its golden roofs![6] where those who dared to build?

110

Tully[7] was not so eloquent as thou,
Thou nameless column[8] with the buried base!
What are the laurels of the Caesar's brow?
Crown me with ivy from his dwelling-place.   985
Whose arch or pillar meets me in the face,
Titus or Trajan's?[9] No—'tis that of Time:
Triumph, arch, pillar, all he doth displace
Scoffing; and apostolic statues climb
To crush the imperial urn, whose ashes slept sublime,[1]   990

111

Buried in air, the deep blue sky of Rome,
And looking to the stars: they had contain'd
A spirit which with these would find a home,
The last of those who o'er the whole earth reign'd,
The Roman globe, for after none sustain'd,   995
But yielded back his conquests:—he was more
Than a mere Alexander,[2] and, unstain'd
With household blood and wine, serenely wore
His sovereign virtues—still we Trajan's name adore.[3]

5. Gaudy trinkets.
6. The *Domus Aurea* (Golden House), comprised of a series of villas, built by Nero, emperor 54–68 C.E.
7. Cicero; see p. 309, n. 6.
8. The column in the Forum of the seventh-century emperor (or Caesar) Phocas, first identified in 1813.
9. Roman emperors of the first and second centuries C.E.
1. "The column of Trajan is surmounted by St. Peter; that of Aurelius by St. Paul."
2. Alexander the Great (356–323 B.C.E.).
3. "Trajan was *proverbially* the best of the Roman princes; and it would be easier to find a sovereign uniting exactly the opposite characteristics, than one possessed of all the happy qualities ascribed to this emperor. 'When he mounted the throne,' says the historian Dion, 'he was strong in body, he was vigorous in mind; age had impaired none of his faculties; he was altogether free from envy and from detraction; he honoured all the good, and he advanced them; and on this account they could not be the objects of his fear, or of his hate; he never listened to informers; he gave not way to his anger; he abstained equally from unfair exactions and unjust punishments; he had rather be loved as a man than honoured as a sovereign; he was affable with his people, respectful to the senate, and universally beloved by both; he inspired none with dread but the enemies of his country.'"

112

Where is the rock of Triumph,[4] the high place   1000
Where Rome embraced her heroes? where the steep
Tarpeian? fittest goal of Treason's race,
The promontory whence the Traitor's Leap
Cured all ambition. Did the conquerors heap
Their spoils here? Yes; and in yon field below,   1005
A thousand years of silenced factions sleep—
The Forum, where the immortal accents glow,
And still[5] the eloquent air breathes—burns with Cicero!

113

The field of freedom, faction, fame, and blood:
Here a proud people's passions were exhaled,   1010
From the first hour of empire in the bud
To that when further worlds to conquer fail'd;
But long before had Freedom's face been veil'd,
And Anarchy assumed her attributes;
Till every lawless soldier who assail'd   1015
Trod on the trembling senate's slavish mutes,
Or raised the venal voice of baser prostitutes.

114

Then turn we to her latest tribune's name,
From her ten thousand tyrants turn to thee,
Redeemer of dark centuries of shame—   1020
The friend of Petrarch—hope of Italy—
Rienzi![6] last of Romans! While the tree
Of freedom's wither'd trunk puts forth a leaf,
Even for thy tomb a garland let it be—
The forum's champion, and the people's chief—   1025
Her new-born Numa[7] thou—with reign, alas! too brief.

115

Egeria![8] sweet creation of some heart
Which found no mortal resting-place so fair
As thine ideal breast; whate'er thou art
Or wert,—a young Aurora[9] of the air,   1030

4. The temple of Jupiter Optimus Maximus, on the Capitoline hill; the Tarpeian Rocks (line 1002) on the western edge of the hill face the Tiber River; Byron identifies this as the place where traitors were thrown ("Traitor's Leap"), though that may have been another side of the hill that faces the Forum, ancient' Rome's market and meeting-place.
5. A note by Byron on the proof reads: "I don't [know] how the devil *still* came there—an error in the copying."
6. For a brief period during the fourteenth century, Cola di'Rienzi was hailed as a liberator of Rome and tribune of the Holy Roman Republic.
7. Numa Pompilius, legendary king and lawgiver of Rome, successor to Romulus.
8. Roman water nymph said to have loved and aided Numa.
9. Roman goddess of the dawn.

The nympholepsy[1] of some fond despair;
Or, it might be, a beauty of the earth,
Who found a more than common votary there
Too much adoring; whatsoe'er thy birth,
Thou wert a beautiful thought, and softly bodied forth.   1035

116

The mosses of thy fountain still are sprinkled
With thine Elysian[2] water-drops; the face
Of thy cave-guarded spring, with years unwrinkled,
Reflects the meek-eyed genius of the place,
Whose green, wild margin now no more erase   1040
Art's works; nor must the delicate waters sleep,
Prison'd in marble, bubbling from the base
Of the cleft statue, with a gentle leap
The rill runs o'er, and round, fern, flowers, and ivy creep,

117

Fantastically tangled; the green hills   1045
Are clothed with early blossoms, through the grass
The quick-eyed lizard rustles, and the bills
Of summer-birds sing welcome as ye pass;
Flowers fresh in hue, and many in their class,
Implore the pausing step, and with their dyes   1050
Dance in the soft breeze in a fairy mass;
The sweetness of the violet's deep blue eyes,
Kiss'd by the breath of heaven, seems colour'd by its skies.

118

Here didst thou dwell, in this enchanted cover,
Egeria! thy all heavenly bosom beating   1055
For the far footsteps of thy mortal lover;
The purple Midnight veiled that mystic meeting
With her most starry canopy, and seating
Thyself by thine adorer, what befel?
This cave was surely shaped out for the greeting   1060
Of an enamour'd Goddess, and the cell
Haunted by holy Love—the earliest oracle!

119

And didst thou not, thy breast to his replying,
Blend a celestial with a human heart;
And Love, which dies as it was born, in sighing,   1065
Share with immortal transports? could thine art
Make them indeed immortal, and impart

1. Being possessed or enthralled by the ecstatic vision of having seen a nymph—longing for an impossible love ideal.
2. Of Elysium, the blissful abode of the dead in classical myth. The description of the Grotto of Egeria (stanzas 116–118) recalls Coleridge's "Kubla Khan," published in 1816 at Byron's suggestion.

The purity of heaven to earthly joys,
Expel the venom and not blunt the dart—
The dull satiety which all destroys—   1070
And root from out the soul the deadly weed which cloys?

120

Alas! our young affections run to waste,
Or water but the desert; whence arise
But weeds of dark luxuriance, tares[3] of haste,
Rank at the core, though tempting to the eyes,   1075
Flowers whose wild odours breathe but agonies,
And trees whose gums are poison; such the plants
Which spring beneath her steps as Passion flies
O'er the world's wilderness, and vainly pants
For some celestial fruit forbidden to our wants.   1080

121

Oh Love! no habitant of earth thou art—
An unseen seraph, we believe in thee,
A faith whose martyrs are the broken heart,
But never yet hath seen, nor e'er shall see
The naked eye, thy form, as it should be;   1085
The mind hath made thee, as it peopled heaven,
Even with its own desiring phantasy,
And to a thought such shape and image given,
As haunts the unquench'd soul—parch'd—wearied—
          wrung—and riven.

122

Of its own beauty is the mind diseased,   1090
And fevers into false creation:—where,
Where are the forms the sculptor's soul hath seized?
In him alone. Can Nature show so fair?
Where are the charms and virtues which we dare
Conceive in boyhood and pursue as men,   1095
The unreach'd Paradise of our despair,
Which o'er-informs the pencil and the pen,
And overpowers the page where it would bloom again?

123

Who loves, raves—'tis youth's frenzy—but the cure
Is bitterer still; as charm by charm unwinds   1100
Which robed our idols, and we see too sure
Nor worth nor beauty dwells from out the mind's
Ideal shape of such; yet still it binds
The fatal spell, and still it draws us on,
Reaping the whirlwind from the oft-sown winds;   1105

3. Noxious weeds.

The stubborn heart, its alchemy begun,
Seems ever near the prize—wealthiest when most undone.

124

We wither from our youth, we gasp away—
Sick—sick; unfound the boon—unslaked the thirst,
Though to the last, in verge of our decay,   1110
Some phantom lures, such as we sought at first—
But all too late,—so are we doubly curst.
Love, fame, ambition, avarice—'tis the same,
Each idle—and all ill—and none the worst—
For all are meteors with a different name,   1115
And Death the sable smoke where vanishes the flame.

125

Few—none—find what they love or could have loved,
Though accident, blind contact, and the strong
Necessity of loving, have removed
Antipathies—but to recur, ere long,   1120
Envenom'd with irrevocable wrong;
And Circumstance, that unspiritual god
And miscreator, makes and helps along
Our coming evils with a crutch-like rod,
Whose touch turns Hope to dust,—the dust we all have trod.   1125

126

Our life is a false nature—'tis not in
The harmony of things,—this hard decree,
This uneradicable taint of sin,
This boundless upas,[4] this all-blasting tree,
Whose root is earth, whose leaves and branches be   1130
The skies which rain their plagues on men like dew—
Disease, death, bondage—all the woes we see—
And worse, the woes we see not—which throb through
The immedicable soul, with heart-aches ever new.

127

Yet let us ponder boldly—'tis a base   1135
Abandonment of reason[5] to resign

---

4. Pronounced yoo´-pas: a tree yielding poisonous sap.
5. "'At all events,' says the author of the *Academical Questions* [Sir William Drummond], 'I trust, whatever may be the fate of my own speculations, that philosophy will regain that estimation which it ought to possess. The free and philosophic spirit of our nation has been the theme of admiration to the world. This was the proud distinction of Englishmen, and the luminous source of all their glory. Shall we then forget the manly and dignified sentiments of our ancestors, to prate in the language of the mother or the nurse about our good old prejudices? This is not the way to defend the cause of truth. It was not thus that our fathers maintained it in the brilliant periods of our history. Prejudice may be trusted to guard the outworks for a short space of time, while reason slumbers in the citadel; but if the latter sink into a lethargy, the former will quickly erect a standard for herself. Philosophy, wisdom, and liberty support each other: he who will not reason is a bigot; he who cannot, is a fool; and he who dares not, is a slave.'"

Our right of thought—our last and only place
Of refuge; this, at least, shall still be mine:
Though from our birth the faculty divine
Is chain'd and tortured—cabin'd, cribb'd, confined,   1140
And bred in darkness, lest the truth should shine
Too brightly on the unprepared mind,
The beam pours in, for time and skill will couch[6] the blind.

128

Arches on arches![7] as it were that Rome,
Collecting the chief trophies of her line,   1145
Would build up all her triumphs in one dome,
Her Coliseum stands; the moonbeams shine
As 'twere its natural torches, for divine
Should be the light which streams here, to illume
This long-explored but still exhaustless mine   1150
Of contemplation; and the azure gloom
Of an Italian night, where the deep skies assume

129

Hues which have words, and speak to ye of heaven,
Floats o'er this vast and wondrous monument,
And shadows forth its glory. There is given   1155
Unto the things of earth, which Time hath bent,
A spirit's feeling, and where he hath leant
His hand, but broke his scythe, there is a power
And magic in the ruin'd battlement,
For which the palace of the present hour   1160
Must yield its pomp, and wait till ages are its dower.

130

Oh Time! the beautifier of the dead,
Adorner of the ruin, comforter
And only healer when the heart hath bled—
Time! the corrector where our judgments err,   1165
The test of truth, love,—sole philosopher,
For all beside are sophists, from thy thrift,
Which never loses though it doth defer—
Time, the avenger! unto thee I lift
My hands, and eyes, and heart, and crave of thee a gift: 1170

131

Amidst this wreck, where thou hast made a shrine
And temple more divinely desolate,
Among thy mightier offerings here are mine,

6. Remove a cataract.
7. The Colosseum: the grand oval amphitheater in Rome, constructed during the first century c.e.,
   several stories of which were built on arches.

Ruins of years—though few, yet full of fate:—
If thou hast ever seen me too elate,   1175
Hear me not; but if calmly I have borne
Good, and reserved my pride against the hate
Which shall not whelm me, let me not have worn
This iron in my soul in vain—shall *they*[8] not mourn?

132

And thou, who never yet of human wrong   1180
Left the unbalanced scale, great Nemesis![9]
Here, where the ancient[1] paid thee homage long—
Thou, who didst call the Furies from the abyss,
And round Orestes bade them howl and hiss
For that unnatural retribution—just,   1185
Had it but been from hands less near—in this
Thy former realm, I call thee from the dust!
Dost thou not hear my heart?—Awake! thou shalt, and must.

133

It is not that I may not have incurr'd
For my ancestral faults or mine the wound   1190
I bleed withal, and, had it been conferr'd
With a just weapon, it had flow'd unbound;
But now my blood shall not sink in the ground;
To thee I do devote it—*thou* shalt take
The vengeance, which shall yet be sought and found,   1195
Which if *I* have not taken for the sake——
But let that pass—I sleep, but thou shalt yet awake.

134

And if my voice break forth, 'tis not that now
I shrink from what is suffer'd: let him speak
Who hath beheld decline upon my brow,   1200
Or seen my mind's convulsion leave it weak;
But in this page a record will I seek.
Not in the air shall these my words disperse,
Though I be ashes; a far hour shall wreak
The deep prophetic fulness of this verse,   1205
And pile on human heads the mountain of my curse!

8. Byron's wife, Annabella Milbanke, and her supporters in their social circle during the separation scandal. Stanzas 131–137 are illuminated by this autobiographical context.
9. See p. 322, n. 3.
1. Aeschylus (525–456 B.C.E.), Athenian dramatist, author of the *Oresteia*, a trilogy about revenge and justice in which the Furies pursue Orestes for killing Clytemnestra, his mother, because she had killed her husband (Agamemnon), Orestes' father; Byron (like the Furies) pronounces Orestes' act an "unnatural retribution" (line 1185) because of the close bond between the avenger and his victim, intending a comparison between Orestes and Lady Byron—though in another poem he refers to her as his "moral Clytemnestra ("Lines On Hearing that Lady Byron Was Ill," *CPW* 4:43).

135

That curse shall be Forgiveness.—Have I not—
Hear me, my mother Earth! behold it, Heaven!—
Have I not had to wrestle with my lot?
Have I not suffer'd things to be forgiven?   1210
Have I not had my brain sear'd, my heart riven,
Hopes sapp'd, name blighted, Life's life lied away?
And only not to desperation driven,
Because not altogether of such clay
As rots into the souls of those whom I survey.   1215

136

From mighty wrongs to petty perfidy
Have I not seen what human things could do?
From the loud roar of foaming calumny
To the small whisper of the as paltry few,
And subtler venom of the reptile crew,   1220
The Janus² glance of whose significant eye,
Learning to lie with silence, would *seem* true,
And without utterance, save the shrug or sigh,
Deal round to happy fools its speechless obloquy.³

137

But I have lived, and have not lived in vain: 1225
My mind may lose its force, my blood its fire,
And my frame perish even in conquering pain;
But there is that within me which shall tire
Torture and Time, and breathe when I expire;
Something unearthly, which they deem not of,   1230
Like the remember'd tone of a mute lyre,
Shall on their soften'd spirits sink, and move
In hearts all rocky now the late remorse of love.

138

The seal is set.—Now welcome, thou dread power!
Nameless, yet thus omnipotent, which here   1235
Walk'st in the shadow of the midnight hour
With a deep awe, yet all distinct from fear;
Thy haunts are ever where the dead walls rear
Their ivy mantles, and the solemn scene
Derives from thee a sense so deep and clear   1240
That we become a part of what has been,
And grow unto the spot, all-seeing but unseen.

---

2. Ancient Roman god of doorways and beginnings, having two faces, back to back, and thus a conventional symbol of hypocrisy.
3. Blame.

139

And here the buzz of eager nations ran,
In murmur'd pity, or loud-roar'd applause,
As man was slaughter'd by his fellow man.[4]   1245
And wherefore slaughter'd? wherefore, but because
Such were the bloody Circus' genial laws,
And the imperial pleasure.—Wherefore not?
What matters where we fall to fill the maws
Of worms—on battle-plains or listed spot?   1250
Both are but theatres where the chief actors rot.

140

I see before me the Gladiator lie:
He leans upon his hand—his manly brow
Consents to death, but conquers agony,
And his droop'd head sinks gradually low—   1255
And through his side the last drops, ebbing slow
From the red gash, fall heavy, one by one,
Like the first of a thunder-shower; and now
The arena swims around him—he is gone,
Ere ceased the inhuman shout which hail'd the wretch
who won.   1260

141

He heard it, but he heeded not—his eyes
Were with his heart, and that was far away;[5]
He reck'd not of the life he lost nor prize,
But where his rude hut by the Danube[6] lay,
There were his young barbarians all at play,   1265
There was their Dacian mother—he, their sire,
Butcher'd to make a Roman holiday—
All this rush'd with his blood—Shall he expire
And unavenged?—Arise! ye Goths, and glut your ire!

4. The Colosseum was one of the arenas where the gladiators of ancient Rome, often slaves or captives, were armed with swords and fought each other (or a wild animal) to death.
5. "Whether the wonderful statue which suggested this image be a laquearian gladiator, which, in spite of Winkelmann's criticism, has been stoutly maintained; or whether it be a Greek herald, as that great antiquary positively asserted*; or whether it is to be thought a Spartan or barbarian shield-bearer, according to the opinion of his Italian editor; it must assuredly seem a *copy* of that masterpiece of Ctesilaus which represented 'a wounded man dying, who perfectly expressed what there remained of life in him.' Montfaucon and Maffei thought it the identical statue; but that statue was of bronze. The gladiator was once in the Villa Ludovizi, and was bought by Clement XII. The right arm is an entire restoration of Michael Angelo. *Either Polifontes, herald of Laius, killed by Oedipus or Cepreas, herald of Euritheus, killed by the Athenians when he endeavoured to drag the Heraclidae from the altar of mercy, and in whose honour they instituted annual games, continued to the time of Hadrian; or Anthemocritus, the Athenian herald, killed by the Megarenses, who never recovered the impiety. See Storia delle Arti, &c. tom. ii. pag. 203, 204, 205, 206, 207. lib. ix. cap. 11."
6. River in central Europe; it lies near the conquered provinces of the Roman Empire, such as Dacia (line 1266), bordering the Teutonic people ("Goths," line 1269) who would invade Rome during the third to fifth centuries—which Byron suggests is a just revenge.

142

But here, where Murder breathed her bloody steam;   1270
And here, where buzzing nations choked the ways,
And roar'd or murmur'd like a mountain stream
Dashing or winding as its torrent strays;
Here, where the Roman millions' blame or praise
Was death or life, the playthings of a crowd,   1275
My voice sounds much—and fall the stars' faint rays
On the arena void—seats crush'd—walls bow'd—
And galleries, where my steps seem echoes strangely loud.

143

A ruin—yet what ruin! from its mass
Walls, palaces, half-cities, have been rear'd;   1280
Yet oft the enormous skeleton ye pass,
And marvel where the spoil could have appear'd.
Hath it indeed been plunder'd, or but clear'd?
Alas! developed, opens the decay,
When the colossal fabric's form is near'd: 1285
It will not bear the brightness of the day,
Which streams too much on all years, man, have reft away.

144

But when the rising moon begins to climb
Its topmost arch, and gently pauses there;
When the stars twinkle through the loops of time,   1290
And the low night-breeze waves along the air
The garland forest, which the gray walls wear,
Like laurels on the bald first Caesar's head;[7]
When the light shines serene but doth not glare,
Then in this magic circle raise the dead: 1295
Heroes have trod this spot—'tis on their dust ye tread.

145

"While stands the Coliseum, Rome shall stand;[8]
"When falls the Coliseum, Rome shall fall;
"And when Rome falls—the World." From our own land
Thus spake the pilgrims o'er this mighty wall   1300
In Saxon times,[9] which we are wont to call
Ancient; and these three mortal things are still
On their foundations, and unalter'd all;

---

7. "Suetonius informs us that Julius Caesar was particularly gratified by that decree of the senate which enables him to wear a wreath of laurel on all occasions. He was anxious, not to show that he was the conqueror of the world, but to hide that he was bald. A stranger at Rome would hardly have guessed at the motive, nor should we without the help of the historian."
8. "This is quoted in the 'Decline and Fall of the Roman Empire,' as a proof that the Coliseum was entire, when seen by the Anglo-Saxon pilgrims at the end of the seventh, or the beginning of the eighth, century. A notice on the Coliseum may be seen in the 'Historical Illustrations,' p. 263."
9. Fifth- and sixth-century Britain was invaded by the Saxons, a Germanic people.

Rome and her Ruin past Redemption's skill,
The World, the same wide den—of thieves, or what ye will.   1305

146

Simple, erect, severe, austere, sublime—
Shrine of all saints and temple of all gods,[1]
From Jove to Jesus—spared and blest by time;
Looking tranquillity, while falls or nods
Arch, empire, each thing round thee, and man plods   1310
His way through thorns to ashes—glorious dome!
Shalt thou not last? Time's scythe and tyrant's rods
Shiver upon thee—sanctuary and home
Of art and piety—Pantheon!—pride of Rome!

147

Relic of nobler days, and noblest arts!   1315
Despoil'd yet perfect, with thy circle spreads
A holiness appealing to all hearts—
To art a model; and to him who treads
Rome for the sake of ages, Glory sheds
Her light through thy sole aperture;[2] to those   1320
Who worship, here are altars for their beads;
And they who feel for genius may repose
Their eyes on honour'd forms, whose busts around them close.[3]

148

There is a dungeon, in whose dim drear light[4]
What do I gaze on? Nothing: Look again!   1325
Two forms are slowly shadow'd on my sight—
Two insulated phantoms of the brain:
It is not so; I see them full and plain—
An old man, and a female young and fair,
Fresh as a nursing mother, in whose vein   1330
The blood is nectar:—but what doth she there,
With her unmantled neck, and bosom white and bare?

1. The Pantheon, domed Roman temple completed during the second century. "Though plundered of all its brass, except the ring which was necessary to preserve the aperture above; though exposed to repeated fires; though sometimes flooded by the river, and always open to the rain, no monument of equal antiquity is so well preserved as this rotundo. It passed with little alteration from the Pagan into the present worship; and so convenient were its niches for the Christian altar, that Michael Angelo, ever studious of ancient beauty, introduced their design as a model in the Catholic church.'—*Forsyth's Italy,* p. 137."
2. The opening in the center of the dome.
3. "The Pantheon has been made a receptacle for the busts of modern great, or, at least, distinguished, men. The flood of light which once fell through the large orb above on the whole circle of divinities, now shines on a numerous assemblage of mortals, some one or two of whom have been almost deified by the veneration of their countrymen."
4. "This and the three next stanzas allude to the story of the Roman daughter, which is recalled to the traveller by the site, or pretended site, of that adventure, now shown at the church of St. Nicholas *in Carcere.* The difficulties attending the full belief of the tale are stated in 'Historical Illustrations,' p. 295." In the story of the "Caritas Romana," a woman kept her imprisoned father alive by secretly allowing him to take the milk from her breast; as a reward for her deed upon its discovery, her father was pardoned and freed.

149

Full swells the deep pure fountain of young life,
Where *on* the heart and *from* the heart we took
Our first and sweetest nurture, when the wife,   1335
Blest into mother, in the innocent look,
Or even the piping cry of lips that brook
No pain and small suspense, a joy perceives
Man knows not, when from out its cradled nook
She sees her little bud put forth its leaves—   1340
What may the fruit be yet?—I know not—Cain was Eve's.

150

But here youth offers to old age the food,
The milk of his own gift:—it is her sire
To whom she renders back the debt of blood
Born with her birth. No; he shall not expire   1345
While in those warm and lovely veins the fire
Of health and holy feeling can provide
Great Nature's Nile, whose deep stream rises higher
Than Egypt's river:—from that gentle side
Drink, drink and live, old man! Heaven's realm holds no
    such tide.   1350

151

The starry fable of the milky way[5]
Has not thy story's purity; it is
A constellation of a sweeter ray,
And sacred Nature triumphs more in this
Reverse of her decree, than in the abyss   1355
Where sparkle distant worlds:—Oh, holiest nurse!
No drop of that clear stream its way shall miss
To thy sire's heart, replenishing its source
With life, as our freed souls rejoin the universe.

152

Turn to the Mole which Hadrian rear'd on high,[6]   1360
Imperial mimic of old Egypt's piles,
Colossal copyist of deformity,
Whose travell'd phantasy from the far Nile's
Enormous model, doom'd the artist's toils
To build for giants, and for his vain earth,   1365
His shrunken ashes, raise this dome: How smiles
The gazer's eye with philosophic mirth,
To view the huge design which sprung from such a birth!

---

5. In one legend, the spilled milk from Hera's breast, when she pushed aside the nursing infant Heracles, formed the Milky Way.
6. "The castle of St. Angelo."

153

But lo! the dome—the vast and wondrous dome,[7]
To which Diana's marvel[8] was a cell—   1370
Christ's mighty shrine above his martyr's tomb!
I have beheld the Ephesian's miracle—
Its columns strew the wilderness, and dwell
The hyaena and the jackall in their shade;
I have beheld Sophia's bright roofs[9] swell   1375
Their glittering mass i' the sun, and have survey'd
Its sanctuary the while the usurping Moslem pray'd;

154

But thou, of temples old, or altars new,
Standest alone—with nothing like to thee—
Worthiest of God, the holy and the true.   1380
Since Zion's desolation,[1] when that He
Forsook his former city, what could be,
Of earthly structures, in his honour piled,
Of a sublimer aspect? Majesty,
Power, Glory, Strength, and Beauty, all are aisled   1385
In this eternal ark of worship undefiled.

155

Enter: its grandeur overwhelms thee not;
And why? it is not lessen'd; but thy mind,
Expanded by the genius of the spot,
Has grown colossal, and can only find   1390
A fit abode wherein appear enshrined
Thy hopes of immortality; and thou
Shalt one day, if found worthy, so defined,
See thy God face to face, as thou dost now
His Holy of Holies, nor be blasted by his brow.[2]   1395

156

Thou movest—but increasing with the advance,
Like climbing some great Alp, which still doth rise,
Deceived by its gigantic elegance;
Vastness which grows—but grows to harmonise—
All musical in its immensities;   1400
Rich marbles—richer painting—shrines where flame
The lamps of gold—and haughty dome which vies
In air with Earth's chief structures, though their frame
Sits on the firm-set ground—and this the clouds must claim.

---

7. "The church of St. Peter's."
8. The Temple of Diana, one of the seven wonders of the world, which Byron mistakenly took for the ruins that he saw at Ephesus in 1810.
9. The Hagia (or Santa) Sophia at Constantinople, originally a Christian church, later a mosque.
1. The destruction of Jerusalem and its temple by the Romans in 70 C.E.
2. Referring to an Old Testament idea that no living person may look upon the face of God.

157

Thou seest not all; but piecemeal thou must break,   1405
To separate contemplation, the great whole;
And as the ocean many bays will make,
That ask the eye—so here condense thy soul
To more immediate objects, and control
Thy thoughts until thy mind hath got by heart   1410
Its eloquent proportions, and unroll
In mighty graduations, part by part,
The glory which at once upon thee did not dart,

158

Not by its fault—but thine: Our outward sense
Is but of gradual grasp—and as it is   1415
That what we have of feeling most intense
Outstrips our faint expression; even so this
Outshining and o'erwhelming edifice
Fools our fond gaze, and greatest of the great
Defies at first our Nature's littleness,   1420
Till, growing with its growth, we thus dilate
Our spirits to the size of that they contemplate.

159

Then pause, and be enlighten'd; there is more
In such a survey than the sating gaze
Of wonder pleased, or awe which would adore   1425
The worship of the place, or the mere praise
Of art and its great masters, who could raise
What former time, nor skill, nor thought could plan;
The fountain of sublimity displays
Its depth, and thence may draw the mind of man   1430
Its golden sands, and learn what great conceptions can.

160

Or, turning to the Vatican,[3] go see
Laocoön's[4] torture dignifying pain—
A father's love and mortal's agony
With an immortal's patience blending:—Vain   1435
The struggle; vain, against the coiling strain
And gripe, and deepening of the dragon's grasp,
The old man's clench; the long envenom'd chain
Rivets the living links,—the enormous asp
Enforces pang on pang, and stifles gasp on gasp.   1440

---

3. The palatial residence of the pope in Rome.
4. A magnificent Greek statue of Apollo's priest Laocoön with his two sons, who were crushed by serpents (*Aeneid* 2.199–227).

161

Or view the Lord of the unerring bow,[5]
The God of life, and poesy, and light—
The Sun in human limbs array'd, and brow
All radiant from his triumph in the fight;
The shaft hath just been shot—the arrow bright   1445
With an immortal's vengeance; in his eye
And nostril beautiful disdain, and might
And majesty, flash their full lightnings by,
Developing in that one glance the Deity.

162

But in his delicate form—a dream of Love,   1450
Shaped by some solitary nymph, whose breast
Long'd for a deathless lover from above,
And madden'd in that vision—are exprest
All that ideal beauty ever bless'd
The mind with in its most unearthly mood,   1455
When each conception was a heavenly guest—
A ray of immortality—and stood,
Starlike, around, until they gather'd to a god!

163

And if it be Prometheus[6] stole from Heaven
The fire which we endure, it was repaid   1460
By him to whom the energy was given
Which this poetic marble hath array'd
With an eternal glory—which, if made
By human hands, is not of human thought;
And Time himself hath hallow'd it, nor laid   1465
One ringlet in the dust—nor hath it caught
A tinge of years, but breathes the flame with which 'twas wrought.

164

But where is he, the Pilgrim of my song,[7]
The being who upheld it through the past?
Methinks he cometh late and tarries long.   1470
He is no more—these breathings are his last;
His wanderings done, his visions ebbing fast,
And he himself as nothing:—if he was
Aught but a phantasy, and could be class'd
With forms which live and suffer—let that pass—   1475
His shadow fades away into Destruction's mass,

---

5. The statue Apollo Belvedere in the Vatican.
6. The Titan Prometheus stole fire from the gods and gave it to mankind; Promethean fire is associ-
   ated with godlike ability, creativity, and life.
7. This is the first reference to Harold in Canto IV.

165

Which gathers shadow, substance, life, and all
That we inherit in its mortal shroud,
And spreads the dim and universal pall
Through which all things grow phantoms,[8] and the cloud   1480
Between us sinks and all which ever glow'd,
Till Glory's self is twilight, and displays
A melancholy halo scarce allow'd
To hover on the verge of darkness; rays
Sadder than saddest night, for they distract the gaze,   1485

166

And send us prying into the abyss,
To gather what we shall be when the frame
Shall be resolved to something less than this
Its wretched essence; and to dream of fame,
And wipe the dust from off the idle name   1490
We never more shall hear,—but never more,
Oh, happier thought! can we be made the same:
It is enough in sooth that *once* we bore
These fardels[9] of the heart—the heart whose sweat was gore.

167

Hark! forth from the abyss a voice proceeds,[1]   1495
A long low distant murmur of dread sound,
Such as arises when a nation bleeds
With some deep and immedicable wound;
Through storm and darkness yawns the rending ground,
The gulf is thick with phantoms, but the chief   1500
Seems royal still, though with her head discrown'd,
And pale, but lovely, with maternal grief
She clasps a babe, to whom her breast yields no relief.

168

Scion of chiefs and monarchs, where art thou?
Fond hope of many nations, art thou dead?   1505
Could not the grave forget thee, and lay low
Some less majestic, less beloved head?
In the sad midnight, while thy heart still bled,
The mother of a moment, o'er thy boy,
Death hush'd that pang for ever: with thee fled   1510
The present happiness and promised joy
Which fill'd the imperial isles so full it seem'd to cloy.

8. Lines 1477–80: cf. Shakespeare, *The Tempest* 4.1.151–56.
9. Burdens; cf. Shakespeare, *Hamlet* 3.1.78.
1. Princess Charlotte, only daughter of the Prince Regent (eventually King George IV), died after giving birth to a stillborn son in November 1817, while Byron was writing Canto IV; she had been wed for one year to Leopold of Saxe-Coburg (the "lonely lord" of lines 1519–21), and her death caused general mourning throughout England, inspiring elegies by nearly all the poets of the period.

169

Peasants bring forth in safety.—Can it be,
Oh thou that wert so happy, so adored!
Those who weep not for kings shall weep for thee,   1515
And Freedom's heart, grown heavy, cease to hoard
· Her many griefs for ONE; for she had pour'd
Her orisons[2] for thee, and o'er thy head
Beheld her Iris.[3]—Thou, too, lonely lord,
And desolate consort—vainly wert thou wed!   1520
The husband of a year! the father of the dead!

170

Of sackcloth[4] was thy wedding garment made;
Thy bridal's fruit is ashes: in the dust
The fair-hair'd Daughter of the Isles is laid,
The love of millions! How we did intrust   1525
Futurity to her! and, though it must
Darken above our bones, yet fondly deem'd
Our children should obey her child, and bless'd
Her and her hoped-for seed, whose promise seem'd
Like stars to shepherds' eyes:—'twas but a meteor beam'd.   1530

171

Woe unto us, not her; for she sleeps well:
The fickle reek of popular breath, the tongue
Of hollow counsel, the false oracle,
Which from the birth of monarchy hath rung
Its knell in princely ears, 'till the o'erstung   1535
Nations have arm'd in madness, the strange fate[5]
Which tumbles mightiest sovereigns, and hath flung
Against their blind omnipotence a weight
Within the opposing scale, which crushes soon or late,—

172

These might have been her destiny; but no,   1540
Our hearts deny it: and so young, so fair,
Good without effort, great without a foe;
But now a bride and mother—and now *there!*
How many ties did that stern moment tear!
From thy Sire's to his humblest subject's breast   1545
Is link'd the electric chain of that despair,

2. Prayers. The sense here seems to be that Freedom (personified) had prayed for Charlotte, who sym-
   pathized with Whigs (liberals) and therefore represented Freedom's hope.
3. Rainbow, a representation of the messenger goddess, Iris, in classical myth, and symbol of hope or
   promise.
4. Traditional garment of mourning (biblical).
5. "Mary died on the scaffold; Elizabeth of a broken heart; Charles V. a hermit; Louis XIV. a bank-
   rupt in means and glory; Cromwell of anxiety; and, 'the greatest is behind,' Napoleon lives a pris-
   oner. To these sovereigns a long but superfluous list might be added of names equally illustrious
   and unhappy."

Whose shock was as an earthquake's, and opprest
The land which loved thee so that none could love thee best.

173

Lo, Nemi![6] navell'd in the woody hills
So far, that the uprooting wind which tears   1550
The oak from his foundation, and which spills
The ocean o'er its boundary, and bears
Its foam against the skies, reluctant spares
The oval mirror of thy glassy lake;
And, calm as cherish'd hate, its surface wears   1555
A deep cold settled aspect nought can shake,
All coil'd into itself and round, as sleeps the snake.

174

And near Albano's scarce divided waves
Shine from a sister valley;—and afar
The Tiber winds, and the broad ocean laves   1560
The Latian coast where sprang the Epic war,[7]
"Arms and the Man," whose re-ascending star
Rose o'er an empire:—but beneath thy right
Tully[8] reposed from Rome;—and where yon bar
Of girdling mountains intercepts the sight   1565
The Sabine[9] farm was till'd, the weary bard's delight.[1]

175

But I forget.—My Pilgrim's shrine is won,
And he and I must part,—so let it be,—
His task and mine alike are nearly done;
Yet once more let us look upon the sea;   1570
The midland ocean breaks on him and me,
And from the Alban Mount we now behold
Our friend of youth, that ocean, which when we
Beheld it last by Calpe's rock[2] unfold
Those waves, we follow'd on till the dark Euxine[3] roll'd   1575

---

6. "The village of Nemi was near the Arician retreat of Egeria, and, from the shades which embosomed the temple of Diana, has preserved to this day its distinctive appellation of *The Grove*. Nemi is but an evening's ride from the comfortable inn of Albano." The basin of the Lago di Nemi is the crater of an extinct volcano, hence the imagery at the end of the stanza.
7. The conquest of Rome as told in Virgil's *Aeneid* (19 B.C.E.), which opens with "Arms and the Man" (line 1562).
8. See p. 309, n. 6.
9. Ancient people of northern Italy subjugated by the Romans.
1. "The whole declivity of the Alban hill is of unrivalled beauty, and from the convent on the highest point, which has succeeded to the temple of the Latian Jupiter, the prospect embraces all the objects alluded to in this stanza; the Mediterranean; the whole scene of the latter half of the Aeneid, and the coast from beyond the mouth of the Tiber to the headland of Circaeum and the Cape of Terracina."
2. Gibraltar.
3. The Black Sea, between Europe and Asia; in classical myth, the Clashing Rocks ("Symplegades," line 1576) barred ships from entering the Euxine.

176

Upon the blue Symplegades: long years—
Long, though not very many, since have done
Their work on both; some suffering and some tears
Have left us nearly where we had begun:
Yet not in vain our mortal race hath run,   1580
We have had our reward—and it is here;
That we can yet feel gladden'd by the sun,
And reap from earth, sea, joy almost as dear
As if there were no man to trouble what is clear.

177

Oh! that the Desert were my dwelling-place,   1585
With one fair Spirit for my minister,[4]
That I might all forget the human race,
And, hating no one, love but only her!
Ye Elements!—in whose ennobling stir
I feel myself exalted—Can ye not   1590
Accord me such a being? Do I err
In deeming such inhabit many a spot?
Though with them to converse can rarely be our lot.

178

There is a pleasure in the pathless woods,
There is a rapture on the lonely shore,
There is society, where none intrudes,   1595
By the deep Sea, and music in its roar:
I love not Man the less, but Nature more,
From these our interviews, in which I steal
From all I may be, or have been before,   1600
To mingle with the Universe, and feel
What I can ne'er express, yet can not all conceal.

179

Roll on, thou deep and dark blue Ocean—roll!
Ten thousand fleets sweep over thee in vain;
Man marks the earth with ruin—his control   1605
Stops with the shore;—upon the watery plain
The wrecks are all thy deed, nor doth remain
A shadow of man's ravage, save his own,
When, for a moment, like a drop of rain,
He sinks into thy depths with bubbling groan,   1610
Without a grave, unknell'd, uncoffin'd, and unknown.

4. Lines 1585–88 suggest Byron's thoughts of his sister; cf. "Epistle to Augusta" (p. 241) and *Manfred*, 2.2 *passim* (p. 261).

180

His steps are not upon thy paths,—thy fields
Are not a spoil for him,—thou dost arise
And shake him from thee; the vile strength he wields
For earth's destruction thou dost all despise,   1615
Spurning him from thy bosom to the skies,
And send'st him, shivering in thy playful spray
And howling, to his Gods, where haply lies
His petty hope in some near port or bay,
And dashest him again to earth:—there let him lay.   1620

181

The armaments which thunderstrike the walls
Of rock-built cities, bidding nations quake,
And monarchs tremble in their capitals,
The oak leviathans,[5] whose huge ribs make
Their clay creator the vain title take   1625
Of lord of thee, and arbiter of war;
These are thy toys, and, as the snowy flake,
They melt into thy yeast of waves, which mar
Alike the Armada's[6] pride or spoils of Trafalgar.

182

Thy shores are empires, changed in all save thee—   1630
Assyria, Greece, Rome, Carthage,[7] what are they?
Thy waters wash'd them[8] power while they were free,
And many a tyrant since; their shores obey
The stranger, slave, or savage; their decay
Has dried up realms to deserts:—not so thou,   1635
Unchangeable save to thy wild waves' play—
Time writes no wrinkle on thine azure brow—
Such as creation's dawn beheld, thou rollest now.

183

Thou glorious mirror, where the Almighty's form
Glasses itself in tempests; in all time,   1640
Calm or convulsed—in breeze, or gale, or storm,
Icing the pole, or in the torrid clime
Dark-heaving;—boundless, endless, and sublime—
The image of Eternity—the throne
Of the Invisible; even from out thy slime   1645
The monsters of the deep are made; each zone
Obeys thee; thou goest forth, dread, fathomless, alone.

5. I.e., great ships; "leviathans" refers to huge sea creatures (biblical).
6. The Spanish fleet launched against England in 1588; at Cape Trafalgar (southwest Spain) in 1805, the English navy defeated the allied French and Spanish fleets.
7. *Assyria . . .* : the great empires of the ancient world.
8. *washed them power*: misprinted as "wasted them" in the first and subsequent editions, including 1832.

184

And I have loved thee, Ocean! and my joy
Of youthful sports was on thy breast to be
Borne, like thy bubbles, onward: from a boy   1650
I wanton'd with thy breakers—they to me
Were a delight; and if the freshening sea
Made them a terror—'twas a pleasing fear,
For I was as it were a child of thee,
And trusted to thy billows far and near,   1655
And laid my hand upon thy mane—as I do here.

185

My task is done—my song hath ceased—my theme
Has died into an echo; it is fit
The spell should break of this protracted dream.
The torch shall be extinguish'd which hath lit   1660
My midnight lamp—and what is writ, is writ,—
Would it were worthier! but I am not now
That which I have been—and my visions flit
Less palpably before me—and the glow
Which in my spirit dwelt is fluttering, faint, and low.   1665

186

Farewell! a word that must be, and hath been—
A sound which makes us linger;—yet—farewell!
Ye! who have traced the Pilgrim to the scene
Which is his last, if in your memories dwell
A thought which once was his, if on ye swell   1670
A single recollection, not in vain
He wore his sandal-shoon, and scallop-shell;
Farewell! with *him* alone may rest the pain,
If such there were—with *you*, the moral of his strain!

Beppo   Byron wrote a first draft of *Beppo* on October 9–10, 1817, while he was staying at La Mira. Over the next several months he continued to write additional stanzas, revise, copy, and eventually correct proofs for the poem, which was published, anonymously, in February 1818. With *Beppo* Byron simultaneously broke away from the emotionally fraught poems of 1816–17 (of which he, his publisher and, they feared, his readers were beginning to tire) and discovered a genre and stanza that he would use with consummate virtuosity in his great final comic works, *Don Juan* and *The Vision of Judgment*. The genre is, broadly, narrative satire, only the traditionally reformative goals of social satire continually compete, on the one hand, with the poet's irrepressible impulse "to giggle and make giggle" (*BLJ* 6:208) and, on the other, with a sense of the pervasiveness of human foibles, self-deception, and the irony of human ideals. The narrative, moreover, is perpetually interrupted by a chatty, cosmopolitan, and facetious narrator, whose opinions and digressions upstage the story—as in fact does the sheer verbal ingenuity of the verse. The stanza form is *ottava rima*, eight iambic pentameter lines rhyming abababcc, which, though it is used in an overtly clever and highly artful way, still manages to give the effect of conversation. The origins of Byron's satiro-comic *ottava rima* poems are traceable to the Italian tradition of Francesco Berni (1497?–1535), Luigi Pulci (1432–1484), and Giambattista Casti (1724–1803), with whose works Byron was familiar; however, the most immediate influence on his use of this form in *Beppo* was an English adaptation of the Italian model by John Hookham Frere, *The Monks and the Giants*, published by Murray in 1817 pseudonymously as the work of William and Robert Whistlecraft. At the same time, one should note that satire was not, in 1817, a new medium for Byron, whose poetic career was essentially launched with *English Bards and Scotch Reviewers* (1809), which was followed by *Hints From Horace* and *The Curse of Minerva* (1811) and *Waltz* (1812). Moreover, in *Childe Harold* Byron had already developed a "technique of associational elaboration" that is directly related to the digressive manner of the later, comic poems (Steffan, 65).

The story of *Beppo* was inspired by an amusing bit of gossip that Byron heard from the husband of one of his Venetian mistresses, Marianna Segati. As transformed into the story of the poem, it involves the pretty wife "of a certain age" (Laura), who is married to a considerably older man (Beppo, short for Giuseppe), a merchant seaman, who leaves her for several years while he travels abroad; not knowing what has become of her husband, Laura takes a Count as a *cavalier servente*—in Italy, the socially accepted, nearly ritualized role of a married woman's lover. The story is set on the day that Beppo returns, which happens to be during Carnival—in certain Catholic countries a period of feasting and partying prior to Lent. Arriving disguised as a Turk and after observing the situation between his wife and the Count, Beppo finally discloses his identity; the ensuing mutual questions and accusations between husband and wife conclude in mutual forgiveness and in Beppo's befriending the Count. The story, involving erring and forgiving spouses, played off in indirect and comic ways of Byron's own circumstances both in Venice and England. However, the main interest, as in the other *ottava rima* poems, lies in the comic and satiric treatment of the modes of human self-deception (observed in the defensive gossip of Laura and the other women), of the deficiencies in English society, politics, language, women, and climate (noted in the contrast between Italy and England), and even of poets in general ("One hates an author that's *all author*" [line 593]) and himself in particular ("a broken Dandy, lately on my travels" [line 410]).

The popularity of *Beppo* made it a marketing coup for publisher John Murray: the poem went into five editions by April 1818. Critical reaction ranged from high praise for its good humor and verbal virtuosity to more moralistic considerations that it is "a tale of pollution, dipped in the deepest die [*sic*] of Italian debauchery, relieved and recommended by a vivacity and grace of colouring that takes from the mischief its apparent turpitude, and disarms the vigilance of virtue" (William Roberts, *The British Review*, May 1818). The astute critic Francis Jeffrey was not entirely condemnatory in calling *Beppo* "absolutely a thing of nothing" (*Edinburgh Review*, February 1818), though he could not of course be aware of the postmodernist implications of a poem so described.

Criticism: In addition to Giuliano, "Marginal Discourse: the Authority of Gossip in *Beppo*," (p. 933), see: Beaty, *Byron the Satirist*; Bone, "*Beppo*: The Liberation of Fiction"; Cochran, "Why We Need a New Text of *Beppo*" (in *Cochran*); Elledge, "Byron and the Dynamics of Metaphor"; Keach, "Political Inflection in Byron's *Ottava Rima*"; McGann, Introduction to a *Beppo* manuscript, *Shelley and His Circle*, Vol. 7; Steffan, "The Devil a Bit of Our *Beppo*."

Beppo

A VENETIAN STORY

Rosalind. Farewell, Monsieur Traveller: Look, you lisp, and wear strange
suits: disable all the benefits of your own country; be out of love with your
Nativity, and almost chide God for making you that countenance you are;
or I will scarce think that you have swam in a Gondola.
As You Like It, Act IV. Sc. 1

Annotation of the Commentators
That is, been at *Venice*, which was much visited by the young English
gentlemen of those times, and was then what *Paris* is *now*—the seat of all
dissoluteness.   S. A. [Samuel Ayscough][1]

1

'Tis known, at least it should be, that throughout
    All countries of the Catholic persuasion,
Some weeks before Shrove Tuesday[2] comes about,
    The people take their fill of recreation,
And buy repentance, ere they grow devout,[3]   5
    However high their rank, or low their station,
With fiddling, feasting, dancing, drinking, masquing,
And other things which may be had for asking.

2

The moment night with dusky mantle covers
    The skies (and the more duskily the better),   10
The time less liked by husbands than by lovers
    Begins, and prudery flings aside her fetter;
And gaiety on restless tiptoe hovers,
    Giggling with all the gallants who beset her;
And there are songs and quavers,[4] roaring, humming,   15
Guitars, and every other sort of strumming.[5]

3

And there are dresses splendid, but fantastical,
    Masks of all times and nations, Turks and Jews,
And harlequins[6] and clowns, with feats gymnastical,
    Greeks, Romans, Yankee-doodles, and Hindoos;   20
All kinds of dress, except the ecclesiastical,
    All people, as their fancies hit, may choose,

1. *The Dramatic Works of William Shakespeare, with Explanatory Notes, by Samuel Ayscough* (1807).
2. Day before Ash Wednesday, which marks the beginning of Lent, the forty days of fasting and penitence prior to Easter.
3. I.e., their self-indulgence and sensualism during Carnival, a period of "recreation" prior to Lent (see stanzas 6–7), give people something to repent for.
4. Musical notes or trills.
5. Sexual innuendo.
6. Masked clowns in bright diamond-patterned attire.

But no one in these parts may quiz[7] the clergy,—
Therefore take heed, ye Freethinkers![8] I charge ye.

4

You'd better walk about begirt with briars,   25
    Instead of coat and smallclothes,[9] than put on
A single stitch reflecting upon friars,
    Although you swore it only was in fun;
They'd haul you o'er the coals, and stir the fires
    Of Phlegethon[1] with every mother's son,   30
Nor say one mass to cool the caldron's bubble
That boil'd your bones, unless you paid them double.

5

But saving this, you may put on whate'er
    You like by way of doublet,[2] cape, or cloak,
Such as in Monmouth-street, or in Rag Fair,[3]   35
    Would rig you out in seriousness or joke;
And even in Italy such places are,
    With prettier name in softer accents spoke,
For, bating Covent Garden, I can hit on
No place that's call'd "Piazza" in Great Britain.[4]   40

6

This feast is named the Carnival,—which being
    Interpreted, implies "farewell to flesh:"[5]
So call'd, because the name and thing agreeing,
    Through Lent they live on fish both salt and fresh.
But why they usher Lent with so much glee in,   45
    Is more than I can tell, although I guess
'Tis as we take a glass with friends at parting,
In the stage-coach or packet,[6] just at starting.

7

And thus they bid farewell to carnal dishes,
    And solid meats, and highly spiced ragouts,   50
To live for forty days on ill-dress'd fishes,
    Because they have no sauces to their stews,
A thing which causes many "poohs" and "pishes,"

7. Mock.
8. Atheists.
9. Undergarments.
1. In classical myth, a river of fire in Hades.
2. Close-fitting jacket or vest.
3. *Monmouth-street . . . Rag Fair*: in London, noted throughout the eighteenth century for the sale of second-hand clothes.
4. An arcade, called "Piazza," ran alongside the Square of Covent Garden, in London, site of the Royal Opera House and until 1974 of the city's principal fruit and garden market.
5. Latin: *carnis* (flesh) and *vale* (farewell).
6. Small ship.

And several oaths (which would not suit the Muse),
From travellers accustom'd from a boy   55
To eat their salmon, at the least, with soy;

8

And therefore humbly I would recommend
"The curious in fish-sauce," before they cross
The sea, to bid their cook, or wife, or friend,
    Walk or ride to the Strand, and buy in gross   60
(Or if set out beforehand, these may send
    By any means least liable to loss),
Ketchup, Soy, Chili-vinegar, and Harvey,[7]
Or, by the Lord! a Lent will well nigh starve ye;

9

That is to say, if your religion's Roman,   65
    And you at Rome would do as Romans do,
According to the proverb,—although no man,
    If foreign, is obliged to fast; and you,
If Protestant, or sickly, or a woman,
    Would rather dine in sin on a ragout—   70
Dine and be d—d! I dont mean to be coarse,
But that's the penalty, to say no worse.

10

Of all the places where the Carnival
    Was most facetious in the days of yore,
For dance, and song, and serenade, and ball,   75
.   And masque, and mime, and mystery, and more
Than I have time to tell now, or at all,
    Venice the bell from every city bore,—
And at the moment when I fix my story,
That sea-born city was in all her glory.[8]   80

11

They've pretty faces yet, those same Venetians,
    Black eyes, arch'd brows, and sweet expressions still,
Such as of old were copied from the Grecians,
    In ancient arts by moderns mimick'd ill;
And like so many Venuses of Titian's[9]   85

---

7. Harvey's Fish Sauce, popular in Byron's day.
8. This stanza seems to contradict the time period of the story given in lines 161–62 (i.e., "some years ago . . . thirty, forty, more or less"); Venice was certainly not by the eighteenth century "in all her glory" as a commercial, political, and cultural center as "in the days of yore" (line 74).
9. Major Venetian painter (c. 1490–1576); line 86 refers to a painting in the Medici Gallery that Byron admired (see *Childe Harold* IV, stanza 49). The painting referred to in stanzas 12 and 13 is probably the *Triple Portrait* attributed to Giorgione but actually by Titian. Byron describes his visit to galleries in Florence and the Manfrini Palace in Venice (line 90) in letters to Murray, April 14 and 26, 1817 (*BLJ* 5:212–14, 217–19).

(The best's at Florence—see it, if ye will)
They look when leaning over the balcony,
Or stepp'd from out a picture by Giorgione,

12

Whose tints are truth and beauty at their best;
    And when you to Manfrini's palace go,   90
That picture (howsoever fine the rest)
    Is loveliest to my mind of all the show;
It may perhaps be also to *your* zest,
    And that's the cause I rhyme upon it so:
'Tis but a portrait of his son, and wife,   95
And self; but *such* a woman! love in life!

13

Love in full life and length, not love ideal,
    No, nor ideal beauty, that fine name,
But something better still, so very real,
    That the sweet model must have been the same;   100
A thing that you would purchase, beg, or steal,
    Wer't not impossible, besides a shame:
The face recalls some face, as 'twere with pain,
You once have seen, but ne'er will see again;

14

One of those forms which flit by us, when we   105
    Are young, and fix our eyes on every face;
And, oh! the loveliness at times we see
    In momentary gliding, the soft grace,
The youth, the bloom, the beauty which agree,
    In many a nameless being we retrace,   110
Whose course and home we knew not, nor shall know,
Like the lost Pleiad[1] seen no more below.

15

I said that like a picture by Giorgione
    Venetian women were, and so they *are*,
Particularly seen from a balcony   115
    (For beauty's sometimes best set off afar)
And there, just like a heroine of Goldoni,[2]
    They peep from out the blind, or o'er the bar;
And, truth to say, they're mostly very pretty,
And rather like to show it, more's the pity!   120

---

1. "'Quae septem dici sex tamen esse solent.'—Ovid." "They are called seven but normally are six" (*Fasti* 4.170.); refers to the hidden star of the constellation Pleiades, also called the Seven Sisters.
2. Carlo Goldoni (1707–1793), Venetian writer of stage comedies.

16

For glances beget ogles, ogles sighs,
   Sighs wishes, wishes words, and words a letter,
Which flies on wings of light-heel'd Mercuries,[3]
   Who do such things because they know no better;
And then, God knows, what mischief may arise,   125
   When love links two young people in one fetter,
Vile assignations, and adulterous beds,
Elopements, broken vows, and hearts, and heads.

17

Shakspeare described the sex in Desdemona[4]
   As very fair, but yet suspect in fame,   130
And to this day from Venice to Verona
   Such matters may be probably the same,
Except that since those times was never known a
   Husband whom mere suspicion could inflame
To suffocate a wife no more than twenty,   135
Because she had a "cavalier servente."[5]

18

Their jealousy (if they are ever jealous)
   Is of a fair complexion altogether,
Not like that sooty devil of Othello's[6]
   Which smothers women in a bed of feather,   140
But worthier of these much more jolly fellows;
   When weary of the matrimonial tether
His head for such a wife no mortal bothers,
But takes at once another, or another's.

19

Didst ever see a Gondola? For fear   145
   You should not, I'll describe it you exactly:
'Tis a long cover'd boat that's common here,
   Carved at the prow, built lightly, but compactly,
Row'd by two rowers, each call'd "Gondolier,"
   It glides along the water looking blackly,   150
Just like a coffin clapt in a canoe,
Where none can make out what you say or do.

20

And up and down the long canals they go,
   And under the Rialto[7]—shoot along,

---

3. Refers to the ancient Roman messenger god.
4. In Shakespeare's *Othello*, Othello's wife.
5. Socially accepted lover of a married woman. See stanzas 36–37 and 40, and letter to Augusta
   Leigh, p. 720.
6. Cf. *Othello* 1.2.71.
7. Famed marble bridge spanning the Grand Canal, built in 1590, early center of the city.

By night and day, all paces, swift or slow,   155
    And round the theatres, a sable throng,
They wait in their dusk livery of woe,—
    But not to them do woful things belong,
For sometimes they contain a deal of fun,
Like mourning coaches when the funeral's done.   160

21

But to my story.—'Twas some years ago,
    It may be thirty, forty, more or less,
The carnival was at its height, and so
    Were all kinds of buffoonery and dress;
A certain lady went to see the show,   165
    Her real name I know not, nor can guess,
And so we'll call her Laura, if you please,
Because it slips into my verse with ease.[8]

22

She was not old, nor young, nor at the years
    Which certain people call a *"certain age,"*   170
Which yet the most uncertain age appears,
    Because I never heard, nor could engage
A person yet by prayers, or bribes, or tears,
    To name, define by speech, or write on page,
The period meant precisely by that word,—   175
Which surely is exceedingly absurd.

23

Laura was blooming still, had made the best
    Of time, and time return'd the compliment,
And treated her genteelly, so that, dress'd,
    She look'd extremely well where'er she went;   180
A pretty woman is a welcome guest,
    And Laura's brow a frown had rarely bent;
Indeed she shone all smiles, and seem'd to flatter
Mankind with her black eyes for looking at her.

24

She was a married woman; 'tis convenient,   185
    Because in Christian countries 'tis a rule
To view their little slips with eyes more lenient;
    Whereas if single ladies play the fool,
(Unless within the period intervenient
    A well-timed wedding makes the scandal cool)   190
I don't know how they ever can get over it,
Except they manage never to discover it.

---

8. Laura happens also to be the name of the young woman to whom Petrarch (1304–1374) addressed his sonnets.

25

Her husband sail'd upon the Adriatic,
   And made some voyages, too, in other seas,[9]
And when he lay in quarantine for pratique[1]   195
   (A forty days' precaution 'gainst disease),
His wife would mount, at times, her highest attic,
   For thence she could discern the ship with ease:
He was a merchant trading to Aleppo,[2]
   His name Giuseppe, call'd more briefly, Beppo.[3]   200

26

He was a man as dusky as a Spaniard,
   Sunburnt with travel, yet a portly figure;
Though colour'd, as it were, within a tanyard,[4]
   He was a person both of sense and vigour—
A better seaman never yet did man yard: 205
   And *she*, although her manners show'd no rigour,
Was deem'd a woman of the strictest principle,
So much as to be thought almost invincible.

27

But several years elapsed since they had met;
   Some people thought the ship was lost, and some   210
That he had somehow blunder'd into debt,
   And did not like the thought of steering home;
And there were several offer'd any bet,
   Or that he would, or that he would not come,
For most men (till by losing render'd sager)   215
Will back their own opinions with a wager.

28

'Tis said that their last parting was pathetic,
   As partings often are, or ought to be,
And their presentiment was quite prophetic
   That they should never more each other see   220
(A sort of morbid feeling, half poetic,
   Which I have known occur in two or three),
When kneeling on the shore upon her sad knee,
He left this Adriatic Ariadne.[5]

9. A ribald double entendre.
1. License to use a port following quarantine for disease.
2. An important city (in present northwest Syria) of the Ottoman Empire; it is mentioned by Othello (5.2.361).
3. "Beppo is the *Joe* of the Italian *Joseph*" (Byron's note on the fair copy).
4. Tannery.
5. In classical myth, Ariadne loved, rescued, and was betrothed to Theseus, who deserted her at Naxos; in one version of the myth, Dionysus comforted her and became her lover.

29

And Laura waited long, and wept a little,   225
    And thought of wearing weeds, as well she might;
She almost lost all appetite for victual,
    And could not sleep with ease alone at night;
She deem'd the window-frames and shutters brittle
    Against a daring housebreaker or sprite,   230
And so she thought it prudent to connect her
With a vice-husband, *chiefly* to *protect her*.

30

She chose (and what is there they will not choose,
    If only you will but oppose their choice?)
Till Beppo should return from his long cruise,   235
    And bid once more her faithful heart rejoice,
A man some women like, and yet abuse—
    A coxcomb[6] was he by the public voice;
A Count of wealth, they said, as well as quality,
And in his pleasures of great liberality.   240

31

And then he was a Count, and then he knew
    Music, and dancing, fiddling, French and Tuscan;
The last not easy, be it known to you,
    For few Italians speak the right Etruscan.[7]
He was a critic upon operas, too,   245
    And knew all niceties of the sock and buskin;[8]
And no Venetian audience could endure a
Song, scene, or air, when he cried "seccatura!"[9]

32

His "bravo" was decisive, for that sound
    Hush'd "Academie" sigh'd in silent awe;   250
The fiddlers trembled as he look'd around,
    For fear of some false note's detected flaw.
The "prima donna's" tuneful heart would bound,
    Dreading the deep damnation of his "bah!"
Soprano, basso, even the contra-alto,   255
Wish'd him five fathom under the Rialto.

33

He patronised the Improvisatori,[1]
    Nay, could himself extemporise some stanzas,

---

6. Vain, foolish man.
7. I.e., pure Italian—from Etruria, the ancient region of Tuscany (as opposed to the Venetian dialect).
8. Sock and buskin: comedy and tragedy—deriving from the kinds of footwear used by the actors in ancient Greece and Rome.
9. Annoyance, bore; "a devilish good word, by the way" (*BLJ* 5:125).
1. Improvising poets.

Wrote rhymes, sang songs, could also tell a story,
  Sold pictures, and was skilful in the dance as   260
Italians can be, though in this their glory
  Must surely yield the palm to that which France has;
In short, he was a perfect cavaliero,
And to his very valet seem'd a hero.[2]

34

Then he was faithful, too, as well as amorous;   265
  So that no sort of female could complain,
Although they're now and then a little clamorous,
  He never put the pretty souls in pain;
His heart was one of those which most enamour us,
  Wax to receive, and marble to retain.   270
He was a lover of the good old school,
Who still become more constant as they cool.

35

No wonder such accomplishments should turn
  A female head, however sage and steady—
With scarce a hope that Beppo could return,   275
  In law he was almost as good as dead, he
Nor sent, nor wrote, nor show'd the least concern,
  And she had waited several years already;
And really if a man won't let us know
That he's alive, he's *dead*, or should be so.   280

36

Besides, within the Alps, to every woman
  (Although, God knows, it is a grievous sin)
'Tis, I may say, permitted to have *two* men;
  I can't tell who first brought the custom in,
But "Cavalier Serventes" are quite common,   285
  And no one notices nor cares a pin;
And we may call this (not to say the worst)
A *second* marriage which corrupts the *first*.

37

The word was formerly a "Cicisbeo,"
  But *that* is now grown vulgar and indecent;   290
The Spaniards call the person a "*Cortejo*,"[3]
  For the same mode subsists in Spain, though recent;

---

2. Cf. "No man is a hero to his valet." ("Il n'y a point de héros pour son valet de chambre": Mme. Cornuel [1605–1694]).
3. "'*Cortejo*' is pronounced 'Corteho,' with an aspirate, according to the Arabesque guttural. It means what there is as yet no precise name for in England, though the practice is as common as in any tramontane country whatever."

In short it reaches from the Po to Teio,[4]
And may perhaps at last be o'er the sea sent.
But Heaven preserve Old England from such courses!   295
Or what becomes of damage and divorces?

38

However, I still think, with all due deference
To the fair *single* part of the Creation,
That married ladies should preserve the preference
In *tête-à-tête* or general conversation—   300
And this I say without peculiar reference
To England, France, or any other nation—
Because they know the world, and are at ease,
And being natural, naturally please.

39

'Tis true, your budding Miss is very charming,   305
But shy and awkward at first coming out,
So much alarm'd, that she is quite alarming,
All Giggle, Blush; half Pertness, and half Pout;
And glancing at *Mamma*, for fear there's harm in
What you, she, it, or they, may be about,   310
The Nursery still lisps out in all they utter—
Besides, they always smell of bread and butter.

40

But "Cavalier Servente" is the phrase
Used in politest circles to express
This supernumerary slave, who stays   315
Close to the lady as a part of dress,
Her word the only law which he obeys.
His is no sinecure, as you may guess;
Coach, servants, gondola, he goes to call,
And carries fan and tippet,[5] gloves and shawl.   320

41

With all its sinful doings, I must say,
That Italy's a pleasant place to me,
Who love to see the Sun shine every day,
And vines (not nail'd to walls) from tree to tree
Festoon'd, much like the back scene of a play,   325
Or melodrame,[6] which people flock to see,
When the first act is ended by a dance
In vineyards copied from the south of France.

---

4. *Po . . . Teio* (Tagus): rivers in Italy and Portugal, respectively.
5. Short cape.
6. In the seventeenth and eighteenth centuries, a romantic drama with musical interludes.

42

I like on Autumn evenings to ride out,
    Without being forced to bid my groom be sure   330
My cloak is round his middle strapp'd about,
    Because the skies are not the most secure;
I know too that, if stopp'd upon my route,
    Where the green alleys windingly allure,
Reeling with *grapes* red waggons choke the way,—   335
In England 'twould be dung, dust, or a dray.[7]

43

I also like to dine on becaficas,[8]
    To see the Sun set, sure he'll rise to-morrow,
Not through a misty morning twinkling weak as
    A drunken man's dead eye in maudlin sorrow,   340
But with all Heaven t'himself; that day will break as
    Beauteous as cloudless, nor be forced to borrow
That sort of farthing[9] candlelight which glimmers
Where reeking London's smoky caldron simmers.

44

I love the language, that soft bastard Latin,   345
    Which melts like kisses from a female mouth,
And sounds as if it should be writ on satin,
    With syllables which breathe of the sweet South,
And gentle liquids gliding all so pat in,
    That not a single accent seems uncouth,   350
Like our harsh northern whistling, grunting guttural,
Which we're obliged to hiss, and spit, and sputter all.

45

I like the women too (forgive my folly),
    From the rich peasant cheek of ruddy bronze,
And large black eyes that flash on you a volley   355
    Of rays that say a thousand things at once,
To the high dama's brow, more melancholy,
    But clear, and with a wild and liquid glance,
Heart on her lips, and soul within her eyes,
Soft as her clime, and sunny as her skies.   360

46

Eve of the land which still is Paradise!
    Italian beauty! didst thou not inspire

---

7. Cart for heavy loads.
8. Small European birds, considered a delicacy.
9. Former English coin worth one-fourth penny.

Raphael,[1] who died in thy embrace, and vies
  With all we know of Heaven, or can desire,
In what he hath bequeath'd us?—in what guise,   365
  Though flashing from the fervour of the lyre,
Would *words* describe thy past and present glow,
  While yet Canova[2] can create below?[3]

47

"England! with all thy faults I love thee still,"[4]
  I said at Calais,[5] and have not forgot it;   370
I like to speak and lucubrate[6] my fill;
  I like the government (but that is not it);
I like the freedom of the press and quill;
  I like the Habeas Corpus[7] (when we've got it);
I like a parliamentary debate,   375
  Particularly when 'tis not too late;

48

I like the taxes, when they're not too many;
  I like a seacoal fire, when not too dear;
I like a beef-steak, too, as well as any;
  Have no objection to a pot of beer;   380
I like the weather, when it is not rainy,
  That is, I like two months of every year.
And so God save the Regent,[8] Church, and King!
  Which means that I like all and every thing.

49

Our standing army, and disbanded seamen,   385
  Poor's rate, Reform, my own, the nation's debt,
Our little riots just to show we are free men,
  Our trifling bankruptcies in the Gazette,[9]

---

1. "For the received accounts of the cause of Raphael's death, see his lives." Raffaello Santi (or Sanzio) (1483–1520), major Italian Renaissance painter; he was rumored to have died from excessive lovemaking, though the actual causes of his death were malaria and exhaustion from overwork.
2. Antonio Canova (1757–1822), Italian sculptor.
3.   "(In talking thus, the writer, more especially
        Of women, would be understood to say,
    He speaks as a spectator, not officially,
        And always, reader, in a modest way;
    Perhaps, too, in no very great degree shall he
        Appear to have offended in this lay,
    Since, as all know, without the sex, our sonnets
    Would seem unfinish'd, like their untrimm'd bonnets.)
        (Signed)   PRINTER'S DEVIL."
A "printer's devil" was a printer's apprentice, whose skin and clothes were often blackened by ink.
4. William Cowper, *The Task* (1784), 2.205–06.
5. Port in northern France where Byron first arrived upon leaving England.
6. Give especially scholarly or pretentious speeches.
7. A legal writ intended to protect against false imprisonment; *habeas corpus* was suspended in England in 1817 but restored the next year. Like this reference, lines 375–76 and 385–88 allude to contemporary political issues.
8. The Prince of Wales, eventually King George IV, who served as England's ruler during the last eight years of his father's life (1811–20), when insanity prevented George III from ruling.
9. The *London Gazette*, English newspaper.

Our cloudy climate, and our chilly women,
    All these I can forgive, and those forget,   390
And greatly venerate our recent glories,[1]
    And wish they were not owing to the Tories.

50

But to my tale of Laura,—for I find
    Digression is a sin, that by degrees
Becomes exceeding tedious to my mind,   395
    And, therefore, may the reader too displease—
The gentle reader, who may wax unkind,
    And caring little for the author's ease,
Insist on knowing what he means, a hard
    And hapless situation for a bard.   400

51

Oh that I had the art of easy writing
    What should be easy reading! could I scale
Parnassus,[2] where the Muses sit inditing
    Those pretty poems never known to fail,
How quickly would I print (the world delighting)   405
    A Grecian, Syrian, or Assyrian tale;
And sell you, mix'd with western sentimentalism,
    Some samples of the finest Orientalism.

52

But I am but a nameless sort of person,
    (A broken Dandy[3] lately on my travels)   410
And take for rhyme, to hook my rambling verse on,
    The first that Walker's Lexicon[4] unravels,
And when I can't find that, I put a worse on,
    Not caring as I ought for critics' cavils;
I've half a mind to tumble down to prose,   415
    But verse is more in fashion—so here goes.

53

The Count and Laura made their new arrangement,
    Which lasted, as arrangements sometimes do,

---

1. Facetious, if not sarcastic: the line suggests above all the victory at Waterloo, but Byron scarcely considered the defeat of his one-time idol, Napoleon, and reestablishment of European monarchies to be "glories." The conservative Tory party, referred to in line 392, dominated throughout Byron's lifetime, to his dismay.
2. In classical myth, the mountain residence of the nine Muses, goddesses who inspire poets and other artists.
3. One of a socially recognized group of fashion-conscious men, led by Beau Brummel (1778–1840), friend of the Prince Regent. Byron wrote: "I liked the Dandies—they were always very civil to *me*— though in general they disliked literary people. . . . I had a tinge of Dandyism in my minority—and probably retained enough of it—to conciliate the great ones—at four & twenty.—I had gamed—& drank—& taken my degrees in most dissipations—and having no pedantry & not being overbearing— we ran quietly together." ("Detached Thoughts," October 15, 1821–May 18, 1822 [*BLJ* 9:22]).
4. John Walker's *Rhyming Dictionary* (1775).

For half a dozen years without estrangement;
   They had their little differences, too;   420
Those jealous whiffs, which never any change meant:
   In such affairs there probably are few
Who have not had this pouting sort of squabble,
From sinners of high station to the rabble.

54

But, on the whole, they were a happy pair,   425
   As happy as unlawful love could make them;
The gentleman was fond, the lady fair,
   Their chains so slight, 'twas not worth while to break them:
The world beheld them with indulgent air;
   The pious only wish'd "the devil take them!"   430
He took them not; he very often waits,
And leaves old sinners to be young ones' baits.

55

But they were young:[5] Oh! what without our youth
   Would love be! What would youth be without love!
Youth lends it joy, and sweetness, vigour, truth,   435
   Heart, soul, and all that seems as from above;
But, languishing with years, it grows uncouth—
   One of few things experience don't improve,
Which is, perhaps, the reason why old fellows
Are always so preposterously jealous.   440

56

It was the Carnival, as I have said
   Some six and thirty stanzas back, and so
Laura the usual preparations made,
   Which you do when your mind's made up to go
To-night to Mrs. Boehm's[6] masquerade,   445
   Spectator, or partaker in the show;
The only difference known between the cases
Is—*here*, we have six weeks of "varnish'd faces."

57

Laura, when dress'd, was (as I sang before)
   A pretty woman as was ever seen,   450
Fresh as the Angel o'er a new inn door,
   Or frontispiece of a new Magazine,
With all the fashions which the last month wore,
   Colour'd, and silver paper leaved between
That and the title-page, for fear the press   455
Should soil with parts of speech the parts of dress.

5. Inconsistent with earlier descriptions of the Count and Laura, especially lines 169–70.
6. Her "Grand Masquerade" was a London society event in 1817.

58

They went to the Ridotto;—'tis a hall
    Where people dance, and sup, and dance again;
Its proper name, perhaps, were a masqued ball,
    But that's of no importance to my strain;   460
'Tis (on a smaller scale) like our Vauxhall,[7]
    Excepting that it can't be spoilt by rain:
The company is "mix'd" (the phrase I quote is
As much as saying, they're below your notice);

59

For a "mix'd company" implies that, save   465
    Yourself and friends, and half a hundred more,
Whom you may bow to without looking grave,
    The rest are but a vulgar set, the bore
Of public places, where they basely brave
    The fashionable stare of twenty score   470
Of well-bred persons, call'd "*the World;*" but I,
Although I know them, really don't know why.[8]

60

This is the case in England; at least was
    During the dynasty of Dandies, now
Perchance succeeded by some other class   475
    Of imitated imitators:—how
Irreparably soon decline, alas!
    The demagogues of fashion: all below
Is frail; how easily the world is lost
By love, or war, and now and then by frost!   480

61

Crush'd was Napoleon by the northern Thor,[9]
    Who knock'd his army down with icy hammer,
Stopp'd by the *elements,* like a whaler, or
    A blundering novice in his new French grammar;
Good cause had he to doubt the chance of war,   485
    And as for Fortune—but I dare not d—n her,
Because, were I to ponder to infinity,
The more I should believe in her divinity.

62

She rules the present, past, and all to be yet,
    She gives us luck in lotteries, love, and marriage;   490

---

7. A place of public entertainment, music, and dancing, Vauxhall in London was open-aired. Cf. *Don Juan* XI, stanza 45 (p. 590).
8. Cf. *Don Juan* XI, stanza 45 (p. 590).
9. In Nordic myth, god of thunder: a reference to Napoleon's Russian defeat, often attributed to the cold weather; in lines 483–84, Byron puns on "elements" as referring both to weather and parts of speech (see *BLJ* 9:21–22).

I cannot say that she's done much for me yet;
   Not that I mean her bounties to disparage,
We've not yet closed accounts, and we shall see yet
   How much she'll make amends for past miscarriage;
Meantime the goddess I'll no more importune,   495
   Unless to thank her when she's made my fortune.

63

To turn,—and to return;—the devil take it!
   This story slips for ever through my fingers,
Because, just as the stanza likes to make it,
   It needs must be—and so it rather lingers;   500
This form of verse began[1] I can't well break it,
   But must keep time and tune like public singers;
But if I once get through my present measure,
I'll take another when I'm next at leisure.

64

They went to the Ridotto ('tis a place   505
   To which I mean to go myself to-morrow,
Just to divert my thoughts a little space,
   Because I'm rather hippish,[2] and may borrow
Some spirits, guessing at what kind of face
   May lurk beneath each mask; and as my sorrow   510
Slackens its pace sometimes, I'll make, or find,
Something shall leave it half an hour behind.)

65

Now Laura moves along the joyous crowd,
   Smiles in her eyes, and simpers on her lips:
To some she whispers, others speaks aloud;   515
   To some she curtsies, and to some she dips,
Complains of warmth, and this complaint avow'd,
   Her lover brings the lemonade, she sips;
She then surveys, condemns, but pities still
Her dearest friends for being dress'd so ill.   520

66

One has false curls, another too much paint,
   A third—where did she buy that frightful turban?
A fourth's so pale she fears she's going to faint,
   A fifth's look's vulgar, dowdyish, and suburban,
A sixth's white silk has got a yellow taint,   525
   A seventh's thin muslin surely will be her bane,

---

1. began (in all editions); however, Byron's draft and fair copy give "begun," which is supported by
   the sense and grammar of lines 501–02.
2. Low-spirited.

And lo! an eighth appears,—"I'll see no more!"
For fear, like Banquo's kings,[3] they reach a score.

67

Meantime, while she was thus at others gazing,
　　Others were levelling their looks at her;　　　　　　　530
She heard the men's half-whisper'd mode of praising,
　　And, till 'twas done, determined not to stir;
The women only thought it quite amazing
　　That, at her time of life, so many were
Admirers still,—but men are so debased,　　　　　　　535
Those brazen creatures always suit their taste.

68

For my part, now, I ne'er could understand
　　Why naughty women—but I won't discuss
A thing which is a scandal to the land,
　　I only don't see why it should be thus;　　　　　　　540
And if I were but in a gown and band,
　　Just to entitle me to make a fuss,
I'd preach on this till Wilberforce and Romilly[4]
Should quote in their next speeches from my homily.

69

While Laura thus was seen and seeing, smiling,　　　　　545
　　Talking, she knew not why and cared not what,
So that her female friends, with envy broiling,
　　Beheld her airs and triumph, and all that;
And well dress'd males still kept before her filing,
　　And passing bow'd and mingled with her chat;　　　550
More than the rest one person seem'd to stare
With pertinacity that's rather rare.

70

He was a Turk, the colour of mahogany;
　　And Laura saw him, and at first was glad,
Because the Turks so much admire philogyny,[5]　　　　555
　　Although their usage of their wives is sad;
'Tis said they use no better than a dog any
　　Poor woman, whom they purchase like a pad:[6]
They have a number, though they ne'er exhibit 'em,
Four wives by law, and concubines "ad libitum."[7]　　　560

---

3. *Macbeth* 4.1.128–40.
4. William Wilberforce (1759–1833) and Sir Samuel Romilly (1757–1818) were social reformers.
5. Love of women.
6. Bed (slang).
7. As many as one wants.

71

They lock them up, and veil, and guard them daily,
  They scarcely can behold their male relations,
So that their moments do not pass so gaily
  As is supposed the case with northern nations;
Confinement, too, must make them look quite palely: 565
  And as the Turks abhor long conversations,
Their days are either pass'd in doing nothing,
Or bathing, nursing, making love, and clothing.

72

They cannot read, and so don't lisp in criticism;
  Nor write, and so they don't affect the muse;   570
Were never caught in epigram or witticism,
  Have no romances, sermons, plays, reviews,—
In harams learning soon would make a pretty schism!
  But luckily these beauties are no "Blues,"[8]
No bustling Botherbys[9] have they to show 'em   575
  "That charming passage in the last new poem."

73

No solemn, antique gentleman of rhyme,
  Who having angled all his life for fame,
And getting but a nibble at a time,
  Still fussily keeps fishing on, the same   580
Small "Triton[1] of the minnows," the sublime
  Of mediocrity, the furious tame,
The echo's echo, usher of the school
Of female wits, boy bards—in short, a fool!

74

A stalking oracle of awful phrase,   585
  The approving "Good!" (by no means GOOD in law)
Humming like flies around the newest blaze,
  The bluest of bluebottles[2] you e'er saw,
Teasing with blame, excruciating with praise,
  Gorging the little fame he gets all raw,   590
Translating tongues he knows not even by letter,
And sweating plays so middling, bad were better.

8. I.e., bluestockings: in Byron's day, derisive term for literary women; frequent target of Byron's satiric barbs.
9. Satiric reference to the poet William Sotheby (1757–1833), whom Byron (wrongly) believed was the author of an anonymous note criticizing *The Prisoner of Chillon*; Byron's publisher unsuccessfully urged him to delete his ridicule of Sotheby (stanzas 73–74).
1. In classical myth, a sea god; *Triton of the minnows*: Shakespeare, *Coriolanus* 3.1.92.
2. Policemen (British slang).

75

One hates an author that's *all author*, fellows
    In foolscap[3] uniforms turn'd up with ink,
So very anxious, clever, fine, and jealous,   595
    One don't know what to say to them, or think,
Unless to puff them with a pair of bellows;
    Of coxcombry's[4] worst coxcombs e'en the pink
Are preferable to these shreds of paper,
These unquench'd snuffings of the midnight taper.   600

76

Of these same we see several, and of others,
    Men of the world, who know the world like men,
Scott, Rogers, Moore,[5] and all the better brothers,
    Who think of something else besides the pen;
But for the children of the "mighty mother's,"[6]   605
    The would-be wits and can't-be gentlemen,
I leave them to their daily "tea is ready,"
Smug coterie, and literary lady.

77

The poor dear Mussulwomen[7] whom I mention
    Have none of these instructive pleasant people,   610
And *one* would seem to them a new invention,
    Unknown as bells within a Turkish steeple;
I think 'twould almost be worth while to pension
    (Though best-sown projects very often reap ill)
A missionary author, just to preach   615
Our Christian usage of the parts of speech.

78

No chemistry for them unfolds her gasses,
    No metaphysics are let loose in lectures,
No circulating library amasses
    Religious novels, moral tales, and strictures   620
Upon the living manners, as they pass us;
    No exhibition glares with annual pictures;
They stare not on the stars from out their attics,
Nor deal (thank God for that!) in mathematics.[8]

---

3. Writing paper approximately 13 inches by 17 inches.
4. See note to line 238.
5. Walter Scott (1771–1832), Samuel Rogers (1763–1855), Thomas Moore (1779–1852): writers Byron admired.
6. Pope, *The Dunciad* 1.1.
7. Muslim women.
8. Byron's estranged wife excelled in mathematics.

79

Why I thank God for that is no great matter,   625
  I have my reasons, you no doubt suppose,
And as, perhaps, they would not highly flatter,
  I'll keep them for my life (to come) in prose;[9]
I fear I have a little turn for satire,
  And yet methinks the older that one grows   630
Inclines us more to laugh than scold, though laughter
Leaves us so doubly serious shortly after.

80

Oh, Mirth and Innocence! Oh, Milk and Water![1]
  Ye happy mixtures of more happy days!
In these sad centuries of sin and slaughter,   635
  Abominable Man no more allays
His thirst with such pure beverage. No matter,
  I love you both, and both shall have my praise:
Oh, for old Saturn's[2] reign of sugar-candy!—
Meantime I drink to your return in brandy.   640

81

Our Laura's Turk still kept his eyes upon her,
  Less in the Mussulman than Christian way,
Which seems to say, "Madam, I do you honour,
  And while I please to stare, you'll please to stay:"
Could staring win a woman, this had won her,   645
  But Laura could not thus be led astray;
She had stood fire too long and well, to boggle
Even at this stranger's most outlandish ogle.

82

The morning now was on the point of breaking,
  A turn of time at which I would advise   650
Ladies who have been dancing, or partaking
  In any other kind of exercise,
To make their preparations for forsaking
  The ball-room ere the sun begins to rise,
Because when once the lamps and candles fail,   655
His blushes make them look a little pale.

9. About the time of the publication of *Beppo*, Byron began writing his Memoirs, burned by his publisher and friends after his death.
1. *Mirth . . . Water!*: phrases Byron used in letter to Moore (see p. 722).
2. Titan whose reign, prior to Jupiter's, was often thought of as a golden age in Italy, commemorated by annual feasts.

83

I've seen some balls and revels in my time,
　　And stay'd them over for some silly reason,
And then I look'd (I hope it was no crime)
　　To see what lady best stood out the season;   660
And though I've seen some thousands in their prime,
　　Lovely and pleasing, and who still may please on,
I never saw but one (the stars withdrawn)
　　Whose bloom could after dancing dare the dawn.

84

The name of this Aurora[3] I'll not mention,   665
　　Although I might, for she was nought to me
More than that patent work of God's invention,
　　A charming woman, whom we like to see;
But writing names would merit reprehension,
　　Yet if you like to find out this fair *she*,   670
At the next London or Parisian ball
You still may mark her cheek, out-blooming all.

85

Laura, who knew it would not do at all
　　To meet the daylight after seven hours sitting
Among three thousand people at a ball,   675
　　To make her curtsy thought it right and fitting;
The Count was at her elbow with her shawl,
　　And they the room were on the point of quitting,
When lo! those cursed gondoliers had got
Just in the very place where they *should not*.   680

86

In this they're like our coachmen, and the cause
　　Is much the same—the crowd, and pulling, hauling,
With blasphemies enough to break their jaws,
　　They make a never intermitting bawling.
At home, our Bow-street gemmen[4] keep the laws,   685
　　And here a sentry stands within your calling;
But for all that, there is a deal of swearing,
And nauseous words past mentioning or bearing.

87

The Count and Laura found their boat at last,
　　And homeward floated o'er the silent tide,   690

3. Roman goddess of dawn. This name recurs in Byron's works to signify an ideal woman: e.g., Egeria
　in *Childe Harold* IV.1030, Haidee in *Don Juan* II.1132, Aurora Raby in *Don Juan* XV–XVI.
4. Bow Street Runners, i.e., the London police, who were connected with the court in Bow Street.

Discussing all the dances gone and past;
  The dancers and their dresses, too, beside;
Some little scandals eke: but all aghast
  (As to their palace stairs the rowers glide)
Sate Laura by the side of her Adorer,   695
When lo! the Mussulman was there before her.

88

"Sir," said the Count, with brow exceeding grave,
  "Your unexpected presence here will make
"It necessary for myself to crave
  "Its import? But perhaps 'tis a mistake;   700
"I hope it is so; and at once to wave
  "All compliment, I hope so for *your* sake;
"You understand my meaning, or you *shall.*"
"Sir," (quoth the Turk) "'tis no mistake at all.

89

"That lady is *my wife!*" Much wonder paints   705
  The lady's changing cheek, as well it might;
But where an Englishwoman sometimes faints,
  Italian females don't do so outright;
They only call a little on their saints,
  And then come to themselves, almost or quite;   710
Which saves much hartshorn,[5] salts, and sprinkling faces,
And cutting stays, as usual in such cases.

90

She said,—what could she say? Why, not a word:
  But the Count courteously invited in
The stranger, much appeased by what he heard: 715
  "Such things, perhaps, we'd best discuss within,"
Said he; "don't let us make ourselves absurd
  In public, by a scene, nor raise a din,
For then the chief and only satisfaction
Will be much quizzing on the whole transaction."   720

91

They enter'd, and for coffee call'd—it came,
  A beverage for Turks and Christians both,
Although the way they make it's not the same.
  Now Laura, much recover'd, or less loth
To speak, cries "Beppo! what's your pagan name   725
  Bless me! your beard is of amazing growth!
And how came you to keep away so long?
Are you not sensible 'twas very wrong?

---

5. Ammonia (used as smelling salt) taken from the antler of a hart.

92

"And are you *really, truly,* now a Turk?
    With any other women did you wive?   730
Is't true they use their fingers for a fork?
    Well, that's the prettiest shawl—as I'm alive!
You'll give it me? They say you eat no pork.
    And how so many years did you contrive
To—Bless me! did I ever? No, I never   735
    Saw a man grown so yellow! How's your liver?

93

"Beppo! that beard of yours becomes you not;
    It shall be shaved before you're a day older:
Why do you wear it? Oh! I had forgot—
    Pray don't you think the weather here is colder?   740
How do I look? You shan't stir from this spot
    In that queer dress, for fear that some beholder
Should find you out, and make the story known.
How short your hair is! Lord! how grey it's grown!"

94

What answer Beppo made to these demands   745
    Is more than I know. He was cast away
About where Troy stood once, and nothing stands;
    Became a slave of course, and for his pay
Had bread and bastinadoes,[6] till some bands
    Of pirates landing in a neighbouring bay,   750
He join'd the rogues and prosper'd, and became
A renegado of indifferent fame.

95

But he grew rich, and with his riches grew so
    Keen the desire to see his home again,
He thought himself in duty bound to do so,   755
    And not be always thieving on the main;
Lonely he felt, at times, as Robin Crusoe,[7]
    And so he hired a vessel come from Spain,
Bound for Corfu: she was a fine polacca,[8]
Mann'd with twelve hands, and laden with tobacco.   760

96

Himself, and much (heaven knows how gotten) cash,
    He then embark'd, with risk of life and limb,
And got clear off, although the attempt was rash;

---

6. Beatings with a stick as a punishment.
7. In Daniel Defoe's *Robinson Crusoe* (1719).
8. A type of sailing vessel used in the Mediterranean Sea; *Corfu*: island off northwest Greece.

He said that *Providence* protected him—
    For my part, I say nothing—lest we clash   765
In our opinions:—well, the ship was trim,
    Set sail, and kept her reckoning fairly on,
Except three days of calm when off Cape Bonn.[9]

97

They reach'd the island, he transferr'd his lading,
    And self and live stock, to another bottom,   770
And pass'd for a true Turkey-merchant, trading
    With goods of various names, but I've forgot 'em.
However, he got off by this evading,
    Or else the people would perhaps have shot him;
And thus at Venice landed to reclaim   775
His wife, religion, house, and Christian name.

98

His wife received, the patriarch re-baptized him
    (He made the church a present, by the way);
He then threw off the garments which disguised him,
    And borrow'd the Count's smallclothes for a day: 780
His friends the more for his long absence prized him,
    Finding he'd wherewithal to make them gay,
With dinners, where he oft became the laugh of them,
For stories—but *I* don't believe the half of them.

99

Whate'er his youth had suffer'd, his old age   785
    With wealth and talking make him some amends;
Though Laura sometimes put him in a rage,
    I've heard the Count and he were always friends.
My pen is at the bottom of a page,
    Which being finish'd, here the story ends;   790
'Tis to be wish'd it had been sooner done,
But stories somehow lengthen when begun.

To the Po. June 2nd 1819[1]

River! that rollest by the ancient walls,
    Where dwells the Lady of my Love, when She
Walks by thy brink and there perchance recalls

---

9. In north Tunisia.
1. Written in June 1819 and first published posthumously, untitled, in Medwin's *Journal of the Conversations of Lord Byron* (1824). In this poem Byron expresses his love for Teresa Guiccioli, a nineteen-year-old married countess with whom he began an affair in Venice in April 1819. Though he sometimes referred to himself with mock chagrin as her *cavalier servente* (a somewhat formalized and accepted role for the lover of a married woman), Byron's attachment to Teresa, as hers to him, was a deep one that continued throughout the rest of their lives. Shortly after their affair began, Teresa had to leave Venice and return with her husband to their home in Ravenna. "To the Po" reflects Byron's "private feelings and passions" during this early separation (*BLJ* 7:97).

A faint and fleeting memory of me,
What if thy deep and ample stream should be   5
A mirror of my heart, where she may read
The thousand thoughts I now betray to thee,
Wild as thy wave and headlong as thy speed?
What do I say? "a mirror of my heart":
Are not thy waters sweeping, dark, and strong?   10
Such as my feelings were and are thou art,
And such as thou art were my passions long.
Time may have somewhat tamed them; not forever
Thou overflow'st thy banks, and not for aye
The bosom overboils, congenial River!   15
Thy floods subside, and mine have sunk away,
But left long wrecks behind us, yet again
Borne on our old career unchanged we move;
Thou tendest wildly to the wilder main,
And I to loving one I should not love.   20
The current I behold will sweep beneath
Her palace walls and murmur at her feet;
Her eyes will look on thee, when She shall breathe
The twilight air unchain'd from Summer's heat.
She will look on thee,—I have look'd on thee,   25
Full of that thought, and from this moment ne'er
Thy waters could I name, hear named, or see
Without the inseparable Sigh for her.
Her bright eyes will be imaged in thy Stream—
Yes, they will meet the wave I gaze on now,   30
But mine can not even witness in a dream
That happy wave repass me in its flow.
The wave that bears my tear returns no more:
Will She return by whom that wave shall sweep?
Both tread thy bank, both wander by thy shore,   35
I near thy source, and She by the blue deep.
But that which keepeth us apart is not
Distance, nor depth of wave, nor space of earth,
But the distractions of a various lot,
Ah! various as the climates of our birth!   40
A Stranger loves a lady of the land,

For a full discussion of the biographical and textual complexities of the poem, see *CPW* 4:497–99 and Stauffer, "The Career of Byron's 'To the Po.'"

Textual Note: All collected editions prior to *CPW* derive from Medwin's printing, which unfortunately was based on an intermediate copy of Byron's draft and not on Byron's fair copy. The present edition is based on the fair copy (Berg Collection, New York Public Library), which has been collated with Byron's draft (Pierpont Morgan Library), *1832*, *C*, and *CPW*. The familiar title "Stanzas to the Po" (in *1832* and all editions prior to *CPW*) has been replaced with the title on the fair copy, and the traditional division of the poem into numbered quatrains has been replaced by Byron's continuous lines. Indeed, the stanza subdivisions, aside from being unauthorized, impede the flow of passionate thoughts that is the essence of the poem and is objectively correlated by the river. *Substantive variants* (by line number; unless otherwise noted, the *1832* wording is given after the bracket)—17: *behind us, yet*] behind, and now.   18: *career unchanged*] unchanged career.   19: *to the wilder*] onwards to.   26: *this*] that.   27: *name, hear named*] dream of, name.   36: I by thy source, she by the dark-blue deep.   39: *distractions*] distraction.   40: *Ah!*] As.   41: *a lady*] the lady.   45: *heart*] blood.   46: *suffered now*] left my clime.   47: *Despite old*] In spite of (*1832*); Despite of (*CPW*).   48: *Oh! Love!*] of love.   49–52: 'Tis vain to struggle—let me perish young— / Live as I lived, and love as I have loved; / To dust if I return, from dust I sprung, / And then, at least, my heart can ne'er be moved.

Born far beyond the Mountains, but his blood
Is all meridian as if never fann'd
By the bleak wind that chills the Polar flood.
My heart is all meridian; were it not   45
I had not suffer'd now, nor should I be,
Despite old tortures ne'er to be forgot,
The Slave again, Oh! Love! at least of thee!
'Tis vain to struggle—I have struggled long
To love again no more as once I loved.   50
Oh! Time! why leave this earliest Passion strong,
To tear a heart which pants to be unmoved?

FROM DON JUAN   "I have finished the First Canto . . . of a poem in the
style and manner of 'Beppo,' encouraged by the good success of the same. It is
called 'Don Juan,' and is meant to be a little quietly facetious upon everything.
But I doubt whether it is not . . . too free for these very modest days" (p. 733).
Thus Byron explained to Thomas Moore the inauguration of a poetic project
that would result in one of the most important long poems in English and the
greatest English comic poem since the *Canterbury Tales.* Influenced by John
Hookham Frere's *The Monks and the Giants* (1817–18), a mock-heroic poem
written in the *ottava rima* stanza, and by the Italian burlesque poets who were
Frere's models—Luigi Pulci (1432–1484), Francesco Berni (1497?–1535), and
Giambattista Casti (1724–1803)—Byron began *Don Juan* in Venice in July
1818, publishing the first two cantos as a unit on July 15, 1819. From the out-
set, the poem's indecent humor and its sharp anti-Tory politics—including
unrestrained, personal attacks on Castlereagh, secretary of war, among other
public figures—troubled his conservative publisher, John Murray. After the
publication of Cantos III, IV, and V in 1821, tired of acquiescing to Murray's
"damned cutting and slashing" (p. 735), Byron gave the succeeding cantos to
the radical publisher John Hunt, who published them in the following
sequence of volumes: Cantos VI–VIII, Cantos IX–XI, and Cantos XII–XIV, all
in 1823, and Cantos XV–XVI in 1824. Though attacked in the periodicals
largely on moral grounds, *Don Juan* was an instant and widespread success
(Hunt's initial print run for each volume was more than 20,000 copies) and
found its way to a wide range of readers through inexpensive printings, piracies,
and translations. The sixteen cantos were issued all together for the first time,
by Murray, in 1828. At the time of his death, Byron had drafted fourteen stan-
zas of a seventeenth canto, which remained unpublished until C (1903).
    "A poem totally of its own species . . . a drama, such as England has not yet
seen," as Percy Shelley observed in a letter to Byron, *Don Juan* is impossible to
contain within a single literary classification. Its starting point is mock epic,
which Byron establishes partly through humorous allusions to the epic con-
ventions "of Virgil and of Homer, / So that my name of Epic's no misnomer"
(I.1599–1600). On a more profound level, the poem undoes the high-minded
seriousness of epic, its underlying belief in the values, people, heroes, leaders,
and gods of a society. To begin with, Byron chose an anti-hero. The heartless
seducer, rapist, and killer of Spanish legend and *El burlador de Sevilla*, the early
seventeenth-century drama by Tirso de Molina, Don Juan became widely
familiar to Byron's readers from Thomas Shadwell's play *The Libertine* (1676)
and Mozart's *Don Giovanni* (1787), as well as from popular theatrical enter-
tainment ("We all have seen him, in the pantomime, / Sent to the devil some-
what ere his time" [I.7–8]). In fact, Byron's choice of hero was partly a reaction
to Coleridge's criticism in *Biographia Literaria* of the "jacobinical" dramas in
which such irrepressible rakes are allowed to escape punishment. However,
while Byron's Juan (the pronunciation is anglicized: Joo´-un) shares with his

legendary namesake an aristocratic lineage, instinctive courage, and a pica-
resque series of sexual encounters, he is hardly the threatening presence that
his literary ancestor is. A youth, rather than a mature man, Byron's hero is typ-
ically in the position of an unempowered (if exceptionally good-looking, capa-
ble, and likable) outsider and is more of a sexual victim (or, in the better
circumstances, beneficiary) than aggressor; he is endowed with natural virtues
of kindness and sympathy, bearing greater resemblance to Fielding's Tom Jones
than to the legendary Spanish villain. The hero, however, is not the poem's cen-
tral character. As in *Childe Harold*, the narrator consistently upstages both the
hero and the narrative with his chatty commentaries. These digressions in fact
form the larger substance and interest of both poems, but in *Don Juan* are used
with the self-conscious playfulness and proto-postmodernism of one of its lit-
erary models, Laurence Sterne's novel *Tristram Shandy* (1759–67).

Byron began the poem, he said, without a plan, but after completing the fifth
canto he outlined a course for Don Juan that highlights both the poem's satir-
ical purpose and autobiographical frame of reference:

> I meant to take him the tour of Europe—with a proper mixture of siege—
> battle—and adventure—and to make him finish as *Anacharsis Cloots* [an
> aristocratic revolutionary guillotined in 1793]—in the French Revolu-
> tion. . . . I meant to have made him a Cavalier Servente in Italy and a
> cause for a divorce in England—and a Sentimental 'Werther-faced man'
> in Germany—so as to show the different ridicules of the society in each
> of those countries. . . . But I had not quite fixed whether to make him end
> in Hell—or an unhappy marriage,—not knowing which would be the
> severest.—The Spanish tradition says Hell—but it is probably only an Alle-
> gory of the other state" (*BLJ* 8:78).

Byron's hero is situated in the "epic" period of Revolution, as he travels eastward
from Europe (from his native Spain) and then back to Europe (to a country manor
in Byron's native England). Along the way he experiences life on a Greek isle, at
a Turkish slave market, harem, and battle (the Russian siege of Ismail), and at
the Russian court. The poet-narrator, however, inhabits the mock-heroic world
of post-Waterloo Europe, with its entrenched conservatism and complacent aris-
tocracy. As "a *satire* against the *abuses* of the present *states* of Society" (*BLJ* 10:68),
the poem has four principle targets: the reactionary Tory government, embodied
in Castlereagh; contemporary poetry, or the Lake poets, chiefly Wordsworth,
Coleridge, and Southey, whose style Byron found mannered and monotonous
and whose Platonism reflected an unworldliness, or "narrowness," that made him
wish they would "change [their] lakes for ocean" (Dedication, 40); the social and
religious codes and mores, especially surrounding love and marriage, that belie
"the controlless core / Of human hearts" (I.924–25); and finally, the sign of all
these abuses, "cant"—jargon and pious clichés that often mask selfish interests.
In Byron's view (expressed in his 1820 "Letter to Bowles" defending the poetry
of Pope) "cant political, cant poetical, cant moral, cant religious" was "the grand
'primum mobile' of England," and among its worst perpetrators was the recipient
of the poem's mock dedication, England's poet laureate, Robert Southey, a one-
time reformer whose "turncoat" politics was reflected in the mediocrity of his
poetry (fiercely derided, too, in *The Vision of Judgment*). Worse than straightfor-
ward lying (which relies on an awareness of truth), cant involves a kind of self-
deception, evasion, or hypocrisy that convinces its user of his own virtue and
conveys such conviction that "the very truth seems falsehood to it" (XI.288).
Responding to the poem's recurrent message that "they lie, we lie, all lie"
(VI.150), the contemporary critic Francis Jeffrey charged *Don Juan* with "the ten-
dency to destroy all belief in the reality of virtue." However, the morality of the
poem is its holding truth to be "the grand desideratum" (VII.642), and the sense
of being undeceived constitutes both its pleasure and its salutariness.

At the same time, *Don Juan* lacks the positive, reformative goal of satire and is in fact something more subversive: comedy. Its ostentatious irreverence and Wildean reversal of clichés turn the most ordinary matters (like steam engines or wrinkles) and the most serious matters (like religion or love) into opportunities "to giggle and make giggle" (p.750). Its facetiousness is unflinching even when confronting disturbing subjects like adultery ("The world . . . / Whisper'd he had a mistress, some said two / But for domestic quarrels one will do" [I.149–52]) or cannibalism ("The surgeon, as there was no other fee, / Had his first choice of morsels for his pains; / But being thirstiest at the moment, he / Preferr'd a draught from the fast-flowing veins" [II.609–12]), not to mention piracy, tyranny, rape, slavery, war, and death. Byron acknowledged that his turn of mind was "given to taking things in the absurd point of view" (*BLJ* 9:123), but flippancy is also a defense (or weapon) against cant moral and cant sentimental. Moreover, charged with scoffing at everything, Byron expressed the deep paradox of comedy by acknowledging, "I laugh . . . that I may not weep" (IV.25–26). With lines like that, too, and with its many thoughtful and lyrical passages, *Don Juan* even eludes classification as comedy. To critical attacks on the poem's heterogeneous materials, blatant contradictions, and frequent unsettling contrasts in tone and feeling, Byron would merely reply: "But if a writer should be quite consistent, / How could he possibly show things existent?" (XV.695–96).

Ottava rima—a stanza of eight iambic pentameter lines rhyming ababacc—provided Byron with a swift-moving poetic vehicle well suited to his temperament and fluent wit. Through this artful stanza, compact and tightly controlled by its numerous rhymes, Byron creates the semblance of a gentleman "rattl[ing] on exactly as I'd talk" (XV.151), an effect that derives from a combination of quotidian content, colloquial diction, feminine rhymes (i.e., rhyme words ending with an unstressed syllables), and often an inventive use of listing:

> A scolding wife, a sullen son, a bill
> To pay, unpaid, protested, or discounted
> At a per-centage; a child cross, dog ill,
> A favourite horse fallen lame just as he's mounted,
> A bad old woman making a worse will,
> Which leaves you minus of the cash you counted
> As certain;—these are paltry things, and yet
> I've rarely seen the man they did not fret. (VI, stanza 2).

Throughout the poem, comic effects are often traceable to sense-wrenching enjambments (as in the stanza above), as well as to rhymes and slant rhymes that rely on distorted pronunciations (Milan/villain), the hudibrastic rhyming of one polysyllabic word against three words (as in "intellectual/henpeck'd you all"), and anti-climactic, irrelevant, or inconclusive concluding couplets. Humor is also achieved through wordplay and odd or inappropriate juxtapositions, particularly those characterized by bathos—a sudden drop in emotional significance:

> Sad thought! to lose the spouse that was adorning
> Our days, and put one's servants into mourning. (III.55–56)

With the *ottava rima* stanza Byron discovered the freedom to go wherever he wanted to go (no subject too big or too small, too high or too low for his "pedestrian Muses" [Dedication, 57]), thus creating the poem's "elastic shape which will hold whatever you choose to put into it," in the words of Virginia Woolf. Byron's own defense of the poem's content was bound up with his awareness of its linguistic achievement:

> . . . it is the sublime of *that there* sort of writing—it may be bawdy—but is it not good English—it may be profligate—but is it not *life*, is it not *the thing*?—
> Could any man have written it—who has not lived in the world?—and tooled

in a post-chaise? in a hackney coach? in a Gondola? against a wall? in a court carriage? in a vis a vis?—on a table?—and under it? (p. 753).

Criticism: The following reviews and essays included in this Norton Critical Edition focus wholly or substantially on *Don Juan*: Wilson or Lockhart (?), review in *Blackwood's Magazine* (p. 790); Jeffrey, review in *Edinburgh Review* (p. 796); Barton, "Byron and the Mythology of Fact" (p. 812); McGann, "The Book of Byron and the Book of a World" (p. 828); Stabler, "Byron, Postmodernism and Intertextuality" (p. 864); Graham, "Nothing So Difficult" (p. 943); Wolfson, "'Their She Condition': Cross-Dressing and the Politics of Gender in *Don Juan*" (p. 955). Lang, "Narcissus Jilted: Byron, *Don Juan* and the Biographical Imperative" (p. 972); Chandler, "'Man fell with apples': The Moral Mechanics of *Don Juan*" (p. 993). Among book-length studies that offer important contributions to the understanding of *Don Juan* are the following: Barton, *Byron: Don Juan*; Beatty, *Byron's Don Juan*; Beaty, *Byron the Satirist*; Boyd, *Byron's Don Juan: A Critical Study*; England, *Byron's Don Juan and Eighteenth-Century Literature*; Franklin, *Byron's Heroines*; Graham, *Don Juan and Regency England*; Haslett, *Byron's Don Juan and the Don Juan Legend*; McGann, *Don Juan in Context*; Ridenour, *The Style of Don Juan*; Vassallo, *Byron: The Italian Literary Influence*. A vast array of editions, manuscript facsimiles, contemporary reviews, source studies, and criticism exists for *Don Juan*, some of which are included in the Selected Bibliography. For a useful listing of bibliographies, concordances, websites, editions, and criticism, see the "Further Reading" compilation by Susan J. Wolfson and Peter J. Manning in *Don Juan*, edited by T. G. Steffan, E. Steffan and W. W. Pratt (Penguin, 2004).

Textual Notes: The 1832 text of *Don Juan*, especially of Cantos I–II, contains unauthorized textual changes, many of which persisted in all editions prior to *DJV* or *CPW*. For the complex transmission history of the text of *Don Juan*, see *CPW* 5. Based on a comparison of 1832 with *CPW*, *DJV*, *More*, *Cochran*, and in some cases the draft manuscript, the present edition generally corrects the wording of the copy text, although in some cases the wording from 1832 has been retained though it differs from *CPW* (e.g., when 1832 is clearly supported by the manuscript or corrects an ungrammatical or illogical reading). In the Textual Notes below, the line number and word(s) from the present edition are given to the left of the bracket and conform to *CPW* unless otherwise indicated; to the right of the bracket is the wording as given in 1832, or in *More* for Canto XVII, unless otherwise indicated. Special mention should be made of the spelling of the name "Haidee," which occurs in Cantos II, III, and IV, and once in Canto XV. 1832 and nearly all editions prior to *CPW* and *Cochran* give the name as Haidée. However, the fact that in the manuscripts of Cantos II, III, and IV the name is written without an accent and that all rhymes with the name are "ee" rhymes almost irrefutably indicates that Byron pronounced the second syllable "dee"; moreover, the earliest editions of Cantos I–II lack the accent, which was added in the 1821 edition of Cantos III, IV, and V (*DJV* 2:224). For the sake of consistency both within the present excerpts and with Byron's manuscripts and apparent pronunciation, the Norton Critical Edition omits the accent throughout.

Dedication

    3:   true you] true that you.
    9:   pie] pye.
   49:   baldness] boldness.

Canto I

  124:   search] quest.
  131:   beyond] above.

156:    so] such.
251:    say] tell.
273:    Yes] Yet.
323:    made] raised.
508:    Francis back] Anthony.
1516:   At least since the retirement of the Vandals.
1520:   embark'd at] shipp'd off from.
1523:   or] and.
1526:   nunnery] convent she.
1527:   And there] Grieved, but.
1544:   nor] or.
1545:   his] man's.
1553–60: Stanzas 195–96 printed in reverse order in *1832* and all editions before *CPW*.
1554:   I struggle but cannot] But still I think I can.
1557:   brain] heart.
1558:   your] one.
1559–60: So shakes the needle, and so stands the pole, / As vibrates my fond heart to my fix'd soul.
1561:   beauty] pleasure.
1574:   flies] shuns.
1578:   crow-quill, rather hard, but new] little crow-quill, slight and new.
1579:   fingers scarce could] hand could hardly.
1580:   But] It.

Canto II

160:    retching (*1832, DJV*)] reaching (*CPW* and MSS.—an alternative spelling of the word in Byron's day).
494:    Was] were.
590:    shock] shook.
890:    he thought (*1832, DJV, More*)] methought (*CPW*).
1547:   hers] her.

Canto V

487:    printing] writing.
492:    Line dropped in the printing of *1832*.

Canto IX

379:    room] not room.
519:    hatch] batch.

Canto X

61:     reach] reach'd.

Canto XI

432:    its] it's.
454:    Cambyses Crowley] Rowley Powley.
456:    these] the.
457–64: First printed in 1837.

Canto XII

20:     holds] hold (*CPW, DJV*)

Canto XVI

    137:   frowns] forms.
    284:   by the bye] by and by.
    780:   smiles bespeak] smile bespeaks.
    855:   the] their.
    893:   Further] Farther.
    915:   wane] fade.

Canto XVII

    14:   just] great.
    29:   can] can't (*CPW*).
    34:   every vulgar] every.
    48:   as bear witness] witness.
    54:   slightly] lightly.
    75:   To] In.
    105:   best is] best it is.

FROM DON JUAN

Difficile est proprie communia dicere.[1]

Hor, *Epist. ad Pison.*

Fragment[2]

On the back of the Poet's MS. of Canto I

I would to heaven that I were so much clay,
    As I am blood, bone, marrow, passion, feeling—
Because at least the past were pass'd away—
    And for the future—(but I write this reeling,
Having got drunk exceedingly to-day,
    So that I seem to stand upon the ceiling)
I say—the future is a serious matter—
And so—for God's sake—hock[3] and soda-water!

DEDICATION

1

Bob Southey![4] You're a poet—Poet-laureate,
    And representative of all the race,

---

1. It is difficult to speak of common subjects in one's own way (Horace, *Ars Poetica*, line 128). For Byron's rendering of this line in *Hints from Horace* (181–82) and his long note on its disputed meaning, see *CPW* 1: 296 and 433–34. Byron had canceled his original motto, "Domestica facta . . . Horace," at Hobhouse's suggestion because of its allusion to the biographical dimension of the poem.
2. Byron canceled this stanza, first used as the poem's headpiece in *1832. CPW* includes it among Unincorporated Material for Canto I, along with a prose preface that Byron drafted but never completed.
3. A dry white wine; Byron refers to a hangover cure.
4. Robert Southey (1774–1843), like Wordsworth and Coleridge, was one of the "Lake Poets" ("Lakers," line 6), who lived in and wrote about the Lake District in northwest England. Liberal in his youth, he became an enthusiastic Tory (hence, "Renegade," line 5) and was made poet laureate in 1813. Byron's particular animus against Southey (see also *The Vision of Judgment* [p. 684]) was fueled by Southey's remark that Byron and Shelley were "in a league of incest" (a reference

Although 'tis true you turn'd out a Tory at
　　Last,—yours has lately been a common case,—
And now, my Epic Renegade! what are ye at? 5
　　With all the Lakers, in and out of place?
A nest of tuneful persons, to my eye
　　Like "four and twenty blackbirds in a pie;[5]

2

Which pie being open'd, they began to sing"
　　(This old song and new simile holds good), 10
"A dainty dish to set before the King,"
　　Or Regent,[6] who admires such kind of food;—
And Coleridge, too, has lately taken wing,
　　But like a hawk encumber'd with his hood,—
Explaining metaphysics to the nation— 15
　　I wish he would explain his Explanation.[7]

3

You, Bob! are rather insolent, you know,
　　At being disappointed in your wish
To supersede all warblers here below,
　　And be the only Blackbird in the dish; 20
And then you overstrain yourself, or so,
　　And tumble downward like the flying fish
Gasping on deck, because you soar too high, Bob,
And fall, for lack of moisture quite a-dry, Bob![8]

4

And Wordsworth, in a rather long "Excursion"[9] 25
　　(I think the quarto[1] holds five hundred pages),
Has given a sample from the vasty version
　　Of his new system to perplex the sages;
'Tis poetry—at least by his assertion,
　　And may appear so when the dog-star[2] rages— 30
And he who understands it would be able
To add a story to the Tower of Babel.[3]

---

to the close relationships among Byron, the Shelleys, and Claire Clairmont, a stepsister of Mary
　　Shelley and lover of Byron during the summer of 1816). Byron's contempt for the Lake poets (see
　　stanzas 5–7), however, was based on aesthetic principles and consistently held throughout his life.
5. A pun on the deceased poet laureate Henry James Pye (1745–1813).
6. Before he became king, George IV served as Prince Regent from 1811 to 1820 due to the insan-
　　ity of his father, George III.
7. A reference to Coleridge's *Biographia Literaria* (1817), an account of his philosophical and liter-
　　ary opinions. Byron's hostile reaction to this work inspired not only the attack on the Lake Poets
　　but other features of *Don Juan* as well (see *CPW* 5: 668).
8. A "dry bob" was slang for orgasm without emission.
9. *The Excursion* (1814).
1. Typical size (approx. 12½ inches by 9½ inches) of an expensive book, formed by folding printed
　　sheets twice to form four leaves (eight pages).
2. Sirius, the Dog Star, thought in folklore to cause insanity while it was in the ascendant.
3. Genesis 11.

5

You—Gentlemen! by dint of long seclusion
   From better company, have kept your own
At Keswick,[4] and, through still continued fusion   35
   Of one another's minds, at last have grown
To deem as a most logical conclusion
   That Poesy has wreaths for you alone:
There is a narrowness in such a notion,
Which makes me wish you'd change your lakes for ocean.   40

6

I would not imitate the petty thought,
   Nor coin my self-love to so base a vice,
For all the glory your conversion brought,
   Since gold alone should not have been its price.
You have your salary; was't for that you wrought?   45
   And Wordsworth has his place in the Excise.[5]
You're shabby fellows—true—but poets still,
And duly seated on the immortal hill.[6]

7

Your bays[7] may hide the baldness of your brows—
   Perhaps some virtuous blushes;—let them go—   50
To you I envy neither fruit nor boughs—
   And for the fame you would engross below,
The field is universal, and allows
   Scope to all such as feel the inherent glow:
Scott, Rogers, Campbell, Moore, and Crabbe,[8] will try   55
'Gainst you the question with posterity.

8

For me, who, wandering with pedestrian Muses,
   Contend not with you on the winged steed,[9]
I wish your fate may yield ye, when she chooses,
   The fame you envy, and the skill you need;   60
And recollect a poet nothing loses
   In giving to his brethren their full meed
Of merit, and complaint of present days
Is not the *certain* path to future praise.

4. Town in the Lake District where Southey resided and near Wordsworth's home.
5. "Wordsworth's place may be in the Customs—it is, I think, in that or the Excise—besides another at Lord Lonsdale's table, where this poetical charlatan and political parasite licks up the crumbs with a hardened alacrity; the converted Jacobin having long subsided into the clownish sycophant of the worst prejudices of the aristocracy." Byron's note refers to Wordsworth's appointment as Distributor or Stamps for the county of Westmoreland in March 1813, through Lord Lonsdale's patronage. The Excise was the branch of the government that collects certain taxes.
6. Mount Parnassus, home of the Muses in classical myth.
7. An honorary garland signifying victory or poetic eminence.
8. Walter Scott, Samuel Rogers, Thomas Moore, George Crabbe: contemporary poets that Byron admired (see journal entry of November 24, 1813, [p. 181]).
9. The winged horse Pegasus, in classical myth, was associated with the Muses and poetic inspiration.

9

He that reserves his laurels for posterity   65
    (Who does not often claim the bright reversion?)[1]
Has generally no great crop to spare it, he
    Being only injured by his own assertion;
And although here and there some glorious rarity
    Arise like Titan[2] from the sea's immersion,   70
The major part of such appellants go
To—God knows where—for no one else can know.

10

If, fallen in evil days on evil tongues,
    Milton[3] appeal'd to the Avenger, Time,
If Time, the Avenger, execrates his wrongs,   75
    And makes the word *"Miltonic"* mean *"sublime,"*
He deign'd not to belie his soul in songs,
    Nor turn his very talent to a crime;
He did not loathe the Sire to laud the Son,
But closed the tyrant-hater he begun.   80

11

Think'st thou, could he—the blind Old Man[4]—arise
    Like Samuel[5] from the grave, to freeze once more
The blood of monarchs with his prophecies,
    Or be alive again—again all hoar
With time and trials, and those helpless eyes,   85
    And heartless daughters—worn—and pale[6]—and poor;
Would he adore a sultan? he obey
The intellectual eunuch Castlereagh?[7]

12

Cold-blooded, smooth-faced, placid miscreant!
    Dabbling its sleek young hands in Erin's gore,   90
And thus for wider carnage taught to pant,
    Transferr'd to gorge upon a sister shore,
The vulgarest tool that Tyranny could want,
    With just enough of talent, and no more,

1. In law, the return of an estate to its grantor or his heirs; "bright reversion" refers to honor given at a later time and is from Alexander Pope's "Elegy to the Memory of an Unfortunate Lady" (line 9).
2. Helios, the ancient Greek sun-god, arising out of the ocean at dawn.
3. After the restoration of the monarchy in 1660, John Milton (1608–1674), author of *Paradise Lost*, was in peril of his life for having supported the Puritan commonwealth. He did not change his politics to praise Charles II, however, and remained a fierce civil libertarian.
4. Milton was blind in his old age.
5. The biblical prophet, who rebukes King Saul for conjuring up his spirit (I Samuel 28.15–20).
6. "Pale, but not cadaverous." Milton's two elder daughters are reputed to have defrauded him.
7. Robert Stewart, Viscount Castlereagh (1769–1822), a highly influential Tory statesman and England's foreign secretary from 1812 until his suicide in 1822. Byron's hatred of him is expressed throughout his works. Stanza 12 refers to Castlereagh's responsibility for the imprisonment of leaders of the Irish rebellion ("Erin's gore," line 90).

To lengthen fetters by another fix'd,   95
And offer poison long already mix'd.

13

An orator of such set trash of phrase[8]
  Ineffably—legitimately vile,
That even its grossest flatterers dare not praise,
  Nor foes—all nations—condescend to smile,—   100
Not even a *sprightly* blunder's spark can blaze
  From that Ixion grindstone's ceaseless toil,
That turns and turns to give the world a notion
Of endless torments and perpetual motion.

14

A bungler even in its disgusting trade,   105
  And botching, patching, leaving still behind
Something of which its masters are afraid,
  States to be curb'd, and thoughts to be confined,[9]
Conspiracy or Congress to be made—
  Cobbling at manacles for all mankind—   110
A tinkering slave-maker, who mends old chains,
With God and man's abhorrence for its gains.

15

If we may judge of matter by the mind,
  Emasculated to the marrow *It*
Hath but two objects, how to serve, and bind,   115
  Deeming the chain it wears even men may fit,
Eutropius[1] of its many masters,—blind
  To worth as freedom, wisdom as to wit,
Fearless—because *no* feeling dwells in ice,
Its very courage stagnates to a vice.   120

16

Where shall I turn me not to *view* its bonds,
  For I will never *feel* them;—Italy!
Thy late reviving Roman soul desponds
  Beneath the lie[2] this State-thing breathed o'er thee—
Thy clanking chain, and Erin's yet green wounds,   125
  Have voices—tongues to cry aloud for me.

---

8. Castlereagh was a notoriously bad orator; hence, the allusion to the Greek myth of Ixion (line 102), one of the great sinners of Hades, where he is eternally bound to a revolving wheel as a symbol of dull, grinding monotony.
9. Lines 108–12 refer to the alliance formed in 1814 by England, Russia, Austria, and Prussia in order to defeat Napoleon, and the Congress of Vienna (1814–15), which restored the monarchies after Napoleon's defeat.
1. A eunuch in the court of the Roman emperor Arcadius. Byron's various sexual slurs regarding Castlereagh hint at his homosexuality.
2. Castlereagh first seemed to support the liberation of Genoa but then favored its annexation by Piedmont.

Europe has slaves—allies—kings—armies still,
And Southey lives to sing them very ill.

17

Meantime—Sir Laureate—I proceed to dedicate,
    In honest simple verse, this song to you.   130
And, if in flattering strains I do not predicate,
    'Tis that I still retain my "buff and blue;"[3]
My politics as yet are all to educate:
    Apostasy's so fashionable, too,
To keep *one* creed's a task grown quite Herculean;   135
Is it not my Tory, ultra-Julian?[4]

                    Venice, September 16, 1818.

CANTO THE FIRST

1

I want a hero: an uncommon want,
    When every year and month sends forth a new one,
Till, after cloying the gazettes with cant,
    The age discovers he is not the true one;
Of such as these I should not care to vaunt,[1]   5
    I'll therefore take our ancient friend Don Juan—
We all have seen him, in the pantomime,[2]
Sent to the devil somewhat ere his time.

2[3]

Vernon, the butcher Cumberland, Wolfe, Hawke,
    Prince Ferdinand, Granby, Burgoyne, Keppel, Howe,   10
Evil and good, have had their tithe of talk,
    And fill'd their sign-posts then, like Wellesley now;
Each in their turn like Banquo's monarchs[4] stalk,
    Followers of fame, "nine farrow" of that sow:
France, too, had Buonaparté and Dumourier   15
Recorded in the Moniteur and Courier.[5]

3. Colors of the Whig party.
4. "I allude not to our friend Landor's hero, the traitor Count Julian, but to Gibbon's hero, vulgarly
    yclept 'The Apostate.'" Julian the Apostate (331–63) was a Roman emperor who renounced Chris-
    tianity to reinstate pagan worship (see *Decline and Fall*, chap. 23).
1. Boast of.
2. Pantomimes and puppet shows of the eighteenth and early nineteenth centuries frequently pre-
    sented the legend of Don Juan, who is dragged to hell when he locks hands with the statue of a
    man he had killed.
3. Stanzas 2 and 3 give a catalogue of English military leaders and French generals and revolution-
    aries.
4. In *Macbeth* 4.1.126ff. the witches show Macbeth the future kings of Scotland, the offspring of
    Banquo, whom Macbeth has killed; the witches' chant in lines 80–81 of this scene refers to the
    sow (female pig) that had eaten her litter (nine farrow [line 14]).
5. French newspapers.

3

Barnave, Brissot, Condorcet, Mirabeau,
    Petion, Clootz, Danton, Marat, La Fayette,
Were French, and famous people, as we know;
    And there were others, scarce forgotten yet,   20
Joubert, Hoche, Marceau, Lannes, Desaix, Moreau,
    With many of the military set,
Exceedingly remarkable at times,
But not at all adapted to my rhymes.

4

Nelson[6] was once Britannia's god of war,   25
    And still should be so, but the tide is turn'd;
There's no more to be said of Trafalgar,
    'Tis with our hero quietly inurn'd;[7]
Because the army's grown more popular,
    At which the naval people are concern'd;   30
Besides, the Prince[8] is all for the land-service,
Forgetting Duncan, Nelson, Howe, and Jervis.

5

Brave men were living before Agamemnon[9]
    And since, exceeding valorous and sage,
A good deal like him too, though quite the same none;   35
    But then they shone not on the poet's page,
And so have been forgotten:—I condemn none,
    But can't find any in the present age
Fit for my poem (that is, for my new one);
So, as I said, I'll take my friend Don Juan.   40

6

Most epic poets plunge "in medias res"[1]
    (Horace makes this the heroic turnpike road),
And then your hero tells, whene'er you please,
    What went before—by way of episode,
While seated after dinner at his ease,   45
    Beside his mistress in some soft abode,
Palace, or garden, paradise, or cavern,
Which serves the happy couple for a tavern.

---

6. Horatio, Lord Nelson (1758–1805), England's greatest naval hero, who defeated Napoleon's navy
   at Trafalgar in 1805.
7. *Hamlet* 1.4.30.
8. Son of George III and the Prince Regent (1811–1820) during the insanity of his father; he allot-
   ted greater funds to the army than to the navy. The names in line 32 are those of British naval fig-
   ures.
9. Horace, *Odes* 4.9.25. Agamemnon was the leader of the Greek army in the Trojan War.
1. In the middle of things (Latin); epics begin in the middle of the story, according to Horace in *Ars
   Poetica*.

7

That is the usual method, but not mine—
    My way is to begin with the beginning;   50
The regularity of my design
    Forbids all wandering as the worst of sinning,
And therefore I shall open with a line
    (Although it cost me half an hour in spinning)
Narrating somewhat of Don Juan's father,   55
And also of his mother, if you'd rather.

8

In Seville was he born, a pleasant city,
    Famous for oranges and women—he
Who has not seen it will be much to pity,
    So says the proverb[2]—and I quite agree;   60
Of all the Spanish towns is none more pretty,
    Cadiz perhaps—but that you soon may see:—
Don Juan's parents lived beside the river,
A noble stream, and call'd the Guadalquivir.

9

His father's name was Jóse—*Don*, of course,   65
    A true Hidalgo,[3] free from every stain
Of Moor or Hebrew blood, he traced his source
    Through the most Gothic gentlemen of Spain;
A better cavalier ne'er mounted horse,
    Or, being mounted, e'er got down again,   70
Than Jóse, who begot our hero, who
Begot—but that's to come——Well, to renew:

10

His mother was a learned lady, famed
    For every branch of every science known—
In every Christian language ever named,   75
    With virtues equall'd by her wit alone,
She made the cleverest people quite ashamed,
    And even the good with inward envy groan,
Finding themselves so very much exceeded
In their own way by all the things that she did.   80

11

Her memory was a mine: she knew by heart
    All Calderon and greater part of Lopé,[4]

2. Spanish proverb, "Quien no ha visto Sevilla, no ha visto una maravilla" (who has not seen Seville has not seen a wonder).
3. Spanish nobleman.
4. Pedro Calderón de la Barca (1600–1681) and Félix Lope de Vega (1562–1635), the prolific originators of classical Spanish drama.

So that if any actor miss'd his part
  She could have served him for the prompter's copy;
For her Feinagle's[5] were an useless art,   85
  And he himself obliged to shut up shop—he
Could never make a memory so fine as
That which adorn'd the brain of Donna Inez.

12

Her favourite science was the mathematical,[6]
  Her noblest virtue was her magnanimity,   90
Her wit (she sometimes tried at wit) was Attic all,[7]
  Her serious sayings darken'd to sublimity;
In short, in all things she was fairly what I call
  A prodigy—her morning dress was dimity,[8]
Her evening silk, or, in the summer, muslin,   95
And other stuffs, with which I won't stay puzzling.

13

She knew the Latin—that is, "the Lord's prayer,"
  And Greek—the alphabet—I'm nearly sure;
She read some French romances here and there,
  Although her mode of speaking was not pure;   100
For native Spanish she had no great care,
  At least her conversation was obscure;
Her thoughts were theorems, her words a problem,
As if she deem'd that mystery would ennoble 'em.

14

She liked the English and the Hebrew tongue,   105
  And said there was analogy between 'em;
She proved it somehow out of sacred song,
  But I must leave the proofs to those who've seen 'em,
But this I heard her say, and can't be wrong,
  And all may think which way their judgments learn 'em,   110
" 'Tis strange—the Hebrew noun which means 'I am,'[9]
The English always use to govern d—n."

15

Some women use their tongues—she look'd a lecture
  Each eye a sermon, and her brow a homily,

---

5. Gregor von Feinagle (1765–1819) developed a system, popular in Byron's day, for improving the memory.
6. An obvious reference to Byron's wife, whom Byron dubbed the "Princess of Parallelograms" (*BLJ* 4:48) and whom the entire description of Inez caricatures.
7. Classical Greek; "Attic wit" is presumably delicate, refined.
8. A thin, cotton fabric.
9. JHVH (or Jahveh), the name of God as given in Exodus 3.14, translated in the King James Version as "I Am."

An all-in-all-sufficient self-director,   115
  Like the lamented late Sir Samuel Romilly,[1]
The Law's expounder, and the State's corrector,
  Whose suicide was almost an anomaly—
One sad example more, that "All is vanity,"[2]—
  (The jury brought their verdict in "Insanity.")   120

16

In short, she was a walking calculation,
  Miss Edgeworth's[3] novels stepping from their covers,
Or Mrs. Trimmer's books on education,
  Or "Coelebs' Wife" set out in search of
Morality's prim personification,   125
  In which not Envy's self a flaw discovers;
To others' share let "female errors fall,"[4]
For she had not even one—the worst of all.

17

Oh! she was perfect past all parallel—
  Of any modern female saint's comparison;   130
So far beyond the cunning powers of hell,
  Her guardian angel had given up his garrison;
Even her minutest motions went as well
  As those of the best time-piece made by Harrison:[5]
In virtues nothing earthly could surpass her,   135
Save thine "incomparable oil," Macassar![6]

18

Perfect she was, but as perfection is
  Insipid in this naughty world of ours,
Where our first parents never learn'd to kiss
  Till they were exiled from their earlier bowers,   140
Where all was peace, and innocence, and bliss
  (I wonder how they got through the twelve hours)
Don José, like a lineal son of Eve,
Went plucking various fruit without her leave.

---

1. A liberal reformer, Samuel Romilly (1757–1818), originally represented Byron in his separation from his wife but later shifted loyalty to Lady Byron. Romilly committed suicide after the death of his own wife.
2. Ecclesiastes 1.2.
3. The first of the stanza's three references to the works of contemporary women writers: Maria Edgeworth (1767–1848) was the author of sentimental novels; Sarah Trimmer (1741–1810) was the author of tracts on moral education; *Coelebs in Search of a Wife* is a book of moral instruction by the bluestocking Hannah Moore (1745–1833).
4. Pope, *Rape of the Lock*, 2.17.
5. John Harrison (1693–1776), famous English watchmaker.
6. "'Description des *vertus incomparables* de l'Huile de Macassar.' See the Advertisement." Hair oil from the Isle of Macassar was a popular commodity, advertised as possessing all manner of healthful qualities.

19

He was a mortal of the careless kind,   145
    With no great love for learning, or the learn'd,
Who chose to go where'er he had a mind,
    And never dream'd his lady was concern'd;
The world, as usual, wickedly inclined
    To see a kingdom or a house o'erturn'd,   150
Whisper'd he had a mistress, some said *two*,
But for domestic quarrels *one* will do.

20

Now Donna Inez had, with all her merit,
    A great opinion of her own good qualities;
Neglect, indeed, requires a saint to bear it,   155
    And so, indeed, she was in her moralities;
But then she had a devil of a spirit,
    And sometimes mix'd up fancies with realities,
And let few opportunities escape
Of getting her liege lord into a scrape.   160

21

This was an easy matter with a man
    Oft in the wrong, and never on his guard;
And even the wisest, do the best they can,
    Have moments, hours, and days, so unprepared,
That you might "brain them with their lady's fan;"[7]   165
    And sometimes ladies hit exceeding hard,
And fans turn into falchions[8] in fair hands,
And why and wherefore no one understands.

22

'Tis pity learned virgins ever wed
    With persons of no sort of education,
Or gentlemen, who, though well born and bred,   170
    Grow tired of scientific conversation:
I don't choose to say much upon this head,
    I'm a plain man, and in a single station,
But—Oh! ye lords of ladies intellectual,   175
Inform us truly, have they not hen-peck'd you all?

23

Don Jóse and his lady quarrell'd—*why*,
    Not any of the many could divine,
Though several thousand people chose to try,
    'Twas surely no concern of theirs nor mine;   180

7. *1 Henry IV* 2.3.19.
8. Swords.

I loathe that low vice—curiosity;
   But if there's any thing in which I shine,
'Tis in arranging all my friends' affairs,
Not having, of my own, domestic cares.

24

And so I interfered, and with the best   185
   Intentions, but their treatment was not kind;
I think the foolish people were possess'd,
   For neither of them could I ever find,
Although their porter afterwards confess'd—
   But that's no matter, and the worst's behind,   190
For little Juan o'er me threw, down stairs,
A pail of housemaid's water unawares.

25

A little curly-headed, good-for-nothing,
   And mischief-making monkey from his birth;
His parents ne'er agreed except in doting   195
   Upon the most unquiet imp on earth;
Instead of quarrelling, had they been but both in
   Their senses, they'd have sent young master for
To school, or had him soundly whipp'd at home,
To teach him manners for the time to come.   200

26

Don Jóse and the Donna Inez led
   For some time an unhappy sort of life,
Wishing each other, not divorced, but dead;
   They lived respectably as man and wife,
Their conduct was exceedingly well-bred,   205
   And gave no outward signs of inward strife,
Until at length the smother'd fire broke out,
And put the business past all kind of doubt.

27[9]

For Inez call'd some druggists, and physicians,
   And tried to prove her loving lord was *mad*,   210
But as he had some lucid intermissions,
   She next decided he was only *bad*;
Yet when they ask'd her for her depositions,
   No sort of explanation could be had,
Save that her duty both to man and God   215
Required this conduct—which seem'd very odd.

---

9. Stanzas 27–32 reflect Byron's view of the events and behaviors of various people involved in his
  and Lady Byron's separation proceedings.

28

She kept a journal, where his faults were noted,
  And open'd certain trunks of books and letters,
All which might, if occasion served, be quoted;
  And then she had all Seville for abettors,   220
Besides her good old grandmother (who doted);
  The hearers of her case became repeaters,
Then advocates, inquisitors, and judges,
Some for amusement, others for old grudges.

29

And then this best and meekest woman bore   225
  With such serenity her husband's woes,
Just as the Spartan[1] ladies did of yore,
  Who saw their spouses kill'd, and nobly chose
Never to say a word about them more——
  Calmly she heard each calumny that rose,   230
And saw *his* agonies with such sublimity,
That all the world exclaim'd, "What magnanimity!

30

No doubt this patience, when the world is damning us,
  Is philosophic in our former friends;
'Tis also pleasant to be deem'd magnanimous,
  The more so in obtaining our own ends;   235
And what the lawyers call a "*malus animus*"[2]
  Conduct like this by no means comprehends:
Revenge in person's certainly no virtue,
But then 'tis not *my* fault, if *others* hurt you.   240

31

And if our quarrels should rip up old stories,
  And help them with a lie or two additional,
I'm not to blame, as you well know—no more is
  Any one else—they were become traditional;
Besides, their resurrection aids our glories   245
  By contrast, which is what we just were wishing all:
And science profits by this resurrection—
Dead scandals form good subjects for dissection.

32

Their friends had tried at reconciliation,
  Then their relations, who made matters worse: 250
('Twere hard to say upon a like occasion
  To whom it may be best to have recourse—

---

1. The natives of Sparta, in ancient Greece, were renowned for their stoic impassivity to grief.
2. Bad intent (Latin).

I can't say much for friend or yet relation):
　The lawyers did their utmost for divorce,[3]
But scarce a fee was paid on either side　　　　　255
　Before, unluckily, Don Jóse died.

33

He died: and most unluckily, because,
　According to all hints I could collect
From counsel learned in those kinds of laws,
　(Although their talk's obscure and circumspect)　　260
His death contrived to spoil a charming cause;
　A thousand pities also with respect
To public feeling, which on this occasion
Was manifested in a great sensation.

34

But ah! he died; and buried with him lay　　　　265
　The public feeling and the lawyers' fees:
His house was sold, his servants sent away,
　A Jew took one of his two mistresses,
A priest the other—at least so they say:
　I ask'd the doctors after his disease—　　　　270
He died of the slow fever call'd the tertian,[4]
And left his widow to her own aversion.

35

Yes Jóse was an honourable man,
　That I must say, who knew him very well;
Therefore his frailties I'll no further scan,　　　275
　Indeed there were not many more to tell:
And if his passions now and then outran
　Discretion, and were not so peaceable
As Numa's (who was also named Pompilius),[5]
He had been ill brought up, and was born bilious.　280

36

Whate'er might be his worthlessness or worth,
　Poor fellow! he had many things to wound him.
Let's own—since it can do no good on earth—
　It was a trying moment that which found him
Standing alone beside his desolate hearth,　　　285
　Where all his household gods lay shiver'd round him:
No choice was left his feelings or his pride,
Save death or Doctors' Commons[6]—so he died.

3. The satiric references to divorce law in stanzas 32–36 are humorously transported from England
　to Spain, where in the eighteenth century divorce was nearly unheard of.
4. A fever that recurs every other day.
5. Early king of Rome, legendary for patience and moderation.
6. Divorce court.

37

Dying intestate, Juan was sole heir
    To a chancery suit, and messuages,[7] and lands,   290
Which, with a long minority and care,
    Promised to turn out well in proper hands:
Inez became sole guardian, which was fair,
    And answer'd but to nature's just demands;
An only son left with an only mother   295
Is brought up much more wisely than another.

38

Sagest of women, even of widows, she
    Resolved that Juan should be quite a paragon,
And worthy of the noblest pedigree:
    (His sire was of Castile, his dam from Aragon.)[8]   300
Then for accomplishments of chivalry,
    In case our lord the king should go to war again,
He learn'd the arts of riding, fencing, gunnery,
And how to scale a fortress—or a nunnery.[9]

39

But that which Donna Inez most desired,   305
    And saw into herself each day before all
The learned tutors whom for him she hired,
    Was, that his breeding should be strictly moral:
Much into all his studies she enquired,
    And so they were submitted first to her, all,   310
Arts, sciences, no branch was made a mystery
To Juan's eyes, excepting natural history.

40

The languages, especially the dead,
    The sciences, and most of all the abstruse,
The arts, at least all such as could be said   315
    To be the most remote from common use,
In all these he was much and deeply read;
    But not a page of any thing that's loose,
Or hints continuation of the species,
Was ever suffer'd, lest he should grow vicious.   320

41

His classic studies made a little puzzle,
    Because of filthy loves of gods and goddesses,

---

7. A legal term for estates; *chancery*: court that probated wills and tried legacy disputes, famous for long delays.
8. *Castile . . . Aragon*: the two great noble houses of Spain.
9. In Thomas Shadwell's drama *The Libertine* (1675), Don Juan rapes nuns in their convent.

Who in the earlier ages made a bustle,
    But never put on pantaloons or bodices;
His reverend tutors had at times a tussle,   325
    And for their Aeneids, Iliads, and Odysseys,
Were forced to make an odd sort of apology,
For Donna Inez dreaded the Mythology.

42[1]

Ovid's a rake, as half his verses show him,
    Anacreon's morals are a still worse sample,   330
Catullus scarcely has a decent poem,
    I don't think Sappho's Ode a good example,
Although Longinus[2] tells us there is no hymn
    Where the sublime soars forth on wings more ample;
But Virgil's songs are pure, except that horrid one   335
Beginning with "Formosum Pastor Corydon."

43

Lucretius' irreligion is too strong
    For early stomachs, to prove wholesome food;
I can't help thinking Juvenal was wrong,
    Although no doubt his real intent was good,   340
For speaking out so plainly in his song,
    So much indeed as to be downright rude;
And then what proper person can be partial
To all those nauseous epigrams of Martial?

44

Juan was taught from out the best edition,   345
    Expurgated by learned men, who place,
Judiciously, from out the schoolboy's vision,
    The grosser parts; but fearful to deface
Too much their modest bard by this omission,
    And pitying sore his mutilated case,   350
They only add them all in an appendix,[3]
Which saves, in fact, the trouble of an index;

---

1. In this and the next stanza Byron mentions some of his favorite Greek and Roman poets, many of whose works he translated, imitated, or alluded to in his poetry. Ovid (43 B.C.E.–C.E. 17) wrote of erotic love in the *Art of Love* and the *Metamorphoses*; Catullus (84–54 B.C.E.) and Anacreon (570–485 B.C.E.) wrote passionate, sexual lyric poems; Sappho (sixth-century B.C.E.) created an erotic masterpiece in her ode "Phainetai moi"; Longinus (d. C.E. 273) in his treatise *On the Sublime* praised Sappho's Ode; Virgil's Fourth Eclogue (*Formosum pastor Corydon*) is a homoerotic lyric; Lucretius (100–55 B.C.E.) in *De rerum natura (On the Nature of Things)* argued for a materialistic and Epicurean world view; Juvenal (60–140 C.E.) and Martial (40–104 C.E.) were the most vitriolic satirists of ancient Rome.
2. "See Longinus, [*On the Sublime*] Section 10." Byron's note continues with a quotation in Greek, which translates as follows: "The effect desired is that not one passion only should be seen in her, but a concourse of passions" (trans. W. Rhys Roberts, 1899, pp. 70–71).
3. "Fact. There is, or was, such an edition, with all the obnoxious epigrams of Martial placed by themselves at the end."

45

For there we have them all "at one fell swoop,"[4]
Instead of being scatter'd through the pages;
They stand forth marshall'd in a handsome troop,   355
To meet the ingenuous youth of future ages,
Till some less rigid editor shall stoop
To call them back into their separate cages,
Instead of standing staring altogether,
Like garden gods[5]—and not so decent either.   360

46

The Missal[6] too (it was the family Missal)
Was ornamented in a sort of way
Which ancient mass-books often are, and this all
Kinds of grotesques illumined; and how they,
Who saw those figures on the margin kiss all,   365
Could turn their optics to the text and pray
Is more than I know—but Don Juan's mother
Kept this herself, and gave her son another.

47

Sermons he read, and lectures he endured,
And homilies, and lives of all the saints;
To Jerome and to Chrysostom[7] inured,   370
He did not take such studies for restraints;
But how faith is acquired, and then ensured,
So well not one of the aforesaid paints
As Saint Augustine in his fine Confessions,   375
Which make the reader envy his transgressions.[8]

48

This, too, was a seal'd book to little Juan—
I can't but say that his mamma was right,
If such an education was the true one.
She scarcely trusted him from out her sight;   380
Her maids were old, and if she took a new one,
You might be sure she was a perfect fright;
She did this during even her husband's life—
I recommend as much to every wife.

---

4. *Macbeth* 4.3.220.
5. The statues of gods (usually nude or semi-nude figures) assembled in a classical English garden.
6. Roman Catholic liturgical text.
7. St. Jerome (348–420) and St. John Chrysostom (345–407) were two important fathers of the early Christian church.
8. "See his *Confessions*, lib. I. cap. ix [lib. ii. cap. ii., *et passim*]. By the representation which Saint Augustine gives of himself in his youth, it is easy to see that he was what we should call a rake. He avoided the school as the plague; he loved nothing but gaming and public shows; he robbed his father of everything he could find; he invented a thousand lies to escape the rod, which they were obliged to make use of to punish his irregularities." St. Augustine (345–430), one of the greatest figures in church history. His *Confessions* (ca. 397) describe in detail his dissolute life prior to his conversion.

49

Young Juan wax'd in goodliness and grace;   385
  At six a charming child, and at eleven
With all the promise of as fine a face
  As e'er to man's maturer growth was given:
He studied steadily, and grew apace,
  And seem'd, at least, in the right road to heaven,   390
For half his days were pass'd at church, the other
Between his tutors, confessor, and mother.

50

At six, I said, he was a charming child,
  At twelve he was a fine, but quiet boy;
Although in infancy a little wild,   395
  They tamed him down amongst them: to destroy
His natural spirit not in vain they toil'd,
  At least it seem'd so; and his mother's joy
Was to declare how sage, and still, and steady,
Her young philosopher was grown already.   400

51

I had my doubts, perhaps I have them still,
  But what I say is neither here nor there:
I knew his father well, and have some skill
  In character—but it would not be fair
From sire to son to augur good or ill: 405
  He and his wife were an ill-sorted pair—
But scandal's my aversion—I protest
Against all evil speaking, even in jest.

52

For my part I say nothing—nothing—but
  This I will say—my reasons are my own—   410
That if I had an only son to put
  To school (as God be praised that I have none),
'Tis not with Donna Inez I would shut
  Him up to learn his catechism[9] alone,
No—no—I'd send him out betimes to college,   415
For there it was I pick'd up my own knowledge.

53

For there one learns—'tis not for me to boast,
  Though I acquired—but I pass over *that*,
As well as all the Greek I since have lost:
  I say that there's the place—but *"Verbum sat,"*[1]   420

9. A summary of the principles of the Christian religion as taught by a particular church.
1. Latin proverb, *Verbum sat sapienti*: A word is enough to the wise.

I think I pick'd up too, as well as most,
    Knowledge of matters—but no matter *what*—
I never married—but, I think, I know
That sons should not be educated so.

54

Young Juan now was sixteen years of age,   425
    Tall, handsome, slender, but well knit: he seem'd
Active, though not so sprightly, as a page;
    And every body but his mother deem'd
Him almost man; but she flew in a rage
    And bit her lips (for else she might have scream'd)   430
If any said so, for to be precocious
Was in her eyes a thing the most atrocious.

55

Amongst her numerous acquaintance, all
    Selected for discretion and devotion,
There was the Donna Julia, whom to call   435
    Pretty were but to give a feeble notion
Of many charms in her as natural
    As sweetness to the flower, or salt to ocean,
Her zone to Venus,[2] or his bow to Cupid,
(But this last simile is trite and stupid.)   440

56

The darkness of her Oriental eye
    Accorded with her Moorish[3] origin;
(Her blood was not all Spanish, by the by;
    In Spain, you know, this is a sort of sin.)
When proud Granada fell, and, forced to fly,   445
    Boabdil wept, of Donna Julia's kin
Some went to Africa, some stay'd in Spain,
Her great great grandmamma chose to remain.

57

She married (I forget the pedigree)
    With an Hidalgo, who transmitted down   450
His blood less noble than such blood should be;
    At such alliances his sires would frown,
In that point so precise in each degree
    That they bred *in and in*, as might be shown,

2. The zone, or belt, of Venus, Roman goddess of love, was believed to give its wearer the power of instilling passion in others. Cupid, Roman god of love, is usually depicted with his bow, from which he shoots the arrows that instill passionate love in those they hit.
3. The Moors, African Muslims, dominated much of Spain from the eighth to the fifteenth centuries and deeply influenced its culture; when they were driven from Granada in 1492, the warrior prince Boabdil (line 446) wept at leaving the city.

Marrying their cousins—nay, their aunts, and nieces,   455
Which always spoils the breed, if it increases.

58

This heathenish cross restored the breed again,
    Ruin'd its blood, but much improved its flesh;
For from a root the ugliest in Old Spain
    Sprung up a branch as beautiful as fresh;   460
The sons no more were short, the daughters plain:
    But there's a rumour which I fain would hush,
'Tis said that Donna Julia's grandmamma
Produced her Don more heirs at love than law.

59

However this might be, the race went on   465
    Improving still through every generation,
Until it centred in an only son,
    Who left an only daughter; my narration
May have suggested that this single one
    Could be but Julia (whom on this occasion   470
I shall have much to speak about), and she
Was married, charming, chaste, and twenty-three.

60

Her eye (I'm very fond of handsome eyes)
    Was large and dark, suppressing half its fire
Until she spoke, then through its soft disguise   475
    Flash'd an expression more of pride than ire,
And love than either; and there would arise
    A something in them which was not desire,
But would have been, perhaps, but for the soul
Which struggled through and chasten'd down the whole.   480

61

Her glossy hair was cluster'd o'er a brow
    Bright with intelligence, and fair, and smooth;
Her eyebrow's shape was like th' aërial bow,
    Her cheek all purple with the beam of youth,
Mounting, at times, to a transparent glow,   485
    As if her veins ran lightning; she, in sooth,
Possess'd an air and grace by no means common:
Her stature tall—I hate a dumpy woman.

62

Wedded she was some years, and to a man
    Of fifty, and such husbands are in plenty;   490
And yet, I think, instead of such a ONE
    'Twere better to have TWO of five-and-twenty,

Especially in countries near the sun:
  And now I think on't, "mi vien in mente,"[4]
Ladies even of the most uneasy virtue   495
Prefer a spouse whose age is short of thirty.

63

'Tis a sad thing, I cannot choose but say,
  And all the fault of that indecent sun,
Who cannot leave alone our helpless clay,
  But will keep baking, broiling, burning on,   500
That howsoever people fast and pray,
  The flesh is frail,[5] and so the soul undone:
What men call gallantry, and gods adultery,
Is much more common where the climate's sultry.

64

Happy the nations of the moral North!   505
  Where all is virtue, and the winter season
Sends sin, without a rag on, shivering forth
  ('Twas snow that brought St. Francis[6] back to reason);
Where juries cast up what a wife is worth,
  By laying whate'er sum, in mulct,[7] they please on   510
The lover, who must pay a handsome price,
Because it is a marketable vice.

65

Alfonso was the name of Julia's lord,
  A man well looking for his years, and who
Was neither much beloved nor yet abhorr'd: 515
  They lived together, as most people do,
Suffering each other's foibles by accord,
  And not exactly either *one* or *two;*
Yet he was jealous, though he did not show it,
For jealousy dislikes the world to know it.   520

66

Julia was—yet I never could see why—
  With Donna Inez quite a favourite friend;
Between their tastes there was small sympathy,
  For not a line had Julia ever penn'd:

---

4. It comes to mind (Italian).
5. Matthew 26.41.
6. Byron originally had written St. Anthony, with the note, "For the particulars of St. Anthony's recipe
for hot blood in cold weather, see Mr. Alban Butler's *Lives of the Saints*"; on the proof, he wrote, "I
am not sure that it was not St. Francis who had the 'wife of snow' in that case the line must run
'St. Francis back to reason.'" In fact, the reference applies to St. Francis, but the line was not cor-
rected until the Penguin edition of Steffan and Pratt (1973).
7. A fine (i.e., for adultery).

Some people whisper (but, no doubt, they lie,   525
    For malice still imputes some private end)
That Inez had, ere Don Alfonso's marriage,
Forgot with him her very prudent carriage;

67

And that still keeping up the old connection,
    Which time had lately render'd much more chaste,   530
She took his lady also in affection,
    And certainly this course was much the best:
She flatter'd Julia with her sage protection,
    And complimented Don Alfonso's taste;
And if she could not (who can?) silence scandal,   535
At least she left it a more slender handle.

68

I can't tell whether Julia saw the affair
    With other people's eyes, or if her own
Discoveries made, but none could be aware
    Of this, at least no symptom e'er was shown;   540
Perhaps she did not know, or did not care,
    Indifferent from the first, or callous grown:
I'm really puzzled what to think or say,
She kept her counsel in so close a way.

69

Juan she saw, and, as a pretty child,   545
    Caress'd him often—such a thing might be
Quite innocently done, and harmless styled,
    When she had twenty years, and thirteen he;
But I am not so sure I should have smiled
    When he was sixteen, Julia twenty-three;   550
These few short years make wondrous alterations,
Particularly amongst sun-burnt nations.

70

Whate'er the cause might be, they had become
    Changed; for the dame grew distant, the youth shy,
Their looks cast down, their greetings almost dumb,   555
    And much embarrassment in either eye;
There surely will be little doubt with some
    That Donna Julia knew the reason why,
But as for Juan, he had no more notion
Than he who never saw the sea of ocean.   560

71

Yet Julia's very coldness still was kind,
    And tremulously gentle her small hand

Withdrew itself from his, but left behind
A little pressure, thrilling, and so bland
And slight, so very slight, that to the mind   565
    'Twas but a doubt; but ne'er magician's wand
Wrought change with all Armida's[8] fairy art
Like what this light touch left on Juan's heart.

72

And if she met him, though she smiled no more,
    She look'd a sadness sweeter than her smile,   570
As if her heart had deeper thoughts in store
    She must not own, but cherish'd more the while
For that compression in its burning core;
    Even innocence itself has many a wile,
And will not dare to trust itself with truth,   575
And love is taught hypocrisy from youth.

73

But passion most dissembles, yet betrays
    Even by its darkness; as the blackest sky
Foretells the heaviest tempest, it displays
    Its workings through the vainly guarded eye,   580
And in whatever aspect it arrays
    Itself, 'tis still the same hypocrisy;
Coldness or anger, even disdain or hate,
Are masks it often wears, and still too late.

74

Then there were sighs, the deeper for suppression,   585
    And stolen glances, sweeter for the theft,
And burning blushes, though for no transgression,
    Tremblings when met, and restlessness when left;
All these are little preludes to possession,
    Of which young Passion cannot be bereft,   590
And merely tend to show how greatly Love is
Embarrass'd at first starting with a novice.

75

Poor Julia's heart was in an awkward state;
    She felt it going, and resolved to make
The noblest efforts for herself and mate,   595
    For honour's, pride's, religion's, virtue's sake;
Her resolutions were most truly great,
    And almost might have made a Tarquin[9] quake:
She pray'd the Virgin Mary for her grace,
As being the best judge of a lady's case.   600

---

8. Sorceress and temptress in Tasso's epic *Jerusalem Delivered* (1575).
9. Legendary early king of Rome, famous for rigor and cruelty.

76

She vow'd she never would see Juan more,
    And next day paid a visit to his mother,
And look'd extremely at the opening door,
    Which, by the Virgin's grace, let in another;
Grateful she was, and yet a little sore—   605
    Again it opens, it can be no other,
'Tis surely Juan now—No! I'm afraid
That night the Virgin was no further pray'd.

77

She now determined that a virtuous woman
    Should rather face and overcome temptation,   610
That flight was base and dastardly, and no man
    Should ever give her heart the least sensation;
That is to say, a thought beyond the common
    Preference, that we must feel upon occasion,
For people who are pleasanter than others,   615
But then they only seem so many brothers.

78

And even if by chance—and who can tell?
    The devil's so very sly—she should discover
That all within was not so very well,
    And, if still free, that such or such a lover   620
Might please perhaps, a virtuous wife can quell
    Such thoughts, and be the better when they're over;
And if the man should ask, 'tis but denial:
I recommend young ladies to make trial.

79

And then there are such things as love divine,   625
    Bright and immaculate, unmix'd and pure,
Such as the angels think so very fine,
    And matrons, who would be no less secure,
Platonic,[1] perfect, "just such love as mine:"
    Thus Julia said—and thought so, to be sure;   630
And so I'd have her think, were I the man
On whom her reveries celestial ran.

80

Such love is innocent, and may exist
    Between young persons without any danger.
A hand may first, and then a lip be kist;   635
    For my part, to such doings I'm a stranger,

---

1. Referring to Plato's concept of ideal love and implying spiritual as opposed to sexual love (though Plato's idea is more complex and does not exclude sexual desire).

But *hear* these freedoms form the utmost list
  Of all o'er which such love may be a ranger:
If people go beyond, 'tis quite a crime,
  But not my fault—I tell them all in time.   640

81

Love, then, but love within its proper limits,
  Was Julia's innocent determination
In young Don Juan's favour, and to him its
  Exertion might be useful on occasion;
And, lighted at too pure a shrine to dim its   645
  Ethereal lustre, with what sweet persuasion
He might be taught, by love and her together—
I really don't know what, nor Julia either.

82

Fraught with this fine intention, and well fenced
  In mail of proof[2]—her purity of soul,   650
She, for the future of her strength convinced,
  And that her honour was a rock, or mole,
Exceeding sagely from that hour dispensed
  With any kind of troublesome control;
But whether Julia to the task was equal   655
Is that which must be mention'd in the sequel.

83

Her plan she deem'd both innocent and feasible,
  And, surely, with a stripling of sixteen
Not scandal's fangs could fix on much that's seizable,
  Or if they did so, satisfied to mean   660
Nothing but what was good, her breast was peaceable—
  A quiet conscience makes one so serene!
Christians have burnt each other, quite persuaded
That all the Apostles[3] would have done as they did.

84

And if in the mean time her husband died,   665
  But Heaven forbid that such a thought should cross
Her brain, though in a dream! (and then she sigh'd)
  Never could she survive that common loss;
But just suppose that moment should betide,
  I only say suppose it—*inter nos.*[4]   670
(This should be *entre nous*, for Julia thought
In French, but then the rhyme would go for nought.)

2. Strong armor—a conventional metaphor for the soul in Catholic tracts.
3. In the New Testament, the twelve disciples sent by Christ to preach the gospel.
4. Just between us (Latin; given in French in line 671).

85

I only say suppose this supposition:
    Juan being then grown up to man's estate
Would fully suit a widow of condition,   675
    Even seven years hence it would not be too late;
And in the interim (to pursue this vision)
    The mischief, after all, could not be great,
For he would learn the rudiments of love,
    I mean the seraph[5] way of those above.   680

86

So much for Julia. Now we'll turn to Juan,
    Poor little fellow! he had no idea
Of his own case, and never hit the true one;
    In feelings quick as Ovid's Miss Medea,[6]
He puzzled over what he found a new one,   685
    But not as yet imagined it could be a
Thing quite in course, and not at all alarming,
Which, with a little patience, might grow charming.

87

Silent and pensive, idle, restless, slow,
    His home deserted for the lonely wood,   690
Tormented with a wound he could not know,
    His, like all deep grief, plunged in solitude:
I'm fond myself of solitude or so,
    But then, I beg it may be understood,
By solitude I mean a sultan's, not   695
A hermit's, with a haram for a grot.

88

"Oh Love! in such a wilderness as this,
    Where transport and security entwine,
Here is the empire of thy perfect bliss,
    And here thou art a god indeed divine."   700
The bard[7] I quote from does not sing amiss,
    With the exception of the second line,
For that same twining "transport and security"
Are twisted to a phrase of some obscurity.

89

The poet meant, no doubt, and thus appeals   705
    To the good sense and senses of mankind,

---

5. The highest order of angels.
6. Medea, described by Ovid in *Metamorphoses* 7.10–12 and *Art of Love* 1.11, is one of the most violently passionate figures in classical mythology.
7. "[Thomas] Campbell's *Gertrude of Wyoming*—(I think)—the opening of Canto Second—but quote from memory." The quotation is the opening of Canto III.

The very thing which every body feels,
　　As all have found on trial, or may find,
That no one likes to be disturb'd at meals
　　Or love.—I won't say more about "entwined"   710
Or "transport," as we knew all that before,
But beg "Security" will bolt the door.

90

Young Juan wander'd by the glassy brooks
　　Thinking unutterable things; he threw
Himself at length within the leafy nooks   715
　　Where the wild branch of the cork forest grew;
There poets find materials for their books,
　　And every now and then we read them through,
So that their plan and prosody are eligible,
Unless, like Wordsworth, they prove unintelligible.   720

91

He, Juan, (and not Wordsworth) so pursued
　　His self-communion with his own high soul,
Until his mighty heart, in its great mood,
　　Had mitigated part, though not the whole
Of its disease; he did the best he could   725
　　With things not very subject to control,
And turn'd, without perceiving his condition,
Like Coleridge, into a metaphysician.

92

He thought about himself, and the whole earth,
　　Of man the wonderful, and of the stars,   730
And how the deuce they ever could have birth;
　　And then he thought of earthquakes, and of wars,
How many miles the moon might have in girth,
　　Of air-balloons, and of the many bars
To perfect knowledge of the boundless skies;—   735
And then he thought of Donna Julia's eyes.

93

In thoughts like these true wisdom may discern
　　Longings sublime, and aspirations high,
Which some are born with, but the most part learn
　　To plague themselves withal, they know not why: 740
'Twas strange that one so young should thus concern
　　His brain about the action of the sky;
Do *you* think 'twas philosophy that this did,
I can't help thinking puberty assisted.

94

He pored upon the leaves, and on the flowers,   745
   And heard a voice in all the winds; and then
He thought of wood-nymphs and immortal bowers,
   And how the goddesses came down to men:
He miss'd the pathway, he forgot the hours,
   And when he look'd upon his watch again,   750
He found how much old Time had been a winner—
He also found that he had lost his dinner.

95

Sometimes he turn'd to gaze upon his book,
   Boscan, or Garcilasso;[8]—by the wind
Even as the page is rustled while we look,   755
   So by the poesy of his own mind
Over the mystic leaf his soul was shook,
   As if 'twere one whereon magicians bind
Their spells, and give them to the passing gale,
According to some good old woman's tale.   760

96

Thus would he while his lonely hours away
   Dissatisfied, nor knowing what he wanted;
Nor glowing reverie, nor poet's lay,
   Could yield his spirit that for which it panted.
A bosom whereon he his head might lay,   765
   And hear the heart beat with the love it granted,
With——several other things, which I forget,
Or which, at least, I need not mention yet.

97

Those lonely walks, and lengthening reveries,
   Could not escape the gentle Julia's eyes;   770
She saw that Juan was not at his ease;
   But that which chiefly may, and must surprise,
Is, that the Donna Inez did not tease
   Her only son with question or surmise;
Whether it was she did not see, or would not,   775
Or, like all very clever people, could not.

98

This may seem strange, but yet 'tis very common;
   For instance—gentlemen, whose ladies take
Leave to o'erstep the written rights of woman,
   And break the——Which commandment is't they break?[9]   780

---

8. Juan Bóscan Almogáver and Garcilaso de la Vega, sixteenth-century Spanish lyric poets; they wrote imitations of Petrarch's sonnets.
9. The seventh (sixth in the Roman Catholic numbering), "Thou shalt not commit adultery."

(I have forgot the number, and think no man
  Should rashly quote, for fear of a mistake.)
I say, when these same gentlemen are jealous,
They make some blunder, which their ladies tell us.

99

A real husband always is suspicious,   785
  But still no less suspects in the wrong place,
Jealous of some one who had no such wishes,
  Or pandering blindly to his own disgrace,
By harbouring some dear friend extremely vicious;
  The last indeed's infallibly the case: 790
And when the spouse and friend are gone off wholly,
He wonders at their vice, and not his folly.

100

Thus parents also are at times short-sighted;
  Though watchful as the lynx, they ne'er discover,
The while the wicked world beholds delighted,   795
  Young Hopeful's mistress, or Miss Fanny's lover,
Till some confounded escapade has blighted
  The plan of twenty years, and all is over;
And then the mother cries, the father swears,
And wonders why the devil he got heirs.   800

101

But Inez was so anxious, and so clear
  Of sight, that I must think, on this occasion,
She had some other motive much more near
  For leaving Juan to this new temptation;
But what that motive was, I sha'n't say here;   805
  Perhaps to finish Juan's education,
Perhaps to open Don Alfonso's eyes,
In case he thought his wife too great a prize.

102

It was upon a day, a summer's day;—
  Summer's indeed a very dangerous season,   810
And so is spring about the end of May;
  The sun, no doubt, is the prevailing reason;
But whatsoe'er the cause is, one may say,
  And stand convicted of more truth than treason,
That there are months which nature grows more merry in,—   815
March has its hares, and May must have its heroine.

103

'Twas on a summer's day—the sixth of June:—
  I like to be particular in dates,

Not only of the age, and year, but moon;
   They are a sort of post-house, where the Fates   820
Change horses, making history change its tune,
   Then spur away o'er empires and o'er states,
Leaving at last not much besides chronology,
   Excepting the post-obits[1] of theology.

104

'Twas on the sixth of June, about the hour   825
   Of half-past six—perhaps still nearer seven—
When Julia sate within as pretty a bower
   As e'er held houri[2] in that heathenish heaven
Described by Mahomet, and Anacreon Moore,[3]
   To whom the lyre and laurels have been given,   830
With all the trophies of triumphant song—
He won them well, and may he wear them long!

105

She sate, but not alone; I know not well
   How this same interview had taken place,
And even if I knew, I should not tell—   835
   People should hold their tongues in any case;
No matter how or why the thing befell,
   But there were she and Juan, face to face—
When two such faces are so, 'twould be wise,
But very difficult, to shut their eyes.   840

106

How beautiful she look'd! her conscious heart
   Glow'd in her cheek, and yet she felt no wrong.
Oh Love! how perfect is thy mystic art,
   Strengthening the weak, and trampling on the strong,
How self-deceitful is the sagest part   845
   Of mortals whom thy lure hath led along—
The precipice she stood on was immense,
So was her creed in her own innocence.

107

She thought of her own strength, and Juan's youth
   And of the folly of all prudish fears,   850
Victorious virtue, and domestic truth,
   And then of Don Alfonso's fifty years:
I wish these last had not occurr'd, in sooth,
   Because that number rarely much endears,

---

1. Literally, legal bonds owed after a death; here, facetious reference to the promise of an afterlife.
2. One of the beautiful virgins promised in paradise for all faithful Muslims.
3. Byron's friend, the Irish poet Thomas Moore (1779–1852), was frequently called this because he had written loose translations of the Odes of Anacreon; Moore's "Paradise and the Peri" in *Lalla Rookh* (1817) describes the "heathenish" (i.e., Muslim) heaven. Moore was one of the most popular poets of the day.

And through all climes, the snowy and the sunny,   855
Sounds ill in love, whate'er it may in money.

108

When people say, "I've told you *fifty* times,"
     They mean to scold, and very often do;
When poets say, "I've written *fifty* rhymes,"
     They make you dread that they'll recite them too;   860
In gangs of *fifty*, thieves commit their crimes;
     At *fifty* love for love is rare, 'tis true,
But then, no doubt, it equally as true is,
A good deal may be bought for *fifty* Louis.[4]

109

Julia had honour, virtue, truth, and love,   865
     For Don Alfonso; and she inly swore,
By all the vows below to powers above,
     She never would disgrace the ring she wore,
Nor leave a wish which wisdom might reprove;
     And while she ponder'd this, besides much more,   870
One hand on Juan's carelessly was thrown,
Quite by mistake—she thought it was her own;

110

Unconsciously she lean'd upon the other,
     Which play'd within the tangles of her hair;
And to contend with thoughts she could not smother   875
     She seem'd, by the distraction of her air.
'Twas surely very wrong in Juan's mother
     To leave together this imprudent pair,
She who for many years had watch'd her son so—
I'm very certain *mine* would not have done so.   880

111

The hand which still held Juan's, by degrees
     Gently, but palpably confirm'd its grasp,
As if it said, "Detain me, if you please;"
     Yet there's no doubt she only meant to clasp
His fingers with a pure Platonic squeeze;   885
     She would have shrunk as from a toad, or asp,
Had she imagined such a thing could rouse
A feeling dangerous to a prudent spouse.

112

I cannot know what Juan thought of this,
     But what he did, is much what you would do;   890

---

4. The *louis d'or*, French gold coin of the seventeenth and eighteenth centuries.

His young lip thank'd it with a grateful kiss,
  And then, abash'd at its own joy, withdrew
In deep despair, lest he had done amiss,
  Love is so very timid when 'tis new:
She blush'd, and frown'd not, but she strove to speak,   895
And held her tongue, her voice was grown so weak.

113

The sun set, and up rose the yellow moon:
  The devil's in the moon for mischief; they
Who call'd her CHASTE,[5] methinks, began too soon
  Their nomenclature; there is not a day,   900
The longest, not the twenty-first of June,
  Sees half the business in a wicked way
On which three single hours of moonshine smile—
And then she looks so modest all the while.

114

There is a dangerous silence in that hour,   905
  A stillness, which leaves room for the full soul
To open all itself, without the power
  Of calling wholly back its self-control;
The silver light which, hallowing tree and tower,
  Sheds beauty and deep softness o'er the whole,   910
Breathes also to the heart, and o'er it throws
A loving languor, which is not repose.

115

And Julia sate with Juan, half embraced
  And half retiring from the glowing arm,
Which trembled like the bosom where 'twas placed;   915
  Yet still she must have thought there was no harm,
Or else 'twere easy to withdraw her waist;
  But then the situation had its charm,
And then——God knows what next—I can't go on;
I'm almost sorry that I e'er begun.   920

116

Oh Plato! Plato! you have paved the way,
  With your confounded fantasies,[6] to more
Immoral conduct by the fancied sway
  Your system feigns o'er the controulless core
Of human hearts, than all the long array   925
  Of poets and romancers:—You're a bore,

---

5. From classical myth, the moon is traditionally a chaste goddess.
6. I.e., that love can be ideal and non-sexual; see line 629 and note.

A charlatan, a coxcomb[7]—and have been,
At best, no better than a go-between.[8]

117

And Julia's voice was lost, except in sighs,
  Until too late for useful conversation;   930
The tears were gushing from her gentle eyes,
  I wish, indeed, they had not had occasion,
But who, alas! can love, and then be wise?
  Not that remorse did not oppose temptation,
A little still she strove, and much repented,   935
And whispering "I will ne'er consent"—consented.

118

'Tis said that Xerxes[9] offer'd a reward
  To those who could invent him a new pleasure:
Methinks, the requisition's rather hard,
  And must have cost his majesty a treasure: 940
For my part, I'm a moderate-minded bard,
  Fond of a little love (which I call leisure);
I care not for new pleasures, as the old
Are quite enough for me, so they but hold.

119

Oh Pleasure! you are indeed a pleasant thing,   945
  Although one must be damn'd for you, no doubt:
I make a resolution every spring
  Of reformation, ere the year run out,
But somehow, this my vestal[1] vow takes wing,
  Yet still, I trust, it may be kept throughout: 950
I'm very sorry, very much ashamed,
And mean, next winter, to be quite reclaim'd.

120

Here my chaste Muse a liberty must take—
  Start not! still chaster reader—she'll be nice hence-
Forward, and there is no great cause to quake;   955
  This liberty is a poetic licence,
Which some irregularity may make
  In the design, and as I have a high sense
Of Aristotle and the Rules,[2] 'tis fit
To beg his pardon when I err a bit.   960

---

7. Pretentious fool.
8. Someone who helps bring lovers together.
9. Fifth-century B.C.E. Persian king and famous voluptuary.
1. In ancient Rome, priestesses of the goddess Vesta took a vow of virginity.
2. Aristotle's *Poetics*.

121

This licence is to hope the reader will
    Suppose from June the sixth (the fatal day,
Without whose epoch my poetic skill
    For want of facts would all be thrown away),
But keeping Julia and Don Juan still   965
    In sight, that several months have pass'd; we'll say
'Twas in November, but I'm not so sure
About the day—the era's more obscure.

122

We'll talk of that anon.—'Tis sweet to hear
    At midnight on the blue and moonlit deep   970
The song and oar of Adria's[3] gondolier,
    By distance mellow'd, o'er the waters sweep;
'Tis sweet to see the evening star appear;
    'Tis sweet to listen as the night-winds creep
From leaf to leaf; 'tis sweet to view on high   975
The rainbow, based on ocean, span the sky.

123

'Tis sweet to hear the watch-dog's honest bark
    Bay deep-mouth'd welcome as we draw near home;
'Tis sweet to know there is an eye will mark
    Our coming, and look brighter when we come;   980
'Tis sweet to be awaken'd by the lark,
    Or lull'd by falling waters; sweet the hum
Of bees, the voice of girls, the song of birds,
The lisp of children, and their earliest words.

124

Sweet is the vintage, when the showering grapes   985
    In Bacchanal[4] profusion reel to earth
Purple and gushing: sweet are our escapes
    From civic revelry to rural mirth;
Sweet to the miser are his glittering heaps,
    Sweet to the father is his first-born's birth,   990
Sweet is revenge—especially to women,
Pillage to soldiers, prize-money to seamen.

125

Sweet is a legacy, and passing sweet
    The unexpected death of some old lady
Or gentleman of seventy years complete,   995
    Who've made "us youth" wait too—too long already

---

3. Venice (on the Adriatic Sea).
4. Drunken revel or orgy, originally celebrations of Bacchus, Roman god of wine and fertility.

For an estate, or cash, or country-seat,
   Still breaking, but with stamina so steady,
That all the Israelites are fit to mob its
   Next owner for their double-damn'd post-obits.[5]   1000

126

'Tis sweet to win, no matter how, one's laurels,
   By blood or ink; 'tis sweet to put an end
To strife; 'tis sometimes sweet to have our quarrels,
   Particularly with a tiresome friend:
Sweet is old wine in bottles, ale in barrels;   1005
   Dear is the helpless creature we defend
Against the world; and dear the schoolboy spot
We ne'er forget, though there we are forgot.

127

But sweeter still than this, than these, than all,
   Is first and passionate love—it stands alone,   1010
Like Adam's recollection of his fall;
   The tree of knowledge has been pluck'd—all's known—
And life yields nothing further to recall
   Worthy of this ambrosial sin, so shown,
No doubt in fable, as the unforgiven   1015
Fire which Prometheus[6] filch'd for us from heaven.

128

Man's a strange animal, and makes strange use
   Of his own nature, and the various arts,
And likes particularly to produce
   Some new experiment to show his parts;   1020
This is the age of oddities let loose,
   Where different talents find their different marts;
You'd best begin with truth, and when you've lost your
Labour, there's a sure market for imposture.

129

What opposite discoveries we have seen!   1025
   (Signs of true genius, and of empty pockets.)
One makes new noses, one a guillotine,
   One breaks your bones, one sets them in their sockets;
But vaccination certainly has been
   A kind antithesis to Congreve's rockets,[7]   1030

---

5. I.e., the money-lenders ("Israelites") will collect from the heir.
6. In classical myth, the Titan Prometheus stole fire from the gods to share it with mankind and was
   consequently subjected to a torturous punishment.
7. Sir William Congreve (1772–1828) perfected a military rocket that was used in the Battle of
   Leipzig (1813).

With which the Doctor[8] paid off an old pox,
By borrowing a new one from an ox.

130

Bread has been made (indifferent) from potatoes;
  And galvanism[9] has set some corpses grinning,
But has not answer'd like the apparatus   1035
  Of the Humane Society's[1] beginning
By which men are unsuffocated gratis:
  What wondrous new machines have late been spinning!
I said the small-pox has gone out of late;
  Perhaps it may be follow'd by the great.[2]   1040

131

'Tis said the great came from America;[3]
  Perhaps it may set out on its return,—
The population there so spreads, they say
  'Tis grown high time to thin it in its turn,
With war, or plague, or famine, any way,   1045
  So that civilisation they may learn;
And which in ravage the more loathsome evil is—
  Their real lues,[4] or our pseudo-syphilis?

132

This is the patent-age of new inventions
  For killing bodies, and for saving souls,   1050
All propagated with the best intentions;
  Sir Humphry Davy's lantern,[5] by which coals
Are safely mined for in the mode he mentions,
  Tombuctoo travels, voyages to the Poles,
Are ways to benefit mankind, as true,   1055
Perhaps, as shooting them at Waterloo.

133

Man's a phenomenon, one knows not what,
  And wonderful beyond all wondrous measure;
'Tis pity though, in this sublime world, that
  Pleasure's a sin, and sometimes sin's a pleasure;   1060

---

8. Edward Jenner (1749–1823) developed a vaccine against smallpox which is produced from infected cattle.
9. Luigi Galvani (1737–1798) discovered that motion could be induced in dead bodies by passing an electric current through them.
1. The Royal Humane Society was founded in 1774 to resuscitate drowning persons.
2. The "great pox" was syphilis.
3. Popular legend was that syphilis was brought to Europe by Columbus's sailors, who had caught it from Native Americans. This stanza, along with the final couplets of stanzas 129 and 130, was thought too shocking by Byron's publisher and friends and was not printed in the early editions. Hobhouse's comment on the proof alongside stanza 131 reads: "Oh did I ever—no I never."
4. Lues venerea: syphilis (Latin).
5. Davy (1778–1829) invented the safety lamp for coal miners.

Few mortals know what end they would be at,
   But whether glory, power, or love, or treasure,
The path is through perplexing ways, and when
The goal is gain'd, we die, you know—and then——

134

What then?—I do not know, no more do you—   1065
   And so good night.—Return we to our story:
'Twas in November, when fine days are few,
   And the far mountains wax a little hoary,
And clap a white cape on their mantles blue;
   And the sea dashes round the promontory,   1070
And the loud breaker boils against the rock,
And sober suns must set at five o'clock.

135

'Twas, as the watchmen say, a cloudy night;
   No moon, no stars, the wind was low or loud
By gusts, and many a sparkling hearth was bright   1075
   With the piled wood, round which the family crowd;
There's something cheerful in that sort of light,
   Even as a summer sky's without a cloud:
I'm fond of fire, and crickets, and all that,
A lobster salad, and champagne, and chat.   1080

136

'Twas midnight—Donna Julia was in bed,
   Sleeping, most probably,—when at her door
Arose a clatter might awake the dead,
   If they had never been awoke before,
And that they have been so we all have read,   1085
   And are to be so, at the least, once more;[6]—
The door was fasten'd, but with voice and fist
First knocks were heard, then "Madam—Madam—hist!

137

"For God's sake, Madam—Madam—here's my master,
   With more than half the city at his back—   1090
Was ever heard of such a curst disaster!
   'Tis not my fault—I kept good watch—Alack!
Do pray undo the bolt a little faster—
   They're on the stair just now, and in a crack
Will all be here; perhaps he yet may fly—   1095
Surely the window's not so *very* high!"

---

6. A reference to the Second Coming of Christ, at which all the dead would awaken.

138

By this time Don Alfonso was arrived,
  With torches, friends, and servants in great number;
The major part of them had long been wived,
  And therefore paused not to disturb the slumber   1100
Of any wicked woman, who contrived
  By stealth her husband's temples to encumber:⁷
Examples of this kind are so contagious,
Were *one* not punish'd, *all* would be outrageous.

139

I can't tell how, or why, or what suspicion   1105
  Could enter into Don Alfonso's head;
But for a cavalier of his condition
  It surely was exceedingly ill-bred,
Without a word of previous admonition,
  To hold a levee⁸ round his lady's bed,   1110
And summon lackeys, arm'd with fire and sword,
To prove himself the thing he most abhorr'd.

140

Poor Donna Julia! starting as from sleep,
  (Mind—that I do not say—she had not slept)
Began at once to scream, and yawn, and weep;   1115
  Her maid Antonia, who was an adept,
Contrived to fling the bed-clothes in a heap,
  As if she had just now from out them crept:
I can't tell why she should take all this trouble
To prove her mistress had been sleeping double.   1120

141

But Julia mistress, and Antonia maid,
  Appear'd like two poor harmless women, who
Of goblins, but still more of men afraid,
  Had thought one man might be deterr'd by two,
And therefore side by side were gently laid,   1125
  Until the hours of absence should run through,
And truant husband should return, and say,
"My dear, I was the first who came away."

142

Now Julia found at length a voice, and cried,
  "In heaven's name, Don Alfonso, what d' ye mean?   1130

---

7. I.e., to cuckold him; a cuckold, a man whose wife committed adultery, was said to have been given horns by his unfaithful wife.
8. Morning reception of callers on a celebrated person, often held in the bedroom.

Has madness seized you? would that I had died
　　Ere such a monster's victim I had been!
What may this midnight violence betide,
　　A sudden fit of drunkenness or spleen?
Dare you suspect me, whom the thought would kill?   1135
Search, then, the room!"—Alfonso said, "I will."

143

He search'd, *they* search'd, and rummaged every where,
　　Closet and clothes' press, chest and window-seat,
And found much linen, lace, and several pair
　　Of stockings, slippers, brushes, combs, complete,   1140
With other articles of ladies fair,
　　To keep them beautiful, or leave them neat:
Arras they prick'd and curtains with their swords,
And wounded several shutters, and some boards.

144

Under the bed they search'd, and there they found—   1145
　　No matter what—it was not that they sought;
They open'd windows, gazing if the ground
　　Had signs or footmarks, but the earth said nought;
And then they stared each others' faces round:
　　'T is odd, not one of all these seekers thought,   1150
And seems to me almost a sort of blunder,
Of looking *in* the bed as well as under.

145

During this inquisition, Julia's tongue
　　Was not asleep—"Yes, search and search," she cried,
"Insult on insult heap, and wrong on wrong!   1155
　　It was for this that I became a bride!
For this in silence I have suffer'd long
　　A husband like Alfonso at my side;
But now I'll bear no more, nor here remain,
If there be law, or lawyers, in all Spain.   1160

146

"Yes, Don Alfonso! husband now no more,
　　If ever you indeed deserved the name,
Is't worthy of your years?—you have threescore—
　　Fifty, or sixty, it is all the same—
Is't wise or fitting, causeless to explore   1165
　　For facts against a virtuous woman's fame?
Ungrateful, perjured, barbarous Don Alfonso,
How dare you think your lady would go on so?

147

"Is it for this I have disdain'd to hold
    The common privileges of my sex?   1170
That I have chosen a confessor so old
    And deaf, that any other it would vex,
And never once he has had cause to scold,
    But found my very innocence perplex
So much, he always doubted I was married—   1175
    How sorry you will be when I've miscarried!

148

"Was it for this that no Cortejo⁹ e'er
    I yet have chosen from out the youth of Seville?
Is it for this I scarce went any where,
    Except to bull-fights, mass, play, rout, and revel?   1180
Is it for this, whate'er my suitors were,
    I favour'd none—nay, was almost uncivil?
Is it for this that General Count O'Reilly,¹
Who took Algiers, declares I used him vilely?

149

"Did not the Italian Musico Cazzani²   1185
    Sing at my heart six months at least in vain?
Did not his countryman, Count Corniani,
    Call me the only virtuous wife in Spain?
Were there not also Russians, English, many?
    The Count Strongstroganoff I put in pain,   1190
And Lord Mount Coffeehouse, the Irish peer,
Who kill'd himself for love (with wine) last year.

150

"Have I not had two bishops at my feet?
    The Duke of Ichar, and Don Fernan Nunez,
And is it thus a faithful wife you treat?   1195
    I wonder in what quarter now the moon is:³
I praise your vast forbearance not to beat
    Me also, since the time so opportune is—
Oh, valiant man! with sword drawn and cock'd trigger,
Now, tell me, don't you cut a pretty figure?   1200

---

9. "The Spanish 'Cortejo' is much the same as the Italian 'Cavalier Servente.' " I.e., an accepted, publicly acknowledged lover of a noble lady.
1. "Donna Julia here made a mistake. Count O'Reilly did not take Algiers—but Algiers very nearly took him: he and his army and fleet retreated with great loss, and not much credit, from before that city, in the year 1775." Alexander O'Reilly (1722–1794) was a Spanish general of Irish descent.
2. Cazzani and Corniani (line 1187) are made-up names that play on vulgar Italian slang: *cazzo* is the equivalent of "prick"; *cornuto* means horned, i.e., cuckolded.
3. A suggestion that Don Alfonso is behaving like a lunatic.

151

"Was it for this you took your sudden journey,
   Under pretence of business indispensable
With that sublime of rascals your attorney,
   Whom I see standing there, and looking sensible
Of having play'd the fool? though both I spurn, he   1205
   Deserves the worst, his conduct's less defensible,
Because, no doubt, 'twas for his dirty fee,
And not from any love to you nor me.

152

"If he comes here to take a deposition,
   By all means let the gentleman proceed;   1210
You've made the apartment in a fit condition:—
   There's pen and ink for you, sir, when you need—
Let every thing be noted with precision,
   I would not you for nothing should be fee'd—
But, as my maid's undrest, pray turn your spies out."   1215
"Oh!" sobb'd Antonia, "I could tear their eyes out."

153

"There is the closet, there the toilet, there
   The antechamber—search them under, over;
There is the sofa, there the great arm-chair,
   The chimney—which would really hold a lover.   1220
I wish to sleep, and beg you will take care
   And make no further noise, till you discover
The secret cavern of this lurking treasure—
And when 't is found, let me, too, have that pleasure.

154

"And now, Hidalgo! now that you have thrown   1225
   Doubt upon me, confusion over all,
Pray have the courtesy to make it known
   Who is the man you search for? how d'ye call
Him? what's his lineage? let him but be shown—
   I hope he's young and handsome—is he tall?   1230
Tell me—and be assured, that since you stain
My honour thus, it shall not be in vain.

155

"At least, perhaps, he has not sixty years,
   At that age he would be too old for slaughter,
Or for so young a husband's jealous fears—   1235
   (Antonia! let me have a glass of water.)
I am ashamed of having shed these tears,
   They are unworthy of my father's daughter;

My mother dream'd not in my natal hour
That I should fall into a monster's power.   1240

156

"Perhaps 'tis of Antonia you are jealous,
    You saw that she was sleeping by my side
When you broke in upon us with your fellows:
    Look where you please—we've nothing, sir, to hide;
Only another time, I trust, you'll tell us,   1245
    Or for the sake of decency abide
A moment at the door, that we may be
Drest to receive so much good company.

157

"And now, sir, I have done, and say no more;
    The little I have said may serve to show   1250
The guileless heart in silence may grieve o'er
    The wrongs to whose exposure it is slow:—
I leave you to your conscience as before,
    'Twill one day ask you *why* you used me so?
God grant you feel not then the bitterest grief!—   1255
Antonia! where's my pocket-handkerchief?"

158

She ceased, and turn'd upon her pillow; pale
    She lay, her dark eyes flashing through their tears,
Like skies that rain and lighten; as a veil,
    Waved and o'ershading her wan cheek, appears   1260
Her streaming hair; the black curls strive, but fail,
    To hide the glossy shoulder, which uprears
Its snow through all;—her soft lips lie apart,
And louder than her breathing beats her heart.

159

The Senhor Don Alfonso stood confused;   1265
    Antonia bustled round the ransack'd room,
And, turning up her nose, with looks abused
    Her master, and his myrmidons,[4] of whom
Not one, except the attorney, was amused;
    He, like Achates,[5] faithful to the tomb,   1270
So there were quarrels, cared not for the cause,
Knowing they must be settled by the laws.

160

With prying snub-nose, and small eyes, he stood,
    Following Antonia's motions here and there,

4. Achilles' troops in Homer's *Iliad*.
5. Aeneas's faithful companion in Virgil's *Aeneid*.

With much suspicion in his attitude;   1275
    For reputations he had little care;
So that a suit or action were made good,
    Small pity had he for the young and fair,
And ne'er believed in negatives, till these
Were proved by competent false witnesses.   1280

161

But Don Alfonso stood with downcast looks,
    And, truth to say, he made a foolish figure;
When, after searching in five hundred nooks,
    And treating a young wife with so much rigour,
He gain'd no point, except some self-rebukes,   1285
    Added to those his lady with such vigour
Had pour'd upon him for the last half-hour,
Quick, thick, and heavy—as a thunder-shower.

162

At first he tried to hammer an excuse,
    To which the sole reply was tears, and sobs,   1290
And indications of hysterics, whose
    Prologue is always certain throes, and throbs,
Gasps, and whatever else the owners choose:
    Alfonso saw his wife, and thought of Job's;[6]
He saw too, in perspective, her relations,   1295
And then he tried to muster all his patience.

163

He stood in act to speak, or rather stammer,
    But sage Antonia cut him short before
The anvil of his speech received the hammer,
    With "Pray, sir, leave the room, and say no more,   1300
Or madam dies."—Alfonso mutter'd, "D—n her,"
    But nothing else, the time of words was o'er;
He cast a rueful look or two, and did,
He knew not wherefore, that which he was bid.

164

With him retired his *"posse comitatus,"*[7]   1305
    The attorney last, who linger'd near the door,
Reluctantly, still tarrying there as late as
    Antonia let him—not a little sore
At this most strange and unexplain'd *"hiatus"*
    In Don Alfonso's facts, which just now wore   1310
An awkward look; as he revolved the case,
The door was fasten'd in his legal face.

6. Job's wife has been traditionally regarded as a scold (Job 2:9–10).
7. Power of the county (Latin), i.e., "posse": a group of citizens empowered to act as temporary enforcers of the law.

165

No sooner was it bolted, than—Oh shame!
    Oh sin! Oh sorrow! and Oh womankind!
How can you do such things and keep your fame,   1315
    Unless this world, and t'other too, be blind?
Nothing so dear as an unfilch'd good name!
    But to proceed—for there is more behind:
With much heartfelt reluctance be it said,
Young Juan slipp'd, half-smother'd, from the bed.   1320

166

He had been hid—I don't pretend to say
    How, nor can I indeed describe the where—
Young, slender, and pack'd easily, he lay,
    No doubt, in little compass, round or square;
But pity him I neither must nor may   1325
    His suffocation by that pretty pair;
'Twere better, sure, to die so, than be shut
With maudlin Clarence in his Malmsey butt.[8]

167

And, secondly, I pity not, because
    He had no business to commit a sin,   1330
Forbid by heavenly, fined by human laws,
    At least 'twas rather early to begin;
But at sixteen the conscience rarely gnaws
    So much as when we call our old debts in
At sixty years, and draw the accompts of evil,   1335
And find a deuced balance with the devil.

168

Of his position I can give no notion:
    'Tis written in the Hebrew Chronicle,[9]
How the physicians, leaving pill and potion,
    Prescribed, by way of blister,[1] a young belle,   1340
When old King David's blood grew dull in motion,
    And that the medicine answer'd very well;
Perhaps 'twas in a different way applied,
For David lived, but Juan nearly died.

169

What's to be done? Alfonso will be back   1345
    The moment he has sent his fools away.
Antonia's skill was put upon the rack,
    But no device could be brought into play—

8. In *Richard III* 1.4.258, the Duke of Clarence is drowned in a cask of malmsey wine.
9. Kings 1.1–3.
1. Cure or treatment.

And how to parry the renew'd attack?
   Besides, it wanted but few hours of day: 1350
Antonia puzzled; Julia did not speak,
   But press'd her bloodless lip to Juan's cheek.

170

He turn'd his lip to hers, and with his hand
   Call'd back the tangles of her wandering hair;
Even then their love they could not all command,   1355
   And half forgot their danger and despair:
Antonia's patience now was at a stand—
   "Come, come, 'tis no time now for fooling there,"
She whisper'd, in great wrath—"I must deposit
   This pretty gentleman within the closet: 1360

171

"Pray, keep your nonsense for some luckier night—
   Who can have put my master in this mood?
What will become on't—I'm in such a fright,
   The devil's in the urchin, and no good—
Is this a time for giggling? this a plight?   1365
   Why, don't you know that it may end in blood?
You'll lose your life, and I shall lose my place,
My mistress all, for that half-girlish face.

172

"Had it but been for a stout cavalier
   Of twenty-five or thirty—(Come, make haste)   1370
But for a child, what piece of work is here!
   I really, madam, wonder at your taste—
(Come, sir, get in)—my master must be near:
   There, for the present, at the least, he's fast,
And if we can but till the morning keep   1375
   Our counsel—(Juan, mind, you must not sleep.)"

173

Now, Don Alfonso entering, but alone,
   Closed the oration of the trusty maid:
She loiter'd, and he told her to be gone,
   An order somewhat sullenly obey'd;   1380
However, present remedy was none,
   And no great good seem'd answer'd if she staid:
Regarding both with slow and sidelong view,
She snuff'd the candle, curtsied, and withdrew.

174

Alfonso paused a minute—then begun   1385
   Some strange excuses for his late proceeding;

He would not justify what he had done,
   To say the best, it was extreme ill-breeding;
But there were ample reasons for it, none
   Of which he specified in this his pleading: 1390
His speech was a fine sample, on the whole,
   Of rhetoric, which the learn'd call "*rigmarole*."

175

Julia said nought; though all the while there rose
   A ready answer, which at once enables
A matron, who her husband's foible knows, 1395
   By a few timely words to turn the tables,
Which, if it does not silence, still must pose,—
   Even if it should comprise a pack of fables;
'Tis to retort with firmness, and when he
   Suspects with *one*, do you reproach with *three*. 1400

176

Julia, in fact, had tolerable grounds,—
   Alfonso's loves with Inez were well known;
But whether 'twas that one's own guilt confounds—
   But that can't be, as has been often shown,
A lady with apologies abounds;— 1405
   It might be that her silence sprang alone
From delicacy to Don Juan's ear,
To whom she knew his mother's fame was dear.

177

There might be one more motive, which makes two;
   Alfonso ne'er to Juan had alluded,— 1410
Mention'd his jealousy, but never who
   Had been the happy lover, he concluded,
Conceal'd amongst his premises; 'tis true,
   His mind the more o'er this its mystery brooded;
To speak of Inez now were, one may say, 1415
Like throwing Juan in Alfonso's way.

178

A hint, in tender cases, is enough;
   Silence is best, besides there is a *tact*
(That modern phrase appears to me sad stuff,
   But it will serve to keep my verse compact)— 1420
Which keeps, when push'd by questions rather rough,
   A lady always distant from the fact:
The charming creatures lie with such a grace,
There's nothing so becoming to the face.

179

They blush, and we believe them; at least I   1425
    Have always done so; 'tis of no great use,
In any case, attempting a reply,
    For then their eloquence grows quite profuse;
And when at length they're out of breath, they sigh,
    And cast their languid eyes down, and let loose   1430
A tear or two, and then we make it up;
    And then—and then—and then—sit down and sup.

180

Alfonso closed his speech, and begg'd her pardon,
    Which Julia half withheld, and then half granted,
And laid conditions, he thought, very hard on,   1435
    Denying several little things he wanted:
He stood like Adam lingering near his garden,
    With useless penitence perplex'd and haunted,
Beseeching she no further would refuse,
When, lo! he stumbled o'er a pair of shoes.   1440

181

A pair of shoes!—what then? not much, if they
    Are such as fit with ladies' feet, but these
(No one can tell how much I grieve to say)
    Were masculine; to see them, and to seize,
Was but a moment's act.—Ah! well-a-day!   1445
    My teeth begin to chatter, my veins freeze—
Alfonso first examined well their fashion,
And then flew out into another passion.

182

He left the room for his relinquish'd sword,
    And Julia instant to the closet flew.   1450
"Fly, Juan, fly! for heaven's sake—not a word—
    The door is open—you may yet slip through
The passage you so often have explored—
    Here is the garden-key—Fly—fly—Adieu!
Haste—haste! I hear Alfonso's hurrying feet—   1455
Day has not broke—there's no one in the street."

183

None can say that this was not good advice,
    The only mischief was, it came too late;
Of all experience 'tis the usual price,
    A sort of income-tax laid on by fate: 1460
Juan had reach'd the room-door in a trice,
    And might have done so by the garden-gate,

But met Alfonso in his dressing-gown,
Who threaten'd death—so Juan knock'd him down.

184

Dire was the scuffle, and out went the light;   1465
Antonia cried out "Rape!" and Julia "Fire!"
But not a servant stirr'd to aid the fight.
Alfonso, pommell'd to his heart's desire,
Swore lustily he'd be revenged this night;
And Juan, too, blasphemed an octave higher;   1470
His blood was up: though young, he was a Tartar,[2]
And not at all disposed to prove a martyr.

185

Alfonso's sword had dropp'd ere he could draw it,
And they continued battling hand to hand,
For Juan very luckily ne'er saw it;   1475
His temper not being under great command,
If at that moment he had chanced to claw it,
Alfonso's days had not been in the land
Much longer.—Think of husbands', lovers' lives!
And how ye may be doubly widows—wives!   1480

186

Alfonso grappled to detain the foe,
And Juan throttled him to get away,
And blood ('twas from the nose) began to flow;
At last, as they more faintly wrestling lay,
Juan contrived to give an awkward blow,   1485
And then his only garment quite gave way;
He fled, like Joseph, leaving it;[3] but there,
I doubt, all likeness ends between the pair.

187

Lights came at length, and men, and maids, who found
An awkward spectacle their eyes before;   1490
Antonia in hysterics, Julia swoon'd,
Alfonso leaning, breathless, by the door;
Some half-torn drapery scatter'd on the ground,
Some blood, and several footsteps, but no more:
Juan the gate gain'd, turn'd the key about,   1495
And liking not the inside, lock'd the out.

---

2. Tartars, Muslims from the area of Mongolia, were renowned for their ferocity as warriors.
3. Genesis 39.11–19; in fleeing the sexual advances of Potiphar's wife, Joseph leaves his garment in her hand.

188

Here ends this canto.—Need I sing, or say,
　　How Juan, naked, favour'd by the night,
Who favours what she should not, found his way,
　　And reach'd his home in an unseemly plight?　　　1500
The pleasant scandal which arose next day,
　　The nine days' wonder which was brought to light,
And how Alfonso sued for a divorce,
Were in the English newspapers, of course.

189

If you would like to see the whole proceedings,　　　1505
　　The depositions, and the cause at full,
The names of all the witnesses, the pleadings
　　Of counsel to nonsuit, or to annul,[4]
There's more than one edition, and the readings
　　Are various, but they none of them are dull;　　　1510
The best is that in short-hand ta'en by Gurney,[5]
Who to Madrid on purpose made a journey.

190

But Donna Inez, to divert the train
　　Of one of the most circulating scandals
That had for centuries been known in Spain,　　　1515
　　Since Roderic's Goths, or older Genseric's Vandals,[6]
First vow'd (and never had she vow'd in vain)
　　To Virgin Mary several pounds of candles;
And then, by the advice of some old ladies,
She sent her son to be embark'd at Cadiz.　　　1520

191

She had resolved that he should travel through
　　All European climes, by land or sea,
To mend his former morals, or get new,
　　Especially in France and Italy
(At least this is the thing most people do).　　　1525
　　Julia was sent into a nunnery
And there, perhaps, her feelings may be better
Shown in the following copy of her letter:—

192

"They tell me 'tis decided; you depart:
　　'Tis wise—'tis well, but not the less a pain;　　　1530

---

4. *nonsuit . . . annul*: in law, ways to end a case.
5. William Gurney was a famous shorthand reporter frequently employed by the English press.
6. The Vandals were a German tribe that ravaged Spain in the fifth century, becoming since then a byword for wanton destructiveness.

I have no further claim on your young heart,
　　Mine is the victim, and would be again;
To love too much has been the only art
　　I used;—I write in haste, and if a stain
Be on this sheet, 'tis not what it appears; 　　　　1535
　　My eyeballs burn and throb, but have no tears.

193

"I loved, I love you, for that love have lost
　　State, station, heaven, mankind's, my own esteem,
And yet can not regret what it hath cost,
　　So dear is still the memory of that dream; 　　　　1540
Yet, if I name my guilt, 'tis not to boast,
　　None can deem harshlier of me than I deem:
I trace this scrawl because I cannot rest—
I've nothing to reproach, nor to request.

194

"Man's love is of his life a thing apart, 　　　　1545
　　'Tis woman's whole existence; man may range
The court, camp, church, the vessel, and the mart,
　　Sword, gown, gain, glory, offer in exchange
Pride, fame, ambition, to fill up his heart,
　　And few there are whom these can not estrange; 　　　　1550
Men have all these resources, we but one,
To love again, and be again undone.

195[7]

"My breast has been all weakness, is so yet;
　　I struggle, but cannot collect my mind;
My blood still rushes where my spirit's set, 　　　　1555
　　As roll the waves before the settled wind;
My brain is feminine, nor can forget—
　　To all, except your image, madly blind;
As turns the needle trembling to the pole
It ne'er can reach, so turns to you, my soul. 　　　　1560

196

"You will proceed in beauty, and in pride,
　　Beloved and loving many; all is o'er
For me on earth, except some years to hide
　　My shame and sorrow deep in my heart's core;
These I could bear, but cannot cast aside 　　　　1565
　　The passion which still rages as before,—
And so farewell—forgive me, love me—No,
That word is idle now—but let it go.

7. Stanzas 195–196 were transposed in all editions prior to *CPW*.

197

"I have no more to say, but linger still,
    And dare not set my seal upon this sheet,   1570
And yet I may as well the task fulfil,
    My misery can scarce be more complete:
I had not lived till now, could sorrow kill;
    Death flies the wretch who fain the blow would meet,
And I must even survive this last adieu,   1575
And bear with life, to love and pray for you!"

198

This note was written upon gilt-edged paper
    With a neat crow-quill, rather hard, but new;
Her small white fingers scarce could reach the taper,[8]
    But trembled as magnetic needles do,   1580
And yet she did not let one tear escape her;
    The seal a sun-flower; *"Elle vous suit partout,"*[9]
The motto, cut upon a white cornelian;
The wax was superfine, its hue vermilion.

199

This was Don Juan's earliest scrape; but whether   1585
    I shall proceed with his adventures is
Dependent on the public altogether;
    We'll see, however, what they say to this,
Their favour in an author's cap's a feather,
    And no great mischief's done by their caprice;   1590
And if their approbation we experience,
Perhaps they'll have some more about a year hence.

200

My poem's epic, and is meant to be
    Divided in twelve books; each book containing,
With love, and war, a heavy gale at sea,   1595
    A list of ships, and captains, and kings reigning,
New characters; the episodes are three:
    A panoramic view of hell's in training,
After the style of Virgil and of Homer,
So that my name of Epic's no misnomer.   1600

201

All these things will be specified in time,
    With strict regard to Aristotle's rules,

---

8. Candle, for hot wax with which to seal the letter.
9. She follows you everywhere (French); Byron had a seal with this motto. The cornelian in the next line recalls Byron's 1806 poem "The Cornelian" (p. 4).

The *Vade Mecum*[1] of the true sublime,
  Which makes so many poets, and some fools:
Prose poets like blank-verse, I'm fond of rhyme,   1605
  Good workmen never quarrel with their tools;
I've got new mythological machinery,
  And very handsome supernatural scenery.

202

There's only one slight difference between
  Me and my epic brethren gone before,
And here the advantage is my own, I ween;   1610
  (Not that I have not several merits more,
But this will more peculiarly be seen;)
  They so embellish, that 'tis quite a bore
Their labyrinth of fables to thread through,   1615
  Whereas this story's actually true.

203

If any person doubt it, I appeal
  To history, tradition, and to facts,
To newspapers, whose truth all know and feel,
  To plays in five, and operas in three acts;   1620
All these confirm my statement a good deal,
  But that which more completely faith exacts
Is, that myself, and several now in Seville,
Saw Juan's last elopement with the devil.

204

If ever I should condescend to prose,   1625
  I'll write poetical commandments, which
Shall supersede beyond all doubt all those
  That went before; in these I shall enrich
My text with many things that no one knows,
  And carry precept to the highest pitch: 1630
I'll call the work "Longinus[2] o'er a Bottle,
Or, Every Poet his *own* Aristotle."

205

Thou shalt believe in Milton, Dryden, Pope;
  Thou shalt not set up Wordsworth, Coleridge, Southey;
Because the first is crazed beyond all hope,   1635
  The second drunk, the third so quaint and mouthy:

---

1. Literally, "Go with me" (Latin): an indispensable book which one carries everywhere. Byron is ridiculing the obsession of neoclassical critics and poets with observing Aristotle's rules as set forth in the *Poetics*.
2. Dionysius Longinus, third-century Greek rhetorician whose treatise *On the Sublime* influenced Romantic poetics.

With Crabbe[3] it may be difficult to cope,
  And Campbell's Hippocrene is somewhat drouthy:
Thou shalt not steal from Samuel Rogers, nor
  Commit—flirtation with the muse of Moore.   1640

206

Thou shalt not covet Mr. Sotheby's[4] Muse,
  His Pegasus,[5] nor any thing that's his;
Thou shalt not bear false witness like "the Blues"[6]—
  (There's one, at least, is very fond of this);
Thou shalt not write, in short, but what I choose: 1645
  This is true criticism, and you may kiss—
Exactly as you please, or not,—the rod;
  But if you don't, I'll lay it on, by G—d!

207

If any person should presume to assert
  This story is not moral, first, I pray,   1650
That they will not cry out before they're hurt,
  Then that they'll read it o'er again, and say,
(But, doubtless, nobody will be so pert)
  That this is not a moral tale, though gay;
Besides, in Canto Twelfth, I mean to show   1655
  The very place where wicked people go.

208

If, after all, there should be some so blind
  To their own good this warning to despise,
Led by some tortuosity of mind,
  Not to believe my verse and their own eyes,   1660
And cry that they "the moral cannot find,"
  I tell him, if a clergyman, he lies;
Should captains the remark, or critics, make,
  They also lie too—under a mistake.

209

The public approbation I expect,   1665
  And beg they'll take my word about the moral,

---

3. Byron generally rated the contemporary poets George Crabbe, Thomas Campbell, Samuel Rogers, and Thomas Moore higher than Wordsworth and the "Lakers" (e.g., see Dedication, line 55, and I.829); here, however, he devalues even these poets when judged against the standard of Milton, Dryden, and Pope. "Hippocrene" (line 1638) is a spring on Mt. Helicon sacred to the Muses, while "drouthy" means dry.
4. William Sotheby (1757–1833), a minor poet Byron recurrently mocked (see *Beppo*, stanzas 72–76 (pp. 367–68), and his letter of May 30, 1817 [p. 930]); earlier in his life, Byron admired Sotheby's poetry (see *English Bards*, line 818).
5. In classical myth, winged horse associated with the Muses and poetic inspiration.
6. Bluestockings: one of several attacks in *Don Juan* on this coterie of intellectual women, of whom his estranged wife was one.

Which I with their amusement will connect
   (So children cutting teeth receive a coral);
Meantime, they'll doubtless please to recollect
   My epical pretensions to the laurel: 1670
For fear some prudish readers should grow skittish,
I've bribed my grandmother's review—the British.[7]

210

I sent it in a letter to the Editor,
   Who thank'd me duly by return of post—
I'm for a handsome article his creditor;   1675
   Yet, if my gentle Muse he please to roast,
And break a promise after having made it her,
   Denying the receipt of what it cost,
And smear his page with gall instead of honey,
All I can say is—that he had the money.   1680

211

I think that with this holy new alliance
   I may ensure the public, and defy
All other magazines of art or science,
   Daily, or monthly, or three monthly; I
Have not essay'd to multiply their clients,   1685
   Because they tell me 'twere in vain to try,
And that the Edinburgh Review and Quarterly
Treat a dissenting author very martyrly.

212

"Non ego hoc ferrem calida juventâ
   Consule Planco,"[8] Horace said, and so   1690
Say I; by which quotation there is meant a
   Hint that some six or seven good years ago
(Long ere I dreamt of dating from the Brenta)[9]
   I was most ready to return a blow,
And would not brook at all this sort of thing   1695
In my hot youth—when George the Third was King.

213

But now at thirty years my hair is grey—
   (I wonder what it will be like at forty?
I thought of a peruke[1] the other day—)
   My heart is not much greener; and, in short, I   1700

7. The *British Review* mounted a strong attack upon the immorality of *Don Juan*. Missing the humor
   of these lines, the editor printed a denial, which Byron, delighted, answered in a "Letter to the Edi-
   tor of *My Grandmother's Review*," printed in the first number of the *Liberal* (1822).
8. I would not have stood for this when I was a hot youth, during the consulship of Planco (Horace,
   Odes 3.14.27–28, slightly misquoted).
9. The river Brenta, near where Byron stayed before living in Venice, where he began *Don Juan*.
1. Wig.

Have squander'd my whole summer while 'twas May,
And feel no more the spirit to retort; I
Have spent my life, both interest and principal,
And deem not, what I deem'd, my soul invincible.

214

No more—no more—Oh! never more on me   1705
The freshness of the heart can fall like dew,
Which out of all the lovely things we see
    Extracts emotions beautiful and new,
Hived in our bosoms like the bag o' the bee:
    Think'st thou the honey with those objects grew?   1710
Alas! 'twas not in them, but in thy power
To double even the sweetness of a flower.

215

No more—no more—Oh! never more, my heart,
    Canst thou be my sole world, my universe!
Once all in all, but now a thing apart,   1715
    Thou canst not be my blessing or my curse:
The illusion's gone for ever, and thou art
    Insensible, I trust, but none the worse,
And in thy stead I've got a deal of judgment,
Though heaven knows how it ever found a lodgement.   1720

216

My days of love are over; me no more[2]
    The charms of maid, wife, and still less of widow,
Can make the fool of which they made before,—
    In short, I must not lead the life I did do;
The credulous hope of mutual minds is o'er,   1725
    The copious use of claret is forbid too,
So for a good old-gentlemanly vice,
I think I must take up with avarice.

217

Ambition was my idol, which was broken
    Before the shrines of Sorrow, and of Pleasure;   1730
And the two last have left me many a token
    O'er which reflection may be made at leisure:
Now, like Friar Bacon's brazen head, I've spoken,
    "Time is, Time was, Time's past:"[3]—a chymic treasure
Is glittering youth, which I have spent betimes—   1735
My heart in passion, and my head on rhymes.

2. "Me nec femina, nec puer / Jam, nec spes animi credula mutui, / Nec certare juvat mero; / Nec vincire novis tempora floribus." Horace, *Odes* 4.1.29–32.
3. From *Friar Bacon and Friar Bungay*, by the Elizabethan dramatist Robert Greene. "Chymic" means alchemistic, or magic.

218

What is the end of Fame? 'tis but to fill
   A certain portion of uncertain paper:
Some liken it to climbing up a hill,
   Whose summit, like all hills, is lost in vapour;   1740
For this men write, speak, preach, and heroes kill,
   And bards burn what they call their "midnight taper,"
To have, when the original is dust,
A name, a wretched picture, and worse bust.[4]

219

What are the hopes of man? Old Egypt's King   1745
   Cheops erected the first pyramid
And largest, thinking it was just the thing
   To keep his memory whole, and mummy hid;
But somebody or other rummaging,
   Burglariously broke his coffin's lid: 1750
Let not a monument give you or me hopes,
Since not a pinch of dust remains of Cheops.

220

But I being fond of true philosophy,
   Say very often to myself, "Alas!
All things that have been born were born to die,   1755
   And flesh (which Death mows down to hay) is grass;[5]
You've pass'd your youth not so unpleasantly,
   And if you had it o'er again—'twould pass—
So thank your stars that matters are no worse,
And read your Bible, sir, and mind your purse."   1760

221

But for the present, gentle reader! and
   Still gentler purchaser! the bard—that's I—
Must, with permission, shake you by the hand,
   And so your humble servant, and good-b'ye!
We meet again, if we should understand   1765
   Each other; and if not, I shall not try
Your patience further than by this short sample—
'Twere well if others follow'd my example.

222

"Go, little book, from this my solitude!
   I cast thee on the waters—go thy ways!   1770
And if, as I believe, thy vein be good,
   The world will find thee after many days."[6]

---

4. Byron was disappointed with the bust made of him by Bertel Thorwaldsen in 1817.
5. Isaiah 40.6.
6. These lines quote the final stanza of Southey's "L'Envoy" to *The Lay of the Laureate* (1816).

When Southey's read, and Wordsworth understood,
   I can't help putting in my claim to praise—
The four first rhymes are Southey's every line: 1775
   For God's sake, reader! take them not for mine.

FROM CANTO THE SECOND

*   *   *

11

Juan embark'd—the ship got under way,
   The wind was fair, the water passing rough:
A devil of a sea rolls in that bay,[1]
   As I, who've cross'd it oft, know well enough;
And, standing upon deck, the dashing spray   85
   Flies in one's face, and makes it weather-tough:
And there he stood to take, and take again,
His first—perhaps his last—farewell of Spain.

12

I can't but say it is an awkward sight
   To see one's native land receding through   90
The growing waters; it unmans one quite,
   Especially when life is rather new:
I recollect Great Britain's coast looks white,
   But almost every other country's blue,
When gazing on them, mystified by distance,   95
We enter on our nautical existence.

13

So Juan stood, bewilder'd, on the deck:
   The wind sung, cordage[2] strain'd, and sailors swore,
And the ship creak'd, the town became a speck,
   From which away so fair and fast they bore.   100
The best of remedies is a beef-steak
   Against sea-sickness: try it, sir, before
You sneer, and I assure you this is true,
For I have found it answer—so may you.

14

Don Juan stood, and, gazing from the stern,   105
   Beheld his native Spain receding far:
First partings form a lesson hard to learn,
   Even nations feel this when they go to war;
There is a sort of unexprest concern,
   A kind of shock that sets one's heart ajar: 110

1. Bay of Cadiz.
2. Rigging of a ship.

At leaving even the most unpleasant people
And places, one keeps looking at the steeple.

15

But Juan had got many things to leave,
   His mother, and a mistress, and no wife,
So that he had much better cause to grieve   115
   Than many persons more advanced in life;
And if we now and then a sigh must heave
   At quitting even those we quit in strife,
No doubt we weep for those the heart endears—
That is, till deeper griefs congeal our tears.   120

16

So Juan wept, as wept the captive Jews
   By Babel's waters, still remembering Sion:
I'd weep,[3]—but mine is not a weeping Muse,
   And such light griefs are not a thing to die on;
Young men should travel, if but to amuse   125
   Themselves; and the next time their servants tie on
Behind their carriages their new portmanteau,[4]
Perhaps it may be lined with this my canto.

17

And Juan wept, and much he sigh'd and thought,
   While his salt tears dropp'd into the salt sea,   130
"Sweets to the sweet"[5] (I like so much to quote;
   You must excuse this extract, 'tis where she,
The Queen of Denmark, for Ophelia brought
   Flowers to the grave); and, sobbing often, he
Reflected on his present situation,   135
And seriously resolved on reformation.

18

"Farewell, my Spain! a long farewell!" he cried,
   "Perhaps I may revisit thee no more,
But die, as many an exiled heart hath died,
   Of its own thirst to see again thy shore: 140
Farewell, where Guadalquivir's waters glide!
   Farewell, my mother! and, since all is o'er,
Farewell, too, dearest Julia!—(Here he drew
Her letter out again, and read it through.)

---

3. "By Babel's waters . . . weep" echoes Psalm 137; also, cf. "Oh! Weep for Those!" and "By the Rivers
   of Babylon We Sat Down and Wept" from *Hebrew Melodies* (1815). Babel is Babylon; Sion (or
   Zion) is Jerusalem (biblical, from the Hebrew).
4. Large suitcase or trunk.
5. *Hamlet* 5.1.227.

19

"And, oh! if e'er I should forget, I swear—   145
    But that's impossible, and cannot be—
Sooner shall this blue ocean melt to air,
    Sooner shall earth resolve itself to sea,
Than I resign thine image, oh, my fair!
    Or think of any thing excepting thee;   150
A mind diseased no remedy can physic
    (Here the ship gave a lurch, and he grew sea-sick).

20

"Sooner shall heaven kiss earth (here he fell sicker),
    Oh, Julia! what is every other woe?
(For God's sake let me have a glass of liquor,   155
    Pedro, Battista, help me down below.)
Julia, my love! (you rascal, Pedro, quicker)—
    Oh, Julia! (this curst vessel pitches so)—
Beloved Julia, hear me still beseeching!"
    (Here he grew inarticulate with retching)   160

21

He felt that chilling heaviness of heart,
    Or rather stomach, which, alas! attends,
Beyond the best apothecary's art,
    The loss of love, the treachery of friends,
Or death of those we dote on, when a part   165
    Of us dies with them as each fond hope ends:
No doubt he would have been much more pathetic,
    But the sea acted as a strong emetic.

22

Love's a capricious power: I've known it hold
    Out through a fever caused by its own heat,   170
But be much puzzled by a cough and cold,
    And find a quinsy[6] very hard to treat;
Against all noble maladies he's bold,
    But vulgar illnesses don't like to meet,
Nor that a sneeze should interrupt his sigh,   175
    Nor inflammations redden his blind eye.

23

But worst of all is nausea, or a pain
    About the lower region of the bowels;
Love, who heroically breathes a vein,
    Shrinks from the application of hot towels,   180
And purgatives are dangerous to his reign,

---

6. Severe tonsillitis.

Sea-sickness death: his love was perfect, how else
Could Juan's passion, while the billows roar,
Resist his stomach, ne'er at sea before?

24

The ship, call'd the most holy "Trinidada,"   185
    Was steering duly for the port Leghorn;[7]
For there the Spanish family Moncada[8]
    Were settled long ere Juan's sire was born:
They were relations, and for them he had a
    Letter of introduction, which the morn   190
Of his departure had been sent him by
    His Spanish friends for those in Italy.

25

His suite consisted of three servants and
    A tutor, the licentiate[9] Pedrillo,
Who several languages did understand,   195
    But now lay sick and speechless on his pillow,
And rocking in his hammock, long'd for land,
    His headache being increased by every billow;
And the waves oozing through the port-hole made
    His berth a little damp, and him afraid.   200

*   *   *

[Following a gale, the ship springs a leak, then capsizes, only a small number
of the original crew escaping in longboats.]

52[1]

Then rose from sea to sky the wild farewell—
    Then shriek'd the timid, and stood still the brave,—   410
Then some leap'd overboard with dreadful yell,
    As eager to anticipate their grave;
And the sea yawn'd around her like a hell,
    And down she suck'd with her the whirling wave,
Like one who grapples with his enemy,   415
    And strives to strangle him before he die.

53

And first one universal shriek there rush'd,
    Louder than the loud ocean, like a crash

7. Seaport in western Italy.
8. One of the noble families of Sicily and Naples in the early seventeenth century.
9. Holding a university degree.
1. Byron, who valued truth to fact in poetry and criticized poets when they departed from it, was
   proud of his accuracy in describing the shipwreck incident (stanzas 52–93 of the excerpted canto
   in this Norton Critical Edition), which he based on the following sources: *Shipwrecks and Disas-
   ters at Sea*, edited by Sir. J. G. Dalyell (1812); *Remarkable Shipwrecks* (Hartford, 1813); *A Narra-
   tive of the Honourable John Byron* (1768); and *A Narrative of the Mutiny of the Bounty* by William
   Bligh (1790).

Of echoing thunder; and then all was hush'd,
    Save the wild wind and the remorseless dash   420
Of billows; but at intervals there gush'd,
    Accompanied with a convulsive splash,
A solitary shriek, the bubbling cry
Of some strong swimmer in his agony.

54

The boats, as stated, had got off before,   425
    And in them crowded several of the crew;
And yet their present hope was hardly more
    Than what it had been, for so strong it blew
There was slight chance of reaching any shore;
    And then they were too many, though so few—   430
Nine in the cutter,[2] thirty in the boat,
Were counted in them when they got afloat.

55

All the rest perish'd; near two hundred souls
    Had left their bodies;[3] and what's worse, alas!
When over Catholics the ocean rolls,   435
    They must wait several weeks before a mass
Takes off one peck of purgatorial coals,
    Because, till people know what's come to pass,
They won't lay out their money on the dead—
It costs three francs for every mass that's said.   440

56

Juan got into the long-boat, and there
    Contrived to help Pedrillo to a place;
It seem'd as if they had exchanged their care,
    For Juan wore the magisterial face
Which courage gives, while poor Pedrillo's pair   445
    Of eyes were crying for their owner's case:
Battista, though (a name call'd shortly Tita)
Was lost by getting at some aqua-vita.[4]

57

Pedro, his valet, too, he tried to save,
    But the same cause, conducive to his loss,   450
Left him so drunk, he jump'd into the wave
    As o'er the cutter's edge he tried to cross,
And so he found a wine-and-watery grave;
    They could not rescue him although so close,

---

2. Single-masted sailing vessel.
3. *near . . . bodies*: one of several echoes throughout the shipwreck passage of Coleridge's "Rime of the Ancient Mariner" (1798).
4. Liquor.

Because the sea ran higher every minute,   455
And for the boat—the crew kept crowding in it.

58

A small old spaniel,—which had been Don Jóse's,
    His father's, whom he loved, as ye may think,
For on such things the memory reposes
    With tenderness—stood howling on the brink,   460
Knowing (dogs have such intellectual noses!)
    No doubt, the vessel was about to sink;
And Juan caught him up, and ere he stepp'd
Off, threw him in, then after him he leap'd.

59

He also stuff'd his money where he could   465
    About his person, and Pedrillo's too,
Who let him do, in fact, whate'er he would,
    Not knowing what himself to say, or do,
As every rising wave his dread renew'd;
    But Juan, trusting they might still get through,   470
And deeming there were remedies for any ill,
Thus re-embark'd his tutor and his spaniel.

60

'Twas a rough night, and blew so stiffly yet,
    That the sail was becalm'd between the seas,
Though on the wave's high top too much to set,   475
    They dared not take it in for all the breeze:
Each sea curl'd o'er the stern, and kept them wet,
    And made them bale without a moment's ease,
So that themselves as well as hopes were damp'd,
And the poor little cutter quickly swamp'd.   480

61

Nine souls more went in her: the long-boat still
    Kept above water, with an oar for mast,
Two blankets stitch'd together, answering ill
    Instead of sail, were to the oar made fast:
Though every wave roll'd menacing to fill,   485
    And present peril all before surpass'd,
They grieved for those who perish'd with the cutter,
And also for the biscuit-casks and butter.

62

The sun rose red and fiery, a sure sign
    Of the continuance of the gale: to run   490
Before the sea until it should grow fine
    Was all that for the present could be done:

A few tea-spoonfuls of their rum and wine
   Was served out to the people, who begun
To faint, and damaged bread wet through the bags,   495
   And most of them had little clothes but rags.

63

They counted thirty, crowded in a space
   Which left scarce room for motion or exertion;
They did their best to modify their case,
   One half sate up, though numb'd with the immersion,   500
While t'other half were laid down in their place,
   At watch and watch; thus, shivering like the tertian[5]
Ague in its cold fit, they fill'd their boat,
With nothing but the sky for a great coat.

64

'Tis very certain the desire of life   505
   Prolongs it: this is obvious to physicians,
When patients, neither plagued with friends nor wife,
   Survive through very desperate conditions,
Because they still can hope, nor shines the knife
   Nor shears of Atropos[6] before their visions: 510
Despair of all recovery spoils longevity,
And makes men's miseries of alarming brevity.

65

'Tis said that persons living on annuities[7]
   Are longer lived than others,—God knows why,
Unless to plague the grantors,—yet so true it is,   515
   That some, I really think, *do* never die;
Of any creditors the worst a Jew it is,
   And *that's* their mode of furnishing supply:
In my young days they lent me cash that way,
Which I found very troublesome to pay.   520

66

'Tis thus with people in an open boat,
   They live upon the love of life, and bear
More than can be believed, or even thought,
   And stand like rocks the tempest's wear and tear;
And hardship still has been the sailor's lot,   525
   Since Noah's ark went cruising here and there;
She had a curious crew as well as cargo,
Like the first old Greek privateer, the Argo.[8]

---

5. Fever that recurs every other day.
6. In Greek myth, of the three Fates, Atropos cuts the thread of life.
7. A specified income lasting the lifetime of the recipient.
8. In classical myth, the ship in which Jason sailed in quest of the Golden Fleece.

67

But man is a carnivorous production,
    And must have meals, at least one meal a day;   530
He cannot live, like woodcocks, upon suction,
    But, like the shark and tiger, must have prey;
Although his anatomical construction
    Bears vegetables, in a grumbling way,
Your labouring people think beyond all question,   535
Beef, veal, and mutton, better for digestion.

68

And thus it was with this our hapless crew,
    For on the third day there came on a calm,
And though at first their strength it might renew,
    And lying on their weariness like balm,   540
Lull'd them like turtles sleeping on the blue
    Of ocean, when they woke they felt a qualm,
And fell all ravenously on their provision,
Instead of hoarding it with due precision.

69

The consequence was easily foreseen—   545
    They ate up all they had, and drank their wine,
In spite of all remonstrances, and then
    On what, in fact, next day were they to dine?
They hoped the wind would rise, these foolish men!
    And carry them to shore; these hopes were fine,   550
But as they had but one oar, and that brittle,
It would have been more wise to save their victual.

70

The fourth day came, but not a breath of air,
    And Ocean slumber'd like an unwean'd child:
The fifth day, and their boat lay floating there,   555
    The sea and sky were blue, and clear, and mild—
With their one oar (I wish they had had a pair)
    What could they do? and hunger's rage grew wild:
So Juan's spaniel, spite of his entreating,
Was kill'd, and portion'd out for present eating.   560

71

On the sixth day they fed upon his hide,
    And Juan, who had still refused, because
The creature was his father's dog that died,
    Now feeling all the vulture in his jaws,
With some remorse received (though first denied)   565
    As a great favour one of the fore-paws,

Which he divided with Pedrillo, who
Devour'd it, longing for the other too.

72

The seventh day, and no wind—the burning sun
   Blister'd and scorch'd, and, stagnant on the sea,   570
They lay like carcasses; and hope was none,
   Save in the breeze that came not; savagely
They glared upon each other—all was done,
   Water, and wine, and food,—and you might see
The longings of the cannibal arise   575
   (Although they spoke not) in their wolfish eyes.

73

At length one whisper'd his companion, who
   Whisper'd another, and thus it went round,
And then into a hoarser murmur grew,
   An ominous, and wild, and desperate sound;   580
And when his comrade's thought each sufferer knew,
   'Twas but his own, suppress'd till now, he found:
And out they spoke of lots for flesh and blood,
And who should die to be his fellow's food.

74

But ere they came to this, they that day shared   585
   Some leathern caps, and what remain'd of shoes;
And then they look'd around them, and despair'd,
   And none to be the sacrifice would choose;
At length the lots were torn up, and prepared,
   But of materials that much shock the Muse—   590
Having no paper, for the want of better,
They took by force from Juan Julia's letter.

75

The lots were made, and mark'd, and mix'd, and handed,
   In silent horror, and their distribution
Lull'd even the savage hunger which demanded,   595
   Like the Promethean vulture, this pollution;
None in particular had sought or plann'd it,
   'Twas nature gnaw'd them to this resolution,
By which none were permitted to be neuter—
And the lot fell on Juan's luckless tutor.   600

76

He but requested to be bled to death:
   The surgeon had his instruments, and bled
Pedrillo, and so gently ebb'd his breath,
   You hardly could perceive when he was dead.

He died as born, a Catholic in faith,   605
    Like most in the belief in which they're bred,
And first a little crucifix he kiss'd,
    And then held out his jugular and wrist.

77

The surgeon, as there was no other fee,
    Had his first choice of morsels for his pains;   610
But being thirstiest at the moment, he
    Preferr'd a draught from the fast-flowing veins:
Part was divided, part thrown in the sea,
    And such things as the entrails and the brains
Regaled two sharks, who follow'd o'er the billow—   615
The sailors ate the rest of poor Pedrillo.

78

The sailors ate him, all save three or four,
    Who were not quite so fond of animal food;
To these was added Juan, who, before
    Refusing his own spaniel, hardly could   620
Feel now his appetite increased much more;
    'Twas not to be expected that he should,
Even in extremity of their disaster,
Dine with them on his pastor and his master.

79

'Twas better that he did not; for, in fact,   625
    The consequence was awful in the extreme;
For they, who were most ravenous in the act,
    Went raging mad—Lord! how they did blaspheme!
And foam and roll, with strange convulsions rack'd,
    Drinking salt-water like a mountain-stream,   630
Tearing, and grinning, howling, screeching, swearing,
And, with hyaena-laughter, died despairing.

80

Their numbers were much thinn'd by this infliction,
    And all the rest were thin enough, Heaven knows;
And some of them had lost their recollection,   635
    Happier than they who still perceived their woes;
But others ponder'd on a new dissection,
    As if not warn'd sufficiently by those
Who had already perish'd, suffering madly,
For having used their appetites so sadly.   640

81

And next they thought upon the master's mate,
    As fattest; but he saved himself, because,

Besides being much averse from such a fate,
  There were some other reasons: the first was,
He had been rather indisposed of late;   645
  And that which chiefly proved his saving clause,
Was a small present[9] made to him at Cadiz,
  By general subscription of the ladies.

82

Of poor Pedrillo something still remain'd,
  But was used sparingly,—some were afraid,   650
And others still their appetites constrain'd,
  Or but at times a little supper made;
All except Juan, who throughout abstain'd,
  Chewing a piece of bamboo, and some lead:
At length they caught two boobies, and a noddy,[1]   655
And then they left off eating the dead body.

83

And if Pedrillo's fate should shocking be,
  Remember Ugolino[2] condescends
To eat the head of his arch-enemy
  The moment after he politely ends   660
His tale: if foes be food in hell, at sea
  'Tis surely fair to dine upon our friends,
When shipwreck's short allowance grows too scanty,
Without being much more horrible than Dante.

84

And the same night there fell a shower of rain,   665
  For which their mouths gaped, like the cracks of earth
When dried to summer dust; till taught by pain,
  Men really know not what good water's worth;
If you had been in Turkey or in Spain,
  Or with a famish'd boat's-crew had your berth,   670
Or in the desert heard the camel's bell,
You'd wish yourself where Truth is—in a well.[3]

85

It pour'd down torrents, but they were no richer
  Until they found a ragged piece of sheet,
Which served them as a sort of spongy pitcher,   675
  And when they deem'd its moisture was complete,
They wrung it out, and though a thirsty ditcher[4]

---

9. I.e., syphilis.
1. *boobies . . . noddy*: sea birds.
2. "Quandò ebbe detto ciò, con gli occhi torti / Riprese il teschio misero co' denti, / Che furo all'osso, dome d'un can forti." Dante's *Inferno* 33.76–78.
3. A saying of the Greek philosopher Democritus (460–370 B.C.E.).
4. Ditchdigger.

Might not have thought the scanty draught so sweet
As a full pot of porter, to their thinking
They ne'er till now had known the joys of drinking.   680

86

And their baked lips, with many a bloody crack,
    Suck'd in the moisture, which like nectar stream'd;
Their throats were ovens, their swoln tongues were black,
    As the rich man's in hell, who vainly scream'd
To beg the beggar, who could not rain back   685
    A drop of dew, when every drop had seem'd
To taste of heaven—If this be true, indeed,
Some Christians have a comfortable creed.

87

There were two fathers in this ghastly crew,
    And with them their two sons, of whom the one   690
Was more robust and hardy to the view,
    But he died early; and when he was gone,
His nearest messmate told his sire, who threw
    One glance on him, and said, "Heaven's will be done!
I can do nothing," and he saw him thrown   695
Into the deep without a tear or groan.

88

The other father had a weaklier child,
    Of a soft cheek, and aspect delicate;
But the boy bore up long, and with a mild
    And patient spirit held aloof his fate;   700
Little he said, and now and then he smiled,
    As if to win a part from off the weight
He saw increasing on his father's heart,
With the deep deadly thought that they must part.

89

And o'er him bent his sire, and never raised   705
    His eyes from off his face, but wiped the foam
From his pale lips, and ever on him gazed,
    And when the wish'd-for shower at length was come,
And the boy's eyes, which the dull film half glazed,
    Brighten'd, and for a moment seem'd to roam,   710
He squeezed from out a rag some drops of rain
Into his dying child's mouth—but in vain.

90

The boy expired—the father held the clay,
    And look'd upon it long, and when at last
Death left no doubt, and the dead burthen lay   715

Stiff on his heart, and pulse and hope were past,
He watch'd it wistfully, until away
     'Twas borne by the rude wave wherein 'twas cast;
Then he himself sunk down all dumb and shivering,
And gave no sign of life, save his limbs quivering.   720

91

Now overhead a rainbow, bursting through
     The scattering clouds, shone, spanning the dark sea,
Resting its bright base on the quivering blue;
     And all within its arch appear'd to be
Clearer than that without, and its wide hue   725
     Wax'd broad and waving, like a banner free,
Then changed like to a bow that's bent, and then
Forsook the dim eyes of these shipwreck'd men.

92

It changed, of course; a heavenly cameleon,
     The airy child of vapour and the sun,   730
Brought forth in purple, cradled in vermilion,
     Baptized in molten gold, and swathed in dun,
Glittering like crescents o'er a Turk's pavilion,
     And blending every colour into one,
Just like a black eye in a recent scuffle   735
(For sometimes we must box without the muffle[5]).

93

Our shipwreck'd seamen thought it a good omen—
     It is as well to think so, now and then;
'Twas an old custom of the Greek and Roman,
     And may become of great advantage when   740
Folks are discouraged; and most surely no men
     Had greater need to nerve themselves again
Than these, and so this rainbow look'd like hope—
Quite a celestial kaleidoscope.

*   *   *

[A current directs the boat (now carrying only Juan, three other living men, and three corpses) toward the shore.]

103

As they drew nigh the land, which now was seen
     Unequal in its aspect here and there,
They felt the freshness of its growing green,
     That waved in forest-tops, and smooth'd the air,   820
And fell upon their glazed eyes like a screen

---

5. Boxing glove.

From glistening waves, and skies so hot and bare—
Lovely seem'd any object that should sweep
Away the vast, salt, dread, eternal deep.

104

The shore look'd wild, without a trace of man,   825
   And girt by formidable waves; but they
Were mad for land, and thus their course they ran,
   Though right ahead the roaring breakers lay:
A reef between them also now began
   To show its boiling surf and bounding spray,   830
But finding no place for their landing better,
They ran the boat for shore,—and overset her.

105

But in his native stream, the Guadalquivir,
   Juan to lave his youthful limbs was wont;
And having learnt to swim in that sweet river,   835
   Had often turn'd the art to some account:
A better swimmer you could scarce see ever,
   He could, perhaps, have pass'd the Hellespont,
As once (a feat on which ourselves we prided)
Leander, Mr. Ekenhead, and I did.[6]   840

106

So here, though faint, emaciated, and stark,
   He buoy'd his boyish limbs, and strove to ply
With the quick wave, and gain, ere it was dark,
   The beach which lay before him, high and dry:
The greatest danger here was from a shark,   845
   That carried off his neighbour by the thigh;
As for the other two, they could not swim,
So nobody arrived on shore but him.

107

Nor yet had he arrived but for the oar,
   Which, providentially for him, was wash'd   850
Just as his feeble arms could strike no more,
   And the hard wave o'erwhelm'd him as 'twas dash'd
Within his grasp; he clung to it, and sore
   The waters beat while he thereto was lash'd;
At last, with swimming, wading, scrambling, he   855
Roll'd on the beach, half senseless, from the sea:

6. "Mr. Ekenhead—the Lieutenant of marines on board the Salsette—was my companion in swim-
   ming across the Dardanelles May the 10th (I think the date) 1810. See Hobhouse's travels"
   (Byron's note on the draft). In several letters written during May 1810, Byron boasts of his swim
   across the Dardanelles (or Hellespont, the strait separating Greece and Turkey); see also "Written
   After Swimming from Sestos to Abydos" (p. 19). The Salsette was the name of the ship on which
   Byron traveled from Smyrna to Constantinople in April 1810.

108

There, breathless, with his digging nails he clung
    Fast to the sand, lest the returning wave,
From whose reluctant roar his life he wrung,
    Should suck him back to her insatiate grave: 860
And there he lay, full length, where he was flung,
    Before the entrance of a cliff-worn cave,
With just enough of life to feel its pain,
And deem that it was saved, perhaps, in vain.

109

With slow and staggering effort he arose,   865
    But sunk again upon his bleeding knee
And quivering hand; and then he look'd for those
    Who long had been his mates upon the sea;
But none of them appear'd to share his woes,
    Save one, a corpse from out the famish'd three,   870
Who died two days before, and now had found
An unknown barren beach for burial ground.

110

And as he gazed, his dizzy brain spun fast,
    And down he sunk; and as he sunk, the sand
Swam round and round, and all his senses pass'd: 875
    He fell upon his side, and his stretch'd hand
Droop'd dripping on the oar (their jury-mast[7]),
    And, like a wither'd lily, on the land
His slender frame and pallid aspect lay,
As fair a thing as e'er was form'd of clay.   880

111

How long in his damp trance young Juan lay
    He knew not, for the earth was gone for him,
And Time had nothing more of night nor day
    For his congealing blood, and senses dim;
And how this heavy faintness pass'd away   885
    He knew not, till each painful pulse and limb,
And tingling vein, seem'd throbbing back to life,
For Death, though vanquish'd, still retired with strife.

112

His eyes he open'd, shut, again unclosed,
    For all was doubt and dizziness; he thought   890
He still was in the boat, and had but dozed,
    And felt again with his despair o'erwrought,
And wish'd it death in which he had reposed,

7. A replacement mast of a ship.

And then once more his feelings back were brought,
And slowly by his swimming eyes was seen 895
A lovely female face of seventeen.

113

'Twas bending close o'er his, and the small mouth
Seem'd almost prying into his for breath;
And chafing him, the soft warm hand of youth
Recall'd his answering spirits back from death; 900
And, bathing his chill temples, tried to soothe
Each pulse to animation, till beneath
Its gentle touch and trembling care, a sigh
To these kind efforts made a low reply.

114

Then was the cordial pour'd, and mantle flung 905
Around his scarce-clad limbs; and the fair arm
Raised higher the faint head which o'er it hung;
And her transparent cheek, all pure and warm,
Pillow'd his death-like forehead; then she wrung
His dewy curls, long drench'd by every storm; 910
And watch'd with eagerness each throb that drew
A sigh from his heaved bosom—and hers, too.

115

And lifting him with care into the cave,
The gentle girl, and her attendant,—one
Young, yet her elder, and of brow less grave, 915
And more robust of figure,—then begun
To kindle fire, and as the new flames gave
Light to the rocks that roof'd them, which the sun
Had never seen, the maid, or whatsoe'er
She was, appear'd distinct, and tall, and fair. 920

116

Her brow was overhung with coins of gold,
That sparkled o'er the auburn of her hair,
Her clustering hair, whose longer locks were roll'd
In braids behind, and though her stature were
Even of the highest for a female mould, 925
They nearly reach'd her heel; and in her air
There was a something which bespoke command,
As one who was a lady in the land.

117

Her hair, I said, was auburn; but her eyes
Were black as death, their lashes the same hue, 930
Of downcast length, in whose silk shadow lies

Deepest attraction, for when to the view
Forth from its raven fringe the full glance flies,
  Ne'er with such force the swiftest arrow flew;
'Tis as the snake late coil'd, who pours his length,   935
And hurls at once his venom and his strength.

118

Her brow was white and low, her cheek's pure dye
  Like twilight rosy still with the set sun;
Short upper lip—sweet lips! that make us sigh
  Ever to have seen such; for she was one   940
Fit for the model of a statuary,
  (A race of mere impostors, when all's done—
I've seen much finer women, ripe and real,
Than all the nonsense of their stone ideal).

119

I'll tell you why I say so, for 'tis just   945
  One should not rail without a decent cause:
There was an Irish lady,[8] to whose bust
  I ne'er saw justice done, and yet she was
A frequent model; and if e'er she must
  Yield to stern Time and Nature's wrinkling laws,   950
They will destroy a face which mortal thought
Ne'er compass'd, nor less mortal chisel wrought.

120

And such was she, the lady of the cave:
  Her dress was very different from the Spanish,
Simpler, and yet of colours not so grave;   955
  For, as you know, the Spanish women banish
Bright hues when out of doors, and yet, while wave
  Around them (what I hope will never vanish)
The basquina and the mantilla,[9] they
Seem at the same time mystical and gay.   960

121

But with our damsel this was not the case:
  Her dress was many-colour'd, finely spun;
Her locks curl'd negligently round her face,
  But through them gold and gems profusely shone:
Her girdle sparkled, and the richest lace   965
  Flow'd in her veil, and many a precious stone
Flash'd on her little hand; but, what was shocking,
Her small snow feet had slippers, but no stocking.

---

8. Probably Lady Adelaide Forbes (1789–1858); see *BLJ* 3:75 and 5:227.
9. A lace headscarf or light cloak; *basquiña*: a short-sleeved over-dress.

122

The other female's dress was not unlike,
　But of inferior materials: she　　　　　　　　　970
Had not so many ornaments to strike,
　Her hair had silver only, bound to be
Her dowry; and her veil, in form alike,
　Was coarser; and her air, though firm, less free;
Her hair was thicker, but less long; her eyes　　975
As black, but quicker, and of smaller size.

123

And these two tended him, and cheer'd him both
　With food and raiment, and those soft attentions,
Which are—(as I must own)—of female growth,
　And have ten thousand delicate inventions:　　980
They made a most superior mess of broth,
　A thing which poesy but seldom mentions,
But the best dish that e'er was cook'd since Homer's
Achilles order'd dinner for new comers.[1]

124

I'll tell you who they were, this female pair,　　985
　Lest they should seem princesses in disguise;
Besides, I hate all mystery, and that air
　Of clap-trap, which your recent poets prize;
And so, in short, the girls they really were
　They shall appear before your curious eyes,　　990
Mistress and maid; the first was only daughter
Of an old man, who lived upon the water.

125

A fisherman he had been in his youth,
　And still a sort of fisherman was he;
But other speculations were, in sooth,　　　　　995
　Added to his connection with the sea,
Perhaps not so respectable, in truth:
　A little smuggling, and some piracy,
Left him, at last, the sole of many masters
Of an ill-gotten million of piastres.[2]　　　　　1000

126

A fisher, therefore, was he,—though of men,
　Like Peter the Apostle,[3]—and he fish'd
For wandering merchant-vessels, now and then,

1. See Homer's *Iliad* 9.193ff.
2. Former coins of Turkey.
3. Matthew 4.18–19.

And sometimes caught as many as he wish'd;
   The cargoes he confiscated, and gain   1005
      He sought in the slave-market too, and dish'd
Full many a morsel for that Turkish trade,
   By which, no doubt, a good deal may be made.

127

He was a Greek, and on his isle had built
      (One of the wild and smaller Cyclades[4])   1010
A very handsome house from out his guilt,
   And there he lived exceedingly at ease;
Heaven knows, what cash he got, or blood he spilt,
   A sad old fellow was he, if you please;
But this I know, it was a spacious building,   1015
   Full of barbaric carving, paint, and gilding.

128

He had an only daughter, call'd Haidee,
   The greatest heiress of the Eastern Isles;
Besides, so very beautiful was she,
   Her dowry was as nothing to her smiles: 1020
Still in her teens, and like a lovely tree
   She grew to womanhood, and between whiles
Rejected several suitors, just to learn
How to accept a better in his turn.

129

And walking out upon the beach, below   1025
   The cliff, towards sunset, on that day she found,
Insensible,—not dead, but nearly so,—
   Don Juan, almost famish'd, and half drown'd;
But being naked, she was shock'd, you know,
   Yet deem'd herself in common pity bound,   1030
As far as in her lay, "to take him in,
A stranger" dying, with so white a skin.

130

But taking him into her father's house
   Was not exactly the best way to save,
But like conveying to the cat the mouse,   1035
   Or people in a trance into their grave;
Because the good old man had so much "γους,"[5]
   Unlike the honest Arab thieves so brave,
He would have hospitably cured the stranger,
And sold him instantly when out of danger.   1040

---

4. Group of Greek islands in the south Aegean.
5. Pronounced nōōs, Greek for mind or intellect.

131

And therefore, with her maid, she thought it best
   (A virgin always on her maid relies)
To place him in the cave for present rest:
   And when, at last, he open'd his black eyes,
Their charity increased about their guest;   1045
   And their compassion grew to such a size,
It open'd half the turnpike-gates to heaven—
(St. Paul says, 'tis the toll which must be given.)[6]

132

They made a fire,—but such a fire as they
   Upon the moment could contrive with such   1050
Materials as were cast up round the bay,—
   Some broken planks, and oars, that to the touch
Were nearly tinder, since so long they lay,
   A mast was almost crumbled to a crutch;
But, by God's grace, here wrecks were in such plenty,   1055
That there was fuel to have furnish'd twenty.

133

He had a bed of furs, and a pelisse,[7]
   For Haidee stripp'd her sables off to make
His couch; and, that he might be more at ease,
   And warm, in case by chance he should awake,   1060
They also gave a petticoat apiece,
   She and her maid,—and promised by daybreak
To pay him a fresh visit, with a dish
For breakfast, of eggs, coffee, bread, and fish.

134

And thus they left him to his lone repose: 1065
   Juan slept like a top, or like the dead,
Who sleep at last, perhaps (God only knows),
   Just for the present; and in his lull'd head
Not even a vision of his former woes
   Throbb'd in accursed dreams, which sometimes spread   1070
Unwelcome visions of our former years,
Till the eye, cheated, opens thick with tears.

135

Young Juan slept all dreamless:—but the maid,
   Who smooth'd his pillow, as she left the den
Look'd back upon him, and a moment stay'd,   1075
   And turn'd, believing that he call'd again.

---

6. Colossians 3.14 and 1 Corinthians 13.
7. Woman's outer garment often lined with furs.

He slumber'd; yet she thought, at least she said
   (The heart will slip, even as the tongue and pen),
He had pronounced her name—but she forgot
   That at this moment Juan knew it not.   1080

136

And pensive to her father's house she went,
   Enjoining silence strict to Zoe, who
Better than her knew what, in fact, she meant,
   She being wiser by a year or two:
A year or two's an age when rightly spent,   1085
   And Zoe spent hers, as most women do,
In gaining all that useful sort of knowledge
Which is acquired in Nature's good old college.

137

The morn broke, and found Juan slumbering still
   Fast in his cave, and nothing clash'd upon   1090
His rest; the rushing of the neighbouring rill,
   And the young beams of the excluded sun,
Troubled him not, and he might sleep his fill;
   And need he had of slumber yet, for none
Had suffer'd more—his hardships were comparative   1095
To those related in my grand-dad's "Narrative."[8]

138

Not so Haidee: she sadly toss'd and tumbled,
   And started from her sleep, and, turning o'er,
Dream'd of a thousand wrecks, o'er which she stumbled,
   And handsome corpses strew'd upon the shore;   1100
And woke her maid so early that she grumbled,
   And call'd her father's old slaves up, who swore
In several oaths—Armenian, Turk, and Greek—
They knew not what to think of such a freak.

139

But up she got, and up she made them get,   1105
   With some pretence about the sun, that makes
Sweet skies just when he rises, or is set;
   And 'tis, no doubt, a sight to see when breaks
Bright Phoebus, while the mountains still are wet
   With mist, and every bird with him awakes,   1110
And night is flung off like a mourning suit
Worn for a husband,—or some other brute.

---

8. One of the sources for the shipwreck sequence; see note to stanza 52.

140

I say, the sun is a most glorious sight,
   I've seen him rise full oft, indeed of late
I have sat up on purpose all the night,   1115
   Which hastens, as physicians say, one's fate;
And so all ye, who would be in the right
   In health and purse, begin your day to date
From daybreak, and when coffin'd at fourscore,
Engrave upon the plate, you rose at four.   1120

141

And Haidee met the morning face to face;
   Her own was freshest, though a feverish flush
Had dyed it with the headlong blood, whose race
   From heart to cheek is curb'd into a blush,
Like to a torrent which a mountain's base,   1125
   That overpowers some Alpine river's rush,
Checks to a lake, whose waves in circles spread;
Or the Red Sea—but the sea is not red.

142

And down the cliff the island virgin came,
   And near the cave her quick light footsteps drew,   1130
While the sun smiled on her with his first flame,
   And young Aurora[9] kiss'd her lips with dew,
Taking her for a sister; just the same
   Mistake you would have made on seeing the two,
Although the mortal, quite as fresh and fair,   1135
Had all the advantage, too, of not being air.

143

And when into the cavern Haidee stepp'd
   All timidly, yet rapidly, she saw
That like an infant Juan sweetly slept;
   And then she stopp'd, and stood as if in awe   1140
(For sleep is awful), and on tiptoe crept
   And wrapt him closer, lest the air, too raw,
Should reach his blood, then o'er him still as death
Bent, with hush'd lips, that drank his scarce-drawn breath.

144

And thus like to an angel o'er the dying   1145
   Who die in righteousness, she lean'd; and there
All tranquilly the shipwreck'd boy was lying,

---

9. Roman goddess of dawn; a name in Byron's poetry associated with significant female figures: compare Aurora Raby in Cantos XV–XVI and Egeria described as "a young Aurora of the air" in *Childe Harold* IV.1030.

As o'er him lay the calm and stirless air:
But Zoe the meantime some eggs was frying,
Since, after all, no doubt the youthful pair   1150
Must breakfast, and betimes—lest they should ask it,
She drew out her provision from the basket.

145

She knew that the best feelings must have victual,
And that a shipwreck'd youth would hungry be;
Besides, being less in love, she yawn'd a little,   1155
And felt her veins chill'd by the neighbouring sea;
And so, she cook'd their breakfast to a tittle;
I can't say that she gave them any tea,
But there were eggs, fruit, coffee, bread, fish, honey,
With Scio[1] wine,—and all for love, not money.   1160

146

And Zoe, when the eggs were ready, and
The coffee made, would fain have waken'd Juan;
But Haidee stopp'd her with her quick small hand,
And without word, a sign her finger drew on
Her lip, which Zoe needs must understand;   1165
And, the first breakfast spoilt, prepared a new one,
Because her mistress would not let her break
That sleep which seem'd as it would ne'er awake.

147

For still he lay, and on his thin worn cheek
A purple hectic[2] play'd like dying day   1170
On the snow-tops of distant hills; the streak
Of sufferance yet upon his forehead lay,
Where the blue veins look'd shadowy, shrunk, and weak;
And his black curls were dewy with the spray,
Which weigh'd upon them yet, all damp and salt,   1175
Mix'd with the stony vapours of the vault.

148

And she bent o'er him, and he lay beneath,
Hush'd as the babe upon its mother's breast,
Droop'd as the willow when no winds can breathe,
Lull'd like the depth of ocean when at rest,   1180
Fair as the crowning rose of the whole wreath,
Soft as the callow cygnet in its nest;
In short, he was a very pretty fellow,
Although his woes had turn'd him rather yellow.

---

1. Italian for Chios, an Aegean island.
2. Feverish flush.

149

He woke and gazed, and would have slept again,   ₁₁₈₅
   But the fair face which met his eyes forbade
Those eyes to close, though weariness and pain
   Had further sleep a further pleasure made;
For woman's face was never form'd in vain
   For Juan, so that even when he pray'd   ₁₁₉₀
He turn'd from grisly saints, and martyrs hairy,
To the sweet portraits of the Virgin Mary.

150

And thus upon his elbow he arose,
   And look'd upon the lady, in whose cheek
The pale contended with the purple rose,   ₁₁₉₅
   As with an effort she began to speak;
Her eyes were eloquent, her words would pose,
   Although she told him, in good modern Greek,
With an Ionian[3] accent, low and sweet,
That he was faint, and must not talk, but eat.   ₁₂₀₀

151

Now Juan could not understand a word,
   Being no Grecian; but he had an ear,
And her voice was the warble of a bird,
   So soft, so sweet, so delicately clear,
That finer, simpler music ne'er was heard;   ₁₂₀₅
   The sort of sound we echo with a tear,
Without knowing why—an overpowering tone,
Whence Melody descends as from a throne.

152

And Juan gazed as one who is awoke
   By a distant organ, doubting if he be   ₁₂₁₀
Not yet a dreamer, till the spell is broke
   By the watchman, or some such reality,
Or by one's early valet's cursed knock;
   At least it is a heavy sound to me,
Who like a morning slumber—for the night   ₁₂₁₅
Shows stars and women in a better light.

153

And Juan, too, was help'd out from his dream,
   Or sleep, or whatsoe'er it was, by feeling
A most prodigious appetite: the steam
   Of Zoe's cookery no doubt was stealing   ₁₂₂₀
Upon his senses, and the kindling beam

---

3. Of the western coast of Asia Minor that had been colonized by the Greeks in ancient times.

Of the new fire, which Zoe kept up, kneeling,
To stir her viands, made him quite awake
And long for food, but chiefly a beef-steak.

154

But beef is rare within these oxless isles;   1225
  Goat's flesh there is, no doubt, and kid, and mutton;
And, when a holiday upon them smiles,
  A joint upon their barbarous spits they put on:
But this occurs but seldom, between whiles,
  For some of these are rocks with scarce a hut on;   1230
Others are fair and fertile, among which
This, though not large, was one of the most rich.

155

I say that beef is rare, and can't help thinking
  That the old fable of the Minotaur[4]—
From which our modern morals, rightly shrinking,   1235
  Condemn the royal lady's taste who wore
A cow's shape for a mask—was only (sinking
  The allegory) a mere type, no more,
That Pasiphae promoted breeding cattle,
To make the Cretans bloodier in battle.   1240

156

For we all know that English people are
  Fed upon beef—I won't say much of beer,
Because 'tis liquor only, and being far
  From this my subject, has no business here;
We know, too, they are very fond of war,   1245
  A pleasure—like all pleasures—rather dear;
So were the Cretans—from which I infer
That beef and battles both were owing to her.[5]

157

But to resume. The languid Juan raised
  His head upon his elbow, and he saw   1250
A sight on which he had not lately gazed,
  As all his latter meals had been quite raw,
Three or four things, for which the Lord he praised,
  And, feeling still the famish'd vulture gnaw,
He fell upon whate'er was offer'd, like   1255
A priest, a shark, an alderman, or pike.[6]

---

4. In Greek myth, Queen Pasiphae, wife of Minos of Crete, conceived a sexual passion for a white
bull. Disguising herself as a cow, she had intercourse with him and gave birth to the Minotaur—
half man, half bull.
5. Pasiphae.
6. A voracious fish; *alderman*: a chief magistrate of a county.

158

He ate, and he was well supplied: and she,
  Who watch'd him like a mother, would have fed
Him past all bounds, because she smiled to see
  Such appetite in one she had deem'd dead: 1260
But Zoe, being older than Haidee,
  Knew (by tradition, for she ne'er had read)
That famish'd people must be slowly nurst,
And fed by spoonfuls, else they always burst.

159

And so she took the liberty to state,   1265
  Rather by deeds than words, because the case
Was urgent, that the gentleman, whose fate
  Had made her mistress quit her bed to trace
The sea-shore at this hour, must leave his plate,
  Unless he wish'd to die upon the place—   1270
She snatch'd it, and refused another morsel,
Saying, he had gorged enough to make a horse ill.

160

Next they—he being naked, save a tattered
  Pair of scarce decent trowsers—went to work,
And in the fire his recent rags they scattered,   1275
  And dressed him, for the present, like a Turk.
Or Greek—that is, although it not much matter'd,
  Omitting turban, slippers, pistol, dirk,[7]—
They furnish'd him, entire, except some stitches,
With a clean shirt, and very spacious breeches.   1280

161

And then fair Haidee tried her tongue at speaking,
  But not a word could Juan comprehend,
Although he listen'd so that the young Greek in
  Her earnestness would ne'er have made an end;
And, as he interrupted not, went eking   1285
  Her speech out to her protégé and friend,
Till pausing at the last her breath to take,
She saw he did not understand Romaic.[8]

162

And then she had recourse to nods, and signs,
  And smiles, and sparkles of the speaking eye,   1290
And read (the only book she could) the lines
  Of his fair face, and found, by sympathy,

7. Dagger.
8. Modern Greek; correctly pronounced Rō-mā'-ik.

The answer eloquent, where the soul shines
   And darts in one quick glance a long reply;
And thus in every look she saw exprest   1295
   A world of words, and things at which she guess'd.

163

And now, by dint of fingers and of eyes,
   And words repeated after her, he took
A lesson in her tongue; but by surmise,
   No doubt, less of her language than her look: 1300
As he who studies fervently the skies
   Turns oftener to the stars than to his book,
Thus Juan learn'd his alpha beta better
From Haidee's glance than any graven letter.

164

'Tis pleasing to be school'd in a strange tongue   1305
   By female lips and eyes—that is, I mean,
When both the teacher and the taught are young,
   As was the case, at least, where I have been;
They smile so when one's right, and when one's wrong
   They smile still more, and then there intervene   1310
Pressure of hands, perhaps even a chaste kiss;—
I learn'd the little that I know by this:

165

That is, some words of Spanish, Turk, and Greek,
   Italian not at all, having no teachers;[9]
Much English I cannot pretend to speak,   1315
   Learning that language chiefly from its preachers,
Barrow, South, Tillotson,[1] whom every week
   I study, also Blair, the highest reachers
Of eloquence in piety and prose—
I hate your poets, so read none of those.   1320

166

As for the ladies, I have nought to say,
   A wanderer from the British world of fashion,
Where I, like other "dogs, have had my day,"[2]
   Like other men, too, may have had my passion—
But that, like other things, has pass'd away,   1325
   And all her fools whom I *could* lay the lash on:
Foes, friends, men, women, now are nought to me
But dreams of what has been, no more to be.

9. Humorous: Byron's letters document his numerous Italian liaisons.
1. Isaac Barrow (1630–1677), Robert South (1634–1716), and John Tillotson (1630–1694) were theologians and preachers; in the next line, Hugh Blair (1718–1800) wrote *Lectures on Rhetoric*.
2. Cf. *Hamlet* 5.1.277.

167

Return we to Don Juan. He begun
   To hear new words, and to repeat them; but   1330
Some feelings, universal as the sun,
   Were such as could not in his breast be shut
More than within the bosom of a nun:
   He was in love,—as you would be, no doubt,
With a young benefactress,—so was she,   1335
Just in the way we very often see.

168

And every day by daybreak—rather early
   For Juan, who was somewhat fond of rest—
She came into the cave, but it was merely
   To see her bird reposing in his nest;   1340
And she would softly stir his locks so curly,
   Without disturbing her yet slumbering guest,
Breathing all gently o'er his cheek and mouth,
As o'er a bed of roses the sweet south.[3]

169

And every morn his colour freshlier came,   1345
   And every day help'd on his convalescence;
'Twas well, because health in the human frame
   Is pleasant, besides being true love's essence,
For health and idleness to passion's flame
   Are oil and gunpowder; and some good lessons   1350
Are also learnt from Ceres and from Bacchus,[4]
Without whom Venus will not long attack us.

170

While Venus fills the heart (without heart really
   Love, though good always, is not quite so good,)
Ceres presents a plate of vermicelli,—   1355
   For love must be sustain'd like flesh and blood,—
While Bacchus pours out wine, or hands a jelly:
   Eggs, oysters, too, are amatory food;
But who is their purveyor from above
Heaven knows,—it may be Neptune, Pan, or Jove.[5]   1360

171

When Juan woke he found some good things ready,
   A bath, a breakfast, and the finest eyes
That ever made a youthful heart less steady,

---

3. I.e., south wind.
4. In Roman myth, Ceres was goddess of grain, Bacchus, god of wine, and Venus, goddess of love.
5. Ancient gods who reign, respectively, in the sea, on the earth, and in the heavens.

Besides her maid's, as pretty for their size;
But I have spoken of all this already—   1365
    And repetition's tiresome and unwise,—
Well—Juan, after bathing in the sea,
Came always back to coffee and Haidee.

172

Both were so young, and one so innocent,
    That bathing pass'd for nothing; Juan seem'd   1370
To her, as 'twere, the kind of being sent,
    Of whom these two years she had nightly dream'd,
A something to be loved, a creature meant
    To be her happiness, and whom she deem'd
To render happy; all who joy would win   1375
    Must share it,—Happiness was born a twin.

173

It was such pleasure to behold him, such
    Enlargement of existence to partake
Nature with him, to thrill beneath his touch,
    To watch him slumbering, and to see him wake: 1380
To live with him for ever were too much;
    But then the thought of parting made her quake:
He was her own, her ocean-treasure, cast
Like a rich wreck—her first love, and her last.

174

And thus a moon roll'd on, and fair Haidee   1385
    Paid daily visits to her boy, and took
Such plentiful precautions, that still he
    Remain'd unknown within his craggy nook;
At last her father's prows put out to sea,
    For certain merchantmen upon the look,   1390
Not as of yore to carry off an Io,[6]
But three Ragusan vessels, bound for Scio.

175

Then came her freedom, for she had no mother,
    So that, her father being at sea, she was
Free as a married woman, or such other   1395
    Female, as where she likes may freely pass,
Without even the incumbrance of a brother,
    The freest she that ever gazed on glass:
I speak of Christian lands in this comparison,
Where wives, at least, are seldom kept in garrison.   1400

6. According to Persian legend, the maiden Io, loved by Zeus in the Greek myth, was carried off by
Phoenician merchants. Ragusa is the Italian name of the modern-day Dubrovnik (Croatia).

176

Now she prolong'd her visits and her talk
   (For they must talk), and he had learnt to say
So much as to propose to take a walk,—
   For little had he wander'd since the day
On which, like a young flower snapp'd from the stalk,   1405
   Drooping and dewy on the beach he lay,—
And thus they walk'd out in the afternoon,
And saw the sun set opposite the moon.

177

It was a wild and breaker-beaten coast,
   With cliffs above, and a broad sandy shore,   1410
Guarded by shoals and rocks as by an host,
   With here and there a creek, whose aspect wore
A better welcome to the tempest-tost;
   And rarely ceased the haughty billow's roar,
Save on the dead long summer days, which make   1415
The outstretch'd ocean glitter like a lake.

178

And the small ripple spilt upon the beach
   Scarcely o'erpass'd the cream of your champagne,
When o'er the brim the sparkling bumpers reach,
   That spring-dew of the spirit! the heart's rain!   1420
Few things surpass old wine; and they may preach
   Who please,—the more because they preach in vain,—
Let us have wine and women, mirth and laughter,
Sermons and soda-water the day after.

179

Man, being reasonable, must get drunk;   1425
   The best of life is but intoxication:
Glory, the grape, love, gold, in these are sunk
   The hopes of all men, and of every nation;
Without their sap, how branchless were the trunk
   Of life's strange tree, so fruitful on occasion: 1430
But to return,—Get very drunk; and when
You wake with headach, you shall see what then.

180

Ring for your valet—bid him quickly bring
   Some hock[7] and soda-water, then you'll know
A pleasure worthy Xerxes[8] the great king;   1435
   For not the blest sherbet, sublimed with snow,

7. Hocheimer wine, used in a hangover cure.
8. Xerxes I, King of Persia (486?–465 B.C.E.), renowned for his opulence.

Nor the first sparkle of the desert-spring,
　Nor Burgundy in all its sunset glow,
After long travel, ennui, love, or slaughter,
　Vie with that draught of hock and soda-water.　　　1440

181

The coast—I think it was the coast that I
　Was just describing—Yes, it *was* the coast—
Lay at this period quiet as the sky,
　The sands untumbled, the blue waves untost,
And all was stillness, save the sea-bird's cry,　　　1445
　And dolphin's leap, and little billow crost
By some low rock or shelve, that made it fret
Against the boundary it scarcely wet.

182

And forth they wander'd, her sire being gone,
　As I have said, upon an expedition;　　　1450
And mother, brother, guardian, she had none,
　Save Zoe, who, although with due precision
She waited on her lady with the sun,
　Thought daily service was her only mission,
Bringing warm water, wreathing her long tresses,　　　1455
And asking now and then for cast-off dresses.

183

It was the cooling hour, just when the rounded
　Red sun sinks down behind the azure hill,
Which then seems as if the whole earth it bounded,
　Circling all nature, hush'd, and dim, and still,　　　1460
With the far mountain-crescent half surrounded
　On one side, and the deep sea calm and chill
Upon the other, and the rosy sky,
With one star sparkling through it like an eye.

184

And thus they wander'd forth, and hand in hand,　　　1465
　Over the shining pebbles and the shells,
Glided along the smooth and harden'd sand,
　And in the worn and wild receptacles
Work'd by the storms, yet work'd as it were plann'd,
　In hollow halls, with sparry roofs and cells,　　　1470
They turn'd to rest; and, each clasp'd by an arm,
Yielded to the deep twilight's purple charm.

185

They look'd up to the sky, whose floating glow
　Spread like a rosy ocean, vast and bright;

They gazed upon the glittering sea below,   1475
    Whence the broad moon rose circling into sight;
They heard the wave's splash, and the wind so low,
    And saw each other's dark eyes darting light
Into each other—and, beholding this,
    Their lips drew near, and clung into a kiss;   1480

186

A long, long kiss, a kiss of youth and love
    And beauty, all concentrating like rays
Into one focus, kindled from above;
    Such kisses as belong to early days,
Where heart, and soul, and sense, in concert move,   1485
    And the blood's lava, and the pulse a blaze,
Each kiss a heart-quake,—for a kiss's strength,
    I think, it must be reckon'd by its length.

187

By length I mean duration; theirs endured
    Heaven knows how long—no doubt they never reckon'd;   1490
And if they had, they could not have secured
    The sum of their sensations to a second:
They had not spoken; but they felt allured,
    As if their souls and lips each other beckon'd,
Which, being join'd, like swarming bees they clung—   1495
    Their hearts the flowers from whence the honey sprung.

188

They were alone, but not alone as they
    Who shut in chambers think it loneliness;
The silent ocean, and the starlight bay,
    The twilight glow, which momently grew less,   1500
The voiceless sands, and dropping caves, that lay
    Around them, made them to each other press,
As if there were no life beneath the sky
Save theirs, and that their life could never die.

189

They fear'd no eyes nor ears on that lone beach,   1505
    They felt no terrors from the night, they were
All in all to each other: though their speech
    Was broken words, they *thought* a language there,—
And all the burning tongues the passions teach
    Found in one sigh the best interpreter   1510
Of nature's oracle—first love,—that all
Which Eve has left her daughters since her fall.

190

Haidee spoke not of scruples, ask'd no vows,
    Nor offer'd any; she had never heard
Of plight and promises to be a spouse,   1515
    Or perils by a loving maid incurr'd;
She was all which pure ignorance allows,
    And flew to her young mate like a young bird;
And, never having dreamt of falsehood, she
Had not one word to say of constancy.   1520

191

She loved, and was beloved—she adored,
    And she was worshipp'd; after nature's fashion,
Their intense souls, into each other pour'd,
    If souls could die, had perish'd in that passion,—
But by degrees their senses were restored,   1525
    Again to be o'ercome, again to dash on;
And, beating 'gainst *his* bosom, Haidee's heart
Felt as if never more to beat apart.

192

Alas! they were so young, so beautiful,
    So lonely, loving, helpless, and the hour   1530
Was that in which the heart is always full,
    And, having o'er itself no further power,
Prompts deeds eternity can not annul,
    But pays off moments in an endless shower
Of hell-fire—all prepared for people giving   1535
Pleasure or pain to one another living.

193

Alas! for Juan and Haidee! they were
    So loving and so lovely—till then never,
Excepting our first parents, such a pair
    Had run the risk of being damn'd for ever;   1540
And Haidee, being devout as well as fair,
    Had, doubtless, heard about the Stygian[9] river,
And hell and purgatory—but forgot
Just in the very crisis she should not.

194

They look upon each other, and their eyes   1545
    Gleam in the moonlight; and her white arm clasps
Round Juan's head, and his around hers lies
    Half buried in the tresses which it grasps;

---

9. In classical myth, the River Styx borders the underworld.

She sits upon his knee, and drinks his sighs,
  He hers, until they end in broken gasps;   1550
And thus they form a group that's quite antique,
  Half naked, loving, natural, and Greek.

195

And when those deep and burning moments pass'd,
  And Juan sunk to sleep within her arms,
She slept not, but all tenderly, though fast,   1555
  Sustain'd his head upon her bosom's charms;
And now and then her eye to heaven is cast,
  And then on the pale cheek her breast now warms,
Pillow'd on her o'erflowing heart, which pants
With all it granted, and with all it grants.   1560

196

An infant when it gazes on a light,
  A child the moment when it drains the breast,
A devotee when soars the Host[1] in sight,
  An Arab with a stranger for a guest,[2]
A sailor when the prize has struck in fight,   1565
  A miser filling his most hoarded chest,
Feel rapture; but not such true joy are reaping
As they who watch o'er what they love while sleeping.

197

For there it lies so tranquil, so beloved,
  All that it hath of life with us is living;   1570
So gentle, stirless, helpless, and unmoved,
  And all unconscious of the joy 'tis giving;
All it hath felt, inflicted, pass'd, and proved,
  Hush'd into depths beyond the watcher's diving;
There lies the thing we love with all its errors   1575
And all its charms, like death without its terrors.

198

The lady watch'd her lover—and that hour
  Of Love's, and Night's, and Ocean's solitude,
O'erflow'd her soul with their united power;
  Amidst the barren sand and rocks so rude   1580
She and her wave-worn love had made their bower,
  Where nought upon their passion could intrude,
And all the stars that crowded the blue space
Saw nothing happier than her glowing face.

---

1. Heavenly army of angels.
2. Hospitality being one of the chief Arabian virtues.

199

Alas! the love of women! it is known   1585
  To be a lovely and a fearful thing;
For all of theirs upon that die is thrown,
  And if 'tis lost, life hath no more to bring
To them but mockeries of the past alone,
  And their revenge is as the tiger's spring,   1590
Deadly, and quick, and crushing; yet, as real
Torture is theirs, what they inflict they feel.

200

They are right; for man, to man so oft unjust,
  Is always so to women; one sole bond
Awaits them, treachery is all their trust;   1595
  Taught to conceal, their bursting hearts despond
Over their idol, till some wealthier lust
  Buys them in marriage—and what rests beyond?
A thankless husband, next a faithless lover,
Then dressing, nursing, praying, and all's over.   1600

201

Some take a lover, some take drams or prayers,
  Some mind their household, others dissipation,
Some run away, and but exchange their cares,
  Losing the advantage of a virtuous station;
Few changes e'er can better their affairs,   1605
  Theirs being an unnatural situation,
From the dull palace to the dirty hovel:
Some play the devil, and then write a novel.[3]

202

Haidee was Nature's bride, and knew not this;
  Haidee was Passion's child, born where the sun   1610
Showers triple light, and scorches even the kiss
  Of his gazelle-eyed[4] daughters; she was one
Made but to love, to feel that she was his
  Who was her chosen: what was said or done
Elsewhere was nothing.—She had nought to fear,   1615
Hope, care, nor love, beyond, her heart beat *here.*

203

And oh! that quickening of the heart, that beat!
  How much it costs us! yet each rising throb
Is in its cause as its effect so sweet,

---

3. A reference to *Glenarvon* (1816), Lady Caroline Lamb's fictional version of her tempestuous affair with Byron in 1812.
4. Having the lustrous dark eyes of this type of small antelope (a description and a feature Byron favored).

That Wisdom, ever on the watch to rob   1620
Joy of its alchymy and to repeat
    Fine truths, even Conscience, too, has a tough job
To make us understand each good old maxim,
So good—I wonder Castlereagh don't tax 'em.

204

And now 'twas done—on the lone shore were plighted   1625
    Their hearts; the stars, their nuptial torches, shed
Beauty upon the beautiful they lighted:
    Ocean their witness, and the cave their bed,
By their own feelings hallow'd and united,
    Their priest was Solitude, and they were wed: 1630
And they were happy, for to their young eyes
Each was an angel, and earth paradise.

205[5]

Oh, Love! of whom great Caesar was the suitor,
    Titus the master, Antony the slave,
Horace, Catullus, scholars, Ovid tutor,   1635
    Sappho the sage blue-stocking, in whose grave
All those may leap who rather would be neuter—
    (Leucadia's rock still overlooks the wave)—
Oh, Love! thou art the very god of evil,
For, after all, we cannot call thee devil.   1640

206

Thou mak'st the chaste connubial state precarious,
    And jestest with the brows of mightiest men:
Caesar and Pompey, Mahomet, Belisarius,[6]
    Have much employ'd the muse of history's pen;
Their lives and fortunes were extremely various,   1645
    Such worthies Time will never see again;
Yet to these four in three things the same luck holds,
They all were heroes, conquerors, and cuckolds.

207

Thou mak'st philosophers; there's Epicurus[7]
    And Aristippus, a material crew!   1650
Who to immoral courses would allure us
    By theories quite practicable too;

---

5. This stanza is a mini-history of classical attitudes toward love. Julius Caesar was the "suitor" of the young Cleopatra; the emperor Titus "mastered" his passion for Berenice, wife of King Herod of Chalcis; Marc Antony was the "slave" of his love for Cleopatra; Horace, Catullus, and Ovid were Roman poets who wrote love lyrics; the ancient Greek poet Sappho conducted a school for girls (hence, "blue-stocking") on the island of Lesbos and reputedly leaped to her death on the island of Leucadia after having been jilted by a lover.
6. The wives of all these men were suspected of infidelity.
7. Third-century B.C.E. Greek philosopher, who, like Aristippus (fourth-century B.C.E.), held that pleasure (hence, "material" existence) is the highest goal of life.

If only from the devil they would insure us,
    How pleasant were the maxim (not quite new),
"Eat, drink, and love, what can the rest avail us?"   1655
So said the royal sage Sardanapalus.[8]

208

But Juan! had he quite forgotten Julia?
    And should he have forgotten her so soon?
I can't but say it seems to me most truly a
    Perplexing question; but, no doubt, the moon   1660
Does these things for us, and whenever newly a
    Palpitation rises, 'tis her boon,
Else how the devil is it that fresh features
Have such a charm for us poor human creatures?

209

I hate inconstancy—I loathe, detest,   1665
    Abhor, condemn, abjure the mortal made
Of such quicksilver clay that in his breast
    No permanent foundation can be laid;
Love, constant love, has been my constant guest,
    And yet last night, being at a masquerade,   1670
I saw the prettiest creature, fresh from Milan,
Which gave me some sensations like a villain.

210

But soon Philosophy came to my aid,
    And whisper'd, "Think of every sacred tie!"
"I will, my dear Philosophy!" I said,   1675
    "But then her teeth, and then, oh, Heaven! her eye!
I'll just enquire if she be wife or maid,
    Or neither—out of curiosity."
"Stop!" cried Philosophy, with air so Grecian,
(Though she was masqued then as a fair Venetian).[9]   1680

211

"Stop!" so I stopp'd.—But to return: that which
    Men call inconstancy is nothing more
Than admiration due where nature's rich
    Profusion with young beauty covers o'er
Some favour'd object; and as in the niche   1685
    A lovely statue we almost adore,
This sort of adoration of the real
Is but a heightening of the "beau ideal."[1]

---

8. Ninth-century B.C.E. warrior king of Assyria, a famous voluptuary. In 1821 Byron made him the
   subject of his drama *Sardanapalus*.
9. I.e., a pretty Venetian woman at the masquerade, having observed the narrator's attraction to a
   pretty young woman from Milan, uses a moral argument to try to dissuade him from pursuing her.
1. The concept of ideal beauty.

212

'Tis the perception of the beautiful,
   A fine extension of the faculties,   1690
Platonic,[2] universal, wonderful,
   Drawn from the stars, and filter'd through the skies,
Without which life would be extremely dull;
   In short, it is the use of our own eyes,
With one or two small senses added, just   1695
   To hint that flesh is form'd of fiery dust.

213

Yet 'tis a painful feeling, and unwilling,
   For surely if we always could perceive
In the same object graces quite as killing
   As when she rose upon us like an Eve,   1700
'Twould save us many a heartache, many a shilling
   (For we must get them any how, or grieve),
Whereas if one sole lady pleased for ever,
How pleasant for the heart, as well as liver!

214

The heart is like the sky, a part of heaven,   1705
   But changes night and day, too, like the sky;
Now o'er it clouds and thunder must be driven,
   And darkness and destruction as on high:
But when it hath been scorch'd, and pierced, and riven,
   Its storms expire in water-drops; the eye   1710
Pours forth at last the heart's blood turn'd to tears,
Which make the English climate of our years.

215

The liver is the lazaret[3] of bile,
   But very rarely executes its function,
For the first passion stays there such a while,   1715
   That all the rest creep in and form a junction,
Like knots of vipers on a dunghill's soil,
   Rage, fear, hate, jealousy, revenge, compunction,
So that all mischiefs spring up from this entrail,
Like earthquakes from the hidden fire call'd "central."   1720

216

In the mean time, without proceeding more
   In this anatomy, I've finish'd now

---

2. Contrast the attitude toward Platonic, or ideal, love here with that given in Canto I, stanzas 79, 111, and 116.
3. Literally, quarantine building; i.e., the liver isolates "bile," which was believed to cause anger, jealousy, and a bitter disposition. Because of the complexity of human emotions, however, nothing can really prevent outbursts of these feelings.

Two hundred and odd stanzas as before,
That being about the number I'll allow
Each canto of the twelve, or twenty-four;   1725
And, laying down my pen, I make my bow,
Leaving Don Juan and Haidee to plead
For them and theirs with all who deign to read.

CANTO THE THIRD[1]

1

Hail, Muse! *et cetera.*—We left Juan sleeping,
   Pillow'd upon a fair and happy breast,
And watch'd by eyes that never yet knew weeping,
   And loved by a young heart, too deeply blest
To feel the poison through her spirit creeping,   5
   Or know who rested there; a foe to rest
Had soil'd the current of her sinless years,
And turn'd her pure heart's purest blood to tears!

2

Oh, Love! what is it in this world of ours
   Which makes it fatal to be loved? Ah why   10
With cypress[2] branches hast thou wreathed thy bowers,
   And made thy best interpreter a sigh?
As those who dote on odours pluck the flowers,
   And place them on their breast—but place to die—
Thus the frail beings we would fondly cherish   15
Are laid within our bosoms but to perish.

3

In her first passion woman loves her lover,
   In all the others all she loves is love,[3]
Which grows a habit she can ne'er get over,
   And fits her loosely—like an easy glove,   20
As you may find, whene'er you like to prove her:
   One man alone at first her heart can move;
She then prefers him in the plural number,
Not finding that the additions much encumber.

4

I know not if the fault be men's or theirs;   25
   But one thing's pretty sure; a woman planted[4]—
(Unless at once she plunge for life in prayers)—
   After a decent time must be gallanted;

---

1. Cantos III and IV were drafted as one long unit between September and November 1819; they were divided into two separate cantos and published with Canto V on August 8, 1821.
2. Symbolic of death and mourning.
3. La Rochefoucauld, *Réflexions* (1665–78), no. 471; lines 31–32 echo *Réflexions*, no. 73.
4. Betrayed (from the Italian *piantare*).

Although, no doubt, her first of love affairs
   Is that to which her heart is wholly granted;   30
Yet there are some, they say, who have had *none*,
   But those who have ne'er end with only *one*.

5

'Tis melancholy, and a fearful sign
   Of human frailty, folly, also crime,
That love and marriage rarely can combine,   35
   Although they both are born in the same clime;
Marriage from love, like vinegar from wine—
   A sad, sour, sober beverage—by time
Is sharpen'd from its high celestial flavour
Down to a very homely household savour.   40

6

There's something of antipathy, as 'twere,
   Between their present and their future state;
A kind of flattery that's hardly fair
   Is used until the truth arrives too late—
Yet what can people do, except despair?   45
   The same things change their names at such a rate;
For instance—passion in a lover's glorious,
But in a husband is pronounced uxorious.[5]

7

Men grow ashamed of being so very fond;
   They sometimes also get a little tired   50
(But that, of course, is rare), and then despond:
   The same things cannot always be admired,
Yet 'tis "so nominated in the bond,"[6]
   That both are tied till one shall have expired.
Sad thought! to lose the spouse that was adorning   55
Our days, and put one's servants into mourning.

8

There's doubtless something in domestic doings
   Which forms, in fact, true love's antithesis;
Romances paint at full length people's wooings,
   But only give a bust of marriages;   60
For no one cares for matrimonial cooings,
   There's nothing wrong in a connubial kiss:
Think you, if Laura[7] had been Petrarch's wife,
He would have written sonnets all his life?

---

5. Excessive fondness for or submissiveness to one's wife.
6. *The Merchant of Venice* 4.1.254.
7. The woman who inspired the numerous love sonnets by the Italian poet and humanist Petrarch (1304–1374).

9

All tragedies are finish'd by a death,   65
    All comedies are ended by a marriage;
The future states of both are left to faith,
    For authors fear description might disparage
The worlds to come of both, or fall beneath,
    And then both worlds would punish their miscarriage;   70
So leaving each their priest and prayer-book ready,
They say no more of Death or of the Lady.[8]

10

The only two that in my recollection
    Have sung of heaven and hell, or marriage, are
Dante and Milton, and of both the affection   75
    Was hapless in their nuptials, for some bar
Of fault or temper ruin'd the connection
    (Such things, in fact, it don't ask much to mar);
But Dante's Beatrice and Milton's Eve
Were not drawn from their spouses, you conceive.[9]   80

11

Some persons say that Dante meant theology
    By Beatrice, and not a mistress—I,
Although my opinion may require apology,
    Deem this a commentator's phantasy,
Unless indeed it was from his own knowledge he   85
    Decided thus, and show'd good reason why;
I think that Dante's more abstruse ecstatics
Meant to personify the mathematics.[1]

12

Haidee and Juan were not married, but
    The fault was theirs, not mine: it is not fair,   90
Chaste reader, then, in any way to put
    The blame on me, unless you wish they were;
Then if you'd have them wedded, please to shut
    The book which treats of this erroneous pair,
Before the consequences grow too awful;   95
'Tis dangerous to read of loves unlawful.[2]

---

8. "Death and the Lady" is the title of a ballad printed in 1736.
9. "Milton's first wife ran away from him within the first month. If she had not, what would John Mil-
   ton have done?" Moore's note, printed as Byron's in 1832. Beatrice, whom Dante writes about in
   both *La Vita Nuova* (1293) and *La Commedia Divina* (1321), was inspired by Beatrice Portinari,
   with whom he fell in love when he was nine years old, she eight, and whom he met with only once
   again on a street in Florence.
1. A traditional Neoplatonic interpretation of the formal organization of the *Commedia*.
2. E.g., the tale of Paolo and Francesca, who succumb to adulterous desires upon reading about the
   love of Launcelot and Guinevere (see *Inferno*, Canto V, and Byron's translation of lines 97–142,
   "Francesca of Rimini" [p. 683]).

13

Yet they were happy,—happy in the illicit
    Indulgence of their innocent desires;
But more imprudent grown with every visit,
    Haidee forgot the island was her sire's;   100
When we have what we like, 'tis hard to miss it,
    At least in the beginning, ere one tires;
Thus she came often, not a moment losing,
Whilst her piratical papa was cruising.

14

Let not his mode of raising cash seem strange,   105
    Although he fleeced the flags of every nation,
For into a prime minister but change
    His title, and 'tis nothing but taxation;
But he, more modest, took an humbler range
    Of life, and in an honester vocation   110
Pursued o'er the high seas his watery journey,
And merely practised as a sea-attorney.

15

The good old gentleman had been detain'd
    By winds and waves, and some important captures;
And, in the hope of more, at sea remain'd,   115
    Although a squall or two had damp'd his raptures,
By swamping one of the prizes; he had chain'd
    His prisoners, dividing them like chapters
In number'd lots; they all had cuffs and collars,
And averaged each from ten to a hundred dollars.   120

16

Some he disposed of off Cape Matapan,[3]
    Among his friends the Mainots; some he sold
To his Tunis correspondents, save one man
    Toss'd overboard unsaleable (being old);
The rest—save here and there some richer one,   125
    Reserved for future ransom—in the hold
Were link'd alike, as for the common people he
Had a large order from the Dey[4] of Tripoli.

17

The merchandise was served in the same way,
    Pieced out for different marts in the Levant,[5]   130

3. The southernmost point of mainland Greece and Europe. The Mainotes were notorious pirates;
   see *The Giaour* (Advertisement [p. 123]) and *BLJ* 2:30–31, 36.
4. Governor, or ruler.
5. Countries bordering the eastern shores of the Mediterranean Sea.

Except some certain portions of the prey,
  Light classic articles of female want,
French stuffs, lace, tweezers, toothpicks, teapot, tray,
  Guitars and castanets from Alicant,[6]
All which selected from the spoil he gathers,   135
Robb'd for his daughter by the best of fathers.

18

A monkey, a Dutch mastiff, a mackaw,[7]
  Two parrots, with a Persian cat and kittens,
He chose from several animals he saw—
  A terrier, too, which once had been a Briton's,   140
Who dying on the coast of Ithaca,
  The peasants gave the poor dumb thing a pittance:
These to secure in this strong blowing weather,
He caged in one huge hamper altogether.

19

Then having settled his marine affairs,   145
  Despatching single cruisers here and there,
His vessel having need of some repairs,
  He shaped his course to where his daughter fair
Continued still her hospitable cares;
  But that part of the coast being shoal and bare,   150
And rough with reefs which ran out many a mile,
His port lay on the other side o' the isle.

20

And there he went ashore without delay,
  Having no custom-house nor quarantine
To ask him awkward questions on the way   155
  About the time and place where he had been:
He left his ship to be hove down next day,
  With orders to the people to careen;[8]
So that all hands were busy beyond measure,
In getting out goods, ballast,[9] guns, and treasure.   160

21

Arriving at the summit of a hill
  Which overlook'd the white walls of his home,
He stopp'd.—What singular emotions fill
  Their bosoms who have been induced to roam!
With fluttering doubts if all be well or ill—   165

6. Port in southeastern Spain.
7. Lines 137–40 reflect Byron's fondness for pets and tendency to keep an unusual assortment of animals in his residences. See Knight, *Lord Byron: Christian Virtues*, chap. 1, excerpted in this volume p. 803.
8. *hove down . . . careen*: refers to the positioning of a ship (often laying it on its side on a beach) for the purpose of repairing or cleaning it.
9. The heavily weighted items carried aboard a ship for the purpose of stability.

With love for many, and with fears for some;
All feelings which o'erleap the years long lost,
And bring our hearts back to their starting-post.

22

The approach of home to husbands and to sires,
   After long travelling by land or water,   170
Most naturally some small doubt inspires—
   A female family's a serious matter
(None trusts the sex more, or so much admires—
   But they hate flattery, so I never flatter);
Wives in their husbands' absences grow subtler,   175
And daughters sometimes run off with the butler.

23

An honest gentleman at his return
   May not have the good fortune of Ulysses;[1]
Not all lone matrons for their husbands mourn,
   Or show the same dislike to suitors' kisses;   180
The odds are that he finds a handsome urn
   To his memory—and two or three young misses
Born to some friend, who holds his wife and riches—
And that his Argus bites him by—the breeches.

24

If single, probably his plighted fair   185
   Has in his absence wedded some rich miser;
But all the better, for the happy pair
   May quarrel, and the lady growing wiser,
He may resume his amatory care
   As cavalier servente,[2] or despise her;   190
And that his sorrow may not be a dumb one,
Write odes on the Inconstancy of Woman.

25

And oh! ye gentlemen who have already
   Some chaste *liaison* of the kind—I mean
An honest friendship with a married lady—   195
   The only thing of this sort ever seen
To last—of all connections the most steady,
   And the true Hymen[3] (the first's but a screen)—
Yet for all that keep not too long away,
I've known the absent wrong'd four times a day.   200

---

1. Latin name for Odysseus, hero of Homer's epic *The Odyssey*. Odysseus's loyal wife, Penelope,
   spurns the many suitors who pursue her during her husband's absence. Upon his return, though
   disguised, Odysseus is recognized and greeted by his old dog, Argus.
2. Italian phrase meaning the socially accepted lover of a married woman.
3. In classical myth, god of marriage.

26

Lambro,[4] our sea-solicitor, who had
　　Much less experience of dry land than ocean,
On seeing his own chimney-smoke, felt glad;
　　But not knowing metaphysics, had no notion
Of the true reason of his not being sad,　　　　　　　205
　　Or that of any other strong emotion;
He loved his child, and would have wept the loss of her,
But knew the cause no more than a philosopher.

27

He saw his white walls shining in the sun,
　　His garden trees all shadowy and green;　　　　　210
He heard his rivulet's light bubbling run,
　　The distant dog-bark; and perceived between
The umbrage of the wood so cool and dun
　　The moving figures, and the sparkling sheen
Of arms (in the East all arm)—and various dyes　　　215
Of colour'd garbs, as bright as butterflies.

28

And as the spot where they appear he nears,
　　Surprised at these unwonted signs of idling,
He hears—alas! no music of the spheres,
　　But an unhallow'd, earthly sound of fiddling!　　　220
A melody which made him doubt his ears,
　　The cause being past his guessing or unriddling;
A pipe, too, and a drum, and shortly after,
A most unoriental roar of laughter.

29

And still more nearly to the place advancing,　　　　225
　　Descending rather quickly the declivity,
Through the waved branches o'er the green-sward glancing,
　　'Midst other indications of festivity,
Seeing a troop of his domestics dancing
　　Like dervises, who turn as on a pivot, he　　　　　230
Perceived it was the Pyrrhic dance[5] so martial,
To which the Levantines are very partial.

30

And further on a group of Grecian girls,
　　The first and tallest her white kerchief waving,
Were strung together like a row of pearls,　　　　　235

---

4. For Haidée's father, Byron uses the name of a Greek pirate, Lambros Katzones; Lambro is also modeled on Ali Pasha, the despot of western Greece and Albania whom Byron met in 1809.
5. Ancient Grecian warlike dance named for Pyrrhus, King of Epirus. See also lines 743–44.

Link'd hand in hand, and dancing; each too having
Down her white neck long floating auburn curls—
  (The least of which would set ten poets raving);
Their leader sang—and bounded to her song,
With choral step and voice, the virgin throng.   240

31

And here, assembled cross-legg'd round their trays,
  Small social parties just begun to dine;
Pilaus and meats of all sorts met the gaze,
  And flasks of Samian and of Chian[6] wine,
And sherbet cooling in the porous vase;   245
  Above them their dessert grew on its vine,
The orange and pomegranate nodding o'er,
Dropp'd in their laps, scarce pluck'd, their mellow store.

32

A band of children, round a snow-white ram,[7]
  There wreathe his venerable horns with flowers;   250
While peaceful as if still an unwean'd lamb,
  The patriarch of the flock all gently cowers
His sober head, majestically tame,
  Or eats from out the palm, or playful lowers
His brow, as if in act to butt, and then   255
Yielding to their small hands, draws back again.

33

Their classical profiles, and glittering dresses,
  Their large black eyes, and soft seraphic cheeks,
Crimson as cleft pomegranates, their long tresses,
  The gesture which enchants, the eye that speaks,   260
The innocence which happy childhood blesses,
  Made quite a picture of these little Greeks;
So that the philosophical beholder
Sigh'd for their sakes—that they should e'er grow older.

34

Afar, a dwarf buffoon stood telling tales   265
  To a sedate grey circle of old smokers
Of secret treasures found in hidden vales,
  Of wonderful replies from Arab jokers,
Of charms to make good gold, and cure bad ails,
  Of rocks bewitch'd that open to the knockers,   270

---

6. From the Greek islands of Samos and Chios.
7. A note here in C quotes Samuel Taylor Coleridge: "Upon the whole, I think the part of *Don Juan*
   in which Lambro's return to his home, and Lambro himself, are described, is the best, that is the
   most individual thing in all I know of Lord B's works. The festal abandonment puts one in mind of
   Nicolas Poussin's pictures" (*Table Talk*, June 7, 1824).

Of magic ladies who, by one sole act,
Transform'd their lords to beasts, (but that's a fact).

35

Here was no lack of innocent diversion
    For the imagination or the senses,
Song, dance, wine, music, stories from the Persian,   275
    All pretty pastimes in which no offence is;
But Lambro saw all these things with aversion,
    Perceiving in his absence such expenses,
Dreading that climax of all human ills,
The inflammation of his weekly bills.   280

36

Ah! what is man? what perils still environ
    The happiest mortals even after dinner—
A day of gold from out an age of iron
    Is all that life allows the luckiest sinner;
Pleasure (whene'er she sings, at least) 's a siren,   285
    That lures to flay alive the young beginner;
Lambro's reception at his people's banquet
Was such as fire accords to a wet blanket.

37

He—being a man who seldom used a word
    Too much, and wishing gladly to surprise   290
(In general he surprised men with the sword)
    His daughter—had not sent before to advise
Of his arrival, so that no one stirr'd;
    And long he paused to re-assure his eyes,
In fact much more astonish'd than delighted,   295
To find so much good company invited.

38

He did not know (alas! how men will lie)
    That a report (especially the Greeks)
Avouch'd his death (such people never die),
    And put his house in mourning several weeks,—   300
But now their eyes and also lips were dry;
    The bloom, too, had return'd to Haidee's cheeks.
Her tears, too, being return'd into their fount,
She now kept house upon her own account.

39

Hence all this rice, meat, dancing, wine, and fiddling,   305
    Which turn'd the isle into a place of pleasure;
The servants all were getting drunk or idling,
    A life which made them happy beyond measure.

Her father's hospitality seem'd middling,
   Compared with what Haidee did with his treasure;   310
'Twas wonderful how things went on improving,
   While she had not one hour to spare from loving.

40

Perhaps you think in stumbling on this feast
   He flew into a passion, and in fact
There was no mighty reason to be pleased;   315
   Perhaps you prophesy some sudden act,
The whip, the rack, or dungeon at the least,
   To teach his people to be more exact,
And that, proceeding at a very high rate,
He show'd the royal *penchants* of a pirate.   320

41

You're wrong.—He was the mildest manner'd man
   That ever scuttled ship or cut a throat;
With such true breeding of a gentleman,
   You never could divine his real thought;
No courtier could, and scarcely woman can   325
   Gird more deceit within a petticoat;
Pity he loved adventurous life's variety,
He was so great a loss to good society.

42

Advancing to the nearest dinner tray,
   Tapping the shoulder of the nighest guest,   330
With a peculiar smile, which, by the way,
   Boded no good, whatever it express'd,
He ask'd the meaning of this holiday;
   The vinous Greek to whom he had address'd
His question, much too merry to divine   335
The questioner, fill'd up a glass of wine,

43

And without turning his facetious head,
   Over his shoulder, with a Bacchant[8] air,
Presented the o'erflowing cup, and said,
   "Talking's dry work, I have no time to spare."   340
A second hiccup'd, "Our old master's dead,
   You'd better ask our mistress who's his heir."
"Our mistress!" quoth a third: "Our mistress!—pooh!—
You mean our master—not the old, but new."

---

8. Pertaining to the drunken revelry of worshipers of Bacchus, classical god of wine.

44

These rascals, being new comers, knew not whom   345
They thus address'd—and Lambro's visage fell—
And o'er his eye a momentary gloom
Pass'd, but he strove quite courteously to quell
The expression, and endeavouring to resume
His smile, requested one of them to tell   350
The name and quality of his new patron,
Who seem'd to have turn'd Haidee into a matron.

45

"I know not," quoth the fellow, "who or what
He is, nor whence he came—and little care;
But this I know, that this roast capon's fat,   355
And that good wine ne'er wash'd down better fare;
And if you are not satisfied with that,
Direct your questions to my neighbour there;
He'll answer all for better or for worse,
For none likes more to hear himself converse."[9]   360

46

I said that Lambro was a man of patience,
And certainly he show'd the best of breeding,
Which scarce even France, the paragon of nations,
E'er saw her most polite of sons exceeding;
He bore these sneers against his near relations,   365
His own anxiety, his heart too bleeding,
The insults too of every servile glutton,
Who all the time was eating up his mutton.

47

Now in a person used to much command—
To bid men come, and go, and come again—   370
To see his orders done too out of hand—
Whether the word was death, or but the chain—
It may seem strange to find his manners bland;
Yet such things are, which I can not explain,
Though doubtless he who can command himself   375
Is good to govern—almost as a Guelf.[1]

9. "'Rispose allor Margutte: a dirtel tosto, / Io non credo più al nero ch'all' azzurro; / Ma nel cappone,
o lesso, o vuogli arrosto, / E credo alcuna volta anche nel burro; / Nella cervogia, e quanto io n'ho
nel mosto, / E molto più nell' aspro che il manguro; / Ma sopra tutto nel buon vino ho fede, / E
credo che sia salvo chi gli crede.' Pulci, *Morgante Maggiore*, Canto 18, Stanza 151." Stanza 45
freely adapts the Pulci quotation.
1. Byron's ironic reference to the House of Hanover, the family of King George III, descendants of
the German royal family of Guelph.

48

Not that he was not sometimes rash or so,
　　But never in his real and serious mood;
Then calm, concentrated, and still, and slow,
　　He lay coil'd like the boa in the wood;　　　　　380
With him it never was a word and blow,
　　His angry word once o'er, he shed no blood,
But in his silence there was much to rue,
And his *one* blow left little work for *two*.

49

He ask'd no further questions, and proceeded　　　385
　　On to the house, but by a private way,
So that the few who met him hardly heeded,
　　So little they expected him that day;
If love paternal in his bosom pleaded
　　For Haidee's sake, is more than I can say,　　　390
But certainly to one deem'd dead, returning,
This revel seem'd a curious mode of mourning.

50

If all the dead could now return to life,
　　(Which God forbid!) or some, or a great many,
For instance, if a husband or his wife　　　　　395
　　(Nuptial examples are as good as any),
No doubt whate'er might be their former strife,
　　The present weather would be much more rainy—
Tears shed into the grave of the connection
Would share most probably its resurrection.　　　400

51

He enter'd in the house no more his home,
　　A thing to human feelings the most trying,
And harder for the heart to overcome,
　　Perhaps, than even the mental pangs of dying;
To find our hearthstone turn'd into a tomb,　　　405
　　And round its once warm precincts palely lying
The ashes of our hopes, is a deep grief,
Beyond a single gentleman's belief.

52

He enter'd in the house—his home no more,
　　For without hearts there is no home;—and felt　　410
The solitude of passing his own door
　　Without a welcome; *there* he long had dwelt,
There his few peaceful days Time had swept o'er,
　　There his worn bosom and keen eye would melt

Over the innocence of that sweet child,   415
His only shrine of feelings undefiled.

53

He was a man of a strange temperament,
  Of mild demeanour though of savage mood,
Moderate in all his habits, and content
  With temperance in pleasure, as in food,   420
Quick to perceive, and strong to bear, and meant
  For something better, if not wholly good;
His country's wrongs and his despair to save her
Had stung him from a slave to an enslaver.

54

The love of power, and rapid gain of gold,   425
  The hardness by long habitude produced,
The dangerous life in which he had grown old,
  The mercy he had granted oft abused,
The sights he was accustom'd to behold,
  The wild seas, and wild men with whom he cruised,   430
Had cost his enemies a long repentance,
And made him a good friend, but bad acquaintance.

55

But something of the spirit of old Greece
  Flash'd o'er his soul a few heroic rays,
Such as lit onward to the Golden Fleece[2]   435
  His predecessors in the Colchian days;
'Tis true he had no ardent love for peace—
  Alas! his country show'd no path to praise
Hate to the world and war with every nation
He waged, in vengeance of her degradation.   440

56

Still o'er his mind the influence of the clime
  Shed its Ionian[3] elegance, which show'd
Its power unconsciously full many a time,—
  A taste seen in the choice of his abode,
A love of music and of scenes sublime,   445
  A pleasure in the gentle stream that flow'd
Past him in crystal, and a joy in flowers,
Bedew'd his spirit in his calmer hours.

---

2. In classical myth, Jason and the Argonauts sailed to Colchis in quest of the Golden Fleece.
3. From the part of the ancient Greek world on the eastern coast of the Aegean Sea.

57

But whatsoe'er he had of love reposed
   On that beloved daughter; she had been   450
The only thing which kept his heart unclosed
   Amidst the savage deeds he had done and seen;
A lonely pure affection unopposed:
   There wanted but the loss of this to wean
His feelings from all milk of human kindness,[4]   455
And turn him like the Cyclops[5] mad with blindness.

58

The cubless tigress in her jungle raging
   Is dreadful to the shepherd and the flock;
The ocean when its yeasty war is waging[6]
   Is awful to the vessel near the rock;   460
But violent things will sooner bear assuaging,
   Their fury being spent by its own shock,
Than the stern, single, deep, and wordless ire
Of a strong human heart, and in a sire.

59

It is a hard although a common case   465
   To find our children running restive—they
In whom our brightest days we would retrace,
   Our little selves re-form'd in finer clay,
Just as old age is creeping on apace,
   And clouds come o'er the sunset of our day,   470
They kindly leave us, though not quite alone,
But in good company—the gout or stone.[7]

60

Yet a fine family is a fine thing
   (Provided they don't come in after dinner);
'T is beautiful to see a matron bring   475
   Her children up (if nursing them don't thin her);
Like cherubs round an altar-piece they cling
   To the fire-side (a sight to touch a sinner).
A lady with her daughters or her nieces
Shine like a guinea and seven-shilling pieces.   480

61

Old Lambro pass'd unseen a private gate,
   And stood within his hall at eventide;
Meantime the lady and her lover sate

4. *Macbeth* 1.5.18.
5. In classical myth, a giant with a single eye.
6. *Macbeth* 4.1.53.
7. Gallstone or kidney stone.

At wassail in their beauty and their pride:
An ivory inlaid table spread with state   485
  Before them, and fair slaves on every side;
Gems, gold, and silver, form'd the service mostly,
Mother of pearl and coral the less costly.

62

The dinner made about a hundred dishes;
  Lamb and pistachio nuts—in short, all meats,   490
And saffron soups, and sweetbreads; and the fishes
  Were of the finest that e'er flounced in nets,
Drest to a Sybarite's[8] most pamper'd wishes;
  The beverage was various sherbets
Of raisin, orange, and pomegranate juice,   495
Squeezed through the rind, which makes it best for use.

63

These were ranged round, each in its crystal ewer,
  And fruits, and date-bread loaves closed the repast,
And Mocha's berry, from Arabia pure,
  In small fine China cups, came in at last;   500
Gold cups of filigree made to secure
  The hand from burning underneath them placed,
Cloves, cinnamon, and saffron too were boil'd
Up with the coffee, which (I think) they spoil'd.

64

The hangings of the room were tapestry, made   505
  Of velvet panels, each of different hue,
And thick with damask flowers of silk inlaid;
  And round them ran a yellow border too;
The upper border, richly wrought, display'd,
  Embroider'd delicately o'er with blue,   510
Soft Persian sentences, in lilac letters,
From poets, or the moralists their betters.

65

These Oriental writings on the wall,
  Quite common in those countries, are a kind
Of monitors adapted to recall,   515
  Like skulls at Memphian[9] banquets, to the mind
The words which shook Belshazzar[1] in his hall,
  And took his kingdom from him: You will find,
Though sages may pour out their wisdom's treasure,
There is no sterner moralist than Pleasure.   520

8. One devoted to pleasure and luxury (Sybaris was an ancient Greek city in southern Italy).
9. Egyptian.
1. A king of Babylon who, in Daniel 5, sees the writing on the wall, which announces his sin and pun-
  ishment; see Byron's "To Belshazzar" and "Vision of Belshazzar" from *Hebrew Melodies* (1815).

66

A beauty at the season's close grown hectic,
 A genius who has drunk himself to death,
A rake turn'd methodistic, or Eclectic[2]—
 (For that's the name they like to pray beneath)—
But most, an alderman[3] struck apoplectic,   525
 Are things that really take away the breath,—
And show that late hours, wine, and love are able
To do not much less damage than the table.

67

Haidee and Juan carpeted their feet
 On crimson satin, border'd with pale blue;   530
Their sofa occupied three parts complete
 Of the apartment—and appear'd quite new;
The velvet cushions—(for a throne more meet)—
 Were scarlet, from whose glowing centre grew
A sun emboss'd in gold, whose rays of tissue,   535
Meridian-like, were seen all light to issue.

68

Crystal and marble, plate and porcelain,
 Had done their work of splendour; Indian mats
And Persian carpets, which the heart bled to stain,
 Over the floors were spread; gazelles and cats, 540
And dwarfs and blacks, and such like things, that gain
 Their bread as ministers and favourites—(that's
To say, by degradation)—mingled there
As plentiful as in a court, or fair.

69

There was no want of lofty mirrors, and   545
 The tables, most of ebony inlaid
With mother of pearl or ivory, stood at hand,
 Or were of tortoise-shell or rare woods made,
Fretted with gold or silver:—by command,
 The greater part of these were ready spread 550
With viands and sherbets in ice—and wine—
Kept for all comers, at all hours to dine.

70

Of all the dresses I select Haidee's:
 She wore two jelicks[4]—one was of pale yellow;
Of azure, pink, and white was her chemise— 555

---

2. Referring to the *Eclectic Review*, which printed hostile critiques of Byron's character and works.
3. Chief magistrate.
4. Vest or bodice worn by Turkish women.

'Neath which her breast heaved like a little billow;
With buttons form'd of pearls as large as peas,
  All gold and crimson shone her jelick's fellow,
And the striped white gauze baracan[5] that bound her,
Like fleecy clouds about the moon, flow'd round her.   560

71

One large gold bracelet clasp'd each lovely arm,
  Lockless—so pliable from the pure gold
That the hand stretch'd and shut it without harm,
  The limb which it adorn'd its only mould;
So beautiful—its very shape would charm,   565
  And clinging as if loath to lose its hold,
The purest ore enclosed the whitest skin
That e'er by precious metal was held in.[6]

72

Around, as princess of her father's land,
  A like gold bar above her instep roll'd[7]   570
Announced her rank; twelve rings were on her hand;
  Her hair was starr'd with gems; her veil's fine fold
Below her breast was fasten'd with a band
  Of lavish pearls, whose worth could scarce be told;
Her orange silk full Turkish trousers furl'd   575
About the prettiest ankle in the world.

73

Her hair's long auburn waves down to her heel
  Flow'd like an Alpine torrent which the sun
Dyes with his morning light,—and would conceal
  Her person[8] if allow'd at large to run,   580
And still they seem resentfully to feel
  The silken fillet's[9] curb, and sought to shun
Their bonds whene'er some Zephyr[1] caught began
To offer his young pinion as her fan.

---

5. Understood by Byron to be a garment of fine cloth, but actually a coarse woollen garment common in Spain and Morocco.
6. "This dress is Moorish, and the bracelets and bar are worn in the manner described. The reader will perceive hereafter, that as the mother of Haidee was of Fez, her daughter wore the garb of the country."
7. "The bar of gold above the instep is a mark of sovereign rank in the women of the families of the deys, and is worn as such by their female relatives."
8. "This is no exaggeration: there were four women whom I remember to have seen, who possessed their hair in this profusion; of these, three were English, the other was a Levantine. Their hair was of that length and quantity that, when let down, it almost entirely shaded the person, so as nearly to render dress a superfluity. Of these, only one had dark hair; the Oriental's had, perhaps, the lightest colour of the four." A Levantine (also, here, Oriental) is a person from one of the countries or islands along the eastern coast of the Mediterranean and Aegean Seas.
9. Lace.
1. Breeze: from Zephyrus, personification of the west wind in classical myth.

74

Round her she made an atmosphere of life,   585
    The very air seem'd lighter from her eyes,
They were so soft and beautiful, and rife
    With all we can imagine of the skies,
And pure as Psyche ere she grew a wife[2]—
    Too pure even for the purest human ties;   590
Her overpowering presence made you feel
It would not be idolatry to kneel.

75

Her eyelashes, though dark as night, were tinged
    (It is the country's custom), but in vain;
For those large black eyes were so blackly fringed,   595
    The glossy rebels mock'd the jetty stain,
And in their native beauty stood avenged:
    Her nails were touch'd with henna; but again
The power of art was turn'd to nothing, for
They could not look more rosy than before.   600

76

The henna should be deeply dyed to make
    The skin relieved appear more fairly fair;
She had no need of this, day ne'er will break
    On mountain tops more heavenly white than her:
The eye might doubt if it were well awake,   605
    She was so like a vision; I might err,
But Shakspeare also says 'tis very silly
"To gild refined gold, or paint the lily."[3]

77

Juan had on a shawl of black and gold,
    But a white baracan, and so transparent   610
The sparkling gems beneath you might behold,
    Like small stars through the milky way apparent;
His turban, furl'd in many a graceful fold,
    An emerald aigrette[4] with Haidee's hair in 't
Surmounted as its clasp—a glowing crescent,   615
Whose rays shone ever trembling, but incessant.

78

And now they were diverted by their suite,
    Dwarfs, dancing girls, black eunuchs, and a poet,
Which made their new establishment complete;

2. In classical myth, Psyche, or spirit, weds Cupid, god of love.
3. *King John* 4.2.
4. Hair ornament made from feathers.

The last was of great fame, and liked to show it:[5]   620
His verses rarely wanted their due feet—
And for his theme—he seldom sung below it,
He being paid to satirise or flatter,
As the psalm says, "inditing a good matter."[6]

79

He praised the present, and abused the past,   625
Reversing the good custom of old days,
An Eastern anti-jacobin[7] at last
He turn'd, preferring pudding to *no* praise—
For some few years his lot had been o'ercast
By his seeming independent in his lays,   630
But now he sung the Sultan and the Pacha
With truth like Southey, and with verse like Crashaw.[8]

80

He was a man who had seen many changes,
And always changed as true as any needle;
His polar star being one which rather ranges,   635
And not the fix'd—he knew the way to wheedle:
So vile, he 'scaped the doom which oft avenges;
And being fluent (save indeed when fee'd ill),
He lied with such a fervour of intention—
There was no doubt he earn'd his laureate pension.   640

81

But he had genius,—when a turncoat has it,
The "Vates irritabilis"[9] takes care
That without notice few full moons shall pass it;
Even good men like to make the public stare:—
But to my subject—let me see—what was it?—   645
Oh!—the third canto—and the pretty pair—
Their loves, and feasts, and house, and dress, and mode
Of living in their insular abode.

82

Their poet, a sad trimmer,[1] but no less
In company a very pleasant fellow,   650
Had been the favourite of full many a mess
Of men, and made them speeches when half mellow;

---

5. The poet's characteristics in stanzas 79–86 are based largely on Byron's view of the poet laureate, Robert Southey, whom Byron detested, but ironically also on Byron himself.
6. Psalm 45.
7. A reactionary (the Jacobins during and after the French Revolution were extreme adherents of its cause).
8. Richard Crashaw (1612?–1649), writer of baroque verse.
9. Literally, irritable seer (Latin): the idea of the temperamental genius.
1. According to McGann, "Byron is punning on the word, which can refer to a tailor's or milliner's assistant, or to one who plays both sides in politics" (*CPW* 5:700).

And though his meaning they could rarely guess,
   Yet still they deign'd to hiccup or to bellow
The glorious meed of popular applause,   655
   Of which the first ne'er knows the second cause.

83

But now being lifted into high society,
   And having pick'd up several odds and ends
Of free thoughts in his travels for variety,
   He deem'd, being in a lone isle, among friends,   660
That without any danger of a riot, he
   Might for long lying make himself amends;
And singing as he sung in his warm youth,
Agree to a short armistice with truth.

84

He had travell'd 'mongst the Arabs, Turks, and Franks,[2]   665
   And knew the self-loves of the different nations;
And having lived with people of all ranks,
   Had something ready upon most occasions—
Which got him a few presents and some thanks.
   He varied with some skill his adulations;   670
To "do at Rome as Romans do,"[3] a piece
Of conduct was which he observed in Greece.

85

Thus, usually, when he was ask'd to sing,
   He gave the different nations something national;
'Twas all the same to him—"God save the king,"   675
   Or "Ça ira,"[4] according to the fashion all:
His muse made increment of any thing,
   From the high lyric down to the low rational:
If Pindar[5] sang horse-races, what should hinder
Himself from being as pliable as Pindar?   680

86

In France, for instance, he would write a chanson;
   In England a six canto quarto[6] tale;
In Spain, he'd make a ballad or romance on
   The last war—much the same in Portugal;
In Germany, the Pegasus[7] he'd prance on   685

---

2. Europeans.
3. Proverbial; the source may be the *Epistles* of St. Augustine (345–430) and/or Robert Burton's *Anatomy of Melancholy* (1621).
4. *It will be*: famous song of the French Revolution.
5. Greek poet (522?–443? B.C.E.) known especially for odes written for particular occasions.
6. A rather large book.
7. In classical myth, the winged horse associated with the Muses.

Would be old Goethe's—(see what says De Staël)[8]
In Italy he'd ape the "Trecentisti;"[9]
In Greece, he'd sing some sort of hymn like this t'ye:

1

The isles of Greece, the isles of Greece!
  Where burning Sappho[1] loved and sung,   690
Where grew the arts of war and peace,—
  Where Delos[2] rose, and Phoebus sprung!
Eternal summer gilds them yet,
But all, except their sun, is set.

2

The Scian and the Teian muse,[3]   695
  The hero's harp, the lover's lute,
Have found the fame your shores refuse;
  Their place of birth alone is mute
To sounds which echo further west
Than your sires' "Islands of the Blest."[4]   700

3

The mountains look on Marathon[5]—
  And Marathon looks on the sea;
And musing there an hour alone,
  I dream'd that Greece might still be free;
For standing on the Persians' grave,   705
I could not deem myself a slave.

4

A king sate on the rocky brow
  Which looks o'er sea-born Salamis;
And ships, by thousands, lay below,
  And men in nations;—all were his!   710
He counted them at break of day—
And when the sun set where were they?

5

And where are they? and where art thou,
  My country? On thy voiceless shore

---

8. Madame de Staël (1766–1817), leading French intellectual and novelist, remarked that Johann
  Wolfgang von Goethe (1749–1832) "represented the entire literature of Germany."
9. Writers of the 1300s.
1. Greek woman poet (seventh century B.C.E.), whose principal subject was passionate love.
2. Presumed to have been raised from the sea by Poseidon and the birthplace of Phoebus Apollo.
3. Referring to the great Greek poets of epic (the heroic) and of love, respectively: Homer, believed
  to be born at Chios (Scio, in Italian), and Anacreon, born at Teos.
4. Note by Moore: "The Μακάρων νῆςοι of the Greek poets were supposed to have been the Cape
  de Verd Islands or the Canaries."
5. Site in 490 B.C.E. of the Greek victory over the Persians, whom they defeated decisively in 480
  B.C.E. at the battle at Salamis (line 705).

The heroic lay is tuneless now—   715
    The heroic bosom beats no more!
And must thy lyre, so long divine,
    Degenerate into hands like mine?

6

'Tis something, in the dearth of fame,
    Though link'd among a fetter'd race,   720
To feel at least a patriot's shame,
    Even as I sing, suffuse my face;
For what is left the poet here?
For Greeks a blush—for Greece a tear.

7

Must *we* but weep o'er days more blest?   725
    Must *we* but blush?—Our fathers bled.
Earth! render back from out thy breast
    A remnant of our Spartan dead!
Of the three hundred grant but three,
To make a new Thermopylae![6]   730

8

What, silent still? and silent all?
    Ah! no;—the voices of the dead
Sound like a distant torrent's fall,
    And answer, "Let one living head,
But one arise,—we come, we come!"   735
'Tis but the living who are dumb.

9

In vain—in vain: strike other chords;
    Fill high the cup with Samian[7] wine!
Leave battles to the Turkish hordes,
    And shed the blood of Scio's vine!   740
Hark! rising to the ignoble call—
How answers each bold Bacchanal![8]

10

You have the Pyrrhic dance as yet,
    Where is the Pyrrhic phalanx gone?[9]
Of two such lessons, why forget   745
    The nobler and the manlier one?

6. Where the Spartans lost a heroic battle against the Persians.
7. From Samos, an Aegean island; Anacreon (line 751) lived there.
8. Drunken reveler.
9. Refers to a victory won at the cost of devastating losses during Greek wars of the third century B.C.E.

You have the letters Cadmus[1] gave—
Think ye he meant them for a slave?

11

Fill high the bowl with Samian wine!
　We will not think of themes like these!　　　750
It made Anacreon's song divine:
　He served—but served Polycrates—
A tyrant; but our masters then
Were still, at least, our countrymen.

12

The tyrant of the Chersonese[2]　　　755
　Was freedom's best and bravest friend;
That tyrant was Miltiades!
　Oh! that the present hour would lend
Another despot of the kind!
Such chains as his were sure to bind.　　　760

13

Fill high the bowl with Samian wine!
　On Suli's rock, and Parga's shore,[3]
Exists the remnant of a line
　Such as the Doric mothers bore;
And there, perhaps, some seed is sown,　　　765
The Heracleidan blood might own.

14

Trust not for freedom to the Franks—
　They have a king who buys and sells:
In native swords, and native ranks,
　The only hope of courage dwells;　　　770
But Turkish force, and Latin fraud,
Would break your shield, however broad.

15

Fill high the bowl with Samian wine!
　Our virgins dance beneath the shade—
I see their glorious black eyes shine;　　　775
　But gazing on each glowing maid,
My own the burning tear-drop laves,
To think such breasts must suckle slaves.

1. In classical myth, a Phoenician prince, founder of Thebes; he is believed to have introduced the alphabet into Greece.
2. Ancient Greek colony (Chersonesus); its tyrant Miltiades led the Greeks to victory at Marathon.
3. *Suli's . . . Parga's:* towns in Albania; Byron believed the Suliotes were descendants of the Spartans, who in turn were believed to descend from Hercules ("Heracleidan") and the early ("Doric") settlers of Greece.

16

Place me on Sunium's[4] marbled steep,
    Where nothing, save the waves and I,   780
May hear our mutual murmurs sweep;
    There, swan-like, let me sing and die:
A land of slaves shall ne'er be mine—
Dash down yon cup of Samian wine!

87

Thus sung, or would, or could, or should have sung,   785
    The modern Greek, in tolerable verse;
If not like Orpheus[5] quite, when Greece was young,
    Yet in these times he might have done much worse:
His strain display'd some feeling—right or wrong;
    And feeling, in a poet, is the source   790
Of others' feeling; but they are such liars,
And take all colours—like the hands of dyers.[6]

88

But words are things,[7] and a small drop of ink,
    Falling like dew, upon a thought, produces
That which makes thousands, perhaps millions, think;   795
    'Tis strange, the shortest letter which man uses
Instead of speech, may form a lasting link
    Of ages; to what straits old Time reduces
Frail man, when paper—even a rag like this,
Survives himself, his tomb, and all that's his.   800

89

And when his bones are dust, his grave a blank,
    His station, generation, even his nation,
Become a thing, or nothing, save to rank
    In chronological commemoration,
Some dull MS. oblivion long has sank,   805
    Or graven stone found in a barrack's station
In digging the foundation of a closet,
May turn his name up, as a rare deposit.

90

And glory long has made the sages smile;
    'Tis something, nothing, words, illusion, wind—   810
Depending more upon the historian's style
    Than on the name a person leaves behind:

4. Cape Colonna, southwest of Athens, overlooking the sea.
5. In Greek legend, consummate poet and musician.
6. Echoing Shakespeare's Sonnet 111.
7. This saying is taken from the French statesman Comte de Mirabeau (1749–1791); see *BLJ* 4:74.

Troy owes to Homer what whist owes to Hoyle:[8]
The present century was growing blind
To the great Marlborough's[9] skill in giving knocks,   815
Until his late Life by Archdeacon Coxe.

91

Milton's the prince of poets—so we say;
  A little heavy, but no less divine:
An independent being in his day—
  Learn'd, pious, temperate in love and wine;   820
But his life falling into Johnson's way,
  We're told this great high priest of all the Nine[1]
Was whipt at college—a harsh sire—odd spouse,
For the first Mrs. Milton left his house.

92[2]

All these are, *certes*, entertaining facts,   825
  Like Shakspeare's stealing deer, Lord Bacon's bribes;
Like Titus' youth, and Caesar's earliest acts;
  Like Burns (whom Doctor Currie well describes);
Like Cromwell's pranks;—but although truth exacts
  These amiable descriptions from the scribes,   830
As most essential to their hero's story,
They do not much contribute to his glory.

93[3]

All are not moralists, like Southey, when
  He prated to the world of "Pantisocrasy;"[4]
Or Wordsworth unexcised,[5] unhired, who then   835
  Season'd his pedlar poems[6] with democracy;
Or Coleridge, long before his flighty pen
  Let to the Morning Post its aristocracy;
When he and Southey, following the same path,
Espoused two partners (milliners of Bath).[7]   840

94

Such names at present cut a convict figure,
  The very Botany Bay[8] in moral geography;

---

8. Edmund Hoyle, *A Short Treatise on Whist* (1742).
9. John Churchill, Duke of Marlborough (1650–1722). Coxe's *Life* (line 816) was published in 1818–19.
1. Muses.
2. The stanza refers to foibles and inglorious acts imputed by biographers to Shakespeare and other important men, including the recently imprisoned Lord Chancellor Bacon, the Roman emperors Julius Caesar and Titus, the poet Robert Burns, and the Puritan statesman and Lord Protector of England (1653–58), Oliver Cromwell.
3. In stanzas 93–100 Byron resumes his attack on Southey, Wordsworth, and Coleridge (see Headnote and Dedication).
4. The utopian society envisioned by Southey and Coleridge.
5. The time prior to Wordsworth's appointment in 1813 as distributor of stamps.
6. Poems about the poor that Wordsworth wrote between 1798–1804.
7. Coleridge contributed poems to the *Morning Post*, and he married Southey's sister-in-law.
8. A penal colony in Australia.

Their loyal treason, renegado[9] rigour,
  Are good manure for their more bare biography.
Wordsworth's last quarto, by the way, is bigger   845
  Than any since the birthday of typography;
A drowsy frowzy poem, call'd the "Excursion,"[1]
  Writ in a manner which is my aversion.

95

He there builds up a formidable dyke
  Between his own and others' intellect;   850
But Wordsworth's poem, and his followers, like
  Joanna Southcote's Shiloh,[2] and her sect,
Are things which in this century don't strike
  The public mind,—so few are the elect;
And the new births of both their stale virginities   855
Have proved but dropsies, taken for divinities.

96

But let me to my story: I must own,
  If I have any fault, it is digression—
Leaving my people to proceed alone,
  While I soliloquize beyond expression;   860
But these are my addresses from the throne,
  Which put off business to the ensuing session:
Forgetting each omission is a loss to
The world, not quite so great as Ariosto.[3]

97

I know that what our neighbours call "*longueurs*,"[4]   865
  (We've not so good a *word*, but have the *thing*
In that complete perfection which ensures
  An epic from Bob Southey every spring—)
Form not the true temptation which allures
  The reader; but 't would not be hard to bring   870
Some fine examples of the *épopée*,[5]
To prove its grand ingredient is *ennui*.

98

We learn from Horace, "Homer sometimes sleeps;"[6]
  We feel without him, Wordsworth sometimes wakes,—
To show with what complacency he creeps,   875

---

9. Refers again to Wordsworth's and Southey's becoming Tories.
1. A nine-book philosophical poem in blank verse (1814).
2. Joanna Southcott (1740–1814) was a religious fanatic and writer of doggerel prophecies, who
   claimed that she had supernatural powers and was pregnant with a special being named Shiloh;
   however, the imagined pregnancy may have been due to illnesses that cause internal swelling
   ("dropsies," line 856). Southcott died of brain disease.
3. Ludovico Ariosto (1474–1533), Italian poet who influenced Byron.
4. Tediousness (French).
5. Epic (French).
6. *Ars Poetica*, line 359.

With his dear "*Waggoners*,"[7] around his lakes.
He wishes for "a boat" to sail the deeps—
Of ocean?—No, of air; and then he makes
Another outcry for "a little boat,"
And drivels seas to set it well afloat.[8]   880

99

If he must fain sweep o'er the etherial plain,
  And Pegasus runs restive in his "Waggon,"
Could he not beg the loan of Charles's Wain?[9]
  Or pray Medea[1] for a single dragon?
Or if too classic for his vulgar brain,   885
  He fear'd his neck to venture such a nag on,
And he must needs mount nearer to the moon,
Could not the blockhead ask for a balloon?

100

"Pedlars," and "Boats," and "Waggons!" Oh! ye shades
  Of Pope and Dryden, are we come to this?   890
That trash of such sort not alone evades
  Contempt, but from the bathos' vast abyss
Floats scumlike uppermost, and these Jack Cades[2]
  Of sense and song above your graves may hiss—
The "little boatman" and his "Peter Bell"   895
Can sneer at him who drew "Achitophel!"

101

T'our tale.—The feast was over, the slaves gone,
  The dwarfs and dancing girls had all retired;
The Arab lore and poet's song were done,
  And every sound of revelry expired;   900
The lady and her lover, left alone,
  The rosy flood of twilight's sky admired;—
Ave Maria! o'er the earth and sea,
That heavenliest hour[3] of Heaven is worthiest thee!

102

Ave Maria! blessed be the hour!   905
  The time, the clime, the spot, where I so oft
Have felt that moment in its fullest power
  Sink o'er the earth so beautiful and soft,

---

7. "The Waggoner" (1819).
8. Byron mocks Wordsworth's *Peter Bell*: "There's something in a flying horse, / There's something in
   a huge balloon; / But through the clouds I'll never float / Until I have a little boat." Byron's abuse
   of Wordsworth's poems continues through line 896, where they are contrasted with John Dryden's
   political satire *Absalom and Achitophel* (1681), much admired by Byron.
9. I.e., Charlemagne's Wain, the constellation known as the Great Bear or Big Dipper.
1. At the end of the *Medea* of Euripides (480–406 B.C.E.), the ferociously vengeful Medea escapes in
   a dragon-drawn chariot.
2. Leader of a rebellious mob against Henry VI in 1450.
3. Vespers (evening prayer).

While swung the deep bell in the distant tower,
   Or the faint dying day-hymn stole aloft,   910
And not a breath crept through the rosy air,
And yet the forest leaves seem'd stirr'd with prayer.

103

Ave Maria! 'tis the hour of prayer!
   Ave Maria! 'tis the hour of love!
Ave Maria! may our spirits dare   915
   Look up to thine and to thy Son's above!
Ave Maria! oh that face so fair!
   Those downcast eyes beneath the Almighty dove—
What though 'tis but a pictured image strike—
That painting is no idol,—'tis too like.   920

104

Some kinder casuists are pleased to say,
   In nameless print—that I have no devotion;
But set those persons down with me to pray,
   And you shall see who has the properest notion
Of getting into heaven the shortest way;   925
   My altars are the mountains and the ocean,
Earth, air, stars,—all that springs from the great Whole,
Who hath produced, and will receive the soul.

105

Sweet hour of twilight!—in the solitude
   Of the pine forest, and the silent shore   930
Which bounds Ravenna's immemorial wood,
   Rooted where once the Adrian[4] wave flow'd o'er,
To where the last Caesarean fortress stood,[5]
   Evergreen forest! which Boccaccio's lore
And Dryden's lay[6] made haunted ground to me,   935
How have I loved the twilight hour and thee!

106

The shrill cicalas,[7] people of the pine,
   Making their summer lives one ceaseless song,
Were the sole echoes, save my steed's and mine,
   And vesper bell's that rose the boughs along;   940
The spectre huntsman of Onesti's line,
   His hell-dogs, and their chase, and the fair throng
Which learn'd from this example not to fly
From a true lover,—shadow'd my mind's eye.

---

4. Adriatic.
5. The last emperor of the West, Honorius, died in 423 at the fortress in Ravenna.
6. Dryden's "Theodore and Honoria" is an adaptation of "Nastagio degli Onesti," one of the tales in
   Boccaccio's *Decameron*.
7. Cicadas.

107

Oh, Hesperus![8] thou bringest all good things[9]—   945
  Home to the weary, to the hungry cheer,
To the young bird the parent's brooding wings,
  The welcome stall to the o'erlabour'd steer;
Whate'er of peace about our hearthstone clings,
  Whate'er our household gods protect of dear,   950
Are gather'd round us by thy look of rest;
Thou bring'st the child, too, to the mother's breast.

108

Soft hour! which wakes the wish and melts the heart
  Of those who sail the seas, on the first day
When they from their sweet friends are torn apart;   955
  Or fills with love the pilgrim on his way
As the far bell of vesper makes him start,
  Seeming to weep the dying day's decay;
Is this a fancy which our reason scorns?
Ah! surely nothing dies but something mourns![1]   960

109

When Nero[6] perish'd by the justest doom
  Which ever the destroyer yet destroy'd,
Amidst the roar of liberated Rome,
  Of nations freed, and the world overjoy'd,
Some hands unseen strew'd flowers upon his tomb:[7]   965
  Perhaps the weakness of a heart not void
Of feeling for some kindness done when power
Had left the wretch an uncorrupted hour.

110

But I'm digressing; what on earth has Nero,
  Or any such like sovereign buffoons,   970
To do with the transactions of my hero,
  More than such madmen's fellow man—the moon's?
Sure my invention must be down at zero,

---

8. The evening star.
9.   "Έσπεζε παντα φεζεις,
    Φεζεις οινον—φεζεις αινα,
    Φεζεις ματεζι παιδα.'
       Fragment of Sappho"
    ("Evening, all things thou bringest / Which dawn spread apart from each other; / The lamb and
    the kid thou bringest, / Thou bringest the boy to his mother." Translated by J. A. Symonds.)
1. "'Era già l'ora che volge il disio, / Ai naviganti, e intenerisce il cuore; / Lo di ch'han detto ai dolci
    amici addio; / E che lo nuovo peregrin' d'amore / Punge, se ode Squilla di lontano, / Che paia il
    giorno pianger che si muore.' Dante's *Purgatory*, canto viii [lines 1–6]. This last line [line 960] is
    the first of Gray's Elegy ["Elegy in a Country Churchyard" (1750)], taken by him without acknow-
    ledgment."
6. Nero Claudius Caesar, Roman emperor (54–68 c.e.), a notoriously depraved and violent tyrant;
    facing execution, he is said to have committed forced sucide.
7. "See Suetonius for this fact."

And I grown one of many "wooden spoons"[8]
Of verse (the name with which we Cantabs please   975
To dub the last of honours in degrees).

111

I feel this tediousness will never do—
    'Tis being *too* epic, and I must cut down
(In copying) this long canto into two;
    They'll never find it out, unless I own   980
The fact, excepting some experienced few;
    And then as an improvement 'twill be shown:
I'll prove that such the opinion of the critic is
From Aristotle *passim.*—See Ποιητικης.[9]

FROM CANTO THE FOURTH[1]

1

Nothing so difficult as a beginning
    In poesy, unless perhaps the end;
For oftentimes when Pegasus[2] seems winning
    The race, he sprains a wing, and down we tend,
Like Lucifer when hurl'd from heaven for sinning;[3]   5
    Our sin the same, and hard as his to mend,
Being pride, which leads the mind to soar too far,
Till our own weakness shows us what we are.

2

But Time, which brings all beings to their level,
    And sharp Adversity, will teach at last   10
Man,—and, as we would hope,—perhaps the devil,
    That neither of their intellects are vast:
While youth's hot wishes in our red veins revel,
    We know not this—the blood flows on too fast;
But as the torrent widens towards the ocean,   15
We ponder deeply on each past emotion.

3

As boy, I thought myself a clever fellow,
    And wish'd that others held the same opinion;
They took it up when my days grew more mellow,
    And other minds acknowledged my dominion: 20
Now my sere fancy 'falls into the yellow

---

8. Awarded to the lowest on the honors list in mathematics among the students of Cambridge University (i.e., *Cantabs*).
9. *Poetics*: Aristotle's study of the principles of epic and other literary forms. *passim*: indicates "here and there throughout" rather than on a specific page.
1. For dates of composition and publication, see note to Canto III.
2. See Dedication, line 58 and note.
3. Isaiah 14.12ff. and *Paradise Lost* 4.39–41.

Leaf,'[4] and Imagination droops her pinion,
And the sad truth which hovers o'er my desk
Turns what was once romantic to burlesque.

4

And if I laugh at any mortal thing,   25
    'Tis that I may not weep; and if I weep,
'Tis that our nature cannot always bring
    Itself to apathy, for we must steep
Our hearts first in the depths of Lethe's[5] spring,
    Ere what we least wish to behold will sleep: 30
Thetis baptized her mortal son in Styx;
A mortal mother would on Lethe fix.

5

Some have accused me of a strange design
    Against the creed and morals of the land,[6]
And trace it in this poem every line: 35
    I don't pretend that I quite understand
My own meaning when I would be *very* fine;
    But the fact is that I have nothing plann'd,
Unless it were to be a moment merry,
A novel word in my vocabulary.[7]   40

6

To the kind reader of our sober clime
    This way of writing will appear exotic;
Pulci[8] was sire of the half-serious rhyme,
    Who sang when chivalry was more Quixotic,[9]
And revell'd in the fancies of the time,   45
    True knights, chaste dames, huge giants, kings despotic;
But all these, save the last, being obsolete,
I chose a modern subject as more meet.

7

How I have treated it, I do not know;
    Perhaps no better than they have treated me   50

4. *'falls . . . Leaf'*: cf. *Macbeth* 5.3.24.
5. In Greek myth, the river of forgetfulness in Hades; the river Styx (line 31), also in Hades, is where
   the nymph Thetis baptized her son Achilles in order to make him invulnerable.
6. See the reviews of *Don Juan* I–II in, for example, *Gentleman's Magazine* (LXXXIX, Aug. 1819),
   Blackwood's (Aug. 1819, V.512–18), and *Edinburgh Monthly Magazine* (September 1819).
7. The line refers to Byron's reputation for brooding, an image popularized by the poems most widely
   associated with him before he wrote *Don Juan*, such as *Childe Harold, Manfred, The Giaour*, and
   The Corsair.
8. Luigi Pulci (1432–1484), author of *Morgante Maggiore*, the first canto of which Byron translated
   (1819), wrote mock-heroic verse that provided one of the models for *Beppo* and *Don Juan*.
9. A witty double entendre: the logic of the context suggests that "Quixotic" refers to Don Quixote,
   the epitome of chivalry in Cervantes' early-seventeenth-century satirical romance; however,
   because of Cervantes' satirical treatment of Quixote's chivalry, "quixotic" has come to mean fool-
   ish, extravagant idealism. Although the effect here is humorous, in XIII.65, Byron refers to *Don
   Quixote* as "the saddest tale ever told."

Who have imputed such designs as show
　　Not what they saw, but what they wish'd to see:
But if it gives them pleasure, be it so;
　　This is a liberal age, and thoughts are free:
Meantime Apollo[1] plucks me by the ear,　　　　　　55
And tells me to resume my story here.

8

Young Juan and his lady-love were left
　　To their own hearts' most sweet society;
Even Time the pitiless in sorrow cleft
　　With his rude scythe such gentle bosoms; he　　60
Sigh'd to behold them of their hours bereft,
　　Though foe to love; and yet they could not be
Meant to grow old, but die in happy spring,
Before one charm or hope had taken wing.

9

Their faces were not made for wrinkles, their　　65
　　Pure blood to stagnate, their great hearts to fail;
The blank grey was not made to blast their hair,
　　But like the climes that know nor snow nor hail
They were all summer: lightning might assail
　　And shiver them to ashes, but to trail　　　　　70
A long and snake-like life of dull decay
Was not for them—they had too little clay.

10

They were alone once more; for them to be
　　Thus was another Eden; they were never
Weary, unless when separate: the tree　　　　　75
　　Cut from its forest root of years—the river
Damm'd from its fountain—the child from the knee
　　And breast maternal wean'd at once for ever,—
Would wither less than these two torn apart;
Alas! there is no instinct like the heart—　　　80

11

The heart—which may be broken: happy they!
　　Thrice fortunate! who of that fragile mould,
The precious porcelain of human clay,
　　Break with the first fall: they can ne'er behold
The long year link'd with heavy day on day,　　85
　　And all which must be borne, and never told;
While life's strange principle will often lie
Deepest in those who long the most to die.

1. Greek god of poetry.

12

"Whom the gods love die young," was said of yore,[2]
  And many deaths do they escape by this: 90
The death of friends, and that which slays even more—
  The death of friendship, love, youth, all that is,
Except mere breath; and since the silent shore
  Awaits at last even those who longest miss
The old archer's[3] shafts, perhaps the early grave   95
Which men weep over may be meant to save.

                        *   *   *

26

Juan and Haidee gazed upon each other
  With swimming looks of speechless tenderness,
Which mix'd all feelings, friend, child, lover, brother,
  All that the best can mingle and express
When two pure hearts are pour'd in one another,   205
  And love too much, and yet can not love less;
But almost sanctify the sweet excess
By the immortal wish and power to bless.

27

Mix'd in each other's arms, and heart in heart,
  Why did they not then die?—they had lived too long   210
Should an hour come to bid them breathe apart;
  Years could but bring them cruel things or wrong;
The world was not for them, nor the world's art
  For beings passionate as Sappho's song;[4]
Love was born *with* them, *in* them, so intense,   215
It was their very spirit—not a sense.

28

They should have lived together deep in woods,
  Unseen as sings the nightingale; they were
Unfit to mix in these thick solitudes
  Call'd social, haunts of Hate, and Vice, and Care: 220
How lonely every freeborn creature broods!
  The sweetest song-birds nestle in a pair;
The eagle soars alone; the gull and crow
Flock o'er their carrion, just like men below.

29

Now pillow'd cheek to cheek, in loving sleep,   225
  Haidee and Juan their siesta took,

2. "See Herodotus [*Cleobis and Biton* 1.31–32]."
3. Death's.
4. See *Don Juan* I.332 and note.

A gentle slumber, but it was not deep,
  For ever and anon a something shook
Juan, and shuddering o'er his frame would creep;
  And Haidée's sweet lips murmur'd like a brook   230
A wordless music, and her face so fair
Stirr'd with her dream, as rose-leaves with the air.

30

Or as the stirring of a deep clear stream
  Within an Alpine hollow, when the wind
Walks o'er it, was she shaken by the dream,   235
  The mystical usurper of the mind—
O'erpowering us to be whate'er may seem
  Good to the soul which we no more can bind;
Strange state of being! (for 'tis still to be)
Senseless to feel, and with seal'd eyes to see.   240

31

She dream'd of being alone on the sea-shore,
  Chain'd to a rock; she knew not how, but stir
She could not from the spot, and the loud roar
  Grew, and each wave rose roughly, threatening her;
And o'er her upper lip they seem'd to pour,   245
  Until she sobb'd for breath, and soon they were
Foaming o'er her lone head, so fierce and high—
Each broke to drown her, yet she could not die.

32

Anon—she was released, and then she stray'd
  O'er the sharp shingles with her bleeding feet,   250
And stumbled almost every step she made;
  And something roll'd before her in a sheet,
Which she must still pursue howe'er afraid:
  'T was white and indistinct, nor stopp'd to meet
Her glance nor grasp, for still she gazed, and grasp'd,   255
And ran, but it escaped her as she clasp'd.

33

The dream changed:—in a cave she stood, its walls
  Were hung with marble icicles, the work
Of ages on its water-fretted halls,
  Where waves might wash, and seals might breed and lurk;   260
Her hair was dripping, and the very balls
  Of her black eyes seem'd turn'd to tears, and murk
The sharp rocks look'd below each drop they caught,
Which froze to marble as it fell,—she thought.

34

And wet, and cold, and lifeless at her feet,   265
    Pale as the foam that froth'd on his dead brow,
Which she essay'd in vain to clear (how sweet
    Were once her cares, how idle seem'd they now!),
Lay Juan, nor could aught renew the beat
    Of his quench'd heart; and the sea dirges low   270
Rang in her sad ears like a mermaid's song,
And that brief dream appear'd a life too long.

35

And gazing on the dead, she thought his face
    Faded, or alter'd into something new—
Like to her father's features, till each trace   275
    More like and like to Lambro's aspect grew—
With all his keen worn look and Grecian grace;
    And starting, she awoke, and what to view?
Oh! Powers of Heaven! what dark eye meets she there?
'T is—'t is her father's—fix'd upon the pair!   280

36

Then shrieking, she arose, and shrieking fell,
    With joy and sorrow, hope and fear, to see
Him whom she deem'd a habitant where dwell
    The ocean-buried, risen from death, to be
Perchance the death of one she loved too well: 285
    Dear as her father had been to Haidee,
It was a moment of that awful kind—
I have seen such—but must not call to mind.

37

Up Juan sprung to Haidee's bitter shriek,
    And caught her falling, and from off the wall   290
Snatch'd down his sabre, in hot haste to wreak
    Vengeance on him who was the cause of all:
Then Lambro, who till now forbore to speak,
    Smiled scornfully, and said, "Within my call,
A thousand scimitars await the word;   295
Put up, young man, put up your silly sword."

38

And Haidee clung around him; "Juan, 'tis—
    'Tis Lambro—'tis my father! Kneel with me—
He will forgive us—yes—it must be—yes.
    Oh! dearest father, in this agony   300
Of pleasure and of pain—even while I kiss
    Thy garment's hem with transport, can it be

That doubt should mingle with my filial joy?
Deal with me as thou wilt, but spare this boy."

39

High and inscrutable the old man stood,   305
 Calm in his voice, and calm within his eye—
Not always signs with him of calmest mood:
 He look'd upon her, but gave no reply;
Then turn'd to Juan, in whose cheek the blood
 Oft came and went, as there resolved to die;   310
In arms, at least, he stood, in act to spring
On the first foe whom Lambro's call might bring.

40

"Young man, your sword;" so Lambro once more said:
 Juan replied, "Not while this arm is free."
The old man's cheek grew pale, but not with dread,   315
 And drawing from his belt a pistol, he
Replied, "Your blood be then on your own head."
 Then look'd close at the flint, as if to see
'Twas fresh—for he had lately used the lock—
And next proceeded quietly to cock.   320

41

It has a strange quick jar upon the ear,
 That cocking of a pistol, when you know
A moment more will bring the sight to bear
 Upon your person, twelve yards off, or so;
A gentlemanly distance, not too near,   325
 If you have got a former friend for foe;
But after being fired at once or twice,
The ear becomes more Irish, and less nice.[5]

42

Lambro presented, and one instant more
 Had stopp'd this Canto, and Don Juan's breath,   330
When Haidee threw herself her boy before;
 Stern as her sire: "On me," she cried, "let death
Descend—the fault is mine; this fatal shore
 He found—but sought not. I have pledged my faith;
I love him—I will die with him: I knew   335
Your nature's firmness—know your daughter's too."

43

A minute past, and she had been all tears,
 And tenderness, and infancy; but now

5. *more . . . nice*: quicker to react and less discerning of subtlety.

She stood as one who champion'd human fears—
    Pale, statue-like, and stern, she woo'd the blow;   340
And tall beyond her sex, and their compeers,[6]
    She drew up to her height, as if to show
A fairer mark; and with a fix'd eye scann'd
    Her father's face—but never stopp'd his hand.

44

He gazed on her, and she on him; 'twas strange   345
    How like they look'd! the expression was the same;
Serenely savage, with a little change
    In the large dark eye's mutual-darted flame;
For she, too, was as one who could avenge,
    If cause should be—a lioness, though tame.   350
Her father's blood before her father's face
Boil'd up, and proved her truly of his race.

45

I said they were alike, their features and
    Their stature, differing but in sex and years;
Even to the delicacy of their hand   355
    There was resemblance, such as true blood wears;
And now to see them, thus divided, stand
    In fix'd ferocity, when joyous tears
And sweet sensations should have welcomed both,
Show what the passions are in their full growth.   360

46

The father paused a moment, then withdrew
    His weapon, and replaced it; but stood still,
And looking on her, as to look her through,
    "Not *I*," he said, "have sought this stranger's ill;
Not *I* have made this desolation: few   365
    Would bear such outrage, and forbear to kill;
But I must do my duty—how thou hast
Done thine, the present vouches for the past.

47

"Let him disarm; or, by my father's head,
    His own shall roll before you like a ball!"   370
He raised his whistle, as the word he said,
    And blew; another answer'd to the call,
And rushing in disorderly, though led,
    And arm'd from boot to turban, one and all,
Some twenty of his train came, rank on rank;   375
He gave the word,—"Arrest or slay the Frank."[7]

6. Equals.
7. European.

48

Then, with a sudden movement, he withdrew
   His daughter; while compress'd within his clasp,
'Twixt her and Juan interposed the crew;
   In vain she struggled in her father's grasp—   380
His arms were like a serpent's coil: then flew
   Upon their prey, as darts an angry asp,
The file of pirates; save the foremost, who
Had fallen, with his right shoulder half cut through.

49

The second had his cheek laid open; but   385
   The third, a wary, cool old sworder, took
The blows upon his cutlass, and then put
   His own well in; so well, ere you could look,
His man was floor'd, and helpless at his foot,
   With the blood running like a little brook   390
From two smart sabre gashes, deep and red—
One on the arm, the other on the head.

50

And then they bound him where he fell, and bore
   Juan from the apartment: with a sign
Old Lambro bade them take him to the shore,   395
   Where lay some ships which were to sail at nine.
They laid him in a boat, and plied the oar
   Until they reach'd some galliots,[8] placed in line;
On board of one of these, and under hatches,
They stow'd him, with strict orders to the watches.   400

51

The world is full of strange vicissitudes,
   And here was one exceedingly unpleasant:
A gentleman so rich in the world's goods,
   Handsome and young, enjoying all the present,
Just at the very time when he least broods   405
   On such a thing is suddenly to sea sent,
Wounded and chain'd, so that he cannot move,
And all because a lady fell in love.

52

Here I must leave him, for I grow pathetic,
   Moved by the Chinese nymph of tears, green tea!   410
Than whom Cassandra[9] was not more prophetic;
   For if my pure libations exceed three,

8. Small sailing vessels.
9. In Greek myth, a prophetess.

I feel my heart become so sympathetic,
  That I must have recourse to black Bohea:[1]
'Tis pity wine should be so deleterious,   415
For tea and coffee leave us much more serious,

53

Unless when qualified with thee, Cogniac!
  Sweet Naïad[2] of the Phlegethontic rill!
Ah! why the liver wilt thou thus attack,
  And make, like other nymphs, thy lovers ill?   420
I would take refuge in weak punch, but *rack*[3]
  (In each sense of the word), whene'er I fill
My mild and midnight beakers to the brim,
Wakes me next morning with its synonym.

54

I leave Don Juan for the present, safe—   425
  Not sound, poor fellow, but severely wounded;
Yet could his corporal pangs amount to half
  Of those with which his Haidee's bosom bounded?
She was not one to weep, and rave, and chafe,
  And then give way, subdued because surrounded;   430
Her mother was a Moorish maid, from Fez,[4]
Where all is Eden, or a wilderness.

55

There the large olive rains its amber store
  In marble fonts; there grain, and flower, and fruit,
Gush from the earth until the land runs o'er;   435
  But there, too, many a poison-tree has root,
And midnight listens to the lion's roar,
  And long, long deserts scorch the camel's foot,
Or heaving whelm the helpless caravan,
And as the soil is, so the heart of man.   440

56

Afric is all the sun's, and as her earth
  Her human clay is kindled; full of power
For good or evil, burning from its birth,
  The Moorish blood partakes the planet's hour,
And like the soil beneath it will bring forth: 445
  Beauty and love were Haidee's mother's dower;
But her large dark eye show'd deep Passion's force,
Though sleeping like a lion near a source.

1. An inferior grade of black tea.
2. In classical myth, a nymph of rivers and streams; Phlegethon was a river of fire in Hades.
3. Both a distilled liquor ("arrack") and physical torment.
4. City in Morocco. Haidee is shown to have inherited some of her beauty and passion from her mother's North African ("Numidian," line 455) ethnicity.

57

Her daughter, temper'd with a milder ray,
    Like summer clouds all silvery, smooth, and fair,   450
Till slowly charged with thunder they display
    Terror to earth, and tempest to the air,
Had held till now her soft and milky way;
    But overwrought with passion and despair,
The fire burst forth from her Numidian veins,   455
Even as the Simoom[5] sweeps the blasted plains.

58

The last sight which she saw was Juan's gore,
    And he himself o'ermaster'd and cut down;
His blood was running on the very floor
    Where late he trod, her beautiful, her own;   460
Thus much she view'd an instant and no more,—
    Her struggles ceased with one convulsive groan;
On her sire's arm, which until now scarce held
Her writhing, fell she like a cedar fell'd.

59

A vein had burst,[6] and her sweet lips' pure dyes   465
    Were dabbled with the deep blood which ran o'er;
And her head droop'd as when the lily lies
    O'ercharged with rain: her summon'd handmaids bore
Their lady to her couch with gushing eyes;
    Of herbs and cordials they produced their store,   470
But she defied all means they could employ,
Like one life could not hold, nor death destroy.

60

Days lay she in that state unchanged, though chill—
    With nothing livid, still her lips were red;
She had no pulse, but death seem'd absent still;   475
    No hideous sign proclaim'd her surely dead;
Corruption came not in each mind to kill
    All hope; to look upon her sweet face bred
New thoughts of life, for it seem'd full of soul—
She had so much, earth could not claim the whole.   480

---

5. Strong, hot desert wind (compare *The Giaour*, line 282 [p. 130], and *Manfred* 3.1.128 [p. 276]).
6. "This is no very uncommon effect of the violence of conflicting and different passions. The Doge Francis Foscari, on his deposition in 1457, hearing the bells of St. Mark announce the election of his successor, 'mourut subitement d'une hemorragie causée par une veine qui s'éclata dans sa poitrine,' at the age of eighty years, when 'Who would have thought the old man had so much blood in him?' [*Macbeth* 5.1.42–44]. Before I was sixteen years of age, I was witness to a melancholy instance of the same effect of mixed passions upon a young person; who, however, did not die in consequence, at that time, but fell a victim some years afterwards to a seizure of the same kind, arising from causes intimately connected with agitation of the mind." The note refers to Sismondi's *Histoire des Républiques Italiennes* . . . (1815) and Daru's *Histoire de la République de Venise* (1821).

61

The ruling passion, such as marble shows
   When exquisitely chisell'd, still lay there,
But fix'd as marble's unchanged aspect throws
   O'er the fair Venus, but for ever fair;
O'er the Laocoon's[7] all eternal throes,   485
   And ever-dying Gladiator's air,
Their energy like life forms all their fame,
Yet looks not life, for they are still the same.

62

She woke at length, but not as sleepers wake,
   Rather the dead, for life seem'd something new,   490
A strange sensation which she must partake
   Perforce, since whatsoever met her view
Struck not on memory, though a heavy ache
   Lay at her heart, whose earliest beat still true
Brought back the sense of pain without the cause,   495
   For, for a while, the furies[8] made a pause.

63

She look'd on many a face with vacant eye,
   On many a token without knowing what;
She saw them watch her without asking why,
   And reck'd not who around her pillow sat;   500
Not speechless, though she spoke not; not a sigh
   Relieved her thoughts; dull silence and quick chat
Were tried in vain by those who served; she gave
No sign, save breath, of having left the grave.

64

Her handmaids tended, but she heeded not;   505
   Her father watch'd, she turn'd her eyes away;
She recognized no being, and no spot,
   However dear or cherish'd in their day;
They changed from room to room—but all forgot—
   Gentle, but without memory she lay;   510
At length those eyes, which they would fain be weaning
Back to old thoughts, wax'd full of fearful meaning.

7. In Greek legend and as told in Book Two of Virgil's *Aeneid*, the Trojan priest Laocoön, uttering the famous line, "Beware of Greeks even when they bear gifts," expressed suspicion of the Greeks' giant wooden horse; to punish Laocoön and as a sign to the Trojans to ignore his warning and take the deceptive gift into their city, Poseidon sent two serpents out of the sea to strangle Laocoön and his two sons in their huge coils. This scene is represented in a magnificent statue (circa first-century B.C.E. or C.E.) in the Vatican. The *Dying Gladiator* (line 486) is another famous statue in Rome.
8. In Greek myth, female vengeful spirits.

65

And then a slave bethought her of a harp;
    The harper came, and tuned his instrument;
At the first notes, irregular and sharp,   515
    On him her flashing eyes a moment bent,
Then to the wall she turn'd as if to warp
    Her thoughts from sorrow through her heart re-sent;
And he begun a long low island song
Of ancient days, ere tyranny grew strong.   520

66

Anon her thin wan fingers beat the wall
    In time to his old tune; he changed the theme,
And sung of love; the fierce name struck through all
    Her recollection; on her flash'd the dream
Of what she was, and is, if ye could call   525
    To be so being; in a gushing stream
The tears rush'd forth from her o'erclouded brain,
Like mountain mists at length dissolved in rain.

67

Short solace, vain relief!—thought came too quick,
    And whirl'd her brain to madness; she arose   530
As one who ne'er had dwelt among the sick,
    And flew at all she met, as on her foes;
But no one ever heard her speak or shriek,
    Although her paroxysm drew towards its close;—
Hers was a phrensy which disdain'd to rave,   535
Even when they smote her, in the hope to save.

68

Yet she betray'd at times a gleam of sense;
    Nothing could make her meet her father's face,
Though on all other things with looks intense
    She gazed, but none she ever could retrace;   540
Food she refused, and raiment; no pretence
    Avail'd for either; neither change of place,
Nor time, nor skill, nor remedy, could give her
Senses to sleep—the power seem'd gone for ever.

69

Twelve days and nights she wither'd thus; at last,   545
    Without a groan, or sigh, or glance, to show
A parting pang, the spirit from her past:
    And they who watch'd her nearest could not know
The very instant, till the change that cast
    Her sweet face into shadow, dull and slow,   550

Glazed o'er her eyes—the beautiful, the black—
Oh! to possess such lustre—and then lack!

70

She died, but not alone; she held within
   A second principle of life, which might
Have dawn'd a fair and sinless child of sin;   555
   But closed its little being without light,
And went down to the grave unborn, wherein
   Blossom and bough lie wither'd with one blight;
In vain the dews of Heaven descend above
The bleeding flower and blasted fruit of love.   560

71

Thus lived—thus died she; never more on her
   Shall sorrow light, or shame. She was not made
Through years or moons the inner weight to bear,
   Which colder hearts endure till they are laid
By age in earth: her days and pleasures were   565
   Brief, but delightful—such as had not staid
Long with her destiny; but she sleeps well
By the sea-shore, whereon she loved to dwell.

72

That isle is now all desolate and bare,
   Its dwellings down, its tenants pass'd away;
None but her own and father's grave is there,   570
   And nothing outward tells of human clay;
Ye could not know where lies a thing so fair,
   No stone is there to show, no tongue to say
What was; no dirge, except the hollow sea's,   575
Mourns o'er the beauty of the Cyclades.[9]

73

But many a Greek maid in a loving song
   Sighs o'er her name; and many an islander
With her sire's story makes the night less long;
   Valour was his, and beauty dwelt with her: 580
If she loved rashly, her life paid for wrong—
   A heavy price must all pay who thus err,
In some shape; let none think to fly the danger,
For soon or late Love is his own avenger.

*   *   *

---

9. A group of Greek islands.

[In Canto IV, Lambro had Juan bound and sent to Turkey to be sold into slavery.]

CANTO THE FIFTH[1]

1

When amatory poets sing their loves
    In liquid lines mellifluously bland,
And pair their rhymes as Venus yokes her doves,
    They little think what mischief is in hand;
The greater their success the worse it proves,   5
    As Ovid's verse may give to understand;
Even Petrarch's[2] self, if judged with due severity,
Is the Platonic pimp of all posterity.[3]

2

I therefore do denounce all amorous writing,
    Except in such a way as not to attract;   10
Plain—simple—short, and by no means inviting,
    But with a moral to each error tack'd,
Form'd rather for instructing than delighting,
    And with all passions in their turn attack'd;
Now, if my Pegasus[4] should not be shod ill,   15
This poem will become a moral model.

3

The European with the Asian shore
    Sprinkled with palaces; the ocean stream[5]
Here and there studded with a seventy-four;[6]
    Sophia's cupola[7] with golden gleam;   20
The cypress groves; Olympus[8] high and hoar;
    The twelve isles,[9] and the more than I could dream,
Far less describe, present the very view
Which charm'd the charming Mary Montagu.[1]

1. Composed October and November 1820 and published with Cantos III and IV on August 8, 1821.
2. Ovid . . . Petrarch: poets of passionate love referred to frequently in Don Juan; see, for example, Canto I, stanza 42, and Canto III, stanza 8.
3. The idea of this stanza is that amatory poetry has an erotic and therefore immoral effect on its readers (compare Canto III, stanza 96), and therefore the better it is as poetry "the worse it proves." The reference to Plato is a continuation of the poem's attack on the self-deception and sentimentality of Romantic idealism (compare Canto I, stanza 116). However, the tone is facetious, and the first two lines of the next stanza are a retort to the critics who charged Don Juan with immorality and tending to corrupt its readers.
4. In classical myth, winged horse associated with poetic inspiration.
5. This expression of Homer has been much criticised. It hardly answers to our Atlantic ideas of the ocean, but is sufficiently applicable to the Hellespont, and the Bosphorus, with the Aegean intersected with islands."
6. A warship.
7. Santa (or Hagia) Sophia, the splendid Byzantine church of Constantinople (present Istanbul), later used as a mosque by the Turks.
8. Mt. Olympus, dwelling of the Greek gods.
9. Probably the Princes' Islands (of which there are nine).
1. Lady Mary Wortley Montagu (1689–1762), whose Turkish Letters were written in 1716, when she lived in Constantinople as the wife of the Turkish ambassador.

4

I have a passion for the name of "Mary,"[2]   25
    For once it was a magic sound to me;
And still it half calls up the realms of fairy,
    Where I beheld what never was to be;
All feelings changed, but this was last to vary,
    A spell from which even yet I am not quite free: 30
But I grow sad—and let a tale grow cold,
Which must not be pathetically told.

5

The wind swept down the Euxine,[3] and the wave
    Broke foaming o'er the blue Symplegades;
'Tis a grand sight from off "the Giant's Grave"[4]   35
    To watch the progress of those rolling seas
Between the Bosphorus, as they lash and lave
    Europe and Asia, you being quite at ease;
There's not a sea the passenger e'er pukes in,
Turns up more dangerous breakers than the Euxine.   40

6

'Twas a raw day of Autumn's bleak beginning,
    When nights are equal, but not so the days;
The Parcae[5] then cut short the further spinning
    Of seamen's fates, and the loud tempests raise
The waters, and repentance for past sinning   45
    In all, who o'er the great deep take their ways:
They vow to amend their lives, and yet they don't;
Because if drown'd, they can't—if spared, they won't.

7

A crowd of shivering slaves of every nation,
    And age, and sex, were in the market ranged;   50
Each bevy with the merchant in his station:
    Poor creatures! their good looks were sadly changed;
All save the blacks seem'd jaded with vexation,
    From friends, and home, and freedom far estranged;
The negroes more philosophy display'd,—   55
Used to it, no doubt, as eels are to be flay'd.

---

2. At the age of seven, Byron became infatuated with a distant cousin, Mary Duff; his youthful love for Mary Chaworth was to remain, in his memory, one of the most passionate experiences of his life. See his letter to Francis Hodgson, November 3, 1808 (*BLJ* 1:173–74).
3. The Black Sea. The Symplegades ("Wandering Rocks," line 34) of classical legend, are a formation in the Bosporus Strait, which connects the Black Sea and the Sea of Marmara.
4. "The 'Giant's Grave' is a height on the Asiatic shore of the Bosphorus, much frequented by holiday parties: like Harrow and Highgate."
5. The three Fates of ancient Rome.

8

Juan was juvenile, and thus was full,
  As most at his age are, of hope, and health;
Yet I must own, he look'd a little dull,
  And now and then a tear stole down by stealth;   60
Perhaps his recent loss of blood might pull
  His spirit down; and then the loss of wealth,
A mistress, and such comfortable quarters,
To be put up for auction amongst Tartars,[6]

9

Were things to shake a stoic; ne'ertheless,   65
  Upon the whole his carriage was serene:
His figure, and the splendour of his dress,
  Of which some gilded remnants still were seen,
Drew all eyes on him, giving them to guess
  He was above the vulgar by his mien;   70
And then, though pale, he was so very handsome;
And then—they calculated on his ransom.

10

Like a backgammon board the place was dotted
  With whites and blacks, in groups on show for sale,
Though rather more irregularly spotted: 75
  Some bought the jet, while others chose the pale.
It chanced amongst the other people lotted,
  A man of thirty,[7] rather stout and hale,
With resolution in his dark grey eye,
Next Juan stood, till some might choose to buy.   80

11

He had an English look; that is, was square
  In make, of a complexion white and ruddy,
Good teeth, with curling rather dark brown hair,
  And, it might be from thought, or toil, or study,
An open brow a little mark'd with care: 85
  One arm had on a bandage rather bloody;
And there he stood with such *sang-froid*[8] that greater
Could scarce be shown even by a mere spectator.

12

But seeing at his elbow a mere lad,
  Of a high spirit evidently, though   90

6. Descendants of the Mongolian and Turkish tribes that overran Asia and eastern Europe in the Middle Ages.
7. His name, Johnson, is first given in Canto VII, line 473.
8. Cool composure (literally, cold blood [French]).

At present weigh'd down by a doom which had
    O'erthrown even men, he soon began to show
A kind of blunt compassion for the sad
    Lot of so young a partner in the woe,
Which for himself he seem'd to deem no worse   95
Than any other scrape, a thing of course.

13

"My boy!"—said he, "amidst this motley crew
    Of Georgians, Russians, Nubians,[9] and what not,
All ragamuffins differing but in hue,
    With whom it is our luck to cast our lot,   100
The only gentlemen seem I and you;
    So let us be acquainted, as we ought:
If I could yield you any consolation,
'Twould give me pleasure.—Pray, what is your nation?

14

When Juan answer'd "Spanish!" he replied,   105
    "I thought, in fact, you could not be a Greek;
Those servile dogs are not so proudly eyed:
    Fortune has play'd you here a pretty freak,
But that's her way with all men, till they're tried;
    But never mind,—she'll turn, perhaps, next week;   110
She has served me also much the same as you,
Except that I have found it nothing new."

15

"Pray, sir," said Juan, "if I may presume,
    What brought you here?"—"Oh! nothing very rare—
Six Tartars and a drag-chain——"—"To this doom   115
    But what conducted, if the question's fair,
Is that which I would learn."—"I served for some
    Months with the Russian army here and there,
And taking lately, by Suwarrow's[1] bidding,
A town, was ta'en myself instead of Widdin."   120

16

"Have you no friends?"—"I had—but, by God's blessing,
    Have not been troubled with them lately. Now
I have answer'd all your questions without pressing,
    And you an equal courtesy should show."
"Alas!" said Juan, "'twere a tale distressing,   125
    And long besides."—"Oh! if 'tis really so,

---

9. Georgia was a nation of Caucasia on the edge of the Black Sea. Nubia was a region in North Africa
   (present-day Sudan).
1. Russian Field Marshall Suvarov (1729–1800) led the campaign against the Turks at Ismail on
   December 22, 1790 (the subject of *Don Juan* VII–VIII) and in 1799 fought against the French
   army in Italy.

You're right on both accounts to hold your tongue;
A sad tale saddens doubly, when 'tis long.

17

"But droop not: Fortune at your time of life,
  Although a female moderately fickle,   130
Will hardly leave you (as she's not your wife)
  For any length of days in such a pickle.
To strive, too, with our fate were such a strife
  As if the corn-sheaf should oppose the sickle:[2]
Men are the sport of circumstances, when   135
  The circumstances seem the sport of men."

18

" 'Tis not," said Juan, "for my present doom
  I mourn, but for the past;—I loved a maid:"—
He paused, and his dark eye grew full of gloom;
  A single tear upon his eyelash staid   140
A moment, and then dropp'd; "but to resume,
  'Tis not my present lot, as I have said,
Which I deplore so much; for I have borne
Hardships which have the hardiest overworn,

19

"On the rough deep. But this last blow—" and here   145
  He stopp'd again, and turn'd away his face.
"Ay," quoth his friend, "I thought it would appear
  That there had been a lady in the case;
And these are things which ask a tender tear,
  Such as I, too, would shed if in your place: 150
I cried upon my first wife's dying day,
And also when my second ran away:

20

"My third——"—"Your third!" quoth Juan, turning round;
  "You scarcely can be thirty: have you three?"
"No—only two at present above ground: 155
  Surely 'tis nothing wonderful to see
One person thrice in holy wedlock bound!"
  "Well, then, your third," said Juan; "what did she?
She did not run away, too,—did she, sir?"
"No, faith."—"What then?"—"I ran away from her."   160

21

"You take things coolly, sir," said Juan. "Why,"
  Replied the other, "what can a man do?

2. Deuteronomy 10.9 and Mark 4.26.

There still are many rainbows in your sky,
　　But mine have vanish'd. All, when life is new,
Commence with feelings warm, and prospects high   165
　　But time strips our illusions of their hue,
And one by one in turn, some grand mistake
Casts off its bright skin yearly like the snake.

22

" 'Tis true, it gets another bright and fresh,
　　Or fresher, brighter; but the year gone through,   170
This skin must go the way, too, of all flesh,
　　Or sometimes only wear a week or two;—
Love's the first net which spreads its deadly mesh;
　　Ambition, Avarice, Vengeance, Glory, glue
The glittering lime-twigs[3] of our latter days,   175
Where still we flutter on for pence or praise."

23

"All this is very fine, and may be true,"
　　Said Juan; "but I really don't see how
It betters present times with me or you."
　　"No?" quoth the other; "yet you will allow   180
By setting things in their right point of view,
　　Knowledge, at least, is gain'd; for instance, now,
We know what slavery is, and our disasters
May teach us better to behave when masters."

24

"Would we were masters now, if but to try   185
　　Their present lessons on our Pagan friends here,"
Said Juan—swallowing a heart-burning sigh:
　　"Heaven help the scholar whom his fortune sends here!"
"Perhaps we shall be one day, by and by,"
　　Rejoin'd the other, "when our bad luck mends   190
Meantime (yon old black eunuch seems to eye us)
I wish to G—d that somebody would buy us!

25

"But after all, what *is* our present state?
　　'Tis bad, and may be better—all men's lot:
Most men are slaves, none more so than the great,   195
　　To their own whims and passions, and what not;
Society itself, which should create
　　Kindness, destroys what little we had got:
To feel for none is the true social art
Of the world's stoics—men without a heart."   200

---

3. To catch birds, branches or twigs were smeared with birdlime, a sticky substance prepared from
holly or mistletoe; hence, a "lime-twig" is a snare or trap.

26

Just now a black old neutral personage
  Of the third sex[4] stept up, and peering over
The captives seem'd to mark their looks and age,
  And capabilities, as to discover
If they were fitted for the purposed cage: 205
  No lady e'er is ogled by a lover,
Horse by a blackleg,[5] broadcloth by a tailor,
Fee by a counsel, felon by a jailor,

27

As is a slave by his intended bidder.
  'Tis pleasant purchasing our fellow-creatures;   210
And all are to be sold, if you consider
  Their passions, and are dext'rous; some by features
Are bought up, others by a warlike leader,
  Some by a place—as tend their years or natures;
The most by ready cash—but all have prices,   215
From crowns to kicks,[6] according to their vices.

28

The eunuch having eyed them o'er with care,
  Turn'd to the merchant, and begun to bid
First but for one, and after for the pair;
  They haggled, wrangled, swore, too—so they did!   220
As though they were in a mere Christian fair
  Cheapening an ox, an ass, a lamb, or kid;
So that their bargain sounded like a battle
For this superior yoke of human cattle.

29

At last they settled into simple grumbling,   225
  And pulling out reluctant purses, and
Turning each piece of silver o'er, and tumbling
  Some down, and weighing others in their hand,
And by mistake sequins with paras[7] jumbling,
  Until the sum was accurately scann'd,   230
And then the merchant giving change, and signing
Receipts in full, began to think of dining.

30

I wonder if his appetite was good?
  Or, if it were, if also his digestion?

4. *neutral . . . sex*: eunuch.
5. Horserace swindler.
6. *crowns . . . kicks*: both are puns—"crowns" meaning royal headgear or five-shilling coins, kicks
   being either a blow with the foot or sixpences.
7. Turkish coins.

Methinks at meals some odd thoughts might intrude,   235
    And conscience ask a curious sort of question,
About the right divine how far we should
    Sell flesh and blood. When dinner has opprest one,
I think it is perhaps the gloomiest hour
Which turns up out of the sad twenty-four.   240

31

Voltaire[8] says "No:" he tells you that Candide
    Found life most tolerable after meals;
He's wrong—unless man were a pig, indeed,
    Repletion rather adds to what he feels,
Unless he's drunk, and then no doubt he's freed   245
    From his own brain's oppression while it reels.
Of food I think with Philip's son,[9] or rather
Ammon's (ill pleased with one world and one father);

32

I think with Alexander, that the act
    Of eating, with another act or two,   250
Makes us feel our mortality in fact
    Redoubled; when a roast and a ragout,
And fish, and soup, by some side dishes back'd,
    Can give us either pain or pleasure, who
Would pique himself on intellects, whose use   255
Depends so much upon the gastric juice?

33

The other evening ('twas on Friday last)—
    This is a fact, and no poetic fable—
Just as my great coat was about me cast,
    My hat and gloves still lying on the table,   260
I heard a shot—'twas eight o'clock scarce past—
    And, running out as fast as I was able,[1]
I found the military commandant
Stretch'd in the street, and able scarce to pant.

34

Poor fellow! for some reason, surely bad,   265
    They had slain him with five slugs; and left him there
To perish on the pavement: so I had

---

8. François Marie Arouet (Voltaire) (1644–1778), brilliant satirist of the French Enlightenment. His
Candide (1759) is a bitter attack upon philosophical optimism; the book's hero, the innocent, trust-
ing Candide, is one of the literary ancestors of Byron's Juan.
9. Alexander the Great (356–323 B.C.E.), the conqueror of the ancient world, was the son of Philip
of Macedon. In the course of his conquests, Alexander claimed (for political reasons) descent from
Ammon (or Amen), the high god of Egypt. Stanza 32 refers to Alexander's reputed view of the
depressive aftereffect of eating, sleeping, and sex.
1. "The assassination alluded to took place on the 8th of December, 1820, in the streets of Ravenna,
not a hundred paces from the residence of the writer. The circumstances were as described."

Him borne into the house and up the stair,
And stripp'd, and look'd to,——But why should I add
      More circumstances? vain was every care;   270
The man was gone: in some Italian quarrel
Kill'd by five bullets from an old gun-barrel.[2]

35

I gazed upon him, for I knew him well;
      And though I have seen many corpses, never
Saw one, whom such an accident befell,   275
      So calm; though pierced through stomach, heart, and liver,
He seem'd to sleep,—for you could scarcely tell
      (As he bled inwardly, no hideous river
Of gore divulged the cause) that he was dead:
So as I gazed on him, I thought or said—   280

36

"Can this be death? then what is life or death?
      Speak!" but he spoke not: "wake!" but still he slept:—
"But yesterday and who had mightier breath?
      A thousand warriors by his word were kept
In awe: he said, as the centurion saith,   285
      'Go,' and he goeth; 'come,' and forth he stepp'd.[3]
The trump and bugle till he spake were dumb—
And now nought left him but the muffled drum."

37

And they who waited once and worshipp'd—they
      With their rough faces throng'd about the bed   290
To gaze once more on the commanding clay
      Which for the last, though not the first, time bled:
And such an end! that he who many a day
      Had faced Napoleon's foes until they fled,—
The foremost in the charge or in the sally,   295
Should now be butcher'd in a civic alley.

38

The scars of his old wounds were near his new,
      Those honourable scars which brought him fame;
And horrid was the contrast to the view——
      But let me quit the theme; as such things claim   300
Perhaps even more attention than is due
      From me: I gazed (as oft I have gazed the same)
To try if I could wrench aught out of death
Which should confirm, or shake, or make a faith;

2. "There was found close by him an old gun barrel, sawn half off: it had just been discharged and
   was still warm."
3. Matthew 8.9.

39

But it was all a mystery. Here we are,   305
    And there we go:—but *where?* five bits of lead,
Or three, or two, or one, send very far!
    And is this blood, then, form'd but to be shed?
Can every element our elements mar?
    And air—earth—water—fire live—and we dead?   310
We, whose minds comprehend all things? No more;
But let us to the story as before.

40

The purchaser of Juan and acquaintance
    Bore off his bargains to a gilded boat,
Embark'd himself and them, and off they went thence   315
    As fast as oars could pull and water float;
They look'd like persons being led to sentence,
    Wondering what next, till the caïque[4] was brought.
Up in a little creek below a wall
O'ertopp'd with cypresses, dark-green and tall.   320

41

Here their conductor tapping at the wicket[5]
    Of a small iron door, 'twas open'd, and
He led them onward, first through a low thicket
    Flank'd by large groves, which tower'd on either hand:
They almost lost their way, and had to pick it—   325
    For night was closing ere they came to land.
The eunuch made a sign to those on board,
Who row'd off, leaving them without a word.

42

As they were plodding on their winding way
    Through orange bowers, and jasmine, and so forth   330
(Of which I might have a good deal to say,
    There being no such profusion in the North
Of oriental plants, "et cetera,"
    But that of late your scribblers think it worth
Their while to rear whole hotbeds in *their* works   335
Because one poet[6] travell'd 'mongst the Turks)—

43

As they were threading on their way, there came
    Into Don Juan's head a thought, which he
Whisper'd to his companion:—'twas the same

---

4. "The light and elegant wherries [boats] plying about the quays of Constantinople are so called"
(note by Byron or Moore).
5. Window part of a door.
6. Byron himself.

Which might have then occurr'd to you or me.   340
"Methinks,"—said he,—"it would be no great shame
    If we should strike a stroke to set us free;
Let's knock that old black fellow on the head,
    And march away—'twere easier done than said."

44

"Yes," said the other, "and when done, what then?   345
    How get out? how the devil got we in?
And when we once were fairly out, and when
    From Saint Bartholomew[7] we have saved our skin,
To-morrow'd see us in some other den,
    And worse off than we hitherto have been;   350
Besides, I'm hungry, and just now would take,
Like Esau, for my birthright a beef-steak.[8]

45

"We must be near some place of man's abode;—
    For the old negro's confidence in creeping,
With his two captives, by so queer a road,   355
    Shows that he thinks his friends have not been sleeping;
A single cry would bring them all abroad:
    'Tis therefore better looking before leaping—
And there, you see, this turn has brought us through,
By Jove, a noble palace!—lighted too."   360

46

It was indeed a wide extensive building
    Which open'd on their view, and o'er the front
There seem'd to be besprent[9] a deal of gilding
    And various hues, as is the Turkish wont,—
A gaudy taste; for they are little skill'd in   365
    The arts of which these lands were once the font:[1]
Each villa on the Bosphorus looks a screen
New painted, or a pretty opera-scene.

47

And nearer as they came, a genial savour
    Of certain stews, and roast-meats, and pilaus,[2]   370
Things which in hungry mortals' eyes find favour,
    Made Juan in his harsh intentions pause,
And put himself upon his good behaviour:

---

7. This early saint was said to have been flayed alive.
8. Esau sold his birthright to his brother, Jacob, for "bread and pottage of lentiles" (Genesis 25.29–34).
9. Bestrewn (archaic).
1. The architecture of Greece and Byzantium.
2. Dishes consisting primarily of rice.

His friend, too, adding a new saving clause,
Said, "In Heaven's name let's get some supper now,   375
And then I'm with you, if you're for a row."

48

Some talk of an appeal unto some passion,
    Some to men's feelings, others to their reason;
The last of these was never much the fashion,
    For reason thinks all reasoning out of season.   380
Some speakers whine, and others lay the lash on,
    But more or less continue still to tease on,
With arguments according to their "forte;"
But no one ever dreams of being short.—

49

But I digress: of all appeals,—although   385
    I grant the power of pathos, and of gold,
Of beauty, flattery, threats, a shilling,—no
    Method's more sure at moments to take hold
Of the best feelings of mankind, which grow
    More tender, as we every day behold,   390
Than that all-softening, overpowering knell,
The tocsin[3] of the soul—the dinner-bell.

50

Turkey contains no bells, and yet men dine;
    And Juan and his friend, albeit they heard
No Christian knoll to table, saw no line   395
    Of lackeys usher to the feast prepared,
Yet smelt roast-meat, beheld a huge fire shine,
    And cooks in motion with their clean arms bared,
And gazed around them to the left and right
With the prophetic eye of appetite.   400

51

And giving up all notions of resistance,
    They follow'd close behind their sable guide,
Who little thought that his own crack'd existence
    Was on the point of being set aside:
He motion'd them to stop at some small distance,   405
    And knocking at the gate, 'twas open'd wide,
And a magnificent large hall display'd
The Asian pomp of Ottoman[4] parade.

---

3. Bell used to send a signal or sound an alarm.
4. Turkish.

52

I won't describe; description is my forte,
　　But every fool describes in these bright days　　410
His wondrous journey to some foreign court,
　　And spawns his quarto, and demands your praise—
Death to his publisher, to him 'tis sport;
　　While Nature, tortured twenty thousand ways,
Resigns herself with exemplary patience　　415
To guide-books, rhymes, tours, sketches, illustrations.

53

Along this hall, and up and down, some, squatted
　　Upon their hams, were occupied at chess;
Others in monosyllable talk chatted,
　　And some seem'd much in love with their own dress.　　420
And divers smoked superb pipes decorated
　　With amber mouths of greater price or less;
And several strutted, others slept, and some
Prepared for supper with a glass of rum.[5]

54

As the black eunuch enter'd with his brace　　425
　　Of purchased Infidels, some raised their eyes
A moment without slackening from their pace;
　　But those who sate, ne'er stirr'd in any wise:
One or two stared the captives in the face,
　　Just as one views a horse to guess his price;　　430
Some nodded to the negro from their station,
But no one troubled him with conversation.

55

He leads them through the hall, and, without stopping,
　　On through a farther range of goodly rooms,
Splendid but silent, save in *one*, where, dropping,[6]　　435
　　A marble fountain echoes through the glooms
Of night, which robe the chamber, or where popping
　　Some female head most curiously presumes
To thrust its black eyes through the door or lattice,
As wondering what the devil noise that is.　　440

5. "In Turkey nothing is more common than for the Mussulmans to take several glasses of strong spir-
　　its by way of appetizer. I have seen them take as many as six of raki before dinner, and swear that
　　they dined the better or it: I tried the experiment, but fared like the Scotchman, who having heard
　　that the birds called kittiwakes were admirable whets, ate six of them, and complained that 'he was
　　no hungrier than when he began.'"
6. "A common furniture. I recollect being received by Ali Pacha, in a large room, paved with marble,
　　containing a marble basin, and fountain playing in the centre, &c, &c." Compare *Childe Harold*
　　II.62.

56

Some faint lamps gleaming from the lofty walls
   Gave light enough to hint their farther way,
But not enough to show the imperial halls
   In all the flashing of their full array;
Perhaps there's nothing—I'll not say appals,   445
   But saddens more by night as well as day,
Than an enormous room without a soul
To break the lifeless splendour of the whole.

57

Two or three seem so little, *one* seems nothing:
   In deserts, forests, crowds, or by the shore,   450
There solitude, we know, has her full growth in
   The spots which were her realms for evermore;
But in a mighty hall or gallery, both in
   More modern buildings and those built of yore,
A kind of death comes o'er us all alone,   455
Seeing what's meant for many with but one.

58

A neat, snug study on a winter's night,
   A book, friend, single lady, or a glass
Of claret, sandwich, and an appetite,
   Are things which make an English evening pass;   460
Though *certes*[7] by no means so grand a sight
   As is a theatre lit up by gas.
I pass my evenings in long galleries solely,
And that's the reason I'm so melancholy.

59

Alas! man makes that great which makes him little: 465
   I grant you in a church 'tis very well:
What speaks of Heaven should by no means be brittle,
   But strong and lasting, till no tongue can tell
Their names who rear'd it; but huge houses fit ill—
   And huge tombs worse—mankind, since Adam fell: 470
Methinks the story of the tower of Babel[8]
Might teach them this much better than I'm able.

7. Certainly (archaic).
8. Genesis 11.1–9.

60[9]

Babel was Nimrod's hunting-box, and then
    A town of gardens, walls, and wealth amazing,
Where Nabuchadonosor, king of men,   475
    Reign'd, till one summer's day he took to grazing,
And Daniel tamed the lions in their den,
    The people's awe and admiration raising;
'Twas famous, too, for Thisbe and for Pyramus,
And the calumniated queen Semiramis.—   480

61[1]

That injured Queen, by chroniclers so coarse
    Has been accused (I doubt not by conspiracy)
Of an improper friendship for her horse
    (Love, like religion, sometimes runs to heresy):
This monstrous tale had probably its source   485
    (For such exaggerations here and there I see)
In printing "Courser" by mistake for "Courier":
I wish the case could come before a jury here.

62

But to resume,—should there be (what may not
    Be in these days?) some infidels, who don't,   490
Because they can't find out the very spot
    Of that same Babel, or because they won't
(Though Claudius Rich, Esquire,[2] some bricks has got,
    And written lately two memoirs upon 't),
Believe the Jews, those unbelievers, who   495
Must be believed, though they believe not you.

63

Yet let them think that Horace has exprest
    Shortly and sweetly the masonic folly
Of those, forgetting the great place of rest,
    Who give themselves to architecture wholly;   500
We know where things and men must end at best:

9. Stanza 60 cites legendary figures associated with Babylon. Nimrod, king and hunter, attempted to
   build the Tower of Babel, Byron jests, as a "hunting-box," or platform from which to shoot at game.
   Nebuchadnezzar, king of Babylon (sixth-century B.C.E.) and conqueror of Jerusalem, punished the
   prophet Daniel for refusing to abjure the God of Israel (Daniel 6.21–22); for this impiety Neb-
   uchadnezzar was driven mad and forced to eat grass like the beasts of the field (Daniel 4.1–37).
   Thisbe and Pyramus were legendary star-crossed lovers. Queen Semiramis was the legendary
   founder of Babylon.
1. After the first printing of Canto V, Byron marked this stanza for deletion, undoubtedly due to the
   impropriety of its humor and its indirect but unmistakable glance at Queen Caroline, the scandal-
   prone wife of George IV, who in 1820 was brought to public trial for adultery with her chamber-
   lain, formerly a courier. In a note to line 481 by Moore (attributed to Byron in 1832): "Babylon
   was enlarged by Nimrod, strengthened and beautified by Nabuchadonosor, and rebuilt by Semi-
   ramis."
2. Claudius James Rich, Esq. published two volumes (1815, 1818) attempting to establish the loca-
   tion of the ruins of Babylon.

A moral (like all morals) melancholy,
And "Et sepulchri immemor struis domos"[3]
Shows that we build when we should but entomb us.

64

At last they reach'd a quarter most retired,   505
    Where echo woke as if from a long slumber;
Though full of all things which could be desired,
    One wonder'd what to do with such a number
Of articles which nobody required;
    Here wealth had done its utmost to encumber   510
With furniture an exquisite apartment,
Which puzzled Nature much to know what Art meant.

65

It seem'd, however, but to open on
    A range or suite of further chambers, which
Might lead to heaven knows where; but in this one   515
    The moveables were prodigally rich:
Sofas 'twas half a sin to sit upon,
    So costly were they; carpets every stitch
Of workmanship so rare, they made you wish
You could glide o'er them like a golden fish.   520

66

The black, however, without hardly deigning
    A glance at that which wrapt the slaves in wonder,
Trampled what they scarce trod for fear of staining,
    As if the milky way their feet was under
With all its stars; and with a stretch attaining   525
    A certain press or cupboard niched in yonder—
In that remote recess which you may see—
Or if you don't the fault is not in me,—

67

I wish to be perspicuous; and the black,
    I say, unlocking the recess, pull'd forth   530
A quantity of clothes fit for the back
    Of any Mussulman,[4] whate'er his worth;
And of variety there was no lack—
    And yet, though I have said there was no dearth,—
He chose himself to point out what he thought   535
Most proper for the Christians he had bought.

3. While we yet live we should not worry about our funeral monuments (Horace, *Carmina*
    2.18.18–19).
4. Muslim.

68

The suit he thought most suitable to each
  Was, for the elder and the stouter, first
A Candiote[5] cloak, which to the knee might reach,
  And trousers not so tight that they would burst,   540
But such as fit an Asiatic breech;
  A shawl, whose folds in Cashmire[6] had been nurst,
Slippers of saffron, dagger rich and handy;
In short, all things which form a Turkish Dandy.

69

While he was dressing, Baba, their black friend,   545
  Hinted the vast advantages which they
Might probably obtain both in the end,
  If they would but pursue the proper way
Which Fortune plainly seem'd to recommend;
  And then he added, that he needs must say,   550
" 'Twould greatly tend to better their condition,
If they would condescend to circumcision.[7]

70

"For his own part, he really should rejoice
  To see them true believers, but no less
Would leave his proposition to their choice."   555
  The other, thanking him for this excess
Of goodness, in thus leaving them a voice
  In such a trifle, scarcely could express
"Sufficiently" (he said) "his approbation
Of all the customs of this polish'd nation.   560

71

"For his own share—he saw but small objection
  To so respectable an ancient rite;
And, after swallowing down a slight refection,
  For which he own'd a present appetite,
He doubted not a few hours of reflection   565
  Would reconcile him to the business quite."
"Will it?" said Juan, sharply: "Strike me dead,
But they as soon shall circumcise my head!

72

"Cut off a thousand heads, before——"—"Now, pray,"
  Replied the other, "do not interrupt: 570
You put me out in what I had to say.

5. Cretan; native to the Mediterranean island of Crete (Candia), southeast of Greece.
6. A state in southeast Asia, known for the especially soft fleece of its goats.
7. A ritual practiced by Muslims.

Sir!—as I said, as soon as I have supt,
I shall perpend if your proposal may
   Be such as I can properly accept;
Provided always your great goodness still   575
Remits the matter to our own free-will."

73

Baba eyed Juan, and said, "Be so good
   As dress yourself—" and pointed out a suit
In which a Princess with great pleasure would
   Array her limbs; but Juan standing mute,   580
As not being in a masquerading mood,
   Gave it a slight kick with his Christian foot;
And when the old negro told him to "Get ready,"
Replied, "Old gentleman, I'm not a lady."

74

"What you may be, I neither know nor care,"   585
   Said Baba; "but pray do as I desire:
I have no more time nor many words to spare."
   "At least," said Juan, "sure I may enquire
The cause of this odd travesty?"—"Forbear,"
   Said Baba, "to be curious; 'twill transpire,   590
No doubt, in proper place, and time, and season:
I have no authority to tell the reason."

75

"Then if I do," said Juan, "I'll be——"—"Hold!"
   Rejoin'd the negro, "pray be not provoking;
This spirit's well, but it may wax too bold,
   And you will find us not too fond of joking."   595
"What, sir!" said Juan, "shall it e'er be told
   That I unsex'd my dress?" But Baba, stroking
The things down, said, "Incense me, and I call
Those who will leave you of no sex at all.   600

76

"I offer you a handsome suit of clothes:
   A woman's, true; but then there is a cause
Why you should wear them."—"What, though my soul loathes
   The effeminate garb?"—thus, after a short pause,
Sigh'd Juan, muttering also some slight oaths,   605
   "What the devil shall I do with all this gauze?
Thus he profanely term'd the finest lace
Which e'er set off a marriage-morning face.

77

And then he swore; and, sighing, on he slipp'd
    A pair of trousers of flesh-colour'd silk;   610
Next with a virgin zone[8] he was equipp'd,
    Which girt a slight chemise as white as milk;
But tugging on his petticoat, he tripp'd,
    Which—as we say—or, as the Scotch say, *whilk*,
(The rhyme obliges me to this; sometimes   615
Monarchs are less imperative than rhymes)—

78

Whilk, which (or what you please), was owing to
    His garment's novelty, and his being awkward:
And yet at last he managed to get through
    His toilet,[9] though no doubt a little backward: 620
The negro Baba help'd a little too,
    When some untoward part of raiment stuck hard;
And, wrestling both his arms into a gown,
He paused, and took a survey up and down.

79

One difficulty still remain'd—his hair   625
    Was hardly long enough; but Baba found
So many false long tresses all to spare,
    That soon his head was most completely crown'd,
After the manner then in fashion there;
    And this addition with such gems was bound   630
As suited the *ensemble* of his toilet,
While Baba made him comb his head and oil it.

80

And now being femininely all array'd,
    With some small aid from scissors, paint, and tweezers,
He look'd in almost all respects a maid,   635
    And Baba smilingly exclaim'd, "You see, sirs,
A perfect transformation here display'd;
    And now, then, you must come along with me, sirs,
That is—the Lady:" clapping his hands twice,
Four blacks were at his elbow in a trice.   640

81

"You, sir," said Baba, nodding to the one,
    "Will please to accompany those gentlemen
To supper; but you, worthy Christian nun,
    Will follow me: no trifling, sir; for when

8. Belt.
9. The process of getting dressed or one's attire (as in line 631).

I say a thing, it must at once be done.   645
    What fear you? think you this a lion's den?
Why, 'tis a palace; where the truly wise
Anticipate the Prophet's paradise.[1]

82

"You fool! I tell you no one means you harm."
    "So much the better," Juan said, "for them;   650
Else they shall feel the weight of this my arm,
    Which is not quite so light as you may deem.
I yield thus far; but soon will break the charm
    If any take me for that which I seem:
So that I trust for every body's sake,   655
That this disguise may lead to no mistake."

83

"Blockhead! come on, and see," quoth Baba; while
    Don Juan, turning to his comrade, who
Though somewhat grieved, could scarce forbear a smile
    Upon the metamorphosis in view,—   660
"Farewell!" they mutually exclaim'd: "this soil
    Seems fertile in adventures strange and new;
One's turn'd half Mussulman, and one a maid,
By this old black enchanter's unsought aid.

84

"Farewell!" said Juan: "should we meet no more.   665
    I wish you a good appetite."—"Farewell!"
Replied the other; "though it grieves me sore;
    When we next meet, we'll have a tale to tell:
We needs must follow when Fate puts from shore.
    Keep your good name; though Eve herself once fell."   670
"Nay," quoth the maid, "the Sultan's self shan't carry me,
Unless his highness promises to marry me."

85

And thus they parted, each by separate doors;
    Baba led Juan onward room by room
Through glittering galleries, and o'er marble floors,   675
    Till a gigantic portal through the gloom,
Haughty and huge, along the distance lowers;
    And wafted far arose a rich perfume:
It seem'd as though they came upon a shrine,
For all was vast, still, fragrant, and divine.   680

---

1. In the Muslim idea of paradise, seventy beautiful virgins await each worthy man.

86

The giant door was broad, and bright, and high,
　　Of gilded bronze, and carved in curious guise;
Warriors thereon were battling furiously;
　　Here stalks the victor, there the vanquish'd lies;
There captives led in triumph droop the eye,   685
　　And in perspective many a squadron flies:
It seems the work of times before the line
Of Rome transplanted fell with Constantine.[2]

87

This massy portal stood at the wide close
　　Of a huge hall, and on its either side   690
Two little dwarfs, the least you could suppose,
　　Were sate, like ugly imps, as if allied
In mockery to the enormous gate which rose
　　O'er them in almost pyramidic pride:
The gate so splendid was in all its *features*,[3]   695
You never thought about those little creatures,

88

Until you nearly trod on them, and then
　　You started back in horror to survey
The wondrous hideousness of those small men,
　　Whose colour was not black, nor white, nor grey,   700
But an extraneous mixture, which no pen
　　Can trace, although perhaps the pencil may;
They were mis-shapen pigmies, deaf and dumb—
Monsters, who cost a no less monstrous sum.

89

Their duty was—for they were strong, and though   705
　　They look'd so little, did strong things at times—
To ope this door, which they could really do,
　　The hinges being as smooth as Rogers'[4] rhymes;
And now and then, with tough strings of the bow,
　　As is the custom of those Eastern climes,   710
To give some rebel Pacha a cravat;[5]
For mutes are generally used for that.

---

2. In 330 Constantine I had moved the capital of the Roman empire to Byzantium, rebuilt as Constantinople (present-day Istanbul), where the action of this canto takes place. Constantinople fell in 1453, under Constantine XI.
3. "*Features* of a gate—a ministerial metaphor: 'the *feature* upon which this question hinges.' See the 'Fudge Family,' or hear Castlereagh." Referring to Moore's *The Fudge Family in Paris* (1818), Byron's note mocks a mixed metaphor from a speech by foreign minister Castlereagh, who was known for his dull and inept oratory.
4. Samuel Rogers (1763–1855), a friend of Byron's and a writer Byron admired.
5. Literally, necktie, but here meaning that the dwarves were sometimes employed to strangle rivals of the Sultan.

90

They spoke by signs—that is, not spoke at all;
    And looking like two incubi,[6] they glared
As Baba with his fingers made them fall   715
    To heaving back the portal folds: it scared
Juan a moment, as this pair so small,
    With shrinking serpent optics on him stared;
It was as if their little looks could poison
Or fascinate whome'er they fix'd their eyes on.   720

91

Before they enter'd, Baba paused to hint
    To Juan some slight lessons as his guide:
"If you could just contrive," he said, "to stint
    That somewhat manly majesty of stride,
'Twould be as well, and,—(though there's not much in't)   725
    To swing a little less from side to side,
Which has at times an aspect of the oddest;—
And also could you look a little modest,

92

" 'Twould be convenient; for these mutes have eyes
    Like needles, which may pierce those petticoats;   730
And if they should discover your disguise,
    You know how near us the deep Bosphorus floats;
And you and I may chance, ere morning rise,
    To find our way to Marmora without boats,
Stitch'd up in sacks—a mode of navigation   735
A good deal practised here upon occasion."[7]

93

With this encouragement, he led the way
    Into a room still nobler than the last;
A rich confusion form'd a disarray
    In such sort, that the eye along it cast   740
Could hardly carry any thing away,
    Object on object flash'd so bright and fast;
A dazzling mass of gems, and gold, and glitter,
Magnificently mingled in a litter.

---

6. Evil demons supposed to descend upon people while they sleep.
7. "A few years ago the wife of Muchtar Pacha complained to his father of his son's supposed infidelity: he asked with whom, and she had the barbarity to give in a list of the twelve handsomest women in Yanina. They were seized, fastened up in sacks, and drowned in the lake the same night. One of the guards who was present informed me, that not one of the victims uttered a cry, or showed a symptom of terror at so sudden a 'wrench from all we knew, from all we love.'" (Compare *The Giaour*, line 1334n. [p.156].) Marmora (line 734): the sea connected by the Bosporus with the Black Sea.

94

Wealth had done wonders—taste not much; such things   745
    Occur in Orient palaces, and even
In the more chasten'd domes of Western kings
    (Of which I have also seen some six or seven)
Where I can't say or gold or diamond flings
    Great lustre, there is much to be forgiven;   750
Groups of bad statues, tables, chairs, and pictures,
On which I cannot pause to make my strictures.

95

In this imperial hall, at distance lay
    Under a canopy, and there reclined
Quite in a confidential queenly way,   755
    A lady; Baba stopp'd, and kneeling sign'd
To Juan, who though not much used to pray,
    Knelt down by instinct, wondering in his mind
What all this meant: while Baba bow'd and bended
His head, until the ceremony ended.   760

96

The lady rising up with such an air
    As Venus rose with from the wave, on them
Bent like an antelope a Paphian[8] pair
    Of eyes, which put out each surrounding gem;
And raising up an arm as moonlight fair,   765
    She sign'd to Baba, who first kiss'd the hem
Of her deep purple robe, and speaking low,
Pointed to Juan, who remain'd below.

97

Her presence was as lofty as her state;
    Her beauty of that overpowering kind,   770
Whose force description only would abate:
    I'd rather leave it much to your own mind,
Than lessen it by what I could relate
    Of forms and features; it would strike you blind
Could I do justice to the full detail;   775
So, luckily for both, my phrases fail.

98

Thus much however I may add,—her years
    Were ripe, they might make six-and-twenty springs,
But there are forms which Time to touch forbears,
    And turns aside his scythe to vulgar things,   780

---

8. The island of Paphos was sacred to Aphrodite, Greek goddess of love. Hence, "Paphian" came to suggest illicit love and prostitution. See *Childe Harold* I.61 (p. 28).

Such as was Mary's Queen of Scots;[9] true—tears
And love destroy; and sapping sorrow wrings
Charms from the charmer, yet some never grow
Ugly; for instance—Ninon de l'Enclos.[1]

99

She spake some words to her attendants, who   785
   Composed a choir of girls, ten or a dozen,
And were all clad alike; like Juan, too,
   Who wore their uniform, by Baba chosen:
They form'd a very nymph-like looking crew,
   Which might have call'd Diana's[2] chorus "cousin,"   790
As far as outward show may correspond;
I won't be bail for any thing beyond.

100

They bow'd obeisance and withdrew, retiring,
   But not by the same door through which came in
Baba and Juan, which last stood admiring,   795
   At some small distance, all he saw within
This strange saloon, much fitted for inspiring
   Marvel and praise; for both or none things win;
And I must say, I ne'er could see the very
Great happiness of the "Nil Admirari."[3]   800

101

"Not to admire is all the art I know
   (Plain truth, dear Murray, needs few flowers of speech)
To make men happy, or to keep them so;"
   (So take it in the very words of Creech).[4]
Thus Horace wrote we all know long ago;   805
   And thus Pope quotes the precept to re-teach
From his translation; but had *none admired,*
Would Pope have sung, or Horace been inspired?

102

Baba, when all the damsels were withdrawn,
   Motion'd to Juan to approach, and then   810
A second time desired him to kneel down,

---

9. Mary Stuart (1542–1587), queen of Scotland. She was imprisoned and later beheaded by her half sister and rival for power, Queen Elizabeth.
1. The most celebrated courtesan of the seventeenth century, reputed to have had lovers into her eighties.
2. Roman goddess of the hunt and patroness of young virgins.
3. To wonder at (admire) nothing (Latin): a formula for happiness arrived at by Horace in *Epistles* 1.6.1.
4. Thomas Creech (1659–1701), translator of Horace. The first four lines of stanza 101 quote (with some alterations) *Imitations of Horace* (1.6.1–4, "To Mr. Murray") by Alexander Pope (1688–1744). Pope's Mr. Murray is Lord Mansfield, while in Byron's quotation, the name applies to John Murray, his publisher.

And kiss the lady's foot; which maxim when
He heard repeated, Juan with a frown
   Drew himself up to his full height again,
And said, "It grieved him, but he could not stoop   815
To any shoe, unless it shod the Pope."

103

Baba, indignant at this ill-timed pride,
   Made fierce remonstrances, and then a threat
He mutter'd (but the last was given aside)
   About a bow-string[5]—quite in vain; not yet   820
Would Juan bend, though 'twere to Mahomet's bride:
   There's nothing in the world like *etiquette*
In kingly chambers or imperial halls,
As also at the race and county balls.

104

He stood like Atlas, with a world of words   825
   About his ears, and nathless would not bend;
The blood of all his line's Castilian lords
   Boil'd in his veins, and rather than descend
To stain his pedigree a thousand swords
   A thousand times of him had made an end;   830
At length perceiving the "*foot*" could not stand,
Baba proposed that he should kiss the hand.

105

Here was an honourable compromise,
   A half-way house of diplomatic rest,
Where they might meet in much more peaceful guise;   835
   And Juan now his willingness exprest,
To use all fit and proper courtesies,
   Adding, that this was commonest and best,
For through the South, the custom still commands
The gentleman to kiss the lady's hands.   840

106

And he advanced, though with but a bad grace,
   Though on more *thorough-bred*[6] or fairer fingers
No lips e'er left their transitory trace:
   On such as these the lip too fondly lingers,
And for one kiss would fain imprint a brace,   845
   As you will see, if she you love shall bring hers
In contact; and sometimes even a fair stranger's
An almost twelvemonth's constancy endangers.

---

5. I.e., strangulation.
6. "There is nothing, perhaps, more distinctive of birth than the hand. It is almost the only sign of blood which aristocracy can generate."

107

The lady eyed him o'er and o'er, and bade
   Baba retire, which he obey'd in style,   850
As if well-used to the retreating trade;
   And taking hints in good part all the while,
He whisper'd Juan not to be afraid,
   And looking on him with a sort of smile,
Took leave, with such a face of satisfaction,   855
As good men wear who have done a virtuous action

108

When he was gone, there was a sudden change:
   I know not what might be the lady's thought,
But o'er her bright brow flash'd a tumult strange,
   And into her clear cheek the blood was brought,   860
Blood-red as sunset summer clouds which range
   The verge of Heaven; and in her large eyes wrought
A mixture of sensations, might be scann'd,
Of half-voluptuousness and half command.

109

Her form had all the softness of her sex,   865
   Her features all the sweetness of the devil,
When he put on the cherub[7] to perplex
   Eve, and paved (God knows how) the road to evil;
The sun himself was scarce more free from specks
   Than she from aught at which the eye could cavil;   870
Yet, somehow, there was something somewhere wanting,
As if she rather *order'd* than was *granting.*—

110

Something imperial, or imperious, threw
   A chain o'er all she did; that is, a chain
Was thrown as 'twere about the neck of you,—   875
   And rapture's self will seem almost a pain
With aught which looks like despotism in view:
   Our souls at least are free, and 'tis in vain
We would against them make the flesh obey—
The spirit in the end will have its way.   880

111

Her very smile was haughty, though so sweet;
   Her very nod was not an inclination;
There was a self-will even in her small feet,
   As though they were quite conscious of her station—
They trod as upon necks; and to complete   885

7. In early paintings of the Fall, the serpent is given a cherubic face.

Her state (it is the custom of her nation),
A poniard deck'd her girdle, as the sign
She was a sultan's bride (thank Heaven, not mine!).

112

'To hear and to obey' had been from birth
    The law of all around her; to fulfil   890
All phantasies which yielded joy or mirth,
    Had been her slaves' chief pleasure, as her will;
Her blood was high, her beauty scarce of earth:
    Judge, then, if her caprices e'er stood still;
Had she but been a Christian, I've a notion   895
We should have found out the "perpetual motion."

113

Whate'er she saw and coveted was brought;
    Whate'er she did *not* see, if she supposed
It might be seen, with diligence was sought,
    And when 'twas found straightway the bargain closed: 900
There was no end unto the things she bought,
    Nor to the trouble which her fancies caused;
Yet even her tyranny had such a grace,
The women pardon'd all except her face.

114

Juan, the latest of her whims, had caught   905
    Her eye in passing on his way to sale;
She order'd him directly to be bought,
    And Baba, who had ne'er been known to fail
In any kind of mischief to be wrought,
    At all such auctions knew how to prevail: 910
She had no prudence, but he had; and this
Explains the garb which Juan took amiss.

115

His youth and features favour'd the disguise,
    And, should you ask how she, a sultan's bride,
Could risk or compass such strange phantasies,   915
    This I must leave sultanas to decide:
Emperors are only husbands in wives' eyes,
    And kings and consorts oft are mystified,
As we may ascertain with due precision,
Some by experience, others by tradition.   920

116

But to the main point, where we have been tending:—
    She now conceived all difficulties past,
And deem'd herself extremely condescending

When, being made her property at last,
　　Without more preface, in her blue eyes blending   925
　　Passion and power, a glance on him she cast,
And merely saying, 'Christian, canst thou love?'
Conceived that phrase was quite enough to move.

117

And so it was, in proper time and place;
　　But Juan, who had still his mind o'er-flowing   930
With Haidee's isle and soft Ionian face,
　　Felt the warm blood, which in his face was glowing,
Rush back upon his heart, which fill'd apace,
　　And left his cheeks as pale as snowdrops blowing;
These words went through his soul like Arab-spears,   935
So that he spoke not, but burst into tears.

118

She was a good deal shock'd; not shock'd at tears,
　　For women shed and use them at their liking;
But there is something when man's eye appears
　　Wet, still more disagreeable and striking;   940
A woman's tear-drop melts, a man's half sears,
　　Like molten lead, as if you thrust a pike in
His heart to force it out, for (to be shorter)
To them 'tis a relief, to us a torture.

119

And she would have consoled, but knew not how: 945
　　Having no equals, nothing which had e'er
Infected her with sympathy till now,
　　And never having dreamt what 'twas to bear
Aught of a serious, sorrowing kind, although
　　There might arise some pouting petty care   950
To cross her brow, she wonder'd how so near
Her eyes another's eye could shed a tear.

120

But nature teaches more than power can spoil,
　　And, when a *strong* although a strange sensation
Moves—female hearts are such a genial soil   955
　　For kinder feelings, whatsoe'er their nation,
They naturally pour the "wine and oil,"
　　Samaritans[8] in every situation;
And thus Gulbeyaz, though she knew not why,
Felt an odd glistening moisture in her eye.   960

---

8. Doers of good deeds; see Luke 10.29–37.

121

But tears must stop like all things else; and soon
    Juan, who for an instant had been moved
To such a sorrow by the intrusive tone
    Of one who dared to ask if "he *had* loved,"
Call'd back the stoic to his eyes, which shone   965
    Bright with the very weakness he reproved;
And although sensitive to beauty, he
Felt most indignant still at not being free.

122

Gulbeyaz, for the first time in her days,
    Was much embarrass'd, never having met   970
In all her life with aught save prayers and praise;
    And as she also risk'd her life to get
Him whom she meant to tutor in love's ways
    Into a comfortable tête-à-tête,
To lose the hour would make her quite a martyr,   975
And they had wasted now almost a quarter.

123

I also would suggest the fitting time,
    To gentlemen in any such like case,
That is to say—in a meridian clime,
    With us there is more law given to the chase,   980
But here a small delay forms a great crime:
    So recollect that the extremest grace
Is just two minutes for your declaration—
A moment more would hurt your reputation.

124

Juan's was good; and might have been still better,   985
    But he had got Haidee into his head:
However strange, he could not yet forget her,
    Which made him seem exceedingly ill-bred.
Gulbeyaz, who look'd on him as her debtor
    For having had him to her palace led,   990
Began to blush up to the eyes, and then
Grow deadly pale, and then blush back again.

125

At length, in an imperial way, she laid
    Her hand on his, and bending on him eyes,
Which needed not an empire to persuade,   995
    Look'd into his for love, where none replies:
Her brow grew black, but she would not upbraid,
    That being the last thing a proud woman tries;

She rose, and pausing one chaste moment, threw
Herself upon his breast, and there she grew.   1000

126

This was an awkward test, as Juan found,
  But he was steel'd by sorrow, wrath, and pride
With gentle force her white arms he unwound,
  And seated her all drooping by his side.
Then rising haughtily he glanced around,   1005
  And looking coldly in her face, he cried,
"The prison'd eagle will not pair, nor I
Serve a sultana's sensual phantasy.

127

"Thou ask'st, if I can love? be this the proof
  How much I *have* loved—that I love not *thee!*   1010
In this vile garb, the distaff, web, and woof,[9]
  Were fitter for me: Love is for the free!
I am not dazzled by this splendid roof;
  Whate'er thy power, and great it seems to be,
Heads bow, knees bend, eyes watch around a throne,   1015
And hands obey—our hearts are still our own."

128

This was a truth to us extremely trite;
  Not so to her, who ne'er had heard such things:
She deem'd her least command must yield delight,
  Earth being only made for queens and kings.   1020
If hearts lay on the left side or the right
  She hardly knew, to such perfection brings
Legitimacy its born votaries, when
Aware of their due royal rights o'er men.

129

Besides, as has been said, she was so fair   1025
  As even in a much humbler lot had made
A kingdom or confusion any where,
  And also, as may be presumed, she laid
Some stress on charms which seldom are, if e'er,
  By their possessors thrown into the shade: 1030
She thought hers gave a double "right divine;"
And half of that opinion's also mine.

---

9. *distaff . . . woof:* related to the occupation of weaving and associated, therefore, with women; the distaff is a tool for spinning thread; web (or warp) and woof are the vertical and lateral patterns of a woven fabric.

130

Remember, or (if you can not) imagine,
  Ye! who have kept your chastity when young,
While some more desperate dowager has been waging   1035
  Love with you, and been in the dog-days stung
By your refusal, recollect her raging!
  Or recollect all that was said or sung
On such a subject; then suppose the face
Of a young downright beauty in this case.   1040

131

Suppose,—but you already have supposed,
  The spouse of Potiphar, the Lady Booby,
Phaedra,¹ and all which story has disclosed
  Of good examples; pity that so few by
Poets and private tutors are exposed,   1045
  To educate—ye youth of Europe—you by!
But when you have supposed the few we know,
You can't suppose Gulbeyaz' angry brow.

132

A tigress robb'd of young, a lioness,
  Or any interesting beast of prey,   1050
Are similes at hand for the distress
  Of ladies who can not have their own way;
But though my turn will not be served with less,
  These don't express one half what I should say:
For what is stealing young ones, few or many,   1055
To cutting short their hopes of having any?

133

The love of offspring's nature's general law,
  From tigresses and cubs to ducks and ducklings;
There's nothing whets the beak, or arms the claw
  Like an invasion of their babes and sucklings;   1060
And all who have seen a human nursery, saw
  How mothers love their children's squalls and chucklings;
This strong extreme effect (to tire no longer
Your patience) shows the cause must still be stronger.

134

If I said fire flash'd from Gulbeyaz' eyes,   1065
  'Twere nothing—for her eyes flash'd always fire;
Or said her cheeks assumed the deepest dyes,

---

1. *spouse . . . Phaedra*: three unsuccessful seductresses. For the story of Joseph and Potiphar's wife, see Genesis 39.7–20 and *Don Juan* I.1487; Lady Booby fails in her attempts to seduce the hero of Fielding's *Joseph Andrews* (1742); in Euripides' *Hippolytus*, Phaedra, wife of Theseus, fell tragically in love with Hippolytus, her stepson, who rejects her.

I should but bring disgrace upon the dyer,
So supernatural was her passion's rise;
    For ne'er till now she knew a check'd desire: 1070
Even ye who know what a check'd woman is
(Enough, God knows!) would much fall short of this.

135

Her rage was but a minute's, and 'twas well—
    A moment's more had slain her; but the while
It lasted 'twas like a short glimpse of hell: 1075
    Nought's more sublime than energetic bile,
Though horrible to see yet grand to tell,
    Like ocean warring 'gainst a rocky isle;
And the deep passions flashing through her form
Made her a beautiful embodied storm.   1080

136

A vulgar tempest 'twere to a typhoon
    To match a common fury with her rage,
And yet she did not want to reach the moon,
    Like moderate Hotspur[2] on the immortal page;
Her anger pitch'd into a lower tune,   1085
    Perhaps the fault of her soft sex and age—
Her wish was but to "kill, kill, kill,"[3] like Lear's,
And then her thirst of blood was quench'd in tears.

137

A storm it raged, and like the storm it pass'd,
    Pass'd without words—in fact she could not speak;   1090
And then her sex's shame broke in at last,
    A sentiment till then in her but weak,
But now it flow'd in natural and fast,
    As water through an unexpected leak,
For she felt humbled—and humiliation   1095
Is sometimes good for people in her station.

138

It teaches them that they are flesh and blood,
    It also gently hints to them that others,
Although of clay, are yet not quite of mud;
    That urns and pipkins are but fragile brothers,   1100
And works of the same pottery, bad or good,
    Though not all born of the same sires and mothers:
It teaches—Heaven knows only what it teaches,
But sometimes it may mend, and often reaches.[4]

2. Henry Percy, the irascible claimant to the English throne in *1 Henry IV*.
3. *King Lear* 4.5.177.
4. Influences, convinces.

139

Her first thought was to cut off Juan's head;   1105
     Her second, to cut only his—acquaintance;
Her third, to ask him where he had been bred;
     Her fourth, to rally him into repentance;
Her fifth, to call her maids and go to bed;
     Her sixth, to stab herself; her seventh, to sentence   1110
The lash to Baba:—but her grand resource
Was to sit down again, and cry of course.

140

She thought to stab herself, but then she had
     The dagger close at hand, which made it awkward;
For Eastern stays are little made to pad,   1115
     So that a poniard pierces if 'tis stuck hard:
She thought of killing Juan—but, poor lad!
     Though he deserved it well for being so backward,
The cutting off his head was not the art
Most likely to attain her aim—his heart.   1120

141

Juan was moved: he had made up his mind
     To be impaled, or quarter'd as a dish
For dogs, or to be slain with pangs refined,
     Or thrown to lions, or made baits for fish,
And thus heroically stood resign'd,   1125
     Rather than sin—except to his own wish:
But all his great preparatives for dying
Dissolved like snow before a woman crying.

142

As through his palms Bob Acres'[5] valour oozed,
     So Juan's virtue ebb'd, I know not how;   1130
And first he wonder'd why he had refused;
     And then, if matters could be made up now;
And next his savage virtue he accused,
     Just as a friar may accuse his vow,
Or as a dame repents her of her oath,   1135
Which mostly ends in some small breach of both.

143

So he began to stammer some excuses;
     But words are not enough in such a matter,
Although you borrow'd all that e'er the muses

---

5. Character in Sheridan's *The Rivals*, whose "courage" is his perspiration.

Have sung, or even a Dandy's[6] dandiest chatter,   1140
Or all the figures Castlereagh abuses;[7]
    Just as a languid smile began to flatter
His peace was making, but before he ventured
Further, old Baba rather briskly enter'd.

144

"Bride of the Sun! and Sister of the Moon!"   1145
    ('Twas thus he spake) "and Empress of the Earth!
Whose frown would put the spheres all out of tune,
    Whose smile makes all the planets dance with mirth,
Your slave brings tidings—he hopes not too soon—
    Which your sublime attention may be worth: 1150
The Sun himself has sent me like a ray
To hint that he is coming up this way."

145

"Is it," exclaim'd Gulbeyaz, "as you say?
    I wish to heaven he would not shine till morning!
But bid my women form the milky way.   1155
    Hence, my old comet! give the stars due warning—
And, Christian! mingle with them as you may,
    And as you'd have me pardon your past scorning——"
Here they were interrupted by a humming
Sound, and then by a cry, "The Sultan's coming!"   1160

146

First came her damsels, a decorous file,
    And then his Highness' eunuchs, black and white;
The train might reach a quarter of a mile:
    His majesty was always so polite
As to announce his visits a long while   1165
    Before he came, especially at night;
For being the last wife of the Emperour,
She was of course the favourite of the four.

147

His Highness was a man of solemn port,
    Shawl'd to the nose, and bearded to the eyes,   1170
Snatch'd from a prison to preside at court,
    His lately bowstrung brother caused his rise;
He was as good a sovereign of the sort
    As any mention'd in the histories

---

6. One of a socially recognized group of fashion-conscious men, with whom Byron for a while asso-
ciated. See *Beppo*, line 410 and note (p. 362).
7. See note to line 695.

Of Cantemir, or Knōllĕs,[8] where few shine   1175
    Save Solyman, the glory of their line.[9]

148

He went to mosque in state, and said his prayers
    With more than "Oriental scrupulosity;"[1]
He left to his vizier all state affairs,
    And show'd but little royal curiosity: 1180
I know not if he had domestic cares—
    No process proved connubial animosity;
Four wives and twice five hundred maids, unseen,
Were ruled as calmly as a Christian queen.

149

If now and then there happen'd a slight slip,   1185
    Little was heard of criminal or crime;
The story scarcely pass'd a single lip—
    The sack and sea had settled all in time,
From which the secret nobody could rip:
    The Public knew no more than does this rhyme;   1190
No scandals made the daily press a curse—
Morals were better, and the fish no worse.

150

He saw with his own eyes the moon was round,
    Was also certain that the earth was square,
Because he had journey'd fifty miles, and found   1195
    No sign that it was circular any where;
His empire also was without a bound:
    'Tis true, a little troubled here and there,
By rebel pachas, and encroaching giaours,
But then they never came to "the Seven Towers;"[2]   1200

151

Except in shape of envoys, who were sent
    To lodge there when a war broke out, according
To the true law of nations, which ne'er meant
    Those scoundrels, who have never had a sword in
Their dirty diplomatic hands, to vent   1205

8. Cantemir and Knolles were eighteenth-century historians of the Turkish Empire.
9. "It may not be unworthy of remark, that Bacon, in his essay on 'Empire,' hints that Solyman was
   the last of his line; on what authority, I know not. These are his words:—'The destruction of
   Mustapha was so fatal to Solyman's line, as the succession of the Turks from Solyman, until this
   day, is suspected to be untrue, and of strange blood; for that Solyman the second was thought to
   be supposititious.' But Bacon, in his historical authorities, is often inaccurate. I could give half a
   dozen instances from his Apophthegms only." The reference is to Suleiman the Magnificent
   (1520–1566), most renowned of all the sultans of Turkey. Byron's entire note, including the list of
   Bacon's errors, is given in 1832 in an Appendix to Canto V and in CPW 5:710–12.
1. From Samuel Johnson's life of Jonathan Swift.
2. In Constantinople, Turkish prison for political enemies.

Their spleen in making strife, and safely wording
Their lies, yclep'd[3] despatches, without risk or
The singeing of a single inky whisker.

152

He had fifty daughters and four dozen sons,
    Of whom all such as came of age were stow'd,   1210
The former in a palace, where like nuns
    They lived till some Bashaw was sent abroad,
When she, whose turn it was, was wed at once,
    Sometimes at six years old—though this seems odd,
'Tis true; the reason is, that the Bashaw[4]   1215
Must make a present to his sire in law.

153

His sons were kept in prison, till they grew
    Of years to fill a bowstring or the throne,
One or the other, but which of the two
    Could yet be known unto the fates alone;   1220
Meantime the education they went through
    Was princely, as the proofs have always shown:
So that the heir apparent still was found
No less deserving to be hang'd than crown'd.

154

His Majesty saluted his fourth spouse   1225
    With all the ceremonies of his rank,
Who clear'd her sparkling eyes and smooth'd her brows,
    As suits a matron who has play'd a prank;
These must seem doubly mindful of their vows,
    To save the credit of their breaking bank: 1230
To no men are such cordial greetings given
As those whose wives have made them fit for heaven.[5]

155

His Highness cast around his great black eyes,
    And looking, as he always look'd, perceived
Juan amongst the damsels in disguise,   1235
    At which he seem'd no whit surprised nor grieved,
But just remark'd with air sedate and wise,
    While still a fluttering sigh Gulbeyaz heaved,
"I see you've bought another girl; 'tis pity
That a mere Christian should be half so pretty."   1240

---

3. Called.
4. Pasha, an honorary title given a high-ranking Turk.
5. By having cuckolded them (a traditional idea).

156

This compliment, which drew all eyes upon
    The new-bought virgin, made her blush and shake.
Her comrades, also, thought themselves undone:
    Oh! Mahomet! that his Majesty should take
Such notice of a giaour, while scarce to one   1245
    Of them his lips imperial ever spake!
There was a general whisper, toss, and wriggle,
But etiquette forbade them all to giggle.

157

The Turks do well to shut—at least, sometimes—
    The women up—because, in sad reality,   1250
Their chastity in these unhappy climes
    Is not a thing of that astringent quality
Which in the North prevents precocious crimes,
    And makes our snow less pure than our morality;
The sun, which yearly melts the polar ice,   1255
Has quite the contrary effect on vice.

158

Thus in the East they are extremely strict,
    And *Wedlock* and a *Padlock* mean the same;
Excepting only when the former's pick'd
    It ne'er can be replaced in proper frame;   1260
Spoilt, as a pipe of claret is when prick'd:[6]
    But then their own Polygamy's to blame;
Why don't they knead two virtuous souls for life
Into that moral centaur, man and wife?

159

Thus far our chronicle; and now we pause,   1265
    Though not for want of matter; but 'tis time,
According to the ancient epic laws,
    To slacken sail, and anchor with our rhyme.
Let this fifth canto meet with due applause,
    The sixth shall have a touch of the sublime;   1270
Meanwhile, as Homer sometimes sleeps, perhaps
You'll pardon to my muse a few short naps.

[Canto VI continues the harem episode begun in Canto V: disguised as one of the harem women with the purpose of evading the jealous suspicions of Gulbayez' husband, the Sultan, "Juanna" sleeps with one of the other odalisques, incurring the wrath of Gulbayez, who orders the traditional punishment for sexual betrayal—sacking and drowning. Baba sees to their escape, however, and

6. The cork is punctured.

in Cantos VII–VIII, Juan has joined with the Russian army in its siege and sack
of Ismail, acquitting himself with such "courage and humanity" (VIII. 1114)
that he is entrusted to deliver the news of Russia's victory to empress Cather-
ine the Great.]

FROM CANTO THE NINTH[1]

1

Oh, Wellington! (or "Vilainton"[2]—for Fame
　　Sounds the heroic syllables both ways;
France could not even conquer your great name,
　　But punn'd it down to this facetious phrase—
Beating or beaten she will laugh the same),   5
　　You have obtain'd great pensions and much praise:
Glory like yours should any dare gainsay,
Humanity would rise, and thunder "Nay!"[3]

2

I don't think that you used Kinnaird quite well
　　In Marinèt's affair[4] —in fact, 'twas shabby,   10
And like some other things won't do to tell
　　Upon your tomb in Westminster's old abbey.[5]
Upon the rest 'tis not worth while to dwell,
　　Such tales being for the tea-hours of some tabby;
But though your years as *man* tend fast to zero,   15
In fact your Grace is still but a *young Hero*.[6]

1. In 1821, after completing Canto V, Byron withdrew from his *Don Juan* project, explaining that his
decision to do so was the result of a promise that he made to Teresa Guiccioli (see letter to Mur-
ray, July 6, 1821 [p. 765]). However, when he resumed work on the poem early in 1822, he had
renewed clarity of its design (intending to write twenty-four books, consistent with his epic model,
and to end Juan's life on the guillotine) and of its serious purpose as a critique of contemporary
politics and society. Cantos VII–VIII not only situate the narrative historically, with the Siege of
Ismail having taken place in November–December 1790, but Byron's treatment of war and the tri-
umph of a powerful monarchy pointedly reflects on Anglo-European politics. Not surprisingly,
Byron decided to restore to the poem stanzas critical of the Duke of Wellington, which he had orig-
inally drafted in 1819 as part of Canto III but withdrew. Except for those first eight stanzas, Canto
IX was written in the summer and early fall of 1822. It was published together with Cantos X and
XI by John Hunt on August 29, 1823.
2. Arthur Wellesley, Duke of Wellington (1769–1852), led the victory at Waterloo (1815). Byron's
hatred of Wellington is motivated by the fact that in defeating Napoleon Wellington ensured the
reestablishment of repressive monarchies throughout Europe. "Villainton" ("nasty style") was a
popular French satirical pun on Wellington's name.
3. "Query—*Ney?*—Printer's Devil." Marshall Michel Ney (1769–1815) was one of the bravest and
most brilliant of Napoleon's generals. A "printer's devil" is an apprentice in a printing office who
often becomes black with ink.
4. In 1818, a Frenchman named Marinet tried to assassinate Wellington. Lord Kinnaird had warned
Wellington of the attempt; but since Kinnaird refused to divulge the identity of his informant, Welling-
ton accused him of treason.
5. Wellington is buried in St. Paul's. A "tabby" (line 14) is a spiteful gossip, and lines 11–14 refer to Welling-
ton's affairs with women, particularly, perhaps, with Lady Frances Wedderburn Webster (see *BLJ*
10:48).
6. I.e., only recently a hero; or perhaps a reference to Wellington as a lover.

3

Though Britain owes (and pays you too) so much,
  Yet Europe doubtless owes you greatly more;
You have repair'd Legitimacy's crutch,
  A prop not quite so certain as before: 20
The Spanish, and the French, as well as Dutch,
  Have seen, and felt, how strongly you *restore*;[7]
And Waterloo has made the world your debtor
(I wish your bards[8] would sing it rather better).

4

You are "the best of cut-throats:"[9]—do not start;   25
  The phrase is Shakspeare's, and not misapplied:—
War's a brain-spattering, windpipe-slitting art,
  Unless her cause by right be sanctified.
If you have acted *once* a generous part,
  The world, not the world's masters, will decide,   30
And I shall be delighted to learn who,
Save you and yours, have gain'd by Waterloo?

5

I am no flatterer—you've supp'd full of flattery:
  They say you like it too—'tis no great wonder.
He whose whole life has been assault and battery,   35
  At last may get a little tired of thunder;
And swallowing eulogy much more than satire, he
  May like being praised for every lucky blunder,
Call'd "Saviour of the Nations"—not yet saved,
And "Europe's Liberator"—still enslaved.[1]   40

6

I've done. Now go and dine from off the plate
  Presented by the Prince of the Brazils,[2]
And send the sentinel before your gate
  A slice or two from your luxurious meals:
He fought, but has not fed so well of late.   45
  Some hunger, too, they say the people feels:—
There is no doubt that you deserve your ration,
But pray give back a little to the nation.

---

7. After Waterloo, the Congress of Vienna restored the Spanish and Bourbon monarchies and the Kingdom of the United Netherlands.
8. Southey, among others, wrote poems praising Wellington's victory.
9. *Macbeth* 3.4.16.
1. "*Vide* Speeches in Parliament, after the battle of Waterloo."
2. "'I at this time got a post, being for fatigue, with four others. We were sent to break biscuit, and make a mess for Lord Wellington's hounds. I was very hungry, and thought it a good job at the time, as we got our own fill while we broke the biscuit,—a thing I had not got for some days. When thus engaged, the Prodigal Son was never once out of my mind; and I sighed, as I fed the dogs, over my humble situation and my ruined hopes.'—*Journal of a Soldier of the 71st Regiment during the War in Spain.*"

7

I don't mean to reflect—a man so great as
   You, my Lord Duke! is far above reflection: 50
The high Roman fashion, too, of Cincinnatus,[3]
   With modern history has but small connection:
Though as an Irishman you love potatoes,
   You need not take them under your direction;
And half a million for your Sabine[4] farm   55
   Is rather dear!—I'm sure I mean no harm.

8

Great men have always scorn'd great recompenses:
   Epaminondas[5] saved his Thebes, and died,
Not leaving even his funeral expenses:
   George Washington had thanks and nought beside,   60
Except the all-cloudless glory (which few men's is)
   To free his country: Pitt[6] too had his pride,
And, as a high-soul'd minister of state is,
   Renown'd for ruining Great Britain gratis.

9

Never had mortal man such opportunity,   65
   Except Napoleon, or abused it more:
You might have freed fallen Europe from the unity
   Of tyrants, and been blest from shore to shore:
And *now*—what *is* your fame? Shall the Muse tune it ye?
   Now—that the rabble's first vain shouts are o'er?   70
Go! hear it in your famish'd country's cries!
   Behold the world! and curse your victories!

10

As these new cantos touch on warlike feats,
   To *you* the unflattering Muse deigns to inscribe
Truths, that you will not read in the Gazettes,   75
   But which 't is time to teach the hireling tribe
Who fatten on their country's gore and debts,
   Must be recited, and—without a bribe.
You *did great* things; but not being *great* in mind,
   Have left *undone* the *greatest*—and mankind.   80

✷   ✷   ✷

3. Roman general and dictator (519–439 B.C.E.) renowned for his humility and courage; in "Ode to Napoleon Buonaparte," line 168 [p. 161], Byron refers to George Washington as the "Cincinnatus of the West."
4. Ancient region in central Italy, subjugated by the Romans; referring to the Sabine farm given to Horace by his patron.
5. Theban general and philosopher (418–362 B.C.E.) who helped save Greece from Persian invasion in 371 B.C.E.
6. William Pitt the Younger (1759–1806), twice prime minister (1783–1801, 1804–06), who in the years following the French Revolution adopted extremely repressive measures against political dissenters in England.

22

'Tis time we should proceed with our good poem,—
    For I maintain that it is really good,   170
Not only in the body but the proem,
    However little both are understood
Just now,—but by and by the Truth will show 'em
    Herself in her sublimest attitude:
And till she doth, I fain must be content   175
To share her beauty and her banishment.

23

Our hero (and, I trust, kind reader! yours)
    Was left upon his way to the chief city
Of the immortal Peter's polish'd boors,
    Who still have shown themselves more brave than witty.   180
I know its mighty empire now allures
    Much flattery—even Voltaire's,[7] and that's a pity.
For me, I deem an absolute autocrat
Not a barbarian, but much worse than that.

24

And I will war, at least in words (and—should   185
    My chance so happen—deeds) with all who war
With Thought;—and of Thought's foes by far most rude,
    Tyrants and sycophants have been and are.
I know not who may conquer: if I could
    Have such a prescience, it should be no bar   190
To this my plain, sworn, downright detestation
Of every despotism in every nation.

25

It is not that I adulate the people:
    Without *me*, there are demagogues enough,
And infidels, to pull down every steeple,   195
    And set up in their stead some proper stuff.
Whether they may sow scepticism to reap hell,
    As is the Christian dogma rather rough,
I do not know;—I wish men to be free
As much from mobs as kings—from you as me.   200

26

The consequence is, being of no party,
    I shall offend all parties:—never mind!
My words, at least, are more sincere and hearty
    Than if I sought to sail before the wind.

---

7. Voltaire had praised Catherine's brilliance effusively. After the French Revolution, however, Catherine forbade the printing or circulation of Voltaire's books in Russia.

He who has nought to gain can have small art: he   205
   Who neither wishes to be bound or bind,
May still expatiate freely, as will I,
Nor give my voice to Slavery's jackall cry.

* * *

41

But I am apt to grow too metaphysical:
   "The time is out of joint,"[8]—and so am I;
I quite forget this poem's merely quizzical,
   And deviate into matters rather dry.
I ne'er decide what I shall say, and this I call ·   325
   Much too poetical: men should know why
They write, and for what end; but, note or text,
I never know the word which will come next.

42

So on I ramble, now and then narrating,
   Now pondering:—it is time we should narrate.   330
I left Don Juan with his horses baiting—
   Now we'll get o'er the ground at a great rate.
I shall not be particular in stating
   His journey, we've so many tours of late:
Suppose him then at Petersburgh; suppose   335
That pleasant capital of painted snows;

43

Suppose him in a handsome uniform;
   A scarlet coat, black facings, a long plume,
Waving, like sails new shiver'd in a storm,
   Over a cock'd hat in a crowded room,   340
And brilliant breeches, bright as a Cairn Gorme,[9]
   Of yellow casimire[1] we may presume,
White stockings drawn uncurdled as new milk
O'er limbs whose symmetry set off the silk;

44

Suppose him sword by side, and hat in hand,   345
   Made up by youth, fame, and an army tailor—
That great enchanter, at whose rod's command
   Beauty springs forth, and Nature's self turns paler,
Seeing how Art can make her work more grand
   (When she don't pin men's limbs in like a gaoler),— 350

8. *Hamlet* 1.5.189.
9. Yellowish quartz stone, named for the Scottish mountain range where it is found.
1. Cashmere.

Behold him placed as if upon a pillar! He
Seems Love turn'd a Lieutenant of Artillery!

45

His bandage slipp'd down into a cravat;
　His wings subdued to epaulettes; his quiver
Shrunk to a scabbard, with his arrows at　　　　　　　　355
　His side as a small sword, but sharp as ever;
His bow converted into a cock'd hat;
　But still so like, that Psyche[2] were more clever
Than some wives (who make blunders no less stupid),
　If she had not mistaken him for Cupid.　　　　　　360

46

The courtiers stared, the ladies whisper'd, and
　The Empress smiled: the reigning favourite frown'd—
I quite forget which of them was in hand
　Just then; as they are rather numerous found,
Who took by turns that difficult command　　　　　　365
　Since first her Majesty was singly crown'd:[3]
But they were mostly nervous six-foot fellows,
　All fit to make a Patagonian[4] jealous.

47

Juan was none of these, but slight and slim,
　Blushing and beardless; and yet ne'ertheless　　　　370
There was a something in his turn of limb,
　And still more in his eye, which seem'd to express
That though he look'd one of the Seraphim,
　There lurk'd a man beneath the spirit's dress.
Besides, the Empress sometimes liked a boy,　　　　　375
　And had just buried the fair-faced Lanskoi.[5]

48

No wonder then that Yermoloff, or Momonoff,
　Or Scherbatoff, or any other *off*
Or *on*, might dread her Majesty had room enough
　Within her bosom (which was not too tough)　　　　380
For a new flame; a thought to cast of gloom enough
　Along the aspect, whether smooth or rough,
Of him who, in the language of his station,
　Then held that "high official situation."

---

2. In classical myth, the Soul, beloved of Cupid, god of love.
3. Catherine was crowned Czarina of all the Russias in 1762, after the death of her husband, Czar
　　Peter III.
4. From "Patagonia" (Argentina), fabled to be inhabited by giants.
5. "He was the grande passion of the grande Catherine. See her Lives under the head of 'Lanskoi.'"
　　Lanskoi, Yermoloff, and the others named in the next stanza were all believed to be lovers of
　　Catherine's.

49

O, gentle ladies! should you seek to know   385
   The import of this diplomatic phrase,
Bid Ireland's Londonderry's Marquess[6] show
   His parts of speech; and in the strange displays
Of that odd string of words, all in a row,
   Which none divine, and every one obeys,   390
Perhaps you may pick out some queer *no*-meaning,
Of that weak wordy harvest the sole gleaning.

50

I think I can explain myself without
   That sad inexplicable beast of prey—
That Sphinx, whose words would ever be a doubt,   395
   Did not his deeds unriddle them each day—
That monstrous Hieroglyphic—that long Spout
   Of blood and water, leaden Castlereagh!
And here I must an anecdote relate,
But luckily of no great length or weight.   400

51

An English lady ask'd of an Italian,
   What were the actual and official duties
Of the strange thing, some women set a value on,
   Which hovers oft about some married beauties,
Called "Cavalier servente?" a Pygmalion[7]   405
   Whose statues warm (I fear, alas! too true 'tis)
Beneath his art. The dame, press'd to disclose them,
Said—"Lady, I beseech you to *suppose them*."

52

And thus I supplicate your supposition,
   And mildest, matron-like interpretation,   410
Of the imperial favourite's condition.
   'Twas a high place, the highest in the nation
In fact, if not in rank; and the suspicion
   Of any one's attaining to his station,
No doubt gave pain, where each new pair of shoulders,   415
If rather broad, made stocks rise and their holders.

53

Juan, I said, was a most beauteous boy,
   And had retain'd his boyish look beyond

---

6. "This was written long before the suicide of that person." I.e., Castlereagh; see Dedication, stanzas 11–16.
7. In Greek myth, the sculptor Pygmalion fell in love with the female statue he had created, and the gods, granting his prayers, brought the statue to life. *"Cavalier servente"*: in Italian society, the semiaccepted lover of a married woman.

The usual hirsute seasons which destroy,
　　With beards and whiskers, and the like, the fond   420
Parisian[8] aspect which upset old Troy
　　And founded Doctors' Commons:[9]—I have conn'd
The history of divorces, which, though chequer'd,
　　Calls Ilion's the first damages on record.

54

And Catherine, who loved all things (save her lord,   425
　　Who was gone to his place) and pass'd for much,
Admiring those (by dainty dames abhorr'd)
　　Gigantic gentlemen, yet had a touch
Of sentiment; and he she most adored
　　Was the lamented Lanskoi, who was such   430
A lover as had cost her many a tear,
And yet but made a middling grenadier.

55

Oh thou "teterrima causa" of all "belli"[1]—
　　Thou gate of Life and Death—thou nondescript!
Whence is our exit and our entrance,—well I   435
　　May pause in pondering how all souls are dipt
In thy perennial fountain:—how man *fell*, I
　　Know not, since Knowledge saw her branches stript
Of her first fruit; but how he falls and rises
　　Since, thou hast settled beyond all surmises.   440

56

Some call thee "the worst cause of war," but I
　　Maintain thou art the *best*: for after all
From thee we come, to thee we go, and why
　　To get at thee not batter down a wall,
Or waste a world? since no one can deny   445
　　Thou dost replenish worlds both great and small:
With, or without thee, all things at a stand
Are, or would be, thou Sea of Life's dry Land!

57

Catherine, who was the grand epitome
　　Of that great cause of war, or peace, or what   450
You please (it causes all the things which be,
　　So you may take your choice of this or that)—

---

8. A pun. In Greek legend Paris of Troy (Ilion) seduced and abducted the wife of king Menelaus, caus-
　　ing the Trojan War.
9. The English divorce court.
1. "Hor. *Sat*. lib. I. sat. iii." The ribald humor of stanzas 55–56 derives from Horace's verse: "cunnus
　　teterrima belli causa," which may euphemistically be rendered "woman is the worst cause of war";
　　in line 433, "cunnus" is coyly omitted, though it is the obvious key to the two stanzas, the
　　antecedent to all the second-person pronouns.

Catherine, I say, was very glad to see
  The handsome herald, on whose plumage sat
Victory; and, pausing as she saw him kneel   455
With his despatch, forgot to break the seal.

58

Then recollecting the whole Empress, nor
  Forgetting quite the woman (which composed
At least three parts of this great whole), she tore
  The letter open with an air which posed   460
The court, that watch'd each look her visage wore,
  Until a royal smile at length disclosed
Fair weather for the day. Though rather spacious,
Her face was noble, her eyes fine, mouth gracious.

59

Great joy was hers, or rather joys: the first   465
  Was a ta'en city, thirty thousand slain.
Glory and triumph o'er her aspect burst,
  As an East Indian sunrise on the main.
These quench'd a moment her ambition's thirst—
  So Arab deserts drink in summer's rain: 470
In vain!—As fall the dews on quenchless sands,
Blood only serves to wash Ambition's hands!

60

Her next amusement was more fanciful;
  She smiled at mad Suwarrow's rhymes, who threw
Into a Russian couplet rather dull   475
  The whole gazette of thousands whom he slew.
Her third was feminine enough to annul
  The shudder which runs naturally through
Our veins, when things call'd sovereigns think it best
To kill, and generals turn it into jest.   480

61

The two first feelings ran their course complete,
  And lighted first her eye, and then her mouth:
The whole court look'd immediately most sweet,
  Like flowers well water'd after a long drouth:—
But when on the Lieutenant at her feet   485
  Her Majesty, who liked to gaze on youth
Almost as much as on a new despatch,
Glanced mildly, all the world was on the watch.

62

Though somewhat large, exuberant, and truculent,
  When *wroth*—while *pleased*, she was as fine a figure   490

As those who like things rosy, ripe, and succulent,
Would wish to look on, while they are in vigour.
She could repay each amatory look you lent
With interest, and in turn was wont with rigour
To exact of Cupid's bills the full amount   495
At sight, nor would permit you to discount.

63

With her the latter, though at times convenient,
Was not so necessary; for they tell
That she was handsome, and though fierce *look'd* lenient,
And always used her favourites too well.   500
If once beyond her boudoir's precincts in ye went,
Your "fortune" was in a fair way "to swell
A man" (as Giles says[2]); for though she would widow all
Nations, she liked man as an individual.

64

What a strange thing is man![3] and what a stranger   505
Is woman! What a whirlwind is her head,
And what a whirlpool full of depth and danger
Is all the rest about her! Whether wed,
Or widow, maid or mother, she can change her
Mind like the wind: whatever she has said   510
Or done, is light to what she'll say or do;—
The oldest thing on record, and yet new!

65

Oh Catherine! (for of all interjections,
To thee both *oh!* and *ah!* belong of right
In love and war) how odd are the connections   515
Of human thoughts, which jostle in their flight!
Just now *yours* were cut out in different sections:
First Ismail's capture caught your fancy quite;
Next of new knights, the fresh and glorious hatch;
And *thirdly* he who brought you the despatch!   520

66

Shakspeare talks of "the herald Mercury
New lighted on a heaven-kissing hill;"
And some such visions cross'd her Majesty,
While her young Herald knelt before her still.
'Tis very true the hill seem'd rather high   525
For a Lieutenant to climb up; but skill

2. "'His fortune swells him, it is rank, he's married.'—*Sir Giles Overreach*; Massinger's '*New Way to pay old Debts.*'"
3. Cf. *Hamlet* 2.2.293–94.

Smooth'd even the Simplon's[4] steep, and by God' blessing
With Youth and Health all kisses are "heaven-kissing."

67

Her Majesty look'd down, the Youth look'd up—
    And so they fell in love;—she with his face,   530
His grace, his God-knows-what: for Cupid's cup
    With the first draught intoxicates apace,
A quintessential laudanum or "black drop,"[5]
    Which makes one drunk at once, without the base
Expedient of full bumpers; for the eye   535
In love drinks all life's fountains (save tears) dry.

68

He, on the other hand, if not in love,
    Fell into that no less imperious passion,
Self-love—which, when some sort of Thing above
    Ourselves, a singer, dancer, much in fashion,   540
Or duchess, princess, Empress, "deigns to prove"
    ('Tis Pope's phrase[6]) a great longing, though a rash one,
For one especial person out of many,
Makes us believe ourselves as good as any.

69

Besides, he was of that delighted age   545
    Which makes all female ages equal—when
We don't much care with whom we may engage,
    As bold as Daniel in the lion's den,[7]
So that we can our native sun assuage
    In the next ocean, which may flow just then,   550
To make a twilight in, just as Sol's[8] heat is
Quench'd in the lap of the salt sea, or Thetis.[9]

70

And Catherine (we must say thus much for Catherine),
    Though bold and bloody, was the kind of thing
Whose temporary passion was quite flattering,   555
    Because each lover look'd a sort of king,
Made up upon an amatory pattern,
    A royal husband in all save the *ring*—
Which, being the damn'dest part of matrimony,
Seem'd taking out the sting to leave the honey.   560

---

4. Mountain in the Alps.
5. *laudanum* . . . *"black drop"*: liquid forms of opium, intended for medicinal use.
6. In *Eloisa to Abelard* (1717).
7. Daniel 6.17–23. The erotic wit of this simile and the lines that follow is consistent with the ribald
   humor throughout this canto.
8. The ancient Roman god of the sun.
9. In Homer's *Iliad*, sea nymph and mother of Achilles.

71

And when you add to this, her womanhood
    In its meridian,[1] her blue eyes or gray—
(The last, if they have soul, are quite as good,
    Or better, as the best examples say:
Napoleon's, Mary's (Queen of Scotland), should   565
    Lend to that colour a transcendent ray;
And Pallas[2] also sanctions the same hue,
Too wise to look through optics black or blue)—

72

Her sweet smile, and her then majestic figure,
    Her plumpness, her imperial condescension,   570
Her preference of a boy to men much bigger
    (Fellows whom Messalina's[3] self would pension),
Her prime of life, just now in juicy vigour,
    With other *extras*, which we need not mention,—
All these, or any one of these, explain   575
Enough to make a stripling very vain.

73

And that's enough for love is vanity,
    Selfish in its beginning as its end,
Except where 'tis a mere insanity,
    A maddening spirit which would strive to blend   580
Itself with Beauty's frail inanity,
    On which the passion's self seems to depend:
And hence some heathenish philosophers
Make Love the main spring of the universe.

74

Besides Platonic[4] love, besides the love   585
    Of God, the love of sentiment, the loving
Of faithful pairs—(I needs must rhyme with dove,
    That good old steam-boat which keeps verses moving
'Gainst reason—Reason ne'er was hand-and-glove
    With rhyme, but always leant less to improving   590
The sound than sense)—besides all these pretences
To Love, there are those things which words name senses;

75

Those movements, those improvements in our bodies
    Which make all bodies anxious to get out

---

1. Catherine was sixty-two in 1791.
2. Athena, Greek goddess of wisdom, often referred to by Homer as "gray-eyed Athena."
3. Wife of the Roman emperor Claudius (died 48 c.e.), known for her greed and lustfulness.
4. See also: line 601; I.629 and note, 885, 921; V.7-8.

Of their own sand-pits, to mix with a goddess,   595
    For such all women are at first no doubt.
How beautiful that moment! and how odd is
    That fever which precedes the languid rout
Of our sensations! What a curious way
The whole thing is of clothing souls in clay!   600

76

The noblest kind of love is Love Platonical,
    To end or to begin with; the next grand
Is that which may be christen'd Love Canonical,
    Because the clergy take the thing in hand;
The third sort to be noted in our Chronicle   605
    As flourishing in every Christian land,
Is, when chaste matrons to their other ties
Add what may be call'd *marriage in disguise*.

77

Well, we won't analyse—our story must
    Tell for itself: the sovereign was smitten,   610
Juan much flatter'd by her love, or lust;—
    I cannot stop to alter words once written,
And the two are so mix'd with human dust,
    That he who *names one*, both perchance may hit on:
But in such matters Russia's mighty Empress   615
Behaved no better than a common Sempstress.

78

The whole court melted into one wide whisper,
    And all lips were applied unto all ears!
The elder ladies' wrinkles curl'd much crisper
    As they beheld; the younger cast some leers   620
On one another, and each lovely lisper
    Smiled as she talk'd the matter o'er; but tears
Of rivalship rose in each clouded eye
Of all the standing army who stood by.

79

All the ambassadors of all the powers   625
    Enquired, Who was this very new young man,
Who promised to be great in some few hours?
    Which is full soon (though life is but a span).
Already they beheld the silver showers
    Of rubles rain, as fast as specie can,   630
Upon his cabinet, besides the presents
Of several ribands, and some thousand peasants.[5]

---

5. "A Russian estate is always valued by the number of the slaves upon it."

80

Catherine was generous,—all such ladies are:
  Love, that great opener of the heart and all
The ways that lead there, be they near or far,   635
  Above, below, by turnpikes great or small,—
Love—(though she had a cursed taste for war,
  And was not the best wife, unless we call
Such Clytemnestra,[6] though perhaps 'tis better
That one should die, than two drag on the fetter)—   640

81

Love had made Catherine make each lover's fortune,
  Unlike our own half-chaste Elizabeth,[7]
Whose avarice all disbursements did importune,
  If history, the grand liar, ever saith
The truth; and though grief her old age might shorten,   645
  Because she put a favourite to death,
Her vile, ambiguous method of flirtation,
And stinginess, disgrace her sex and station.

82

But when the levee rose, and all was bustle
  In the dissolving circle, all the nations'   650
Ambassadors began as 'twere to hustle
  Round the young man with their congratulations.
Also the softer silks were heard to rustle
  Of gentle dames, among whose recreations
It is to speculate on handsome faces,   655
Especially when such lead to high places.

83

Juan, who found himself, he knew not how,
  A general object of attention, made
His answers with a very graceful bow,
  As if born for the ministerial trade.   660
Though modest, on his unembarrass'd brow
  Nature had written "gentleman." He said
Little, but to the purpose; and his manner
Flung hovering graces o'er him like a banner.

84

An order from her Majesty consign'd   665
  Our young Lieutenant to the genial care

6. Wife of Agamemnon, whom she murders when he returns to Argos at the end of the Trojan War. Byron referred to his wife as his "moral Clytemnestra" (*BLJ* 5:144, 198).
7. Queen Elizabeth I (1558–1603); line 646 refers to her ordering the execution of Robert Devereux, earl of Essex, in 1601.

Of those in office: all the world look'd kind
   (As it will look sometimes with the first stare,
Which Youth would not act ill to keep in mind),
   As also did Miss Protasoff[8] then there,   670
Named from her mystic office "l'Eprouveuse,"
   A term inexplicable to the Muse.

85

With *her* then, as in humble duty bound,
   Juan retired,—and so will I, until
My Pegasus[9] shall tire of touching ground.   675
   We have just lit on a "heaven-kissing hill,"
So lofty that I feel my brain turn round,
   And all my fancies whirling like a mill;
Which is a signal to my nerves and brain,
To take a quiet ride in some green lane.   680

FROM CANTO THE TENTH[1]

1

When Newton[2] saw an apple fall, he found
   In that slight startle from his contemplation—
'Tis *said* (for I'll not answer above ground
   For any sage's creed or calculation)—
A mode of proving that the earth turn'd round   5
   In a most natural whirl, called "gravitation;"
And this is the sole mortal who could grapple,
Since Adam, with a fall, or with an apple.

2

Man fell with apples, and with apples rose,
   If this be true; for we must deem the mode   10
In which Sir Isaac Newton could disclose
   Through the then unpaved stars the turnpike road,
A thing to counterbalance human woes:
   For ever since immortal man hath glow'd
With all kinds of mechanics, and full soon   15
Steam-engines will conduct him to the moon.

3

And wherefore this exordium?[3]—Why, just now,
   In taking up this paltry sheet of paper,

---

8. Anna Stepanovna Protassova (1744–1826); she would oversee the medical examinations of
   Catherine's favorites, hence, "L'Eprouveuse," meaning "the tester" (sexual innuendo).
9. In classical myth, winged horse associated with artistic inspiration and the Muses.
1. Begun at Pisa, September 1822, finished at Genoa, in October; published with Cantos IX and XI
   on August 29, 1823.
2. Sir Isaac Newton (1642–1727) formulated the laws of gravity.
3. Introduction.

My bosom underwent a glorious glow,
    And my internal spirit cut a caper: 20
And though so much inferior, as I know,
    To those who, by the dint of glass and vapour,
Discover stars, and sail in the wind's eye,
I wish to do as much by Poesy.

4

In the wind's eye I have sail'd, and sail; but for   25
    The stars, I own my telescope is dim;
But at the least I have shunn'd the common shore,
    And leaving land far out of sight, would skim
The Ocean of Eternity: the roar
    Of breakers has not daunted my slight, trim,   30
But *still* sea-worthy skiff; and she may float
Where ships have founder'd, as doth many a boat.

5

We left our hero, Juan, in the *bloom*
    Of favouritism, but not yet in the *blush*;—
And far be it from my *Muses* to presume   35
    (For I have more than one Muse at a push)
To follow him beyond the drawing-room:
    It is enough that Fortune found him flush
Of youth, and vigour, beauty, and those things
Which for an instant clip Enjoyment's wings.   40

6

But soon they grow again and leave their nest.
    "Oh!" saith the Psalmist, "that I had a dove's
Pinions to flee away, and be at rest!"[4]
    And who that recollects young years and loves,—
Though hoary now, and with a withering breast,   45
    And palsied fancy, which no longer roves
Beyond its dimm'd eye's sphere,—but would much rather
Sigh like his son, than cough like his grandfather?

7

But sighs subside, and tears (even widows') shrink,
    Like Arno[5] in the summer, to a shallow,   50
So narrow as to shame their wintry brink,
    Which threatens inundations deep and yellow!
Such difference doth a few months make.[6] You'd think
    Grief a rich field which never would lie fallow;

---

4. Psalm 55.6; for Byron's particular appreciation of this psalm, see his note to "I Would I Were a Careless Child" (p. 7).
5. River in central Italy, visible from Byron's residence in Pisa, where he began this canto.
6. Lines 53–64 recall the recent deaths of Byron's daughter Allegra and close friend Percy Shelley.

No more it doth, its ploughs but change their boys,   55
Who furrow some new soil to sow for joys.

                              8

But coughs will come when sighs depart—and now
     And then before sighs cease; for oft the one
Will bring the other, ere the lake-like brow
     Is ruffled by a wrinkle, or the sun   60
Of life reach ten o'clock: and while a glow,
     Hectic and brief as summer's day nigh done,
O'erspreads the cheek which seems too pure for clay,
Thousands blaze, love, hope, die,—how happy they!

                              9

But Juan was not meant to die so soon.   65
     We left him in the focus of such glory
As may be won by favour of the moon
     Or ladies' fancies—rather transitory
Perhaps; but who would scorn the month of June,
     Because December, with his breath so hoary,   70
Must come? Much rather should he court the ray,
To hoard up warmth against a wintry day.

                              10

Besides, he had some qualities which fix
     Middle-aged ladies even more than young:
The former know what's what; while new-fledged chicks   75
     Know little more of Love than what is sung
In rhymes, or dreamt (for fancy will play tricks)
     In visions of those skies from whence Love sprung.
Some reckon women by their suns or years,
I rather think the moon should date the dears.   80

                              11

And why? because she's changeable and chaste.
     I know no other reason, whatsoe'er
Suspicious people, who find fault in haste,
     May choose to tax me with; which is not fair,
Nor flattering to "their temper or their taste,"[7]   85
     As my friend Jeffrey writes with such an air:
However, I forgive him, and I trust
He will forgive himself;—if not, I must.

---

7. Quoted from criticism of *Don Juan* (especially its "too savage" attack on Southey) by Francis Jeffrey (1773–1858) in the *Edinburgh Review* (February 1822). The lines that follow, as well as stanzas 16–17, refer to Byron's relationship with Jeffrey. Having initially believed that Jeffrey had written the review ridiculing *Hours of Idleness* (1807), Byron satirized him in *English Bards and Scotch Reviewers* (1809); however, after Byron learned that Jeffrey was not the person who had written that review, they became friends, and Byron always respected Jeffrey's critical judgment.

12

Old enemies who have become new friends
  Should so continue—'tis a point or honour;   90
And I know nothing which could make amends
  For a return to hatred: I would shun her
Like garlic, howsoever she extends
  Her hundred arms and legs, and fain outrun her.
Old flames, new wives, become our bitterest foes—   95
Converted foes should scorn to join with those.

13

This were the worst desertion:—renegadoes,
  Even shuffling Southey, that incarnate lie,
Would scarcely join again the "reformadoes,"[8]
  Whom he forsook to fill the Laureate's sty: 100
And honest men from Iceland to Barbadoes,
  Whether in Caledon or Italy,
Should not veer round with every breath, nor seize
To pain, the moment when you cease to please.

14

The lawyer and the critic but behold   105
  The baser sides of literature and life,
And nought remains unseen, but much untold,
  By those who scour those double vales of strife.
While common men grow ignorantly old,
  The lawyer's brief is like the surgeon's knife,   110
Dissecting the whole inside of a question,
And with it all the process of digestion.

15

A legal broom's[9] a moral chimney-sweeper,
  And that's the reason he himself's so dirty;
The endless soot[1] bestows a tint far deeper   115
  Than can be hid by altering his shirt; he
Retains the sable stains of the dark creeper,
  At least some twenty-nine do out of thirty,
In all their habits;—not so *you*, I own;
As Caesar wore his robe you wear your gown.   120

16

And all our little feuds, at least all *mine*,
  Dear Jeffrey, once my most redoubted foe

---

8. "'Reformers,' or rather 'Reformed.' The Baron Bradwardine, in Waverley, is authority for the word."
9. A pun on the name of Henry Brougham, a lawyer whom Byron detested.
1. "Query, *suit?*—Printer's Devil." A printer's devil is a printer's apprentice, often blackened by ink stains.

(As far as rhyme and criticism combine
To make such puppets of us things below),
Are over: Here's a health to "Auld Lang Syne!"[2]   125
I do not know you, and may never know
Your face—but you have acted on the whole
Most nobly, and I own it from my soul.

17

And when I use the phrase of "Auld Lang Syne!"
'Tis not address'd to you—the more's the pity   130
For me, for I would rather take my wine
    With you, than aught (save Scott) in your proud city.
But somehow,—it may seem a schoolboy's whine,
    And yet I seek not to be grand nor witty,
But I am half a Scot by birth, and bred   135
A whole one,[3] and my heart flies to my head,—

18

As "Auld Lang Syne" brings Scotland, one and all,
    Scotch plaids, Scotch snoods,[4] the blue hills, and clear
        streams,
The Dee, the Don, Balgounie's brig's *black wall*,[5]
    All my boy feelings, all my gentler dreams   140
Of what I *then dreamt*, clothed in their own pall,
    Like Banquo's offspring;[6]—floating past me seems
My childhood in this childishness of mine:
I care not—'tis a glimpse of 'Auld Lang Syne.'

19

And though, as you remember, in a fit   145
    Of wrath and rhyme, when juvenile and curly,
I rail'd at Scots to show my wrath and wit,
    Which must be own'd was sensitive and surly,
Yet 'tis in vain such sallies to permit,
    They cannot quench young feelings fresh and early: 150
I "*scotch'd* not kill'd"[7] the Scotchman in my blood,
And love the land of "mountain and of flood."

2. Scots phrase (literally, "Old Long Since"), well known from the poem written by Robert Burns in 1788.
3. Byron's mother was a Scot, and she raised Byron in Aberdeen, Scotland, from the time he was three years old until he was ten, when they moved to London.
4. Headband worn by unmarried women in Scotland.
5. "The brig of Don, near the 'auld toun' of Berdeen, with its one arch, and its black deep salmon stream below, is in my memory as yesterday. I still remember, though perhaps I may misquote, the awful proverb which made me pause to cross it, and yet lean over it with a childish delight, an only son, at least by the mother's side. The saying as recollected by me was this, but I have never heard or seen it since I was nine years of age:—'Brig of Balgounie, *black's* your wa', / Wi' a wife's *ae son*, and a mear's *ae foal*, / Doun ye shall fa'!' " Line 139 and Byron's note refer to two rivers, the Dee and the Don, that flow through Aberdeen, and the bridge ("brig") over the Don.
6. *Macbeth* 4.1.84–110.
7. *Scotch'd*: wounded, rendered harmless. Cf. *Macbeth* 3.2.15. In the line that follows Byron quotes from Walter Scott's *Lay of the Last Minstrel* 6.2.

20

Don Juan, who was real, or ideal,—
　For both are much the same, since what men think
Exists when the once thinkers are less real
　Than what they thought, for mind can never sink,
And 'gainst the body makes a strong appeal;
　And yet 'tis very puzzling on the brink
Of what is call'd Eternity, to stare,
And know no more of what is here, than there;—

21

Don Juan grew a very polish'd Russian—
　How we won't mention, *why* we need not say:
Few youthful minds can stand the strong concussion
　Of any slight temptation in their way;
But *his* just now were spread as is a cushion
　Smooth'd for a monarch's seat of honour: gay
Damsels, and dances, revels, ready money,
Made ice seem paradise, and winter sunny.

22

The favour of the Empress was agreeable;
　And though the duty wax'd a little hard,[8]
Young people at his time of life should be able
　To come off handsomely in that regard.
He was now growing up like a green tree, able
　For love, war, or ambition, which reward
Their luckier votaries, till old age's tedium
Make some prefer the circulating medium.

23

About this time, as might have been anticipated,
　Seduced by youth and dangerous examples,
Don Juan grew, I fear, a little dissipated;
　Which is a sad thing, and not only tramples
On our fresh feelings, but—as being participated
　With all kinds of incorrigible samples
Of frail humanity—must make us selfish,
And shut our souls up in us like a shell-fish.

24

This we pass over. We will also pass
　The usual progress of intrigues between
Unequal matches, such as are, alas!
　A young Lieutenant's with a *not old* Queen,

---

8. Lines 170–72 contain sexual double entendres.

But one who is not so youthful as she was
   In all the royalty of sweet seventeen.   190
Sovereigns may sway materials, but not matter,
   And wrinkles, the d——d democrats, won't flatter.

25

And Death, the sovereign's sovereign, though the great
   Gracchus of all mortality, who levels
With his *Agrarian* laws[9] the high estate   195
   Of him who feasts, and fights, and roars, and revels,
To one small grass-grown patch (which must await
   Corruption for its crop) with the poor devils
Who never had a foot of land till now,—
   Death's a reformer, all men must allow.   200

26

He lived (not Death, but Juan) in a hurry
   Of waste, and haste, and glare, and gloss, and glitter,
In this gay clime of bear-skins black and furry—
   Which (though I hate to say a thing that's bitter)
Peep out sometimes, when things are in a flurry,   205
   Through all the "purple and fine linen,"[1] fitter
For Babylon's than Russia's royal harlot—
   And neutralise her outward show of scarlet.

27

And this same state we won't describe: we would
   Perhaps from hearsay, or from recollection;   210
But getting nigh grim Dante's "obscure wood,"[2]
   That horrid equinox, that hateful section
Of human years, that half-way house, that rude
   Hut, whence wise travellers drive with circumspection
Life's sad post-horses o'er the dreary frontier   215
   Of age, and looking back to youth, give *one* tear;—

28

I won't describe,—that is, if I can help
   Description; and I won't reflect,—that is,
If I can stave off thought, which—as a whelp
   Clings to its teat—sticks to me through the abyss   220

---

9. "Tiberius Gracchus, being tribune of the people, demanded in their name the execution of the Agrarian law; by which all persons possessing above a certain number of acres were to be deprived of the surplus for the benefit of the poor citizens." (Moore's note.)
1. Luke 16.19; excessive luxuriousness, more suited, as the next line indicates, to the pagan queen Semiramis than the Christian Catherine.
2. "'Mi retrovai per un selva oscura.'—*Inferno, Canto I.*" Byron refers to the famous opening line of the Inferno: "Midway through the journey of life, I found myself at a dark woods." Byron is thirty-four years old when he writes this stanza, one year younger than the age that Dante is supposed to have begun his journey through hell.

Of this odd labyrinth; or as the kelp
   Holds by the rock; or as a lover's kiss
Drains its first draught of lips:—but, as I said,
I *won't* philosophise, and *will* be read.

29

Juan, instead of courting courts, was courted,—   225
   A thing which happens rarely: this he owed
Much to his youth, and much to his reported
   Valour; much also to the blood he show'd,
Like a race-horse; much to each dress he sported,
   Which set the beauty off in which he glow'd,   230
As purple clouds befringe the sun; but most
He owed to an old woman and his post.

30

He wrote to Spain:—and all his near relations,
   Perceiving he was in a handsome way
Of getting on himself, and finding stations   235
   For cousins also, answer'd the same day.
Several prepared themselves for emigrations;
   And eating ices, were o'erheard to say,
That with the addition of a slight pelisse,[3]
Madrid's and Moscow's climes were of a piece.   240

31

His mother, Donna Inez, finding, too,
   That in the lieu of drawing on his banker,
Where his assets were waxing rather few,
   He had brought his spending to a handsome anchor,—
Replied, "that she was glad to see him through   245
   Those pleasures after which wild youth will hanker;
As the sole sign of man's being in his senses
Is, learning to reduce his past expenses.

32

"She also recommended him to God,
   And no less to God's Son, as well as Mother,   250
Warn'd him against Greek worship,[4] which looks odd
   In Catholic eyes; but told him, too, to smother
Outward dislike, which don't look well abroad;
   Inform'd him that he had a little brother
Born in a second wedlock; and above   255
All, praised the empress's *maternal* love.

3. Fur-lined cloak.
4. I.e., the Russian Orthodox religion.

33

"She could not too much give her approbation
　Unto an Empress, who preferr'd young men
Whose age, and what was better still, whose nation
　And climate, stopp'd all scandal (now and then):—   260
At home it might have given her some vexation;
　But where thermometers sunk down to ten,
Or five, or one, or zero, she could never
Believe that virtue thaw'd before the river."

34

Oh for a *forty-parson power*[5] to chant   265
　Thy praise, Hypocrisy! Oh for a hymn
Loud as the virtues thou dost loudly vaunt,
　Not practise! Oh for trumps of cherubim!
Or the ear-trumpet of my good old aunt,
　Who, though her spectacles at last grew dim,   270
Drew quiet consolation through its hint,
When she no more could read the pious print.

35

She was no hypocrite at least, poor soul,
　But went to heaven in as sincere a way
As any body on the elected roll,   275
　Which portions out upon the judgment day
Heaven's freeholds, in a sort of doomsday scroll,
　Such as the conqueror William did repay
His knights with, lotting others' properties
Into some sixty thousand[6] new knights' fees.   280

36

I can't complain, whose ancestors are there,
　Erneis, Radulphus[7]—eight-and-forty manors
(If that my memory doth not greatly err)
　Were their reward for following Billy's banners;
And though I can't help thinking 'twas scarce fair   285
　To strip the Saxons of their *hydes*,[8] like tanners;
Yet as they founded churches with the produce,
You'll deem, no doubt, they put it to a good use.

---

5. "A metaphor taken from the 'fortyhorse power' of a steam-engine. That mad wag, the Reverend Sydney Smith, sitting by a brother clergyman at dinner, observed afterwards that his dull neighbour had a 'twelve-parson power' of conversation."
6. A traditional exaggeration of the force that invaded England under William the Conqueror in 1066.
7. Ancestors of Byron's, perhaps, who came to England with William and overwhelmed the Saxons (line 286).
8. "'Hyde.'—I believe a hyde of land to be a legitimate word, and, as such, subject to the tax of a quibble." A "hyde" was about 120 acres.

37

The gentle Juan flourish'd, though at times
    He felt like other plants called sensitive,   290
Which shrink from touch, as monarchs do from rhymes,
    Save such as Southey can afford to give.
Perhaps he long'd in bitter frosts for climes
    In which the Neva's[9] ice would cease to live
Before May-day: perhaps, despite his duty,   295
In royalty's vast arms he sigh'd for beauty:

38

Perhaps—but, sans perhaps, we need not seek
    For causes young or old: the canker-worm
Will feed upon the fairest, freshest cheek,
    As well as further drain the wither'd form: 300
Care, like a housekeeper, brings every week
    His bills in, and however we may storm,
They must be paid: though six days smoothly run,
The seventh will bring blue devils or a dun.[1]

39

I don't know how it was, but he grew sick: 305
    The Empress was alarm'd, and her physician
(The same who physick'd Peter) found the tick
    Of his fierce pulse betoken a condition
Which augur'd of the dead, however *quick*
    Itself, and show'd a feverish disposition;   310
At which the whole court was extremely troubled,
The sovereign shock'd, and all his medicines doubled.

40

Low were the whispers, manifold the rumours:
    Some said he had been poison'd by Potemkin;[2]
Others talk'd learnedly of certain tumours,   315
    Exhaustion, or disorders of the same kin;
Some said 'twas a concoction of the humours,
    Which with the blood too readily will claim kin;
Others again were ready to maintain,
" 'Twas only the fatigue of last campaign."[3]   320

41

But here is one prescription out of many:[4]
    "Sodae sulphat. ʒvj. ʒfs. Mannae optim.

---

9. River in czarist Russia's capital city, St. Petersburg.
1. *blue devils . . . dun*: depression or alcoholic delirium . . . bill collector.
2. Renowned Russian field marshal (1739–1791) and a favorite of Catherine II.
3. Sexual suggestion.
4. The Latin prescription satirized in this stanza is for a strong laxative and emetic (vomit-inducing compound)—all-purpose treatments in Byron's day. For a full translation, see *DJV* 4:210 or *CPW* 5:744.

Aq. fervent. f. ℥ifs. ℥ij. tinct. Sennae
    Haustus" (And here the surgeon came and cupp'd him)
"℞ Pulv. Com. gr. iij. Ipecacuanhae"   325
    (With more beside if Juan had not stopp'd 'em).
"Bolus Potassae Sulphuret, sumendus,
Et haustus ter in die capiendus."

42

This is the way physicians mend or end us,
    Secundum artem:[5] but although we sneer   330
In health—when ill, we call them to attend us,
    Without the least propensity to jeer:
While that "hiatus maxime deflendus"[6]
    To be fill'd up by spade or mattock's near,
Instead of gliding graciously down Lethe,[7]   335
We tease mild Baillie, or soft Abernethy.[8]

43

Juan demurr'd at this first notice to
    Quit; and though Death had threaten'd an ejection,
His youth and constitution bore him through,
    And sent the doctors in a new direction.   340
But still his state was delicate: the hue
    Of health but flicker'd with a faint reflection
Along his wasted cheek, and seem'd to gravel
The faculty—who said that he must travel.

44

The climate was too cold, they said, for him,   345
    Meridian-born, to bloom in. This opinion
Made the chaste Catherine look a little grim,
    Who did not like at first to lose her minion:
But when she saw his dazzling eye wax dim,
    And drooping like an eagle's with clipt pinion,   350
She then resolved to send him on a mission,
But in a style becoming his condition.

45

There was just then a kind of a discussion,
    A sort of treaty or negotiation
Between the British cabinet and Russian,   355
    Maintain'd with all the due prevarication

---

5. According to their art.
6. "That great gap much to be regretted": here, the grave, though the phrase was generally used to indicate a literary gap.
7. In Greek myth, river of forgetfulness in Hades over which the dead had to be ferried.
8. *Baillie . . . soft Abernethy*: doctors noted for their bluntness.

With which great states such things are apt to push on;
   Something about the Baltic's navigation,
Hides, train-oil, tallow, and the rights of Thetis,
   Which Britons deem their "uti possidetis."[9]   360

46

So Catherine, who had a handsome way
   Of fitting out her favourites, conferr'd
This secret charge on Juan, to display
   At once her royal splendour, and reward
His services. He kiss'd hands the next day,   365
   Received instructions how to play his card,
Was laden with all kinds of gifts and honours,
Which show'd what great discernment was the donor's.

47

But she was lucky, and luck's all. Your queens
   Are generally prosperous in reigning;   370
Which puzzles us to know what Fortune means.
   But to continue: though her years were waning
Her climacteric[1] teased her like her teens;
   And though her dignity brook'd no complaining,
So much did Juan's setting off distress her,   375
She could not find at first a fit successor.

48

But time, the comforter, will come at last;[2]
   And four-and-twenty hours, and twice that number
Of candidates requesting to be placed,
   Made Catherine taste next night a quiet slumber:—   380
Not that she meant to fix again in haste,
   Nor did she find the quantity encumber,
But always choosing with deliberation,
Kept the place open for their emulation.

49

While this high post of honour's in abeyance,   385
   For one or two days, reader, we request
You'll mount with our young hero the conveyance
   Which wafted him from Petersburgh: the best
Barouche,[3] which had the glory to display once
   The fair czarina's autocratic crest,   390

---

9. Lines 358–60: England considered that it had the right to rule the seas (like the ancient Greek sea
nymph, Thetis), including access to the Baltic Sea's trade goods, by virtue of possession ("uti pos-
sidetis"), i.e., as a result of its great naval victory at Trafalgar (1805).
1. Menopause.
2. The stanza contains some crude wordplay.
3. Horse-drawn carriage.

When, a new Iphigene, she went to Tauris,[4]
Was given to her favourite, and now *bore his*.

* * *

CANTO THE ELEVENTH[1]

1

When Bishop Berkeley said "there was no matter,"[2]
And proved it—'twas no matter what he said:
They say his system 'tis in vain to batter,
  Too subtle for the airiest human head;
And yet who can believe it? I would shatter   5
  Gladly all matters down to stone or lead,
Or adamant, to find the world a spirit,
And wear my head, denying that I wear it.

2

What a sublime discovery 'twas to make the
  Universe universal egotism,   10
That all's ideal—*all ourselves*: I'll stake the
  World (be it what you will) that *that's* no schism.
Oh Doubt!—if thou be'st Doubt, for which some take thee,
  But which I doubt extremely—thou sole prism
Of the Truth's rays, spoil not my draught of spirit! 15
Heaven's brandy, though our brain can hardly bear it.

3

For ever and anon comes Indigestion,
  (Not the most "dainty Ariel"[3]) and perplexes
Our soarings with another sort of question:
  And that which after all my spirit vexes,   20
Is, that I find no spot where man can rest eye on,
  Without confusion of the sorts and sexes,
Of beings, stars, and this unriddled wonder,
The world, which at the worst's a glorious blunder—

4

If it be chance; or if it be according   25
  To the Old Text,[4] still better:—lest it should

---

4. "The empress went to the Crimea, accompanied by the Emperor Joseph, in the year—I forget which." It was 1787. The line refers to the Greek myth of Iphigenia, who was transported by Artemis to Tauris, located in modern-day Crimea (a region in southwest Russia on the Black Sea).
1. Canto XI was written in October 1822; for publication information, see note to Canto IX.
2. In *On the Principles of Human Knowledge* (1734), George Berkeley (1685–1753), Anglican bishop and philosopher, held that reality was spiritual and that matter does not exist. Byron's satirical retort to Berkeley in stanzas 1–5 is consistent with the poem's recurrent critique of Platonic idealism and with the poem's assertion of the force of historical and physical reality.
3. *The Tempest* 5.1.97.
4. The Bible.

Turn out so, we'll say nothing 'gainst the wording,
    As several people think such hazards rude.
They're right; our days are too brief for affording
    Space to dispute what *no one* ever could   30
Decide, and *every body one day* will
    Know very clearly—or at least lie still.

5

And therefore will I leave off metaphysical
    Discussion, which is neither here nor there:
If I agree that what is, is; then this I call   35
    Being quite perspicuous and extremely fair;
The truth is, I've grown lately rather phthisical:[5]
    I don't know what the reason is—the air
Perhaps; but as I suffer from the shocks
Of illness, I grow much more orthodox.   40

6

The first attack at once proved the Divinity
    (But *that* I never doubted, nor the Devil);
The next, the Virgin's mystical virginity;
    The third, the usual Origin of Evil;
The fourth at once established the whole Trinity   45
    On so uncontrovertible a level,
That I devoutly wish'd the three were four,
On purpose to believe so much the more.

7

To our theme.—The man who has stood on the Acropolis,[6]
    And look'd down over Attica; or he   50
Who has sail'd where picturesque Constantinople is,
    Or seen Timbuctoo, or hath taken tea
In small-eyed China's crockery-ware metropolis,
    Or sat amidst the bricks of Nineveh,
May not think much of London's first appearance—   55
But ask him what he thinks of it a year hence?

8

Don Juan had got out on Shooter's Hill;[7]
    Sunset the time, the place the same declivity
Which looks along that vale of good and ill
    Where London streets ferment in full activity;   60

---

5. Consumptive.
6. Hill in Athens (*Attica*) where the Parthenon was built. The stanza names centers of other ancient
    empires: *Constantinople*, the Ottoman Empire; *Timbuctoo*, in northwest Africa and once an impor-
    tant center of the Muslim world; and *Nineveh*, the Babylonian Empire.
7. Eight miles south of London, offering an expansive view of London and the surrounding country-
    side; a reputed haunt for robbers.

While every thing around was calm and still,
    Except the creak of wheels, which on their pivot he
Heard,—and that bee-like, bubbling, busy hum
Of cities, that boil over with their scum:—

9

I say, Don Juan, wrapt in contemplation,   65
    Walk'd on behind his carriage, o'er the summit,
And lost in wonder of so great a nation,
    Gave way to't, since he could not overcome it.
"And here," he cried, "is Freedom's chosen station;
    Here peals the people's voice, nor can entomb it   70
Racks, prisons, inquisitions; resurrection
Awaits it, each new meeting or election.

10

"Here are chaste wives, pure lives; here people pay
    But what they please; and if that things be dear,
'Tis only that they love to throw away   75
    Their cash, to show how much they have a-year.
Here laws are all inviolate; none lay
    Traps for the traveller; every highway's clear:
Here—" he was interrupted by a knife,
With,—"Damn your eyes! your money or your life!"—   80

11

These freeborn sounds proceeded from four pads[8]
    In ambush laid, who had perceived him loiter
Behind his carriage; and, like handy lads,
    Had seized the lucky hour to reconnoitre,[9]
In which the heedless gentleman who gads   85
    Upon the road, unless he prove a fighter,
May find himself within that isle of riches
Exposed to lose his life as well as breeches.

12

Juan, who did not understand a word
    Of English, save their shibboleth,[1] "God damn!"   90
And even that he had so rarely heard,
    He sometimes thought 'twas only their "Salām,"[2]
Or "God be with you!"—and 'tis not absurd
    To think so: for half English as I am[3]
(To my misfortune) never can I say   95
I heard them wish "God with you," save that way;—

8. Footpads: muggers.
9. Inspect or survey (the enemy).
1. A catchword or phrase adopted by a group, party, or sect.
2. Peace be with you (Islamic greeting).
3. Byron is half Scottish.

13

Juan yet quickly understood their gesture,
  And being somewhat choleric and sudden,
Drew forth a pocket pistol from his vesture,
  And fired it into one assailant's pudding—   100
Who fell, as rolls an ox o'er in his pasture,
  And roar'd out, as he writhed his native mud in,
Unto his nearest follower or henchman,
"Oh Jack! I'm floor'd by that 'ere bloody Frenchman!"

14

On which Jack and his train set off at speed,   105
  And Juan's suite, late scatter'd at a distance,
Came up, all marvelling at such a deed,
  And offering, as usual, late assistance.
Juan, who saw the moon's late minion[4] bleed
  As if his veins would pour out his existence,   110
Stood calling out for bandages and lint,
And wish'd he had been less hasty with his flint.

15

"Perhaps," thought he, "it is the country's wont
  To welcome foreigners in this way: now
I recollect some innkeepers who don't   115
  Differ, except in robbing with a bow,
In lieu of a bare blade and brazen front.
  But what is to be done? I can't allow
The fellow to lie groaning on the road:
So take him up; I'll help you with the load."   120

16[5]

But ere they could perform this pious duty,
  The dying man cried, "Hold! I've got my gruel!
Oh! for a glass of *max!* We've miss'd our booty;
  Let me die where I am!" And as the fuel
Of life shrunk in his heart, and thick and sooty   125
  The drops fell from his death-wound, and he drew ill
His breath,—he from his swelling throat untied
A kerchief, crying, "Give Sal that!"—and died.

17

The cravat stain'd with bloody drops fell down
  Before Don Juan's feet: he could not tell   130

<hr>

4. Follower (Falstaff's euphemism for thieves, "minions of the moon," in *1 Henry IV* 1.2.23.)
5. In stanzas 16, 17, and 19, Byron uses "flash" language, the low-life slang that was nonetheless con-
sidered chic in Regency society. Thus, in stanza 16: *got my gruel* means to be punished or killed;
max is gin. In stanza 17: *kiddy* is a low-class thief who affects gentility; *varmint* is a skilled ama-
teur; *swell* is a well-dressed person; *full-flash* means affecting a manner in order to be noticed; *did-
dled* means cheated.

Exactly why it was before him thrown,
    Nor what the meaning of the man's farewell.
Poor Tom was once a kiddy upon town,
    A thorough varmint, and a *real* swell,
Full flash, all fancy, until fairly diddled,   135
His pockets first and then his body riddled.

18

Don Juan, having done the best he could
    In all the circumstances of the case,
As soon as "Crowner's quest"⁶ allow'd, pursued
    His travels to the capital apace;—   140
Esteeming it a little hard he should
    In twelve hours' time, and very little space,
Have been obliged to slay a freeborn native
In self-defence: this made him meditative.

19

He from the world had cut off a great man,   145
    Who in his time had made heroic bustle.
Who in a row like Tom could lead the van,
    Booze in the ken, or at the spellken hustle?
Who queer a flat? Who (spite of Bow-street's ban)
    On the high toby-spice so flash the muzzle?   150
Who on a lark, with black-eyed Sal (his blowing),
So prime, so swell, so nutty, and so knowing?⁷

20

But Tom's no more—and so no more of Tom.
    Heroes must die; and by God's blessing 'tis

---

6. Coroner's inquest.
7. "The advance of science and of language has rendered it unnecessary to translate the above good
and true English, spoken in its original purity by the select mobility and their patrons. The fol-
lowing is a stanza of a song which was very popular, at least in my early days:—

> 'On the high toby-spice flash the muzzle,
>   In spite of each gallows old scout;
> If you at the spellken can't hustle,
>   You'll be hobbled in making a Clout.
>
> 'Then your Blowing will wax gallows haughty,
>   When she hears of your scaly mistake,
> She'll surely turn snitch for the forty—
>   That her Jack may be regular weight.'

If there be any gemman so ignorant as to require a traduction, I refer him to my old friend and
corporeal pastor and master, John Jackson, Esq., Professor of Pugilism; who, I trust, still retains
the strength and symmetry of his model of a form, together with his good humour, and athletic as
well as mental accomplishments."

Moore provides the following translations: "*ken*, a house that harbors thieves; *spellken*, the play-
house; *queer a flat*, to puzzle or confound a gull, or silly fellow; *high toby-spice*, robbery on horse-
back; *flash the muzzle*, to swagger openly; *lark*, fun or sport of any kind; *his blowing*, a pickpocket's
trull [prostitute]; *so swell*, so gentlemanly; *To be nuts upon*, is, to be very much pleased or gratified
with, any thing: thus, a person who conceived a strong inclination for another of the opposite sex
is said to be quite *nutty* upon him or her.—*Slang Dictionary*." *Bow-street* was the location of Mag-
istrates' Court.

Not long before the most of them go home.   155
   Hail! Thamis,[8] hail! Upon thy verge it is
That Juan's chariot, rolling like a drum
   In thunder, holds the way it can't well miss,
Through Kennington[9] and all the other "tons,"
Which make us wish ourselves in town at once;—   160

21

Through Groves, so call'd as being void of trees,
   (Like *lucus*[1] from *no* light; through prospects named
Mount Pleasant,[2] as containing nought to please,
   Nor much to climb; through little boxes framed
Of bricks, to let the dust in at your ease,   165
   With "To be let," upon their doors proclaim'd;
Through "Rows" most modestly call'd "Paradise,"
Which Eve might quit without much sacrifice;—

22

Through coaches, drays,[3] choked turnpikes, and a whirl
   Of wheels, and roar of voices, and confusion;   170
Here taverns wooing to a pint of "purl,"[4]
   There mails fast flying off like a delusion;
There barbers' blocks with periwigs in curl
   In windows; here the lamplighter's infusion
Slowly distill'd into the glimmering glass   175
(For in those days we had not got to gas—);

23

Through this, and much, and more, is the approach
   Of travellers to mighty Babylon:
Whether they come by horse, or chaise, or coach,
   With slight exceptions, all the ways seem one.   180
I could say more, but do not choose to encroach
   Upon the Guide-book's privilege. The sun
Had set some time, and night was on the ridge
Of twilight, as the party cross'd the bridge.

24

That's rather fine, the gentle sound of Thamis—   185
   Who vindicates a moment, too, his stream—
Though hardly heard through multifarious "damme's."

8. The Thames River, which flows through London.
9. Stylish section of London, with a pun on *ton*, French for élite style.
1. Grove or dense wood (Latin). *Lucus* is ironically related to the Latin word meaning bright or shining.
2. Note in C: "Don Juan must have driven by *Pleasant Row*, and passed within hail of *Paradise Row*, on the way from Kennington to Westminster Bridge."
3. Carts.
4. Moore: "A kind of medicated malt liquor. . . ."

The lamps of Westminster's[5] more regular gleam,
The breadth of pavement, and yon shrine where Fame is
  A spectral resident—whose pallid beam   190
In shape of moonshine hovers o'er the pile—
Make this a sacred part of Albion's[6] isle.

25

The Druids'[7] groves are gone—so much the better:
  Stone-Henge is not—but what the devil is it?—
But Bedlam[8] still exists with its sage fetter,   195
  That madmen may not bite you on a visit;
The Bench[9] too seats or suits full many a debtor;
  The Mansion House[1] too (though some people quiz it)
To me appears a stiff yet grand erection;
But then the Abbey's worth the whole collection.   200

26

The line of lights too up to Charing Cross,
  Pall Mall, and so forth, have a coruscation[2]
Like gold as in comparison to dross,
  Match'd with the Continent's illumination,
Whose cities Night by no means deigns to gloss.   205
  The French were not yet a lamp-lighting nation,
And when they grew so—on their new-found lantern,
Instead of wicks, they made a wicked man turn.[3]

27

A row of gentlemen along the streets
  Suspended, may illuminate mankind,   210
As also bonfires made of country seats;
  But the old way is best for the purblind:
The other looks like phosphorus on sheets,
  A sort of ignis fatuus[4] to the mind,
Which, though 'tis certain to perplex and frighten,   215
Must burn more mildly ere it can enlighten.

28

But London's so well lit, that if Diogenes[5]
  Could recommence to hunt his *honest man*,

---

5. Westminster Abbey; *yon shrine* (line 189): the Abbey's Poets' Corner.
6. England (archaic and poetic).
7. Ancient sect of pre-Christian priests, who worshiped at the prehistoric monument Stonehenge.
8. Bethlehem Royal Hospital, first insane asylum in England.
9. The court of Common Pleas at Westminster.
1. Official residence of the Lord Mayor.
2. Flash of light. *Charing Cross, Pall Mall*: fashionable locations in London.
3. During the Revolution in France, aristocrats were sometimes hanged from lampposts.
4. Literally, foolish fire (Latin); also called will-o'-the-wisp: spectral lighting effects over marshland that play tricks on travelers.
5. The Greek Cynic philosopher (412?–323? B.C.E.) who, it is told, searched throughout Athens with a lantern trying to find an honest man.

And found him not amidst the various progenies
   Of this enormous city's spreading spawn,   220
'Twere not for want of lamps to aid his dodging his
   Yet undiscover'd treasure. What *I* can,
I've done to find the same throughout life's journey,
But see the world is only one attorney.

29

Over the stones still rattling, up Pall Mall,   225
   Through crowds and carriages, but waxing thinner
As thunder'd knockers[6] broke the long seal'd spell
   Of doors 'gainst duns, and to an early dinner
Admitted a small party as night fell,—
   Don Juan, our young diplomatic sinner,   230
Pursued his path, and drove past some hotels,
St. James's Palace and St. James's "Hells."[7]

30

They reach'd the hotel: forth stream'd from the front door
   A tide of well-clad waiters, and around
The mob stood, and as usual several score   235
   Of those pedestrian Paphians[8] who abound
In decent London when the daylight's o'er;
   Commodious but immoral, they are found
Useful, like Malthus,[9] in promoting marriage.—
   But Juan now is stepping from his carriage   240

31

Into one of the sweetest of hotels,
   Especially for foreigners—and mostly
For those whom favour or whom fortune swells,
   And cannot find a bill's small items costly.
There many an envoy either dwelt or dwells   245
   (The den of many a diplomatic lost lie),
Until to some conspicuous square they pass,
And blazon o'er the door their names in brass.

32

Juan, whose was a delicate commission,
   Private, though publicly important, bore   250
No title to point out with due precision
   The exact affair on which he was sent o'er.

6. Aggressive bill-collectors; *duns* (line 228): creditors.
7. "'Hells,' gaming-houses. What their number may now be in this life, I know not. Before I was of age I knew them pretty accurately, both 'gold' and 'silver.' I was nearly called out by an acquaintance, because when he asked me where I thought that his soul would be found hereafter, I answered, 'In Silver Hell.'"
8. Lovers (from Paphos, island in Crete having a temple to Aphrodite).
9. Thomas Malthus (1766–1834), in his *Essay on the Principle of Population*, favored marriage only among the wealthy in order to check population growth.

'Twas merely known, that on a secret mission
   A foreigner of rank had graced our shore,
Young, handsome, and accomplish'd, who was said   255
   (In whispers) to have turn'd his sovereign's head.

33

Some rumour also of some strange adventures
   Had gone before him, and his wars and loves;
And as romantic heads are pretty painters,
   And, above all, an Englishwoman's roves   260
Into the excursive, breaking the indentures
   Of sober reason, wheresoe'er it moves,
He found himself extremely in the fashion,
Which serves our thinking people for a passion.

34

I don't mean that they are passionless, but quite   265
   The contrary; but then 'tis in the head;
Yet as the consequences are as bright
   As if they acted with the heart instead,
What after all can signify the site
   Of ladies' lucubrations?[1] So they lead   270
In safety to the place for which you start,
What matters if the road be head or heart?

35

Juan presented in the proper place,
   To proper placemen, every Russ credential;
And was received with all the due grimace,   275
   By those who govern in the mood potential,[2]
Who, seeing a handsome stripling with smooth face,
   Thought (what in state affairs is most essential)
That they as easily might *do* the youngster,
As hawks may pounce upon a woodland songster.   280

36

They err'd, as aged men will do; but by
   And by we'll talk of that; and if we don't,
'Twill be because our notion is not high
   Of politicians and their double front,
Who live by lies, yet dare not boldly lie:—   285
   Now what I love in women is, they won't
Or can't do otherwise than lie, but do it
So well, the very truth seems falsehood to it.

---

1. Intensive study or scholarly writing.
2. I.e., not actual rulers, but those who have political influence, i.e., *placemen* (line 274).

37

And, after all, what is a lie? 'Tis but
 The truth in masquerade; and I defy   290
Historians, heroes, lawyers, priests, to put
 A fact without some leaven of a lie.
The very shadow of true Truth would shut
 Up annals, revelations, poesy,
And prophecy—except it should be dated   295
Some years before the incidents related.

38

Praised be all liars and all lies! Who now
 Can tax my mild Muse with misanthropy?
She rings the world's "Te Deum,"[3] and her brow
 Blushes for those who will not:—but to sigh   300
Is idle; let us like most others bow,
 Kiss hands, feet, any part of majesty,
After the good example of "Green Erin,"[4]
Whose shamrock now seems rather worse for wearing.

39

Don Juan was presented, and his dress   305
 And mien excited general admiration—
I don't know which was more admired or less:
 One monstrous diamond drew much observation,
Which Catherine in a moment of "ivresse"[5]
 (In love or brandy's fervent fermentation)   310
Bestow'd upon him, as the public learn'd;
And, to say truth, it had been fairly earn'd.

40

Besides the ministers and underlings,
 Who must be courteous to the accredited
Diplomatists of rather wavering kings,   315
 Until their royal riddle's fully read,
The very clerks,—those somewhat dirty springs
 Of office, or the house of office,[6] fed
By foul corruption into streams,—even they
Were hardly rude enough to earn their pay: 320

41

And insolence no doubt is what they are
 Employ'd for, since it is their daily labour,
In the dear offices of peace or war;

3. Ancient Latin hymn of praise beginning *Te Deum laudamus* (We praise thee, God).
4. Ireland; a reference to the welcome extended to George IV when he visited Ireland in 1820.
5. Rapture (literally, intoxication [French]).
6. *house of office*: a pun on this colloquial phrase for latrine.

And should you doubt, pray ask of your next neighbour,
When for a passport, or some other bar   325
    To freedom, he applied (a grief and ā bore),
If he found not this spawn of taxborn riches,
Like lap-dogs, the least civil sons of b——s.

42

But Juan was received with much "empressement:"[7]—
    These phrases of refinement I must borrow   330
From our next neighbours' land, where, like a chessman,
    There is a move set down for joy or sorrow
Not only in mere talking, but the press. Man
    In islands is, it seems, downright and thorough,
More than on continents—as if the sea   335
(See Billingsgate[8]) made even the tongue more free.

43

And yet the British "Damme" 's rather Attic:[9]
    Your continental oaths are but incontinent.
And turn on things which no aristocratic
    Spirit would name, and therefore even I won't anent[1]   340
This subject quote; as it would be schismatic
    In politesse, and have a sound affronting in't:—
But "Damme" 's quite ethereal, though too daring—
Platonic blasphemy, the soul of swearing.

44

For downright rudeness, ye may stay at home;   345
    For true or false politeness (and scarce *that*
Now) you may cross the blue deep and white foam—
    The first the emblem (rarely though) of what
You leave behind, the next of much you come
    To meet. However, 'tis no time to chat   350
On general topics: poems must confine
Themselves to unity, like this of mine.

45

In the great world,—which, being interpreted,
    Meaneth the west or worst end[2] of a city,
And about twice two thousand people bred   355
    By no means to be very wise or witty,
But to sit up while others lie in bed,
    And look down on the universe with pity,—

---

7. Eager attention (French).
8. The London fishmarket.
9. I.e., refined, because spoken by the aristocrats.
1. "'Anent' was a Scotch phrase meaning 'concerning'—'with regard to:' it has been made English by the Scotch novels; and, as the Frenchman said, 'If it *be not, ought to be* English.'"
2. The west end of London was where the aristocracy lived.

Juan, as an inveterate patrician,
Was well received by persons of condition.   360

46

He was a bachelor, which is a matter
    Of import both to virgin and to bride,
The former's hymeneal hopes to flatter;
    And (should she not hold fast by love or pride)
'Tis also of some moment to the latter: 365
    A rib's a thorn in a wed gallant's side,
Requires decorum, and is apt to double
The horrid sin—and what's still worse, the trouble.

47

But Juan was a bachelor—of arts,
    And parts, and hearts: he danced and sung, and had   370
An air as sentimental as Mozart's
    Softest of melodies; and could be sad
Or cheerful, without any "flaws or starts,"[3]
    Just at the proper time; and though a lad,
Had seen the world—which is a curious sight,   375
And very much unlike what people write.

48

Fair virgins blush'd upon him; wedded dames
    Bloom'd also in less transitory hues;
For both commodities dwell by the Thames,
    The painting and the painted; youth, ceruse,[4]   380
Against his heart preferr'd their usual claims,
    Such as no gentleman can quite refuse:
Daughters admired his dress, and pious mothers
Enquired his income, and if he had brothers.

49

The milliners who furnish "drapery Misses"[5]   385
    Throughout the season, upon speculation
Of payment ere the honey-moon's last kisses
    Have waned into a crescent's coruscation,

---

3. *Macbeth* 3.4.62.
4. Powder used in paints.
5. " 'Drapery Misses.'—This term is probably any thing now but a *mystery*. It was, however, almost so to me when I first returned from the East in 1811–1812. It means a pretty, a high-born, a fashionable young female, well instructed by her friends, and furnished by her milliner with a wardrobe upon credit, to be repaid, when married, by the *husband*. The riddle was first read to me by a young and pretty heiress, on my praising the 'drapery' of the '*untochered*' but 'pretty virginities' (like Mrs. Anne Page) of the *then* day, which has now been some years yesterday: she assured me that the thing was common in London; and as her own thousands, and blooming looks, and rich simplicity of array, put any suspicion in her own case out of the question, I confess I gave some credit to the allegation. If necessary, authorities might be cited; in which case I could quote both 'drapery' and the wearers. Let us hope, however, that it is now obsolete."

Thought such an opportunity as this is,
   Of a rich foreigner's initiation,   390
Not to be overlook'd—and gave such credit,
   That future bridegrooms swore, and sigh'd, and paid it.

50

The Blues,[6] that tender tribe, who sigh o'er sonnets,
   And with the pages of the last Review
Line the interior of their beads or bonnets,   395
   Advanced in all their azure's highest hue:
They talk'd bad French or Spanish, and upon its
   Late authors ask'd him for a hint or two;
And which was softest, Russian or Castilian?
And whether in his travels he saw Ilion?[7]   400

51

Juan, who was a little superficial,
   And not in literature a great Drawcansir,[8]
Examined by this learned and especial
   Jury of matrons, scarce knew what to answer:
His duties warlike, loving or official,   405
   His steady application as a dancer,
Had kept him from the brink of Hippocrene,[9]
Which now he found was blue instead of green.

52

However, he replied at hazard, with
   A modest confidence and calm assurance,   410
Which lent his learned lucubrations pith,
   And pass'd for arguments of good endurance.
That prodigy, Miss Araminta Smith
   (Who at sixteen translated "Hercules Furens"
Into as furious English), with her best look,   415
Set down his sayings in her common-place book.[1]

53

Juan knew several languages—as well
   He might—and brought them up with skill, in time
To save his fame with each accomplish'd belle,
   Who still regretted that he did not rhyme.   420
There wanted but this requisite to swell
   His qualities (with them) into sublime:

---

6. Bluestockings; i.e., literary women.
7. Troy (Greek).
8. Braggart (after a character in George Villiers's *The Rehearsal* [1671]).
9. The Muses' spring on Mt. Helicon.
1. A notebook in which favorite poems, quotations, or comments are written down. *Herules Furens*
   (line 414) was an ancient Roman drama by Seneca.

Lady Fitz-Frisky, and Miss Maevia Mannish,
Both long'd extremely to be sung in Spanish.

54

However, he did pretty well, and was   425
  Admitted as an aspirant to all
The coteries, and, as in Banquo's glass,[2]
  At great assemblies or in parties small,
He saw ten thousand living authors pass,
  That being about their average numeral;   430
Also the eighty "greatest living poets,"
As every paltry magazine can show *its*.

55

In twice five years the "greatest living poet,"
  Like to the champion in the fisty ring,
Is call'd on to support his claim, or show it,   435
  Although 'tis an imaginary thing.
Even I—albeit I'm sure I did not know it,
  Nor sought of foolscap[3] subjects to be king,—
Was reckon'd a considerable time,
The grand Napoleon of the realms of rhyme.   440

56[4]

But Juan was my Moscow, and Faliero
  My Leipsic, and my Mont Saint Jean seems Cain:
"La Belle Alliance" of dunces down at zero,
  Now that the Lion's fall'n, may rise again:
But I will fall at least as fell my hero;   445
  Nor reign at all, or as a *monarch* reign;
Or to some lonely isle of gaolers go,
With turncoat Southey for my turnkey Lowe.

57

Sir Walter[5] reign'd before me; Moore and Campbell
  Before and after; but now grown more holy,   450
The Muses upon Sion's hill[6] must ramble
  With poets almost clergymen, or wholly;

---

2. *Macbeth* 4.1.128–40.
3. Large sheets of manuscript or printers' paper.
4. A crucial, moving, and witty stanza, in which Byron relates some of the works he wrote since his exile from England to several defeats of Napoleon Bonaparte, his lifelong alter ego. In lines 443–44: *"La Belle Alliance" of dunces* refers to the Quadruple Alliance of England, Austria, Prussia, and Russia, and the *Lion's fall'n* refers to Napoleon. In line 448, *Turncoat Southey* is one of the poem's recurrent references to the poet-laureate's having turned from a reformer to a Tory; Sir Hudson *Lowe* was the governor of St. Helena during Napoleon's exile there.
5. Sir Walter Scott, along with Thomas Moore and Thomas Campbell: contemporary poets Byron admired.
6. Where the temple at Jerusalem (*Sion*) was built.

And Pegasus hath a psalmodic amble
  Beneath the very Reverend Cambyses Croly,[7]
Who shoes the glorious animal with stilts,   455
  A modern Ancient Pistol—by these hilts![8]

58[9]

Still he excels that artificial hard
  Labourer in the same vineyard, though the vine
Yields him but vinegar for his reward,—
  That neutralised dull Dorus of the Nine;   460
That swarthy Sporus, neither man nor bard;
  That ox of verse, who *ploughs* for every line:—
Cambyses' roaring Romans beat at least
The howling Hebrews of Cybele's priest.—

59

Then there's my gentle Euphues;[1] who, they say,   465
  Sets up for being a sort of *moral me;*
He'll find it rather difficult some day
  To turn out both, or either, it may be.
Some persons think that Coleridge hath the sway;
  And Wordsworth has supporters, two or three;   470
And that deep-mouth'd Boeotian "Savage Landor"[2]
Has taken for a swan rogue Southey's gander.

60

John Keats, who was kill'd off by one critique,[3]
  Just as he really promised something great,
If not intelligible, without Greek   475
  Contrived to talk about the gods of late,
Much as they might have been supposed to speak.
  Poor fellow! His was an untoward fate;
'Tis strange the mind, that very fiery particle,[4]
  Should let itself be snuff'd out by an article.   480

---

7. Reverend George Croly (1780–1860); *Cambyses*: name of two Persian kings; perhaps suggesting energetic oratorical style.
8. *I Henry VI* 2.4.190.
9. This stanza was not printed in *1832* and was first published in 1837. It concerns Henry Hart Milman (1791–1868), whom Byron believed was the author of John Wilson Croker's harsh critique of Keats's *Endymion* that appeared in the *Quarterly Review* in April 1818. Through various classical references Byron satirizes Croly and Milman; see *DJV* 3:226. After copying this stanza, Mary Shelley wrote to Byron, "I have nearly finished copying your *savage* Canto. You will cause Milman to hang himself. . . ."
1. Bryan Waller Procter (1787–1874) wrote a poem on a Spanish subject in ottava rima but considerably milder than *Don Juan.*
2. Landor was a friend of Southey's; see Byron's Preface to *The Vision of Judgment. Boeotian*: boorish, deriving from the ancient Athenians' view of the Boetians, a people from central Greece.
3. In his Preface to *Adonais*, Shelley is largely responsible for generating the Romantic myth that it was Croker's stinging review that precipitated the fatal illness of Keats, who died on February 23, 1821.
4. "Divinae Particulum Aurae." A fragment of the divine spirit (Latin; see Horace, *Satires* 2.2.79).

61

The list grows long of live and dead pretenders
    To that which none will gain—or none will know
The conqueror at least; who, ere Time renders
    His last award, will have the long grass grow
Above his burnt-out brain, and sapless cinders.   485
    If I might augur, I should rate but low
Their chances;—they're too numerous, like the thirty
Mock tyrants, when Rome's annals wax'd but dirty.[5]

62

This is the literary *lower* empire,
    Where the praetorian[6] bands take up the matter;—   490
A "dreadful trade," like his who "gathers samphire,"[7]
    The insolent soldiery to soothe and flatter,
With the same feelings as you'd coax a vampire.
    Now, were I once at home, and in good satire,
I'd try conclusions with those Janizaries,[8]   495
And show them *what* an intellectual war is.

63

I think I know a trick or two, would turn
    Their flanks;—but it is hardly worth my while
With such small gear to give myself concern:
    Indeed I've not the necessary bile;   500
My natural temper's really aught but stern,
    And even my Muse's worst reproof's a smile;
And then she drops a brief and modern curtsy,
And glides away, assured she never hurts ye.

64

My Juan, whom I left in deadly peril   505
    Amongst live poets and blue ladies, past
With some small profit through that field so sterile.
    Being tired in time, and neither least nor last
Left it before he had been treated very ill;
    And henceforth found himself more gaily class'd   510
Amongst the higher spirits of the day,
The sun's true son, no vapour, but a ray.

65

His morns he pass'd in business—which dissected,
    Was like all business, a laborious nothing,

---

5. *Decline and Fall* (1776–88) 1.250–51.
6. According to Gibbon, the Praetorian Guard proclaimed the public sale of the Roman Empire to the highest bidder (*Decline and Fall*, chap. 5).
7. A succulent herb; cf. *King Lear* 4.5.15.
8. Turkish soldiers.

That leads to lassitude, the most infected   515
   And Centaur Nessus[9] garb of mortal clothing,
And on our sofas makes us lie dejected,
   And talk in tender horrors of our loathing
All kinds of toil, save for our country's good—
Which grows no better, though 'tis time it should.   520

66

His afternoons he pass'd in visits, luncheons,
   Lounging, and boxing; and the twilight hour
In riding round those vegetable puncheons
   Call'd "Parks," where there is neither fruit nor flower
Enough to gratify a bee's slight munchings;   525
   But after all it is the only "bower"
(In Moore's phrase[1]) where the fashionable fair
Can form a slight acquaintance with fresh air.

67

Then dress, then dinner, then awakes the world!
   Then glare the lamps, then whirl the wheels, then roar   530
Through street and square fast flashing chariots hurl'd
   Like harness'd meteors; then along the floor
Chalk mimics painting; then festoons[2] are twirl'd;
   Then roll the brazen thunders of the door,
Which opens to the thousand happy few   535
An earthly Paradise of "Or Molu."[3]

68

There stands the noble hostess, nor shall sink
   With the three-thousandth curtsy; there the waltz,
The only dance which teaches girls to think,
   Makes one in love even with its very faults.   540
Saloon, room, hall, o'erflow beyond their brink,
   And long the latest of arrivals halts,
'Midst royal dukes and dames condemn'd to climb,
And gain an inch of staircase at a time.

69

Thrice happy he who, after a survey   545
   Of the good company, can win a corner,
A door that's *in* or boudoir *out* of the way,
   Where he may fix himself like small "Jack Horner,"
And let the Babel[4] round run as it may,
   And look on as a mourner, or a scorner,   550

9. Hercules was poisoned by a garment soaked in the blood of the Centaur Nessus.
1. In Moore's poem "Come to me, love, I've wander'd far."
2. Garlands of flowers.
3. Gilded bronze decorations for furniture.
4. Genesis 11.1–9; here, the chattering, self-important world.

Or an approver, or a mere spectator,
Yawning a little as the night grows later.

70

But this won't do, save by and by; and he
    Who, like Don Juan, takes an active share,
Must steer with care through all that glittering sea   555
    Of gems and plumes and pearls and silks, to where
He deems it is his proper place to be;
    Dissolving in the waltz to some soft air,
Or proudlier prancing with mercurial skill
Where Science marshals forth her own quadrille.   560

71

Or, if he dance not, but hath higher views
    Upon an heiress or his neighbour's bride,
Let him take care that that which he pursues
    Is not at once too palpably descried.
Full many an eager gentleman oft rues   565
    His haste: impatience is a blundering guide
Amongst a people famous for reflection,
Who like to play the fool with circumspection.

72

But, if you can contrive, get next at supper;
    Or, if forestalled, get opposite and ogle:—   570
Oh, ye ambrosial Moments! always upper
    In mind, a sort of sentimental bogle,[5]
Which sits for ever upon Memory's crupper,
    The ghost of vanish'd pleasures once in vogue! Ill
Can tender souls relate the rise and fall   575
Of hopes and fears which shake a single ball.

73

But these precautionary hints can touch
    Only the common run, who must pursue,
And watch, and ward; whose plans a word too much
    Or little overturns; and not the few   580
Or many (for the number's sometimes such)
    Whom a good mien, especially if new,
Or fame, or name, for wit, war, sense, or nonsense,
Permits whate'er they please, or *did* not long since.

74

Our hero, as a hero, young and handsome,   585
    Noble, rich, celebrated, and a stranger,

---

5. Goblin (Scottish).

Like other slaves of course must pay his ransom
   Before he can escape from so much danger
As will environ a conspicuous man. Some
   Talk about poetry, and "rack and manger,"[6]   590
And ugliness, disease, as toil and trouble;—
   I wish they knew the life of a young noble.

75

They are young, but know not youth—it is anticipated;
   Handsome but wasted, rich without a sou;
Their vigour in a thousand arms is dissipated;   595
   Their cash comes *from*, their wealth goes *to* a Jew;
Both senates see their nightly votes participated
   Between the tyrant's and the tribunes' crew;
And having voted, dined, drank, gamed, and whored,
   The family vault receives another lord.   600

76

"Where is the world?" cries Young,[7] at *eighty*—"Where
   The world in which a man was born?" Alas!
Where is the world of *eight* years past? *'Twas there*—
   I look for it—'tis gone, a Globe of Glass!
Crack'd, shiver'd, vanish'd, scarcely gazed on, ere   605
   A silent change dissolves the glittering mass.
Statesmen, chiefs, orators, queens, patriots, kings,
And dandies,[8] all are gone on the wind's wings.

77[9]

Where is Napoleon the Grand? God knows:
   Where little Castlereagh? The devil can tell: 610
Where Grattan, Curran, Sheridan, all those
   Who bound the bar or senate in their spell?
Where is the unhappy Queen, with all her woes?
   And where the Daughter, whom the Isles loved well?
Where are those martyr'd saints the Five per cents?[1]   615
And where—oh, where the devil are the rents?[2]

---

6. Waste and destruction (cf. rack and ruin).
7. Edward Young's *Resignation* (1762), published when he was eighty years old.
8. The Dandies, a prominent social group of fashionable men; cf. *Beppo*, line 474 (p. 364).
9. Besides *Napoleon*, finally defeated in 1815 and exiled to St. Helena, stanzas 77–80 name various
   people in Regency society with whom Byron was acquainted before he left England in 1816, many
   of whom had since died or experienced a reversal of fortune. In stanza 77: *Castlereagh* was the for-
   mer foreign minister whom Byron detested and who committed suicide on August 12, 1822 (see
   the headnote, p. 376, and Dedication, stanzas 11–16); Henry *Grattan* and John Philpot *Curran*
   were deceased statesmen; Richard Brinsley *Sheridan* was the renowned dramatist and orator; *the
   unhappy Queen* is Caroline, who died in 1821, having outlived her *Daughter*, Princess Charlotte,
   who had died in childbirth in 1817.
1. A kind of British bond.
2. Income Byron expected from his lands.

78³

Where's Brummel? Dish'd. Where's Long Pole Wellesley? Diddled.
Where's Whitbread? Romilly? Where's George the Third?
Where is his will? (That's not so soon unriddled.)
And where is "Fum" the Fourth, our "royal bird?"   620
Gone down, it seems, to Scotland to be fiddled
Unto by Sawney's violin, we have heard:
"Caw me, caw thee"—for six months hath been hatching.
This scene of royal itch and loyal scratching.

79

Where is Lord This? And where my Lady That?   625
The Honourable Mistresses and Misses?
Some laid aside like an old opera hat,
Married, unmarried, and remarried: (this is
An evolution oft performed of late.)
Where are the Dublin shouts—and London hisses?   630
Where are the Grenvilles?⁴ Turn'd as usual. Where
My friends the Whigs?⁵ Exactly where they were.

80

Where are the Lady Carolines and Franceses?⁶
Divorced or doing thereanent. Ye annals
So brilliant, where the list of routs and dances is,—   635
Thou Morning Post, sole record of the panels
Broken in carriages, and all the phantasies
Of fashion,—say what streams now fill those channels?
Some die, some fly, some languish on the Continent,
Because the times have hardly left them *one* tenant.   640

81

Some who once set their caps at cautious dukes,
Have taken up at length with younger brothers:
Some heiresses have bit at sharpers' hooks:
Some maids have been made wives, some merely mothers;
Others have lost their fresh and fairy looks: 645
In short, the list of alterations bothers.

---

3. Stanza 78 contains the following references: Beau *Brummel*, leader of the Dandies, became impoverished; *William Pole Tylney Long Wellesley* was another dandy who wasted his property on high living; Samuel *Whitbread*, a Whig politician, and Samuel *Romilly*, a legal reformer, committed suicide; the ambiguity surrounding the *will* (or, rather, two wills) of George III led to a dispute between George IV and his brother, the Duke of York; *'Fum' the Fourth, our 'royal bird'* echoes a satire by Moore of George IV, whose visit to Scotland is mocked in the remaining lines of the stanza; *Sawney* is a derogatory name for a Scot; *Caw me, caw thee* alludes to the old saying meaning "you scratch my back and I'll scratch yours."
4. George Grenville and one of his sons, William Wyndham, Baron Grenville, originally supported reform but became Tories.
5. The party of reform, to which Byron was loyal throughout his life.
6. Lady Caroline Lamb and Lady Frances Wedderburn Webster, with whom Byron had romantic involvements.

There's little strange in this, but something strange is
The unusual quickness of these common changes.

82

Talk not of seventy years as age! in seven
   I have seen more changes, down from monarchs to   650
The humblest individual under heaven,
   Than might suffice a moderate century through.
I knew that nought was lasting, but now even
   Change grows too changeable, without being new:
Nought's permanent among the human race,   655
   Except the Whigs *not* getting into place.

83

I have seen Napoleon, who seem'd quite a Jupiter,
   Shrink to a Saturn. I have seen a Duke[7]
(No matter which) turn politician stupider,
   If that can well be, than his wooden look.   660
But it is time that I should hoist my "blue Peter,"[8]
   And sail for a new theme:—I have seen—and shook
To see it—the king hiss'd, and then carest;[9]
   But don't pretend to settle which was best.

84

I have seen the Landholders without a rap—   665
   I have seen Joanna Southcote[1]—I have seen
The House of Commons turn'd to a tax-trap—
   I have seen that sad affair of the late Queen—
I have seen crowns worn instead of a fool's cap—
   I have seen a Congress doing all that's mean—   670
I have seen some nations like o'erloaded asses
Kick off their burthens—meaning the high classes.

85

I have seen small poets, and great prosers, and
   Interminable—*not eternal*—speakers—
I have seen the funds at war with house and land—   675
   I have seen the country gentlemen turn squeakers—
I have seen the people ridden o'er like sand
   By slaves on horseback[2]—I have seen malt liquors

---

7. The Duke of Wellington; *Saturn*: in classical myth, the old Titan Saturn was deposed and replaced
   by his son, Jupiter, the foremost Olympian deity.
8. Ship's flag indicating immediate departure.
9. *hiss'd . . . carest*: the King's unpopularity during the divorce trials, then his adulation when he vis-
   ited Ireland in 1822.
1. A religious fanatic and self-proclaimed prophet, who at one time claimed to be pregnant with a spir-
   itual being; she died in 1814 of a brain disease.
2. A likely reference to "Peterloo": a workers' demonstration in St. Peter's Field, Manchester, on
   August 16, 1819, which was dispersed when a charge of drunken cavalry killed or injured many of
   the people gathered there.

Exchanged for "thin potations" by John Bull[3]—
I have seen John half detect himself a fool.—   680

86

But "carpe diem,"[4] Juan, "carpe, carpe!"
    To-morrow sees another race as gay
And transient, and devour'd by the same harpy.[5]
    "Life's a poor player,"—then "play out the play,[6]
Ye villains!" and above all keep a sharp eye   685
    Much less on what you do than what you say:
Be hypocritical, be cautious, be
Not what you *seem*, but always what you *see*.

87

But how shall I relate in other cantos
    Of what befell our hero in the land,   690
Which 'tis the common cry and lie to vaunt as
    A moral country? But I hold my hand—
For I disdain to write an Atalantis;[7]
    But 'tis as well at once to understand
You are *not* a moral people, and you know it   695
Without the aid of too sincere a poet.

88

What Juan saw and underwent shall be
    My topic, with of course the due restriction
Which is required by proper courtesy;
    And recollect the work is only fiction,   700
And that I sing of neither mine nor me,
    Though every scribe, in some slight turn of diction,
Will hint allusions never *meant*. Ne'er doubt
This—when I speak, I *don't hint*, but *speak out*.

89

Whether he married with the third or fourth   705
    Offspring of some sage husband-hunting countess,
Or whether with some virgin of more worth
    (I mean in Fortune's matrimonial bounties)
He took to regularly peopling Earth,
    Of which your lawful awful wedlock fount is,—   710
Or whether he was taken in for damages,
For being too excursive in his homages,—

3. An epithet for an Englishman. *Malt liquors . . . "thin potations"*: cf. *2 Henry IV* 4.3.111. Brewers attempted to avoid the malt tax by diluting their product.
4. Seize the day (Latin, Horace, *Odes* 1.11.8).
5. In classical myth, rapacious female monster.
6. *Macbeth* 5.5.23, and *1 Henry IV* 2.4.442.
7. Referring to a 1709 work by Mrs. Mary de la Riviere Manley, in which she revenged herself on her enemies.

90

Is yet within the unread events of time.
   Thus far, go forth, thou Lay! which I will back
Against the same given quantity of rhyme,   715
   For being as much the subject of attack
As ever yet was any work sublime,
   By those who love to say that white is black.
So much the better!—I may stand alone,
But would not change my free thoughts for a throne.   720

FROM CANTO THE TWELFTH[1]

1

Of all the barbarous middle ages, that
   Which is most barbarous is the middle age
Of man; it is—I really scarce know what;
   But when we hover between fool and sage,
And don't know justly what we would be at—   5
   A period something like a printed page,
Black letter upon foolscap,[2] while our hair
Grows grizzled, and we are not what we were,—

2

Too old for youth,—too young, at thirty-five,
   To herd with boys, or hoard with good threescore,—   10
I wonder people should be left alive;
   But since they are, that epoch is a bore:
Love lingers still, although 'twere late to wive;
   And as for other love, the illusion's o'er;
And money, that most pure imagination,   15
Gleams only through the dawn of its creation.

3

O Gold! Why call we misers miserable?
   Theirs is the pleasure that can never pall;
Theirs is the best bower anchor,[3] the chain cable
   Which holds fast other pleasures great and small.   20
Ye who but see the saving man at table,
   And scorn his temperate board, as none at all,
And wonder how the wealthy can be sparing,
Know not what visions spring from each cheese-paring.

---

1. Composed in late 1822; published with Cantos XIII–XIV by John Hunt on December 17, 1823.
2. Large sheets of printer's paper.
3. Anchor carried at the bow of a ship.

4

Love or lust makes man sick, and wine much sicker;   25
    Ambition rends, and gaming gains a loss;
But making money, slowly first, then quicker,
    And adding still a little through each cross
(Which *will* come over things), beats love or liquor,
    The gamester's counter, or the statesman's *dross*.[4]   30
O Gold! I still prefer thee unto paper,
Which makes bank credit like a bark of vapour.[5]

5

Who hold the balance of the world? Who reign
    O'er congress, whether royalist or liberal?
Who rouse the shirtless patriots of Spain?[6]   35
    (That make old Europe's journals squeak and gibber[7] all.)
Who keep the world, both old and new, in pain
    Or pleasure? Who make politics run glibber all?
The shade of Buonaparte's noble daring?—
Jew Rothschild, and his fellow Christian Baring.[8]   40

6

Those, and the truly liberal Lafitte,[9]
    Are the true lords of Europe. Every loan
Is not a merely speculative hit,
    But seats a nation or upsets a throne.
Republics also get involved a bit;   45
    Columbia's[1] stock hath holders not unknown
On 'Change;"[2] and even thy silver soil, Peru,
Must get itself discounted by a Jew.

7

Why call the miser miserable? as
    I said before: the frugal life is his,   50
Which in a saint or cynic ever was
    The theme of praise: a hermit would not miss
Canonization for the self-same cause,
    And wherefore blame gaunt Wealth's austerities?
Because, you'll say, nought calls for such a trial;—   55
Then there's more merit in his self-denial.

---

4. *gamester's . . . dross*: the gambler's chip or the statesman's wasted or worthless efforts.
5. Steamboat. The irony is that steamships, regarded skeptically in Byron's day, like paper currency, would soon dominate the world of commerce. Byron was undoubtedly conscious of the irony; see Canto X, line 16.
6. The *Descimados* of the Spanish Revolution (1820–23).
7. *Hamlet* 1.1.106.
8. Nathan Meyer Rothschild (1777–1836), London member of the international banking family; Alexander Baring, Baron Ashburton (1774–1848), of the banking house of Baring Brothers.
9. Jacques Lafitte (1767–1844), governor of the Bank of France and a liberal government Deputy.
1. America's.
2. The London Stock Exchange.

8

He is your only poet;—passion, pure
    And sparkling on from heap to heap, displays,
Possess'd, the ore, of which *mere hopes* allure
    Nations athwart the deep: the golden rays   60
Flash up in ingots[3] from the mine obscure;
    On him the diamond pours its brilliant blaze,
While the mild emerald's beam shades down the dyes
Of other stones, to soothe the miser's eyes.

9

The lands on either side are his: the ship   65
    From Ceylon, Inde, or far Cathay,[4] unloads
For him the fragrant produce of each trip;
    Beneath his cars of Ceres[5] groan the roads,
And the vine blushes like Aurora's lip;
    His very cellars might be kings' abodes;   70
While he, despising every sensual call,
Commands—the intellectual lord of all.

10

Perhaps he hath great projects in his mind,
    To build a college, or to found a race,
A hospital, a church,—and leave behind   75
    Some dome surmounted by his meagre face:
Perhaps he fain would liberate mankind
    Even with the very ore which makes them base;
Perhaps he would be wealthiest of his nation,
Or revel in the joys of calculation.   80

11

But whether all, or each, or none of these
    May be the hoarder's principle of action,
The fool will call such mania a disease:—
    What is his *own?* Go—look at each transaction,
Wars, revels, loves—do these bring men more ease   85
    Than the mere plodding through each "vulgar fraction?"[6]
Or do they benefit mankind? Lean miser!
Let spendthrifts' heirs enquire of yours—who's wiser?

12

How beauteous are rouleaus![7] how charming chests
    Containing ingots, bags of dollars, coins   90

3. Masses of metal.
4. China.
5. Ancient goddess of agriculture, grain and food; *Aurora* (line 69) was the ancient Roman goddess of the dawn.
6. Common fractions (as opposed to decimals), but a pun is obviously intended.
7. Rolls of gold coins.

(Not of old victors, all whose heads and crests
   Weigh not the thin ore where their visage shines,
But) of fine unclipt gold, where dully rests
   Some likeness, which the glittering cirque confines,
Of modern, reigning, sterling, stupid stamp:—   95
Yes! ready money *is* Aladdin's lamp.

*   *   *

CANTO THE THIRTEENTH[1]

1

I now mean to be serious;—it is time,
   Since laughter now-a-days is deem'd too serious.
A jest at Vice by Virtue's call'd a crime,
   And critically held as deleterious:
Besides, the sad's a source of the sublime,   5
   Although when long a little apt to weary us;
And therefore shall my lay soar high and solemn
As an old temple dwindled to a column.

2

The Lady Adeline Amundeville
   ('Tis an old Norman[2] name, and to be found   10
In pedigrees by those who wander still
   Along the last fields of that Gothic[3] ground)
Was high-born, wealthy by her father's will,
   And beauteous, even where beauties most abound,
In Britain—which of course true patriots find   15
The goodliest soil of body and of mind.

3

I'll not gainsay them; it is not my cue;
   I'll leave them to their taste, no doubt the best:
An eye's an eye, and whether black or blue,
   Is no great matter, so 'tis in request: 20
'Tis nonsense to dispute about a hue—
   The kindest may be taken as a test.
The fair sex should be always fair, and no man,
Till thirty, should perceive there's a plain woman.

4

And after that serene and somewhat dull   25
   Epoch, that awkward corner turn'd for days

---

1. Canto XIII was written in February 1823; it was published along with Cantos XII and XIV by John
   Hunt on December 17, 1823.
2. The Normans conquered England in 1066.
3. Refers to the Middle Ages.

More quiet, when our moon's no more at full,
   We may presume to criticise or praise;
Because indifference begins to lull
   Our passions, and we walk in Wisdom's ways;   30
Also because the figure and the face
Hint, that 'tis time to give the younger place.

5

I know that some would fain postpone this era,
   Reluctant as all placemen[4] to resign
Their post; but theirs is merely a chimera,   35
   For they have pass'd life's equinoctial line:
But then they have their claret and Madeira
   To irrigate the dryness of decline;
And county meetings, and the parliament,
And debt, and what not, for their solace sent.   40

6

And is there not Religion, and Reform,
   Peace, War, the taxes, and what's call'd the "Nation"?
The struggle to be pilots in a storm?[5]
   The landed and the monied speculation?
The joys of mutual hate to keep them warm,   45
   Instead of love, that mere hallucination?
Now hatred is by far the longest pleasure;
Men love in haste, but they detest at leisure.

7

Rough Johnson, the great moralist, profess'd,
   Right honestly, "he liked an honest hater"[6]—   50
The only truth that yet has been confest
   Within these latest thousand years or later.
Perhaps the fine old fellow spoke in jest:—
   For my part, I am but a mere spectator,
And gaze where'er the palace or the hovel is,   55
Much in the mode of Goethe's Mephistopheles;[7]

8

But neither love nor hate in much excess;
   Though 'twas not once so. If I sneer sometimes,
It is because I cannot well do less,
   And now and then it also suits my rhymes.   60
I should be very willing to redress
   Men's wrongs, and rather check than punish crimes,

4. Someone who was given an official position in return for political support.
5. Echoes "The Pilot," song by British statesman George Canning (1770–1827).
6. "'Sir, I love a good hater.'—See Boswell's *Johnson*." Slightly misquoted from a note by John Wilson Croker to James Boswell's *Life of Johnson* (1791), 1.104.
7. The devil in *Faust*, by Johann Wolfgang von Goethe (1749–1832).

Had not Cervantes,[8] in that too true tale
Of Quixote, shown how all such efforts fail.

9

Of all tales 'tis the saddest—and more sad,   65
  Because it makes us smile: his hero's right,
And still pursues the right;—to curb the bad,
  His only object, and 'gainst odds to fight,
His guerdon: 'tis his virtue makes him mad!
  But his adventures form a sorry sight;—   70
A sorrier still is the great moral taught
By that real epic unto all who have thought.

10

Redressing injury, revenging wrong,
  To aid the damsel and destroy the caitiff;[9]
Opposing singly the united strong,   75
  From foreign yoke to free the helpless native:—
Alas! must noblest views, like an old song,
  Be for mere Fancy's sport a theme creative,
A jest, a riddle, Fame through thick and thin sought?
And Socrates himself but Wisdom's Quixote?   80

11

Cervantes smiled Spain's chivalry away;
  A single laugh demolish'd the right arm
Of his own country;—seldom since that day
  Has Spain had heroes. While Romance could charm,
The world gave ground before her bright array;   85
  And therefore have his volumes done such harm,
That all their glory, as a composition,
Was dearly purchased by his land's perdition.

12

I'm "at my old lunes"[1]—digression, and forget
  The Lady Adeline Amundeville;   90
The fair most fatal Juan ever met,
  Although she was not evil nor meant ill;
But Destiny and Passion spread the net
  (Fate is a good excuse for our own will)
And caught them;—what do they *not* catch, methinks?   95
But I'm not Oedipus, and life's a Sphinx.[2]

---

8. Miguel de Cervantes Saavedra (1547–1616), great Spanish writer. His *Don Quixote* (1605, 1615), the subject of stanzas 9–11, is often regarded as the first novel; it is simultaneously a satire of the romances of chivalry, a sharp criticism of society, and a tragic portrayal of idealism in a corrupt world.
9. Base, despicable person (archaic).
1. Fits of madness; *The Merry Wives of Windsor* 4.2.16.
2. In the Greek tragedy *Oedipus the King* by Sophocles, Oedipus solves the riddle of the Sphinx.

13

I tell the tale as it is told, nor dare
   To venture a solution: "Davus sum!"[3]
And now I will proceed upon the pair.
   Sweet Adeline, amidst the gay world's hum,   100
Was the Queen-Bee, the glass of all that's fair;
   Whose charms made all men speak, and women dumb.
The last's a miracle, and such was reckon'd,
And since that time there has not been a second.

14

Chaste was she, to detraction's desperation,   105
   And wedded unto one she had loved well—
A man known in the councils of the nation,
   Cool, and quite English, imperturbable,
Though apt to act with fire upon occasion,
   Proud of himself and her: the world could tell   110
Nought against either, and both seem'd secure—
She in her virtue, he in his hauteur.

15

It chanced some diplomatical relations,
   Arising out of business, often brought
Himself and Juan in their mutual stations   115
   Into close contact. Though reserved, nor caught
By specious seeming, Juan's youth, and patience,
   And talent, on his haughty spirit wrought,
And form'd a basis of esteem, which ends
In making men what courtesy calls friends.   120

16

And thus Lord Henry, who was cautious as
   Reserve and pride could make him, and full slow
In judging men—when once his judgment was
   Determined, right or wrong, on friend or foe,
Had all the pertinacity pride has,   125
   Which knows no ebb to its imperious flow,
And loves or hates, disdaining to be guided,
Because its own good pleasure hath decided.

17

His friendships, therefore, and no less aversions,
   Though oft well founded, which confirm'd but more   130
His prepossessions, like the laws of Persians

---

3. The slave Davus, in *Andria* by the second-century B.C.E. Roman playwright Terence, replies to a question with "Davus sum, non Oedipus," referring to the fact that only Oedipus could solve the riddle of the Sphinx.

And Medes,[4] would ne'er revoke what went before.
His feelings had not those strange fits, like tertians,[5]
    Of common likings, which make some deplore
What they should laugh at—the mere ague still   135
Of men's regard, the fever or the chill.

18

" 'Tis not in mortals to command success:
    But *do you more*, Sempronius—*don't* deserve it,"[6]
And take my word, you won't have any less.
    Be wary, watch the time, and always serve it;   140
Give gently way, when there's too great a press;
    And for your conscience, only learn to nerve it,
For, like a racer, or a boxer training,
'Twill make, if proved, vast efforts without paining.

19

Lord Henry also liked to be superior,   145
    As most men do, the little or the great;
The very lowest find out an inferior,
    At least they think so, to exert their state
Upon: for there are very few things wearier
    Than solitary Pride's oppressive weight,   150
Which mortals generously would divide,
By bidding others carry while they ride.

20

In birth, in rank, in fortune likewise equal,
    O'er Juan he could no distinction claim;
In years he had the advantage of time's sequel;   155
    And, as he thought, in country much the same—
Because bold Britons have a tongue and free quill,
    At which all modern nations vainly aim;
And the Lord Henry was a great debater,
So that few members kept the House[7] up later.   160

21

These were advantages: and then he thought—
    It was his foible, but by no means sinister—
That few or none more than himself had caught
    Court mysteries, having been himself a minister:
He liked to teach that which he had been taught.   165
    And greatly shone whenever there had been a stir;

---

4. An ancient people of western Asia.
5. Fevers that recur every other day.
6. Echoes Joseph Addison's *Cato* (1713).
7. The House of Lords.

And reconciled all qualities which grace man,
Always a patriot, and sometimes a placeman.

22

He liked the gentle Spaniard for his gravity;
    He almost honour'd him for his docility,   170
Because, though young, he acquiesced with suavity,
    Or contradicted but with proud humility.
He knew the world, and would not see depravity
    In faults which sometimes show the soil's fertility,
If that the weeds o'erlive not the first crop—   175
For then they are very difficult to stop.

23

And then he talk'd with him about Madrid,
    Constantinople, and such distant places;
Where people always did as they were bid,
    Or did what they should not with foreign graces.   180
Of coursers also spake they: Henry rid
    Well, like most Englishmen, and loved the races;
And Juan, like a true-born Andalusian,[8]
Could back a horse, as despots ride a Russian.

24

And thus acquaintance grew, at noble routs,   185
    And diplomatic dinners, or at other—
For Juan stood well both with Ins and Outs,
    As in Freemasonry[9] a higher brother.
Upon his talent Henry had no doubts;
    His manner show'd him sprung from a high mother;   190
And all men like to show their hospitality
To him whose breeding matches with his quality.

25

At Blank-Blank Square;—for we will break no squares[1]
    By naming streets: since men are so censorious,
And apt to sow an author's wheat with tares,[2]   195
    Reaping allusions private and inglorious,
Where none were dreamt of, unto love's affairs,
    Which were, or are, or are to be notorious,
That therefore do I previously declare,
Lord Henry's mansion was in Blank-Blank Square.   200

---

8. From Andalusia, a region of southern Spain on the Mediterranean Sea.
9. A secret order focusing on brotherly love.
1. I.e., violate decorum.
2. Weeds (Matthew 13.25).

26

Also there bin³ another pious reason
    For making squares and streets anonymous;
Which is, that there is scarce a single season
    Which doth not shake some very splendid house
With some slight heart-quake of domestic treason—   205
    A topic Scandal doth delight to rouse:
Such I might stumble over unawares,
Unless I knew the very chastest squares.

27

'Tis true, I might have chosen Piccadilly,⁴
    A place where peccadillos are unknown;   210
But I have motives, whether wise or silly,
    For letting that pure sanctuary alone.
Therefore I name not square, street, place, until I
    Find one where nothing naughty can be shown,
A vestal shrine of innocence of heart: 215
Such are——but I have lost the London Chart.

28

At Henry's mansion then, in Blank-Blank Square,
    Was Juan a *recherché*,⁵ welcome guest,
As many other noble scions were;
    And some who had but talent for their crest;   220
Or wealth, which is a passport every where;
    Or even mere fashion, which indeed's the best
Recommendation; and to be well drest
Will very often supersede the rest.

29

And since "there's safety in a multitude   225
    Of counsellors"⁶ as Solomon has said,
Or some one for him, in some sage, grave mood;—
    Indeed we see the daily proof display'd
In senates, at the bar, in wordy feud,
    Where'er collective wisdom can parade,   230
Which is the only cause that we can guess
Of Britain's present wealth and happiness;—

30

But as "there's safety" grafted in the number
    "Of counsellors" for men,—thus for the sex

---

3. "'With every thing that pretty *bin*, / My lady sweet, arise.'" *Cymbeline* 2.3.22.
4. Lines 209–12: Byron lived at No. 13 Piccadilly Terrace in 1815–16; *peccadillos*: petty sins or offenses.
5. Very rare, carefully sought out (French).
6. Proverbs 11.14 and 24.6.

A large acquaintance lets not Virtue slumber;   235
  Or should it shake, the choice will more perplex—
Variety itself will more encumber.
  'Midst many rocks we guard more against wrecks;
And thus with women: howsoe'er it shocks some's
Self-love, there's safety in a crowd of coxcombs.[7]   240

31

But Adeline had not the least occasion
  For such a shield, which leaves but little merit
To virtue proper, or good education.
  Her chief resource was in her own high spirit,
Which judged mankind at their due estimation;   245
  And for coquetry, she disdain'd to wear it:
Secure of admiration, its impression
Was faint, as of an every-day possession.

32

To all she was polite without parade;
  To some she show'd attention of that kind   250
Which flatters, but is flattery convey'd
  In such a sort as cannot leave behind
A trace unworthy either wife or maid;—
  A gentle, genial courtesy of mind,
To those who were, or pass'd for meritorious,   255
Just to console sad Glory for being glorious;

33

Which is in all respects, save now and then,
  A dull and desolate appendage. Gaze
Upon the shades of those distinguish'd men
  Who were or are the puppet-shows of praise,   260
The praise of persecution; gaze again
  On the most favour'd; and amidst the blaze
Of sunset halos o'er the laurel-brow'd,
What can ye recognise?—a gilded cloud.

34

There also was of course in Adeline   265
  That calm patrician polish in the address
Which ne'er can pass the equinoctial line
  Of any thing which Nature would express;
Just as a mandarin[8] finds nothing fine,—
  At least his manner suffers not to guess   270
That any thing he views can greatly please.
  Perhaps we have borrow'd this from the Chinese—

---

7. Conceited, vain man.
8. A ranking officer in the Chinese Empire.

35

Perhaps from Horace: his '*Nil admirari*'[9]
   Was what he call'd the 'Art of Happiness;'
An art on which the artists greatly vary,   275
   And have not yet attain'd to much success.
However, 'tis expedient to be wary:
   Indifference certes don't produce distress;
And rash enthusiasm in good society
Were nothing but a moral inebriety.   280

36

But Adeline was not indifferent: for
   (*Now* for a common-place!) beneath the snow,
As a volcano holds the lava more
   Within—*et cetera*. Shall I go on?—No!
I hate to hunt down a tired metaphor,   285
   So let the often-used volcano go.
Poor thing! How frequently, by me and others,
It hath been stirr'd up till its smoke quite smothers!

37

I'll have another figure in a trice:—
   What say you to a bottle of champagne?   290
Frozen into a very vinous ice,
   Which leaves few drops of that immortal rain,
Yet in the very centre, past all price,
   About a liquid glassful will remain;
And this is stronger than the strongest grape   295
Could e'er express in its expanded shape:

38

'Tis the whole spirit brought to a quintessence;
   And thus the chilliest aspects may concentre
A hidden nectar under a cold presence.
   And such are many—though I only meant her   300
From whom I now deduce these moral lessons,
   On which the Muse has always sought to enter.
And your cold people are beyond all price,
When once you have broken their confounded ice.

39

But after all they are a North-West Passage[1]   305
   Unto the glowing India of the soul;

---

9. See Canto V, stanza 100 and note.
1. A route to India via the Arctic coast of Canada and Alaska; Sir William Parry (1790–1855; mentioned in line 309) commanded several expeditions seeking the Northwest Passage.

And as the good ships sent upon that message
  Have not exactly ascertain'd the Pole
(Though Parry's efforts look a lucky presage),
  Thus gentlemen may run upon a shoal;   310
For if the Pole's not open, but all frost
  (A chance still), 'tis a voyage or vessel lost.

40

And young beginners may as well commence
  With quiet cruising o'er the ocean woman;
While those who are not beginners should have sense   315
  Enough to make for port, ere Time shall summon
With his grey signal-flag; and the past tense,
  The dreary "*Fuimus*"[2] of all things human,
Must be declined, while life's thin thread's spun out
Between the gaping heir and gnawing gout.   320

41

But heaven must be diverted; its diversion
  Is sometimes truculent—but never mind:
The world upon the whole is worth the assertion
  (If but for comfort) that all things are kind:
And that same devilish doctrine of the Persian,[3]   325
  Of the two Principles, but leaves behind
As many doubts as any other doctrine
Has ever puzzled Faith withal, or yoked her in.

42

The English winter—ending in July,
  To recommence in August—now was done,   330
'Tis the postilion's paradise: wheels fly;
  On roads, east, south, north, west, there is a run.
But for post-horses who finds sympathy?
  Man's pity's for himself, or for his son,
Always premising that said son at college   335
Has not contracted much more debt than knowledge.

43

The London winter's ended in July—
  Sometimes a little later. I don't err
In this: whatever other blunders lie
  Upon my shoulders, here I must aver   340
My Muse a glass of weatherology;
  For parliament is our barometer:

2. We have been (Latin).
3. Zoroaster, Persian religious teacher (sixth-century B.C.E.), whose creed, according to Walter Scott, "supposes the co-existence of a benevolent and malevolent principle, which contend together without either being able decisively to prevail over his antagonist" (*Letters on Demonology*, 1830).

Let radicals its other acts attack,
Its sessions form our only almanack.

44

When its quicksilver's down at zero,—lo!   345
   Coach, chariot, luggage, baggage, equipage!
Wheels whirl from Carlton palace to Soho,[4]
   And happiest they who horses can engage;
The turnpikes glow with dust; and Rotten Row[5]
   Sleeps from the chivalry of this bright age;   350
And tradesmen, with long bills and longer faces,
Sigh—as the postboys fasten on the traces.

45

They and their bills, 'Arcadians both,'[6] are left
   To the Greek kalends[7] of another session.
Alas! to them of ready cash bereft,   355
   What hope remains? Of *hope* the full possession,
Or generous draft, conceded as a gift,
   At a long date—till they can get a fresh one—
Hawk'd about at a discount, small or large;
Also the solace of an overcharge.   360

46

But these are trifles. Downward flies my lord
   Nodding beside my lady in his carriage.
Away! away! "Fresh horses!" are the word,
   And changed as quickly as hearts after marriage;
The obsequious landlord hath the change restored;   365
   The postboys have no reason to disparage
Their fee; but ere the water'd wheels[8] may hiss hence,
The ostler[9] pleads too for a reminiscence.

47

'Tis granted; and the valet mounts the dickey[1]—
   That gentleman of lords and gentlemen;   370
Also my lady's gentlewoman, tricky,
   Trick'd out, but modest more than poet's pen
Can paint,—"*Cosi viaggino i Ricchi!*"[2]
   (Excuse a foreign slipslop now and then,

---

4. A fashionable quarter in London during the Regency period. *Carlton palace*: then the palace of the Prince of Wales.
5. A fashionable road between Kensington Palace and St. James's Palace.
6. "Arcades ambo." From Virgil's *Eclogues*, 7.4. Arcadia was a place of pastoral innocence in ancient Greece.
7. I.e., never—since kalends are part of the Roman and not the Greek calendar.
8. Watered to keep them from rattling.
9. Someone who takes care of horses.
1. Seat at the front or the rear of a carriage.
2. Thus the rich travel (Italian).

If but to show I've travell'd; and what's travel,   375
Unless it teaches one to quote and cavil?)

48

The London winter and the country summer
   Were well nigh over. 'Tis perhaps a pity,
When Nature wears the gown that doth become her,
   To lose those best months in a sweaty city,   380
And wait until the nightingale grows dumber,
   Listening debates not very wise or witty,
Ere patriots their true *country* can remember;—
But there's no shooting (save grouse) till September.

49

I've done with my tirade. The world was gone;   385
   The twice two thousand, for whom earth was made,
Were vanish'd to be what they call alone—
   That is, with thirty servants for parade,
As many guests, or more; before whom groan
   As many covers, duly, daily laid.   390
Let none accuse Old England's hospitality—
Its quantity is but condensed to quality.

50

Lord Henry and the Lady Adeline
   Departed like the rest of their compeers,
The peerage, to a mansion very fine;   395
   The Gothic Babel[3] of a thousand years.
None than themselves could boast a longer line,
   Where Time through heroes and through beauties steers;
And oaks as olden as their pedigree
Told of their sires, a tomb in every tree.   400

51

A paragraph in every paper told
   Of their departure: such is modern fame:
'Tis pity that it takes no farther hold
   Than an advertisement, or much the same;
When, ere the ink be dry, the sound grows cold.   405
   The Morning Post was foremost to proclaim—
"Departure, for his country seat, to-day,
Lord H. Amundeville and Lady A.

52

"We understand the splendid host intends
   To entertain, this autumn, a select   410

---

3. Large structure (after the Tower of Babel in Genesis 11) of a medieval architectural style.

And numerous party of his noble friends;
   Midst whom we have heard, from sources quite correct,
The Duke of D—— the shooting season spends,
   With many more by rank and fashion deck'd;
Also a foreigner of high condition,   415
The envoy of the secret Russian mission."

53

And thus we see—who doubts the Morning Post?
   (Whose articles are like the "Thirty-nine,"[4]
Which those most swear to who believe them most)—
   Our gay Russ Spaniard was ordain'd to shine,   420
Deck'd by the rays reflected from his host,
   With those who, Pope says, "greatly daring dine."[5]—
'Tis odd, but true,—last war the News abounded
More with these dinners than the kill'd or wounded;—

54

As thus: "On Thursday there was a grand dinner;   425
   Present, Lords A.B.C."—Earls, dukes, by name
Announced with no less pomp than victory's winner:
   Then underneath, and in the very same
Column: date, "Falmouth.[6] There has lately been here
   The Slap-dash regiment, so well known to fame;   430
Whose loss in the late action we regret:
The vacancies are fill'd up—see Gazette."

55

To Norman Abbey[7] whirl'd the noble pair,—
   An old, old monastery once, and now
Still older mansion,—of a rich and rare   435
   Mix'd Gothic, such as artists all allow
Few specimens yet left us can compare
   Withal: it lies perhaps a little low,
Because the monks preferr'd a hill behind,
To shelter their devotion from the wind.   440

56

It stood embosom'd in a happy valley,
   Crown'd by high woodlands, where the Druid[8] oak
Stood like Caractacus[9] in act to rally

---

4. The Thirty-nine Articles to which Anglican priests subscribe.
5. Cf. Alexander Pope's *Dunciad* (1728), 4.318.
6. Seaport in southwest England.
7. The name and description of Norman Abbey (stanzas 55–72) are drawn from Byron's own ancestral mansion, Newstead Abbey; see also "On Leaving Newstead Abbey" and "Elegy on Newstead Abbey" in *Hours of Idleness* (1806).
8. Ancient, pre-Christian religion.
9. Also known as Caradoc: first-century C.E. British king who resisted the Roman invasion for several years.

His host, with broad arms 'gainst the thunder-stroke;
And from beneath his boughs were seen to sally   445
The dappled foresters[1]—as day awoke,
The branching stag swept down with all his herd,
To quaff a brook which murmur'd like a bird.

57

Before the mansion lay a lucid lake,
Broad as transparent, deep, and freshly fed   450
By a river, which its soften'd way did take
In currents through the calmer water spread
Around: the wildfowl nestled in the brake
And sedges, brooding in their liquid bed:
The woods sloped downwards to its brink, and stood   455
With their green faces fix'd upon the flood.

58

Its outlet dash'd into a deep cascade,
Sparkling with foam, until again subsiding,
Its shriller echoes—like an infant made
Quiet—sank into softer ripples, gliding   460
Into a rivulet; and thus allay'd,
Pursued its course, now gleaming, and now hiding
Its windings through the woods; now clear, now blue,
According as the skies their shadows threw.

59

A glorious remnant of the Gothic pile   465
(While yet the church was Rome's) stood half apart
In a grand arch, which once screen'd many an aisle.
These last had disappear'd—a loss to art:
The first yet frown'd superbly o'er the soil,
And kindled feelings in the roughest heart,   470
Which mourn'd the power of time's or tempest's march,
In gazing on that venerable arch.

60

Within a niche, nigh to its pinnacle,
Twelve saints had once stood sanctified in stone;
But these had fallen, not when the friars fell,   475
But in the war which struck Charles from his throne,[2]
When each house was a fortalice[3]—as tell
The annals of full many a line undone,—

---

1. Spotted animals, i.e., deer.
2. In the English Civil Wars, 1642–46 and 1648–51, Byron's ancestors were Cavaliers, who faithfully
   supported Charles I.
3. Small fort.

The gallant Cavaliers, who fought in vain
For those who knew not to resign or reign.   480

61

But in a higher niche, alone, but crown'd,
   The Virgin Mother of the God-born Child,
With her Son in her blessed arms, look'd round,
   Spared by some chance when all beside was spoil'd;
She made the earth below seem holy ground.   485
   This may be superstition, weak or wild,
But even the faintest relics of a shrine
Of any worship wake some thoughts divine.

62

A mighty window, hollow in the centre,
   Shorn of its glass of thousand colourings,   490
Through which the deepen'd glories once could enter,
   Streaming from off the sun like seraph's wings,
Now yawns all desolate: now loud, now fainter,
   The gale sweeps through its fretwork, and oft sings
The owl his anthem, where the silenced quire   495
Lie with their hallelujahs quench'd like fire.

63

But in the noontide of the moon, and when
   The wind is winged from one point of heaven,
There moans a strange unearthly sound, which then
   Is musical—a dying accent driven   500
Through the huge arch, which soars and sinks again.
   Some deem it but the distant echo given
Back to the night wind by the waterfall,
And harmonised by the old choral wall:

64

Others, that some original shape, or form   505
   Shaped by decay perchance, hath given the power
(Though less than that of Memnon's statue,[4] warm
   In Egypt's rays, to harp at a fix'd hour)
To this grey ruin, with a voice to charm.
   Sad, but serene, it sweeps o'er tree or tower;   510
The cause I know not, nor can solve; but such
The fact:—I've heard it,—once perhaps too much.

65

Amidst the court a Gothic fountain play'd,
   Symmetrical, but deck'd with carvings quaint—

---

4. The statue in Egypt of the mythic Ethiopian king Memnon is said to emit musical sounds at dawn.

Strange faces, like to men in masquerade,   515
    And here perhaps a monster, there a saint:
The spring gush'd through grim mouths of granite made,
    And sparkled into basins, where it spent
Its little torrent in a thousand bubbles,
Like man's vain glory, and his vainer troubles.   520

66

The mansion's self was vast and venerable,
    With more of the monastic than has been
Elsewhere preserved: the cloisters still were stable,
    The cells, too, and refectory, I ween:
An exquisite small chapel had been able,   525
    Still unimpair'd, to decorate the scene;
The rest had been reform'd, replaced, or sunk,
And spoke more of the baron than the monk.

67

Huge halls, long galleries, spacious chambers, join'd
    By no quite lawful marriage of the arts,   530
Might shock a connoisseur; but when combined,
    Form'd a whole which, irregular in parts,
Yet left a grand impression on the mind,
    At least of those whose eyes are in their hearts:
We gaze upon a giant for his stature,   535
Nor judge at first if all be true to nature.

68

Steel barons, molten the next generation
    To silken rows of gay and garter'd earls,
Glanced from the walls in goodly preservation:
    And Lady Marys blooming into girls,   540
With fair long locks, had also kept their station:
    And countesses mature in robes and pearls:
Also some beauties of Sir Peter Lely,[5]
Whose drapery hints we may admire them freely.

69

Judges in very formidable ermine   545
    Were there, with brows that did not much invite
The accused to think their lordships would determine
    His cause by leaning much from might to right:
Bishops, who had not left a single sermon:
    Attorneys-general, awful to the sight,   550

---

5. Dutch portrait painter in England (1618–1680).

As hinting more (unless our judgments warp us)
Of the "Star Chamber" than of "Habeas Corpus."[6]

70

Generals, some all in armour, of the old
    And iron time, ere lead had ta'en the lead;
Others in wigs of Marlborough's martial fold,[7]   555
    Huger than twelve of our degenerate breed:
Lordlings, with staves of white or keys of gold:[8]
    Nimrods,[9] whose canvass scarce contain'd the steed;
And here and there some stern high patriot stood,
Who could not get the place for which he sued.   560

71[1]

But ever and anon, to soothe your vision,
    Fatigued with these hereditary glories,
There rose a Carlo Dolce or a Titian,
    Or wilder group of savage Salvatore's:
Here danced Albano's boys, and here the sea shone   565
    In Vernet's ocean lights; and there the stories
Of martyrs awed, as Spagnoletto tainted
His brush with all the blood of all the sainted.

72

Here sweetly spread a landscape of Lorraine;
    There Rembrandt made his darkness equal light,   570
Or gloomy Caravaggio's gloomier stain
    Bronzed o'er some lean and stoic anchorite:—
But, lo! a Teniers woos, and not in vain,
    Your eyes to revel in a livelier sight:
His bell-mouth'd goblet makes me feel quite Danish[2]   575
Or Dutch with thirst—What, ho! a flask of Rhenish.

73

O reader! if that thou canst read,—and know,
    'Tis not enough to spell, or even to read,
To constitute a reader; there must go
    Virtues of which both you and I have need.   580

---

6. Lines 551–52: more of a secret court than of an open court that guarantees against unjust imprisonment; perhaps a reference to the suspension of Habeas Corpus in England in 1817–18.
7. The Duke of Marlborough led victories against the French in the War of the Spanish Succession (1701–08).
8. Symbols of office.
9. Nimrod was a great hunter (Genesis 10.8–10).
1. Stanzas 71–72 continue to describe the painters and subjects represented in the portraits of Norman Abbey; these descriptions are based on many of the paintings Byron admired in galleries at Venice and Milan (see *DJV* 4:251–52). *Salvatore's*: refers to Salvator Rosa.
2. "If I err not, 'your Dane,' is one of Iago's catalogue of nations 'exquisite in their drinking.'" *Othello* 2.3.68–73.

Firstly, begin with the beginning—(though
   That clause is hard); and secondly, proceed;
Thirdly, commence not with the end—or, sinning
In this sort, end at least with the beginning.

74

But, reader, thou hast patient been of late,   585
   While I, without remorse of rhyme, or fear,
Have built and laid out ground at such a rate,
   Dan Phoebus[3] takes me for an auctioneer.
That poets were so from their earliest date,
   By Homer's "Catalogue of ships"[4] is clear;   590
But a mere modern must be moderate—
I spare you then the furniture and plate.

75

The mellow autumn came, and with it came
   The promised party, to enjoy its sweets.
The corn is cut, the manor full of game;   595
   The pointer ranges, and the sportsman beats
In russet jacket:—lynx-like is his aim,
   Full grows his bag, and wonder*ful* his feats.
Ah, nutbrown partridges! Ah, brilliant pheasants!
And ah, ye poachers!—'Tis no sport for peasants.   600

76

An English autumn, though it hath no vines,
   Blushing with Bacchant[5] coronals along
The paths, o'er which the far festoon entwines
   The red grape in the sunny lands of song,
Hath yet a purchased choice of choicest wines;   605
   The claret light, and the Madeira strong.
If Britain mourn her bleakness, we can tell her,
The very best of vineyards is the cellar.

77

Then, if she hath not that serene decline
   Which makes the southern autumn's day appear   610
As if 'twould to a second spring resign
   The season, rather than to winter drear,—
Of in-door comforts still she hath a mine,—
   The sea-coal fires, the "earliest of the year;"[6]
Without doors, too, she may compete in mellow,   615
As what is lost in green is gain'd in yellow.

---

3. Phoebus Apollo, Greek god of poetry; *Dan*: title of honor, like Don or Sir.
4. In the second book of *The Iliad*.
5. Celebrations of the Roman god of wine, Bacchus.
6. Echoing *2 Henry IV* 2.1.81.

78

And for the effeminate *villeggiatura*[7]—
    Rife with more horns than hounds—she hath the chase,
So animated that it might allure a
    Saint from his beads to join the jocund race;   620
Even Nimrod's self might leave the plains of Dura,[8]
    And wear the Melton[9] jacket for a space:
If she hath no wild boars, she hath a tame
Preserve of bores, who ought to be made game.

79

The noble guests, assembled at the Abbey,   625
    Consisted of—we give the sex the pas[1]—
The Duchess of Fitz-Fulke; the Countess Crabby;
    The Ladies Scilly, Busey;—Miss Eclat,
Miss Bombazeen, Miss Mackstay, Miss O'Tabby,
    And Mrs. Rabbi, the rich banker's squaw;   630
Also the honourable Mrs. Sleep,
Who look'd a white lamb, yet was a black sheep:

80

With other Countesses of Blank—but rank;
    At once the "lie"[2] and the "élite" of crowds;
Who pass like water filter'd in a tank,   635
    All purged and pious from their native clouds;
Or paper turn'd to money by the Bank:
    No matter how or why, the passport shrouds
The "passée" and the past; for good society
Is no less famed for tolerance than piety,—   640

81

That is, up to a certain point; which point[3]
    Forms the most difficult in punctuation.
Appearances appear to form the joint
    On which it hinges in a higher station;
And so that no explosion cry "Aroint   645
    Thee, witch!"[4] or each Medea has her Jason;
Or (to the point with Horace and with Pulci)
"*Omne tulit punctum, quae miscuit utile dulci.*"[5]

---

7. A stay in the country.
8. "In Assyria."
9. From Melton Mowbray, headquarters of the English chase.
1. We let the ladies go first.
2. Lee (dregs).
3. A pun: *point* in punctuation is a period.
4. *Macbeth* 1.3.5 (Go away, witch). In Euripides' *Medea*, the witch Medea takes brutal revenge against
   her husband, Jason, for his infidelity.
5. He who mixes profit with pleasure has carried every vote (Horace, *Ars Poetica*, line 343). He wrote
   for pleasure and Augustus Caesar, as Luigi Pulci (1432–1484), writer of *Morgante Maggiore*,
   received the favors of Lorenzo de Medici.

82

I can't exactly trace their rule of right,
    Which hath a little leaning to a lottery.   650
I've seen a virtuous woman put down quite
    By the mere combination of a coterie;
Also a so-so matron boldly fight
    Her way back to the world by dint of plottery,
And shine the very *Siria*[6] of the spheres,   655
Escaping with a few slight, scarless sneers.

83

I have seen more than I'll say:—but we will see
    How our *villeggiatura* will get on.
The party might consist of thirty-three
    Of highest caste—the Brahmins of the ton.[7]   660
I have named a few, not foremost in degree,
    But ta'en at hazard as the rhyme may run.
By way of sprinkling, scatter'd amongst these
There also were some Irish absentees.[8]

84

There was Parolles,[9] too, the legal bully,   665
    Who limits all his battles to the bar
And senate: when invited elsewhere, truly,
    He shows more appetite for words than war.
There was the young bard Rackrhyme, who had newly
    Come out and glimmer'd as a six weeks' star.   670
There was Lord Pyrrho, too, the great freethinker;
And Sir John Pottledeep, the mighty drinker.

85

There was the Duke of Dash, who was a—duke,
    "Ay, every inch a" duke;[1] there were twelve peers
Like Charlemagne's[2]—and all such peers in look   675
    And intellect, that neither eyes nor ears
For commoners had ever them mistook.
    There were the six Miss Rawbolds—pretty dears!
All song and sentiment; whose hearts were set
Less on a convent than a coronet.   680

---

6. "Siria, *i.e.* bitch-star." (Sirius is the dog-star.)
7. I.e., the most high-toned of society; the Brahmins are the highest caste of Hindus.
8. Irish landowners who lived in England.
9. Reference to Henry Brougham, a lawyer Byron hated; Parolles (name of a boasting coward in *All's Well That Ends Well*) derives from the French word for "words." For conjectures about the actual individuals in Byron's former English circle to whom his satiric portraits might refer, see *DJV* 4:254–57 and *CPW* 5:758.
1. *King Lear* 4.6.104.
2. King of the Franks and the Emperor of the West in the first-century C.E.

86

There were four Honourable Misters, whose
  Honour was more before their names than after;
There was the preux Chevalier de la Ruse,[3]
  Whom France and Fortune lately deign'd to waft here,
Whose chiefly harmless talent was to amuse;   685
  But the clubs found it rather serious laughter,
Because—such was his magic power to please—
The dice seem'd charm'd, too, with his repartees.

87

There was Dick Dubious, the metaphysician,
  Who loved philosophy and a good dinner;   690
Angle, the soi-disant[4] mathematician;
  Sir Henry Silvercup, the great race-winner.
There was the Reverend Rodomont Precisian,
  Who did not hate so much the sin as sinner;
And Lord Augustus Fitz-Plantagenet,   695
Good at all things, but better at a bet.

88

There was Jack Jargon, the gigantic guardsman;
  And General Fireface, famous in the field,
A great tactician, and no less a swordsman,
  Who ate, last war, more Yankees than he kill'd.   700
There was the waggish[5] Welsh Judge, Jefferies Hardsman,
  In his grave office so completely skill'd,
That when a culprit came for condemnation,
He had his judge's joke for consolation.

89

Good company's a chess-board—there are kings,   705
  Queens, bishops, knights, rooks, pawns; the world's a game;
Save that the puppets pull at their own strings,
  Methinks gay Punch hath something of the same.
My Muse, the butterfly hath but her wings,
  Not stings, and flits through ether without aim,   710
Alighting rarely:—were she but a hornet,
Perhaps there might be vices which would mourn it.

90

I had forgotten—but must not forget—
  An orator, the latest of the session,
Who had deliver'd well a very set   715

3. Gallant knight of trickery; i.e., Casimir Compte de Montand, exiled in London 1812–14.
4. Self-styled.
5. Good-humored, jocular.

Smooth speech, his first and maidenly transgression
Upon debate:[6] the papers echo'd yet
    With his début, which made a strong impression,
And rank'd with what is every day display'd—
"The best first speech that ever yet was made."   720

91

Proud of his "Hear hims!" proud, too, of his vote
    And lost virginity of oratory,
Proud of his learning (just enough to quote),
    He revell'd in his Ciceronian[7] glory:
With memory excellent to get by rote,   725
    With wit to hatch a pun or tell a story,
Graced with some merit and with more effrontery,
"His country's pride," he came down to the country.

92

There also were two wits by acclamation,
    Longbow from Ireland, Strongbow from the Tweed,[8]   730
Both lawyers and both men of education;
    But Strongbow's wit was of more polish'd breed:
Longbow was rich in an imagination
    As beautiful and bounding as a steed,
But sometimes stumbling over a potato,—   735
While Strongbow's best things might have come from Cato.[9]

93

Strongbow was like a new-tuned harpsichord;
    But Longbow wild as an Aeolian harp,[1]
With which the winds of heaven can claim accord,
    And make a music, whether flat or sharp.   740
Of Strongbow's talk you would not change a word:
    At Longbow's phrases you might sometimes carp:
Both wits—one born so, and the other bred,
This by his heart—his rival by his head.

94

If all these seem an heterogeneous mass   745
    To be assembled at a country seat,
Yet think, a specimen of every class
    Is better than a humdrum tête-à-tête.

6. Byron alludes to his own maiden (i.e., first) speech in the House of Lords in 1812.
7. Pertaining to the great Roman orator Marcus Tullius Cicero (106–43 B.C.E.).
8. *Longbow . . . Strongbow*: John Philpot Curran (1750–1817); Lord Thomas Erskine (1750–1823), of Scotland. See *BLJ* 10:26–27 and 44).
9. Cato (234–149 B.C.E.), Roman soldier, statesman, and writer.
1. A favorite image for Romantic poets, an aeolian harp is left out of doors and produces musical sounds as the wind passes over it.

The days of Comedy are gone, alas!
    When Congreve's fool could vie with Molière's *bête*:[2]   750
Society is smooth'd to that excess,
    That manners hardly differ more than dress.

95

Our ridicules are kept in the back-ground—
    Ridiculous enough, but also dull;
Professions, too, are no more to be found   755
    Professional; and there is nought to cull
Of folly's fruit: for though your fools abound,
    They're barren, and not worth the pains to pull.
Society is now one polish'd horde,
Form'd of two mighty tribes, the *Bores* and *Bored*.   760

96

But from being farmers, we turn gleaners, gleaning
    The scanty but right-well thresh'd ears of truth;
And, gentle reader! when you gather meaning,
    You may be Boaz, and I—modest Ruth.[3]
Farther I'd quote, but Scripture intervening   765
    Forbids. A great impression in my youth
Was made by Mrs. Adams, where she cries
"That Scriptures out of church are blasphemies."[4]

97

But what we can we glean in this vile age
    Of chaff, although our gleanings be not grist.   770
I must not quite omit the talking sage,
    Kit-Cat, the famous conversationist,
Who, in his common-place book, had a page
    Prepared each morn for evenings. "List, oh list!"—
"Alas, poor ghost!"[5]—What unexpected woes   775
Await those who have studied their bons-mots![6]

98

Firstly, they must allure the conversation
    By many windings to their clever clinch;
And secondly, must let slip no occasion,
    Nor *bate* (abate) their hearers of an *inch*,   780

---

2. Sir Joseph Wittol in William Congreve's *The Old Bachelor* (1693) and Monsieur Jourdain in Molière's *Le Bourgeois Gentilhomme* (1670). *Bête* is French for fool.
3. In the Book of Ruth, the wealthy Boaz tells his gleaners to leave over some of the barley so Ruth may take it.
4. "'Mrs. Adams answered Mr. Adams, that it was blasphemous to talk of Scripture out of church.' This dogma was broached to her husband—the best Christian in any book.—See *Joseph Andrews*." Book IV, chap. 11, 1742, by Henry Fielding.
5. *Hamlet* 1.5.22, 4.
6. Clever sayings.

But take an ell—and make a great sensation,
    If possible; and thirdly, never flinch
When some smart talker puts them to the test,
But seize the last word, which no doubt's the best.

99

Lord Henry and his lady were the hosts;   785
    The party we have touch'd on were the guests:
Their table was a board to tempt even ghosts
    To pass the Styx[7] for more substantial feasts.
I will not dwell upon ragoûts or roasts,
    Albeit all human history attests   790
That happiness for man—the hungry sinner!—
Since Eve ate apples, much depends on dinner.

100

Witness the lands which "flow'd with milk and honey"[8]
    Held out unto the hungry Israelites:
To this we have added since, the love of money,   795
    The only sort of pleasure which requites.
Youth fades, and leaves our days no longer sunny;
    We tire of mistresses and parasites;
But oh, ambrosial cash! Ah! who would lose thee?
When we no more can use, or even abuse thee!   800

101

The gentlemen got up betimes to shoot,
    Or hunt: the young, because they liked the sport—
The first thing boys like, after play and fruit;
    The middle-aged, to make the day more short;
For *ennui* is a growth of English root,   805
    Though nameless in our language:—we retort
The fact for words, and let the French translate
That awful yawn which sleep can not abate.

102

The elderly walk'd through the library,
    And tumbled books, or criticised the pictures,   810
Or saunter'd through the gardens piteously,
    And made upon the hot-house several strictures,
Or rode a nag which trotted not too high,
    Or on the morning papers read their lectures,
Or on the watch their longing eyes would fix,   815
Longing at sixty for the hour of six.

---

7. In Greek myth, one of the rivers bordering the underworld.
8. Cf. Exodus 3.8.

103

But none were "gêné:"[9] the great hour of union
　Was rung by dinner's knell; till then all were
Masters of their own time—or in communion,
　Or solitary, as they chose to bear　　　　　　　820
The hours, which how to pass is but to few known.
　Each rose up at his own, and had to spare
What time he chose for dress, and broke his fast
When, where, and how he chose for that repast.

104

The ladies—some rouged, some a little pale—　　　825
　Met the morn as they might. If fine, they rode,
Or walk'd; if foul, they read, or told a tale,
　Sung, or rehearsed the last dance from abroad;
Discuss'd the fashion which might next prevail,
　And settled bonnets by the newest code,　　　　830
Or cramm'd twelve sheets into one little letter,
To make each correspondent a new debtor.

105

For some had absent lovers, all had friends.
　The earth has nothing like a She epistle,
And hardly heaven—because it never ends.　　　　835
　I love the mystery of a female missal,
Which, like a creed, ne'er says all it intends,
　But full of cunning as Ulysses' whistle,
When he allured poor Dolon:[1]—you had better
Take care what you reply to such a letter.　　　　840

106

Then there were billiards; cards, too, but *no* dice;—
　Save in the clubs no man of honour plays;—
Boats when 'twas water, skating when 'twas ice,
　And the hard frost destroy'd the scenting days:
And angling, too, that solitary vice,　　　　　　845
　Whatever Izaak Walton sings or says:[2]

9. Put out, inconvenienced (French).
1. In Homer's *Iliad*, 10, a Trojan who is tricked and then killed by Odysseus and Diomedes.
2. "It would have taught him humanity at least. This sentimental savage, whom it is a mode to quote (amongst the novelists) to show their sympathy for innocent sports and old songs, teaches how to sew up frogs, and break their legs by way of experiment, in addition to the art of angling, the cruellest, the coldest, and the stupidest of pretended sports. They may talk about the beauties of nature, but the angler merely thinks of his dish of fish; he has no leisure to take his eyes from off the streams, and a single *bite* is worth to him more than all the scenery around. Besides, some fish bite best on a rainy day. The whale, the shark, and the tunny fishery have somewhat of noble and perilous in them; even net fishing, trawling, &c. are more humane and useful—but angling! No angler can be a good man. [MS note ends here.]
　'One of the best men I ever knew;—as humane, delicate-minded, generous, and excellent a creature as any in the world, was an angler: true he angled with painted flies, and would have been incapable of the extravagances of I. Walton.'

The quaint, old, cruel coxcomb, in his gullet
Should have a hook, and a small trout to pull it.

107

With evening came the banquet and the wine;
   The *conversazione*; the duet,   850
Attuned by voices more or less divine
   (My heart or head aches with the memory yet).
The four Miss Rawbolds in a glee would shine;
   But the two youngest loved more to be set
Down to the harp—because to music's charms   855
They added graceful necks, white hands and arms.

108

Sometimes a dance (though rarely on field days,
   For then the gentlemen were rather tired)
Display'd some sylph-like figures in its maze;
   Then there was small-talk ready when required;   860
Flirtation—but decorous; the mere praise
   Of charms that should or should not be admired.
The hunters fought their fox-hunt o'er again,
And then retreated soberly—at ten.

109

The politicians, in a nook apart,   865
   Discuss'd the world, and settled all the spheres;
The wits watch'd every loop-hole for their art,
   To introduce a bon-mot head and ears:
Small is the rest of those who would be smart,
   A moment's good thing may have cost them years   870
Before they find an hour to introduce it,
And then, even *then*, some bore may make them lose it.

110

But all was gentle and aristocratic
   In this our party; polish'd, smooth, and cold,
As Phidian[3] forms cut out of marble Attic.   875
   There now are no Squire Westerns[4] as of old;
And our Sophias are not so emphatic,
   But fair as then, or fairer to behold.
We have no accomplish'd blackguards, like Tom Jones,[5]
But gentlemen in stays, as stiff as stones.   880

   The above addition was made by a friend in reading over the MS.—*"Audi alteram partem"*—I
leave it to counterbalance my own observation."
   Izaac Walton (1593–1683) wrote *The Compleat Angler: or, the Contemplative Man's Recreation*
(1653).
3. Relating to the Athenian ("Attic") sculptor Phidias (500–432 B.C.E.).
4. Coarse and robust landowner in Henry Fielding's satiric novel *Tom Jones*. Squire Western's daugh-
ter, Sophia, is the novel's heroine.
5. Facetious: Tom Jones is similar to, if not a model for, Byron's Juan.

111

They separated at an early hour;
    That is, ere midnight—which is London's noon:
But in the country ladies seek their bower
    A little earlier than the waning moon.
Peace to the slumbers of each folded flower—   885
    May the rose call back its true colour soon!
Good hours of fair cheeks are the fairest tinters,
And lower the price of rouge—at least some winters.

FROM CANTO THE FOURTEENTH[1]

*   *   *

9

The world is all before me—or behind;[2]   65
    For I have seen a portion of that same,
And quite enough for me to keep in mind;—
    Of passions, too, I have proved enough to blame,
To the great pleasure of our friends, mankind,
    Who like to mix some slight alloy with fame;   70
For I was rather famous in my time,
Until I fairly knock'd it up with rhyme.

10

I have brought this world about my ears, and eke
    The other; that's to say, the clergy—who
Upon my head have bid their thunders break   75
    In pious libels by no means a few.
And yet I can't help scribbling once a week,
    Tiring old readers, nor discovering new.
In youth I wrote because my mind was full,
And now because I feel it growing dull.   80

11

But "why then publish?"[3]—There are no rewards
    Of fame or profit when the world grows weary.
I ask in turn,—Why do you play at cards?
    Why drink? Why read?—To make some hour less dreary.
It occupies me to turn back regards   85
    On what I've seen or ponder'd, sad or cheery;
And what I write I cast upon the stream,
To swim or sink—I have had at least my dream.

---

1. Composed in February and March of 1823; published along with Cantos XII and XIII by John Hunt on December 17, 1823.
2. Cf. *Paradise Lost,* "The World was all before them" (12.646), describing Adam and Eve's departure from Eden.
3. Alexander Pope, *Epistle to Dr. Arbuthnot* (1735), 135.

12

I think that were I *certain* of success,
    I hardly could compose another line: 90
So long I've battled either more or less,
    That no defeat can drive me from the Nine.[4]
This feeling 'tis not easy to express
    And yet 'tis not affected, I opine.
In play, there are two pleasures for your choosing—   95
The one is winning, and the other losing.[5]

13

Besides, my Muse by no means deals in fiction:
    She gathers a repertory of facts,
Of course with some reserve and slight restriction,
    But mostly sings of human things and acts—   100
And that's one cause she meets with contradiction;
    For too much truth, at first sight, ne'er attracts;
And were her object only what's call'd glory,
With more ease too she'd tell a different story.

14

Love, war, a tempest—surely there's variety;   105
    Also a seasoning slight of lucubration;[6]
A bird's eye view, too, of that wild, Society;
    A slight glance thrown on men of every station.
If you have nought else, here's at least satiety
    Both in performance and in preparation;   110
And though these lines should only line portmanteaus,[7]
Trade will be all the better for these Cantos.

15

The portion of this world which I at present
    Have taken up to fill the following sermon,
Is one of which there's no description recent: 115
    The reason why, is easy to determine:
Although it seems both prominent and pleasant,
    There is a sameness in its gems and ermine,
A dull and family likeness through all ages,
Of no great promise for poetic pages.   120

16

With much to excite, there's little to exalt;
    Nothing that speaks to all men and all times;

---

4. The nine Muses, daughters of Zeus and Mneomsyne (Memory), who inspire poets and other creative artists and thinkers.
5. I.e., the game, or gambling, itself is pleasurable (see *BLJ* 9:23).
6. Profound, difficult writing, usually done at night.
7. Trunks or large suitcases.

A sort of varnish over every fault;
    A kind of common-place, even in their crimes;
Factitious passions, wit without much salt,   125
    A want of that true nature which sublimes
Whate'er it shows with truth; a smooth monotony
Of character, in those at least who have got any.

17

Sometimes, indeed, like soldiers off parade,
    They break their ranks and gladly leave the drill;   130
But then the roll-call draws them back afraid,
    And they must be or seem what they were: still
Doubtless it is a brilliant masquerade;
    But when of the first sight you have had your fill,
It palls—at least it did so upon me,   135
This Paradise of Pleasure and Ennui.

18

When we have made our love, and gamed our gaming,
    Drest, voted, shone, and, may be, something more;
With dandies dined; heard senators declaiming;
    Seen beauties brought to market by the score,   140
Sad rakes to sadder husbands chastely taming;
    There's little left but to be bored or bore.
Witness those "*ci-devant jeunes hommes*"[8] who stem
The stream, nor leave the world which leaveth them.

19

'Tis said—indeed a general complaint—   145
    That no one has succeeded in describing
The *Monde*,[9] exactly as they ought to paint:
    Some say, that authors only snatch, by bribing
The porter, some slight scandals strange and quaint,
    To furnish matter for their moral gibing;   150
And that their books have but one style in common—
My lady's prattle, filter'd through her woman.

20

But this can't well be true, just now; for writers
    Are grown of the *Beau Monde* a part potential:
I've seen them balance even the scale with fighters,   155
    Especially when young, for that's essential.
Why do their sketches fail them as inditers
    Of what they deem themselves most consequential,

8. Formerly young men.
9. Literally, the world (French); i.e., society. Cf. *beau monde* (line 154): the so-called beautiful people.

The *real* portrait of the highest tribe?
'Tis that, in fact, there's little to describe.   160

21

"*Haud ignara loquor;*" these are *Nugae*, "*quarum
Pars* parva *fui,*"[1] but still art and part.
Now I could much more easily sketch a harem,
    A battle, wreck, or history of the heart,
Than these things; and besides, I wish to spare 'em,   165
    For reasons which I choose to keep apart.
"*Vetabo Cereris sacrum qui vulgarit*"[2]—
Which means, that vulgar people must not share it.

22

And therefore what I throw off is ideal—
    Lower'd, leaven'd, like a history of Freemasons;[3]   170
Which bears the same relation to the real,
    As Captain Parry's voyage may do to Jason's.[4]
The grand arcanum's[5] not for men to see all;
    My music has some mystic diapasons;[6]
And there is much which could not be appreciated   175
In any manner by the uninitiated.

23

Alas! Worlds fall—and Woman, since she fell'd
    The World (as, since that history less polite
Than true, hath been a creed so strictly held)
    Has not yet given up the practice quite.   180
Poor Thing of Usages! coerced, compell'd,
    Victim when wrong, and martyr oft when right,
Condemn'd to child-bed, as men for their sins
Have shaving too entail'd upon their chins,—

24

A daily plague, which in the aggregate   185
    May average on the whole with parturition.
But as to women, who can penetrate
    The real sufferings of their she condition?
Man's very sympathy with their estate
    Has much of selfishness and more suspicion.   190
Their love, their virtue, beauty, education,
But form good housekeepers, to breed a nation.

1. I speak of things I know; trifling matters in which I have played a small part. Slightly altered from
   Virgil's *Aeneid* 2.91, 6.
2. I shall forbid the man who has divulged the sacred rites of mystic Ceres. Horace, *Odes* 3.2.26.
3. Secret fraternal order.
4. *Captain Parry's voyage . . . Jason's*: Sir William Parry's early-nineteenth-century Arctic expeditions;
   the legendary voyage of Jason in pursuit of the Golden Fleece.
5. Great secret.
6. Melodies, sound qualities.

25

All this were very well, and can't be better;
    But even this is difficult, Heaven knows!
So many troubles from her birth beset her,   195
    Such small distinction between friends and foes,
The gilding wears so soon from off her fetter,
    That——but ask any woman if she'd choose
(Take her at thirty, that is) to have been
Female or male? a schoolboy or a Queen?   200

*   *   *

31

Juan—in this respect, at least, like saints—
    Was all things unto people of all sorts,
And lived contentedly, without complaints,
    In camps, in ships, in cottages, or courts—
Born with that happy soul which seldom faints,   245
    And mingling modestly in toils or sports.
He likewise could be most things to all women,
Without the coxcombry[7] of certain *she* men.

32

A fox-hunt to a foreigner is strange;
    'Tis also subject to the double danger   250
Of tumbling first, and having in exchange
    Some pleasant jesting at the awkward stranger:
But Juan had been early taught to range
    The wilds, as doth an Arab turn'd avenger,
So that his horse, or charger, hunter, hack,   255
Knew that he had a rider on his back.

33

And now in this new field, with some applause,
    He clear'd hedge, ditch, and double post, and rail,
And never *craned*,[8] and made but few *"faux pas,"*[9]
    And only fretted when the scent 'gan fail.   260
He broke, 'tis true, some statutes of the laws
    Of hunting—for the sagest youth is frail;
Rode o'er the hounds, it may be, now and then,
And once o'er several country gentlemen.

---

7. Conceited dandyism.
8. "*Craning.*—'To *crane*' is, or was, an expression used to denote a gentleman's stretching out his neck over a hedge, 'to look before he leaped':—a pause in his 'vaulting ambition' [*Macbeth* 1.7.27], which in the field doth occasion some delay and execration in those who may be immediately behind the equestrian sceptic. 'Sir, if you don't choose to take the leap, let me!'—was a phrase which generally sent the aspirant on again; and to good purpose: for though 'the horse and rider' might fall, they made a gap, through which, and over him and his steed, the field might follow."
9. Social missteps.

34

But on the whole, to general admiration   265
   He acquitted both himself and horse: the squires
Marvell'd at merit of another nation;
   The boors cried "Dang it! who'd have thought it?"—Sires,
The Nestors[1] of the sporting generation,
   Swore praises, and recall'd their former fires;   270
The huntsman's self relented to a grin,
And rated him almost a whipper-in.[2]

35

Such were his trophies—not of spear and shield,
   But leaps, and bursts, and sometimes foxes' brushes;
Yet I must own,—although in this I yield   275
   To patriot sympathy a Briton's blushes,—
He thought at heart like courtly Chesterfield,[3]
   Who, after a long chase o'er hills, dales, bushes,
And what not, though he rode beyond all price,
Ask'd next day, "If men ever hunted *twice?*"   280

36

He also had a quality uncommon
   To early risers after a long chase,
Who wake in winter ere the cock can summon
   December's drowsy day to his dull race,—
A quality agreeable to woman,   285
   When her soft, liquid words run on apace,
Who likes a listener, whether saint or sinner,—
He did not fall asleep just after dinner;

37

But, light and airy, stood on the alert,
   And shone in the best part of dialogue,   290
By humouring always what they might assert,
   And listening to the topics most in vogue;
Now grave, now gay, but never dull or pert;
   And smiling but in secret—cunning rogue!
He ne'er presumed to make an error clearer;—   295
In short, there never was a better hearer.

38

And then he danced;—all foreigners excel
   The serious Angles[4] in the eloquence

---

1. Nestor is the old, wise Greek adviser in Homer's *Iliad* and *Odyssey*.
2. Huntsman's assistant.
3. Philip Dormer Stanhope, Earl of Chesterfield (1694–1773), English statesman and author.
4. I.e., the English, named after the Germanic people that settled in west Britain in the fifth century.

Of pantomime;—he danced, I say, right well,
  With emphasis, and also with good sense—   300
A thing in footing indispensable;
  He danced without theatrical pretence,
Not like a ballet-master in the van
  Of his drill'd nymphs, but like a gentleman.

39

Chaste were his steps, each kept within due bound,   305
  And elegance was sprinkled o'er his figure;
Like swift Camilla,[5] he scarce skimm'd the ground,
  And rather held in than put forth his vigour;
And then he had an ear for music's sound,
  Which might defy a crotchet critic's rigour.   310
Such classic *pas—sans*[6] flaws—set off our hero,
He glanced like a personified Bolero;[7]

40

Or, like a flying Hour before Aurora,
  In Guido's famous fresco,[8] which alone
Is worth a tour to Rome, although no more a   315
  Remnant were there of the old world's sole throne.
The "*tout ensemble*" of his movements wore a
  Grace of the soft ideal, seldom shown,
And ne'er to be described; for to the dolour
Of bards and prosers, words are void of colour.   320

41

No marvel then he was a favourite;
  A full-grown Cupid,[9] very much admired;
A little spoilt, but by no means so quite;
  At least he kept his vanity retired.
Such was his tact, he could alike delight   325
  The chaste, and those who are not so much inspired.
The Duchess of Fitz-Fulke, who loved "*tracasserie*,"
Began to treat him with some small "*agacerie*."[1]

42

She was a fine and somewhat full-blown blonde,
  Desirable, distinguish'd, celebrated   330
For several winters in the grand, *grand Monde*.[2]

---

5. Alexander Pope's *Essay on Criticism* (1711), 372–73.
6. *pas—sans*: step—without.
7. Lively Spanish dance.
8. Refers to the ceiling fresco of the Italian painter Guido Reni (1575–1642) in Palazzo Rospigliosi
   in Rome (see *BLJ* 5:216 and 6.148).
9. Roman god of love.
1. *tracasserie . . . agacerie*: mischief making . . . flirtatiousness.
2. Great world, high society.

I'd rather not say what might be related
Of her exploits, for this were ticklish ground;
   Besides there might be falsehood in what's stated:
Her late performance had been a dead set[3]   335
At Lord Augustus Fitz-Plantagenet.[4]

43

This noble personage began to look
   A little black upon this new flirtation;
But such small licences must lovers brook,
   Mere freedoms of the female corporation.   340
Woe to the man who ventures a rebuke!
   'Twill but precipitate a situation
Extremely disagreeable, but common
To calculators when they count on woman.

44

The circle smiled, then whisper'd, and then sneer'd;   345
   The Misses bridled, and the matrons frown'd;
Some hoped things might not turn out as they fear'd;
   Some would not deem such women could be found;
Some ne'er believed one half of what they heard;
   Some look'd perplex'd, and others look'd profound;   350
And several pitied with sincere regret
Poor Lord Augustus Fitz-Plantagenet.

45

But what is odd, none ever named the duke,
   Who, one might think, was something in the affair:
True, he was absent, and 'twas rumour'd, took   355
   But small concern about the when, or where,
Or what his consort did: if he could brook
   Her gaieties, none had a right to stare:
Theirs was that best of unions, past all doubt,
Which never meets, and therefore can't fall out.   360

46

But, oh! that I should ever pen so sad a line!
   Fired with an abstract love of virtue, she,
My Dian[5] of the Ephesians, Lady Adeline,
   Began to think the duchess' conduct free;
Regretting much that she had chosen so bad a line,   365
   And waxing chiller in her courtesy,

---

3. Determination to gain someone's interest.
4. The name suggests an ancient and royal line of descent, from the Roman emperor Augustus and the Plantagenet kings of England.
5. The Roman goddess of chastity and the hunt, Diana was worshipped as a nature goddess at Ephesus in Asia Minor.

Look'd grave and pale to see her friend's fragility,
For which most friends reserve their sensibility.

* * *

85

Our gentle Adeline had one defect—
　　Her heart was vacant, though a splendid mansion;
Her conduct had been perfectly correct,　　　　　675
　　As she had seen nought claiming its expansion.
A wavering spirit may be easier wreck'd,
　　Because 'tis frailer, doubtless, than a stanch one;
But when the latter works its own undoing,
Its inner crash is like an earthquake's ruin.　　680

86

She loved her lord, or thought so; but *that* love
　　Cost her an effort, which is a sad toil,
The stone of Sysiphus,[6] if once we move
　　Our feelings 'gainst the nature of the soil.
She had nothing to complain of, or reprove,　　685
　　No bickerings, no connubial turmoil:
Their union was a model to behold,
Serene, and noble,—conjugal, but cold.

87

There was no great disparity of years,
　　Though much in temper; but they never clash'd:　690
They moved like stars united in their spheres,
　　Or like the Rhone by Leman's waters wash'd,[7]
Where mingled and yet separate appears
　　The river from the lake, all bluely dash'd
Through the serene and placid glassy deep,　　695
Which fain would lull its river-child to sleep.

* * *

91

She knew not her own heart; then how should I?
　　I think not she was *then* in love with Juan:
If so, she would have had the strength to fly
　　The wild sensation, unto her a new one:
She merely felt a common sympathy　　　　　725
　　(I will not say it was a false or true one)
In him, because she thought he was in danger,—
Her husband's friend, her own, young, and a stranger.

6. King Sisyphus, in Greek myth, was given the eternal punishment of having to roll to the top of a
　hill a heavy stone, which as it neared the top rolled down again.
7. Lake Geneva (Leman) lies across the Rhone River, its source.

92

She was, or thought she was, his friend—and this
   Without the farce of friendship, or romance   730
Of Platonism, which leads so oft amiss
   Ladies who have studied friendship but in France,
Or Germany, where people *purely* kiss.
   To thus much Adeline would not advance;
But of such friendship as man's may to man be   735
She was as capable as woman can be.

93

No doubt the secret influence of the sex
   Will there, as also in the ties of blood,
An innocent predominance annex,
   And tune the concord to a finer mood.   740
If free from passion, which all friendship checks,
   And your true feelings fully understood,
No friend like to a woman earth discovers,
So that you have not been nor will be lovers.

94

Love bears within its breast the very germ   745
   Of change; and how should this be otherwise?
That violent things more quickly find a term
   Is shown through nature's whole analogies;
And how should the most fierce of all be firm?
   Would you have endless lightning in the skies?   750
Methinks Love's very title says enough:
How should "the *tender* passion" e'er be *tough*?

95

Alas! by all experience, seldom yet
   (I merely quote what I have heard from many)
Had lovers not some reason to regret   755
   The passion which made Solomon a zany.
I've also seen some wives (not to forget
   The marriage state, the best or worst of any)
Who were the very paragons of wives,
Yet made the misery of at least two lives.[8]   760

96

I've also seen some female *friends* ('tis odd,
   But true—as, if expedient, I could prove)

---

8. A reference to Lady Byron. The next stanza refers to the women, such as his sister Augusta Leigh
   and his confidante Lady Melbourne, who remained loyal to Byron throughout and following the
   separation scandal.

That faithful were through thick and thin, abroad,
　At home, far more than ever yet was Love—
Who did not quit me when Oppression trod　　　　　765
　Upon me; whom no scandal could remove;
Who fought, and fight, in absence, too, my battles,
Despite the snake Society's loud rattles.

97

Whether Don Juan and chaste Adeline
　Grew friends in this or any other sense,　　　　770
Will be discuss'd hereafter, I opine:
　At present I am glad of a pretence
To leave them hovering, as the effect is fine,
　And keeps the atrocious reader in *suspense*;
The surest way for ladies and for books　　　　　775
To bait their tender, or their tenter, hooks.

98

Whether they rode, or walk'd, or studied Spanish
　To read Don Quixote in the original,
A pleasure before which all others vanish;
　Whether their talk was of the kind call'd "small,"　780
Or serious, are the topics I must banish
　To the next Canto; where perhaps I shall
Say something to the purpose, and display
Considerable talent in my way.

99

Above all, I beg all men to forbear　　　　　　785
　Anticipating aught about the matter:
They'll only make mistakes about the fair,
　And Juan too, especially the latter.
And I shall take a much more serious air
　Than I have yet done, in this epic satire.　　　790
It is not clear that Adeline and Juan
Will fall; but if they do, 'twill be their ruin.

100

But great things spring from little:—Would you think,
　That in our youth, as dangerous a passion
As e'er brought man and woman to the brink　　　795
　Of ruin, rose from such a slight occasion,
As few would ever dream could form the link
　Of such a sentimental situation?
You'll never guess, I'll bet you millions, milliards—
It all sprung from a harmless game at billiards.[9]　　800

9. A reference to Byron's flirtation with Lady Frances Wedderburn Webster (see letter to Lady Melbourne, p. 178).

101

'Tis strange,—but true; for Truth is always strange;
   Stranger than Fiction; if it could be told,
How much would novels gain by the exchange!
   How differently the world would men behold!
How oft would vice and virtue places change!   805
   The new world would be nothing to the old,
If some Columbus of the moral seas
Would show mankind their souls' antipodes.

102

What "antres vast and deserts idle" then
   Would be discover'd in the human soul!   810
What icebergs in the hearts of mighty men,
   With self-love in the centre as their Pole!
What Anthropophagi are nine of ten
   Of those who hold the kingdoms in control!
Were things but only call'd by their right name,   815
Caesar himself would be ashamed of Fame.

FROM CANTO THE FIFTEENTH[1]

*   *   *

10

Fair Adeline, the more ingenuous[2]
   Where she was interested (as was said),
Because she was not apt, like some of us,   75
   To like too readily, or too high bred
To show it (points we need not now discuss)—
   Would give up artlessly both heart and head
Unto such feelings as seem'd innocent,
For objects worthy of the sentiment.   80

11

Some parts of Juan's history, which Rumour,
   That live gazette, had scatter'd to disfigure,
She had heard; but women hear with more good humour
   Such aberrations than we men of rigour:
Besides, his conduct, since in England, grew more   85
   Strict, and his mind assumed a manlier vigour;
Because he had, like Alcibiades,[3]
The art of living in all climes with ease.

---

1. Canto XV was written in March 1823 and published with Canto XVI by John Hunt on March 26, 1824.
2. Artless, innocently straightforward.
3. Athenian statesman and general (450–404 B.C.E.); see Plutarch's *Life of Alcibiades*, sec. 23.

12

His manner was perhaps the more seductive,
   Because he ne'er seem'd anxious to seduce;   90
Nothing affected, studied, or constructive
   Of coxcombry[4] or conquest: no abuse
Of his attractions marr'd the fair perspective,
   To indicate a Cupidon[5] broke loose,
And seem to say, "Resist us if you can"—   95
Which makes a dandy[6] while it spoils a man.

13

They are wrong—that's not the way to set about it;
   As, if they told the truth, could well be shown.
But, right or wrong, Don Juan was without it;
   In fact, his manner was his own alone;   100
Sincere he was—at least you could not doubt it,
   In listening merely to his voice's tone.
The devil hath not in all his quiver's choice
An arrow for the heart like a sweet voice.

14

By nature soft, his whole address held off   105
   Suspicion: though not timid, his regard
Was such as rather seem'd to keep aloof,
   To shield himself than put you on your guard:
Perhaps 'twas hardly quite assured enough,
   But Modesty's at times its own reward,   110
Like Virtue; and the absence of pretension
Will go much farther than there's need to mention.

15

Serene, accomplish'd, cheerful but not loud;
   Insinuating without insinuation;
Observant of the foibles of the crowd,   115
   Yet ne'er betraying this in conversation;
Proud with the proud, yet courteously proud,
   So as to make them feel he knew his station
And theirs:—without a struggle for priority,
He neither brook'd nor claim'd superiority.   120

16

That is, with men: with women he was what
   They pleased to make or take him for; and their

---

4. Foppishness; pretentiousness in appearance and gesture.
5. An Adonis, lover (from the French diminutive for Cupid).
6. Vain man of fashion; one of a recognized social group of fashionable men during the Regency (see *Beppo*, lines 410 and 474 [pp. 362, 364]).

Imagination's quite enough for that:
   So that the outline's tolerably fair,
They fill the canvass up—and "verbum sat."[7]   125
   If once their phantasies be brought to bear
Upon an object, whether sad or playful,
They can transfigure brighter than a Raphael.[8]

17

Adeline, no deep judge of character,
   Was apt to add a colouring from her own: 130
'Tis thus the good will amiably err,
   And eke the wise, as has been often shown.
Experience is the chief philosopher,
   But saddest when his science is well known:
And persecuted sages[9] teach the schools   135
Their folly in forgetting there are fools.

18

Was it not so, great Locke? and greater Bacon?
   Great Socrates? And thou, Diviner still,[1]
Whose lot it is by man to be mistaken,
   And thy pure creed made sanction of all ill?   140
Redeeming worlds to be by bigots shaken,
   How was thy toil rewarded? We might fill
Volumes with similar sad illustrations,
But leave them to the conscience of the nations.

19

I perch upon an humbler promontory,   145
   Amidst life's infinite variety:[2]
With no great care for what is nicknamed glory,
   But speculating as I cast mine eye
On what may suit or may not suit my story,
   And never straining hard to versify,   150
I rattle on exactly as I'd talk
With any body in a ride or walk.

7. *Verbum sat sapienti* (Latin): A word to the wise is sufficient (proverbial).
8. Refers to the *Transfiguration* by the major Italian Renaissance painter Raphael (1483–1520).
9. Some of the philosophers persecuted either for their ideas or for political reasons are mentioned
   in lines 137–38: John Locke (1632–1704), Francis Bacon (1561–1626), and Socrates (469–399
   B.C.E.).
1. "As it is necessary in these times to avoid ambiguity, I say that I mean, by 'Diviner still,' CHRIST.
   If ever God was man—or man God—he was *both*. I never arraigned his creed, but the use—or
   abuse—made of it. Mr. Canning one day quoted Christianity to sanction negro slavery, and Mr.
   Wilberforce had little to say in reply. And was Christ crucified, that black men might be scourged?
   If so, he had better been born a Mulatto, to give both colours an equal chance of freedom, or at
   least salvation."
2. Echoes *Antony and Cleopatra* 2.2.241.

20

I don't know that there may be much ability
  Shown in this sort of desultory rhyme;
But there's a conversational facility,   155
  Which may round off an hour upon a time.
Of this I'm sure at least, there's no servility
  In mine irregularity of chime,
Which rings what's uppermost of new or hoary,
Just as I feel the "Improvvisatore."[3]   160

21

"Omnia vult *belle* Matho dicere—dic aliquando
  Et *bene*, dic *neutrum*, dic aliquando *male*."[4]
The first is rather more than mortal can do;
  The second may be sadly done or gaily;
The third is still more difficult to stand to;   165
  The fourth we hear, and see, and say too, daily:
The whole together is what I could wish
To serve in this conundrum of a dish.

22

A modest hope—but modesty's my forte,
  And pride my feeble:—let us ramble on.   170
I meant to make this poem very short,
  But now I can't tell where it may not run.
No doubt, if I had wish'd to pay my court
  To critics, or to hail the *setting* sun
Of tyranny of all kinds, my concision   175
Were more;—but I was born for opposition.

23

But then 'tis mostly on the weaker side;
  So that I verily believe if they
Who now are basking in their full-blown pride
  Were shaken down, and "dogs had had their day,"[5]   180
Though at the first I might perchance deride
  Their tumble, I should turn the other way,
And wax an ultra-royalist in loyalty,
Because I hate even democratic royalty.

24

I think I should have made a decent spouse,   185
  If I had never proved the soft condition;

3. While living in Venice, Byron admired the skill of the Italian *Improvvisatori*, who would improvise verses in public.
4. Maltho, if you want to express everything beautifully, sometimes speak well, sometimes in a neutral way, and sometimes badly (Martial, *Epigrams* 10.46).
5. Cf. *Hamlet* 5.1.277.

I think I should have made monastic vows,
   But for my own peculiar superstition:
'Gainst rhyme I never should have knock'd my brows,
   Nor broken my own head, nor that of Priscian,[6]   190
Nor worn the motley mantle of a poet,
If some one had not told me to forego it.[7]

*   *   *

28

When Adeline, in all her growing sense
   Of Juan's merits and his situation,
Felt on the whole an interest intense,—
   Partly perhaps because a fresh sensation,   220
Or that he had an air of innocence,
   Which is for innocence a sad temptation,—
As women hate half measures, on the whole,
She 'gan to ponder how to save his soul.

29

She had a good opinion of advice,   225
   Like all who give and eke[8] receive it gratis,
For which small thanks are still the market price,
   Even where the article at highest rate is:
She thought upon the subject twice or thrice,
   And morally decided, the best state is   230
For morals, marriage; and this question carried,
She seriously advised him to get married.

30

Juan replied, with all becoming deference,
   He had a predilection for that tie;
But that, at present, with immediate reference   235
   To his own circumstances, there might lie
Some difficulties, as in his own preference,
   Or that of her to whom he might apply:
That still he'd wed with such or such a lady,
If that they were not married all already.   240

*   *   *

40

But Adeline determined Juan's wedding
   In her own mind, and that's enough for woman:

---

6. Famed Latin grammarian of the early sixth century.
7. A reference to Henry Brougham's harsh critique of *Hours of Idleness* (1807) in the *Edinburgh Review.* For excerpts from Brougham's review, see p. 784.
8. Also (archaic).

But then, with whom? There was the sage Miss Reading, 315
    Miss Raw, Miss Flaw, Miss Showman, and Miss Knowman,
And the two fair co-heiresses Giltbedding.
    She deem'd his merits something more than common:
All these were unobjectionable matches,
And might go on, if well wound up, like watches. 320

41[9]

There was Miss Millpond, smooth as summer's sea,
    That usual paragon, an only daughter,
Who seem'd the cream of equanimity,
    Till skimm'd—and then there was some milk and water,
With a slight shade of blue[1] too, it might be, 325
    Beneath the surface; but what did it matter?
Love's riotous, but marriage should have quiet,
And being consumptive, live on a milk diet.

42

And then there was the Miss Audacia Shoestring,
    A dashing demoiselle of good estate, 330
Whose heart was fix'd upon a star or blue string;[2]
    But whether English dukes grew rare of late,
Or that she had not harp'd upon the true string,
    By which such sirens can attract our great,
She took up with some foreign younger brother, 335
A Russ or Turk—the one's as good as t'other.

43

And then there was—but why should I go on,
    Unless the ladies should go off?—there was
Indeed a certain fair and fairy one,
    Of the best class, and better than her class,— 340
Aurora Raby,[3] a young star who shone
    O'er life, too sweet an image for such glass,
A lovely being, scarcely form'd or moulded,
A rose with all its sweetest leaves yet folded;

44

Rich, noble, but an orphan; left an only 345
    Child to the care of guardians good and kind;
But still her aspect had an air so lonely!

9. The stanza caricatures Annabella Milbanke, Byron's ex-wife.
1. Reference to the Bluestockings, a tag for intellectual or literary women.
2. *star . . . string*: honorific emblems of aristocratic orders.
3. Although her portrait and role in Juan's life were left incomplete in the unfinished poem, Aurora
   seems an ideal type of woman in society, as Haidee is an ideal type in nature; in Canto II, stanza 42,
   the name Aurora appears in connection with Haidee, and the comparison and contrast between
   them are explicitly made in stanza 58 of the present canto. On similarities between Aurora and
   Byron's wife, see Cecil Lang's essay "Narcissus Jilted" in this volume, p. 972.

Blood is not water; and where shall we find
Feelings of youth like those which overthrown lie
    By death, when we are left, alas! behind,   350
To feel, in friendless palaces, a home
Is wanting, and our best ties in the tomb?

45

Early in years, and yet more infantine
    In figure, she had something of sublime
In eyes which sadly shone, as seraphs' shine.   355
    All youth—but with an aspect beyond time;
Radiant and grave—as pitying man's decline;
    Mournful—but mournful of another's crime,
She look'd as if she sat by Eden's door,
And grieved for those who could return no more.   360

46

She was a Catholic, too, sincere, austere,
    As far as her own gentle heart allow'd,
And deem'd that fallen worship far more dear
    Perhaps because 'twas fallen: her sires were proud
Of deeds and days when they had fill'd the ear   365
    Of nations, and had never bent or bow'd
To novel power; and as she was the last,
She held their old faith and old feelings fast.

47

She gazed upon a world she scarcely knew
    As seeking not to know it; silent, lone,   370
As grows a flower, thus quietly she grew,
    And kept her heart serene within its zone.
There was awe in the homage which she drew;
    Her spirit seem'd as seated on a throne
Apart from the surrounding world, and strong   375
In its own strength—most strange in one so young!

48

Now it so happen'd, in the catalogue
    Of Adeline, Aurora was omitted,
Although her birth and wealth had given her vogue
    Beyond the charmers we have already cited;   380
Her beauty also seem'd to form no clog
    Against her being mention'd as well fitted,
By many virtues, to be worth the trouble
Of single gentlemen who would be double.

49

And this omission, like that of the bust   385
   Of Brutus at the pageant of Tiberius,[4]
Made Juan wonder, as no doubt he must.
   This he express'd half smiling and half serious;
When Adeline replied with some disgust,
   And with an air, to say the least, imperious,   390
She marvell'd "what he saw in such a baby
As that prim, silent, cold Aurora Raby?"

50

Juan rejoin'd—"She was a Catholic,
   And therefore fittest, as of his persuasion;
Since he was sure his mother would fall sick,   395
   And the Pope thunder excommunication,
If——" But here Adeline, who seem'd to pique
   Herself extremely on the inoculation
Of others with her own opinions, stated—
As usual—the same reason which she late did.   400

51

And wherefore not? A reasonable reason,
   If good, is none the worse for repetition;
If bad, the best way's certainly to tease on,
   And amplify: you lose much by concision,
Whereas insisting in or out of season   405
   Convinces all men, even a politician;
Or—what is just the same—it wearies out.
So the end's gain'd, what signifies the route?

52

Why Adeline had this slight prejudice—
   For prejudice it was—against a creature   410
As pure as sanctity itself from vice,
   With all the added charm of form and feature,
For me appears a question far too nice,
   Since Adeline was liberal by nature;
But nature's nature, and has more caprices   415
Than I have time, or will, to take to pieces.

53

Perhaps she did not like the quiet way
   With which Aurora on those baubles look'd,
Which charm most people in their earlier day:
   For there are few things by mankind less brook'd,   420

---

4. See Tacitus, *Annals* 3.76, and cf. *Childe Harold* IV, stanza 59 [p. 314].

And womankind too, if we so may say,
   Than finding thus their genius stand rebuked,
Like "Anthony's by Caesar,"[5] by the few
Who look upon them as they ought to do.

54

It was not envy—Adeline had none;   425
   Her place was far beyond it, and her mind.
It was not scorn—which could not light on one
   Whose greatest *fault* was leaving few to find.
It was not jealousy, I think: but shun
   Following the "ignes fatui"[6] of mankind.   430
It was not——but 'tis easier far, alas!
To say what it was not than what it was.

55

Little Aurora deem'd[7] she was the theme
   Of such discussion. She was there a guest,
A beauteous ripple of the brilliant stream   435
   Of rank and youth, though purer than the rest,
Which flow'd on for a moment in the beam
   Time sheds a moment o'er each sparkling crest.
Had she known this, she would have calmly smiled—
She had so much, or little, of the child.   440

56

The dashing and proud air of Adeline
   Imposed not upon her: she saw her blaze
Much as she would have seen a glow-worm shine,
   Then turn'd unto the stars for loftier rays.
Juan was something she could not divine,   445
   Being no sibyl[8] in the new world's ways;
Yet she was nothing dazzled by the meteor,
Because she did not pin her faith on feature.

57

His fame too,—for he had that kind of fame
   Which sometimes plays the deuce with womankind,   450
A heterogeneous mass of glorious blame,
   Half virtues and whole vices being combined;
Faults which attract because they are not tame;
   Follies trick'd out so brightly that they blind:[9]—

5. Cf. *Macbeth* 3.1.55–58.
6. The lighting effects that appear over marshes (also called will-o'-the-wisps), here meaning illusions or delusory attractions. The term occurs a number of times in Byron's poems: e.g., Canto XI.214–16 and *Manfred* 1.1.195 (p. 254).
7. I.e., Little did Aurora deem. . . .
8. Prophetess.
9. Lines 449–54 are autobiographical.

These seals upon her wax made no impression,   455
　　Such was her coldness or her self-possession.

58

Juan knew nought of such a character—
　　High, yet resembling not his lost Haidee;
Yet each was radiant in her proper sphere:
　　The island girl, bred up by the lone sea,   460
More warm, as lovely, and not less sincere,
　　Was Nature's all: Aurora could not be,
Nor would be thus:—the difference in them
Was such as lies between a flower and gem.

*　　*　　*

77

Aurora sat with that indifference
　　Which piques a preux chevalier[1]—as it ought: 610
Of all offences that's the worst offence,
　　Which seems to hint you are not worth a thought.
Now Juan, though no coxcomb in pretence,
　　Was not exactly pleased to be so caught;
Like a good ship entangled among ice,   615
And after so much excellent advice.

78

To his gay nothings, nothing was replied,
　　Or something which was nothing, as urbanity
Required. Aurora scarcely look'd aside,
　　Nor even smiled enough for any vanity.   620
The devil was in the girl! Could it be pride?
　　Or modesty, or absence, or inanity?
Heaven knows! But Adeline's malicious eyes
Sparkled with her successful prophecies,

79

And look'd as much as if to say, "I said it;"   625
　　A kind of triumph I'll not recommend,
Because it sometimes, as I have seen or read it,
　　Both in the case of lover and of friend,
Will pique a gentleman, for his own credit,
　　To bring what was a jest to a serious end: 630
For all men prophesy what *is* or *was*,
And hate those who won't let them come to pass.

1. Gallant (or valiant) knight.

80

Juan was drawn thus into some attentions,
   Slight but select, and just enough to express,
To females of perspicuous comprehensions,   635
   That he would rather make them more than less.
Aurora at the last (so history mentions,
   Though probably much less a fact than guess)
So far relax'd her thoughts from their sweet prison,
As once or twice to smile, if not to listen.   640

81

From answering she began to question: this
   With her was rare; and Adeline, who as yet
Thought her predictions went not much amiss,
   Began to dread she'd thaw to a coquette—
So very difficult, they say, it is   645
   To keep extremes from meeting, when once set
In motion; but she here too much refined—
Aurora's spirit was not of that kind.

82

But Juan had a sort of winning way,
   A proud humility, if such there be,   650
Which show'd such deference to what females say,
   As if each charming word were a decree.
His tact, too, temper'd him from grave to gay,
   And taught him when to be reserved or free:
He had the art of drawing people out,   655
Without their seeing what he was about.

83

Aurora, who in her indifference
   Confounded him in common with the crowd
Of flatterers, though she deem'd he had more sense
   Than whispering foplings, or than witlings loud— 660
Commenced (from such slight things will great commence)
   To feel that flattery which attracts the proud
Rather by deference than compliment,
And wins even by a delicate dissent.

84

And then he had good looks;—that point was carried   665
   Nem. con.[2] amongst the women, which I grieve
To say leads oft to *crim. con.* with the married—

---

2. *Nemine contradicenti*: unanimously; compare *crim. con.* (line 667), "criminal conversation," i.e., adultery.

A case which to the juries we may leave,
Since with digressions we too long have tarried.
  Now though we know of old that looks deceive,   670
And always have done, somehow these good looks
Make more impression than the best of books.

85

Aurora, who look'd more on books than faces,
  Was very young, although so very sage,
Admiring more Minerva than the Graces,[3]   675
  Especially upon a printed page.
But Virtue's self, with all her tightest laces,
  Has not the natural stays of strict old age;
And Socrates, that model of all duty,
Own'd to a penchant, though discreet, for beauty.   680

86

And girls of sixteen are thus far Socratic,
  But innocently so, as Socrates;
And really, if the Sage sublime and Attic[4]
  At seventy years had phantasies like these,
Which Plato in his dialogues dramatic   685
  Has shown, I know not why they should displease
In virgins—always in a modest way,
Observe; for that with me's a "sine quâ."[5]

87

Also observe, that, like the great Lord Coke
  (See Littleton),[6] whene'er I have express'd   690
Opinions two, which at first sight may look
  Twin opposites, the second is the best.
Perhaps I have a third too, in a nook,
  Or none at all—which seems a sorry jest:
But if a writer should be quite consistent,   695
How could he possibly show things existent?

88

If people contradict themselves, can I
  Help contradicting them, and every body,
Even my veracious self?—But that's a lie;
  I never did so, never will—how should I?   700
He who doubts all things nothing can deny:
  Truth's fountains may be clear—her streams are muddy,

3. The ancient Greek goddesses of beauty; *Minerva*: the ancient Roman goddess of wisdom.
4. Athenian (i.e., Socrates).
5. "Subauditur '*non*;' omitted for the sake of euphony." I.e., *sine qua non*: without equal; essential.
6. Sir Edward Coke's *Institutes of the Laws of England* (1628–44), part of which is a commentary on Sir Thomas Littleton's "Tenures."

And cut through such canals of contradiction,
That she must often navigate o'er fiction.

89

Apologue, fable, poesy, and parable,   705
   Are false, but may be render'd also true
By those who sow them in a land that's arable.
   'Tis wonderful what fable will not do!
'Tis said it makes reality more bearable:
   But what's reality? Who has its clue?   710
Philosophy? No: she too much rejects.
Religion? *Yes*; but which of all her sects?

90

Some millions must be wrong, that's pretty clear;
   Perhaps it may turn out that all were right.
God help us! Since we have need on our career   715
   To keep our holy beacons always bright,
'Tis time that some new prophet should appear,
   Or old indulge man with a second sight.
Opinions wear out in some thousand years,
Without a small refreshment from the spheres.   720

91

But here again, why will I thus entangle
   Myself with metaphysics? None can hate
So much as I do any kind of wrangle;
   And yet, such is my folly, or my fate,
I always knock my head against some angle   725
   About the present, past, or future state:
Yet I wish well to Trojan and to Tyrian,[7]
For I was bred a moderate Presbyterian.

92

But though I am a temperate theologian,
   And also meek as a metaphysician,   730
Impartial between Tyrian and Trojan,
   As Eldon[8] on a lunatic commission,—
In politics my duty is to show John
   Bull something of the lower world's condition.
It makes my blood boil like the springs of Hecla,[9]   735
To see men let these scoundrel sovereigns break law.

---

7. Echoing Virgil's *Aeneid* 1.574.
8. Lord Eldon, Lord Chancellor (1801–27) and a favorite satiric target for Byron, had recently presided over a sanity hearing.
9. Hecla is a famous hot-spring in Ireland.

93

But politics, and policy, and piety,
    Are topics which I sometimes introduce,
Not only for the sake of their variety,
    But as subservient to a moral use;   740
Because my business is to *dress* society,
    And stuff with *sage* that very verdant goose.
And now, that we may furnish with some matter all
Tastes, we are going to try the supernatural.

94

And now I will give up all argument;   745
    And positively henceforth no temptation
Shall "fool me to the top up of my bent:"[1]—
    Yes, I'll begin a thorough reformation.
Indeed, I never knew what people meant
    By deeming that my Muse's conversation   750
Was dangerous;—I think she is as harmless
As some who labour more and yet may charm less.

95

Grim reader! did you ever see a ghost?
    No; but you have heard—I understand—be dumb!
And don't regret the time you may have lost,   755
    For you have got that pleasure still to come:
And do not think I mean to sneer at most
    Of these things, or by ridicule benumb
That source of the sublime and the mysterious:—
For certain reasons, my belief is serious.   760

96

Serious? You laugh;—you may: that will I not;
    My smiles must be sincere or not at all.
I say I do believe a haunted spot
    Exists—and where? That shall I not recall,
Because I'd rather it should be forgot,   765
    "Shadows the soul of Richard"[2] may appal.
In short, upon that subject I've some qualms very
Like those of the Philosopher of Malmsbury.[3]

97

The night—(I sing by night—sometimes an owl,
    And now and then a nightingale)—is dim,   770

1. "Hamlet, Act III, sc. ii.[374–75]." (Cf. *Hamlet* 3.2.353.)
2. *Richard III* 5.5.170–71.
3. "Hobbes: who, doubting of his own soul, paid that compliment to the souls of other people as to decline their visits, of which he had some apprehension." Malmsbury was the birthplace of Thomas Hobbes.

And the loud shriek of sage Minerva's fowl
   Rattles around me her discordant hymn:
Old portraits from old walls upon me scowl—
   I wish to heaven they would not look so grim;
The dying embers dwindle in the grate—   775
   I think too that I have sate up too late:

98

And therefore, though 'tis by no means my way
   To rhyme at noon—when I have other things
To think of, if I ever think—I say
   I feel some chilly midnight shudderings,   780
And prudently postpone, until mid-day,
   Treating a topic which, alas, but brings
Shadows;—but you must be in my condition
Before you learn to call this superstition.

99

Between two worlds life hovers like a star,   785
   'Twixt night and morn, upon the horizon's verge.
How little do we know that which we are!
   How less what we may be![4] The eternal surge
Of time and tide rolls on, and bears afar
   Our bubbles; as the old burst, new emerge,   790
Lash'd from the foam of ages; while the graves
Of empires heave but like some passing waves.

FROM CANTO THE SIXTEENTH[1]

1

The antique Persians taught three useful things,
   To draw the bow, to ride, and speak the truth.[2]
This was the mode of Cyrus, best of kings—
   A mode adopted since by modern youth.
Bows have they, generally with two strings;   5
   Horses they ride without remorse or ruth;
At speaking truth perhaps they are less clever,
But draw the long bow[3] better now than ever.

2

The cause of this effect, or this defect,—
   "For this effect defective comes by cause,"[4]—   10
Is what I have not leisure to inspect;

---

4. Cf. *Hamlet* 4.5.43–44.
1. Canto XVI was written between March and May 1823 and published by John Hunt with Canto XV
   on March 26, 1824.
2. Cyrus the Great (558–529 B.C.E.) was founder of the Persian empire.
3. To exaggerate.
4. *Hamlet* 2.2.104.

But this I must say in my own applause,
Of all the Muses that I recollect,
　　Whate'er may be her follies or her flaws
In some things, mine's beyond all contradiction 15
The most sincere that ever dealt in fiction.

3

And as she treats all things, and ne'er retreats
　　From any thing, this epic will contain
A wilderness of the most rare conceits,
　　Which you might elsewhere hope to find in vain. 20
'Tis true there be some bitters with the sweets,
　　Yet mix'd so slightly, that you can't complain,
But wonder they so few are, since my tale is
"De rebus cunctis et quibusdam aliis."[5]

4

But of all truths which she has told, the most 25
　　True is that which she is about to tell.
I said it was a story of a ghost—
　　What then? I only know it so befell.
Have you explored the limits of the coast,
　　Where all the dwellers of the earth must dwell? 30
'Tis time to strike such puny doubters dumb as
The sceptics who would not believe Columbus.

5

Some people would impose now with authority,
　　Turpin's or Monmouth Geoffry's[6] Chronicle;
Men whose historical superiority 35
　　Is always greatest at a miracle.
But Saint Augustine has the great priority,
　　Who bids all men believe the impossible,
Because 'tis so. Who nibble, scribble, quibble, he
Quiets at once with "*quia* impossibile."[7] 40

6

And therefore, mortals, cavil not at all;
　　Believe:—if 'tis improbable, you *must*;
And if it is impossible, you *shall*:
　　'Tis always best to take things upon trust.
I do not speak profanely, to recall 45
　　Those holier mysteries which the wise and just

5. About all things, and a few additional things; from *De omnibus rebus* and *De quibusdam aliis*, two treatises by the theologian St. Thomas Aquinas (d. 1274).
6. Medieval historians.
7. It was actually the Roman theologian Tertullian (160–230), not St. Augustine (354–430), who uttered the famous profession of faith, *certum est quia impossibile est* ("I believe because it is impossible").

Receive as gospel, and which grow more rooted,
As all truths must, the more they are disputed:

7

I merely mean to say what Johnson[8] said,
    That in the course of some six thousand years,   50
All nations have believed that from the dead
    A visitant at intervals appears;
And what is strangest upon this strange head,
    Is, that whatever bar the reason rears
'Gainst such belief, there's something stronger still   55
In its behalf, let those deny who will.

8

The dinner and the soirée too were done,
    The supper too discuss'd, the dames admired,
The banqueteers had dropp'd off one by one—
    The song was silent, and the dance expired: 60
The last thin petticoats were vanish'd, gone
    Like fleecy clouds into the sky retired,
And nothing brighter gleam'd through the saloon
Than dying tapers—and the peeping moon.

9

The evaporation of a joyous day   65
    Is like the last glass of champagne, without
The foam which made its virgin bumper gay;
    Or like a system coupled with a doubt;
Or like a soda bottle when its spray
    Has sparkled and let half its spirit out;   70
Or like a billow left by storms behind,
Without the animation of the wind;

10

Or like an opiate which brings troubled rest,
    Or none; or like—like nothing that I know
Except itself;—such is the human breast;   75
    A thing, of which similitudes can show
No real likeness,—like the old Tyrian vest
    Dyed purple, none at present can tell how,
If from a shell-fish or from cochineal.[9]
So perish every tyrant's robe piece-meal!   80

---

8. Dr. Samuel Johnson (1709–1784), the great writer and literary critic of the late eighteenth cen-
   tury, throughout his life retained an open mind on the possibility of supernatural visitations.
9. "The composition of the old Tyrian purple, whether from a shell-fish, or from cochineal, or from
   kermes, is still an article of dispute; and even its colour—some say purple, others scarlet; I say noth-
   ing." Cochineal and kermes both refer to a red dye made from insect scales.

11

But next to dressing for a rout or ball,
    Undressing is a woe; our robe de chambre
May sit like that of Nessus,[1] and recall
    Thoughts quite as yellow, but less clear than amber.
Titus exclaim'd, "I've lost a day!"[2] Of all   85
    The nights and days most people can remember
(I have had of both, some not to be disdain'd),
I wish they'd state how many they have gain'd.

12

And Juan, on retiring for the night,
    Felt restless, and perplex'd, and compromised: 90
He thought Aurora Raby's eyes more bright
    Than Adeline (such is advice) advised;
If he had known exactly his own plight,
    He probably would have philosophised;
A great resource to all, and ne'er denied   95
Till wanted; therefore Juan only sigh'd.

13

He sigh'd;—the next resource is the full moon,
    Where all sighs are deposited; and now
It happen'd luckily, the chaste orb shone
    As clear as such a climate will allow;   100
And Juan's mind was in the proper tone
    To hail her with the apostrophe—"O thou!"
Of amatory egotism the *Tuism*,[3]
Which further to explain would be a truism.

14

But lover, poet, or astronomer,   105
    Shepherd, or swain, whoever may behold,
Feel some abstraction when they gaze on her:
    Great thoughts we catch from thence (besides a cold
Sometimes, unless my feelings rather err);
    Deep secrets to her rolling light are told;   110
The ocean's tides and mortals' brains she sways,
And also hearts, if there be truth in lays.

15

Juan felt somewhat pensive, and disposed
    For contemplation rather than his pillow:

1. The centaur whose blood was used to poison the shirt which killed Hercules; *robe de chambre*: dressing gown (French).
2. The emperor Titus exclaimed this, according to Suetonius (c. 69–140; *Lives of the Twelve Caesars*), when once he realized that he had let a day go by without acting on the petitions of any of his suppliants.
3. Play on words: *tu* is the French intimate second-person form (in English, "thou").

The Gothic chamber, where he was enclosed, 115
  Let in the rippling sound of the lake's billow,
With all the mystery by midnight caused:
  Below his window waved (of course) a willow;
And he stood gazing out on the cascade
That flash'd and after darken'd in the shade. 120

16

Upon his table or his toilet,[4]—*which*
  Of these is not exactly ascertained,—
(I state this, for I am cautious to a pitch
  Of nicety, where a fact is to be gain'd,)
A lamp burn'd high, while he leant from a niche, 125
  Where many a Gothic ornament remain'd,
In chisell'd stone and painted glass, and all
That time has left our fathers of their hall.

17

Then, as the night was clear though cold, he threw
  His chamber door wide open—and went forth 130
Into a gallery, of a sombre hue,
  Long, furnish'd with old pictures of great worth,
Of knights and dames heroic and chaste too,
  As doubtless should be people of high birth.
But by dim lights the portraits of the dead 135
Have something ghastly, desolate, and dread.

18

The frowns of the grim knight and pictured saint
  Look living in the moon; and as you turn
Backward and forward to the echoes faint
  Of your own footsteps—voices from the urn 140
Appear to wake, and shadows wild and quaint
  Start from the frames which fence their aspects stern,
As if to ask how you can dare to keep
A vigil there, where all but death should sleep.

19

And the pale smile of beauties in the grave, 145
  The charms of other days, in starlight gleams,
Glimmer on high; their buried locks still wave
  Along the canvass; their eyes glance like dreams
On ours, or spars within some dusky cave,
  But death is imaged in their shadowy beams. 150
A picture is the past; even ere its frame
Be gilt, who sate hath ceased to be the same.

4. Dressing table.

20

As Juan mused on mutability,
   Or on his mistress—terms synonymous—
No sound except the echo of his sigh   155
   Or step ran sadly through that antique house;
When suddenly he heard, or thought so, nigh,
   A supernatural agent—or a mouse,
Whose little nibbling rustle will embarrass
Most people as it plays along the arras.   160

21

It was no mouse, but lo! a monk, array'd
   In cowl and beads, and dusky garb, appear'd,
Now in the moonlight, and now lapsed in shade,
   With steps that trod as heavy, yet unheard;
His garments only a slight murmur made;   165
   He moved as shadowy as the sisters weird,[6]
But slowly; and as he passed Juan by,
Glanced, without pausing, on him a bright eye.

22

Juan was petrified; he had heard a hint
   Of such a spirit in these halls of old,[5]   170
But thought, like most men, there was nothing in't
   Beyond the rumour which such spots unfold,
Coin'd from surviving superstition's mint,
   Which passes ghosts in currency like gold,
But rarely seen, like gold compared with paper.   175
And *did* he see this? or was it a vapour?

23

Once, twice, thrice pass'd, repass'd—the thing of air,
   Or earth beneath, or heaven, or t'other place;
And Juan gazed upon it with a stare,
   Yet could not speak or move; but, on its base   180
As stands a statue, stood: he felt his hair
   Twine like a knot of snakes around his face;
He tax'd his tongue for words, which were not granted,
To ask the reverend person what he wanted.

24

The third time, after a still longer pause,   185
   The shadow pass'd away—but where? the hall
Was long, and thus far there was no great cause

5. There was a legend about such a ghostly monk haunting Newstead Abbey.
6. The three witches in *Macbeth*.

To think his vanishing unnatural:
  Doors there were many, through which, by the laws
    Of physics, bodies whether short or tall   190
Might come or go; but Juan could not state
Through which the spectre seem'd to evaporate.

25

He stood—how long he knew not, but it seem'd
  An age—expectant, powerless, with his eyes
Strain'd on the spot where first the figure gleam'd;   195
    Then by degrees recall'd his energies,
And would have pass'd the whole off as a dream,
  But could not wake; he was, he did surmise,
Waking already, and return'd at length
Back to his chamber, shorn of half his strength.[7]   200

26

All there was as he left it: still his taper
  Burnt, and not *blue*,[8] as modest tapers use,
Receiving sprites with sympathetic vapour;
    He rubb'd his eyes, and they did not refuse
Their office; he took up an old newspaper;   205
    The paper was right easy to peruse;
He read an article the king attacking,
And a long eulogy of "patent blacking."[9]

27

This savour'd of this world; but his hand shook—
  He shut his door, and after having read   210
A paragraph, I think about Horne Tooke,[1]
    Undrest, and rather slowly went to bed.
There, couch'd all snugly on his pillow's nook,
  With what he had seen his phantasy he fed;
And though it was no opiate, slumber crept   215
Upon him by degrees, and so he slept.

28

He woke betimes; and, as may be supposed,
  Ponder'd upon his visitant or vision,
And whether it ought not to be disclosed,
  At risk of being quizz'd for superstition.   220
The more he thought, the more his mind was posed:

---

7. A reference to the biblical Samson (cf. Judges 16.19).
8. In Gothic fiction and in folklore, the presence of a ghost or devil caused candles to burn blue.
9. Rhyming advertisements for shoe polish were common in Byron's day.
1. John Horne Tooke (1736–1812), English radical writer whom Byron admired; see *Vision of Judgment*, stanza 84 (p. 708).

In the mean time, his valet, whose precision
Was great, because his master brook'd no less,
Knock'd to inform him it was time to dress.

29

He dress'd; and like young people he was wont   225
    To take some trouble with his toilet, but
This morning rather spent less time upon't;
    Aside his very mirror soon was put;
His curls fell negligently o'er his front,
    His clothes were not curb'd to their usual cut,   230
His very neckcloth's Gordian knot² was tied
Almost an hair's breadth too much on one side.

30

And when he walk'd down into the saloon,
    He sate him pensive o'er a dish of tea,
Which he perhaps had not discover'd soon,   235
    Had it not happen'd scalding hot to be,
Which made him have recourse unto his spoon;
    So much distrait he was, that all could see
That something *was* the matter—Adeline
The first—but *what* she could not well divine.   240

31

She look'd, and saw him pale, and turn'd as pale
    Herself; then hastily look'd down, and mutter'd
Something, but what's not stated in my tale.
    Lord Henry said, his muffin was ill butter'd;
The Duchess of Fitz-Fulke play'd with her veil,   245
    And look'd at Juan hard, but nothing utter'd.
Aurora Raby with her large dark eyes
Survey'd him with a kind of calm surprise.

32

But seeing him all cold and silent still,
    And every body wondering more or less,   250
Fair Adeline enquired, "If he were ill?"
    He started, and said, "Yes—no—rather—yes."
The family physician had great skill,
    And being present, now began to express
His readiness to feel his pulse and tell   255
The cause, but Juan said, "He was quite well."

---

2. An extremely complicated knot. In legend, the Gordian knot was loosed by the single stroke of the
sword of Alexander the Great.

33

"Quite well; yes,—no."—These answers were mysterious,
  And yet his looks appear'd to sanction both,
However they might savour of delirious;
  Something like illness of a sudden growth   260
Weigh'd on his spirit, though by no means serious:
  But for the rest, as he himself seem'd loth
To state the case, it might be ta'en for granted
It was not the physician that he wanted.

34

Lord Henry, who had now discuss'd his chocolate,   265
  Also the muffin whereof he complain'd,
Said, Juan had not got his usual look elate,
  At which he marvell'd, since it had not rain'd;
Then ask'd her Grace what news were of the duke of late?
  Her Grace replied, *his* Grace was rather pain'd   270
With some slight, light, hereditary twinges
Of gout,[3] which rusts aristocratic hinges.

35

Then Henry turn'd to Juan, and address'd
  A few words of condolence on his state:
"You look," quoth he, "as if you had had your rest   275
  Broke in upon by the Black Friar of late."[4]
"What friar?" said Juan; and he did his best
  To put the question with an air sedate,
Or careless; but the effort was not valid
To hinder him from growing still more pallid.   280

36

"Oh! have you never heard of the Black Friar?
  The spirit of these walls?"—"In truth not I."
"Why Fame—but Fame you know's sometimes a liar—
  Tells an odd story, of which by the bye:
Whether with time the spectre has grown shyer,   285
  Or that our sires had a more gifted eye
For such sights, though the tale is half believed,
The Friar of late has not been oft perceived.

37

"The last time was——"—"I pray," said Adeline—
  (Who watch'd the changes of Don Juan's brow,   290
And from its context thought she could divine

---

3. An arthritic type of ailment that was believed to be caused by overindulgence in rich food and drink.
4. The final stanza of this canto elucidates the innuendo in Lord Henry's remark.

Connections stronger than he chose to avow
With this same legend)—"if you but design
   To jest, you'll choose some other theme just now,
Because the present tale has oft been told,   295
And is not much improved by growing old."

38

"Jest!" quoth Milor; "why, Adeline, you know
   That we ourselves—'twas in the honey moon—
Saw:——"—"Well, no matter, 'twas so long ago;
   But, come, I'll set your story to a tune."   300
Graceful as Dian, when she draws her bow,
   She seized her harp, whose strings were kindled soon
As touch'd, and plaintively began to play
The air of "'Twas a Friar of Orders Gray."[5]

39

"But add the words," cried Henry, "which you made;   305
   For Adeline is half a poetess,"
Turning round to the rest, he smiling said.
   Of course the others could not but express
In courtesy their wish to see display'd
   By one *three* talents, for there were no less—   310
The voice, the words, the harper's skill, at once
Could hardly be united by a dunce.

40

After some fascinating hesitation,—
   The charming of these charmers, who seem bound,
I can't tell why, to this dissimulation,—   315
   Fair Adeline, with eyes fix'd on the ground
At first, then kindling into animation,
   Added her sweet voice to the lyric sound,
And sang with much simplicity,—a merit
Not the less precious, that we seldom hear it.   320

1

Beware! beware! of the Black Friar,
   Who sitteth by Norman stone,
For he mutters his prayer in the midnight air,
   And his mass of the days that are gone.
When the Lord of the Hill, Amundeville,   325
   Made Norman Church his prey,
And expell'd the friars, one friar still
   Would not be driven away.

5. Late-eighteenth-century song, "I am a friar of orders grey," music by William Reeve, words by John O'Keefe.

2

Though he came in his might, with King Henry's right,
 To turn church lands to lay,   330
With sword in hand, and torch to light
 Their walls, if they said nay,
A monk remain'd, unchased, unchain'd,
 And he did not seem form'd of clay,
For he's seen in the porch, and he's seen in the church, 335
 Though he is not seen by day.

3

And whether for good, or whether for ill,
 It is not mine to say;
But still with the house of Amundeville
 He abideth night and day.   340
By the marriage-bed of their lords, 'tis said,
 He flits on the bridal eve;
And 'tis held as faith, to their bed of death
 He comes—but not to grieve.

4

When an heir is born, he's heard to mourn, 345
 And when aught is to befall
That ancient line, in the pale moonshine
 He walks from hall to hall.
His form you may trace, but not his face,
 'Tis shadow'd by his cowl;   350
But his eyes may be seen from the folds between,
 And they seem of a parted soul.

5

But beware! beware! of the Black Friar,
 He still retains his sway,
For he is yet the church's heir   355
 Whoever may be the lay.
Amundeville is lord by day,
 But the monk is lord by night;
Nor wine nor wassail could raise a vassal
 To question that friar's right.   360

6

Say nought to him as he walks the hall,
 And he'll say nought to you;
He sweeps along in his dusky pall,
 As o'er the grass the dew.
Then Grammercy! for the Black Friar; 365

Heaven sain[6] him! fair or foul,
And whatsoe'er may be his prayer,
Let ours be for his soul.

41

The lady's voice ceased, and the thrilling wires
    Died from the touch that kindled them to sound;   370
And the pause follow'd, which when song expires
    Pervades a moment those who listen round;
And then of course the circle much admires,
    Nor less applauds, as in politeness bound,
The tones, the feeling, and the execution,   375
To the performer's diffident confusion.

42

Fair Adeline, though in a careless way,
    As if she rated such accomplishment
As the mere pastime of an idle day,
    Pursued an instant for her own content,   380
Would now and then as 'twere *without* display,
    Yet *with* display in fact, at times relent
To such performances with haughty smile,
To show she *could*, if it were worth her while.

43

Now this (but we will whisper it aside)   385
    Was—pardon the pedantic illustration—
Trampling on Plato's pride with greater pride,
    As did the Cynic on some like occasion;
Deeming the sage would be much mortified,
    Or thrown into a philosophic passion,   390
For a spoilt carpet—but the "Attic Bee"
Was much consoled by his own repartee.[7]

44

Thus Adeline would throw into the shade
    (By doing easily, whene'er she chose,
What dilettanti do with vast parade)   395
    Their sort of *half profession*; for it grows
To something like this when too oft display'd;
    And that it is so, every body knows,

6. Bless.
7. "I think that it *was* a *carpet* on which Diogenes trod, with—'Thus I trample on the pride of Plato!'—
'With greater pride,' as the other replied. But as *carpets* are *meant* to be trodden upon, my mem-
ory probably misgives me, and it might be a robe, or tapestry, or table-cloth, or some other expensive
and uncynical piece of furniture." The Cynic philosopher Diogenes is supposed once to have
stamped upon Plato's couch, exclaiming, "So much for the pride of Plato!" Plato (the "Attic Bee")
replied, "And how much for the pride of Diogenes?" The point of the anecdote is that proclaiming
one's contempt of arrogance is often the highest form of arrogance.

Who have heard Miss That or This, or Lady T'other,
Show off—to please their company or mother.   400

45

Oh! the long evenings of duets and trios!
    The admirations and the speculations;
The "Mamma Mia's!" and the "Amor Mio's!"[8]
    The "Tanti palpiti's" on such occasions:
The "Lasciami's," and quavering "Addio's!"   405
    Amongst our own most musical of nations;
With "Tu mi chamas's" from Portingale,
To soothe our ears, lest Italy should fail.[9]

46

In Babylon's bravuras[1]—as the home
    Heart-ballads of Green Erin or Gray Highlands,[2]   410
That bring Lochaber back to eyes that roam
    O'er far Atlantic continents or islands,
The calentures[3] of music which o'ercome
    All mountaineers with dreams that they are nigh lands,
No more to be beheld but in such visions—   415
Was Adeline well versed, as compositions.

47

She also had a twilight tinge of "*Blue*,"[4]
    Could write rhymes, and compose more than she wrote,
Made epigrams occasionally too
    Upon her friends, as every body ought.   420
But still from that sublimer azure hue,
    So much the present dye, she was remote;[5]
Was weak enough to deem Pope a great poet,
And what was worse, was not ashamed to show it.

---

8. The Italian phrases in this stanza are to represent opening lines of pieces sung by the dilettanti or amateurs. Their opening lines—"My mother," "My love!" "So many heartbeats," "Leave me" and "Farewell"—indicate that they are sentimental love songs. "Tu mi chamas" is a Portugese song, which Byron translated ("From the Portuguese," 1812, pub. 1814).
9. "I remember that the mayoress of a provincial town, somewhat surfeited with a similar display from foreign parts, did rather indecorously break through the applauses of an intelligent audience—intelligent, I mean, as to music,—for the words, besides being in recondite languages (it was some years before the peace, ere all the world had travelled, and while I was a collegian)—were sorely disguised by the performers;—this mayoress, I say, broke out with, 'Rot your Italianos! for my part, I loves a simple ballat!' Rossini will go a good way to bring most people to the same opinion, some day. Who would imagine that he was to be the successor of Mozart? However, I state this with diffidence, as a liege and loyal admirer of Italian music in general, and of much of Rossini's: but we may say, as the connoisseur did of painting, in The Vicar of Wakefield, 'that the picture would be better painted if the painter had taken more pains.'"
1. Perhaps florid arias from *Semiramide*, Rossini's opera about Semiramis, queen of Babylon.
2. *Green Erin or Gray Highlands*: Ireland or Scotland. Lines 410–13 recall the Irish ballads of Moore and the Scottish ballads of Walter Scott and Allan Ramsay.
3. Fevers associated with delirium.
4. She was at least partly a "bluestocking," or literary female.
5. Adeline was not an enthusiast of Romantic poetry and was an admirer of Pope—points in her favor in Byron's view.

48

Aurora—since we are touching upon taste,   425
    Which now-a-days is the thermometer
By whose degrees all characters are class'd—
    Was more Shakspearian, if I do not err.
The worlds beyond this world's perplexing waste
    Had more of her existence, for in her   430
There was a depth of feeling to embrace
Thoughts, boundless, deep, but silent too as Space.

49

Not so her gracious, graceful, graceless Grace,
    The full-grown Hebe[6] of Fitz-Fulke, whose mind,
If she had any, was upon her face,   435
    And that was of a fascinating kind.
A little turn for mischief you might trace
    Also thereon,—but that's not much;[7] we find
Few females without some such gentle leaven,
For fear we should suppose us quite in heaven.   440

50

I have not heard she was at all poetic,
    Though once she was seen reading the "Bath Guide,"
And "Hayley's Triumphs,"[8] which she deem'd pathetic,
    Because she said *her temper* had been tried
So much, the bard had really been prophetic   445
    Of what she had gone through with—since a bride.
But of all verse, what most ensured her praise
Were sonnets to herself, or "bouts rimés."[9]

51

'Twere difficult to say what was the object
    Of Adeline, in bringing this same lay   450
To bear on what appear'd to her the subject
    Of Juan's nervous feelings on that day.
Perhaps she merely had the simple project
    To laugh him out of his supposed dismay;
Perhaps she might wish to confirm him in it,   455
Though why I cannot say—at least this minute.

---

6. Classical goddess of youth, who filled the cups of the gods.
7. *but that's not much*: Othello 3.3.270.
8. William Hayley's *The Triumphs of Temper* (1781) is a sentimental verse novel on a sexual theme. Christopher Anstey's *New Bath Guide* (1766) is a bawdy verse novel.
9. Rhymed endings: a parlor entertainment in which a guest is given the rhyming words and has to fill in the rest of the lines.

52

But so far the immediate effect
   Was to restore him to his self-propriety,
A thing quite necessary to the elect,
   Who wish to take the tone of their society: 460
In which you cannot be too circumspect,
   Whether the mode be persiflage or piety,
But wear the newest mantle of hypocrisy,
On pain of much displeasing the gynocracy.[1]

53

And therefore Juan now began to rally   465
   His spirits, and without more explanation
To jest upon such themes in many a sally.
   Her Grace, too, also seized the same occasion,
With various similar remarks to tally,
   But wish'd for a still more detail'd narration   470
Of this same mystic Friar's curious doings,
About the present family's deaths and wooings.

54

Of these few could say more than has been said;
   They pass'd as such things do, for superstition
With some, while others, who had more in dread   475
   The theme, half credited the strange tradition;
And much was talk'd on all sides on that head:
   But Juan, when cross-question'd on the vision,
Which some supposed (though he had not avow'd it)
Had stirr'd him, answer'd in a way to cloud it.   480

55

And then, the mid-day having worn to one,
   The company prepared to separate;
Some to their several pastimes, or to none,
   Some wondering 'twas so early, some so late.
There was a goodly match too, to be run   485
   Between some greyhounds on my lord's estate,
And a young race-horse of old pedigree,
Match'd[2] for the spring, whom several went to see.

*   *   *

87

Dully past o'er the dinner of the day;
   And Juan took his place, he knew not where,

1. Government by women (written "Gynocrasy" by Byron).
2. Entered in the list of matches or races.

Confused, in the confusion, and distrait,[3]
  And sitting as if nail'd upon his chair: 740
Though knives and forks clang'd round as in a fray,
  He seem'd unconscious of all passing there,
Till some one, with a groan, exprest a wish
(Unheeded twice) to have a fin of fish.

88

On which, at the *third* asking of the banns,[4] 745
  He started; and perceiving smiles around
Broadening to grins, he colour'd more than once,
  And hastily—as nothing can confound
A wise man more than laughter from a dunce—
  Inflicted on the dish a deadly wound, 750
And with such hurry, that ere he could curb it,
He had paid his neighbour's prayer with half a turbot.

89

This was no bad mistake, as it occurr'd,
  The supplicator being an amateur;
But others, who were left with scarce a third, 755
  Were angry—as they well might, to be sure.
They wonder'd how a young man so absurd
  Lord Henry at his table should endure;
And this, and his not knowing how much oats
Had fallen last market, cost his host three votes. 760

90

They little knew, or might have sympathised,
  That he the night before had seen a ghost,
A prologue which but slightly harmonised
  With the substantial company engross'd
By matter, and so much materialised, 765
  That one scarce knew at what to marvel most
Of two things—how (the question rather odd is)
Such bodies could have souls, or souls such bodies.

91

But what confused him more than smile or stare
  From all the 'squires and 'squiresses around, 770
Who wonder'd at the abstraction of his air,
  Especially as he had been renown'd
For some vivacity among the fair,
  Even in the country circle's narrow bound—

3. Distraught, preoccupied.
4. In the Anglican Church, a couple would have to announce their intention to marry (the "banns" of marriage) three times on three successive weeks before the wedding could take place—so as to allow anyone having a legitimate objection to the marriage time to come forward.

(For little things upon my lord's estate 775
Were good small talk for others still less great)—

92

Was, that he caught Aurora's eye on his,
  And something like a smile upon her cheek.
Now this he really rather took amiss:
  In those who rarely smile, their smiles bespeak 780
A strong external motive; and in this
  Smile of Aurora's there was nought to pique
Or hope, or love, with any of the wiles
Which some pretend to trace in ladies' smiles.

93

'Twas a mere quiet smile of contemplation, 785
  Indicative of some surprise and pity;
And Juan grew carnation with vexation,
  Which was not very wise, and still less witty,
Since he had gain'd at least her observation,
  A most important outwork of the city— 790
As Juan should have known, had not his senses
By last night's ghost been driven from their defences.

94

But what was bad, she did not blush in turn,
  Nor seem embarrass'd—quite the contrary;
Her aspect was as usual, still—*not* stern— 795
  And she withdrew, but cast not down, her eye,
Yet grew a little pale—with what? concern?
  I know not; but her colour ne'er was high—
Though sometimes faintly flush'd—and always clear,
As deep seas in a sunny atmosphere. 800

95

But Adeline was occupied by fame
  This day; and watching, witching, condescending
To the consumers of fish, fowl, and game,
  And dignity with courtesy so blending,
As all must blend whose part it is to aim 805
  (Especially as the sixth year is ending)[5]
At their lord's, son's, or similar connection's
Safe conduct through the rocks of re-elections.

---

5. Lord Henry's Parliamentary term is ending. He has invited these guests to help him stand for
reelection.

96

Though this was most expedient on the whole,
    And usual—Juan, when he cast a glance   810
On Adeline while playing her grand rôle,
    Which she went through as though it were a dance,
Betraying only now and then her soul
    By a look scarce perceptibly askance
(Of weariness or scorn), began to feel   815
Some doubt how much of Adeline was *real*;

97

So well she acted all and every part
    By turns—with that vivacious versatility,
Which many people take for want of heart.
    They err—'tis merely what is call'd mobility,[6]   820
A thing of temperament and not of art,
    Though seeming so, from its supposed facility;
And false—though true; for surely they're sincerest
Who are strongly acted on by what is nearest.

98

This makes your actors, artists, and romancers,   825
    Heroes sometimes, though seldom—sages never;
But speakers, bards, diplomatists, and dancers,
    Little that's great, but much of what is clever;
Most orators, but very few financiers,
    Though all Exchequer chancellors[7] endeavour,   830
Of late years, to dispense with Cocker's[8] rigours,
And grow quite figurative with their figures.

99

The poets of arithmetic[9] are they
    Who, though they prove not two and two to be
Five, as they might do in a modest way,   835
    Have plainly made it out that four are three,
Judging by what they take, and what they pay.
    The Sinking Fund's unfathomable sea,
That most unliquidating liquid, leaves
The debt unsunk, yet sinks all it receives.   840

6. "In French, 'mobilité.' I am not sure that mobility is English, but it is expressive of a quality which rather belongs to other climates, though it is sometimes seen to a great extent in our own. It may be defined as an excessive susceptibility of immediate impressions—at the same time without *losing* the past; and is, though sometimes apparently useful to the possessor, a most painful and unhappy attribute."
7. Treasurers.
8. Cocker's *Arithmetic* (1677) was still a standard textbook in Byron's day.
9. Government economists whose scheme to eliminate the British national debt, the Sinking Fund (line 838), proved a financial disaster.

100

While Adeline dispensed her airs and graces,
　　The fair Fitz-Fulke seem'd very much at ease;
Though too well bred to quiz[1] men to their faces,
　　Her laughing blue eyes with a glance could seize
The ridicules of people in all places—   845
　　That honey of your fashionable bees—
And store it up for mischievous enjoyment;
And this at present was her kind employment.

101

However, the day closed, as days must close;
　　The evening also waned—and coffee came.   850
Each carriage was announced, and ladies rose,
　　And curtsying off, as curtsies country dame,
Retired: with most unfashionable bows
　　Their docile esquires also did the same,
Delighted with the dinner and their host,   855
But with the Lady Adeline the most.

102

Some praised her beauty: others her great grace;
　　The warmth of her politeness, whose sincerity
Was obvious in each feature of her face,
　　Whose traits were radiant with the rays of verity.   860
Yes; *she* was truly worthy *her* high place!
　　No one could envy her deserved prosperity.
And then her dress—what beautiful simplicity
Draperied her form with curious felicity![2]

103

Meanwhile sweet Adeline deserved their praises,   865
　　By an impartial indemnification
For all her past exertion and soft phrases,
　　In a most edifying conversation,
Which turn'd upon their late guests' miens and faces,
　　And families, even to the last relation;   870
Their hideous wives, their horrid selves and dresses,
And truculent distortion of their tresses.

104

True, *she* said little—'twas the rest that broke
　　Forth into universal epigram;
But then 'twas to the purpose what she spoke: 875

---

1. Mock.
2. "'Curiosa felicitas.'—PETRONIUS ARBITER." See *Satyricon*, chap. 18.

Like Addison's "faint praise," so wont to damn,[3]
Her own but served to set off every joke,
    As music chimes in with a melodrame.
How sweet the task to shield an absent friend!
I ask but this of mine, to—*not* defend.   880

105

There were but two exceptions to this keen
    Skirmish of wits o'er the departed; one
Aurora, with her pure and placid mien;
    And Juan, too, in general behind none
In gay remark on what he had heard or seen,   885
    Sate silent now, his usual spirits gone:
In vain he heard the others rail or rally,
He would not join them in a single sally.

106

'Tis true he saw Aurora look as though
    She approved his silence; she perhaps mistook   890
Its motive for that charity we owe
    But seldom pay the absent, nor would look
Further, it might or it might not be so.
    But Juan, sitting silent in his nook,
Observing little in his reverie,   895
Yet saw this much, which he was glad to see.

107

The ghost at least had done him this much good,
    In making him as silent as a ghost,
If in the circumstances which ensued
    He gain'd esteem where it was worth the most.   900
And certainly Aurora had renew'd
    In him some feelings he had lately lost
Or harden'd; feelings which, perhaps ideal,
Are so divine, that I must deem them real:—

108

The love of higher things and better days;   905
    The unbounded hope, and heavenly ignorance
Of what is call'd the world, and the world's ways;
    The moments when we gather from a glance
More joy than from all future pride or praise,
    Which kindle manhood, but can ne'er entrance   910
The heart in an existence of its own,
Of which another's bosom is the zone.

---

3. Alexander Pope's *Epistle to Dr. Arbuthnot* (1735), line 201: "Damn with faint praise."

109

Who would not sigh Αι *αι ταν Κυθερειαν*![4]
　　That *hath* a memory, or that *had* a heart?
Alas! *her* star must wane like that of Dian:[5]　　　　915
　　Ray fades on ray, as years on years depart.
Anacreon[6] only had the soul to tie an
　　Unwithering myrtle round the unblunted dart
Of Eros: but though thou hast play'd us many tricks,
Still we respect thee, "Alma Venus Genetrix!"[7]　　　　920

110

And full of sentiments, sublime as billows
　　Heaving between this world and worlds beyond,
Don Juan, when the midnight hour of pillows
　　Arrived, retired to his; but to despond
Rather than rest. Instead of poppies, willows[8]　　　　925
　　Waved o'er his couch; he meditated, fond
Of those sweet bitter thoughts which banish sleep,
And make the worldling sneer, the youngling weep.

111

The night was as before: he was undrest,
　　Saving his night-gown, which is an undress;　　　　930
Completely "sans culotte,"[9] and without vest;
　　In short, he hardly could be clothed with less:
But apprehensive of his spectral guest,
　　He sate with feelings awkward to express
(By those who have not had such visitations),　　　　935
Expectant of the ghost's fresh operations.

112

And not in vain he listen'd;—Hush! what's that?
　　I see—I see—Ah, no!—'tis not—yet 'tis—
Ye powers! it is the—the—the—Pooh! the cat!
　　The devil may take that stealthy pace of his!　　　　940
So like a spiritual pit-a-pat,
　　Or tiptoe of an amatory Miss,
Gliding the first time to a rendezvous,
And dreading the chaste echoes of her shoe.

---

4. *Ai, ai, tan Kytherian* ("Woe, woe, for Cytherea [Aphrodite]"). From *Lament for Adonis* by the early
　Greek pastoral poet Bion (c. 100 B.C.E.); in his elegy, Aphrodite is grief-stricken over the death of
　Adonis, the young man whom she loved.
5. The ascendancy of Cytherea (Love) wanes like the moon (Dian).
6. Greek poet (570–480 B.C.E.), author of drinking and erotic songs; Byron was especially fond of his
　lyrics and translated several of them.
7. Opening words of Lucretius's first-century B.C.E. philosophical poem *De rerum natura* (*On the
　Nature of Things*): "Hail, life-giving, beneficent Venus!"
8. Poppies bring sleep; willows are associated with sorrow.
9. Without trousers; *sans-coulottes* was the term applied to the popular masses during the French Rev-
　olution.

113

Again—what is't? The wind? No, no,—this time   945
　　It is the sable Friar as before,
With awful footsteps regular as rhyme,
　　Or (as rhymes may be in these days) much more.
Again through shadows of the night sublime,
　　When deep sleep fell on men,[1] and the world wore   950
The starry darkness round her like a girdle
Spangled with gems—the monk made his blood curdle.

114

A noise like to wet fingers drawn on glass,[2]
　　Which sets the teeth on edge; and a slight clatter
Like showers which on the midnight gusts will pass,   955
　　Sounding like very supernatural water,
Came over Juan's ear, which throbb'd, alas!
　　For immaterialism's a serious matter;
So that even those whose faith is the most great
In souls immortal, shun them tête-à-tête.   960

115

Were his eyes open?—Yes! and his mouth too.
　　Surprise has this effect—to make one dumb,
Yet leave the gate which Eloquence slips through
　　As wide as if a long speech were to come.
Nigh and more nigh the awful echoes drew,   965
　　Tremendous to a mortal tympanum:
His eyes were open, and (as was before
Stated) his mouth. What open'd next?—the door.

116

It open'd with a most infernal creak,
　　Like that of hell. "Lasciate ogni speranza   970
Voi che entrate!"[3] The hinge seemed to speak,
　　Dreadful as Dante's rima,[4] or this stanza;
Or—but all words upon such themes are weak:
　　A single shade's sufficient to entrance a
Hero—for what is substance to a spirit?   975
Or how is't *matter* trembles to come near it?

---

1. Cf. Job 4.13.
2. "See the account of the ghost of the uncle of Prince Charles of Saxony, raised by Schroepfer—
   'Karl—Karl—was wollst du mit mich?'"
3. Abandon all hope, ye who enter here: the words written over the Gate of Hell in Dante's *Inferno*
   (3.9).
4. Terza rima is the distinctive verse of the *Divine Comedy*. It is "dreadful" in that Dante's poem
   explores the awe-inspiring themes of hell, purgatory, and heaven.

117

The door flew wide, not swiftly,—but, as fly
   The sea-gulls, with a steady, sober flight—
And then swung back; nor close—but stood awry,
   Half letting in long shadows on the light,   980
Which still in Juan's candlesticks burn'd high,
   For he had two, both tolerably bright,
And in the door-way, darkening Darkness, stood
The sable Friar in his solemn hood.

118

Don Juan shook, as erst he had been shaken   985
   The night before; but being sick of shaking,
He first inclined to think he had been mistaken;
   And then to be ashamed of such mistaking;
His own internal ghost began to awaken
   Within him, and to quell his corporal quaking—   990
Hinting that soul and body on the whole
Were odds against a disembodied soul.

119

And then his dread grew wrath, and his wrath fierce,
   And he arose, advanced—the shade retreated;
But Juan, eager now the truth to pierce,   995
   Follow'd, his veins no longer cold, but heated,
Resolved to thrust the mystery carte and tierce,[5]
   At whatsoever risk of being defeated:
The ghost stopp'd, menaced, then retired, until
He reach'd the ancient wall, then stood stone still.   1000

120

Juan put forth one arm—Eternal Powers!
   It touch'd no soul, nor body, but the wall,
On which the moonbeams fell in silvery showers,
   Chequer'd with all the tracery of the hall;
He shudder'd, as no doubt the bravest cowers   1005
   When he can't tell what 'tis that doth appal.
How odd, a single hobgoblin's non-entity
Should cause more fear than a whole host's identity.[6]

121

But still the shade remain'd: the blue eyes glared,
   And rather variably for stony death: 1010
Yet one thing rather good the grave had spared,

---

5. *carte and tierce*: positions of attack in fencing.
6. "'—*Shadows* to-night / Have struck more terror to the soul of Richard, / Than could the *substance* of ten thousand soldiers,' &c.—*Rich. III* [5.5.170–71]."

The ghost had a remarkably sweet breath.
A straggling curl show'd he had been fair-hair'd;
  A red lip, with two rows of pearls beneath,
Gleam'd forth, as through the casement's ivy shroud   1015
The moon peep'd, just escaped from a grey cloud.

122

And Juan, puzzled, but still curious, thrust
  His other arm forth—Wonder upon wonder!
It press'd upon a hard but glowing bust,
  Which beat as if there was a warm heart under.   1020
He found, as people on most trials must,
  That he had made at first a silly blunder,
And that in his confusion he had caught
Only the wall, instead of what he sought.

123

The ghost, if ghost it were, seem'd a sweet soul   1025
  As ever lurk'd beneath a holy hood:
A dimpled chin, a neck of ivory, stole
  Forth into something much like flesh and blood;
Back fell the sable frock and dreary cowl,
  And they reveal'd—alas! that e'er they should!   1030
In full, voluptuous, but *not o'er*grown bulk,
The phantom of her frolic Grace—Fitz-Fulke!

CANTO THE SEVENTEENTH[1]

1

THE world is full of orphans: firstly, those
  Who are so in the strict sense of the phrase;
But many a lonely tree the loftier grows
  Than others crowded in the Forest's maze.—
The next are such as are not doomed to lose   5
  Their tender parents in their budding days,
But, merely, their parental tenderness,
Which leaves them orphans of the heart no less.

2

The next are "*only* Children," as they are styled,
  Who grow up *Children* only, since the old saw   10
Pronounces that an "only"'s a spoilt child—
  But not to go too far, I hold it law,
That where their education, harsh or mild,
  Transgresses the just bounds of love or awe,

---

1. The final, incomplete canto is dated on the manuscript "May 8th 1823." Byron regretfully aban-
doned composition of *Don Juan* during his preparations to sail for Greece. This fragment was first
published in C (1903).

The sufferers—be't in heart or intellect—   15
Whate'er the *cause*, are orphans in *effect*.

3

But to return unto the stricter rule—
    As far as words make rules—our common notion
Of orphan paints at once a parish school,
    A half-starved babe, a wreck upon Life's ocean,   20
A human (what the Italians nickname) "Mule"![2]
    A theme for Pity or some worse emotion;
Yet, if examined, it might be admitted
The wealthiest orphans are to be more pitied.

4

Too soon they are Parents to themselves: for what   25
    Are Tutors, Guardians, and so forth, compared
With Nature's genial Genitors? so that
    A child of Chancery,[3] that Star-Chamber ward
(I'll take the likeness I can first come at),
    Is like—a duckling by Dame Partlett[4] rear'd,   30
And frights—especially if 'tis a daughter,
Th' old Hen—by running headlong to the water.

5

There is a common-place book[5] argument,
    Which glibly glides from every vulgar tongue;
When any dare a new light to present,   35
    "If you are right, then everybody's wrong!"
Suppose the converse of this precedent
    So often urged, so loudly and so long;
"If you are wrong, then everybody's right!"
Was ever everybody yet so quite?   40

6

Therefore I would solicit free discussion
    Upon all points—no matter what, or whose—
Because as Ages upon Ages push on,
    The last is apt the former to accuse
Of pillowing its head on a pin-cushion,   45
    Heedless of pricks because it was obtuse:
What *was* a paradox becomes a truth or
A something like it—as bear witness Luther![6]

2. "The Italians, at least in some parts of Italy, call bastards and foundlings the *mules*—*why*, I cannot see, unless they mean to infer that the offspring of matrimony are asses."
3. Courts of Chancery and of the Star Chamber settled matters of inheritance.
4. Traditional name for a hen and a talkative woman.
5. Notebook used for lessons and personal thoughts.
6. Martin Luther (1483–1546), theologian who initiated the Protestant Reformation.

7

The Sacraments have been reduced to two,
    And Witches unto none, though somewhat late   50
Since burning aged women (save a few—
    Not witches only b——ches—who create
Mischief in families, as some know or knew,
    Should still be singed, but slightly, let me state),
Has been declared an act of inurbanity,   55
Malgré Sir Matthew Hales's[7] great humanity.

8

Great Galileo was debarr'd the Sun,[8]
    Because he fix'd it; and, to stop his talking,
How Earth could round the solar orbit run,
    Found his own legs embargo'd from mere walking: 60
The man was well-nigh dead, ere men begun
    To think his skull had not some need of caulking;
But now, it seems, he's right—his notion just:
No doubt a consolation to his dust.

9

Pythagoras, Locke, Socrates[9]—but pages   65
    Might be fill'd up, as vainly as before,
With the sad usage of all sorts of sages,
    Who, in his life-time, each, was deem'd a Bore!
The loftiest minds outrun their tardy ages:
    This they must bear with and, perhaps, much more; .   70
The wise man's sure when he no more can share it, he
Will have a firm Post Obit[1] on posterity.

10

If such doom waits each intellectual Giant,
    We little people in our lesser way,
To Life's small rubs should surely be more pliant,   75
    And so for one will I—as well I may—
Would that I were less bilious—but, oh, fie on't!
    Just as I make my mind up every day,
To be a "totus, teres," Stoic,[2] Sage,
The wind shifts and I fly into a rage.   80

---

7. Sir Matthew Hale (1609–1676), presiding officer at witchcraft trial in 1662, which convicted two women, who were subsequently executed. Malgré: in spite of (French).
8. Galileo Galilei (1564–1642), Italian astronomer, was imprisoned for his heretical claim that the earth circled around the sun and not vice versa.
9. Philosophers noted for their enlightened ideas. Pythagoras (born ca. 580 B.C.E.) and Socrates (469?–399 B.C.E.) were martyred; Locke was temporarily expelled from England in 1684 for political reasons.
1. A legal term involving a promise to pay a large sum of money upon the death of someone from whom the payer expects an inheritance.
2. The Stoics were ancient Greek philosophers who believed in mastering one's passions through reason; totus, teres: whole, smooth (Horace, Satires 2.7.86).

11

Temperate I am—yet never had a temper;
  Modest I am—yet with some slight assurance;
Changeable too—yet somehow *"Idem semper"*:[3]
  Patient—but not enamour'd of endurance;
Cheerful—but, sometimes, rather apt to whimper;   85
  Mild—but at times a sort of *'Hercules furens"*:[4]
So that I almost think that the same skin
For one without—has two or three within.

12

Our Hero was, in Canto the Sixteenth,
  Left in a tender moonlight situation,   90
Such as enables Man to show his strength
  Moral or physical: on this occasion
Whether his virtue triumph'd—or, at length,
  His vice—for he was of a kindling nation—
Is more than I shall venture to describe;—   95
Unless some Beauty with a kiss should bribe.

13

I leave the thing a problem, like all things:—
  The morning came—and breakfast, tea and toast,
Of which most men partake, but no one sings.
  The company whose birth, wealth, worth, has cost   100
My trembling Lyre already several strings,
  Assembled with our hostess, and mine host;
The guests dropp'd in—the last but one, Her Grace,
The latest, Juan, with his virgin face.

14

Which best is to encounter—Ghost, or none,   105
  'Twere difficult to say—but Juan look'd
As if he had combated with more than one,
  Being wan and worn, with eyes that hardly brook'd
The light that through the Gothic window shone:
  Her Grace, too, had a sort of air rebuked—   110
Seem'd pale and shiver'd, as if she had kept
A vigil, or dreamt rather more than slept.

---

3. Always the same (Latin).
4. Hercules mad (Latin); in Greek legend and in Euripides' tragedy (*Heracles*), Hercules was driven
  to a murderous madness by Hera, his mother.

Francesca of Rimini[1]

From the Inferno of Dante, Canto the Fifth

"The land where I was born sits by the seas,[2]
Upon that shore to which the Po descends,
With all his followers, in search of peace.
Love, which the gentle heart soon apprehends,
Seized him for the fair person which was ta'en   5
From me, and me even yet the mode offends.
Love, who to none beloved to love again
Remits, seized me with wish to please so strong
That, as thou seest, yet, yet it doth remain.
Love to one death conducted us along: 10
But Caina[3] waits for him our life who ended."
These were the accents utter'd by her tongue.
Since I first listen'd to these souls offended
I bow'd my visage, and so kept it till—
"What think'st thou?" said the bard; when[4] I unbended   15
And recommenced: "Alas! unto such ill
How many sweet thoughts, what strong ecstasies
Led these their evil fortune to fulfil!"
And then I turn'd unto their side my eyes,
And said, "Francesca, thy sad destinies   20
Have made me sorrow till the tears arise.
But tell me, in the season of sweet sighs
By what and how thy love to passion rose,
So as his dim desires to recognise?"
Then she to me: "The greatest of all woes   25
Is to remind us of[5] our happy days

---

1. From Ravenna, near the port of Rimini in northeast Italy, Byron sent a manuscript of "Francesca of Rimini" on March 20, 1820, to John Murray with a note: "Enclosed you will find *line for line* in third rhyme (*terza rima*) . . . Fanny of Rimini—you know that She was born here—and married and slain . . . —I have done it into *cramp* English line for line and rhyme for rhyme to try the possibility" (*BLJ* 7:58). However, Byron's translation of this famous passage from Dante's *Inferno* remained unpublished during his lifetime and was first published in *Life* (1830).
   The passage tells of the adulterous love between Paolo and Francesca, whose desire overwhelmed them one day as they were reading about the legendary adulterous lovers Lancelot and Guinevere; Paolo and Francesca were subsequently murdered for their adultery. Dante based the story on an incident that occurred during his lifetime, involving a young woman forced by her father into a loveless, politically advantageous marriage with Paolo's brother. The pathos of Dante's rendering of the story has made it one of the most widely known and loved parts of *The Inferno*—especially among the Romantics, who responded not only to its sentiment but to its political, anti-Royalist implications. For Byron, the lover of the Countess Guiccioli, who lived in Ravenna with her much older husband, the story had serious personal significance—though he connected it as well to his relationship with Augusta (see letter of May 17, 1819 [p. 741]) and facetiously alluded to it in *Don Juan*, which warns the reader, "'Tis dangerous to read of loves unlawful" (III. 96). Byron took considerable pains over his "*literal* translation word for word" (*BLJ* 7:59), but accuracy proved elusive, resulting in several manuscripts with alternative wordings (*CPW* 4:514–16). C gives some of the variants (4:313–22), also printing, as Byron had wished, the Italian original as a parallel text, and *CPW* prints two separate versions of the poem; variants in the notes below are from the *CPW* text based on *Proof* S (4:280–82). For Byron's thoughts on Dante, see his Ravenna Journal entry of January 29, 1821 (*BLJ* 8:39–40); see also Marchand, *Byron: A Biography* 2, 794–95. *Criticism:* Frederick L. Beaty, "Byron and Francesca da Rimini."
2. "Ravenna." Francesca narrates the story to Dante and Virgil, the "bard" referred to in line 15.
3. The name (after the biblical Cain) of the first part of the ninth circle in Dante's hell, where traitors to blood relatives are punished.
4. then (*CPW*).
5. *remind us of*: recal to mind (*CPW*).

In misery, and that thy teacher knows.
But if to learn our passion's first root preys
Upon thy spirit with such sympathy,
I will do even[6] as he who weeps and says.   30
We read one day for pastime, seated nigh,
Of Lancilot, how love enchain'd him too.
We were alone, quite unsuspiciously.
But oft our eyes met, and our cheeks in hue
All o'er discolour'd by that reading were;   35
But one point only wholly us o'erthrew.
When we read the long-sigh'd-for smile of her
To be thus kiss'd by such devoted[7] lover,
He, who from me can be divided ne'er,
Kiss'd my mouth, trembling in the act all over.   40
Accursed was the book and he who wrote;
That day no further leaf we did uncover."—
While thus one spirit told us of their lot,
The other wept so, that with pity's thralls
I swoon'd as if by death I had been smote,   45
And fell down even as a dead body falls.

THE VISION OF JUDGMENT   Byron began *The Vision of Judgment* in May 1821, but put it aside for a few months, drafting most of it in September. He sent a manuscript to John Murray on October 4, but when the conservative Murray, after preparing a proof of the poem, balked at publishing it fearing prosecution for sedition, Byron demanded that the poem be handed over to the radical publisher John Hunt for publication in the *Liberal*, a periodical conceived by Byron, Shelley, and John and his brother Leigh Hunt the previous summer. *Vision* was published on October 15, 1823, in the inaugural issue of *The Liberal* (though it lacked the prose preface, which, along with Byron's corrected proof, Murray seems to have withheld from Hunt). Hunt, consequently, was prosecuted for a publication charged with calumniating the late king, offending the new one, and endangering the public peace. After Byron's offer to return to England to stand trial in Hunt's stead was disallowed, he engaged a renowned lawyer for Hunt and, after Hunt's conviction, which followed Byron's death, Byron's estate covered the cost of the fine. Though printed anonymously, *Vision* was immediately recognized as Byron's and was widely pirated; Murray first published it in the collected edition of 1831.

Byron's *Vision of Judgment* is a parody of *A Vision of Judgement* by Robert Southey. Published on April 11, 1821, a little more than a year after the death of King George III, the poem by Southey, England's poet laureate, is a grandiose depiction of the heavenly apotheosis of George III, along with the beatification of Tory statesmen and the damnation of Whigs and revolutionaries. The combined magniloquence and mediocrity of Southey's poem might in themselves have been sport for Byron's satiric pen—not less because of Byron's inveterate contempt for Southey's political apostasy, his having

---

6. *do even*: relate (*CPW*). In a note to line 126 of the Italian, Byron wrote "In some of the editions it is 'diro,' in others 'faro';—an essential difference between 'saying' and 'doing,' which I know not how to decide . . . the damned editors drive me mad." According to E. H. Coleridge, the reading is *faro* (*C* 4:319), though according to McGann, "the accepted reading now is *diro*" (*CPW* 4:517).
7. a fervent (*CPW*).

started out an idealistic Godwinian liberal and ending a Tory and flatterer of power. Additionally, however, in a preface to his *Vision* Southey attacked the poetry and morals of Byron and his coterie, including the radical poets Percy Shelley and Leigh Hunt, dubbing them, famously, "the Satanic school." Byron counterattacked in his preface to *The Two Foscari* (1821), and Southey rejoined in a letter published in the *Courier*—a letter that so incensed Byron that he sent Southey, via his friend Douglas Kinnaird, a challenge to a duel, which Kinnaird judiciously neglected to deliver. But in the *Courier* letter Southey, to what must be his eternal chagrin, made Byron an offer he could not refuse: "one word of advice to Lord Byron—When he attacks me again, let it be in rhyme." *The Vision of Judgment*, a withering and brilliant satire of the poet laureate, as well as of the past and present kings George and the Tory ministers that Southey's poem celebrates, has provoked nearly two centuries of laughter at Southey's work.

In addition to the expressed satirical intent of Byron's *Vision*—"to put the said George's Apotheosis in a Whig point of view, not forgetting the Poet Laureate for his preface and his other demerits" (*BLJ* 8:229)—the poem critiques the simplistic heaven-or-hell morality that Byron (like Blake) understood to be a tool of power: "I cannot help thinking that the *menace* of Hell makes as many devils as the severe penal codes of inhuman humanity make villains" (*BLJ* 9:46). Or, as the poem offers more playfully but no less pointedly: "I know this is unpopular; I know / 'Tis blasphemous; I know one may be damn'd / For hoping no one else may e'er be so" (105–07). Southey consigns his enemies to hell, but Byron's vision deconstructs Southey's moral code by acknowledging that, in fact, "the angels all are Tories," guardians of the law and "singing out of tune" (line 9)—while the Whigs, along with the likes of George Washington and Benjamin Franklin, bear witness for Sathan (Byron uses the medieval spelling), leader of the opposition. In that role, Sathan is a spokesman for Byron, who thus ironically disarms Southey's "Satanic school" accusation. But the poem is no allegory; instead, relentless ridicule and virtuosic versifying expose and upstage the contemporary political and moral charade. Thus, after something of a send-up of the courtesies of parliamentary debate, the deranged king of England—like the literally headless (i.e., guillotined) king of France before him—slips into heaven, while his mean and corrupt ministers must suffer the eternal purgatory of an adored poet's parody. The poem, moreover, is layered with biographical, historical, and literary references, the latter drawn not only from Southey's *Vision* but from the broad range of Byron's reading, especially the Bible and *Paradise Lost*. *Vision* has been regarded by many of Byron's readers as his consummate poetic achievement, a view shared, for example, by Goethe and by Swinburne, who in his 1866 edition of Byron's works wrote: "it stands alone, not in Byron's work only, but in the work of the world" (380).

Textual Note: For the complex and problematic editorial history of *Vision*, see *CPW* 6:669–71 and *Cochran*. The present edition corrects the 1832 text in lines 62, 96, 301, and 470, based on *CPW*; a footnote in each case gives the 1832 wording. Also departing from 1832, the medieval spelling of Sathan, as it appears in the manuscript and first edition, has been restored in this Norton Critical Edition (as in *CPW* and *Cochran*).

Criticism: In addition to Kelsall, "Byron's Politics" (p. 855) and Peterfreund, "The Politics of 'Neutral Space' in Byron's *Vision of Judgment*" (p. 1008), see: Jones, "Byron's Visions of Judgment"; Rutherford, *Byron: A Critical Study*; Wolfson, "*The Vision of Judgment* and the Visions of 'Author.'"

The Vision of Judgment

by Quevedo Redivivus[1]

suggested by the composition so entitled by the author of "wat tyler"[2]

"A Daniel come to judgment! yea, a Daniel!
I thank thee, Jew, for teaching me that word."[3]

Preface[4]

It hath been wisely said, that "One fool makes many;" and it hath been poetically observed,

"That fools rush in where angels fear to tread."—*Pope.*[5]

If Mr. Southey had not rushed in where he had no business, and where he never was before, and never will be again, the following poem would not have been written. It is not impossible that it may be as good as his own, seeing that it cannot, by any species of stupidity, natural or acquired, be *worse.* The gross flattery, the dull impudence, the renegado intolerance and impious cant, of the poem by the author of "Wat Tyler," are something so stupendous as to form the sublime of himself—containing the quintessence of his own attributes.

So much for his poem—a word on his preface. In this preface it has pleased the magnanimous Laureate to draw the picture of a supposed "Satanic School," the which he doth recommend to the notice of the legislature; thereby adding to his other laurels the ambition of those of an informer. If there exists any where, excepting in his imagination, such a School, is he not sufficiently armed against it by his own intense vanity? The truth is, that there are certain writers whom Mr. S. imagines, like Scrub, to have "talked of *him;* for they laughed consumedly."[6]

I think I know enough of most of the writers to whom he is supposed to allude,[7] to assert, that they, in their individual capacities, have done more good in the charities of life, to their fellow-creatures in any one year, than Mr. Southey has done harm to himself by his absurdities in his whole life; and this is saying a great deal. But I have a few questions to ask.

1stly, Is Mr. Southey the author of "Wat Tyler?"

2dly, Was he not refused a remedy at law by the highest judge of his beloved England, because it was a blasphemous and seditious publication?

3dly, Was he not entitled by William Smith, in full parliament, "a rancorous renegado?"

---

1. Quevedo Reborn. Francisco Gomez de Quevedo y Villegas (1580–1645) was a Spanish satirist whose "Vision of the Last Judgment" (1607) attacked social corruption during the reign of Phillip III (1598–1621).
2. Robert Southey's radical drama of 1794, celebrating the leader of the Peasants' Revolt of 1381; the poem was an embarrassment to Southey after his conversion to Tory conservatism and, to Byron, was a reminder of Southey's turncoat politics.
3. Shakespeare, *The Merchant of Venice* 4.1.218, 336.
4. First printed with the second edition of the poem (January 1823).
5. Alexander Pope, *Essay on Criticism* (1711), line 625.
6. Cf. George Farquhar, *The Beaux' Stratagem* (1707), 3.66–67.
7. E.g., Percy Shelley.

4thly, Is he not poet laureate, with his own lines on Martin the regicide staring him in the face?

And, 5thly, Putting the four preceding items together, with what conscience dare *he* call the attention of the laws to the publications of others, be they what they may?

I say nothing of the cowardice of such a proceeding; its meanness speaks for itself; but I wish to touch upon the *motive*, which is neither more nor less than that Mr. S. has been laughed at a little in some recent publications, as he was of yore in the "Anti-jacobin"[8] by his present patrons. Hence all this "skimble scamble stuff"[9] about "Satanic," and so forth. However, it is worthy of him—"*quatis ab incepto.*"[1]

If there is any thing obnoxious to the political opinions of a portion of the public in the following poem, they may thank Mr. Southey. He might have written hexameters, as he has written every thing else, for aught that the writer cared—had they been upon another subject. But to attempt to canonise a monarch, who, whatever were his household virtues, was neither a successful nor a patriot king,—inasmuch as several years of his reign passed in war with America and Ireland, to say nothing of the aggression upon France,—like all other exaggeration, necessarily begets opposition. In whatever manner he may be spoken of in this new "Vision," his *public* career will not be more favourably transmitted by history. Of his private virtues although a little expensive to the nation) there can be no doubt.

With regard to the supernatural personages treated of, I can only say that I know as much about them, and (as an honest man) have a better right to talk of them than Robert Southey. I have also treated them more tolerantly. The way in which that poor insane creature, the Laureate, deals about his judgments in the next world, is like his own judgment in this. If it was not completely ludicrous, it would be something worse. I don't think that there is much more to say at present.

QUEVEDO REDIVIVUS.

P.S.—It is possible that some readers may object, in these objectionable times, to the freedom with which saints, angels, and spiritual persons discourse in this "Vision." But, for precedents upon such points, I must refer him to Fielding's "Journey from this World to the next," and to the Visions of myself, the said Quevedo, in Spanish or translated. The reader is also requested to observe, that no doctrinal tenets are insisted upon or discussed; that the person of the Deity is carefully withheld from sight, which is more than can be said for the Laureate, who hath thought proper to make him talk, not "like a school divine," but like the unscholarlike Mr. Southey. The whole action passes on the outside of heaven; and Chaucer's Wife of Bath, Pulci's Morgante Maggiore, Swift's Tale of a Tub, and the others works above referred to, are cases in point of the freedom with which saints, &c. may be permitted to converse in works not intended to be serious.

Q.R.

---

8. A journal founded in the late eighteenth century to combat subversive politics and philosophy; it printed a parody of Southey called "The Needy Knife-grinder."
9. Shakespeare, *I Henry IV* 3.1.150.
1. As (he was) from the start (Latin), from Horace, *Ars Poetica*, line 127.

*** Mr. Southey being, as he says, a good Christian and vindictive, threatens, I understand, a reply to this our answer. It is to be hoped that his visionary faculties will in the mean time have acquired a little more judgment, properly so called: otherwise he will get himself into new dilemmas. These apostate jacobins furnish rich rejoinders. Let him take a specimen. Mr. Southey laudeth grievously "one Mr. Landor," who cultivates much private renown in the shape of Latin verses; and not long ago, the poet laureate dedicated to him, it appeareth, one of his fugitive lyrics, upon the strength of a poem called *Gebir*. Who could suppose, that in this same Gebir the aforesaid Savage Landor (for such is his grim cognomen) putteth into the infernal regions no less a person than the hero of his friend Mr. Southey's heaven,—yea, even George the Third! See also how personal Savage becometh, when he hath a mind. The following is his portrait of our late gracious sovereign:—

> (Prince Gebir having descended into the infernal regions, the shades of his royal ancestors are, at his request, called up to his view; and he exclaims to his ghostly guide)—

> "Aroar, what wretch that nearest us? what wretch
> Is that with eyebrows white and slanting brow?
> Listen! him yonder, who, bound down supine,
> Shrinks yelling from that sword there, engine-hung.
> He too amongst my ancestors! I hate
> The despot, but the dastard I despise.
> Was he our countryman?"
>   "Alas, O king!
> Iberia bore him, but the breed accurst
> Inclement winds blew blighting from north-east."
> "He was a warrior then, nor fear'd the gods?"
> Gebir, he fear'd the demons, not the gods,
> Though them indeed his daily face adored;
> And was no warrior, yet the thousand lives
> Squander'd, as stones to exercise a sling,
> And the tame cruelty and cold caprice—
> Oh madness of mankind! address'd, adored!"—*Gebir*, p. 28.

I omit noticing some edifying Ithyphallics of Savagius,[2] wishing to keep the proper veil over them, if his grave but somewhat indiscreet worshipper will suffer it; but certainly these teachers of "great moral lessons" are apt to be found in strange company.

1

> Saint Peter[1] sat by the celestial gate:
> His keys were rusty, and the lock was dull,
> So little trouble had been given of late;
> Not that the place by any means was full,

---

2. Indecent verse by Walter Savage Landor (1775–1864).
1. Christ gave the apostle Peter the "keys of the Kingdom of Heaven" (Matthew 16.17–19).

But since the Gallic era "eighty-eight"[2]   5
   The devils had ta'en a longer, stronger pull,
And "a pull altogether," as they say
At sea—which drew most souls another way.

2

The angels all were singing out of tune,
   And hoarse with having little else to do,
Excepting to wind up the sun and moon,   10
   Or curb a runaway young star or two,
Or wild colt of a comet, which too soon
   Broke out of bounds o'er the ethereal blue,
Splitting some planet with its playful tail,   15
As boats are sometimes by a wanton whale.

3

The guardian seraphs[3] had retired on high,
   Finding their charges past all care below;
Terrestrial business fill'd nought in the sky
   Save the recording angel's black bureau;[4]   20
Who found, indeed, the facts to multiply
   With such rapidity of vice and woe,
That he had stripp'd off both his wings in quills,
And yet was in arrear of human ills.[5]

4

His business so augmented of late years,   25
   That he was forced, against his will, no doubt,
(Just like those cherubs, earthly ministers,)
   For some resource to turn himself about
And claim the help of his celestial peers,
   To aid him ere he should be quite worn out   30
By the increased demand for his remarks;
Six angels and twelve saints were named his clerks.

5

This was a handsome board—at least for heaven;
   And yet they had even then enough to do,
So many conquerors' cars[6] were daily driven,   35
   So many kingdoms fitted up anew;
Each day too slew its thousands six or seven,
   Till at the crowning carnage, Waterloo,

---

2. 1788 was the last year of "the Gallic era," or the Old Regime of France, i.e., France prior to the Revolution, at which point the revolutionaries, or "devils" (line 6), took the lead.
3. The highest of the nine traditional orders of angels; cf. "cherubs" (line 27).
4. Desk.
5. That is, he could not keep up with recording all the evil done by men.
6. Triumphal processions of the conquerors, especially the monarchs who triumphed after Napoleon's defeat at Waterloo (line 38) on June 18, 1815.

They threw their pens down in divine disgust—
The page was so besmear'd with blood and dust.   40

6

This by the way; 'tis not mine to record
   What angels shrink from: even the very devil
On this occasion his own work abhorr'd,
   So surfeited with the infernal revel:
Though he himself had sharpen'd every sword,   45
   It almost quench'd his innate thirst of evil.
(Here Sathan's[7] sole good work deserves insertion—
'Tis, that he has both generals in reversion.)[8]

7

Let's skip a few short years of hollow peace,
   Which peopled earth no better, hell as wont,   50
And heaven none—they form the tyrant's lease,
   With nothing but new names subscribed upon't;
'Twill one day finish: meantime they increase,
   "With seven heads and ten horns," and all in front,
Like Saint John's foretold beast;[9] but ours are born   55
Less formidable in the head than horn.

8

In the first year of freedom's second dawn[1]
   Died George the Third; although no tyrant, one
Who shielded tyrants, till each sense withdrawn
   Left him nor mental nor external sun:[2]   60
A better farmer[3] ne'er brush'd dew from lawn,
   A weaker king ne'er[4] left a realm undone!
He died—but left his subjects still behind,
One half as mad—and t' other no less blind.

9

He died!—his death made no great stir on earth;   65
   His burial made some pomp; there was profusion
Of velvet, gilding, brass, and no great dearth
   Of aught but tears—save those shed by collusion.[5]

---

7. Satan (1832). On the spelling of Sathan, see the Textual Note (p. 685).
8. The return of an estate to its owner after the grant for its use has expired; i.e., both Wellington and Napoleon belong to Satan after they die.
9. Revelation 12.3, 13.1, 17.3.
1. 1820, the year of George III's death and of revolutionary activities in Greece, Spain, Portugal, and Italy.
2. George III in his last illness was both deranged and blind.
3. Having deliberately espoused conventionally modest English habits and values, George III was referred to as "farmer George."
4. *weaker king ne'er*: worse king never (1832) and in all editions before *CPW*, where the correction is based on the errata printed in the second issue of the first edition (see also lines 96, 397, and 470).
5. I.e., insincerely, with an ulterior purpose.

For these things may be bought at their true worth;
    Of elegy there was the due infusion—   70
Bought also; and the torches, cloaks, and banners,
Heralds, and relics of old Gothic manners,

10

Form'd a sepulchral melodrame. Of all
    The fools who flock'd to swell or see the show,
Who cared about the corpse? The funeral   75
    Made the attraction, and the black the woe.
There throbb'd not there a thought which pierced the pall;[6]
    And when the gorgeous coffin was laid low,
It seem'd the mockery of hell to fold
The rottenness of eighty years in gold.   80

11

So mix his body with the dust! It might
    Return to what it *must* far sooner, were
The natural compound left alone to fight
    Its way back into earth, and fire, and air;
But the unnatural balsams[7] merely blight   85
    What nature made him at his birth, as bare
As the mere million's base unmummied clay—
Yet all his spices but prolong decay.

12

He's dead—and upper earth with him has done;
    He's buried; save the undertaker's bill,   90
Or lapidary scrawl,[8] the world is gone
    For him, unless he left a German will;[9]
But where's the proctor[1] who will ask his son?
    In whom his qualities are reigning still,
Except that household virtue, most uncommon,   95
Of constancy to an unhandsome[2] woman.

13

"God save the king!" It is a large economy[3]
    In God to save the like; but if he will
Be saving, all the better; for not one am I
    Of those who think damnation better still: 100
I hardly know too if not quite alone am I

---

6. Coffin or cloth that drapes the coffin.
7. Embalming fluids.
8. Tombstone inscription.
9. The will of George I (written in German) was hidden by his son, George II.
1. Someone in a managerial or supervisory role.
2. *an unhandsome*: a bad, ugly (1832); see note to line 62. In contrast to his father (see lines
    358–65), George IV was notorious for his many extramarital affairs and constant bickering with
    Queen Caroline, his physically unattractive and promiscuous wife.
3. A jibe at George IV, who was fat.

In this small hope of bettering future ill
By circumscribing, with some slight restriction,
The eternity of hell's hot jurisdiction.

14

I know this is unpopular; I know   105
   'Tis blasphemous; I know one may be damn'd
For hoping no one else may e'er be so;
   I know my catechism; I know we are cramm'd
With the best doctrines till we quite o'erflow;
   I know that all save England's church have shamm'd,   110
And that the other twice two hundred churches
And synagogues have made a *damn'd* bad purchase.

15

God help us all! God help me too! I am,
   God knows, as helpless as the devil can wish,
And not a whit more difficult to damn   115
   Than is to bring to land a late-hook'd fish,
Or to the butcher to purvey the lamb;
   Not that I'm fit for such a noble dish
As one day will be that immortal fry
Of almost every body born to die.   120

16

Saint Peter sat by the celestial gate,
   And nodded o'er his keys; when, lo! there came
A wondrous noise he had not heard of late—
   A rushing sound of wind, and stream, and flame;
In short, a roar of things extremely great,   125
   Which would have made aught save a saint exclaim;
But he, with first a start and then a wink,
Said, "There's another star gone out, I think!"

17

But ere he could return to his repose,
   A cherub flapp'd his right wing o'er his eyes—   130
At which Saint Peter yawn'd, and rubb'd his nose:
   "Saint porter," said the Angel, "prithee rise!"
Waving a goodly wing, which glow'd, as glows
   An earthly peacock's tail, with heavenly dyes:
To which the Saint replied, "Well, what's the matter?   135
"Is Lucifer come back with all this clatter?"

18

"No," quoth the Cherub; "George the Third is dead."
   "And who *is* George the Third?" replied the apostle:
"*What George? what Third?*" "The king of England," said

The Angel. "Well! he won't find kings to jostle   140
Him on his way; but does he wear his head?
    Because the last[4] we saw here had a tussle,
And ne'er would have got into heaven's good graces,
Had he not flung his head in all our faces.

19

"He was, if I remember, king of France;   145
    That head of his, which could not keep a crown
On earth, yet ventured in my face to advance
    A claim to those of martyrs—like my own:
If I had had my sword, as I had once
    When I cut ears off,[5] I had cut him down;   150
But having but my *keys*, and not my brand,
I only knock'd his head from out his hand.

20

"And then he set up such a headless howl,
    That all the saints came out and took him in;
And there he sits by St. Paul, cheek by jowl;   155
    That fellow Paul—the parvenù![6] The skin
Of Saint Bartholomew,[7] which makes his cowl
    In heaven, and upon earth redeem'd his sin
So as to make a martyr, never sped[8]
Better than did this weak and wooden head.   160

21

"But had it come up here upon its shoulders,
    There would have been a different tale to tell:
The fellow-feeling in the saint's beholders
    Seems to have acted on them like a spell;
And so this very foolish head heaven solders   165
    Back on its trunk: it may be very well,
And seems the custom here to overthrow
Whatever has been wisely done below."

22

The Angel answer'd, "Peter! do not pout:
    The king who comes has head and all entire,   170
And never knew much what it was about—
    He did as doth the puppet—by its wire,

---

4. Louis XVI of France, beheaded in 1793.
5. In a rage, Peter had cut off the ear of one of the officers who arrested Christ on the eve of the Crucifixion (John 18.10).
6. One who has newly acquired a position or wealth but lacks the background and breeding; Byron imagines St. Peter resenting St. Paul because the latter was converted only after being, in his early years, a persecutor of Christians—and then rapidly becoming the most influential of early members of the faith (Paul's extreme change of allegiance thus resembling Southey's).
7. One of the apostles; he was martyred by flaying.
8. Succeeded.

And will be judged like all the rest, no doubt:
　My business and your own is not to enquire
Into such matters, but to mind our cue—　　　　　　　175
Which is to act as we are bid to do."

23

While thus they spake, the angelic caravan,
　Arriving like a rush of mighty wind,
Cleaving the fields of space, as doth the swan
　Some silver stream (say Ganges, Nile, or Inde,　　180
Or Thames, or Tweed),⁹ and 'midst them an old man
　With an old soul, and both extremely blind,
Halted before the gate, and in his shroud
Seated their fellow-traveller on a cloud.

24

But bringing up the rear of this bright host　　　　185
　A Spirit of a different aspect waved
His wings, like thunder-clouds above some coast
　Whose barren beach with frequent wrecks is paved;
His brow was like the deep when tempest-toss'd;
　Fierce and unfathomable thoughts engraved　　　190
Eternal wrath on his immortal face,
And *where* he gazed a gloom pervaded space.

25

As he drew near, he gazed upon the gate
　Ne'er to be enter'd more by him or sin,
With such a glance of supernatural hate,　　　　　195
　As made Saint Peter wish himself within;
He patter'd with his keys at a great rate,
　And sweated through his apostolic skin:
Of course his perspiration was but ichor,¹
Or some such other spiritual liquor.　　　　　　　200

26

The very cherubs huddled all together,
　Like birds when soars the falcon; and they felt
A tingling to the tip of every feather,
　And form'd a circle like Orion's belt²
Around their poor old charge; who scarce knew whither　　205
　His guards had led him, though they gently dealt
With royal manes³ (for by many stories,
And true, we learn the angels all are Tories).⁴

9. Rivers in India, Egypt, Germany, England, and Scotland.
1. In classical myth, the fluid that flows in the veins of the gods.
2. The constellation Orion.
3. Spirits (pronounce mā´-nēz).
4. Royalists; the reactionary Tory party dominated British politics throughout Byron's lifetime.

27

As things were in this posture, the gate flew
    Asunder, and the flashing of its hinges   210
Flung over space an universal hue
    Of many-colour'd flame, until its tinges
Reach'd even our speck of earth, and made a new
    Aurora borealis[5] spread its fringes
O'er the North Pole; the same seen, when ice-bound,   215
By Captain Parry's crews,[6] in "Melville's Sound."

28

And from the gate thrown open issued beaming
    A beautiful and mighty Thing of Light,
Radiant with glory, like a banner streaming
    Victorious from some world-o'erthrowing fight: 220
My poor comparisons must needs be teeming
    With earthly likenesses, for here the night
Of clay[7] obscures our best conceptions, saving
Johanna Southcote,[8] or Bob Southey raving.

29

'Twas the archangel Michael:[9] all men know   225
    The make of angels and archangels, since
There's scarce a scribbler has not one to show,
    From the fiends' leader to the angels' prince.
There also are some altar-pieces,[1] though
    I really can't say that they much evince   230
One's inner notions of immortal spirits;
But let the connoisseurs explain *their* merits.

30

Michael flew forth in glory and in good;
    A goodly work of him from whom all glory
And good arise; the portal past—he stood;   235
    Before him the young cherubs and saints hoary—
(I say *young*, begging to be understood
    By looks, not years; and should be very sorry
To state, they were not older than St. Peter,
But merely that they seem'd a little sweeter).   240

---

5. The Northern Lights.
6. crew (*1832* and in all other editions except first edition, *CPW*, and *Cochran*). In 1819 the English explorer William Edward Parry (1790–1855) led two ships to the inlet in Greenland called Melville's Sound.
7. Mortal flesh.
8. Joanna Southcott (1750–1814), religious fanatic who claimed supernatural gifts and wrote visionary verse.
9. The greatest and leader, or ruler ("Hierarch," line 242), of the archangels, who defeated Satan when he rebelled against God.
1. Painted screen behind or above the altar, common in Catholic churches of the Middle Ages and Renaissance.

31

The cherubs and the saints bow'd down before
   That arch-angelic Hierarch, the first
Of essences angelical, who wore
   The aspect of a god; but this ne'er nursed
Pride in his heavenly bosom, in whose core   245
   No thought, save for his Maker's service, durst
Intrude, however glorified and high;
He knew him but the viceroy[2] of the sky.

32

He and the sombre silent Spirit met—
   They knew each other both for good and ill;   250
Such was their power, that neither could forget
   His former friend and future foe; but still
There was a high, immortal, proud regret
   In either's eye, as if 'twere less their will
Than destiny to make the eternal years   255
Their date of war, and their "champ clos" the spheres.[3]

33

But here they were in neutral space: we know
   From Job,[4] that Sathan hath the power to pay
A heavenly visit thrice a year or so;
   And that "the sons of God,"[5] like those of clay,   260
Must keep him company; and we might show,
   From the same book, in how polite a way
The dialogue is held between the Powers
Of Good and Evil—but 'twould take up hours.

34

And this is not a theologic tract,   265
   To prove with Hebrew and with Arabic
If Job be allegory or a fact,
   But a true narrative; and thus I pick
From out the whole but such and such an act
   As sets aside the slightest thought of trick.   270
'Tis every tittle true, beyond suspicion,
And accurate as any other vision.

35

The spirits were in neutral space, before
   The gate of heaven; like eastern thresholds is

---

2. Ruler who serves a yet higher power.
3. The planets; "champ clos": an enclosed space for a tournament.
4. The Book of Job in the Hebrew Bible, chaps. 1–2.
5. Genesis 6.2 and Job 1.6.

The place where Death's grand cause is argued o'er,[6]   275
  And souls despatch'd to that world or to this;
And therefore Michael and the other wore
  A civil aspect: though they did not kiss,
Yet still between his Darkness and his Brightness
There pass'd a mutual glance of great politeness.   280

36

The Archangel bow'd, not like a modern beau,[7]
  But with a graceful oriental bend,
Pressing one radiant arm just where below
  The heart in good men is supposed to tend.
He turn'd as to an equal, not too low,   285
  But kindly; Sathan met his ancient friend
With more hauteur, as might an old Castilian[8]
Poor noble meet a mushroom rich civilian.[9]

37

He merely bent his diabolic brow
  An instant; and then raising it, he stood   290
In act to assert his right or wrong, and show
  Cause why King George by no means could or should
Make out a case to be exempt from woe
  Eternal, more than other kings, endued
With better sense and hearts, whom history mentions,   295
Who long have "paved hell with their good intentions."[1]

38

Michael began: "What wouldst thou with this man,
  Now dead, and brought before the Lord? What ill
Hath he wrought since his mortal race began,
  That thou canst claim him? Speak! and do thy will,   300
If it be just: if in his[2] earthly span
  He hath been greatly failing to fulfil
His duties as a king and mortal, say,
And he is thine; if not, let him have way."

39

"Michael!" replied the Prince of Air, "even here,   305
  Before the gate of him thou servest, must

6. In the ancient near east, a city's gate was the customary location for judicial hearings.
7. In early-nineteenth-century parlance, a dandified or affectedly elegant gentleman.
8. Native of Castile, one of the most ancient provinces of Spain; hence, Satan's "hauteur," or haughtiness.
9. Someone who practiced civil, as opposed to common or statute law; a likely reference to Lord Eldon, who through his law practice rose from a modest background to become Lord Chancellor (see essay by Peterfreund, p. 1008); *mushroom*: newly sprung up.
1. Proverbial; i.e., "the road to hell is paved with good intentions."
2. this (*1832*); see note to line 62.

I claim my subject: and will make appear
   That as he was my worshipper in dust,
So shall he be in spirit, although dear
   To thee and thine, because nor wine nor lust   310
Were of his weaknesses; yet on the throne
He reign'd o'er millions to serve me alone.

40

"Look to *our* earth, or rather *mine*; it was,
   Once, more thy master's: but I triumph not
In this poor planet's conquest; nor, alas!   315
   Need he thou servest envy me my lot:
With all the myriads[3] of bright worlds which pass
   In worship round him, he may have forgot
Yon weak creation of such paltry things:
   I think few worth damnation save their kings,—   320

41

"And these but as a kind of quit-rent,[4] to
   Assert my right as lord; and even had
I such an inclination, 'twere (as you
   Well know) superfluous; they are grown so bad,
That hell has nothing better left to do   325
   Than leave them to themselves: so much more mad
And evil by their own internal curse,
Heaven cannot make them better, nor I worse.

42

"Look to the earth, I said, and say again:
   When this old, blind, mad, helpless, weak, poor worm[5]   330
Began in youth's first bloom and flush to reign,
   The world and he both wore a different form,
And much of earth and all the watery plain
   Of ocean call'd him king: through many a storm
His isles had floated on the abyss of time;   335
For the rough virtues chose them for their clime.

43

"He came to his sceptre young; he leaves it old:
   Look to the state in which he found his realm,
And left it; and his annals too behold,
   How to a minion[6] first he gave the helm;   340
How grew upon his heart a thirst for gold,
   The beggar's vice, which can but overwhelm

---

3. Thousands.
4. Small sum paid to a landlord to satisfy certain property laws.
5. Cf. Shelley's sonnet "England in 1819," line 1: "An old, mad, blind, despised and dying King."
6. A subordinate, or minor official: a reference to John Stuart, prime minister 1762–63 (George III came to the throne in 1760).

The meanest hearts; and for the rest, but glance
Thine eye along America and France.

44

" 'Tis true, he was a tool from first to last   345
  (I have the workmen[7] safe); but as a tool
So let him be consumed. From out the past
  Of ages, since mankind have known the rule
Of monarchs—from the bloody rolls amass'd
  Of sin and slaughter—from the Caesars' school,[8]   350
Take the worst pupil; and produce a reign
More drench'd with gore, more cumber'd[9] with the slain.

45

"He ever warr'd with freedom and the free:
  Nations as men, home subjects, foreign foes,[1]
So that they utter'd the word 'Liberty!'   355
  Found George the Third their first opponent. Whose
History was ever stain'd as his will be
  With national and individual woes?
I grant his household abstinence; I grant
  His neutral virtues, which most monarchs want;   360

46

"I know he was a constant consort; own
  He was a decent sire, and middling lord.
All this is much, and most upon a throne;
  As temperance, if at Apicius[2] board,
Is more than at an anchorite's[3] supper shown.   365
  I grant him all the kindest can accord;
And this was well for him, but not for those
Millions who found him what oppression chose.

47

"The New World shook him off; the Old yet groans
  Beneath what he and his prepared, if not   370
Completed: he leaves heirs on many thrones
  To all his vices, without what begot
Compassion for him—his tame virtues; drones
  Who sleep, or despots who have now forgot
A lesson which shall be re-taught them, wake   375
Upon the thrones[4] of earth; but let them quake!

---

7. Unable to escape; *workmen*: the various councilors who influenced George III.
8. The line of Roman emperors, many of whom were remarkable for their cruelty.
9. Encumbered.
1. Lines 353–54 glance at the aggressive or repressive foreign and domestic policies of George III,
   e.g., in response to American independence, Catholic emancipation, and workers' rights.
2. Famous first-century Roman gourmet.
3. Religious hermit; his table would have only the simplest fare.
4. throne (*CPW*).

48

"Five millions of the primitive, who hold
   The faith which makes ye great on earth, implored
A *part* of that vast *all* they held of old,—
   Freedom to worship—not alone your Lord,   380
Michael, but you, and you, Saint Peter! Cold
   Must be your souls, if you have not abhorr'd
The foe to Catholic participation[5]
In all the license of a Christian nation.

49

"True! he allow'd them to pray God; but as   385
   A consequence of prayer, refused the law
Which would have placed them upon the same base
   With those who did not hold the saints in awe."
But here Saint Peter started from his place,
   And cried, "You may the prisoner withdraw: 390
Ere heaven shall ope her portals to this Guelph,[6]
   While I am guard, may I be damn'd myself!

50

"Sooner will I with Cerberus[7] exchange
   My office (and *his* is no sinecure)[8]
Than see this royal Bedlam[9] bigot range   395
   The azure fields of heaven, of that be sure!"
"Saint!" replied Sathan, "you do well to avenge
   The wrongs he made your satellites endure;
And if to this exchange you should be given,
   I'll try to coax *our* Cerberus up to heaven."   400

51

Here Michael interposed: "Good saint! and devil!
   Pray, not so fast; you both outrun discretion.
Saint Peter! you were wont to be more civil:
   Sathan! excuse this warmth of his expression,
And condescension to the vulgar's level: 405
   Even saints sometimes forget themselves in session.
Have you got more to say?"—"No."—"If you please,
I'll trouble you to call your witnesses."

---

5. The cause of Catholic Emancipation—allowing Catholics ("the primitive" [line 377], or original,
   Christians) to hold office in Parliament and enjoy all the freedoms ("license") of citizenship—was
   squelched by George III in 1795, 1801, and 1807.
6. Original family name of the House of Hanover.
7. Three-headed dog that guarded the classical underworld.
8. Position for which one is paid but does little or no work.
9. Madhouse; popular contraction of the Hospital of St. Mary of Bethlehem, famous London asylum.

52

Then Sathan turn'd and waved his swarthy hand,
   Which stirr'd with its electric qualities   410
Clouds farther off than we can understand,
   Although we find him sometimes in our skies;
Infernal thunder shook both sea and land
   In all the planets, and hell's batteries
Let off the artillery, which Milton[1] mentions   415
As one of Sathan's most sublime inventions.

53

This was a signal unto such damn'd souls
   As have the privilege of their damnation
Extended far beyond the mere controls
   Of worlds past, present, or to come; no station   420
Is theirs particularly in the rolls
   Of hell assign'd; but where their inclination
Or business carries them in search of game,
They may range freely—being damn'd the same.

54

They are proud of this—as very well they may,   425
   It being a sort of knighthood, or gilt key
Stuck in their loins;[2] or like to an "entré"
   Up the back stairs, or such free-masonry.[3]
I borrow my comparisons from clay,
   Being clay myself. Let not those spirits be   430
Offended with such base low likenesses;
We know their posts are nobler far than these.

55

When the great signal ran from heaven to hell—
   About ten million times the distance reckon'd
From our sun to its earth, as we can tell   435
   How much time it takes up, even to a second,
For every ray that travels to dispel
   The fogs of London, through which, dimly beacon'd,
The weathercocks are gilt some thrice a year,
If that the *summer* is not too severe:—   440

56

I say that I can tell—'twas half a minute:
   I know the solar beams take up more time

---

1. In *Paradise Lost* 6.482 *ff*. Milton describes Satan and the rebellious angels inventing firearms.
2. A gold key worn in the belt was one of the insignia of the Lord Chamberlain and other court officials; the stanza contains sexual innuendoes.
3. The secret society of Freemasons, dating back to the Middle Ages, was celebrated for its elaborate and arcane symbols of membership.

Ere, pack'd up for their journey, they begin it;
    But then their telegraph[4] is less sublime,
And if they ran a race, they would not win it   445
    'Gainst Sathan's couriers bound for their own clime.
The sun takes up some years for every ray
To reach its goal—the devil not half a day.

57

Upon the verge of space, about the size
    Of half-a-crown, a little speck appear'd   450
(I've seen a something like it in the skies
    In the Aegean, ere a squall); it near'd,
And, growing bigger, took another guise;
    Like an aërial ship it tack'd, and steer'd,
Or *was* steer'd (I am doubtful of the grammar   455
Of the last phrase, which makes the stanza stammer;—

58

But take your choice); and then it grew a cloud;
    And so it was—a cloud of witnesses.
But such a cloud! No land e'er saw a crowd
    Of locusts numerous as the heavens saw these;   460
They shadow'd with their myriads space; their loud
    And varied cries were like those of wild geese
(If nations may be liken'd to a goose).
And realised the phrase of "hell broke loose."[5]

59

Here crash'd a sturdy oath of stout John Bull,[6]   465
    Who damn'd away his eyes as heretofore:[7]
There Paddy[8] brogued "By Jasus!"—"What's your wull?"
    The temperate Scot exclaim'd: the French ghost swore
In certain terms I sha'n't translate in full,
    As the first coachman will; and 'midst the roar,[9]   470
The voice of Jonathan[1] was heard to express,
"*Our* president is going to war, I guess."

60

Besides there were the Spaniard, Dutch, and Dane;
    In short, an universal shoal of shades,

---

4. A network of semaphore signals from London to Portsmouth.
5. *Paradise Lost* 4.918.
6. Name for the blunt, straightforward Englishman.
7. As he did when he was alive; "damn your [or his] eyes" was a common English profanity.
8. I.e., an Irishman. "Wull" is the slurred (brogue) pronunciation of "will."
9. war (*1832*); see note to line 62.
1. I.e., an American; the "president," in this case, being Satan.

From Otaheite's isle to Salisbury Plain,[2]   475
    Of all climes and professions, years and trades,
Ready to swear against the good king's reign,
    Bitter as clubs in cards are against spades:
All summon'd by this grand "subpoena," to
Try if kings mayn't be damn'd like me or you.   480

61

When Michael saw this host, he first grew pale,
    As angels can; next, like Italian twilight,
He turn'd all colours—as a peacock's tail,
    Or sunset streaming through a Gothic skylight
In some old abbey, or a trout not stale,   485
    Or distant lightning on the horizon *by* night,
Or a fresh rainbow, or a grand review
Of thirty regiments in red, green, and blue.

62

Then he address'd himself to Sathan: "Why—
    My good old friend, for such I deem you, though   490
Our different parties make us fight so shy,
    I ne'er mistake you for a *personal* foe;
Our difference is *political*, and I
    Trust that, whatever may occur below,
You know my great respect for you: and this   495
Makes me regret whate'er you do amiss—

63

"Why, my dear Lucifer, would you abuse
    My call for witnesses? I did not mean
That you should half of earth and hell produce;
    'Tis even superfluous, since two honest, clean,   500
True testimonies are enough: we lose
    Our time, nay, our eternity, between
The accusation and defence: if we
Hear both, 'twill stretch our immortality."

64

Sathan replied, "To me the matter is   505
    Indifferent, in a personal point of view:
I can have fifty better souls than this
    With far less trouble than we have gone through
Already; and I merely argued his
    Late Majesty of Britain's case with you   510
Upon a point of form: you may dispose
Of him; I've kings enough below, God knows!"

2. The Stonehenge area of England; *Otaheite*: Tahiti.

65

Thus spoke the Demon (late call'd "multifaced"
　　By multo-scribbling Southey).[3] "Then we'll call
One or two persons of the myriads placed　　　　　　　　515
　　Around our congress, and dispense with all
The rest," quoth Michael: "Who may be so graced
　　As to speak first? there's choice enough—who shall
It be?" Then Sathan answer'd, "There are many;
　　But you may choose Jack Wilkes[4] as well as any."　　520

66

A merry, cock-eyed, curious-looking Sprite[5]
　　Upon the instant started from the throng,
Dress'd in a fashion now forgotten quite;
　　For all the fashions of the flesh stick long
By people in the next world; where unite　　　　　　　　525
　　All the costumes since Adam's, right or wrong,
From Eve's fig-leaf down to the petticoat,
Almost as scanty, of days less remote.

67

The Spirit look'd around upon the crowds
　　Assembled, and exclaim'd, "My friends of all　　　　　530
The spheres, we shall catch cold amongst these clouds;
　　So let's to business: why this general call?
If those are freeholders[6] I see in shrouds,
　　And 'tis for an election that they bawl,
Behold a candidate with unturn'd coat!　　　　　　　　535
Saint Peter, may I count upon your vote?"

68

"Sir," replied Michael, "you mistake; these things
　　Are of a former life, and what we do
Above is more august; to judge of kings
　　Is the tribunal met: so now you know."　　　　　　　540
"Then I presume those gentlemen with wings,"
　　Said Wilkes, "are cherubs; and that soul below
Looks much like George the Third, but to my mind
A good deal older—Bless me! is he blind?"

3. Southey had called the Devil "multifaced" in his *Vision of Judgement*.
4. John Wilkes (1727–1797), the most influential radical opponent of George III; he was elected to Parliament three times and, in 1774, lord mayor of London; in his last years, however, he "turn'd to half a courtier" (line 570) by voting consistently against the Whig policies he had done so much to form.
5. Spirit.
6. Independent land and or property holders, hence empowered to vote in an election.

69

"He is what you behold him, and his doom   545
   Depends upon his deeds," the Angel said.
"If you have aught to arraign in him, the tomb
   Gives license to the humblest beggar's head
To lift itself against the loftiest."—"Some,"
   Said Wilkes, "don't wait to see them laid in lead,   550
For such a liberty—and I, for one,
Have told them what I thought beneath the sun."

70

"*Above* the sun repeat, then, what thou hast
   To urge against him," said the Archangel. "Why,"
Replied the Spirit, "since old scores are past,   555
   Must I turn evidence? In faith, not I.
Besides, I beat him hollow at the last,
   With all his Lords and Commons:[7] in the sky
I don't like ripping up old stories, since
His conduct was but natural in a prince.   560

71

"Foolish, no doubt, and wicked, to oppress
   A poor unlucky devil without a shilling;
But then I blame the man himself much less
   Than Bute and Grafton,[8] and shall be unwilling
To see him punish'd here for their excess,   565
   Since they were both damn'd long ago, and still in
Their place below: for me, I have forgiven,
And vote his 'habeas corpus'[9] into heaven."

72

"Wilkes," said the Devil, "I understand all this;
   You turn'd to half a courtier ere you died,   570
And seem to think it would not be amiss
   To grow a whole one on the other side
Of Charon's ferry;[1] you forget that *his*
   Reign is concluded; whatsoe'er betide,
He won't be sovereign more: you've lost your labour,   575
For at the best he will but be your neighbour.

---

7. The two houses of the English Parliament.
8. Earl of Bute (1713–1792) and Earl of Grafton (1735–1811): two ministers of George III and ene-
   mies of Wilkes.
9. Literally, have the body (Latin). A writ of law requiring a person accused of a crime to be brought
   before a judge; its purpose is to prevent unlawful imprisonment and it is therefore regarded as a
   cornerstone of liberty. Habeas corpus was suspended for a time in George III's reign; cf. "I like the
   Habeas Corpus (when we've got it)" (*Beppo,* line 374).
1. Charon, in classical myth, ferried the souls of the dead across the River Styx into Hades.

73

"However, I knew what to think of it,
     When I beheld you in your jesting way.
Flitting and whispering round about the spit
     Where Belial,[2] upon duty for the day,   580
With Fox's lard was basting William Pitt,[3]
     His pupil; I knew what to think, I say:
That fellow even in hell breeds farther ills;
I'll have him *gagg'd*—'twas one of his own bills.

74

"Call Junius!"[4] From the crowd a Shadow stalk'd,   585
     And at the name there was a general squeeze,
So that the very ghosts no longer walk'd
     In comfort, at their own aërial ease,
But were all ramm'd, and jamm'd (but to be balk'd,
     As we shall see), and jostled hands[5] and knees,   590
Like wind compress'd and pent within a bladder,
Or like a human colic,[6] which is sadder.

75

The Shadow came—a tall, thin, grey-hair'd figure,
     That look'd as it had been a shade on earth;
Quick in its motions, with an air of vigour,   595
     But nought to mark its breeding or its birth:
Now it wax'd little, then again grew bigger,
     With now an air of gloom, or savage mirth;
But as you gazed upon its features, they
Changed every instant—to *what*, none could say.   600

76

The more intently the ghosts gazed, the less
     Could they distinguish whose the features were;
The Devil himself seem'd puzzled even to guess;
     They varied like a dream—now here, now there;
And several people swore from out the press,   605
     They knew him perfectly; and one could swear
He was his father; upon which another
Was sure he was his mother's cousin's brother:

---

2. One of the traditional devils in hell; mentioned in *Paradise Lost.*
3. Charles James Fox (1749–1806) was an important—and very fat—Whig statesman. His lifelong opponent, William Pitt the Younger (1759–1806) was prime minister 1783–1801 and 1804–06. Pitt was the agent of highly repressive measures against political dissenters in England, including the so-called "gagging" laws (see line 584), which drastically restricted freedom of speech and the press.
4. The pseudonym of the author of a series of public letters attacking George III's policies; his identity has never been conclusively determined. "Shadow" is a further allusion to this person (see line 650 and note and line 667).
5. heads (*Cochran,* manuscript).
6. Severe abdominal pain.

77

Another, that he was a duke, or knight,
   An orator, a lawyer, or a priest,   610
A nabob,[7] a man-midwife; but the wight[8]
   Mysterious changed his countenance at least
As oft as they their minds: though in full sight
   He stood, the puzzle only was increased;
The man was a phantasmagoria[9] in   615
Himself—he was so volatile and thin!

78

The moment that you had pronounced him *one*,
   Presto! his face changed, and he was another;
And when that change was hardly well put on,
   It varied, till I don't think his own mother   620
(If that he had a mother) would her son
   Have known, he shifted so from one to t'other;
Till guessing from a pleasure grew a task,
At this epistolary "Iron Mask."[1]

79

For sometimes he like Cerberus would seem—   625
   "Three gentlemen at once" (as sagely says
Good Mrs. Malaprop);[2] then you might deem
   That he was not even *one*; now many rays
Were flashing round him; and now a thick steam
   Hid him from sight—like fogs on London days: 630
Now Burke,[3] now Tooke, he grew to people's fancies,
And certes often like Sir Philip Francis.

80

I've an hypothesis—'tis quite my own;
   I never let it out till now, for fear
Of doing people harm about the throne,
   And injuring some minister or peer.   635
On whom the stigma might perhaps be blown:
   It is—my gentle public, lend thine ear!
'Tis, that what Junius we are wont to call
Was *really, truly*, nobody at all.   640

7. In this case, an Englishman who has made a large fortune in the east.
8. Person (archaic).
9. Shifting series or scenes of phantoms.
1. Referring to the so-called "man in the iron mask," a nobleman who was masked and imprisoned in the Bastille by Louis XIV; he died in 1703, and his identity (Ercole Mattioli) was not known until after Byron's death.
2. Character in Richard Brinsley Sheridan's play *The Rivals* (1775), who has a habit of comically mis-forming and misusing words.
3. Edmund Burke (1729–1797), John Horne Tooke (1736–1812), and Sir Philip Francis (1740–1818) were all believed at one time or another to be the author of the "Junius" letters. Burke was the great Irish statesman and conservative political theorist; Tooke was an English radical; Francis was a political reformer and pamphleteer.

81

I don't see wherefore letters should not be
   Written without hands, since we daily view
Them written without heads; and books, we see,
   Are fill'd as well without the latter too:
And really till we fix on somebody   645
   For certain sure to claim them as his due,
Their author, like the Niger's mouth,[4] will bother
The world to say if *there* be mouth or author.

82

"And who and what art thou?" the Archangel said.
   "For *that* you may consult my title-page,"[5]   650
Replied this mighty Shadow of a Shade:
   "If I have kept my secret half an age,
I scarce shall tell it now."—"Canst thou upbraid,"
   Continued Michael, "George Rex,[6] or allege
Aught further?" Junius answer'd, "You had better   655
First ask him for *his* answer to my letter:

83

"My charges upon record will outlast
   The brass of both his epitaph and tomb."
"Repent'st thou not," said Michael, "of some past
   Exaggeration? something which may doom   660
Thyself if false, as him if true? Thou wast
   Too bitter—is it not so?—in thy gloom
Of passion?"—"Passion!" cried the Phantom dim,
"I loved my country, and I hated him.

84

"What I have written, I have written:[7] let   665
   The rest be on his head or mine!" So spoke
Old "Nominis Umbra;" and while speaking yet,
   Away he melted in celestial smoke.
Then Sathan said to Michael, "Don't forget
   To call George Washington, and John Horne Tooke,   670
And Franklin;"[8]—but at this time there was heard
A cry for room, though not a phantom stirr'd.

---

4. The mouth of the River Niger in west Africa, covered with dense forests, had not yet been discovered.
5. The title page of each of the Junius letters read, "Letters of Junius, *Stat Nominis Umbra*" (Latin, meaning "it is the shadow of a name"); see line 667.
6. George the King.
7. John 19.22.
8. George Washington, John Horne Tooke (see line 631 note), and Benjamin Franklin would naturally be called upon to bear witness against George III.

85

At length with jostling, elbowing, and the aid
   Of cherubim appointed to that post,
The devil Asmodeus[9] to the circle made   675
   His way, and look'd as if his journey cost
Some trouble. When his burden[1] down he laid,
   "What's this?" cried Michael; "why, 'tis not a ghost?"
"I know it," quoth the incubus;[2] "but he
Shall be one, if you leave the affair to me.   680

86

"Confound the Renegado![3] I have sprain'd
   My left wing, he's so heavy; one would think
Some of his works about his neck were chain'd.[4]
   But to the point; while hovering o'er the brink
Of Skiddaw[5] (where as usual it still rain'd),   685
   I saw a taper,[6] far below me, wink,
And stooping, caught this fellow at a libel—
No less on History than the Holy Bible.

87

"The former is the devil's scripture, and
   The latter yours, good Michael; so the affair   690
Belongs to all of us, you understand.
   I snatch'd him up just as you see him there,
And brought him off for sentence out of hand:
   I've scarcely been ten minutes in the air—
At least a quarter it can hardly be: 695
I dare say that his wife is still at tea."

88

Here Sathan said, "I know this man of old,
   And have expected him for some time here;
A sillier fellow you will scarce behold,
   Or more conceited in his petty sphere: 700
But surely it was not worth while to fold
   Such trash below your wing, Asmodeus dear:
We had the poor wretch safe (without being bored
With carriage) coming of his own accord.

9. One of the traditional devils in Hell.
1. Southey.
2. Demon that visits people while they sleep.
3. Renegade or outlaw; the word was actually used against Southey when he was attacked in Parliament in 1817 (see Preface).
4. A joking reference to the size of some of Southey's books.
5. Mountain in the Lake District of England, near Southey's home.
6. I.e., the candle on Southey's writing desk.

89

"But since he's here, let's see what he has done."   705
    "Done!" cried Asmodeus, "he anticipates
The very business you are now upon,
    And scribbles as if head clerk to the Fates.
Who knows to what his ribaldry may run,
    When such an ass as this, like Balaam's,[7] prates?"   710
"Let's hear," quoth Michael, "what he has to say;
You know we're bound to that in every way."

90

Now the Bard, glad to get an audience, which
    By no means often was his case below,
Began to cough, and hawk, and hem, and pitch   715
    His voice into that awful note of woe
To all unhappy hearers within reach
    Of poets when the tide of rhyme's in flow;
But stuck fast with his first hexameter,[8]
Not one of all whose gouty feet would stir.   720

91

But ere the spavin'd[9] dactyls could be spurr'd
    Into recitative,[1] in great dismay
Both cherubim and seraphim were heard
    To murmur loudly through their long array;
And Michael rose ere he could get a word   725
    Of all his founder'd verses under way,
And cried, "For God's sake stop, my friend! 'twere best—
Non Di, non homines[2]—you know the rest."

92

A general bustle spread throughout the throng,
    Which seem'd to hold all verse in detestation;   730
The angels had of course enough of song
    When upon service; and the generation
Of ghosts had heard too much in life, not long
    Before, to profit by a new occasion;

---

7. In Numbers 22.28-30, the Lord speaks to the Canaanite priest Balaam through Balaam's ass (beast of burden).
8. Southey's *Vision of Judgement* is written in dactylic hexameter, a six-foot poetic line comprised of one stressed then two unstressed syllables—the meter of the great epics of Homer and Virgil. The final three words of line 720 should be read as a dactyl, which parodies the awkwardness of Southey's verse.
9. Crippled (literally).
1. Intoned or sung verse.
2. *Mediocribus esse poetis / Non homines, non di, non concessere columnae* ("Neither gods nor men can tolerate mediocre poets"), from *Ars Poetica* (*The Art of Poetry*, lines 372–73) by Horace (65–8 B.C.E.), Rome's great lyric poet and satirist, highly admired by and an important influence on Byron.

The Monarch, mute till then, exclaim'd, "What! what!   735
Pye³ come again? No more—no more of that!"

93

The tumult grew; an universal cough
   Convulsed the skies, as during a debate,
When Castlereagh⁴ has been up long enough
   (Before he was first minister of state,   740
I mean—the *slaves hear now*); some cried "Off, off!"
   As at a farce; till, grown quite desperate,
The Bard Saint Peter pray'd to interpose
(Himself an author)⁵ only for his prose.

94

The varlet⁶ was not an ill-favour'd knave;   745
   A good deal like a vulture in the face,
With a hook nose and a hawk's eye, which gave
   A smart and sharper-looking sort of grace
To his whole aspect, which, though rather grave,
   Was by no means so ugly as his case;   750
But that indeed was hopeless as can be,
Quite a poetic felony *"de se."*⁷

95

Then Michael blew his trump, and still'd the noise
   With one still greater, as is yet the mode
On earth besides; except some grumbling voice,   755
   Which now and then will make a slight inroad
Upon decorous silence, few will twice
   Lift up their lungs when fairly overcrow'd;
And now the bard could plead his own bad cause,
With all the attitudes of self-applause.   760

96

He said—(I only give the heads)—he said,
   He meant no harm in scribbling; 'twas his way
Upon all topics; 'twas, besides, his bread,
   Of which he butter'd both sides; 'twould delay
Too long the assembly (he was pleased to dread),   765
   And take up rather more time than a day,
To name his works—he would but cite a few—
"Wat Tyler"—"Rhymes on Blenheim"—"Waterloo."

3. Henry James Pye (1745–1813), a notoriously mediocre poet and poet laureate before Southey. The repetitions in lines 735–36 imitates a speech mannerism of George III.
4. Robert Stewart, Viscount Castlereagh (1769–1822), England's foreign secretary, a highly influential Tory statesman, dull orator, and, along with Southey, consistent object of Byron's detestation and sharpest satire (see "Dedication" to *Don Juan* and headnote to that poem).
5. Referring to his Epistles in the New Testament.
6. Rascal, knave; originally an attendant or servant.
7. *Felo de se* (Latin, felon of himself), an archaic legal term for someone who commits suicide.

97

He had written praises of a regicide;[8]
 He had written praises of all kings whatever;   770
He had written for republics far and wide,
 And then against them bitterer than ever;
For pantisocracy[9] he once had cried
 Aloud, a scheme less moral than 'twas clever;
Then grew a hearty anti-jacobin[1]—   775
Had turn'd his coat—and would have turn'd his skin.

98

He had sung against all battles, and again
 In their high praise and glory; he had call'd
Reviewing "the ungentle craft,"[2] and then
 Become as base a critic as e'er crawl'd—   780
Fed, paid, and pamper'd by the very men
 By whom his muse and morals had been maul'd:
He had written much blank verse, and blanker prose,
And more of both than any body knows.

99

He had written Wesley's life:[3]—here turning round 785
 To Sathan, "Sir, I'm ready to write yours,
In two octavo[4] volumes, nicely bound,
 With notes and preface, all that most allures
The pious purchaser; and there's no ground
 For fear, for I can choose my own reviewers: 790
So let me have the proper documents,
That I may add you to my other saints."

100

Sathan bow'd, and was silent. "Well, if you,
 With amiable modesty, decline
My offer, what says Michael? There are few   795
 Whose memoirs could be render'd more divine.
Mine is a pen of all work; not so new
 As it was once, but I would make you shine
Like your own trumpet. By the way, my own
Has more of brass in it, and is as well blown. 800

8. Someone who kills or would kill a king; referring to "Lines on Marten the Regicide" (1797). The rest of this stanza focuses on Southey's turncoat politics as represented by the contradictory values of his various works.
9. The name of the ideal society based on Godwinian principles of justice that Southey (with Coleridge) had hoped to found in Pennsylvania in 1794.
1. Someone opposed to the goals and supporters of the French Revolution.
2. "See 'Life of Henry Kirke White.'"
3. *Life of John Wesley* (1703–1791), who was the founder of Methodism.
4. A book size, about six-by-nine inches.

101

"But talking about trumpets, here's my Vision![5]
    Now you shall judge, all people; yes, you shall
Judge with my judgment! and by my decision
    Be guided who shall enter heaven or fall.
I settle all these things by intuition,   805
    Times present, past, to come, heaven, hell, and all,
Like King Alfonso.[6] When I thus see double,
I save the Deity some worlds of trouble."

102

He ceased, and drew forth an MS.;[7] and no
    Persuasion on the part of devils, or saints,   810
Or angels, now could stop the torrent; so
    He read the first three lines of the contents;
But at the fourth, the whole spiritual show
    Had vanish'd, with variety of scents,
Ambrosial and sulphureous,[8] as they sprang,   815
Like lightning, off from his "melodious twang."[9]

103

Those grand heroics acted as a spell;
    The angels stopp'd their ears and plied their pinions;[1]
The devils ran howling, deafen'd, down to hell;
    The ghosts fled, gibbering, for their own dominions—   820
(For 'tis not yet decided where they dwell,
    And I leave every man to his opinions);
Michael took refuge in his trump—but, lo!
His teeth were set on edge, he could not blow!

104

Saint Peter, who has hitherto been known   825
    For an impetuous saint, upraised his keys,
And at the fifth line knock'd the Poet down;
    Who fell like Phaeton,[2] but more at ease,
Into his lake, for there he did not drown;
    A different web being by the Destinies   830

---

5. Southey's *Vision of Judgement* (1820).
6. "Alfonso [Alphonso X, king of Castile (1221–1284)], speaking of the Ptolomean system, said, that 'had he been consulted at the creation of the world, he would have spared the Maker some absurdities.'"
7. Manuscript.
8. Ambrosia is the food of the gods in classical myth; sulfur is a traditional ingredient of hell-fire.
9. "See Aubrey's account of the apparition which disappeared 'with a curious perfume and a *most melodious twang;*' or see the '*Antiquary,*' vol. 1.p. 225." Byron's note refers to John Aubrey's *Miscellanies* (1696) and Scott's *The Antiquary* (1816).
1. Wings.
2. In classical myth Phaeton, son of Apollo, attempted to drive the chariot of the sun across the heavens for one day but lost control of it, caught fire from flying too close to the sun, and fell to earth all aflame.

Woven for the Laureate's final wreath, whene'er
Reform shall happen either here or there.

105

He first sank to the bottom—like his works,
    But soon rose to the surface—like himself;
For all corrupted things are buoy'd like corks,[3]   835
    By their own rottenness, light as an elf,
Or wisp that flits o'er a morass: he lurks,
    It may be, still, like dull books on a shelf,
In his own den, to scrawl some "Life" or "Vision,"
As Welborn[4] says—"the devil turn'd precisian."   840

106

As for the rest, to come to the conclusion
    Of this true dream, the telescope is gone
Which kept my optics[5] free from all delusion,
    And show'd me what I in my turn have shown;
All I saw farther, in the last confusion,   845
    Was, that King George slipp'd into heaven for one;
And when the tumult dwindled to a calm,
I left him practising the hundredth psalm.[6]

On This Day I Complete My Thirty-Sixth Year[1]

Missolonghi, Jan. 22, 1824.

1

'Tis time this heart should be unmoved,
    Since others it hath ceased to move,
Yet though I cannot be beloved,
    Still let me love!

---

3. "A drowned body lies at the bottom till rotten; it then floats, as most people know."
4. A Puritan ("precisian") character in Philip Massinger's comedy *A New Way to Pay Old Debts* (1626).
5. Eyesight.
6. The psalm begins, "Make a joyful noise unto the Lord," and includes the verse, "Enter into his gates with thanksgiving, and into his courts with praise."
1. Byron arrived at Missolonghi on January 4, 1824, to take charge of a Greek army of liberation that he intended to lead against the Turks. According to the brother of Teresa Guiccioli, Pietro Gamba, who accompanied Byron to Greece, on the morning of January 22, Byron presented this poem to his friends with the words, "You were complaining, the other day, that I never write any poetry now:—this is my birthday, and I have just finished something, which, I think, is better than what I usually write" (*Narrative of Lord Byron's Last Journey to Greece*). It was first printed posthumously in the *Morning Chronicle* on October 29, 1824. The subject of the poem may have been Byron's feelings for two young people, his page Loukas Chalandratsanos and a Turkish girl whom he had taken into his care (see Crompton, *Byron and Greek Love* [pp. 318–28], and Moore, *The Late Lord Byron* [pp. 175–78]). In view of Byron's death from a fever three months after writing this poem, stanzas 9–10 lend it a premonitory quality.
    Textual Note: The poem's problematic textual history is summarized in *CPW* 7:150–52. The poem's title in *CPW*, following Byron's fair copies, is given as "January 22nd 1824. / Messalonghi. / On this day I complete my thirty sixth year."

2

My days are in the yellow leaf;[2]   5
   The flowers and fruits of Love are gone;
The worm, the canker, and the grief
    Are mine alone!

3

The fire that on my bosom preys
   Is lone as some volcanic isle;   10
No torch is kindled at its blaze—
    A funeral pile!

4

The hope, the fear, the jealous care,
   The exalted portion of the pain
And power of Love I cannot share,   15
    But wear the chain.

5

But 'tis not *thus*—and 'tis not *here*
   Such thoughts should shake my Soul, nor *now*,
Where Glory decks the hero's bier
    Or binds his brow.   20

6

The Sword—the Banner—and the Field—
   Glory and Greece around us[3] see!
The Spartan borne upon his shield[4]
    Was not more free!

7

Awake! (not Greece—she *is* awake!)   25
   Awake, my Spirit! think through *whom*
Thy life-blood tracks its parent lake
    And then strike home!

8

Tread those reviving passions down,
   Unworthy Manhood;—unto thee   30
Indifferent should the smile or frown
    Of Beauty be.

2. *Macbeth* 5.3.24.
3. me (*1832*) and in all subsequent editions prior to *BLJ* and *CPW*.
4. "The slain were borne on their shields—witness the Spartan mother's speech to her son, delivered with his buckler—'Either *with* this or *on* this.'" (Byron's manuscript note.)

9

If thou regret'st thy youth, *why live?*
The land of honourable Death
Is here:—up to the Field! and give   35
    Away thy Breath.

10

Seek out—less often sought than found—
A Soldier's Grave, for thee the best;
Then look around and choose thy ground
    And take thy Rest.   40

LETTERS AND JOURNALS

To Thomas Moore

Venice, November 17th, 1816

    I wrote to you from Verona the other day in my progress hither, which letter I hope you will receive. Some three years ago, or it may be more, I recollect your telling me that you had received a letter from our friend Sam, dated "On board his gondola". *My* gondola is, at this present, waiting for me on the canal; but I prefer writing to you in the house, it being autumn— and rather an English autumn than otherwise. It is my intention to remain at Venice during the winter, probably, as it has always been (next to the East) the greenest island of my imagination. It has not disappointed me; though its evident decay would, perhaps, have that effect upon others. But I have been familiar with ruins too long to dislike desolation. Besides, I have fallen in love, which, next to falling into the canal, (which would be of no use, as I can swim.) is the best or the worst thing I could do. I have got some extremely good apartments in the house of a "Merchant of Venice," who is a good deal occupied with business, and has a wife in her twenty-second year. Marianna (that is her name)[1] is in her appearance altogether like an antelope. She has the large, black, oriental eyes, with that peculiar expression in them which is seen rarely among *Europeans*—even the Italians—and which many of the Turkish women give themselves by tinging the eyelid,—an art not known out of that country, I believe. This expression she has *naturally*,—and something more than this. In short, I cannot describe the effect of this kind of eye,—at least upon me. Her features are regular, and rather aquiline—mouth small—skin clear and soft, with a kind of hectic colour—forehead remarkably good: her hair is of the dark gloss, curl, and colour of Lady J**'s [Jersey's]: her figure is light and pretty, and she is a famous songstress—scientifically so; her natural voice (in conversation, I mean) is very sweet; and the naiveté of the Venetian dialect is always pleasing in the mouth of a woman.

---

1. Marianna Segati; her husband was a draper.

November 23.

You will perceive that my description, which was proceeding with the minuteness of a passport, has been interrupted for several days. In the meantime *
* *
December 5

Since my former dates, I do not know that I have much to add on the subject, and, luckily, nothing to take away; for I am more pleased than ever with my Venetian, and begin to feel very serious on that point—so much so, that I shall be silent. *

By way of divertisement, I am studying daily, at an Armenian monastery,[2] the Armenian language. I found that my mind wanted something craggy to break upon; and this—as the most difficult thing I could discover here for an amusement—I have chosen, to torture me into attention. It is a rich language, however, and would amply repay any one the trouble of learning it. I try, and shall go on;—but I answer for nothing, least of all for my intentions or my success. There are some very curious MSS. in the monastery, as well as books; translations also from Greek originals, now lost, and from Persian and Syriac, &c.; besides works of their own people. Four years ago the French instituted an Armenian professorship. Twenty pupils presented themselves on Monday morning, full of noble ardour, ingenuous youth, and impregnable industry. They persevered, with a courage worthy of the nation and of universal conquest, till Thursday; when *fifteen* of the *twenty* succumbed to the six-and-twentieth letter of the alphabet. It is, to be sure, a Waterloo of an Alphabet—that must be said for them. But it is so like these fellows, to do by it as they did by their sovereigns—abandon both; to parody the old rhymes, "Take a thing and give a thing"—"Take a King and give a King". They are the worst of animals, except their conquerors.

I hear that H[odgso]n is your neighbour, having a living in Derbyshire. You will find him an excellent-hearted fellow, as well as one of the cleverest; a little, perhaps, too much japanned by preferment in the church and the tuition of youth, as well as inoculated with the disease of domestic felicity, besides being over-run with fine feelings about women and *constancy* (that small change of Love, which people exact so rigidly, receive in such counterfeit coin, and repay in baser metal); but, otherwise, a very worthy man, who has lately got a pretty wife, and (I suppose) a child by this time. Pray remember me to him, and say that I know not which to envy most— his neighbourhood, him, or you.

Of Venice I shall say little. You must have seen many descriptions; and they are most of them like. It is a poetical place; and classical, to us, from Shakespeare and Otway. I have not yet sinned against it in verse, nor do I know that I shall do so, having been tuneless since I crossed the Alps, and feeling, as yet, no renewal of the "estro".[3] By the way, I suppose you have seen "Glenarvon".[4] Madame de Stael lent it me to read from Copet last autumn. It seems to me that, if the authoress had written the *truth*, and

---

2. On the island of San Lazzaro.
3. Inspiration.
4. Published in May 1816, Caroline Lamb's tell-all novel about her love affair with Byron.

nothing but the truth—the whole truth—the romance would not only have
been more *romantic*, but more entertaining. As for the likeness, the picture
can't be good—I did not sit long enough. When you have leisure, let me
hear from and of you, believing me,

Ever and truly yours most affectionately,

B

.   .   .

To John Murray

Venice Novr. 25th. 1816

Dear Sir—It is some months since I have heard from or of you—I
think—*not* since I left Diodati[1]—From Milan I wrote once or twice;—but
have been here some little time—and intend to pass the winter without
removing.—I was much pleased with the Lago di Garda & with Verona—
particularly the amphitheatre—and a sarcophagus in a Convent garden—
which they show as Juliet's—they insist on the *truth* of her history.—Since
my arrival at Venice—the Lady of the Austrian Governor told me that
between Verona & Vicenza there are still ruins of the Castle of the *Mon-
tecchi*[2]—and a chapel once appertaining to the Capulets—Romeo seems to
have been of *Vicenza* by the tradition—but I was a good deal surprized to
find so firm a faith in Bandello's novel[3]—which seems really to have been
founded on a fact.— —Venice pleases me as much as I expected—and I
expected much—it is one of those places which I know before I see them—
and has always haunted me the most—after the East.— —I like the gloomy
gaiety of their gondolas—and the silence of their canals—I do not even dis-
like the evident decay of the city—though I regret the singularity of it's van-
ished costume—however there is much left still;—the Carnival too is
coming.— —St. Mark's[4]—and indeed Venice—is most alive at night—the
theatres are not open till *nine*—and the society is proportionably late—all
this is to my taste—but most of your countrymen miss & regret the rattle
of hackney coaches—without which they can't sleep.— —I have got
remarkably good apartments in a private house—I see something of the
inhabitants (having had a good many letters to some of them) I have got my
gondola—I read a little—& luckily could speak Italian (more fluently
though than accurately) long ago;—I am studying out of curiosity the
Venetian dialect—which is very naive—soft & peculiar—though not at all
classical—I go out frequently—and am in very good contentment.— —The
Helen of Canova[5]—(a bust which is in the house of M[adam]e the Count-
ess d'Albrizzi whom I know) is without exception to my mind the most per-
fectly beautiful of human conceptions—and far beyond my ideas of human
execution.—

---

1. The villa on lake Geneva where Byron stayed during the summer of 1816.
2. Montagues (Italian).
3. Matteo Bandello (1450–1562); his story of Romeo and Juliet was a source for Shakespeare.
4. Piazza San Marco, the large central square of Venice.
5. A sculpture of Helen of Troy by the Italian sculptor Antonio Canova (1757–1822). The lines "In
   this beloved marble view" were first published in *Life* (2:61) and collected (as "On the Bust of
   Helen by Canova") in *1831*.

> In this beloved marble view
>> Above the works & thoughts of Man—
> What Nature *could*—but *would not* do—
>> And Beauty and Canova *can*!
> Beyond Imagination's power—
>> Beyond the Bard's defeated art,
> With immortality her dower—
>> Behold the *Helen* of the *heart*!

Talking of the "heart" reminds me that I have fallen in love—which except falling into the Canal—(and that would be useless as I swim) is the best (or worst) thing I could do.— —I am therefore in love—fathomless love—but lest you should make some splendid mistake—& envy me the possession of some of those Princesses or Countesses with whose affections your English voyagers are apt to invest themselves—I beg leave to tell you—that my Goddess is only the wife of a "Merchant of Venice"—but then she is pretty as an Antelope,—is but two & twenty years old—has the large black Oriental eyes—with the Italian countenance—and dark glossy hair of the curl & colour of Lady Jersey's—then she has the voice of a lute—and the song of a Seraph (though not quite so sacred) besides a long postscript of graces— virtues and accomplishments—enough to furnish out a new Chapter for Solomon's song.—But her great merit is finding out mine—there is nothing so amiable as discernment.—Our little arrangement is completed—the usual oaths having been taken—and everything fulfilled according to the "understood relations" of such liaisons. The general race of women appear to be handsome—but in Italy as on almost all the Continent—the highest orders are by no means a well looking generation—and indeed reckoned by their countrymen very much otherwise.—Some are exceptions but most of them as ugly as Virtue herself.—If you write—address to me *here Poste Restante*—as I shall probably stay the winter over.—I never see a newspaper & know nothing of England—except in a letter now & then from my Sister.—Of the M.S. sent you I know nothing except that you have received it—& are to publish it &c. &c. but when—where—& how—you leave me to guess—. But it don't much matter.— —I suppose you have a world of works passing through your process for next year—when does Moore's poem appear?—I sent a letter for him addressed to your care the other day.—So— Mr. *Frere*[6] is married—and you tell me in a former letter that he had "nearly forgotten that he was so—"—he is fortunate.— —

yrs ever & very truly
B

To Augusta Leigh

Venice. Decr. 19th. 1816

My dearest Augusta—I wrote to you a few days ago.—Your letter of the 1st. is arrived—and you have "a *hope*" for me—it seems—what "hope"—child?—my dearest Sis. I remember a methodist preacher who on perceiving a profane grin on the faces of part of his congregation—exclaimed "no *hopes* for *them* as

---

6. John Hookham Frere, diplomat and author, whose *The Monks and the Giants* (1821) published under the pseudonym Whistlecraft was a model for the mock-heroic style of *Beppo* and *Don Juan*.

laughs" and thus it is—with us—we laugh too much for hopes—and so even let them go—I am sick of sorrow—& must even content myself as well as I can—so here goes—I won't be woeful again if I can help it.—My letter to my moral Clytemnestra[1] required no answer—& I would rather have none—I was wretched enough when I wrote it—& had been so for many a long day & month—at present I am less so—for reasons explained in my late letter (a few days ago) and as I never pretend to *be* what I am not you may tell her if you please that I am recovering—and the reason also if you like it.—I do not agree with you about Ada—there was *equivocation* in the answer—and it shall be settled one way or the other—I wrote to Hanson[2] to take proper steps to prevent such a removal of my daughter—and even the probability of it—you do not know the woman so well as I do—or you would perceive in her *very negative answer*—that she *does intend* to take Ada with her—if she should go abroad.—
—I have heard of Murray's squabble with one of his brethren—who is an impudent impostor—and should be trounced.— —You do not say whether the *true po's* are out—I hope you like them.—You are right in saying that I like Venice—it is very much what you would imagine it—but I have no time just now for description;—the Carnival is to begin in a week—and with it the mummery of masking.— —I have not been out a great deal—but quite as much as I like—I am going out this evening—in my *cloak* & *Gondola*—there are two nice Mrs. Radcliffe[3] words for you—and then there is the place of St Mark—and conversaziones—and various fooleries—besides many *nau*[ghty]. indeed every body is *nau.* so much so that a lady with only *one lover* is not reckoned to have overstepped the modesty of marriage—that being a regular thing;—some have two—three—and so on to twenty beyond which they don't account—but they generally begin by one.— —The husbands of course belong to any body's wives—but their own:— —My present beloved[4]—is aged two & twenty—with remarkably fine black eyes—and very regular & pretty features—figure light & pretty—hair dark—a mighty good singer—as they all are—she is married (of course) & has one child—a girl.—Her temper very good—(as you know it had need to be) and lively—she is a Venetian by birth—& was never further from Venice than Milan in her days—her lord is about five years older than me—an exceeding good kind of a man.—That amatory appendage called by us a lover—is here denominated variously—sometimes an "Amoroso" (which is the same thing) and sometimes a Cavaliero servente—which I need not tell you—is a serving Cavalier.— —I told my fair one—at setting out—that as to the love and the Cavaliership—I was quite of accord—*but as to the servitude*—it would not suit me at all—so I begged to hear no more about it.—You may easily suppose I should not at all shine in the ceremonious department—so little so—that instead of handing the Lady as in duty bound into the Gondola—I as nearly as possible conveyed her into the Canal—and this at midnight—to be sure it was as dark as pitch—but if you could have seen the gravity with which I was committing her to the waves—thinking all the time of something or other not to the purpose;—I always forget that the streets are canals—and was going to walk her over the water—if the servants & the Gondoliers had not awakened me.— — So much for love & all that.— —The music here is famous—and there will be a whole tribe of singers & dancers during the Carnival—besides the usual theatres.—The Society here is something like our own—except that the women sit in a semicircle at one end of the room—& the men stand at the other.—I

1. I.e., Byron's wife, Annabella Milbanke. In Aeschylus's *Agamemnon*, Clytemnestra takes revenge against her husband, Agamemnon, by killing him; unlike Byron's "moral" wife, Clytemnestra is having an adulterous affair.
2. John Hanson (17?–1841), Byron's solicitor, business agent, and friend. Ada: Byron and Annabella's daughter, then one year old.
3. Ann Radcliffe (1764–1823), writer of Gothic novels.
4. Marianna Segati.

pass my mornings at the Armenian convent studying Armenian. My evenings here & there—tonight I am going to the Countess Albrizzi's—one of the noblesse—I have also been at the Governor's—who is an Austrian—& whose wife the Countess Goetz appeared to me in the little I have seen of her a very amiable & pleasing woman—with remarkably good manners—as many of the German women have.— —There are no English here—except birds of passage—who stay a day & then go on to Florence—or Rome.—I mean to remain here till Spring.—When you write address *directly* here—as in your present letter.—

ever dearest yrs.
B

To Thomas Moore[1]

Venice, December 24th, 1816

. . .

The day after to-morrow (to-morrow being Christmas-day) the Carnival begins. I dine with the Countess Albrizzi and a party, and go to the opera. On that day the Phenix, (not the Insurance Office, but) the theatre of that name, opens: I have got me a box there for the season, for two reasons, one of which is, that the music is remarkably good. The Contessa Albrizzi, of whom I have made mention, is the De Stael of Venice; not young, but a very learned, unaffected, good-natured woman; very polite to strangers, and, I believe not at all dissolute, as most of the women are. She has written very well on the works of Canova, and also a volume of Characters, besides other printed matter. She is of Corfu, but married a dead Venetian—that is, dead since he married.

My flame (my "Donna" whom I spoke of in my former epistle, my Marianna) is still my Marianna, and I her—what she pleases. She is by far the prettiest woman I have seen here, and the most loveable I have met with any where—as well as one of the most singular. I believe I told you the rise and progress of our *liaison* in my former letter. Lest that should not have reached you, I will merely repeat, that she is a Venetian, two-and-twenty years old, married to a merchant well to do in the world, and that she has great black oriental eyes, and all the qualities which her eyes promise. Whether being in love with her has steeled me or not, I do not know; but I have not seen many other women who seem pretty. The nobility, in particular, are a sad-looking race—the gentry rather better. And now, what art *thou* doing?

> What are you doing now,
>   Oh Thomas Moore?
> What are you doing now,
>   Oh Thomas Moore?
> Sighing or suing now,
> Rhyming or wooing now,
> Billing or cooing now,
>   Which, Thomas Moore?

---

1. The two lyrics Byron included in this letter were first published in *Life*.

Are you not near the Luddites?[2] By the Lord! if there's a row, but I'll be among ye! How go on the weavers—the breakers of frames—the Lutherans of politics—the reformers?

> As the Liberty lads o'er the sea
> Bought their freedom, and cheaply, with blood,
> > So we, boys, we
> > Will *die* fighting, or *live* free,
> And down with all kings but King Ludd!
>
> When the web that we weave is complete,
> And the shuttle exchanged for the sword,
> > We will fling the winding-sheet
> > O'er the despot at our feet,
> And dye it deep in the gore he has pour'd.
>
> Though black as his heart its hue,
> Since his veins are corrupted to mud,
> > Yet this is the dew
> > Which the tree shall renew
> Of Liberty, planted by Ludd!

There's an amiable *chanson* for you—all impromptu. I have written it principally to shock your neighbour * * [Hodgson?], who is all clergy and loyalty—mirth and innocence—milk and water.

> But the Carnival's coming,
> > Oh Thomas Moore,
> The Carnival's coming,
> > Oh Thomas Moore,
>
> Masking and humming,
> Fifing and drumming,
> Guitarring and strumming,
> > Oh Thomas Moore.

The other night I saw a new play,—and the author. The subject was the sacrifice of Isaac.[3] The play succeeded, and they called for the author—according to continental custom—and he presented himself, a noble Venetian, Mali—or Malapiero, by name. Mala was his name, and *pessima* his production,—at least, I thought so; and I ought to know, having read more or less of five hundred Drury Lane[4] offerings, during my coadjutorship with the sub-and-super Committee.

When does your Poem of Poems come out? I hear that the E[dinburgh] R[eview] has cut up Coleridge's Christabel, and declared against me for praising it.[5] I praised it, firstly, because I thought well of it; secondly, because Coleridge was in great distress, and after doing what little I could

---

2. Workers who, protesting poor working conditions, stole into factories at night to break machinery; Byron's maiden speech in the House of Lords (February 27, 1812) opposed a bill to make "frame breaking" a capital offense. The lyric that follows is entitled "[Song for the Luddites]" in *CPW*.
3. Based on Genesis 22.
4. The London theater where Byron had served as one of the managing directors.
5. Byron had praised *Christabel* in a note to line 522 of *The Siege of Corinth* (1816).

for him in essentials, I thought that the public avowal of my good opinion might help him further, at least with the booksellers. I am very sorry that J[effrey] has attacked him, because, poor fellow, it will hurt him in mind and pocket. As for me, he's welcome—I shall never think less of J[effrey] for any thing he may say against me or mine in future.

I suppose Murray has sent you, or will send (for I do not know whether they are out or no) the poem, or poesies, of mine, of last summer. By the mass! they're sublime—"Ganion Coheriza"[6]—gainsay who dares! Pray, let me hear from you, and of you, and, at least, let me know that you have received these three letters. Direct right *here, poste restante.*

Ever and ever, &c.

P.S.—I heard the other day of a pretty trick of a bookseller, who has published some d[amne]d nonsense, swearing the bastards to me, and saying he gave me five hundred guineas for them. He lies—I never wrote such stuff, never saw the poems, nor the publisher of them, in my life, nor had any communication, directly or indirectly, with the fellow. Pray say as much for me, if need be. I have written to Murray, to make him contradict the imposter.

To Thomas Moore

Venice, January 28th, 1817

. . .

I rejoice to hear of your forthcoming in February—though I tremble for the "magnificence," which you attribute to the new Childe Harold.[1] I am glad you like it; it is a fine indistinct piece of poetical desolation, and my favourite. I was half mad during the time of its composition, between metaphysics, mountains, lakes, love unextinguishable, thoughts unutterable, and the nightmare of my own delinquencies. I should, many a good day, have blown my brains out, but for the recollection that it would have given pleasure to my mother-in-law; and, even *then*, if I could have been certain to haunt her—but I won't dwell upon these trifling family matters.

Venice is in the *estro* of her carnival, and I have been up these last two nights at the ridotto and the opera, and all that kind of thing. Now for an adventure. A few days ago a gondolier brought me a billet without a subscription, intimating a wish on the part of the writer to meet me either in gondola or at the island of San Lazaro, or at a third rendezvous, indicated in the note. "I know the country's disposition well"—in Venice "they do let Heaven see those tricks they dare not show,"[2] &c. &c.; so, for all response, I said that neither of the three places suited me; but that I would either be at home at ten at night *alone*, or at the ridotto at midnight, where the writer might meet me masked. At ten o'clock I was at home and alone (Marianna was gone with her husband to a conversazione), when the door of my apartment opened, and in walked a well-looking and (for an Italian) *bionda* girl of about nineteen, who informed me that she was married to the brother

6. Motto of the Macdonalds (probably taken from Scott's novel *Waverley* [1814]).
1. Canto III, published November 18, 1816; *forthcoming*: Moore's *Lallah Rooke* (1817).
2. Echoing *Othello* 3.3.206–07.

of my *amorosa*, and wished to have some conversation with me. I made a decent reply, and we had some talk in Italian and Romaic (her mother being a Greek of Corfu), when lo! in a very few minutes, in marches, to my very great astonishment, Marianna S[egati], *in propria persona,* and after making polite courtesy to her sister-in-law and to me, without a single word seizes her said sister-in-law by the hair, and bestows upon her some sixteen slaps, which would have made your ear ache only to hear their echo. I need not describe the screaming which ensued. The luckless visitor took flight. I seized Marianna, who, after several vain efforts to get away in pursuit of the enemy, fairly went into fits in my arms; and, in spite of reasoning, eau de Cologne, vinegar, half a pint of water, and God knows what other waters beside, continued so till past midnight.

After damning my servants for letting people in without apprizing me, I found that Marianna in the morning had seen her sister-in-law's gondolier on the stairs, and, suspecting that his apparition boded her no good, had either returned of her own accord, or been followed by her maids or some other spy of her people to the conversazione, from whence she returned to perpetrate this piece of pugilism. I had seen fits before, and also some small scenery of the same genus in and out of our island: but this was not all. After about an hour, in comes—who? why, Signor S[egati], her lord and husband, and finds me with his wife fainting upon the sofa, and all the apparatus of confusion, dishevelled hair, hats, handkerchiefs, salts, smelling-bottles—and the lady as pale as ashes without sense or motion. His first question was, "What is all this?" The lady could not reply—so I did. I told him the explanation was the easiest thing in the world; but in the mean time it would be as well to recover his wife—at least, her senses. This came about in due time of suspiration and respiration.

You need not be alarmed—jealousy is not the order of the day in Venice, and daggers are out of fashion; while duels, on love matters, are unknown—at least, with the husbands. But, for all this, it was an awkward affair; and though he must have known that I made love to Marianna, yet I believe he was not, till that evening, aware of the extent to which it had gone. It is very well known that almost all the married women have a lover; but it is usual to keep up the forms, as in other nations. I did not, therefore, know what the devil to say. I could not out with the truth, out of regard to her, and I did not choose to lie for my sake;—besides, the thing told itself. I thought the best way would be to let her explain it as she chose (a woman being never at a loss—the devil always sticks by them)—only determining to protect and carry her off, in case of any ferocity on the part of the Signor. I saw that he was quite calm. She went to bed, and next day—how they settled it, I know not, but settle it they did. Well—then I had to explain to Marianna about this never to be sufficiently confounded sister-in-law; which I did by swearing innocence, eternal constancy, &c. &c. * * * But the sister-in-law, very much discomposed with being treated in such wise, has (not having her own shame before her eyes) told the affair to half Venice, and the servants (who were summoned by the fight and the fainting) to the other half. But, here, nobody minds such trifles, except to be amused by them. I don't know whether you will be so, but I have scrawled a long letter out of these follies.

Believe me ever. &c

To Thomas Moore

Venice, February 28th, 1817

You will, perhaps, complain as much of the frequency of my letters now, as you were wont to do of their rarity. I think this is the fourth within as many moons. I feel anxious to hear from you, even more than usual, because your last indicated that you were unwell. At present, I am on the invalid regimen myself. The Carnival—that is, the latter part of it—and sitting up late o'nights, had knocked me up a little. But it is over,—and it is now Lent, with all its abstinence and Sacred Music.

The mumming closed with a masked ball at the Fenice,[1] where I went, as also to most of the ridottos, etc., etc.; and, though I did not dissipate much upon the whole, yet I find "the sword wearing out the scabbard," though I have but just turned the corner of twenty-nine.

> So we'll go no more a roving
>   So late into the night,
> Though the heart be still as loving,
>   And the moon be still as bright.
>
> For the sword outwears its sheath,
>   And the soul wears out the breast,
> And the heart must pause to breathe,
>   And Love itself have rest.
>
> Though the night was made for loving,
>   And the day returns too soon,
> Yet we'll go no more a roving
>   By the light of the moon.[2]

I have lately had some news of litter*atoor*, as I heard the editor of the Monthly[3] pronounce it once upon a time. I hear that W. W. has been publishing and responding to the attacks of the Quarterly, in the learned Perry's Chronicle. I read his poesies last autumn, and amongst them found an epitaph on his bull-dog, and another on *myself*. But I beg to assure him (like the astrologer Partridge) that I am not only alive now but was alive also at the time he wrote it. * * * * Hobhouse has (I hear, also) expectorated a letter against the Quarterly, addressed to me. I feel awkwardly situated between him and Gifford, both being my friends.

And this is your month of going to press—by the body of Diana! (a Venetian oath,) I feel as anxious—but not fearful for you—as if it were myself coming out in a work of humour, which would, you know, be the antipodes of all my previous publications. I don't think you have any thing to dread but your own reputation. You must keep up to that. As you never showed me a line of your work, I do not even know your measure; but you must

---

1. The opera house.
2. As McGann notes, this well-known lyric is "best read as part of B's letter to Moore" (*CPW* 4:476), as it was first published (*Life* 2:79); the stanza divisions were added in Murray's edition of 1831, the first printing of the poem by itself. The first four lines of the poem echo the Scottish ballad "The Jolly Beggar" (see David Herd, ed., *Ancient and Modern Scottish Songs*, 2nd ed. [1776], II. 26).
3. The *Monthly Review* and the *Quarterly Review* were journals featuring reviews of contemporary literature. The *Morning Chronicle*, published by James Perry, was the daily newspaper.

send me a copy by Murray forthwith, and then you shall hear what I think. I dare say you are in a pucker. Of all authors, you are the only really *modest* one I ever met with,—which would sound oddly enough to those who recollect your morals when you were young—that is, when you were *extremely* young—I don't mean to stigmatise you either with years or morality.

I believe I told you that the E[dinburgh] R[eview] had attacked me, in an article on Coleridge (I have not seen it)—"*Et tu*, Jeffrey?"—"there is nothing but roguery in villanous man."[4] But I absolve him of all attacks, present and future; for I think he had already pushed his clemency in my behoof to the utmost, and I shall always think well of him. I only wonder he did not begin before, as my domestic destruction was a fine opening for all the world, of which all, who could, did well to avail themselves.

If I live ten years longer, you will see, however, that it is not over with me—I don't mean in literature, for that is nothing; and it may seem odd enough to say, I do not think it my vocation. But you will see that I will do something or other—the times and fortune permitting—that, "like the cosmogony, or creation of the world, will puzzle the philosophers of all ages."[5] But I doubt whether my constitution will hold out. I have, at intervals, ex*or*cised it most devilishly.

I have not yet fixed a time of return, but I think of the spring. I shall have been away a year in April next. You never mention Rogers, nor Hodgson, your clerical neighbour, who has lately got a living near you. Has he also got a child yet?—his desideratum, when I saw him last. * * * * * * * *

Pray let me hear from you, at your time and leisure, believing me ever and truly and affectionately, &c.

To John Murray

Venice May 30th 1817

Dear Sir—I returned from Rome two days ago—& have received your letter but no sign nor tidings of the parcel sent through Sir——Stuart[1] which you mention;—after an interval of months a packet of "Tales," &c. found me at Rome—but this is all—& may be all that ever will find me—the post seems to be the only sane conveyance—& *that only for letters.*—From Florence I sent you a poem on Tasso[2]—and from Rome the new third act of "Manfred," & by Dr. Polidori two pictures for my sister. I left Rome & made a rapid journey home.—You will continue to direct here as usual.—Mr. Hobhouse is gone to Naples—I should have run down there too for a week—but for the quantity of English whom I heard of there—I prefer hating them at a distance—unless an Earthquake or a good real eruption of

4. 1 *Henry IV* 2.5.113; *E[dinburgh] R[eview] attacked me*: for praising Coleridge's *Christabel* in a note to *The Siege of Corinth* (1816). Echoing "Et tu, Brute" (*Julius Caesar* 3.1.85), Byron refers to Lord Francis Jeffrey (1773–1850), founder of the *Edinburgh Review*, who often wrote favorably about Byron's poems. Jeffrey disliked the poetry of Wordsworth and the Lake Poets—an opinion generally shared by Byron who, nonetheless, admired some of Coleridge's poetry. (For more about Byron's relationship with Jeffrey, see *English Bards and Scotch Reviewers*, line 82 n.)
5. *Vicar of Wakefield*, chap. 14.
1. Charles Stuart (1779–1845), an English diplomat.
2. Torquato Tasso (1544–1595), Italian Renaissance poet, whose tragic life is the subject of Byron's *Lament of Tasso*, published July 17, 1817.

Vesuvius were insured to reconcile me to their vicinity.—I know no other situation except Hell which I should feel inclined to participate with them—as a race—always excepting several individuals.—There were few of them in Rome—& I believe none whom you know—except that old Blue-*bore* Sotheby[3]—who will give a fine account of Italy in which he will be greatly assisted by his total ignorance of Italian—& yet this is the translator of Tasso.—The day before I left Rome I saw three robbers guillotined— the ceremony—including the *masqued* priests—the half-naked executioners—the bandaged criminals—the black Christ & his banner— the scaffold—the soldiery—the slow procession—& the quick rattle and heavy fall of the axe—the splash of the blood—& the ghastliness of the exposed heads—is altogether more impressive than the vulgar and ungentlemanly dirty "new drop" & dog-like agony of infliction upon the sufferers of the English sentence. Two of these men—behaved calmly enough—but the first of the three—died with great terror and reluctance— which was very horrible—he would not lie down—then his neck was too large for the aperture—and the priest was obliged to drown his exclamations by still louder exhortations—the head was off before the eye could trace the blow—but from an attempt to draw back the head— notwithstanding it was held forward by the hair—the first head was cut off close to the ears—the other two were taken off more cleanly;—it is better than the Oriental way—& (I should think) than the axe of our ancestors.— The pain seems little—& yet the effect to the spectator—& the preparation to the criminal—is very striking & chilling.—The first turned me quite hot and thirsty—& made me shake so that I could hardly hold the opera-glass (I was close—but was determined to see—as one should see every thing once—with attention) the second and third (which shows how dreadfully soon things grow indifferent) I am ashamed to say had no effect on me— as a horror—though I would have saved them if I could.— —It is some time since I heard from you—the *12th April* I believe.—

yrs. ever truly,
B

To Thomas Moore

La Mira, Venice, July 10th, 1817

Murray, the Mokanna[1] of booksellers, has contrived to send me extracts from Lalla Rookh by the post. They are taken from some magazine, and contain a short outline and quotations from the two first Poems. I am very much delighted with what is before me, and very thirsty for the rest. You have caught the colours as if you had been in the rainbow, and the tone of the East is perfectly preserved; so that [Ilderim?] and its author must be somewhat in the back-ground, and learn that it required something more than to have been upon the hunch of a dromedary to compose a good oriental story. I am glad you have changed the title from "Persian Tale." * * * * * * *

---

3. William Sotheby (1757–1833), minor English poet, whom Byron satirizes in *Beppo* (stanzas 72–75), in part for his association with the intellectual and literary women known as Bluestockings.
1. Referring to a figure in Moore's Oriental epic *Lalla Rookh* (1817).

I suspect you have written a devilish fine composition, and I rejoice in it from my heart; because "the Douglas and the Percy both together are confident against a world in arms."[2] I hope you won't be affronted at my looking on us as "birds of a feather;" though, on whatever subject you had written, I should have been very happy in your success.

There is a simile of an orange-tree's "flowers and fruits," which I should have liked better, if I did not believe it to be a reflection on * * * * * * * *

Do you remember Thurlow's poem to Sam—"*When* Rogers[3];" and that d—d supper at Rancliffe's that ought to have been a *dinner*? "Ah, Master Shallow, we have heard the chimes at midnight."[4] But,

> My boat is on the shore,
>   And my bark is on the sea;
> But, before I go, Tom Moore,
>   Here's a double health to thee!
>
> Here's a sigh to those who love me,
>   And a smile to those who hate;
> And, whatever sky's above me,
>   Here's a heart for every fate.
>
> Though the ocean roar around me,
>   Yet it still shall bear me on;
> Though a desert should surround me,
>   It hath springs that may be won.
>
> Were't the last drop in the well,
>   As I gasp'd upon the brink,
> Ere my fainting spirit fell,
>   'Tis to thee that I would drink.
>
> With that water, as this wine,
>   The libation I would pour
> Should be—peace with thine and mine,
>   And a health to thee, Tom Moore.

This should have been written fifteen moons ago—the first stanza was. I am just come out from an hour's swim in the Adriatic; and I write to you with a black-eyed Venetian girl before me, reading Boccac[c]io. * * * *

Last week I had a row on the road (I came up to Venice from my casino, a few miles on the Paduan road, this blessed day, to bathe) with a fellow in a carriage, who was impudent to my horse. I gave him a swinging box on the ear, which sent him to the police, who dismissed his complaint. Witnesses had seen the transaction. He first shouted, in an unseemly way, to frighten my palfry. I wheeled round, rode up to the window, and asked him what he meant. He grinned, and said some foolery, which produced him an immediate slap in the face, to his utter discomfiture. Much blasphemy ensued, and some menace, which I stopped by dismounting and opening

---

2. *1 Henry IV* 5.1.116–17 (slightly misquoted).
3. Poem by Lord Thurlow to the poet Samuel Rogers (1763–1855), which was the subject of Byron's, Moore's and Rogers's mockery (see *BLJ* 3:54n).
4. *2 Henry IV* 3.2.197. "My boat is on the shore" was first published with sheet music by Henry R. Bishop (1818).

the carriage door, and intimating an intention of mending the road with his immediate remains, if he did not hold his tongue. He held it.

Monk Lewis is here—"how pleasant!" He is a very good fellow, and very much yours. So is Sam—so is every body—and amongst the number,

Yours ever,

B

P.S.—What think you of Manfred? * * * *

To John Murray

Sept 15th. 1817

Dear Sir—I enclose a sheet for correction if ever you get to another edition—you will observe that the blunder in printing makes it appear as if the Chateau was *over* St. Gingo—instead of being on the opposite shore of the lake over Clarens—so—separate the paragraphs otherwise my *topog*raphy will seems as inaccurate as your *typ*ography on this occasion.[1]— — The other day I wrote to convey my proposition with regard to the 4th & concluding Canto—I have gone over—& extended it to one hundred and fifty stanzas which is almost as long as the two first were originally—& longer by itself—than any of the smaller poems except the "Corsair"—Mr. Hobhouse has made some very valuable & accurate notes of considerable length—& you may be sure I will do for the text all that I can to finish with decency.—I look upon C[hild]e Harold as my best—and as I begun—I think of concluding with it—but I make no resolutions on that head—as I broke my former intention with regard to "the Corsair"—however—I fear that I shall never do better—& yet—not being thirty years of age for some moons to come—one ought to be progressive as far as Intellect goes for many a good year—but I have had a devilish deal of wear & tear of mind and body—in my time—besides having published too often & much already. God grant me some judgement! to do what may be most fitting in that & every thing else—for I doubt my own exceedingly.— —I have read "Lallah Rookh"—but not with sufficient attention yet—for I ride about— & lounge—& ponder &—two or three other things—so that my reading is very desultory & not so attentive as it used to be.—I am very glad to hear of its popularity—for Moore is a very noble fellow in all respects—& will enjoy it without any of the bad feelings which Success—good or evil— sometimes engenders in the men of rhyme.—Of the poem itself I will tell you my opinion when I have mastered it—I say of the *poem*—for I don't like the *prose* at all—at all—and in the mean time the "Fire-worshippers" is the best and the "Veiled Prophet" the worst, of the volume.— —With regard to poetry in general I am convinced the more I think of it—that he and *all* of us—Scott—Southey—Wordsworth—Moore—Campbell—I—are all in the wrong—one as much as another—that we are upon a wrong revolutionary poetical system—or systems—not worth a damn in itself—& from which none but Rogers and Crabbe are free—and that the present & next generations will finally be of this opinion.—I am the more confirmed in this—by having lately gone over some of our Classics—particularly *Pope*—whom I tried in this way—I took Moore's poems & my own & some others—& went

---

1. The third canto of *Childe Harold*.

over them side by side with Pope's—and I was really astonished (I ought not
to have been so) and mortified—at the ineffable distance in point of
sense—harmony—effect—and even *Imagination* Passion—& *Invention*—
between the little Queen Anne's Man—& us of the lower Empire—depend
upon it [it] is all Horace then, and Claudian[2] now among us—and if I had
to begin again—I would model myself accordingly—Crabbe's the man—
but he has got a coarse and impracticable subject—& Rogers the Grandfa-
ther of living Poetry—is retired upon half-pay, (I don't mean as a Banker)—

> Since pretty Miss Jaqueline
> With her nose aquiline

and has done enough—unless he were to do as he did formerly.—

To John Murray[1]

Venice, January 8th. 1818

1

My dear Mr. Murray,
You're in a damned hurry
To set up this ultimate Canto,[2]
But (if they don't rob us)
You'll see Mr. Hobhouse
Will bring it safe in his portmanteau.—

2

For the Journal you hint of.[3]
As ready to print off;
No doubt you do right to commend it
But as yet I have writ off
The devil a bit of
Our "Beppo", when copied—I'll send it.—

3

In the mean time you've "Gally"[4]
Whose verses all tally,
Perhaps you may say he's a Ninny,
But if you abashed are
Because of "Alashtar"
He'll piddle another "Phrosine".—

---

2. *Horace . . . Claudian:* Roman poets Quintus Horatius Flaccus (65–68 B.C.E.), greatly revered by
   Byron, and Claudius Claudianus (c. 370–404 C.E.).
1. Stanzas 3, 5, 6, 10–11 of this verse epistle were first published in *Life* (1830); stanzas 1–11 were
   first published in Murray's collected edition of 1831 as "Epistle to Mr. Murray"; stanzas 12–14 were
   not published until Marchand's *Byron: A Biography* (2:722) (1957).
2. Canto IV of *Childe Harold's Pilgrimage*, which Hobhouse brought with him from Venice to deliver
   to Murray.
3. Murray had contemplated publishing a new periodical.
4. Henry Gally Knight, who wrote the oriental verse tales *Alashtar* and *Phrosine.*

4

Then you've Sotheby's tour,[5]
No great things to be sure—
You could hardly begin with a less work,
For the pompous rascallion
Who don't speak Italian
Nor French, must have scribbled by guesswork.

5

No doubt he's a rare man
Without knowing German
Translating his way up Parnassus,
And now still absurder
He meditates Murder
As you'll see in the trash he calls *Tasso's*

6

But you've others his betters
The real men of letters—
Your Orators—critics—and wits—
And I'll bet that your Journal
(Pray is it diurnal?)
Will pay with your luckiest hits.—

7

You can make any loss up—
With "Spence"[6] and his Gossip,
A work which must surely succeed,
Then Queen Mary's Epistle-craft,[7]
With the new "Fytte" of "Whistlecraft"[8]
Must make people purchase and read.—

8

Then you've General Gordon[9]
Who "girded his sword on"
To serve with a Muscovite Master
And help him to polish
A ⟨people⟩ Nation so *owlish*,
They thought shaving their beards a disaster.

5. *Farewell to Italy* (1818) by William Sotheby, British poet and translator frequently mocked by Byron (see letter to Murray of May 30, 1817 [p. 730] and *Beppo*, stanzas 72–75 [pp. 367–68]).
6. Rev. Joseph Spence, *Observations, Anecdotes, and Characters of Books and Men*, ed. Edmund Malone (1820).
7. George Chalmers, *The Life of Mary Queen of Scots* (1819).
8. See p. 723, n. 6.
9. Thomas Gordon (1788–1841) traveled widely in the East and served for several years in the Russian army.

9

For the man *"poor and shrewd"**
With whom you'd conclude
A Compact without more delay.
Perhaps some such pen is
            *(Vide your letter)
Still extant in Venice,
But ⟨pray⟩ please Sir to mention *your pay?*—

10

Now tell me some news
Of your friends and the Muse
Of the Bar,—or the Gown—or the House,[1]
From Canning the tall wit
To Wilmot the small wit
Ward's creeping Companion and *Louse.*—

11

⟨He's⟩ Who's so damnably bit
With fashion and Wit
That ⟨still a⟩ he crawls on the surface like Vermin
But an Insect in both,—
By his Intellect's growth
Of what *size* you may quickly determine.

12

Now, I'll put out my taper
(I've finished my paper
For these stanzas you see on the *brink* stand)
There's a whore on my right
For I rhyme best at Night
When a C—t is tied close to *my Inkstand.*

13

It was Mahomet's notion   (See his life in
That comical motion   Gibbon's abstract)
Increased his "devotion in prayer"—
If that tenet holds good
In a Prophet, it should
In a poet be equally fair.—

14

For, in rhyme or in love
(Which both come from above)

---

1. *Bar . . . Gown . . . House*: referring to the law—to barristers, their court attire, and the House of Lords. The lines that follow refer to the British statesman George Canning (1770–1827), Byron's cousin Sir John Wilmot (1784–1841), and an old friend, John William Ward (1781–1833).

> I'll *stand* with our *"Tommy"* or *"Sammy"* ("Moore" and
>   "Rogers")
> But the Sopha and lady
> Are both of them ready
> And so, here's "Good Night to you dammee!"

To Thomas Moore

Venice, September 19th, 1818

. . .

I have finished the First Canto (a long one, of about 180 octaves)[1] of a poem in the style and manner of "Beppo," encouraged by the good success of the same. It is called "Don Juan", and is meant to be a little quietly facetious upon every thing. But I doubt whether it is not—at least, as far as it has yet gone—too free for these very modest days. However, I shall try the experiment, anonymously, and if it don't take, it will be discontinued. It is dedicated to S[outhey] in good, simple, savage verse, upon the [Laureate's] politics, and the way he got them. But the bore of copying it out is intolerable; and if I had an amanuensis he would be of no use, as my writing is so difficult to decipher.

> My poem's Epic, and is meant to be
>   Divided in twelve books, each book containing,
> With love and war, a heavy gale at sea—
>   A list of ships, and captains, and kings reigning—
> New characters, &c. &c.

The above are two [*sic*] stanzas, which I send you as a brick of my Babel, and by which you can judge of the texture of the structure.

. . .

I wish you a good night, with a Venetian benediction, "Benedetto te, e la terra che ti fara!"—"May you be blessed, and the *earth* which you will *make*" is it not pretty? You would think it still prettier if you had heard it, as I did two hours ago, from the lips of a Venetian girl,[2] with large black eyes, a face like Faustina's, and the figure of a Juno—tall and energetic as a Pythoness, with eyes flashing, and her dark hair streaming in the moonlight—one of those women who may be made any thing. I am sure if I put a poniard into the hand of this one, she would plunge it where I told her,—and into *me*, if I offended her. I like this kind of animal, and am sure that I should have preferred Medea to any woman that ever breathed. You may, perhaps, wonder that I don't in that case. * * * * * * *
* * * * * * * * * * * * * * * *
I could have forgiven the dagger or the bowl, any thing, but the deliberate desolation piled upon me, when I stood alone upon my hearth, with my household gods shivered around me, * * * * * * * Do you suppose I have forgotten or forgiven it? It has comparatively swallowed up in me every

---

1. Byron continued adding stanzas after completing the first draft; the first canto contains 222 stanzas.
2. Probably Margarita Cogni; see letter to Murray, August 1, 1819 (p. 745).

other feeling, and I am only a spectator upon earth, till a tenfold opportunity offers. It may come yet. There are others more to be blamed than * * * *, and it is on these that my eyes are fixed unceasingly.

To Hobhouse and Kinnaird

Venice January 19th. 1819

Dear H. and dear K.—I approve and sanction all your legal proceedings with regard to my affairs, and can only repeat my thanks & approbation—if you put off the payments of debts "till *after* Lady Noel's death"—it is well—if till *after* her damnation—better—for that will last forever—yet I hope not:—for her sake as well as the Creditors'—I am willing to believe in Purgatory.——With regard to the Poeshie—I will have no "cutting & slashing" as Perry calls it—you may omit the stanzas on Castlereagh—indeed it is better—& the two "*Bobs*" at the end of the 3d. stanza of the dedication—which will leave "high" & "adry" good rhymes without any "*double* (or Single) Entendre"[1]—but no more—I appeal—not "to Philip fasting" but to Alexander drunk—I appeal to Murray at his ledger—to the people—in short, Don Juan shall be an entire horse or none.—If the objection be to the indecency, the Age which applauds the "Bath Guide" & Little's poems—& reads Fielding & Smollett still—may bear with that;—if to the poetry—I will take my chance.—I will not give way to all the Cant of Christendom—I have been cloyed with applause & sickened with abuse;—at present—I care for little but the Copyright,—I have imbibed a great love for money—let me have it—if Murray loses this time—he won't the next—he will be cautious—and I shall learn the decline of his customers by his epistolary indications.— — But in no case will I submit to have the poem mutilated.—There is another Canto written—but not copied—in two hundred & odd Stanzas,—if this succeeds—as to the prudery of the present day—what is it? are we more moral than when Prior wrote—is there anything in Don Juan so strong as in Ariosto—or Voltaire—or Chaucer?—Tell Hobhouse—his letter to De Breme has made a great Sensation—and is to be published in the Tuscan & other Gazettes—Count R[izzo] came to consult with me about it last Sunday—we think of Tuscany—for Florence and Milan are in literary war—but the Lombard league is headed by Monti[2]—& would make a difficulty of insertion in the Lombard Gazettes—once published in the Pisan—it will find its way through Italy—by translation or reply.——So Lauderdale has been telling a story!—I suppose this is my reward for presenting him at Countess Benzone's—& shewing him—what attention I could.——Which "piece" does he mean?—since last year I have run the Gauntlet;—is it the Tarruscelli—the Da Mosti—the Spineda—the Lotti—the Rizzato—the Eleanora—the Carlotta—the Giulietta—the Alvisi—the Zambieri—The Eleanora da Bezzi—(who was the King of Naples' Gioaschino's mistress—at least one of them) the Theresina of Mazzurati—the Glettenheimer—& her Sister—the Luigia & her mother—the Fornaretta—the Santa—the

---

1. Refers to the British slang sexual pun on "a dry Bob" (line 24); *dedication*: in the Dedication to *Don Juan*, Byron subjects Castlereagh, the powerful foreign secretary, and Robert Southey, the poet laureate, to humiliating invective. As the first edition of the poem was anonymous, Byron withdrew the Dedication, "for I won't be shabby—& attack Southey under Cloud of night" (*BLJ* 6:127).
2. Vicenzo Monti, Italian poet.

Caligari—the Portiera [Vedova?]—the Bolognese figurante—the Tentora and her sister—cum multis aliis?—some of them are Countesses—& some of them Cobblers wives—some noble—some middling—some low—& all whores—which does the damned old "Ladro—& porco fottuto"[3] mean?—I have had them all & thrice as many to boot since 1817—Since *he* tells a story about me—I will tell one about him;—when he landed at the *Custom house* from *Corfu*—he called for *"Post horses—directly"*—he was told that there were no horses except mine nearer than the Lido—unless he wished for the four bronze Coursers of St. Mark[4]—which were at his Service.—

I am yrs. ever—

Let me have H's Election immediately—I mention it *last* as being what I was least likely to forget.— —

P.S.—Whatever Brain-money—you get on my account from Murray—pray remit me—I will never consent to pay away what I *earn*—that is *mine*—& what I get by my brains—I will spend on my b— —ks—as long as I have a tester or a testicle remaining.—I shall not live long—& for that Reason—I must live while I can—so—let him disburse—& me receive—"for the Night cometh."— —If I had but had twenty thousand a year I should not have been living now—but all men are not born with a silver or Gold Spoon in their mouths.— —My balance—also—my balance—& a Copyright—I have another Canto—too—ready—& then there will be my half year in June—recollect—*I* care for nothing but "monies".—January 20th. 1819.—You say nothing of Mazeppa[5]—did it arrive—with one other—besides that you mention?— —

To John Murray

Venice April 6 1819

Dear Sir—The Second Canto of Don Juan was sent on Saturday last by post in 4 packets—two of 4—& two of three sheets each—containing in all two hundred & seventeen stanzas octave measure.—But I will permit no curtailments except those mentioned about Castlereagh & the two *"Bobs"* in the introduction.[1]—You sha'n't make *Canticles* of my Cantos. The poem will please if it is lively—if it is stupid it will fail—but I will have none of your damned cutting & slashing.—If you please you may publish *anonymously*[;] it will perhaps be better;—but I will battle my way against them all—like a Porcupine.—So you and Mr. Foscolo &c. want me to undertake what you call a "great work" an Epic poem I suppose or some such pyramid.—I'll try no such thing—I hate tasks—and then "seven or eight years!" God send us all well this day three months—let alone years—if one's years can't be better employed than in sweating poesy—a man had better be a ditcher.—And works too!—is Childe Harold nothing? you have so many *"divine"* poems, is it nothing to have written a *Human* one? without any of your worn out machinery.—Why—man—I could have spun the

---

3. Italian insult, literally "thief—fucked-up swine."
4. The famous four bronze horses at the San Marco Basilica; *Lido*: the island beach of Venice.
5. Narrative poem by Byron, published June 28, 1819.
1. See note 1 to previous letter.

thought of the four cantos of that poem into twenty—had I wanted to book-make—& it's passion into as many modern tragedies—since you want *length* you shall have enough of *Juan* for I'll make 50 cantos.—And Foscolo too! why does *he* not do something more than the letters of Ortis—and a tragedy—and pamphlets—he has good fifteen years more at his command than I have—what has he done all that time?—proved his Genius doubtless—but not fixed it's fame—nor done his utmost.—Besides I mean to write my best work in *Italian*—& it will take me nine years more thoroughly to master the language—& then if my fancy exists & I exist too—I will try what I *can* do really.—As to the Estimation of the English which you talk of, let them calculate what it is worth—before they insult me with their insolent condescension.—I have not written for their pleasure;—if they are pleased—it is that they chose to be so,—I have never flattered their opinions—nor their pride—nor will I.—Neither will I make "Ladies books" "al dilettar le femine e la plebe"—I have written from the fullness of my mind, from passion—from impulse—from many motives—but not for their "sweet voices."—I know the precise worth of popular applause—for few Scribblers have had more of it—and if I chose to swerve into their paths—I could retain it or resume it—or increase it—but I neither love ye—nor fear ye—and though I buy with ye—and sell with ye—and talk with ye—I will neither eat with ye—drink with ye—nor pray with ye.[2]—They made me without my search a species of popular Idol—they—without reason or judgement beyond the caprice of their Good pleasure—threw down the Image from it's pedestal—it was not broken with the fall—and they would it seems again replace it—but they shall not. You ask about my health—about the beginning of the year—I was in a state of great exhaustion—attended by such debility of Stomach—that nothing remained upon it—and I was obliged to reform my "way of life" which was conducting me from the "yellow leaf" to the Ground with all deliberate speed.—I am better in health and morals—and very much yrs. ever,

[scrawl]

P.S.—Tell Mrs. Leigh I never had "my Sashes" and I want some tooth-powder—the red—by all or any means.—

To John Cam Hobhouse

Venice April 6. 1819

My dear Hobhouse—I have not derived from the Scriptures of Rochfou-cault that consolation which I expected "in the misfortunes of our best friends".[1]— —I had much at heart your gaining the Election[2]—but from "the filthy puddle" into which your Patriotism had run you—I had like Croaker my bodings but like old "Currycomb" you make so "handsome a Corpse"[3]—that my wailing is changed into admiration.—With the Burdet-tites divided—and the Whigs & Tories united—what else could be

---

2. *Merchant of Venice* 1.3.31–32.
1. Referring to the well-known maxim of La Rochefoucauld (1613–1680), "There is something in the misfortunes of our best friends which does not displease us."
2. Hobhouse ran for a seat in the House of Commons but lost to George Lamb, brother-in-law of Byron's former mistress, Lady Caroline Lamb.
3. *The Good-Natured Man* (end of first act), by Oliver Goldsmith (1730?–1774).

expected? If I had guessed at your *opponent*[4]—I would have made one among you Certes—and have f— —d Caroline Lamb out of her "two hundred votes" although at the expence of a testicle.— —I think I could have neutralized her zeal with a little management—but alas! who could have thought of that Cuckoldy family's ⟨sitting⟩ *standing* for a *member*—I suppose it is the first time that George Lamb ever *stood* for any thing—& William with his "Corni Cazzo da Seno!" (as we Venetians say—it means— Penis *in earnest*—a sad way of swearing) but that you who know them should have to con*cur* with such dogs—well—did I ever—no I never &c. &c. &c.— —I have sent my second Canto—but I will have no gelding.— — Murray has my order of the day.—Douglas Kinnaird with more than usual politeness writes me vivaciously that Hanson or I willed the *three per cents* instead of the five—as if I could prefer *three* to *five* per Cent!—death & fiends!—and then *he* lifts up his leg against the publication of Don Juan— et "tu *Brute*"[5] (the *e mute* recollect) I shall certainly hitch our dear friend into some d— —d story or other—"my dear Mr. Sneer—Mr. Sneer—my dear"— —I must write again in a few days—it being now past four in the morning—it is Passion week—& rather dull.—I am dull too for I have fallen in love with a Romagnuola Countess[6] from Ravenna—who is nineteen years old & has a Count of fifty—whom She seems disposed to qualify the first year of marriage being just over.—I knew her a little last year at her starting, but they always wait a year—at least generally.—I met her first at the Albrizzi's, and this Spring at the Benzone's—and I have hopes Sir— hopes—but She wants me to come to Ravenna—& then to Bologna—now this would be all very well for certainties—but for mere hopes—if She should plant[7] me—and I should make a "fiasco" never could I show my face on the Piazza.— —It is nothing that Money can do—for the Conte is awfully rich—& would be so even in England—but he is fifty and odd—has had two wives & children before this his third—(a pretty fair-haired Girl last year out of a Convent—now making her second tour of the Venetian Conversazioni—) and does not seem so jealous this year as he did last— when he stuck close to her side even at the Governor's.— —She is pretty— but has no tact—answers aloud—when she should whisper—talks of age to old ladies who want to pass for young—and this blessed night horrified a correct company at the Benzona's—by calling out to me "Mio Byron" in an audible key during a dead Silence of pause in the other prattlers, who stared & whispered [to] their respective Serventi.—One of her preliminaries is that I must never leave Italy;—I have no desire to leave it—but I should not like to be frittered down into a regular Cicisbeo[8]—What shall I do! I am in love—and tired of promiscuous concubinage—& have now an opportunity of settling for life.—

[ever yours]

·   ·   ·

4. Caroline Lamb campaigned for her brother-in-law.
5. *Julius Caesar* 3.1.76.
6. Teresa Guiccioli.
7. Abandon (from the Italian *piantare*).
8. Gigolo, kept man.

To Douglas Kinnaird

Venice April 24th. 1819

Dear Douglas—

. . . —Damn *"the Vampire,"*[1]—what do I know of Vampires? it must be some bookselling imposture—contradict it in a solemn paragraph.—I sent off on April 3rd. the 2nd. Canto of "Don Juan" addressed to Murray—I hope it is arrived—by the Lord! it is a Capo d'Opera—so "full of pastime and prodigality"—but you shan't decimate nor mutilate—no—"rather than that come Critics into the list—and champion me to the uttermost."—Nor you nor that rugged rhinoceros Murray have ever told me in answer to fifty times the question—if he ever received the additions to Canto *first* entitled "Julia's letter" and also some four stanzas for the beginning.—I have fallen in love within the last month with a Romagnuola Countess from Ravenna—the Spouse of a year of Count Guiccioli—who is sixty—the Girl twenty—he has eighty thousand ducats of rent—and has had two wives before—but he is Sixty—he is the first of Ravenna Nobles—but he is sixty—She is fair as Sunrise—and warm as Noon—we had but ten days—to manage all our little matters in beginning middle and end. & we managed them;—and I have done my duty—with the proper consummation.—But She is young—and was not content with what she had done—unless it was to be turned to the advantage of the public—and so She made an eclat which rather astonished even the Venetians—and electrified the Conversazioni of the Benzone—the Albrizzi—& the Michelli—and made her ⟨Lord⟩ husband look embarrassed.—They have been gone back to Ravenna—some time—but they return in the Winter.—She is the queerest woman I ever met with—for in general they cost one something in one way or other—whereas by an odd combination of circumstances—I have proved an expence to HER—which is not my custom,—but an accident—however it don't matter.—She is a sort of an Italian Caroline Lamb, except that She is much prettier, and not so savage.—But She has the same red-hot head—the same noble dis*dain* of public opinion—with the superstructure of all that Italy can add to such natural dispositions.—To be sure they may go much further here with impunity—as her husband's rank ensured their reception at all societies including the Court—and as it was her first outbreak since Marriage—the Sympathizing world was liberal.—She is also of the Ravenna noblesse—educated in a convent—sacrifice to Wealth—filial duty and all that.—I am damnably in love—but they are gone—gone—for many months—and nothing but Hope—keeps me alive seriously.

yrs. [scrawl]

---

1. *The Vampyre,* by Byron's doctor, John William Polidori, which he based on the tale Byron began at the Villa Diodati in 1816; published anonymously in 1819, it was widely believed to have been written by Byron.

To Teresa Guiccioli[1]

Venice, April 25th, 1819

My Love,—I hope you have received my letter of the 22nd, addressed to the person in Ravenna of whom you told me, before leaving Venice. You scold me for not having written to you in the country—but—how could I? My sweetest treasure, you gave me no other address but that of Ravenna. If you knew how great is the love I feel for you, you would not believe me capable of forgetting you for a single instant; you must become better acquainted with me—perhaps one day you will know that although I do not deserve you—I do indeed love you.

You want to know whom I most enjoy seeing, since you have gone away, who makes me tremble and feel—not what you alone can arouse in my soul—but something like it? Well, I will tell you—it is the *old porter* whom Fanny used to send with your notes when you were in Venice—and who now brings your letters—still dear, but not so dear as those which brought the hope of seeing you that same day at the usual time. My Teresa, where are you? Everything here reminds me of you—everything is the same, but you are not here and I still am. In separation the one who goes away suffers less than the one who stays behind. The distraction of the journey, the change of scene, the landscape, the movement, perhaps even the separation, distracts the mind and lightens the heart. But the one who stays behind is surrounded by the same things; tomorrow is like yesterday—while only She is lacking who made him forget that a tomorrow would ever come. When I go to the Conversazione, I give myself up to Tedium, too happy to suffer ennui rather than grief. I see the same faces—hear the same voices—but no longer dare to look towards the sofa where I shall not see *you* any more—but instead some old crone who might be Calumny personified. I hear, without the slightest emotion, the opening of that door which I used to watch with so much anxiety when I was there before you, hoping to see you come in. I will not speak of *much dearer* places still, for *there* I shall not go—*until* you return. I have no other pleasure than thinking of you, but I do not see how I could see again the places where we have been together—especially those most consecrated to our love—without dying of grief.

Fanny is now in Treviso—and God knows when I shall have any more letters from you—but meanwhile I have received three; you must by now have arrived in Ravenna—I long to hear of your arrival; my fate depends upon your decision. Fanny will be back in a few days—but tomorrow I shall send her a note by a friend's hand to ask her not to forget to send me your news, if she receives any letters before returning to Venice.

My Treasure—my life has become most monotonous and sad; neither books, nor music, nor *Horses* (rare things in Venice—but you know that mine are at the Lido)—nor dogs—give me any pleasure; the society of women does not attract me; I won't speak of the society of men, for that I have always despised. For some years I have been trying systematically to avoid strong passions, having suffered too much from the tyranny of Love.

---

1. Byron wrote this letter in Italian; like most of his letters to her, it was translated by Iris Origo (*The Last Attachment*).

Never to feel admiration[2]—and to enjoy myself without giving too much importance to the enjoyment in itself—to feel indifference toward human affairs—contempt for many, but hatred for none,—this was the basis of my philosophy. I did not mean to love any more, nor did I hope to receive Love. You have put to flight all my resolutions—now I am all yours—I will become what you wish—perhaps happy in your love, but never at peace again. You should not have re-awakened my heart—for (at least in my own country) my love has been fatal to those I love—and to myself. But these reflections come too late. You have been mine—and whatever the outcome—I am, and eternally shall be, entirely yours. I kiss you a thousand and a thousand times—but—

> What does it profit you, my heart to be beloved?
> What good to me to have so dear a lover?
> Why should a cruel fate
> Separate those whom love has once united?[3]

Love me—as always your tender and faithful,

B

To John Murray

Venice. May 15th. 1819

Dear Sir—I have received & return by this post under cover—the first proof of "Don Juan."—Before the second can arrive it is probable that I may have left Venice—and the length of my absence is so uncertain—that you had better proceed to the publication without boring me with more proofs—I sent by last post an addition—and a new copy of "Julia's letter," perceiving or supposing the former one in Winter did not arrive.—Mr. Hobhouse is at it again about indelicacy—there is *no indelicacy*—if he wants *that*, let him read Swift—his great Idol—but his Imagination must be a dunghill with a Viper's nest in the middle—to engender such a supposition about this poem.—For my part I think you are all crazed.—What does he mean about "G—d damn"—there is "*damn*" to be sure—but no "G—d" whatever.[1]—And as to what he calls "a p—ss bucket"—it is nothing but simple water—as I am a Sinner—pray tell him so—& request him not "to put me in a phrenzy," as Sir Anthony Absolute says—"though he was not the indulgent father that I am."[2]—I have got yr. extract, & the "Vampire". I need not say it is *not mine*—there is a rule to go by—you are my publisher (till we quarrel) and what is not published by you is not written by me.—The Story of Shelley's agitation is true[3]—I can't tell what seized him—for he don't want courage. He was once with me in a Gale of Wind in a small boat right under the rocks

---

2. A reference to the "Nil admirari" dictum of Horace ("To admire nothing is perhaps the one and only thing . . . that can make and keep a man happy," *Epistles* 6.1); see *Don Juan* V, stanzas 100–01, and XIII, stanza 35 (pp. 540, 613).

3. Guarini, *Il Pastor Fido* 3.4.

1. Probably a reference to Canto I, lines 111–12 (p. 388).

2. Richard Brinsley Sheridan (1751–1816), *The Rivals* 2.1.

3. Marchand's note reads: "Dr. Polidori in the Preface to *The Vampyre* told of an evening at the Villa Diodati when Shelley was so agitated while ghost stories were being told that he rushed out of the room and later confessed that his imagination had been so stirred that he conceived that one of the ladies (Mary Godwin) had eyes in her breasts" (*BLJ* 6:125).

between Meillerie & St. Gingo—we were five in the boat—a servant—two boatmen—& ourselves. The Sail was mismanaged & the boat was filling fast—he can't swim.—I stripped off my coat—made him strip off his—& take hold of an oar—telling him that I thought (being myself an expert swimmer) I could save him if he would not struggle when I took hold of him—unless we got smashed against the rocks which were high & sharp with an awkward Surf on them at that minute;—we were then about a hundred yards from shore—and the boat in peril.—He answered me with the greatest coolness—"that he had no notion of being saved—& that I would have enough to do to save myself, and begged not to trouble me".—Luckily the boat righted & baling [sic] we got round a point into St. Gingo—where the Inhabitants came down and embraced the boatmen on their escape—the Wind having been high enough to tear up some huge trees from the Alps above us as we saw next day.—And yet the same Shelley who was as cool as it was possible to be in such circumstances—(of which I am no judge myself as the chance of swimming naturally gives self-possession when near shore) certainly had the fit of phantasy which P[olidori] describes—though *not exactly* as he describes it. The story of the agreement to write the Ghost-books is true—but the ladies are *not Sisters*—one is Godwin's daughter by Mary Wolstonecraft—and the other the *present* Mrs. Godwin's daughter by a former husband. So much for Scoundrel Southey's Story of "*incest*"—neither was there *any promiscuous intercourse* whatever—both are an invention of the execrable villain Southey—whom I will term so as publicly as he deserves.—Mary Godwin (now Mrs. Shelley) wrote "Frankenstein"—which you have reviewed thinking it Shelley's—methinks it is a wonderful work for a Girl of nineteen—*not* nineteen indeed—at that time.—I enclose you the beginning of mine—by which you will see how far it resembles Mr. Colburn's publication.—If you choose to publish it in the Edinburgh Magazine (*Wilsons & Blackwoods*) you may—*stating why*, & with such explanatory proem as you please.—I never went on with it—as you will perceive by the date.—I began it in an old account-book of Miss Milbanke's which I kept because it contains the word "*Household*" written by her twice on the inside blank page of the Covers—being the only two Scraps I have in the world in her writing, except her name to the deed of Separation—Her letters I sent back—except those of the quarrelling correspondence—and those being documents are placed in possession of a third person (Mr. Hobhouse) with copies of several of my own,—so that I have no kind of memorial whatever of her but these *two* words—and her actions. I have torn the leaves containing the part of the tale out of the book & enclose them with this sheet.—Next week—I set out for Romagna—at least in all probability. . . .

. . .

I am yrs. very truly
B

To Augusta Leigh

Venice [Monday] May 17th. 1819
My dearest Love—I have been negligent in not writing, but what can I say[.] Three years absence—& the total change of scene and habit make

such a difference—that we have now nothing in common but our affections & our relationship.—

But I have never ceased nor can cease to feel for a moment that perfect & boundless attachment which bound & binds me to you—which renders me utterly incapable of *real* love for any other human being—what could they be to me after *you*? My own XXXX [short word crossed out] we may have been very wrong—but I repent of nothing except that cursed marriage—& your refusing to continue to love me as you had loved me—I can neither forget nor *quite forgive* you for that precious piece of reformation.—but I can never be other than I have been—and whenever I love anything it is because it reminds me in some way or other of yourself—for instance I not long ago attached myself to a Venetian for no earthly reason (although a pretty woman) but because she was called XXXX [short word crossed out] and she often remarked (without knowing the reason) how fond I was of the name.—It is heart-breaking to think of our long Separation—and I am sure more than punishment enough for all our sins—Dante is more humane in his "Hell" for he places his unfortunate lovers (Francesca of Rimini & Paolo whose case fell a good deal short of *ours*—though sufficiently naughty) in company—and though they suffer—it is at least together.—If ever I return to England—it will be to see you—and recollect that in all time—& place—and feelings—I have never ceased to be the same to you in heart—Circumstances may have ruffled my manner—& hardened my spirit—you may have seen me harsh & exasperated with all things around me; grieved & tortured with *your new resolution*,—& the soon after persecution of that infamous fiend who drove me from my Country & conspired against my life—by endeavouring to deprive me of all that could render it precious—but remember that even then *you* were the sole object that cost me a tear? and *what tears!* do you remember *our* parting? I have not spirits now to write to you upon other subjects—I am well in health—and have no cause of grief but the reflection that we are not together—When you write to me speak to me of yourself—& say that you love me—never mind common-place people & topics—which can be in no degree interesting—to me who see nothing in England but the country which holds *you*—or around it but the sea which divides us.—They say absence destroys weak passions—& confirms strong ones—Alas! *mine* for you is the union of all passions & of all affections—Has strengthened itself but will destroy me—I do not speak of *physical* destruction—for I have endured & can endure much—but of the annihilation of all thoughts feelings or hopes—which have not more or less a reference to you & to *our recollections*—

Ever dearest
[Signature erased]

To John Murray

Venice, May 18, 1819

Dear Sir—Yesterday I wrote to Mr. Hobhouse and returned the proof under cover to you. Tell Mr. Hobhouse that in the Ferrara story I told him, the phrase was *Vi riveresco Signor Cognato* and *not Cognato mio* as I stated yesterday by mistake. I write to you in haste and at past two in the morning—having besides had an accident. In going, about an hour and a half ago, to a rendezvous with a Venetian Girl (unmarried and the daughter of one of their nobles), I tumbled into the Grand Canal—and not choosing to miss my appointment by the delays of changing—I have been perched in a balcony with my wet clothes on ever since—till this minute that on my return I have slipped into my dressing gown. My foot slipped in getting into my Gondola to set out (owing to the cursed slippery steps of their palaces) and in I flounced like a Carp—and went dripping like a Triton to my Sea-nymph—and had to scramble up to a Grated window

> "Fenced with iron within and without
> Lest the Lover get in, or the Lady get out."

She is a very dear friend of mine—and I have undergone some trouble on her account—for last winter the truculent tyrant her flinty-hearted father—having been informed by an infernal German Countess Vorsperg (their next neighbour) of our meetings—they sent a priest to me—and a Commissary of police—and they locked the Girl up—and gave her prayers and bread and water—and our connection was cut off for some time—but the father hath lately been laid up—and the brother is at Milan—and the mother falls asleep—and the Servants are naturally on the wrong side of the question—and there is no Moon at Midnight just now—so that we have lately been able to recommence;—the fair one is eighteen—her name Angelina—the family name of course I don't tell you. She proposed to me to divorce my mathematical wife—and I told her that in England we can't divorce except for *female* infidelity—"and pray, (said she), how do you know what she may have been doing these last three years?"—I answered *that* I could not tell—but that the status of Cuckoldom was not quite so flourishing in Great Britain as with us here.—But—She said—"can't you get rid of her?"—"not more than is done already" (I answered)—"you would not have me *poison her?*"—would you believe it? She made me *no answer*—is not that a true and odd national trait?—it spoke more than a thousand words—and yet this is a little—pretty—sweet-tempered,—quiet, feminine being as ever you saw—but the Passions of a Sunny Soil are paramount to all other considerations;—an unmarried Girl naturally wishes to be married—if she can marry & love at the same time it is well—but at any rate She must love;—I am not sure that my pretty paramour was herself fully aware of the inference to be drawn from her dead Silence—but even the unconsciousness of the latent idea was striking to an Observer of the Passions—and I never strike out a thought of another's or of my own—without trying to trace it to it's Source. . . .

. . .

very truly yrs. ever
B

To Augusta Leigh

Ravenna. July 26th. 1819

My dearest Augusta—I am at too great a distance to scold you—but I *will* ask you—whether *your* letter of the *1st*. July *is an answer* to the letter I wrote you before I quitted Venice?—What? is it come to *this*?—Have you no memory? or no heart?—You *had* both—and I *have* both—at least for *you*.— —I write this presuming that you received *that* letter—is it that you fear? do not be afraid of the post—the World has it's own affairs without thinking of *ours* and you may write safely—if you do—address as usual to *Venice*.—My house is not in St. Marc's but on the Grand Canal—within sight of the Rialto Bridge.— —I do not like at all this pain in your side and always think of your mother's constitution—you must always be to me the first consideration in the World.—Shall I come to *you*?—or would a warm climate do you good?—if so say the word—and I will provide you & your whole family (including that precious baggage your Husband) with the means of making an agreeable journey—you need not fear about *me*—I am much altered—and should be little trouble to you—nor would I give you more of my company than you like.— —I confess after three years and a half—and *such years*! and *such a year* as preceded those three years! it would be a relief to see you again—and if it would be so to you—I will come to you.— —Pray—answer me—and recollect that I will do as you like in everything—even to returning to England—which is *not* the pleasantest of residences were *you* out of it.— —I write from Ravenna—I came here on account of a Countess Guiccioli—a Girl of Twenty married to a very rich old man of Sixty—about a year ago;—with her last Winter I had a *liaison* according to the good old Italian custom—she miscarried in May—and sent for me here—and here I have been these two months.— She is pretty—a great Coquette—extremely vain—excessively affected— clever enough—without the smallest principle—with a good deal of imagination and some passion;—She had set her heart on carrying me off from Venice out of vanity—and succeeded—and having made herself the subject of general conversation has greatly contributed to her recovery.— Her husband is one of the richest Nobles of Ravenna—threescore years of age—this is his third wife.— —You may suppose what *esteem* I entertain for *her*—perhaps it is about equal on both sides.—I have my saddle-horses here and there is good riding in the forest—with these—and my carriage which is here also—and the Sea—and my books—and the lady—the time passes—I am very fond of riding and always *was out* of England—but I hate your Hyde Park—and your turnpike roads—& must have forests— downs—or deserts to expatiate in—I detest *knowing* the road—one is to go,—and being interrupted by your damned fingerposts, or a blackguard roaring for twopence at a turnpike.— —I send you a sonnet which this faithful Lady had made for the nuptials of one of her relations in which she swears the most *alarming constancey* to her husband—is not this good? you may suppose my *face* when she showed it to me—I could not help laughing—one of *our* laughs.— —All this is very absurd—but you see that I have good morals at bottom.— —She is an Equestrian too—but a bore in her rides—for she can't guide her horse—and he runs after mine— and tries to bite him—and then she begins screaming in a high hat and Sky-blue habit—making a most absurd figure—and embarrassing me and both our grooms—who have the devil's own work to keep her from tumbling—or having her clothes torn off by the trees and thickets of the Pine forest.— —I fell a little in love with her intimate friend—a certain Geltruda—(that is *Gertrude*) who is very young & seems very well disposed to be perfidious—but alas!—*her* husband is jealous—and the G. also detected me in an illicit squeezing of hands, the consequence of which was that the friend was whisked off to Bologna for a few days—and since her return I have never been able to see her but twice—with a dragon of a mother in law—and a barbarous husband by her side—besides my own dear precious *Amica*—who hates all flirting but her own.—But I have a Priest who befriends me—and the Gertrude says a good deal with her great black eyes, so that perhaps—but Alas! I mean to give up these things altogether.— —I have now given you some account of my present state— the Guide-book will tell you about Ravenna—I can't tell how long or short may be my stay—write to me—love me—as ever

yrs. most affectly.
B

P.S.—*This* affair is *not* in the least expensive—being all in the wealthy line—but troublesome—for the lady is imperious—and exigeante— however there are hopes that we may quarrel—when we do you shall hear [In margin of printed sonnet enclosed]
Ask Hobhouse to translate this to you—and tell him the reason.— —

To John Murray

Ravenna. August 1st. 1819

Address yr. answer to Venice however

Dear Sir—
. . . You have bought Harlow's drawings of Margarita and me rather dear methinks—but since you desire the story of Margarita Cogni—you shall be told it—though it may be lengthy.— —Her face is of the fine Venetian cast of the old Time—and her figure though perhaps too tall not less fine— taken altogether in the national dress.— —In the summer of 1817, Hob-house and myself were sauntering on horseback along the Brenta[1] one evening—when amongst a group of peasants we remarked two girls as the prettiest we had seen for some time.—About this period there had been great distress in the country—and I had a little relieved some of the people.—Generosity makes a great figure at very little cost in Venetian livres—and mine had probably been exaggerated—as an Englishman's— — Whether they remarked us looking at them or no—I know not—but one of them called out to me in Venetian—"Why do not you who relieve others— think of us also?"—I turned round and answered her—"Cara—tu sei troppo bella e giovane per aver' bisogno del' soccorso mio"[2]—she answered—[" if you saw my hut and my food—you would not say so["]— All this passed half jestingly—and I saw no more of her for some days—A few evenings after—we met with these two girls again—and they addressed us more seriously—assuring us of the truth of their statement.—They were cousins—Margarita married—the other single.—As I doubted still of the circumstances—I took the business up in a different light—and made an appointment with them for the next evening.—Hobhouse had taken a fancy to the single lady—who was much shorter—in stature—but a very pretty girl also.— —They came attended by a third woman—who was cursedly in

1. River near Venice, in the vicinity of Byron's home during the summer of 1817.
2. "Dear—you are too beautiful and young to need my help."

the way—and Hobhouse's charmer took fright (I don't mean at Hobhouse but at not being married—for here no woman will do anything under adultery), and flew off—and mine made some bother—at the propositions—and wished to consider of them.—I told her "if you really are in want I will relieve you without any conditions whatever—and you may make love with me or no just as you please—*that* shall make no difference—but if you are not in absolute necessity—this is naturally a rendezvous—and I presumed that you understood this—when you made the appointment".——She said that she had no objection to make love with me—as she was married—and all married women did it—but that her husband (a baker) was somewhat ferocious—and would do her a mischief.—In short—in a few evenings we arranged our affairs—and for two years—in the course of which I had ⟨almost two⟩ more women than I can count or recount—she was the only one who preserved over me an ascendancy—which was often disputed & never impaired.—As she herself used to say publicly—"It don't matter—he may have five hundred—but he will always come back to me".——The reasons of this were firstly—her person—very dark—tall—the Venetian face—very fine black eyes—and certain other qualities which need not be mentioned.—She was two & twenty years old—and never having had children—had not spoilt her figure—nor *anything else*—which is I assure you—a great desideration in a hot climate where they grow relaxed and doughy and *flumpity* in a short time after breeding.——She was besides a thorough Venetian in her dialect—in her thoughts—in her countenance—in every thing—with all their naïveté and Pantaloon humour.—Besides she could neither read nor write—and could not plague me with letters—except twice that she paid sixpence to a public scribe under the piazza—to make a letter for her—upon some occasion when I was ill and could not see her.——In other respects she was somewhat fierce and "prepotente" that is—overbearing—and used to walk in whenever it suited her—with no very great regard to time, place, nor persons—and if she found any women in her way she knocked them down.—When I first knew her I was in "relazione" (liaison) with la Signora Segati—who was silly enough one evening at Dolo—accompanied by some of her female friends—to threaten her—for the Gossips of the Villeggiatura—had already found out by the neighing of my horse one evening—that I used to "ride late in the night" to meet the Fornarina[3]——Margarita threw back her veil (fazziolo) and replied in very explicit Venetian—"*You* are *not* his *wife*: I am *not* his *wife*—*you* are his Donna—and *I* am his *donna*—*your* husband is a cuckold—and mine is another;—for the rest, what *right* have you to reproach me?—if he prefers what is mine—to what is yours—is it my fault? if you wish to secure him—tie him to your petticoat-string—but do not think to speak to me without a reply because you happen to be richer than I am."——Having delivered this pretty piece of eloquence (which I translate as it was related to me by a byestander) she went on her way—leaving a numerous audience with Madame Segati—to ponder at her leisure on the dialogue between them.—When I came to Venice for the Winter she followed:—I never had any regular *liaison* with her—but whenever she came I never allowed any other connection to interfere with her—and as she found herself out to be

3. The little baker girl, or (here) baker's wife.

a favourite she came pretty often.—But She had inordinate Self-love—and was not tolerant of other women—except of the Segati—who was as she said my regular "Amica"—so that I being at that time somewhat promiscuous—there was great confusion—and demolition of head dresses and handkerchiefs—and sometimes my servants in "redding the fray" between her and other feminine persons—received more knocks than acknowledgements for their peaceful endeavours.— —At the "Cavalchina" the masqued ball on the last night of the Carnival—where all the World goes—she snatched off the mask of Madame Contarini—a lady noble by birth—and decent in conduct—for no other reason but because she happened to be leaning on my arm.—You may suppose what a cursed noise this made—but this is only one of her pranks.—At last she quarrelled with her husband—and one evening ran away to my house.—I told her this would not do—she said she would lie in the street but not go back to him—that he beat her (the gentle tigress) spent her money—and scandalously neglected his Oven. As it was Midnight—I let her stay—and next day there was no moving her at all.— —Her husband came roaring & crying—& entreating her to come back, *not* She!—He then applied to the Police—and they applied to me—I told them and her husband to *take* her—I did not want her—she had come and I could not fling her out of the window—but they might conduct her through that or the door if they chose it— —She went before the Commissary—but was obliged to return with that "becco Ettico" (consumptive cuckold), as she called the *poor* man who had a Ptisick.—In a few days she ran away again.—After a precious piece of work she fixed herself in my house—really & truly without my consent—but owing to my indolence—and not being able to keep my countenance—for if I began in a rage she always finished by making me laugh with some Venetian pantaloonery or other—and the Gipsy knew this well enough—as well as her other powers of persuasion—and exerted them with the usual tact and success of all She-things—high and low—they are all alike for that.—Madame Benzone also took her under her protection—and then her head turned.— She was always in extremes either crying or laughing—and so fierce when angered that she was the terror of men women and children—for she had the strength of an Amazon with the temper of Medea. She was a fine animal—but quite untameable. *I* was the only person that could at all keep her in any order—and when she saw me really angry—(which they tell me is rather a savage sight), she subsided.—But she had a thousand fooleries— in her fazziolo—the dress of the lower orders—she looked beautiful—but alas! she longed for a hat and feathers and all I could say or do (and I said much) could not prevent this travestie.—I put the first into the fire—but I got tired of burning them before she did of buying them—so that she made herself a figure—for they did not at all become her.—Then she would have her gowns with a *tail*—like a lady forsooth—nothing would serve her—but "l'abito colla *coua*", or *cua*, (that is the Venetian for "la *Coda*" the tail or train) and as her cursed pronunciation of the word made me laugh—there was an end of all controversy—and she dragged this diabolical tail after her every where.— —In the mean time she beat the women—and stopped my letters.—I found her one day pondering over one—she used to try to find out by their shape whether they were feminine or no—and she used to lament her ignorance—and actually studied her Alphabet—on purpose (as she declared) to open all letters addressed to me and read their contents.— —I must not omit to do justice to her housekeeping qualities— after she came into my house as "donna di governo" the expences were reduced to less than half—and every body did their duty better—the apartments were kept in order—and every thing and every body else except herself.— —That she had a sufficient regard for me in her wild way I had many reasons to believe—I will mention one.— —In the autumn one day going to the Lido with my Gondoliers—we were overtaken by a heavy Squall and the Gondola put in peril—hats blown away—boat filling—oar lost—tumbling sea—thunder—rain in torrents—night coming—& wind increasing.—On our return—after a tight struggle: I found her on the open steps of the Mocenigo palace on the Grand Canal—with her great black eyes flashing though her tears and the long dark hair which was streaming drenched with rain over her brows & breast;—she was perfectly exposed to the storm—and the wind blowing her hair & dress about her tall thin figure—and the lightning flashing round her—with the waves rolling at her feet—made her look like Medea alighted from her chariot—or the Sibyl of the tempest that was rolling around her—the only living thing within hail at that moment except ourselves.—On seeing me safe—she did not wait to greet me as might be expected—but calling out to me—"Ah! Can' della Madonna xe esto il tempo per andar' al' Lido?" (ah! Dog of the Virgin!—is this a time to go to Lido?) ran into the house—and solaced herself with scolding the boatmen for not foreseeing the "temporale".—I was told by the servants that she had only been prevented from coming in a boat to look after me—by the refusal of all the Gondoliers of the Canal to put out into the harbour in such a moment and that then she sate down on the steps in all the thickest of the Squall—and would neither be removed nor comforted. Her joy at seeing me again—was moderately mixed with ferocity— and gave me the idea of a tigress over her recovered Cubs.— —But her reign drew near a close.—She became quite ungovernable some months after—and a concurrence of complaints some true and many false—"a favourite has no friend"—determined me to part with her.—I told her quietly that she must return home—(she had acquired a sufficient provision for herself and mother, &c. in my service,) and She refused to quit the house.—I was firm—and she went—threatening knives and revenge.—I told her—that I had seen knives drawn before her time—and that if she chose to begin—there was a knife—and fork also at her service on the table and that intimidation would not do.—The next day while I was at dinner— she walked in, (having broke open a glass door that led from the hall below to the staircase by way of prologue) and advancing strait up to the table snatched the knife from my hand—cutting me slightly in the thumb in the operation.—Whether she meant to use this against herself or me I know not—probably against neither—but Fletcher seized her by the arms—and disarmed her.—I then called my boatmen—and desired them to get the Gondola ready and conduct her to her own house again—seeing carefully that she did herself no mischief by the way.—She seemed quite quiet and walked down stairs.—I resumed my dinner.—We heard a great noise—I went out—and met them on the staircase—carrying her up stairs.—She had thrown herself into the Canal.—That she intended to destroy herself I do not believe—but when we consider the fear women and men who can't swim have of deep or even of shallow water—(and the Venetians in particular though they live on the waves) and that it was also night—and dark—

& very cold—it shows that she had a devilish spirit of some sort within her.—They had got her out without much difficulty or damage except the salt water she had swallowed and the wetting she had undergone.—I foresaw her intention to refix herself, and sent for a Surgeon—enquiring how many hours it would require to restore her from her agitation, and he named the time.—I then said—"I give you that time—and more if you require it—but at the expiration of the prescribed period—if *She* does not leave the house—*I* will".— —All my people were consternated—they had always been frightened at her—and were now paralyzed—they wanted me to apply to the police—to guard myself—&c. &c.—like a pack of sniveling servile boobies as they were— —I did nothing of the kind—thinking that I might as well end that way as another—besides—I had been used to savage women and knew their ways.—I had her sent home quietly after her recovery—and never saw her since except twice at the opera—at a distance amongst the audience.—She made many attempts to return—but no more violent ones.—And this is the story of Margharita Cogni—as far as it belongs to me.—I forgot to mention that she was very devout—and would cross herself if she heard the prayer-time strike—sometimes—when that ceremony did not appear to be much in unison with what she was then about.—She was quick in reply—as for instance;—one day when she had made me very angry with beating somebody or other—I called her a *Cow* (*Cow* in Italian is a sad affront and tantamount to the feminine of dog in English) I called her "Vacca" she turned round—curtsied—and answered "Vacca *tua*—'Celenza" (i.e. Eccelenza) *your* Cow—please your Excellency.— In short—she was—as I said before—a very fine Animal—of considerable beauty and energy—with many good & several amusing qualities—but wild as a witch—and fierce as a demon.—She used to boast publicly of her ascendancy over me—contrasting it with that of other women—and assigning for it sundry reasons physical and moral which did more credit to her person than her modesty.— —True it was that they all tried to get her away—and no one succeeded—till her own absurdity helped them.—Whenever there was a competition, and sometimes—one would be shut in one room and one in another—to prevent battle—she had generally the preference.— —

yrs. very truly and affectly
B

P.S.—The Countess G[uiccioli] is much better than she was.—I sent you before leaving Venice—a letter containing the real original sketch—which gave rise to the "Vampire"[4]&c. did you get it?—

To John Murray

Bologna. August 12th. 1819

Dear Sir—

. . .

. . . Cut me up root and branch—quarter me in the Quarterly—send round my "disjecti membra poetae" like those of the Levite's Concubine—

---

4. See letters to Kinnaird of April 24, 1819 and note (p. 738) and to Murray of May 15, 1819 (p. 740).

make—if you will—a spectacle to men and angels—but don't ask me to alter for I can't—I am obstinate and lazy—and there's the truth.—But nevertheless—I will answer your friend C. V.[1] who objects to the quick succession of fun and gravity—as if in that case the gravity did not (in intention at least) heighten the fun.—His metaphor is that "we are never scorched and drenched at the same time!"—Blessings on his experience!—Ask him these questions about "scorching and drenching".—Did he never play at Cricket or walk a mile in hot weather?—did he never spill a dish of tea over his testicles in handing the cup to his charmer to the great shame of his nankeen breeches?—did he never swim in the sea at Noonday with the Sun in his eyes and on his head—which all the foam of ocean could not cool? did he never draw his foot out of a tub of too hot water damning his eyes & his valet's? did he never inject for a Gonorrhea?—or make water through an ulcerated Urethra?—was he ever in a Turkish bath—that marble paradise of sherbet and sodomy?—was he ever in a cauldron of boiling oil like St. John?—or in the sulphureous waves of hell? (where he ought to be for his "scorching and drenching at the same time") did he never tumble into a river or lake fishing—and sit in his wet cloathes in the boat—or on the bank afterwards "scorched and drenched" like a true sportsman?——"Oh for breath to utter"[2]——but make him my compliments—he is a clever fellow for all that—a very clever fellow.——You ask me for the plan of Donny Johnny—I *have* no plan—I *had* no plan—but I had or have materials—though if like Tony Lumpkin—I am "to be snubbed so when I am in spirits"[3] the poem will be naught—and the poet turn serious again.—If it don't take I will leave it off where it is with all due respect to the Public—but if continued it must be in my own way—you might as well make Hamlet (or Diggory)[4] "act mad" in a strait waistcoat—as trammel my buffoonery—if I am to be a buffoon—their gestures and my thoughts would only be pitiably absurd—and ludicrously constrained.—Why Man the Soul of such writing is it's licence?—at least the *liberty* of that *licence* if one likes—*not* that one should abuse it—it is like trial by Jury and Peerage—and the Habeas Corpus—a very fine thing—but chiefly in the *reversion*—because no one wishes to be tried for the mere pleasure of proving his possession of the privilege.——But a truce with these reflections;—you are too earnest and eager about a work never intended to be serious;—do you suppose that I could have any intention but to giggle and make giggle?—a playful satire with as little poetry as could be helped—was what I meant—and as to the indecency—do pray read in Boswell—what *Johnson* the sullen moralist—says of *Prior*[5] and Paulo Purgante——Will you get a favour done for me?—*you* can by your Government friends—Croker—Canning—or my old Schoolfellow Peel[6]—and I can't.—Here it is—will you ask them to appoint (*without salary or emolument*) a noble Italian (whom I will name afterwards) Consul or Vice Consul for Ravenna.—He is a man of very large property—noble too—but he wishes to have a British protection in case of

1. The reviewer was Francis Cohen.
2. *1 Henry IV* 2.5.227.
3. Echoing *She Stoops to Conquer* (act 2), by Oliver Goldsmith (1730?–1774).
4. In a contemporary farce, a stage-struck servant who offers to take the part of a madman.
5. Matthew Prior (1664–1721). Samuel Johnson said, "there is nothing in Prior that will excite to lewdness" (James Boswell, *Life of Johnson* [1791], 3:192).
6. Robert Peel (1788–1850), John Wilson Croker (1780–1857), George Canning (1770–1827). Canning and Peel became prime ministers in 1827 and 1841, respectively.

changes—Ravenna is near the Sea—he wants *no emolument* whatever;—
that his office might be useful—I know—as I lately sent off from Ravenna
to Trieste—a poor devil of an English Sailor—who had remained there sick
sorry and penniless (having been set ashore in 1814) from the want of any
accredited agent able or willing to help him homewards.—Will you get this
done?—it will be the greatest favour to me?—if you do—I will then send
his name and condition—subject of course to rejection if *not* approved—
when known.— —I know that in the Levant—you make consuls—and Vice
Consuls perpetually—of foreigners—this man is a Patrician and has twelve
thousand a year.—His motive is a British protection in case of new
Invasions.— —Don't you think Croker would do it for us? to be sure *my
interest* is rare!!—but perhaps a brother-wit in the Tory line might do a good
turn at the request of so harmless and long absent a Whig—particularly as
there is no *salary* nor *burthen* of any sort to be annexed to the office.— —
I can assure you I should look upon it as a great obligation—but Alas! that
very circumstance may very probably operate to the contrary—indeed it
ought.—But I have at least been an honest and an open enemy.— —
Amongst your many splendid Government Connections—could not you
think you? get our Bibulus[7] made a Consul?—Or make me one that I may
make him my Vice.—You may be assured that in case of accidents in Italy—
he would be no feeble adjunct—as you would think if you knew his
property.— — . . .

· · ·

yrs. [scrawl]

To John Cam Hobhouse

Bologna. August 23d. 1819

My dear Hobhouse—I have received a letter from Murray containing the
"British review's" eleventh article.[1]—Had you any conception of a man's
tumbling into such a trap as Roberts has done? why it is precisely what he
was wished to do.—I have enclosed an epistle for publication with a queer
signature (to Murray who should keep the anonymous still about D Juan)
in answer to Roberts—which pray approve if you can—it is written in an
evening & morning in haste—with ill health & worse nerves.—I am so
bilious—that I nearly lose my head—and so nervous that I cry for
nothing—at least today I burst into tears all alone by myself over a cistern
of Gold fishes—which are not pathetic animals.—I can assure you it is not
Mr. Roberts or any of his crew that can affect me;—but I have been
excited—and agitated and exhausted mentally and bodily all this summer—
till I really sometimes begin to think not only "that I shall die at top first"[2]—
but that the moment is not very remote.—I have had no particular cause
of grief—except the usual accompaniments of all unlawful passions;—I

---

7. Consul with Julius Caesar in 59 B.C.E.
1. The *British Review*, a periodical with Tory and Evangelical leanings, printed a review of *Don Juan*
   by William Roberts (1767–1849), who took seriously Byron's jesting line in Canto I, "I've bribed
   My Grandmother's Review—the British" (line 209). Byron's "Letter to the Editor of 'My Grand-
   mother's Review,'" signed "Wortley Clutterbuck," was printed in the first number of the *Liberal*
   (1822).
2. Suffering from deafness and aware of his incipient mental decay, Jonathan Swift (1667–1745)
   once remarked: "I shall be like that tree, I shall die from the top."

have to do with a woman rendered perfectly disinterested by her situation in life—and young and amiable and pretty—in short as good and at least as attractive as anything of the sex can be with all the advantages and disadvantages of being scarcely twenty years old—and only two out of her Romagnuolo Convent at Faenza.— —But I feel & I feel it bitterly—that a man should not consume his life at the side and on the bosom—of a woman—and a stranger—that even the recompense and it is much—is not enough—and that this Cisisbean[3] existence is to be condemned.—But I have neither the strength of mind to break my chain, nor the insensibility which would deaden it's weight.—I cannot tell what will become of me— to leave or to be left would at present drive me quite out of my senses—and yet to what have I conducted myself?—I have luckily or unluckily no ambition left—it would be better if I had—it would at least awake me—whereas at present I merely start in my sleep.— —I think I wrote to you last week— but really (Like Lord Grizzle)[4] cannot positively tell.—Why don't you write, pray do—never mind "Don Juan"—let him tumble—and let me too—like Jack and Gill.— —Write—and believe me—as long as I can keep my sanity

ever yrs. most truly & affectly.

B

To Douglas Kinnaird

Venice. Octr. 26th. 1818 [*1819*]

My dear Douglas—My late expenditure has arisen from living at a distance from Venice and being obliged to keep up two establishments, from frequent journeys—and buying some furniture and books as well as a horse or two—and not from any renewal of the EPICUREAN[1] system as you suspect. I have been faithful to my honest liaison with Countess Guiccioli— and I can assure you that *She* has never cost me directly or indirectly a sixpence—indeed the circumstances of herself and family render this no merit.—I never offered her but one present—a broach of brilliants—and she sent it back to me with her *own hair* in it (I shall *not* say of *what part* but *that* is an Italian custom) and a note to say that she was not in the habit of receiving presents of that value—but hoped that I would not consider her sending it back as an affront—nor the value diminished by the enclosure.—I have not had a whore this half-year—confining myself to the strictest adultery.— —Why should you prevent Hanson from making a *peer* if he likes it—I think the "*Garretting*"[2] would be by far the best parliamentary privilege—I know of.— —Damn your delicacy.—It is a low commercial quality—and very unworthy a man who prefixes "honourable" to his nomenclature. If you say that I must sign the bonds—I suppose that I must—but it is very iniquitous to make me pay my debts—you have no idea of the pain it gives one.—Pray do three things—get my property out of the *funds*—get Rochdale sold—get me some information from Perry about *South America*—and 4thly. ask Lady Noel[3] not to live so very long.—

3. Like a *cavalier servente*, a woman's lover or kept man.
4. Character in *Tom Thumb*, a burlesque opera based on a work of Henry Fielding (1707–1754).
1. The ancient Greek philosophical system that advocates living for pleasure.
2. Referring to the garret, or apartment, provided to Members of Parliament.
3. Byron's mother-in-law, part of whose estate Byron expected to inherit.

—As to Subscribing to Manchester—if I do that—I will write a letter to Burdett—for publication—to accompany the Subscription—which shall be more radical than anything yet rooted—but I feel lazy.—I have thought of this for some time—but alas! the air of this cursed Italy enervates—and disfranchises the thoughts of a man after nearly four years of respiration— to say nothing of emission.—As to "Don Juan"—confess—confess—you dog—and be candid—that it is the sublime of *that there* sort of writing— it may be bawdy—but is it not good English?—it may be profligate—but is it not *life*, is it not *the thing*?—Could any man have written it—who has not lived in the world?—and tooled in a post-chaise? in a hackney coach? in a Gondola? against a wall? in a court carriage? in a vis a vis?—on a table?—and under it?—I have written about a hundred stanzas of a third Canto—but it is damned modest—the outcry has frightened me.—I had such projects for the Don—but the *Cant* is so much stronger than *Cunt*— now a days,—that the benefit of experience in a man who had well weighed the worth of both monosyllables—must be lost to despairing posterity.—After all what stuff this outcry is—Lalla Rookh and Little[4]— are more dangerous than my burlesque poem can be—Moore has been here—we got tipsy together—and were very amicable—he is gone on to Rome—I put my life (in M.S.) into his hands—(*not* for publication) you— or any body else may see it—at his return.—It only comes up to 1816.— —He is a noble fellow—and looks quite fresh and poetical—nine years (the age of a poem's education) my Senior—he looks younger—this comes of marriage and being settled in the Country. I want to go to South America—I have written to Hobhouse all about it.[5]—I wrote to my wife— three months ago—under care to Murray—has she got the letter—or is the letter got into Blackwood's magazine?— —You ask after my Christmas pye—Remit it any how—*Circulars* is the best—you are right about *income*—I must have it all—how the devil do I know that I may live a year or a month?—I wish I knew that I might regulate my spending in more ways than one.—As it is one always thinks that there is but a span.—A man may as well break or be damned for a large sum as a small one—I should be loth to pay the devil or any other creditor more than sixpence in the pound.—

[scrawl for signature]

. . .

---

4. Works by Thomas Moore: *The Poetical Works of Thomas Little* (1801) and *Lallah Rookh* (1817).
5. On October 3, Byron had written to Hobhouse of his interest in settling in Venezuela: "The Anglo-Americans are a little too coarse for me—and their climate too cold—and I should prefer the others.—I could soon grapple with the Spanish language.— —Ellice or others could get me letters to Bolivar and his government—and if men of little or of no property are encouraged there—surely with present income—and if I could sell Rochdale—and with some capital—I might be suffered as a landholder there—or at least a tenant—and if possible and legal—a Citizen. . . . You must not talk to me of England—that is out of the question.—I had a house—and lands—and a wife and child—and a name there—once—but all these things are transmuted or sequestered. . . . My taste for revolution is abated—with my other passions.— —Yet I want a country—and a home—and if possible—a free one— . . . There is no freedom in Europe—that's certain—it is besides a worn out portion of the globe" (*BLJ* 6:225–27).

To John Murray

Venice. Octr. 29th. 1819

Dear Murray—Yours of the 15th. came yesterday. I am sorry that you do not mention a large letter addressed to *your care* for Lady Byron—from me at Bologna—two months ago. Pray tell me was this letter received and forwarded?— —You say nothing of the Vice Consulate for the Ravenna patrician—from which it is to be inferred that the thing will not be done.— —I had written about a hundred stanzas of a *third* Canto to Don Juan— but the reception of the two first is no encouragement to you nor me to proceed.— —I had also written about 600 lines of a poem—the Vision (or Prophecy) of Dante[1]—the subject a view of Italy in the ages down to the present—supposing Dante to speak in his own person—previous to his death—and embracing all topics in the way of prophecy—like Lycophron's Cassandra.[2] But this and the other are both at a standstill—for the present.— —I gave Moore who is gone to Rome—my Life in M.S. in 78 folio sheets brought down to 1816.[3]— —But this I put into his hands for *his* care—as he has some other M.S.S. of mine—a journal kept in 1814— &c.—Neither are for publication during my life—but when I am cold—you may do what you please.— —In the mean time—if you like to read them— you may—and show them to any body you like—I care not.— —The life is *Memoranda*—and not *Confessions*—I have left out all my *loves* (except in a general way) and many other of the most important things—(because I must not compromise other people) so that it is like the play of Hamlet— "the part of Hamlet omitted by particular desire".— —But you will find many opinions—and some fun—with a detailed account of my marriage and it's consequences—as true as a party concerned can make such accounts—for I suppose we are all prejudiced.— —I have never read over this life since it was written—so that I know not exactly what it may repeat—or contain.— —Moore and I passed some merry days together— but so far from "seducing me to England" as you suppose—the account he gave of me and mine—was of any thing but a nature to make me wish to return;—it is not such opinions of the public that would weigh with me one way or the other—but I think they should weigh with others of my friends before they ask me to return to a place for which I have no great inclination.— —I probably must return for business—or in my way to America—pray—did you get a letter for Hobhouse—who will have told you the contents.—I understood that the Venezuelan commissioners had orders to treat with emigrants—now I want to go there—I should not make a bad South-American planter, and I should take my natural daughter Allegra with me and settle.— —I wrote at length to Hobhouse to get information from Perry who I suppose is the best topographer and trumpeter of the new Republicans. Pray write—

yrs. ever
[Scrawl]

---

1. *The Prophecy of Dante* was written in June 1819 but not published until 1821.
2. Lycophron was an Alexandrian poet of the third century B.C.E.; his *Cassandra* is a long poem prophesying events in Greek history.
3. Byron's memoirs, eventually sold by Moore to Murray, were burned at Murray's house on May 17, 1824, three days after the news of Byron's death reached England. For an account of this event, see Doris Langley Moore, *The Late Lord Byron*.

P.S.—Moore and I did nothing but laugh—he will tell you of "my where-abouts" and all my proceedings at this present—they are as usual.— —You should not let those fellows publish false "Don Juans"[4]—but do not put *my name* because I mean to cut Roberts up like a gourd—in the ⟨anonymous⟩ preface—if I continue the poem.

To Richard Belgrave Hoppner

October 29th. 1819

My dear Hoppner—The Ferrara Story is of a piece with all the rest of the Venetian manufacture—you may judge.—I only changed horses there since I wrote to you after my visit in June last.—"*Convent*"—and "*carry off*" quotha!—and "*girl*"— —I should like to know *who* has been carried off—except poor dear *me*—I have been more ravished myself than anybody since the Trojan war—but as to the arrest and it's causes—one is as true as the other—and I can account for the invention of neither.—I suppose it is some confusion of the tale of the For[narina]—and of M[adam]e Guiccioli—and half a dozen more—but it is useless to unravel the web—when one has only to brush it away.—I shall settle with Master Edgecombe who looks very blue at your indecision—and swears that he is the best arith-matician in Europe—and so I think also—for he makes out two and two to be five.— —You may see me next week—I have a horse or two more (five in all) and I shall repossess myself of Lido—and I will rise earlier—and we will go and shake our livers over the beach as heretofore—if you like—and we will make the Adriatic roar again with our hatred of that now empty Oys-ter shell—without it's pearl—the city of Venice.—Murray sent me a letter yesterday—the impostors have published—*two* new *third* Cantos of *Don Juan*—the devil take the impudence of some blackguard bookseller or other there*for*.—Perhaps I did not make myself understood—he told me the sale had not been great—1200 out of 1500 quarto I believe (which is nothing after selling 13000 of the Corsair in one day) but that the "best Judges &c." had said it was very fine and clever and particularly good English & poetry and all those consolatory things which are not however worth a single copy to a bookseller—and as to the author—of course I am in a damned passion at the bad taste of the times—and swear there is nothing like posterity—who of course must know more of the matter than their Grandfathers.——There has been an eleventh commandment to the women not to read it—and what is still more extraordinary they seem not to have broken it.——But that can be of little import to them poor things—for the reading or non-reading a book—will never keep down a single petticoat;—but it is of import to Murray—who will be in scandal for his aiding as publisher.— — He is bold howsomedever—wanting two more cantos against the winter—I think that he had better not—for by the larkins!—it will only make a new row for him. . . .

. . .

yrs. ever
Byron

---

4. See letter to Hobhouse of August 23, 1819 (p. 751) and note; *false "Don Juans"*: piracies and for-geries of *Don Juan* were common from the time of its earliest publication.

To John Murray

Ravenna. February 21st. 1820

Dear Murray—The Bulldogs will be very agreeable—I have only those of this country who though good—& ready to fly at any thing—yet have not the tenacity of tooth and Stoicism in endurance of my canine fellow citizens, then pray send them—by the readiest conveyance, perhaps best by Sea.— —Mr. Kinnaird will disburse for them & deduct from the amount on your application or on that of Captain Fyler.—I see the good old King is gone to his place—one can't help being sorry—though blindness—and age and insanity are supposed to be drawbacks—on human felicity—but I am not at all sure that the latter at least—might not render him happier than any of his subjects.— —I have no thoughts of coming to the Coronation— though I should like to see it—and though I have a right to be a puppet in it—but my division with Lady Byron which has drawn an equinoctial line between me and mine in all other things—will operate in this also to prevent my being in the same procession.

— —By Saturday's post—I sent you four packets containing Cantos third and fourth of D[on] J[uan]—recollect that these two cantos reckon only as *one* with you and me—being in fact the third Canto cut into two—because I found it too long.—Remember this—and don't imagine that there could be any other motive.—The whole is about 225 Stanzas more or less—and a lyric of 96 lines—so that they are no longer than the first *single* cantos— but the truth is—that I made the first too long—and should have cut those down also had I thought better.— —Instead of saying in future for so many cantos—say so many *Stanzas* or pages—it was Jacob Tonson's way—and certainly the best—it prevents mistakes—I might have sent you a dozen cantos of 40 Stanzas each—those of "the Minstrel" (Beatties's) are no longer—and ruined you at once—if you don't suffer as it is;—but recollect you are not *pinned down* to anything you say in a letter and that calculating even these two cantos as *one* only (which they were and are to be reckoned) you are not bound by your offer,—act as may seem fair to all parties.— —I have finished my translation of the first Canto of the "Morgante Maggiore" of Pulci[1]—which I will transcribe and send—it is the parent not only of Whistlecraft—but of all jocose Italian poetry.— —You must print it side by side with the original Italian because I wish the reader to judge of the fidelity—it is stanza for stanza—and often line for line if not word for word.— —

You ask me for a volume of manners &c.—on Italy; perhaps I am in the case to know more of them than most Englishmen—because I have lived among the natives—and in parts of the country—where Englishmen never resided before—(I speak of Romagna and this place particularly) but there are many reasons why I do not choose to touch in print on such a subject— I have lived in their houses and in the heart of their families—sometimes merely as "amico di casa" and sometimes as "Amico di cuore" of the Dama—and in neither case do I feel myself authorized in making a book of

---

1. *Morgante Maggiore di Messer Luigi Pulci* was published in 1823 by John Hunt in the *Liberal*. Pulci's *Morgante* (1483) was both directly and through its influence on Frere's "Whistlecraft" (1817–18) one of the main influences on the form and style of *Beppo, Don Juan,* and *The Vision of Judgment.*

them.— —Their moral is not your moral—their life is not your life—you would not understand it—it is not English nor French—nor German— which you would all understand—the Conventual education—the Cavalier Servitude—the habits of thought and living are so entirely different—and the difference becomes so much more striking the more you live intimately with them—that I know not how to make you comprehend a people—who are at once temperate and profligate—serious in their character and buf- foons in their amusements—capable of impressions and passions which are at once *sudden* and *durable* (what you find in no other nation) and who *actually* have *no society* (what we would call so) as you may see by their Comedies—they have no real comedy not even in Goldoni—and that is because they have no society to draw it from.— —

Their Conversazioni are not Society at *all.*—They go to the theatre to talk—and into company to hold their tongues—The *women* sit in a circle and the men gather into groupes [sic]—or they play at dreary Faro—or "Lotto reale"—for small sums.—Their Academie are Concerts like our own—with better music—and more form.—Their best things are the Carnival balls—and masquerades—when every body runs mad for six weeks.— —After their dinners and suppers they make extempore verses— and buffoon one another—but it is in a humour which you would not enter into—ye of the North.— —

In their houses it is better—I should know something of the matter— having had a pretty general experience among their women—[from] the fisherman's wife—up to the Nobil' Donna whom I serve.— —Their system has it's rules—and it's fitnesses—and decorums—so as to be reduced to a kind of discipline—or game at hearts—which admits few deviations unless you wish to lose it.— —They are extremely tenacious—and jealous as furies—not permitting their Lovers even to marry if they can help it—and keeping them always close to them in public as in private whenever they can.— —In short they transfer marriage to adultery—and strike the *not* out of that commandment.—The reason is that they marry for their parents and love for themselves.—They exact fidelity from a lover as a debt of honour—while they pay the husband as a tradesman—that is not at all.— —You hear a person's character—male or female—canvassed—not as depending on their conduct to their husbands or wives—but to their mis- tress or lover.— —And—and—that's all.—If I wrote a quarto—I don't know that I could do more than amplify what I have here noted.— —

It is to be observed that while they do all this—the greatest outward respect is to be paid to the husbands—and not only by the ladies but by their Serventi—particularly if the husband serves no one himself—(which is not often the case however) so that you would often suppose them relations—the Servente making the figure of one adopted into the family.— Sometimes the ladies run a little restive—and elope—or divide—or make a scene—but this is at starting generally—when they know no better—or when they fall in love with a foreigner—or some such anomaly—and is always reckoned unnecessary and extravagant.— —

. . .

To John Cam Hobhouse

Ravenna. March 3d. 1820

. . .

William Bankes[1] came to see me twice—once at Venice—and he since came a second time from Bologna to Ravenna on purpose—so I took him to a Ball here and presented him to all the Ostrogothic Nobility—and to the Dama whom I serve;—I have settled into regular Serventismo—and find it the happiest state of all—always excepting Scarmentado's.[2]—I double a shawl with considerable alacrity—but have not yet arrived at the perfection of putting it on the right way—and I hand in and out and know my post in a Conversazione—and theatre—and play at cards as well as [a] man can do who of all the Italian pack can only distinguish "Asso" and "Re" the rest for me are hieroglyphics.—Luckily the play is limited to "Papetti" that is pieces of four Pauls—somewhere in or about two shillings. I am in favour & respect with the Cardinal and the Vice-legato—and in decent intercourse with the Gonfaloniere—and all the Nobiltà of the middle ages.—Nobody has been stabbed this winter—and few new liaisons formed—there is a Sposa Fiorentina—a pretty Girl yet in abeyance—but no one can decide yet who is to be her Servente—most of the men being already adulterated—and she showing no preferences to any who are not.—There is a certain Marchese who I think would run a good chance—if he did not take matters rather too philosophically.—Sgricci is here improvising away with great success—he is also a celebrated Sodomite a character by no means so much respected in Italy as it should be; but they laugh instead of burning—and the Women talk of it as a pity in a man of talent—but with greater tolerance than could be expected—and only express their hopes that he may yet be converted to Adultery.— —He is not known to have b———d anybody here as yet but he has paid his addresses "fatto la corte" to two or three.— —

[scrawl]

To Richard Belgrave Hoppner

Ravenna. Septr. 10th. 1820

My dear Hoppner—Ecco Advocate Fossati's letter.—No paper has nor will be signed.—Pray—*draw* on me for the Napoleons—for I have no mode of remitting them—otherwise. Missiaglia would empower some one here to receive them for you—as it is not a *piazza bancale.*—I regret that you have such a bad opinion of Shiloh[1]—you used to have a good one.—Surely he has talent—honour—but is crazy against religion and morality.—His tragedy[2] is sad work—but the subject renders it so.—His Islam had much poetry.—You seem lately to have got some notion against him.—Clare[3]

1. One of Byron's Trinity College friends.
2. Hero of Voltaire's *Historie des Voyages de Scarmentado Ecrite par lui-même* (1756); at the end of his travels, Scarmentado concludes: "I married in my home town, I was cuckolded, and I saw that this was the sweetest state of life."
1. Byron's nickname for Shelley (from the name of the savior that the fanatic prophet Joanna South-cott claimed would be born to her).
2. *The Cenci* (1819). The next sentence refers to Shelley's *Revolt of Islam* (1818).
3. Claire Clairmont, Mary Shelley's stepsister, whose affair with Byron in the summer of 1816 resulted in the birth of their daughter, Allegra, in 1817. In 1821, Byron sent Allegra to be raised in a convent not far from Ravenna, where she died in 1823 at the age of five.

writes me the most insolent letters about Allegra—see what a man gets by taking care of natural children!—Were it not for the poor little child's sake—I am almost tempted to send her back to her atheistical mother—but that would be too bad;—you cannot conceive the excess of her insolence and I know not why—for I have been at great care and expence—taking a house in the country on purpose for her—she has *two* maids & every possible attention.—If Clare thinks that she shall ever interfere with the child's morals or education—she mistakes—she never shall—The girl shall be a Christian and a married woman—if possible.—As to seeing her—she may see her—under proper restrictions—but She is not to throw every thing into confusion with her Bedlam behaviour.—To express it delicately—I think Madame Clare is a damned bitch—what think you?

To Thomas Moore

Ravenna, November 5th, 1820

. . .

I am glad of your epigram. It is odd that we should both let our wits run away with our sentiments; for I am sure that we are both Queen's men at bottom. But there is no resisting a clinch—it is so clever! Apropos of that— we have a "diphthong" also in this part of the world—not a *Greek*, but a *Spanish* one[1]—do you understand me?—which is about to blow up the whole alphabet. It was first pronounced at Naples, and is spreading;—but we are nearer the Barbarians; who are in great force on the Po, and will pass it, with the first legitimate pretext.

There will be the devil to pay, and there is no saying who will or who will not be set down in his bill. If "honour should come unlooked for"[2] to any of your acquaintance, make a Melody of it, that his ghost, like poor Yorick's, may have the satisfaction of being plaintively pitied—or still more nobly commemorated, like "Oh breathe not his name."[3] In case you should not think him worth it, here is a Chant for you instead—

> When a man hath no freedom to fight for at home,
>   Let him combat for that of his neighbours;
> Let him think of the glories of Greece and of Rome,
>   And get knock'd on the head for his labours.
>
> To do good to mankind is the chivalrous plan,
>   And is always as nobly requited;
> Then battle for freedom wherever you can,
>   And, if not shot or hang'd, you'll get knighted.[4]

So you have gotten the letter of "Epigrams"—I am glad of it. You will not be so, for I shall send you more. Here is one I wrote for the endorsement of "the Deed of Separation" in 1816; but the lawyers objected to it, as superfluous. It was written as we were getting up the signing and sealing. * * has the original.

---

1. Probably referring to the Bourbon rule in southern Italy, while the next few lines allude to the Italian uprisings and their suppression by Austria ("the Barbarians").
2. *1 Henry IV* 5.3.58–59 (freely quoted).
3. A song from Moore's *Irish Melodies*.
4. This poem was first published in 1831.

Endorsement to the Deed of Separation, in the April of 1816.[5]

A year ago you swore, fond she!
  "To love, to honour," and so forth:
Such was the vow you pledged to me,
  And here's exactly what 'tis worth.

For the anniversary of January 2, 1821, I have a small grateful anticipation, which, in case of accident, I add—

To Penelope, January 2, 1821.

This day, of all our days, has done
  The worst for me and you:—
'Tis just *six* years since we were *one*,
  And *five* since we were *two*.

Pray excuse all this nonsense; for I must talk nonsense just now, for fear of wandering to more serious topics, which, in the present state of things, is not safe by a foreign post.

I told you in my last, that I had been going on with the "Memoirs," and have got as far as twelve more sheets. But I suspect they will be interrupted. In that case I will send them on by post, though I feel remorse at making a friend pay so much for postage, for we can't frank here beyond the frontier.

I shall be glad to hear of the event of the Queen's concern. As to the ultimate effect, the most inevitable one to you and me (if they and we live so long) will be that the Miss Moores and Miss Byrons will present us with a great variety of grandchildren by different fathers.

Pray, where did you get hold of Goethe's Florentine husband-killing story?[6] Upon such matters, in general, I may say, with Beau Clincher, in reply to Errand's wife—

"Oh the villain, he hath murdered my poor Timothy!
"*Clincher.* Damn your Timothy!—I tell you, woman,
your husband has *murdered me*—he has carried away
my fine jubilee clothes."[7]

So Bowles has been telling a story, too ('tis in the *Quarterly*), about the woods of "Madeira," and so forth. I shall be at Bowles again, if he is not quiet. He misstates, or mistakes, in a point or two. The paper is finished, and so is the letter.

Yours, &c.

5. Both lyrics on this page were first published in *Life*.
6. Goethe tells this story in his review of *Manfred* (see *BLJ* 7:220 and *LJ* 5:503 ff.).
7. George Farquhar, *The Constant Couple, or a Trip to the Jubilee* (1700).

To John Murray

R[avenn]a. 9bre. 9.o 1820

Dear Moray— . . .

Hobhouse writes me a facetious letter about my *indolence*—and love of Slumber.—It becomes him—he is in active life—he writes pamphlets against Canning to which he does not put his name—he gets into Newgate—and into Parliament—both honourable places of refuge—and he "greatly daring dines" at all the taverns—(why didn't he set up a *tap room* at once?) and then writes to quiz my laziness.— —Why I do like one or two vices to be sure—but I can back a horse and fire a pistol without "winking or blinking" like Major Sturgeon—I have fed at times for two months together on *sheer* biscuit & water (without metaphor) I can get over seventy or eighty miles a day *riding* post and *swim five* at a Stretch taking a *piece* before & after as at Venice in 1818 or at least I *could do* & have done [it] *once* & I never was ten minutes in my life over a *solitary* dinner.—Now my friend Hobhouse—when we were wayfaring men used to complain grievously of hard beds and sharp insects—while I slept like a top—and to awaken me with his swearing at them—he used to damn his dinners daily both quality & cookery and quantity—& reproach me for a sort of "brutal" indifference as he called it to these particulars—& now he writes me facetious sneerings because I *do not* get up early in a morning—when there is no occasion—if there were—*he* knows that I was always *out* of bed before him—though it is true that my ablutions detained me longer in dressing—than his noble contempt for that "oriental scrupulosity" permitted.—Then he is still sore about "*the ballad*"—he!! why he lampooned me at Brighton in 1808—about Jackson the boxer and bold Webster &c.—in 1809—he turned the death of my friend Ed. *Long* into ridicule & rhyme because his name was susceptible of a *pun*—and although he saw that I was distressed at it—before I left England in 1816—he wrote rhymes upon D. *Kinnaird— you*—and *myself*—and at Venice he parodied the lines "Though the day of my destiny's over"[1] in a comfortable quizzing way—and now he harps on my ballad about his election!—Pray tell him all this—for I will have no underhand work with my "old Cronies".—If he can deny the facts let him.—I maintain that he is more *carnivorously* & *carnally sensual* than I am— though I am bad enough too for that matter—but not in eating & haranguing at the Crown and Anchor—where I never was but twice—and those were at "Whore's Hops" when I was a younker in my teens; and Egad—I think them the most respectable meetings of the two.— —

But he is a little wroth that I would not come over to the *Queen's* trial— *lazy—quotha!*—it is so true that he should be ashamed of asserting it.— — He counsels me not to "get into a scrape" but as Beau Clincher says—"How melancholy are Newgate reflections!"[2]— —To be sure his advice is worth following—for experience teacheth—he has been in a dozen within these last two years.—*I pronounce me the more temperate of the two.* Have you gotten "the Hints"[3] yet?— —

. . .

---

1. "Stanzas to Augusta" (1816) (*CPW* 4:33–35).
2. Farquhar, *The Constant Couple.*
3. Byron wrote *Hints from Horace* in 1811, but it was not published in its entirety till 1831.

Rose's[4] *lines* must be at his own option—*I* can have no objection to their publication.—Pray salute him from me.— —Mr. Keats whose poetry you enquire after—appears to me what I have already said;—such writing is a sort of mental masturbation—he is always f—gg—g his *Imagination*.—I don't mean that he is *indecent* but viciously soliciting his own ideas into a state which is neither poetry nor any thing else but a Bedlam vision produced by raw pork and opium[5]— — . . .

[Scrawl]

To John Murray

Ravenna. 9bre. 18.o 1820

. . .

I remand you the preface—*don't forget* that the Italian extract from the Chronicle must *be translated*. With regard to what you say of retouching the Juans—and the Hints—it is all very well—but I can't *furbish*.—I am like the tyger (in poesy) if I miss my first Spring—I go growling back to my Jungle.—There is no second.—I can't correct—I can't—& I won't.—Nobody ever succeeds in it great or small.—Tasso remade the whole of his Jerusalem but who ever reads that version?—all the world goes to the first.—Pope *added* to the "Rape of the Lock"—but did not reduce it.— —You must take my things as they happen to be—if they are not likely to suit—reduce their *estimate* then accordingly—I would rather give them away than hack & hew them.—I don't say that you are not right—I merely assert that I can not better them.—I must either "make a spoon or spoil a horn".—And there's an end.— — . . .

yrs. ever
[Scrawl]

To John Murray

Ravenna. Decr. 9th. 1820

Dear Murray—I intended to have written to you at some length by this post,—but as the Military Commandant is now lying dead in my house— on Fletcher's bed—I have other things to think of.— —He was shot at 8 o Clock this evening about two hundred paces from our door.—I was putting on my great Coat to pay a visit to the Countess G[uiccioli]—when I heard a shot—and on going into the hall—found all my servants on the balcony—exclaiming that "a Man was murdered".— —As it is the custom here to let people fight it through—they wanted to hinder me from going

---

4. William Stewart Rose (1775–1843), British poet and translator; it was Rose who in 1817 had given Byron a copy of Frere's *The Monks and the Giants*, the most immediate model for Byron's *ottava rima* poems.
5. The sexual focus of Byron's criticism of Keats's poetry echoes an earlier letter to Murray: "Jack Keats or Ketch or whatever his names are;—why his is the *Onanism* of Poetry—something like the pleasure an Italian fiddler extracted out of being suspended daily by a Street Walker in Drury Lane—this went on for some weeks—at last the Girl went to get a pint of Gin—met another, chatted too long—and Cornelli was *hanged outright* before she returned. Such like is the trash they praise—and such will be the end of the *outstretched* poesy of this miserable Self-polluter of the human mind" (*BLJ* 7:217).

out—but I ran down into the Street—Tita the bravest of them followed me—and we made our way to the Commandant who was lying on his back with five wounds—of which three in the body—one in the heart.— —There were about him—Diego his Adjutant—crying like a Child—a priest howling—a Surgeon who dared not touch him—two or three confused & frightened Soldiers—one or two of the boldest of the mob—and the Street dark as pitch—with the people flying in all directions.—As Diego could only cry and wring his hands—and the Priest could only pray—and nobody seemed able or willing to do anything except exclaim shake and stare—I made my Servant & one of the mob take up the body—sent off Diego crying to the Cardinal—the Soldiers for the Guard—& had the Commandant carried up Stairs to my own quarters.—But he was quite gone.—I made the Surgeon examine him & examined him myself.—He had bled inwardly, & very little external blood was apparent.—One of the Slugs had gone quite through—all but the Skin, I felt it myself.—Two more shots in the body—one in a finger—and another in the arm.—His face not at all disfigured—he seems asleep—but is growing livid.—The Assassin has not been taken—but the gun was found—a gun filed down to half the barrel.— —

He said nothing—but "O Dio!" and "O Gesu" two or three times. The house was filled at last with Soldiers—officers—police—and military—but they are clearing away—all but the Sentinels—and the [body] is to be removed tomorrow.—It seems [that] if I had not had him taken into my house he might have lain in the Street till morning—for here nobody meddles with such things—for fear of the consequences—either of public suspicion, or private revenge on the part of the Slayers.—They may do as they please—I shall never be deterred from a duty of humanity by all the assassins of Italy—and that is a wide word.— —He was a brave officer—but an unpopular man.—The whole town is in confusion.—You may judge better of things here by this detail than by anything which I could add on the Subject—communicate this letter to Hobhouse & Douglas K[innair]d—and believe me

yrs. truly
B

P.S.—The poor Man's wife is not yet aware of his death—they are to break it to her in the morning.—The Lieutenant who is watching the body is smoking with the greatest Sangfroid—a strange people.—

To Percy Bysshe Shelley

Ravenna, April 26th, 1821

The child[1] continues doing well, and the accounts are regular and favourable. It is gratifying to me that you and Mrs. Shelley do not disapprove of the step which I have taken, which is merely temporary.

I am very sorry to hear what you say of Keats[2]—is it *actually* true? I did

---

1. Allegra, Byron's four-year-old natural daughter with Claire Clairmont, whom Byron decided to send to a convent to be raised.
2. Keats died on February 23, 1821. Shelley was among those who believed that the hostile reviews of Keats's poetry, particularly John Wilson Croker's review in the April 1818 issue of the *Quarterly Review*, precipitated his death. Byron's ironic stance towards this theory (e.g., "*poor Keats* now slain by the Quarterly Review" [*BLJ* 8:172]) is echoed in *Don Juan* XI, stanza 60 [p. 594].

not think criticism had been so killing. Though I differ from you essentially in your estimate of his performances, I so much abhor all unnecessary pain, that I would rather he had been seated on the highest peak of Parnassus than have perished in such a manner. Poor fellow! though with such inordinate self-love he would probably have not been very happy. I read the review of "Endymion" in the Quarterly. It was severe,—but surely not so severe as many reviews in that and other journals upon others.

I recollect the effect on me of the Edinburgh on my first poem; it was rage, and resistance, and redress—but not despondency nor despair. I grant that those are not amiable feelings; but, in this world of bustle and broil, and especially in the career of writing, a man should calculate upon his powers of *resistance* before he goes into the arena.

> "Expect not life from pain nor danger free,
> Nor deem the doom of man reversed for thee."[3]

You know my opinion of *that second-hand* school of poetry. You also know my high opinion of your own poetry,—because it is of *no* school. I read Cenci[4]—but, besides that I think the *subject* essentially *un*dramatic, I am not an admirer of our old dramatists *as models*. I deny that the English have hitherto had a drama at all. Your Cenci, however, was a work of power, and poetry. As to *my* drama, pray revenge yourself upon it, by being as free as I have been with yours.

I have not yet got your Prometheus,[5] which I long to see. I have heard nothing of mine, and do not know that it is yet published. I have published a pamphlet on the Pope controversy, which you will not like. Had I known that Keats was dead—or that he was alive and so sensitive—I should have omitted some remarks upon his poetry, to which I was provoked by his *attack* upon *Pope*,[6] and my disapprobation of *his own* style of writing.

You want me to undertake a great Poem—I have not the inclination nor the power. As I grow older, the indifference—*not* to life, for we love it by instinct—but to the stimuli of life, increases. Besides, this late failure of the Italians has latterly disappointed me for many reasons,—some public, some personal. My respects to Mrs. S.

> Yours ever,
> B

P.S.—Could not you and I contrive to meet this summer? Could not you take a run *alone*?

To John Murray

R[avenn]a July 6th. 1821

Dear Sir/—In agreement with a wish expressed by Mr. Hobhouse—it is my determination to omit the Stanza upon the *horse* of *Semiramis*[1]—in the fifth Canto of D[on] J[uan].—I mention this in case you are or intend to be

3. Samuel Johnson's *Vanity of Human Wishes* (1749), lines 155–56.
4. *The Cenci* (1819).
5. *Prometheus Unbound* (1820); Byron's "Prometheus" (pp. 239–41), written and published in 1816.
6. In Keats's *Sleep and Poetry* (1817), lines 193–206.
1. See *Don Juan* V, stanza 61 (p. 531).

the publisher of the remaining Cantos.—By yesterday's post I ought in point of [time] to have had an acknowledgement of the [arrival] of the M.S.S. of "Sardanapalus"[2]—If it *has* arrived & you have delayed the few lines necessary for this—I can only say that you are keeping two people in hot water—the postmaster here—because the packet was insured—& myself because I had but that one copy.—I am in the *fifth* act of a play on the subject of the Foscaris—father and son.—Foscolo can tell you their story.

I am yrs. [Scrawl]

P.S.—At the particular request of the Countess G[uiccioli] I have promised *not* to continue Don Juan.—You will therefore look upon these 3 cantos as the last of that poem.—She had read the two first in the French translation—& never ceased beseeching me to write no more of it.—The reason of this is not at first obvious to a superficial observer of FOREIGN manners[,] but it arises from the wish of all women to exalt the *sentiment* of the passions—& to keep up the illusion which is their empire.—Now D. J. strips off this illusion—& laughs at that & most other things.—I never knew a woman who did not protect *Rousseau*—not one who did not dislike de Grammont—Gil Blas & all the *comedy* of the passions—when brought out naturally.—But "King's blood must keep word" as Serjeant Bothwell says.[3]—Write you Scamp! Your parcel of *extracts* never came & never will— you should have sent it by the post—but you are growing a sad fellow and some fine day we shall have to dissolve partnership. Some more *Soda* powders.—

To John Murray

R[avenn]a August 31st. 1821

Dear Sir/—I have received the Juans—which are printed so *carelessly* especially the 5th. Canto—as to be disgraceful to me—& not creditable to you.—It really must be *gone over again* with the *Manuscript*—the errors are so gross—words added—changed—so as to make cacophony & nonsense.— —You have been careless of this poem because some of your Synod don't approve of it—but I tell you—it will be long before you see any thing half so good as poetry or writing.— —Upon what principle have you omitted the *note* on Bacon & Voltaire? and one of the concluding stanzas sent as an addition? because it ended I suppose—with—

> "And do not link two virtuous souls for life
> Into that *moral Centaur* man & wife?["]

Now I must say once for all—that I will not permit any human being to take such liberties with my writings—because I am absent.—I desire the omissions to be replaced (except the stanza on Semiramis) particularly the stanza upon the Turkish marriages—and I request that the whole be carefully *gone over* with the M.S.S.—I never saw such stuff as is printed— Gulleyaz—instead of Gul*beyaz* &c. Are you aware that Gul*beyaz* is a real name—and the other nonsense?—I copied the *Cantos* out carefully—so

2. *Sardanapalus* was published together with *Cain* and *The Two Foscari* on December 19, 1821.
3. Walter Scott, *Old Mortality* (1816), chap. 6.

that there is *no* excuse—as the Printer reads or at least *prints* the M.S.S. of the plays without error.— —If you have no feeling for your own reputation pray have some little for mine.— —I have read over the poem carefully—and I tell you *it is poetry.*—Your little envious knot of parson-poets may say what they please—time will show that I am not in this instance mistaken.— —

Desire my friend Hobhouse to correct the press especially of the last Canto from the Manuscript—as it is—it is enough to drive one out of one's senses—to see the infernal torture of words from the original.—For instance the line

>   "And pair their rhymes as Venus yokes her doves["]

is printed—

>   "and *praise* their rhymes &c.—["]

also "precarious" for "precocious"—and this line stanza 133.—

>   *"And this strong extreme effect—to tire no longer."*

Now do turn to the Manuscript—& see—if I ever made such a *line*—it is *not verse.*— —No wonder the poem should fail—(which however *it wont* you will see)[1] with such things allowed to creep about it.— —Replace what is omitted—& correct what is so shamefully misprinted,—and let the poem have fair play—and I fear nothing.— —I see in the last two Numbers of the Quarterly—a strong itching to assail me—(see the review of the "*Etonian*")[2] let it—and see if they shan't have enough of it.— —I don't allude to Gifford—who has always been my friend—& whom I do not consider as responsible for the articles written by others.—But if I do not give Mr. Milman—⟨Mr. Southey⟩—& others of the crew something that shall occupy their dreams!—[line crossed out] I have *not* begun with *the* Quarterers—but let them look to it.—As for *Milman*[3] (*you* well know I have not been unfair to his poetry ever) but I have lately had some information of his critical proceedings in the Quarterly which may bring that on him which he will be sorry for.—I happen to know *that* of him—which would annihilate him—when he pretends to preach *morality—not* that *he* is immoral—because he *isn't*—having in early life been once too much so.— And dares he set up for a preacher? let him go and be priest to *Cybele.*— —

You will publish the plays—when ready—I am in such a humour about this printing of D[on] J[uan] so inaccurately—that I must close this.

>   yrs. [Scrawl]

>   . . .

---

1. Indeed, the success of Cantos III, IV, and V, published on August 8, 1821, was immediate: "The booksellers' messengers filled the street in front of [John Murray's establishment], and the parcels of books were given out the window to their obstreperous demands" (Smiles, *A Publisher and His Friends* . . . , 1.413).
2. *Quarterly Review,* XXV.106.
3. Henry Hart Milman (1791–1868), whom Byron mistakenly believed to be the reviewer whose harsh critique of Keats in the *Quarterly* was thought to have caused his death. (The reviewer was John Wilson Croker.) Innuendoes about Milman's sexuality that follow in this letter are echoed in *Don Juan* XI, stanza 58 (p. 594).

To John Murray

Ravenna Septr. 24th. 1821

Dear Murray/—I have been thinking over our late correspondence and wish to propose the following articles for our future.—1stly—That you shall write to me of yourself—of the health wealth and welfare of all friends—but of *me* (*quoad me*) little or nothing.—

2dly—That you shall send me Soda powders—tooth-paste—tooth-brushes—or any such anti-odontalgic or chemical articles as heretofore "ad libitum" upon being re-imbursed for the same.—

3dly—That you shall *not* send me any modern or (as they are called) *new* publications in *English*—*whatsoever*—save and excepting any writing prose or verse of (or reasonably presumed to be of) Walter Scott—Crabbe—Moore—Campbell—Rogers—Gifford—Joanna Baillie—*Irving* (the American) Hogg—Wilson (Isle of Palms Man) or any especial *single* work of fancy which is thought to be of considerable merit.—*Voyages* and *travels*—provided that they are *neither in Greece Spain Asia Minor Albania nor Italy* will be welcome—having travelled the countries mentioned—I know that what is said of them can convey nothing further which I desire to know about them.—No other *English* works whatsoever.— —

4thly—That you send me *no periodical works* whatsoever—*no* Edinburgh—Quarterly—Monthly—nor any Review—Magazine—Newspaper English or foreign of any description— —

5thly—That you send me *no* opinions whatsoever either *good*—*bad*—or *indifferent*—of yourself or your friends or others—concerning any work or works of mine—past—present—or to come.—

6thly—That all Negotiations in matters of business between you and me pass through the medium of the Hon[oura]ble Douglas Kinnaird—my friend and trustee, or Mr. Hobhouse—as "Alter Ego" and tantamount to myself during my absence.—or presence.— —

Some of these propositions may at first seem strange—but they are founded.—The quantity of trash I have received as books is incalculable, and neither amused nor instructed.—Reviews & Magazines—are at the best but ephemeral & superficial reading—*who thinks* of the *grand article* of *last year* in any *given review*? in the next place—if they regard *myself*—they tend to increase *Egotism*,—if favourable—I do not deny that the praise *elates*—and if unfavourable that the abuse *irritates*—the latter may conduct me to inflict a species of Satire—which would neither do good to you nor to your friends—*they* may smile *now*, and so may *you* but if I took you all in hand—it would not be difficult to cut you up like gourds. I did as much by as powerful people at nineteen years old[1]—& I know little as yet in three & thirty—which should prevent me from making all your ribs—Gridirons for your hearts—if such were my propensity.—But it is *not*.—Therefore let me hear none of your provocations—if anything occurs so very *gross* as to require my notice—I shall hear of it from my personal friends.—For the rest—I merely request to be left in ignorance.—

The same applies to opinions *good*—*bad* or *indifferent* of persons in conversation or correspondence; these do not *interrupt* but they *soil* the *current* of my *Mind*;—I am sensitive enough—but *not* till I am *touched & here*

---

1. A reference to *English Bards and Scotch Reviewers* (1809).

I am beyond the touch of the short arms of literary England—except the few feelers of the Polypus that crawl over the Channel in the way of Extract.— —All these precautions *in* England would be useless—the libeller or the flatterer would there reach me in spite of all—but in Italy we know little of literary England & think less except what reaches us through some garbled & brief extract in some miserable Gazette.— —For *two years* (except two or three articles cut out & sent by *you*—by the post) I never read a newspaper—which was not forced upon me by some accident—& know upon the whole as little of England—as you all do of Italy—& God knows—*that* is little enough with all your travels &c. &c. &c.—The English travellers *know Italy* as *you* know Guernsey—how much is *that*?—If any thing occurs so violently gross or personal as to require notice, Mr. D[ougla]s Kinnaird will let me *know*—but of *praise* I desire to hear *nothing*.— —You will say—"to what tends all this?—" I will answer THAT— — to keep my mind *free and* unbiased—by all paltry and personal irritabilities of praise or censure;—To let my Genius take it's natural direction,—while my feelings are like the dead—who know nothing and feel nothing of all or aught that is said or done in their regard.— —If you can observe these conditions you will spare yourself & others some pain—let me not be worked upon to rise up—for if I do—it will not be for a little;—if you can *not* observe these conditions we shall cease to be correspondents,—but *not friends*—for I shall always be yrs. ever & truly

BYRON

P.S.—I have taken these resolutions not from any irritation against *you* or *yours* but simply upon reflection that all reading either praise or censure of myself has done me harm.—When I was in Switzerland and Greece I was out of the way of hearing either—& *how I wrote there!*—In Italy I am out of the way of it too—but latterly partly through my fault—& partly through your kindness in wishing to send me the *newest* & most periodical publications— I have had a crowd of reviews &c. thrust upon me—which have bored me with their jargon of one kind or another—& taken off my attention from greater objects.— —You have also sent me a parcel of trash of poetry for no reason that I can conceive—unless to provoke me to write a new "English Bards"—Now *this* I wish to avoid—for if ever I *do*—it will be a strong production—and I desire peace as long as the fools will keep their nonsense out of my way.— —

From Detached Thoughts

October 15, 1821–May 18, 1822

. . .

73

People have wondered at the Melancholy which runs through my writings.—Others have wondered at my personal gaiety— —but I recollect once after an hour in which I had been sincerely and particularly gay—and rather brilliant in company—my wife replying to me when I said (upon her remarking my high spirits) "and yet Bell—I have been called and mis-called Melancholy—you must have seen how falsely frequently." "No—B—(she answered) it is not so—at *heart* you are the most melancholy of mankind, and often when apparently gayest. ["]— —

74

If I could explain at length the *real* causes which have contributed to increase this perhaps *natural* temperament of mine—this Melancholy which hath made me a bye-word—nobody would wonder— —but this is impossible without doing much mischief.— —I do not know what other men's lives have been—but I cannot conceive anything more strange than some of the earlier parts of mine— —I have written my memoirs—but omitted *all* the really *consequential & important* parts—from deference to the dead—to the living—and to those who must be both.—

75

I sometimes think that I should have written the *whole*—as a *lesson*— — but it might have proved a lesson to be *learnt*—rather than *avoided*—for passion is a whirlpool, which is not to be viewed nearly without attraction from it's Vortex.— —

76

I must not go on with these reflections—or I shall be letting out some secret or other—to paralyze posterity.—

To Thomas Moore

Pisa, March 4th, 1822

. . .

With respect to "Religion," can I never convince you that *I* have no such opinions as the characters in that drama,[1] which seems to have frightened every body? Yet *they* are nothing to the expressions in Goethe's Faust (which are ten times hardier), and not a whit more bold than those of Milton's Satan. My ideas of a character may run away with me: like all imaginative men, I, of course, embody myself with the character while I *draw* it, but not a moment after the pen is from off the paper.

I am no enemy to religion, but the contrary. As a proof, I am educating my natural daughter a strict Catholic in a convent of Romagna; for I think people can never have *enough* of religion, if they are to have any. I incline, myself, very much to the Catholic doctrines; but if I am to write a drama, I must make my characters speak as I conceive them likely to argue.

As to poor Shelley, who is another bugbear to you and the world, he is, to my knowledge, the *least* selfish and the mildest of men—a man who has made more sacrifices of his fortune and feelings for others than any I ever heard of. With his speculative opinions I have nothing in common, nor desire to have.

---

1. *Cain*, published December 1821.

The truth is, my dear Moore, you live near the *stove* of society, where you are unavoidably influenced by its heat and its vapours. I did so once—and too much—and enough to give a colour to my whole future existence. As my success in society was *not* inconsiderable, I am surely not a prejudiced judge upon the subject, unless in its favour; but I think it, as now constituted, *fatal* to all great original undertakings of every kind. I never courted it *then*, when I was young and high in blood, and one of its "curled darlings;"[2] and do you think I would do so *now*, when I am living in a clearer atmosphere? One thing *only* might lead me back to it, and that is, to try once more if I could do any good in *politics*; but *not* in the petty politics I see now preying upon our miserable country.

Do not let me be misunderstood, however. If you speak your *own* opinions, they ever had, and will have, the greatest weight with *me*. But if you merely *echo* the "monde", (and it is difficult not to do so, being in its favour and its ferment,) I can only regret that you should ever repeat any thing to which I cannot pay attention.

But I am prosing. The gods go with you, and as much immortality of all kinds as may suit your present and all other existence.

Yours, &c.

To Henri Beyle[1]

Genoa, May 29, 1823

Sir,—At present, [now?] that I know to whom I am indebted for a very flattering mention in the "Rome, Naples, and Florence in 1817, by Mons. Stendhal," it is fit that I should return my thanks (however undesired or undesirable) to Mons. Beyle, with whom I had the honour of being acquainted at Milan in 1816. You only did me too much honour in what you were pleased to say in that work; but it has hardly given me less pleasure than the praise itself, to become at length aware (which I have done by mere accident) that I am indebted for it to one of whose good opinion I was really ambitious. So many changes have taken place since that period in the Milan circle, that I hardly dare recur to it;—some dead, some banished, and some in the Austrian dungeons.—Poor Pellico![2] I trust that, in his iron solitude, his Muse is consoling him in part—one day to delight us again, when both she and her Poet are restored to freedom.

Of your works I have seen only "Rome", etc., the Lives of Haydn and Mozart, and the *brochure* on Racine and Shakespeare. The "Histoire de la Peinture" I have not yet the good fortune to possess.

There is one part of your observations in the pamphlet which I shall venture to remark upon;—it regards Walter Scott. You say that "his character is little worthy of enthusiasm," at the same time that you mention his productions in the manner they deserve. I have known Walter Scott long and well, and in occasional situations which call forth the *real* character—and I can assure you that his character *is* worthy of admiration—that of all men

2. *Othello* 1.2.69.
1. The French novelist (1783–1842) known by his pen name, Stendhal, whom Byron met at La Scala opera house in Milan in October 1816.
2. Silvio Pellico (1788–1854), Italian writer arrested in 1820 by the Austrian government and held in jail for nine years because of his connection with a liberal newspaper.

he is the most *open*, the most *honourable*, the most *amiable*. With his politics I have nothing to do: they differ from mine, which renders it difficult for me to speak of them. But he is *perfectly sincere* in them; and Sincerity may be humble, but she cannot be servile. I pray you, therefore, to correct or soften that passage. You may, perhaps, attribute this officiousness of mine to a false affectation of *candour*, as I happen to be a writer also. Attribute it to what motive you please, but *believe* the *truth*. I say that Walter Scott is as nearly a thorough good man as man can be, because I *know* it by experience to be the case.

If you do me the honour of an answer—may I request a speedy one—because it is possible (though not yet decided) that Circumstances may conduct me once more to Greece;—my present address is *Genoa*—where an answer will reach me in a short time, or be forwarded to me wherever I may be.

I beg you to believe me with a lively recollection of our brief acquaintance—and the hope of one day renewing it.—

your ever obliged and obedt. humble Servt.
NOEL BYRON

I make no excuse for writing to you in English, as I understand you are well acquainted with that language.

To Johann Wolfgang von Goethe

Leghorn. July 22d. 1823

Illustrious Sir—I cannot thank you as you ought to be thanked for the lines which my young friend Mr. Sterling[1] sent me of yours,—and it would but ill become me to pretend to exchange verses with him who for fifty years has been the undisputed Sovereign of European literature.—You must therefore accept my most sincere acknowledgements in prose—and in hasty prose too—for I am at present on my voyage to Greece once more—and surrounded by hurry and bustle which hardly allow a moment even to Gratitude and Admiration to express themselves.— —I sailed from Genoa some days ago—was driven back by a Gale of Wind—and have since sailed again—and arrived here (Leghorn) this morning to receive on board some Greek passengers for their struggling Country.— —*Here* also I found your lines and Mr. Sterling's letter—and I could not have had a more favourable Omen or more agreeable surprise than a word from Goethe written by his own hand.— —I am returning to Greece to see if I can be of any little use there;—if ever I come back I will pay a visit to Weimar to offer the sincere homage of one of the many Millions of your admirers.—I have the honour to be ever & most respectfully

yr. obliged adm[irer] & Se[rvant]
NOEL BYRON

Aux Soins de Monsieur Sterling.

---

1. Charles Sterling, son of the British Consul at Genoa, delivered this letter to Goethe. The lines Goethe had sent Byron are printed in *Life* 2:676.

From Journal in Cephalonia[1]

June 19th. 1823

The Dead have been awakened—shall I sleep?
The World's at war with tyrants—shall I crouch?
The harvest's ripe—and shall I pause to reap?
   I slumber not—the thorn is in my Couch—
   Each day a trumpet soundeth in mine ear—
   It's Echo in my heart— —

Metaxata—Cephalonia—Septr. 28th. 1823

On the sixteenth (I think) of July I sailed from Genoa on the English Brig Hercules—Jno. Scott Master—on the 17th. a Gale of wind occasioning confusion and threatening damage to the horses in the hold—we bore up again for the same port—where we remained four and twenty hours longer and then put to sea—touched at Leghorn—and pursued our voyage by the straits of Messina for Greece—passing within sight of Elba—Corsica—the Lipari islands including Stromboli Sicily Italy &c.—about the 4th of August we anchored off Argostoli, the chief harbour of the Island of Cephalonia.— —

. . .

In the island of Cephalonia Colonel Napier commanded in chief as Resident—and Col. Duffie the 8th. a King's regiment then forming the Garrison. We were received by both those Gentlemen—and indeed by all the Officers as well as the Civilians with the greatest kindness and hospitality—which if we did not deserve—I still hope that we have done nothing to forfeit—and it has continued unabated—even since the Gloss of new acquaintance has been worn away by frequent intercourse.— —We have learned what has since been fully confirmed—that the Greeks are in a state of political dissention amongst themselves—that Mavrocordato was dismissed or had resigned (L'Un vaut bien l'autre) and that Colocotroni with I know not what or whose party was paramount in the Morea.—The Turks were in force in Acarnania &c. and the Turkish fleet blockaded the coast from Missolonghi to Chiarenza—and subsequently to Navarino— —the Greek Fleet from the want of means or other causes remained in port in Hydra—Ipsara and Spezas[?]—and for aught that is yet certainly known may be there still. As rather contrary to my expectations I had no advices from Peloponnesus—and had also letters to receive from England from the Committee I determined to remain for the interim in the Ionian Islands—especially as it was difficult to land on the opposite coast without risking the confiscation of the Vessel and

---

1. Byron arrived at Cephalonia on August 3, 1823, having set sail for Greece on July 15, determined to assist its war of liberation against Turkey. The lines dated June 19 head the first page of the Journal; they were first published in *LJ*. Once in Greece, ". . . Byron showed himself to be a great statesman and a born leader of men. The work of advocating unity among the various Greek tribes was no easy task for him, and he laboured tirelessly in the malarial climate of the gulf of Patras in the furtherance of this aim. His military project was to lead an expedition against the Turkish stronghold of Lepanto, and, with this in view, he enlisted the services of five hundred Suliotes. But mutiny broke out among the soldiers, and, at a critical moment, an epileptic fit threatened Byron's life. For a time, he recovered; but, early in April, he caught a severe chill when sailing, wet to the skin, in an open boat; rheumatic fever set in, and, on the nineteenth day of the month, he died" (*Cambridge History of English and American Literature*, vol. 12).

her Contents—which Capt. Scott naturally enough declined to do—unless I would insure to him the full amount of his possible damage.— —

. . .

. . . Soon after my arrival I took into my own pay a body of forty Suliotes[2] under the Chiefs Photomara—Giavella—and Drako—and would probably have increased the number—but I found them not quite united among themselves in any thing except raising their demands on me—although I had given a dollar per man more each month—than they could receive from the G[ree]k Gov[ernmen]t and they were destitute[,] at the time I took them[,] of every thing.— —I had acceded too to their own demand— and paid them a month in advance.— —But set on probably by some of the trafficking shopkeepers with whom they were in the habit of dealing on credit—they made various attempts at what I thought extortion—so that I called them together stating my view of the case—and declining to take them on with me—but I offered them another month's pay—and the price of their passage to Acarnania—where they could now easily go as the Turk- ish fleet was gone—and the blockade removed.—This part of them accepted—and they went accordingly.—Some difficulty arose about restor- ing their arms by the Septinsular Gov[ernmen]t but these were at length obtained—and they are now with their compatriots in Etolia or Acarnania.— —

. . .

As I did not come here to join a faction but a nation—and to deal with honest men and not with speculators or peculators—(charges bandied about daily by the Greeks of each other) it will require much circumspec- tion ⟨for me⟩ to avoid the character of a partizan—and I perceive it to be the more difficult—as I have already received invitations from more than one of the contending parties—always under the pretext that *they* are the "real Simon Pure"[2]— —After all—one should not despair—though all the foreigners that I have hitherto met with from amongst the Greeks—are going or gone back disgusted.—

Whoever goes into Greece at present should do it as Mrs. Fry went into Newgate—not in the expectation of meeting with any especial indication of existing probity—but in the hope that time and better treatment will reclaim the present burglarious and larcenous tendencies which have fol- lowed this General Gaol delivery.—When the limbs of the Greeks are a little less stiff from the shackles of four centuries—they will not march so much "as if they had gyves on their legs".[3]— —At present the Chains are broken indeed—but the links are still clanking—and the Saturnalia is still too recent to have converted the Slave into a sober Citizen.—The worst of them is—that (to use a coarse but the only expression that will not fall short of the truth) they are such d– – – –d liars;—there never was such an inca- pacity for veracity shown since Eve lived in Paradise.—One of them found fault the other day with the English language—because it had so few shades of a Negative—whereas a Greek can so modify a No—to a yes—and vice versa—by the slippery qualities of his language—that prevarication

2. The Suliotes were an Albanian tribe, whose warlike prowess Byron celebrated in *Childe Harold II*.
2. Mrs. Centlivre (1667?–1723), *A Bold Stroke for a Wife*.
3. *1 Henry IV* 4.2.36.

may be carried to any extent and still leave a loop-hole through which perjury may slip without being perceived.— —This was the Gentleman's own talk—and is only to be doubted because in the words of the Syllogism— "Now Epimenides was a Cretan".[4] But they may be mended by and bye.—

To Yusuff Pasha[1]

J[anuar]y 23d. 1824

Highness—A ship with some of my friends and servants on board was brought under the turrets of a Turkish frigate. It was then released on the order of Your Highness. I thank you, not for having released the ship—since it had a neutral flag and was under English protection, so that no one had the right to detain it—but for having treated my friends with the utmost courtesy—while they were at your disposition.— —In the hope of performing an action not displeasing to Your Highness I have asked the Greek Government here to place four Mussulman prisoners in my hands.—I now release them to Your Highness in recompense, as far as is possible, for your Courtesy.—They are sent without conditions—but if the circumstances could win a place in your memory I would only beg Your Highness to treat with humanity any Greek who may be [captured?] or fall into the hands of the Mussulmans—Since the horrors of war are sufficient in themselves without adding cold-blooded ruthlessness on either side.—

I have the honour to be etc. etc. etc.

From Journal in Cephalonia

February 15th. 1824

Upon February 15th—(I write on the 17th. of the same month) I had a strong shock of a Convulsive description but whether Epileptic—Paralytic— or Apoplectic is not yet decided by the two medical men who attend me— or whether it be of some other nature (if such there be) it was very painful and had it lasted a moment longer must have extinguished my mortality— if I can judge by sensations.—I was speechless with the features much distorted—but *not* foaming at the mouth—they say—and my struggles so violent that several persons—two of whom—Mr. Parry the Engineer—and my Servant Tita the Chasseur are very strong men—could not hold me—it lasted about ten minutes—and came on immediately after drinking a tumbler of Cider mixed with cold water in Col. Stanhope's apartments.—This is the first attack that I have had of this kind to the best of my belief. I never heard that any of my family were liable to the same—though my mother was subject to *hysterical* affections. Yesterday (the 16th.) Leeches were applied to my temples. I had previously recovered a good deal—but with some feverish and variable symptoms;—I bled profusely—and as they went too near the temporal Artery—there was some difficulty in stopping the blood—even with the Lunar Caustic—this however after some hours was

---

4. A reference to Epimenides' paradox: whether the truth or falsehood of Epimenides' statement "all Cretans are liars" can be determined since Epimenides was a Cretan.
1. One of the Turkish commanders during the Greek war of independence. Byron wrote the letter in Italian; the translation is by Antony Peattie for Leslie Marchand (*BLJ* 11:2, 98–99).

accomplished about eleven o'clock at night—and this day (the 17th.) though weakly I feel tolerably convalescent.— —

With regard to the presumed cause of this attack—as far as I know there might be several—the state of the place and of the weather permits little exercise at present;—I have been violently agitated with more than one passion recently—and a good deal occupied politically as well as privately— and amidst conflicting parties—politics—and (as far as regards public matters) circumstances;—I have also been in an anxious state with regard to things which may be only interesting to my own private feelings—and perhaps not uniformly so temperate as I may generally affirm that I was wont to be—how far any or all of these may have acted on the mind or body of One who had already undergone many previous changes of place and passion during a life of thirty six years I cannot tell—nor— —but I am interrupted by the arrival of a report from a party returned from reconnoitring a Turkish Brig of War just stranded on the Coast—and which is to be attacked the moment we can get some guns to bear upon her.—I shall hear what Parry says about it—here he comes.—

To Mr. Mayer[1]

[*Feb. 21, 1824?*] [*Undated*]

Sir,—Coming to Greece, one of my principal objects was to alleviate as much as possible the miseries incident to a warfare so cruel as the present. When the dictates of humanity are in question, I know no difference between Turks and Greeks. It is enough that those who want assistance are men, in order to claim the pity and protection of the meanest pretender to humane feelings. I have found here twenty-four Turks, including women and children, who have long pined in distress, far from the means of support and the consolations of their home. The Government has consigned them to me: I transmit them to Prevesa, whither they desire to be sent. I hope you will not object to take care that they may be restored to a place of safety, and that the Governor of your town may accept of my present. The best recompense I can hope for would be to find that I had inspired the Ottoman commanders with the same sentiments towards those unhappy Greeks who may hereafter fall into their hands. I beg you to believe me, &c.

[N BYRON]

1. The English Consul in Prevesa, Greece.

CRITICISM

One artistic frustration that Byron never had to face was critical neglect. Critical reaction to his published poetry throughout his lifetime was immediate, emphatic, and highly public. Although the earliest review, by Henry Brougham in the *Edinburgh Review*, stingingly berated the weaknesses and pretensions of the young peer's *Hours of Idleness* (1808), critical reaction became more respectful following the publication of *English Bards and Scotch Reviewers*, *Childe Harold* I–II, and the immensely popular Eastern tales. In 1817, Francis Jeffrey would pronounce *Manfred* "undoubtedly a work of genius and originality," while critics began to note that the same darkly brooding Byronic hero—outcast, guilt-ridden, beyond the reaches of human consolation—reappeared in each work as essentially a single, unvarying subject, a feature that elicited the censure of some critics and the pity of others (who identified these heroes with the poet). The publication of *Don Juan*, however, beginning with the first two cantos in 1819, precipitated a vehement moralistic backlash, as illustrated by the famous review in *Blackwood's Magazine* (p. 790). Despite, or perhaps because of Byron's fame and *Don Juan's* popularity, no words were spared to warn of the poem's, and the poet's, moral depravity and harmfulness to literature and society. The year after Byron's death, the influential essayist and critic William Hazlitt published *The Spirit of the Age*, which included an essay further delineating Byron's numerous flaws: "He is like a solitary peak, all access to which is cut off not more by elevation than distance. . . . He scorns all things . . . Lord Byron's verse glows like a flame, consuming every thing in its way . . . his Lordship's Muse spurns *the olden time*, and affects all the supercilious airs of a modern fine lady and an upstart. . . . Lord Byron, who in his politics is a *liberal*, in his genius is haughty and aristocratic . . ." and so forth. Later in the century, however, the poets Algernon Charles Swinburne and Matthew Arnold praised Byron's "sincerity and strength" and, along with other Victorian writers like Tennyson, Browning, and Ruskin, began to establish Byron's importance alongside Wordsworth as one of England's two leading poets of the recent past. Even Thomas Carlyle, whose eventual rejection of Romantic solipsism in *Sartor Resartus*—"Close thy Byron, open thy Goethe!"—is well known, observed in 1826 that the news of Byron's death "came down upon my heart like a mass of lead; and yet, the thought of it sends a painful twinge through all my being, as if I had lost a Brother!" (letter to Jane Baillie Welsh, his future wife, May 19, 1824).

A measure of Byron's cultural significance in nineteenth-century Europe is his distinction as the only poet to whom Bertrand Russell devoted a chapter in *A History of Western Philosophy* (1945). However, during the first half of the twentieth century, academic criticism veered away from popular opinion and, if anything, Byron's former popularity was considered an indication of his lack of poetic substance, complexity, and nuance. This view was not shared by James Joyce, who admired Byron; in *Portrait of the Artist As a Young Man*, Stephen Daedalus takes a beating defending Byron as "the greatest poet" against his schoolmate's charges that Byron was a heretic, immoral, and a poet for uneducated people. Virginia Woolf, however, was "much impressed by the extreme badness" of Byron's poetry, though allowing *Don Juan* to be "the most readable poem of its length ever written" (*A Writer's Diary*, Wednesday, August 7 and 8, 1918). Important early twentieth century Byron scholarship includes the invaluable scholarly edition of the complete poetry and prose by E. H. Coleridge and Rowland Prothero, and critical and biographical studies by Samuel Chew, André Maurois, Ethel Colburn Mayne, Harold Nicholson, and

Peter Quennell. But practitioners of the New Criticism did not find in Byron's works the ideals of form, internally coherent image patterns, and, with the exception of the satires, irony that rewarded close reading and therefore deserved critical attention. W. H. Auden, who greatly admired *Don Juan*, wrote in the introduction to his selected edition of Byron's poetry and letters: "I have no idea how many readers he still has, but, as one of them, I find the poems that made his reputation among his contemporaries, *Childe Harold* and the Tales, unreadable" (New American Library, 1966).

Even throughout this period of Byron's frequent disparagement by writers and critics, however, isolated but important books about Byron, such as those by Samuel Chew and Ernest Lovell, reflected continued awareness of his significance. In 1937, T. S. Eliot, while concurring with Woolf on the matter of Byron's "imperceptiveness to the English word" and observing that as a poet Byron was "the most nearly remote from the sympathies of every living critic," wrote an illuminating and largely appreciative essay in which he called for a critical reassessment of Byron, recognizing his skill as a narrative poet and observing that in the longer poems Byron "did something that no one else has ever equalled." Indeed, while noting that in his day poetry was expected to be something distilled, Eliot did not particularly denigrate Byron's poetry by observing that "bulk is inevitable in a poet of Byron's type" and that "if Byron had distilled his verse, there would have been nothing whatever left"— observations that Byron's admirers now, as then, would not be inclined to contradict. Yet if Byron appeared to be at a remove from certain modernist aesthetics, his omission from M. H. Abrams's influential study of English Romantic poetry published in 1971, *Natural Supernaturalism*, indicated the degree to which Byron also stood apart (as he himself knew) from the Romantic prophetic mode, and hardly, at that point in time, signified critical neglect. The critical reevaluation that reflected and promoted awareness of Byron's unique poetic achievement has largely been the province of two generations of British and American scholars, following the publication in 1957 of Leslie Marchand's warmly respectful, scrupulously researched three-volume biography. The 1960s saw a significant rise in critical attention, with insightful studies by, among others, Michael Cooke, W. Paul Elledge, Robert Gleckner, M. K. Joseph, G. Wilson Knight, William Marshall, Doris Langley Moore, Andrew Rutherford, Peter Thorslev, Paul Trueblood, and Paul West. With the editor's extreme regret, so much excellent criticism from the 1960s and 1970s, some of which was printed in the previous Norton Critical Edition, has been omitted from the present edition in order to leave room for a wider array of more recent essays, most of which build on the earlier work. Important textual scholarship during the 1970s and 1980s—particularly Marchand's edition of the complete letters and journals and the Clarendon Press scholarly edition of the complete poetical works edited by Jerome McGann—has been the springboard to an active critical dialogue about Byron. Enormously influential since the 1970s has been the criticism of McGann, whose two books devoted to Byron (*Fiery Dust* and *Don Juan in Context*) and numerous essays provide trenchant revisionary critiques of Byron's poetry, which emphasize the relevance of textual documents, biography, literary influences, and Byron's anti-Romantic rhetorical strategies. The recent criticism included in this Norton Critical Edition illustrates the range of theoretical approaches to Byron by today's critics, including biographical, new historicist, psychoanalytic, poststructuralist, and gender studies.

Nineteenth-Century Responses

JOHN KEATS

To Lord Byron[†]

Byron, how sweetly sad thy melody,
   Attuning still the soul to tenderness,
   As if soft Pity with unusual stress
Had touch'd her plaintive lute; and thou, being by,
Hadst caught the tones, nor suffered them to die.
   O'ershading sorrow doth not make thee less
   Delightful: thou thy griefs dost dress
With a bright halo, shining beamily;
As when a cloud a golden moon doth veil,
   Its sides are tinged with a resplendent glow,
Through the dark robe oft amber rays prevail,
   And like fair veins in sable marble flow.
Still warble, dying swan,—still tell the tale,
   The enchanting tale—the tale of pleasing woe.

Written December 1814

From Letter to George and Georgiana Keats (February 19, 1819)[‡]

* * * A Man's life of any worth is a continual allegory—and very few eyes can see the Mystery of his life—a life like the scriptures, figurative—which such people can no more make out than they can the hebrew Bible. Lord Byron cuts a figure—but he is not figurative—Shakespeare led a life of Allegory; his works are the comments on it. * * *

From Letter to George and Georgiana Keats (September 20, 1819)

* * * You speak of Lord Byron and me—There is this great difference between us. He describes what he sees—I describe what I imagine—Mine is the hardest task. * * *

---

† From *The Poems of John Keats,* ed. Jack Stillinger (Cambridge, MA: Harvard University Press, 1978).
‡ This and the letter below are from *The Letters of John Keats, 1814–1821,* ed. H. E. Rollins (Cambridge, MA: Harvard University Press, 1958).

WILLIAM WORDSWORTH

From Letter to John Scott (April 18, 1816)[†]

* * * Let me only say one word upon Lord B. The man is insane. * * * You yourself appear to me to labour under some delusion as to the merits of Lord B's Poetry, and treat those wretched verses, "The Farewell" [i.e., "Fare Thee Well"], with far too much respect. They are disgusting in sentiment, and in execution contemptible. "Though my many faults deface me" etc. Can worse doggrel be written than such a stanza? One verse is commendable, "All my madness none can know" * * *

From Letter to Henry Crabb Robinson(?) (January 1820)[‡]

* * * You will probably see Gifford, the Editor of the *Quarterly Review*; tell him from me, if you think proper, that every true-born Englishman will regard the pretensions of the Review to the character of a faithful defender of the institutions of the country, as *hollow*, while it leaves that infamous publication *Don Juan* unbranded; I do not mean by a formal Critique, for it is not worth it; it would also tend to keep it in memory; but by some decisive words of reprobation, both as to the damnable tendency of such works, and as to [the] despicable quality of the powers requisite for their production. What avails it to hunt down Shelley, whom few read, and leave Byron untouched?

I am persuaded that *Don Juan* will do more harm to the English character, than anything of our time * * *

PERCY BYSSHE SHELLEY

From Letter to Thomas Love Peacock (July 17, 1816)[*]

* * * Lord Byron is an exceedingly interesting person, and as such is it not to be regretted that he is a slave to the vilest and most vulgar prejudices, and as mad as the winds?

From Letter to Byron (May 26, 1820)

* * * I have read your *Don Juan* in print, and I observe that the *murrain* has killed some of the finest of the flock, i.e. that your bookseller has omitted certain passages. The personal ones, however, though I thought them

† From *The Letters of William and Dorothy Wordsworth: The Middle Years*, ed. Ernest de Selincourt, vol. 2 (Oxford: Oxford University Press, 1937).
‡ From *The Correspondence of Henry Crabb Robinson with the Wordsworth Circle*, ed. Edith J. Morely, vol. 2 (Oxford: Oxford University Press, 1927). This letter was most likely written to Robinson.
* From *The Letters of Percy Bysshe Shelley*, ed. Frederick L. Jones (Oxford: Oxford University Press, 1964).

wonderfully strong, I do not regret. What a strange and terrible storm is that at sea, and the two fathers, how true, yet how strong a contrast! Dante hardly exceeds it. With what flashes of divine beauty have you not illuminated the familiarity of your subject towards the end! The love letter, and the account of its being written, is altogether a masterpiece of portraiture; of human nature laid with the eternal colours of the feeling of humanity. Where did you learn all these secrets? I should like to go to school there. I cannot say I equally approve of the service to which this letter was appropriated; or that I altogether think the bitter mocking of our common nature, of which this is one of the expressions, quite worthy of your genius. The power and the beauty and the wit, indeed, redeem all this—chiefly because they belie and refute it. Perhaps it is foolish to wish that there had been nothing to redeem.

From Letter to Thomas Love Peacock (August [10?], 1821)

* * * Lord Byron is in excellent cue both of health and spirits. He has got rid of all those melancholy and degrading habits which he indulged at Venice. He lives with one woman, a lady of rank here, to whom he is attached, and who is attached to him, and is in every respect an altered man. He has written three more cantos of *Don Juan*. I have yet only heard the fifth, and I think that every word of it is pregnant with immortality. I have not seen his late plays except *Marino Faliero*, which is very well, but not so transcendently fine as the *Don Juan*. * * *

JOHANN WOLFGANG VON GOETHE

From Review of *Don Juan* (1819)[†]

Don Juan is a work of boundless genius, manifesting the bitterest and most savage hatred of humanity, and then again penetrated with the deepest and tenderest love for mankind. And as we already know and esteem the author and would not have him other than he is, we gratefully enjoy what with excessive licence, nay with audacity, he dares to set before us. The technical handling of the verse is quite in harmony with the strange, wild, ruthless content; the poet spares his language as little as he spares humanity; and as we approach closer we become aware that English poetry is already in possession of something we Germans totally lack: a cultured comic language.

---

† From *Goethes Werke* (Weimar, 1888–1919, XLI.I.245–49); trans. E. M. Butler, *Byron and Goethe: Analysis of a Passion* (London: Bowes & Bowes, 1956). The review was published in 1821.

HENRY P. BROUGHAM

From Review of *Hours of Idleness*[†]

The poesy of this young lord belongs to the class which neither gods nor men are said to permit.[1] Indeed, we do not recollect to have seen a quantity of verse with so few deviations in either direction from that exact standard. His effusions are spread over a dead flat, and can no more get above or below the level, than if they were so much stagnant water. As an extenuation of this offence, the noble author is peculiarly forward in pleading minority. We have it in the title-page, and on the very back of the volume; it follows his name like a favourite part of his *style*. Much stress is laid upon it in the preface, and the poems are connected with this general statement of his case, by particular dates, substantiating the age at which each was written.

* * *

His other plea of privilege, our author rather brings forward in order to waive it. He certainly, however, does allude frequently to his family and ancestors—sometimes in poetry, sometimes in notes; and while giving up his claim on the score of rank, he takes care to remember us of Dr Johnson's saying, that when a nobleman appears as an author, his merit should be handsomely acknowledged. In truth, it is this consideration only, that induces us to give Lord Byron's poems a place in our review, beside our desire to counsel him, that he do forthwith abandon poetry, and turn his talents, which are considerable, and his opportunities, which are great, to better account.

With this view, we must beg leave seriously to assure him, that the mere rhyming of the final syllable, even when accompanied by the presence of a certain number of feet,—nay, although (which does not always happen) those feet should scan regularly, and have been all counted accurately upon the fingers,—is not the whole art of poetry. We would entreat him to believe, that a certain portion of liveliness, somewhat of fancy, is necessary to constitute a poem; and that a poem in the present day, to be read, must contain at least one thought, either in a little degree different from the ideas of former writers, or differently expressed. * * *

* * *

It is a sort of privilege of poets to be egotists; but they should "use it as not abusing it"; and particularly one who piques himself (though indeed at the ripe age of nineteen), of being "an infant bard"—("The artless Helicon I boast is youth")—should either not know, or should seem not to know, so much about his own ancestry. Besides a poem above cited on the family seat of the Byrons, we have another of eleven pages on the self-same subject, introduced with an apology, "he certainly had no intention of inserting

† From Brougham's unsigned review, *Edinburgh Review* (February 1808). Stung by this review of his first publicly issued collection of poems, Byron retaliated with the satire *English Bards and Scotch Reviewers* (1809). As late as 1823, he alluded to this review when, as the narrator of *Don Juan*, he claimed that he would never have "worn the motley mantle of a poet, / If some one had not told me to forego it" (Canto XV.191–92).

1. Alluding to Horace's *Art of Poetry*, lines 372–73. (*Editor's note.*)

it;" but really, "the particular request of some friends," &c. &c. It concludes with five stanzas on himself, "the last and youngest of a noble line." There is a good deal also about his maternal ancestors, in a poem on Lachin-y-gair, a mountain where he spent part of his youth, and might have learnt that *pibroch* is not a bagpipe, any more than duet means a fiddle.

✣   ✣   ✣

But whatever judgment may be passed on the poems of this noble minor, it seems we must take them as we find them, and be content; for they are the last we shall ever have from him. He is at best, he says, but an intruder into the groves of Parnassus; he never lived in a garret, like thorough-bred poets; and "though he once roved a careless mountaineer in the Highlands of Scotland," he has not of late enjoyed this advantage. Moreover, he expects no profit from his publication; and whether it succeeds or not, "it is highly improbable, from his situation and pursuits hereafter," that he should again condescend to become an author.[2] Therefore, let us take what we get and be thankful. What right have we poor devils to be nice? We are well off to have got so much from a man of this Lord's station, who does not live in a garret, but "has the sway" of Newstead Abbey. Again, we say, let us be thankful; and, with honest Sancho, bid God bless the giver, nor look the gift horse in the mouth.

FRANCIS JEFFREY

From Review of *Childe Harold's Pilgrimage* I–II[†]

Lord Byron has improved marvellously since his last appearance at our tribunal;—and this, though it bear a very affected title, is really a volume of very considerable power, spirit and originality—which not only atones for the evil works of his nonage, but gives promise of a further excellence here-after; to which it is quite comfortable to look forward.

The most surprising thing about the present work, indeed, is, that it should please and interest so much as it does, with so few of the ordinary ingredients of interest or poetical delight. There is no story or adventure—and, indeed, no incident of any kind; the whole poem—to give a very short account of it—consisting of a series of reflections made in travelling through a part of Spain and Portugal, and in sailing up the Mediterranean to the shores of Greece. These reflections, too, and the descriptions out of which they arise, are presented without any regular order or connexion—being sometimes strung upon the slender thread of Childe Harold's Pilgrimage, and sometimes held together by the still slighter tie of the author's local situation at the time of writing. As there are no incidents, there cannot well be any characters;—and accordingly, with the exception of a few national sketches, which form part of the landscape of his pilgrimage, that of the hero himself is the only delineation of the kind that is offered to the reader of this volume;—and this hero, we must say, appears to us as oddly

---

2. Referring to the earliest of Byron's several announcements in the course of his poetic career that he would write no more poetry. (*Editor's note.*)

† From Jeffrey's unsigned review in *Edinburgh Review* (May 1812).

chosen as he is imperfectly employed. Childe Harold is a sated epicure—sickened with the very fulness of prosperity—oppressed with ennui, and stung with occasional remorse;—his heart hardened by a long course of sensual indulgence, and his opinion of mankind degraded by his acquaintance with the baser part of them. In this state he wanders over the fairest and most interesting parts of Europe, in the vain hope of stimulating his palsied sensibility by novelty, or at least of occasionally forgetting his mental anguish in the toils and perils of his journey. Like Milton's fiend, however, he "sees undelighted all delight," and passes on through the great wilderness of the world with a heart shut to all human sympathy—sullenly despising the stir both of its business and its pleasures—but hating and despising himself most of all, for beholding it with so little emotion.

Lord Byron takes the trouble to caution his readers against supposing that he meant to shadow out his own character under the dark and repulsive traits of that which we have just exhibited; a caution which was surely unnecessary—though it is impossible not to observe, that the mind of the noble author has been so far tinged by his strong conception of this Satanic personage, that the sentiments and reflections which he delivers in his own name, have all received a shade of the same gloomy and misanthropic colouring which invests those of his imaginary hero. The general strain of those sentiments, too, is such as we should have thought very little likely to attract popularity, in the present temper of this country. They are not only complexionally dark and disdainful, but run directly counter to very many of our national passions, and most favoured propensities. Lord Byron speaks with the most unbounded contempt of the Portuguese—with despondence of Spain—and in a very slighting and sarcastic manner of wars, and victories, and military heroes in general. Neither are his religious opinions more orthodox, we apprehend, than his politics; for he not only speaks without any respect of priests, and creeds, and dogmas of all descriptions, but doubts very freely of the immortality of the soul, and other points as fundamental.

Such are some of the disadvantages under which this poem lays claim to the public favour; and it will be readily understood that we think it has no ordinary merit, when we say, that we have little doubt that it will find favour, in spite of these disadvantages. Its chief excellence is a singular freedom and boldness, both of thought and expression, and a great occasional force and felicity of diction, which is the more pleasing that it does not appear to be the result either of long labour or humble imitation. There is, indeed, a tone of self-willed independence and originality about the whole composition—a certain plain manliness and strength of manner, which is infinitely refreshing after the sickly affectations of so many modern writers; and reconciles us not only to the asperity into which it sometimes degenerates, but even in some degree to the unamiableness upon which it constantly borders. We do not know, indeed, whether there is not something *piquant* in the very novelty and singularity of that cast of misanthropy and universal scorn, which we have already noticed as among the repulsive features of the composition. It excites a kind of curiosity, at least, to see how objects, which have been usually presented under so different an aspect, appear through so dark a medium; and undoubtedly gives great effect to the flashes of emotion and suppressed sensibility that occasionally burst through the gloom. The best parts of the poem, accordingly, are those which embody those stern and disdainful reflexions, to which the author seems to recur with unfeigned cordiality and eagerness—and through which we think we can sometimes discern the strugglings of a gentler feeling, to which he is afraid to abandon himself. There is much strength, in short, and some impetuous feeling in this poem—but very little softness; some pity for mankind—but very little affection; and no enthusiasm in the cause of any living men, or admiration of their talents or virtues. The author's inspiration does not appear to have brought him any beatific visions, nor to have peopled his fancy with any forms of loveliness; and though his lays are often both loud and lofty, they neither "lap us in Elysium," nor give us any idea that it was in Elysium that they were framed.

The descriptions are often exceedingly good; and the diction, though unequal and frequently faulty, has on the whole a freedom, copiousness and vigour, which we are not sure that we could match in any contemporary poet. Scott alone, we think, possesses a style equally strong and natural; but Scott's is more made up of imitations, and indeed is frequently a mere cento of other writers—while Lord Byron's has often a nervous simplicity and manly freshness which reminds us of Dryden, and an occasional force and compression, in some of the smaller pieces especially, which afford no unfavourable resemblance of Crabbe.

※   ※   ※

FRANCIS JEFFREY

From Review of *Childe Harold's Pilgrimage* III and Other Poems of 1816[†]

If the finest poetry be that which leaves the deepest impression on the minds of its readers—and this is not the worst test of its excellence—Lord Byron, we think, must be allowed to take precedence of all his distinguished contemporaries. He has not the variety of Scott—nor the delicacy of Campbell—nor the absolute truth of Crabbe—nor the polished sparkling of Moore; but in force of diction, and inextinguishable energy of sentiment, he clearly surpasses them all. 'Words that breathe, and thoughts that burn,' are not merely the ornaments, but the common staple of his poetry; and he is not inspired or impressive only in some happy passages, but through the whole body and tissue of his composition. It was an unavoidable condition, perhaps, of this higher excellence, that his scene should be narrow, and his persons few. To compass such ends as he had in view, it was necessary to reject all ordinary agents, and all trivial combinations. He could not possibly be amusing, or ingenious, or playful; or hope to maintain the requisite pitch of interest by the recitation of sprightly adventures, or the opposition of common characters. To produce great

---

[†] From Jeffrey's unsigned review (*Edinburgh Review*, February 1817) of *Childe Harold's Pilgrimage* III, "Fare Thee Well," and poems published in *The Prisoner of Chillon and Other Poems* ("Darkness," "The Dream," "Prometheus," etc.). About the review, Byron wrote to Moore: "I was not, and, indeed, am not even *now*, the misanthropical and gloomy gentleman he takes me for, but a facetious companion, well to do with those with whom I am intimate, and as loquacious and laughing as if I were a much cleverer fellow. I suppose now I shall never be able to shake off my sables in public imagination" (*BLJ* 6:186).

effects, he felt that it was necessary to deal only with the greater passions—
with the exaltations of a daring fancy, and the errors of a lofty intellect—
with the pride, the terrors, and the agonies of strong emotion—the fire and
air alone of our human elements.

*   *   *

With all these undoubted claims to our admiration, however, it is impos-
sible to deny that the Noble author before us has still something to learn,
and a good deal to correct. He is frequently abrupt and careless, and some-
times obscure. There are marks, occasionally, of effort and straining after
an emphasis which is generally spontaneous;—and, above all, there is far
too great a monotony in the moral colouring of his pictures, and too much
repetition of the same sentiments and maxims. He delights too exclusively
in the delineation of a certain morbid exaltation of character and of
feeling,—a sort of demoniacal sublimity, not without some traits of the
ruined Archangel. He is haunted almost perpetually with the image of a
being feeding and fed upon by violent passions, and the recollections of the
catastrophes they have occasioned: And, though worn out by their past
indulgence, unable to sustain the burden of an existence which they do not
continue to animate—full of pride and revenge and obduracy—disdaining
life and death, and mankind and himself—and trampling, in his scorn, not
only upon the falsehood and formality of polished life, but upon its tame
virtues and slavish devotion: Yet envying, by fits, the selfish beings he
despises, and melting into mere softness and compassion when the help-
lessness of childhood or the frailty of woman make an appeal to his gen-
erosity. Such is the person with whom we are called upon almost exclusively
to sympathize in all the greater productions of this distinguished writer:—
In *Childe Harold*—in *The Corsair*—in *Lara*—in *The Siege of Corinth*—in
Parisina, and in most of the smaller pieces.

It is impossible to represent such a character better than Lord Byron has
done in all these productions,—or indeed to represent anything more terri-
ble in its anger, or more attractive in its relenting. In point of effect, we read-
ily admit, that no one character can be more poetical or impressive.—But it
is really too much to find the scene perpetually filled by one character—not
only in all the acts, but in all the different pieces;—and, grand and impres-
sive as it is, we feel at last that these very qualities make some relief more
indispensable, and oppress the spirits of ordinary mortals with too deep an
impression of awe and repulsion. There is too much guilt in short, and too
much gloom, in the leading character. *   *   *

*   *   *

*   *   * We do not consider it as unfair, therefore, to say that Lord Byron
appears to us to be the zealous apostle of a certain fierce and magnificent
misanthropy, which has already saddened his poetry with too deep a shade,
and not only led to a great misapplication of great talents, but contributed
to render popular some very false estimates of the constituents of human
happiness and merit. *   *   *

*   *   *

*   *   * Of the verses entitled "Fare thee well",—and some others of a sim-
ilar character, we shall say nothing but that, in spite of their beauty, it is

painful to read them—and infinitely to be regretted that they should have been given to the public. It would be a piece of idle affectation to consider them as mere effusions of fancy, or to pretend ignorance of the subjects to which they relate—and with the knowledge which all the world has of these subjects, we must say, that not even the example of Lord Byron can persuade us that they are fit for public discussion. We come, therefore, to the consideration of the Noble author's most recent publications.

The most considerable of these, is the Third Canto of *Childe Harold*, a work which has the disadvantage of all continuations in admitting of little absolute novelty in the plan of the work, or the cast of its character, and must, besides, remind all Lord Byron's readers of the extraordinary effect produced by the sudden blazing forth of his genius upon their first introduction to that title. In spite of all this, however, we are persuaded that this Third Part of the poem will not be pronounced inferior to either of the former; and, we think, will probably be ranked above them by those who have been most delighted with the whole. The great success of this singular production, indeed, has always appeared to us an extraordinary proof of its merits; for, with all its genius, it does not belong to a sort of poetry that rises easily to popularity.—It has no story or action—very little variety of character—and a great deal of reasoning and reflection of no very attractive tenor. It is substantially a contemplative and ethical work, diversified with fine description, and adorned or overshaded by one emphatic person, who is sometimes the author, and sometimes the object of the reflections on which the interest is chiefly rested. It required, no doubt, great force of writing, and a decided tone of originality to recommend a performance of this sort so powerfully as this has been recommended to public notice and admiration—and those high characteristics belong perhaps still more eminently to the part that is now before us, than to any of the former. There is the same stern and lofty disdain of mankind, and their ordinary pursuits and enjoyments, with the same bright gaze on nature, and the same magic power of giving interest and effect to her delineations—but mixed up, we think, with deeper and more matured reflections, and a more intense sensibility to all that is grand or lovely in the external world.—Harold, in short, is somewhat older since he last appeared upon the scene—and while the vigour of his intellect has been confirmed, and his confidence in his own opinions increased, his mind has also become more sensitive; and his misanthropy, thus softened over by habits of calmer contemplation, appears less active and impatient, even although more deeply rooted than before. Undoubtedly the finest parts of the poem before us are those which thus embody the weight of his moral sentiments, or disclose the lofty sympathy which binds the despiser of Man to the glorious aspects of Nature. It is in these, we think, that the great attractions of the work consist, and the strength of the author's genius is seen. The narrative and description are of far inferior interest. With reference to the sentiments and opinions, however, which thus give its distinguishing character to the piece, we must say, that it seems no longer possible to ascribe them to the ideal person whose name it bears, or to any other than the author himself.—Lord Byron, we think, has formerly complained of those who identified him with his hero, or supposed that Harold was but the expositor of his own feelings and opinions;—and in noticing the former portions of the work, we thought it unbecoming to give any countenance to such a supposition.—In this last part, however, it is really impracticable to distinguish them.—Not only do the author and his hero travel and reflect together—but, in truth, we scarcely ever have any notice to which of them the sentiments so energetically expressed are to be ascribed; and in those which are unequivocally given as those of the Noble author himself, there is the very same tone of misanthropy, sadness and scorn, which we were formerly willing to regard as a part of the assumed costume of the Childe. We are far from supposing, indeed, that Lord Byron would disavow any of these sentiments; and though there are some which we must ever think it most unfortunate to entertain, and others which it appears improper to have published, the greater part are admirable, and cannot be perused without emotion even by those to whom they may appear erroneous.

* * *

Beautiful as this poetry is, it is relief at last to close the volume. We cannot maintain our accustomed tone of levity, or even speak like calm literary judges, in the midst of these agonizing traces of a wounded and distempered spirit. Even our admiration is at last swallowed up in a most painful feeling of pity and of wonder. It is impossible to mistake these for fictitious sorrows, conjured up for the purpose of poetical effect. There is a dreadful tone of sincerity, and an energy that cannot be counterfeited in the expression of wretchedness and alienation from human kind, which occurs in every page of this publication; and as the author has at last spoken out in his own person, and unbosomed his griefs a great deal too freely to his readers, the offence now would be to entertain a doubt of their reality. We certainly have no hope of preaching him into philanthropy and cheerfulness; but it is impossible not to mourn over such a catastrophe of such a mind, or to see the prodigal gifts of Nature, Fortune, and Fame, thus turned to bitterness, without an oppressive feeling of impatience, mortification and surprise. Where there are such elements, however, it is equally impossible to despair that they may yet enter into happier combinations,—or not to hope that "this puissant spirit"

> yet shall reascend
> Self-raised, and repossess its native seat.

JOHN WILSON OR JOHN GIBSON LOCKHART(?)

Remarks on *Don Juan* in *Blackwood's Magazine*[†]

It has not been without much reflection and overcoming many reluctancies, that we have at last resolved to say a few words more to our readers concerning this very extraordinary poem. The nature and causes of our difficulties will be easily understood by those of them who have read any part of *Don Juan*—but we despair of standing justified as to the conclusion at which we have arrived, in the opinion of any but those who have read and

---

† From *Blackwood's Magazine* (August 1819); tentatively ascribed to John Wilson or John Gibson Lockhart. In response to this review, Byron wrote "Some Observations upon an Article in *Blackwood's Magazine*" on March 15, 1820, but it was not published in his lifetime (see *Lord Byron: The Complete Miscellaneous Prose*, ed. Andrew Nicholson).

understood the whole of a work, in the composition of which there is unquestionably a more thorough and intense infusion of genius and vice— power and profligacy—than in any poem which had ever before been writ- ten in the English, or indeed in any other modern language. Had the wickedness been less inextricably mingled with the beauty and the grace, and the strength of a most inimitable and incomprehensible muse, our task would have been easy: But SILENCE would be a very poor and a very use- less chastisement to be inflicted by us, or by any one, on a production, whose corruptions have been so effectually embalmed—which, in spite of all that critics can do or refrain from doing, nothing can possibly prevent from taking a high place in the literature of our country, and remaining to all ages a perpetual monument of the exalted intellect, and the depraved heart, of one of the most remarkable men to whom that country has had the honour and the disgrace of giving birth.

That Lord Byron has never written any thing more decisively and tri- umphantly expressive of the greatness of his genius, will be allowed by all who have read this poem. That (laying all its manifold and grievous offences for a moment out of our view) it is by far the most admirable spec- imen of the mixture of ease, strength, gayety, and seriousness extant in the whole body of English poetry, is a proposition to which, we are almost as well persuaded, very few of them will refuse their assent. With sorrow and humiliation do we speak it—the poet has devoted his powers to the worst of purposes and passions; and it increases his guilt and our sorrow, that he has devoted them entire. What the immediate effect of the poem may be on contemporary literature, we cannot pretend to guess—too happy could we hope that its lessons of boldness and vigour in language, and versifica- tion, and conception, might be attended to, as they deserve to be—without any stain being suffered to fall on the purity of those who minister to the general shape and culture of the public mind, from the mischievous insults against all good principle and all good feeling, which have been unworthily embodied in so many elements of fascination.

The moral strain of the whole poem is pitched in the lowest key—and if the genius of the author lifts him now and then out of his pollution, it seems as if he regretted the elevation, and made all haste to descend again. To particularize the offences committed in its pages would be worse than vain—because the great genius of the man seems to have been throughout exerted to its utmost strength, in devising every possible method of pour- ing scorn upon every element of good or noble nature in the hearts of his readers. Love—honour—patriotism—religion, are mentioned only to be scoffed at and derided, as if their sole resting-place were, or ought to be, in the bosoms of fools. It appears, in short, as if this miserable man, having exhausted every species of sensual gratification—having drained the cup of sin even to its bitterest dregs, were resolved to shew us that he is no longer a human being, even in his frailties,—but a cool unconcerned fiend, laugh- ing with a detestable glee over the whole of the better and worse elements of which human life is composed—treating well nigh with equal derision the most pure of virtues, and the most odious of vices—dead alike to the beauty of the one, and the deformity of the other—a mere heartless despiser of that frail but noble humanity, whose type was never exhibited in a shape of more deplorable degradation than in his own contemptuously distinct delineation of himself. To confess in secret to his Maker, and weep over in secret agonies the wildest and most phantastic transgressions of heart and mind, is the part of a conscious sinner, in whom sin has not become the sole principle of life and action—of a soul for which there is yet hope. But to lay bare to the eye of man and of *woman* all the hidden convulsions of a wicked spirit—thoughts too abominable, we would hope, to have been imagined by any but him that has expressed them—and to do all this without one symptom of pain, contrition, remorse, or hesitation, with a calm careless ferociousness of contented and satisfied depravity— this was an insult which no wicked man of genius had ever before dared to put upon his Creator or his Species. This highest of all possible exhibitions of self-abandonment has been set forth in mirth and gladness, by one whose name was once pronounced with pride and veneration by every English voice. This atrocious consummation was reserved for Byron.

It has long been sufficiently manifest, that this man is devoid of religion. At times, indeed, the power and presence of the Deity, as speaking in the sterner workings of the elements, seems to force some momentary consciousness of their existence into his labouring breast;—a spirit in which there breathes so much of the divine, cannot always resist the majesty of its Maker. But of true religion terror is a small part—and of all religion, that founded on mere terror, is the least worthy of such a man as Byron. We may look in vain through all his works for the slightest evidence that his soul had ever listened to the *gentle voice* of the oracles. His understanding has been subdued into conviction by some passing cloud; but his heart has never been touched. He has never written one line that savours of the spirit of meekness. His faith is but for a moment—"he believes and trembles," and relapses again into his gloom of unbelief—a gloom in which he is at least as devoid of HOPE and CHARITY as he is of FAITH.—The same proud hardness of heart which makes the author of *Don Juan* a despiser of the Faith for which his fathers bled, has rendered him a scorner of the better part of woman; and therefore it is that his love poetry is a continual insult to the beauty that inspires it. The earthy part of the passion is all that has found a resting place within his breast—His idol is all of clay— and he dashes her to pieces almost in the moment of his worship. Impiously railing against his God—madly and meanly disloyal to his Sovereign and his country,—and brutally outraging all the best feelings of female honour, affection, and confidence—How small a part of chivalry is that which remains to the descendant of the Byrons—a gloomy vizor, and a deadly weapon!

Of these offences, however, or of such as these, Lord Byron had been guilty abundantly before, and for such he has before been rebuked in our own, and in other more authoritative pages. There are other and newer sins with which the author of *Don Juan* has stained himself—sins of a class, if possible, even more despicable than any he had before committed; and in regard to which it is matter of regret to us, that as yet our periodical critics have not appeared to express themselves with any seemly measure of manly and candid indignation.

Those who are acquainted, (as who is not?) with the main incidents in the private life of Lord Byron,—and who have not seen this production, (and we are aware, that very few of our Northern readers have seen it),— will scarcely believe, that the odious malignity of this man's bosom should have carried him so far, as to make him commence a filthy and impious poem, with an elaborate satire on the character and manners of his wife—from whom, even by his own confession, he has been separated only in consequence of his own cruel and heartless misconduct. * * * To offend the love of such a woman was wrong—but it might be forgiven; to desert her was unmanly—but he might have returned and wiped for ever from her eyes the tears of her desertion;—but to injure, and to desert, and then to turn back and wound her widowed privacy with unhallowed strains of cold-blooded mockery—was brutally, fiendishly, inexpiably mean. For impurities there might be some possibility of pardon, were they supposed to spring only from the reckless buoyancy of young blood and fiery passions,—for impiety there might at least be pity, were it visible that the misery of the impious soul were as great as its darkness;—but for offences such as this, which cannot proceed either from the madness of sudden impulse, or the bewildered agonies of self-perplexing and self-despairing doubt—but which speak the wilful and determined spite of an unrepenting, unsoftened, smiling, sarcastic, joyous sinner—for such diabolical, such slavish vice, there can be neither pity nor pardon.[1] Our knowledge that it is committed by one of the most powerful intellects our island ever has produced, lends intensity a thousand fold to the bitterness of our indignation. Every high thought that was ever kindled in our breasts by the muse of Byron—every pure and lofty feeling that ever responded from within us to the sweep of his majestic inspirations—every remembered moment of admiration and enthusiasm is up in arms against him. * * * It is indeed a sad and an humiliating thing to know, that in the same year there proceeded from the same pen two productions, in all things so different, as the Fourth Canto of *Childe Harold* and this loathsome *Don Juan*.

*　*　*

Perhaps there are not a few women who may profit from seeing in what a style of contemptuous coldness the sufferings to which licentious love exposes them are talked of by such people as the author of *Don Juan*. The many fine eyes that have wept dangerous tears over his descriptions of the Gulnares and Medoras cannot be the worse for seeing the true side of *his* picture.

*　*　*

But the best and the worst part of the whole is without doubt the description of the shipwreck. As a piece of terrible painting, it is as much superior as can be to every description of the kind—not even excepting that in the *Aeneid*—that ever was created. In comparison with the fearful and intense reality of its horrors, every thing that any former poet had thrown together to depict the agonies of that awful scene, appears chill and tame. [Quotes *Don Juan* II, stanzas 52–53.]

---

1. Lady Byron's response to the satirical resemblence between herself and Donna Inez was impressively magnanimous: "In the first place I am very much relieved to find that there is not anything which I can be expected to notice. As for myself, I don't think that my sins are in the pharisaical or pedantic line, and I am very sure that he does not think they are, but avails himself of the prejudices which some may entertain against me, to give a plausible colouring to his accusations. I must however confess that the quizzing in one or two passages was so good as to make me smile at myself—therefore others are heartily welcome to laugh" (as quoted in Ethel Colburn Mayne, *The Life and Letters of Anne Isabella Lady Noel Byron, from Unpublished Papers in the Possession of the Late Ralph, Earl of Lovelace* [1929], p. 283). (*Editor's note.*)

But even here the demon of his depravity does not desert him. We dare not stain our pages with quoting any specimens of the disgusting merriment with which he has interspersed his picture of human suffering. He paints it well, only to shew that he scorns it the more effectually; and of all the fearful sounds which ring in the ears of the dying, the most horrible is the demoniacal laugh with which this unpitying brother exults over the contemplation of their despair. Will our readers believe that the most innocent of all his odious sarcasms is contained in these two lines?

> They grieved for those that perished in the cutter.
> And also for the biscuit casks, and butter.

ROBERT SOUTHEY

[On *Don Juan* and the "Satanic School" of Poetry][†]

* * *

* * * I am well aware that the public are peculiarly intolerant of such innovations [i.e., Southey's own metrical experiments]. * * * Would that this literary intolerance were under the influence of a saner judgement, and regarded the morals more than the manner of a composition; the spirit rather than the form! Would that it were directed against those monstrous combinations of horrors and mockery, lewdness and impiety, with which English poetry has, in our days, first been polluted! For more than half a century English literature had been distinguished by its moral purity, the effect, and, in its turn, the cause of an improvement in national manners. A father might, without apprehension of evil, have put into the hands of his children any book which issued from the press, if it did not bear, either in its title-page or frontispiece, manifest signs that it was intended as furniture for the brothel. There was no danger in any work which bore the name of a respectable publisher, or was to be procured at any respectable booksellers. This was particularly the case with regard to our poetry. It is now no longer so; and woe to those by whom the offence cometh! The greater the talents of the offender, the greater is his guilt, and the more enduring will be his shame. Whether it be that the laws are in themselves unable to abate an evil of this magnitude, or whether it be that they are remissly administered, and with such injustice that the celebrity of an offender serves as a privilege whereby he obtains impunity, individuals are bound to consider that such pernicious works would neither be published nor written, if they were discouraged as they might, and ought to be, by public feeling; every person, therefore, who purchases such books, or admits them into his house, promotes the mischief, and thereby, as far as in him lies, becomes an aider and abettor of the crime.

The publication of a lascivious book is one of the worst offences which can be committed against the well-being of society. It is a sin, to the con-

---

† From Preface to *A Vision of Judgement* (April 1821). Southey's grandiloquent ode on the heavenly apotheosis of King George III—with its preface attacking Byron, Shelley and their coterie—became the basis for Byron's satiric masterpiece *The Vision of Judgment* (1822).

sequences of which no limits can be assigned, and those consequences no after repentance in the writer can counteract. Whatever remorse of conscience he may feel when his hour comes (and come it must!) will be of no avail. The poignancy of a death-bed repentance cannot cancel one copy of the thousands which are sent abroad; and as long as it continues to be read, so long is he the pander of posterity, and so long is he heaping up guilt upon his soul in perpetual accumulation.

These remarks are not more severe than the offence deserves, even when applied to those immoral writers who have not been conscious of any evil intention in their writings, who would acknowledge a little levity, a little warmth of colouring, and so forth, in that sort of language with which men gloss over their favourite vices, and deceive themselves. What then should be said of those for whom the thoughtlessness and inebriety of wanton youth can no longer be pleaded, but who have written in sober manhood and with deliberate purpose? Men of diseased hearts and depraved imaginations, who, forming a system of opinions to suit their own unhappy course of conduct, have rebelled against the holiest ordinances of human society, and hating that revealed religion which, with all their efforts and bravadoes, they are unable entirely to disbelieve, labour to make others as miserable as themselves, by infecting them with a moral virus that eats into the soul! The school which they have set up may properly be called the Satanic school; for though their productions breathe the spirit of Belial in their lascivious parts, and the spirit of Moloch in those loathsome images of atrocities and horrors which they delight to represent, they are more especially characterized by a Satanic spirit of pride and audacious impiety, which still betrays the wretched feeling of hopelessness wherewith it is allied.

This evil is political as well as moral, for indeed moral and political evils are inseparably connected.[1] * * *

* * *

No apology is offered for these remarks. The subject led to them; and the occasion of introducing them was willingly taken, because it is the duty of every one, whose opinion may have any influence, to expose the drift and aim of those writers who are labouring to subvert the foundations of human virtue, and of human happiness. * * *

1. In a letter Southey had written on February 20, 1820, to Walter Savage Landor, he referred to *Don Juan* as "a foul blot on the literature of his country, an act of high treason on English poetry" (*The Life and Correspondence of the late Robert Southey*, ed. C. C. Southey [1849–50]). (*Editor's note.*)

FRANCIS JEFFREY

[On *Don Juan*]†

* * *

The charge we bring against Lord B. in short is, that his writings have a tendency to destroy all belief in the reality of virtue—and to make all enthusiasm and constancy of affection ridiculous; and that this is effected, not merely by direct maxims and examples, of an imposing or seducing kind, but by the constant exhibition of the most profligate heartlessness in the persons of those who had been transiently represented as actuated by the purest and most exalted emotions—and in the lessons of that very teacher who had been, but a moment before, so beautifully pathetic in the expression of the loftiest conceptions. * * *

* * *

This is the charge which we bring against Lord Byron. We say that, under some strange misapprehension as to the truth, and the duty of proclaiming it, he has exerted all the powers of his powerful mind to convince his readers, both directly and indirectly, that all ennobling pursuits, and disinterested virtues, are mere deceits or illusions—hollow and despicable mockeries for the most part, and, at best, but laborious follies. Love, patriotism, valour, devotion, constancy, ambition—all are to be laughed at, disbelieved in, and despised!—and nothing is really good, so far as we can gather, but a succession of dangers to stir the blood, and of banquets and intrigues to sooth it again! If this doctrine stood alone, with its examples, it would revolt, we believe, more than it would seduce:—but the author of it has the unlucky gift of personating all those sweet and lofty illusions, and that with such grace and force and truth to nature, that it is impossible not to suppose, for the time, that he is among the most devoted of their votaries—till he casts off the character with a jerk—and, the moment after he has moved and exalted us to the very height of our conception, resumes his mockery at all things serious or sublime—and lets us down at once on some coarse joke, hard-hearted sarcasm, or fierce and relentless personality—as if on purpose to show

Whoe'er was edified, himself was not—

or to demonstrate practically as it were, and by example, how possible it is to have all fine and noble feelings, or their appearance, for a moment, and yet retain no particle of respect for them—or of belief in their intrinsic worth or permanent reality. Thus, we have an indelicate but very clever scene of the young Juan's concealment in the bed of an amorous matron, and of the torrent of "rattling and audacious eloquence" with which she repels the too just suspicions of her jealous lord. All this is merely comic, and a little coarse:—But then the poet chuses to make this shameless and abandoned woman address to her young gallant, an epistle breathing the very spirit of warm, devoted, pure and unalterable love—thus profaning the holiest language of the heart, and indirectly associating it with the most hateful and degrading sensuality. In like manner, the sublime and terrific

---

† From his unsigned review of *Sardanapalus, The Two Foscari,* and *Cain* in the *Edinburgh Review* (February 1822).

description of the Shipwreck is strangely and disgustingly broken by traits of low humour and buffoonery;—and we pass immediately from the moans of an agonizing father fainting over his famished son, to facetious stories of Juan's begging a paw of his father's dog—and refusing a slice of his tutor!—as if it were a fine thing to be hard-hearted—and pity and compassion were fit only to be laughed at. In the same spirit, the glorious Ode on the aspirations of Greece after Liberty, is instantly followed up by a strain of dull and cold-blooded ribaldry;—and we are hurried on from the distraction and death of Haidee to merry scenes of intrigue and masquerading in the seraglio. Thus all good feelings are excited only to accustom us to their speedy and complete extinction; and we are brought back, from their transient and theatrical exhibition, to the staple and substantial doctrine of the work—the non-existence of constancy in women or honour in men, and the folly of expecting to meet with any such virtues, or of cultivating them, for an undeserving world;—and all this mixed up with so much wit and cleverness, and knowledge of human nature, as to make it irresistibly pleasant and plausible—while there is not only no antidote supplied, but everything that might have operated in that way has been anticipated, and presented already in as strong and engaging a form as possible—but under such associations as to rob it of all efficacy, or even turn it into an auxiliary of the poison.

*　*　*

There is a minor blemish, of which we meant to say something also—but it is scarcely worth while—we mean the outrageous, and, till he set the example, the unprecedented *personalities* in which this noble author indulges. We have already noticed the ferocity of his attacks on Mr. Southey. The Laureate had railed at him indeed before; but he had railed 'in good set terms;'—and, if we recollect right, had not even mentioned his Lordship's name. It was all, in his exquisite way, by innuendo. In spite of this, we do not mean to deny that Lord B. had a right to name Mr. Southey—but he had no right to say any thing of Mr. Southey's wife; and the mention of her, and of many other people, is cruel, coarse, and unhandsome. If his Lordship's sense of propriety does not cure him of his propensity, we hope his pride may. For the practice has gone down to such imitators, as can do him no honour in pointing to him as their original. We rather think it would be better after all, to be called the founder of the Satanic School, than the Master of the John Bulls, Beacons, and Sentinels.[1]

ALGERNON CHARLES SWINBURNE

From Preface to *Selections from the Works of Lord Byron*[†]

* * *The time was when all boys and girls who paddled in rhyme and dabbled in sentiment were wont to adore the presence or the memory of Byron with foolish faces of praise. It is of little moment to him or to us that they have long since ceased to cackle and begun to hiss. They have become used

---

1. Newspapers noted for printing vicious political and personal attacks. (*Editor's note.*)
† From *Selections from The Works of Lord Byron* (1866); reprinted in *Essays and Studies* (London: Chatto and Windus, 1875).

to better verse and carefuller workmen; and must be forgiven if after such training they cannot at once appreciate the splendid and imperishable excellence which covers all his offences and outweighs all his defects: the excellence of sincerity and strength. Without these no poet can live; but few have ever had so much of them as Byron. His sincerity indeed is difficult to discover and define; but it does in effect lie at the root of all his good works: deformed by pretension and defaced by assumption, masked by folly and veiled by affectation; but perceptible after all, and priceless.

*　　*　　*

Thus much however we may safely assert: that no man's work was ever more influenced by his character; and that no man's character was ever more influenced by his circumstances. Rather from things without than from things within him did the spirit of Byron assume colour and shape. His noblest verse leapt on a sudden into life after the heaviest evils had fallen upon him which even he ever underwent. From the beginning indeed he had much to fight against; and three impediments hung about him at starting, the least of which would have weighed down a less strong man: youth, and genius, and an ancient name.[1] In spite of all three he made his way; and suffered for it. At the first chance given or taken, every obscure and obscene thing that lurks for pay or prey among the fouler shallows and thickets of literature flew against him; every hound and every hireling lavished upon him the loathsome tribute of their abuse; all nameless creatures that nibble and prowl, upon whom the serpent's curse has fallen, to go upon his belly and eat dust all the days of his life, assailed him with their foulest venom and their keenest fangs. And the promise given of old to their kind was now at least fulfilled: they did bruise his heel. But the heads of such creatures are so small that it is hard to bruise them in return; it would first be necessary to discern them.

That Byron was able to disregard and to outlive the bark and the bite of such curs as these is small praise enough: the man who cannot do as much is destructible, and therefore contemptible. He did far more than this; he withstood the weight of circumstances to the end; not always without complaint, but always without misgiving. His glorious courage, his excellent contempt for things contemptible, and hatred of hateful men, are enough of themselves to embalm and endear his memory in the eyes of all who are worthy to pass judgment upon him. And these qualities gave much of their own value to verse not otherwise or not always praiseworthy. Even at its best, the serious poetry of Byron is often so rough and loose, so weak in the screws and joints which hold together the framework of verse, that it is not easy to praise it enough without seeming to condone or to extenuate such faults as should not be overlooked or forgiven. No poet is so badly represented by a book of selections. It must show something of his weakness; it cannot show all of his strength. Often, after a noble overture, the last note struck is either dissonant or ineffectual. His magnificent masterpiece, which must endure for ever among the precious relics of the world, will not bear dissection or extraction. The merit of *Don Juan* does not lie in any part, but in the whole. There is in that great poem an especial and exquisite balance and sustenance of alter-

---

1. That his youth and his rank were flung in his face with vulgar insolence on the publication of his first little book it can hardly be necessary to remind any reader of Byron; but possibly even these offences might have been condoned in a scribbler whose work had given no offensive promise of greatness yet to be. In the verse on Lochnagar at least an ominous threat or presage of something new and splendid must have been but too perceptible to the discerning eye of criticism.

nate tones which cannot be expressed or explained by the utmost ingenuity of selection. Haidée is supplanted by Dudù, the shipwreck by the siege, the Russian court by the English household; and this perpetual change, this tidal variety of experience and emotion, gives to the poem something of the breadth and freshness of the sea. Much of the poet's earlier work is or seems unconsciously dishonest; this, if not always or wholly unaffected, is as honest as the sunlight, as frank as the sea-wind. Here, and here alone, the student of his work may recognise and enjoy the ebb and flow of actual life. Here the pulse of vital blood may be felt in tangible flesh, Here for the first time the style of Byron is beyond all praise or blame: a style at once swift and supple, light and strong, various and radiant. Between *Childe Harold* and *Don Juan* the same difference exists which a swimmer feels between lake-water and sea-water: the one is fluent, yielding, invariable; the other has in it a life and pulse, a sting and a swell, which touch and excite the nerves like fire or like music. Across the stanzas of *Don Juan* we swim forward as over "the broad backs of the sea"; they break and glitter, hiss and laugh, murmur and move, like waves that sound or that subside. There is in them a delicious resistance, an elastic motion, which salt water has and fresh water has not. There is about them a wide wholesome air, full of vivid light and constant wind, which is only felt at sea. Life undulates and death palpitates in the splendid verse which resumes the evidence of a brave and clear-sighted man concerning life and death. Here, as at sea, there is enough and too much of fluctuation and intermission; the ripple flags and falls in loose and lazy lines: the foam flies wide of any mark, and the breakers collapse here and there in sudden ruin and violent failure. But the violence and weakness of the sea are preferable to the smooth sound and equable security of a lake: its buoyant and progressive impulse sustains and propels those who would sink through weariness in the flat and placid shallows. There are others whom it sickens, and others whom it chills; these will do well to steer inshore.

* * *

JOHN MORLEY

From Fortnightly Review[†]

It is one of the singular facts in the history of literature, that the most rootedly conservative country in Europe should have produced the poet of the Revolution. Nowhere is the antipathy to principles and ideas so profound, nor the addiction to moderate compromise so inveterate, nor the reluctance to advance away from the past so unconquerable, as in England; and nowhere in England is there so settled an indisposition to regard any thought or sentiment except in the light of an existing social order, nor so firmly passive a hostility to generous aspirations, as in the aristocracy. Yet it was precisely an English aristocrat who became the favourite poet of all the most high-minded conspirators and socialists of continental Europe for half a century; of the best of those, that is to say, who have borne the most unsparing testimony against the present ordering of society, and against the theological and moral conceptions which have guided and maintained it. The rank and file of the

† From *Fortnightly Review* (December 1870); reprinted in *Critical Miscellanies* (London: Macmillan and Co., 1871). Morley (1838–1923) was a British statesman, historian, and writer.

army has been equally inspired by the same fiery and rebellious strains against the order of God and the order of man. "The day will come," wrote Mazzini;[1] thirty years ago, "when Democracy will remember all that it owes to Byron. England, too, will, I hope, one day remember the mission—so entirely English, yet hitherto overlooked by her—which Byron fulfilled on the Continent; the European rôle given by him to English literature, and the appreciation and sympathy for England which he awakened amongst us. Before he came, all that was known of English literature was the French translation of Shakespeare, and the anathema hurled by Voltaire against the 'intoxicated barbarian.' It is since Byron that we Continentalists have learned to study Shakespeare and other English writers. From him dates the sympathy of all the true-hearted amongst us for this land of liberty, whose true vocation he so worthily represented among the oppressed. He led the genius of Britain on a pilgrimage throughout all Europe."[2]

MATTHEW ARNOLD

From Memorial Verses. April 27, 1850[†]

> When Byron's eyes were shut in death,
> We bow'd our head and held our breath.
> He taught us little; but our soul
> Had *felt* him like the thunder's roll.
> With shivering heart the strife we saw
> Of Passion with Eternal Law;
> And yet with reverential awe
> We watch'd the fount of fiery life
> Which flow'd for that Titanic strife.

From Preface to *Poetry of Byron*[‡]

* * *

Byron found our nation, after its long and victorious struggle with revolutionary France, fixed in a system of established facts and dominant ideas which revolted him. The mental bondage of the most powerful part of our nation, of its strong middle-class, to a narrow and false system of this kind, is what we call British Philistinism. That bondage is unbroken to this hour, but in Byron's time it was even far more deep and dark than it is now. Byron was an aristocrat, and it is not difficult for an aristocrat to look on the prejudices and habits of the British Philistine with scepticism and disdain. Plenty of young men of his own class Byron met at Almack's or at Lady Jersey's, who regarded the established facts and reigning beliefs of the England of that day

---

1. Giuseppe Mazzini (1805–1872), Italian patriot and revolutionary. (*Editor's note*).
2. The number of translations that have appeared in Germany since 1830 proves the coincidence of Byronic influence with revolutionary movement in that country.
† First published in *Fraser's Magazine* XLI (June 1850): 630. Excerpted here are lines 6–14 of the 74-line poem.
‡ From Preface to *Poetry of Byron*, ed. Matthew Arnold (1881); reprinted in *Essays in Criticism*: Second Series (London: Macmillan and Co., 1888).

with as little reverence as he did. But these men, disbelievers in British Philis-
tinism in private, entered English public life, the most conventional in the
world, and at once they saluted with respect the habits and ideas of British
Philistinism as if they were a part of the order of creation, and as if in pub-
lic no sane man would think of warring against them. With Byron it was
different. What he called the *cant* of the great middle part of the English
nation, what we call its Philistinism, revolted him; but the cant of his own
class, deferring to this Philistinism and profiting by it, while they disbelieved
in it, revolted him even more. "Come what may," are his own words," "I will
never flatter the million's canting in any shape." His class in general, on the
other hand, shrugged their shoulders at this cant, laughed at it, pandered to
it, and ruled by it. The falsehood, cynicism, insolence, misgovernment,
oppression, with their consequent unfailing crop of human misery, which
were produced by this state of things, roused Byron to irreconcilable revolt
and battle. They made him indignant, they infuriated him; they were so
strong, so defiant, so maleficent,—and yet he felt that they were doomed.
"You have seen every trampler down in turn," he comforts himself with say-
ing, "from Buonaparte to the simplest individuals." The old order, as after
1815 it stood victorious, with its ignorance and misery below, its cant, self-
ishness, and cynicism above, was at home and abroad equally hateful to him.
"I have simplified my politics," he writes, "into an utter detestation of all exist-
ing governments." And again: "Give me a republic. The king-times are fast
finishing; there will be blood shed like water and tears like mist, but the peo-
ples will conquer in the end. I shall not live to see it, but I foresee it."

Byron himself gave the preference, he tells us, to politicians and doers, far
above writers and singers. But the politics of his own day and of his own
class,—even of the Liberals of his own class,—were impossible for him.
Nature had not formed him for a Liberal peer, proper to move the Address in
the House of Lords to pay compliments to the energy and self-reliance of
British middle-class Liberalism, and to adapt his politics to suit it. Unfitted
for such politics, he threw himself upon poetry as his organ; and in poetry his
topics were not Queen Mab, and the Witch of Atlas, and the Sensitive
Plant—they were the upholders of the old order, George the Third and Lord
Castlereagh and the Duke of Wellington and Southey, and they were the can-
ters and tramplers of the great world, and they were his enemies and himself.

Such was Byron's personality, by which "he is different from all the rest of
English poets, and in the main greater." But he posed all his life, says M.
Scherer.[1] Let us distinguish. There is the Byron who posed, there is the Byron
with his affectations and silliness, the Byron whose weakness Lady Bless-
ington, with a woman's acuteness, so admirably seized: "His great defect is
flippancy and a total want of self-possession." But when this theatrical and
easily criticised personage betook himself to poetry, and when he had fairly
warmed to his work, then he became another man; then the theatrical per-
sonage passed away; then a higher power took possession of him and filled
him; then at last came forth into light that true and puissant personality, with
its direct strokes, its ever-welling force, its satire, its energy, and its agony.
This is the real Byron; whoever stops at the theatrical preluding does not
know him. And this real Byron may well be superior to the stricken Leopardi,
he may well be declared "different from all the rest of English poets, and in

1. Edmond Scherer (1815–1889), French critic. (*Editor's note.*)

the main greater," in so far as it is true of him, as M. Taine[2] well says, that "all other souls, in comparison with his, seem inert"; in so far as it is true of him that with superb, exhaustless energy, he maintained, as Professor Nichol well says, "the struggle that keeps alive, if it does not save, the soul;" in so far, finally, as he deserves (and he does deserve) the noble praise of him which I have already quoted from Mr. Swinburne; the praise for "the splendid and imperishable excellence which covers all his offences and outweighs all his defects: *the excellence of sincerity and strength.*"

True, as a man, Byron could not manage himself, could not guide his ways aright, but was all astray. True, he has no light, cannot lead us from the past to the future; "the moment he reflects, he is a child."[3] The way out of the false state of things which enraged him he did not see,—the slow and laborious way upward; he had not the patience, knowledge, self-discipline, virtue, requisite for seeing it. True, also, as a poet, he has no fine and exact sense for word and structure and rhythm; he has not the artist's nature and gifts. Yet a personality of Byron's force counts for so much in life, and a rhetorician of Byron's force counts for so much in literature! But it would be most unjust to label Byron, as M. Scherer is disposed to label him, as a rhetorician only. Along with his astounding power and passion he had a strong and deep sense for what is beautiful in nature, and for what is beautiful in human action and suffering. When he warms to his work, when he is inspired, Nature herself seems to take the pen from him as she took it from Wordsworth, and to write for him as she wrote for Wordsworth, though in a different fashion, with her own penetrating simplicity. Goethe has well observed of Byron, that when he is at his happiest his representation of things is as easy and real as if he were improvising. * * *

* * *

Wordsworth's value is of another kind. Wordsworth has an insight into permanent sources of joy and consolation for mankind which Byron has not; his poetry gives us more which we may rest upon than Byron's,—more which we can rest upon now, and which men may rest upon always. I place Wordsworth's poetry, therefore, above Byron's on the whole, although in some points he was greatly Byron's inferior, and although Byron's poetry will always, probably, find more readers than Wordsworth's, and will give pleasure more easily. But these two, Wordsworth and Byron, stand, it seems to me, first and pre-eminent in actual performance, a glorious pair, among the English poets of this century. Keats had probably, indeed, a more consummate poetic gift than either of them; but he died having produced too little and being as yet too immature to rival them. I for my part can never even think of equalling with them any other of their contemporaries;— either Coleridge, poet and philosopher wrecked in a mist of opium; or Shelley, beautiful and ineffectual angel, beating in the void his luminous wings in vain. Wordsworth and Byron stand out by themselves. When the year 1900 is turned, and our nation comes to recount her poetic glories in the century which has then just ended, the first names with her will be these.

---

2. Hippolyte Taine (1828–1893), French critic, philosopher, and historian; in his *Histoire de la littérature anglaise* (1863) Byron is featured more prominently than any of the other English Romantic poets. (*Editor's note.*)
3. Often-quoted statement by Johann Wolfgang von Goethe (*Conversations with Eckermann,* [1822–32]). (*Editor's note.*)

Twentieth-Century and Recent Criticism

GENERAL STUDIES

G. WILSON KNIGHT

From Lord Byron: Christian Virtues[†]

This is a work on Byron as a man in whom poetry has become incarnate. Of the poetry I have already published a preliminary study,[1] and intend a more thorough investigation later on. With our current assessment I disagree totally. Byron appears to me our greatest poet in the widest sense of the term since Shakespeare; and I do not know where we shall look for his master in prose. But, great though the literature be, it is out-distanced by Byron's importance as a man; an importance, I believe, so great that it has been difficult to focus, like the large letters on a map. * * *

* * *

* * * In a letter to his sister dated 22 May 1809, C. S. Matthews tells of the dangers of a visit to Newstead.[2] On entering the hall you may run into a bear—or wolf. The animals are fierce, and roam freely (LJ, I, 154, note). Nor was this a mere youthful whim: whatever the pressure of his later fortunes or misfortunes, Byron loved having animals round him. Newton Hanson describes his visit to Byron at Venice in the year 1818, observing that 'the basement contained his lordship's carriages, two or three kinds of dogs, birds, monkeys, a fox, a wolf, in different cages', and that, 'as his lordship passed to his gondola, he used to stop and amuse himself with watching their antics, or would feed them himself occasionally' (LJ, IV, 266, note). When he moved to Ravenna Byron took his menagerie with him, and on such occasions the cavalcade of carriages, servants, horses and animals made an amazing spectacle (Medwin, 1–2; Galt, XL). On 15 August 1821 Shelley gave Peacock his first impressions of Byron's Ravenna establishment, noting that it 'consists, besides servants, of ten horses, eight enormous dogs, three monkeys, five cats, an eagle, a crow and a falcon; and all those, except the horses, walk

† From *Lord Byron: Christian Virtues* (London: Routledge and Kegan Paul, 1953; reissued, New York: Barnes & Noble, 1967). Copyright © 1953. Reprinted by permission of Taylor and Francis Books UK.
1. "The Two Eternities: an Essay on Byron," in *The Burning Oracle: Studies in the Poetry of Action* (Oxford: Oxford University Press, 1939) (*Editor's note*).
2. Newstead Abbey, Byron's ancestral home, where he resided between 1798 and 1803. (*Editor's note*).

about the house, which every now and then resounds with their unarbitrated quarrels, as if they were the masters of it'. In a postscript he adds: 'I find that my enumeration of the animals in this Circeaean Palace was defective, and that in a material point. I have just met, on the grand staircase, five peacocks, two guinea-hens and an Egyptian crane. I wonder who all these animals were before they were changed into these shapes' (LJ, V, 339, note). The phrase 'as if they were the masters of it' is important: the human inmates of such a household were certainly in part dependent on the *beasts'* behaviour. Such establishments, with all the appalling trouble of transporting the creatures concerned from place to place as Byron changed his residences, might be considered a reasonable test of 'love of animals'.

Byron's prose writings bear out his extraordinary regard for his often ferocious and undisciplined pets. His innate sympathy is shown in a note from his Swiss Journal for Augusta, 20 September 1816: 'Strolled to river: saw boy and kid; kid followed him like a dog; kid could not get over a fence, and bleated piteously; tried myself to help kid, but nearly overset both self and kid into the river' (LJ, III, 356). The same sympathetic care is given to his own charges: 'The crow is lame of a leg—wonder how it happened—some fool trod upon his toe, I suppose. The falcon pretty brisk—the cats large and noisy—the monkeys I have not looked to since the cold weather, as they suffer by being brought up. Horses must be gay—get a ride as soon as weather serves.' That is purely a piece of self-communing, written for his own private satisfaction (Journal, 6 Jan. 1821; LJ, V, 155). But his affection is not limited to an oppressive care; he does not humanize the relation: 'Fed the two cats, the hawk, and the tame (though *not tamed*) crow' (Journal, 5 Jan. 1821; LJ, V, 152). Byron's italics here are important.

He seems to have liked his animals fierce. Pigot tells us that at Harrogate in the year 1806, Byron, then a young man of nineteen, possessed a very ferocious bull-mastiff, Nelson, as well as his Newfoundland, Boatswain. Nelson always wore a muzzle, though sometimes Byron sent for him into his room and to Pigot's embarrassment had the muzzle removed. The dog and his master amused themselves by 'throwing the room into disorder'. Nelson and Boatswain sometimes fought and then everyone, hotel waiters included, had to assist in parting them. Finally, Nelson attacked the horses and was shot by a stable-boy (Moore, IV, 37–8). Byron was never afraid of animals. On sailing from Genoa in 1823 he spent the night controlling the horses who had broken loose and were kicking each other in terror during a storm (Gamba, I, 11–12). Indeed, his pets were in part loved for their ferocity and forgiven for any hurts received. He had a bulldog called 'Savage', 'the finest puppy I ever saw', and dangerous: 'In his great and manifold kindness he has already bitten my fingers, and disturbed the *gravity* of old Boatswain, who is *grievously discomposed'* (Elizabeth Pigot, 11 June 1807; LJ, I, 129). Much later, included in a letter to Murray from Ravenna, is a request for some bulldogs to be sent from England (1 March 1820; LJ, IV, 415). That Byron's fondness for animals was not, as Mr. Quennell suggests (VIII, 252),[3] capricious and self-centred', may be further supposed from another attacking creature, a parrot. James Nathan tells of the 'beautiful parrots' with which Byron amused himself during composition, and especially notes his patience when once, on leaving the room, he was so

---

3. Peter Quennell, *Byron in Italy* (New York: Viking Press, 1941), p. 238. (*Editor's note*).

fiercely attacked that the blood flowed 'copiously': 'Instead of being excited by the pain produced, his Lordship was only lost in admiration at the strong attachment of the bird, which he instantly caressed, and, in the words of Macheath, exclaimed, "Was this well done, Jenny?"' (LJ, III, 75–6, note).

To Byron animals were half-human; they are not humanized, they are their own wild selves; but even so he feels their kinship with the wild selves of mankind. Such touches, though often light, are significant enough. Here is one, from a letter to Moore, 24 May 1820: 'I have just been scolding my monkey for tearing the seal of her letter, and spoiling a mock book, in which I put rose leaves. I had a civet-cat the other day, too; but it ran away, after scratching my monkey's cheek, and I am in search of it still. It was the fiercest beast I ever saw, and like——in the face and manner' (LJ, V, 31). He could visualize Count Guiccioli as a pig (Teresa, 15 July 1820; Origo, v, 193) and Italian peasants as 'a fine, savage, race of two-legged leopards' (Journal, 24 Jan. 1821; LJ, v, 185). After visiting a zoo he compares the beasts to his various acquaintances:

> 'Two nights ago I saw the tigers sup at Exeter 'Change. Except Veli Pasha's lion in the Morea—who followed the Arab keeper like a dog—the fondness of the hyaena for her keeper amused me most. Such a conversazione!—There was a "hippopotamus", like Lord Liverpool in the face; and the "Ursine Sloth" had the very voice and manner of my valet—but the tiger talked too much. The elephant took and gave me my money again—took off my hat—opened a door—*trunked* a whip—and behaved so well, that I wish he was my butler. The handsomest animal on earth is one of the panthers; but the poor antelopes were dead. I should hate to see one *here*:—the sight of the *camel* made me pine again for Asia Minor. "O quando te aspiciam?"' (Journal, 14 Nov. 1813; LJ, II, 319.)

Later, writing from Venice to Murray on 14 April 1817 on his response to painting, Byron notes that most things in his life have proved disappointing with the exception of mountains and seas, 'two or three women', 'some horses', 'a lion (at Veli Pasha's) in the Morea'; and 'a tiger at supper in Exeter 'Change' (LJ, IV, 107).

To Byron animals radiated vivid significances. He admired especially their energies and strength. From Venice he described the breaking loose of an elephant who 'ate up a fruit shop, killed his keeper, broke into a church', and eventually had to be killed by cannon. Approaching him in a gondola, Byron was greeted by a shower of hurled beams—his strength was 'extraordinary'—and later saw him dead, 'a stupendous fellow' (Kinnaird, 6 March 1819; C, II, 105). This admiration of animal power was one with Byron's interest in the vital stuff of men and nations. He enjoys using terms of warfare to describe a fight between his great dog Matz and a mountain pig: 'The Pig was first thrown into confusion, and compelled to retire with great disorder', but later faced about and 'drove Matz from all his positions, with such slaughter that nothing but night prevented a total defeat' (Hobhouse, 22 April 1817; C, II, 50). We hear of Matz again: 'I have got two monkeys, a fox, and two new mastiffs. Matz is still in high old age. The monkeys are charming' (Kinnaird, 6 March 1819; C, II, 106). One of Byron's most lovable characteristics is his habit of referring to his dependants' well-being, whether servants (e.g. Fletcher) or animals.

Animals were felt as close, intimate beings, like lovers: he compared his first Italian mistress to an antelope (Moore, 17 Nov. 1816; LJ, IV, 7) and his second to a pythoness and tigress: 'I like this kind of animal', he says, and calls her 'a fine animal but quite untameable' (Moore, 19 Sept. 1818; Murray, 1 Aug. 1819; LJ, IV, 262, 332). Animals resembled himself: 'I am like the tyger (in poesy), if I miss my first Spring, I go growling back to my Jungle. There is no second. I can't correct. I can't and I won't' (Murray, 18 Nov. 1820; LJ, V, 120). He saw himself when attacked by his enemies as a bear or a bull being baited, and possessing the 'united energies of those amiable animals' (Murray, 1 Aug. 1819; LJ, IV, 326). Driven from London, he compared himself to a hunted stag that 'betakes him to the waters' (*Blackwood's* Defence, LJ, IV, 479). He was, from the start, a lonely animal ('The lion is alone and so am I', *Manfred*, III, i), and the friend of animals: 'I have got a new friend, the finest in the world, a *tame bear*' (Elizabeth Pigot, 26 Oct. 1807; LJ, I, 147). He had a painter down to Newstead to do its and his wolf's portrait (LJ, II, 57, note; Finlay, quoted Edgcumbe, I, VIII, 99); and some people thought the *Thyrza* poems recorded a perverted love for it (Medwin, 277, note). From his early travels he brought back four live tortoises and a greyhound which died on the passage (Drury, 17 July 1811; LJ, I, 318). Strangers made him 'sick': 'For my part (since I lost my Newfoundland dog) I like nobody except his successor, a Dutch Mastiff, and three land Tortoises brought with me from Greece' (Augusta, 9 Sept. 1811; LJ, II, 31). To make a friend of a dog is natural; but to find romance in tortoises is rarer. He was deeply concerned about them: 'My tortoises (all Athenians), my hedge-hog, my mastiff and the other live Greek, are all purely (poorly?). The tortoises lay eggs, and I have hired a hen to hatch them' (Hodgson, 25 Sept. 1811; LJ, II, 46). He was often in the mood of a hermit, of a Robinson Crusoe, a Timon, alone among the beasts: 'I am now', he writes to Lady Melbourne, 'quite alone with my books and my Maccaw' (17 Oct. 1814; C, I, 281). Again, he tells Murray that he couldn't write, his vein being gone: 'my principal conversation is with my Maccaw and Bayle' (26 April 1814; LJ, III, 75).

We have already observed Byron's reference to his Newfoundland, Boatswain. 'Byron', writes Maurois, 'nursed him like a friend, and with his own bare hands sponged the froth that ran from his gaping jaws' (I, XII, 99). The dog's death was a severe blow to him. To Hodgson he wrote on 18 November 1808: 'Boatswain is dead! He expired in a state of madness on the 10th after suffering much, yet retaining all the gentleness of his nature to the last, never attempting to do the least injury to any one near him. I have now lost everything except Old Murray' (LJ, III, 171, note); and added, on 27 November (LJ, I, 200), that he 'is to be buried in a vault waiting for myself', and that he has composed an epitaph. The epitaph is in both verse and prose. The verse, published originally with *The Corsair* in 1815, is entitled *Inscription on the Monument of a Newfoundland Dog*. A titled man, whatever his worth, receives honour in burial—

> But the poor dog, in life the firmest friend,
> The first to welcome, foremost to defend,
> Whose honest heart is still his master's own,
> Who labours, fights, lives, breathes for him alone,
> Unhonour'd falls, unnotic'd all his worth,
> Denied in heaven the soul he held on earth:
> While man, vain insect! hopes to be forgiven,
> And claims himself a sole exclusive heaven.

Next the poet, in the manner of Timon, denounces man's insincerity and vice in direct comparison with the integrity of the brute creation. The conclusion runs:

> Ye! who perchance behold this simple urn,
> Pass on—it honours none you wish to mourn.
> To mark a friend's remains these stones arise;
> I never knew but one—and here he lies.

The prose inscription is in similar vein:

> Near this spot
> Are deposited the Remains of one
> Who possessed Beauty without Vanity,
> Strength without Insolence,
> Courage without Ferocity,
> And all the Virtues of Man without his Vices.
> This Praise, which would be unmeaning Flattery
> If inscribed over human ashes,
> Is but a just tribute to the Memory of
> Boatswain, a Dog
> Who was born at Newfoundland, May 1803,
> And died at Newstead Abbey, November 18, 1808.
>
> (Moore, VII, 73.)

The thoughts of this inscription recur in Byron's remark, when visiting the house of Petrarch and seeing the embalmed body of his cat, 'that the hearts of animals were often better than ours, and that this animal's affection may well have put Laura's coldness to shame' (Teresa, quoted Origo, III, 116). In setting out directions for his will (12 Aug. 1811) Byron stated that he was to be buried without ceremony or service and that no inscription except his name and age was to be written on his tomb, adding: 'it is my will that my faithful dog may not be removed from the said vault'. This was his 'particular desire'. Though his solicitor urged that the request be left as a letter and not in the will, Byron insisted: 'It must stand' (LJ, I, 329–30).

He probably had Boatswain in mind when, on 5 May 1823, just before his last expedition, he wrote from the Villa Saluzzo to Edward Le Mesurier expressing great gratitude for the gift of a Newfoundland dog, a breed for which he asserted his especial fondness (LJ, VI, 203). This was, presumably, Lyon, the dog Byron took with him to Missolonghi and of which Parry writes:

> 'With Lyon Lord Byron was accustomed, not only to associate, but to commune very much, and very often. His most usual phrase was, "Lyon, you are no rogue, Lyon"; or "Lyon", his Lordship would say, "thou art an honest fellow, Lyon." The dog's eyes sparkled, and his tail swept the floor, as he sat with his haunches on the ground. "Thou art more faithful than men, Lyon; I trust thee more." Lyon sprang up, and barked and bounded round his master, as much as to say, "You may trust me, I will watch actively on every side." "Lyon, I love thee, thou art my faithful dog," and Lyon jumped and kissed his master's hand, as an acknowledgment of his homage. In this sort of mingled talk and gambol Lord Byron passed a good deal of time, and seemed more contented,

more calmly self-satisfied, on such occasions, than almost on any other. In conversation and in company he was animated and brilliant; but with Lyon and in stillness he was pleased and perfectly happy' (Parry, IV, 75).

At Missolonghi Byron told George Finlay that Newfoundland dogs had twice saved his life, and that 'he could not live without one' (Finlay, quoted Edgcumbe, I, VIII, 99).

Byron's sympathy with animals was one with his sympathy with men and peoples. 'Lord Byron', wrote Gamba, 'never could be an idle spectator of any calamity. . . . The slightest appearance of injustice or cruelty, not only to his own species, but to animals, roused his indignation and compelled his interference, and personal consequences never for one moment entered into his calculations' (quoted Edgcumbe, I, VIII, 80 and Teresa, I; IX, 387; no refs.). Once, thinking of an execution, he soliloquized on his own reluctance to attend: 'Now, could I *save* him, or a fly even, from the same catastrophe, I would out-match years . . .' (*Detached Thoughts,* Oct. 1821; LJ, V, 439). 'Tears of mental or physical suffering', wrote Teresa, 'make him almost ill—the dread of treading on an ant makes him go out of his way— a scene at the play, a sad story or a melodious tune bring tears to his eyes' (quoted Origo, II, 87). When, after the failure of the rising in Ravenna, Teresa was imploring Byron to join her at Pisa, his continued delay was prompted by his concern for certain delicate 'Dutch horses' for whom the condition of the roads was regarded as unsatisfactory. To the last he showed, says Iris Origo, a 'greater concern for the Dutch horses than for his mistress' impatience' (Teresa, 12, 23, 26 Oct. 1821; Origo, VI, 288—90). Byron loved horses and liked comparing himself with Alfieri, whose tastes likewise included a love of liberty and a fondness for animals, 'and above all, for horses' (Blessington, 96–7).

His menagerie caused him continual anxiety: 'It is troublesome' he told Medwin, 'to travel so far with so much live and dead stock as I do; and I don't like to leave behind me any of my pets that have been accumulating since I came on the Continent. One cannot trust to strangers to take care of them. You will see at the farmer's some of my pea-fowls *en pension*' (Medwin, 8). Medwin tells us that he bought a monkey in Pisa in the street, because he saw it ill-used (9, note); and quotes *Don Juan,* where Juan's love of pets ('let deeper sages the true cause determine') is emphasized:

> He had a kind of inclination, or
> Weakness, for what most people deem mere vermin,
> Live animals . . .
>
> (X, 50.)

There is, too, the interesting affair with the geese. Byron believed that one should eat a goose at Michaelmas (Gamba, quoted Origo, IX, 365). Nevertheless the phraseology of a letter to Teresa on 11 October 1820, 'Pray do not have such a massacre of geese as I cannot come for several days' (Origo, V, 228), subtly suggests a reluctance. On his journey from Pisa to Genoa, he had some geese with him for Michaelmas. I follow Teresa's account, drawing variously on her two studies. The geese 'swung in a cage behind his carriage, punctuating the journey with their cackling'. But Byron, says Teresa, 'felt sorry for them', and 'when the time came to wring their necks, he would not give the order, and decided instead to keep them, "to test the theory of their longevity"'. On arriving in Genoa, 'they at once became the guardians and mistresses of the yard, as sacred as those of the Capitol, and waddled about in the garden and the lower floor of the house, accompanying Byron wherever he went'. Notice Byron's rationalization of his instincts in 'in order to test their longevity': it happens elsewhere. Byron was always 'caressing' the birds and when he left for Greece boarded them with his banker, Mr. Barry, who was told to take good care of them, it being Byron's intention 'to keep them as long as they lived' (Origo, VIII, 325, 344; Notes, 513; Teresa, I; IX, 388–9).

Naturally enough, Byron repudiated field-sports. Teresa notes how he regularly refused the 'pleasures of the chase' (X; IX, 387). As early as 2 April 1804, he complained to Augusta that the sole pleasure of some of his neighbours, themselves 'only one degree removed from the brute creation', consisted in 'field sports' (LJ, I, 25). As he grew older, his antipathy hardened. On 14 December 1808—again to Augusta—he wrote: 'I hate all field sports' (LJ, I, 205). He kept no guns at Newstead (Dallas, 27 Aug. 1811; LJ, II, 9). Once, in supporting the values of paganism, he asked: 'Is there a Talapoin or a Bonze who is not superior to a fox-hunting curate?' (Hodgson, 3 Sept. 1811; II, 22). He sensed a hideous discrepancy in the conception, his revulsion from the cruelty involved being the clearer from his lines on angling in *Don Juan*:

> And angling, too, that solitary vice,
> Whatever Isaak Walton sings or says;
> The quaint, old, cruel coxcomb, in his gullet
> Should have a hook, and a small trout to pull it.
>
> (XIII, 106.)

On the last line his own note reads:

> 'It would have taught him humanity at least. This sentimental savage . . . teaches how to sew up frogs, and break their legs by way of experiment, in addition to the art of angling, the cruelest, the coldest, and the stupidest of pretended sports. . . . The whale, the shark and the tunny fishery have somewhat of noble and perilous in them; even net fishing, trawling, etc. are more humane and useful. But angling!— No angler can be a good man.'

His dislike of blood-sports started early and continued throughout his life. His clearest statement occurs in his Journal of 20 March 1814:

> 'I remember, in riding from Chrisso to Castri (Delphos), along the sides of Parnassus, I saw six eagles in the air. It is uncommon to see so many together; and it was the number—not the species, which is common enough—that excited my attention.
>
> 'The last bird I ever fired at was an *eaglet,* on the shore of the Gulf of Lepanto, near Vostitza. It was only wounded, and I tried to save it, the eye was so bright; but it pined, and died in a few days; and I never did since, and never will, attempt the death of another bird' (LJ, II, 404).

We have a letter to Moore on 15 September 1814 (LJ, III, 136), written at a time of mental 'confusion' when distraction was apparently sought in fishing and 'firing at the fowls of the air' as well as at 'soda-water bottles', probably without much expectation of catching or hitting anything; both the phraseology and 'bottles'—Byron's usual target—suggesting a random and haphazard activity with pistols. The action was certainly exceptional. Witness after witness records Byron's love of pistol practice, and each in turn notes his use of inanimate targets (bottles, coins, etc.). The only exception is one recorded by Trelawny (xviii) whose reminiscences are notoriously unreliable (see Nicolson's reference to 'his usual inaccuracy' (vi, 130)). When associating with Teresa Guiccioli and the Gambas near Ravenna in the year 1820, at a time when it was in his interests, both as lover and revolutionary, to appear among his foreign friends as a man of iron, he stuck to his principles: 'From the bowling-green the company passed to a trial of marksmanship—a sport, Teresa added, in which Byron excelled, but in which he refused to take part whenever the target was a living bird.' The guests were later taken to the river and 'provided with fishing nets', but 'before then Byron had had enough of it' and returned to Ravenna. His behaviour must have surprised his friends, Teresa noting it as 'a weakness, but the weakness of a great heart!' (Origo, following Teresa, v, 217).

Among the various causes that raised British society against Byron, Jeaffreson (xvii, 225–6) listed his aversion from blood-sports (and see *Don Juan,* xiii, 75). Like his own Cain, Byron suffered for his sympathies with the animal creation.

Among Byron's challenging eccentricities, Jeaffreson lists also the poet's alienation of social feeling by his habit of 'sustaining life on biscuits and soda-water' (xvii, 225). There were various causes for Byron's almost suicidal diet maintained, with intermissions, throughout; but his ingrained sympathy with animal life clearly played its part. 'He ate little,' says Galt, describing the voyage from Gibraltar; 'no animal food, but only bread and vegetables' (viii). It is not my purpose to prove Byron a theorizing or consistent vegetarian, but merely to observe a tendency noted by every one who knew him; together with his instinct for living, as well as writing, his convictions.

He could, however, and did, write them too. That Byron is our greatest poet of animal life can scarcely be disputed. In revelation of animal energy and animal pathos—for his animals are regularly felt *tragically*—he has no equal in English poetry; and in deliberately putting much of his major work *at the service of* animals, he probably stands alone in the literatures of the world.

Beside our prose description of the elephant at Venice we can set the magnificent Bull of the bull-fight in *Childe Harold* (i, 74–9). In each there is *both* a delight in the beast's strength *and* awe at its agony and destruction. Each outlines the other, as again in the brilliant miniature of the dying war-horse in *The Destruction of Sennacherib;* or the fire-eye'd buffalo attacked by wolves, together with the packed stanza of distraught animals at the poem's conclusion, in *The Siege of Corinth* (xxiii, xxxiii). In close relation we have the fascinating horror of biological energy in the quivering fragments of the severed viper in *Marino Faliero* (iii, ii); and the agony of the scorpion ringed with fire and twisting round to inject itself with its own poison in *The Giaour.* No poet is so appallingly aware of animal suffering; the lioness robbed of her young in *The Giaour;* the over-worked post-horses in England in *Don Juan* (XIII, 42); the lamb 'bleating' before the butcher in *Marino Faliero* (V, I). The power of *Heaven and Earth* derives from its extraordinary realization of the Flood's impact on animals and birds (see pp. 111–12). Small creatures get equal notice with the greater: the wounded butterfly in *The Giaour*, the insect stinging in defence of its own in *The Corsair* (I, 13); most exquisite of all, that wonderful penetration of human psychology and animal companionship when the dungeoned Bonnivard, after years of solitary durance, is anguished at leaving his long-loved friends, the spiders at their 'sullen trade'—the spiders' victims being also remembered—and the little mice at their moonlit play (*The Prisoner of Chillon*, XIV).

Three of Byron's late works—and two of them among his greatest—mature from this peculiar sympathy. We have, first, the nightmare ride and wild mustangs of *Mazeppa*, a narrative of suspended, sickening excitement, based on a vivid apprehension of horses. Horses are, indeed, Byron's peculiar favourites, as with the magnificent, supernatural, coal-black horses of *The Deformed Transformed*:

> The mighty steam, which volumes high
> From their proud nostrils, burns the very air;
> And sparks of flame, like dancing fire-flies, wheel
> Around their manes as common insects swarm
> Round common steeds at sunset.
>
> (I, i.)

Our second is *Cain*, the impressions ranging from the tiniest to the most vast forms of animal life:

> The little shining fire-fly in its flight,
> And the immortal star in its great course,
> Must both be guided. . . .
>
> (II, i.)

From this we move to sight of great prehistoric monsters, mammoths tenfold greater than the forested roaring beasts of earth; to leviathans and the gigantic, dripping serpent rising from the abyss. This serpent may be felt as the archetype of other Byronic serpents; and indeed the drama is at pains to assert that the serpent, not Lucifer, tempted Adam. The action, moreover, revolves precisely round the theme of animal slaughter. Cain instances a lamb stung by a serpent in accusation of Jehovah's cruel creation (II, ii); and his crime is, like Byron's, a refusal to participate in the accepted code. He will offer fruits, but not blood, to Jehovah:

> *His pleasure!* What was his high pleasure in
> The fumes of scorching flesh and smoking blood,
> To the pain of the bleating mothers, which
> Still yearn for their dead offspring? Or the pangs
> Of the sad ignorant victims underneath
> Thy pious knife? Give way! This bloody record
> Shall not stand in the sun to shame creation!
>
> (III, i.)

Abel's sacrifice is accepted, Cain's rejected. Biblical authority is closely followed. This drama, Byron's final statement of revolt against the religious and social traditions of Europe, specifically levels its indictment in terms of animal slaughter. Our third work is the lucid and compact *Sardanapalus,* probably Byron's most exquisite single creation, wherein all past themes of his life and poetry are beautifully and exactly harmonized.[4] The action shows us an enlightened emperor who refuses, like Byron himself, to conform to current standards regarding (i) blood-sports and (ii) imperial conquest; of which the respective symbols are his grim ancestors, Nimrod and Semiramis, whose ghosts in nightmare objectify the hero's sense of guilt:

> Hence—hence—
> Old hunter of the earliest brutes! and ye,
> Who hunted fellow-creatures as if brutes!
> Once bloody mortals—and now bloodier idols,
> If your priests lie not! And thou, ghastly beldame!
> Dripping with dusky gore, and trampling on
> The carcasses of Inde—away! away!
>
>   (IV, i.)

As so often, no distinction is drawn between the sufferings of men and those of animals.

I have presented my case. Byron's interest in animals cannot be called 'capricious and self-centred'.[5] It is probable that no great man on record has left stronger evidence to the contrary.

*   *   *

ANNE BARTON
Byron and the Mythology of Fact[†]

In 1821, acting against the advice of all his friends, Byron published *Cain: A Mystery.* The uproar which resulted was impressive. By reviewers, the play was described as immoral and blasphemous, a scandal and an offence. Sermons were preached against it from church pulpits, and it was rumoured that at least one reader had been so distressed by Byron's questioning of the goodness of God that he shot himself. John Murray, who printed the play, was threatened with prosecution, and frightened so effectively, that Byron subsequently had to take his work to another publisher. In his Italian exile, Byron himself adopted an attitude of humorous resignation. He was entirely aware that everything he published now diminished his popularity, that his poetic empire of a few years before was vanishing as irrevocably as Napoleon's. To Canto XI of *Don Juan,* a work he had also been begged to suppress, he appended at characteristically wry assessment of the situation:

> Even I—albeit I'm sure I did not know it,
>   Nor sought of foolscap subjects to be king—
> Was reckon'd a considerable time,

---

4. My study appears in *The Burning Oracle. Sardanapalus* is unfortunately omitted from the *Everyman* Byron. (*Sardanapalus* [1821] is printed in *CPW* 6 and in *Lord Byron: Selected Poems* [Penguin, 1966] [*Editor's note*].)
5. See p. 808 and note quotes (*Editor's note*).
† University of Nottingham Byron Lecture (1968). Copyright © 1968 Anne Barton. Reprinted by permission of the author.

The grand Napoleon of the realms of rhyme.
But Juan was my Moscow, and Faliero
My Leipsic, and my Mount Saint Jean seems Cain.

Among Byron's readers in 1821 was a man of whom he had almost certainly never heard: William Blake. Blake's reaction to *Cain* was also unfavourable, but not on moral or Christian grounds. In the following year, he expressed his criticism by way of a dramatic poem of his own, *The Ghost of Abel: A Revelation in the Visions of Jehovah Seen by William Blake*. *The Ghost of Abel* was Blake's last poem, and it is the only one which has a dedication:

To Lord Byron in the Wilderness:

What doest thou here, Elijah?
Can a poet doubt the Visions of Jehovah? Nature has no Outline,
But Imagination has. Nature has no Tune, but Imagination has.
Nature has no Supernatural, and dissolves: Imagination is Eternity.

For Blake, the wilderness in which Byron wandered was not only that of exile, but of error. He was a potential poet-prophet destroyed by his allegiance to false gods of realism and rationality: a man clinging to a world of fact when he should look beyond it. Even in *Cain*, a work apparently concerned with the supernatural, Blake recognized (and quite rightly) Byron's distrust of the visionary, his stubborn insistence that however truth is to be reached, it is not by way of the imagination.

'There is this great difference between us', Keats once wrote of Byron. 'He describes what he sees; I describe what I imagine. You see which is the harder task'. In an age which was rapidly turning Shakespeare into a kind of Messiah, in which Shelley could claim that poets were "the unacknowledged legislators of the world", and Coleridge speak of the imagination as 'the living power and prime agent of all human perception . . . a repetition in the finite mind of the eternal act of creation', Byron stands apart. In 1817, Keats wrote his famous letter to Bailey:

I am certain of nothing but of the holiness of the Heart's affections and the truth of Imagination—What the imagination seizes as Beauty must be truth—whether it existed before or not.

Byron, in the very same year, told his publisher Murray:

I hate things all fiction; and therefore the Merchant and Othello have no great associations to me: but Pierre [in Otway's *Venice Preserv'd*] has. There should always be some foundation of fact for the most airy fabric, and pure invention is but the talent of a liar.[1]

Byron's statement is not only the polar opposite of Keats's; it reaches back to undermine the assertion of Sir Philip Sidney, advanced against Gosson and his school, that 'of all writers under the sun the poet is the least liar; and, though he would, as a poet can scarcely be a liar'. The fact was that at a time when the value placed on poetry and the imagination was reaching a height inconceivable in the sixteenth, seventeenth or eighteenth centuries, the most celebrated poet of Europe—the grand Napoleon of the

---

1. To Murray, April 2, 1817.

realms of rhyme—regarded his art with a suspicion amounting at times to contempt.

> I by no means rank poetry or poets high in the scale of intellect. This may look like affectation, but it is my real opinion . . . I prefer the talents of action—of war, of the senate, or even of science—to all the speculations of those mere dreamers of another existence.[2]

This passage comes from a letter to Annabella Milbanke, dated November 10, 1813. Similar remarks are scattered liberally throughout Byron's correspondence. 'No one should be a rhymer who could be anything better',[3] he announces at one point. And again: 'Who would write who had anything better to do?' 'As to defining what a poet should be, it is not worth while, for what are they worth? What have they done?'[4]

✳   ✳   ✳

For all his self-obsession, Byron was far more closely connected with Moneta's 'great world'[5] than either Wordsworth or Keats. He was in touch all his life with an objective reality that was wider, more various and also more insistent in its claims than the one normally available to them. The American poet Wallace Stevens once defined the artist's task as that of returning—not evading—the pressure of reality through imaginative means.[6] He pointed out that this pressure tends to be stronger in some periods than in others. One might add to this the observation that certain individuals in a given moment of historical time may feel the force of fact, of a denotative as opposed to a connotative world, more urgently than others. The range of Byron's experience, social, political, geographical, was enormous. He did not merely wish to be a man of action: a traveller, a lover, an orator, a revolutionary. He was all these things, and more. He participated fully in the world of fact. It was scarcely surprising that he should develop a respect for this world, as opposed to its less substantial, fictional twin, which sets him apart from most of his poetic contemporaries. Byron distrusted art. It was a distrust which not only led him to adopt some singular aesthetic positions. It also meant that he himself tried continually, and sincerely, to renounce the writing of verse.

Declarations that his literary career had come to an end were characteristic of Byron throughout most of his life. He published *Hours of Idleness* in 1807 with the announcement that this juvenile collection was his first and would be his last. *English Bards and Scotch Reviewers*, the poem which represented the breaking of this vow, imprudently promised in its turn never again 'to stun Mankind with Poesy, or Prose'. Just two years later, Byron was to find this second promise as embarrassing as the first. On January 14, 1811 he announced in a letter from Athens that he had 'done with Authourship . . . I have a famous Bavarian artist taking some views of Athens for me. This will be better than scribbling, a disease I hope myself cured of'.[7] How imperfect the cure was is revealed by a later paragraph in

---

2. To Annabella, Nov. 10, 1813.
3. *Journal*, Nov. 23, 1813.
4. *Journal*, Nov. 24, 1813; *Journal*, Jan. 31, 1821.
5. A reference to Keats's *The Fall of Hyperion* (1819) (*Editor's note*).
6. Wallace Stevens 'The Noble Rider and the Sound of Words', in *The Necessary Angel*, London, 1960.
7. To his mother, Jan. 14, 1811.

the same letter: he had already completed Cantos I and II of *Childe Harold*. This, of course, was the poem which virtually overnight made Byron famous. He was firm, however, in his refusal to continue it once he was back in England. In a letter written early in 1813, he claimed that 'the days of Authourship are over with me altogether',[8] but the statement was belied by the fact that he had already embarked on the Oriental Tales. He published *The Corsair* in 1814 with a preface insisting that this would be his last literary work for some years. To his friends, he went even further: it was absolutely the last forever. Like his earlier renunciations, this vow did not survive the year in which he recorded it. Byron was, for all his faults, a man remarkably honest with himself and others and he never recovered from a feeling of shame about the swiftness with which he had violated this published promise in *The Corsair*. He did not abandon the effort to stop writing. Like a lame man who believes that he will surely be able to walk naturally if only he tries hard enough, he was perpetually flinging away the crutch. After 1814, however, the struggle was one that he conducted in private, in his journals and in letters to close friends. There were to be no further public declarations.

In his heart, one suspects, Byron recognized the essential hopelessness of the attempt. During the years that followed, he would in fact succeed in giving up poetry for brief periods. His poetic works may be considerable in volume: they were produced spasmodically. Periods of literary activity coincide with periods of idleness, often of disgust and frustration, in his personal life. When he felt himself to be truly and happily engaged in the events of the world around him, he was able to stop writing. It was when revolutions or passions had failed him that he was drawn back, inevitably, to his 'poeshie' as he mockingly called it. 'And now let us be literary', he wrote to Thomas Moore after the collapse of the Italian uprising in 1821,

> A sad falling off, but it is always a consolation. If Othello's occupation be gone, let us take to the next best; and if we cannot contribute to make mankind more free and wise, we may amuse ourselves and those who like it. What are you writing? I have been scribbling at intervals.[9]

Even *Don Juan*, a poem which had become necessary to him in a profound and complex way, was laid aside when he went to Greece. Byron took the unfinished seventeenth canto with him, but he added nothing to it, despite a multitude of opportunities. To one of his companions who reproached him, he declared: 'Poetry should only occupy the idle. In more serious affairs it would be ridiculous.'[1] The remark itself is quite characteristic; that Byron could make it of *Don Juan* at this point in time testifies eloquently to the underlying strength of his conviction about the relative worth of art and life.

———

Why, then, did Byron against his own will and beliefs continue to write poetry? The answers to this question became more complicated and also more interesting as his life unfolded. It is obvious enough why he broke his

8. To Hodgson, Feb. 3, 1813.
9. To Moore, April 28, 1821.
1. Remark made to Gamba at Missolonghi, quoted in Leslie A. Marchand, *Byron: A Biography*, New York 1957. Vol. III, p. 1125.

first resolution and composed *English Bards and Scotch Reviewers*. His pride had been deeply wounded by the attack on *Hours of Idleness* and he wanted revenge. The publication of the first two cantos of *Childe Harold*, on the other hand, had no such justification. In effect, the poem represents Byron's indirect admission that, for all his protestations to the contrary, the efforts of the Bavarian scene-painter were not enough. That objective record of the English nobleman's grand tour which these views were intended to provide sufficed for most travellers of the period. It could not content Byron. The impersonal images of the scene-painter left out, per-force, all that mattered most to him. Only poetry could order the tumult of his experiences in Greece and in the East, relating his own complex, half-understood self to the external scenes through which he passed. Reluc-tantly, shamefacedly, he resorted to creation because in no other way was he able to link those twin intensities, an objective and a private world.

Byron returned to England in July, 1811. The Oriental Tales, which he began to write in 1812, are the products of a situation far more desperate than the one which lay behind Cantos I and II of *Childe Harold*, although their settings and some of their characters are obviously derived from things seen and noted down in the course of the same journey. *Childe Harold* could at least shelter under the pretence that it was a verse guide-book, a useful compendium of information for anyone intending to retrace Byron's steps in the regions described. The poem was much more than this, of course, or Byron would not have had to write it at all, let alone in the form he chose, but the excuse was convenient in the light of his expressed contempt for fiction. The verse tales, on the other hand, strike a balance between reality and the imagination very different from that of *Childe Harold*. They are much more obviously works of fiction, invented histories in which the important truth is not literal but psychological. There is some-thing almost pathetic about Byron's reiterated concern with the accuracy of his facts in these poems. Had he presented a faithful picture of Eastern manners? Were his costumes correct down to the last detail? Could he be faulted in the least circumstance by an observer who knew these countries and their people? It is an attempt to justify what Byron felt to be a bad cause, to prop up fiction with a basis of demonstrable fact, more or less as a sop to a bad conscience. The reason for this new dependence upon the imagination in the verse tales is worth exploring.

The Giaour, the first of the tales, stands slightly apart from the others. It is an exorcism, a kind of magic spell. Feverishly, it re-enacts on the level of art a real incident. Byron would never talk openly about the episode; in the 1813 Journal he claimed that even to recollect how he had felt at that moment was 'icy'.[2] From the contemporary testimony collected, however, in Professor Marchand's biography, it seems clear that the original of Leila, the heroine of *The Giaour* who is sewn up in a sack and drowned in the Bospho-rus because she gave herself to a foreign lover, was in fact a young Turkish girl narrowly rescued by Byron from just this fate in March 1810. He had encountered her, purely by chance, as she was being haled along by her exe-cutioners near the sea's edge at Athens. The meeting was particularly for-tunate in view of the fact that Byron himself, almost certainly, had been the forbidden lover. Luck, a few threats, and the plentiful administration of

2. *Journal*, Dec. 1813.

bribes freed the prisoner from her fate, and Byron from responsibility for what would have been a peculiarly reproachful death. It is one of those incidents in which what did not happen, the disaster so miraculously averted, is likely to overshadow in retrospect the actual happy ending. Back in England, the hair's-breadth rescue came to seem for Byron, as well it might, like the false consolation of fiction and the weighted sack swaying with the tide on the sea-bottom like the real conclusion of the story. This is the stuff out of which nightmares are made, the hauntings of a lifetime. Troubled by phantoms, Byron sought assistance from poetry. He wrote *The Giaour*, a poem in which the tragedy is allowed to happen. Fortune does not send the foreigner riding down the beach at the crucial moment, and Leila dies. In visualizing this catastrophe down to the last, grim detail Byron obtained a curious sense of relief. He had forced a ghost to materialize and to identify itself clearly as fiction, a creature of the imagination, not of fact.

'All convulsions', Byron wrote in 1813, 'end with me in rhyme.'[3] Like *Don Juan* later, *The Giaour* is oddly shapeless according to any normal criterion of artistic form. Nervously, Byron kept returning to the poem as it sped through its various editions, adding more and more until, by the time he finally forced himself to desist—with the fifth edition—he had virtually doubled its length. Incorporated in *The Giaour* by this time was another and more recent guilt: his fear that his half-sister Augusta could not possibly have escaped unharmed from a situation for which he again was responsible: their perilous summer affair. In the Journals for 1813 and 1814, Byron recorded on several occasions his conviction that the composition of the Oriental Tales during this period preserved his sanity. 'I believe the composition of [*The Bride of Abydos*] kept me alive—for it was written to drive my thoughts from the recollection of.'[4] The cautious blank, transparently, is a symbol for Augusta and it is no accident that the subject of *The Bride of Abydos* is the ill-fated love of a brother and his half-sister. The conscious purpose of this poem, and of its companions, as he stated in the Journals, was 'to withdraw *myself* from *myself* . . . to wring my thoughts from reality, and take refuge in "imaginings", however "horrible".'[5] These imaginings were demonstrable shadowings of fact, and not just the neutral, innocent fact of scimitars and Arab horses, Koran-chanters and the Turkish national dress; the stories of Leila and the Giaour, of Selim and Zuleika or the Corsair were incarnations of a much more dangerous personal truth. Byron's fables are far from being identical with the reality which gave them birth, but in their very discrepancies from actual fact there resided now, for him, a peculiar value.

*   *   *

Byron's various statements, then, about poetry as 'the lava of the imagination, whose eruption prevents an earthquake' are far from standing alone in their period. Many of the later and more important works which he produced after his exile from England in 1816, *Manfred* or Cantos III and IV of *Childe Harold*, are shaped in part by this psychological necessity. By 1816, however, another impulse had joined with it.

3. To Moore, Nov. 30, 1813.
4. *Journal* Nov. 1813.
5. *Journal* Nov. 27, 1813; To Moore, Nov. 30, 1813.

> 'Tis to create, and in creating live
> A being more intense, that we endow
> With form our fancy, gaining as we give
> The life we image, even as I do now.

This extraordinary statement, an artistic credo of a very individual kind, appears at the beginning of *Childe Harold*, Canto III. It is, in effect, an admission that life is inadequate, that it needs to borrow from art an intensity and shapeliness not really its own. Nothing, it would seem, could be further from Byron's normal belief, his conviction that poetry is only reality's poor relation. I have tried to indicate already that what may appear at first like the diametric opposition between Keats and Byron with regard to the issue of poetic truth conceals an underlying affinity. The *Childe Harold* declaration is also, I think, best seen in its relation to contradiction elsewhere as a kind of amphisbaena: Shelley's beloved image of the serpent with a head at either end, moving in one direction and in the reverse with equal ease. It is a question of seeming extremities which, looked at closely, are one.

In his book *Byron: Christian Virtues*, Professor G. Wilson Knight has claimed that Byron was a man continually trying to exact from life itself the qualities of great poetry. This, I think, is true. Byron needed to mythologize fact. Hence the quite extraordinary quality of his pleasure when he came to stand upon what he thought was the site of Troy: when he was shown the grass-grown mounds which must contain the bones of the heroes. He had rescued a fiction for reality. His pride in swimming the Hellespont from Sestos to Abydos belongs here too; it proved the truth of a legend. Both in Italy and in Greece, Byron's revolutionary principles were strongly reinforced by a desire to realize myth, to create in a manner which, as Professor Knight puts it, 'used mankind itself rather than ink and paper for its materials.'[6] He pinned his hopes that the world's great age might begin again, the golden years return, not to any Shelleyan metaphysic but to the possibility of re-incarnating, initially in political terms, the fables of the past. As a very young man, he tried to see Napoleon as a creator in these terms, and admired him as the hero of an epic performed. Disillusion followed, and not simply because Byron began to suspect that his hero, when successful, would be a tyrant as clumsy as the legitimacy he replaced. Napoleon's exile at St. Helena grieved him beyond measure. This was not the way a hero, a man who had gambled for the world and lost, should end: acquiescing in defeat, accommodating himself humbly to the petty, day by day routine of captivity. By declining a fifth act suicide, a tragedy in the grand manner, Napoleon had failed to live up to the standards of art.

In his own political involvements, in his friendships, even in his love affairs, Byron tried throughout his existence to re-make reality in artistic terms. In this sense, he carried Romanticism to a further extreme than any of his contemporaries, was in fact the arch-Romantic among them. It is a little like Anselm's ontological argument for the existence of God. God is a Being predicated as perfect, altogether admirable. Therefore, He must exist, because non-existence would fatally flaw this perfection. The very terms of the description enforce reality upon the thing described. For all his

6. G. Wilson Knight, *Byron: Christian Virtues*, London 1952. p. 176.

expressed scorn of fiction, Byron in a way took art more seriously than its orthodox worshippers, valued it more highly. The golden world of the imagination mattered so much to him that he was continually trying to impose its qualities upon the brazen world of fact, to make poetry come true. It was quite characteristic of the weary, cynical Byron who set out on the last journey to Greece fully expecting not to return, perfectly aware of the struggle with factions and with greedy, pseudo-patriots which awaited him, that he should nonetheless include in his baggage two ferocious war-helmets in what he imagined to be the Homeric style. A foolishly theatrical gesture on one level, and as such the object of Trelawny's malice, it was on another level something more.

Oddly enough, it was Goethe among Byron's contemporaries who seems to have understood most clearly this insistence upon ploughing art back into reality. He did not approve. Most people, hearing of Byron's death at Missolonghi, thought that nothing in his life became him like the leaving it. Only Goethe was dismayed. The whole Greek enterprise, he declared bitterly,

> had something impure about it, and could never have ended well. It is a real misfortune when minds so rich in ideas insist on realising their ideal and bringing it to life. That simply will not do. The ideal and ordinary reality must be kept strictly apart.[7]

It was only afterwards, when he had transformed Byron into Euphorion, the child of Faust and Helen—of the medieval and the antique world—and made of his sacrifice in Greece a symbol of the death-wish of the modern artist, not the consequence of a preference for action of a very special kind as opposed to pure poetry, that Goethe was able to accept it.

By dying in Greece, Byron did manage to transform himself into a symbol of peculiar political potency: an almost mythological liberator. His death accomplished what his actual leadership almost certainly could not, in terms of foreign aid and support for the cause. He himself seems to have suspected, even before leaving Italy, that something drastic of this kind was going to be necessary. After all, by this point in his existence, he had had a good deal of experience with the refractory nature of life, the fact that it does not accommodate itself willingly to the patterns of art. It is true, of course, that sometimes reality co-operated with him. Of the Carnival in Venice, Byron wrote delightedly in 1818: 'Life becomes for the moment a drama without the fiction.'[8] That brilliant sequence of letters which he wrote to Lady Melbourne between the 21st of September and the end of October 1813 presents an extremely interesting aesthetic problem in just this sense. These letters, a kind of blow by blow account of his attempted seduction of Lady Frances Webster, in whose country house he was staying for much of the period, were posted every day as written. Byron never re-shaped them, never tidied up the earlier letters in the light of the somewhat surprising end of the story. Many of them were dashed off secretly, in the unsuspecting presence of other participants in the comedy. They are absolutely truthful. If you ask yourself what differentiates these letters from the ones contrived so carefully by Laclos in *Les Liaisons Dangereuses*, or by

---

7. E. M. Butler, *Goethe and Byron* (The Nottingham Byron Lecture, 1949/50).
8. Prose fragment of 1818 printed in the Prothero edition of the Letters and Journals, Vol. VI, 440.

Richardson in his epistolary novels, the answer I think must be that we are being presented on the one hand with a factual record and on the other with the constructions of the imagination, but that effectively there is no way of telling them apart. Unplanned, unretouched as they are, the Byron letters confront us like a formal work of art.

Life was not always, however, so obliging. It tended to become less and less co-operative as Byron grew older, with the result that he depended increasingly upon poetry proper. The heightenings of art might be sec-ondbest, but they were preferable to real banality. The problem at this point became one, essentially, of finding a form, a form which could bestow upon life some of the qualities of art without betraying Byron's basic convictions about the relative value of the two. Cantos III and IV of *Childe Harold*, poetically more accomplished though they are, did not represent much of an advance over his earlier work in this respect. The real break-through came with *Don Juan*. It has become something of a critical fashion to cas-tigate Byron for taking so long to arrive at the solution of *Don Juan*, to rec-ognize that this was the poem he was born to write. The real wonder, I think, is not that the formulation should have been so late in coming, but that he should have been able to work it out at all. When the moment of decision came, Byron put *Don Juan* aside and went to Greece. This was predictable. What was not predictable was the degree to which the poem almost made this action unnecessary by healing (for a little while) the breach between life and art.

> If in the course of such a life as was
>   At once adventurous and contemplative,
> Men, who partake all passions as they pass,
>   Acquire the deep and bitter power to give
> Their images again as in a glass,
>   And in such colours that they seem to live;
> You may do right forbidding them to show 'em,
> But spoil (I think) a very pretty poem.

This is *Don Juan's* equivalent to that statement from the third canto of *Childe Harold* ("'Tis to create, and in creating live / A being more intense . . .') which I quoted earlier. The *Don Juan* declaration occurs in Canto IV. In Canto XIV, he added to it a wry confession:

> And yet I can't help scribbling once a week,
>   Tiring old readers, nor discovering new.
> In youth I wrote because my mind was full,
> And now because I feel it growing dull.
>
> But 'why then publish?'—There are no rewards
>   Of fame or profit when the world grows weary.
> I ask in turn,—Why do you play at cards?
>   Why drink? Why read?—To make some hour less dreary.
> It occupies me to turn back regards
>   On what I've seen or ponder'd.

Some new factors have appeared here in Byron's attitude towards his art.

Don Juan is very much a poem of retrospect, the work of an extraordi-nary, lonely man looking back not only upon his own vanished life, but upon that of an era. It is, in a way, Byron's *A la Recherche du Temps Perdu*. 'Almost all *Don Juan* is real life', Byron wrote to his publisher in 1821. 'Either my own or from people I knew'.[9] Within the poem itself, he declared stubbornly that

> my Muse by no means deals in fiction:
> She gathers a repertory of facts,
> Of course with some reserve and slight restriction,
> But mostly sings of human things and acts.
>
>   (Canto XIV)

The characteristic passion for fact as the saving grace of fiction is still in play. Indeed, Byron took great pains over his research for *Don Juan*: the shipwreck scene is accurate down to the last nautical detail; the siege of Ismail is faithful to historical record; there is an almost pedantic concern for truth in his description of Eastern modes of life. Both personally, and in more general terms, Byron's poetry had always contained a strong documentary element. *Childe Harold* and the Oriental Tales were poems about actual places and occurrences, as well as being vehicles of emotional release, a means of ordering his own passions and guilts. Now, towards the end of his life, poetry served Byron less as *catharsis* than as a device for rescuing the reality of people and events from time. The *ubi sunt* theme in *Don Juan* takes in Egypt, Troy, Greece and Rome. This had been more or less its range in *Childe Harold* as well. *Don Juan*, however, also reflects that impulse which in 1818 made Byron decide to write a prose autobiography, a record of his existence up to that point. Hobhouse, Thomas Moore and John Murray burned Byron's Memoirs, unforgivably, in a panic after his death. Only in *Don Juan* does a shadow image of the autobiography survive. The poem is a lament for Byron's own youth, for friends and enemies, even for casual acquaintances—boxers and actresses—who made up a unique personal world.

'Troy owes to Homer what whist owes to Hoyle'; beneath the surface facetiousness of this comment in the third canto of *Don Juan* lies a reluctant but serious admission. Life may be superior to art. This basic superiority does not prevent reality from being dependent upon its secondhand and artificial cousin for survival in time.

> 'Tis strange, the shortest letter which man uses
> Instead of speech, may form a lasting link
> Of ages; to what straits old Time reduces
> Frail man, when paper—even a rag like this,
> Survives himself, his tomb, and all that's his.
>
>   (Canto III)

The position which Shakespeare had taken up with deliberate arrogance in the *Sonnets*—'So long as men can breathe, or eyes can see / So long lives this, and this gives life to thee'—the whole idea of immortality through verse, was one that Byron adopted against his will and deepest convictions. It seemed monstrous to him that art, the frozen figures on the urn, should outlast the warm and breathing reality from which they derived their parasitic existence.

9. To Murray, Aug. 23, 1821.

Nonetheless, he had been forced not only to concede the paradox, but actually to hope that in his own case it might prove true.

In Canto III of *Don Juan*, Byron introduces a fictitious poet, that pliable Greek who obligingly shapes his verses to please all parties. The man is a trimmer, in Dante's sense, utterly contemptible, but the song he sings is not. This lyric, 'The Isles of Greece', is a plea for Greek independence from Turkish rule and, as such, not only true but useful.

> His strain display'd some feeling—right or wrong;
>   And feeling, in a poet, is the source
> Of others' feeling; but they are such liars,
>   And take all colours—like the hands of dyers.
>
> But words are things, and a small drop of ink,
>   Falling like dew, upon a thought, produces
> That which makes thousands, perhaps millions, think.

The conflict of attitude in this passage is obvious. The Greek poet is himself despicable, a common liar. Byron uses him as a means of venting his customary spleen against literary men. Yet the verses which this scoundrel produces become a sword in the hands of revolution. They have power to change men's minds, to make them think and so, ultimately, to provoke action. 'But words are things': the equivalence which Byron admits here between imaginative language and fact is new in his work.

> Apologue, fable, poesy and parable,
>   Are false, but may be render'd also true,
> By those who sow them in a land that's arable.
>   'Tis wonderful what fable will not do!
>   (Canto XV)

Also new, is the resulting sense of moral purpose with which Byron began to invest *Don Juan*. At first, he treated the poem cavalierly, in the old manner: it was a trifle, intended only 'to giggle and make giggle'.[1] Long before the end of those five years during which he worked on his epic, he had come to regard it in quite another light. The popular and critical reception accorded to Cantos I and II was, on the whole, disastrous. After the death of Shelley, there was almost no one to encourage Byron, to assure him that what he was writing mattered. Indeed, there were a great many people, some of them whose opinion he valued, urging him to destroy the cantos he had already published and to abandon the poem. Stubbornly, he went on with it, in what came to be an increasing artistic isolation. It is an interesting reversal of the state of affairs in Byron's earlier life, when the public, his publishers and his friends were all begging for more poetry from him and Byron, sceptical of the value of this activity in any but the most momentary, personal sense, was resisting their demands. He was writing now against the wishes of virtually everyone but himself, but he had come to believe in *Don Juan*. 'I maintain', he wrote angrily to John Murray, 'that it is the most moral of poems; but if people won't discover the moral, that is their fault, not mine.'[2]

---

1. To Murray, Aug. 12, 1819.
2. To Murray, Feb. 1, 1819.

Professor Helen Gardner once described *Don Juan* as a poem about 'the salutariness of being undeceived'.[3] This seems to me a remarkably just summation, and one with which Byron himself would have agreed. The poem aims to destroy imaginary certainties of all kinds, hollow ideals, hypocrisy and cant. In this sense, it is a celebration of truth against the distortions of fiction and perfectly in accord with Byron's lifelong suspicion of the latter. The extraordinary thing about *Don Juan*, however, is the way in which as a work of art it contrives to honour fact in its very structure, not simply in its material or in the social and moral judgements it makes. Byron's various jokes about the shapelessness of his epic, the fact that he might (or might not) canter gently through one hundred cantos, are not altogether flippant. The poem deliberately rejects a closed, and thereby explicitly literary, form. When he began *Don Juan*, Byron may have thought of it as an enterprise with definite limits: eight cantos, or perhaps twelve. As he went on writing, the other end of the poem began to recede into the infinite distance in a way we do not ordinarily associate with works of art. *Don Juan* is not really, of course, as haphazard as some of Byron's comments would suggest. The claim that 'Note or text, I never know the word which will come next' (Canto IX) constitutes a bit of play-acting on the part of the narrator. The poem does, however, catch up and reflect in its organization something of the random nature of life itself. Its rhythms are the rhythms of reality, not of art in any normal sense. You cannot, as a result, say that it is unfinished, as Keats's *Hyperion* or Shelley's *Triumph of Life* are unfinished. A rainstorm and a pair of murderously incompetent doctors killed Byron and Don Juan together in the middle of breakfast at Norman Abbey in Canto XVII. It was the natural end of the poem, in that its form was really co-terminous with Byron's life, both destined to conclude together.

Childe Harold too had been indefinitely extendable, and so had *The Giaour*. A preference for poetic forms which echo the diffuse and sprawling pattern of human existence is the natural consequence of Byron's attitude towards art, and one of the reasons why he was generally unsuccessful with lyric verse. The neo-classical concentration of plays like *Marino Faliero* and *Sardanapalus* was something he imposed upon himself experimentally, but it is no accident that subsequent dramas gradually became more and more open in their weave until, with *The Deformed Transformed*, dramatic structure deliquesced into a rhythm so like that of *Don Juan* that Byron himself seems to have recognized the similarity of the two works, and abandoned the play as redundant. *Don Juan*, however, distinguishes itself from his earlier, permissive forms by the complexity of its reconciliation between fact and fiction, the success with which it marries life and art. It is a success largely dependent upon its construction as a story set within a frame.

Where *Childe Harold* had blurred the lines between narrator and hero, *Don Juan* by contrast is absolutely clear. We are, on the one hand, following a story: a series of picaresque incidents involving harems and enchanted islands, warfare and love betrayed. The hero of these deliberately heightened adventures is a young man who, contrary to the 'lies' told about him by previous literary men, is not the world's seducer, but its prey. He is not even a complicated character. Generosity, affection, a capacity to

3. Helen Gardner, 'Don Juan', in *The London Magazine*, July 1958.

form strong attachments, a strain of slightly ludicrous idealism, sway his actions. He is handsome, energetic, kind—and that is about all. In a poem filled with brilliant dialogue, we rarely hear Juan speak. Compared with most of the characters in his story: Julia, Lambro, Johnson or Lady Adeline, he has no personality at all. Only Haidee is as simple in outline as he, and this is one reason why she is his true love. Their very construction as characters unites them.

Byron's reasons for keeping Juan in this half-light owe something to the picaresque tradition, to Smollett and Fielding. They derive chiefly, however, from the fact that Juan must stand opposite the narrator in that strange dialectic between fiction and reality, art and life, which the poem sustains. Where Juan is simple, Byron as narrator is complex. Where the hero is passive, swept along on a tide of events, the narrator is the source of action: a Prospero-like contriver. Juan rarely reflects; his various involvements leave him no time. Byron has time on his hands, and reflects constantly. In the plot, Juan is surrounded with characters whose personalities are all more vivid than his own. Byron, in his historical present, dwarfs all the real people he summons up in his digressions, from Castlereagh and Southey, to Napoleon and George III. By a curious process of inversion, he is as dominant a figure in the commentary—many-sided, brilliant, individual—as Juan himself is colourless, simple and subdued in the story.

Juan and the narrator, the invented character and the real one, may represent the opposite poles of the poem, but their two worlds of fiction and of fact are linked in a number of ways. A surprising amount of the Juan story is actually true, either historically, or because it includes scenes and characters from Byron's own past. It is a fictional world with a heavy ballast of fact.

> 'tis the part
> Of a true poet to escape from fiction
> Whene'er he can; for there is little art
> In leaving verse more free from the restriction
> Of truth than prose, unless to suit the mart
> For what is sometimes called poetic diction.
> (Canto VIII)

Conversely, the narrator is not above fictional impersonation. Again and again, he invents attitudes, fanciful responses for the benefit of the reader. He poses, and then parodies his own assumed role, creates as well as records a complex personality.

Most important of all perhaps is the link provided by the common factor of time. As we read, real time is running out for Byron, in Venice, in Ravenna and Pisa. Revolutions take shape in Italy and England and then peter out. Keats and Shelley die, and so does Byron's natural daughter Allegra; an Italian officer is suddenly and inexplicably shot dead in the street outside his house. All these events find their way into the narrator's part of the poem, as they might into a journal. This is real time, which the writer can describe, but over which he has no control. Poised against it is the more malleable time of fiction. According to this second clock, Juan grows up in Seville, seduces Julia, is sent abroad, shipwrecked, lives on the island, is sold into slavery, and embarks on a number of adventures in Turkey, Russia and (finally) England. This narrative time, unlike the other, is in the writer's control and what Byron did was to run it parallel with the time of fact. Both narrator and hero age side by side as the poem proceeds. The young man who arrives in England as Catherine's ambassador in Canto X may be no more complex as a character than he was at the beginning: he is a far sadder and more worldly figure. Even so, the Byron who placed Juan in Norman Abbey between Lady Adeline and her frolic Grace Fitz-Fulke was not the same man as the one who devised the bedroom farce of Canto I, a few years before. He too is older, concerned with his own apathy, his inability to feel. It is not the least of the poem's accomplishments that it can reveal to us this bitter process of ageing as it affects the writer, side by side with Juan's gradual accommodation to the way of a corrupt world. Fictional time grows out of the time of fact.

Ultimately, the unity of *Don Juan* is that of Byron's personality, a personality manifesting itself both as commentator and as creative agent. If it is a unity which sometimes seems based more upon the principle of contradiction pushed to an extreme than upon anything else, this is not really surprising. Byron's mind was neither orderly nor of a synthesizing kind. He recognized that his own nature was paradoxical, made up of opposites, and it seemed to him that experience itself, insofar as he could understand it, was the same. He himself was both melancholy and gay, cynical and sentimental, endlessly amused by life and a prey to ennui. These qualities might clash with one another, but they were all of them genuine. To try and suppress one reaction in favour of its opposite, even to insist upon relating them, represented for him a tampering with facts, a tidying up of reality which made it false. Always, for Byron, two honest fragments, even if incompatible, were preferable to an artificially adjusted, and therefore half-true, whole. In life and in art, he mistrusted the shaping spirit of imagination, and this mistrust created serious problems for him, both as a person and as a writer.

Poetry after all is an ordering of experience. It implies choice, whether it is a discrimination among words, or that gradual elimination of the superfluous and discordant which expresses, and ultimately defines, form. Byron came to believe in *Don Juan* as he had believed in no previous poem partly because he had at last developed a structure which was like life itself in that, potentially at least, it excluded nothing. Irrelevance becomes a term without meaning; all contradictions can be allowed to stand. *Don Juan* is a poem which affirms in one stanza to deny in the next, which insists simultaneously upon conflicting points of view. Byron has been castigated by more than one modern critic for undercutting the love of Juan and Haidee, the idyll of the island, with mockery. The truth is, of course, that his treatment of the episode brilliantly incorporates both his own longing for life lived as an absolute, raised to the condition of art, and his realistic awareness of the basic impossibility of the attempt. Isolated on the island, Juan and Haidee manage for a little while to realize myth.

> This is in others a factitious state,
>   An opium dream of too much youth and reading,
> But was in them their nature or their fate:
>   No novels e'er had set their young hearts bleeding.
>   (Canto IV)

The miracle, however, is precarious. Lambro destroys it on his return, but he only does violently what Time would have accomplished, more slowly, without him. Already, in the palace scenes of Canto III there is a note of corruption in that new profusion of sherbets and sweetmeats, dwarfs, black eunuchs and dancing girls. Haidee herself, although "tis very silly / To gild refined gold, or paint the lily' adds unnecessary, artificial aids to a beauty which effortlessly corresponds to the sculptor's most cherished ideal. In the great, tapestried chamber, with the stern words of the Persian moralists confronting the lovers from the walls, the mythic simplicity of those earlier, Praxitelian, embraces by the sea vanishes. Gradually, life descends from the level of art. Haidee, given death as the best gift of the gods, does not live out this bitter transformation. Juan, who survives, is sold into a treble slavery: he is bound to the service of his purchaser, but also and more permanently to that of Time and a world in which ideal love, perfect beauty, are only diseases of the mind.

> Who loves, raves—'tis youth's frenzy; but the cure
> Is bitterer still. As charm by charm unwinds
> Which robed our idols, and we see too sure
> Nor worth nor beauty dwells from out the mind's
> Ideal shape of such; yet still it binds
> The fatal spell, and still it draws us on.
> Reaping the whirlwind from the oft-sown winds.
> (*Childe Harold*, Canto IV)

It was Byron's respect for truth, no matter how unpalatable, which made him treat the Juan and Haidee episode as he did. Even so, it is entirely characteristic of him that, for all the anger of the anti-war cantos, he can still insist that Catherine's general Suwarrof was in certain respects admirable as well as despicable. He included the grotesque anecdote of the Russian officer who found his heel gripped firmly between the teeth of a severed head, because it was something which really happened in this campaign and, in the midst of his indignation over the needless sufferings of Ismail, he permitted himself a comic side-glance at those middle-aged ladies in the city who were 'heard to wonder in the din . . . Wherefore the ravishing did not begin.' (Canto VIII). For the Texas editors of the Variorum *Don Juan*, blatant incongruities and lapses in tone of this kind blunt the force of the satire, even render it suspect.[4] Byron would almost certainly have replied to this criticism that he did indeed wish to persuade his readers that war is wrong, but that he could not do so by falsifying reality, by altering the heterogeneous facts of experience so that they all pointed artificially in one direction. The poet may wish to use a battle like Ismail as a piece of propaganda, but he has no right to forget that in its complex reality, for the people on both sides who lived through it, it could not be a unified, or singly-directed experience of this kind. To forget this is to lie, and thereby destroy something Byron was now, in rather special terms, willing to concede: the validity of poetry.

4. T. G. Steffan, *Byron's Don Juan: The Making of a Masterpiece*. University of Texas Press, 1957. Vol. I, pp. 226–8.

After Byron's death, there came to light a curious fragment of verse which he had composed at Cephalonia, the island where he waited before establishing himself on the mainland of Greece. This fragment, which bears the title 'Aristomenes' is dated by Byron September 10, 1823. It was first published in the *Collected Poems* of 1901. Aristomenes was an historical person. He was a general of Messenia, that province of the ancient Peloponesus which lay between Arcadia and the sea. He lived in the 7th century B.C., at a time when this province had, for some thirty years, been enslaved by Sparta and he became the hero of the Second Messenien War for freedom. His exploits are recorded in a number of Greek sources, including Pausanias and Diodorus of Sicily. A brilliant military commander, Aristomenes (like Aristides) also earned the epithet, 'the Just'. He was famed for his compassion, even to the enemy. Offered a crown by his people, he magnanimously refused it. He was a lover, and he is said to have written verse. On all these grounds, Aristomenes might naturally appeal to Byron at this moment of his own life, might confront him with new meaning from the almost forgotten past of his classical reading. Aristomenes is also, however, one of those historical figures whose life trespasses upon the territory of fiction. Much of his story is obviously invented: hair's breadth escapes in which he is aided by a fox and an eagle, legends about the women who loved him, or about his magical power to aid and advise his country from the tomb. Indeed, he became the hero of an Alexandrian epic, and it is said that even in the second century A.D. ballads were still being written about him, and sung, in Messenia. He is a creature half of fact, half of myth.

Byron seems to have intended a long poem about Aristomenes, because the fragment is headed 'Canto the First'. Only eleven lines were completed:

> The Gods of old are silent on their shore,
> Since the great Pan expired, and through the roar
> Of the Ionian waters broke a dread
> Voice which proclaim'd 'the mighty Pan is dead.'
> How much died with him! false or true—the dream
> Was beautiful which peopled every stream
> With more than finny tenants, and adorn'd
> The woods and waters with coy nymphs that scorn'd
> Pursuing Deities, or in the embrace
> Of gods brought forth the high heroic race
> Whose names are on the hills and o'er the seas.

They are, I think, an extraordinary and unjustly neglected eleven lines. In them, Byron refers to that legend of the Greek sailor who, at the time of the birth of Christ, heard from the deck of his ship a great cry go up from the shores of the Mediterranean: 'The god Pan is dead!' It is a story about the moment in which classical myth ceased to exist as part of the real world. What is remarkable about the Byron fragment—apart from the fact that the verse movement is totally different from anything in his previous work—is the relaxed confidence that 'false or true' the beauty of the dream, of fable, was its own excuse for being: a sufficient justification. Almost, he accepts the point of view of Keats in the opening lines of *Endymion*. What Byron would have made of 'Aristomenes' had he lived, we cannot know. From the lines which survive, and from the nature of the hero he had selected, it looks as though he planned a poetic construct more formal than *Don Juan*. He could afford to do this now, afford to honour fiction and to admit that, between them, reality and the imagination can work out something of which neither is capable alone. The road which leads to this final position was long and difficult, but 'Aristomenes' is the work of a man who had at last made his peace with art.

JEROME J. McGANN

The Book of Byron and the Book of a World[†]

Thought is no longer theoretical. As soon as it functions it offends or reconciles, attacks or repels, breaks, dissociates, unites or reunites; it cannot help but liberate or enslave.

(Michel Foucault)

I

Byron's popularity—the fact that he was a bestseller and 'famous in [his] time'—has always focused certain literary problems not least of all at the outset for Byron himself. 'Lord Byron cuts a figure—but he is not figurative,'[1] Keats waspishly observed in a letter to the George Keatses. This is an envious and illuminating remark which reveals as much about Keats and his ambitions for a successful career as it does about the character of Byron's verse, the phenomenon of Byronism, and the changing structure of the institution of letters at the beginning of the nineteenth century. Later writers have sometimes condescended to Byron, particularly to the Byron of the pre-exilic period, as a factitious writer who had merely seized the main chance during the Years of Fame. Of course it is true that he was himself largely responsible for creating the enormous popularity of the Oriental and Byronic Tales. Nevertheless—so the story goes—he cranked out verse between 1812–15 to various formulas and audience expectations. In this activity he was not so much a poet as he was a pander and whore to public taste. It passes without saying that those tastes were corrupt. (The non-malicious version of this general view is that Byron invented the myth of himself as The Romantic Poet, thereby creating a new structure of authorship which answered to the changing conditions that were rapidly transforming the English literary institution.)

Byron himself was well aware of these events and social formations. His letters and his poetry alike reflect on these matters often. In May, 1813, for example, at the peak of his London years, Byron writes to Thomas Moore about projects in poetry: 'Stick to the East;—the oracle, Staël, told me it was the only poetical policy . . . The little I have done in that way is merely a "voice in the wilderness" for you; and, if it has had any success, that also will prove that the public are orientalizing, and pave the path for you.'[2] Later, of course, he came to speak more critically, even disparagingly, of this

† From *The Beauty of Inflections: Literary Investigations in Historical Method and Theory* (Oxford: Clarendon Press, 1985). Copyright © 1985 Jerome J. McGann. Reprinted with permission of Oxford University Press.
1. *The Letters of John Keats*, ed. H. E. Rollins, Cambridge, Mass., 1958, ii. 67.
2. *Byron's Letters and Journals*, ed. Leslie A. Marchand, Cambridge, Mass., 1973–82, iii. 101 (cited below as *BLJ*).

kind of careerist calculation. In January 1822 he tells Douglas Kinnaird that '*my* object is not *immediate* popularity in my present productions which are written on a different system from the rage of the day'; and in another letter three days later: 'Now once and for all about publication—I [*n*]*ever courted the* public—and I will never yield to it.—As long as I can find a *single* reader I will publish my Mind . . . and write while I feel the impetus'.[3]

Byron arrived at this changed position largely because of the Separation Controversy and its aftermath, which exposed to critical analysis a whole train of Byron's most cherished ideas and illusions. The idea which dominates his 'Epistle to Augusta'—that 'I have been cunning in mine overthrow, / The careful pilot of my proper woe' (lines 23–4)—has its deepest filiations with Byron's public life and poetical career between 1807 and 1816:

> With false Ambition what had I to do?
> Little with Love, and least of all with Fame;
> And yet they came unsought; and with me grew;
> And made me all which they can make—a Name.
> Yet this was not the end I did pursue;
> Surely I once beheld a nobler aim.
> ('Epistle to Augusta', lines 97–102)[4]

This critical examination of himself, his public life, and his poetical/moral goals will dominate most of his later years and will affect all aspects of his work in the most profound ways.

I have sketched this brief history in order to recollect the most salient aspect of Byron's work: that he wrote about *himself*, and that his books, like God's human creatures, are all made in his image and likeness. The most dramatic example of this biographical/historical imperative in his work is perhaps to be found in the amusing stanzas 51–2 of *Beppo*.[5]

> Oh! that I had the art of easy writing,
>   What should be easy reading! could I scale
> Parnassus, where the Muses sit inditing
>   Those pretty poems never known to fail,
> How quickly would I print (the World delighting)
>   A Grecian, Syrian, or *Assyrian* tale;
> And sell you, mixed with western Sentimentalism,
> Some samples of the *finest Orientalism*.
>
> But I am but a nameless sort of person,
>   (A broken Dandy lately on my travels) . . .

Part of the genius of this passage is that it manages to be at once critical and sympathetic toward Byron's career, his own earlier work, and the audience which found (and which continues to find) an interest and profit in

---

3. *BLJ* ix. 92, 94.
4. The texts of Byron's poems which were printed after 1816—with the exception of the last two cantos of *Childe Harold* and all of *Don Juan*—are here taken from *Byron's Works. Poetry*, ed. E. H. Coleridge, London, 1898–1904. For the other texts, see below.
5. Similar autobiographical references abound in *Don Juan* (see e.g. Canto XI sts. 55–85). Quotations from *Don Juan* below are taken from the *Variorum* edition of T. G. Steffan and W. W. Pratt, Austin, Tex., 1957 (cited here as *DJV*).

such things. This poetry institutes a benevolent critique of itself and its World, on the one hand, and on the other of the verse which fashion will cultivate at various times, as well as the very concept and event of 'the fashionable'.

This pointed and personal quality in Byron's work is apparent from the beginning. His first book, *Fugitive Pieces*, was privately printed in 1806 for an audience of friends and acquaintances who were privy to its local references and biographical connections—many of which were connections with themselves. *Hours of Idleness*, his first published work, appeared the following year, and it sought to extend the range of Byron's intimacies to a somewhat larger book-purchasing audience. Here, Byron projected himself before his English audience as a recognizable figure whom, he trusted, they would be happy to take to their breasts. Here, the English world at large met, for the first time, not the Man but the Lord of Feeling, a carefully constructed self-image which was fashioned to launch him on his public career. This was not conceived, at the time, as a literary career.[6]

Byron succeeded in his effort, though not precisely as he had expected. Certain hostile reviews—most notoriously Brougham's in the highly visible and influential *Edinburgh Review*—interrupted Byron's initial, unruffled expectations. Had he reflected more critically on the hostile reception which *Fugitive Pieces* had provoked in certain narrow quarters of its local (Southwell) society, he might have foreseen some trouble for his next book.[7] But he did not, apparently, and seems only to have realized later that he was destined to be both the darling and the demon of his age.

The attack on *Hours of Idleness* was another opportunity for Byron to produce yet a third Book of Himself: this time, *English Bards and Scotch Reviewers*, the fiery counter-attack on his persecutors and the culture which supported such beings.[8] If it is true that Byron was 'born for opposition', this book revealed that fact, for the first time unmistakably.

And so it went on. In 1809 Byron left benighted England to chew over the high rhetoric of his last book, and he plunged into Europe and the Levant, where his next productions began to accumulate their materials in the much larger context of European affairs. He wrote a continuation, or sequel, to *English Bards and Scotch Reviewers* called *Hints from Horace*, which was not published in his lifetime, and he composed the first two cantos of that unsurpassed act of literary self-creation, *Childe Harold's Pilgrimage. A Romaunt.*[9]

This book is worth pausing over—not the poem, but the book.[1] It is a handsome and rather expensive (30s.) quarto volume beautifully printed on

---

6. For a discussion of these matters see my *Fiery Dust. Byron's Poetic Development*, Chicago, 1968, chap. 1, and *Lord Byron. Complete Poetical Works*, ed. Jerome J. McGann, Oxford, 1980– i. 360–3. The latter work is hereafter referred to as *CPW*. The best single piece of work on the biographical dimensions of Byron's poetry—it is one of the most important essays on Byron ever written, as well as a crucial work on the methodology of biographical studies—is 'Narcissus Jilted', by Cecil Lang, first given in an abbreviated version as a lecture at the 1984 Caltech/Weingart Conference in Humanities.
7. See *CPW*, ibid. and poems 24, 25, 28 in *CPW*.
8. *CPW* i. 398–9.
9. *CPW* i. 426–7 and ii. 268–71.
1. For complete bibliographical details see *Byron's Works. Poetry*, ed. E. H. Coleridge, London, 1901–4, vii. 180–4 and T.J. Wise, *Byron. A Bibliography . . .* , London, 1932–3, i. 50–4. The history of the book's publication is discussed in *CPW* ii. 268–9. The prose quotations below from *Childe Harold's Pilgrimage. A Romaunt* are taken from the first edition, and page nos. are given in the text.

heavy paper. It comprises four distinct parts: 1. The title poem in two cantos (pp. iii–109); 2. The extensive notes to these cantos (pp. 111–61); 3. A section headed 'Poems' which included fourteen short pieces (pp. 163–200); 4. An Appendix containing bibliographical materials, translations, Romaic transcriptions and one facsimile manuscript, all having to do with the current state of the literary culture of modern Greece (pp. 201–[27]). Its publisher conceived its audience to be a wealthy one, people interested in travel books and topographical poems, people with a classical education and with a taste for antiquarian lore and the philosophical musings of a young English lord. As it turned out, all of England and Europe were to be snared by this book's imaginations. It went through a dozen (cheaper) editions in three years and established all of the principal features of that imaginative (but not imaginary) world-historical figure known as Byron. Later circumstances would only provide the public with slightly different perspectives on this figure.

The book of *Childe Harold* published in 1812 picks up the autobiographical myth which Byron had left *in medias res* when he left England in 1809.[2] The notes specifically recall the controversy surrounding *English Bards and Scotch Reviewers*, the section of 'Poems' is so arranged as to mirror the personal tale narrated through the title poem, and the latter presents a dramatic picture of a young lord who leaves his local home and friends, as well as his country, in a condition of psychic and cultural alienation. Simply, he is disgusted with himself and the world as he has thus far seen it. He finds, when he flees to other lands and in particular to the fabulous Levantine seat of western culture, that his own personal *anomie*, experienced in the tight little island of Britain, mirrors the condition of Europe (or, in Byron's startling and important variation on this ancient topos, that Europe and the entire world mirrors *his* personal condition). Thus does Byron force himself—and the individual person through himself—to the centre of attention. What his book says is not simply that we should deplore the condition of western culture in this critical time, but that we should deplore it because its debasement has poisoned its chief, indeed, its only, value: the individual human life. In particular, Byron's life.

Byron inserts his personal history into the latest phase of the European crisis which began in 1789. The outbreak of the Peninsular War in 1809 initiated the last act in the drama of the Napoleonic Wars, which would end in the defeat of Napoleon and the restoration of the European monarchies under the hegemony of England. In *Childe Harold* (1812) Byron's itinerary takes him first to the very heart of the Peninsular events, where his initial mood of disgust at his English existence acquires its European dimension. When he moves to the East and the dominions of the Turkish Empire, including Greece, his cynicism is confirmed: Greece, the very symbol of the west's highest ideals and self-conceptions, lies in thrall not merely to the military rule of the Porte, but to the contest of self-serving political interests of the English, French, and Russians.

This is the context which explains Byron's peculiar Appendix, with its heterogenous body of Romaic materials. *Childe Harold* (1812) is obsessed with the idea of the renewal of human culture in the west at a moment of

---

2. For a more detailed discussion of the context and meaning of the poem see *CPW* ii, ibid. and *Fiery Dust*, Part II.

its deepest darkness. This means for Byron the renewal of the value of the individual person, and the renewal of Greece as an independent political entity becomes Byron's 'objective correlative' for this idea. *Childe Harold* (1812) is thus, on one hand, a critique of present European society and politics, and, on the other, a pronouncement of the crucial need, throughout Europe, for the independence of Greece. As Byron would later say: 'There is *no* freedom—even for *Masters*—in the midst of slaves.'[3] The question of Greece thus becomes for Byron a way of focusing the central questions which bear upon the present European epoch. The Europeans normally date this epoch from 1789, and rightly so, but in this book (as well as in his next two books, *The Giaour* and *The Bride of Abydos*) Byron argues that the conflict of European self-interests can be best and most clearly understood in terms of the recent history of Greece, whose abortive efforts for independence in the late eighteenth century were either neglected by the European powers or actively betrayed.

Thus, in *Childe Harold* (1812) Byron enlarged his personal myth, which he had already begun to develop in his earlier books, by inserting it into the wider context of the European political theatre as it appeared to him in 1809–12; and the central ideological focus of the entire myth involves the question of personal and political freedom in the oppressive and contradictory circumstances which Byron observed in the world of his experience. More than anything else this book says that the most personal and intimate aspects of an individual's life are closely involved with, and affected by, the social and political context in which the individual is placed. Byron goes further to say that such a context is more complex and extensive than one ordinarily thinks, that each person is more deeply affected by (as it were) invisible people, places, and events than we customarily imagine. Ali Pacha and his Albanians may appear far removed from England and the Napoleonic Wars, but to the perspicacious European they will have more than a merely exotic interest. Similarly, Byron's use of antiquarian and classical materials, though ostentatious, is not merely a clumsy display of learning and artistic pendantry. On the contrary, he invokes the classical world and the later history of Europe's investment in that world because this complex ideological and political network exerts a powerful effect upon current European affairs, and hence on the experience of each single person living in Europe. A powerful and illuminating irony runs through Byron's flight from contemporary England and Europe and his pursuit of ancient Greek ideals:

> Of the ancient Greeks we know more than enough; at least the younger men of Europe devote much of their time to the study of Greek writers and history, which would be more usefully spent in mastering their own. Of the moderns, we are perhaps more neglectful than they deserve; and while every man of any pretensions to learning is tiring out his youth, and often his age, in the study of the language and the harangues of the Athenian demogogues in favour of freedom, the real or supposed descendants of these sturdy republicans are left to the actual tyranny of their masters . . . (*Childe Harold's Pilgrimage. A Romaunt* (1812), p. 173)

3. *BLJ* ix. 41.

Byron's proposal in his book is to look at England, Europe, and Greece not as these political entities appear in their ideological self-representations, but 'as they are' (p. 174) in fact. The reality reveals an Islam and a modern Greece very different from what they are commonly represented to be in English and European commentaries; it also reveals the hypocritical fault lines which run through the high-minded and Greek-derived ideologies of liberty to which the major European powers give lip-service. In Byron's book, the image of the young European gentleman acquiring a classical education is contradictory and deeply satiric. Such a person's mind is filled with self-serving and self-deluding ideas which permit him to identify with the dream of ancient Greece even as they also allow him to remain blind to certain important actualities: that the Russians 'have twice . . . deceived and abandoned' the Greeks, that the French seek the deliverance of continental Greece' as part of their policy for 'the subjugation of the rest of Europe', and that the English, in addition to the pursuit of their economic self-interests, profess to seek the freedom of Greece even as they subjugate the rights of 'our Irish Helots' (p. 201) and 'Catholic brethren' (p. 172).

In Byron's books—*Childe Harold* (1812) is merely prototypical in this respect—the variety of materials often conveys an image of heterogeneity, but in fact this image is no more than the sign of intrinsic connections which are not normally perceived, of connections between 'opposite and discordant' matters which only *appear* to be separated, but which are in fact fundamentally related. The soon-to-be published Oriental Tales are not merely a set of exotic adventure stories. They constitute a series of symbolic historical and political meditations on current European ideology and politics in the context of the relations between East and West after the break-up of the Roman Empire and the emergence of Islam.[4] That later readers and critics have often taken Byron's Levantine materials as a sign of a (presumptively shallow) poetic interest in local colour and oriental ornamentation merely testifies to a failure of critical intelligence and historical consciousness. Byron was deeply interested in these social and political questions and he used his poetry to probe their meaning and their roots. Later criticism has too often translated *its* lack of interest into a myth of the intellectual poverty of Byron's verse.

Byron's skill at manipulating his publications produced some of the strangest and most interesting books of poetry ever printed in England. *The Giaour* may stand as one example out of many.[5] Like the other tales which were soon to follow, this poem is a political allegory told from the point of view of those 'younger men of Europe' whom Byron described in the notes to *Childe Harold* (1812). The subject of the poem, at the plot level, is the state of modern Greece around 1780. At the narrative level, the poem is a contemporary (1809–13) meditation on the meaning of the European (and especially the English) understanding of Levantine politics between 1780 and 1813. The poem's story (its plot level) is a nihilistic tragedy in which all parties are involved, and destroyed. The meditation on the story is carried most dramatically in the introductory (167) lines, which appear as the 'original' work of the poem's redactor (Byron himself), as well as in the

---

4. See the commentaries to the Oriental Tales in *CPW* iii.
5. *CPW* iii. 406–15. For an excellent discussion of the political aspects of two of the books of Byron's tales see Peter Manning, 'Tales and Politics: *The Corsair, Lara, The White Doe of Rylstone*', in *Byron. Poetry and Politics . . .* , ed. E. A. Stürzl and James Hogg, Salzburg, 1981, pp. 204–30.

poem's 'Advertisement' and its many prose notes, also represented in *The Giaour* as the 'original' work of the editor/redactor Byron. The entire significance of this excellent work does not appear unless one responds to the interplay between the poem's two 'levels'. Briefly, the 'original' work of the editor/redactor comprises a set of deeply contradictory materials: on one hand, a complete romantic sympathy with the characters and events as well as an absorption in the heroic ideology which they exhibit; on the other, a mordant series of comical remarks on Eastern mores and commonplace European ideas about such matters. This radical split in the poem's attitude at its meditative level reflects, and interprets, the European understanding of the Levant between 1780–1813. The interpretation which Byron produces is a critical one: the European understanding is self-deluded and helpless, and Byron's own exposure to this failed understanding is represented as the vision of the one-eyed man in the kingdom of the blind. The comedy of the poem's notes, apparently so urbane, is in fact a flinching away, the laughter, spoken of in *Don Juan*, which serves to hold back weeping and bleaker realities.

All of Byron's works, and especially his published books, exhibit intersections of these kinds. Thus, his bibliography is more than a scholar's guide and resource, it is also a graphic display of his life in books, and of the extension of his life through books. The piracies, the huge number of translations, the numerous printings all attest and perpetuate the poetic explorations of reality which he initially set in motion. And it is the 'books', rather than the 'poems' (or least of all the 'texts'), which draw attention to the central quality of Byron's poetical work; for when we study the works through their material existences we are thereby helped to see and understand the social and historical ground which defines their human meanings.

II

Nowhere is this fact about Byron's work more clear than in the case of his masterwork, *Don Juan*. We respond to its name as if it were one thing, as indeed it is; but it is also, like the world which it expresses and represents, incredibly various and heterogeneous. Readers have of course always responded to that variety, but we must do so even as we also bear in mind that the variety is of a determinate and specifiable sort. *Don Juan* is, formally, a romantic fragment poem comprising six authorized and published volumes, along with a body of material published only after Byron's death, at different times and with various justifications. The first two volumes were published by John Murray in a certain way, and the next four volumes were published by John Hunt in a very different way. Important aspects of the meaning of the poem are bound up with these interesting events in the work's publication history.[6]

Most important to see is that when Byron began publishing the poem with John Hunt he was released from certain constraints which he had to struggle against when he was publishing with the conservative house of Murray. *Don Juan*'s (rejected) Preface and (suppressed) Dedication emphasize the political and social critique which is finally so fundamental to the

6. For a discussion of the history of the poem's publication see *DJV* i. 25–52.

poem.[7] But Murray and his allies forced Byron to revise the published version of the first five cantos so as to *de*-emphasize this aspect of the epic. As a consequence, the original Cantos I–V (the first two published volumes of the poem) preserve the poem's social and political critique as a peripheral and subsidiary matter, an incidental topic that seems to appear and disappear in the poem in a random way. The suppressed Dedication was not published until 1832, and the rejected Preface did not appear until 1901.

With the appearance of Cantos VI–VIII, published by Hunt, the situation changes radically. These cantos are introduced with a prose Preface where the social and political issues are finally raised to great, even to a dominant, position; and the poetic materials as well undergo a shift in emphasis toward more explicitly social and political matters. This change in the poem has been recognized for some time and critics have described the differences between the earlier and the later cantos in various (often useful) ways. What has not been seen, however, is the structural change brought about in the poem as a whole when Byron began his epic 'again' (as it were) with Cantos VI–VIII and John Hunt.

We can begin to see what is involved here by looking briefly at the original Preface to Cantos I–II. Byron never completed this Preface, which descends to us in his fragmentary draft manuscript. Nevertheless, what he completed gives us some interesting information about his initial conception of the work. In the course of satirizing Wordsworth Byron tells his readers that 'the following epic Narrative' is to be regarded as the work of a certain 'Story-teller' who is living, and delivering his narrative, at a certain place and time: specifically, 'in a village in the Sierra Morena on the road between Monasterio and Seville' sometime during the Peninsular War (the reference to the village in the Sierra Morena is autobiographical and specifies the date as 1809). As for the narrator himself, 'The Reader is . . . requested to suppose him . . . either an Englishman settled in Spain—or a Spaniard who had travelled in England—perhaps one of the Liberals who have subsequently been so liberally rewarded by Ferdinand of grateful memory—for his restoration.'[8] This passage establishes a second point of view on the events treated in the poem: that is, one subsequent to 1814 and the early years of the period of European restoration following the fall of Napoleon. As it turns out, the reader inevitably places this historical vantage-point at that moment of contemporaneity which attaches to the poem's date of composition and/or publication (in this case, 1818–19).

Byron finally dropped his Preface with its specific historical perspectives, and he did not fully exploit the structural advantages of his poem's double perspectivism until he began to reconceive the project of *Don Juan* in 1822–3. Before considering that act of reconception, however, we should reflect upon the double historical perspective in terms of which the work was initially conceived and set in motion. Like the later cantos, Cantos I–V organize their materials in two dialectically functioning historical frames of

---

7. See *DJV* ii. 3–20 and iv. 4–15. The Preface is placed at the beginning of the text of *Don Juan* in *DJV* as well as its sequel, the Penguin modernized edition. Leslie A. Marchand's school edition also places it at the poem's beginning. Such a placement is seriously misleading, however, for Byron not only left this Preface in an uncompleted state, he discarded it and meant originally to replace it with the verse Dedication. The latter he reluctantly removed from Cantos I–II under pressure from his publisher and friends. The conjecture of *DJV* (see ibid.), that the fragmentary Preface was written after the verse Dedication and then abandoned, is almost certainly not right.
8. *DJV* ii. 4–5.

reference: on the one hand, the frame of the poem's plot or 'story', which contains the narrated events of Juan's life; and, on the other hand, the frame of the poem's narrating voice, which comprises Byron speaking to his world between 1818–24 via the six published volumes of *Don Juan*. Byron's rejected and incomplete Preface to Cantos I–II reminds us that he initially had some idea of using the plot and the narrative to comment on each other, and that he thought of Juan's life in specific historical terms. As it turned out, he rejected the idea of setting the poem's narrative frame in the complicated way suggested by the initial Preface, where it is unclear whether the narrator speaks from the vantage of 1809 or 1818, or both. In Cantos I–V Byron also neglected to specify clearly the historical frame in which Juan's career is placed. When he published Cantos VI–VIII with John Hunt, however, he finally let his contemporary readers see very clearly the exact relation between the history of Juan's career and the history of the poem's narrator, Byron *in propria persona*.

We can date Byron's reconception of his epic with some precision: in January and February 1822, which is the period when Byron resumed his composition of *Don Juan* (he left off his poem when he finished Canto V at the end of 1820). Byron wrote to Murray on 16 Feb. 1821 and outlined a projected plot for Juan's adventures.[9] This outline, however, only corresponds in a loose and general way to the episodes of the poem that he was soon to write, and hence shows that Byron had not yet fixed on a definite plan. Byron first articulated this plan to Medwin between December 1821 and March 1822:

> I left him [Juan] in the seraglio. There I shall make one of the favourites, a Sultana . . . fall in love with him, and carry him off from Constantinople . . . Well, they make good their escape to Russia; where, if Juan's passion cools, and I don't know what to do with the lady, I shall make her die of the plague . . . As our hero can't do without a mistress, he shall next become man-mistress to Catherine the Great . . . I shall . . . send him, when he is *hors de combat*, to England as her ambassador. In his suite he shall have a girl whom he shall have rescued during one of his northern campaigns, who shall be in love with him, and he not with her . . . I shall next draw a town and country life at home . . . He shall get into all sorts of scrapes, and at length end his career in France. Poor Juan shall be guillotined in the French Revolution! What do you think of my plot? It shall have twenty-four books too . . . [1]

This scheme corresponds fairly closely to the poem as we now have it, and it holds to the general plan which Byron gave to Murray at the beginning of 1821 (though not to the particular details of the episodes). The most important episode missing from Byron's outline is the siege of Ismail, though it is clear from this and Byron's immediately preceding discussion that he planned to send Juan into war. But in the first few months of 1822 Byron seems not yet to have decided on the Ismail episode, as he had not yet worked out how to separate Juan and Gulbeyaz. These decisions would be made in the next few months. The idea of having Juan die on the guillotine in the French Revolution was certainly fundamental to the plot of the poem from the earliest stages of its conception as a plotted sequence.

9. *BLJ* viii. 78.
1. *Medwin's Conversations of Lord Byron*, ed. Ernest J. Lovell Jr., Princeton, 1966, pp. 164–5.

The Preface to Cantos VI–VIII, written in September 1822, calls attention, on one hand, to the historical immediacy of the poem as Byron's act of discourse with his world, and, on the other, to the specific (past) historical nexus in which Byron's story of Juan's career is imbedded. The second part of the Preface is a bitter diatribe against Castlereagh, who had recently taken his own life, against the present condition of Europe under the restored thrones and their allied policies, and against those like Southey who were at once supporters of these institutions and detractors of Byron's recent work. The opening sentences of the Preface, however, tell us that the material in Cantos VII and VIII is based upon an actual event: the siege of Ismail by the Russians in Nov.–Dec. 1790. The latter was the chief episode in the (latest) Russo-Turkish War, which had been renewed in 1787. The Preface tells the reader, in other words, that Juan's career in Byron's poem is unfolding within real historical time, and—specifically— that we are to map his career in terms of specific places, dates, and events. When Juan goes to Catherine's court after the siege of Ismail the date is early 1791. Shortly afterwards he goes to England.

Clearly, then, Byron's projected scheme for the plot of Juan's career was actually being implemented when Byron renewed the poem's composition at the beginning of 1822. That he was preparing Juan for a trip to Paris and death on the guillotine in 1793 at the end of the poem is borne out by the fulfilment of the other details which he gave to Medwin, as well as by the chronology of Juan's exploits established in the siege of Ismail episode.[2] We should note that this precise dating of Juan's life in the poem accommodates the events of Cantos I–VI. Before the Preface to Cantos VI–VIII, Byron had not forced his audience to read the events of Cantos I–VI within a specific historical frame of reference. After the Preface, however, those events are drawn into the poem's newly defined historical scheme. Juan's career in Byron's poem begins in Seville just as the French Revolution has broken out, or is about to break out. He is then sixteen years old. His life will end at the end of Byron's poem, and the date for him will be 1793.

Lacking the precise historical frame which Byron established for his poem in 1822, Juan's career would appear episodic, the verse equivalent of the fictional careers of characters in Smollett, Sterne, and Fielding.[3] The exact historical placement changes the situation radically. Juan at first appears to move through Byron's poem in a picaresque fashion, but as the poem develops and his life is brought into ever closer relations with the great and epochal events shaking Europe in the early 1790s, the reader begins to glimpse an order, or perhaps a fate, which was not at first evident or even suspected. Having Juan die in the Reign of Terror at the end of Byron's poem is a daring conception: on the one hand, it seems a surprising, even an arbitrary,

---

2. Some of Byron's marginal jottings in Canto XIV schematize two of the poem's episodes, including the death of Juan. These marginalia appear on a scrap of manuscript (not known to the *DJV* editors) now in the Murray archives. The notations occur on a MS carrying a variant version of lines 479–80.

3. Critics have frequently drawn attention to *Don Juan*'s parallels with eighteenth-century picaresque novels. See Elizabeth Boyd, *Byron's 'Don Juan'*, New Brunswick, NJ, 1945, esp. chaps. 4–7; Andras Horn, *Byron's 'Don Juan' and the 18th Century Novel*, Bern, 1962, and A. B. England, *Byron's 'Don Juan' and Eighteenth Century Literature*, Lewisburg, Pa., 1975, esp. chap. 3. In fact, however, Scott's example in the Waverley novels was perhaps even more important for *Don Juan*. For it was Scott who showed Byron how to incorporate historical events into a fictional narrative in a significant and illuminating way.

end for Byron's inoffensive hero, but on the other it calls attention to a hidden constellation of forces drawing together far-flung and apparently unrelated people and events. History proceeds 'according to the mighty working' of forces which gather up the odd and the disparate, and historical explanation, in Byron, proceeds according to the mighty working of a poem which *reveals* these odd and unapparent connections.

Not least of all does it reveal the connections which hold between the pan-European world of 1787–93 and its counterpart in 1818–24. The revolutionary epoch in which Juan's career begins and ends is explicitly examined from the vantage of the period of Europe's restoration. Juxtaposing these two worlds allows each to comment on the other. More crucially for the poem, however, the juxtaposition gives Byron the opportunity to expose certain congruences between these periods, and to suggest that the second period is a variant repetition of the first. These congruences are established via the third historical frame which gives a structure to *Don Juan*: the period in which the Book of Byron was initally composed, and more especially the central years of that period, 1809–17/18.

The congruences appear most dramatically as a series of related and repeating sequences of gain and loss, rise and fall, triumph and disaster. Juan's career illustrates this pattern both in its particular episodes and in the larger scheme which Byron projected for his hero. Adversative forces of various kinds interrupt and thwart Juan's plans and hopes. Some of these are represented as his responsibility while others originate in external circumstances over which he can have no control. In both cases, the pattern of an early promise which later fails or is betrayed appears in Juan's life as well as in the course of the French Revolution. Juan's life follows the moral arc of the revolution even as his career follows its early chronological development. But what is most important, so far as Byron's poem is concerned, is that both of these sequences recur in the next generation. The second phase of the revolution is dominated by the rise and fall of Napoleon, whose professed aim (at any rate) was to establish the revolution on a secure European footing. The consequence of his career was, on the contrary, the final defeat of the revolution's historic agenda. This repetition, in Napoleon's life, of the historical course of the early years of the revolution appears in Byron's poem through its autobiographical analogue: the meteoric rise and subsequent fall of Lord Byron, a series of events which we—following Byron—associate with the years 1809–17/18. In Byron's and Napoleon's careers the reader of *Don Juan* observes, once again, the pattern established in Juan's life and in the course of the early revolution.

Following his self-exile from England in 1816 Byron meditated on the meaning of this pattern in his life and on its relation to similar patterns in past and contemporary history. The most important of the meditations comes down to us as *Childe Harold's Pilgrimage*, Canto IV, which Byron completed shortly before he began *Don Juan*. Here Byron decides that all history, when judged by meliorist or revolutionary standards, is a story of disaster and unsuccess. What he also decides, however, is that against this fatal and repeating story may be, and has been, placed the deed of the opposing mind and will, the individual voice which, while it recognizes the evil pattern, refuses to accept or assent to it.

Yet, Freedom! yet thy banner, torn, but flying,
   Streams like the thunder-storm *against* the wind;
Thy trumpet voice, though broken now and dying,
   The loudest still the tempest leaves behind . . .
                          (*CHP* iv, stanza 98)

Yet let us ponder boldly—'tis a base
   Abandonment of reason to resign
Our right of thought—our last and only place
   Of refuge . . .
                          (*CHP* iv, stanza 127)

These attitudes establish the ground on which *Don Juan* comes to judge the patterns of historical repetition. Byron begins the poem from the vantage of 1818, a point in European history when time appears to have rolled back upon itself. Thirty years have passed, yet the enormous upheavals which marked those years seem to have returned the European world virtually to the same political position that it occupied in 1788. Furthermore, Byron observes in this period a series of repetitions which suggest that the cycle of revolutionary disappointment is a general pattern which is found in many historical periods and which is replicated for the individual as well as for society. In terms of the narrator's historical frame (1818–24), *Don Juan* is yet another revolutionary undertaking begun in a period of darkness. As such, the bleak patterns of repetition over which the Byron of 1818–24 will brood—the pattern of Juan's career and the early phase of the revolution, the pattern of Byron's career and the Napoleonic wars— threaten the narrative project of 1818–24 with a fearful end.

III

The early cantos of *Don Juan* represent this threat most dramatically, perhaps, in connection with the 'Isles of Greece' lyric in Canto III. Within the Juan/Haidée/Lambro cantos this passage focuses the most self-conscious episode from an historical and political standpoint. The passage involves a complex act of poetic ventriloquism through which Byron is able to develop, simultaneously, a polemical analysis of recent European history and a self-conscious critique of his own character and professed social ideals. To understand how this is managed we will have to recall briefly Byron's famous ideas about poetic 'mobility'.

The discussion of this concept comes up in Canto XVI when Byron is describing Lady Adeline Amundeville. Her mobility, Byron says, is a characteristic of a certain type of person, and in particular of artists.

This makes your actors, artists, and romancers,
   Heroes sometimes, though seldom—sages never;
But speakers, bards, diplomatists, and dancers,
   Little that's great, but much of what is clever;
Most orators, but very few financiers . . .
                          (stanza 98, lines 1–5)

In other words, people whose work or life demands that they treat with others in a broadly public or spectacular field.

In a note to this passage Byron defines mobility as follows: 'an excessive susceptibility of immediate impressions—at the same time without *losing* the past; and is, though sometimes apparently useful to the possessor, a most painful and unhappy attribute.' Lady Adeline Amundeville shows that she possesses this equivocal virtue when she is observed dealing with her guests at Norman Abbey.

95

But Adeline was occupied by fame
   This day; and watching, witching, condescending
To the consumers of fish, fowl and game,
   And dignity with courtesy so blending,
As all must blend whose part it is to aim
   (Especially as the sixth year is ending)
At their lord's son's, or similar connection's
Safe conduct through the rocks of re-elections.

96

Though this was most expedient on the whole,
   And usual—Juan, when he cast a glance
On Adeline while playing her grand role,
   Which she went through as though it were a dance,
(Betraying only now and then her soul
   By a look scarce perceptibly askance
Of weariness or scorn) began to feel
Some doubt how much of Adeline was *real*;

97

So well she acted, all and every part
   By turns—with that vivacious versatility,
Which many people take for want of heart.
   They err—'tis merely what is called mobility,
A thing of temperament and not of art,
   Though seeming so, from its supposed facility;
And false—though true; for surely they're sincerest,
Who are strongly acted on by what is nearest.

These lines deserve some attention. If mobility is 'an excessive susceptibility to immediate impressions', the passage also suggests that it is not *simply* a psychological attribute. Lady Adeline is at home in this social world; indeed, her entire life in the poem shows that she is governed by a *social* 'susceptibility' to this kind of structure. She has at once a taste and a gift for managing social affairs of these kinds with brilliance. In the end, however, the passage shows that the psychological attribute and the social formation call out to each other, that they are, indeed, symbiotic and interdependent.

When Byron says that such mobility is 'a most painful and unhappy attribute' we will understand what he means when we meditate on Lady Adeline's barely perceptible 'look . . . Of weariness or scorn'. Juan glimpses an important aspect of her character and its social determinants when he

observes her 'now and then'—in the very midst of her social brilliance—
'Betraying . . . her soul' in those looks of scorn and weariness. 'Playing her
grand role' involves, within a Romantic Ideology, a reciprocal danger: lack
of authenticity. Thus Lady Adeline 'betrays' her soul in at least two senses
when she inadvertently reveals her mobility to Juan and ourselves.

What is crucial to see in all this is that mobility involves a structure of
social relations and not simply a psychological characteristic. Byron *inter-
prets* mobility in psychological terms, but his verse exposes this interpreta-
tion as a special (ultimately, a Romantic) view of what is clearly a much
more complex state of affairs. Scarcely less important is an interesting par-
adox which Byron calls attention to. Mobility appears as a set of social
graces, a capacity to charm and to be all things to all men. But it arises,
apparently, from a ground of 'sincerity' in those kinds of people 'Who are
strongly acted on by what is nearest'. Yet it *appears* the very height of insin-
cerity and calculation. Which is it: 'a thing of' one's spontaneous 'tem-
perament', or of one's role-playing and 'art'? Is it 'false' or is it 'true'?

This set of paradoxes and contradictions gets registered for us in Lady
Adeline's looks of weariness and scorn, and in Byron's remark that mobility
is painful and a source of unhappiness. Lady Adeline's 'soul' is rent by these
paradoxes which her situation reflects but which her consciousness does not
appear to understand (or even try to understand). When Byron reflects upon
her situation he gains a clearer knowledge of the contradictions, but he too
remains incapable of producing anything more than a demonstrative and
aesthetic explanation (which is itself supplemented by the psychological
explanation of his note). Reading Byron's verse we *see* it all much more
clearly than Lady Adeline does, for we are provided with a much more com-
prehensive vantage of the field of relations being played out.

The connection of social mobility to the Romantic artist's ideal of spon-
taneity and sincerity has often been noted by scholars, most trenchantly,
perhaps, by George Ridenour.[4] Thus we now commonly equate the 'conver-
sational facility' (xv, stanza 20) of *Don Juan*, or the 'strain of passionate
improvisation' in Byron's High Romantic mode,[5] with the mobility of Lady
Adeline and the 'actors, artists, and romancers' who are her equivalents.
What is less often noted is the negative dimension which Byron sees in the
artist of mobility. It is mildly shocking, but quite necessary, to understand that
the dark shadow cast by the mobility of the spontaneous Romantic poet is
called (in *Don Juan*) Robert Southey, and sometimes William Wordsworth.
Byron calls Southey an 'Epic Renegade' at the very outset of the poem
('Dedication', stanza 1) and he links the recent laureate with Wordsworth as
instances of poets who apostasized their early republican principles in their
later years. Southey's 'conversion' ('Dedication', stanza 6) 'has lately been a
common case' ('Dedication', stanza 1), Byron says, but if such 'Apostasy's . . .
fashionable' now ('Dedication', stanza 17), it was not always so. Milton rises
up in Byron's 'Dedication' as one who 'deigned not to belie his soul in songs'
('Dedication', stanza 10) which swerved from his initial ground and princi-
ples. Byron, of course, justifies himself with such an ideal of poetic and
ideological behaviour: 'And, if in flattering strains I do not predicate, / 'Tis
that I still retain my "buff and blue"' ('Dedication', stanza 17).

---

4. George Ridenour, *The Style of Don Juan*, New Haven, 1960.
5. H. J. C. Grierson, 'Lord Byron: Arnold and Swinburne', *Wharton Lecture on English Poetry* no. 11
(1920), p. 11.

In Byron's 'Vision of Judgment' Southey's political apostasy is elaborated into a general 'literary character', a Grub Street avatar formed in the image of his own time.

96

He said—(I only give the heads)—he said,
   He meant no harm in scribbling; 'twas his way
Upon all topics; 'twas, besides, his bread,
   Of which he buttered both sides; 'twould delay
Too long the assembly (he was pleased to dread),
   And take up rather more time than a day,
To name his works—he would but cite a few—
'Wat Tyler'—'Rhymes on Blenheim'—'Waterloo.'

97

He had written praises of a Regicide;
   He had written praises of all kings whatever;
He had written for republics far and wide,
   And then against them bitterer than ever;
For pantisocracy he once had cried
   Aloud, a scheme less moral than 'twas clever;
Then grew a heavy anti-jacobin—
Had turned his coat—and would have turned his skin.

98

He had sung against all battles, and again
   In their high praise and glory; he had called
Reviewing 'the ungentle craft,' and then
   Became as base a critic as e'er crawled—
Fed, paid, and pampered by the very men
   By whom his muse and morals had been mauled;
He had written much blank verse, and blanker prose,
And more of both than any body knows.

99

He had written Wesley's life:—here turning round
   To Satan, 'Sir, I'm ready to write yours,
In two octavo volumes, nicely bound,
   With notes and preface, all that most allures
The pious purchaser; and there's no ground
   For fear, for I can choose my own reviewers:
So let me have the proper documents,
That I may add you to my other saints.'

Like Lady Adeline when she is 'occupied by fame' (xvi, stanza 95), Southey too is ever 'watching, witching, condescending' with those who might advance his literary career and projects. He will write on any topic, from any point of view, in any style or medium. He is, besides, keenly aware of all that is most current, and anxious to be borne along by that current. Finally, he understands how the institutions of literary production operate in his day. In his own summing up, Southey's is 'a pen of all work' (stanza 100) and he is a poet of skill and industry, without malice (or conscience), good-natured (and culpably unscrupulous). He has all of Lady Adeline's (and by extension Byron's) gifts, and would be an exact literary reflection but for one thing: his looks never betray that telltale glance 'Of weariness or scorn'. His mobility is complete but, in the end, unByronic, for Southey does not feel it as a 'most painful and unhappy attribute'.[6]

IV

Byron's most profound presentation of his idea of Romantic mobility comes, as we might expect, when he draws himself and his own practice into the analysis. 'Changeable too—yet somehow *"idem semper"*' (xvii, stanza 11): thus Byron sought to describe both himself and his poem in his last, fragmentary canto. The characterization intersects with the entire constellation of ideas related to the concept of mobility, and thereby also gestures toward the similarities and differences which link Byron to his dark double Robert Southey. In Canto III these similarities and differences are fully elaborated in the figure of the poet who comes to sing at Juan and Haidée's lavish banquet and festival.

Byron's introductory stanzas (78–86) describe the character of this poet as 'a sad trimmer' (stanza 82). This passage distinctly recalls what Byron had said earlier about Southey in the (abandoned) 'Preface' to *Don Juan* and the (reluctantly cancelled) 'Dedication'. There the tone is much more savage, however, resembling in this respect the satiric passage cited earlier from 'Vision of Judgment'. All the (by now) familiar charges are brought forward—for example, in stanzas 80 and 85.

80

He was a man who had seen many changes,
    And always changed as true as any needle,
His polar star being one which rather ranges,
    And not the fix'd—he knew the way to wheedle:
So vile he 'scaped the doom which oft avenges;
    And being fluent (save indeed when fee'd ill),
He lied with such a fervour of intention—
There was no doubt he earn'd his laureate pension.

85

Thus, usually, when he was ask'd to sing,
    He gave the different nations something national;
'Twas all the same to him—'God save the king,'
    Or 'Ca ira', according to the fashion all;
His muse made increment of any thing,

6. I suppose it does not need to be remarked that this representation of the laureate is a travesty of his actual character. In fact, the worst truth one might say of Southey would be the opposite—that he was self-righteous and absolutist (Byron of course accused him of these vices as well). For a good assessment of his character see Geoffrey Carnall, *Southey and His Age*, Oxford, 1960.

> From the high lyric down to the low rational:
> If Pindar sang horse-races, what should hinder
> Himself from being as pliable as Pindar?

These stanzas epitomize Byron's usual critique of the poet as renegade and unscrupulous time-server, and they sum up the general tone of Byron's presentation in the passage as a whole. But two other stanzas in the sequence disturb the proprieties which customarily govern Byron's satire in these situations. In stanza 84 Byron tells us that this poet

> had travell'd 'mongst the Arabs, Turks, and Franks,
> And knew the self-loves of the different nations;
> And having lived with people of all ranks,
>   Had something ready upon most occasions—
> Which got him a few presents and some thanks.
> He varied with some skill his adulations;
> To 'do at Rome as Romans do,' a piece
> Of conduct was which he observed in Greece.

These lines recall nothing so much as Byron himself: first, as the Levantine cruiser of 1809–11, and second, as the poet and social lion of 1812–14. Byron had fun at Southey's laureate expense, and while he sometimes protested that he never courted his immense popularity or flattered his adulators, he knew that he had in fact 'filed [his] mind' (*Childe Harold* iii, stanza 113) during his Years of Fame. For Byron himself, those years were far from innocent of the 'adulations' for which he denounced Southey. Of himself he could say, with far more certainty than he could of Southey, that he had written verse to foster his image and advance his career. Like Lady Adeline, however, such work was produced side by side with those self-revelatory looks (or poems) 'Of weariness or scorn' which reflected critically on the 'adulations'. Indeed, the 'adulations' themselves frequently displayed their own internal self-contradictions.

In the 'sad trimmer' poet, then, we glimpse the face of Robert Southey, and this is no great surprise; but in the allusion to Southey the outlines of another, unexpected face are also glimpsed. This palimpsest produces an unstable and apparently self-contradicted text whose true biographical subject—Byron himself—emerges from beneath the layers of his own normal satiric displacements.

83

> But now being lifted into high society,
>   And having picked up several odds and ends
> Of free thoughts in his travels, for variety,
>   He deem'd, being in a lone isle, among friends,
> That without any danger of a riot, he
>   Might for long lying make himself amends;
> And singing as he sung in his warm youth,
> Agree to a short armistice with truth.

This could be, and is in part, an oblique thrust at Southey's renegado turn from his youthful republicanism to his later apostasy. It is also, however, an even more oblique glimpse of Byron's political and poetical career up to

1816, which was marked by its own definite, if much less apparent, forms of ideological backsliding and dishonesty. Byron was much more 'cunning in [his] own overthrow' than Southey was, but that he had pursued 'False Ambition' and betrayed his soul's 'nobler aim' he could not, and would not, deny (see 'Epistle to Augusta' lines 97, 102). And so 'for long lying' he aimed, in this passage, to 'make himself amends' in the form of an imitation revolutionary Greek ballad, the famous 'Isles of Greece'.[7]

The poem is at once an admonishment, or call, and a fulfilment of his highest poetical ideals. And the fulfilment lies precisely in this: that when he *now* sings 'as he sung in his warm youth' he reveals, self-consciously and deliberately, both his utopian goals (to which he rededicates himself) as well as his understanding that he has been the worst betrayer of those goals. He is the worst because he appeared, to himself and to others, as one of their staunchest supporters.

The ballad's subtle mastery emerges when this network of allusions, intertexts, and subtexts is fully comprehended. In general, Byron's fiction is that the ballad is sung by a Romaic poet in the late 1780s to an audience of his fellows who live quiescently under Turkish rule. It calls them from their lives of pleasure and political degeneracy to take up a more strenuous and principled course of action. At this level, it is a poem determined to raise the Greek national consciousness. Consequently, though its fictive date is the late 1780s, and though it recalls the Greek patriotic songs of the late eighteenth century (like Rhiga's War Song), its 1820 context is equally operative. In fact, the Greek war for independence was to commence in 1821, and Byron's early attachment to that cause would draw him in 1823 from Italy to western Greece and his famous death in 1824.

Don Juan's fictive level—that is, the plot of Juan's career in the poem's imagined time-scheme stretching from about 1787 to its (unreached) conclusion in 1793—is always calling attention to its narrative (or 'real') level: that is, to the poem as a continuing historical event which unfolds before its European audience between 1818 and 1824, and which makes that context part of its subject. This interplay between a fictive and a narrative time-scheme throws into relief a dominant fact about *Don Juan*: that it is fundamentally an autobiographical poem which comments upon and interprets the course of European history between 1787 and 1824. In the case of 'The Isles of Greece', Byron's fictional Greek poet masks only to reveal more clearly the poem's true author. As always in *Don Juan*, Byron reveals and thereby manipulates his poetical machinery in a self-conscious drama of his own mind. We therefore observe this ballad as a vehicle for satirizing Southey and all other republican turncoats, for satirizing generally those who have betrayed the cause of the European political ideal of liberty which had its origin in ancient Greece and which appeared once again in various revolutionary movements during the late eighteenth and early nineteenth centuries (paradigmatically in America and France). So, when we read 'The Isles of Greece' we are also to *see* Lord Byron satirizing Robert Southey in 1820.

At the poem's most complex level, we also *see through* Lord Byron's satire of Southey into the innermost drama of his own mind. Consider the ballad's fifth stanza.

---

7. For an excellent discussion of the poem's Greek context, both classical and modern, see Kiriakoula Solomou, *Byron and Greek Poetry*, PhD Thesis, U. of Aberdeen, 1980, pp. 294–9.

> And where are they? and where art thou,
>   My country? On thy voiceless shore
> The heroic lay is tuneless now—
>   The heroic bosom beats no more!
> And must thy lyre, so long divine,
> Degenerate into hands like mine?

An act of poetic ventriloquism multiplies the pronominal references in these lines. The Romaic poet sings here of himself and of Greece, but the English poet sings of England and Lord Byron. The ideal of Greece calls out to Byron's, and England's, identification with the ideal, just as the degeneracy of present-day Greece (whether conceived in the context of 1787 or 1820) reflects upon England's, and Byron's, betrayals of their most cherished, and Greek-derived, ideals.

Two fictive voices sing 'The Isles of Greece'—the imaginary Romaic poet of 1787 and the imaginative Robert Southey of 1820; and they sing of the ideals and betrayals of themselves and their respective countries. In the end, however, the two voices are incorporated as the poetically 'actual' voice of Lord Byron, who sings of his own immediate psychic and political situation and the context in which it had developed.

> 'Tis something, in the dearth of fame,
>   Though link'd among a fetter'd race,
> To feel at least a patriot's shame,
>   Even as I sing, suffuse my face;
> For what is left the poet here!
> For Greeks a blush, for Greece a tear.

A passage like this dramatically reveals the complex voicing techniques of the ballad, along with the related and equally complex network of references and levels of statement. In these lines the 'Fame' is Greece's, England's, and Byron's; the 'fettered race' is Greek, but also Italian (Byron is writing his poem in the Italian dominions of the Austrian Empire), and—even more generally—European ('There is *no* freedom—even for *Masters*—in the midst of slaves'). Thus, when Byron gestures to 'the poet here', his words resonate in the widest European context of 1787–1824.

The ballad plays itself out as a contest between the rival claims of 'The Scian and the Teian muse, / The hero's harp, the lover's lute.' Representing a poetical career and its goals as a dialectic between the shifting claims of heroic and amatory verse—here, specifically, between Homer and Anacreon—is a pre-eminently Byronic structure of thought.[8] His entire life's work as a poet develops as a self-lacerating experience of their rival claims. Whenever Byron moves too definitively toward one of these poetical and political ideals he will call upon the other to limit, criticize, and judge its illusions and appeals. Byron's great lyric 'On This Day I Complete My Thirty-Sixth Year' culminates this conflict by representing it as (by itself) a hopeless one. 'On This Day' calls for its cessation by invoking the option of suicide.

This is also the option toward which 'The Isles of Greece' makes its final gesture.

---

8. We should recall Byron's many early translations of Anacreontic verse.

> Place me on Sunium's marbled steep,
>   Where nothing, save the waves and I,
> May hear our mutual murmurs sweep;
>   There, swan-like, let me sing and die:
> A land of slaves shall ne'er be mine—
> Dash down yon cup of Samian wine.
>
> (stanza 16)

As in the later lyric, when the poet here chooses death to break the impasse of his life, his choice involves a decision for the claims of heroism. What is important to see is that this is an historical choice, one demanded by time, place, and circumstance. The voice of the Scian muse plays through 'The Isles of Greece' to remind us of the essential virtues of a truly civilized life, which would not include war and violence. But no such life is possible when the social structure is degenerate at its ground.

> Fill high the bowl with Samian wine!
>   Our virgins dance beneath the shade—
> I see their glorious black eyes shine;
>   But gazing on each glowing maid,
> My own the burning tear-drop laves,
> To think such breasts must suckle slaves.
>
> (stanza 15)

In such times the image of love itself becomes an occasion for swerving toward heroic values. Nevertheless, we have to see that the move toward the heroic is now regarded as deeply equivocal, a fate or doom embraced by those who are willing to sacrifice themselves by choosing an heroic life in order to secure, at some future date, the restoration of a civilized order.

Thus the ideological structures of 'On This Day' and 'The Isles of Greece' are all but exact equivalents. However, 'On This Day' is a much more interiorized poem, and that difference is crucial. The fact that Byron's voice in 'The Isles of Greece' is explicitly mixed with the voices of Southey and the modern Greek patriot, and implicitly with the entire Anacreontic and Homeric traditions, socializes the lyric in a number of important and specific ways. The history imbedded in 'On This Day' is Byron's personal history and the drama is fundamentally psychic. In 'The Isles of Greece', on the other hand, the complex voicing extends the world of which and for which the poem is speaking. 'On This Day' is set in 1824, in Greece, and in Byron's mind—finally, in the relations which the poem establishes between these three *loci* and all that each implicitly involves. The layered voices in 'The Isles of Greece' dramatically enlarge the poem's network of references, forcing the reader to consider the complex *relations* of those references. In the end—like *Don Juan* itself—the lyric implies that European history between 1787 and 1820 is all of a piece, and that the condition of Greece during the period is the very symbol of the condition of Europe. At the end of the eighteenth century Greece looked for freedom from Turkish rule as Europe looked for a revolutionary emancipation from inherited and archaic political orders; in 1820, despite the intervening years of turmoil and promise, the *status quo* has been (at least formally and materially) preserved. Even more telling, however, is the poem's revelation of all of Europe's—including England's—complicity in this state of affairs. In 1809–11 Byron began to fear the truth of such complicity and he expressed his fears in *Childe Harold's Pilgrimage* I–II.[9] In 1820 his fears have been fully realized. 'The Isles of Greece' exposes, analyses, and judges this complicity. The English Lord speaks as and for the failed Greek patriot and the turncoat jacobin Southey. In *Don Juan's* 'Dedication' and elsewhere Byron will separate himself from Southey, Castlereagh, Metternich, and the forgers of Europe's spiritual slavery. Here, by contrast, he speaks with their voices and says, of himself and for all those who have judged themselves innocent: '*Hypocrite lecteur, mon semblable, mon frère.*'

In 'The Isles of Greece' Byron's voice does, however, gain a certain frail integrity through its aspiration toward the whole truth, toward complete freedom from cant. The ballad reveals and denounces the canting life of its age by constructing a poem which gives lip-service to the traditional western ideas of love and honour. Its honesty appears as a double understanding: first, that these ideals, in their inherited forms at any rate, are conflicted and self-contradictory; and second, that lip-service, in Byron's age, is the most which history could expect. Byron everywhere speaks of the degeneracy of his period, a condition he deplored in the cant political, poetical, and moral which was being delivered by contemporary ideologues like Southey. These are the voices who speak with authority of what is right and wrong, good and evil, angelic and satanic. Byron's voice, by contrast, undercuts and ironizes every voice which pretends to assume this kind of authority. The shock and even the genius of this procedure lies in the poetry's final level of irony, where Byron deliberately assumes the *rhetoric* of a total and dependable authority. Byron's high style—which appears once again in this famous ballad—projects the ideal of the poet and hero *manqué*, the figure who alone (in both senses) can speak in an unbetrayed voice of his age's persistent betrayals:

> Thus sung, or would, or could, or should have sung,
>   The modern Greek, in tolerable verse;
> If not like Orpheus quite, when Greece was young,
>   Yet in these times he might have done much worse:
> His strain display'd some feeling—right or wrong;
>   And feeling, in a poet, is the source
> Of others' feeling; but they are such liars,
> And take all colours—like the hands of dyers.
>
> (III, stanza 87)

Thus Byron sums up the significance of the ballad he has just presented. The statement displays the ironic equivocalness engineered in 'these times', but it equally and forthrightly says that a poet 'might have done much worse' than this. The remark recalls Southey's laureate performances as well as Byron's earlier work in which the truth he is fundamentally committed to had been subtly, cunningly betrayed. Like the several stanzas which follow, this one concludes in that typical Byronic gesture of resolute

9. The whole of this book comprises a commentary on Greece and Europe's relation to Greece's political condition under Turkish rule. Byron was deeply critical of the hypocrisy of English, French, and Russian philhellenism, as we see most clearly in that book's notes and appendices. Most telling of all—and almost never remarked upon—is Byron's reference to, and partial translation of, the Romaic satire on Greece, England, Russia, and France: the so-called 'Rossanglogallos'. See Solomou's discussion, pp. 186–90, 218–21, 310–318; and see also *CPW* ii. 213–15.

irresolution: an equivocal affirmation of the power of poetry, on the one hand, and an equally equivocal pronouncement upon its unreliability.

The Shakespeare echo at the end of the stanza recalls Byron's views on poetic mobility. The cynical tone in which the echo is made, however—so unlike the original passage—reminds us, in this case, that Byron's ventriloquism, or mobility, is everywhere marked by the 'weariness or scorn' which Juan glimpsed in Adeline's accommodating looks. Paradoxically, Byron's cynicism is a liberating rather than a defeatist move because Byron is aware that the past—its deeds, its voices, its ideas—cannot be appropriated to the present through simple gestures of mobility or chameleonic acts. Byron turns a mordant eye on the inheritance of greatness (especially poetic greatness) because he knows that its ideal apparitions conceal human, equivocal truths. Indeed, when those equivocal human forms do not appear, the ideals enter the world as monsters.

In the ballad, the temptation to accept an idealized view of the voices and deeds of the past appears most clearly in the call to heroic action—for example, in stanza eight:

> What, silent still? and silent all?
>   Ah! no;—the voices of the dead
> Sound like a distant torrent's fall,
>   And answer, 'Let one living head,
> But one arise,—we come, we come!'
> 'Tis but the living who are dumb.

But the fact is that these martial voices from the dead may (and have) issued calls to freedom *and* to tyranny. The 'Turkish hordes' of stanza nine have answered that call as surely as did the three hundred who fell at Thermopylae. If 'the living . . . are dumb' now to that call, their silence may be the honesty of Keats's aesthetic escapism, or the critical judgement of the sybarite Sardanapalus. Besides, Byron has seen the call answered too often and too well by the poets and ideologues of European imperialism: by a Southey in his Waterloo hymns, and by a Wordsworth who could proclaim that the carnage of battle is the daughter of God.

So in the ballad the voice of the Scian muse repeatedly undercuts the voice of the Teian—but not definitively. Anacreon's role, in this respect, is to introduce the note of 'weariness or scorn' into the poem's act of heroic ventriloquism. In this way Byron tries to insure that he will raise up from the past a human rather than a demonic figure; and in this way he also manages to compose, in 1820, a song on behalf of human freedom which escapes incorporation by the Age of Cant. The crowning wit of the poem is that the song is offered to the reader as a familiar Byronic *tour de force* in which his identity is submerged in a network of competing voices. Byron appears, in the end, as the self-conscious creator and observer of his own verse: the man who finds his identity and freedom when he acknowledges the constellation of his own social determinants, the man who discovers his voice in a conscious and dialectical act of poetic ventriloquism.

V

The episode which incorporates the 'Isles of Greece' displays the continuities which hold between Byron's past life and career and his present concerns as they are revealed and activated in *Don Juan*. The episode also shows the place which his life and career occupy within the larger social and political framework of European affairs between 1788 and 1820. Finally, the mordant critical view which he takes toward himself and this period of European history involves an important set of revolutionary ideological judgements which comprise an integrated and comprehensive interpretation of his age.

Byron begins *Don Juan* already knowing that individual and social history, from a revolutionary point of view, always follows a curve of disappointment or disaster. In this sense (but only in this sense) is the poem 'nihilistic'. In every other respect the poem is a great work of hope, for it insists that projects of change and renewal must continue to be raised up despite the fact of absolute adversity. The Byron who set *Don Juan* in motion understands that the eye begins to see only in a dark time, and— more crucially—that there never is a time which is or was not dark. Those who seek not merely to understand the world, but to change it, strive toward an ideal of human life which will have to be 'anywhere out of the world'. This is the strife of *Don Juan*'s hope, the deed of its mind—the fact of its books. The poem begins its quest for renewal under its own prophecy of failure, and it seeks to persuade its readers that one begins in this way simply because there is no other place *to* begin, that the renewal arrives with the event, not in the end. For in the end you lose, always.

Thus Byron begins his poem in 1818 by calling for a new hero to take the place of all the failed heroes of the past, and in particular of all the failed heroes of the preceding revolutionary epoch. Byron catalogues their names in Canto I only to toss them aside in favour of 'our friend, Don Juan', whose history he purposes to tell. As we have seen, however, and as every reader of the poem has always recognized, that fictive history recollects and alludes, at every point, to the actual history of Lord Byron, who is the poem's true 'hero' and central figure. Juan's progress from Seville to the Levant, and thence via Russia to England and (prospectively) to Paris and his death, is shadowed by the actual career of Byron. In fact, Juan's career is no more than a displaced re-presentation of Byron's, a coded fiction through which the reader may glimpse the friends, enemies, and the incidents of Byron's life, as well as the patterns and epochs of that life. The English Cantos, at the level of the poem's plot, should be located in the summer and early autumn of 1791; at the level of the poem's recollective autobiographical structure, as everyone knows, these cantos reflect Byron's life in England during his Years of Fame.

When Byron reinitiated his *Don Juan* project at the beginning of 1822, therefore, he did so with two objects clearly in his mind. The first of these involved structural matters: specifying a precise chronology for Juan's life in the poem. This move entailed, as a consequence, a dramatic refocusing of the poem's materials. Because of the move readers would be better able to see the tripartite organization of the poem's historical vision. *Don Juan* examines the period 1789–1824 in terms of its three dominant phases: the early years of the French Revolution (the poem's displaced fiction); the epoch of the Napoleonic Wars (viewed through Byron's analogous and contemporary experience of those years); and the epoch of the European restoration (dramatically fashioned and presented at the poem's immediate narrative level).

Byron's second object, which is related to the first, aimed at reasserting in an unmistakeable way the socio-political character of his work. When he began *Don Juan* he spoke of it as 'bitter in politics',[1] but as he struggled to get Murray to publish his cantos he was gradually led to de-emphasize both the bitterness and the politics. The de-emphasis appeared in the published work itself—the removal of the 'Dedication', the decision not to print the Wellington stanzas in Canto III, and so forth—as well as in Byron's letters back to England in which he raised his defence of the poem against his publisher's and his friends' objections.[2] During 1819–21 these letters take a conciliating and mollifying line. Byron tried to get his poem accepted by assuring his friends that it was actually a harmless thing, an elaborate *jeu d'esprit* conceived more in a comic than a satiric mode, 'to giggle and make giggle'.[3] In 1822 the structural changes are accompanied by an uncompromising and candid political stance. In his resumed poem, he told Moore in July, 1822, he meant to 'throw away the scabbard' and make open ideological war with the new reactionary spirit of the age. By December he was equally clear on the subject in a letter to Murray: *Don Juan* 'is intended [as] a *satire* on *abuses* of the present *states* of Society'.[4] Cantos VI–VIII, issued by the liberal Hunt rather than the conservative Murray, are prefaced with Byron's prose declaration of mental war, and the next volume—Cantos IX–XI—begins with the diatribe against war and Wellington which Byron, in 1819, had withdrawn from Canto III.

Byron's purposes with his poem, then, are accompanied by important changes in his aesthetic and political consciousness. Not the least of these was his new and clearer understanding of the *wholeness* of the period 1789–1824, of the intimate relations which held between the three major phases of this period, and of the connections between people and events which might appear, at first, to have little do do with each other. No episode in the poem reveals more clearly Byron's increased understanding of these historical repetitions and relations than the Siege of Ismail, the episode in which Byron initially focused the historical and political restructuring of his epic.

The siege is, at least in part, what it appears to be: a satire on war and its violence. Byron was not a pacifist, however. He supported patriotic struggles and wars of liberation, and he eventually went to serve in the Greek effort to break free of the Turkish Empire. We have to specify, therefore, the ground of Byron's satire. This ground begins to emerge when we reflect upon Byron's chief source for his details. He used the account in Marquis Gabriel de Castelnau's *Essai sur l'Histoire ancienne et moderne de la nouvelle Russie* (3 vols., Paris, 1800).[5] The ideology of this book is reactionary and monarchist, and its narrative of the siege is largely based on the first-hand details supplied to Castelnau from the diary of Armand Emmanuel du Plessis, Duc de Richelieu (1767–1822). Byron mentions Castelnau's *Essai* in the Preface to Cantos VI–VIII, where he also speaks of the Duc de Richelieu as 'a young volunteer in the Russian service, and afterwards the founder and benefactor of Odessa'.[6] The irony and satire implicit in these

1. *BLJ* vi. 76–7.
2. See *DJV* i. 13–24; Samuel C. Chew, *Byron in England,* London, 1924, chap. 4; and J. J. McGann, *Don Juan in Context,* Chicago, 1976, pp. 51–67.
3. See *BLJ* vi. 208; see also vi. 67.
4. *BLJ* ix. 191 and x. 68.
5. See Boyd, pp. 148–50 and Nina Diakonova. 'The Russian Episode in Byron's "Don Juan"' *The Ariel* iii (1972), pp. 51–7.
6. *DJV* iii. 3.

remarks arises from Byron's negative approach to Castelnau's glorifying account of the siege, as well as from his ironic sense of the young Richelieu's benefactions.

Reading Castelnau Byron saw that many of the officers in Catherine's army at the siege of Ismail were 'distinguished strangers' (Canto VII, line 254), a wickedly oblique phrase calling attention to the fact that these men, like the young Duc de Richelieu, were *émigrés* from France and the revolution. Richelieu and the other distinguished strangers are not patriots fighting for their country, they are military adventurers. That Byron intended this line of attack on the French *émigrés* at Ismail is perfectly plain from the letter to Moore in which he said that his new cantos (the siege cantos, that is) constitute an attack upon 'those butchers in large business, your mercenary soldiery'.[7] Lying behind the satire of this battle and the entire Russian episode in the poem is the idea, commonly found in liberal thought of the period, that monarchists like Richelieu have no other business in life except to fight in wars (any wars will do) and intrigue at court. The fact that Juan's rescue of Leila is based upon an actual incident in Richelieu's life only underscores Byron's mordant comments on the indiscriminate militarism of aristocratic ideology:

> If here and there some transient trait of pity
>   Was shown, and some more noble heart broke through
> Its bloody bond, and saved perhaps some pretty
>   Child, or an aged, helpless man or two—
> What's this in one annihilated city . . . ?
>
> (VIII, stanza 124)

These lines, and the larger passage from which they are drawn, cut back against Castelnau's account of the war, on one hand, and the supposed 'noble heart' of the young duke. The man celebrated by reactionaries like Castelnau as 'the founder and benefactor of Odessa' is as well one of those who destroyed a city in which he had no personal or political interest whatsoever, who fled his own country at a moment of crisis, and who later—after the fall of Napoleon—returned to France to become minister for foreign affairs in the restored monarchy.[8]

Richelieu merely epitomizes what Byron wishes to attack in his narrative of the siege and in the Russian cantos generally: the character of monarchist régimes. He is even more important in Byron's poem, however, as a focus for the political filiations which connect, on one hand, such apparently separated events as the siege of Ismail and the events in France in 1789–90, and, on the other, the strange twists and eventualities of European history between 1789 and 1818. Richelieu and the other distinguished strangers do not find their way into Catherine's army merely by chance, nor is it chance that brings him back, at the Bourbon restoration, to serve as an important functionary in the reactionary alliance. Neither is it chance which leads Byron in 1822 to expose this pattern of relations through his narrative of the siege. Byron had been well aware, at least since 1809, of the imperialist stake which various European powers had in

---

7. *BLJ* ix. 191.
8. Byron's critique of the contemporary world of the restoration operates as well in his treatment of 'Suwarrow' in the Russian cantos. For a good discussion see Philip W. Martin, *Byron. A Poet. Before His Public*, Cambridge, 1982, pp. 213–17.

Balkan and Levantine affairs. The narrative of the siege of Ismail forces the reader to recall to mind that network of political and economic interests, as well as to see that the power and self-interests of the monarchies has not been broken by the revolutionary and Napoleonic years. When Byron looks at the siege from the vantage of the restoration, then, he integrates it into the pattern of pan-European affairs of 1789–93 (that is to say, the event is integrated into the order and fate of Juan's fictional-historical career), and he also uses it to comment upon current European conditions. In effect, Byron's employment of his sources involves him in a massive critical-revolutionary reinterpretation of the history of Europe from the outbreak of the French Revolution to the early years of the restoration.

VI

Thus, in 1822 Byron transforms *Don Juan* into a book of the European world, a comprehensive survey and explanation of the principal phases of the epoch 1789–1824. The period is dominated by repetitions, by the violence which has accompanied them, and by the ignorance and indifferences which have abetted these repetitions and their violences. Against these things Byron sets the project of *Don Juan*, which is itself finally recognized to be involved in, to be a part of, the epoch and its repetitions. *Don Juan* becomes a book of the European world by becoming, finally, the Book of Byron, an integrated meditation and commentary upon his own life as it is and was and continues to be a revelation of the meaning of his age.

Don Juan is the Book of Byron because he is its hero, because the poem gives the reader a history of 1789–1824 which is set and framed, at all points, in terms of Byron's history. Juan's fictional movements retraverse actual places and scenes which Byron once passed through, and their details recollect persons and events in his past. In addition, the digressive narration often ruminates Byron's career to comment on and finally to judge it. In short, the poem repeatedly gives the reader views of Byron's past life in the coded sequence of its fictional level as well as in the memorial sequence of its narrative level. All this is widely recognized, as is the related fact that the history of an entire epoch is to be glimpsed in the reflective details of the poem.

Less apparent is the significance of the narrative as it is an *immediate* rather than a recollective event. Cantos I–V constitute the fictional level and the narrative level through two volumes of verse issued by John Murray in 1819 and 1821, and the remaining cantos constitute themselves through the four succeeding volumes issued by Hunt in 1823 and 1824. In addition, however, the last four volumes reconstitute what was originally printed in the first two volumes (*a*) by forcing the reader to place the whole of the fictional level in a specified historical frame of reference, and (*b*) by making this important interpretive shift a part of the poem's developing structure, a part of its own self-criticism. Byron begins the Hunt volumes of his poem, Cantos VI–XVI, with a Preface announcing his ideological purposes, and describing the key elements in the historical restructuring of the poem. Cantos VI–XVI then carry out these changes of direction, and thereby force Cantos I–V to accommodate the changes. The structural accommodations we have already discussed. The ideological changes appear as a more comprehensive understanding of the subjects taken up by the project of *Don Juan*. Most noticeable here is Byron's effort to present a totalized interpretation and critique of his age: to compel his readers to understand how the several phases of the period 1789–1824 hang together, and to persuade them that his critical-revolutionary reading of the period is the correct one. Related to this polemic is the poem's vision of self-judgement, its critical-revolutionary reading of the limits and blindnesses of Cantos I–V. Byron's revisionary turn on the first five cantos is not, of course, a repudiation of them. Though an act of self-criticism, the change of direction in Cantos VI–XVI assumes—indeed, it demonstrates—a dialectical continuity with its objects of criticism. The advances and the retreats of Cantos I–V, their boldness and timidity, accumulate a set of dynamic contradictions which eventually generate Cantos VI–XVI.

In this way *Don Juan* represents not merely a comprehensive interpretation of the period 1789–1824 but a comprehensive critical interpretation which incorporates its own acts of consciousness in its critique as part of a developing and changing act of interpretation. All readers have recognized this quality of the poem's digressive and shifting style, but it is important to see that this stylistic feature is grounded in the work's ideological structure. Even more important to see, however, is that the ground of this ideological structure is not in some definable form of critical interpretation which we may educe from the work. Rather, it lies in the act of the poem, the social and historical deeds of its consciousness which appear to us, most immediately, as a set of specific acts of publication. Of course, the fragmentary character of the work has heretofore obscured somewhat the comprehensiveness of its historical argument. Scholarship helps to bring that argument into sharper focus, to lift it from the sphere of a reader's intuition into a more explicit and defined frame of reference.

Late in the poem, we recall, Byron said of himself that like his own work *Don Juan* he is 'Changeable too—yet somehow "*Idem semper*"' (xvii, stanza 11). Readers have not found it easy to say what exactly in the poem is 'changeable' and what exactly stands resistant to change. I think we can now make an attempt to isolate these factors. What changes in the poem are its ideas; these are continually subjected to qualification, revision, even repudiation. What remains the same is the perpetual dialectic of the individual mind in its social world, the active deed of its committed intelligence. Fichte called this ground of permanence '*Tat*', Schopenhauer '*Wille*'. These are of course nothing more than conceptual markers for an act of social consciousness which can only be *carried out* in words but which cannot be defined in them. The act of the poem's mind, then, is an understanding that changes and brings about change. In *Don Juan*—to adapt a contemporary formulation of a fragment from Herakleitos—'What does not change / is the will to change.'[9]

---

9. This is Charles Olson's translation of Herakleitos, frag. 23, which appears as the first line of Olson's poem 'The Kingfishers'.

MALCOLM KELSALL

Byron's Politics[†]

'Ambition was my idol', Byron wrote, looking back to his 'hot youth—when George the Third was King' (*Don Juan*, 1.212.8). That ambition had been political. As an hereditary legislator of the British Empire, he had hoped to sway the destiny of nations by the power of oratory. His classical education offered the examples of men like Demosthenes in Greece and Cicero in Rome. Among his elder contemporaries were figures such as Henry Grattan, a founding father of the Irish 'patriot' parliament, and Byron's friends, Richard Brinsley Sheridan, the eloquent manager of the impeachment of Warren Hastings, and Thomas Erskine, the famous advocate of freedom of speech. A greater ambition yet might move a young man called by the duty of rank to public service. The statesman might also be a war leader and a maker of nations. The pre-eminent example for the age was George Washington and, for a European aristocrat, the example of Washington's ally, the Marquis de la Fayette, was close behind. More dangerously dazzling was the career of the disastrous comet, Napoleon Bonaparte, and the meteoric disaster of the Irish revolutionary, Lord Edward Fitzgerald.

Byron's political affiliations were to the Whig party in opposition and began at Cambridge where he was a member of a small and intimate political circle including the Duke of Devonshire, Lord Tavistock, John Cam Hobhouse (the future Lord Broughton), and Douglas Kinnaird. In London he was recruited by the Holland House circle where he was indoctrinated in the hagiography of the great dead Whig leader, Charles James Fox, Lord Holland's uncle and mentor. It was Lord Holland who was instrumental in promoting Byron's inaugural speech in the House of Lords. In the circle of Lady Oxford, he moved towards the more radical wing of the party represented by Sir Francis Burdett and John Horne Tooke (who had been tried for high treason and acquitted, 1794). That radicalism was demonstrated by his symbolic action in visiting Leigh Hunt in jail (imprisoned for libelling the Prince Regent). Hunt was to be his future collaborator on the political journal *The Liberal* (in which *The Vision of Judgment* was first published).

Byron's association with the Whigs provided him with both an ideology and a discourse of 'liberty'. His political position was rooted in the mythology of the 'Glorious Revolution' of 1688/9. As a political party, the Whigs had originated in opposition to what was described as Stuart 'tyranny'. They drew upon a teleological view of history in which the forces of liberty (enshrined in the 'ancient constitution' of the free Saxon peoples) were locked in a long struggle with the powers of oppression (now represented by those adherents of 'passive obedience' to the Crown nominated as 'Tories'). Certain great historical landmarks had recorded the advance of the principles of liberty, witness the acceptance by King John of Magna Carta, or John Hampden's refusal to pay the tax of ship money to Charles I on the emergent principle of 'no taxation without representation'. The revolution of 1688/9 had guaranteed the rule of law as sanctioned by parliament (with the monarch as the chief 'magistrate' in a 'balanced'

† From *The Cambridge Companion to Byron*, ed. Drummond Bone. Copyright © 2004 Cambridge University Press. Reprinted by permission of Cambridge University Press.

constitution of King, Lords, and Commons). A Bill of Rights guaranteed the life, liberty, and the property of the subject. Among such essential 'rights' (it was claimed) were freedom of speech, the freedom of the subject to petition for redress of grievances, freedom from arbitrary arrest (habeas corpus) and trial by jury. In practice many of these rights were to prove extremely fragile (Roman Catholics, for instance, were excluded from the body politic) but the foundational principles of 'resistance' to the arbitrary power of the Crown and of the 'rights' of the subject continued to shape the Whig thinking during the eighteenth century. The classic formulation of party principle was John Dunning's motion passed in the House of Commons (1780): 'The power of the Crown has increased, is increasing, and ought to be diminished.' Famous among Byron's older contemporaries had been the case of the Whig hero, John Wilkes, imprisoned for criticising the Crown as 'prostitute' (*The North Briton*, 45, 23 April 1763) and the attacks on the abuses of power by George III and his ministers in the 'Junius' *Letters* (1769–72).

Whig principles were internationalised by the revolt of the British colonists in North America. The men of property who led the revolution (great plantation owners like Washington) used (and applied) the by then well-established discourse of Whig opposition. They drew their examples from the classic authorities of the Glorious Revolution (figures like Hampden and Algernon Sydney) but radically linked with more obviously republican figures such as John Milton and John Harrington. Thomas Jefferson's vitriolic abuse of the tyranny of George III in the Declaration of Independence is directly in the tradition of Whig polemic, as was his declaration, inscribed in his Memorial in Washington, DC: 'I have sworn upon the altar of God eternal hostility against every form of tyranny over the mind of man.' The first ten amendments to the American Constitution derive from the Whig Bill of Rights and, historically, led to the Declaration of the Rights of Man and of the Citizen of the French Revolution.

It was the impact upon the Whig party of the revolution in France which provided the last great moments of heroic opposition (of which Byron was the late heir) and which broke the Whigs as a political force. The rise of Jacobinism in France, and the consequent 'radicalisation' of British politics, fundamentally changed the signification of Whig opposition to 'the Crown'. There was a substantial gap between the claim of great Whig lords to act as 'the friends of the people' (and the defenders of property) and, in France, the execution of the monarch and the aristocracy, the confiscation of property and the proclamation of universal republican war. Meantime, in Britain, the political establishment was challenged by a developing working-class movement, philosophically based on Thomas Paine's *The Rights of Man*, and, in practical terms, demanding a 'democracy' based on universal male suffrage and the delegation of members to annual parliaments. This threatened the established constitution with what the 'Tories' called 'anarchy'.

The dilemma for the Whigs was that the ideology and discourse of the party was potentially republican in its application (as the North American revolution had shown), but, in practice, their power and property was intrinsically interwoven with the maintenance of the so-called 'balanced' constitution between King, Lords, and Commons. They were caught, therefore, between the upper and nether millstones of 'Tory' reactionism and the Jacobinical 'radicals' (the political use of the word originates about this time). In keeping with the 'principles' of 1688/9 the party leader, Charles James Fox, welcomed both the American and the French revolutions. Accordingly, the Foxite wing of the Whigs opposed war with France. Sir James Mackintosh's defence of the revolution, *Vindiciae Gallicae* (1791), and Erskine's criticism of British war policy, *On the Causes and Consequences of the War with France* (1797), were to become key texts underpinning Byron's subsequent support for Napoleon. But this theoretical position became increasingly difficult to sustain. The threat from France (militarily and ideologically) caused the overwhelming majority of the Whig opposition to adopt the 'Tory' position. Eventually, the rump of the Foxite Whigs in 1797 seceded in despair from parliament. Apart from a brief spell in coalition after the death of the great war leader, William Pitt, the Whigs no longer existed as a force.

This was the party which Byron joined in 1812. It seemed an opportune moment. The establishment of the Regency because of the insanity of George III appeared to open a window of opportunity for the Whigs, for the Prince Regent had numerous friends among the opposition. Byron himself had assiduously prepared himself for a political career. Before embarking on his Grand Tour in 1809, he had already attended the House of Lords seven times, and his list of essential reading had included the parliamentary debates from the heartland of the Whig/Tory struggles of 1688 to 1745. On his return to Britain he attended all the major debates between January and July 1812 and also some of the minor work of committees. His maiden speech was on 27 February 1812, when he was chosen to lead a debate for the opposition on industrial unrest in his home county of Nottinghamshire. Unemployment among the stocking-knitters had provoked major civil disorder (the 'Luddite' riots) and the government was in process of introducing a Bill to make the breaking of the new manufacturing machinery a capital offence. The Whig position, as 'friends of the people', was that conciliation of grievances would be more effective than hanging workers. They proposed instead a committee of enquiry.

Byron spoke again on two other classic Whig issues. On 21 April 1812, in conjunction with his party, he advocated the removal of the residual constitutional disabilities from Roman Catholic subjects of the United Kingdom (Byron concentrated upon the position of the Catholic majority in Ireland). Finally, on 1 June 1813, he briefly presented a plea for freedom to petition on behalf of the veteran campaigner for parliamentary reform, Major John Cartwright. Cartwright claimed to have been harassed by the authorities during one of his campaigns. Consideration of his petition might have led to debate on the perennial Whig topic of reform of parliament (by a moderate extension of the franchise among men of property). Thereafter Byron's most significant action was to vote with the forty-four peers, led by Lord Grey, who on 23 May 1815 opposed renewal of war against Napoleon after the emperor's escape from Elba (the 'Hundred Days' which culminated in the battle of Waterloo).

The two major speeches (on the 'Luddites' and on the position of Roman Catholics in Ireland) are characterised by deep compassion for the sufferings of the common people and by an eloquent invective against the tyranny of the government. In context of the normal manner of proceeding of the House, however, they are out of kilter. The established mode of the

Lords was formal and proceeded by 'mutual politeness' (to adopt Byron's own description in *The Vision of Judgment*, line 280). It was not the custom of the House, for instance, to liken Lord Liverpool to 'that Athenian lawgiver [Draco] whose edicts were said to be written . . . in blood' (in the Luddite debate), nor to warn the government (in the Catholic debate) that they were traitors to the people whose heads might end up on 'the greedy niches' of Temple Bar. This kind of invective in the House was supported by a series of poetical squibs, some anonymous or not written *in propria persona*. Of the latter kind, the 'Song for the Luddites' (1816) is the most violent:

> As the Liberty lads o'er the sea
> Bought their freedom, and cheaply, with blood,
> So we, boys, we
> Will die fighting, or live free,
> And down with all kings but King Ludd!

This was way off the scale of acceptable Whig polemic and unpublishable. It flirts dangerously with 'Jacobinism'. The argument, ultimately, is that the 'anarchy' which the government seeks to repress was, in fact, justly provoked by the very tyranny of the government.

How seriously did Byron subscribe to the revolutionary tendency of what he said? Thomas Moore, in his *Life* of Byron, tells how the poet came to see him 'in a state of the most humorous exaltation' after delivering the Cartwright petition.

> 'I told them', he said, 'that it was a most flagrant violation of the Constitution—that, if such things were permitted, there was an end of English freedom, and that—'—'but what was this dreadful grievance?' I asked . . . 'the grievance?' he repeated, pausing as if to consider—Oh, *that* I forget'.
>
> (Moore, *Life*, 1832, 11, 207)

Such flippancy is hard to reconcile with the passion of the parliamentary rhetoric. It suggests that Byron saw his invective as a kind of superheated discourse of 'English freedom' easily turned on or off. Alternatively, the self-subversion suggests that by the summer of 1813 Byron was already disenchanted with what he called the 'mummeries' of parliamentary government.

There was reason for the disenchantment. Whig reliance on the patronage of the Prince Regent proved unfounded. He continued with his father's administration. Meantime, Byron had been unsuccessful on every major issue on which he had spoken. Machine-breaking had been made a capital offence; Catholic emancipation was rejected (and not fully achieved until after Byron's death); Cartwright's petition was rejected. In the Luddite debate, Byron was studiously insulted by the administration, which did not deign even to respond to his speech; in the affair of the Cartwright petition, even members of his own party spoke against him. Perhaps most symptomatic of the gap between rhetoric and reality were the results of his one partial success. The Whig proposal for enquiry into the Luddite disturbances was accepted. Consequentially, 'A Bill for Preventing Fraud and Abuses in the Frame-work Knitting Manufacture, and in the Payment of Persons Employed Therein' was introduced in the summer of 1812. It was totally emasculated. One of the leading opponents of this 'mistaken and mischievous' Bill was Lord Holland, Byron's mentor who had put him up to lead for the Whigs in February. Embarrassing the administration was one thing; interference in the conditions of trade was something quiet alien to the aristocrats at Holland House. Byron himself did not speak in the debate. He relieved his feelings in a poem to Lady Melbourne, 21 September 1813:

> 'Tis said—*Indifference* marks the present time,
> Then hear the reason—though 'tis told in rhyme—
> A King who *can't*—a Prince of Wales who *don't*—
> Patriots who *shan't*—and Ministers who *won't*—
> What matters who are *in* or *out* of place
> The *Mad*—the *Bad*—the *Useless*—or the *Base?*
>
> (*BLJ*, III, 117)

But the nadir of Byron's political career was marked by his paralysis during the Napoleonic Hundred Days. Although he voted with the rump of forty-four Whigs against renewal of the war, he remained silent in the House of Lords. How might one explain that silence? He had always admired the French emperor from the time when he had fought for his bust of Napoleon while a schoolboy at Harrow. Moreover, it is with great issues of European politics that Byron's name is associated both as a poet and a man of action. In addition, there was substantial pressure exerted on the poet to go public in support of Napoleon. Byron's friend, Hobhouse, was in Paris during the Hundred Days and in correspondence with the poet and parliamentarian. Hobhouse's letters were classically Whig. The events of 1688/9 were being repeated in France. The Bourbons, held in power by the bayonets of the monarchical powers of Europe, were like the tyrannical Stuarts of old. Napoleon was a liberator like William III, called to govern by the mandate of the people. As a great European statesman, now become a Constitutional ruler, he represented the best hope for the establishment of liberal policies in his country. It was unacceptable for Britain to interfere in the internal affairs of France. Hobhouse's letters were written to move Byron and public opinion and were subsequently collected (and revised) as *The Substance of Some Letters Written by an Englishman Resident at Paris during the Last Reign of the Emperor Napoleon* (1816). The second edition (1817) eventually revealed Byron's name as the principal recipient. But during the entire crisis of the Napoleonic restoration, Byron did no more than leak some of the correspondence anonymously to Leigh Hunt's opposition journal *The Examiner*. He voted against renewal of the war but otherwise kept his head down. In verse, nothing appeared until after Waterloo, and then in squibs published anonymously in *The Examiner* and *The Morning Chronicle* (the standard Whig newspaper). He only went public in the *Poems* of 1816 and *in propria persona* in the famous Waterloo stanzas of *Childe Harold* III.

The reasons for Byron's paralysis in 1815 are complex (not least the sexual and financial mess of his personal life). As far as party politics are concerned, however, the Hundred Days provide the clearest of indications of the impasse to which the Whig opposition had been brought. Hobhouse's historical Whig paradigm was irrelevant. The simple fact was that restoration of Napoleon meant war. If the emperor were defeated, the *ancien régime* would be restored. That had always been the war aim of the Allies. If Napoleon won, then, in Lord Holland's words, 'we must have twenty years more war'. It was, on the European scene, the same aporia between 'tyranny' or 'anarchy' which paralysed Whig attempts on the domestic front. It is a reasonable guess that Byron, after three years in politics, was sufficiently astute to perceive the cause of the paralysis. There was nothing he could say. But there is another possibility for his silence. He did not have the guts to get up in the House of Lords and speak out.

Byron's political career, therefore, is a record of failure ending in inarticulateness. There are a couple of exciting 'burns' of humanitarian rhetoric and indignant invective in the Luddite and Catholic debates, but they resemble a kind of hot-air ballooning. He was not fit for the long haul. In part this was the result of circumstance. The Whigs could offer nothing more than a rhetoric of opposition; and there were elements in the party who preferred it that way. But there is also an element of wilful nihilism in Byron's political career, as if the external impasse found a correspondent psychological response. His journal for 16 January 1814 provides a typical example:

> I have simplified my politics into an utter detestation of all existing governments; and, as it is the shortest and most agreeable and summary feeling imaginable, the first moment of an universal republic would convert me into an advocate for single and uncontradicted despotism. The fact is, riches are power, and poverty is slavery all over the earth, and one sort of establishment is no better, nor worse, for a *people* than another.

Even more nihilistic is his explosion of tragic rage of 19 April 1814:

> the Bourbons are restored!!!—'Hang up philosophy'. To be sure, I have long despised myself and man, but I never spat in the face of my species before—'O fool! I shall go mad'.

The tragic role he would assume here is that of the dispossessed and powerless monarch, King Lear (a fantastic and gross exaggeration of his role as a statesman). More provocative, and utterly self-destructive in relation to domestic politics, was his pretence of being the British equivalent of Napoleon Bonaparte. His post-Waterloo departure into 'exile' (provoked in fact by debts and sexual scandal) was marked by his commissioning of a replica of Napoleon's own coach in which Byron embarked on Childe Harold's second European tour (of necessity avoiding France). It was an analogy he was to develop later by signing his letters N[oel] B[yron] and by his claim to be the 'grand Napoleon of the realms of rhyme' (*Don Juan*, XI. 55.8). This myth-building suggests a form of self-fashioning developed as a compensation for the utter failure, in the real world, of the 'idol' of his own political 'ambition'.

Although Byron's role in British party politics was insignificant, yet, as part of the education of a poet's mind his experiences were fundamental. They provided a schooling in scepticism about idealistic rhetoric and a bitter experience of failure. This experience might be readily generalised as paradigmatic of the age itself. This was a time which Shelley called in the Preface to *The Revolt of Islam* (1818) the 'age of despair', and Shelley, in *Julian and Maddalo* (written 1818, published 1824), dramatised Byron as the voice of that despair. Byron himself in a late, bitter political satire nominated the epoch, *The Age of Bronze* (1823). There had been a giant race before the flood, and he names as heroes the American Whigs Patrick Henry ('give me liberty, or give me death'), Benjamin Franklin, and George

Washington. He associated these men with the Continental Congress of the American founding fathers. The American republic was now parodied by the reactionary Congress of the monarchical powers of Europe. Meantime, in Britain, the one preoccupation of the governing caste (the landed self-interest) was the preservation of their rents. Reform was a dead letter. The poem contains a long disquisition on the fall of Napoleon:

> A single step into the right had made
> This man the Washington of worlds betrayed;
> A single step into the wrong has given
> His name a doubt to all the winds of heaven.
> (*The Age of Bronze*, 233–6)

In a 'betrayed' Britain and Europe, it is little wonder that Byron's *Don Juan* begins with the demand 'I want a hero'.

Byron's personal attempt to reconstitute his own heroic status is associated with his commitment to direct-action anti-colonial politics in Italy and then in Greece. It is commonplace to describe Byron as a Foxite Whig at home (which is a party affiliation) and a constitutional nationalist abroad (to which the name 'Liberal' was given). The obvious attraction of direct-action politics in Europe was that they were freed (for Byron) from the class and party complexities of Britain. Single-issue demonstrations—Austrians 'out'; Turks 'out—are much easier than, for instance, finding a *modus vivendi* for competing Catholic and Protestant interests in Ireland. But much of Byron's political verse remained more concerned with British political affairs (home thoughts from abroad) than the simplified, heart-on-sleeve, militant nationalism for which he is famous.

His writing after his 'exile' repeatedly revisits the topics and the problems of his years in the House of Lords either to rewrite the record as he would wish it to have been, or to come to terms with issues which still deeply perplexed him. As soon as he was abroad Byron relieved himself of some of the feelings suppressed during the Hundred Days. His account of the battle of Waterloo in *Childe Harold* III (1816) laments the fall of the flawed tragic hero, Napoleon, and declines to lend support to the triumphalist celebrations of the Duke of Wellington, represented, for instance, by Walter Scott's *The Field of Waterloo*, Robert Southey's *The Poet's Pilgrimage to Waterloo*, or William Wordsworth's *Ode* (1815). The poem, accordingly, might be read as a complaint by an anti-war Whig faced with a Tory victory. In Canto IV (1818), Hobhouse's notes radicalised the historical generalities of Byron's seemingly remote historical reflections on the fall of the Venetian and Roman republics. Britain's collusion with the reactionary continental imperial powers, it is claimed, had betrayed the cause of national revival in Italy (as elsewhere in Europe).

Subsequently, the Venetian plays, *Marino Faliero* and *The Two Foscari* (1821), were directly applied to British affairs. Byron's portrayal of the clash between a corrupt Senate and a disaffected populace was seized upon during the anti-monarchical turmoil generated by George IV's divorce proceedings against Queen Caroline. Domestic politics, and Whig party preoccupations, therefore, remained pervasive. Even the European cantos of *Don Juan* (1819–23) might be interpreted as loosely veiled allegories of what the original epigraph called in transparent Latin *domestica facta*. The domestic scene emerges directly in the derisive satire of the subsequent English cantos.

These are concerned with the fundamental basis of establishment power, for Lord Henry Amundeville's country-house gathering (the central subject of the cantos) is not just a 'party' but is party political. The great landowner and placeman consolidates his electoral support by entertaining men of influence from London and in the locality. Equally essential is the 'marriage market' which operates at Norman Abbey, Lord Henry's home (ironically modelled on Byron's former estate at Newstead Abbey). It is upon dynastic relationships among the ruling caste that the political power of both Tories and Whigs depends, and Lord Henry claims that he nicely hits the mean between 'place' (support for the Tories) and 'patriotism' (the rhetoric of Whig opposition). As an astute politician he speaks for 'middle' England (and, in fact, pursues his selfish interests in the name of the public weal).

In many respects, therefore, Byron's verse after his 'exile' is a continuation of the original adversarial stance he had taken in the House of Lords. He even characterised himself in *Don Juan* as a man 'born for opposition' (*Don Juan*, XIV.22.8). He had not deserted his earlier principles by leaving the country, so his apologetic claimed. It was apostate Britain which had left those principles of liberty enunciated by the successive revolutions of 1688/9, 1776 and 1789. On one side stood the hypocritical Lord Henrys of the age, against them are the working words of the spokesman of freedom. The great declarations of Byron's commitment to the historic Whig principle of 'liberty' were to become the most potent political elements in his writing. Moreover, in poetic utterance, the principle itself becomes liberated from the specifics of time and place, acquiring in Byron's provocative utterance a numinous and transhistorical resonance. Witness the sonnet on *The Prisoner of Chillon* (1816):

> Eternal Spirit of the chainless mind!
> Brightest in dungeons, Liberty! thou art,
> For there thy habitation is the heart—

These words are not specific merely to the case of one political prisoner, but apply to all the oppressed of the earth. It is essential, if Byron's politics are to be understood, that the power of poetry to free the spirit be recognised. He wrote that he warred with words because all other courses of action were closed to him (*Don Juan*, IX.24.1). Wherever 'Tyrants' or their 'Sycophants' exist, Byron's verse opposes the abuses of power. He is, in that respect, Jeffersonian in his 'eternal hostility against every form of tyranny over the mind of man'.

That concept of 'liberty', however, requires always something to oppose. Underlying the great utterances about the flag of 'Freedom' streaming like the thunderstorm against the wind (*CHP*, IV.98.2) there is a philosophy of history which depends upon the polarisation of events to extremes. (George III must be always nothing less than a tyrant, his laureate Southey always a sycophant.) These extremes, philosophically considered, always exist. The party political words 'Tory' and 'Whig', accordingly, acquire a universal signification in which they are bonded by mutual, transhistorical necessity. The Whig theorist, Thomas Jefferson, summarised the essential interrelationship between 'Tory' and 'Whig' in a letter to John Adams, 27 June 1813:

> Men have differed in opinion, and been divided into parties by these
> opinions, from the first origin of societies; and in all governments

where they have been permitted freely to think and to speak. The same political parties . . . have existed thro' all time. Whether the power of the people, or that of the *aristoi* should prevail, were questions which kept the states of Greece and Rome in eternal convulsions: as they now schismatize every people whose minds and mouths are not shut up by the gag of a despot. And in fact the terms of whig and tory belong to natural, as well as to civil history.

This is an heroic (and convulsive) philosophy of history which functions by polarities, and, as Jefferson describes it, is necessary because it is intrinsic in the human psyche and, thus, in all human societies. It is, accordingly, a profoundly ironic philosophy because the liberationist ethic requires the hegemonic tendency to justify its opposition. You cannot have one without the other.

Hence the importance of the Satanic figure in Byron's verse, for Satan in rebellion against the power of God was the first 'Whig' and also, in Goethe's characterisation, eternally 'der Geist der stets verneint' ('the spirit that always denies', *Faust*, Part I, 'Studierzimmer'). Whatever is must always be opposed. This Satanic irony structures Byron's profoundest political satire, *The Vision of Judgment* (1822). Here, George III is made to stand as the type of tyranny and the case against him is put by Satan with Jeffersonian fervour: 'The new world shook him off; the old yet groans / Beneath what he and his prepared' (*The Vision of Judgment*, 369–70). Yet it remains essential that Satanic rebellion does not succeed universally, for that would be to substitute the tyranny of the revolutionary ruler of hell for the tyranny of the status quo. Byron's poem, accordingly, creates a 'neutral space' (*The Vision of Judgment*, 257) between heaven and hell in which the forces of Tory and Whig remain perpetually suspended in unresolvable and necessary opposition.

Hence the irony of Byron's gloss in *Don Juan* on his existential dilemma as a man 'born for opposition':

> But then 'tis mostly on the weaker side:
> So that I verily believe if they
> Who now are basking in their full-blown pride,
> Were shaken down, and 'dogs had had their day',
> Though at the first I might perchance deride
> Their tumble, I should turn the other way,
> And wax an Ultra-royalist in loyalty,
> Because I hate even democratic royalty.
> (*Don Juan*, XV.23)

The price of liberty is eternal denial of all forms of hegemonic power whether of government or opposition. The aphorism 'Power tends to corrupt and absolute power corrupts absolutely' applies to Whig as much as to Tory. Ultimately it is not merely a philosophical theory but an existential imperative for the poet:

> I wish men to be free
> As much from mobs as kings, from you as me.
> (*Don Juan*, IX.25.7–8)

These lines seem proleptic of John Stuart Mill *On Liberty* (1859). But that is a history of liberalism which Byron did not live to see.

JANE STABLER

Byron, Postmodernism and Intertextuality[†]

* * *

* * * Postmodernism has been defined variously as a continuation of modernism or late modernism and also as a break with modernist abstraction. It has been categorised both as nostalgic and rootless: as an offshoot of cynical capitalism and as playing a part in the defence of minority cultures and communities; enervated, parasitic and playfully courageous. All these terms (including a suspicion that the writer and his publisher were exploiting the market) have been applied to literature produced long before the twenty-first century. Ihab Hassan observes that we now detect 'postmodern features in *Tristram Shandy* precisely because our eyes have learned to recognise postmodern features'.[1]

Following delightedly in the wake of Laurence Sterne's infamous 'oddity', Byron's work—especially *Don Juan*, the work he called his 'poetical T[ristram] Shandy'—supports the view that the postmodern is a genre coexistent with the rise of print culture as well as a late twentieth- and twenty-first-century epoch.[2] This chapter is concerned with generic features rather than political and economic contexts, but it is obvious that the technological developments which have mediated the reception of genre since the early nineteenth century are significant phenomena. In particular, developing journalistic coverage of daily—or hourly—events (as noted in Wordsworth's 1800 Preface) has contributed to an increasingly self-reflexive vein in literature. We need to take account of this shift as well as many other aspects of historical difference when we discuss Byron's (and Sterne's) literary forms of disruption as a proto-postmodernism.

Mazeppa's wry closing reflection on a capricious and thankless audience acknowledges the vagaries of reception which had always shaped Byron's career.[3] The poem belongs to the period when Byron had ceased to be at the centre of fashionable London society, and was living in self-imposed exile in Italy. He began *Mazeppa* in April 1817 in Venice, abandoned it for a while (in the meantime starting and finishing *Beppo* and *Childe Harold's Pilgrimage* Canto IV), then returned to it in the summer of 1818 when he was again living in Venice, and finished it during a visit by the Shelleys. On this occasion Percy Shelley heard Byron read the first canto of *Don Juan*. Shelley greeted the *ottava rima* work enthusiastically, discerning a much-needed reform of Byron's philosophy. After the visit to Venice, Shelley wrote to Peacock:

> I entirely agree with what you say about Childe Harold. The spirit in
> which it is written is . . . a kind of obstinate and selfwilled folly, in

---

† From *The Cambridge Companion to Byron*, ed. Drummond Bone. Copyright © 2004 Cambridge University Press. Reprinted by permission of Cambridge University Press.

1. Ihab Hassan, *The Postmodern Turn: Essays in Postmodern Theory and Culture* (Columbus: Ohio State University Press, 1987), p. xvi.
2. *BLJ*, x, 150.
3. In *Mazeppa* (1819), King Charles requests the tale but falls asleep almost as soon as it begins: "And if ye marvel Charles forgot / To thank his tale, *he* wonder'd not,— / The king had been an hour asleep" (lines 867–69). (*Editor's note.*)

which he hardens himself. I remonstrated with him in vain on the tone of mind from which such a view of things alone arises. For its real root is very different from its apparent one. Nothing can be less sublime than the true source of these expressions of contempt and desperation . . . He allows fathers and mothers to bargain with him for their daughters . . . He associates with wretches who seem almost to have lost the gait and physiognomy of man, and who do not scruple to avow practices which are not only not named, but I believe seldom even conceived in England. He says he disapproves, but he endures.[4]

Shelley's remonstrance takes a more generous form in *Julian and Maddalo*, but this letter recoils (somewhat squeamishly) from Byron's surrender to an 'orgasm of Buffoonery', a sort of negative sublime, as he submerged himself in the hectic carnality of Venice.[5] Byron's accommodation of what Shelley and others 'seldom even conceived' extended to art as well as life. Shelley, to take a revealing instance of their difference in taste, could not abide the Restoration comedies that Byron loved to quote. Byron's appreciation of artistic licentiousness grew out of a cosmopolitan Regency dandy pose, but by the time of *Mazeppa* it had matured into a more politically aware, ironic use of artifice.

Between 1817 and 1819 Byron's immersion in Venetian culture with its intricate social conventions (including Carnival and the male role of the *cavalier servente*) informed the conjunction of the homely and the exotic, the marginal and the sublime in his work. For many critics this matrix defines the conditions of postmodern writing. While T. S. Eliot's High Modernism flinched from the chaotic details of ordinary life and sought to transcend them with new artistic wholes, postmodern art accepts with Byron and Beckett that 'Existence may be borne' (*CHP*, IV.21.1). It builds on the foundations of modernism's 'unreal city', but emphasises an intermingling with (not distance from) quotidian particularity. If carnivalisation is one of the hallmarks of postmodernist writing, Byron is the Romantic poet most hospitable to the 'periodic Saturnalia' with all its 'laughing—flirting—tormenting—pleasant' plurality.[6] *Childe Harold's Pilgrimage* Canto IV dazzled its first readers by rapid shifts between different categories of existence: 'the transitions are so quickly performed . . . from Venice to Rome, from Rome to Greece . . . from Mr. Hobhouse to politics, and back again to Lord Byron; that our head is absolutely bewildered by the want of connexion', complained the *Literary Gazette*, anticipating the reading public's shock at the violent juxtapositions of *Don Juan*.[7]

Well before the first appearance of Byron's *ottava rima* verse, however, reviewers felt that Byron was misleading his readers about the genre of his poems. By the time they reached *Childe Harold's Pilgrimage* Canto IV, the progression implied by the word 'pilgrimage' had dissolved completely into an eclectic flux of 'fantastically tangled' (*CHP*, IV.17.1) Spenserian stanzas which came as close as any nineteenth-century poem had come to suggesting the simultaneity of modern life:

---

4. P. B. Shelley, *The Complete Works*, ed. Roger Ingpen and Walter E. Peck, 10 vols. (London: Ernest Benn; New York: Gordian Press, 1965), x, 12.
5. 'An Italian Carnival', *CMP*, 191. [In the notes to this essay *CMP* refers to *Lord Byron: The Complete Miscellaneous Prose*, ed. Andrew Nicholson (Oxford: Clarendon Press, 1991) (*Editor's note*).]
6. *CMP*, 192.
7. Reiman (ed.), *Romantics Reviewed*, B, v, 1399.

                                                    still teems
                    My mind with many a form which aptly seems
                    Such as I sought for, and at moments found;
                    Let these too go—for waking Reason deems
                    Such over-weening phantasies unsound,
              And other voices speak, and other sights surround.
                                                    (*CHP*, IV.7.4–9)

Whereas Shelley believed that 'poetry defeats the curse which binds us
to be subjected to the accident of surrounding impressions', Byron's poetry
draws attention to the mystery of an ever-shifting surface and involves the
reader in the formation of that surface.[8] In the footsteps of Childe Harold
on a journey through Italy, William Hazlitt viewed the waterfall at Terni and
felt that this rather tame cascade ought to have been captured by the genial
sparkle of a poet like Thomas Moore rather than the troubling force of
Byronic textuality. The waterfall, he said:

> has nothing of the texture of Lord Byron's terzains, twisted, zigzag,
> pent up and struggling for a vent, broken off at the end of a line, or
> point of a rock, diving under ground, or out of the reader's compre-
> hension, and pieced on to another stanza or shelving rock.[9]

This passage reveals the physicality of Hazlitt's (and other people's) reading
experience of Byron's poetry. Byron's most subversive aesthetic technique
was abrupt transition between different modes, a juxtaposition of types and
qualities which was perceived first as Whiggish aristocratic caprice and later
as more offensively radical disruption. Early readers of *Don Juan* were
stunned by the callousness of a narrative which could veer between high sen-
timent and vomit, and yet, the reception of *Don Juan* was continuous with
objections to the fragmentary form of *The Giaour*, the dangerous intermix-
ture of satire in the notes to *Childe Harold* and the other Turkish Tales.
Byron's sudden poetic breaks and gulfs were a form of sublimity, but they also
violated the law of genre and the expectation that sublime poetic boundless-
ness would disturb its readers only within certain acceptable parameters.
Above all, the sublime was supposed to sustain a mood of seriousness or rev-
erence before God or Nature and Byron's infringement of this rule frequently
took the form of casual, quotidian or comic interruptions to lyrical passages.
His poetry allowed all that had been repressed by genre to return.

'The more enlightened our houses are, the more their walls ooze ghosts',
Italo Calvino remarked as he contemplated the position of the writer in
1967.[1] Byron's texts comprehend an enlightened, unillusioned world in
which 'spectres' and 'things familiar' jostle together as in Childe Harold's
Venice. For Shelley the Lido offered 'The pleasure of believing what we see /
Is boundless, as we wish our souls to be', whereas Byron's sinking and
deserted city was endlessly 'peopled' by the texts of what the poet has read
and done before in a place where 'Curiosity is always excited' (*Julian and
Maddalo*, II.16–17).[2] Such inclusiveness lends his account of this Italian

---

8. Shelley, *Complete Works*, VII, 37.
9. William Hazlitt, *The Complete Works*, ed. P. P. Howe, 21 vols. (London: J. M. Dent, 1930–4), x, 258.
1. Italo Calvino, 'Cybernetics and Ghosts', in Malcolm Bradbury (ed.), *The Novel Today: Contempo- rary Writers in Modern Fiction* (London: Fontana, 1977; repr. 1990), pp. 223–41; p. 235.
2. *CMP*, 192.

city an indeterminacy more unsettling than the melting loveliness of a Shel-
leyan sunset because it embraces not only idealised forms, but the multi-
ple dislocated particulars (animal, vegetable and mineral) associated with
'Venice' as a place much over-written about by earlier artists, tourists and
conquests: 'Shylock and the Moor, / And Pierre' (*CHP*, IV.4.6–7); 'The
Bucentaur . . . rotting unrestored' (*CHP*, IV.II.3); 'blind old Dandolo' (*CHP*,
IV.12.8); 'The "Planter of the Lion"' (*CHP*, IV.14.3); 'The camel . . . with the
heaviest load' (*CHP*, IV.21.4). Both poets were wary (as Lacanian theory
would be) of fantasies of wholeness, but while Shelleyan poetry reaches
towards 'The One' which remains, Byron's verse follows 'the many' which
'change and pass', contemplating nostalgically or sardonically the prospect
of ideal resolution.

Shelley and Byron's disagreement on the matter of ideal versus 'peopled'
existence offers a way of conceptualising the contested ground between
modernism and postmodernism. Like their conversations on poetry, this is
a difference which can shade into reciprocity ('(I think with you / In some
respects, you know)'[3] as Maddalo tells Julian). A vital point of comparison
is their shared inheritance of earlier literature. Whereas Shelley believed
with the High Modernists that the poet's work was to 'make it new', Byron
was much happier to return to history, and he distrusted literary attempts
to sever the past utterly. About the Pope-Bowles controversy, Shelley argued
'I certainly do not think Pope, or any writer, a fit model for any succeeding
writer . . . it would all come to a question as to under what forms medioc-
rity should perpetually reproduce itself.[4] After helping the oriental verse-
tale to become one of the most popular verse commodities of the day,
Byron, on the other hand, urged his contemporaries to reinstate Pope's
'superartificiality'.[5] This discipline, he argued, would counter the egotisti-
cal experimentation of, for example, Cockney couplets. Byron was notori-
ously dismissive of Keats's early verse with its shibboleth of individual
(adolescent) imagination. By contrast, Byron's imaginative play is more
sporting in that it addresses itself to what is communal rather than what is
'mawkish'. Byron valued cosmopolitan polish above the self-indulgence of
a sect—hence his impatience with the Lake School's insular organicism
and Leigh Hunt's 'system'. Art that plays by only its own self-regarding con-
ventions has no right to expect the audience to stay awake. Byron is clearly
on the side of artistic frame breaking that has mastered traditional disci-
pline first. His postmodernism is certainly not that which prides itself
merely on the efficient vandalism of established forms.

Mary Shelley's report of Byron's and Shelley's debate on Hamlet neatly
encapsulates the way Byron's performative scepticism affronts mystical sys-
tem. After Shelley's eloquent discourse on the 'expressive unity' of *Hamlet*,
we are told, he 'looked up, and found Lord Byron fast asleep'.[6] The physi-
cal presence of a dozing audience ironises the authority of the bard and
comically deflates the transcendent potential of the lyric artist (as in
Byron's aside on Keats's 'Sleep and Poetry': '(an ominous title)').[7] By dis-
playing the artist at the mercy of the material, contingent world Byron

3. Shelley, *Julian and Maddalo: A Conversation*, III 240–1.
4. Shelley, *Complete Works*, X, 265–6.
5. *CMP*, 146–57.
6. Jonathan Bate, *The Romantics on Shakespeare* (Harmondsworth: Penguin, 1992), p. 349.
7. *CMP*, 117.

unravelled the sealed, unified pretensions of the autonomous Romantic or High Modernist work of art. As well as fuelling a debate with Shelley, Byron's suspicion of self-contained poetry also shaped the peculiar dynamic of Romantic irony within his work which is, as Drummond Bone has observed,[8] distinct from both the disillusioned backlash of Irving Babbit's Romantic irony and the transcendental ascension of Friedrich Schlegel's Romantic irony. Byron's Romantic irony is a 'letting in' (or, perhaps, a 'letting be'), rather than an escape or a turning away from; its hospitality to contradiction is both Shakespearean and Negatively Capable as Anne Barton has pointed out.[9]

*   *   *

* * * A cheerful acceptance that his art can be no more than 'telling old tales' (*Mazeppa*, 200) separates the Modernist appropriation of myth from postmodernist palimpsests and helps us to see a continuity between Byron's narrative techniques and those of Sterne, Joyce, Beckett and Nabokov. For them repetition is comically inescapable yet it yields the fraught possibility of finding a way onward. From Sterne's struggle to make headway with the history of his life we recognise Byron's '—the devil take it! / This story slips for ever through my fingers' (*Beppo*, 498), and Malone's frustrated efforts to write:

> The exercise book had fallen to the ground. I took a long time to find it. It was under the bed. How are such things possible? I took a long time to recover it. I had to harpoon it. It is not pierced through and through, but it is in a bad way. It is a thick exercise book. I hope it will see me out. From now on I shall write on both sides of the page.[1]

Malone's prosaic sense of time (and his tragicomical wish to extend it) are shared by Byron's narratives as well as the way physical obstructions, particularly bodily complications, interpose themselves between the tale and the telling. *Beppo* ends, we are told, because Byron has reached 'the bottom of a page' (689). Canto v of *Don Juan* ends because the muse needs 'a few short naps'. Postmodernist writers flag up the difficulty of telling a tale and take neither subject matter nor readers for granted. The materiality of the text is signalled by a variety of textual devices such as puns, parentheses and quotation of other texts. This is not the post-structuralist dream of everything dissolving into pure text, but an opening up of text to the impurities of life. The modernist text cannot bear very much reality, the postmodernist text talks about bearing the unbearable: 'I can't go on. I'll go on.'[2]

The relationship between historical and literary texts in *Mazeppa* was foregrounded when Byron included extracts from his source in Voltaire's *Histoire de Charles XII* in the advertisement. As *Blackwood's* remarked, the tale was 'well-known'. Like his contemporaries, Byron had to draw his poetic material from somewhere, but to a much greater extent, he fretted over historical accuracy. He was peculiarly concerned with the relationship

---

8. J. Drummond Bone, 'Romantic Irony Revisited' in *Byron: East and West*, ed. Martin Procházka (Prague: Charles University Press, 2000), pp. 237–47.

9. See Anne Barton, 'Byron and the Mythology of Fact', Nottingham Byron Foundation Lecture (University of Nottingham, 1968), p. 5.

1. Samuel Beckett, *The Beckett Trilogy: Molloy, Malone Dies, The Unnamable* (London: Picador, 1979), p. 192.

2. *The Unnamable*, p. 382.

between his poetry and 'fact': 'There should always be some foundation of fact for the most airy fabric, and pure invention is but the talent of a liar.'[3] Unlike most of his contemporaries, Byron's use of the word 'pure' here withdraws the word's accustomed ethical value. His insistence on the imperative of fact might seem to undercut postmodern *savoir faire* by suggesting a naive faith in the transparency of language. It is rather, I think, responsiveness to minute detail which answers accusations of nihilism levelled at postmodern modes.

Byron's quotations of earlier authorities and 'fact' are a good place to test contradictory views of postmodernist intertextuality. Does the citation of other works which is a familiar motif in postmodern art and architecture imply a recognition that there is nothing more to say or is something else going on? According to Rosalind Krauss, a critical difference between Modernism and postmodernism is that the former legitimates itself through a cult of originality upholding the 'singularity, authenticity, uniqueness' of art while the latter is more open to forms of repetition.[4] Byron's contemporaries believed in originality as the hallmark of genius and they expressed shock (like Sterne's readers) when Byron's literary borrowings were pointed out. 'They call me "Plagiary"', Byron remarked ruefully, 'I think I now, in my time, have been accused of *every* thing'.[5] Following Sterne's delighted apprehension of the way books become part of experience: 'many, I know, quote the book, who have not read it,—and many have read it who understand it not',[6] Byron's intertextuality diminishes the authority of the author by socialising with earlier texts and accepting the vagaries of readerly interpretation.

Although his Years of Fame (1812–15) made him the most famous poet of the day, Byron grew increasingly aware of the limits of authorial power. There were several reasons for this. First, Byron's aristocratic consciousness made him look down on 'inky-fingered' professional authorship. 'One hates an author that's *all author*', he wrote in *Beppo*, they are 'So very anxious, clever, fine, and jealous, / One don't know what to say to them, or think' (*Beppo*, 595). Secondly, for complex legal reasons, several of his works lost the protection of copyright and circulated freely in widely differing shapes and forms accompanied by spoofs and spin-offs pretending to be from the pen of Lord Byron. Byron exhorted Murray and Kinnaird to limit piracies, but the lack of control over all the various transmutations inevitably complicated his sense of the readership. Finally, geographical and political distance from Murray and John Hunt led to delays and mistakes in proof-correction for most of his poems after 1816.

Byron's rage about these accidents was gradually tempered by an acceptance of the haphazard element in authorship. Risk was enfolded within the verse as part of the dynamic of composition, co-existing with a commitment to the value of publication for which he admits, 'There are no rewards'. The question 'why publish?' in *Don Juan* is answered with a series of other questions, 'why do you play at cards? / Why drink? Why read?':

---

3. *BLJ*, v, 203 (to Murray 2 April 1817). See also Barton, 'Byron and the Mythology of Face', pp. 4–11.
4. Rosalind E. Krauss, *The Originality of the Avant-Garde and Other Modernist Myths* (Cambridge, MIT Press, 1985; repr. 1997), p. 161; discussed in M. Steven Connor, *Postmodernist Culture: An Introduction to Theories of the Contemporary*, 2nd edn (Oxford: Blackwell, 1997), pp. 101–2.
5. *BLJ*, viii, 166.
6. Laurence Sterne, *The Life and Opinions of Tristram Shandy, Gentleman*, ed. Graham Petrie (Harmondsworth: Penguin, 1967; repr. 1986), p. 107.

> Besides, my Muse by no means deals in fiction:
>   She gathers a repertory of facts,
> Of course with some reserve and slight restriction,
>   But mostly sings of human things and acts—
> And that's one cause she meets with contradiction;
>   For too much truth, at first sight, ne'er attracts;
> And were her object only what's call'd glory,
> With more ease too she'd tell a different story.
>   (*Don Juan*, xiv.13)

English *ennui* (which is discussed four stanzas later) is simultaneously courted and held at bay by the *ottava rima* verse. The boredom of the author meets that of his audience and confronts head-on the awkward question of how one continues when everything appears to have been seen and said before. 'One gets tired of everything, my angel', Byron was fond of (mis)quoting from *Les Liaisons Dangereuses*.[7] The last cantos of *Don Juan* present an image of English society as 'a brilliant masquerade' that 'palls'. They are also reminiscent of 'The truth in masquerade' which was Byron's earlier diagnosis of the condition of all art. 'True Truth' (*Don Juan*, xi.37.5) or Truth unmediated by language would lead to silence so appalling it is better to 'play out the play'. An inevitable side-effect of staying with the flotsam and jetsam of experience, however, is that nothing (including the poet) remains intact. By 1821 in *The Vision of Judgment* Byron could envisage an author who was 'really, truly, nobody at all' (*The Vision of Judgment*, 640).[8]

The radical post-structuralist view of authorship explored by Roland Barthes in the late 1960s was that it exists only as a 'function' of the text. Byron's furious outbursts against the 'cutting and slashing' of his work are notable instances of an author's belief in the integrity of his version of the printed page. Despite the commodification of 'Byron' in the nineteenth century, there was a George Gordon (Noel) Byron who set in motion the multiplicity of 'dialogue, parody, contestation' Barthes saw as making up a text.[9] Unexpectedly, perhaps, this author granted his readers considerable freedom in the production of meaning in his work especially after the move to Italy. When Mary Shelley made the fair copy of *Don Juan* Cantos vi and vii, Byron invited her to choose between different couplet endings for a number of stanzas. The published version of the second stanza of Canto vi ends: 'Men with their heads reflect on this and that— / But women with their hearts or heaven knows what!' In the manuscript, this couplet is followed by other variants:

> or
> Man with his head reflects—(as Spurzheim tells)
> But Women with the heart—or something else.—
> or
> Man's pensive part is (now & then) the head
> Woman's the heart—or any thing instead.

All three versions were left standing as equally valid ways of finishing the stanza and in this case Mary Shelley adopted the first one ('what comes

---

7. *BLJ*, III, 220.
8. See Wolfson, 'The Vision of Judgment and the Visions of "Author"', this volume, p. 171.
9. See Roland Barthes, 'The Death of the Author' in *Image. Music. Text*, trans. Stephen Heath (London: Fontana, 1977; repr. 1990), pp. 142–8.

uppermost') for her fair copy. As Peter Cochran remarks, Byron was either 'happy with her decisions' or 'fatalistically indifferent'.[1] His silent relinquishments of authorial control are a much more modest way of opening the work to readerly participation than the activities of later artists who display (and sell) the detritus of their studios, notebooks, beds, or those who, like George Oppen, literally build poems out of manuscript layers.[2]

Byron's ambivalent attitude to the power of the readership is evident in his reflexive and complex modes of intertextuality that are significantly different from the practices of his Romantic contemporaries. Writers like Charlotte Smith, William Wordsworth, Samuel Coleridge, John Keats and the Shelleys drew on a sentimental model of allusion in which the borrowed material harmonised with the affective design of the new poem. Byron could do this as well, but he also experimented with a more disruptive mixture of texts from eighteenth-century satire and stage parody, emphasising the plunder of incongruous material and readerly responsibility for the recognition of lost property. Stanza 158, which Murray left out of the first edition of *Don Juan* Canto v, begins 'Thus in the East they are extremely strict, / And *Wedlock* and a *Padlock* mean the same.' Murray may have been uneasy about the intimations of English marriage, especially about the strict Lady Byron. The italics also serve, however, to nudge the reader to Isaac Bickerstaffe's popular two-act farce, *The Padlock* which plays with the wedlock/padlock joke.[3] As well as italics, other marks of punctuation could signal allusions to classical literature or contemporary culture. One of Byron's early couplet parodies advertised the fact that the poem was 'Half stolen, with acknowledgements . . . Stolen parts marked with inverted commas of quotation'.[4] Byron later applied the omnivorous topicality of newspaper satire or performative parody to the more elevated fields of narrative and lyric poetry. Introduced at the beginning of the eighteenth century and popularised by Samuel Richardson's epistolary novels, quotation marks were a relatively new and showy typographic device. Thomas De Quincey disliked them because they tended to 'break the continuity of the passion by reminding the reader of a printed book'.[5] But Byron revelled in their potential for disruptiveness. The vast majority of quotation marks in his poems are present in the first draft and were not inserted (unlike other marks of syntax) in the editorial process. The effects he achieved through signalled quotation, parenthetical aside and direct address to the reader are remarkably close to the ones defined as 'paratextual conventions' by Linda Hutcheon in her discussion of the postmodern novel:

> What postmodern novels . . . do is to focus in a very self-reflexive way
> on the processes of both the production and the reception of para-
> doxically fictive historical writing. They raise the issue of how the

1. Peter Cochran, 'Mary Shelley's Fair Copying of *Don Juan*', *The Keats-Shelley Review*, 10 (1996), 221–41: 237.
2. See Michael Davidson, 'Palimtexts: Postmodern Poetry and the Material Text', in *Postmodern Genres*, ed. Marjorie Perloff (Norman: University of Oklahoma Press, 1988; repr. New York: Keats-Shelley Association of America, 1995), pp. 75–95.
3. *The Padlock* is included in Elizabeth Inchbald's (1808) *Collection of Farces and Afterpieces* which appears in the 1816 Sale Catalogue of Byron's Library.
4. *CPW*, III, 32.
5. Thomas De Quincey, *Recollections of the Lakes and the Lake Poets*, ed. David Wright (Harmondsworth: Penguin, 1970; repr.1985), p. 38.

intertexts of history, its documents or traces, get incorporated into such an avowedly fictional context, while somehow also retaining their historical documentary value.[6]

Many critics have pointed out that Byron's *ottava rima* poetry is, to some extent, 'novelised'. What is often not recognised is the extent to which historical material had been making repeated incursions across the generic boundary of lyric poetry from the beginning of Byron's career. Even in *Childe Harold* Canto III, obsessive self-exploration is interrupted by a digressive pull towards the curious circumstances of composition. Moments of Shelleyan-Wordsworthian vision are interrupted, literally and graphically on the page, as Byron's scribbled manuscript notes perform an historical dialogue with the lyric stanzas, emphasising the marginal, the haphazard and the contingent.

Immediately after the stanza on the ruined fortress of Ehrenbreitstein, Byron turns from the sublime 'height' of 'A tower of victory' to consider local anecdote:

> I was shown a window where [General Marceau] is said to have been standing—observing the progress of the siege by moonlight—when a ball struck immediately below it.—He was killed not long afterwards at Altenkirchen by a rifleman: it is rather singular—that these narrow escapes have in several instances been followed closely by death:—at Nuremberg shortly before the battle of Lutzen Gustavus Adolphus had his horse killed under him—Falconer but escaped one Shipwreck to perish by another more successful—The Prince of Orange died by the attempt of a *third* assassin—and Nelson rarely came out of action without a wound till the most fatal & glorious of all—which—instead of a scar—left him immortality.[7]

This note draws attention to the fictive contours of history. Bodily scars are a record of what happened and also a ghostly reminder of what might have happened. The allusions that run across Byron's narratives and lyrics have a similarly disconcerting effect. The possibility of different outcomes and the 'singularity' of the way things do turn out energise Byron's art of digression. Whereas the published version of *Childe Harold's Pilgrimage* relegated observations on local historical curiosity to a substantial section of end notes, the capacious *ottava rima* stanza form of *Don Juan* goes out of its way to include digressive trails of association in the text and notes. In Canto V just after Juan has been sold into slavery, Byron diverts to matters closer to home:

> The other evening ('twas on Friday last)—
>   This is a fact and no poetic fable—
> Just as my great coat was about me cast,
>   My hat and gloves still lying on the table,
> I heard a shot—'twas eight o'clock scarce past—
>   And running out as fast as I was able,
> I found the military commandant
> Stretch'd in the street, and able scarce to pant.
>   (*Don Juan*, V.33)

6. Linda Hutcheon, *The Politics of Postmodernism* (London: Routledge, 1989; repr. 1993), p. 82.
7. [Byron], *Childe Harold's Pilgrimage Canto III. A Facsimile of the Autograph Fair Copy*, ed. T. A. J. Burnett (New York and London: Garland, 1988), pp. 106–11.

The digression is one of several retellings of this incident for different audiences. The insistence on 'fact' (the time, the date, the particularity of being in the middle of dressing for the evening) is accompanied by an awareness of helpless human involvement in the stream of history:

> The scars of his old wounds were near his new,
>   Those honourable scars which brought him fame;
> And horrid was the contrast to the view—
>   But let me quit the theme; as such things claim
> Perhaps even more attention than is due
>   From me: I gazed (as oft I have gazed the same)
> To try if I could wrench aught out of death
> Which should confirm, or shake, or make a faith.
>
>   (*Don Juan*, v. 38)

This stanza comprehends the sense of alternative endings: the old scars were survivable, the new wounds not and the contrast is 'horrid' (in its prickly sense) because it is random. The poet questions his own (or any) attempt to invest this randomness with meaning while the stanza gives it a form and wrenches a rhyme out of 'death'. This patterning supplants the orthodox Christian sense of death as a sure return, upholding instead a perilous transitory significance.

In Byron's texts, the ending often happens by accident: Manfred's 'Old man, 'tis not so difficult to die' (*Manfred*, III.iv.151) is a wry acknowledgement of this most arbitrary of processes. As in James Joyce's *Ulysses*, the finality of death in Byron's texts is dispersed by multiplicity. Throughout Dignam's funeral Bloom is distracted by recollections of food, *Hamlet* and *Julius Caesar*, the possibility of sex in graveyards, the different epitaphs on tombstones: 'Eulogy in a country churchyard it ought to be that poem of whose is it Wordsworth or Thomas Campbell'.[8] In the more experimentally fragmented 'Wandering Rocks' episode, large-scale human tragedy (the *General Slocum* steamship disaster on New York City's East River in 1904) is enfolded in gossipy flow. Narrative drift passes over 'A thousand casualties. And heartrending scenes . . . Not a single lifeboat would float and the firehose all burst . . . And America they say is the land of the free.'[9]

Contemplating the commandant's untidy end in Ravenna, Byron rhymes his way through the same sort of bricolage: stomach; heart; liver; what is life or death; the parable of the centurion's daughter; the Napoleonic wars; butchery; 'But it was all a mystery.' There is no closure—only the continuation of narrative: 'No more, / But let us to the story as before' (*Don Juan*, v.39.7–8).

*   *   *

Here, I would argue, lies the difference between Byron's postmodernism and the mixture of trash and high art evident in other varieties of late twentieth- and twenty-first-century postmodern culture. Byron's world of things is inextricably bound up with the work of art and with questions of readerly and writerly responsibility towards those things. *Don Juan* dances

---

8. James Joyce, *Ulysses*, ed. Hans Walter Gabler, with Wolfhard Steppe and Claus Melchior (Harmondsworth: Penguin Books, in association with The Bodley Head, 1986), p. 93.
9. *Ibid.*, pp. 196–7.

along an ever-varying line, but it has its pools of commitment. Byron's fierce defence of Shelley is one and Juan's simple pledge to Leila is another—beautifully crystallised in the rhyme of fourteen syllables which brings Canto VIII to a close: 'And Juan wept, / And made a vow to shield her, which he kept' (*Don Juan*, VIII.141.7–8).

Byron's contemporary readers felt that by mingling sentiment and satire, his texts undermined the possibility of sincerity altogether. But the effect of his poetry is more complex than this as it invites its readers to invest imaginative energy in different and sometimes contradictory directions. In the letter of the Marquise de Merteuil which Byron knew from *Les Liaisons Dangereuses*, the potential of design is treated with disarming negligence:

> I have nothing more to say, but to tell you a trifling story; perhaps you will not have leisure to read it, or to give so much attention to it as to understand it properly? At worst, it will be only a tale thrown away.[1]

This sentiment is invoked in Byron's beguiling aside on the probable fate of what he 'meant to say' in *Don Juan*—'Certes it would have been but thrown away' (*Don Juan*, IX.36.6). It epitomises the mixture of free-play and artfulness which characterises Byron's postmodernism. As Frank Kermode reminds us, 'without routine, without inherited structures, carnival loses its point; without social totalities there are no anti-social fragments'.[2] The patterns of English and Italian verse provide a structure which both energises and throws into relief the most sociable fragments in English Romanticism.

I have been arguing that Byron's intertextuality is inseparable from what we might call his postmodernism because it knowingly takes a risk on the reader to make or mar its effect. No one was more aware than Byron of the way that events could change the impact of a literary work and no one made a more conscious effort to inject biographical and historical detail into the realm of the aesthetic. Putting to one side his scepticism about the relationship between poet and reader, Byron went on writing poetry after his departure for Greece. There, he confided to Lady Blessington, he hoped that successful events would 'give a totally different reading to my thoughts, words, deeds'.[3] In his well-known 'On This Day I Complete My Thirty-Sixth Year', he returned to a favourite borrowing from *Macbeth* ('My days are in the yellow leaf', 5) and dallied for the last time with the image of a slumbering audience ('Awake! (*not* Greece—She *is* awake!)', 25). Irony at the expense of Romantic philhellenism did not, however, corrode the possibility of political commitment. In Byron's last known poem, usually called 'Last Words on Greece', he added to his wide range of poetic and dramatic allusions and the material he recuperated from newspapers a curious instance of self-quotation:

> What are to me those honours or renown
> Past or to come, a new-born people's cry
> Albeit for such I could despise a crown

1. Choderlos de Laclos, *Dangerous Connections; or, Letters Collected in a Society, and Published for the Instruction of other Societies*, by M. C***** de L***, 4 vols. (T. Hookham, 1784), IV, 101.
2. Frank Kermode, *History and Value* (Oxford: Clarendon Press, 1988), p. 143.
3. Lady Blessington's *Conversations of Lord Byron* (London, 1834), p. 227.

> Of aught save Laurel, or for such could die;
> I am the fool of passion—and a frown
>   Of thine to me is as an Adder's eye
> To the poor bird whose pinion fluttering down
>   Wafts unto death the breast it bore so high—
> Such is this maddening fascination grown—
>   So strong thy Magic—or so weak am I.

The poem was addressed to the Greek boy, Loukas Chalandritsanos, who did not love Byron in return. In all the anguish of hopeless infatuation, Byron's poem keeps in mind the possibility of other readers 'Past or to come' and keeps an open mind about the ongoing political cause ('or for such could die'). The a b a b rhyme relentlessly exposes the unanswered nature of Byron's desire and the pathetic image of a bird helpless before a snake threatens a collapse into self-pity before the wry alternative perspective of the last line. Woeful lovers are archetypal stage characters and Byron holds this tendency to self-dramatisation at bay by turning to actual performance. Embedded in the heart of the verse is a quotation from Byron's late tragedy *Werner; or, the Inheritance* (1822). 'I am the fool of passion' echoes a speech by Gabor, a blunt world-weary soldier, who rebukes himself for his faith in the treacherous young Ulric ('—you have vanquish'd me. / I was the fool of passion to conceive that I could cope with you' (II.i.304–6)).[4] The quotation of *Werner* is unsignalled and may be unconscious, but through a memory of this exchange, Byron rewrites his place in history as a marginal character in Loukas's eyes. With a simple shift of tense, Byron turns a dramatic *cri de coeur* into a self-deprecating summary of his new role. It is, however, consistent with his attitude to writing that a single disinterested reader has the power to sideline the most famous poet of the day. Like the Greek helmets Byron had made for his expedition, the allusion helps us to see the value of knowingly playing a role in a desperate situation. Byron was playing at being a soldier while striving to be one and his invocation of an earlier voice of experience reveals the quickening force of intertextual repetition which is not the 'blank' recycling of a spent art form, but an urgent encounter between poet and reader and what they might share in an increasingly alienating world.

---

4. The phrase 'fool of passion' may have been drawn from the eighteenth-century tragedy, *Athelstan*, by John Brown. It was produced in 1766 and was almost certainly in the Drury Lane Theatre Library when Byron was involved in the theatre management subcommittee. Brown's earlier play *Barbarossa* (1765) was included in Elizabeth Inchbald's 1808 collection of *British Theatre* which appears in the 1816 Sale Catalogue of Byron's library.

STUDIES OF INDIVIDUAL WORKS

DONALD H. REIMAN

Byron and the "Other": Poems 1808–1814[†]

* * *

After affirming the *self* in his earliest poetry, published in *Fugitive Pieces, Poems on Various Occasions,* and *Hours of Idleness,* Byron began to distance himself from his origins and selfhood almost as soon as he had clearly defined them.[1] Many of the poems in *Hours of Idleness* comment in a retrospective or even elegiac mood on Byron's brief past and on the traditions of his ancestors. But even as he defines himself as a Scottish youth, the heir to a Norman barony, a student, a lover, and a friend, he records the passing of that self-definition. In "Lachin y Gair," the stanzas beginning "When I rov'd a young Highlander o'er the dark heath," and those beginning "I would I were a careless child," Byron celebrates his youthful innocence in Scotland.[2] In "On Leaving Newstead Abbey," Byron recounts the military exploits of his baronial ancestors (mostly on behalf of lost causes) even as he bids farewell to these "Shades of heroes."[3] In a more elaborate "Elegy on Newstead Abbey" (I, 107–112), Byron traces the history of his seat from its foundation by Henry II, through its monastic days till the "royal sacrilege" of "Another HENRY . . . bids devotion's hallow'd echoes cease" (stanzas 10 and 11). In making Henry VIII's gift of the abbey to his ancestors an act of sacrilege, Byron already begins to distance himself from his Protestant and his baronial heritage. In the subsequent stanzas, he identifies himself with his cavalier ancestors, fighting with Lord Falkland against the "traitors" of the Parliamentary forces, and glories in the restoration of "the legal Ruler" (Charles II), siding with the Stuart monarchy against the Protestant, Hanoverian succession—an opposition to contemporary England that he maintained through *The Vision of Judgment* and *The Age of Bronze.*

Byron's other declared identities, besides a Scot and an English baron, include those of a student at Harrow and Cambridge, a romantic suitor of various girls (and, as Marchand has made clear, of John Edleston[4]), a sentimental friend of his school contemporaries, and—especially in a poem "On the Death of Mr. Fox" (I, 42–43)—as a fair-minded, patriotic liberal Whig. As Byron's letters and poems attest, he spent the rest of his short life transforming both his own and the world's conceptions of what those identities could and should signify.

† From *Intervals of Inspiration: The Skeptical Tradition and the Psychology of Romanticism* (Greenwood, FL: Penkevill Publishing Company, 1988). Copyright © 1988. Reprinted with permission of the author.

1. The publications that I have found most helpful with Byron's early poetry, besides Marchand's *Byron: A Biography,* are these: Willis W. Pratt, *Byron at Southwell* (Austin: Univ. of Texas Press, 1948); Andrew Rutherford, *Byron: A Critical Study* (Edinburgh: Oliver & Boyd, 1961); Robert F. Gleckner, *Byron and the Ruins of Paradise* (The Johns Hopkins Univ. Press, 1967); Gleckner, "From Selfish Spleen to Equanimity: Byron's Satires," *SiR,* 18 (1979), 173–205; and Frederick L. Beaty's *Byron the Satirist* (DeKalb: Northern Illinois Univ. Press, 1985).
2. Byron, *Poetical Works,* I, 103–104, 47–48, 121–123.
3. Byron, *Poetical Works,* I, 35–36.
4. See Marchand, *Byron: A Biography,* I, 107 ff.

Byron, in later life, always felt more attracted by the unlike "other" than by the mirror image of his own nature. The more distant from himself another person or concept was in social status, religion, political tendency, time, and place, the greater the attraction it held for him. This apparent anomaly can be explained psychologically (à la Manning) by Byron's need to assume a *persona* removed from the helpless, lame George Gordon Bryon who had been terrified by the memory of his reckless, violent father and warped by endless emotional quarrels with his passionate, unstable mother. His need to distance his values from himself can be explained sociologically by the disparity between his exalted family connections with the illustrious Gordons and Byrons and his obscure, poverty-stricken boyhood in Aberdeen (1794–98) and among the middle-class provincials at Southwell (1803–05). His Calvinistic sense of guilt probably made him wish to distance himself from his sinful life. These and other formative factors combined to motivate the adult Byron to seek his values outside himself. Like Keats, he was both moved by the "negative capability" to enter into other people's consiousnesses and prevented by a sense of self-preservation from allowing his selfhood to by swallowed up by any parochial context, whether the self-aggrandizing "patriotism" of the Whigs, the urbane nihilism of the Dandies, Lady Byron's narrow moralism, or Shelley's free-thinking speculations.

Byron responded to Henry Brougham's hostile review of *Hours of Idleness* in the *Edinburgh Review* by disavowing his own Scottish heritage.[5] *English Bards and Scotch Reviewers* (1809) was followed by another violent attack on Scots in *The Curse of Minerva* (1811), where Lord Elgin was the ostensible target. (Byron's violent quarrels with his mother during the years just before he left England for Iberia may have provoked additional animus in both these poems toward her Scottish heritage.) In *English Bards and Scotch Reviewers*, Byron describes the Edinburgh reviewers as, among other things, "Northern wolves that still in darkness prowl, / A coward brood, which mangle as they prey, / By brutal instinct, all that cross their way."[6] In *The Curse of Minerva*, Byron's attack becomes even more virulent. The poet answers Minerva's curse on the depredations of "Alaric and Elgin," "the Gothic monarch and the Pictish peer" who have ravaged classical sites, in these words:

> "Daughter of Jove! in Britain's injur'd name,
> A true-born Briton may the deed disclaim.
> Frown not on England; England owns him not:
> Athena! no; thy plunderer was a Scot.

*   *   *

> And well I know within that bastard land
> Hath Wisdom's goddess never held command:
> A barren soil, where Nature's germs confin'd
> To stern sterility can stint the mind,
> Whose thistle well betrays the niggard earth,
> Emblem of all to whom the land gives birth;

---

5. *Edinburgh Review,* XI (January 1808), 285–289; *Romantics Reviewed,* Part B, II, 833–835. In the review, Brougham concentrates on two of Byron's own definitions of himself: the titlepage designations of the author as "George Gordon, *Lord* Byron, a *Minor.*" Neither Byron's minority nor his title, writes Brougham, excuse his publication of poems of such a dead-level of mediocrity.
6. See lines 426–539 (*Poetical Works,* I, 242–246).

Each genial influence nurtur'd to resist,
A land of meanness, sophistry, and mist. . . .
(lines 125–138; I, 324–325)

In *English Bards and Scotch Reviewers*, Byron not only rejected his Scottish heritage, but he also denied any intention of becoming a serious author. Byron carried this denial of self with him to Italy, distinguishing himself from mere men of letters in *Don Juan* and in his prose attacks on Bowles. In *English Bards* he also denied his natural political allegiance by attacking Lord Holland and the Whigs. Finally, that poem contains a subtler and more intimate denial of self when Byron declares William Gifford to be his literary hero. For Byron was honoring not only the editor of the *Quarterly Review*, but the author of *The Baviad* and *The Mæviad*, attacks on the harmless poetasters of the Della Cruscan school, in which Gifford—himself a poetaster—viciously satirized the crutches of lame Mary Robinson ("Perdita").[7] Byron's identification of himself with this harsh, bitter Tory satirist who made fun of the advanced age, ill-health, and physical deformities of powerless people says more to me about Byron's psyche than any other instance of his *mobilité*. Byron clearly chose to renounce any aspect of himself that he thought was vulnerable to attack. Fearing ridicule because of his lameness, he could praise Gifford, a cripple who attacked the lame, as the moral "physician" of his age: "Arouse thee, GIFFORD! be thy promise claimed, / Make bad men better, or at least ashamed" (lines 829–830).

In July 1816, Byron went over a copy of *English Bards and Scotch Reviewers* and wrote a series of notes that show him once again distancing himself from many of his earlier opinions.[8] Between 1810 and 1816, Byron had become close friends with Francis Jeffrey, Walter Scott, "Monk" Lewis, Thomas Moore, John Murray, Lord and Lady Holland, and others he had attacked in the poem. Critics and biographers have been divided as whether to blame Byron for his early critical bad taste or to praise him for his flexibility and the deep-seated congeniality that enabled him to win over or be won over by the enemies he had made by means of this poem. But, in truth, Byron was only doing what came naturally to him. In 1810, when he had attacked the Whigs and Scots, they represented the self he thought he wanted to be; by the time he withdrew his censure in 1816, he had already disavowed and been exiled from that old self. Byron's *mobilité* was, clearly, a psychological compulsion that he only gradually learned to convert into a creative perspective.

Whereas *English Bards and Scotch Reviewers* displays the least attractive side of Byron's tendency to ally himself always with the "other," the four cantos of *Childe Harold's Pilgrimage* develop the positive side of this tendency. *Childe Harold's Pilgrimage* is a unified poem, written in two stages of Byron's life as the two parts of *Don Quixote* and *Faust* were written at different stages of Cervantes' and Goethe's careers. Though the late *ottava*

---

7. See *The Baviad* (1791; facsimile reprint in *Romantic Context: Poetry*, 1978), page 9. Leigh Hunt, Byron's contemporary, alludes to this piece of baseness in several publications, including Chapter XII of his *Autobiography* (London: Smith, Elder, 1850), II, 86–87, and Byron, himself lame, could hardly have overlooked or forgotten it. As a crowning irony, Gifford himself was bent and crippled as the result of a childhood accident.
8. Byron, *Poetry*, I, 381 fn.; *Poetical Works*, ed. McGann, I, 399 ff.

rima poems are greater works of literature, Byron could never have reached that level of artistic discipline, had he not in *Childe Harold's Pilgrimage* transformed the psychic weakness that forced him to disavow the self into an aesthetic strength.[9]

A "pilgrimage," whether viewed literally or figuratively, involves a journey from the sinful (or inadequate) pilgrim's home either to a holy place from which he hopes to derive inspiration, enabling him to live more meaningfully in his everyday world, or (as in Bunyan's *Pilgrim's Progress*) to a new land where the limitations of his unhappy origins will be left behind. The first two cantos of *Childe Harold's Pilgrimage* (1812) recount the journey of "Childe Harold" from his sinful identity in Christian England, through a series of observations and semi-adventures, to the sites of his spiritual inspiration in Classical Greece—particularly Parnassus and Marathon. *Childe Harold,* Karl Kroeber has suggested, is a "mournful *Odyssey,*"[1] and Cantos I–II (especially the association of "Calypso's isles" with Harold's "new Calypso" at Malta[2]) hint that Byron himself conceived of the pilgrim in the first two cantos as a cynical modern Odysseus, returning to his spiritual home, where his idealistic vision is restored.

The narrator represents the rejuvenated self that writes after the pilgrimage, whereas Childe Harold is the protagonist who slowly comes to self-knowledge while undergoing the experiences of the journey. This distinction conforms to the dichotomy between the protagonist (the author's past self) and the narrator (the author's present self) found in all autobiographical writing. "Childe Harold" is, at the beginning of Canto I, far removed from the narrator. Once that distance has been articulated, the archaic style (used to identify the old, unregenerated self) disappears, and by the end of Canto II the narrator's authorial voice permeates the poem as the two personae merge into one.

Byron employs a moral geography and ethnology in all four cantos of *Childe Harold's Pilgrimage.* In Cantos I–II, the action moves from England, which has thrust upon Harold all the vices of a decadent, commercialized Christian tradition; to Portugal, a Christian country of even more corrupt heritage, where every man truly does have his price; thence to Spain, reviving after its own decadence to a renewal of feudal pride. After an interlude at British Gibraltar, in a British man-of-war, and at British Malta (the new Calypso's isle that tempts him to abandon his quest), the poet encounters more honorable natures among the fierce mountaineers in Albania and Turkish Europe. Though classical Greece, the object of the quest, is no longer protected and ruled by such ancient deities as Athena/Minerva and the Muses, but has suffered a bastard Christian-Moslem decadence, both Nature and the remains of ancient art and culture inspire those cognizant of the great Classical past. At last Byron realizes that the true heirs of the

---

9. Among the studies not hitherto mentioned that especially helped to shape my understanding of Byron's art in general and *Childe Harold's Pilgrimage* in particular are: William A. Borst, *Lord Byron's First Pilgrimage* (New Haven: Yale Univ. Press, 1948); Ernest J. Lovell, Jr., *Byron: The Record of a Quest* (Austin: Univ. of Texas Press, 1949); Karl Kroeber, *Romantic Narrative Art* (Madison: Univ. of Wisconsin Press, 1960); Ward Pafford, "Byron and the Mind of Man: *Childe Harold* III–IV and *Manfred,*" in *SiR,* 1 (1962), 105–127; Jerome J. McGann, *Fiery Dust: Byron's Poetic Development* (Chicago: Univ. of Chicago Press, 1968); Carl Woodring, "Nature, Art, Reason, and Imagination in *Childe Harold,*" in *Romantic and Victorian,* ed. W. P. Elledge and R. L. Hoffman (Rutherford, NJ: Fairleigh Dickinson Univ. Press, 1971), pp. 147–157.

1. Kroeber, *Romantic Narrative Art,* p. 137.

2. See *Childe Harold,* II. stanzas 29–33; *Poetical Works,* ed. McGann, II, 53–54.

glory that was Greece are pilgrims like himself who "throng" from the West to "Hail the bright clime of battle and song" (II. stanza 91). Such pilgrims "approach this consecrated land" reverently and refrain from defacing "the scenes, already how defac'd!" (by Lord Elgin and others).

Thus, in a dramatic turn, Byron assumes as his rightful heritage the values of Classical Greece, rather than those of the merry monks or warlike barons of Newstead Abbey, the cynical and stupid British diplomacy of the Convention of Cintra, or the bloody battles against the French at Talavera and Albuera, where "Ambition's honour'd fools!" "feed the crow . . . / And fertilize the field that each pretends to gain" (I. stanzas 41–42). The first two cantos also specifically reject both reckless hedonism and sensual indolence, not only Childe Harold's own earlier experience of "Sin's long labyrinth," but also William Beckford, "England's wealthiest son" (I. stanzas 22–23), Mrs. Spencer Smith, the "new Calypso" or Circe (II. stanzas 30–35), and the Spanish vices of Seville and Cadiz.[3] Finally, the first installment of *Childe Harold* rejects extremes of superstitious piety and asceticism, these examples drawn from various cultures—the hermit Honorius, who hoped "to merit Heaven by making earth a Hell" (I. stanza 20), and the great palace-monastery at Mafra (I. stanza 29). The relative innocence and simplicity of Spanish peasants and Albanian mountaineers is contrasted favorably with the concomitant vices and corruption that accompany any accumulation of wealth or power in these societies at Seville and Cadiz, the capital of Ali Pacha, or Turkish-ruled Athens.

Harold-Byron learns from his first pilgrimage that Classical Greece survives primarily in the minds of educated men from schools such as Harrow and universities such as Cambridge. This idea thematically justifies Byron's late insertion of the final elegiac stanzas commemorating the deaths of John Edleston, John Wingfield, and his own mother.[4] So, too, the disillusioned, world-weary tone of the final stanzas seems appropriate when we consider that Harold-Byron has traveled throughout the world seeking the ideals of Classical Greece, only to find that they exist nowhere more fully than in the Unhappy Valley where his journey began. Though Byron had succeeded in exposing the limitations of his native culture, he had found no living embodiment of the ideal of reason, courage, and integrity he sought to worship in "august Athena" (I. 2). Instead, he had to remain content with the skeptical wisdom of Socrates, "Athena's wisest son! / 'All that we know is, nothing can be known.'"[5]

The experiences reflected in *Childe Harold's Pilgrimage*, I–II, forced Byron to draw values from the somewhat broader spectrum of human nature and the deepened knowledge of himself that he brought back with him from Iberia and the East. But, as Manning demonstrates, Byron continued to try to exorcise the powerful memory of his father by returning compulsively again and again to variants of the Oedipal plot in his poetic romances.[6] Each

---

3. Canto I. stanzas 45–46, 54–59, 71–84, and "To Inez." Byron contrasts the "young-eyed Lewdness" of Seville and the bloody bullfight he saw on his way to Cadiz with the "fooleries" of lower-and middle-class Londoners on their Sunday outings to Highgate. Here the contrasting innocence of the unheroic bourgeois British society is interwoven with the fierce heroism of the rustic Spanish freedom-fighters and the sensual and blood-thirsty entertainments of the Spanish upper classes.

4. Canto II. stanzas 9, 94–96.

5. Canto II. stanza 7. This conception of Socrates's message was the basis of the Academic Skeptics' claim that Socrates was the fountainhead of their philosophy.

6. See Manning, *Byron and His Fictions*, pp. 35–61.

of these poems—*The Giaour* (1813), *The Bride of Abydos* (1813), *The Corsair* (1814), *Lara* (1814), *The Siege of Corinth* and *Parisina* (published together in 1816)—records the vain efforts of a young lover/hero to overcome an older chieftain who is in one way or another his rival for the love of a woman. Either the elder ultimately destroys the younger man, or—if the youth kills the elder—the young protagonist is either totally corrupted (*Lara*) or crushed by unrelieved guilt (*The Giaour*).

＊   ＊   ＊

In *Parisina* and *The Siege of Corinth* Byron took his characters and plots from historical sources. In his *Ode to Napoleon Buonaparte* (1814), Byron seized on his most significant contemporary to illustrate that following one's ungoverned self-will leads only to abject slavery:

> By gazing on thyself grown blind,
> Thou taught'st the rest to see.

＊   ＊   ＊

> Nor till thy fall could mortals guess
> Ambition's less than littleness!

Three additional stanzas, written at Murray's request but never authorized for publication during Byron's lifetime, contrast Napoleon's littleness ("Vain froward child of Empire! say, / Are all thy playthings snatched away?") with the greatness of George Washington:

> The Cincinnatus of the West,
> Whom envy dared not hate,
> Bequeathed the name of Washington,
> To make man blush there was but one![7]

In Napoleon, with whom, he identified his own passions and ambitions, Byron saw the parable of the unruly self; in Washington, whose motivations Byron could only dimly sense, he sought his historical "other," although Byron, like Shelley, seems to have resisted the idea of proclaiming a slave-owner his political ideal.

In 1814 Byron aided two Jewish musicians, John Braham and Isaac Nathan, by contributing a series of lyrics to be set to traditional *Hebrew Melodies*.[8] Though Byron does not actually confront the heritage of the Old Testament, as he does those of ancient Greece and Rome, *Hebrew Melodies* evidences his willingness to identify with the traditions and aspirations of a long-oppressed people just beginning to integrate themselves into British society. The task both expanded his personal range of experience and provided another clear example of Byron's tendency to take the values of his poetry from an "other."

＊   ＊   ＊

7. *Poetical Works*, III, 259–266; 456–458. Byron regarded these additional stanzas—and, indeed, the entire *Ode*—as poetically inferior (see Byron, *Letters*, IV, 103–107).
8. Published January 1815. For a full account of the poems and their context, see Thomas L. Ashton, *Byron's Hebrew Melodies* (London: Routledge and Kegan Paul, 1972).

MARILYN BUTLER

The Orientalism of Byron's *Giaour*[†]

Orientalism is a major theme of English Romanticism. Much, even perhaps most, of the best poetry of Byron and Shelley is set between Greece and the Hindu Kush, a region which in their day signified the crumbling Ottoman empire and the insecure overland route to British India. This was the Debateable Land between a Europe locked in a war involving at one time or another every major state, and the supposedly wealthy empire and trading monopoly which Britain had secured in the East. The geographical significations should be taken at face value, since these are materialist poets, for whom the place of a poem's setting means what it says, and the time is always in some sense the present. Hazlitt came to view Byron's contemporaneity as a reproach: 'his Lordship's Muse spurns the olden time, and affects all the supercilious airs of a modern fine lady and an upstart'.[1] John Hamilton Reynolds thought his friend Keats scored over Byron by getting away from specifics of time and place. Keats 'does not make a home for his mind in one land—its productions are an universal story, not an eastern tale'.[2] Whether these two are right about the value of what Byron did, they are surely not wrong as to the fact. Whatever the East came afterwards to represent as an abstraction—a paradisal religious region of the mind for German academics, a place of sexual release and fantasy for French artists—in English culture in the Napoleonic war period it is also the site of a pragmatic contest among the nations for world power.

When Byron left England for the Mediterranean on 2 July 1809 he surely expected the focus of his trip to be more European than *Childe Harold* I and II, considered as a single poem, actually is. He visited exotic lands now fallen into slavery, but showing symptoms of heroic resistance: first Portugal and Spain, afterwards Albania and Greece. Colourful freedom-fighters, present-day equivalents of Scott's highly saleable Border rievers and Highland chieftains, must have been the bait that took Byron initially to the Iberian peninsula. After the French invaded Spain and Portugal in 1807, some of the Spanish peasantry rose against them in the spring of 1808, and were supported that August by the landing of a British army. Byron a year later arrives not quite as a tourist, more as a literary type of war correspondent, an early Hemingway. The whole of *Childe Harold* I and II in its original form, most of it written in Greece between 31 October 1809 and 28 March 1810, has the stamp of investigative journalism, in which the poetic reporter looks for signs of rebellion and (since he is highly partisan) satirizes the natives when, as in Portugal and Greece, he finds them supine.

For Byron the exercise is decidedly not designed to help the British war effort. Conservative intellectuals had rushed to make capital for Britain out of these uprisings by peasants against the theoretically democratic French. Wordsworth in *The Convention of Cintra* and Coleridge in *The Friend* both

---

† From *Byron and the Limits of Fiction*, ed. Bernard Beatty and Vincent Newey (Liverpool: Liverpool University Press, 1988). Reprinted with permission of Liverpool University Press.
1. William Hazlitt, 'Lord Byron', *The Spirit of the Age* (1825); reprinted in *Byron: The Critical Heritage*, ed. Andrew Rutherford (London, 1970), p. 269.
2. J. H. Reynolds, review of *Endymion* in *The Alfred*, 6 October 1818; reprinted in *Keats: The Critical Heritage*, ed. G. M. Matthews (London, 1971), p. 119.

extolled the Spanish people for confirming Burke's view of human nature as *naturally* religious, traditional, socially bonded to a little platoon rather than to the abstract concepts of liberty and fraternity. Liberals like Byron and Francis Jeffrey were correspondingly embarrassed by Spanish resistance to the French, which had to be acknowledged as popular, but was also rightist, Catholic, and ideologically uncongenial to them. Byron contrives to dilute the topic in his first two Cantos of *Childe Harold* by placing it in a wider context and even trumping it with the yet more glorious possibility of an uprising in Greece, the spiritual home of liberty.

Significantly, Byron was not alone in linking the Spanish struggle with matters further east. Three of the most serious older poets then writing, Landor, Scott and Southey, all chipped in with works on the Peninsula, managing to choose the very same episode, which had a hero, Don Roderick, who could claim to be the father of all Spanish freedom fighters through his resistance to the Moorish invasion in the early eighth century. The subject was made obvious by its analogies with recent events at the Spanish court. The Moors were invited into Spain by a traitor, Count Julian, as an act of revenge after his daughter, la Cava, had been raped by Don Roderick. King Charles IV of Spain, or his Prime Minister Manuel de Godoy, the Queen's paramour, made the Treaty of Fountainebleau which in 1807 brought the French into the Peninsula. Still, and perhaps by chance, by the time Landor published his tragedy *Count Julian* (1812), and Scott and Southey their long narrative poems on Roderick, in 1812 and 1814, the fact that they were describing the Islamic occupation of a Christian country looked up-to-the-minute for a quite new reason. It became increasingly likely that there would be a war of liberation in the eastern Mediterranean, and there, in Greece, the religions of conqueror and conquered were as they had been in eighth-century Spain.

Southey, the most hawkish as a war poet of these three, was also the last to publish, so that his *Roderick, the Last of the Goths* had less topical impact than most of his work. Already by 1809 Southey liked to represent war with Napoleon not simply as a fight against an alien despotism, but, more popularly, as a Christian crusade of later days. In July 1811, when Byron got back to Britain, he found plenty of signs of a more resolute war policy than when he had left, and signs too of a vigorous Evangelical campaign in favour of proselytism in the East. It was in relation to India that the Evangelical pressure-group known as the Clapham Sect first mounted the campaign that for Wilberforce even outdid the abolition of slavery as a national moral crusade. Hitherto it had been the policy of the British East India Company, strongly supported by Parliament, to leave the Indian social structure undisturbed, or if parts were defunct, as was the case with Hindu law, to revive them. It was a cornerstone of Company policy to respect the spheres of influence of Hindu and Moslem religious leaders. But as long ago as 1792 the Evangelical Charles Grant, a servant of the Company first in India, now at its London headquarters in Leadenhall Street, wrote a tract which challenged the old policy of religious coexistence not merely on religious but on moral and social grounds. Writing for the minister under Pitt responsible for Indian affairs, Henry Dundas, Grant argued that Hinduism was not, as Warren Hastings and William Jones had argued in the 1770s and 1780s, a social creed rooted in immemorial village customs which also found expression in an indigenous code of law. In fact the laws of Manu, a code on which Jones as chief justice in Calcutta expended immense labour, were, Grant asserted, chaotic and in their origins despotic, an imposition on the populace from above. The 'cruel genius' which pervaded them was the ethos of Hinduism, and it encouraged fraud, lying and the abuse of people of inferior caste.[3]

Grant's long paper, though not published until admitted as evidence in the parliamentary debates of 1813, was circulated in India House and Evangelical circles in 1797, and frequently seems to have been echoed in the first decade of the new century, as Grant's Evangelical faction struggled for control of the London end of the company's affairs. From 1802 Southey took up the campaign to allow Christian missionaries in among the Indian population, initially in reviews for the Dissenter-owned *Annual Review*, then in 1805 in his epic *Madoc*. The epic first took shape in 1794 as a romantic tale of a twelfth-century quest to the New World in search of social and religious freedom—a historical analogue to the pantisocracy plan—but Southey revamped it extensively between 1803 and 1805. The final version makes a strong case for the mass conversion of native peoples where, as in pre-Conquest Mexico, their own religion was cruel and oppressive. Southey's Mexico worships a serpent cult served by priests who practise human sacrifice and keep a cruel despotism in power. It is a paradigm of a socially unacceptable religion which has close resemblances to Grant's portrayal of Hinduism in 1792, for both these analyses of religions concentrate on their impact on the welfare of the common people, what Grant called the tendency of Hinduism to forge 'a life of abject slavery and unparalleled depravity'. Indeed, in an article written a year before his Hindu epic, *The Curse of Kehama* (1810), Southey draws attention to the similarity between the two religions: 'Except the system of Mexican priestcraft, no fabric of human fraud has ever been discovered so deadly as the Braminical'.[4]

*   *   *

In July 1811 Byron thus found that a topic overlapping that of his new poem—the small Eastern nation absorbed into a foreign empire[5]—had been recently used by a rival poet to advocate a nationalistic religious policy for the British in *their* empire. At first sight it could benefit the Greeks if they engaged the sympathy of a powerful and wealthy stratum of British public opinion. But Byron plainly saw mostly disadvantages in representing Greek liberation as a Christian struggle. One arose from what he knew of Greek politics: in return for religious freedom the leaders of the Greek Orthodox church operated, according to a modern historian, 'as guarantors of the loyalty of the Orthodox populations to the Ottoman empire'.[6] The second was longer-term and more telling. The imminent fall of the Ottoman empire was certain to lead to a scramble for pickings by the Christian European powers, who now in the later war years found the swelling religious revival handing them new moral justifications for annexing East-

3. Charles Grant, 'Observations on the State of Society among the Asiatic Subjects of Great Britain, particularly with respect to Morals, and on the means of Improving It. Written chiefly in the Year 1792', *Parliamentary Papers*, 1812–13, X, Paper 282, p. 66.
4. [Robert Southey], 'Periodical Accounts, relative to the Baptist Missionary Society, &c', *Quarterly Review*, I (1809), 194. Cf. Grant, p. 44.
5. Referring to Southey's *Curse of Kehama*, summarized in the preceding paragraphs omitted here. (*Editor's note*).
6. Richard Clogg, *The Movement for Greek Independence, 1770–1821* (London, 1976), p. xiii.

ern populations. If only to protect Greece's chances of real independence, it was most important for Byron to play down the religious implications of the brewing storm there. Within a month of his return, in August 1811, he sent a new note for *Childe Harold* II, stanzas 3–9, to his friend R. C. Dallas, who was helping him with arrangements for publication. Dallas advised him not to publish it, and Byron agreed; it appears in McGann's new Oxford edition in the version Dallas published in his *Recollections*:

> In this age of bigotry, when the puritan and priest have changed places, and the wretched catholic is visited with the 'sins of his fathers', even unto generations far beyond the pale of the commandment, the cast of opinion in these stanzas will doubtless meet with many a contemptuous anathema. But let it be remembered, that the spirit they breathe is desponding, not sneering, scepticism; that he who has seen the Greek and Moslem superstitions contending for mastery over the former shrines of Polytheism,—who has left in his own country 'Pharisees, thanking God that they are not like Publicans and Sinners', and Spaniards in theirs, abhorring the Heretics, who have holpen them in their need,—will be not a little bewildered, and begin to think, that as only one of them can be right, they may most of them be wrong. With regard to morals, and the effect of religion on mankind, it appears, from all historical testimony, to have had less effect in making them love their neighbours, than inducing that cordial christian abhorrence between sectaries and schismatics. The Turks and Quakers are the most tolerant; if an Infidel pays heratch to the former, he may pray how, when, and where he pleases; and the mild tenets, and devout demeanour of the latter, make their lives the truest commentary on the Sermon of the Mount.[7]

In 1814, two years after publication, Byron added ten new stanzas to *Childe Harold* Canto II, which focus upon the danger that foreign intervention will lead to fresh enslavement, that the Greeks must free themselves, and that religion is not the issue.[8]

The first of Byron's oriental poems written under the influence of the new, more polarized attitudes to the East was *The Giaour*, composed late 1812–March 1813, published in its first state in May 1813, and added to throughout that year. These dates coincide with the height of the Evangelical campaign to mobilize public opinion behind missions to India, a policy still opposed by the majority of directors of the East India Company as well as by the majority of members of Parliament. It was William Wilberforce, an M.P. of great eloquence and great moral authority, who saw that the Administration and the Commons could not be carried without an extra-parliamentary campaign. Wilberforce organized support not merely among Anglicans and old, respectable Dissent, but among enthusiastic popular sectarians more genuinely given to proselytizing, such as the Baptists, who in the teeth of official disapproval had been sending missions to India for a decade and a half.[9] The campaign worked; the volume and the

---

7. Byron, note to *Childe Harold*, II.3–9, published in R. C. Dallas, *Recollections of the Life of Lord Byron* (1824), pp. 171–72; reprinted in *Lord Byron: The Complete Poetical Works*, ed. J. J. McGann (Oxford, 1980–), II, 283.

8. Cf. especially Canto II, stanzas 27, 77–83, 89–90.

9. For the controversy over renewing the Company's charter, and especially over the insertion of the 'pious clause', see Eric Stokes, *English Utilitarians and India* (Oxford, 1959), pp. 28ff., and Ainslie Embree, *Charles Grant and British Rule in India* (London, 1962), especially pp. 141ff.

fervour of public support induced Parliament to include in the Charter Act of 1813 a 'pious clause' which permitted missions to be sent to India and allowed for the establishment of an Anglican bishopric there. Though the practical effects were much slower than enthusiasts expected, the symbolic consequences were great. The secular Enlightenment intellectuals who had advocated governing India by old, Indian ways were now to be steadily driven back by a coalition of middle-class ideologues, Evangelicals and utilitarians, who believed in changing India for something better.

Byron's concept of other nations' independence was that of an Enlightenment intellectual, who respected the autonomy of other cultures, but was inclined to admire them precisely for their otherness, their unreformed feudal 'romantic' features. The decisive shift in the British public's perception of an Eastern population which was signalled in 1813 irked him partly because, like the Spanish uprising, it exposed the fault line in late Enlightenment liberalism, its equivocal attitude to mass movements. By marshalling popular opinion at home, Christians had won permission to go out and teach a populace abroad. Southey, one of the leading advocates of this Christianized and popular form of imperialism, remained Byron's chief literary antagonist throughout his life, and it is of course a great mistake to accept unexamined Byron's portrayals of Southey in *Don Juan* and *The Vision of Judgement* as merely a paid government hack. Southey was the only one of the trio of 'Lake Poets' to remain a genuine populist, the more troubling because by 1810 he was a Tory populist, and Tory populism almost certainly commanded more general British support than 'jacobinism' ever did. His influence, and that of the campaign of 1813, is felt profoundly in *The Giaour*. It is telling for example that Islam in that poem is the religion of leaders as well as followers, and can be illustrated from elegant courtly literature, while Christianity has no spokesmen in the poem but ignorant zealots.

As learned annotated verse, set in part of the Ottoman empire, Byron's *Childe Harold* II and *The Giaour* have often been spoken of as formally indebted to the first of Southey's romance epics, *Thalaba* (1801). Byron does indeed share with this poem by Southey a format, a concern with Islam, and a battery of sources in eighteenth-century learned Western orientalism. J. J. McGann lists other debts, some of them structurally or textually significant, such as the fragment form, which Byron found in Samuel Rogers's *The Vision of Columbus* (1812).[1] But images, phrasing and formalistic details do not necessarily get to the centre of a poem, nor distinguish it from others, nor explain why it had to be written. *The Giaour* opposes two men who love the same woman, one a Moslem, the other a (nominal) Christian, and it is concerned with their creeds' attitudes to sexual love, to death and to an individual afterlife. In his treatment of the social implications of different religions, Byron often seems to be matching the materialism and pragmatism of his newly evangelized opponent Southey, though Byron's tone remains jeeringly, perhaps by implication snobbishly sceptical, and his political drift is quite different. The argument of this paper is that for its central subject, and indeed for much of its power and urgency, *The Giaour* is indebted to a current controversy, in part outside 'literature' as narrowly conceived, but already reflected in literature.

1. McGann, *Complete Poetical Works*, III, 415.

Texts by Grant and Southey, some in verse, represent the ideological attitudes and social interests to which Byron was opposed at a level far more fundamental than his taste for the orientalizing of, say, Beckford.

Unlike *Childe Harold* II, which precedes it, and the Oriental romances to come, *The Giaour*, a love story, appears to have nothing directly to do with Greek independence. The 'Giaour' of the title (the word means foreigner or infidel) tries to save his mistress Leila, a slave in Hassan's harem, from being tied in a sack and thrown into the sea as a ritual, socially-approved punishment for her adultery. When he fails, he joins a band of Albanian brigands in order to ambush Hassan and kill him. In spite of incidental resemblances to (for example) Scott's *Marmion*, *The Giaour* begins very emphatically in the present day and in a mood to reject the romance of history. The first narrator, an educated Westerner, contemplates modern Greeks under Turkish rule, and finds them so enfeebled that he cannot bring himself to tell a story of heroic Greeks in olden times (ll.143–58). At this point indeed his narration fails completely, and we switch to the 'Turkish Fragment' announced in the poem's subtitle, supposedly a popular ballad narrated by a Moslem in a coffee-house. The complex narrational method balances the Western and Eastern points of view and impedes the Western reader from reading Hassan with Western sympathies, since to the Moslem fisherman who witnesses the violent main action it is the Giaour, not Hassan, who is the alien—'I know thee not, I loathe thy race' (l.191). Byron's Oriental tale out-Southeys Southey by being 'naturalistically' anti-Western. This does not prevent him from framing the fisherman in a more educated and cosmopolitan context, or from overlaying his voice with the sardonic commentary provided in Byron's dense, witty and idiosyncratic notes.

Byron's notes, here more personal as well as more generally informative than in any other of the tales, put greater emphasis on the Moslem governors than on the Christian governed, for, in this story of Athens, the native Greeks are virtually invisible. Similarly, though the turbulent, tormented Christian Giaour is the poem's hero, it takes some while for him to become the focus of attention. For at least half the story we are exploring the religion and psyche of Hassan, his Turkish antagonist, and noticing that he is socialized in his world, while the Giaour seems friendless there, except for Leila. The notes convey undisguised admiration for the warlike qualities taught by Mohammedanism—the courage instilled in warriors, for example, by their belief that if they fall in battle they will be welcomed to Paradise by a beautiful woman, or houri. Byron also derives satisfaction from revealing to his readers the dislike with which Christians are regarded in the East. But his respect for Turks does not extend to their regime in Athens, which he roundly abuses—'A pandar and a eunuch . . . now *govern* the *governor* of Athens' (l.151n).

Byron often retains an urbane Voltairean detachment when he writes of the Moslem's conception of the afterlife:

> Monkir and Nekir are the inquisitors of the dead, before whom the corpse undergoes a slight noviciate and preparatory training for damnation. If the answers are none of the clearest, he is hauled up with a scythe and thumped down with a red hot mace till properly seasoned, with a variety of subsidiary probations. The office of these

angels is no sinecure; there are but two; and the number of orthodox deceased being in a small proportion to the remainder, their hands are always full.[2]

But this at least is colourful, and thus, like the other Moslem superstitions Byron treats, relatively attractive. The notes are more consistently derisory where they touch on Christianity. 'The monk's sermon is omitted. It seems to have had so little effect upon the patient, that it could have no hopes from the reader' (l.1207n). It is noticeable, too, that Hassan dies consoled by the knowledge that he can expect rewards in heaven because he is killed by an infidel. The sympathetic Moslem fisherman takes pious pleasure from this fact (though Byron ironically defamiliarizes such piety by his sly emphasis on the non-Hebraic, non-ascetic notion of the houris). Mohammedanism performs at least two useful social functions, it seems: to console people and to draw them together. But from the monk who later in the poem attends the deathbed of the Giaour there is no such fellow-feeling. The monk views the Giaour as a damned soul:

> If ever evil angel bore
> The form of mortal, such he wore.
> (ll.912–13)

Any possibility of Christian solidarity vanishes when the Giaour rejects the monk's half-hearted consolation and takes over the burden of the narration, with a 'confession' as theologically perverse as that of Pope's Eloisa: he will not hear of a Heaven which omits the sexual happiness he has known and lost on earth:

> Who falls from all he knows of bliss
> Cares little into what abyss.
> (ll.1157–58)

In his philosophy it is not the monk's transcendental Deity, but Leila, who is

> My good, my guilt, my weal, my woe,
> My hope on high—my all below.
> (ll.1182–83)

In a dying vision which echoes the Mohammedan belief in the houri, he sees the ghost of the drowned Leila. Unlike Hassan, the ungodly Giaour is loath to believe in apparitions, yet he begs her to stay and let him share her fate, even bodily, rather than leave him to enter some future existence without her:

> But, shape or shade!—whate'er thou art,
> In mercy, ne'er again depart—
> Or farther with thee bear my soul,
> Than winds can waft—or waters roll!
> (ll.1315–18)

As a love story, one of those classic late-Enlightenment triangles of the *Werther* type that oppose the free and intuitive behaviour of illicit lovers to the

---

2. McGann, III, 420: Byron's note to *Giaour*, I.748.

religious propriety of the legal husband, *The Giaour* achieves a greater sim-
plicity and intensity than the tales which succeed it, *The Bride of Abydos* and
The Corsair. However accidentally it was put together, the effect is elegantly
compact. To withhold the Giaour's own voice, to deny us entry to his con-
sciousness, until he comes to utter his fiercely heterodox dying 'confession',
is to give him the special status of one speaking from the grave, the domain
long since of the only people he has cared about, his mistress and his enemy.
As a humane and personal morality, the Giaour's creed is plainly Byron's: he
sincerely hates a religion that instructs a man to tie his wife in a sack and
throw her into the sea for infidelity. Hassan's pious docility puts him in the
same category as two of the Old Testament's Just Men Byron later depicted,
Abel, who loves God better than his brother Cain, and Noah, who lets drown
the girl his son loves, because she is not on the list of those God wants saved
from the Flood. Byron's morality prefers the personal and human to the
abstract and divine, a point he characteristically makes by redeeming a char-
acter technically criminal through the trait of total sexual loyalty to a single
individual. (Women may have this reckless sexual loyalty too, especially in his
later work—Myrrha in *Sardanapalus*, Aholibamah in *Heaven and Earth*.) But
nowhere perhaps is there a study of the Byronic humanist so concentrated,
intense, and personally felt, so skilfully central and unimpeded, as in the last
five hundred lines of *The Giaour*, where the intellectually superior hero con-
fronts the dense priestly bigot trying to prepare him for a Christian afterlife.

For all the elaboration of its fragmented format, the poem achieves sim-
plicity through its ferocious concentration on one moral issue—whether
love between human beings is not superior to and perhaps incompatible
with belief in either of the two great monotheistic religions. The two halves
of the poem can be seen in the end as equally preoccupied with this issue.
Byron enforces the point by symmetrically ending the first 'Moslem' part
with a meditation on the afterlife, first as the pious Hassan will encounter
it, then, anticipating the end, as the Giaour eventually should. The Moslem
section ends with the fisherman's curse, a pronouncement which rises to
the strange fanatical intensity so characteristic of this poem, and, in
Byron's perception, of the discourse of religion itself:

> And fire unquench'd, unquenchable—
> Around—within—thy heart shall dwell,
> Nor ear can hear, nor tongue can tell
> The tortures of that inward hell!—
> But first, on earth as Vampire sent,
> Thy corse shall from its tomb be rent;
> Then ghastly haunt thy native place,
> And suck the blood of all thy race,
> There from thy daughter, sister, wife,
> At midnight drain the stream of life;
> Yet loathe the banquet which perforce
> Must feed thy livid living corse;
> Thy victims ere they yet expire
> Shall know the daemon for their sire,
> As cursing thee, thou cursing them,
> Thy flowers are wither'd on the stem.
> But one that for thy crime must fall—

> The youngest—most belov'd of all,
> Shall bless thee with a *father's* name—
> That word shall wrap thy heart in flame!
> Yet must thou end thy task, and mark
> Her cheek's last tinge, her eye's last spark . . .
> Wet with thine own best blood shall drip,
> Thy gnashing tooth and haggard lip;
> Then stalking to thy sullen grave—
> Go—and with Gouls and Afrits rave.
>   (ll.751–72, 781–84)

In gloating over the Giaour's hell to come, in the arms of human loved ones, the fisherman ironically anticipates his voluntary dying preference of eternity under any conditions with Leila. But the curse is also a religious statement, though it represents the dark underside of religion, its primitive superstition and its cruelty. Rhetorically it makes the centrepiece of the poem, though only Byron's note fully reveals how ideologically appropriate this is. His source for the folk belief in vampirism, common to the Balkans and the Levant, is a note to Book VIII of Southey's *Thalaba*, a work which overall maintains the kindliness and orderliness of monotheistic religions. But the notion of the curse and some of its details, for example the perpetual fire about the victim's heart, also recall the most celebrated moment in the more recent *Curse of Kehama*, where the very same author accused polytheistic religions of a peculiar tendency to superstition and cruelty. (It is strange, all things considered, that the motif of the vampire was released into nineteenth-century Western literature by two competing progressivist critics of regressive religions.)

Poems inevitably take on the ambivalences of the human consciousness in which they are moulded. But, viewed as polemic, *The Giaour* is hardly muddled or likely to be practically ineffectual. The story 'proves' Turkish rule ethically unacceptable to civilized Westerners, without ever showing the Christian church in a more favourable light. The plain fact is that the poem has good Moslems but no good Christians. The poem's villains are the two great monotheistic codes, Christianity and Islam, *comparable* instruments of personal control over the lives of men and women, and potentially of political control by great powers over the destiny of small nations.

*   *   *

In the long run, Byron was to be successfully attacked more as an anti-clerical writer sapping the faith and morals of individuals than as a mis-leader of the riotous masses. After he left England for good in 1816, a sustained campaign began, not ended even with his death, on the Gothic self-projection perhaps most tellingly pioneered in the vampirish Giaour. Coleridge connects Byron with the subversive Gothic taste in *The Courier* in August 1816. This is that curious, deeply revealing and pregnant passage, afterwards absorbed into the *Biographia Literaria* as chapter XXIII, in which Coleridge, by contrasting Byron's self-absorbed and self-absolved demon-heroes with the properly-punished sinners of Christian literature (such as Don Juan), seems incidentally to have incited Byron to reply with his greatest poem. Lesser critics (Coleridge's nephew J. T. Coleridge, Southey, Reginald Heber) from 1818 mounted an intensifying campaign on his Satanism that led equally logically to the most spectacularly heterodox of all his works, *Cain*.[3]

If *The Giaour* represents the aspect of Byron his religious antagonists most wanted to attack, this is not only because of its protagonist, but because of its wholesale critique of Christianity as a social creed, an instrument of government at home as well as abroad. Byron did not often deal with such topics on a level of generality, but he did eventually return to this one in the mythological tragedy which is also a pre-Shavian comedy, *Sardanapalus* (1821). Here the monarch concerned is a debauchee and a divorcee who cavorts with his mistress in a newly-built pavilion. He also has the misfortune, as a secularist and pacifist, to be king of a nation seized with belief in a divine mission to conquer India. Sardanapalus is thus both the newly-crowned George IV, unhappily cast as leader of a serious, professional, efficient middle-class nation, and the equally déraciné Byron, whose role in the public limelight requires him to take up uncongenially responsible positions. A study of a post-religious consciousness, *Sardanapalus* is the most complex and searching of Byron's self-projections. But it is also the most social and political. In returning to the type of national dilemma he first properly confronted in *The Giaour*, how to determine the goals of government among the sometimes contending and sometimes collusive forces of religion, nationalism and progressivism, Byron if nothing else added a dimension to his studies of private disaffection and existential despair.

CAROLINE FRANKLIN

"A Soulless Toy for Tyrant's Lust?": The Heroine as Passive Victim[†]

In the verse tales of Byron's contemporaries, romantic love was minimized or manipulated by the plot to accord with social duty to the heroine's father, the venerable patriarch of beleaguered traditional values. In Byron's tales, however, the heroine has to choose between love and conformity. To her father or husband she is seen as an object of value in the exchange of women by men in a patriarchal social system based on dynastic alliance and male primogeniture. To her Western lover she is the unattainable ideal in his internalized individualistic quest for self-completion.

> My good, my guilt, my weal, my woe,
> My hope on high—my all below.
> (*The Giaour*, 1182–3)

Traditionally, critics have seen the latter view as that of the poet himself. But it will be shown that Byron deconstructs the romantic love of man for woman as the uneasy conjunction of these two impulses, by his ironic comparison of the Eastern and Western male view of women.[1] The series of

3. For this campaign and its implications for Byron's dramas of 1821, see my 'Romantic Manicheism', in *The Sun is God*, ed. J. B. Bullen (Oxford, 1989).
† From *Byron's Heroines*. Copyright © 1992 Caroline Franklin. Reprinted by permission of Oxford University Press.
1. Byron originally intended to portray Hassan and the Giaour with equal emphasis, but his additions gave the latter more weight. See Michael G. Sundell, 'The Development of *The Giaour*', *SEL* 9 (1969), 587–99 (590).

tales evolves through creative ongoing experimentation with the presentation of sexual relationships, rather than (as is sometimes assumed) the repetition of a static dualism resulting either from the poet's own sexual obsessions or from his cynical cashing-in on a successful formula.

Byron's earliest heroines—Leila, Zuleika, Francesca, Medora, and Parisina—are characterized chiefly by their passivity, sensibility, and tragic deaths. Like the muses of Byron's lyric poetry, these heroines are objects of the male gaze—the feminine Other. Examples of the beauty of nature, they are compared to their native land of Greece. The function of such a heroine is to be, not do. Her power lies in her capacity to inspire men to action. The first of these passive heroines functions as an object of differing value to the male characters, and thus is an absence, even a lacuna in the poem.

Leila

The Giaour best illustrates the reification of the heroine, though all the early tales focus her through the male point of view. Like Astarte in *Manfred* and Francesca in *The Siege of Corinth*, Leila is viewed entirely from the vantage point of her death—which is therefore simultaneously the starting-point and climax of the story, and fixes her as an icon. *The Giaour* is presented as a series of fragments to be pieced together, with varying degrees of success, by its readers. Critics interested in Byron's experimentation with point of view have compared the earlier and later texts to elucidate the poem's development.[2] The questions which concern us here are why Byron decided this narrative technique (derived from Rogers's *The Voyage of Columbus* (1812)) to be particularly appropriate to his subject-matter and why he did not use a similar technique in any of the other tales.

The clue is to be found where the 'manuscript' is most dramatically ruptured in the middle of line 373. It is at the very point at which the ceremonial drowning of Leila is being related that the Emir's voice is lost, and the poem resumes with the fisherman's description of the sinking body. The execution of Leila for adultery is the most shocking of any of the heroines' deaths—the manner of the disposal of the live human parcel demonstrates her status as a chattel. Both the fragmentation of the text and the multiple narration are devices to distance the reader from this central event of the poem, and to bring out the mystery and the full horror of the murder as gradually as possible.

The autonomous feminine voice is totally suppressed in *The Giaour*. The heroine's story has to be reconstructed by the reader from various male viewpoints: those of her master, her lover, and the Turkish fisherman who assisted in her execution, as relayed by a Turkish oral bard, and imperfectly pieced together by the modern European poet/editor. Her silent presence vanishes from view like her sinking body, as it recedes from the fisherman's gaze. She dies without protest, hardly moving enough to show she is alive as she drowns (375–9).

The gap in the narrative invites a horrified response from the reader, an eroticized mix of pathos and excitement at this dramatization of male power

---

2. On the accretive composition of *The Giaour* see Sundell; William H. Marshall, 'The Accretive Structure of Byron's *The Giaour*', *MLN* 76 (1961), 502–9; Robert Gleckner, *Byron and the Ruins of Paradise* (Baltimore, 1967), pp. 96–117; Jerome McGann, *Fiery Dust*, pp. 141–8; and David Seed, ' "Disjointed Fragments": Concealment and Revelation in *The Giaour*', *BJ* 18 (1990), 14–27.

of life or death over woman. But the sentimental Gothicism of the poetry is ironically juxtaposed with the caustic tone of the prose Advertisement and the notes, in which the poet assures us that the drowning of alleged adulteresses is still practised by the Turkish Empire, and describes the recent drowning without trial of twelve women on the word of a wronged wife, though the husband apparently went unpunished.[3] Furthermore, Byron toyed with the idea of publishing an account of the personally-experienced event on which the poem was based. As he had returned from swimming in the Piraeus, he had met a procession, and on enquiring found that they were about to throw into the sea, for infidelity, a girl sewn into a sack. Byron interfered, but had to draw his pistol to halt the proceedings. He managed to procure her pardon and helped her to escape to Thebes. The device of quoting Lord Sligo's account of the incident would of course have raised in the reader's mind the very suspicion which it was intended to refute: that Byron himself had been the girl's lover. The evidence for this is inconclusive.[4] The salient fact, however, is that Byron identified his own sexual guilt with the barbarity towards women which he had witnessed. The impression it made on him is evident from his journal:

> L.[Lewis] wondered I did not introduce the situation into *The Giaour*. He may wonder;—he might wonder more at that production being written at all. But to describe the *feelings* of *that situation* were impossible—it is *icy* even to recollect them.[5]

Like Francesca in *The Siege of Corinth* and Astarte in *Manfred*, Leila exists only as a ghostly presence in the consciousness of the hero, her death a riddle only partially solved by the narrative. In these poems, which all had their origin in 1812, even if completed and published later,[6] the male speakers construct the feminine in terms of natural beauty, passivity, and vulnerability. Nostalgia is engendered by the act of projecting these qualities from the self, and defining them as 'feminine' and Other. They are therefore by definition 'lost' to the masculine men of action doomed to an ethos of action and violence.

Anthony Vital has commented how a power relationship between the sexes informed the rhetorical structure of the sentimentalism of the early lyrics, determining how the poems are read: '. . . in the speaker's mind the woman's potential for action is doubly suppressed: not only is she mute, and her powers of expression made over to her body, but her body is there simply to be made over to the language of the feminine for any male to read.'[7]

The bodies of the heroines of the earliest tales are used as mute objects of male reverence in exactly the same way as the subjects of the amorous lyrics. Thus in the account of Leila's beauty (473–518), the poet guides the

---

3. *CPW* iii. 39; 422–3.
4. The inconclusive evidence as to this is summed up by M. K. Joseph, *Byron the Poet* (London, 1964), p. 65 n. 16.
5. *L&J* iii. 230.
6. McGann suggests that *The Siege of Corinth* and *Parisina* developed out of an original MS tale begun in 1812 (*CPW* iii. 479–80). *Manfred* 'was based on an unfinished Witch drama', parts of which were written from 1812–13 (*CPW* iv. 464).
7. Anthony Vital, 'Lord Byron's Embarrassment: Poesy and the Feminine', *Bulletin of Research in the Humanities*, 86:3 (1983–5), 269–90. On the attitudes to women in the early lyrics see also ch. 2 of Gloria T. Hull's unpublished Ph.D. thesis, 'Women in Byron's Poetry: A Biographical and Critical Study', Purdue University, 1972.

subjective reader via the Turkish fisherman, who advises him to 'gaze' on a gazelle to assist him in imagining her eyes. Though the fisherman's religion postulates woman as 'nought but breathing clay', the gazer is promised spiritual inspiration from reading her glance:

> Oh! Who young Leila's glance could read
> And keep that portion of his creed
> Which saith, that woman is but dust,
> A soulless toy for tyrant's lust?
> On her might Muftis gaze, and own
> That through her eye the Immortal shone.   (487–92)

Compared with examples of earthly physical beauty and purity—blossoms, mountain sleet, and swan—Leila is endowed with a natural nobility in spite of her lowly sexual and social status. Even the Turkish fisherman concedes that, like the swan, she remains loyal to her chosen mate—but she did not choose Hassan (515–18). Her stature is such that by the end of the encomium she has come to assume a dominant role over the now-subservient gazer:

> Thus armed with beauty would she check
> Intrusion's glance, till Folly's gaze
> Shrunk from the charms it meant to praise.

She is now 'armed' like a warrior whilst he shows 'feminine' embarrassment and must withdraw his gaze. The half-naked posed body of Leila in Thomas Stothard's illustration of these lines also invites the reader's gaze, which her accusatory eyes simultaneously repel.

The passage brings into ironic juxtaposition the 'Turkish' language of courtly love with the belief of ordinary Muslim men that women have no soul: their only function is to please men on earth as the houris do in the afterlife. Byron's sarcastic note draws attention to the fact that officially Islam does not deny *all* women immortality: 'The Koran allots at least a third of Paradise to well-behaved women.'[8] Here—as in the poem as a whole—the theoretical idealization of women in the Eastern code of chivalry is shown to be conditional on their actual subordination in religio-societal structures. Byron goes on to emphasize in a later note that it is an emir, whose claim to holiness is via male primogeniture as he is a supposed descendant of the prophet, who superintends the drowning of Leila.[9] Byron's irony, of course, depends on his Western reader's Christian belief in the sexual equality of the soul.

The civilization destroyed by Leila's avenger is seen through Turkish eyes in lines 288–351. Hassan's 'deserted bower' is a symbol of 'the fortress of his power' with which it is made to rhyme. The slavery of women is concomitant with this hierarchical society, evoked by references to 'serf' and 'vassal', and to the military life of 'fortress' and 'steed'. Hassan has acted, not sadistically but logically, in his relations to Leila, in complete accor-

---

8. Byron continues: 'but by far the greater number of Mussulmans interpret the text their own way, and exclude their moieties from heaven. Being enemies to Platonics, they cannot discern "any fitness of things" in the souls of the other sex, conceiving them to be superseded by the Houris' (*CPW* iii. 419).

9. In his note on the Emirs Byron comments: 'they are the worst of a very indifferent brood', and that, basing their power on their lineage from the prophet, they enforce strict religious legalism (*CPW* iii. 418).

dance with the mores of his civilization. This is emphasized by the acceptance by his mother of his treatment of women, the disposal and immediate replacement of Leila (689–722). He dies, as he had lived, showing no remorse for her death (1092), and secure in the belief that even the most impressive earthly woman is inconsiderable in comparison with the attainment of a warrior's paradise and the service of the Houris (737–46).

> There sleeps as true an Osmanlie
> As e'er at Mecca bent the knee.   (729–30)

The Turkish view of Leila is patriarchal in the anthropological rather than the generalized feminist sense of the word. Kate Millett quotes the definition of Sir Henry Maine, the nineteenth-century historian of ancient jurisprudence, on the archaic patriarchal family: 'The eldest male parent is absolutely supreme in his household. His dominion extends to life and death and is as unqualified over his children and their houses as over his slaves.'[1] In much of his poetry, Byron's liberal rhetoric is framed by the background of a patriarchal power system of the present or past. Apart from representations of the Turkish Empire in the tales and *Don Juan*, *Parisina*, *Sardanapalus*, and *Heaven and Earth* all depict a male ruler or leader exercising the power of life and death over his household.

Turkish patriarchy, polygamy, and Muslim doubt as to whether women have souls are not contrasted with a specifically Christian alternative view of woman in *The Giaour*, for the eponymous hero is an infidel to both Muslims and Christians (807). While the traditional Christian dogma of an ungendered soul was still available to nineteenth-century 'feminist' discourse asserting sexual equality,[2] the Giaour's depiction of Leila reflects instead the contemporary ideology of a specifically womanly sanctity comprising the quintessence of femininity. Thus while Leila is treated as merely an object of physical lust by Hassan, she has become for the Giaour the complete opposite of this—his sole source of spiritual meaning in earthly life: 'My life's unerring light' (1144).

Byron's poem thus contributes to the cult of womanhood, while at the same time, by combining the roles of adulteress and spiritual icon in the same heroine, he focuses attention on the very contradictions that his male contemporaries sought to minimize. The reader endeavours to piece together not just the story but the versions of Leila offered by the various voices in the poem. At every point the construct of woman is exaggerated in order to interrogate its contradictions. Thus Leila's identification with the beauty of nature both sanctifies her and yet intensifies the traditional association of woman with sinful sexuality, which drives men to destructive violence. As a harem slave she is a fallen woman in Western eyes, yet her complete separation from men and the tainted public arena endows her with an aura of unworldly purity.

However, whereas the heroines of the verse tales of his male contemporaries, like those of the female novelists, were given specifically social roles as inspirers of familial morality in the cult of womanhood, Byron's Leila functions only as the personal inspiration of an individual. For if most Muslims

---

1. Kate Millett, *Sexual Politics* (London, 1969; repr. 1981), p. 76.
2. E.g. 'It is my spirit that addresses your spirit; just as if both had passed through the grave, and we stood at God's feet, equal,—as we are!' (*Jane Eyre*, ch. 23).

think woman soulless, the title of *The Giaour* draws attention to the relationship between the Westerner's abandonment of religion and his substitution of an extremely idealized individualistic romantic love. Love of woman becomes a secular form of Grace and a means of restoring the lost paradise on earth:

> Yes, Love indeed is light from heaven—
> A spark of that immortal fire
> With angels shar'd—by Alla given,
> To lift from earth our low desire.   (1131–4)

As Frederick Beaty has shown, the definition of love as 'light from heaven' is a characteristic Romantic metaphor for endowing earthly emotions with a halo of celestial light.[3] 'A ray of him who formed the whole— / A glory circling round the soul!' (1140)

Byron rejects Scott's and Southey's puritanical concept of love as chaste friendship leading to matrimony. On the other hand, the Giaour despises courtly gallantry: 'I cannot prate in puling strain / Of ladye-love and beauty's chain' (1103–4). This is true, for we notice that in the Giaour's long speech to the Friar he is concerned only with the changes love has wrought in himself, rather than in imaginatively recreating Leila and her situation, or in perceiving her as an autonomous being. For the Giaour, Leila has become part of his way of perceiving the world: '. . . a form of life and light / That seen—became a part of sight' (1127–8). She is part of his consciousness: 'The Morning-star of Memory!' (1130).

Lesley Rabine, writing on the novelistic romantic heroine, compares the use of a heroine as an intermediary between the hero and his self-knowledge with Hegel's 'circle of the self'. For Hegel, the feminine principle is 'eternal love that merely feels', while only the masculine principle is the 'self-driving force of self-conscious existence'.[4] Similarly, McGann sees Byron's heroines as Platonic emanations of the hero's soul:

> The female counterparts of the heroes . . . correspond exactly to the state of the hero's soul which they inhabit. They objectify the passionate impulses in the man whose imagination made them what they are. This is as much to say that none of them are truly 'persons' . . . These women are allegorical figures set in an allegorical framework. Blake's females are of the same order . . . [5]

Irene Tayler and Gina Luria, in their essay on women in Romantic literature, extend the point to all male Romantic poets. Whilst women novelists of the Regency period stress the community and its shared moral values, the aesthetic of the male Romantic poet sanctified the uniquely individual experience. Consequently, his female muse-figure exists as merely the objectified impulse of his ego. This study[6] will show that the heroine's role develops from that of a mere emanation in this series of poems. But certainly the hero's romantic love for the dead heroine in *The Giaour, The Siege of Corinth* and *Manfred* can thus be interpreted as a displaced form of male narcissism.

3. Frederick L. Beaty, *Light from Heaven: Love in British Romantic Literature* (Illinois, 1971).
4. See Lesley Rabine, *Reading the Romantic Heroine: Text, History, Ideology* (Ann Arbor, Mich., 1985), ch.1.
5. McGann, *Fiery Dust*, p. 189. See also Irene Tayler and Gina Luria, 'Gender and Genre', p. 118.
6. I.e., *Byron's Heroines* (later chapters of which focus on stronger female characters). (*Editor's note*).

Byron's tales were not written in Romantic literary isolation, but specifi-
cally to challenge the consensus on female propriety—the shared moral
values—that Tayler and Luria point out were paramount in the female-
authored Regency novel. The Western hero's creed of passionate romantic
love is preferenced in the hierarchy of discourses within the poem by the
adoption of direct speech and by endowing his retrospective view with the
closure of the poem. However, it is insistently questioned as well as drama-
tized. Byron's strong sense of irony asks us to compare and judge Hassan and
the Giaour in their attitude to Leila. We find the egotistical nature of the lat-
ter's internalized quest underlined in the lines which shocked the reviewers:

> 'Tis true, I could not whine nor sigh,
> I knew but to obtain or die.
> I die—but first I have possest.   (1112–14)

The Giaour values love freely given, not extorted: 'To me she gave her heart,
that all / Which tyranny can ne'er enthrall' (1068–9).

Yet he can still judge Leila as 'faithless', and refer to her 'treachery' to
Hassan, thus endorsing the Turkish patriarchal rule of women. The Giaour
respects Hassan: they share the same military ethos. Moreover, both
believe in punishing female adultery with death: 'Yet did he but what I had
done / Had she been false to more than one' (1062–3). The Giaour is a fer-
vent believer in monogamous love, even after the death of his lover,
whereas Hassan practises polygamy: 'The swan that swims upon the lake,
/ One mate, and one alone, will take' (1170–1). Though the adulterous hero
and heroine have both broken society's moral laws, the Giaour's delineation
of the heroine's guilt in his confession to the Friar reinforces conventional
values with regard to female chastity, while reserving for himself a heroic
posture of defiance. Like Manfred, he worries for the consequences of the
woman's 'guilt' (1141–4) more than his own. He even regrets—for her
sake—that she ever returned his love: 'Yet sometimes with remorse in vain /
I wish she had not loved again' (1054–5). However much her doom haunts
him, he sees it as 'deserv'd' (1066).

He recognizes and castigates society's double standard in judging female
adultery more harshly than male (see lines 1172–9), and deplores heartless
seducers. However, rather than postulating a changed attitude towards
female sexuality, he advocates strict monogamy for both sexes. Like the
other heroes of the tales, he prides himself on his own monogamy for life.

Finally, the Giaour's attitude to women is also comparable to Hassan's in
the way he sees the possession of women as a measure of success. As Has-
san's harem is a visible sign of his power, so the Venetian equates Leila with
the lure of booty or property:

> But place again before my eyes
> Aught that I deem a worthy prize;
> The maid I love—the man I hate,
> And I will hunt the steps of fate.   (1016–19)

His passions are forged by the thought of her defence and revenge into an
inflexible weapon in the competitive warfare of men (922–36).

By this deeply ironic point-by-point comparison of the attitudes of Has-
san and the Giaour towards Leila (and their joint guilt for her death), we
see that the Venetian's romantic love retains many of the basic ideological

assumptions of primitive patriarchy. The poem thus is paradoxically both a strongly charged plea for female sexual autonomy, and an acknowledgment that as the fabric of society is built on the foundation of female chastity, woman will always be the chief victim of illegitimate love.

*   *   *

PETER J. MANNING

The Sublime Self and the Single Voice[†]

The ease with which we fall into speaking of his "exile" from England in 1816 marks Byron's power to impose his myth on us; in reality he chose to quit a situation made intolerable by the strain marriage brought to his ingrained conflicts. He announces in the epigraph affixed to Canto III of *Childe Harold* that the motive of the poem is distraction from his troubles: "Afin que cette application vous forçàt de penser à autre chose: il n'y a en vérité de remède que celui-là et le temps." "Long-absent Harold reappears at last" in order that his creator may "fling / Forgetfulness" about himself:

> He, who grown agéd in this world of woe,
> In deeds, not years, piercing the depths of life,
> So that no wonder waits him—nor below
> Can Love or Sorrow, Fame, Ambition, Strife,
> Cut to his heart again with the keen knife
> Of silent, sharp endurance—he can tell
> Why Thought seeks refuge in lone caves, yet rife
> With airy images, and shapes which dwell
> Still unimpaired, though old, in the Soul's haunted cell.
>
> 'Tis to create, and in creating live
> A being more intense that we endow
> With form our fancy, gaining as we give
> The life we image, even as I do now—
> What am I? Nothing: but not so art thou,
> Soul of my thought! with whom I traverse earth,
> Invisible but gazing, as I glow
> Mixed with thy spirit, blended with thy birth,
> And feeling still with thee in my crushed feelings' dearth.
>
> (5–6)

It may seem curious that Byron should have sought relief by reassuming a persona initially intended to express the melancholy aspects of his nature. The language of stanza 5 suggests that Byron now more purposefully intends Harold to embody the "lone caves" and "haunted cells" of the soul, and to make them available for scrutiny by externalizing them, but the program is again unimplemented. The links between Harold and Byron are superficially indicated in the next ten stanzas and then Harold largely vanishes.

The reasons for his disappearance should be considered. Readers have long noted the irony of Byron's having grown into his protagonist, but

---

[†] From *Byron and His Fictions* (Detroit: Wayne State University Press, 1978).

Harold's redundance is also the sign of a reorientation: he becomes redundant because Byron endeavors to repudiate those aspects of the self which he symbolizes. The drive towards exposure baldly stated in Matthew Arnold's remark that Byron dragged the pageant of his bleeding heart across Europe is deceptive: it forms part of the dominant drive toward "forgetfulness" in the poem.[1] As stanza 6 suggests, Harold (and, more inclusively, the writing of Canto III) enables Byron to overcome personal disaster by restoring his response to the outside world, but he is not a means of probing the self. Harold is truly an *alter* ego: the bearer of rejected parts of the self. Like the heroes of his tales, Byron turns from introspection to a stoic denial of grief: "Yet am I changed; though still enough the same / In strength to bear what Time cannot abate, / And feed on bitter fruits without accusing Fate" (7). Declaring to Augusta his confidence in the work, Byron explained: "I am certain in my mind that this Canto is the *best* which I have ever written; there is depth of thought in it throughout and a strength of repressed passion which you must feel before you find" (*BLJ* 5:159).

Canto III of *Childe Harold* displays a wholly natural impulse of recoil from the strivings obliquely recorded in the tales: to evade further bruises by retirement to a less assertive posture. The poem tests the possibility of attitudes not unlike maternal dependence, and these fantasies, if regressive in content, are reparative in function: through them Byron regenerates the values threatened by the bitterness of his separation. Alternately, he seeks to keep his urgent private griefs at a distance by adopting the voice of grave and exalted meditation on grandly public themes. These strategies engender conflicting crosscurrents, and the shape of the canto is determined by Byron's repeated oscillations between them. When either fails he turns to the other, and when it proves unsatisfactory he returns anew to the first. The very essence of the poem is an effort to rehabilitate the self: to read the poem is to watch the process.

The great set piece on Waterloo is symptomatic of Byron's wish to appraise the stresses of his character while yet remaining safely above them. His habitual identification with Napoleon provided a perspective on himself that the device of Harold no longer furnished. Extreme in all things, capable of governing an empire but not his own passions, Napoleon is a paradigm of Byron's Titanic figures:

> But Quiet to quick bosoms is a Hell,
> And *there* hath been thy bane; there is a fire
> And motion of the Soul which will not dwell
> In its own narrow being, but aspire
> Beyond the fitting medium of desire;
> And, but once kindled, quenchless evermore,
> Preys upon high adventure, nor can tire
> Of aught but rest; a fever at the core,
> Fatal to him who bears, to all who ever bore.
> (42)

---

1. Cf. Paul West, *Byron and the Spoiler's Art* (London: Chatto and Windus, 1960): "Reduce everything Byron ever wrote, and you will find an essential act of repulsion: either self-emptying into a *persona*, or a repudiation" (p. 12).

This tyrannical will can issue only in self-destruction. Within three stanzas Byron replaces the metaphors of fire and warmth with those of cold and sterility:

> He who ascends to mountain-tops, shall find
> The loftiest peaks most wrapt in clouds and snow;
> He who surpasses or subdues mankind,
> Must look down on the hate of those below.
> Though high *above* the Sun of Glory glow,
> And far beneath the Earth and Ocean spread,
> *Round* him are icy rocks, and loudly blow
> Contending tempests on his naked head,
> And thus reward the toils to which those summits led.
>
> (45)

The imaginative poverty of these lines is directly related to the attitude they strike. In them the narrator reaches for "the grandeur of generality," presenting himself as the sage moralist contemplating the eternal truths of the human condition. This oratorical voice is the Byron who thrilled a generation, and it is also Byron as he would have liked to see himself, the master of an ideal, impersonal stance. Byron writes about Napoleon because he feels an affinity with him, but in the poem the connection is not acknowledged. None of the self-consuming passion imputed to Napoleon is permitted to disturb the measured tones of the speaker.

The narrator forcefully repudiates the Titans whom Napoleon exemplifies, but the abruptness of the rejection hints at the sympathies being exorcised by the deliberate act of will: "Away with these! true Wisdom's world will be / Within its own creation, or in thine, / Maternal Nature!" (46). The configuration of these stanzas is identical with that of the tales: from the world of destructive masculine aggressiveness Byron turns to a sheltering environment characterized by its womanly overtones. For Byron inquiry into the self and inquiry into history are parallel, and just as Canto III shies away from investigating the turbulent inner life it illustrates, so it seeks to counteract the lessons of history which are the amplified image of that turbulence with an ahistorical, benevolent, feminine nature. "Shelley, when I was in Switzerland," Byron later told Medwin in an apposite phrase, "used to dose me with Wordsworth physic even to nausea,"[2] and Byron briefly tried to heal his wounds according to the prescription:

> Where rose the mountains, there to him were friends,
> Where rolled the ocean, thereon was his home;
> Where a blue sky, and glowing clime, extends,
> He had the passion and the power to roam;
> The desert, forest, cavern, breaker's foam,
> Were unto him companionship; they spake
> A mutual language, clearer than the tome
> Of his land's tongue, which he would oft forsake,
> For Nature's pages glassed by sunbeams on the lake.
>
> (13)

---

2. Medwin, p. 194.

The distinctively maternal qualities of the nature appealed to in the third canto are evident in the associations it evokes. In the midst of beautiful landscape Harold achieves a mood in which his heart can "leap kindly back to kindness, though Disgust / Hath weaned it from all worldlings" (53). The tranquility of nature leads to one specific image: "There was soft Remembrance, and sweet Trust / In one fond breast," continues stanza 53, "And in its tenderer hour on that his bosom dwelt." The literal reference is to Augusta, but the scene half-disclosed by "weaned" points to an earlier memory which is developed in the following stanza:

> And he had learned to love,—I know not why,
> For this in such as him seems strange of mood,—
> The helpless looks of blooming Infancy,
> Even in its earliest nurture; . . .
>
> (54)

In his "Epistle to Augusta" Byron connects his response to nature still more explicitly than he does here with memories of his childhood and of his sister.[3] His nature borrows its power from the intense nostalgic yearnings invested in it, and if the third canto is Wordsworthian it is perhaps because Byron sensed that the descriptive language of the older poet had been made to serve a similar function.[4] The picture Byron gives of Lake Leman implicitly identifies the gratification he hopes to recover by withdrawing into nature with the situation of infant and mother:

> Is it not better, then, to be alone,
> And love Earth only for its earthly sake?
> By the blue rushing of the arrowy Rhone,
> Or the pure bosom of its nursing Lake,
> Which feeds it as a mother who doth make
> A fair but froward infant her own care,
> Kissing its cries away as these awake; . . .
>
> (71)

The interrogative, wishful note of this and succeeding stanzas betrays the contradictions which beset this solution. The unspoiled harmony Byron seeks is repeatedly disrupted by the correlative intrusions of history and his own preoccupations. Wherever he looks, the landscape reveals battlefields and the ruins of past civilizations: it is the book not of God or of womanly fostering but of man's depredations. Like Wordsworth's, the nature he sees

---

3. The "Epistle to Augusta", written at Diodati, begins with an apostrophe to "My Sister! my sweet Sister!" and continues with memories of Newstead. [The note quotes stanzas 7–11 (see pp. 243–44). (*Editor's note*).]

  The long quotation is necessary to illustrate one of Byron's characteristic fusions. The address to Augusta seems to grow out of the recollections of happy childhood" in stanza 7; the invocation of "our own" lake in stanza 8 thus seems to refer to a time spent with Augusta at Newstead before Byron's "mind was sacrificed to books"—that is, before his schooldays. The differences between the biographical evidence and the poetic creation illuminate a particular element of Byron's fictions. Marchand declares that Augusta "did not see her half-brother until he went to Harrow [April, 1801], and then only rarely" (*BLJ* 1:273); he was then thirteen. Elsewhere Marchand comments that although their correspondence in 1804 presumes some previous meeting, it was "possibly during Byron's holidays spent in London" (1:81). The first reference in Marchand placing Byron and Augusta together at Newstead occurs when they were snowbound there in January, 1814 (1:432). The lines therefore both connect Byron's response to landscape with Augusta and reveal the earlier feelings invested in her: that Byron should have conflated his memories of childhood with those of his much later affair with Augusta is further confirmation of the argument of this chapter.

4. On this subject see Richard J. Onorato, *The Character of The Poet: Wordsworth in THE PRELUDE* (Princeton: Princeton Univ. Press, 1971).

is "half-created" by the perceiving mind, but it can therefore never be free of his projected anxieties and ambitions. As the merely analogical use of natural imagery to describe Napoleon suggests, nature for Byron supplies emblems of his already existent condition and not independent, lasting, spiritual solace. The assertive and aspiring elements of his character are exemplified by the fervent (if nominally disciplined) response to Napoleon and the glowing praise of Morat and Marathon, "true Glory's stainless victories" (64). His passionate determination that he must, and would, excel in the world of men calls forth the magnificent description of Waterloo and the elegiac stanzas on Waterloo, but it also strengthens the instinct to place a "silent seal" (8) on any emotions which might make him appear weak. Much as he longed for its contentment, Byron's own heroic temper blocked any final acquiescence in the passive, trusting role of the mother-infant relationship.

This dilemma erupts in oscillations which become more violent as the canto proceeds. It is resolved at last and unstably in the mediating figure of Rousseau, but only after a gradual evolution in his depiction shows with great precision the values involved. The persecuted, outcast author is a model of the control of private suffering in art:

> Here the self-torturing sophist, wild Rousseau,
> The apostle of Affliction, he who threw
> Enchantment over Passion, and from Woe
> Wrung overwhelming eloquence, first drew
> The breath which made him wretched; . . .
>
> (77)

Byron at this point refrains from embracing Rousseau because his political writings associate him too nearly with the *philosophes* and the destructive consequences of the domineering masculine will. The ambivalence is the same as that already noted in his attitude to Napoleon:

> But good with ill they also overthrew,
> Leaving but ruins, wherewith to rebuild
> Upon the same foundation, and renew
> Dungeons and thrones, which the same hour refilled,
> As heretofore, because Ambition was self-willed.
>
> (82)

From this dead end Byron retreats as before to the fantasized peace of nature. The familiar vocabulary of a second apostrophe to Lake Leman, before characterized in maternal terms, enforces the opposition of masculine and feminine and illustrates as well the fusion of sister and mother in Byron's imaginative universe: "thy soft murmuring / Sounds sweet as if a Sister's voice reproved, / That I with *stern* delights should e'er have been so moved" (85; italics added). The calm, complete with a chirping grasshopper "who makes / His life an infancy" (87), is shattered by a nightstorm which corresponds to the resurgence of Byron's inner tensions. As they reassert their power the landscape is transformed into a mirror of the particular griefs of the poet separated from those he loves. The sky becomes ominously lovely "as is the light / Of a dark eye in Woman" (92), and the "arrowy Rhone" of the previous description (71) becomes a malign masculine force confirming the severance of Byron's happiness:

> Now, where the swift Rhone cleaves his way between
> Heights which appear as lovers who have parted
> In hate, whose mining depths so intervene,
> That they can meet no more, though broken-hearted: . . .
>
> (94)

The layers of conflict laid bare by the failure of Byron's marriage and his self-exile from England vividly appear in the conflation of mother, sister, and lover in this scene.

Baffled in his attempt to escape into nature, Byron rises almost to frenzy:

> Sky—Mountains—River—Winds—Lake—Lightnings! ye!
> With night, and clouds, and thunder—and a Soul
> To make these felt and feeling, well may be
> Things that have made me watchful; the far roll
> Of your departing voices, is the knoll
> Of what in me is sleepless,—if I rest.
> But where of ye, O Tempests! is the goal?
> Are ye like those within the human breast?
> Or do ye find, at length, like eagles, some high nest?
>
> Could I embody and unbosom now
> That which is most within me,—could I wreak
> My thoughts upon expression, and thus throw
> Soul—heart—mind—passions—feelings—strong or weak—
> All that I would have sought, and all I seek,
> Bear, know, feel—and yet breathe—into *one* word,
> And that one word were Lightning, I would speak;
> But as it is, I live and die unheard,
> With a most voiceless thought, sheathing it as a sword.
>
> (96–97)

The frantic accumulation and halting syntax imitate a breakdown of which the cause is evident. Byron's feverish longing for "one word" to contain the complexity of his emotions is itself a barrier to his comprehending them: a rough paraphrase of this passage might read: "Since I lack the magic talisman that would open all the locks, why try speaking of myself at all?" The psychological subtext is the reverse of what is stated: the admission of defeat avoids the painful necessity of working through the pressures catalogued in the preceding stanzas. The all-or-nothing terms subconsciously justify to Byron merely reiterating in verse a despairing avowal of silence. This common gambit to reduce stress, however, prolongs and increases its severity, and an art based on such a posture offers no more satisfactory resolution of inner discord than a withdrawal into "maternal nature." The progression of imagery from the ideal maternal/sibling harmony through "lovers who have parted in hate" to the impotence symbolized by the sheathed sword is a miniature of the failure of Byron's resources.

An abrupt shift from the nightstorm in which repressed agonies have surfaced to the "dewy Morn" marks the beginning of resolution (98). It is at this point that Rousseau re-enters the poem, now shorn of his compromising engagement with the world of men. A visit to Clarens, the setting of *La Nouvelle Héloïse,* prepares the new introduction (99). Byron transforms Rousseau into a benign power within the landscape his creations "people," and the strength of his imagination counteracts the reminders of strife which have hitherto dominated Byron's vision. Most important, the novel's celebration of the trials and love of Julie and Saint Preux contrasts with the misery of Byron's separation. In this surrogate who performs what eludes Byron *in propria persona* we can see the outline of an artist figure who incorporates the values of compassion and natural energies previously associated exclusively with women. The agency of Rousseau brings Byron to a tentative utterance of faith:

> I have not loved the World, nor the World me,—
> But let us part fair foes; I do believe,
> Though I have found them not, that there may be
> Words which are things,—hopes which will not deceive,
> And Virtues which are merciful, nor weave
> Snares for the failing; I would also deem
> O'er others' griefs that some sincerely grieve—
> That two, or one, are almost what they seem,—
> That Goodness is no name—and Happiness no dream.
>
> (114)

The fragile assertion is cut across by the experience it records so proudly and resentfully: surrounding echoes of *Coriolanus* characterize Byron's stance more accurately than the moderation here grudgingly conceded.[5] The stanza avows a trust and faith in the possibilities of expression which are desired rather than achieved.

The declaration is followed immediately by Byron's apostrophe to his daughter: "My daughter! with thy name this song begun! / My daughter! with thy name thus much shall end!— / I see thee not—I hear thee not— but none / Can be so wrapt in thee; Thou art the Friend / To whom the shadows of far years extend" (115). Readers generally have judged this conclusion arbitrary, but its suddenness indicates the profound appeal the image of the innocent child holds for Byron. As he muses on the delights which he has been denied of tending Ada's growth the reversal of their positions becomes apparent. It is not the prospect of supervising her ascent to maturity which seizes his imagination, but the hope that she might redeem him: "Fain would I waft such blessing upon thee, / As—with a sigh—I deem thou might'st have been to me!" (118). As in Wordsworth's address to Dorothy at the close of "Tintern Abbey," this shift reveals beneath the overt affirmation a regressive wish. The possibilities brought by a daughter are that she paradoxically regenerates the desired situation in which he is restored by the mother figure in whom he needs to believe: "I know that thou wilt love me . . . I know that thou wilt love me . . . Still thou would'st love me . . ." (117). The configuration of the father nourished by the daughter-mother shall be encountered more dramatically in Canto IV, and its revelation of a mind still obsessed by the past suggests why the forward-looking optimism on which Byron attempts to end could be for him only a vulnerable and impermanent modus vivendi. A poem of failure, however, is not a failed poem: *Childe Harold* III vividly dramatizes the desperate questionings of its author.

---

5. E.g., stanza 113: "I have not loved the World, nor the World me; / I have not flattered its rank breath," to which E. H. Coleridge compares *Coriolanus*: "For the mutable, rank-scented many, let them/ Regard me as I do not flatter" (III, i, 66–67).

Manfred teaches more about the relationship in Byron's work of this period between "forgetfulness," with its two components of stern self-repression and desire to return to an earlier, untroubled stage of existence, and the role of women, or, to give the subject the broad context its complex development deserves, between Titanic aspiration and idealized harmony. The drama has profited less from the revaluation accorded Byron than one might have hoped. The formulation of E. H. Coleridge that "the motif of *Manfred* is remorse—eternal suffering for inexpiable crime" now appears too simple, but other categories limit apprehension of the play even as its stock rises.[6] For E. E. Bostetter and others the play depicts an existential dilemma and proffers a correspondingly existential resolution.[7] In his largely dismissive attitude Andrew Rutherford appears to stand at the opposite pole, but, in this like the favorable criticism, Rutherford assumes that *Manfred* is Byron's "supreme attempt to claim significance and value for the Byronic hero."[8] Rather, *Manfred* is the fullest manifestation of the psychological patterns already traced. Readings that seek to dignify Manfred into an existential hero misconstrue the drama, minimizing the turmoil that constitutes its affective power. Studies of the structure of the play apart from Byron's implication in it fail to convey that sense of uncontrollable pressures which is what engages the reader.[9] "My pang shall find a voice," Manfred exclaims (II, ii, 50), and that impulse to express the inner tensions of "alienation from within"[1] is the surest point of departure.

Yet the drama undeniably invites the grandiose terms applied to it. On the surface its pattern is that of the hero's quest. Defying the spirits he has evoked, Manfred in the very first scene arrogates to himself Promethean status:

> Slaves, scoff not at my will!
> The Mind—the Spirit—the Promethean spark,
> The lightning of my being, is as bright,
> Pervading, and far darting as your own,
> And shall not yield to yours, though cooped in clay!
>   (I, i, 153–157)

Arcane researches and a darkly hinted violation of taboo, conversation with spirits and a descent into the underworld, combine to sound mythic resonances. Manfred's triumph over the infernal powers who demand his submission in the last scene seems to declare the absolute omnipotence of the human will. When Murray omitted Manfred's last line from the first edition Byron protested that he had "destroyed the whole effect & moral of the poem" (*BLJ* 5:257). The line—"Old man! 'tis not so difficult to die"— is Manfred's assertion that he dies unconquered by any force, natural or supernatural. Like Prometheus, he contrives to surmount his oppressive situation.[2]

---

6. *Poetry*, 4: 82.
7. *The Romantic Ventriloquists* (Seattle: Univ. of Washington Press, 1963).
8. *Byron: A Critical Study* (1961; rpt. Edinburgh: Oliver and Boyd, 1965), pp. 89–90.
9. E.g., David Eggenschwiler, "The Tragic and Comic Rhythms of *Manfred*," *SiR* 13 (1974), 63–77.
1. See K. M. Luke, "Lord Byron's *Manfred*: A Study of Alienation from Within," *UTQ*, 40 (1970), 15–26.
2. A paraphrase of Harold Bloom, *The Visionary Company*, rev. and enl. edition (Ithaca: Cornell Univ. Press, 1971), p. 252.

The play nonetheless exposes Manfred's boast. He is no Prometheus seeking a boon for mankind, but a ceaseless self-tormentor whose most insistent desire is absolution from the painful self-consciousness which is the Promethean heritage: "Forgetfulness— . . . Oblivion—self-oblivion!" (I, i, 135–144). Manfred's sorrows are private, not the paradigm of an unjust human condition. Byron called Manfred's speech to the sun "one of the best in the thing" (*BLJ* 5:249), and the apostrophe depicts a benevolent nature:

> Most glorious Orb! that wert a worship, ere
> The mystery of thy making was revealed!
> Thou earliest minister of the Almighty,
> Which gladdened, on their mountain tops, the hearts
> Of the Chaldean shepherds, till they poured
> Themselves in orisons!
>
> (III, ii, 9–14)

Though Manfred again and again bemoans the inability of nature to assuage his suffering, the fault is in him and not in nature.[3] Persistently counterpoised against the gloomily alienated figure who dominates the play are the innocence of the shepherds and the "humble virtues" of the Chamois Hunter (II, i, 63–73). Manfred beholds "pure vales" where "the patriarchal days are not / A pastoral fable" (I, ii, 49–50). Society does not need redemption; Manfred alone, like Milton's Satan, is cut off from joy.

Byron's treatment of the Chamois Hunter who saves Manfred's life reveals the distortions inherent in existential interpretations of the drama. Manfred condescends to his rescuer, but the peasant stoutly refuses to be overawed:

> *Man.*   Preach [patience] to mortals of a dust like thine,—
>   I am not of thine order.
> *C. Hun.*   Thanks to Heaven!
>   I would not be of thine for the free fame
>   Of William Tell; but whatso'er thine ill,
>   It must be borne, and these wild starts are useless.
>
> (II, i, 37–41)

The symbolic topography of the play supports the hunter. He comments that "My way of life leads me but rarely down" to the level of Manfred's castle, and that he habitually occupies higher reaches of the Alps than does Manfred is significant (II, i, 11). The mountains are emblems of Manfred's isolation, but because he dwells peacefully within their majesty they ennoble the hunter. He easily prevents Manfred's purposed suicide; in contrast to him Manfred is "all feebleness" and he tamely accepts the hunter as his guide (I, ii, 114–125).

It is important thus to emphasize the positive elements before which Byron stations Manfred because a proper understanding of the central conflict of the play depends upon recognition of the essential nature of the objects which he approaches with such wistfulness and defiance. The secondary characters do not create dramatic tension, but they are more than foils for the protagonist's self-revelation: they precisely define his dilemma.

---

3. The most comprehensive discussion of Byron's treatment of nature in *Manfred* is that of E. J. Lovell, Jr., "The Wordsworthian Note and the Byronic Hero," *Byron: The Record of a Quest* (1949; rpt. Hamden, Conn.: Archon, 1966).

Byron's pattern of setting Manfred in relief against other male figures culminates in the soliloquy which opens the last scene of the play. Manfred recalls a night he "stood within the Coliseum's wall, / 'Midst the chief relics of almighty Rome":

> And thou didst shine, thou rolling Moon, upon
> All this, and cast a wide and tender light,
> Which softened down the hoar austerity
> Of rugged desolation, and filled up,
> As 'twere anew, the gaps of centuries;
> Leaving that beautiful which still was so,
> And making that which was not—till the place
> Became religion, and the heart ran o'er
> With silent worship of the Great of old,—
> The dead, but sceptred, Sovereigns, who still rule
> Our spirits from their urns.
>
> (III, iv, 31–41)

This passage is usually dismissed as conventionally picturesque, but it merits longer attention.[4] The vision is a memory, and it is about memory; moreover, it is the only remembrance in the play which does not blast Manfred with remorse. He who sought only "forgetfulness" encounters Rome, the potent symbol of history, and bows before it. In the face of achievements that have survived the ages, assimilated to the natural forces which appear to erode them, he who proclaimed the omnipotence of his will acknowledges the sway of "The dead, but sceptred, Sovereigns, who still rule / Our spirits from their urns." In recognizing the supremacy of the "Great of old" Manfred obliquely passes judgment on his own solipsism, and his death immediately thereafter confirms the bankruptcy of his Titanic pretensions.

The new peace in Manfred's voice is purchased by this submission. The legendary Caesars, mentioned three times in the first thirty lines of the soliloquy, are the inclusive symbol of the masculine authority to which he now bows. It may seem strange to suggest that one current of the action is Manfred's struggle to earn a place in the world of men, for the contest is indirect, and spectral; most important, Manfred is in effect defeated before the play begins. To phrase the issue in this way, however, emphasizes the ubiquitous and decisive presence of fathers, father figures, and ancestors in the drama. In Act III the servant Manuel contrasts Manfred unfavorably with his father, "whom he nought resembles":

Manuel. I speak not
  Of features or of form, but mind and habits;
  Count Sigismund was proud, but gay and free,—
  A warrior and a reveller; he dwelt not
  With books and solitude, nor made the night

---

4. For example, by E. J. Lovell in the work just cited: "This is, of course, pictorial composition with the emphasis on the picturesque as it was understood by Byron" (p. 177). G. Wilson Knight is an exception; although his cryptic comment does not explore the significance of the passage, he pointed to it as long ago as 1939 in "The Two Eternities": "the phrases go deep into the acceptances and revolts of Byron's work." The essay is reprinted as "Byron: The Poetry," in *Poets of Action* (London: Methuen, 1967), p. 199.

> A gloomy vigil, but a festal time,
> Merrier than day; . . .
>   (III, iii, 15–23)

Next to the vivid recollection of the "jocund times" of the former count Manfred seems shrunken, and the "patriarchal days" associated with the Chamois Hunter hark back to the same richness of existence from which Manfred sadly feels himself to have declined. His scorn of the hunter springs from resentment at having had to be rescued: as with Gulnare's rescue of Conrad, the act reminds him of his inadequacy, and underscores his failure to achieve independence.

The Chamois Hunter is one of two older men who in the course of the action judge Manfred: the other is the Abbot. His analysis in Act III has the ring of authorial pronouncement; condemnation of Manfred is so absorbed in admiration and pity that Byron seems to be delicately placing the best possible construction on the characterological strains reflected in the play, describing himself to himself and making his apologia to the world:

> This should have been a noble creature: he
> Hath all the energy which would have made
> A goodly frame of glorious elements,
> Had they been wisely mingled; as it is,
> It is an awful chaos—Light and Darkness—
> And mind and dust—and passions and pure thoughts,
> Mixed, and contending without end or order,—
> All dormant or destructive.
>   (III, i, 160–167)

The inner frustration and outer torpor repeat a malady familiar from the tales and *Childe Harold* III, and the reader's interest in the accurate diagnosis is increased by Byron's choice of speaker: the Byronic hero is once more confronted by an older male figure of solid personal authority.

The solicitous Abbot by his very strengths exacerbates the self-doubt Manfred tries to conceal under a show of bravado. In a scene which in configuration and tone virtually duplicates the final confession of the Giaour to a monk, Manfred acknowledges to the Abbot the failure of his hope to have been the benefactor of mankind:

> Aye—father! I have had those early visions,
> And noble aspirations in my youth,
> To make my own the mind of other men,
> The enlightener of nations; . . .
>   (III, i, 104–107)

Manfred rationalizes his disappointment by a prickly integrity—"I could not tame my nature down; for he / Must serve who fain would sway" (III, i, 116–117)—but the grandiloquent manner does not disguise the lack of accomplishment; indeed, the excess of the contempt toward worldly achievement suggests rather its continuing appeal. The Abbot presses Manfred until he is forced to admit the utter sterility of his arrogance:

> *Abbot.*   And why not live and act with other men?
> *Man.*   Because my nature was averse from life;
>   And yet not cruel; for I would not make,

> But find a desolation. Like the Wind,
> The red-hot breath of the most lone Simoom,
> Which dwells but in the desert, and sweeps o'er
> The barren sands which bear no shrubs to blast,
> And revels o'er their wild and arid waves,
> And seeketh not, so that it is not sought,
> But being met is deadly,—such hath been
> The course of my existence; . . .
>
> (III, i, 116–134)

The simile equates ocean and desert as emblems of a psychological waste-land.[5] Since in the great address which completes *Childe Harold* Byron hails the ocean as the primal, vital "Image of Eternity" (IV, 183), the equivalence is at first surprising, but in both works the image of ocean is coordinate with the presence or absence of nurturing womanly energies: here therefore it can connote only infertility. In his initial speech Manfred declares: "Good— or evil—life— / Powers, passions—all I see in other beings, / Have been to me as rain unto the sands, / Since that all-nameless hour" (I, i, 21–24). Though his predicament is unchanging from the start of the play, it is the paternal Abbot who reduces Manfred to this bitterly reductive account of himself, the fullest confession that his vaunts of self-sufficiency are hollow. Manfred perfectly comprehends his situation, but without Astarte he does not possess the resources to change it, and the prideful rhetoric cannot eclipse the greater substance of the Abbot.

A brief consideration of the compositional history of *Manfred* refines insight into his role. In the third act as Byron originally wrote it he is a nar-row and grasping figure who threatens Manfred with damnation unless he donates his lands to the church. Manfred responds to this attempted extor-tion by having the Abbot carried off to a mountain peak by one of the dev-ils in his command, who disappears with him while singing anticlerical doggerel. This crude business is "certainly d——d bad" (*BLJ* 5:211), as Byron was ready enough to agree when it was criticized by his publisher, but the conception is significant. The caricature of the Abbot suggests that Byron, frustrations aggravated by the soul-wearying distractions of a Vene-tian Carnival and an ensuing fever, found violent debasement the sole recourse in answering the reproaches the Abbot embodies, while his removal by the devil seems a patently wish-fulfilling victory over a force too imposing for Byron to contemplate without fantasy. From the frenzy of the repudiation the magnitude of the imagined threat is inferred. In the revi-sions made some weeks later the Abbot "is become a good man," as Byron told Murray (*BLJ* 5:219), but even in his final shape the traces of the dom-inant father before whom Manfred must prove himself can be discerned.[6]

Deeper than the anxieties reflected by the male figures in *Manfred* are those revolving around Astarte. It is obvious that she is the source of Man-fred's despair, but to advance beyond the obvious asks careful discrimina-tion. In an understandable effort to circumvent the scandalmongering that befuddled earlier interpretations, criticism has tended lately to minimize

---

5. Noted by Bostetter, p. 275, and Gleckner, p. 232.
6. The original third act is printed in *Poetry* 4: 121–130. The two versions are compared by M. H. Butler, "An Examination of Byron's Revisions of *Manfred*, Act III, "*SP*, 60 (1963), 627–636.

the importance of incest in the drama.[7] In so doing it has underemphasized the role of Astarte, for she stands at the heart of the drama, although in terms different from those which shocked Byron's contemporaries. Guilt for the commission of sin is not what eats at Manfred, however; incest is mentioned only twice in the play (II, i, 27; III, iii, 44–47), and it occupies a much less prominent place than Manfred's remorse for the death of Astarte, for which he bears the guilt but was not responsible (II, ii, 117–121). It is this paradox which should be investigated.

The vague introduction of Astarte in the first scene, indicating neither her name nor her relationship to Manfred, illustrates that she has symbolic value beyond biographical reference. Manfred asks the "most powerful" of the spirits he has summoned to assume "such aspect/ As unto him may seem most fitting," and the Seventh Spirit then appears as "a beautiful female figure." This spirit has before described himself as Manfred's personal fate:

> The Star which rules thy destiny
> Was ruled, ere earth began, by me:
> It was a World as fresh and fair
> As e'er revolved round Sun in air;
> Its course was free and regular,
> Space bosomed not a lovelier star.
> The Hour arrived—and it became
> A wandering mass of shapeless flame,
> A pathless Comet, and a curse,
> The menace of the Universe;
> Still rolling on with innate force,
> Without a sphere, without a course,
> A bright deformity on high,
> The monster of the upper sky!
>   (I, i, 110–123)

The imagery of this speech has gone largely unnoticed. The first sentence associates the conventional language of cosmic harmony with feminine, generative, energies: "fresh," "fair," "bosomed," "lovelier." After the unspecified disaster the "free and regular" star is transformed into a monstrous "pathless Comet" "rolling on with innate force" which recalls the self-consuming will of Napoleon and Byron's Titans generally. The speech looks back nostalgically from the sterile masculine world of the present to a peacefully fostering feminine world.

---

7. For example, Ward Pafford, "Byron and the Mind of Man: *Childe Harold* III–IV and *Manfred*," *SiR*, 1 (1962), 105–127. Yet in "Byron's *Manfred* and Zoroastrianism," *JEGP*, 57 (1958), 726–738, M. J. Quinlan points out that Astarte, a deity of the early Canaanites, was both bride and mother of Tammuz: the name of this incestuous goddess of sexual love is appropriate for the sister Manfred loves. Quinlan believes that Byron did not have the pagan figure in mind, but took the name rather from Montesquiou's *Persian Letters*, where it is found in a loving brother-sister relationship; the maternal aspects, however, are also relevant. Quinlan notes too that "Ashtaroth," the demon who carries off the Abbot in the original third act, is a variant form of "Astarte," inferring therefrom that Byron must have been ignorant of that fact; it would be a nice touch, however, and consistent with his characteristic patterns, if Byron had used a representative of female sexuality to overcome the chief male authority of his drama. P. L. Thorslev, Jr., discusses the range of the incest motif in "Incest as Romantic Symbol," *CLS* 2 (1965), 41–58.

In requesting "forgetfulness" from the spirits Manfred expresses a desire to reverse the progression outlined by the Seventh Spirit, in effect to undo the being he has become. Ironically, the spirits offer instead total recall: "We are immortal, and do not forget; / We are eternal, and to us the past / Is, as the future, present" (I, i, 149–151). Memory recalls to Manfred the happy state which he passionately wants to re-enter, but because the return is impossible the memory tortures him. His vision of the beautiful female figure for whom he yearns confirms that he longs for death only to end this cruel frustration, his true desire is for her: "Oh God! if it be thus, and *thou* / Art not a madness and a mockery, / I yet might be most happy" (I, i, 188–190). When she vanishes, he faints, and the swoon literalizes his predicament: deprived of her life-giving power, he is inert. The incantation which follows condemns Manfred to suffer the pains of his own hypocrisy and guile, but since these charges are not borne out by any subsequent evidence they must be understood as an externalization of Manfred's self-accusations.[8] By the end of the scene, then, the two chief components of Manfred's character have been presented: his desire for the woman affiliated with the past on whom he depends for healthful life, and the "cold breast" and "shut soul" for which he currently reproaches himself.

Manfred's interview with the Witch of the Alps, whom he calls up after having quit the Chamois Hunter, elaborates the connection between his icy control and his regressive wishes. Their meeting is set beneath a rainbow, the symbol of the covenant between man and God, and Manfred invokes the "Beautiful Spirit" in images that combine purity and fecundity:

> . . . the hues of youth—
> *Carnationed like a sleeping Infant's cheek,*
> *Rocked by the beating of her mother's heart,*
> Or the rose tints, which Summer's twilight leaves
> Upon the lofty Glacier's virgin snow,
> The blush of earth embracing with her Heaven,—
> Tinge thy celestial aspect, and make tame
> The beauties of the Sunbow which bends o'er thee.
>
> (II, ii, 17–24; italics added)

The simile unfolds the tableau whose myriad afterimages are seen throughout Byron's work, affecting testimony that the core of Manfred's grief is a re-enactment of the child's loss of the all-protective mother. The witch, like Astarte whom she duplicates, is a projection of Manfred's desire for the vanished security of the maternal embrace. Her serene maternal presence enables Manfred to unburden himself, and elicits from him the first history of his plight:

---

8. The incantation was published before the drama, on December 5, 1816. Leslie Marchand has challenged the assumption that it reflects Byron's sense of guilt, arguing in *Byron's Poetry* (Boston: Houghton Mifflin, 1965) that it is "obviously directed" against Lady Byron (p. 77). The allusions to the "brotherhood of Cain," however, seem to suggest a male rather than a female subject.

> From my youth upwards
> My spirit walked not with the souls of men,
> Nor looked upon the earth with human eyes;
> The thirst of their ambition was not mine,
> The aim of their existence was not mine,
> My joys—my griefs—my passions—and my powers,
> Made me a stranger; though I wore the form,
> I had no sympathy with breathing flesh,
> Nor midst the Creatures of Clay that girded me
> Was there but One who—but of her anon.
>   (II, ii, 50–59)

So far from being the cause of Manfred's isolation, Astarte represents his one link with humanity; as Manuel tells Herman, she was "The sole companion of his wanderings / And watchings—her, whom of all earthly things / That lived, the only thing he seemed to love . . ." (III, iii, 43–45). This extraordinary intimacy parallels the situation of the child who sees the world through the mediation of his mother; the "Blest Babe" passage in Book II of *The Prelude* is a helpful analogue to clarify the nature of the communion Manfred remembers. In his earliest days the infant does not distinguish between "self" and "other," so it is not surprising that in memory Astarte should appear to Manfred as an idealized extension of himself:

> She was like me in lineaments—her eyes—
> Her hair—her features—all, to the very tone
> Even of her voice, they said were like to mine;
> But softened all, and tempered into beauty:
> She had the same lone thoughts and wanderings,
> The quest of hidden knowledge, and a mind
> To comprehend the Universe: nor these
> Alone, but with them gentler powers than mine,
> Pity and smiles, and tears—which I had not;
> And tenderness—but that I had for her;
> Humility—and that I never had.
>   (II, ii, 105–115)

Basing their interpretations on this portrait, critics have always treated Astarte as a wholly ideal figure, but it is necessary to separate her intrinsic qualities from her function in Manfred's life. The conclusion of his dialogue with the Witch reveals the threatening implications of the mother figure. The witch replies to Manfred's narrative of his miseries by offering assistance:

Witch.   It may be
           That I can aid thee.
Man.   To do this thy power
           Must wake the dead, or lay me low with them
           Do so—in any shape—in any hour
           With any torture—so it be the last.
Witch.   That is not in my province; but if thou
           Wilt swear obedience to my will, and do
           My bidding, it may help thee to thy wishes.
Man.   I will not swear—Obey! and whom? the Spirits

> Whose presence I command, and be the slave
> Of those who served me—Never!
>   (II, ii, 150–159)

Manfred remains adamant despite her hope of a "gentler answer," and his refusal discloses the psychological impasse in which he is trapped. Two related strands of motivation converge in Manfred's vehement denial. Bereft of maternal support, Manfred feels himself too impoverished to be able to give, and because he cannot give, he reacts to any emotional demand made on him by another as if he were in danger of being swallowed up. The witch's sudden insistence on a vow of obedience suggests that the episode is the vehicle of its creator's fears of losing autonomy if he succumbs to the bliss he most desires: when the seductive witch offers him the chance of happiness, Manfred perceives it as the negation of his manhood. He is caught in the dilemma adumbrated in the tales: like the child, he wishes to remain with the mother, but his adult status is predicated precisely on his ability to leave her and establish his independence. To move into the world of men he must reject her, and in so doing he appears to himself to acquire the "cold breast" and "shut soul" for which Manfred feels guilty.

The scorning of the witch shows Manfred's pride to be the outer manifestation of his backward-facing longings. After such a cul-de-sac he can only descend to the underworld and parley with the dead, and in the final scene of Act II Manfred directly encounters the Phantom of Astarte. His six-times-reiterated plea, "Speak to me," affirms that his original request for "oblivion" was only a desperate substitute for his true desire, forgiveness:

> *Man.*   Yet one word more—am I forgiven?
> *Phan.*   Farewell!
> *Man.*   Say, shall we meet again?
> *Phan.*   Farewell!
> *Man.*   One word for mercy! Say thou lovest me.
> *Phan.*   Manfred! [*The spirit of Astarte disappears.*]
>   (II, iv, 152–154)

Astarte announces Manfred's impending death, but does not pardon him. What Manfred wants to be forgiven for is the masculine adult behavior which he values so ambivalently: proud of his authority, yet conscious that his will cannot restore the harmony he prizes and that each exercise of it takes him further from the oneness he knew with Astarte. It is a commonplace of the psychological literature already cited that children often interpret the death of a parent as retribution for some imagined sin of their own, and so it is that Manfred assumes the responsibility for Astarte's death as if his growing away from her were an act of murder. Because he is determined to persist in his independence his growth to manhood is an action for which he cannot imagine forgiveness. It is harshly apposite that Nemesis be the agent to resurrect Astarte, since by continually rejecting the maternal embrace Manfred nullifies the redemptive power of the virtues he attributes to her, while enshrining them as the painful reminders of a wilfully abandoned paradise.

Manfred welcomes the annunciation of his death as "grace" (II, iv, 166) and the anticipated release from his frustrations produces at the opening of

Act III a note of resignation unheard before: "Inexplicable stillness! which till now / Did not belong to what I knew of life" (III, i, 7–8). Astarte's tacit withdrawal from him is the obverse of his arrogant refusal of the Witch of the Alps, and this definitive rejection of the mother is followed by the submission to the masculine forces Manfred acknowledges in his memory of Rome. Michael Cooke has written that "Manfred becomes a hero less for what he can do than for what he can do without," but in the last act he seems to me more exhausted than heroic.[9] Manfred's rejections mark the rhythm of the play of the Spirits, of the Chamois Hunter, of the Witch of the Alps, of the Destinies, and of the Abbot. Each repudiation prepares the next more fundamental one, and each reduces Manfred more severely than its precursor. He defines his position with ever-increasing sharpness, but the process simultaneously guarantees that the stasis which threatens him will become total.

From his first speech Manfred's consciousness is entirely retrospective: "I have essayed . . . I have done men good . . . I have had my foes. . . ." His quest for oblivion is in part a quest for absolution from the past necessary if he is to move forward: "The future, till the past be gulfed in darkness, / It is not of my search" (I, ii, 6–7). By proposing the quest in terms of "forgetfulness," however, Manfred entails upon himself the worst alienation, the alienation from his own history. He is spared this consequence by confessing that it is rather forgiveness he seeks, but his assertiveness prevents the second formulation from being any more fruitful for him than the first.

Torn by remorse for the very qualities of daring which distinguish him, Manfred is paralyzed. He knows that in his radically subjective world the flow of time and the sense of life are measured by human action:

> Think'st thou existence doth depend on time?
> It doth; but actions are our epochs: mine
> Have made my days and nights imperishable,
> Endless, and all alike, as sands on the shore,
> Innumerable atoms; and one desert,
> Barren and cold, on which the wild waves break,
> But nothing rests, save carcasses and wrecks,
> Rocks, and the salt-surf weeds of bitterness.
> (II, i, 51–58)

Only fresh actions can liberate Manfred, but actions require motives and imply objects or others, and these Manfred's fixation on the irrecoverable harmony of infancy systematically eliminates. One way Manfred destroys the past, the other way he precludes a future. The present remains, but the present has been inevitably degraded into an eternity of lifelessness. The two faces of his desire, aspiration and memory, combine to diminish the value of the here-and-now: as he declares, "In life there is no present" (II, ii, 172). Hence the distortion in Manfred's sense of time: great urgency joined to the loss of all sense of time as a medium for living.[1] The Hamlet whom Manfred echoes and who provides the epigraph to the play is finally a hero not only because he perceives and reflects, but also because he cleanses Denmark of the corruption which infects it.[2] Manfred, cut off from valid action,

---

9. *The Blind Man Traces the Circle*, p. 65.

1. On the connection between this phenomenon and "identity diffusion," a useful term for consideration of *Manfred*, see Erik H. Erikson, "The Problem of Ego Identity," *Identity and the Life Cycle*.

2. The allusions to *Hamlet* are especially suggestive in the light of the oedipal content found there by Freud and Ernest Jones, *Hamlet and Oedipus* (1949; rpt. Garden City: Doubleday, 1954).

loses even the physical glamor of Byron's earlier protagonists. W. P. Elledge is right to conclude that "in the vacuum of Manfred's selfhood our traditional interpretations of 'triumph' and 'defeat' are altogether meaningless,"[3] but it is one of the achievements of the play to set forth the psychological grounds of that appalling vacuum.

Unlike the heroes of the tales, Manfred does not compete against a man for a woman: that the struggles of the play are largely two-body rather than triangular marks the depth of their roots. The crisis at the center of *Manfred* reaches back to the crisis of separation and individuation.[4] Manfred does not so much seek for Astarte as a separate, independent being as he searches for a state prior to identity, the state in which mother and child form one organic unit. Astarte is an ideal, mirror image, a reflection in which the self can discover and ground itself, or, in this instance more accurately, a vision of wholeness imagined by a being in discord.[5] It is clear, however, that in these terms Manfred's quest for Astarte can only be, literally, self-defeating: the symbiotic reunion with Astarte Manfred desires so intensely would be the annulment of his individuality, the death of the self. To end the pain of separate identity is his goal: to fuse with another, or to die, are but different avenues to the same destination. Manfred exists only in this tension between two fundamentally identical alternatives: within this static, closed system no development is possible. His dilemma proceeds from the shattering of an independent identity that his yearning for Astarte reveals, a dilemma whose consequences Byron works out with rigorous completeness. The "character" to which Manfred clings is the substitute for this lack, the grandeur of one who, incapable of advance, can only choose to die in his own way.[6]

One objection to the argument that the bottommost stratum of *Manfred* reveals mother-centered conflicts of dependence and autonomy, and beneath that of separation and individuation, may here be anticipated. Manfred implies that Astarte shared in his "crime":

> Thou lovedst me
> Too much, as I loved thee: we were not made
> To torture thus each other—though it were
> The deadliest sin to love as we have loved.
> Say that thou loath'st me not—that I do bear
> This punishment for both— . . .
>
> (II, iv, 120–125)

---

3. *Byron and the Dynamics of Metaphor*, pp. 81–94.
4. The terms are drawn from Margaret S. Mahler. The most inclusive theoretical statement of her work is to be found in Margaret S. Mahler, Fred Pine, and Anni Bergman, *The Psychological Birth of the Human Infant* (New York: Basic Books, 1975).
5. Use is made here of the work of D. W. Winnicott on early parent-infant relations, particularly "Mirror-role of Mother and Family in Child Development," *Playing and Reality*, and of the concept of the *stade du miroir* in the thought of Jacques Lacan, whose theoretical speculations here Winnicott's observations corroborate: see *The Language of the Self*, tr. Anthony Wilden (1968; rpt. New York: Delta, 1975).
6. This account converges with that of Stuart M. Sperry, "Byron and the Meaning of *Manfred*," *Criticism*, 16 (1974), 189–202, insofar as the play is seen as Byron's confrontation with his own persona, his latent realization of the danger of personal domination by the character of his own creating." Sperry's essay is one of the best the play has received, but it is perhaps slightly idealizing. *Manfred* is not quite "*Man Freed*" or "Byron's renunciation" of his Titanic hero, as Sperry suggests: while Byron's exposure of his hero undoubtedly points in that direction, his psychological victories were never that clear-cut.

The passage seems inapplicable to the mother-son relationship, and firmly supports the traditional reading that in Manfred's love for Astarte Byron offers a disguised account of his love for Augusta. A probable affair with Augusta is indeed the immediate cause of *Manfred*, but throughout his time in England Byron sought in his half sister the warmth and stable affection of which he felt deprived by his mother. From the first Augusta was for Byron a substitute object who might compensate for the terrible pressures Mrs. Byron placed on him and sibling incest in the drama contains unmistakable evidences of prior conflicts. The representation of Astarte as having died and her silence in reply to Manfred's appeals for forgiveness argue that interwoven in the drama is the remorse Byron experienced at the death of his mother. Manfred's unremitting sense of guilt for a death he had no part in reflects Byron's guilt for a death he too had no part in except in wishful fantasies. These exacted their price in the unconscious when they were unexpectedly realized.

The nature of the conflict itself is the fundamental evidence of the traces of the mother in *Manfred*, but the secondary testimony of biography corroborates the interpretation. The maternal character which tinges Bryon's sexual attachments throughout his life is pronounced in the period between his mother's death and the composition of *Manfred*. The predilection of Lady Caroline Lamb for page's livery has never gone unnoticed in discussions of her tumultuous affair with Byron in 1812, but that detail is less important to a consideration of her appeal for Byron than the hysterical strain generally permeating her conduct. Byron tired of her instability, but it was not without gratification: her lack of self-control assured him of his greater competence and reliability. He painted himself as he wished to be in the brilliant correspondence describing the affair to Caroline's mother-in-law, Lady Melbourne: the reasonable, patient man superior to the shrill entreaties of a ridiculous woman. In Lady Melbourne, already past sixty, Byron found the wise and indulgent older woman in whom he could confide intimately without risk of entanglement. His sense of loss lent its force to their friendship, as it did to the liaison with the forty-year-old Lady Oxford which succeeded that with Caroline. "'I never felt a stronger passion,'" Byron later said to Medwin of Lady Oxford, "'which she returned with equal ardour. I was as fond of, indeed more attached than I ought to have been, to one who had bestowed her favours on many. . . . Strange as it may seem, she gained (as all women do) an influence over me so strong, that I had great difficulty in breaking with her, even when I knew she had been inconstant to me; and once was on the point of going abroad with her,—and narrowly escaped this folly.'"[7]

Lady Oxford sailed from England without Byron at the end of June 1813, before a planned farewell meeting of the lovers could take place. It was at this moment of renewed loneliness that Augusta re-entered Byron's life. For almost a decade she had been the object of his warmest feelings, but he had not seen her since going abroad in 1809. Married for six years already to Colonel George Leigh, Augusta now came up to London to escape in the company of her celebrated half brother the worries heaped high by three

---

7. Medwin, p. 70. Byron's murmuring against the influence "all women" gained over him is a representative instance of the fear of maternal dominance that runs throughout his life. Compare the remark of his valet Fletcher about his marriage: "It is very odd, but I never yet knew a lady that could not manage my Lord, *except* my Lady" (quoted by Marchand, 2: 547).

unwell children and the improvidence of her husband. For the first time Augusta and Byron had the pleasure of extended contact, their natural delight in rediscovered affinities intensified by circumstances. They saw each other daily for three weeks; when Augusta returned to her home at Six Mile Bottom Byron soon paid her two visits of several days each. After the second of these he brought her back to London with him; by August 5 he was talking again of going abroad—his intended companion, Augusta (*BLJ* 3:85). Before the end of the month he was hinting to Lady Melbourne and others that the relationship had developed into incest. On the vexed question of whether it had actually done so, acrimoniously debated for a hundred and fifty years, the judicious comment of Leslie Marchand must be taken as the final word: "All that can be said is that the circumstantial evidence in Byron's letters can not be ignored, and that certain aspects of his life and correspondence can not be explained sensibly in any other terms."[8] Of the historical actuality there may yet be some doubters, but of the overwhelming psychological reality of Byron's involvement with his half sister, conditioned as it was by his whole life thus far, there can be no denial.

It was partly to extricate himself from the anxieties of this ever-deepening affair with Augusta that Byron turned his thoughts to marriage: "She wished me much to marry," he wrote Lady Melbourne, "because it was the only chance of redemption for *two* persons" (*BLJ* 4:191). No solution could have been more taxing upon the fragile defenses Byron had erected against his fears of maternal suffocation. The particular choice of Annabella Milbanke increased the burden hundredfold, and the fateful quality of the choice marks the strength of the psychic patterns which influenced it. The complacent self-righteousness which Byron mercilessly satirized after the separation constituted much of Annabella's original attraction. A woman so ostentatiously virtuous could scarcely pose a threat, especially not one who virtually signalled her indifference by refusing an offer of marriage, as Annabella did in rejecting Byron's initial proposal in 1812.

When, to his surprise, a second, tentative exploration was treated as a definite proposal and accepted in September 1814, Byron displayed the misgivings which the fears of engulfment reflected in his poems might lead us to expect. Delaying with pretext upon pretext, reluctant to divide himself from Augusta and hesitant to be thus committed, Byron stalled the wedding. He lingered in London until December 24 before setting out for Seaham, his fiancée's home. Hobhouse, who made the journey with him, recorded his friend's unloverlike lack of impatience and "almost aversion." On the day of the ceremony, January 2, 1815, Byron awakened "with the most melancholy reflections, on seeing his wedding-suit spread out before him."[9]

8. Marchand, 1: 404n. John S. Chapman, in *Byron and the Honourable Mrs. Leigh* (New Haven: Yale Univ. Press, 1975), has queried this conclusion, but his reconsideration seems insufficient to reverse the consensus. It is, in any event, the *image* that Byron constructed out of Augusta and earlier strata which matters to his poetry, and its significance cannot be approached through literal facts alone.

9. Moore's recollection of Byron's burnt *Memoirs*, quoted by Marchand, 2: 505. Byron's fatalistic sense that he would repeat the conduct of his father is apparent in a confession made years later to Medwin, part of which has already been quoted: "I was not so young when my father died, but that I perfectly remember him; and had very early a horror of matrimony, from the sight of domestic broils: this feeling came over me very strongly at my wedding. Something whispered me that I was sealing my own death-warrant" (p. 55).

Once wed, Byron was driven to a course of behavior which seems to us, and seemed to him, as laid out in advance as his wedding-suit. Tenderness toward Annabella was followed by icy withdrawal or deliberate insult, as if only by that means could he be sure of his mastery. He ceaselessly baited his unfortunately humorless bride with Augusta, flaunting their closeness; the motive seems less outward, the infliction of pain on Annabella, than inward, the assertion of unbroken fidelity to the mother figure represented by Augusta. All Byron's conflicts of dependence and autonomy inevitably converged on Annabella, and the compulsion to re-enact the model of his parents' marriage inflamed the situation still further. The drama proceeded to its agonizing conclusion: in January 1816 Annabella left London with her infant daughter, Augusta Ada. Byron had sadly conspired against himself to produce the abandonment he suffered; in April he sought relief on the Continent, as his father had done. As Byron candidly confessed in a poem to his sister after the accumulating storms had broken at last: "I have been cunning in mine overthrow, / The careful pilot of my proper woe" ("Epistle to Augusta," 23–24).

From this complex of originally mother-centered tensions, reactivated by Augusta and Annabella, *Manfred* grows. In the last scene of the play Manfred earns his death by conquering the spirits who claim him. The climactic negation is more flamboyant but less substantial than another element of the scene: the respect symbolized by the handclasp between Manfred and the Abbot who shares his final moments. The fragile parity established by that gesture marks an acceptance by the world of men which is Manfred's true, if brief, victory. With the world of women Manfred can reach no similar accommodation. Sundered from Astarte, on whom he utterly depends, it is indeed "not difficult" for Manfred to die: it is really all he can do. While he too sought to bury his past in "oblivion" Byron was equally paralyzed.

The stagnation which envelops and ultimately chokes the exercise of the hero's will is apparent also in two poems contemporary with *Manfred*. Bonnivard, the protagonist of *The Prisoner of Chillon*, explains at the outset of the tale the cause of his imprisonment:

> But this was for my father's faith
> I suffered chains and courted death;
> That father perished at the stake
> For tenets he would not forsake;
> And for the same his lineal race
> In darkness found a dwelling place; . . .
> (11–16)

The substitution of the singular "father's" in the common generic expression "fathers' faith," like Francesca's rebuke of Alp in *The Siege of Corinth* for having renounced his "father's creed" (576), emphasizes a muted familial configuration which connects this story to its forerunners: the suffering son crushed by the father he emulates.

Bonnivard is one of seven brothers, but the paternal legacy has already claimed four of the boys, "dying as their father died," before the tale begins. Two others succumb during its course; first the familiar hunter-warrior figure "formed to combat with his kind"; then the youngest:

> . . . the favourite and the flower,
> Most cherished since his natal hour,
> His mother's image in fair face,
> The infant love of all his race,
> His martyred father's dearest thought,
> My latest care, for whom I sought
> To hoard my life, that his might be
> Less wretched now, and one day free; . . .
> (164–171)

To the perishing boy Bonnivard stands *in loco parentis,* and his inability to preserve his life adds to his woes as son the frustrations of a father whose line is extinguished.

The mood of debility is a worsening of the weakness of the heroes in the tales: Bonnivard's incarceration embodies in severer form the same psychological materials as Conrad in Seyd's prison and the Giaour in the monastery. The imaginative heart of the poem is not the ideal of Liberty celebrated as the "Eternal Spirit of the chainless Mind!" in the prefatory sonnet, but Byron's depiction of Bonnivard's increasing apathy. He greets the arbitrary release he is finally accorded with pathetic reluctance:

> At last men came to set me free;
>   I asked not why, and recked not where;
> It was at length the same to me,
> Fettered or fetterless to be.
>   I learned to love despair.
> And thus when they appeared at last,
> And all my bonds aside were cast,
> These heavy walls to me had grown
> A hermitage—and all my own!
> And half I felt as they were come
> To tear me from a second home: . . .
> (372–380)

"My very chains and I grew friends," Bonnivard confesses, in words that belie the affirmation of the sonnet. The cell that encloses him "below the surface of the lake" has become an appealing retreat from the world of men—a womb, though a forbidding one. Bonnivard's dungeon and Manfred's tower, enforced imprisonment and voluntary isolation, stoic endurance and Titanic assertiveness, are revealed as two faces of the same sterile arrest. Bonnivard is separated from the energies of nature by a barred window, an emblem of the isolated self-consciousness starker even than the parallel representations in *Childe Harold* III and *Manfred.* The self-control Bonnivard achieves is, like Manfred's, a minimal triumph, but it enables him to relate his misfortunes as none of Byron's earlier protagonists can. The moving restraint of his narrative counteracts in the reader's estimation his immobility and tacit admission of defeat. His successful self-presentation draws value out of personal disaster, a transformation that is like Byron's desperate appeal to art for the power to reshape his limited self and circumstances into a more desirable image.

∗   ∗   ∗

ALAN RICHARDSON

Byron and the Theatre[†]

Byron's considerable body of dramatic poetry poses special challenges for literary criticism, and studies of Byron have often had little to say about the plays as plays. In part, this neglect reflects a larger failure to bring the verse drama of the Romantic poets comfortably within the standard categories of literary history. All of the canonical Romantics—Coleridge, Wordsworth, Byron, Shelley, and Keats—wrote at least one verse play, but until the last dozen years or so these have tended to be dismissed as misguided attempts at 'closet drama': plays meant to be read but not performed. The counter-impulse to read at least some works of Romantic verse drama as 'mental theatre' (Byron's term)—innovative and iconoclastic poetic forms rather than stage plays *manqués*—can work well enough for a 'dramatic poem' like *Manfred* or an intellectual drama like *Cain*.[1] It tends, though, to lose sight of the productive tension between the dramatic works of the Romantic poets and the lively and politically fraught theatrical culture of their time.[2] Byron not only produced a larger and more varied canon of verse drama— eight works, if one counts *Manfred* and the fragmentary *Deformed Transformed*—than any of the other canonical poets, but he also stands out as the only one with extensive, practical experience of the stage. This overview of Byron's poetic drama, then, opens with a look at his relation to the contemporary theatre.

To begin with, Byron was a gifted and enthusiastic amateur actor, dating from his schooldays at Harrow, where he recited Lear and other roles to gratifying applause. As late as 1822, Byron attempted to get up an amateur production of *Othello* while living in exile at Pisa. Though the plan fell through, Byron's interpretation of Iago inspired Thomas Medwin to remark that 'perhaps Lord Byron would have made the finest actor in the world'.[3] Medwin was also impressed with Byron's ability to recall and convincingly mimic the actors he had heard on the London stage years before. In a note added to the preface to *Marino Faliero*, Byron professes his admiration for the great actors of the Romantic-era stage: John Philip Kemble, G. F. Cooke, Edmund Kean, Sarah Siddons, and (in comic parts) Robert William Elliston. The 'long complaints of the actual state of the drama arise', he stresses, 'from no fault of the performers' (*CPW*, IV, 563).

Nevertheless, the 'state of the drama' was indeed a favourite subject for adverse criticism at the time, and Byron's most extensive experience with the contemporary stage, his association with the Drury Lane theatre, came about as a direct result of such 'complaints'.

Drury Lane, along with its rival theatre at Covent Garden, held a monop-oly on London productions of all 'legitimate' drama during the regular sea-son: that is, on tragedy and what Byron called 'gentleman's comedy' (*CPW*,

---

† From *The Cambridge Companion to Byron*, ed. Drummond Bone. Copyright © 2004 Cambridge University Press. Reprinted by permission of Cambridge University Press.

1. Alan Richardson, *A Mental Theater: Poetic Drama and Consciousness in the Romantic Age* (University Park: Pennsylvania State University Press, 1988).

2. Julie A. Carlson's *In the Theatre of Romanticism: Coleridge, Nationalism, Women* (Cambridge University Press, 1994) makes this point most forcefully (esp. pp. 1–29).

3. Thomas Medwin, *Conversations of Lord Byron: Noted During a Residence with His Lordship at Pisa, in the Years 1821 and 1822* (London: Henry Colburn, 1824), pp. 99–100.

IV, 563). Despite the efforts of great, even legendary, actors, however, both Drury Lane and Covent Garden were widely viewed as failing in their mission to guarantee the health of what was variously called 'legitimate', 'regular', or 'national' drama. One problem inhered in the design of the theatres themselves: in an effort to increase profits, theatre managers had insisted on an absurdly enlarged house, and many spectators simply could not hear the actors' spoken lines as a result. Gesture, attitude, and declamation were relied on to convey action and emotion, resulting in what was widely seen as a loss of nuance and a constant temptation toward 'ranting' and other forms of overacting. Meanwhile, the unlicensed, 'illegitimate' stage—including pantomime, burlesque, puppet shows, melodrama, spectacle, and extravaganza—had entered an especially lively and inventive era and began drawing audiences away from the two patent theatres. The attempts of beleaguered theatre managers to borrow such innovations for the licensed stage—most notoriously including 'quadruped drama', the incorporation of horses, dogs, camels, and even elephants into the action—only served to deepen the perceived crisis of 'legitimate' theatre.[4] Drury Lane and Covent Garden were constantly running up losses, and various rescue plans were broached to revivify the licensed theatres, or at least to keep them solvent.

One such plan, led by the brewer and Whig politician Samuel Whitbread, came to involve the establishment of an amateur board of directors for the recently rebuilt Drury Lane, with a subcommittee empowered to run the theatre as a renewed centre for 'national' culture. As a titled aristocrat aligned with the liberal Whigs and as an acclaimed poet, Byron was seen as an ideal choice for the subcommittee: his talent, reputation, and social status would help restore confidence in Whitbread's stewardship. Byron duly became a member in June 1815, and his addition was initially seen as a coup for those wishing to restore the 'regular' drama. The arrangement did not work out, however, and by the time Byron had begun his period of exile in April 1816, there was little to regret so far as abandoning the Drury Lane project was concerned. The theatre continued to lose money, and control was eventually given over to a professional, the actor-manager Elliston, who brought back the 'illegitimate' conventions and effects he had mastered in the unlicensed playhouses.[5] The experience, however, gave Byron a full season of active experience behind the scenes of a working stage, a stint that left him both more knowing in the ways of the theatre and more cynical regarding the immediate prospects for serious poetic drama in London.

Byron's special duty—a dreary enough one—involved working through Drury Lane's massive stockpile of unsolicited scripts looking for decent plays, in addition to soliciting new works from noted writers. The 'number of plays upon the shelves were about five hundred', he later recalled; 'I do not think that of those which I saw—there was one which could be conscientiously tolerated' (*BLJ*, IX, 35). Invitations to Coleridge and Scott led nowhere, though Byron did successfully promote the production of Charles Maturin's *Bertram*, which enjoyed a good run some weeks after Byron himself had left England for good. Given the dearth of material suitable to the theatre's

---

4. Jane Moody, *Illegitimate Theatre in London, 1770–1840* (Cambridge University Press, 2000), pp. 10–78.
5. *Ibid.*, p. 127.

renewed 'national' mission, why did Byron not contribute a play himself? He did make a start on one—*Werner*—which he left behind him with only the first act partially finished, eventually writing it over from scratch six years later. (After Byron's death, *Werner* became his one popular stage success.) His published verse plays, however, Byron repeatedly insisted 'were not composed with the most remote view to the stage' (*CPW*, VI, 16). The poet who (in *Hours of Idleness*) had urged Richard Brinsley Sheridan to produce 'One classic drama, and reform the stage' (*Hours of Idleness*, 585) seemed curiously averse to doing so himself.

Byron's disavowal of any wish for theatrical production, in the face of his active interest in a reformed stage, has struck many critics as problematic. David V. Erdman's 1939 essay 'Byron's Stage Fright' is still cited as the definitive statement of the issue, despite serious flaws in its argument. For one, Erdman relies on a crudely applied Adlerian psychology, a (now dated) school of psychoanalysis that stresses adult overcompensation for childhood traumas. In this spirit, Erdman argues that Byron's inordinate sensitivity to public exposure (with dual origins in his lameness and in inadequate mothering) led him to crave popular success in the theatre while dreading the potential humiliation should his plays fail. Any psychopathological explanation for Byron's ambivalence, however, must occlude the larger cultural issues that help account for the similar resistance to stage representation evinced by a number of Romantic-era poets and critics alike.[6] More troubling, perhaps, is Erdman's extensive reliance on carefully selected and sometimes misleadingly pruned quotations from Byron, 'lifted out of context and assembled to support a predetermined theory'.[7] If the 'stage fright' thesis needs rethinking, however, Erdman unquestionably established Byron's intense and long-term interest in acting, theatricals, and the London stage.

Byron's claim that his own dramatic works were written 'without regard to the Stage' but for the 'mental theatre of the reader' (*BLJ*, VIII, 210) is entirely compatible with a wish for their eventual representation on a more suitable stage of the future. Byron's resistance concerns a specific theatrical climate that, as he well knew from his Drury Lane days, would have all but guaranteed failure for the 'regular English drama' (*BLJ*, VIII, 187) he attempted to create with his historical tragedies, *Marino Faliero*, *Sardanapalus*, and *The Two Foscari*. As Margaret Howell demonstrates in amusing detail throughout her study, Byron's verse plays needed major cutting, reworking, and livening up even to imperfectly meet the expectations of nineteenth-century London audiences. Early productions of *Sardanapalus*, for example, were enlivened by musical interludes like the catchy 'Assyrian Cymbal Dance' and most admired for the spectacular fire effects that all but literally brought down the house in the final scene. Yet Byron remained open to the potential revival of his plays on a reformed stage of the future: 'the Stage is not my object—and even interferes with it—as long as it is in it's [*sic*] present state' (*BLJ*, VIII, 210).[8] Writing immediately for 'a mental theatre', however, allowed Byron

6. Carlson, for example, argues that Byron and other male Romantics found the presence of women on the stage problematic for cultural and political reasons, virtually equating women with the theatre (*In the Theatre*, pp. 199–204).

7. Margaret Howell, *Byron Tonight: A Poet's Plays on the Nineteenth Century Stage* (Windlesham: Springwood Books, 1982).

8. Byron's position as a dramatic poet disenchanted with the theatre of his time may productively be compared to that of his admired contemporary Joanna Baillie, especially as Baillie's theory has been delineated by Catherine B. Burrough in *Closet Stages: Joanna Baillie and the Theater Theory of British Romantic Women Writers* (Philadelphia: University of Pennsylvania Press, 1997).

not only to envision a new era of 'regular' drama, but to write dramatic works of a much greater length, and touching on more sensitive political, ideological, and religious issues than would have been allowed on the licensed stage of the time.

The question of Byron's ambivalence toward stage representation does not have a single answer in any case. As Erdman himself concedes, Byron seems not to have intended what he called his 'metaphysical' dramas—*Manfred*, *Cain*, and *Heaven and Earth*—for production on any stage, present or future.[9] Rather, these works are more usefully understood as experiments in poetic form, combining lyric, dialogic, and choric elements and drawing eclectically for inspiration on Aeschylean drama, descriptions of medieval plays, and Gothic melodrama, as well as on contemporary experimental works like Goethe's *Faust* and Shelley's *Prometheus Unbound*. Their relation to the nineteenth-century stage is an axiomatically oblique one. The three historical tragedies, on the other hand, are presented in direct reaction to the crisis of the legitimate London theatre that Byron had experienced first hand, models of what a restored 'regular' drama might look like. These are neo-classical in form: 'It has been my object to be as simple and severe as Alfieri' (*BLJ*, VIII, 152), the Italian neoclassical dramatist whose works Byron greatly admired. *Werner*, in its completed version, has often been seen as Byron's attempt (ironical or not) to craft a play that would succeed on the stage of the time, 'calculated' as Erdman dourly puts it 'to suit the degraded tastes of the contemporary audience'.[1] Byron's final play, *The Deformed Transformed*, which he left as a fragment, draws again on *Faust*, but in a manner of its own. For all their differences in form, style, and stage-worthiness, however, the dramatic works share a number of recurring themes, character types, and plot elements that lend a measure of continuity—if nothing like unity—to Byron's experiments in dramatic writing considered as a group.

Byron subtitled *Manfred* (1816) a 'Dramatic Poem' and described it as a 'sort of metaphysical drama', the 'very Antipodes of the stage and is meant to be so' (*BLJ*, V, 194). If *Manfred* was designed to be unstageable, however, it still borrowed motifs, effects, and even 'mental' scenery from the Gothic melodramas then popular in the London theatres. More than one critic has seen *Manfred* as approaching burlesque in its relation to the witch plays and Gothic shockers of the day. But contemporary reviewers like John Wilson found *Manfred* an 'extraordinary' if flawed work of dramatic poetry; a 'very powerful and most poetical production' in the words of Francis Jeffrey, one of Byron's most astute critics. Jeffrey noted the formal and stylistic daring of the piece, including its incorporation of choric elements and lyrical songs, reminiscent of early Greek drama: *Manfred* 'reminds us much more of the Prometheus of Aeschylus, than of any more modern performance',[2] not least in the character of the title figure, tormented, sleepless, rebellious, larger than life.

Jeffrey also began a long tradition of viewing *Manfred* as a static monodrama: 'It has no action; no plot—and no characters; Manfred merely

9. David V. Erdman, 'Byron's Stage Fright: The History of His Ambition and Fear of Writing for the Stage', *ELH*, 6 (1939), 219–43: 241.
1. *Ibid.*, p. 241.
2. Jeffrey, in Andrew Rutherford (ed.), *Byron: The Critical Heritage* (London: Routledge, 1970; New York: Barnes and Noble, 1970), p. 118.

muses and suffers from beginning to end.'[3] It is true that *Manfred* deals more with reaction than with action. Haunted by a crime committed in the past, recounted with deliberate obscurity but involving violence, incest, bloodshed, and the death of his beloved sister, Astarte, Manfred alternately seeks 'self-oblivion' and renewed contact with Astarte, or at least with her shade. Deploying a 'mixed mythology of [his] own', Byron confronts Manfred with a series of spirits, demons, witches, and deities, including the 'Evil principle' (*BLJ*, v, 195) of Manichaean tradition. These confrontations invariably leave Manfred in the same self-involved, self-tormented state as before. The foreshortening and deflation of one potential dramatic encounter after another is intentional, enacting the 'withering of social life' that ideological critics have located at the poem's thematic core.[4] Having felt 'no sympathy with breathing flesh' in his youth, Manfred finds no more kinship with spirits, however powerful. They inspire a competing show of Manfred's own power—he refuses to worship or to bargain with them—but each attenuated struggle ends in stalemate, and Manfred remains his own master but categorically alone.

The failure to break out of a profoundly isolated self-consciousness finds its ultimate expression in Manfred's memories and invocations of Astarte (a name Byron borrowed from a tale of incestuous siblings in Montesquieu's *Persian Letters*).[5] Astarte is evidently not only Manfred's sister but his twin:

> She was like to me in lineaments—her eyes,
> Her hair, her features, all, to the very tone
> Even of her voice, they said were like to mine
> (*Manfred*, ii.ii.105–7)

The only being with whom Manfred could feel anything like sympathy is virtually a mirror image of Manfred himself. The potential for an idealized androgynous hero gives way to the absorption of a desired feminine counterpart into an aggressively incorporative masculine self: 'I loved her, and destroy'd her!' (ii.ii.117). When he finally confronts her reticent shade, the 'Phantom of Astarte' speaks fragmentary lines, the first and last of which are merely 'Manfred!' (i.iv.150–5). If this is monodrama, it is a monodrama acutely aware of and self-consciously revealing its own formal limitations.

In seeking to restore a serious, 'national', poetic drama, the Romantic poets were constantly aware of the precedent of Shakespeare, who had become an icon both for tragedy at its highest pitch and for the staging of a British national identity. Although Byron held that Shakespeare was the '*worst* of models' (*BLJ*, viii, 152) for a renewed drama and would turn to Alfieri and other neoclassicists for alternative examples of regular dramatic structure, the verbal texture of Byron's dramatic poetry is everywhere interwoven with Shakespearean echoes and allusions. *Macbeth*, with its own brooding, sleepless, criminal protagonist, hovers behind *Manfred*. Byron

---

3. *Ibid.*, p. 116.
4. Daniel Watkins, *A Materialist Critique of English Romantic Drama* (Gainesville: University Press of Florida, 1993), p. 151.
5. Alan Richardson, 'Astarté: Byron's *Manfred* and Montesquieu's *Lettres persanes*', *Keats-Shelley Journal*, 40 (Keats-Shelley Association of America, New York, 1991), 19–22.

echoes the famous banquet scene (made much of in Romantic-era stagings of *Macbeth*) when Manfred, about to drink from a wine goblet, sees 'blood upon the brim' (II.i.21); the entry of the Destinies a bit later (II.iii) is modelled on the entry of the witches in *Macbeth* (I.iii). The final act of *Manfred*, however, makes repeated allusion not to Shakespearean tragedy but to Miltonic epic, borrowing the very terms of Manfred's enduring defiance from Milton's Satan. In lines that reverberate throughout Byron's dramatic writing, Satan had announced a rebellious yet dubious autonomy in the first book of *Paradise Lost*—'the mind is its own place, and in itself / Can make a Heav'n of Hell, a Hell of Heav'n' (I.254–5); the corollary, as Satan discovers in Book IV, is: 'myself am Hell' (IV.75). Resisting the local Abbot's efforts at an eleventh-hour conversion, Manfred grounds his own claim to autonomy on

> The innate tortures of that deep despair,
> Which is remorse without the fear of hell
> But all in all sufficient of itself
> Would make a hell of heaven
> > (*Manfred*, III.i.70–3)

'Back to thy hell!', Manfred commands the demon who arrives to claim his soul:

> The mind which is immortal makes itself
> Requital for its good or evil thoughts,
> Is its own origin of ill and end,
> And its own place and time
> > (*Manfred*, III.iv.389–92)

The presence of quotation within these assertions of psychic independence and absolute self-identity discloses the emptiness of Manfred's radically autonomous pose. In *Manfred*, Byron models an asocial, isolated, heroic self-hood of titanic proportions only to underscore its limitations. The failure of dramatic action does not so much compromise as constitute the fragmented tragic trajectory followed by the work and its hero.

✻   ✻   ✻

JEROME CHRISTENSEN

The Shaping Spirit of Ruin: *Childe Harold* IV†

There can be no limits set to the interest that attaches to a great poet thus going forth, like a spirit, from the heart of a powerful and impassioned people, to range among the objects and events to them most pregnant with passion, who is, as it were, the representative of our most exalted intellect. . . . The consciousness that he is so considered by a great people, must give a kingly power and confidence to a poet. He feels himself entitled, and, as it were, elected to survey the phenomena of the times, and to report upon them in poetry He is the speculator of the passing might and greatness of his generation.

—John Wilson, review of *Childe Harold* IV, *Blackwood's*, June 1818

The fourth canto of *Childe Harold* slouches from nature to culture, from the weather to the weathered: "I stood in Venice on the Bridge of Sighs, / A palace and a prison on each hand" (st. 1). "Power," according to Selim's dictum, "sways but by division." As the Venetian plays will dramatize, splitting society between palace and prison is the technique by which the oligarchy rules. Here Lord Byron's colossal command of both principle and place announces his authority to dictate the moral of civilized history to a captive audience.

England has a special relationship with Venice:

> But unto us she hath a spell beyond
> Her name in story, and her long array
> Of mighty shadows, whose dim forms despond
> Above the dogeless city's vanish'd sway;
> Ours is a trophy which will not decay
> With the Rialto; Shylock and the Moor
> And Pierre can not be swept or worn away,
> The keystones of the arch!—though all were o'er,
> For us repeopled were the solitary shore.

> The beings of the mind are not of clay;
> Essentially immortal, they create
> And multiply in us a brighter ray
> And more beloved existence. That which Fate
> Prohibits to dull life in this our state
> Of mortal bondage, by these spirits supplied,
> First exiles, then replaces what we hate;
> Watering the heart whose early flowers have died,
> And with a fresher growth replenishing the void.

> Such is the refuge of our youth and age,
> The first from Hope, the last from Vacancy;
> And this worn feeling peoples many a page,
> And, may be, that which grows beneath mine eye.
> Yet there are things whose strong reality
> Outshines our fairy-land; in shape and hues
> More beautiful than our fantastic sky,

And the strange constellations; which the Muse
O'er her wild universe is skilful to diffuse:

I saw or dream'd of such,—but let them go,—
They came like truth, and disappear'd like dreams.
                                                    (sts. 4–7)

Bound to Venice by the fascinating literary representations of her that En-
glish writers have spelled out, England dominates the Queen of the Adriatic
more than doge has ever done. Though attributed to Shakespeare, Otway,
and Radcliffe, this empire of the imagination is quintessentially Byronic, for
Lord Byron interprets the displacement of Venetian reality by English liter-
ature in light of the colonization he has already executed in his own Orien-
tal tales, thereby fashioning an identification of Byron's destiny with the
ambitions of post-Napoleonic Britain as audacious and compelling as
Napoleon's earlier identification with the aims of postrevolutionary France.
    The speculative dialectic that galvanizes *Childe Harold III* is here put to
imperial use by means of a thoroughgoing objectification of the image—the
storied past becomes a "trophy"—and a complementary hollowing out of
the subject, described as a clay vessel through which "beloved existences"
pass. The blurry personification of "Fate" allows the poet to mobilize
energy around the act of "exile" without becoming specific about agent or
object. What is exiled is something that "we" hate, but the "we" is a subject
that both includes the poet and notoriously excludes him as well. Lord
Byron imagines himself as both victim and exploiter of the historical pro-
cess that he describes with such Hegelian verve. In the waning stanzas of
the third canto, Lord Byron had exploited nature's fabled abhorrence of a
vacuum (*CH III*, sts. 101–2). Voided, he had, as he notes in his journal,
"repeopled my mind with nature" (*BLJ* 5:99). The enabling discovery of
Childe Harold IV is that commerce makes itself a second nature by creat-
ing vacuums that it can then naturally fill. The way Byron's mind works is
the way British commercial society works. The way British society works is
the way everyone's mind will work. Byronic self-division has become the
model for the recursive machine of Britain's imperial self-division: exiling
a hateful reality *in order* to "multiply" representations that can replenish
the void. *Childe Harold's* momentous "Stop!" can be rationalized as a more
than Malthusian injunction not only against breeding but against all forms
of creaturely life. Depopulation precedes repopulation. Venice becomes a
storied past so that it can be made a trophy and that trophy a page repeo-
pled "for us." The implantation of characters from Shakespeare succeeds
to the implantation of the Venetian lion as the sign for a bloodlessly impe-
rial acquisition and a colonial occupation exempt from erosion by the tides
of history.
    The imperial self-division of Byronism descends from the precedent sen-
timental responses to the depopulation of the English countryside in the
eighteenth century (Goldsmith's *Deserted Village* may stand for all) as well
as to the modernizing imperative memorably demonstrated in the clear-
ances of the Scottish Highlands following the Battle of Culloden in 1745
(the fashionable Ossianism of Byron's *Hours of Idleness* is an apt example).
Locke in boots, Cumberland cleared the landscape of a population and a
political culture as if he were wiping a slate clean. It was on this tabula rasa
that the political economists and conjectural historians of the Scottish

Enlightenment diagrammed the commercial system—a dynamic articulation of cultural representations, social transactions, and economic laws—which promised the elevation of a benighted Scotland to the level of its southern neighbor and which would serve as the pattern for the United Kingdom's global projection of its interests. Although it is true that the identification of English power with commerce had long been a cliché, until Waterloo success had nevertheless been ad hoc; it is a signal extension of that power for the poet to demonstrate that the imperial market has its image and ideological support in the speculative dialectic of literary creation, that the cultural imperialism practiced in Ireland and Scotland could be limitlessly extended, and that depopulation could be bloodless, a mere matter of substituting representations for bodies (Francis Jeffrey's "perpetual stream of thick-coming fancies" [*RR* B:2:865]).

Byron's use of the Spenserian stanza in *Childe Harold IV*, far more technically adept than in any of the earlier cantos, seems a fitting homage to his precursor and peer in the strategic transmutation of a foreign reality. What Byron adds to the Elizabethan romancer is the intervening history of British literature, which has confirmed the Burkean insight that that literature, the fiction of Britain, could stand firm against revolutionary ideology and imperial threat. Thus endowed, Byron can be "comprehensive" (preface) as Spenser was not and aggressive where Burke was defensive; he can render the past as a field inhabited by literary characters fully granted the status of historical persons in order that the past and the foreign might be enclosed in a global discursive space. The sun will never set on a Britain thus Byronized. As John Wilson rhapsodizes in his review of the poem, "Whatever lives now—has perished heretofore—or may exist hereafter—and that has within it a power to kindle passion, may become the material of his all-embracing song" (*RR* B:2:899).

But nothing is got for nothing. The very comprehensiveness of the recharacterization of the world entails that Britain be voided as well: the apocalyptic flood that the dreamer of Wordsworth's *Prelude* fears is the flood that *Childe Harold* presupposes as the historical condition for its imperial stance. Do not say that the flood is merely metaphorical, for it is the material force of that flood to prove that the land, that anchorage of the literal for yeoman and nobleman alike, had never been more than a powerful metaphor, now supplanted by the groundless power to make and impose metaphors. If Great Britain has become an imperial discourse, it is at the cost of the land of the Angles as well as the land of the Celts. Byron takes as fitting reward for performing his ideological service the singular power to ship back, like a planter from the West Indies, his "fresher growth" to the cleared surface of the country that had formerly uprooted him, thereby to dominate a culture and a mode of production now tailored to his figure. This reversal will be simultaneously enacted and parodied in the English Cantos of *Don Juan;* from a station in Venice the poet will repeople the vanished world of Regency England with phantoms from the foreign country of his own exiled past (Juan with an Aurora and an Adeline on each hand).[1] The darker implications of this literary/commercial leg-

---

1. On the general phenomenon of spectralization, which she defines as the "absorption of ghosts into thought," see Terry Castle, "Phantasmagoria: Spectral Technology and the Metaphorics of Modern Reverie," *Critical Inquiry* 14 (Fall 1988): 26–61. Castle refers to Byron's description of George III in *The Vision of Judgment* on p. 44

erdemain, whereby the hateful is bloodlessly replaced by the beloved and the "absence" of real people is supplied by their representations, are explored in *The Two Foscari*. There the villainous Loredano compacts the figures of merchant, ruler, and poet; his enterprise matches that announced here, at the head of Lord Byron's most "comprehensive" poem: he zealously works to eliminate the hateful Foscari one by one so that he can mark them down as figures in his ledger—their dynasty displaced by an account book that their deaths balance. In Loredano's version of the dialectic of enlightenment, "History's purchased page" becomes history's page of purchases.

"Yet there be. . . ." "Strong reality" is the "one word" of *Childe Harold III* elevated from destructive wish to utopian dream. In its original appearance the notion poached its ethic from the Wordsridgean doctrine of the "one life," abbreviated with Byronic negligence: "And thus I am absorb'd and this is life" (*CH III*, st. 73). The line, by all odds the most unconvincing Byron ever wrote, makes Wordsworthian "matter of factness" seem a modest thing. And even when the poet rises to a more plausible sublimity,

> All is concentred in a life intense,
> Where not a beam nor air nor leaf is lost,
> But hath a part of being, and a sense
> Of that which is of all Creator and defence.
>
> Then stirs the feeling infinite, so felt
> In solitude where we are *least* alone;
> A truth, which through our being then doth melt
> And purifies from self.
>
> (CH III, sts. 89–90)

the rite of intensification cannot defend against a sudden storm and the old itch:

> The sky is changed!—and such a change!; Oh night,
> And storm, and darkness, ye are wondrous strong,
> Yet lovely in your strength, as is the light
> Of a dark eye in woman!
>
> (st. 92)

Nature's reality is eclipsed by the simile invoked to celebrate it. Not for this faints the poet, whose career, as we have seen, is elaborated in the studied violence of the shift from one moment of absorption to another. In the opening of the fourth canto the Byronic *yet* introduces yet another lure in sequence, not, as its Wordsworthian counterpart, a revision or a compensation. The perception that the repopulation of the void by a Venetian fairyland will not permanently satisfy the appetite of a reading public does not undermine the speculative model but complicates and extends it.

Setting off from the inaugural image of Venice, the fourth canto iterates the Spenserian stations of Lord Byron's dilatory comprehension of the panorama if not the principles of history. His poem, as his soul, "wanders" until, periodically, he demands it back to "stand." This is a poem where the different connotations of *stand*—poetic, moral, and theatrical—are masterfully condensed. In Italy, he "stand[s] / A ruin amidst ruins; there to track

/ Fall'n states and buried greatness" (*CH IV*, st. 25). And fitly one ruin
addresses another:

> Thou art the garden of the world, the home
> Of all Art yields, and Nature can decree;
> Even in thy desert, what is like to thee?
> Thy very weeds are beautiful, thy waste
> More rich than other climes' fertility;
> Thy wreck a glory, and thy ruin graced
> With an immaculate charm which cannot be defaced.
>
> (st. 26)

Speculating beyond the Napoleonic analogy in an endeavor to claim a trans-
historical integrity, Lord Byron monumentalizes himself by Byronizing all
monuments. To be Byronic has become the universal criterion of unique-
ness and authenticity. And Italy certainly flaunts a Byronic glamour. Its
"desert" is a version of the "sterile track" and the "last sands of life" from
the opening of *Childe Harold III*. Its "weeds" recall Byron's plangent self-
characterization in stanzas 2 and 3 of that poem. A terrible change has
befallen Byron, Italy, and the world—but at least no worse there is.

Despite time's relentless assault, the object, like the corpse of Greece in
the opening of *The Giaour*, retains an inextinguishable allure:

> Time, which hath wrong'd thee with ten thousand rents
> Of thine imperial garment, shall deny,
> And hath denied, to every other sky
> Spirits which soar from ruin: thy decay
> Is still impregnate with divinity,
> Which gilds it with revivifying ray.
>
> (st. 55)

Italy's immunity partakes of the mystery that grounds all claim to privilege
in Byron: the gift of his noble birth. That native assurance underwrites the
poet's Miltonic vaunt that "to the mind / Which is itself, no changes bring
surprise" and permits him not only to stand a ruin amidst ruins but as an
island against the "inviolate island" of his birth.

The island on which the poet ultimately stands is the one word of his
name, the self-sufficiency of which had been the poet's dream at least since
the bold prophecy of "A Fragment" in *Hours of Idleness*:

> My epitaph shall be my name alone;
> If *that* with honour fail to crown my clay,
> Oh may no other fame my deeds repay!
> *That*, only *that*, shall single out the spot;
> By that remember'd or with that forgot.

Following the separation and a taste of celebrity, however, some amend-
ment became necessary:

> With false Ambition what had I to do?
> Little with Love, and least of all with Fame;
> And yet they came unsought, and with me grew,
> And made me all which they can make—a name.
>
> ("Epistle to Augusta," ll. 97–100)

A Byron made not born. Made not making. Indeed, being made and being stabbed or raped have the same traumatic force for Byron: as the ruin is the intersection of the natural and the cultural, so is the name the intersection of the psychic and the historical. The ruin of Lord Byron's name (published abroad by scandal and reviews) does not any more than the ruin of Italy mean extinction but *allegorization: Byron* becomes the name of ruin. Thus circumstanced, the name can be imagined to be the linguistic corollary to the decayed body of a murdered Italy; the immaculate charm that the poet sees in Italy is what he wishes for "Byron." But as the "revivifying ray" of divinity shows that the soul within is indistinguishable from a cosmetic gilding, so is "Byron" suspiciously dependent for its "native" charm on the pathos of those events that have *ostensibly* corrupted it. I stress "ostensibly" because the ruinology of *Childe Harold IV*—its will-to-iconicity—which attempts an elegiac break with the past, looks, in retrospect, like no break at all in a career that has always been elegiac in its mood and always iconic, if only in the modern, commercial sense that the poet's name has always been identifiable with his books and those books have always been vended as commodities. This duplex commodification of the poetic object and of the poet's name does represent a radical break between Byron and those poets of the past—Tasso, Rienzi, Ariosto, Dante—with whom he makes common cause. The commodity is not a ruin: it is neither natural nor subject to natural processes, although it is always being naturalized, as, with exemplary finesse, here in *Childe Harold IV.*

Such a conclusion does not contradict Byron's identification with the ruins of Italy. On the contrary, it suggests that the ruins of the modern age are themselves radically discontinuous with ruins in the past: their suspension between nature and culture reflects denaturalization and deculturation—expresses, that is, their status as commodities subject to extraction from context, whether by *force de main*, as in the cases of Lord Elgin and Napoleon or, more economically, by the representation of the poet. The commodity is not a ruin *in* history because the commodity form is the ruin *of* history.

Made, the poet's name expresses not the metaphysics of blood but the privilege of copyright. Under the commercial magic of John Murray, the charm of "Byron" has become as immaculate as that of a banknote: if soiled, the name can be replaced by its facsimile. Under the poetic magic of Lord Byron the charm of Italy is endowed with the same resiliency. Induction into the cultural system properly named Byronism confers immunity to surprise with the same force as does the formalization of an astronomical system called Ptolemaic or Copernican in Adam Smith's account. This is the immunity offered to the aristocrat (the aristocracy offered to a reader) whose mind must be itself because he has sold his ancestral estate and, who, unlike the floating commercial empire of Venice, cannot even find any soil in which to "plant his lion." Consequently, he must, as image after image in *Childe Harold IV* attests, build his castles (or plant his tannen tree) in the air:

> But from their nature will the tannen grow
> Loftiest on loftiest and least shelter'd rocks,
> Rooted in barrenness, where nought below
> Of soil supports them 'gainst the Alpine shocks

> Of eddying storms; yet springs the trunk, and mocks
> The howling tempest, till its height and frame
> Are worthy of the mountains from whose blocks
> Of bleak, gray granite into life it came,
> And grew a giant tree;—the mind may grow the same.
>
> (*CH IV*, st. 20)

Hardly a Wordsworthian plant (primrose, daffodil, or thorn thrusting up from the ground whose being it becomingly tells), Lord Byron's tannen is the image of an alienated, ungrounded organicism, a plant of the imagination. But it is an organicism all the same, where things develop and grow according to an inner law despite the absence of the soil that had once seemed necessary for life, as for meaning. In the fade of the ground, becoming is a kind of being; growth seems natural and inevitable, without assertion. In typically Byronic fashion, however, that act of identification also discloses its defensive function: one plants oneself in the air, becomes a being, in order to steel a self against shocks.

The mind's turn round on itself in a Satanic / organic closure is metaphor and metonymy for the enclosure of the "inviolate island of the sage and free" (*CH IV*, st. 8). This systematic self-enclosure must pass for virtue in default of the traditional support for autonomy and strength, land. At this historical juncture (that is, in *Childe Harold IV*), when the commercial economy takes on a stoic mien and figures the possibility of surprise (such as a Napoleonic coup d'état or an imperative foreign utterance) as a change without profit, "Lord Byron" preempts real change by *predicting* an inexorable alteration, by representing corruption, decay, and degradation—the ruin of virtue—as part of the routine, *economical* modifications of the superficies that assure novelty and revive taste, extend commerce and engrain its sway:

> But ever and anon of griefs subdued
> There comes a token like a scorpion's sting,
> Scarce seen but with fresh bitterness imbued;
> And slight withal may be the things which bring
> Back on the heart the weight which it would fling
> Aside for ever; it may be a sound,—
> A tone of music, summer's eve, or spring,
> A flower, the wind, the ocean,—which shall wound,
> Striking the electric chain wherewith we are darkly bound;
>
> And how and why we know not, nor can trace
> Home to its cloud this lightning of the mind,
> But feel the shock renew'd, nor can efface
> The blight and blackening which it leaves behind,
> Which out of things familiar, undesign'd,
> When least we deem of such, calls up to view
> The spectres whom no exorcism can bind,
> The cold—the changed—perchance the dead—anew,
> The mourn'd, the lov'd, the lost—too many!—yet how few!
>
> (*CH IV*, sts. 23–24)

No change, whether in the cycles of the market or of empires, may bring surprise, but something—call it the past—shocks the chain by which we have bound our effects to our causes. The analysis here strikes a note, albeit muted, of modernity. It is muted by Byron's sentimental recuperation of the shock in the figures of the "mourn'd, the lov'd, the lost"—a familiarization of the specters in personal terms that echoes the familiarization of the ghosts haunting the unpeopled wastes of the square of St. Mark, the Highlands, or the Russian steppes with characters from Shakespeare, Otway, and Scott. After having denied his ability to "trace home" the "lightning of the mind," the poet ostentatiously proceeds to track it right down. That recuperation abbreviates the scenario of *Manfred*, Byron's earlier, grandiose attempt to dramatize a mind capable of opening itself to those spectral shocks and of portentously connecting their appearance with remembered acts against loved persons. By taking responsibility for his torments, Manfred aspired to bind all shocks to the narrative unfolding of an individual destiny. *Childe Harold IV* follows suit.

CHERYL FALLON GIULIANO

Marginal Discourse: The Authority of Gossip in *Beppo*[†]

For some time it has been known that Byron based his comical satire *Beppo* on a piece of gossip passed to him by Pietro Segati, the elderly husband of Byron's twenty-two-year-old, dark-eyed mistress Marianna. What amuses me in the telling of that story is the gossip that follows it: Hobhouse's reflection on Marianna's response to the tale of the returning Turk. In that tale the Turk, returned after several years at sea without any communication, offers his wife three choices: "either to quit your amoroso and come with me—or to stay with your amoroso, or to accept a pension and live alone."[1] "M Zagati [sic] said I'm sure I would not leave my amoroso for any husband—looking at B. [this] is too gross even for me," Hobhouse records in his diary.[2] Already it is apparent that gossip generates more gossip, the original tale begetting Hobhouse's judgmental disclaimer, Byron's gossiping poem, and this essay, which will engender talk among us about people who are absent or treated as absent. The procreative potential of gossip interests me in this essay because when Byron's poem is fully read as a piece of gossip itself and not just as *Don Juan*'s stylistic forebear, the reading begets new ways of talking about the cultural and biographical contexts of the poem. *Beppo*'s seemingly genial manner conceals the poem's personal and social purposes: more than commemorating the cutting of his ties to England (in particular to Annabella and his previous poetic voice), through the celebration of his relationship with Marianna and his initiation into Venetian mores, *Beppo*, as a piece of self-generated gossip, cleverly manipulates the conventions of gossip, placing Byron, the exile, back in the center of English society. In addition, it aims its dart of gossip not, as is commonly the case,

---

† From *Rereading Byron: Essays Selected from Hofstra University's Byron Bicentennial Conference*, ed. Alice Levine and Robert N. Keane. Copyright © 1993 Hofshra University. Reprinted by permission of Garland Publishing, Inc.
1. Leslie A. Marchand, *Byron. A Biography* (New York: Alfred A. Knopf, 1957), 2:708 (hereafter cited in the text by volume and page number).
2. Ernest J. Lovell, Jr., ed. *Lady Blessington's Conversations of Lord Byron* (Princeton: Princeton University Press, 1969), 28.

at the absent party talked about, because Byron generates the talk about himself, but at the recipients: English society, especially Lady Byron.

Byron was a great proponent of and participator in gossip. By the account of Lady Blessington, one of his few women friends (friend equalling not mistress by Byron's own testimony):

> Byron is very fond of gossiping, and of hearing what is going on in the London fashionable world: his friends keep him au courant, and any little scandal amuses him very much.[3]

When the countess refers to such information as "trifles" beneath him, Byron responds with characteristic charm: "Don't you know that the trunk of an elephant, which can lift the most ponderous weight, disdains not to take up the most minute? This is the case with my *great mind*, (laughing anew) and you must allow the simile is worthy the subject. Jesting apart, I do like a little scandal—I believe all English people do."[4] Simultaneously endorsing and ridiculing gossip by mocking the clever pun on worthy and weighty in his image, Byron goes on to comment more seriously on what he sees as the need of the English for gossip. Taking his cue from the Countess Benzoni, Byron agrees that the severe morals in England caused the English to attack the sins of others so that they could prove an abhorrence of impropriety through words instead of actions, thereby denying their own improprieties and, in fact, allowing them to continue.[5]

Byron was also the target of gossip, some of it extremely malicious. A year after his separation from Annabella, he complained to Douglas Kinnaird that "Caroline Lamb—& Lady B[yron]—my 'Lucy' & 'Polly' have destroyed my *moral* existence amongst you—& I am rather sick of being the theme of their mutual inventions" (5, 162). A man who had fashioned his own image throughout his poetic career, Byron despised others' inventions of him, especially when they contradicted his own. Feeling victimized by gossip that annihilated his moral character, Byron may have realized that he could turn the tables and let gossip speak not only against him but for him as well. Gossip is a powerful mode of discourse for the victim who feels unable to "fight fair." It is also one of the fastest spreading forms of information, pyramidal in its reach.

His letters from Venice, a tissue of news and gossip, often request the same from England. "Since my arrival in Venice I have written to you *twice*. . . . — in these I told you all the gossip I could think of—& shall be glad to have a letter in return," he writes Kinnaird in January 1817. During this period Byron often counted his letters in his letters to his friends, recounting in the process what he saw as their neglect of him through lack of correspondence. Such letters signal how deeply he felt the sting of marginalization from English society: no longer the literary lion in the center, he has become a social outcast. "Life has little left for my curiosity," he writes. . . . "if I could but manage to arrange my pecuniary concerns in England—so as to pay my debts—& leave me what would be here a very fair income . . . you might consider me as posthumous—for I would never willingly dwell in the 'tight little Island.'" Marginality feels to Byron like a kind of living death, living outside

---

3. *Ibid.*
4. *Ibid.* 28–29.
5. *Byron's Letters and Journals*, ed. Leslie A. Marchand (London: John Murray, 1973–82), 5:162 (hereafter cited in the text by volume and page number).

or on the edge of the "tight little Island" (5, 135–36). He wishes to be "dead" to England personally but alive in his writing, a "posthumous" author.

His greatest triumphs of gossip are his stories about himself. He frequently repeats the same story to different people, amazingly, in some of the very same words, as though he has memorized them. The amusing, swaggering tale about Marianna and her sister-in-law fighting over him is a case in point. His rendition of this story emphasizes the physical scuffle between the two women ("sixteen slaps given and received . . . a deal of eau of Cologne—& burnt feathers . . . which ended in the flight of one & the fits of the other" [5, 172–73]). The entertainment value of the tale places Byron in the center of Venetian talk. At the end of January 1817, gleeful about the spread of the story, he writes Thomas Moore:

> . . . the sister-in-law, very much discomposed with being treated in suchwise, has . . . told the affair to half of Venice, and the servants (who were summoned by the fight and the fainting) to the other half. (5, 167)

A whole month later he reports the story to both Kinnaird and Augusta in a strikingly similar fashion. The narrative quality of these letters suggests a somewhat objective stance toward the stories of his life. More than sharing his life's experiences with his friends, Byron turns them into titillating stories, the kind that will be told and retold, like gossip. *Beppo* is told in the same vein. Clearly Byron wants all of England to hear his stories just as all of Venice has heard this one.

Beppo was published anonymously, a strange fact for a poem which repeatedly makes an issue of naming and not naming names. The heroine, nameless at first, is introduced through the process of naming, only to have the significance of naming dismissed.

> A certain lady went to see the show,
>   Her real name I know not, nor can guess,
> And so we'll call her Laura, if you please,
> Because it slips into my verse with ease.[6]

Beppo, as Byron explains in a letter, "(the short name for Giuseppe—that is the *Joe* of the Italian Joseph)" (5,269), disappears for several years only to return home to "reclaim" his "Christian name (97)." Sotheby is called Botherby, though Byron denies the association—"if there are resemblances between Botherby & Sotheby or Sotheby and Botherby the fault is not mine—but in the person who resembles—or the persons who trace a resemblance" (6, 35–36). And the narrator, a palpable presence throughout, is "but a nameless sort of person, / (A broken Dandy lately on my travels)" (52). Perhaps this anonymity is self-protective; perhaps it is protective of Murray as Byron's publication instructions suggest: "it won't do for your journal—being full of political allusions—*print alone—without name*—alter nothing" (6, 7). Perhaps it reflects Byron's feeling that he had lost his "good name." But it seems to me, if not a conscious ploy, an informed subconscious urge, effective in raising questions about authorship and ultimately about Byron's place in the poem, since its autobiography is so thinly disguised. Throughout the first half of 1817, Byron's letters

6. *Lord Byron. The Complete Poetical Works*, ed. Jerome J. McGann (Oxford: Clarendon Press, 1980–), 4:135–36, stanza 21. (Stanzas of *Beppo* are cited from this edition and are given by stanza number.)

are studded with thoughts of returning to England to "settle his affairs." With the sale of Newstead, when his physical return became unnecessary, gossip proved to be the fastest traveling vehicle by which to return to England, if not physically, at least conversationally: he would quickly be in the minds and mouths of English society through gossip. And the early reviews of *Beppo* accomplished exactly that. Byron's identity quickly became known—his name appeared on the title page of the fifth edition in late April—but until the word of his authorship spread, the reviews were littered with speculation. Although Francis Jeffrey refused to "expose [himself] by guessing," he could not help thinking he had seen this author of "loquacious prattle" and "desultory babbling" before. Many were more certain. The *British Review* closed with "wish[ing] we could have parted better friends with the author of *Beppo*, whoever he may be, for we cannot help respecting his genius. We rather hope that those will be found right in their conjecture who have ascribed it to Lord Byron himself; for, under all circumstances, we do not wish for a duplicate of that eccentric nobleman."[7] Byron could not but have been pleased, in spite of the embedded assault on his character.

Although Byron never discussed his psychological motives for writing *Beppo* as a piece of gossip, I think it is clear that he was well acquainted with the literary power of gossip to impel plots, its economic power to sell, and its erotic power to titillate.[8] Much more complex and interesting to a reading of *Beppo* are the sociopolitical functions of gossip. More than idle chatter, which is a nineteenth-century definition, gossip is small talk with a social purpose.[9] It is a powerful mechanism of socialization and social control. Gossip socializes or produces conformity because it focuses group attention on norms and values, causing the members of the group not to deviate from sanctioned behavior—or suffer the consequences: gossip. Gossip about approved behavior preserves cultural standards by allowing norms to be stated and reaffirmed. Gossip about unacceptable behavior, on the contrary, achieves the same goal by taking a disapproving tone. Consequently, gossip can create a measure of social control for the person who circulates information he wants others to have or to judge according to his telling. Byron manipulates these workings of gossip, twisting the conventions to suit his needs. His practice, for example, inverts the sociological theory that people gossip "to obtain information in order to make comparisons between themselves and others,"[1] to reassure themselves, from peoples' reactions, that they haven't strayed too far from acceptable norms. Byron needs no such reassurance. Rather, he spreads gossip to make the listeners draw comparisons between themselves and others, hoping the English will see how moralistic and hypocritical they are in comparison with the Venetians.

As a social phenomenon, gossip draws boundaries and lines of social distance. While a cursory glance may suggest that gossip bonds people

7. *The Romantics Reviewed: Contemporary Reviews of British Romantic Writers*, ed. Donald A. Reiman, Part B, *Byron and the Regency Society Poets* (New York: Garland Publishing, Inc., 1972), 2:893, 1:458.

8. Patricia Meyer Spacks, *Gossip* (New York: Alfred A. Knopf, 1985), 7 ff.

9. Ralph L. Rosnow, "Gossip and Marketplace Psychology," *Journal of Communication* 27 (1977) 158; Jack Levin and Allan J. Kimmel, "Gossip Columns: Media Small Talk," *Journal of Communication* 7 (1977), 169.

1. Jerry M. Suls, "Gossip as Social Comparison," *Journal of Communication* 27 (1977), 164; see also Sissela Bok, *Secrets: On the Ethics of Concealment and Revelation* (New York: Vintage Books, 1984), 92; Spacks, *Gossip*, 22.

together, those bonds, which exclude others, may easily be ruptured or exposed as untrustworthy. One who gossips about others *to you* may just as easily gossip *about you* to others. And the supposed intimacy of the bond is easily mimicked by someone who, understanding the conventions of the shared secret, shares secrets of others rather than his own. Yet gossip can be used to underline similarities among those "in the know," and draw differences between the knowing ones and outsiders. The boundaries drawn by gossip are even more complex than this. To be meaningful and enjoyable, gossip must concern the actions or lives of acquaintances. Gossip about strangers is generally uninteresting. Although it appears that Byron gossips about strangers, the Venetians, to English society, *Beppo* is a thinly disguised representation of his relations with Marianna and Pietro Segati. His letters from Venice are full of references to his position as *cavalier servente* and how he feels about it. What is interesting here is that Byron again twists the conventions of gossip: gossiping about strangers, a practice rarely exercised, teases those in the know to spy the relatively undisguised personal references. The gossiper, then, is an insider—spreading talk about a member of the community—and an outsider at the same time—turning a critical eye on a member of the community and, therefore, not fully coinciding with it.

Gossip's complicated lines of social demarcation trace Byron's position in relation to both English and Venetian society. Self-exiled, outside English society, with an insider's knowledge, Byron could easily use gossip to tie himself to and critique England at the same time.

Much of *Beppo*'s overt critique satirizes "London's smoky cauldron," "chilly" English women, the harsh English language—"whistling, grunting guttural, / Which we're obliged to hiss, and spit, and sputter all" (44)—and English smugness and moral hypocrisy. But a more covert critique lurks below the surface of the satire, a critique of Lady Byron's character. *Beppo* incorporates much forgiveness: "And how came you to keep away so long? / And are you not sensible 'twas very wrong?" With these questions, Laura forgives Beppo; Beppo forgives the Count and Laura ("Though Laura sometimes put him in a rage, / I've heard the Count and he were always friends"); and although he makes all three silly, the narrator forgives them all for their behavior. Yet Lady Byron remains indefatigably unforgiving. Byron supports his position further by endorsing "sinful doings" in Venice:

> . . . 'Cavalier Serventes' are quite common,
>   And no one notices, nor cares a pin;
> And we may call this (not to say the worst)
> A *second* marriage which corrupts the *first*. (36)

Byron salutes constancy in amorous relationships, overlooking the marital infidelity they presuppose. Implicit in his celebration is a condemnation of an opposing, straitlaced moralism, the kind he attributed to Annabella. To the extent that this dart is directed at Lady Byron, *Beppo* is malicious gossip.

I do not think Byron means, through *Beppo*, to extend to Annabella the Venetian right to have two men in her life. Rather, I think he means to show her that a threesome can be congenial. True, in *Beppo* the trio is composed of two men and a woman; however, because at this stage in his life Byron felt like the oppressed party (generally the woman) and because in the poem he uses the gossiping voice of the woman, he remains the person analogically allowed to have two simultaneous relationships.

Gossip is the special province of people on the edge of power: people with little social authority typically hesitate to inquire directly about the personal lives or beliefs of their superiors. Perhaps this is why gossip is traditionally considered women's talk. Originally gossip meant god-related, designating god-parents of either sex who congregated for the birth of a child.[2] The term later narrowed its scope to individual relationships. Applied to men by Samuel Johnson, a gossip was a drinking companion, signifying camaraderie and warm fellow-feeling; as he applied it to women, the term carried the pejorative cast of "one who runs about tattling like women at a lying-in." By 1811, gossip denoted a type of conversation rather than a type of person: "idle talk, trifling or groundless rumor, tittle-tattle" (OED). But it was still associated more with women than men, and it still is, even though sociological studies reveal that members of both sexes gossip. These associations tend to demean women, linking their uncontrolled garrulity to sexual promiscuity, weak and inferior minds, and—perhaps most kindly—to a lack of anything more meaningful to do. But these stereotypical judgments neglect the peculiar, compensatory power of gossip and the solidarity that may result from it.

Patricia Meyer Spacks and Alexander Rysman in their literary and sociological studies of gossip emphasize its positive psychological powers to establish female community, and its subversive political power to strengthen those on the margins through the freedom to critique dominant outsiders within the new community.[3] Rysman's 1940s study of an anonymous small town, "Plainville," suggests that men fear women's gossip because "a patriarchal society resents female solidarity" (179). Spacks's point, less gender specific, is similar: "those nominally in control, the moralists who articulate society's view of itself, may feel nervous about what by definition they cannot govern" (30): the type of gossip such moralists condemn slanders, betrays secrets, and invades privacy.[4] Flaunting his disregard of convention, Byron puts even the reprehensible qualities of gossip to his advantage: he wants to betray the secrets of his private life, not to slander his reputation, of course—he feels that has already been done during the separation proceedings—but to scandalize English society.

Through his strategic use of gossip, Byron partakes in the community this kind of talk renders. *Beppo* is addressed, at least in part, to Byron's circle of Cambridge friends who, Louis Crompton shows in *Byron and Greek Love*, practiced a private mode of writing understood in one way by intimates, another way by outsiders: a coded language.[5] When contemplating adding his name to the published poem, Byron writes to Murray: "If you think that it will do *you* or the work—or *works* any good—you may—or may not put my name to it—*but first consult the knowing ones*" (6, 25). Clearly *Beppo*, as gossip, is meant to solidify Byron's bonds with his inner circle back in England.

2. Jack Levin and Arnold Arluke, *Gossip: The Inside Scoop* (New York: Plenum Press, 1987), 14–42.
3. Spacks, *Gossip*, introductory chapter; Alexander Rysman, "How the 'Gossip' Became a Woman," *Journal of Communication* 27 (1977), 176–80.
4. Spacks, *Gossip*, 33, and Bok, *Secrets*, 98.
5. Louis Crompton, *Byron and Greek Love: Homophobia in 19-Century England* (Berkeley and Los Angeles: University of California Press, 1985); see also Jerome J. McGann "Lord Byron's Twin Opposites of Truth" a chapter in *Towards a Literature of Knowledge* (Chicago: University of Chicago Press, 1989).
6. Karen Chase, " '"Bad" was my commentary'—Propriety, Madness, Independence in Feminist Literary History," in *Victorian Connections*, ed. Jerome J. McGann (Charlottesville: University Press of Virginia, 1989), p. 26.

But more important than this solidarity is the authority Byron gains by reversing the "nominally-accepted, downward-looking gaze of the dominant upon the subordinant: he inspects the inspector."[6] That is to say, through the marginal discourse of gossip, Byron directs his critical gaze at the moral magistrates he feels have judged him, Lady Byron in particular. The reprobate chastizing the judge, Byron neutralizes authority's decree, his satire becoming a form of revenge, a form of self-empowerment.

That Byron was aware of the subversive dynamics of gossip is clear within the poem. At the Ridotto several forms of gossip intermingle:

> Now Laura moves along the joyous crowd,
> . . . .
> She then surveys, condemns, but pities still
> Her dearest friends for being drest so ill.
>
> One has false curls, another too much paint,
>   A third—where did she buy that frightful turban?
> A fourth's so pale she fears she's going to faint,
>   A fifth's look's vulgar, dowdyish, and suburban. . . .
>   (65, 66)

Laura internalizes gossip about women in her circle, thus distancing herself from them—to her advantage. But while Byron ridicules other women through her eyes, he ridicules her as well for her perceptions. Laura's thoughts are petty but harmless.

With Laura placed momentarily in the center of attention, the other women at the masquerade turn their eyes on her examining eye. The risk in any voyeuristic peering is that those who watch will be *seen seeing*:

> Mean time, while she was thus at others gazing,
>   Others were levelling their looks at her;
> . . . .
> The women only thought it quite amazing
>   That at her time of life so many were
> Admirers still,—but men are so debased,
> Those brazen creatures always suit their taste.
>
> . . . Laura thus was *seen* and *seeing*. . . .
>   (emphasis my own; 67, 69)

These women neutralize, with spiteful gossip, their feelings of inferiority by downgrading Laura and the men who appreciate her, enhancing their own position among themselves and subverting, or carnivalizing, the established hierarchy.

Suddenly trivializing women's gossip, Byron cuts himself off from his female voice:

> For my part, now, I ne'er could understand
>   Why naughty women—but I won't discuss
> A thing which is a scandal to the land,
>   I only don't see why it should be thus;
>   (68)

No, he'll not gossip. But, of course, the entire poem is gossip. All writers "gossip" with their readers. Moreover, all writers resemble gossips because all are vulnerable to the fluctuations of popularity reputation confers.

Continuing his stanza, Byron tries to distance himself from the world of gossip further by opposing it to religious discourse:

> And if I were but in a gown and band,
>   Just to entitle me to make a fuss,
> I'd preach on this till Wilberforce and Romilly
> Should quote in their next speeches from my homily.

The problem with gossip is not, then, in disclosing the content of the scandal but choosing the form in which to expose it. The traditional authority of the clergy, Byron suggests, "entitles" them to speak moral judgments with impunity. The gossip, it seems, cannot. The voice of religion also claims an uncontested authority never granted to gossip because the scriptural paradigm, "It is written," does not emanate from the community as gossip does, but descends upon it from above and exists in a written instead of an oral form.[7] Though disembodied and non-human, this paradigmatic voice enters the male guard, the clergy. Thus whereas gossip is associated with female inanity, scripture, at the opposite, more authoritative end of the discourse spectrum, is associated with male power. It is not surprising, then, that when he tries to dissociate himself from the world of female gossip, Byron introduces the clergy.

But try as he may to shed his gossiping persona, Byron is not attracted to the clerical world where sermons "make a fuss," but to women's modes of discourse. Thinking of Lady Byron, for instance, he nearly gossips about their marital difficulties:

> Why I thank God for that [that Mussulwomen don't deal in
>   mathematics] is no great matter,
>   I have my reasons, you no doubt suppose,
> And as, perhaps, they would not highly flatter,
>   I'll keep them for my life (to come) in prose;
>
> (79)

He restrains himself here, but he decides, following another strategy typically associated with women, to keep a secret, another empowering device for those on the margins. The power of a secret here is its inherent threat: that it could at any time be divulged.

At the end of the poem Byron reclaims the traditionally masculine mode of written discourse: "My pen is at the bottom of a page, / Which being finished, here the story ends" and apologizes for going on so long, "stories somehow lengthen when begun" (99), like gossip. He also readmits Beppo to the authoritative male community: "the patriarch re-baptized him, / (He made the Church a present by the way)" and celebrates the male bonding of the Count and Beppo, Beppo even borrowing "the Count's small-clothes for a day" (98).[8] But still, the charm of the poem is its loquaciousness, Byron's appropriation of the female voice of gossip. "I've heard the count and he were always friends," he gossips all too comfortably, a feminine voice finally dominating the poem.

As though he wants no competition from masculine tale-tellers, who are not trivialized with the title of gossips, Byron blocks out Beppo's voice near

---

7. Chase, "'Bad,' was my commentary," p. 26.
8. I heard this fine point in a paper Peter Manning delivered to the UCLA Romantic Study Group in 1988 while I was still in the process of writing my essay.

the end of the poem ("What answer Beppo made to [Laura's] demands, / Is more than I know"), takes exception with it ("*He* said that *Providence* protected him— / For my part, I say nothing, lest we clash"), and denies him reliability ("His friends the more for his long absence prized him, / . . . For stories,—but *I* don't believe the half of them"). His own gossiping voice rises above all others, keeping Byron in the company of women.

Appropriating a female voice grants Byron the authority he feels he cannot attain any other way. Feeling deprived of authority in many important areas of his life—in his marriage and with Ada, for example—Byron writes Annabella in March 1816 about the separation proceedings:

> the World has been with you throughout—the contest has been as unequal to me as it was undesired—and my name has been as completely blasted as if it were branded on my forehead:—
>
> (5, 54)

This statement is telling because it expresses Byron's association of his loss of name, or reputation, his falling in the world's eyes, with Lady Byron's rise. From Italy, one year later, he worries that Annabella and her family are trying to deprive him, as he tells Augusta Leigh, "of all *authority* over my daughter" (emphasis my own; 5, 190). The effect of Lady Byron's tales about her husband's personal life—he attributes his unpopularity to them—align her with regulative marketplace forces that seem to deny his exclusive authority over his work. Her voice, a female voice, he believes, preempts both his outer masculine voice (poetry) and the spontaneous inner literary production he characterizes with the ejaculatory metaphor "the lava of the imagination whose eruption prevents an earthquake." Though he is the prototypical masculinist Romantic poet, Byron knows how to usurp the power of women, even as he feels his authority being usurped by them.

Byron frequently appropriates Augusta Leigh's voice, asking her to speak for him: "I have been too ill to write to Lady Byron myself—but I desire you to repeat what I have said & say" (5, 190); "do not forget to state to Lady B[yron] what I say in this letter" (5, 224). Augusta admits to John Hanson that this upsets her: "He has desired me to write so many things to Lady B. that my head can't hold them, and I'm sure my pen could not write them."[9] Hoping she will gossip to Annabella, Byron writes to Augusta:

> My letter to my moral Clytemnestra required no answer—& I would rather have none—I was wretched enough when I wrote it—& had been so for many a long day & month—at present I am less so—for reasons explained in my late letter (a few days ago) [On 18 December 1816, Byron had written Augusta about his romance with Marianna Segati, "at present I am better—thank Heaven above—& woman beneath."] and as I never pretend to *be* what I am not you may tell her if you please that I am recovering—and the reason also if you like it.—
>
> (5, 144)

With Augusta, he hoped, the power of suggestion could make her repeat the message verbatim. He can make his presence felt by speaking through her, but in the process, he may rob her of her own voice.

9. Malcolm Elwin, *Lord Byron's Wife* (New York: Harcourt, Brace & World, Inc., 1962), 421 ff.

His nickname for his estranged wife resonates with meaning, both repressed and overt. In branding Lady Byron a Clytemnestra, Byron focuses on the figure of the violent, vindictive woman, suggesting, of course, that *he* is Annabella's victim. In his partial reading of this ancient myth, Byron overlooks the Clytemnestra whose voice as queen and king's wife is insufficient to save her daughter from Agamemnon's willful sacrifice to the Trojan War, eliding the figure of the woman silenced. In writing a letter that "required no answer," Byron has his say and denies Lady Byron a response. In effect, he silences her, as Clytemnestra was silenced, appropriating her voice. In *Beppo* Byron's appropriation of a feminine voice does not silence Laura. Nothing could of course: the return of her long lost husband causes her only a momentary pause.

Like Laura, Byron realizes that gossip can serve him, but he will not worship it. He assumes the voice of gossip to set tongues in England wagging, only to retreat to the masculine world of the written word at the close of the poem; "My pen is at the bottom of the page" becomes his signature. The poem does, however, paradoxically enfranchise women's talk: it mocks women's gossip at the same time that it revels in it. Byron joins the company of women to appropriate the authority gossip confers. In refusing to be embarrassed by its gossiping, the poem refuses to be judged. Thus Byron is able to turn his examining eye upon the eyes of his English examiners, and in this reversal of gaze, the poem performs a "radical gesture," an early, unknowing "act of feminism."[1] The danger of gossip—that those spying will be spyed on, that those speaking will be spoken of—becomes its strength. When Byron's English audience reads the poem, succumbs to its gossip, and talks about it, not only do they become gossipers but they also validate the activity of the gossip. Being "overheard" grants the original gossiper the power of speech and puts those overhearing in the traditionally feminine position of eavesdropper. *Beppo*, the gossiping poem, successfully inverts the hierarchical social structure. Its setting, too, provides at least a temporary subversion of cultural norms, Carnival being a time when authority tolerates the breaking of rules knowing order will be reimposed.

Unfortunately, we have no conscious revaluation of gossip in *Beppo*, most likely because Byron would have feared being feminized by attributing value to a feminine mode of communication. But his use of gossip does open the way for the sort of reexamination this paper undertakes. *Beppo* may be gossip, but it is not merely small talk. "I fear I have a little turn for satire," Byron confesses. "And yet methinks the older that one grows / Inclines us more to laugh than scold" (79). Byron's comical poem implies a connection among laughter, gossip, and satire. All can be subversive and all can be used to register criticism of authority. This poem, which makes us laugh so much, can, in fact, leave us "doubly serious shortly after."

---

1. Chase, "'Bad,' was my commentary," p. 27.

PETER W. GRAHAM

Nothing So Difficult
[Opening Signals in *Don Juan*]†

> *Every good poem must be wholly intentional and*
> *wholly instinctive. That is how it becomes ideal.*
> Friedrich Schlegel, *Critical Fragments*

In literature and criticism alike, beginnings are difficult largely because they need to be accurately and efficiently significant. Having adopted as my title one of Byron's openers acknowledging the problem of getting started, I shall continue by taking as my own approach to *Don Juan* his professed method of telling the story, to "begin at the beginning" by giving attention to what Victor Brombert would call "opening signals," the useful and often crucial early hints that alert readers to generic or thematic contexts.[1] In the course of this essay, I shall consider *Don Juan*'s two Horatian epigraphs, the prose Preface, the Dedication, and the first canto. The irony of such an approach is that Byron chose or created a number of these meaningful pre-liminaries only to suppress them: for reasons to be explained later, the orig-inal epigraph, the Preface, and the Dedication did not appear in editions of *Don Juan* published during Byron's lifetime. But before looking at these opening signals, let us examine the two words that precede them all, the poem's title.

"*Don Juan.*" The first thing noticed (and then most likely forgotten) by any-one who does not think in British English is the peculiar pronounciation "Joo-un." Those whose first encounter with the title is a spoken reference, such as a teacher's "Tomorrow we start *Don Juan*" or a friend's "*Don Juan* is the one poem I'd take along to a desert island," will immediately detect the alteration of the expected "Hwan." Readers who have not heard the title pro-nounced do not have much longer to wait. They might suppose the title pro-nounced in the Spanish way, but six lines into the first stanza of the first canto, "Juan" appears as the third *b* rhyme in a pattern thus far established as *a b a b a*. If "Juan" were part of the first trio, there would perhaps be a fur-ther moment of doubt—is the author rhyming a third *a* or setting up a *c*? But because "want," "cant," and "vaunt" have already appeared, it is clear that "Juan" is to rhyme with the preceding *b* words, "new one" and "true one," though the precedent of the *a* group suggests that this rhyme need not be perfect. So whether readers learn before embarking or after arriving at the sixth line that "Juan" is "Joo-un" instead of "Hwan," the awareness of this phonetic mutation comes quickly.

I have spent this much time explaining a small and largely self-evident matter because the point involves more than just humor. Pronouncing "Juan" to rhyme with "new one" is comical, yes. More important, it exem-

---

† From *Don Juan and Regency England*. Copyright © 1990 by the Rector and Visitors of the Uni-versity of Virginia.

1. Victor Brombert, "Opening Signals in Narrative," *New Literary History* 11 (1980): 489–502. Attending to opening signals generally proves rewarding, but especially so in *Don Juan*, which, as Michael G. Cooke and Peter J. Manning have separately but similarly concluded, proceeds by repeating and varying its initial pattern. See Cooke's "Byron's *Don Juan*: The Obsession and Self-Discipline of Spontaneity," *Studies in Romanticism* 14, no. 3 (Summer 1975): 290–300, Manning's *Byron and His Fictions* (Detroit: Wayne State University Press, 1978), 220–24.

plifies a distinctively English habit of speech that in turn suggests a human trait Byron particularly deplored in his countrymen—the tendency to appropriate and then alter (that is, "improve" or "correct") another culture's property, whether a word, a practice, or a product: "Juan," waltzing, or tea. Byron's opposition to the habit of reducing the whole world to the vision that appears through one's own spectacles and his desire to transcend all forms of such narrowness can be seen throughout his poetry, from the biting satire on literary coteries and political camps in *ENGLISH Bards* and *SCOTCH Reviewers* (my emphasis) to *Childe Harold's* restless roving through lands and civilizations and its denunciation of the spirit that thinks packing Grecian marbles off to London will save them, to *Manfred, Cain,* and *Heaven and Earth*, where the highest mortals (if not always the happiest ones) are those ambitious to go beyond the boundaries and values of more complacent human bipeds, to *Beppo's* practical and courteous Venetian counterpoint to English prudery and hypocrisy. I would suggest that insularity in all its protean shapes, but particularly those guises it assumes in Great Britain, is one of *Don Juan's* most important topics. Byron shows it to be so in a number of ways, but first in the pronunciation of his poem's title, his title character's name.

How do we know that "Joo-un" is Byron's meaningful choice rather than his using by default the pronunciation current in his day? First, we can be sure that he was aware of the difference—and that he knew his readers would know of his awareness. Byron had journeyed through Spain during his travels of 1809–11; and his Iberian adventures, transparently fictionalized, had appeared in the first cantos of *Childe Harold*. Ever since publishing that poem he had been a poet who could take it for granted that his readers were interested in him—or in the myth fashioned by the public, then polished and projected by the poet himself.[2]

Second, "Joo-un" is far from being the poem's sole example of this particular comic effect. Byron seems to go out of his way to warp Spanish proper nouns. As meter and shifted accent mark show, the name of Juan's father becomes "Jó-se" rather than "Jo-sé." The name of Juan's mother, "Inez," is made to rhyme with "fine as"; "Lope" with "copy"; "Nunez" with "moon is"; "Seville" with "revel"; "Cadiz" with "ladies"; and, in a stanza where the narrator has just shown himself familiar with a Spanish proverb, "Guadalquivir" with "river." That other literary don grotesquely renamed by English readers, "Don Kwik-zut," is mentioned three times, and never could the verse accommodate the Spanish "Kee-ho-tay."

Spanish is not the only foreign language to receive such treatment in *Don Juan*—for instance, "louis" rhymes with "true is" and "Lyons" with "dying"—and the beginning of canto 1 is not the only starting place where linguistic comedy of this sort is highlighted. Byron applies the strategy to an English name at the beginning of canto 9, in the apostrophe to and denunciation of Arthur Wellesley, created duke of Wellington for his labors at Waterloo but called something else on Napoleon's side of the English Channel:

> Oh, Wellington! (or "Vilainton"—for Fame
> Sounds the heroic syllables both ways;

---

2. Jerome J. McGann, *Fiery Dust* (Chicago: University of Chicago Press, 1968), 285–86.

> France could not even conquer your great name,
> But punned it down to this facetious phrase— (DJ 9.1)

French does to "Wellington" much the same thing that English does to "Don Juan." The joke is funny enough for someone who knows only English, who smiles as Byron looks at a victor and sees a villain, but it becomes yet funnier when taken bilingually. *"Vilainton"* imputes vileness and vulgarity to this newly created duke and utterly fashionable hero—and to the entire Ton (as London's Great World called itself) that toasted him.

Just as Byron can do things with English names as well as Spanish ones, he can also use the device for a closing as well as a commencement. *Don Juan* seems by its own nature and by critical consensus a poem that stops rather than ends,[3] but if Byron had wanted to end his poem at sixteen cantos, the last stanza would have been as good a place as he might easily find to leave Don Juan. At this point we see Don Juan, who is presently involved in different ways with four females (Leila, Aurora, Lady Adeline, and the Duchess of Fitz-Fulke), about to distinguish appearance from reality by unfrocking the Black Friar. The scene at once follows and inverts the traditional Don Juan ending. Byron's Juan, like the others, faces a ghostly visitant—but it is a specter most fleshly, a holy being most profane, a man most womanly: "In full, voluptuous, but *not o'er*grown bulk, / The phantom of her frolic Grace—Fitz-Fulke!" (*DJ* 16.123). If knowing British English hampers recognition of the humorous significance in "Don Joo-un," it is crucial to the comic effect here. "Fulke" and "bulk" look as if they should rhyme, and in *Don Juan* they do. But in regular British pronunciation, "Fulke" would be said "Fook"—much apter for this high priestess of dalliance. The name is brilliantly chosen in and of itself: "Fitz" and "Fulke" when taken together both aurally and visually suggest the duchess's double nature (her sublime pedigree and her earthy preoccupation) and the two chief sources, Norman and Saxon, of her culture and language. In thus rhyming the couplet and mispronouncing the name, Byron gilds his wit. He concludes the last completed canto as he began his poem, by violating a cultural convention. It is delightfully ironic that here he turns the tables and treats his mother tongue to the phonetic imperialism it inflicts on other languages throughout the poem.

This play on pronunciation is a particular manifestation of Byron's international theme—more precisely, his way of viewing narrowly insular values, practices, beliefs, and happenings (especially English ones) from a wider context. Another form the theme takes is discernible in the pair of Latin epigraphs Byron successively chose for *Don Juan*. Both come from Horace,

---

3. The sense that *Don Juan* stops rather than concludes is widespread among critics. For a range of discussion on causes and effects of this incompletion, see, among others, Elizabeth Boyd, *Byron's* Don Juan (New York: Humanities Press, 1968), 30–33; Jerome J. McGann, Don Juan *in Context* (Chicago: University of Chicago Press, 1976), 3–4; George M. Ridenour, *The Style of* Don Juan (Hamden: Archon, 1969, rpt.), 122; Andrew Rutherford, *Byron: A Critical Study* (Stanford, Calif.: Stanford University Press, 1967), 238–41; M. K. Joseph, *Byron the Poet* (London: Victor Gollancz, 1964), 303; Lilian R. Furst, *Fictions of Romantic Irony in European Narrative, 1760–1857* (London: Macmillan, 1980), 116–17; Anne K. Mellor, *English Romantic Irony* (Cambridge: Harvard University Press, 1980), 62; Bernard Beatty, *Byron's* Don Juan (Totowa: Barnes and Noble, 1985), 182; Peter J. Manning, *Byron and His Fictions*, 220–21. Michael Cooke, who sees "the unfinishable poem" as "a signal romantic contribution to the form and vital entelechy of poetry itself," is especially insightful on the rewards of incompletion ("Byron's *Don Juan*," 285–86).

the poet whose urbane jesting sets a style and tone for Byron to emulate.[4] Both place Don Juan's modern story within an ancient tradition whose origins are not English—and in this way implicitly characterize the poem's readership. Only readers who, like Byron, have enjoyed or endured a classical education (the training typically provided ruling-class British men) will begin—without footnotes, that is—to appreciate the relevance of the epigraphs. Only readers who can add some understanding of Byron the poet and the man to acquaintance with Latin in general and Horace in particular can approach "competence" as they venture to interpret the quotations employed as epigraphs. *Domestica facta*, the epigraph Byron rejected after Hobhouse noted "Do not have this motto" on the proofs, is a particularly witty illustration of this point. In a 26 January 1819 letter to Scrope Davies, Byron proclaims his sense of *domestica facta* to be "'*Common life*'—& not one's own adventures" (*LJ* 11:171), a broadened application of "Roman events as opposed to borrowings from Greek legend and history," as Horace meant the phrase in context, "*vestigia Graecr / Ausi deserere et celebrare domestica facta.*"[5] Byron must have known, however, that English readers—especially his contemporary public, notably inclined as it was to project him into his verse—would first see *domestica facta* as its cognate "domestic facts" in the sense of "Lord Byron's affairs." Even the classically educated Hobhouse took it that way.[6] Reducing *domestica facta* to either private affairs or public events would ignore a dimension of *Don Juan*, but taken together the contemporary connotation and the classical one do a good job of signaling how wide *Don Juan*'s range of subjects and perspectives will be.

The epigraph replacing *Domestica facta* is *Difficile est proprie communia dicere,* which Byron had earlier translated as "'Tis no slight task to write on common things" in *Hints from Horace.*[7] Again, the Latin quotation offers a double insight as to what the workings of *Don Juan* will be and how Byron conceives of his poetic task. *Don Juan*'s subjects may be *communia*, common things, ordinary or shared concerns; and as the poet of *communia*, Byron is quick to strike a modest attitude. In the Dedication he pictures himself "wandering with pedestrian Muses" (stanza 8), and this ironically self-deprecatory stance recurs. But Byron also assumes the contrary position, whose elements are evident in the first two words of Horace's phrase, *difficile est.* "To write on common things" is "no slight task" in that doing so calls for considerable skill and having done so can produce estimable results: a clear, honest view of things as they are, a "moral model," an epic. Not just anyone can write on common things— and, as Byron sees it, two English authors woefully lacking the aptitude are William Wordsworth and Robert Southey, brother Lakers and fellow subjects of the Preface.

*   *   *

Let us now turn to the Dedication of *Don Juan*. The Preface at which we have just been looking swings that way on the hinge of "Having supposed

---

4. McGann, Don Juan *in Context*, 69–70.
5. Horace, *Ars Poetica*, lines 286–87. Quoted in C. O. Brink, *Horace on Poetry: The "Ars Poetica"* (Cambridge: Cambridge University Press, 1971), 65.
6. See John Cam Hobhouse, *Byron's Bulldog: The Letters of John Cam Hobhouse to Lord Byron,* ed Peter. W. Graham (Columbus: Ohio State University Press, 1984), 257.
7. McGann, Commentary to *Don Juan*, 670.

as much of this . . . ," at which point the reader must proceed to envision an "English editor" whose work the Dedication is said to be and Byron's attention turns from Wordsworth to Southey, the principal subject of that Dedication.

Writing to Thomas Moore, Byron described the Dedication as "good, simple, savage verse upon the [Laureate's] politics, and the way he got them" (LJ 6:68). This characterization is not entirely accurate. In his seventeen dedicatory stanzas, Byron does not display *Don Juan's* full range of moods and subjects, but his target is not just Southey, his time not only the present, his place not merely England, and his tone not simply savage indignation.[8] The Dedication's first three stanzas take aim at Southey (with a four-line potshot at Coleridge in stanza 2), but the fourth draws a bead on Wordsworth, and the fifth blasts the Lakers as a group. Stanzas 6–8 compare the Lakers with their contemporaries, Byron included; 9 generalizes about the poet who "reserves his laurels for posterity" to make a transition (stanzas 10–11) to Milton, excellent as the Lakers are debased. Stanzas 12–15 confront that personage Anne Mellor perceptively recognizes as the "other Bob" of the Dedication, Robert Stewart, Viscount Castlereagh and foreign secretary of the Tory government.[9] Stanza 16 offers the narrator's reaction to Castlereagh's foul foreign policies and turns in its last line back to Southey, who "lives to sing them very ill," and whose political apostasy is contrasted with the narrator's faithfulness to the "buff and blue" of Whiggery in the final stanza.

Byron's choice of Southey to receive the dedicatory honor is amusing in several ways. At its simplest, the Dedication achieves an ironic reversal, dispensing a slap in the form of a bow. The feat is delicately done in that there are credible reasons for Byron to compliment Southey. Any author might reasonably dedicate his work to the official poet of his nation. If, as I shall go on to suggest in the next chapter, *Don Juan* owes a debt of influence to Robert Southey's prose narrative of a fictive Spaniard traveling in England, Byron might gratefully acknowledge the begetter (though not the "onlie" one) of his verses. Still, Byron has personal and public reasons, much stronger ones, to turn such a Dedication to satire; and these reasons justify the digressions from Southey himself.

In his Dedication Byron announces what we have seen offered by the Preface in the form of *répétition*, the English subject of his poem. The shape this announcement takes shows the aristocratic Byron as keenly aware as the democratic Orwell would be of the close connection between language and politics. Byron denounces the tuneless, foggy ravings of the Lakers and their turncoat Toryism—the repressive Irish and Continental policies of the "slave-maker" Castlereagh and the "set trash of phrase" that marks his oratory. Against all these stands the historical example of Milton, the antithesis to the Regency Tories, a man and poet sublime in his song, uncompromising in his antimonarchical politics: "He did not loathe the sire to laud the son, / But closed the tyrant-hater he begun" (DJ, Dedication, 10). The vision offered here is a highly stylized one. For now, Byron

---

8. The best introduction to the "brilliant, self-contained satire" of the Dedication and its relevance to the main body of *Don Juan* is "Honest Simple Verse," the first chapter of Ridenour's *The Style of* Don Juan.

9. Mellor, *English Romantic Irony*, 56.

does not show us mixed cases: good poets with bad politics, bad poets with good politics, principled but tongue-tied statesmen, or corrupt yet eloquent ones.

Instead, Byron presents what he hates and what he admires in their purest forms. He enhances political and poetical incompetence by linking them and by associating both with sexual inadequacy. Each "Bob" of the Dedication (and it is an iconoclastic gesture to address either the laureate or the minister so familiarly) is depicted as sexually deficient. Castlereagh is an "intellectual eunuch," so vile as to warrant no pronoun but "it." Southey, somewhat more virile, is made the butt of the famous "dry Bob" innuendo and along with the other Lakers is obliquely accused of intellectual incest, a charge enriched by knowledge that Southey and Coleridge were married to sisters, Edith and Sarah Fricker, and that the Coleridges for a long time had shared the Southeys' house at Keswick:

> You, Gentlemen! by dint of long seclusion
>   From better company have kept your own
> At Keswick, and through still continued fusion
>   Of one another's minds at last have grown
> To deem as a most logical conclusion
>   That Poesy has wreaths for you alone;
> There is a narrowness in such a notion
> Which makes me wish you'd change your lakes for ocean.
>
> (*DJ*, Dedication, 5)

One way to look at incest is as a particular variety of provinciality, and it is interesting to see Byron so deftly exploit its metaphorical potential to even the score with the man whom he thought had done as much as anyone to spread through England the tale of Byron and Shelley's Diodati "league of incest"—an unjust charge to which Byron may have been sensitive for reasons outside that precise situation.

Byron's grudge against at least one Laker, Southey, is both principled and personal. The brilliance with which he here can blend the two realms, as he does in the application of *domestica facta*, gives an accurate gauge of *Don Juan*'s soon-to-be-encountered complexity and economy. Likewise, the Dedication faithfully predicts the cosmopolitan freedom of the *Don Juan* narrator, who takes the long view of one who understands history as well as the present, the broad view of one who knows cultures beyond that into which he was born, the lofty view of one generally inclined to magnanimity but not so priggish as to be above yielding to pettiness when it proves entertaining. In subject, opinion, tone, and method, the Dedication informs us that what follows will be a work where English concerns—poetical, political, and the rest—will be a crucial though not single-minded interest of a composing presence that resists authority, undercuts order, and transcends limits: even that authority called the poet, that order called the poem, and those limits called themes and subjects.

We are now ready to look at the opening signals displayed in *Don Juan*'s first canto, though these are not the looming indicators of intent and purpose some works might offer. Byron began *Don Juan*, as his letters say and as McGann rightly stresses, with little forethought and no plans for a poem of length.[1] Thus canto 1 does not shadow forth a coming epic (none being yet envisioned), or trumpet its aspirations (as yet unfelt), or lay out strategy (improvisation being the mode Byron had hit upon). But *Don Juan* is from its first line a felicitous work, and in canto 1 we can see some embryonic features of what will later develop. The poem's habitual reliance on comparison of matters, moods, people, and things and the grounding of these comparisons on English soil are already clear. As we shall see below, the first English readers, who received a sealed manuscript copy Byron had sent from Venice via Lord Lauderdale, reacted to the poem as if the crucial matters in the ostensibly fictive (and Spanish) tale were real (and English) in model and significance.

Those readers were Byron's most intimate Cambridge comrades John Cam Hobhouse and Scrope Davies, his friend and banker Douglas Kinnaird, and John Hookham Frere, author of "Whistlecraft's" *The Monks and the Giants*, the English ottava rima precursor of *Don Juan*. Witty, worldly, well-read, enlightened in their opinions, liberal in their sentiments, familiar with Byron's life, ideas, and manners, these men can be seen as coming as close as any real people could to being the ideal readership for *Don Juan*. Their careful group judgment, relayed by Hobhouse in a long letter of 5 January 1819, is the earliest critique of *Don Juan* and a consistently accurate prediction of the outrage and objections the poem would provoke in some quarters. Despite the Spanish setting of canto 1, Hobhouse and the others immediately saw that its "domestic facts were more English than Spanish."[2] Though Byron took umbrage at their recommendation that he not publish *Don Juan*, there is neither prudery nor detraction in their advice. Fully appreciative of *Don Juan*'s merits, they argued against publication on grounds of expediency.

Hobhouse acknowledges that *Don Juan* demonstrates Byron "as superior in the burlesque as in the heroic to all competitors" and sees that "this singular style" may be Byron's "real forte." But, he says, the transparently veiled digs at Lady Byron and the sarcastic hints at the details of their separation (e.g., stanza 28's lines "She kept a journal, where his faults were noted, / And open'd certain trunks of books and letters") would repulse public opinion, which had begun to turn away from Annabella in Byron's favor. The English readership would confuse Byron with his "half-real hero" Juan; and this blend of author and character would confirm the widely held belief in the exaggerated accounts of Byron's Venetian dissipations, rumors whose flames Byron took care to fan and Hobhouse to extinguish. Such coarse or irreverent passages as the discussion of the pox (*DJ* 1.131) and the parody of the Ten Commandments (*DJ* 1.205–6) would weaken Byron's position as a champion of liberal causes. The ad hominem attacks would be construed as unseemly—the political ones because Byron could not be at hand to fight Castlereagh, the literary ones because the first poet of the age should not condescend to notice such "wretched antagonists" as Southey, Wordsworth, and Coleridge.

Hobhouse's letter shows that the English focus of Byron's narrative was obvious to his contemporaries. Modern readers have little trouble reaching

---

1. McGann, Don Juan *in Context*, x, 3.
2. Hobhouse, *Byron's Bulldog*, 256–61. Subsequent quotations in the paragraph that follows in text are also from this source.

the same conclusion: the Spanish details are too false and the English ones too real for reading any other way. A suspicion that *Don Juan's* Spanish scene is a painted backdrop might start at the moment of noticing "Joo-un," and the rapid buildup of other Spanish mispronunciations should only increase doubts of authenticity. So should the line that follows Juan's appearance: "We all have seen him in the pantomime." Don Juan is not "at" but "in" the show, so our "ancient friend" has to be a stage Spaniard rather than a true one watching the spectacle. What of the "we" who "all have seen him"? Common sense says that this is an English audience—and spelling out the reasons why only strengthens the conviction. Presentations of Don Juan in pantomime and other forms of spectacular theater were highly popular in England during the period spanned by Juan's story and Byron's life. Add to this the fact that the poem's language is English and the further fact that the first string of recent "heroes" to be rejected in the next stanza are English soldiers: it is certain that "we" the characterized readers must be English.

And indeed, quite apart from the contorted names, there are many misrepresentations of things Spanish in canto 1 that take the form of communal fallacies prevailing in England (and other Protestant nations). The canto's two betrayed spouses, Inez and Alfonso, do not react as Spanish Catholics would. At the close of the eighteenth century a Spanish lady— even a prodigious one of Inez's sort—would not be divorcing her husband, on grounds of adultery or anything else. If a marriage were to be ended, the alternatives would not be "death or Doctors' Commons" (*DJ* 1.36) but death or a papal bull, marriage being ultimately a sacrament as well as a legal matter. And should one of the partners in a failing marriage take the former path, a Spanish heir would not be left, as Juan is, with particularly English legal entanglements and rewards, "a chancery suit" and "messuages" (*DJ* 1.37). Likewise, when Don Alfonso divorces Julia (unlikely), the details would not be featured "in the English newspapers, of course" (unlikely) with the best of the transcripts "ta'en by Gurney" [*sic*] the Parliamentary shorthand clerk (most unlikely), and once divorced, Julia would not be "sent into a nunnery" (*DJ* 1.188–91). English Protestant audiences, from Shakespeare's day to Byron's, might suppose convents convenient receptacles for disgraced women; but by the eighteenth century the religious orders typically saw the matter another way.

The *domestica facta* of marriage, inheritance, and separation that seem so wrong for Spain are very like Byron's own English experience, as are some of the principals in these proceedings. Everyone since Hobhouse has noticed many specific similarities between Lady Byron and the "learned lady" who masterminds both separations: the pedantry, mathematical talent, loftiness, cryptic pronouncements, even the choice of dress material. Should a reader miss the specific resemblances to Annabella, Byron sketches Inez with a more general Englishness that can hardly be overlooked. The Prioress of Chaucer's *Canterbury Tales* is evident in the series of accomplishments attributed to Inez and then retracted. When he needs to fashion a comparison to convey something of Inez's "perfection," the narrator always turns to England for his raw materials: to the works of such writers as Maria Edgeworth, Sarah Trimmer, and Hannah More, to the legal career of Sir Samuel Romilly (who had handled Byron affairs and whose 1818 suicide had made recent scandal), to the best English products—such as timepieces by Harrison and Rowlandson's Macassar hair oil.

The associations of these English allusions to high-minded legalism struck down by misfortune and notoriety, female intellectualism and didacticism, the repressive precision of a well-crafted machine, a mundane cosmetic claiming otherworldly powers, can all be seen as relevant to Annabella as Byron might want to present her. But we cannot simply equate the Spanish lady and the English one. Byron denies patterning the former on the latter, though his denial is not without a semiconfessional undertone: "What are you so anxious about Donna Inez for?" he writes to Hobhouse. "She is not meant for Clytemnestra [one of his stock names for Lady Byron]—and if She were—would you protect the fiend?" (*LJ* 6:131). If we are not inclined to take Byron's word on the matter, then his associative ingenuity will thwart a simplistic "this equals that" reading; for the depiction of Don Juan's family situation offers early evidence of a strategy that recurs throughout the poem—fiction-making that braids or weaves two or more realities into a whole that resists reduction into any one of its component strands. Relying on this superbly effective means of frustrating the systematizing, oversimplifying impulse in readers, Byron can facetiously exploit material from his marriage without exactly presenting that marriage, for many details of the "ill-assorted pair" who produced Don Juan are also reminiscent of Byron's own parents, Captain John Byron and Catherine Gordon Byron. Donna Inez's circumspection is the reverse of Mrs. Byron's violent frenzies, but she is equally disagreeable to her husband. And that husband has much in common with Captain Byron. He is a gentleman, though not a titled one. His blood is ancient. He is both a cavalier and a womanizer. His wife characterizes him as *"mad"* and *"bad,"* words at once recalling Annabella's fears at the time of the separation and Lady Caroline Lamb's famous three-attribute summation of Byron *fils* but also evoking Byron *père*, "Mad Jack," in whose paternal shoes the poet, as estranged husband and absent father, found himself. Having given his wife a miserable time of it and one child, a son, Don Jóse dies as Captain Byron did and leaves to his wife the rearing of that only son, whose boyhood education is puritanical. All these details suggest that Byron was thinking of his parents' marital situation as well as his own when he concocted Jóse, Inez, and Juan; but one further detail seems to make the matter certain. That detail is found in a parenthetical reference to Don Juan's pedigree: "(His sire was of Castile, his dam from Arragon)" (*DJ* 1.38).

These particulars of Don Juan's regional background call up an alliance grander than Don Jóse and Donna Inez's, that of the Spanish monarchs Ferdinand and Isabella. But the allusion is either imperfect or deliberately reversed: Ferdinand was from Aragon and Isabella from Castile. Byron was too good an historian for his confusion on such a matter to be likely; and if we see a certain parallel between Don Juan's and Byron's parents there is indeed a good explanation for the reversal. Like Ferdinand and Isabella, Jóse and Inez, Byron's "sire" and "dam" were from different parts of a united kingdom: Catherine Gordon from Scotland, Captain Byron from England. Byron's twisting the Spanish allusion makes Juan's father, like his own, come from the larger, more populous, prosperous, and powerful region, which is also the one whose language (Castilian Spanish) is the literary one of Spain, as English is of Britain.

Ascribing traits of the British Byrons to a Spanish cast of characters is not Byron's sole means of "domesticating" the Don Juan story in canto 1. Although, as we shall see in the third essay, Byron does follow pantomime convention by starting with the enactment of a well-known legend that is transformed and then followed with an improvisational harlequinade, the ways he bends the tradition and highlights certain aspects or details go far toward making the protagonist of *Don Juan* Don Juan with a difference. The poem's recurrent strategy will be to remove Don Juan from his customary, legendary contexts and place his character, despite the extraordinary experiences confronting him, in Byron's and the reader's shared frame, which is ordinary reality, an ordinary reality that contains British references to contemporary life (such as the one in stanza 178 to the "modern phrase" *tact* first used in England in the 1790s and the one in stanza 183 to income tax, first levied in England in 1799)[3] and to literature (such as Juan's near suffocation in Julia's bed being compared to Clarence's fate in the malmsey butt in stanza 166, the quotation of Campbell in stanza 88, the burlesque of Wordsworth in stanza 90, the allusion to Moore in stanza 104, and the possible echo of Jane Austen or Lady Caroline Lamb in stanza 194).

Byron could have started Don Juan's story at any point—and even informs us that "Most epic poets plunge in 'medias res'" (*DJ* 1.6). But his narrative choices in canto 1 present Don Juan not as a full-grown, independent seducer but as a child—a boy whose social background, parents, and education are as plausible as if he were a neighbor instead of an archetype. We have already seen that this Juan's "Spanish" milieu is not particularly Spanish, despite his house being by the Guadalquivir; but it is a densely real and solidly bourgeois realm. Canto 1 unfolds in a world where social connections and personal belongings are more pervasive, tenacious, entangling, and incriminating than are emotional relations—a world filled with people (not just feminine objects of seduction and masculine adversaries but ancestors, family friends, lackeys) and things (erotically illuminated missals, bowdlerized textbooks, doors to stand ajar, shoes for a cuckolded husband to trip over, quills, writing paper, and seals that reveal the letter writer's taste).

It is also a world grounded in time—not historical time at this point, but what we might call practical time, the petty and tyrannical chronology that arranges our days and seasons. The legendary Don Juan's heaven-seeking or heaven-defying ardor is much damped (so it seems to the reader, though not to the lady) when his debut in love is fixed with increasingly laughable precision in this mundane sort of time: "It was upon a day, a summer's day;—" (1.102) and then " 'Twas on a summer's day—the sixth of June:—" (1.103) and finally " 'Twas on the sixth of June, about the hour / Of half past six—perhaps still nearer seven," (*DJ* 1.104).

Similarly, Byron makes the passion of the first canto's young lovers more ordinary, less a part of the mythic Don Juan realm, by revealing exactly how young each party is and, more important, the extent and nature of the gap existing between their ages. Juan is sixteen and "almost a man" (*DJ* 1.54). Julia, "married, charming, chaste, and twenty-three" (*DJ* 1.59), is by both station and age entirely a woman. Knowing her to be Don Juan's senior in years and experience empties the conquest (if such a compound of attrac-

---

3. On "tact" and income tax alike, see McGann's Commentary (*DJ* 680).

tion and self-deception can be called a "conquest" on either side) of masculine rakishness and power. In being older than Juan as well as in taking the initiative in their relationship, Julia sets a pattern to which every woman romantically involved with him conforms in the poem. Only Leila and Aurora, who passively receive Juan's pure and high-minded regard, are explicitly younger than he. Haidée is seventeen (*DJ* 2.112), as is Dudù (*DJ* 6.54)—and depending on when Juan's birthday takes place, he must be more or less the same age. Gulbeyaz's years "might make six and twenty springs" (*DJ* 5.98). Catherine is encountered at that overripe stage when "Her climacteric teased her like her teens" (*DJ* 10.47), and thus should be in her sixties. When Juan comes into the glittering orbit of Lady Adeline Amundeville, he is twenty-one—and six weeks her junior (*DJ* 14.51, 54). It might perhaps be indiscreet for the narrator, a habitué of the English world of fashion, to disclose the years of "her frolic Grace—Fitz-Fulke," but her introduction as "a fine and somewhat full-blown blonde, / Desirable, distinguish'd, celebrated / For several winters in the grand, *grand Monde*" (*DJ* 14.42) certainly characterizes the duchess as a well-preserved woman "of a certain age." The very fact that three of these unconventionally enterprising women are the same age or only minimally older than Juan stresses that the prosaic distinction of age is an important one—and firmly anchors the grand or grandiose legend of the seducer in domestic or domesticated reality. From Don Hwan comes Don Joo-un—and it is worth remembering that if Byron saw his Continental liaisons in the Don Hwan vein (as his epic epistolary catalogue of Venetian mistresses, a distinct echo of Mozart's *Don Giovanni*, suggests),[4] he retrospectively viewed his amorous career among the predatory ladies of the English Great World, some of them his elders by a few years or a good many, as closer to the experience of Don Joo-un.

We have seen how the presentation in canto 1 of Don Juan's story sometimes is, sometimes is not, and sometimes is and is not drawn from Byron's own experiences, whether these are active or contemplative. The English digressions are likewise close to if not perfectly congruent with Byron's opinions. The burlesque of Wordsworthian romanticism in Don Juan's adolescent mopings, the friendly but not utterly admiring references to lyric love à la "Anacreon Moore," the ironic ambiguity of the narrator's fifth literary commandment, "Thou shalt not steal from Samuel Rogers" (*DJ* 1.205), all correspond to personal sentiments Byron expressed at one time or another. As for the narrator whose presence is conspicuous from the first line of the canto, he also is like Byron and of Byron without precisely being Byron. The elusiveness of this playful narrator is perhaps the most genuinely Byronic thing about him. Lady Blessington, whose talents and

---

4. Writing to Hobhouse and Kinnaird on 19 January 1819, Byron enumerates his amours of the recent past in this epic list: "Which 'piece' does he [Lord Lauderdale, who had carried a tale home to England] mean?—since last year I have run the Gauntlet,—is it the Tarruscelli—the Da Mosti—the Spineda—the Lotti—the Rizzato—the Eleanora—the Carlotta—the Giulietta—the Alvisi—the Zambieri—The Eleanora da Bezzi—(who was the King of Naples' Gioschino's mistress—at least one of them) the Theresina of Mazzurati—the Glettenheimer—& her Sister—the Luigia & her mother—the Fornaretta—the Santa—the Caligari—the Portiera [Vedova?]—the Bolognese figurante—the Tentora and her sister—cum multis aliis?—some of them are Countesses—& some of them Cobblers wives—some noble—some middling—some low—& all whores" (*LJ* 6:92). The tone and detail alike are reminiscent of "Madamina! il catalogo e questo," the aria in which Leporello catalogues, for a vengeful Donna Elvira, the international army of women seduced by Don Giovanni—640 Italians, 231 Germans, 100 French, 91 Turks, and 1003 Spaniards.

circumstances equipped her to understand Byron as well as most anyone has ever done, sees him as above all loving to mystify, to feign seriousness. He is for her a man of natural mobility who is fully aware of his nature: "Byron is a perfect chameleon, possessing the fabulous qualities attributed to that animal, of taking the color of whatever touches him. He is conscious of this."[5] This shifting color, at once a reflex and an artifice, is equally characteristic of the *Don Juan* narrator; and because there is "Nothing so difficult as a beginning / In poesy, unless perhaps the end" (*DJ* 4.1), we might do well to end our appraisal of opening signals by seeing how that Byronic narrator ends the opening canto, for the final impression he makes will modify our expectations of canto 2 and all else that follows.

Like the other cantos, 8 and 16 being the sole exceptions, the first one ends with its focus on the narrator, not Don Juan. As the narrator turns from Don Juan's "earliest scrape" in stanza 199, he begins supplying us with professions of his own attitudes and intentions to keep in mind when and if the poem resumes. The claims advanced are wonderfully and deliberately self-contradictory. Their inconsistencies appear in clearest form when we strip away the delicate tissue of poetry and rhetoric from the bones of assertion, as the following series of prose abstracts attempts to do for the canto's last twenty-four stanzas:

—The continuation of Don Juan's adventures is "Dependent on the public altogether" (stanza 199), yet the poem is said to be "epic" (implying continuation with or without popular demand) and then crammed with so many projected "epic" attributes and episodes that its epic nature cannot be taken seriously (200–201).

—Unlike previous epics, this one is "actually true" (202) and proven to be so by reference to such "reliable" sources as history, tradition, facts, newspapers, plays, operas, and, above all, the ever-straightforward narrator's ocular proof (203).

—If the narrator should "condescend to prose," he will write poetical commandments (204), which he then proceeds to do in ottava rima verse (205–6).

—No honest and perceptive reader can assert that this poem is not "a moral tale, though gay" (207–8). But just in case anyone should try, the narrator has assured himself that his public will see the poem as he wishes—he's bribed his "grandmother's review—the British" to guarantee its being understood in these terms (209–10).

—Like Byron, the narrator is not so prone to quarrel with less malleable reviews, such as the *Edinburgh* and the *Quarterly*, as he was back in his "hot youth—when George the Third was King," some six or seven years before he "dreamt of dating from the Brenta" (211–12).

—Now thirty and graying, the narrator is thinking of a wig and (unlike Byron) through with love and wine, left only with that "good old gentlemanly vice," avarice (213–16).

—He's also through with ambition, for fame is futile, as precedent shows (217–19).

5. Lady Blessington, *Conversations of Lord Byron*, Ed. Ernest J. Lovell, Jr. (Princeton: Princeton University Press, 1969), 47, 71.

—Thus, wisely embracing what consolations are possible for one of such advanced decrepitude, he ingratiatingly bids farewell to the "gentle reader" and "Still gentler purchaser" with many a humble platitude (221), which humility is so unnatural to him that he must now resort to Southey's verse to voice it (222) and then, casting off obsequiousness and Southey, make sure that the reader understands that neither the verses nor the attitude could possibly be his: "The first four rhymes are Southey's every line: / For God's sake, reader! Take them not for mine" (222).

In this resourceful way, the supposedly errant storyteller brings his tale full circle and his reader right back to the Dedication and the laureate. The opening arabesque of *Don Juan*, a bravura performance simultaneously demonstrating the poem's pattern and apparent randomness, sincerity and duplicity, revelation and concealment of "Byron" and his attitudes, is now complete. That much seems clear. What the shifting proportions of this arabesque may be at any one point and in any one detail is less clear and best left unsettled—to please, perplex, and tempt the reader on, as Byron, "Byron," and the narrator seem equally inclined to do.

SUSAN J. WOLFSON

"Their She Condition": Cross-Dressing and the Politics of Gender in *Don Juan*†

I

Don Juan, like much Romantic writing, displays numerous demarcations of sexual difference. Indeed, there is a notable contradiction between the poem's social politics, which despite an aristocratic allegiance, tend to satirize prevailing ideologies, and its sexual politics, which often reflect a conventional masculinism.[1] Some have summoned issues of the latter to make categorical claims about Byron and his contemporaries. Questions of gender are certainly fundamental; evidence of Byron's—and many others'—sexism and patriarchal bias is clear and compelling. Yet I wish to revise some of the categories advanced in some recent feminist readings of English Romanticism by showing that Byron's sexual politics are neither persistent nor consistent. Even granting the notoriously adept ironies of *Don Juan*, its politics of sexual difference prove remarkably complex and unstable. At times they are governed by the general satirical perspective of the poem; at other times they clash with Byron's pronounced liberal politics; and at still others they appear scarcely fixed—even within their own frame of reference. Signs that seem clear markers of difference can become

† From *ELH* 54.3 (1987): 585–617. Copyright © The Johns Hopkins University Press, Reprinted with permission of the Johns Hopkins University Press. A later development of this essay appears as chapter 6, "Gender as Cross-Dressing in *Don Juan*: Men & Women / Male & Female / Masculine & Feminine," in *Borderlines: The Shiftings of Gender in British Romanticism* (Stanford University Press, 2006).

1. Leslie A. Marchand, in *Byron: A Biography* (3 vols., New York: Knopf, 1957), remarks that Byron "had always been most successful with girls below his social and intellectual level . . . who flattered his ego and looked up with awe at his title" (1:330). Similarly, Louis Crompton, in *Byron and Greek Love: Homophobia in 19th-Century England* (Berkeley: Univ. of California Press, 1985) suggests that Byron's favoring of the "pederastic" form of homosexuality over the "comrade" form corresponds to an overall sexual politics that "preferred aristocracies to democracy and hierarchies to egalitarianism" (239).

agents of sexual disorientation that break down, invert, and radically call into question the categories designed to discriminate "masculine" from "feminine."

This sense of dislocation is provoked in a variety of ways, but with particular agitation in instances of cross-dressing. Such agitation, not surprisingly, can generate a conservative counterreaction—a series of defensive maneuvers to reinscribe sexual orthodoxy. Even so, the energies released in such instances are central to Byron's writing, not only illuminating the codes that govern the behavior of men and women, but becoming a means of exploring new possibilities as well. The cross-dressings of *Don Juan* also, and undeniably, reflect a more private, and more privately coded, issue: Byron's homoeroticism. Louis Crompton's recent study, *Byron and Greek Love,* offers a lucid and powerful examination of Byron's literary and social behavior from this perspective, especially in relation to Georgian and Regency homophobia. My essay concentrates on Byron's representations of heterosexual politics, which, sensitized by his homosexuality, turn personal experience outward into a critical reading of the discourses of sexual difference and sexual ideology that permeate his age.

II

Traditional distinctions of gender and corresponding habits of judgment are everywhere apparent in Byron's writing. A woman may be written off with the prescription of "a looking-glass and a few sugar plums . . . she will be satisfied."[2] If her gaze turns to man, he must guard against the peril to his security. "Love" in *Don Juan* is personified as a gallant male (9.44), but its female embodiments in the Sultana Gulbeyaz or the Empress Catherine are dangerous; and in Queen Elizabeth, love is so "ambiguous" in method and so incompatible with the exercise of political power, that she disgraces both "her Sex and Station" (9.81).[3] "Hatred," not coincidentally, is pure female treachery, a spidery woman with a "hundred arms and legs" (10.12). Even if "woman" in this poem escapes such extreme representations, it is only towards an unpredictable chaos of activity:

> What a strange thing is man! and what a stranger
> Is woman! What a whirlwind is her head,
> And what a whirlpool full of depth and danger
> Is all the rest about her! (9.64)

Man may be strange, but woman is both stranger than he and ultimately a stranger to him and his world. Thus, if as Peter Manning remarks, "Juan's education is his experience with women," *Don Juan* remains concerned about that economy, for female pedagogy, even when its curriculum is "that useful sort of knowledge . . . acquired in nature's good old college" (2.136), is of dubious value.[4] " 'Tis pity learned virgins ever wed / With persons of

---

2. *Medwin's "Conversations of Lord Byron"*, ed. Ernest J. Lovell, Jr. (Princeton: Princeton Univ. Press, 1966), 73. Hereafter cited as *Medwin.*

3. Quotations of *Don Juan*, as well as of other poems, follow *Lord Byron: The Complete Poetical Works*, 5 vols., ed. Jerome J. McGann (Oxford: Clarendon Press, 1980–86). In the parenthetic references in my text, I note canto and stanza for *Don Juan*; for other poems, I give canto and line number; a number alone, unless the context of the paragraph suggests otherwise, designates stanza number. Citations of the edition itself hereafter are given as *CPW* with volume and page.

4. Peter J. Manning, *Byron and His Fictions* (Detroit: Wayne State Univ. Press, 1978), 180.

no sort of education," the narrator muses, with Byron's line-break momentarily suggesting an even more radical solution to the summary lament, "Oh! ye lords of ladies intellectual, / Inform us truly, have they not henpeck'd you all?" (1.22). This couplet may be Byron's most famous; it is significant that the point of its testy wit is the reduction of women's intellect to an instrument to torture a lord. When it is not so precise, women's learning is treated as an easily exposed pretension: "Men with their heads reflect on this and that— / But women with their hearts or heaven knows what!" (6.2). Their capacity for "sober reason" is so easily compromised that it is impossible, the narrator smirks, to know what "can signify the site / Of ladies' lucubrations" (11.33–34). Those subject to sharpest sarcasm are, predictably, "The Blues"—a "tribe" whom even Juan ("who was a little superficial") can conquer, and with no more than a light continental style "Which lent his learned lucubrations pith, / And passed for arguments of good endurance" (11.50–52). Of the two orders of pretension, Juan's escapes derision because Byron allows him to recognize the hoax, indeed to participate in the self-parodies of his author, who could on occasion refer to "his masterpieces" as "his elucubrations."[5]

Byron shows his narrator preferring women who behave in accord with conventional models—for example, Haidée and Zoe nursing Juan "With food and raiment, and those soft attentions, / Which are (as I must own) of female growth" (2.123). Similarly, the Sultana Gulbeyaz is most affecting, to Juan and the narrator alike, when her "imperial, or imperious" manner (5.110) succumbs to the female heart, as when, for instance, she is moved to tears by Juan's own. If her rage at Juan's refusal to love on command reminds the narrator of King Lear's in intensity, he is struck by how "her thirst of blood was quench'd in tears," which he deems "the fault of her soft sex" and the conduit through which "her sex's shame broke in at last. . . . it flow'd in natural and fast." He is glad to note that on such occasions "she felt humbled," adding that "humiliation / Is sometimes good for people in her station" (5.136–37). For then, "nature teaches more than power can soil, / And, when a *strong* although a strange sensation, / Moves— female hearts are . . . genial soil / For kinder feelings, whatso'er their nation" (5.120). Byron's textual variants imply that tutelage by "nature" yields a political corrective as well: thus moved, Gulbeyaz not only "forgot her station," but may be addressed as a "Poor Girl."[6]

If tears mark the female here, they are still part of that world of woman's strangeness, and not always susceptible to certain interpretation. For what looks "natural" also has the effect of manipulating male sympathy, and we have just heard that women such as Gulbeyaz may "shed and use" tears "at their liking" (5.118). Tellingly, Juan finds that his resistance to sexual exploitation "Dissolved like snow before a woman crying" (5.141). By contrast, men's tears, the narrator is certain, are true "torture," agon rather than art: "A woman's tear-drop melts, a man's half sears, / Like molten lead, as if you thrust a pike in / His heart to force it out" (5.118). Men's tears reflect a wholly unsuspect emotion: when one of the shipwrecked crew "wept at length," the narrator assures us it was "not fears / That made his eyelids as a woman's be"; he weeps in pure pity for "a wife and children" (2.43).

5. *His Very Self and Voice: Collected Conversations of Lord Byron*, ed. Ernest J. Lovell, Jr. (New York: Macmillan, 1954), 249.
6. See *CPW*, 5:279 and 5:284, respectively.

The subject of tears is a synecdoche for the demarcations of gender that inflect the world of *Don Juan,* and one instance of how its narrator generates masculine self-definition by contraries and oppositions. These dynamics are typically represented as a contest between masculine and feminine will, in which female manipulation is represented as inimical to male independence and power. Significantly, the suspicion of calculation in Gulbeyaz's tears and their effect in mastering Juan's resistance recall the arts Donna Julia deploys to deflect interrogation by her husband, even as she conceals her lover in her bed. Byron's narrator, in solidarity with the cuckold, dons a voice of moral outrage at the whole gender. "Oh shame! / Oh sin! Oh sorrow! and Oh womankind! / How can you do such things and keep your fame, / Unless this world, and t'other too, be blind? / Nothing so dear as an unfilch'd good name!" (1.165). Byron, whose own name was tainted by sexual scandal, is perhaps a little irked by the female art of having it both ways. Thus of Lady Adeline, a later variation on Julia, he has his narrator remark, "whatso'er she wished, she acted right; / And whether coldness, pride, or virtue, dignify / A Woman, so she's good, what does it signify?" (14.57). Her security depends on remaining an opaque or perpetually intractable signifier to masculine intelligence, and her social power derives from such finesse: she acts the "amphibious sort of harlot, / 'Couleur de rose,' who's neither white nor scarlet," and who, with a "little genial sprinkling of hypocrisy," may become one of the "loveliest Oligarchs of our Gynocrasy" (12.62, 66). This is a rhyme Byron liked, for he summons it again to advise all who would "take the tone of their society" to "wear the newest mantle of hypocrisy, / On pain of much displeasing the Gynocrasy" (16.52). The hostility that sharpens the point of these pairings can be heard in Byron's self-congratulating claim to be neither surprised nor distressed on hearing of women's aversion to *Don Juan:* "they could not bear it because it took off the *veil* [of their] d[amne]d sentiment. . . . They hated the book because it showed and exposed their hypocrisy," he says, and he seems to have enjoyed provoking Teresa Guiccioli's dislike of "that ugly *Don Juan.*"[7]

Yet if these numerous apostrophes to and declarations about arts of women, as well as the narrator's insistence on "their" hypocrisy, seem to divide the world of *Don Juan* securely along lines of gender, Byron's concentration tugs at a network of affiliations. Even to say *"our Gynocrasy"* implies a certain pride of identification. Indeed, in the stanza from Canto 12 quoted above, the third rhyme word, significantly, is "aristocracy"—as if Byron were signalling his awareness that women are culpable of nothing more than disclosing the master-trope of all social success. The play of rhyme itself is relevant, for if, as the narrator remarks with faint condescension, "There's nothing women love to dabble in / More . . . Than match-making in general: 'tis no sin" (15.31), Byron has him do so in matched words, a sign of his own love of match-making in the general society of language. There is an even more pronounced affinity of interest to challenge the supposition that hypocrisy is all "theirs": hypocrisy may be a moral fault, but it is also artful acting, and the narrator's confessed pleasure in performances both literary and social implicates him in a similar

---

7. *His Very Self and Voice,* 452 and 299 respectively; compare *Byron's Letters and Journals,* 12 vols., ed. Leslie A. Marchand (Cambridge: Harvard Univ. Press, 1973–1982), 8:147–48. Cited hereafter *BLJ* by volume and page.

masquerade. It is interesting that Princess Caroline would apply the same term to Byron that his narrator applies to women: "He was all *couleur de rose* last evening."[8] These cross applications are not exactly "cross-dressing," but they indirectly participate—for the fashion, if not the material, is the same. Thus it is only half-sarcastically that Byron's narrator admits, "What I love in women is, they won't / Or can't do otherwise than lie, but do it / So well, the very truth seems falsehood to it"; their artifice is natural, and so their lies are true. And in a world where all pretenses to truth seem to veil the artifices of ideology, women's hypocrisy may, paradoxically, be the most honest behavior of all: "after all, what is a lie? 'Tis but / The truth in masquerade" (11.36–37). By Canto 16, in fact, Byron's narrator is praising his female muse as "The most sincere that ever dealt in fiction" (2), and reflecting this quality in the "mobility" of women such as Adeline who, in adapting to the performative requirements of any occasion, are not playing "false," but "true; for surely, they're sincerest, / Who are strongly acted on by what is nearest" (97).

Byron makes some attempt to distinguish the male poet and his muse from the behavior of such women, for mobility, his narrator says, is "A thing of temperament and not of art" (16.97), and a habit that may leave its possessor more "acted on" than acting—while his poem, presumably, is a thing of art alone. He implies that distinction elsewhere in his claims that it is "ladies' fancies" that are "rather transitory" (10.9), and "feminine Caprice" that inspires their "indecision, / Their never knowing their own mind two days" (6.119, 117). And of course, the poem's definitive figure of mobility is Lady Adeline. Even so, mobility is not the sure index of gender that tears are. Byron in fact added a note to the poem in Adeline's defense, as if to balance the masculine bias of Juan's external perspective on her "playing her grand role" (and thus prone to "doubt how much of Adeline was *real*" [16.96]) with a more sympathetic assessment: mobility is "an excessive susceptibility of immediate impressions," he explains, and "though sometimes apparently useful to the possessor, a most painful and unhappy attribute" (*CPW*, 5:769). This gloss seems more than sympathy; it has the sound of psychological self-pleading. Thus it is not surprising to hear from Thomas Moore that Byron "was fully aware not only of the abundance of this quality in his own nature, but of the danger in which it placed consistency and singleness of character" (*CPW*, 5:769). Lady Blessington comments that the "mobility of his nature is extraordinary, and makes him inconsistent in his actions as well as in his conversation"—a quality Hazlitt observes in *Don Juan* itself, summoning a term that suggests cross-dressing: the "great power" of this poem, he proposes, lies in Byron's ability to "turn round and *travestie* himself: the drollery is in the utter discontinuity of ideas and feelings."[9]

8. Marchand (note 1), 1:382.
9. *Lady Blessington's "Conversations of Lord Byron"*, ed. Ernest J. Lovell, Jr. (Princeton: Princeton Univ. Press, 1969), 47; hereafter cited as *Blessington*. Hazlitt, "Lord Byron," *The Spirit of The Age* (1825), reprinted in *The Complete Works of William Hazlitt*, ed. P. P. Howe, 21 vols. (London: J. M. Dent, 1930–34), 11:75. *Travestie* (Hazlitt's italics) abbreviates *transvestire* (the OED in fact gives the "odd travesty" of Juan in woman's garb as an instance of *travesty* meaning "alteration of dress"). Shelley is inclined to describe Byron's style in terms that play at a similar sense: of the same canto in which Byron makes Juan an odalisque, he writes, "the language in which the whole is clothed—a sort of chameleon under the changing sky of the spirit that kindles it" (*Letters 1818 to 1822*, ed. Roger Ingpen, 331; vol. 10 of *The Complete Works of Percy Bysshe Shelley*, 10 vols., ed. Roger Ingpen and Walter E. Peck [New York: Charles Scribner's Sons, 1926]).

In Byron's experience, it seems clear, mobility is an epic renegade, loyal to no sex, itself showing mobility across gender lines. George M. Ridenour in fact discerns in Adeline's mobility "another version of that growing urbanity Byron has so praised in his hero himself: 'The art of living in all climes with ease' (15.11)," and he extends this art to include the narrator's acknowledged facility at playing "the *Improvvisatore*" "amidst life's infinite variety" (15.19–20).[1] This last allusion to the arts of Shakespeare's Cleopatra, which in their "infinite variety" defeat the attritions of "custom" (2.2.241), further perplexes discriminations of gender. Not only does Byron have his narrator apply the infinite variety of her art to his own general view of life, but it is worth recalling that Cleopatra's various repertoire includes the fun of cross-dressing: "I . . . put my tires and mantles on him, whilst / I wore his sword" (2.5.21–23).[2] With this borrowing, Byron fashions a kind of psychic cross-dressing for his narrator; not coincidentally, Byron's very language for "mobility" appears to have been converted from Madame de Staël's description of feminine consciousness in her popular novel, *Corinne*.[3]

As the issue of mobility suggests, *Don Juan* at times complicates the language of gender in ways that focus on the definition of self in gendered society, and may even expose the political investments of those definitions. Such preoccupation in Byron's poetry with "the social structures of its rhetoric," as Jerome J. McGann argues, works to reflect "the audience's character . . . back to itself so that it can 'reflect' upon that reflection in a critical and illuminating way."[4] That dynamic is especially active in the social and linguistic cross-dressings of *Don Juan*, for these figures not only concentrate the energies of Byron's satire, but compel our attention to those crucial discriminations through which the masculine and the feminine have been culturally defined, and through which men and women have been psychologically compelled and historically confined. Social cross-dressing includes both the "odd travesty" of Juan in the slave market "femininely all array'd" (5.74, 80) and "her frolic Grace—Fitz-Fulke" disguised as the ghost of the Black Friar (16.123); it also involves the less obvious but equally significant covering of Juan by female clothes—first by Julia, then by Haidée and Zoe. Linguistic cross-dressing materializes in transfers of verbal property, such as the narrator's calling himself "a male Mrs. Fry" (10.84), or Antonia's references to Juan as a "pretty gentleman" with a "half-girlish face" (1.170–71), corroborated by the narrator's descriptions of his hero as "a most beauteous Boy" (9.53), "feminine in feature" (8.52), who dances "like a flying Hour before Aurora, / In Guido's famous fresco" (14.40). These transfers also include the application of masculine-toned terms to women: the Sultan desires a "handsome paramour" (6.91); Empress Catherine is "handsome" and "fierce" (9.63)—her behavior "a kind of travesty" as one critic remarks, and so in the most fun-

---

1. George M. Ridenour, *The Style of Don Juan* (New Haven: Yale Univ. Press, 1960), 164–65.
2. My quotation follows the Arden edition of *Antony and Cleopatra*, ed. M. R. Ridley (Cambridge: Harvard Univ. Press, 1956).
3. Ridenour comments on the similarity, 165–66. See also Jerome J. McGann's discussion of "mobility" in *Don Juan* ("Byron, Mobility and the Poetics of Historical Ventriloquism," *Romanticism, Past and Present* 9 [1985]: 66–82—the terms of which bear on the question of gender, insofar as the poem does not confine this "psychological attribute and [its] social formation" to women such as Adeline, but "specifically calls attention to the relation of mobility to the structure of the artist's life" (69–71).
4. McGann, "Byron, Mobility," 69.

damental sense, for "travesty" is a linguistic kin of "transvestite." (Sugges-
tively, another reader discerns Catherine's origins in a male historical fig-
ure, the Ali Pasha, who implicitly feminized Byron by paying great attention
to his beauty.)[5] An even more complex exchange of the properties of gen-
der plays in the comment that Juan dances "Like swift Camilla" (14.39).
The comparison may appear to feminize Juan, but it actually entertains a
dizzying interchange of properties, for as a hunter and epic warrior, Camilla
is associated with typically male pursuits.

The ambiguous swirl of Juan's sexual composition even spilled over into
the extratextual realm of Regency society. As Byron knew, his hero—that
slender, pretty "stripling of sixteen" (1.83)—was impersonated at a mas-
querade by Caroline Lamb (*BLJ*, 7:169), an early mistress who herself may
have been a model for Juan. She was petite, epicene, and often described
as resembling a young teenage boy: a famous set of portraits shows her in
page's guise, a costume she enjoyed and on occasion adopted for discreet
visits to Byron's apartment. Byron, for his part, sometimes disguised his
female lovers in male attire to avoid gossip, once presenting one of these
as "my brother Gordon"; as a result of such habits, some of the boys in
Byron's circle were at times mistaken for girls in boys' clothes. Byron's own
style of dress also played a part. In Italy he would often appear "holding a
handkerchief, upon which his jewelled fingers lay embedded," so Leigh
Hunt reports, adding that Byron trimmed and oiled his hair "with all the
anxiety of a Sardanapalus. The visible character to which this effeminacy
gave rise appears to have indicated itself as early as his travels in the Lev-
ant, where the Grand Signior is said to have taken him for a woman in dis-
guise."[6] The composition of Juan's intersexual character, along with the
poem's linguistic and social transvestism, is inhabited by these playful dis-
guises and habits of dress, and all were undoubtedly energized by Byron's
homoeroticism, which, in the repressive and punitive atmosphere of
Regency England, could not risk exposure.[7]

The fictions of *Don Juan* serve Byron in part as an outlet for homoerotic
material in disguise, but its cross-dressings accomplish something else as
well, for they put his imagination in touch with heterosexual politics by ani-
mating a set of social signifiers that challenge conventional expectations
and customary boundaries of demarcation. Some of these transfers and
transgressions emerge as farce, but not exclusively, for Byron implicates
them in deep (if not fully sustained) counterplots that perplex the terms
"male" and "female"—both politically and psychologically construed—and

---

5. See Ridenour (140) for the remark about Catherine's "travesty," and Cecil Y. Lang for a discussion
   of Catherine and Juan as "masks" for Ali Pasha and Byron ("Narcissus Jilted: Byron, *Don Juan*, and
   the Biographical Imperative," *Historical Studies and Literary Criticism*, ed. Jerome J. McGann
   [Madison: Univ. of Wisconsin Press, 1985]: 143–79).

6. For the anecdotes, see *Medwin*, 67; Marchand (note 1), 1:156, note 5; Hunt, *Lord Byron and Some
   of His Contemporaries; With Recollections of the Author's Life, and of His Visit to Italy* (1828;
   reprinted, Philadelphia: Carey, Lea & Carey, 1828), 83. One reads Hunt's comments, of course,
   knowing that mutual insinuations of effeminacy were one medium through which mounting
   strains in the friendship of Hunt and Byron were exercised; see also 30, 69–70, 75, 77.

7. For a discussion of the constraints imposed on Byron's range of expression by the punishment of
   homosexuality as a capital crime in Regency England, see Crompton: "in societies where straight-
   foward representation of same-sex love was taboo" female transvestism afforded "homosexual writ-
   ers a chance for surreptitious romance" (210). Crompton reads *Lara* in these terms, as well as the
   linguistic regendering evinced in Byron's "Thyrza" lyrics: their male subject—Byron's early love, the
   choirboy John Edleston—was disguised by feminine names and pronouns, also Byron's practice in
   his translations of Greek and Latin homoerotic lyrics (see 94, 105–6, 177–78).

thereby unsettle, even dismantle, the social structures to which gender has
been assimilated. The result of these transsexual poetics is a qualified but
potent redefinition of conventional sexual politics, for gender symbolism,
as Natalie Zemon Davis remarks, "is always available to make statements
about social experience and to reflect (or conceal) contradictions within
it."[8] Thus the spectacle of Juan "femininely all array'd" in the slave market
works to foreground female restriction and vulnerability, while the figures
of women "masculinized" through social power or costume disguise emerge
with the energy of self-direction and the force of sexual assertiveness.
These transfers allow Byron to inscribe a language of cultural contradiction
and personal self-division in which what has been habitually denied to one
sex gets projected in terms of the other. And while the figures on both sides
of these transfers are often made to seem absurd or anomalous, it is their
very anomaly that makes palpable the ideology by which conventional
codes are invested, maintained, and perpetuated.

*   *   *

III

*   *   *

* * * Fluctuations of compassion and nervous scorn can be read in the
very passage in which Byron has his narrator ponder the "she condition."
He begins in tones of mock sympathy and blame, but within a few lines
these become expressions of genuine sympathy:

> Alas! Worlds fall—and Woman, since she fell'd
> The World (as, since that history, less polite
> Than true, hath been a creed so strictly held)
> Has not yet given up the practice quite.
> Poor Thing of Usages! Coerc'd, compell'd,
> Victim when wrong, and martyr often when right,
> Condemn'd to child-bed . . . (14.23)

His sympathy modulates into a self-conscious contemplation of sexual pol-
itics and policy:

> who can penetrate
> The real sufferings of their she condition?
> Man's very sympathy with their estate
> Has much of selfishness and more suspicion.
> Their love, their virtue, beauty, education,
> But form good housekeepers, to breed a nation. (14.24)

Wollstonecraft herself could have written the next stanza:[9]

> The gilding wears so soon from off her fetter,
> That—but ask any woman if she'd choose
> (Take her at thirty, that is) to have been
> Female or male? a school-boy or a Queen? (14.25)

---

8. Natalie Zemon Davis, "Women on Top," *Society and Culture in Early Modern France* (Stanford:
Stanford Univ. Press, 1975), 127.
9. Mary Wollstonecraft's *A Vindication of the Rights of Woman* is discussed in the preceding portion
of the essay, omitted here. (*Editor's note*).

If Pope's Epistle assumes that "ev'ry Lady would be Queen for life" and shudders at the thought of "a whole Sex of Queens! / Pow'r all their end" (218–20), Byron's summary question guesses that any woman might prefer the lot of a schoolboy—the lowest of males—to that of a queen, the highest of females. But he allows the issue to diffuse as he returns his narrator to the more familiar ground of sexist mocking: "'Petticoat Influence' is a great reproach, / Which even those who obey would fain be thought / To fly from, as from hungry pikes a roach" (14.26). Potential political commentary then evaporates into a digression on the "mystical sublimity" of the petticoat (14.26–27). Yet the evasion itself is revealing; the analogy of hungry pikes and their prey that Peter Manning remarks is indeed worth attention—not the least for renewing an earlier image of Englishwomen as unholy "fishers for men" (12.59).[1] Though the vehicle shifts, the tenor is the same: women are always the predators.

Despite the narrator's reversion to antifeminist bitterness, Byron's willingness to have him meditate on the "she condition" is a striking one, for it not only allows a male voice to confirm the validity of a woman's earlier lament—namely Julia's—but now invests that grievance with intersexual authority. Writing to Juan, Julia had complained that if

> Man's love is of man's life a thing apart,
> 'Tis woman's whole existence; man may range
> The court, camp, church, the vessel, and the mart,
> Sword, gown, gain, glory, offer in exchange
> Pride, fame, ambition, to fill up his heart. . . .
> Man has all these resources, we but one,
> To love again, and be again undone. (1.194)

Not only does Byron's ventriloquy through Julia express a sympathetic understanding of the limits imposed on "woman's whole existence," but Julia's letter may actually have female authority—its voice inhabited by the language of both Jane Austen and (like the meditation on mobility) Madame de Staël.[2] Though still reflecting the terms of difference authorized by his culture, in his effort to address the "she condition," to hear and render its voices, Byron attempts a critical perspective, one that allows him to reveal and explore the ideological implications of those terms.[3]

---

1. Manning (note 4), 247.
2. Truman Guy Steffan and Willis W. Pratt, the editors of *Byron's Don Juan, A Variorum Edition* (4 vols., Austin: Univ. of Texas Press, 1957) cite *De L'influence des passions* (1976) and *Corinne, ou l'Italie* (1807), chapter 5 (1:45). McGann remarks that the same position "is memorably stated by Anne Elliot in Jane Austen's *Persuasion* . . . which [Byron's publisher] Murray published, and which he may very well have sent to Byron, not long before this passage was written" (*CPW*, 5:680).
3. Even *Blackwood's Edinburgh Magazine*, which charges Byron with "brutally outraging all the best feelings of female honour, affection, and confidence," admires Julia's "beautiful letter," printing stanzas 94–97, and regretting only the "style of contemptuous coldness" applied in stanza 98 to "the sufferings to which licentious love exposes" some women ("Remarks on Don Juan," vol. 5 [Aug. 1819]: 512–18; my quotations are from 512, 516–17; Donald Reiman thinks John Gibson Lockhart is the reviewer [*The Romantics Reviewed*, B:143]). Leigh Hunt's brief for Julia focuses on the social criticism implicit in the restriction of women by "custom." . . . (*"Don Juan. Cantos 1st and 2nd,"* Examiner [13 Oct. 1819]:700–02; Reiman identifies the reviewer [B:1004]). Other readers are less sympathetic. . . . Even a modern reader, Bernard Blackstone, refused to hear any "compassionate sigh for poor woman" in Julia's letter, but finds it, instead, "a vampire threat to the whole structure of masculine, rational values painstakingly built up through the civilized centuries" (*Byron: A Survey* [London: Longman, 1975], 299–300). The sexual politics animated by this episode may help explain why, contrary to Byron's assumptions, some women *did* like the poem: "of all my works D[on] Juan is the most popular" in Paris, he reports to John Hunt, "especially amongst the women who send for it the more that it is abused" (April 9, 1823; *BLJ*, 10:146).

That exploration is helped by Byron's capacity for owning what amounts to a "he" complicity in the "she condition": even as the narrator of *Don Juan* rails against marriage, Byron has him admit that not only do women invest "all" in love, but that "man, to man so oft unjust, / Is always so to women" (2.199–200). Byron himself informs an "incredulous" Lady Blessington that "men think of themselves alone, and regard the woman but as an object that administers to their selfish gratification, and who, when she ceases to have this power, is thought of no more, save as an obstruction in their path." His terms for assessing difference still inscribe a hierarchy: men enjoy the privilege of power, women the honor of a higher moral place: "women only know evil from having experienced it through men; whereas men have no criterion to judge of purity or goodness but woman"; "I have a much higher opinion of your sex than I have even now expressed," he adds (*Blessington*, 196)—a remark that his Italian mistress, Countess Teresa Guiccioli, underscored in her own copy of Blessington's *Conversations of Lord Byron*. These critiques reflect ideological myths of course, but their psychological reflex in Byron is revealingly self-critical. In the privacy of his journal he remarks: "There is something to me very softening in the presence of a woman,—some strange influence, even if one is not in love with them,—which I cannot at all account for, having no very high opinion of the sex. But yet,—I always feel in better humour with myself and every thing else, if there is a woman within ken" (*BLJ*, 3:246). Conventional polarities and traces of habitual opinion notwithstanding, one is struck by the implication that "the presence of a woman" seems necessary to Byron, both for his sense of self-completion and for his sense of integration with the world at large. He wants a heroine.

That psychological undercurrent to Byron's critique of the sexual politics that underwrite the "she condition" exerts a nervous force however— especially when that critique is articulated by cross-dressings, for these inversions and reversals not only erode male privilege, but inhabit plots in which such erosion is associated with images and threats of death. The dissolution of male power is apparent enough in the loss of male attire and the quasi-transvestism that ensues in Juan's romances with Julia and Haidée. Julia "half-smother'd" a naked Juan in her bedding to hide him from her husband's posse; it is a naked and half-dead Juan for whom "Haidée stripp'd her sables off" to make a couch—"and, that he might be more at ease, / And warm, in case by chance he should awake," she and Zoe "also gave a petticoat apiece" (2.133). Though not overtly transvestite, these coverings still compromise Juan's manhood, for each, while protective, also marks him as passive and dependent, the property of a woman's design. Significantly, after being discovered by Alfonso, Juan cannot recover his clothes, but must escape "naked" (188) into the night. That reduction is also suggested by the garments Juan, "naked" once again, receives from Haidée, for though these are men's, the apparel does not proclaim the man: the "breeches" in which she "dress'd him" are rather "spacious" (probably her father's) and more tellingly, she neglects to supply the real signifiers of male power—"turban, slippers, pistols, dirk" (2.160). With both Julia and Haidée, Juan remains a "boy" (Catherine too, we learn, "sometimes liked a boy," "slight and slim," preferring such "a boy to men much bigger" [9.47, 72]), and Byron underscores the corresponding impotence not only by confronting Juan with a genuine threat of death from the men betrayed by these affairs, but by masculinizing the women. Julia is given an uncommon bearing of "stature tall," complemented by a "brow / Bright with intelligence" and "handsome eyes" (1.60–61). Haidée's stature is "Even of the highest for a female mould . . . and in her air / There was a something which bespoke command" (2.116). The implicit maleness of this manner is confirmed when she confronts her father: protecting Juan, "Haidée threw herself her boy before"; "Stern as her sire" (Byron revises the adjective from "calm" [*CPW*, 5:216]), "She stood . . . tall beyond her sex . . . and with a fix'd eye scann'd / Her father's face. . . . How like they look'd! the expression was the same. . . . their features and / Their stature differing but in sex and years (4.42–45). Sexual difference is less remarkable than the display of common traits across gender lines, for Haidée and Lambro differ less from each other than both differ from the "boy" Juan—a term applied several times in this episode (2.144, 174; 4.19, 38).

All these inversions of socially prescribed character fuel a lethal economy, as if Byron worried that to indulge such transgressions were to tempt self-cancellation—a psychological updating of the well-known injunction of Deuteronomy dear to Stubbes and other chroniclers of abuses: "The woman shall not wear that which pertaineth unto a man, neither shall a man put on a woman's garment: for all that do so *are* abomination unto the LORD" (22:5). A feminized Juan always invites death into the poem, whether in the form of threats to his own life or to the lives of those implicated in his travesties. "Juan nearly died" (1.168) from affairs with Julia and Haidée, and they exact full wages: the passionate Julia is sentenced to life-in-death in a convent; Haidée's nurturing of Juan is allied with figures of death, and she herself dies.[4] The threat is nearly perpetual: when Gulbeyaz discovers her designs for Juan as odalisque usurped by his harem bedpartner, she issues a warrant for both their deaths, and Catherine's appetites all too soon reduce her "beauteous" favorite to "a condition / Which augured of the dead" (10.39). So, too, after his first sighting of the Black Friar's Ghost—itself a patent spectre of death—Juan and Fitz-Fulke look "pale" (16.31); the morning after discovering her within that "sable frock and dreary cowl" (16.123), Juan appears "wan and worn, with eyes that hardly brooked / The light"; Her Grace seems scarcely better—"pale and shivered" (17.14). Byron's "Memoranda" on the Murray manuscript scrap in fact reveals a suggestive linkage: "The Shade of the / Friar / The D[ea]th of J[uan]" (*CPW*, 5:761). All these presages and figures of death suggest that Byron senses fatal consequences when the law of gender is violated: the annihilation of self in both its social identity and psychological integrity.

* * *

IV

The two most extended episodes of transvestism in *Don Juan*—Juan's conscription as an odalisque and Fitz-Fulke's appropriation of a friar's habit—show Byron's effort to explore the arbitrariness of male privilege in an economy of sexual commodities. Both derive their energy from the inversion of that privilege, and both provoke Byron's ambivalence about the

---

4. For a compelling reading of Haidée in these terms, see Manning: "enveloping protection becomes suffocation, and what were only undertones in Juan's affair with Julia become prominent" (186).

cost. Behind both, too, is Byron's participation in the institution of the "Cavalier Servente," the accepted escort and socially tolerated lover of a married woman. Byron could sometimes comment on the system in quasi-feminist terms, deeming Serventism a byproduct of the way Italian fathers treat their daughters as commodities to be sold "under the market price"—that "portion" of their assets "fixed by law for the dower." The successful bidder was often a man older than the father himself (Teresa Guiccioli's husband, for instance, was about three times her age). With "such a preposterous connexion," Byron exclaims, "no love on either side," extramarital romance was necessary, indeed inevitable (*Medwin,* 22). That is not the whole story, of course, for as Cavalier Servente to Teresa Guiccioli, Byron felt acutely the inversion of sexual privilege to which he was accustomed in England, an inversion that may have been doubly disturbing for bringing into prominence his intrinsic passivity with Regency women: in Venice "the *polygamy* is all on the female side. . . . it is a strange sensation," he remarks (*BLJ,* 6:226).

This wavering between defensiveness and feminist analysis in relation to Serventism thoroughly informs Juan's experience in the Turkish court. Here Byron partly redresses Venetian imbalances, for the polygamy is all on the male side: that Gulbeyaz is one of four wives and fifteen hundred concubines makes her purchase of Juan seem minor in comparison. Yet by placing Juan in women's clothes and in the role of a sex-slave, Byron does more than simply invert the cultural norm; he allows Juan's debasement to reflect in excess the customary status of women as objects of barter and trade in a male-centered economy. Behind Juan's shocked discovery at learning he is the property of a Sultana who asks only "Christian, canst thou love?" and who "conceived that phrase was quite enough to move" (5.116), one senses Byron's own discomfort at having actually become "a piece of female property" in his relationship with Teresa Guiccioli (*BLJ,* 7:28): "the system of *serventism* imposes a thousand times more restraint and slavery than marriage ever imposed," he laments to Lady Blessington (180). And he feels particularly taxed by the erosion of time and autonomy that his "defined duties" required (*BLJ,* 7:195). The mistress's word is "the only law which he obeys. / His is no sinecure. . . . Coach, servants, gondola, he goes to call, / And carries fan, and tippet, gloves, and shawl," the narrator of *Beppo* reports, describing the role of this "supernumerary slave" (the noun was originally "gentleman" [*CPW* 4:141]) in terms that tellingly figure such bondage as a species of transvestism: he "stays / Close to the lady as a part of dress" (40). As if to inflict his own lot on his hero, Byron considered submitting Juan to the "ridicules" of being "a Cavalier Servente in Italy" (*BLJ,* 8:78), a role he has him rehearse in Russia. And when he comments on his hero thus as "man-mistress to Catherine the Great" (*Medwin,* 165), he reveals his agitation about the radical cost of these inversions: degraded to sexual property, Juan has to be regendered.[5]

---

5. The sexual ideology behind remarks such as this is so emphatic that it affects even a reader such as Cecil Lang [note 5, p. 961], who is otherwise impressed by the "revolutionary" aspect of *Don Juan* "in transferring sexual aggression to the female figures"; Lang retains conventional terms of evaluation, speaking of aggressive women as "sexual predators," but crediting aggressive men with "an assertion of sexuality"; similarly, he describes Juan as Catherine's "male whore," as if the role were implicitly female and Juan something of a degenerate transvestite in such a position (152, 153, 158). The politics of this episode are discussed by Katherine Kernberger ("Power and Sex: The Implication of role reversal in Catherine's Russia," *The Byron Journal* 8 [1980]:49).

Juan had, of course, been something of an illicit or smuggled piece of property in his affairs with Julia and Haidée; but the spectacle of him as woman's property is particularly compelling "in his feminine disguise" (6.26) because Byron now makes his loss of power coincide with loss of male identity. The slave market itself is an omen, for in addition to being for sale, the "boy" Juan (5.13)—"an odd male" in more ways than one—gets paired with an "odd female" in an allotment in which everyone else is paired "Lady to lady . . . man to man" (4.91–92). Indeed this odd couple is linked only after the captors decide not to link Juan with one of the *third sex* (86), a castrato who inspires "some discussion and some doubt" if such a "soprano might be deem'd to be a male" (92). The precarious security of Juan's gender in the marketplace becomes yet more vulnerable when he is purchased by a eunuch and ordered to dress himself in "a suit / In which a Princess with great pleasure would / Array her limbs" (5.73). The narrator conspires in this travesty, not only by insisting on referring to Juan as "her"—"Her shape, her hair, her air, her every thing" (6.35; itself a parody of Shakespeare's Troilus on "fair Cressid": "Her eyes, her hair, her cheek, her gait, her voice" [1.1.54])—but also by teasing at Juan's latent affinities with the feminine odalisques "all clad alike" (5.99).[6] For in such company, Juan's difference is scarcely apparent: indeed "his youth and features favour'd the disguise" (5.115), and "no one doubted on the whole, that she / Was what her dress bespoke, a damsel fair, / And fresh, and 'beautiful exceedingly'" (6.36)—that last phrase further dressing Juan in Coleridge's phrase for Christabel's first sight of Geraldine.

Yet Byron's total treatment of Juan cross-dressed, though it exposes the politics of sexual property, ultimately contains its subversive impulses by subsuming them into renewed expressions of male power. That agenda is anticipated by Juan's steadfast adherence to the grounds of his identity: Byron allows him the dignity of protesting to his purchaser "I'm not a lady," and of worrying about his social reputation if "it e'er be told / That I unsexed my dress" (5.73, 75). It is only Baba's threat that he will be left with more unsexed than his dress if he does not cooperate that produces compliance, even as Juan declares his "soul loathes / the effeminate garb" (5.76). Juan's statements of resistance to the effeminate find an even stronger ally in Byron's narrative politics, which, as often happens with male transvestism in literary and theatrical tradition, give the occasion over to farce, yet another means of restabilizing the apparent sexual radicalism of Juan regendered.[7] The political implications of Juan's effeminate garb dissipate into a high-camp parody of the trappings of female subjection. Juan even has to be coached "to stint / That somewhat manly majesty of stride" (5.91). The Englishman who befriends him in the slave market sounds the cue as he favors Juan with a jesting version of Laertes' caution to Ophelia—"Keep your good name"—and Juan and the narrator merrily play along: "Nay," quoth the maid, "the Sultan's self shan't carry me, / Unless his highness promises to marry me" (5.84). And when the Sultan takes a shine to Juan's beauty, Juan shows how well he has learned to mimic feminine manners: "This compliment . . . made her blush and shake"

---

6. My quotation follows the Arden edition of *Troilus and Cressida*, ed. Kenneth Palmer (New York and London: Methuen, 1981).

7. Contemporary reviews were divided over the evaluation of Julia's sexual aggressiveness, but were uniformly amused by Juan's adventures in the harem.

(5.156). And quite beyond such campy playfulness, Byron actually reverses the seeming impotence of Juan's travesty by introducing another kind of potency: Juan discovers he is not so much an unsexed man as a newly powerful woman. "Juanna" immediately becomes the center of attention and rivalry in the harem; all the girls want "her" to share their beds. This turn of events affords Juan a novel indirection by which to find directions out, for as the only phallic woman in the harem, he discovers a world of sexual opportunity. Clothes make the man.[8]

Juan's success as a phallic woman is all the more significant for its relation to a set of psychological and cultural contexts that are particularly potent for Byron. The psychological matrix has been studied by Otto Fenichel, who argues that some forms of transvestism are the behavior of a man who fantasizes about being a woman with a penis. Elaborating this view, Robert J. Stoller claims that the male transvestite "does not question that he is male," nor is he "effeminate when not dressed as a woman"; the transvestite, in fact, "is constantly aware of the penis under his woman's clothes, and, when it is not dangerous to do so, gets great pleasure in revealing that he is a male-woman."[9] In *Don Juan* phallic womanhood is made to seem a lucky effect rather than the premise of Juan's transvestism, but Byron's letters suggest an impetus for such luck. The relevant issue is Stoller's proposal that the transvestite man senses "the biological and social 'inferiority' of women" and knows "that within himself there is a propensity toward being reduced to this 'inferior' state" (215)—a propensity Byron displays in Juan's "feminine" characteristics as well as in his affairs with Julia and Haidée. Both Fenichel and Stoller argue that the transvestite invents the fantasy of a "phallic woman" either to remedy his feminine tendencies, or to assert a superior presence in his relations with strong women. In fact, Stoller goes on to say, the "prototype" for this figure "has actually existed in his life—that is, the fiercely dangerous and powerful woman who has humiliated him as a child" (215), namely his mother, whom the male transvestite at once identifies with and supersedes. This analysis may seem to some to be the myth of a male-authored and male-centered psychoanalytic tradition, but it is for that very reason so appropriate in Byron's case, coinciding remarkably not only with Juan's mother, the tyrannical Donna Inez, but with Byron's picture of his own mother in his letters: "Mrs. Byron furiosa," a "tormentor whose *diabolical* disposition . . . seems to increase with age, and to acquire new force with Time" (*BLJ*, 1:93–94; 1:75). Byron's sense of his vulnerability is clear enough in his reports of her behavior and his own corresponding hostility: "I have never been so *scurrilously* and *violently* abused by any person, as by that woman, whom I think, I am to call mother" (1:66); "she flies into a fit of phrenzy upbraids me as if I was the most undutiful wretch in existence. . . . Am I to call this woman mother? Because by natures law she has authority over me,

---

8. This episode of transvestite opportunity may have been inspired by the resourcefulness of Byron's friend, Colonel Mackinnon: "Byron was much amused by Mackinnon's funny stories, one of which was later supposed to be the basis of *Don Juan*, V: Mackinnon disguised himself as a nun in order to enter a Lisbon convent" (*The Reminiscences of Captain [Rees Howell] Gronow*, [1862], 85–86, quoted in Lovell (note 5), 612 n. 39). The anecdote seems, in addition, to offer a fantasy continuation of Juan's aborted romance with Julia.

9. Otto Fenichel, "The Psychology of Transvestitism" (1930); reprinted in *The Collected Papers of Otto Fenichel*, First Series (New York: Norton, 1953) 1:167–80 (I refer to 169); Robert J. Stoller, *Sex and Gender: On the Development of Masculinity and Femininity* (New York: Science House, 1968), 176–77.

am I to be trampled upon in this manner?" (1:56).[1] Byron's fantasy of Juan-the-phallic-woman at once reclaims "authority" from "natures law" and redresses a psychic grievance by imagining, as Stoller puts it, the possibility of "a better woman than a biological female" (177).[2]

Because the biological female in Juan's case is a Sultana, Byron's promotion of Juan from odalisque to phallic woman invests transvestism with a political significance that exceeds the realm of specific psychic grievance. Such potential is implicit in Stoller's incidental remark that "sanctioned transvestic behavior" is frequent "at carnival times, at masquerade parties" (186), behavior with which Byron was familiar, having attended "masquerades in the year of revelry *1814*" (*BLJ*, 9:168) and the Venice Carnival in 1818 and 1819. Even so sanctioned, the sexual inversions of the carnival, as Davis points out, were ambiguously productive. On the one hand, they could "clarify" the structure of hierarchical society in the very process of reversing it; these occasions offer a controlled "expression of, or a safety valve for, conflicts within the system" that operate, ultimately, to contain energy and reinforce assent. On the other hand, "festive and literary inversions of sex roles" could also excite "new ways of thinking about the system and reacting to it," and so "*undermine* as well as reinforce" assent to authority, and destabilize political structure—especially through "connections with everyday circumstances outside the privileged time of carnival and stage-play." Male transvestism, it turns out, is a particularly potent form of connection: aware that women were deemed susceptible to irrational behavior and so given some legal license for misbehavior, men resorted to transvestite cover, hiding behind the female dress when they wanted to challenge authority or engage in outright rebellion. "Donning female clothes . . . and adopting female titles" could even energize and "validate disobedient and riotous behavior by men." Davis notes a number of "transvestite riots" in Britain between the 1450s and the 1840s.[3] As a member of Parliament whose maiden speech passionately opposed the Frame-breaking bill (which specified the death penalty), and whose sarcastic "Ode to the Framers of the Frame Bill" was published (anonymously) a few days later in the *Morning Chronicle*, Byron knew about at least one such instance: the riot in April 1812 at Stockport, during which steam looms were smashed and a factory burned, led by "two men in women's clothes, calling themselves 'General Ludd's wives.'"[4] He may also have recalled that the Edinburgh Porteous Riots of 1736 featured men in women's clothes, led by one "Madge Wildfire." Certainly by the time he was writing cantos 5 and 6 of *Don Juan*, he knew Scott's representation of these riots in *The Heart of Midlothian* (1818), spearheaded by a "stout

1. For a perceptive discussion of Byron's relationship with his mother and its literary consequences, see Manning, 23–55 and 177–99.
2. Also referring to Stoller, Sandra M. Gilbert studies various "costume drama[s] of misrule" in modern literature with an aim to showing how "the hierarchical principle of an order based upon male dominance/female submission [gets] recovered from transvestite disorder" ("Costumes of the Mind: Transvestism as Metaphor in Modern Literature," *Writing and Sexual Difference*, ed. Elizabeth Abel [Chicago: Univ. of Chicago Press, 1982]: 193–219). Elaine Showalter, too, refers to Stoller in a witty and perceptive essay on how the figure of the "phallic woman" in the male feminism of the 1980s underwrites masculine power, usurping and in effect marginalizing the feminism it seems to endorse ("Critical Cross-Dressing: Male Feminists and The Woman of The Year," *Raritan* 3:2 [Fall 1983]: 130–149).
3. Davis ("Women on Top"), 130–31, 142–43, 147–50.
4. See E. P. Thompson, *The Making of the English Working Class* (London: Victor Gollancz, 1965), 567.

Amazon"—a term Byron applies to "bold and bloody" Catherine, that "modern Amazon" (9.70, 6.96).[5]

The figure of the phallic woman not only redeems the character of Juan in female garb, but reduces Gulbeyaz, the biological woman who would exercise "male" political and sexual power in this episode. For at the same time that Juan is newly empowered by his female attire, Byron's narrative abases the "imperious" woman by whom he had been abased: the episode ends with the Sultana's will subverted and her character refeminized. When we first meet her, she is an interesting "mixture . . . Of half-voluptuousness and half command" (5.108), but the destiny of biology—"Her form had all the softness of her sex" (5.109)—prevails. Not only can she not command Juan, but having been outwitted by him and his harem bedpartner, she is reduced to a caricature of a woman scorned. Her culpability in commanding Juan's sexual service, moreover, is not something Byron cares to impose on the men in his poem who command women's bodies: in a later canto, he makes crude comedy out of geriatric rape. After the sack of Ismail, "six old damsels, each of seventy years, / Were all deflowered by different Grenadiers" (a couplet Mary Shelley refused to copy), and certain "buxom" widows who had not yet met the conquering army, we are told, were "heard to wonder in the din . . . 'Wherefore the ravishing did not begin!'" (8.130, 132).[6]

Nor surprisingly, such a heavy-handed restoration of male power does not settle the sexual politics of the poem. Byron renews the whole question with Fitz-Fulke's impersonation of the Black Friar, an episode that restages and makes more flexible the issues of transvestism and female appropriation of male property. In contrast to the Sultana's thwarted attempt to exercise male sexual prerogative, Fitz-Fulke's transvestism, even in the figure of a friar whose ghost is hostile to the sexual productivity of the House of Amundeville, is a relatively successful strategy. Byron may be recalling the chimerical behavior of Caroline Lamb, who sometimes visited him "in the disguise of a carman. My valet, who did not see through the masquerade, let her in," Byron recalls; when "she put off the man, and put on the woman . . . Imagine the scene" (*Medwin*, 216–17). Fitz-Fulke's disguise carries a similar force of surprise, giving her already aggressive sexuality an opportunity for bold initiative as she temporarily escapes conventional constraints on her behavior. Feminized men in *Don Juan* are typically objects of contempt or subjects for farce, but masculinized women are almost always figures of erotic desire, and Byron's characterization of English society makes it clear why some women might desire male prerogatives: women's whole existence is limited to gossip and social intrigue; marriage is the only game in town and an unmarried man the only game worth the pursuit; and for a woman to wield any kind of power is to risk men's derision as one of the scheming "Oligarchs of Gynocrasy" (12.66). Fitz-Fulke's cross-dressing releases her from these circumscriptions, affords an outlet for desire, and grants her a kind of "male" power of action within the existing social structure. Indeed, it aligns her with male power, for quite

5. For Byron's references to Scott's novel, see *BLJ*, 9:87, 10:146, 11:46. The riots are represented in chapters 6 and 7.
6. Andrew Rutherford (while finding these stanzas "very funny") laments Byron's "abandonment of the standards of morality on which his satire has been based," for he frivolously refuses "to face the horror of mass rape, or even indeed of individual cases. Byron attacked Suvarov for callousness, for seeing men in the gross, but here he is himself prepared to think of women in the same way . . . to withhold in treating rape the moral sensitivity that he had shown in treating deaths in battle" (*Byron: A Critical Study* [Stanford: Stanford Univ. Press, 1961], 179).

beyond her plotting against Juan, Byron allows the art signified by her disguise to operate as a witty deconstruction of the duplicitous political arts practiced by the men of that world—those "Historians, heroes, lawyers, priests" who put "truth in masquerade" (11.37), and whose example inspires the narrator to urge Juan to "Be hypocritical . . . be / Not what you *seem*" (11.86).

Fitz-Fulke's transvestite behavior draws even fuller energy and ideological significance in this respect from the highly popular institution of the masquerade, at which, Terry Castle reports, transvestism was not only frequent, but frequently suspected of encouraging "female sexual freedom, and beyond that, female emancipation generally." Indeed, in the world of the eighteenth-century English novel, Castle argues, the masquerade episode is "the symbolic theater of female power," for here women usurp "not only the costumes but the social and behavioral 'freedoms' of the opposite sex." As in Byron's transvestite episodes, there are conservative checks and balances: from the novelist's overall perspective, Castle suggests, the masquerade offers a way to indulge "the scenery of transgression while seeming to maintain didactic probity. The occasion may be condemned in conventional terms, yet its very representation permits the novelist, like the characters, to assume a different role."[7] Byron's version of such "probity" is typically not a matter of attitude, but an inference of those larger narrative patterns which "correct," or at least remain nervous about, the different roles played out in his episodes of transvestite transgression. Yet because Fitz-Fulke's disguise has less to do with the specific hypocrisies of the Gynocrasy than with the general ways of the world, her manipulations yield an ambiguously potent narrative. If, as Byron's narrator remarks, that "tender moonlight situation" in which she and Juan discover each other "enables Man to show his strength / Moral or physical," he remains coy both about who the "Man" is—the girlish Juan or the transvestite Fitz-Fulke?—and about what actions, and by whom, exemplify "moral or physical" strength. He merely remarks that this is an occasion on which his hero's "virtue" may have "triumphed—or, at length, / His vice." His "or" is not much help either, for insofar as virtue (in the Latin sense of manly power) may reveal itself in "strength / Moral or physical" (even if the bawdiness of "at length" favors physical vice), Byron's phrasing compounds rather than resolves the question. The issue is managed only by a provisional deferral, a decision to retract his narrator's power of speech: this "is more than I shall venture to describe;— / Unless some Beauty with a kiss should bribe" (17.12). That seduction is and remains merely potential, for the narrator soon becomes as silent as Juan himself, who is a thoroughly ambiguous signifier in the wake of his seduction: only his "face" can be called "virgin" and even that looks "as if he had combated" (17.13–14).

With the categories of virtue and vice, strength and weakness, activity and inactivity, male reticence and female determination, male coyness and female arts thus perplexed, Byron has his narrator "leave the thing a problem, like all things" (17.13).[8] If the "masculine tradition" is, as Homans

---

7. I quote, in order, from "Eros and Liberty at the English Masquerade, 1710–90," *Eighteenth-Century Studies* 17 (1983–84): 164, and "The Carnivalization of Eighteenth-Century English Narrative," *PMLA* 99 (1984): 909, 912.

8. If, as Castle argues, the masquerade episode has the effect of introducing "a curious instability into the would-be orderly cosmos of the eighteenth-century English novel" ("Carnivalization," 904), the transvestite episodes of *Don Juan* reflect a world that presumes no such order, but is, as Anne K. Mellor puts it, "founded on abundant chaos; everything moves, changes it shape, becomes something different" (*English Romantic Irony* [Cambridge: Harvard Univ. Press, 1980], 42).

remarks, typically manifested by "the masculine self dominat[ing] and internaliz[ing]" an otherness "identified as feminine," Byron's participation in such a tradition, as is his habit, is animated by critical self-consciousness: the sexual politics that inform *Don Juan* at once expose their ideological underpinnings and qualify the potential subversiveness of these exposures with strategies to contain the risks posed to male privilege.[9] The cross-dressings of *Don Juan* are thus significant not so much for showing the poem's male hero appropriating and internalizing female otherness (indeed, his very name implies a parody of that masculine tradition), as for provoking the poem's readers to attend to what happens—politically, socially and psychologically—when women and men are allowed, or forced, to adopt the external properties and prerogatives of the other. Byron's poem does not, finally, escape the roles fashioned and maintained by his culture, but it does explore the problems of living with and within those roles. And by doing so in the heightened forms of transvestite drama and verbal cross-dressing, Byron foregrounds the artifice that sustains much of what we determine to be "masculine" and "feminine"—a strategy at once cautious and bold, through which he engenders the world of *Don Juan* and generates its elaborate plays against the codes and laws of gender.

CECIL Y. LANG

Narcissus Jilted:
Byron, *Don Juan* and the Biographical Imperative[†]

* * *

It will surprise no one if I say that Byron was obsessed with Byron. It seems to be a fact, and I do not propose to cover such familiar ground more than is necessary for the sake of exposition. Exhibit A in this exposition is of course the four cantos of *Childe Harold's Pilgrimage*, and a major part of their appeal today, as on publication, is their unabashed egotism.

Byron sailed from England on his first foreign tour on June 20, 1809; he returned, two years later, on July 14, 1811. We don't know any specific reasons for the journey, but we know that they were secret and urgent. Leslie Marchand, his biographer and the editor of his letters and journals, suggests that Byron "had a wish to escape his own proclivities towards attachment to boys, or perhaps he feared a closer connection with the Cambridge choirboy Edleston, who had wanted to live with him in London."[1] Doris Langley Moore, as sympathetic, knowledgeable, and judicious a critic as Byron has ever had, allows for the possibility that he was not merely fleeing "some particular temptation" but in fact "fleeing toward a temptation."[2]

---

9. I quote Margaret Homans (*Women Writers and Poetic Identity* [Princeton, Princeton Univ. Press, 1958], p. 12) for a representative description of the masculine tradition.
† From *Historical Studies and Literary Criticism*, ed. Jerome J. McGann. Copyright © 1985 The Board of Regents of the University of Wisconsin System. Reprinted by permission of The University of Wisconsin Press.
1. Leslie A. Marchand, ed., *Byron's Letters and Journals*, 12 vols. (Cambridge: Belknap Press of Harvard University Press, 1973–82), 1:233 n.; hereafter cited in text as *LJ*.
2. Doris Langley Moore, *Lord Byron: Accounts Rendered* (New York: Harper and Row, 1974), pp. 103–4.

In the first two cantos of *Childe Harold*, published in March 1812, the speaker leaves his ancestral home, journeys to Portugal, Spain, Gibraltar, Malta, and then to Albania, where he calls upon Ali Pacha, the virtually autonomous, powerful, ruthless gangster ruler, wooed by both the French and British governments, widely known as the Lion of Jannina, a title conferred upon him by the Sultan, who was in fact much less famous than Ali the Lion. In real life this visit to Ali Pacha began on October 19, 1809, and terminated on the twenty-third, when Byron and his friend John Cam Hobhouse departed. Some time in the next eight days, probably on October 31, Byron began writing *Childe Harold's Pilgrimage*. He also wrote at this time "a very exact journal of every circumstance of his life and many of his thoughts while young." He let "Hobhouse see it in Albania" and Hobhouse "persuaded him to burn it."[3] They quitted Albania on November 3, and on November 6 in Arta (Ambracia) we know that Byron was reading Spenser's *The Faerie Queen* (*Childe Harold* is written in Spenserian stanzas) and that he called Hobhouse's attention to an Albanian reference in Book 3, Canto 12. This reference is interesting and important. It is interesting because, together with other evidence, it leads us to proof that, contrary to received opinion, *Childe Harold's Pilgrimage* was directly and significantly influenced by Spenser's own poem as well as by the eighteenth-century Spenserians named in the Preface. It is important because it led Byron to a way of treating poetically, publicly, and cathartically a radical, intimate aspect of his nature without putting it into plain language. The specific episode in *Childe Harold* must be viewed as a kind of palimpsest with the specific episode in *The Faerie Queen* showing through. Together, these episodes in the palimpsest make possible a new reading of *Don Juan*, a reading that has "real critical importance" and will alter "critical evaluation."

Byron describes the visit to Ali Pacha at length, both in *Childe Harold*, Canto 2, and also in a marvelous letter to his mother written about a fortnight later. Let me quote from the letter:

> In nine days I reached Tepaleen, our Journey was much prolonged by the torrents that had fallen from the mountains and intersected the roads. I shall never forget the singular scene on entering Tepaleen at five in the afternoon as the Sun was going down. . . . I was conducted to a very handsome apartment and my health enquired after by the vizier's secretary "a la mode de Turque."—The next day I was introduced to Ali Pacha, I was dressed in a full suit of Staff uniform with a very magnificent saber, etc.—The vizier received me in a large room paved with marble, a fountain was playing in the centre, the apartment was surrounded by scarlet Ottomans, he received me *standing*, a wonderful compliment from a Musselman, and made me sit down on his right hand. . . . His first question was why, at so early an age, I left my country? . . . He said he was certain I was a man of birth because I had small ears, curling hair, and little white hands, and expressed himself pleased with my appearance and garb.—He told me to consider him as a father whilst I was in Turkey, and said he looked on me as his son.—Indeed, he treated me like a child, sending me almonds and sugared sherbet, fruit and sweetmeats 20 times a day.—He begged me to visit him often, and at night when he was more at leisure—I then after

---

3. Leslie A. Marchand, *Byron: A Biography*, 3 vols. (New York: Knopf, 1957), Vol. 1, Notes p. 22.

coffee and pipes retired for the first time. I saw him thrice after-
wards. . . . His Highness is 60 years old, very fat and not tall, but with
a fine face, light blue eyes and a white beard, his manner is very kind
and at the same time he possesses that dignity which I find universal
amongst the Turks. (*LJ* 1:226–31)

Byron does not say, here or elsewhere, what we learn from Hobhouse's
account forty-six years later, that at this audience they were attended by
"four or five young persons very magnificently dressed in the Albanian
habit, and having their hair flowing half way down their backs: these
brought in the refreshments, and continued supplying us with pipes,
which, though perhaps not half-emptied, were changed three times, as is
the custom when particular honours are intended for a guest." Hobhouse
also refers to the "monstrous sensualities, which were certainly not
invented, although they were practised, by Ali as well as by Tiberius," and
in a footnote to this footnote he quotes (in Latin) a passage from Sueto-
nius's *Life of Titus Vespasianus* mentioning, among other things, the
"swarms of catamites and eunuchs about him."[4]

In *Childe Harold's Pilgrimage*, Canto 2, stanzas 55–72, the same episode
is narrated, with the addition of something new and vital—or, to phrase it
more accurately, with the addition of something explicit that the letter
invites us to infer. In stanza 61 Byron refers to Ali Pacha's harem (after the
first four lines I cite the canceled reading):

> Here, woman's voice is never heard: apart,
> And scarce permitted, guarded, veil'd, to move,
> She yields to one her person and her heart,
> Tam'd to her cage, nor feels a wish to rove:
> For boyish minions of unhallow'd love
> The shameless torch of wild desire is lit,
> Caressed, preferred even to woman's self above,
> Whose forms for Nature's gentler errors fit
> All frailties mote excuse save that which they commit.[5]

The next stanza (62) echoes part of the letter just quoted:

> In marble-pav'd pavilion, where a spring
> Of living water from the centre rose
> Whose bubbling did a genial freshness fling,
> And soft voluptuous couches breath'ed repose
> Ali reclin'd, a man of war and woes;
> Yet in his lineaments ye cannot trace,
> While Gentleness her milder radiance throws
> Along that aged venerable face,
> The deeds that lurk beneath, and stain him with disgrace.

Stanza 63 continues (in the published version):

> It is not that yon hoary lengthening beard
> Ill suits the passions which belong to youth . . .

4. Lord Broughton [John Cam Hobhouse], *Travels in Albania and Other Provinces of Turkey in 1809
   and 1810*, New Edition, 2 vols. (London: John Murray, 1855), 1: 97–98, 112 n.
5. Lord Byron, *The Complete Poetical Works*, ed. Jerome J. McGann (Oxford: Clarendon Press,
   1980), vol. 2. All quotations from Byron's poetry are taken from this edition. Texts of poems not
   yet published in McGann's edition, like *Don Juan*, have been kindly supplied by the editor.

But in the Murray manuscript this reads:

> It is not that yon hoary lengthening beard
> Delights to mingle with the lip of youth . . .

Canto 12 of Book 3 of *The Faerie Queen* begins with a "universall cloud" and then a "hideous storm of winde," with "dreadful thunder and lightning."[6] Byron's journey from Jannina to Tepelene to call on Ali Pacha was interrupted by a nine-hour storm, which is alluded to twice in his letter (*LJ* 1:227, 229) and was in fact the occasion for his poem "Stanzas composed during a Thunder-Storm." Spenser's storm is followed by the theatrical appearance of a "grave personage . . . Yclad in costly garments," standing, whose name, "on his robe in gold letters cyphered," was Ease—which, with the "gold-embroidered garments" four stanzas earlier in *Childe Harold*, is a fair suggestion of Ali. Spenser's fifth and sixth stanzas describe the merrymaking of this masque of Cupid:

> . . . a joyous fellowship issewed
> Of minstrales making goodly merriment,
> With wanton bardes and rymers impudent,
> All which together sung full chearefully
> A lay of loves delight, with sweet concent.

In *Childe Harold*:

> . . . when the lingering twilight hour was past,
> Revel and feast assum'd the rule again:
> Now all was bustle and the menial train
> Prepar'd and spread the plenteous board within;
> The vacant gallery now seem'd made in vain,
> But from the chambers came the mingling din
> As page and slave anon were passing out and in.

In *The Faerie Queen*, stanzas 7 and 8 describe a personified "Fansy," glossed as "the power of the imagination to deceive with false images of love" or as "love of a capricious, casual, and wanton nature":

> . . . Fansy, like a lovely boy,
> Of rare aspect and beauty without peare.

Fansy is likened to Ganymede, beloved of Jove, and to Hylas, beloved of Hercules, and stanza 9 describes his companion, whose appearance, like Ali's, was that of an older man and who, also like Ali, lit "the shameless torch of wild desire":

> And him biside marcht amorous Desire,
> Who seemed of riper years then th'other swayne
>
> .   .   .   .
>
> His garment was disguysed very vayne [fantastically fashioned]
> And his embrodered bonet sat awry;
> Twixt both his hands few sparks he close did strayne,
> Which still he blew and kindled busily,
> That soon they life conceiv'd, and forth in flames did fly.

---

6. Edmund Spenser, *The Faerie Queen*, ed. A. C. Hamilton (London and New York: Longman, 1977); hereafter cited in text as *FQ* with book, canto, and stanza number.

We don't know many particular details about Ali's dress, but Hobhouse, who was present, tells us that he wore a "high turban composed of many small rolls [that] seemed of fine gold muslin, and his ataghan, or long dagger, was studded with brilliants."[7]

What *really* happened at Ali's palace? We don't know, of course, but Byron may have left us a coded confession. In an "Addition to the Preface" published in the fourth edition of *Childe Harold's Pilgrimage* in September 1812 (six months after the first), he says that Harold has been called "*unknightly.*" In this connection Byron limits his brief discussion almost wholly to vows of chastity. The "good old times" of chivalry, he says, were "the most profligate of all possible centuries." For proof he refers us to a book by Lacurne de Sainte Palaye, *Mémoires sur l'ancienne chevalerie,* especially to volume 2, page 69. Well, what do we find there? This: "A Lady who receives in her home a Chevalier is not willing to go to sleep without sending him one of her women to keep him company." Following this are sixteen lines of medieval verse, with marginal glosses:

> The Countess practiced in courtliness is not unhappy to have her guest. Therefore, with great pleasure she had a splendid bed prepared for him in a room to himself. There, he falls asleep easily and rests well, and the Countess at length goes to bed, summons the most courtly and beautiful of her maidens, secretly tells her: "My dear, go at once, without worrying about it, and lie with this Chevalier. . . . Serve him, if need be. I would willingly go myself, I would not refrain out of shame, were it not for Milord the Count who is not yet asleep."[8]

Byron, who loved to live dangerously in many ways, loved most of all to sail close to the wind with words. I think he is doing so here. Specifically, I think he is telling us, with his cunning allusion, what *really* happened at Ali's palace.

I will return to this later with a postscript, but it is apparent already that *something* happened and that it transformed the young Byron in the same way that, twenty-four years later, the death of Arthur Henry Hallam transformed the young Tennyson. Each event endowed for the first time a young poet with subject matter, and in each case the subject was the same, himself. I *surmise* (1) that Byron's companion John Cam Hobhouse had the

---

7. Broughton, *Travels in Albania*, p. 97.
8. "Une dame qui reçoit chez elle un Chevalier, ne veut point s'endormir qu'elle ne lui envoye une de ses femmes pour lui faire compagnie:

> La Comtesse qui fut courtoise,
> De son oste pas ni li poise,
> Ainsi li fist fere à grant delit,
> En un chambre un riche lit.
> Là se dort à aise & repose,
> Et la Comtesse à chief se pose,
> Apele une soue pucelle,
> La plus courtoise & la plus bele,
> A consoil li dist, belle amie,
> Alez tost, ne vous ennuit mie,
> Avec ce Chevalier gesir,
> . . . .
> . . . .
> . . . .
>
> Si le servez, s'il est mestiers.
> Je i alasse volentiers,
> Que ja ne laissasse pour honte;
> Ne fust pour Monseigneur le Conte
> Qui ne pas encore endormiz.

same experience; (2) that Byron described it in the journal that Hobhouse "persuaded him to burn"; (3) that Byron's reading of *The Faerie Queen* was the catalyst perhaps for the idea of writing *Childe Harold*, certainly for the narration of the Ali Pacha episode; and (4) that, finally, chickening out like Wordsworth in Book 9 of *The Prelude*, Byron so muted his language that, even with the publication of the telltale manuscript variants in 1899, the pivotal significance of the experience remained hidden, at least from all but a few contemporaries, until now.

*   *   *

Childe Harold's Pilgrimage, as is well known, is a work of myth-making. *Don Juan* is a work of myth unmaking. What *Childe Harold* mythologizes, *Don Juan* demythologizes. The promise of glory held out in *Childe Harold* is literally ridiculed in *Don Juan*, Canto 7. The Peninsular War, more or less observed by Harold the Pilgrim, *in spite of* all the irony and satire, is nonetheless romanticized, partly by the narrator's ideological bias (one side is wrong, the other is right), partly by the inflated rhetoric. The Russo-Turkish War, observed *and participated in* by Don Juan, *because of* the irony and satire, is exposed as brutal and vain, partly by the *absence* of ideological bias (the Christian Russians are as barbaric as the Moslem Turks), partly by the deft control of tone, and partly by the factual background on which Byron so prided himself. (He used volume 2 of Gabriel de Castelnau's *Essai sur l'histoire ancienne et moderne de la nouvelle Russie*, which incorporated several pages of an eyewitness account by an anonymous Russian lieutenant-general.)

The Russo-Turkish War of Juan is a revision of the Peninsular War of Harold, and in this way Byron begins now his *recherche du temps perdu*. He begins to merge present and past, to transform Harold into Juan.

*   *   *

Canto 9 of *Don Juan*, to which I turn now, was composed in August and September 1822, thirteen years after the visit to Ali Pacha, three months or so after the inspection of the American Mediterranean squadron and the telling allusion to Ali's snuffbox.[9] The subject of Canto 9 is Juan at the court of Catherine the Great. He has been sent there by Marshal Suvarow, who seems to have been attracted to Juan much as the Sultan had been—and in the same way (*DJ* 7.526–27), with the dispatch announcing, in rhyme, the capture of Ismail, with thirty thousand slain. Catherine rejoices (in this order) over the news, over Suvarow's rhymes, and then over Juan. She is of course enchanted by his youth and beauty. She has him vetted—indeed, *tested*—by Miss Protasoff, the Eprouveuse—and Juan becomes the royal favorite, a morsel for a monarch, in the line of Lanskoi, Potemkin, and all the others, about whom Byron knew all there was to know.

This is powerful stuff, but Byron handles it perfectly—as deftly and expertly as Mozart. He had achieved a similar success in Canto 8, in the battle of Ismail, where Juan, "pervaded" by "the thirst/Of glory" (*DJ* 8.412–13), becomes an efficient instrument of war, becomes a killing

---

9. In a letter to Thomas Moore, June 8, 1822, Byron mentions having been invited on board an American warship and comments on his fame in America by remarking that he would rather "have a nod from an American than a snuff-box from an emperor" (*BLJ* 9:171); in a letter written on November 12, 1809, Byron had told his mother of Napoleon's gift of a snuff-box to Ali Pasha (see p. 112). (*Editor's note.*)

machine. Juan's heroism is diminished, precisely, by his courage; his moral stature is degraded, precisely, by his valor. He is redeemed from squalor by a major instance of "humanity" (*DJ* 8.1114)—his rescue of little Leila, the Moslem orphan, who accompanies him throughout the rest of the poem. No such redemption is possible at the court of Catherine. Juan, like Tom Jones with Lady Bellaston, becomes a male whore.

Let's look now at details. The year of the siege of Ismail is 1790, when Catherine, born in 1729, as Byron knew perfectly well, was sixty-one or sixty-two years old. She probably had her husband, Peter III, murdered, and her lechery, even to the end of her life, age sixty-seven, was and remains legendary. Her motto ought to have been: "Trespassers will be violated." She had a succession of official favorites, all of them known to history, all of them young and handsome, and all discussed in Byron's source, Charles François Philibert Masson's *Mémoires secrets sur la Russie pendant les règnes de Catherine II et de Paul Ier* (1800). But I do not think it is true, despite all the commentators, that Don Juan here is a composite portrait made of three of the favorites. Byron is far more subtle, far more profound, far more ironic, far more devious, and far more interesting.

"Man is least himself," said Oscar Wilde, "when he talks in his own person. Give him a mask and he will tell you the truth." Don Juan here is Byron himself and, what is more, Catherine here is Ali Pacha. Juan is clothed in the "full suit of Staff uniform," with magnificent saber, that Byron had had made, for fifty guineas, by a tailor in Gibraltar, in August 1809, two and a half months before he saw Ali. "I have a most superb uniform as a court dress," Byron wrote to his mother, "indispensable in travelling" (*LJ* 1:221). Hobhouse had one also, and they were the uniforms of an aide-de-camp, according to John Galt, who saw them in Gibraltar and later in Sardinia,[1] and of such a "gaudy red"[2] that Galt thought them a ridiculous affectation.

Here is the description of Juan when Catherine receives him:

> Suppose him in a handsome uniform;
> A scarlet coat, black facings, a long plume,
> Waving, like sails new shivered in a storm,
> Over a cocked hat in a crowded room,
> And brilliant breeches, bright as a Cairn Gorme,
> Of yellow cassimere we may presume,
> White stockings drawn, uncurdled as new milk,
> O'er limbs whose symmetry set off the silk:
>
> Suppose him sword by side, and hat in hand,
> Made up by Youth, Fame, and an Army tailor—
> That great Enchanter, at whose rod's command
> Beauty springs forth, and Nature's self turns paler,
> Seeing how Art can make her work more grand,
> (When she don't pin men's limbs in like a gaoler)—
> Behold him placed as if upon a pillar! He
> Seems Love turned a Lieutenant of Artillery!
>
> His Bandage slipped down into a cravāt;
> His Wings subdued to epaulettes; his Quiver

---

1. John Galt, *The Life of Byron* (New York: Fowle, 1900), pp. 65–68.
2. Marchand, *Byron*, 1: 197, and *Notes*, p. 20.

Shrunk to a scabbard, with his Arrows at
His side as a small sword, but sharp as ever;
His Bow converted into a cocked hat;
But still so like, that Psyche were more clever
Than some wives (who make blunders no less stupid)
If she had not mistaken him for Cupid.

(*DJ* 9.337–60)

For the audience with Ali Pacha, Byron's uniform was certainly that gorgeous confection made up by the army tailor in Gibraltar, and there can be no doubt that in his audience with Catherine Juan was wearing the same outfit, though except by necessity Byron would not have appeared in knee breeches. Let me quote Doris Langley Moore, as great an authority on costume as on Byron: "For ceremonial occasions abroad he had a cocked hat with plumes, and a scarlet suit embroidered with gold which was the full dress uniform of an aide-de-camp. I believe it was an admissible dress for peers being presented at foreign courts, and certainly it had a tremendous effect on certain Pashas in Albania and Turkey."[3] One detail, however, is significantly different—the yellow cashmere breeches. Court protocol required breeches, all right, but why yellow? Once more, Hobhouse may have given us the answer. Albanian custom, he reported, required the removal indoors of the "outward shoes." "The rich," he said, "have a thin boot without a sole, reaching a little above their ankles, which, when worn by a Turk or privileged Greek, is yellow or scarlet, but in all other cases blue, or some dark colour."[4]

Ali, in Byron's accounts, was "60 years old, very fat and not tall, but with a fine face, light blue eyes," and with a "very kind" manner (*LJ* 1:228); "Gentleness" throws a "milder radiance" along his face (*CHP* 2.556–57). Catherine is sixty-one or sixty-two, she is plump, has "blue eyes, or grey," and "though fierce *looked* lenient" and "Glanced mildly" on Juan. "Her face was noble, her eyes were fine, mouth gracious" (*DJ* 9.570, 562, 498–99, 464).

Ali was certain that Byron was "a man of birth" because of his "small ears, curling hair, and little white hands." Byron tells us that on Juan's "unembarrassed brow / Nature had written 'gentleman'" (*DJ* 9.661–62). Byron, with Ali, found his "pedigree more regarded than even" his title (*LJ* 1:228), and Juan, with Catherine, owed much "to the blood he show'ed / Like a race-horse" (*DJ* 10.228–29). Ali told Byron "to consider him as a father . . . and said he looked on me as his son" (*LJ* 1: 227–28); Juan's mother, in a letter, praised Catherine's "*maternal* love" (*DJ* 10.256). Byron and Hobhouse saw, and indeed spent their first evening in Ali's palace in the company of, his two physicians; Juan is attended by Catherine's physician (*LJ* 1:227; *DJ* 10.304–52).[5]

The "shameless torch of wild desire is lit," chez Ali, we recall, for "boyish minions." Catherine, we are twice told, "sometimes liked a boy," and preferred "a boy to men much bigger," and Juan is referred to as her "minion" (*DJ* 9.375, 571; 10.348). Ali "Delights to mingle with the lip of youth" (*CHP* 2.506 vl.); Catherine "liked to gaze on youth" (*DJ* 9.486). Ali, with his kind manner and "dignity," has the "appearance of anything but his real

3. Doris Langley Moore, "Byronic Dress," *Costume* 5 (1971): 1–13.
4. Broughton, *Travels in Albania*, p. 46.
5. See also ibid., 1: 94–95.

character, for he is a remorseless tyrant" (*LJ* 1:228); Catherine, "though fierce *looked* lenient" (*DJ* 9.499).

Catherine thinks of Juan as "the herald Mercury / New lighted on a 'Heaven-kissing hill'" (*DJ* 9.521), and Byron, in the same episode, says, "we have just lit on a 'Heaven-kissing hill'" (*DJ* 9.676). The allusion is to *Hamlet* 3.4.58, where Hamlet is bitterly berating his mother for her unnatural act, and Gertrude replies: "Thou turn'st mine eyes into my very soul, / And there I see such black and grained spots / As will not leave their tinct." Juan, at second *Hamlet* reference, "retired" with Miss Protasoff, the "Eprouveuse," and it is interesting that Byron should have used the same word when terminating his initial interview with Ali: "I then after coffee and pipes retired for the first time" (*LJ* 1:228). ("In England," Byron observed in a letter six months later [May 3, 1810], "the vices in fashion are whoring and drinking, in Turkey Sodomy and smoking, we prefer a girl and a bottle, they a pipe and a pathic. They are sensible people," he continues without a break, "Ali Pacha told me he was sure I was a man of rank because I had *small ears* and handsome *curling* hair" [*LJ* 1:238].) In Albania, by Ali's order, Byron was "supplied with every kind of necessary, *gratis*," and "was not permitted to pay for a single article of household consumption" (*LJ* 1:226). In Russia Juan, as his mother's letter says, "brought his spending to a handsome anchor" and reduced his "expenses" (*DJ* 10.244, 248).

Juan and Ali talked of "war and travelling, politics and England," and when Byron left Ali's court, he says, Ali gave him "letters, guards and every possible accommodation" (*LJ* 1:228]. At the Russian court Juan falls ill and Catherine

> . . . resolved to send him on a mission,
> But in a style becoming his condition.

He is sent as her emissary to England, to negotiate

> Something about the Baltic's navigation,
> Hides, train-oil, tallow, and the rights of Thetis,
> Which Britons deem their "uti possidetis."

So she fitted him out "in a handsome way" and sent him to England "laden with all kinds of gifts and honours" (*DJ* 10.361, 367).

The English cantos that follow are praised by everyone, and in due course I will have something to say about them, but there is more to be said about the episode with Catherine the Great, in which there is yet another stratum: once more *The Faerie Queen*.

Let me turn once more to biographical fact, to July 1822, at the Casa Lanfranchi, Byron's palace in Pisa. There, Leigh Hunt and his family arrived about July 1, living in the "ground-floor apartments."[6] All this is a story in itself, and a well-known one, but I am concerned now with only one fact. I quote a paragraph from Leslie Marchand's *Byron: A Biography*:

> Hunt, who had lived among books since his earliest years, thought Byron's collection lopsided and rather poor, consisting chiefly of new ones and English works published on the Continent. "He was anxious to show you that he possessed no Shakespeare and Milton; 'because,'

6. Marchand, *Byron*, 3: 1008.

he said, 'he had been accused of borrowing from them!'" Byron said he could not read Spenser. Hunt recalled: "I lent him a volume of the 'Fairy Queen,' and he said he would try to like it. Next day he brought it to my study-window, and said, 'Here, Hunt, here is your Spenser. I cannot see anything in him:' and he seemed anxious that I should take it out of his hands, as if he was afraid of copying so poor a writer."[7]

In view of what we know about *Childe Harold's Pilgrimage*, this remark is, to say the least, interesting. It is certain that *The Faerie Queen* had recently been in his consciousness to some extent, for in Canto 7 of *Don Juan*, completed on June 28, a couple of days before Hunt's arrival, Byron had wittily distorted a familiar line from the Introduction (line 9) to *The Faerie Queen* to read, "Fierce loves and faithless wars," which, as we have seen, is precisely the subject of Cantos 8 and 9.

In Canto 9 in stanza 42, immediately preceding Juan's appearance at court, Byron says:

> So on I ramble, now and then narrating,
> Now pondering:—it is time we should narrate:
> I left Don Juan with his horses baiting—
> Now we'll get o'er the ground at a great rate.
> I shall not be particular in stating
> His journey, we've so many tours of late:
> Suppose him then at Petersburgh; suppose
> That pleasant capital of painted Snows.

The usual—indeed, the only—gloss of "painted snows" is that of E. H. Coleridge, who quotes a passage from William Tooke's *Life of Catherine*, which does not mention either paint or snow and of which the very point is that the Petersburg winter is only too real.[8] For Byron the snow *is* painted, but it is painted with blood, and the source of his phrase is *The Faerie Queen*, Book 2, Canto 12. And it is this book, and most particularly this canto, that underlies this whole episode. Book 2 of *The Faerie Queen* is "The Legend of Sir Guyon, or Of Temperance," and it is primarily upon Canto 12, with the Bower of Bliss, that Byron draws. Even in Canto 1, however, Guyon rescues an infant orphan in a manner entirely comparable to Juan's rescue of little Leila, the Moslem orphan, in the siege of Ismail. And in Canto 7 (stanzas 53 ff.), the golden apples in the Garden of Proserpina contributed to the wonderful dream of Dudu in the harem scene in *Don Juan* (6.593–616). Guyon is of course beset with every temptation conceivable, all of which are warded off by the Palmer accompanying, and though it is not necessary to identify Guyon and the Palmer with Byron and Hobhouse, the points of resemblance, mutatis mutandis, are striking, and it would be humorless to dismiss the possibility of this delicious nuance.

Guyon and the Palmer enter the Bower of Bliss through a gate of ivory, intricately carved with the story of Jason and Medea and the voyage of the Argo. The ivory of the waves and billows is called a "snowy substance sprent / with vermell," sprinkled with vermilion, "like the boys blood therein shed" (*FQ* 2.12.43–45), and a little later (stanza 58) Spenser refers to the "painted flowers"—all this, of course, the essence of the Bower of Bliss,

---

7. Ibid., 3: 1014.
8. William Tooke, *Life of Catherine II, Empress of All the Russias* (Philadelphia: William Fry, 1802).

created by the "faire enchanteresse" (stanza 81), where, Spenser tells us
several times, art imitated nature and "Art at nature did repine [fret]" (stan-
zas 42, 59), mentioning also "Art, as half in scorne / Of niggard Nature"
(stanza 50). The Bower of Bliss is in a plain (which Byron seems to have
drawn on in *Childe Harold*, 2.442–59, en route to Ali Pacha), in the midst
of which "a fountain stood" (stanza 60).

In Juan's introduction to Catherine, he is in his resplendent uniform,
"made up by . . . an army tailor" who is called

> That great Enchanter, at whose rod's command
> Beauty springs forth, and Nature's self turns paler.

Spenser had earlier (stanza 23) referred to "Dame Nature selfe" and in the
same stanza to the "Great Whirlpoole" that even the fishes flee, which
becomes in *Don Juan* "the whirlpool full of depth and danger" (9.507)
about all women, especially Catherine. Before the gate of the Bower of
Bliss the Palmer brandishes his mighty staff, made up of the same wood as
the Caduceus, the "rod of Mercury" (stanzas 40–41), just as Byron, when
Juan kneels before Catherine, speaks of the "herald Mercury / New lighted
on a Heaven-kissing hill" (9.521).

Guyon and the Palmer penetrate to the depths of the garden and there
view Acrasia lying "upon a bed of roses" (stanza 77) with her young lover,
Verdant. Here is Spenser:

> The young man sleeping by her seemed to bee
> Some goodly swayne of honourable place,
> That certes it great pittie was to see
> Him his nobilitie so foule deface;
> And sweet regard and amiable grace,
> Mixed with manly sternnesse did appeare
> Yet sleeping, in his well-proportioned face,
> And on his tender lip the downy heare
> Did now but freshly spring, and silken blossoms beare.

Here is Byron:

> Juan was . . . slight and slim,
> Blushing and beardless; and yet ne'ertheless
> There was a something is his turn of limb,
> And still more in his eye, which seemed to express
> That though he looked one of the Seraphim,
> There lurked a Man beneath the Spirit's dress.
>   (*DJ* 9.369–74)

And six stanzas later:

> Juan, I said, was a most beauteous Boy,
> And had retained his boyish look beyond
> The usual hirsute seasons . . .
>   (*DJ* 9.417–20)

Following this is next to the bawdiest passage in Byron's works, the apostrophe
to the vulva, especially Catherine's. And after *that*, in stanzas 67 and 68, she
looks down at him, "and so they fell in love—She with his face, / His
grace, his God-knows-what," and Juan—this marks his decisive transformation into

Don Juan—Juan fell into "Self-love." Then, in the next stanza, the ne plus ultra of Byron's bawdry, we are told that all cats are gray in the dark— especially for a lusty young nobleman of twenty-one, handsome, rich, well dressed, willful, far away from home for the first time in his life and in an obscure, remote, exotic, barbarous part of the world, and, what is more, tempted to indulge "to the full," as Hobhouse wrote of Ali, "all the pleasures that are licenced by the custom of the country."[9]

> [Juan] was of that delighted age
> Which makes all female ages equal—when
> We don't much care with whom we may engage,
> As bold as Daniel in the Lion's den,
> So that we can our native sun assuage
> In the next ocean, which may flow just then,
> To make a twilight in, just as Sol's heat is
> Quenched in the lap of the salt Sea, or Thetis.

In the episode at the Sultan's palace Byron had already twice referred to Daniel in the lion's den (*DJ* 5.477, 646). "Assuage" has the sense of "abate, lessen, diminish (esp. anything swollen)" (OED). "Lap" for female puden-dum is familiar in Hamlet's "country matters" bawdry with Ophelia (3.2.116 ff.). "Quenched in the lap of the salt sea, or Thetis" seems to be an allusion to *Hudibras*, 2.2.29 (a poem that Byron knew intimately and quoted at will):

> The sun had long since in the Lap
> Of Thetis, taken out his Nap,
> And . . .   the Morn
> From black to red began to turn.

In the Bower of Bliss Guyon and the Palmer come upon Acrasia and Verdant:

> That wanton Ladie, with her lover lose [loose or wanton]
> Whose sleepie head she in her lap did soft dispose.
> (*FQ* 3.23.76)

Byron had already defined "cunnus" (from Horace's *Satire* 1.3.107) as "Thou sea of life's dry land" (*DJ* 9.448). And to this I add two things: (1) as Byron wrote to his mother, he entered Tepelene, where Ali resided, "at five in the afternoon as the Sun was going down," and (2) in the same letter he remarks: "I bathed in the sea, today" (*LJ* 1:227, 229).

One does not want to be too ingenious, and I do not think I have erred in that direction. There is a conspicuous difference between the received interpretations of this episode and the interpretation you have just heard, a difference as conspicuous and as vital as the difference between night and day. Everyone can tell the difference between night and day, but no one can say exactly where one ends and the other begins, and in the case of this stanza it seems necessary to cite *all* the evidence. The para-phrasable prose meaning, in any event, is beyond dispute, and it is bawdy. The stanza is unquestionably a cryptogram. The context and the resonances imply something beyond plain prose and, this being true, one should not overlook the implications of the fact that the number of the stanza is 69.

---

9. Broughton, *Travels in Albania*, p. 113.

Let me return now for the postscript to *Childe Harold* that I promised earlier. Don Juan has slept with Miss Protasoff before sleeping with Catherine, and in the harem he had slept with Dudu rather than with the Sultana (not to mention the Sultan!). Childe Harold, on the other hand, sleeps with nobody at any time, but Byron thought it desirable to discuss the charge of unknightliness in terms of a medieval French poem (from a book by Ste. Palaye, vol. 2, p. 69) in which a Chevalier sleeps with a maiden deputized by his hostess, the Countess. There *is* a pattern and the outlines are clear, so clear that it would require a scholarship of uncommon severity to resist the inference that it tells us something about Byron's experience chez Ali Pacha.

This reading of Canto 9 has shown definitively that biography has critical importance and can influence critical evaluation. "It has frequently been suggested"—I am quoting Leslie Marchand—"that the Russian cantos of *Don Juan* are the weakest because Byron was writing about what he had not seen and experienced, and by his own confession that always put a damper on his genius."[1] The editor of Byron's poetry calls Juan's affair with Catherine "the poem's least interesting episode."[2] On the basis of the biographical evidence presented here, I myself would call it the poem's *most* interesting episode, and I would affirm additionally that Canto 9 is the very climax of the poem viewed as a whole, with the same structural importance that Canto 9 has in several books of *The Faerie Queen* (especially Books 1 and 2), that Book 9 has in *Paradise Lost* (the temptation and fall), and that Book 9 has in *The Prelude* ("Residence in France"). Moreover, Byron's Canto 9 shares with Book 9 of *Paradise Lost* and of *The Prelude*, and also with Tennyson's "Pelleas and Ettarre," the ninth of the *Idylls of the King*, the same crucial significance, sexual awareness.

The remainder of *Don Juan*, though no less interesting, is clear sailing, for a clear reason. Juan is sent to England as Catherine's emissary—by way of Warsaw, Konigsberg,

> And thence through Berlin, Dresden, and the like,
> Until he reached the castellated Rhine.

Juan reverses Byron's journey of April–May 1816, when he left England for the last time. It is an extraordinary phenomenon and an extraordinary tour-de-force, and the progress of the poem can be measured, easily and in detail, in the letters of that period, in the third canto of *Childe Harold* read backward, so to speak, and in other documents. Mindfully and wittily, Byron draws upon the scenes, the language, and even the inflated rhetoric of *Childe Harold's Pilgrimage*:

> Ye glorious Gothic scenes! how much ye strike
> All phantasies, not even excepting mine:
> A grey wall, a green ruin, rusty pike,
> Make my soul pass the equinoctial line
> Between the present and past worlds, and hover
> Upon their airy confine, half-seas-over.

These few lines in themselves are stunning echoes. The "rusty pike" is, in *Childe Harold*,

1. Leslie A. Marchand, *Byron's Poetry: A Critical Introduction* (Boston: Houghton Mifflin, 1965), p. 206.
2. Jerome J. McGann, *Don Juan in Context* (Chicago: University of Chicago Press, 1976), p. 65.

> . . . the sword laid by
> Which eats into itself and rusts ingloriously,
> (CHP 3.395–96)

symbol of Napoleon in defeat and exile as of Byron himself and all others who are the vampires of their own hearts. The "grey wall, green ruin" reflect the

> . . . chiefless castles breathing stern farewells
> From gray but leafy walls, where Ruin greenly dwells.
> (*CHP* 3.413–14)

Another allusion just as specifically evokes the "castled crag of Drachenfels" lyric in *Childe Harold*, and in this evocation (which also draws upon a letter to Hobhouse of May 16, 1816) Byron is remembering in 1822 his remembering in 1816 of Augusta Leigh:

> But Juan posted on through Mannheim, Bonn,
> Which Drachenfels frowns over like a spectre
> Of the good feudal times for ever gone,
> On which I have not time just now to lecture.
> (*DJ* 10.488–89)

After Drachenfels Juan

> . . . was drawn onwards to Cologne,
> A city which presents to the inspector
> Eleven thousand Maidenheads of bone,
> The greatest number flesh hath ever known.

From the diary of his physician and companion, Polidori, we know that Byron saw the "11,000 virgins' bones,"[3] but it is from the same letter to Hobhouse that we learn of the "German chambermaid—whose red cheeks and white teeth . . . made me venture upon her carnally." But there is another stratum to this letter. In September–October 1822, Byron, writing of Juan's Rhine journey, recalls his own Rhine journey of May 1816. In May 1816, the Rhine valley scenery reminded him of his 1809 journey in Portugal and, much more significant, the Albanian valley on the route to Tepelene, where he saw Ali Pacha (*LJ* 5.76).

In Holland Juan embarks for England in language that echoes the departure in *Childe Harold* from England, and also the very seasickness of that voyage described in a letter: "As a veteran I stomached the sea pretty well— till a damned 'Merchant of Bruges' capsized his breakfast close by me—and made me sick by contagion" (*LJ* 5:71). The customhouse at Dover is in both *Don Juan* (10.567) and the letter to Hobhouse (*LJ* 5:71). Canterbury was a tourist stop, outward-bound in 1816, inward-bound in *Don Juan*.

At Shooter's Hill, eight miles south of London, the poem resumes the psychological development of the character of Juan and no doubt betrays some nostalgia on the part of the author. The dehumanization of Juan proceeds apace. The very smog seemed to Juan a "magic vapour," and, though it "put the sun out like a taper," to him it was "but the natural atmosphere" (*DJ* 10.657–64). In Canto 11 he is ambushed by four pads, and, too "hasty"

---

3. Marchand, *Byron*, 2: 618–19.

in his own defense, draws his pistol and kills one of the assailants. The killing was unnecessary, as Juan admits.

Juan enters London society and is of course there, as elsewhere, a great success. He is invited to Norman Abbey, the countryseat of Lady Adeline Amundeville and Lord Henry, which is of course Byron's own Newstead Abbey, and it is described in some of the very words used to depict that home in the opening stanzas of *Childe Harold*, before the pilgrimage began. In other words, Byron has sent Juan back to the very beginning of *Childe Harold*.

In a couple of stanzas in Canto 14, as nimble witted as anything in all literature, Byron gaily warns us that he writes in code, and even this warning has been ignored or misconstrued by the commentators:

> "*Haud ignara loquor*": these are *Nugae*, "*quarum*
> *Pars* parva *fui*," but still art and part.
> Now I could much more easily sketch a harem,
> A battle, wreck, or history of the heart,
> Than these things; and besides, I wish to spare 'em,
> For reasons which I choose to keep apart.
> '*Vetabo Cereris sacrum qui volgarit*'—
> Which means that vulgar people must not share it.
>
> And therefore what I throw off is ideal—
> Lower'd, leaven'd like a history of Freemasons;
> Which bears the same relation to the real,
> As Captain Parry's voyage may do to Jason's.
> The grand Arcanum's not for men to see all;
> My music has some mystic diapasons;
> And there is much which could not be appreciated
> In any manner by the uninitiated.

This multilayered passage is the richest lode in all *Don Juan* and the most explicit for our purposes here. The first Latin phrases, cleverly adapted from the *Aeneid* (2.91, 6), "Haud ignara loquor" and "these are Nugae, quarum Pars parva fui," can be rendered as "I know whereof I speak" and "'these are trifling matters [which I myself saw and] in which I played a small part." This is not exactly straightforward and viewed in context can induce vertigo, for in the passage in Virgil Aeneas is relating to Dido the story of the Trojan horse. And what *he* said was "These are piteous sights which I myself saw and in which I played a great part." Byron thus warns us that he knows what he is talking about, that he took part in the events related, and that he is deliberately deceptive. But there is yet another layer of biographical evidence, for Byron had quoted the same Virgilian phrase some years earlier (1813–14) in connection with his poem "The Bride of Abydos." This tale, originally conceived as a love affair between brother and sister, everybody (including Byron himself) recognizes as a reflection of his love for his half-sister, Augusta, and his affair with Lady Frances Wedderburn Webster. Byron continues his waggish obfuscation in the next Latin phrase: "Vetabo Cereris sacrum qui volgarit," from Horace's *Odes* (3.2.26), is "I will forbid him who has divulged the sacred rites of mystic Ceres [to abide beneath the same roof or to unmoor with me the sacred bark]." The next stanza says that no one is supposed to penetrate all of what he writes; it has some mysterious ranges of meaning ("diapasons"), and therefore

> There is much which could not be appreciated
> In any manner by the uninitiated.

At Norman Abbey Juan meets a muster of society's darlings, invited from the four thousand 'for whom the world was made' (*DJ* 13.386; 11.355). Everyone agrees that these brilliant sketches are drawn from life, and several convincing identifications have been suggested and are generally accepted. Juan is of course pursued by the ladies as in real life Byron himself was pursued. In real life Byron was conspicuously *not* pursued by one woman, Annabella Milbanke, but for a complex of reasons, which did not include romantic love, Byron proposed marriage to her. She, for her part, for a complex of reasons, which included the absence of romantic love, rejected him. As Leslie Marchand puts it: "When half of the women of London society wore their hearts on their sleeve wherever Byron appeared, and dozens of others who had never seen him were willing to profess their love, Miss Milbanke refused his offer of honorable marriage because she could not feel a sufficiently "strong affection" for him."[4] A couple of years later he proposed again, and after a fair amount of skirmishing she accepted and they were married on January 2, 1815. She left him in January 1816 and they never saw each other again.

In *Don Juan*, at Norman Abbey, one lady conspicuously does not pursue Juan. Her name is Aurora Raby, and, except for two small details—Aurora Raby is an orphan (as Byron wished Annabella!) and, like Juan, Catholic (and Annabella had to be satisfied about Byron's religion [*LJ* 4:177])—her description coincides in every particular with what we know of Annabella Milbanke: of good birth, an only child, bookish, cold, prim, priggish, pensive, pretty, reserved, rich, and silent. In *Don Juan* (16.883) Aurora Raby's "pure and placid mien" is noted; and Byron, speaking of Annabella Milbanke in a letter remarks on her "placid countenance" (*LJ* 2:175) and in another letter on the "serenity" of her countenance.[5] Of Aurora Raby it is said that she had

> . . . a depth of feeling to embrace
> Thoughts, boundless, deep, but silent too as Space.
> (*DJ* 16.431–32)

Of Annabella, Byron wrote to Lady Melbourne: "She seems to have more feeling than we imagined—but is the most *silent* woman I ever encountered" (*LJ* 4:228). And Annabella Milbanke wrote to Byron: "It is my nature to feel long, deeply, and secretly."[6] A full stanza and a half can be documented so completely, phrase by phrase, that there can be no doubt as to the actuality of Byron's recollections:

> Juan was something she could not divine,
> Being no Sybil in the new world's ways;

---

4. Ibid., 1: 370.
5. Malcolm Elwin, *Lord Byron's Wife* (New York: Harcourt, Brace and World, 1963), p. 166.
6. Marchand, *Byron*, 1: 405.

> Yet she was nothing dazzled by the meteor,
> Because she did not pin her faith on feature.
>
> His fame too,—for he had that kind of fame
> Which sometimes plays the deuce with womankind,
> A heterogeneous mass of glorious blame,
> Half virtues and whole vices being combined;
> Faults which attract because they are not tame;
> Follies trick'd out so brightly that they blind:—
> These seals upon her wax made no impression,
> Such was her coldness or her self-possession.
>
> (*DJ* 15.445–56)

Annabella Milbanke wrote a "Character" of Byron,[7] which Byron read and described as "more favourable to her talents than to her discernment" (*LJ* 2:229). The first time she saw Byron, she praised—more accurately, *appraised*—his beauty: "His features are well formed—his upper lip is drawn toward the nose with an impression of impatient disgust. His eye is restlessly thoughtful." And, she goes on, "I did not seek an introduction to him, for all the women were absurdly courting him, and trying to *deserve* the lash of his Satire. . . . I thought that *inoffensiveness* was the most secure conduct. . . . So I made no offering at the shrine of Childe Harold."[8] A few months later (October 1812), she drew up a sort of character of herself for Lady Melbourne, enumerating the qualities she wanted in a husband, one of which was: "I do not regard *beauty* . . ."[9] Later still, in a letter to Byron, she wrote: "Early in our acquaintance . . . I studied your character. . . . My regard for your welfare did not arise from blindness to your errors; I was interested by the strength and generosity of your feelings, and I honored you for that pure sense of moral rectitude, which could not be perverted, though perhaps tried by the practice of Vice. I would have sought to arouse your own virtues to a consistent plan of action, for so directed, they would guide you more surely than any mortal counsel."[1] Moreover, Annabella Milbanke's coldness and self-possession were conspicuous and famous. The duchess of Devonshire called her "cold, prudent and reflecting": "She is really an icicle."[2] In a letter to Byron, she herself refers to the "formality and coldness" observable in her "manners" as well as in her "writing" and admits to "having been repulsively cold towards" Byron each time they had met the year before in London.[3] And earlier, when his first proposal was rejected, Byron, congratulating himself on his "escape," said: "That would have been but a *cold collation*, and I prefer hot suppers" (*LJ* 2:246).

Stanza 45, in this respect, is even more revealing:

> Early in years, and yet more infantine
> In figure, she had something of sublime
> In eyes which sadly shone, as seraphs' shine.
> All youth—but with an aspect beyond time;

7. Elwin, *Lord Byron's Wife*, p. 119.
8. Ibid., pp. 105–6.
9. Mabell, Countess of Airlie, *In Whig Society* (London: Hodder and Stoughton, 1921), p. 138.
1. Elwin, *Lord Byron's Wife*, p. 167.
2. Countess of Airlie, *In Whig Society*, p. 138; Elwin, *Lord Byron's Wife*, p. 116.
3. Elwin, *Lord Byron's Wife*, p. 198.

> Radiant and grave—as pitying man's decline;
> Mournful—but mournful of another's crime,
> She look'd as if she sat by Eden's door,
> And grieved for those who could return no more.

Byron, speaking of Annabella's "disposition," said, "She is like a child in that respect—and quite *caressable* into kindness and good humour" (*LJ* 4.231). But the remainder of the stanza is a puzzling reference, glossed by no one. (In a manuscript variant, by the way, the seventh line, instead of "sat by Eden's door," read "sat by Eden's gate.") The source is, in fact, a poem by one of Byron's oldest and closest friends, Tom Moore: the second tale, "Paradise and the Peri," in *Lalla Rookh* (1817), which Byron read soon after publication and admired (*LJ* 5.252). The reference is to the opening eight lines:

> One morn a Peri at the gate
> Of Eden stood, disconsolate;
> And as she listen'd to the Springs
> Of Life within, like music flowing,
> And caught the light upon her wings
> Through half the open portal glowing,
> She wept to think her recreant race
> Should e'er have lost that glorious place!

This explanation of a difficult allusion would, in itself, justify a paragraph in *Notes and Queries* but not space and time in this essay. What, then, qualifies this stanza for inclusion in a discussion of biographical interpretation?

Two things. One is that in the climactic episode of Moore's story (lines 398 ff.) a Byronic hero, transparently the Giaour or Conrad, comes upon a young boy chasing "damsel-flies" (as in *The Giaour*, lines 388–95, a young boy chases an "insect queen"). The lad tires (as in *The Giaour*), rests, and then prays. That "man of crime" (line 430), whose brow is haggard and fierce and in whose eye can be read "dark tales of many a ruthless deed," whose "memory ran / O'er many a year of guilt and strife," observes the kneeling lad, "lisping th' eternal name of God," and—I'm embarrassed to go on with this—weeps and then joins him, "kneeling there / By the child's side, in humble pray'r" (lines 487–88), and thus experiences the redemption denied all Byronic heroes, save one. I suggest, without further discussion, that in this episode Byron saw himself and his daughter Ada.

The second reason for discussing the allusion to Aurora Raby mourning by Eden's gate is more complicated. Annabella Milbanke had turned down a proposal of marriage from a man named George Eden. The Edens, like the Milbankes, were a Durham family, and George Eden, according to Ethel Colburn Mayne, "was a friend of Annabella's childhood."[4] Now, nothing in Byron's life is simple, and this episode isn't either. For her own reasons (bad ones, as it turned out), Annabella Milbanke "let Byron think she was engaged to [George Eden], and then was embarrassed as to how to undeceive him without admitting to a lie" (*LJ* 2:202 n.). She and her parents visited Eden's parents, at Eden Farm, in Kent, on several occasions. Byron was told by Annabella Milbanke's "great friend" that Eden "would be

---

4. Ethel Colburn Mayne, *The Life and Letters of Anne Isabella Milbanke* (New York: Charles Scribner's Sons, 1929), p. 15.

the *best husband* in the world" and himself its *"Antithesis"* (*LJ* 2.217), and
he said that "she deserves a better heart than mine" (*LJ* 2.222). And imme-
diately after the ceremony that joined him forever to Annabella Milbanke
in unholy matrimony, Byron said in the carriage as they drove away on their
honeymoon: "You had better have married——, he would have made you a
better husband." (This comes from the book *Lord Byron's Wife*, by Malcolm
Elwin, who supplies, in square brackets, the name "Eden.")[5] He certainly
would have made her a better husband, for he was in all respects her male
counterpart. And that is how Byron describes him as Lord Henry, husband
of Lady Adeline Amundeville.

George Eden succeeded his father as second Lord Auckland in 1814, was
created earl of Auckland in 1839, and had a "brilliant political career, being
successively President of the Board of Trade, First Lord of the Admiralty,
and Governor-General of India."[6] When Byron knew him, he was a Whig
member of Parliament and, according to the *DNB*, noted for his "constant
attendance" and "plain commonsense." On his death in 1849 Fulke Gre-
ville, diarist of the nineteenth-century political world, wrote: "He was a
man without shining qualities or showy accomplishments, austere, almost
forbidding in his manner, silent and reserved in society, unpretending both
in private and public life." Greville also mentions his placid temper, his
"apparent gravity," and his "cold exterior."[7] That he was indefatigable the
letters of his sister Emily Eden, the novelist, clearly reveal. "George went
to the opening of some medical college," she writes. "It is the oddest thing,
and shows what he was predestined for: but he never feels tired . . . , and
he goes on working away, filling all the hours fuller than they can hold, and
sleeps like a top at night!"[8] That Lord Henry was the same is equally clear
from the catalogue of his multifarious activities in the country (*DJ*
16.485–656), for Norman Abbey is not merely Newstead Abbey, but also (I
believe) Eden Farm.

Lord Henry, according to Byron, was "cool, and quite English, imper-
turbable" (*DJ* 13.108), cautious, proud, reserved (*DJ* 13.115, 121–22), and
a "cold, good, honourable man" (*DJ* 14.553):

> In birth, in rank, in fortune likewise equal,
> O'er Juan he could no distinction claim;
> In years he had the advantage of time's sequel.
>   (*DJ* 13.153–55)

George Eden succeeded his father as Baron Auckland in 1814. His rank
was thus the same as Byron's, and he was four years older. Lord Henry was
handsome (*DJ* 14.566), knew horses, rode well (*DJ* 13.181–82; 16.487,
489), and hunted (*DJ* 16.586), and we know from the letters of his sister,
who was with him in India, that Auckland was handsome, a connoisseur of
horseflesh, and an expert horseman and hunter.[9] In fact, his death occurred
"on his return from shooting."[1] Byron says that Lord Henry was a privy
councillor (*DJ* 13.537–38) and

---

5. Elwin, *Lord Byron's Wife*, p. 250.
6. Ibid., p. 93.
7. Ibid.
8. Emily Eden, *Letters from India*, 2 vols. (London: Richard Bentley and Son, 1872), 1: 107.
9. Eden, *Letters from India*, 1: 56, 286; Emily Eden, *Up the Country*, ed. Edward Thompson (Lon-
   don: Curzon Press, 1978), passim [first published in 1866].

A figure fit to walk before a king;
Tall, stately, form'd to lead the courtly van
On birth-days, glorious with a star and string;
The very model of a Chamberlain—
And such I mean to make him when I reign.
                                    (*DJ* 14.556–60)

George Eden was also a privy councillor,[2] though certainly not in Byron's
lifetime. But clearly he was the stuff of which privy councillors are made.
In the endless round of formal receptions in India in ceremonial dress,
"stiffly uniformed and cockaded, gold-laced and gold-sworded," we are told,
he "was an imposing figure."[3] "Our first and best energies are devoted to
making a *clinquant* figure of his Excellency," wrote his sister from India, "in
order that he may shine in the eyes of the native princes; and I take it he
will make a pretty considerable figure"; on another occasion, a native dig-
nitary at the Queen's Ball "was very much struck at George's entry, which
is always a pretty sight."[4] Greville wrote of his "calmness and dignity" and
of his "laborious and conscientious administration" in India, and of his
"diligence, his urbanity, his fairness and impartiality" while in office in En-
gland.[5] Byron says of Lord Henry:

> Courteous and cautious therefore in his county,
> He was all things to all men . . .
>
>   (*DJ* 16.609)

In *Up the Country*, by Eden's sister Emily, there is a portrait of him that
could well be of Lord Henry himself. Eden never married and, the parents
having died early on, several of his sisters always shared his home, in India
as in England. Indeed, when he sailed for India in October 1835, accom-
panied by two of his sisters, he had a farewell letter from King William say-
ing "he had always given George credit for his exemplary attachment to his
sisters."[6] In this respect, therefore, it is worth noting that Lord Henry
kissed Lady Adeline "Less like a young wife than an aged sister" (*DJ*
14.552). Byron, in fact, may imply that Lord Henry is not merely passion-
less but sexually neuter (*DJ* 14.567–68, 606–7), and though our sources
are limited and partisan, one has no difficulty forming the same opinion of
George Eden. And, finally, I think Annabella Milbanke must have had Eden
in mind when she wrote to her aunt, Lady Melbourne: "So far from sup-
posing that I could be attached by a character of *dry* Reason, and *cold* Rec-
titude, I am always *repelled* by people of that description."[7]

One thing remains to be said on the subject of Aurora Raby. Everybody
senses her importance and everybody misreads the evidence. Nearly every-
body misreads it utterly—including T. S. Eliot, T. G. Steffan, Andrew
Rutherford, and E. D. Hirsch, Jr., who, pairing her with Haidee as one of
"the two pure spirits" of the poem, says she is introduced "to preserve the

1. *The Greville Memoirs*, ed. Henry Reeve, new edition, 8 vols. (London and New York: Longman's,
   Green, 1896), 6: 260; *DNB*.
2. G. E. Cokayne, *Complete Peerage*; obituary in the *Gentleman's Magazine*, February 1849, p. 201;
   not mentioned in *DNB*.
3. Janet Dunbar, *Golden Interlude: The Edens in India* (London: Murray, 1955), p. 167.
4. Eden, *Letters from India*, 2: 81, 239.
5. *Greville Memoirs*, 6: 262.
6. Eden, *Letters from India*, 1: 3.
7. Countess of Airlie, *In Whig Society*, p. 140.

possibility of the ideal and to renew the imagination of the hero and the narrator as well."[8] There are two partial exceptions. Leslie Marchand surmises that Aurora might be what Byron "had imagined and hoped Annabella might be when he first saw her" but says no more on the subject.[9] Thomas L. Ashton quotes Marchand's shrewd insight, ignores it, and then goes one step further. The name "Aurora" of course suggests not only beauty, youth, and innocence but also, in this poem, their incarnation in Haidee, and it is this suggestion that has led commentators astray. Her name, however, is not only Aurora, it is also Raby, which in no way evokes images of beauty, youth, innocence, and Thomas Ashton, alone among the commentators, has taken note of this.[1]

The Milbankes were from Seaham, County Durham. The lord lieutenant of Durham and "the center of the Durham society patronized by the Milbankes," as Ashton observes, was William Henry Vane (1766–1842), later (1833) first duke of Cleveland but in Byron's lifetime earl of Darlington and—what is more to the point—Baron Raby, of Raby Castle, Durham. Raby was a high liver and a low lifer, and even the *DNB* says he "was more important as a sportsman than as a politician." Thus, in naming her Aurora Raby Byron was once more writing about the impossibility of sustaining an ideal.

> Even Petrarch's self, if judged with due severity,
> Is the Platonic pimp of all posterity.

As a biographical sketch of Annabella Milbanke, the portrait of Aurora is even more ruthlessly honest than any of the others in *Don Juan*, except perhaps that of George Eden. She appeared to be a "Rose with all its sweetest leaves yet folded" (*DJ* 15.344), but that is only half of the portrait. And the only puzzling aspect of it all is why anyone described in some of the language used of her could possibly be regarded as "ideal": prim, silent, cold, indifferent. Moreover, Byron is quite explicit at one point:

> Juan knew nought of such a character—
> High, yet resembling not his lost Haidée;
> Yet each was radiant in her proper sphere:
> The Island girl, bred up by the lone sea,
> More warm, as lovely, and not less sincere,
> Was Nature's all: Aurora could not be,
> Nor would be thus;—the difference in them
> Was such as lies between a flower and gem.
> (*DJ* 15.457–64)

And that is all we know—perhaps more than we know—of Aurora Raby. She appears only in Cantos 15 and 16, and the poem breaks off with the fourteenth stanza of Canto 17. No one knows how the poem would have continued or how it would have ended. Byron suggests, in a letter and elsewhere, that Juan might have finished in the French Revolution, guillotined like Anacharsis Clootz.[2] I myself think, from evidence in the same

8. E. D. Hirsch, Jr., "Byron and the Terrestrial Paradise," in Frederick W. Hilles and Harold Bloom, eds., *From Sensibility to Romanticism* (New York: Oxford University Press, 1965), pp. 483, 477.
9. Marchand, *Byron's Poetry*, p. 229.
1. Thomas L. Ashton, "Naming Byron's Aurora Raby," *English Language Notes* 7 (1969): 114–20.
2. *LJ* 8: 78; *Medwin's Conversations of Lord Byron*, p. 165.

letter, that a different (and better) conclusion is indicated. Byron said he had "not quite fixed whether to make him end in Hell—or in an unhappy marriage,—not knowing which would be the severest.—The Spanish tradition says Hell—but it is probably only an Allegory of the other state."[3] I think Byron would have married Juan to Aurora and that they would have lived unhappily ever after—in the hell of an unhappy marriage.

Narcissus has been punished. The love affair with himself that began with *Childe Harold's Pilgrimage* has led to his jilting in *Don Juan*, and as in mythology he remains as a beautiful flower, the greatest poem of the nineteenth century. Byron spent his professional life trying to learn the truth about himself and trying to tell it. Hobhouse persuaded him to destroy the beginnings of a journal in Albania in 1809, and he aided and abetted the destruction of the final one in May 1824. *Don Juan*, yet another attempt, traces the growth not of the poet's mind, à la Wordsworth, but of the poet's psyche. In *The Prelude* we know that our Redeemer liveth and that his name is Wordsworth, who tells us in thirteen or fourteen books how he achieved that awesome responsibility. The point is that we can all be like Wordsworth. Byron, in *Childe Harold's Pilgrimage*, hyped himself into believing that he had redeemed himself only, but in *Don Juan* he took back even that. Wordsworth's poem is exemplary, Byron's cautionary. *Don Juan* is his memoir in verse, and it would be difficult to conceive of any more direct and forceful contradiction of the idea that "no biographical evidence can change or influence critical evaluation."

JAMES CHANDLER

"Man fell with apples": The Moral Mechanics of *Don Juan*[†]

Epics explain. That much is clear from the narrative convention that has most consistently distinguished the genre: the beginning *in medias res*. The point holds no less obviously for modernized epics, such as *Paradise Lost* and *The Prelude*, than for ancient ones. And it holds no less obviously for *Don Juan* than for these other English examples, in spite of the fact that Byron invokes the marking convention only to insist that he will have no use for it:

> Most epic poets plunge in "medias res,"
>   (Horace makes this the heroic turnpike road)
> And then your hero tells, when'er you please,
>   What went before—by way of episode. . . .
>   (1:6)

3. *LJ* 8: 78.
† From *Rereading Byron: Essays Selected from Hofstra University's Byron Bicentennial Conference*, ed. Alice Levine and Robert N. Keane. Copyright © 1993 Hofshra University. Reprinted by permission of Garland Publishing, Inc. An expanded version of this essay appears as chapter 6, "Byron's Causes: The Moral Mechanics of *Don Juan*," in *England in 1819* (University of Chicago Press, 1998).

That, says Byron, "is the usual method, but not mine— / My way is to begin with the beginning" (1:7). Commenting on this passage in his chapter on "Form" in *Don Juan in Context*—perhaps the most interesting chapter in the best book on the subject—Jerome McGann concludes that Byron's declaration should be taken as a disclaimer of the poem's interest in explanation:

> . . . epic poets continually begin *in medias res* because such a narrative procedure establishes the need for an explicatory context. The convention of *in medias res* puts the reader in suspense, not about what will happen, but about how and why the present state of affairs came to be. *In medias res* enforces the desire to understand events in terms of an orderliness that springs from causes and natural consequences. To begin *in medias res* is to ensure that the events of the epic will be set only in the context of what is relevant to them. It is a probability device.
> *Don Juan* is different. It explicitly does not begin *in medias res* and its arrangement scarcely covets probability.[1]

Don Juan is different—McGann is certainly right about that—and perhaps if we look only at this issue of ordonnance, we can see the poem as uncovetous of "probability." But other indicators suggest that the relation of the poem to explanatory ambition is at the very least one of deep ambivalence, for it sometimes seems to verge on downright obsession.

If we look instead to diction, for example, we can actually go some way toward quantifying the poem's preoccupation with the topic. The conjunction "because" occurs one hundred and fourteen times in *Don Juan*, more than four times the number of its appearances in all of Wordsworth's poetical works. The word "cause" occurs fifty-six times in the poem, a figure that puts it near the top of the poem's most frequently-appearing nouns and verbs—higher, for example than such staples of Byronic diction as *passion, war, word, words, age, sun, light*, and *water. Cause* also happens to appear exactly the same number of times as *women*, a coincidence one might discount as meaningless if it were not that gender categories do so much explanatory work in the poem. There are about a dozen instances of some form of the word "explain" itself, some of which directly thematize explanation as an issue.

Byron wrote to his publisher, John Murray, in 1819 that he had no other intention in the poem than "to giggle and make giggle," and herein lies another way to recognize *Don Juan's* strong interest in explanation (6:208). For the poem's great faculty of pleasure, its celebrated wit, exercises itself most flamboyantly in the making of explanatory jokes. These jokes are not all of the same kind; and they are not all equally funny or pleasurable. There is a range of them, for example, that are not particularly funny or pleasurable because they parody what is itself already a failed effort at explanatory humor in Wordsworth's "The Thorn," the poem invoked as the mock narrative framework for *Don Juan* in Byron's Preface. Wordsworth's jokes appear paradigmatically in response to the whys and wherefores of the poem's internal balladic dialogue:

---

1. Jerome McGann, *Don Juan in Context* (Chicago, 1976), p. 100.

> "Now wherefore thus, by day and night,
> In rain, in tempest, and in snow,
> Thus to the dreary mountain-top
> Does this poor woman go?
> And why sits she beside the thorn
> When the blue day-light's in the sky,
> Or when the whirlwind's on the hill,
> Or frost air is keen and still,
> And wherefore does she cry?—
> Oh wherefore? wherefore? tell me why
> Does she repeat that doleful cry?"
> I cannot tell; I wish I could;
> For the true reason no one knows.
> $(78–90)^2$

The old sea-captain who narrates the poem, and who is the object of Byron's first lampoon in *Don Juan*, offers several such disavowals of his explanatory capacity: "I'll give you the best help I can . . ." (111), "No more I know; I wish I did. . . ." (155). Yet while these comments may be cast in the form of disclaimers of his explanatory authority, their effect is to call attention to the narrator's explanatory obsessions. Indeed, he often succumbs to the temptation to offer surmises in spite of protests about his incapacities. It is in any case clear from Wordsworth's famous note to "The Thorn," a text that comes in for particular ridicule in Byron's Preface, that Wordsworth attempted to frame the poem as an investigation of how causal categories function in what anthropologists such as Lévy-Bruhl came to call the "primitive mentality."[3]

Byron appropriates Wordsworth's disclamatory idiom pervasively in *Don Juan*. When Don Alfonso invades Julia's bedroom during her liaison with Juan, the narrator says he is at a loss to account for it: "I can't tell how or why or what suspicion / Could enter Don Alfonso's head" (1:139). Introducing Juan's premonition of disaster before Lambro's return in Canto 4, which the narrator will go on to describe as "feelings causeless, or at least abstruse," he says:

> I know not why, but in that hour to-night
>   Even as they gazed, a sudden tremor came
> And swept, as 'twere across their hearts delight . . .
> (4:21)

Of Dudù's blush in Canto 6, the narrator says: "I can't tell why she blushed, nor can expound / The mystery of this rupture of their rest" (6:85). Of the disappearance of Juan's infantry corps during the siege of Ismail, he says:

2. This and subsequent citations from 1800 text of the poem as republished in Wordsworth, *Lyrical Ballads*, ed. R.L Brett and A. R. Jones (Edinburgh: T. and A. Constable, 1963).
3. Lucian Lévy-Bruhl, *Primitive Mentality*, trans. Lilian A. Clare (London: Allen & Unwin, 1923); the question of causation is perhaps the central one in Lévy-Bruhl's famous study. For a good discussion of how proto-anthropological discourses shape Wordsworth's major poetry, see Alan Bewell, *Wordsworth and the Enlightenment* (New Haven: Yale University Press, 1988).

> . . . the gods know how. I can't
> Account for everything which may look bad
> In history . . .
>
> (8:31)

And of Juan's sickness during his "service" for Catherine in Canto 10:

> Perhaps—but sans perhaps, we need not seek
> For causes young or old. . . .
> I don't know how it was, but he grew sick.
>
> (10:38–39)

The Wordsworthian *occupatio* remains in play even into the English cantos, as one can see in the review of various speculations on the cause of the unearthly music that occasionally sounds through the arches of Norman Abbey: "The cause I know not, nor can solve; but such / The fact: I've heard it—once perhaps too much" (13:64). The ironies that operate in these jokes are both labile and heterogeneous. While some (like the Norman Abbey joke) seem to indicate skepticism about assigning causes to clear up mysterious events, others (like the joke about Juan's sickness) appear to point to causes that could be inobvious only (it is implied) to the most repressed or obtuse among Byron's readership. Likewise the relation of these jokes to their Wordsworthian target is difficult to ascertain. It is hard to tell if Wordsworth's "I cannot tell" is being mocked as an escape from the responsibilities of explanation or, on the other hand, as a too-simple irony that conceals a concomitantly naive optimism about the poet's ability to explain such matters as the psychology of superstition in the first place. It is hard to tell, indeed, what telling might *mean* in many of these instances.

One can also find in *Don Juan* a second form of causal humor, certainly related to the first but more effective as humor and probably more salient in the poem. These are the jokes of a narrator who is in fact quite cavalier about the problem of identifying causes behind what he observes. The tone is set for these moments early on when, in a pastiche of Montesquieu's climatological analysis, the narrator asserts in Canto 1 that the sexual mores of Southern European countries are "all the fault of that indecent sun, / Who cannot leave alone our helpless clay, / But will keep baking, broiling, burning on" (1:63). Or again in Canto 5:

> The Turks do well to shut—at least sometimes—
> The women up—because in sad reality,
> Their chastity in these unhappy climes
> Is not a thing of that astringent quality,
> Which in the North prevents precocious crimes,
> And makes our snow less pure than our morality.
>
> (5:157)

These are explanations *of* sexuality, but a more common version of this more confident Byronic joke involves an explanation *from* sexuality. For example, in an early episode explicitly satirical of Wordsworthian sublimity, where the narrator has occasion to report Juan's distracted ruminations between encounters with Donna Julia, Juan is said to be wandering and wondering in "self-communion with his own high soul":

'Twas strange that one so young should thus concern
His brain about the action of the sky;
If you think 'twas philosophy that this did,
I can't help thinking puberty assisted.

(1:93)

If one recognizes in these explanatory jokes the stuff out of which the poem is made, one also recognizes that they are characteristically "anti-philosophical," which is to say "materialist" in orientation. The explanations of "philosophy"—which Byron tends to identify with Coleridge, Plato, and Berkeley—lead one to mistake ideas for things. Byron's explanations set out to expose this delusion. They deal in things themselves—material "facts," as Byron likes to stress. Berkeley may be allowed to introduce Canto 11 with his dictum that "there was no matter," but it is met immediately by Byron's witty rejoinder: "'twas no matter what he said" (11:1). When he strikes this posture, Byron seems to presume a certain easy access to his "facts," and he gestures openhandedly toward providing such access for his readers as well. In this role, Byron shows unqualified confidence in his talent for lucid explanation: "I wish to be perspicuous," he says in Canto 5 with no apparent doubts about his ability to do so—no doubts, that is, in spite of the lability of the ironies that attend his use throughout the poem of the "I-know-not-why" idiom from "The Thorn."

Some of the problems about Byron's "materialism" can be illustrated in what is probably his most explicitly formulated meditation on the problem of causality in *Don Juan*, the witty exordium to Canto 10, which contemplates the relation between explanation in natural philosophy and in (what the eighteenth century called) "moral philosophy":

When Newton saw an apple fall, he found
In that slight startle from his contemplation—
'Tis *said* (for I'll not answer above ground
For any sage's creed or calculation)—
A mode of proving that the earth turned round
In a most natural whirl called "Gravitation,"
And this is the sole mortal who could grapple,
Since Adam, with a fall, or with an apple.

Man fell with apples, and with apples rose,
If this be true; for we must deem the mode
In which Sir Isaac Newton could disclose
Through the then unpaved stars the turnpike road,
A thing to counterbalance human woes;
For ever since immortal man hath glowed
With all kinds of mechanics, and full soon
Steam-engines will conduct him to the Moon.

(10: 1–2)

This passage may have the look of perspicuity about it, but its juxtaposition of natural mechanics and moral mechanics could scarcely be more problematically framed. Certain post-Newtonian philosophers, such as Hume, attempted to work out the possibilities of extending the Newtonian method beyond natural science. To accept the Humean premises to which Byron often seems so committed, premises that William Godwin accepted wholesale in *Political Justice* and that for years had Shelley's full endorsement, is to see natural and moral mechanics as analogues of one another, two sciences united by a single method. On this view, the sense of necessity that underwrites an account of the operations of nature—the operations of the stars, for example—is exactly the same *in form* as the sense of necessity that underwrites what can be told about the operations of human nature. Such a picture, however, is Pelasgian in character, and if we take account of Byron's use of Genesis as the framework for the moral side of the question, we find that the analogy no longer seems to hold. For whether one locates the consequences of a fall in the blindness of the subject's understanding or in the corruption of the subject's will—i.e., in the theory of knowledge or the theory of action—the physical-science/moral science analogy breaks down. It is a problem of comparing apples with, well, apples that you just can't compare them with. Thus *Don Juan* both creates and erases the structure of analogy between physical science and moral science, and herein lies the discrepancy in Byron's own "mode of proving" or ". . . showing." This is the glitch in the mechanics with which he glows.[4]

What further raises the stakes on this score is the way in which Byron uses the issue of explanation in attacking his poetic adversaries. Central to this critique is Byron's allegation of the failure of the Lake Poets to achieve perspicuity in their writings. As early as in the second stanza of the poem's Dedication one can find the witty dismissal of some of Coleridge's recent work on the grounds of its opacity. The reference is probably to the *Lay Sermons* (1816–17):

> And Coleridge, too, has lately taken wing,
>   But, like a hawk encumber'd with his hood,
> Explaining metaphysics to the nation—
> I wish he would explain his Explanation.
>
> (D: 2)

Two stanzas after the satirical remarks about Coleridge's opaque self-encumbrances, his poetical partner comes in for criticism along similar lines:

> And Wordsworth, in a rather long 'Excursion',
>   (I think the quarto holds five hundred pages)
> Has given a sample from the vasty version
>   Of his new system to perplex the sages . . .
> And he who understands it would be able
> To add a story to the Tower of Babel.
>
> (D:4)

---

4. Peter Manning's discussion of this passage rightly notes how "the allusions to Prometheus and Adam suggest that *Don Juan* is not only epic action and Romantic introspection but also a version of history." The version of history that Byron has in view, for Manning, is "the history of consciousness seen as a movement from a past hypostatized as univalent, conscious only of the present, hence innocent, to the ambiguities and temporal self-consciousness of the modern era." Manning's *Don Juan*, in other words, is the history of historical consciousness itself, in roughly the sense identified by R. G. Collingwood, to whom Manning specifically refers. See *Byron and his Fictions* (Detroit: Wayne State University Press, 1978), 214–216. I will try below to resituate this interesting claim about the poem, and likewise Manning's observation about Juan's "passivity," when I take up the problem of *Don Juan* as a historical novel.

The pun on "story" would seem to compromise the perspicuity of this very comment about Wordsworth's lack of it and thus to compress into a single line one major pattern of irony in the poem.

There is something else to be noted here. Both of these early keynote passages couch the issue we are investigating in terms of intelligibility (to borrow a distinction from modern philosophy of explanation) rather than those of causality.[5] Coleridge *explicates* metaphysics, one might paraphrase Byron, but needs to explicate his explication; Wordsworth is faulted (this critique derives from Francis Jeffrey) for writing incomprehensible defenses of his poetry in the Preface to *Lyrical Ballads* and other essays. We have already seen that there is a problem, in view of the labile ironies in *Don Juan*, about the poem's own general intelligibility. That is one problem to be addressed. Another, obviously related, is that of how the relation of intelligibility and causation appear in those parts of the poem most involved with the topic or practice of explanation.

The question of intelligibility figures prominently, and even explicitly, in that description of Juan's wanderings in the woods just before his adultery with Donna Julia, a passage in which, as we have seen, causal humor is particularly intense. Juan wanders through "leafy nooks," attempting to imagine his sexual interest in Julia as a merely speculative curiosity:

> He thought about himself and the whole earth,
>   Of man the wonderful and of the stars,
> And how the deuce they ever could have birth;
>   And then he thought of earthquakes, and of wars,
> How many miles the moon might have in girth,
>   Of air balloons and of the many bars
> To perfect knowledge of the boundless skies;
> And then he thought of Donna Julia's eyes.
>
>   (1:92)

In his very act of inquiring into the causes of general ("man") and external ("the stars") objects of his observation, Juan becomes mystified about his own motives, and thus grows unintelligible to himself. The apparently casual disposition of the items in the catalogue would seem to betoken a certain insouciance of disposition *toward* those objects. That *affect*, on the other hand, can be read as an *effect* of Juan's self-deception. We can, that is, read the last object in the catalogue, Julia's eyes, as the one that counts, and the one that provides means of explaining the wandering of his attention in the first place.

The question of intelligibility becomes explicit when Byron likens Juan's confusion in these "leafy nooks" to the sort of confusion to which Wordsworth fell prey during those wanderings in nature that he made the subject of his most celebrated poetry:

5. This distinction has been in play at least since Peter Winch's Wittgensteinian critique of the nomological view of explanation held by Carl Hempel and the Berlin school; see *The Idea of a Social Science and its Relation to Philosophy* (London: Routledge & Kegan Paul, 1958), esp. pp. 18–21. For a more recent formulation, also sympathetic to Wittgenstein, see Anthony Giddens, *Central Problems in Social Theory* (Berkeley and Los Angeles, 1979). Speaking of Hempel's neo-Humian position, Giddens writes: "Explanation, most broadly conceived, can be more appropriately treated as the clearing up of puzzles or queries; seen from this point of view, explanation is the making intelligible of observations of events that cannot be readily interpreted within the context of an existing theory or frame of meaning" (p. 258).

> There poets find materials for their books,
>   And every now and then we read them through,
> So that their plan and prosody are eligible,
> Unless like Wordsworth they prove unintelligible.
>   (1:90)

I find that the line "so that their plan and prosody are eligible" is itself unintelligible here, and conclude that Byron is once again performing the confusion he says he deplores. As for the analogy of the confusions imputed to Juan and Wordsworth, it becomes so strong that it threatens to become a confusion of Juan and Wordsworth themselves, or at least this is a plausible inference from the narrator's having to enter the ensuing semantic clarification: "He, Juan (and not Wordsworth), . . . pursued / His self-communion with his own high soul" (91). Further, the locution that the narrator has taken from the "The Thorn"—"I know not why"—is now modified to apply to the class of persons (such as Juan, and Wordsworth himself) who tend to mistake the effects of philosophy for those of puberty:

> In thoughts like these true wisdom may discern
>   Longings sublime, and aspirations high,
> Which some are born with, but the most part learn
>   To plague themselves withal, *they know not why.*
>   (1:93; my italics)

The Lake poets as a group appear in the poem as writers whose failure to achieve perspicuity in explanation is a function of a failure to acknowledge material causality, especially sexual causality, in everyday life.

To see how much importance *Don Juan* lends to this linkage between one's acknowledgment of certain kinds of causes and the intelligibility of one's writing, we need only consider how it forms the basis, in turn, for a linkage between the Lake Poets and the poem's preeminent bogeyman: the Viscount Castlereagh, England's Foreign Minister and chief negotiator at the Congress of Vienna (and thus a principal architect of the European Restoration after Waterloo). Byron's Castlereagh, two-faced embodiment of tyranny and sycophancy in the poem, is the figure *par excellence* at once of verbal unintelligibility and suppressed sexuality. He appears in the Dedication after the lampoon on Southey, Coleridge, and Wordsworth, and as their master—and thus in the position of one whose character can explain theirs. The set-piece lampoon of Castlereagh with which Byron closes his Dedication is as trenchant as anything that one might find in the satire of, say, Swift and Pope, whom Byron so admired.

The subject of this lampoon is initially called the "intellectual eunuch Castlereagh," and subsequently referred to only with pronouns of neutral gender. Yet Byron's description of Castlereagh does not finally represent him as without sexual passion:

> Cold-blooded, smooth-faced, placid miscreant!
>   Dabbling its sleek young hands in Erin's gore,
> And thus for wider carnage taught to pant,
>   Transferr'd to gorge upon a sister-shore;
> The vulgarest tool that tyranny could want,
>   With just enough of talent, and no more,

To lengthen fetters by another fix'd,
And offer poison long already mix'd.

An orator of such set trash of phrase
   Ineffably, legitimately vile,
That even its grossest flatterers dare not praise,
   Nor foes—all nations—condescend to smile:
Not even a *sprightly* blunder's spark can blaze
   From that Ixion grindstone's ceaseless toil,
That turns and turns, to give the world a notion
Of endless torments, and perpetual motion.

A bungler even in its disgusting trade,
   And botching, patching, leaving still behind
Something of which its masters are afraid,
   States to be curb'd, and thoughts to be confined,
Conspiracy or Congress to be made—
   Cobbling at manacles for all mankind—
A tinkering slavemaker, who mends old chains,
With God and man's abhorrence for its gains.

If we may judge of matter by the mind,
   Emasculated to the marrow, *It*
Hath but two objects—how to serve and how to bind,
   Deeming the chain it wears even men may fit.
                (D:12–15)

Though Byron will go on to say that Castlereagh is "fearless, because *no* feeling dwells in ice," this is a description of one whose sexuality is not inert, but sado-masochistic. It is not that Castlereagh is without desire. Rather, the desire that he has is only to serve and bind. He pants to wreak wider carnage with his sleek hands. The alleged perversion, furthermore, appears as a displacement that comes of a disavowal. It develops as part of a process of self-emasculation understood as sexual self-denial, the denial of the *place* of sexuality in one's life. Castlereagh's language is what it is because he has tried to debar passion from entering it. In this respect, ironically, Byron's implied argument resembles one that Wordsworth had made, though not published, in *The Prelude*, where he describes the theory-justified violence of the Reign of Terror as conduct in which passions exert their power without ever hearing the sound of their own names. Byron's Castlereagh can't manage his language because he doesn't own it, and he doesn't own his language because he doesn't own up to his passion. His phrases are manacles, to recall Blake's terms, not in that they are "mind forg'd" but in that they are unforged by their own user. The chains in which he would sadistically bind others are the same chains in which he himself has been bound, figured here as the "set trash of phrase" that issues in the mechanical operations of his oratory.

The issue of intelligibility in Castlereagh's prose reappears more explicitly in lines that introduce Juan's encounter with Catherine the Great, in Canto 9, after the *Waverley*-styled account of Juan's involvement in the siege of Ismail. Juan is about to achieve cabinet-level status in the Russian state by virtue of Catherine's sexual preference for him, her decision to elevate Juan over "him who, in the language of his station, / Then held that

'high official situation.'" (9:48). Byron takes it upon himself to "explain"
the phrase "high official situation":

> Oh, gentle ladies! should you seek to know
>   The import of this diplomatic phrase,
> Bid Ireland's Londonderry's Marquess show
>   His parts of speech; and in the strange displays
> Of that odd string of words, all in a row,
>   Which none divine, and every one obeys,
> Perhaps you may pick out some queer *no*-meaning,
> Of that weak wordy harvest the sole gleaning.
>
> I think I can explain myself without
>   That sad inexplicable beast of prey—
> That Sphinx, whose words would ever be a doubt,
>   Did not his deeds unriddle them each day—
> That monstrous Hieroglyphic—that long Spout
>   Of blood and water, leaden Castlereagh!
>   (9:49–50)

Here, the figure of the chain made by one's oppressor and inflicted on one's
victim reappears as the meaningless "string of words" in Castlereagh's
prose. Byron thus reformulates the charge against Castlereagh's bureau-
cratic cant explicitly in terms of its unintelligibility—his "queer no
meaning"—and the punning phrase "bid [him] show his parts" (of speech)
articulates a suspicion about the soundness of Castlereagh's grammar as a
suspicion about the soundness of both his sexual parts and intellectual
parts as well.

Byron's own capacity for self-explanation is defined not only by his act of
self-definition against Castlereagh but also, paradoxically, by his claim that
he does not need Castlereagh to make himself "perspicuous." The implicit
contradiction here is only aggravated by the general sense that Byron's
resort to Castlereagh (or Southey, or Coleridge, or Wordsworth) for pur-
poses of invidious self-definition recurs so routinely in this poem as to
become a kind of narrative tic. How else to explain this tic if not by posit-
ing an anxiety about the uncertain state of Byron's and his poem's own
forms of (self-)intelligibility? The labile ironies in the poem's recurrent
explanatory jokes, like the mutual incompatibilities of its deep explanatory
paradigms, already offer ample grounds for such anxieties.

There is a further complication. While the canto 9 passage portrays
Castlereagh in his writings as a Sphinx to be unriddled and thus suggests
a defining antithesis to Byron's self-representation in *Don Juan*, some lines
near the end of Canto 8 take stock of the poem in a way that, even before
the fact, calls such a self-characterization into question:

> Reader! I have kept my word,—at least so far
>   As the first Canto promised. You have now
> Had sketches of love, tempest, travel, war—
>   All very accurate, you must allow,
> And *Epic*, if plain truth should prove no bar;
>   For I have drawn much less with a long bow
> Than my forerunners. Carelessly I sing,
> But Phoebus lends me now and then a string,

With which I still can harp, and carp, and fiddle,
   What further hath befallen or may befall
The Hero of this grand poetic riddle,
   I bye and bye may tell you, if at all.[6] . . .
                                                    (8:138–39)

The riddle of *Don Juan*, then, is perhaps how the poem can be both a riddle and not a riddle—or, if we concede that it is a riddle, how its riddling differs from that of its adversary, who evidently stands for all that the poem professes to abhor.

Byron stresses that his is a "grand poetic"—that is to say, an "Epic"— riddle. Let's suppose that the riddle of *Don Juan* differs from the riddle of Castlereagh's writings by virtue of the way it registers exactly that complex relation—just as we might say that Byron's contradictory deployment of explanatory idiom differs from Wordsworth's by virtue of its registering of *that* relation, the one between him and Wordsworth. The epic dimension of *Don Juan* would then more generally be understood in terms of its capacity for accommodating a variety of such relations. This would be the difference between, on the one hand, the unintelligibility of the local and unmeaning repetitions of cant and (on the other) the unintelligibility that we find in the work of a writer like Whitman, who claims to contain multitudes: Do I contradict myself, very well then I contradict myself. This epic dimension might further be said to lend historical perspective on such relations in the poem, especially the perspective of historical contemporaneity. On such an account, Byron would be inscribing himself into the representation of an epoch in which, much as he might wish to lampoon his fellow representative men, we can make out a dim recognition that he is of their number.

If the supposition seems far fetched, it may be well to recall what Byron said on the subject of contemporaneity at about this time, when he took part in the controversy over the canonical status of Pope. Here again, the issue is broached by way of a problem about intelligibility, though here Byron is more willing to see it as a problem in his own writings. The rhetorical crescendo of his *Letter to* [John Murray], published in 1821, occurs as an elaboration of his charge that the present enemies of Pope "have raised a mosque by the side of a Grecian temple of the purest architecture; and, more barbarous than the barbarians from whose practice I have borrowed the figure, they are not contented with their own grotesque edifice, unless they destroy the prior, and purely beautiful fabric which preceded, and which shames them and theirs for ever and ever." Byron then answers the charge of hypocrisy on this score by conceding its truth:

> I shall be told that amongst those I *have* been (or it may be still *am*) conspicuous—true, and I am ashamed of it. I have been amongst the builders of this Babel, attended by a confusion of tongues. . . . [7]

---

6. This passage offers an example of *syntactic* unintelligibility to go with the other forms that we have noted. The clause, "What further hath befallen or may befall . . . ," constitutes the direct object, incompatibly, of both "fiddle" and "tell."
7. *Works of Lord Byron*, ed. R. E. Prothero and E. H. Coleridge, 13 vols. (London: 1898–1904), 5:559.

What Byron goes on to say in his own defense—i.e., that he has not been among the detractors of the pure classical temple erected by Pope—is less directly relevant here than his acknowledgment that when it comes to the production of romantic unintelligibility he cannot escape being of his age.[8]

And yet there are problems with even this attempt to recuperate Byronic intelligibility in the face of the aporias of his text. I would like to raise just one here. I mentioned the Waverley novels in conjunction with the account of the Siege of Ismail, and any discussion of explanation, contemporaneity, and history in *Don Juan*, must include the crucial role of Scott's epic historical fiction in the making of Byron's attempt to answer it with an epic historical fiction of his own. What properly should follow at this point in the discussion is an extensive analysis of Byron's relation to this writer who was, after all: 1) his most illustrious rival in the literary market; 2) someone whose novels he claimed to have read "fifty times" and for an hour a day while working on *Don Juan*; 3) someone whose work left both explicit and implicit marks all over the poem; and 4) the writer who, in the Waverley novels, created the literary form in which the problem of what it means to "be of one's age" was given the fullest realization. Further, if there is one Romantic project that is as fully absorbed in the problematics of explanation as *Don Juan* is, it is surely Scott's attempt in the Waverley novels to bring Edinburgh's "philosophical history" to bear on the practice of fiction. With space enough for the task, it would not be difficult to show how the epic conception of *Don Juan* is modeled on the Waverley novels, nor how young Juan is Byron's answer to the passive hero from the Waverley series, the character shaped in being buffeted by conflicting historical forces.[9]

Instead, in what space remains I will just look briefly at the representation of Juan's encounter with Catherine the Great, who, like Castlereagh, is a world historical individual in *Don Juan*, and who is perhaps the only character in the poem to surpass him in daemonic power. This episode, perhaps more obviously derivative of one of Scott's inventions than any other in the poem, also points to Byron's crucial departure from Scott's narrative practice in the Waverley novels, especially in regard to explanation. The reason this sort of episode recurs so often in Scott's fiction is that, as Lukács has explained, it follows from the attempt to keep the mediocre character at center of the focus and to stage collisions of this character with the world historical individuals of his culture. One need only think of Edward Waverley's meeting with Bonnie Prince Charles, Henry Morton's with Claverhouse (in *Old Mortality*) or Jeannie Deans's meeting with the Duke of Argyll (in *The Heart of Mid-Lothian*) to recall how this sort of incident is handled by Scott.

---

8. For a more detailed account of Byron's position on this subject see my "The Pope Controversy: Romantic Poetics and the English Canon," *Critical Inquiry* (Spring, 1984) 10:481–509.

9. The topic of Byron's relation to Scott has enjoyed some recent attention. There are two brief biographical essays in *Byron and Scotland*, ed. Angus Calder (Totowa, N.J.: Barnes and Noble, 1989): P.H. Scott, "Byron and Scott," pp. 51–64, and J. Drummond Bone, "Byron, Scott, and Scottish Nostalgia," 119–31. Andrew Rutherford takes up the question of Byron's relation to Scott's fiction toward the latter half of his "Byron, Scott, and Scotland," in *Lord Byron and His Contemporaries*, ed. Charles Robinson (Newark, Del.: Delaware Univ. Press, 1982), 43–65. Perhaps the most provocative discussion of the subject, especially in respect to their mutually constructed relation to the literary market, is Sonia Hofkash's "The Writer's Ravishment: Women and the Romantic Author—the Example of Byron," in *The Romantic Woman*, ed. Anne K. Mellor (Bloomington, Indiana: Indiana University Press), pp. 99–104.

In such episodes, Scott tends to draw the historical figure in such a way as to typify a specifically historical formation or sociological group of the cultural epoch in question; the encounter serves to place the mediocre hero in connection with such forces. Certain residual tendencies of this narrative strategy survive in Byron's handling of the Juan-Catherine episode. Seeing the poem as moving through a series of "stages of society," from the barbarism of the shipwreck episode to the commercial manners of the English cantos, we might say that Catherine and her modernized court typify something about the social structure of Europe's developing nation states in the eighteenth century. Something of this historical particularity is suggested in the way in which Byron dresses Juan for the part he will play in this meeting. We are asked to "suppose" Juan as "Love turned a Lieutenant of Artillery":

> His Bandage slipped down into a cravat;
>> His wings subdued to epaulettes; his Quiver
> Shrunk to a scabbard, with his Arrows at
>> His side as a small sword, but sharp as ever;
> His bow converted into a cocked hat;
>> But still so like, that Psyche were more clever
> Than some wives (who make blunders no less stupid)
> If She had not mistaken him for Cupid.
>
> (9:45)

But just as the particularity of Juan's role as late-eighteenth-century military officer is overshadowed by the mythic type he is said to embody, so Catherine will be made to play Psyche to his Cupid here, as well as Helen to his Paris. And when it comes to issues of explanation and causality, which are intensely foregrounded here, explanation from period specificity tends to give way to an overriding explanatory axis, just as the third-person narrative decorum of the passage gives way to an apostrophe that is extraordinary even by the wide-ranging standards of this poem:

> Oh, thou 'teterrima Causa"' of all 'belli'—
>> Thou gate of Life and Death—thou nondescript!
> Whence is our exit and our entrance,—well I
>> May pause in pondering how all Souls are dipt
> In thy perennial fountain: how man *fell*, I
>> Know not, since Knowledge saw her branches stript
> Of her first fruit, but how he falls and rises
> *Since, thou* has settled beyond all surmises.
>
> Some call thee 'the worst Cause of war,' but I
>> Maintain thou art the *best*: for after all
> From thee we come, to thee we go, and why
>> To get at thee not batter down a wall,
> Or waste a world? Since no one can deny
>> Thou dost replenish worlds both great and small:
> With, or without thee, all things at a stand
> Are, or would be, thou Sea of Life's dry Land!
>
> Catherine, who was the grand Epitome
>> Of that great Cause of war, or peace, or what

> You please (it causes all the things which be,
>   So you may take your choice of this or that)—
> Catherine, I say, was very glad to see
>   The handsome herald, on whose plumage sat
> Victory; and, pausing as she saw him kneel
> With his dispatch, forgot to break the seal.
>
> Then recollecting the whole Empress, nor
>   Forgetting quite the woman (which composed
> At least three parts of this great whole) she tore
>   The letter open with an air which posed
> The Court, that watched each look her visage wore,
>   Until royal smile at length disclosed
> Fair weather for the day. Though rather spacious,
> Her face was noble, her eyes fine, mouth gracious.
>   (9:55–57)

The addressee of the apostrophe in stanzas 55 and 56, as the Latin allusion makes clear, is the Horatian *cunnus*, and Byron's figurings of it at this key juncture in the poem mark some of the most complex poetry he ever composed. Stylistically, these lines comprise one of those rare passages in his work where his Augustan sensibility fully merges with both a Cavalier poetic subject matter and Metaphysical poetic talent for complicating the witty conceit, though style provides only one point of access to these bizarre lines.

Some of the complications of the metonymy in question here are elaborated by an ostentatious logic that seems to call attention to Byron's "wish to be perspicuous." Although the *cunnus* is the worst cause of war, he argues, it is also the best, since of all causes of war this at least can also replenish the populations that war destroys. In stanza 57, which returns from apostrophic to narrative mode, Byron extends the analysis of the *cunnus* as the cause of war by an implicitly syllogistic line of thought that runs thus: if the *cunnus* is the cause of all things, and if war is a thing, then it is necessarily the cause of war as well.

Only, the complications generated here are not so easily held in check. In the passage leading up to these lines, Byron has prepared the undoing of Catherine's historical specificity by the strong suggestion that the Siege of Ismail is a replay of the Homeric account of the Siege of Troy, a siege he represents as carried out on very much, as it were, the same grounds. At first, one might take Byron's dehistoricizing move here as a simplification of Scott's practice in such episodes. Where Scott makes such scenes occasions for the applications of his explanatory frameworks for relating characters to one another, Byron turns one of his characters, Catherine, into the "Epitome" of what he insists on calling the cause of all things, the great (w)hole itself. This is Catherine as Woman, Woman as Eve, Eve as the absent cause (in the meditation on Newton and the apples) of all of Man's fallings and risings. This very reduction, however, is articulated in terms of tropes that seem to defy it and to recomplicate the question with a vengeance. In Kenneth Burke's terms, the passage might be said to conflate the dramatistic functions of scene and agent.[1] For the *cunnus* in this pas-

---

1. Kenneth Burke, *A Grammar of Motives* (New York, 1945), pp. xvii–xxv and 3–15.

sage is figured both as a part of the scene—the gate of our exits and our entrances—and as a part played in the scene, in the person of Catherine, who is said to be epitomized by it.

To unpack this contradiction, let alone this entire sequence in the poem, is beyond my purpose here. A first step in the analysis, however, would point to Byron's deployment of the first person plural pronoun, which seems to wobble along an axis very close to that which can been seen in Byron's self-conscious paranomasia with "man" as marking both gendered and ungendered humanity.[2] In calling the *cunnus* the scene of "our exits and our entrances," he even seems to be giving himself away on this point, since the first "our" indicates a non-gendered first-person plural and the second a gendered one. The relation of what might be called the "grammar of gender" in Byron to the recent work of Louis Crompton on Byron's sexuality is yet another question. Crompton actually deals with the case of Castlereagh at some length in his study, but his concern is chiefly with the "historical" Castlereagh, and with the possibility that his suicide in 1822 was occasioned by attempts to blackmail him for alleged homosexual liaisons.[3] Oddly, Crompton doesn't address the Dedication, where Byron makes an issue of Castlereagh's sexuality three years before either the suicide controversy or the arrest of Bishop Clogher on charges of homosexuality, two events that Byron links in the 1822 preface to Cantos 6–8. Wishing, like Crompton, "that Byron had had the decency not to engage in popular gay-baiting," one can nonetheless feel that the case of *Don Juan* is far more complicated than Crompton's account makes out.[4] Much of the complication is generated out of the relation of Castlereagh and Catherine in the poem. Does Byron's Castlereagh become the epitome of all that lies beyond the causal field of the all-causing *cunnus* of which Catherine is the epitome? In calling Castlereagh an intellectual eunuch, can Byron be suggesting that the explanatory confusions of this monstrous sphinx are what they are because "it" has attempted to place itself beyond the power of what the poem represents as the *primum mobile*? And if so, then where does this sort of placement leave "Byron" himself in the poem's epic framework of erotics and explanations?

The most vexing questions of all for the poem, in the end, have to do precisely with the way in which "Byron" figures as a site of motivation for what we read in *Don Juan*. At the beginning and the end of the long set-piece description of Donna Julia there are editorial interjections: "Her eye (I'm very fond of handsome eyes) / Was large and dark" and "Her stature tall—I hate a dumpy woman" (1:60–61). Causal relations are very much in play here but it is hard to judge how they run: are the editorial

---

2. There are a number of passages in *Don Juan* that acknowledge the problem of the gender-specificity of humanist idiom. Even in the stretch between this encounter with Catherine and the "Man fell with apples" passage at the start of the next canto we find one that marks this semantic wobble, a stanza in which the apothegm in Shakespearean humanist idiom, "What a strange thing is man!," is followed immediately by the qualification: "And what stranger thing is woman!" (9:64). For an even more explicit revision of the Shakespearean idiom, see the use made of Brutus's most famous speech in the opening lines of successive stanzas in canto 6: "There is a tide in the affairs of men. . . . There is a tide in the affairs of women" (6:3–4). For a good recent discussion of related gender questions in the poem see Susan Wolfson, "'Their She-Condition': Cross-Dressing and the Politics of Gender in *Don Juan*," *ELH* (Fall, 1987), 54:585–613.
3. Louis Crompton, *Byron and Greek Love* (Berkeley: Univ. of California Press); the case of Castlereagh is discussed on pp. 301–11.
4. Ibid., p. 310.

comments occasioned by the picture of such charms, or are they meant to explain why the character is drawn that way in the first place? To put it another way, do such comments explain Byron's masquerade of masculinity or does it tend rather to explain them? We are still early in the Byron revival, and criticism has only begun to broach such questions for the perspicuous perplexity of this text. When they are pursued further it may prove that the poem does covet probability after all, but that it is confused by this very desire and quite at a loss to explain it. That is why the task is left to us.

STUART PETERFREUND

The Politics of "Neutral Space" in Byron's *Vision of Judgment*[†]

Byron shares with the other Romantics the need to revise and adjust his relationship to a process of history no longer explained or controlled by Christian, deistic, or humanistic conceptions of the meaning of time.[1] His solution to the problem of time's meaning is, in the words of Jerome J. McGann, "to become a 'historical figure,' and to make that figure identical with the dreams of his own very personal imaginations. . . . Even when we seek the man Byron in the driest historical records we find that a mythological transformation often takes place."[2] Byron, in other words, attempts to "write himself into history," and in doing so attempts either to endow that history with primary meaning or to revise an erroneous, received meaning. The process is similar to the one employed by Blake, although Byron's motives in becoming a "historical figure" are distinctly more modest than are those of the older poet, as McGann observes (p. 40).

While Byron's decision to "write himself into history" is readily evident in autobiographical poems like *Childe Harold's Pilgrimage* and *Don Juan*—is, in fact, documentable, as Nina Diakonova has recently shown[3]—it is less evident but no less responsible for a good deal of the substance of *The Vision of Judgment*. Only in this poem, as Carl Woodring observes, "did Byron achieve such simplicity on the surface with so much complexity beneath. Few poems of equal compactness can boast so many levels of parody, satire, comedy, church-window symbolism, factual history dissolved in comic myth, and moral argument."[4] Because his purpose in *Politics in English Romantic Poetry* is to frame broad historical and political perspectives rather than give a close historical or political reading of Byron's satire, however, Woodring does not amplify the dimension of "factual history dissolved in comic myth." It is to this dimension of the poem that we must return in

---

[†] Modern Language Quarterly 40 (1979): 275–91. Copyright © 1979 University of Washington. All rights reserved. Used by permission of the publisher.

1. For discussions touching on this need in English Romanticism and beyond, see M. H. Abrams, *Natural Supernaturalism* (New York: Norton, 1971), pp. 83–87, 122–40; Hayden V. White, "Romanticism, Historicism, and Realism: Toward a Period Concept for Early 19th Century Intellectual History," in *The Uses of History*, ed. Hayden V. White (Detroit: Wayne State University Press, 1968), pp. 45–58; and Carl Woodring, "Nature and Art in the Nineteenth Century," *PMLA*, 92 (1977), 193–200.

2. *Fiery Dust: Byron's Poetic Development* (Chicago: University of Chicago Press, 1968), p. 27.

3. "Byron's Prose and Byron's Poetry," *SEL*, 16 (1976), 547–61.

4. *Politics in English Romantic Poetry* (Cambridge, Mass.: Harvard University Press, 1970), p. 193.

order to understand the political symbolism entailed in George III's trial and the original identities of the "spirits" responsible for due process of law in "neutral space," the venue of the trial, as we are told in stanza 35.[5] Only in doing so will we begin to recover the full satiric impact of Byron's poem and to understand the subtle but outrageous changes rung by Byron on Southey's original vision of the dead king's arraignment before the Gate of Heaven, as we trace Byron "writing himself into history" in *The Vision of Judgment*.

As a keen admirer and student of the techniques employed by the satirists of the Restoration and eighteenth century, Byron could not have failed to observe that the bite of satire is most mordant when the correspondences between the "world" of the satire and the "world" that is the butt of the satire are as complete as possible. Our sense of what the intrigue is about in *Absalom and Achitophel* of course depends primarily on our knowing that Dryden means for us to associate the Duke of Monmouth with Absalom and Shaftesbury with Achitophel. But a good deal of our delight is contingent upon seeing to what extent Dryden is capable of drawing out his initial premise of correspondence and accommodating fully the history of his own time to the history of King David's. Thus the importance of our being able to identify Queen Catherine as the original of "Michal," Oliver Cromwell as the original of "Saul," and Richard Cromwell as the original of "foolish Ishbosheth." Similarly, in Byron's *Vision of Judgment*, it is important for us to have a certain amount of background on George III, Southey, John Wilkes, and Junius, but it is also important for us to understand that the supposed "spirits" are based on originals living at the time Byron wrote his satire. Like those figures in Byron's poem identified by name, the "spirits" in the poem are political, and learning their real-life identities can help us decipher the dubious politics of "neutral space."

Byron, of course, writes himself into the poem as Satan, in ironic rejoinder to Southey's remarks about the "Satanic School" of poetry. In the preface to his own *Vision of Judgement*, Southey attacks the aesthetics and morals of Byron, Shelley, Hunt, and their circle. And he attacks their politics as well: "This evil is political as well as moral; for, indeed, moral and political evils are inseparably connected."[6] Byron replies to Southey's allegations in his preface. Concerning the politics of the "Satanic School," Byron states:

> I think I know enough of most of the writers to whom he is supposed to allude, to assert, that they, in their individual capacities, have done more good, in the charities of life, to their fellow-creatures, in any one year, than Mr. Southey has done harm to himself by his absurdities in his whole life; and this is saying a great deal. (p. 482)

Evidence in the satire itself also indicates that Byron assumes the role of Satan, and that the assumption of the role has everything to do with politics and little or nothing to do with perverse morality. Byron's wry observation that "we learn the Angels all are Tories" (st. 26) casts Satan as the leader of the Radical Opposition, a parliamentary role Byron had once half-

5. *The Works of Lord Byron: Poetry*, ed. Ernest Hartley Coleridge, 7 vols. (1898–1904; rpt. New York: Octagon, 1966). Quotations from *The Vision of Judgment* are from volume IV of this edition, and will be denoted by page number (prose) and stanza number (poetry).
6. *Poetical Works*, 10 vols. (London: John Murray, 1838), X, 207.

wished for himself.[7] As Michael, the leader of the "Tory" angels, is quick to point out later in the poem, his eloquence moved by the sight of the horde of witnesses summoned by Satan to testify against the dead king, although

> Our different parties make us fight so shy,
> I ne'er mistake you for a *personal* foe;
> Our difference is *political*. . . . (st. 62)

Perhaps the strongest evidence for considering Byron as the original of Satan has to do with the uses that the poem's speaker makes of at least one, and probably two, of Byron's parliamentary speeches. Such uses will be discussed below, once we have made a case for the earthly, political originals of the other "spirits."

Taking a hint from Woodring, who claims that *The Vision of Judgment* parodies, among other things, "the courtesies of lethal Parliamentary debate" (*Politics in English Romantic Poetry*, p. 193), and combining that hint with Michael's claim that the differences between Satan and himself are political rather than personal, we might well expect the originals of Byron's archangelic "spirits" to have been drawn from his brief experience as a radical Member in an overwhelmingly Tory House of Lords. Such is in fact the case. In Parliament as in poetry, Byron singled out those he considered as symbols of an oppressive regime and fixed his attention on them. As will be seen below, a good case can be made for identifying Michael's original as Lord Eldon and Peter's original as Lord Harrowby on the basis of Byron's use of rendering details. But before doing so it would seem wise to make a prima-facie case for Byron's focus on these two members of the Government in particular, a focus arising from the circumstances surrounding Byron's maiden speech in the House of Lords on February 27, 1812.

When Byron rose to address the Woolsack on that day, the issue under debate was the Frame-Work Bill, being pushed by the Government as the antidote to the Luddite sabotage of power looms going on in the North, especially in Nottingham. The bill prescribed hanging as the penalty for such sabotage, and was therefore abhorred alike by the forces of liberalism and human rights. Byron spoke for the Opposition and recorded this account of the speech in a letter to Francis Hodgson (March 5):

> Lds. Holland & Grenville, particularly the latter paid some high compts. in the course of their speeches as you may have seen in the papers, & Ld. Eldon & Harrowby answered me. . . . I spoke very violent sentences with a sort of modest impudence, abused every thing & every body, & put the Ld. Chancellor [i.e., Eldon] very much out of humour, & if I may believe what I hear, have not lost any character by the experiment.[8]

Byron's own description of his speech, "violent sentences with a modest sort of impudence," gives some sense of the fulminations to be found in its text, nor is such a sense disappointed upon a closer look. But the modesty of Byron's impudence is very much in question when one considers the unsigned poem of Byron's that appeared in the *Morning Chronicle* for

---

7. On Byron's aspirations to the leadership of the Radical Opposition, see Leslie A. Marchand, *Byron: A Biography*, 3 vols. (New York: Knopf, 1957), pp. 319 ff.
8. *Byron's Letters and Journals*, ed. Leslie A. Marchand, 9 vols. to date (Cambridge, Mass.: Belknap Press of Harvard University Press, 1972–79), II, 167.

March 2, three days before the letter to Hodgson. In the letter, Byron merely notes that Eldon and Harrowby answered his speech, an unusual response both in terms of the number and eminence of the respondents, to be sure (perhaps even one to be taken as an augury of future political greatness), and that the speech displeased Lord Eldon. What Byron did not tell Hodgson—or anyone of record, for that matter—is that he expressed his displeasure over the passage of the Frame-Work Bill in the unsigned poem. Notwithstanding the youth of its author, the poem shows, in its political focus and wryly humorous prosody, unmistakable intimations of the later Byronic satire. The first stanza will serve to convey the flavor and establish the objects of the poem's address.

> OH well done Lord E——n! and better done R——r!
>   Britannia must prosper with councils like yours;
> Hawkesbury, Harrowby, help you to guide her,
>   Whose remedy only must *kill* ere it cures:
> Those villains; the Weavers, are all grown refractory,
>   Asking some succour for Charity's sake—
> So hang them in clusters round each Manufactory,
>   That will at once put an end to *mistake*.

E——n is of course Lord Eldon; R——r is Ryder, Lord Harrowby's family name. The poem envisions the fate of the weavers under the new law, which was passed in part to quell a situation unintended by the weavers themselves. A note appended to the poem as it appeared in the *Morning Chronicle* reads: "Lord E, on Thursday night, said the riots at Nottingham arose from a 'mistake'" (*Works of Lord Byron: Poetry*, VII, 13–14 n.).

Byron's initial animosity toward Eldon and Harrowby was not likely to be lessened by the fact that they and the Government they supported remained in power throughout the waning years of George III's life, Harrowby in fact improving his lot by being appointed President of the Council in 1815. Byron may even have taken wry comfort from the fact that when it came time to write an Opposition *Vision of Judgment*, he could attack the same figures he had excoriated as a member of the Opposition nine years earlier.

The prima-facie case for the identities of Michael and Peter having been made, it remains now to turn to Byron's poem itself for internal clues to the archangelic identities.

Two of Byron's asides confirm the fact that Eldon is the original of Michael. After Michael has appeared in his capacity as the leader of the Cherubim and Saints (Byron's satiric analogue for the Tory Lords and Commons),[9] he is characterized thus:

> No thought, save for his Maker's service, durst
> Intrude, however glorified and high;
> He [i.e., the Maker] knew him [i.e., Michael] but
>   the Viceroy of the sky.   (st. 31)

Byron is here paying grudging tribute to Eldon. J. M. Rigg has noted Eldon's "urbanity, tact, and dignity," adding, "To the king his loyalty was

---

9. The logic for calling the Cherubim "Lords" and the Saints "Commons" turns on the fact that the Cherubim hold their seats by hereditary right, while the Saints acquire theirs by (pardon the pun) "election."

above suspicion, and it was requited with confidence and affection."[1] The degree of George III's confidence in, and affection for, Eldon can perhaps best be glimpsed in an anecdote recounted by the Lord Chancellor to a Mrs. Forster some thirty years after his investiture as Lord Chief Justice of Common Pleas, a post Eldon held until the collapse of the Pitt Government in 1801. In Eldon's words,

> "I do not know what made George III so fond of me; but he *was* fond of me. Did I ever tell you the manner in which he gave me the seals? When I went to him, he had his coat buttoned thus (one or two buttons fastened at the lower part), and putting his right hand within, he drew them out from the left side, saying, 'I give them to you *from my heart.*'"[2]

With the continued good will of George III to aid him, Eldon did indeed become the "Viceroy" of the Regency and was instrumental in forming a new Government to continue ruling in the stead of the old, blind king after the assassination of Spencer Perceval in 1812, thereby maintaining a continued, if repressive, stability.

Though Byron sets up Michael/Eldon initially with an aura of respect about him, the poet, within five stanzas, inserts a biographical gibe that helps to dissipate that aura. In response to Michael/Eldon's "kindly" greeting, Satan/Byron

> met his ancient friend
> With more hauteur, as might an old Castilian
> Poor Noble meet a mushroom rich civilian.
>   (st. 36)

If the point has not yet been made, unpacking this passage of less than three lines should furnish a full sense of the rich complexity alluded to by Woodring above. The passage is rich with ironically rendered biographical and autobiographical allusions, and it also serves as a recounting of Byron's first actual meeting with Eldon in March of 1809.

Concerning the third word of the passage, Eldon, born in 1751, had lived his allotted threescore and ten by the time Byron wrote his satire, and could, with justice, be considered "ancient." Additionally, Byron had known Eldon for some twelve years at the time of this writing, so their "friendship" could, with some justice, be called "ancient." Thus the double biographical pun on the word, which denotes, in the immediate context of the poem, the age-old opposition of good and evil, however ironic the rendering may be. The likening of Satan to an old and poor Castilian noble is a playful remembrance of Satan/Byron's synonymity with another such Castilian—Don Juan. Byron's parsimony, well known in his time and well-chronicled in ours, stemmed from a fear of living a life of noble poverty such as that of his hidalgo devil; and Byron's fear of growing old, age being another characteristic ascribed to his Satan, is likewise a matter of biographical fact.[3]

What clinches the case for taking Michael to be Eldon in real life is the likening of the archangel to a "mushroom rich civilian." Eldon began his

---

1. *Dictionary of National Biography*, s.v. "Scott, John."
2. Horace Twiss, *The Public and Private Life of Lord Chancellor Eldon*, 3 vols. (London: John Murray, 1844), I, 368.
3. Marchand, *Byron: A Biography*, pp. 821, 1158–59, 880–81, 1163.

political career in the law, choosing equity over common or statute law, was accounted a sound equity lawyer by 1780, and, on the basis of his achievements, was created a D.C.L. (Doctor of Civil Law) by Oxford on October 15, 1801. Thus the appropriateness of the appellation "civilian," the first definition of which is found in the *OED* to read in part, "a practitioner, doctor, professor, or student of Civil Law."

Just as the substantive term alludes to Eldon, so does the adjective. Eldon was in fact "mushroom rich" in the sense that he had obtained his wealth as a consequence of financial adventuring rather than of inheritance. Eldon came from common stock. His father and grandfather pursued the trade of coal-factor in Newcastle-on-Tyne. The father rose to a position of some wealth, no doubt aided by the growing application of steam power to manufacturing, and acquired several coal barges and a public house. At the end of his days, the father was able to settle a considerable sum on each of his children, but while the future Lord Eldon was just plain John Scott, the family circumstances were such that his attendance at Oxford had to be underwritten in part by the award of a fellowship reserved for students from the Northumbrian region (Twiss, I, 51).

Scott's first quantum leap in financial status came when the parents of Elizabeth Surtees, whom he eloped with and married with no regard to dowry arrangements, relented in their objections to the match and settled £3000 upon the couple. Thereafter, Eldon *né* Scott was careful to insure that he never again wanted for money. His retirement as Lord Chief Justice of Common Pleas, for example, necessitated by the collapse of the Pitt regime in 1801, was cushioned considerably by a prudently prearranged retirement annuity of £4000. Shrewd and speculative money management indeed made Eldon "mushroom rich."

Finally, there is the matter of the "choreography" of the encounter between Satan and Michael to be dealt with. The description of Satan/Byron behaving toward Michael/Eldon as would a poor noble to a rich parvenu needs to be looked at in the context of the whole stanza.

> The Archangel bowed, not like a modern beau,
>   But with a graceful oriental bend,
> Pressing one radiant arm just where below
>   The heart in good men is supposed to tend;
> He turned as to an equal, not too low,
>   But kindly; Satan met his ancient friend
> With more hauteur, as might an old Castilian
> Poor Noble meet a mushroom rich civilian.

The Archangel bows in a graceful though ancient manner; he expresses a kindly demeanor. Satan, on the other hand, is cold and haughty in his response, ostensibly to make it clear that old friendships will not restrain him from pressing for advantage in the adversary proceedings about to take place. With the exception of any possible prior friendship, the situation described might well have been that of Byron's first meeting with Eldon, at least in terms of the emotions expressed by the two. In the words of Byron's contemporary Dallas,

> . . . the Chancellor [Eldon] quitted his seat and went towards him, with a smile, putting out his hand warmly to welcome him; and, though I did not catch his words, I saw he paid him some compliment.

This was thrown away on Lord Byron, who made a stiff bow, and put the tips of his fingers into a hand, the amiable offer of which demanded the whole of his. . . . The Chancellor did not press a welcome so received, but resumed his seat, while Lord Byron carelessly seated himself a few minutes on one of the empty benches to the left of the throne, usually occupied by the Lords in opposition. When, on his joining me, I expressed what I had felt, he said, "If I had shaken hands heartily, he would have set me down for one of his party; but I will have nothing to do with them on either side. I have taken my seat and now I will go abroad." (Twiss, II, 73)[4]

The original of Peter, Dudley Ryder, First Earl of Harrowby and Viscount Sandon, rose in response to Byron's maiden speech in the House of Lords (see above). Additionally, Harrowby served the Eldon Administration as President of the Council from 1815 to 1827. The three references in the poem to him as keeper of the celestial gate and keys (sts. 1, 16, 25) would rather tend to make us suspect the original of Peter to be the Lord Chamberlain, but the gold key serves as the symbol of other court officials as well (st. 54, n. 2). It should be noted that the use made by Peter of the celestial keys in stanza 25 is to open the celestial gate, thus allowing Michael/Eldon, newly come from conferring with the celestial ruler whose "Viceroy" he is, to enter and begin the proceedings. Peter, in other words, opens the gate to open the meeting, just as Harrowby, in his capacity as President, would be responsible for opening a meeting of the Chancellor-led Council. Byron may in addition be poking fun at Harrowby's past career as a type of "noble porter," Harrowby having been Chancellor of the Duchy of Lancaster and High Steward at Tiverton.[5] Both jobs would entail the carrying of keys as the badge and instrument of office.

The character traits evident in the glimpses of Peter's behavior allowed us by Byron, as well as Peter's reaction to the question of Catholic Emancipation, also serve to link him with Lord Harrowby as an original. The first glimpse, extremely brief, is given us in stanza 25: "He pottered with his keys at a great rate, / And sweated through his Apostolic skin." The second comes when Peter responds to Satan's description of the consequences wrought by George III's blockage of Catholic Emancipation:

> But here Saint Peter started from his place
>   And cried, "You may the prisoner withdraw:
> Ere Heaven shall ope her portals to this Guelph,[6]
>   While I am guard, may I be damned myself!
>
> "Sooner will I with Cerberus exchange
>   My office (and *his* is no sinecure)
> Than see this royal Bedlam-bigot range
>   The azure fields of Heaven, of that be sure!"
>
>   (sts. 49–50)

---

4. After Robert Charles Dallas, *Recollections of the Life of Lord Byron from the Year 1808 to the End of 1814* (London: Knight, 1824), pp. 53–54.

5. *Dictionary of National Biography*, s.v. "Ryder, Dudley."

6. On the matter of Peter calling George III a "Guelph," thus allying him, ironically, with the Papal party of the Italian Renaissance, see Edmund Miller, "Byron's *The Vision of Judgment*, Stanzas 48–51," *Expl*, 33 (1974), item 4.

The original of Saint Peter in Byron's poem does not exhibit the suave polish we might expect of a representative of His Majesty's Government. His manner is, to say the least, ungracious and feisty. Furthermore, he would seem to be at odds with the Government's position on Catholic Emancipation, since he considers the architect of that position, the King, to be not merely a bigot, but a "Bedlam-bigot," one whose well-publicized fits of insanity are in some essential manner related to his stand on withholding full civil rights for Catholics. Both with regard to the manner and the substance of his politics, at least on this one issue, Harrowby proves to be the perfect match.

Were we to look for a summary of Peter's behavior in the two instances cited above, we probably could not do better than consult *The Greville Memoirs*. For Peter's manner turns out to be very much like Harrowby's. As Greville remembers him,

> Lord Harrowby has all the requisites of disagreeableness, a tart, short, provoking manner, with manners at once pert and rigid. . . . Always acute, but sometimes crotchety, he had the same fault in politics which was the reproach of Lord Eldon in law—indecision; and this in no small degree impaired both his efficacy and authority.[7]

It is also of no small interest to see that Greville associates the name of Harrowby with that of Eldon.

And yet, notwithstanding his manner and his party affiliations, Lord Harrowby was not the arch-Tory that Eldon was. If Harrowby had his anxieties about change, he nevertheless realized that it was inevitable, and could be turned to good account, *if* the Tories supported and directed it instead of opposing it. Eleven years after Byron conferred on Harrowby a dubious immortality, Greville, on the eve of the First Reform Bill, found Harrowby in February of 1832 " 'half dead with a headache and dreadfully irritable' because 'these besotted predestined Tories *will* follow the Duke [Wellington, while] the Duke *will* oppose all Reform because he said he would.' "[8]

Harrowby's acceptance of the inevitability of change may well have conditioned his views on Catholic Emancipation. Greville, whatever he may have thought of Harrowby's personality, gave his character its due, declaring that Harrowby "was always devoid of selfishness and ambition, honourable and conscientious to a degree which rendered him incapable of a sordid or oblique action" (*Memoirs*, III, 53). Translated to the sphere of action on the religious question, Harrowby's essential decency led him to support Catholic claims as early as 1812. He spoke and voted in their favor in 1823 and 1824, and a few years later gave his approval to the repeal of the Test Act. Eldon, on the other hand, first spoke against Catholic claims on May 13, 1805 (Twiss, I, 492–93), opposed the Earl of Donoughmore's petition for redress of Catholic grievances on June 6, 1810 (Twiss, II, 123 ff.), and remained inexorably opposed to any change in the structure of religious privilege in England throughout his lifetime. Byron, who admired Catholicism enough to wish his daughter raised in that faith, and who had

---

7. Charles C. F. Greville, *The Greville Memoirs*, ed. Henry Reeve, 2nd ed., 3 vols. (London: Longmans, Green, 1874), III, 52–53.
8. Charles C. F. Greville, *The Greville Diary*, ed. Philip W. Wilson, 2 vols. (Garden City, N.Y.: Doubleday, 1927), I, 381.

himself spoken in favor of Catholic claims on April 21, 1812, seems to have recognized Harrowby's decency and right-mindedness on the issue, and Harrowby's satiric caricature as Peter comes off as more flattering to its subject than does the caricature of Eldon as Michael. Notwithstanding a display of his "tart, short, provoking manner," Peter/Harrowby is portrayed as unambitious, stating his willingness to give up his office to Cerberus out of a conscientious desire to see justice done. Peter/Harrowby's modesty even leads him to refer, self-deprecatingly, to his position as a "sinecure."

Once the political dimension of Byron's satire is no longer at issue, the earthly original of the devil Asmodeus is easy to uncover. In the actions and speech of Asmodeus, Byron is alluding to the actions proposed and a speech actually delivered in the Commons by William Smith, M.P. Just as Asmodeus hales the cumbersome Laureate and his works before the bar in "neutral space," so had Smith haled the case of Southey before the Commons in 1817, shortly after the publication of the poet's long-suppressed *Wat Tyler*. Written in 1793, when Southey was an anti-Jacobin and a republican, the work brought some question to bear on his loyalty to high Toryism. And just as Smith had accused Southey of possessing "the determined malignity of a *renegade*" (p. 482, n. 2; my italics), so Asmodeus makes his entrance, Southey tucked under his diabolical wing, with the expostulation "Confound the renegado!" (st. 86).

To what purpose all this veiled characterization, all this parliamentary procedure, all this litigation in "neutral space"? Southey's *Vision of Judgement* devotes roughly a quarter of its length—three of twelve sections—to George's arraignment, absolution, and beatification, while Byron's satiric parody devotes roughly two-fifths of its length—forty-six of one hundred six stanzas—to George's arraignment and prosecution, which is never satisfactorily concluded either for conviction or acquittal. Why the discrepancy?

We might begin by looking at the way in which Byron transforms Southey's "vision" of the Gate of Heaven in our effort to answer the questions raised above. Early in his description of the Gate, "on the scene" with the King as he approaches it, Southey says: "Wheresoever I look'd, there was light and glory around me. / Brightest it seem'd in the East, where the New Jerusalem glitter'd" (4.4–5). Byron plays down the attempt to describe the physical aspect of the location, choosing to say what the Gate is like in earthly terms rather than try to capture its ineffable qualities.

> The spirits were in neutral space, before
>   The gate of Heaven; like eastern thresholds is
> The place where Death's grand cause is argued o'er,
>   And souls despatched to that world or to this.
>   (st. 35)

Like the eastern gates of the cities of biblical antiquity—and perhaps like the eastern gates of the cities Byron visited on his tour of the Levant as well—the Gate of Heaven is a place whence souls are sent to salvation or damnation. But there is an additional point to be made about the worldly eastern gates evoked by Byron: they are the places where justice is administered in cases involving capital crimes committed against the inhabitants of the city-state within the walls. The implication of Byron's simile is therefore that the case being decided in the matter of George III has to do with his guilt or innocence of a capital crime.

Of the four "spirits" mentioned in Byron's "proceedings," three are members of the House of Lords. The fourth, Asmodeus, is not a principal litigant; rather, he "approaches the bench" as a "friend of the court." Not only are the other three in the Lords: each functions in some sort of presiding role—Michael/Eldon as Lord Chancellor, Satan/Byron as the self-styled leader of the Radical Opposition, and Peter/Harrowby as the President of the Council.

To sum up: we have three presiding figures of the House of Lords at law over the question of whether George III is guilty of a capital crime. We might expect the earthly analogue of the trial's venue to be the House of Lords, and indeed it is. Byron tips us off to the setting, as well as to the cause of the trial, by including in the speaker's description of Satan's witnesses at least one direct quotation and one remembrance of his speech on the issue of Catholic Emancipation (April 21, 1812) and one remembrance of his maiden speech on the Frame-Work Bill (February 27, 1812). Interestingly enough, the references to the parliamentary speeches are not put in the mouth of Satan/Byron, as we might have expected them to be, nor are they put in mouth of any other "spirit" in the satire. Byron's strategy of making the poem's speaker the agency of these speeches would seem to arise from an intention, in portraying the long train of witnesses summoned to testify against George III in a "celestial" House of Lords, to make the scene nothing more, or less, than the fulfillment of the bitter, often ironic visions he conjured in those speeches. In his use of echoes from his speeches, Byron is attempting to substitute his earlier political vision, articulated on the floor of the House of Lords, for Southey's, articulated in an intellectual vacuum, because Byron's vision has been validated, not so much by the death of George as by the consequences brought down upon itself by the Government that ruled in his name, both during his competence and his incompetence, and for which he was ultimately responsible.

The actual quotation from Byron's speech on Catholic Emancipation, delivered in support of the Earl of Donoughmore's motion for a Committee on Roman Catholic Claims, appears in stanza 58: ". . . and then it grew a cloud; / And so it was—a cloud of witnesses." Attacking the Government for general ineptitude, but especially for the ineptitude shown in the conduct of the Walcheren Expedition (1809), Byron had said:

> If they [George's ministers] look to the army, what wreaths . . . of nightshade are preparing for the heroes of Walcheren! It is true, there are few living deponents left to testify to their merits on that occasion; but a "cloud of witnesses" are gone above from that gallant army which they so generously and piously despatched, to recruit the "noble army of martyrs."[9]

A remembrance of the same speech, at least in terms of its itinerary, occurs in stanza 59:

> Here crashed a sturdy oath of stout John Bull,
>   Who damned away his eyes as heretofore:
> There Paddy brogued "By Jasus!"—"What's your wull?"
>   The temperate Scot exclaimed. . . .

9. *The Works of Lord Byron: Letters and Journals*, ed. Rowland E. Prothero, 6 vols. (1898–1901; rpt. New York: Octagon, 1966), II, 442. Quotations from Byron's speeches are from volume II and will be denoted by page number in the text.

The passage from Byron's speech that the poetry draws on concerns a hypothetical "progress" to be made by the members of the Government.

> If they plunge into the midland counties, there will they be greeted by the manufacturers, with spurned petitions in their hands, and those halters round their necks recently voted in their behalf, imploring blessings on the heads of those who so simply, yet ingeniously, contrived to remove them from their miseries in this to a better world. If they journey on to Scotland, from Glasgow to John o' Groat's, every where will they receive similar marks of approbation. If they take a trip from Portpatrick to Donaghadee, there will they rush at once into the embraces of four Catholic millions, to whom their vote of this night is about to endear them for ever. (pp. 441–42)

What Byron foresees as happening to the Tory Government if it makes such a progress indeed happens to George III on the occasion of this, his final "progress."

Byron's last reference to his parliamentary speeches occurs in stanza 60, where the purpose of the "cloud of witnesses" is duly noted: "All summoned by this grand 'subpoena,' to / Try if kings mayn't be damned like me or you." The echo is of Byron's speech on the Frame-Work Bill: "Is there not blood enough upon your penal code, that more must be poured forth to *ascend to Heaven and testify against you?*" (p. 429; my italics).

It should be clear at this point that Byron's emendation of Southey's "vision" portrays the dead king as being arraigned not merely on the matter of his fitness to enter Heaven. Entry into Heaven is certainly the reward in the event of acquittal, but George III has come to "trial" before the "celestial" House of Lords on what amounts to the charge of treason against his people. There is, of course, a delicious irony at play in George's being tried before this "celestial" analogue of the House of Lords without the slightest idea of what is going on. The decision to leave the deceased king blind and enfeebled, instead of restoring his faculties, as Southey had done in his poem, may stem from Byron's all-out effort to subvert and burlesque Southey's poem, but it may have another, more profound dimension of significance. That George knows nothing of his surroundings because of his blindness and feebleness, that Louis XVI knows nothing of his surroundings because of his beheaded condition, may be the case because of the demands of Byron's slapstick, but it may as well be the case because of Byron's peculiar epistemology, as displayed, for example, in *Cain*, written at the same time that Byron was at work on *The Vision of Judgment*.

In *Cain* II.ii, the play's namesake and protagonist is directed by Lucifer to view the existence of the Pre-Adamite giants. Cain finds the significance of the creatures' existence incomprehensible, and yet he cannot deny that the existence has significance, albeit significance beyond his ability to understand.

> CAIN.   What are these mighty phantoms which I see
> Floating around me? They wear not the form
> Of the intelligences I have seen
> Round our regretted and unentered Eden.
>
> . . . .
> And yet they have an aspect which, though not

Of men nor angels, looks like something which,
If not the last, rose higher than the first.
                                                    (44–53)[1]

The lesson that Byron portrays Cain as learning on his journey through the cosmos is that existence *qua* existence partakes of a process of decline from sphere to sphere. There is no teleology to mitigate this process except for that which the sentient individual—man or the Pre-Adamite—is able to provide through action. More importantly for our reading of *The Vision of Judgment*, the absolutely arbitrary nature of existence is such that there is no connection between higher and lower spheres, no matter how elaborate the correspondences between them may appear. Michael/Eldon, Satan/Byron, and Peter/Harrowby perform precisely the same functions in "neutral space" that they did in the lower, mundane sphere of endeavor. But George, blind though he may be, would not in any case be able to identify them or their significance even if his faculties were intact, any more than Cain is able to decipher the significance of what Lucifer shows him. The ability to intuit order and value is limited in the individual, extending only to his native sphere. The Byronic poet or visionary can know of hierarchies of order beyond his own, but he cannot decipher them, except comically, as in the case of *The Vision.*

The final irony of *The Vision of Judgment* is that the dead king, clearly guilty to Byron's mind, manages to slip into Heaven with the unwitting aid of his Laureate, whose self-interest, not his patriotism, precipitates the dubious moment of triumph.[2] Though he is "glad to get an audience" (st. 90), Southey never notices the true occasion of its being gathered there, nor does he ever acknowledge the king's presence, so eager is he to acquire some living—and, therefore, paying—patrons. The poem Southey reads—his *Vision of Judgement*, naturally—breaks up the treason trial and facilitates the miraculous passage of its subject into Heaven, where he is last seen committing to heart Psalm 100, which in part enjoins him to make "a joyful noise unto the Lord," after the horrendous croakings of Southey have been stilled. The Psalm further enjoins George III to enter "into his gates with thanksgiving, and into his courts with praise: be thankful unto him and bless his name."

Thus in Byron's revision, Southey manages to save the soul of his late master from the realms of brimstone, but by aiding and abetting George in his treasonous acts, Southey becomes the principal defendant in any future litigation, to be conducted after the close of the poem. If history has rendered a verdict, it is indeed that George III and Southey are guilty—but

---

1. *Lord Byron's "Cain": Twelve Essays and a Text with Variants and Annotations*, ed. Truman Guy Steffan (Austin: University of Texas Press, 1968).
2. There is also irony latent in Michael/Eldon's agreeing to hear what Southey has to say for himself: " 'Let's hear,' quoth Michael, 'what he has to say: / You know we're bound to that in every way' " (st. 89). Eldon, as Lord Chancellor, had in fact heard Southey's suit for damages against W. Benbow, the publisher of *Wat Tyler*. The verdict went against Southey on the basis of the principle, laid down by Eldon, that "damages cannot be recovered for a work which is in its nature calculated to do an injury to the public" (p. 482, n. 1). In "neutral space," as on earth, Michael/Eldon quiets Southey by blowing his "trump" (st. 95), but to no avail, as the irrepressible Southey refuses to be stilled, pandering to his distinguished audience with the true instincts of a turncoat. These instincts come through most strongly in stanzas 99–100, where Southey, after failing to interest Satan in having his biography done by the Laureate and thereby added "to my other saints," turns, without batting an eye, to Michael, utterly insensitive to the differences between Satan and Michael, and solicits the latter.

only of provoking the laughter that their absurdities deserve to be greeted with. Byron gracefully enough did not petition Satan to renew the prosecution, and soon shifted his emphasis from fighting *against* tyranny, to fighting *for* freedom, the very thing he was doing at the end of his life in April of 1824, when the case on his part was closed.

Goethe, responding to Riemer's mention of Byron's death almost a month after it had occurred, had a comment about *The Vision of Judgment* that we might do well to end with. Goethe believed that Byron had achieved his full creative potential, and so had died fulfilled.

> "Byron could, in a certain sense, go no farther. He had reached the summit of his creative power, and whatever he might have done in the future, he would have been unable to extend the boundaries of his talent. In the incomprehensible poem, his *Vision of Judgment*, he has done the utmost of which he was capable."[3]

We may agree with Goethe's assessment of the poem's importance, but the recovery of the historical dimension of Byron's poem should go a long way toward making the poem comprehensible—and that much funnier for being so.

---

3. Johann Peter Eckermann, *Conversations with Goethe,* trans. John Oxenford, ed. J. K. Moorhead (London: Dent, 1930), p. 67.

Biographical Register

Beyle, Henri (1783–1842), better known by his pseudonym, Stendhal; Beyle served for a time in the army as secretary to Napoleon and became one of France's greatest novelists, recognized especially for *Le Rouge et le Noir* (1830) and *La Chartreuse de Parme* (1839). In Milan in 1816, he occasionally dined with Byron and Hobhouse and would meet Byron at a mutual friend's box at the opera. In "Lord Byron en Italie" (1854), Stendhal offers an insightful account of Byron's genius and vanities.

Blessington, Lady Marguerite, Countess of (1789–1849), of humble birth, rose in society through beauty, grace, and intellectual charm, and the Blessington home in London became a center for the social elite. During a tour of Europe, she and her husband came to reside in Genoa in 1823, while Byron was staying there. By this time, Byron was happy to have the company of English society (which in earlier years in Italy he had avoided), and his comfortable relationship with Lady Blessington led him to express himself frankly and freely with her. She published her *Journal of the Conversations of Lord Byron* in 1834.

Bonaparte (or Buonaparte), Napoleon (1769–1821), Corsican-born soldier who became emperor of France (as Napoleon I, 1804–15). Through relentless and successful war, he controlled much of western Europe, but after defeats in Russia (1812) and Leipzig (1813), he was forced into exile on the island of Elba (1814). He returned to France in 1815, ruling for the "hundred days," but was finally defeated at the Battle of Waterloo by an alliance of European monarchs whose army was led by the Duke of Wellington, and he was forced into permanent exile on the island of St. Helena. While he was reviled and demonized by most Englishmen, especially the Tories, among groups of liberal thinkers and writers, Napoleon was a much more ambivalent figure, hated for his warmaking but admired as a self-made man of talent, demolisher of monarchies, and enlightened ruler. Byron was "dazzled and overwhelmed by his character and career" and "confounded and baffled" by his defeat, with "the restoration of the despicable Bourbons—the triumph of tameness over talent" (*BLJ* 284, 101). For Byron, moreover, the fascination with Napoleon was that of an alter ego. Before leaving England for Switzerland in 1816, Byron went to considerable expense commissioning a coach replicating one of Napoleon's; in *Childe Harold* III, he contemplated Napoleon's uncontainable, unmistakably Byronic spirit; and in *Don Juan* he dubbed himself "the grand Napoleon of the realms of rhyme" (11.440).

Burns, Robert (1759–1796), popular Scottish poet who spent his early years as a farm laborer, and was well liked for his charm and good humor. His most famous lyrics include "Auld Lang Syne" and "My luve is like a red, red rose."

Byron, Augusta Ada (1815–1852), called Ada, the daughter of Byron and his wife, Annabella Milbanke, was born on December 10, 1815, a few months before her father left England never to return. Some of his thoughts about her at this time are expressed in the first and final stanzas of *Childe Harold* III. Although Byron never saw his daughter again, through correspondence with Lady Byron and his sister Augusta he inquired about her, sent gifts, expressed opinions about her upbringing, and received pictures of her. In 1843, she married the Earl of Lovelace and had three children. Like her mother, she excelled at mathematics and, with Charles Babbage, pioneered one of the earliest computer prototypes. (In 1979, a software language developed by the U.S. Department of Defense was named "Ada" in her honor.) She died of cancer at the age of thirty-six, the same age as her father at his death. The relationship between Byron and Ada is the subject of a play by the American playwright Romulus Linney, *Childe Byron* (1977).

Byron, Clara Allegra (1817–1822), called Allegra, was the daughter of Byron and Claire Claremont. Byron provided for her, insisting that she be sent to a convent near Ravenna to be raised in the Catholic faith, over the strenuous objections of Claire. She died there of a fever, and Byron and Claire were shocked and deeply saddened by her death.

Byron, Augusta See Leigh, Augusta.

Byron, Catherine Gordon (1760–1811), Byron's mother, was a descendent of James I of Scotland; she was the daughter of George Gordon, twelfth laird of Gight, and his second cousin. In 1785, at twenty years of age, she married Captain John Byron, a dashing widower who quickly ran through much of her fortune and left her and their baby son. Portrayed by Byron in his letters as alternating unpredictably between affection and explosive displays of temper, she nonetheless cared consistently for her son and responsibly looked out for his financial interests and the Newstead estate.

Byron, Lady , see Milbanke, Annabella.

Campbell, Thomas (1777–1844), a Scottish poet, best known for *The Pleasures of Hope* (1799) and *Gertrude of Wyoming* (1809). He was a friend of Rogers's and Moore's, and through them, of Byron's, who praised him in *English Bards and Scotch Reviewers*.

Castlereagh, Robert Stewart, second Marquis of Londonderry (1769–1822), called Viscount Castlereagh, was largely responsible for the Act of Union by the Irish parliament and served as England's foreign secretary from 1812 to 1822. He took a lead part at the Congress of Vienna, which reestablished the monarchic powers of Europe after the downfall of Napoleon Bonaparte, and played an important role in restraining the allies from retaliation against France. For his service in the Tory government, perceived reactionary policies abroad, and support of repressive measures at home, he was hated by Shelley (who mercilessly memorialized him in "The Masque of Anarchy" [1819] with the lines "I met Murder on the way— / He had a face like Castlereagh") and by Byron, who viciously attacked him in letters and poems, notably in the "Dedication" to *Don Juan* and a fill-in-the-rhyme epitaph—"Posterity will ne'er survey / A nobler grave than this; / Here lie the bones of Castlereagh: / Stop traveller,—." Even after Castlereagh committed suicide in 1822, possibly a consequence of rumors of homosexuality, Byron was unrelenting in his expressions of contempt for "carotid-artery-cutting Castlereagh," offering the epigram: "So He has cut his throat at last!—He! Who? / The man who cut his country's long ago."

Chalandritsanos, Loukas (1809–1824?), the son of a Greek family of refugees during the war of independence from Turkey whom Byron had rescued in the summer of 1823. Byron became romantically attached to him, employed him at Missolonghi as his page, and lavished gifts on him and his family. However, Byron's passionate feelings were unrequited, and the pathos of his situation is recorded in the three last poems he wrote in Greece, most notably in "On This Day I Complete My Thirty-Sixth Year."

Clairmont, Clara Mary Jane (1798–1879), who took the name of Claire, was stepsister to Mary Godwin (eventually Mary Shelley) after William Godwin married Mrs. Mary Jane Clairmont. When she was seventeen years old she initiated an affair with Byron, which he ended before he left for Switzerland in April 1816. She then accompanied Mary Godwin and Percy Shelley to Lake Geneva, where she renewed the affair with Byron. He did not love her then ("but," as he explained to Augusta, "could not exactly play the Stoic with a woman who had scrambled eight hundred miles to unphilosophise me" [*BLJ* 5:92]) and later grew to dislike her more. All the same, it was Claire who introduced Byron to Shelley, thus beginning one of Byron's most important friendships. On January 12, 1817, Claire gave birth to their daughter, Allegra. Byron supported the child but consistently attempted to cut off his relationship with Claire, with Shelley becoming their intermediary and perhaps (as has been conjectured) Claire's lover. In Italy, Byron insisted over Claire's objections on Allegra's being sent to a convent to be educated, and they both were devastated by her death there in 1822. Claire Clairmont's story inspired Henry James's novella *The Aspern Papers* (1888).

Cogni, Margarita (c. 1795), twenty-two years old when Byron met her in the summer of 1817 at La Mira, near Venice, and called "La Fornarina," as she was the wife of a baker. She was unperturbed by Byron's involvement at the time with Marianna Segati, and though she and Byron never had "any regular *liaison*," she became "a favourite" during 1817–18. Her animal fierceness and possessiveness towards Byron are the subject of his letter to Murray of August 1, 1819 (p. 745).

Coleridge, Samuel Taylor (1772–1834), like Wordsworth, belonged to the school of "Lake poets," which Byron derided in *Don Juan*, where he also mocked Coleridge's metaphysical speculations. However, Byron responded to Coleridge's poetry in a way that he did not to Wordsworth's, and his poems contain echoes of passages from Coleridge's great poems of 1797–1800, "The Rime of the Ancient Mariner," *Christabel*, and "Kubla Khan"—the last work published eighteen years after it was written on Byron's advice. In 1813, as a managing director of the Drury Lane Theatre and out of sympathy for Coleridge's personal difficulties, Byron helped produce Coleridge's drama *Remorse*. In moral, religious, and political understanding, the two men could not be further apart, and on those grounds Coleridge was highly critical of *Don Juan*.

Crabbe, George (1754–1832), in his collection of poetic tales *The Borough* (1810), which includes the well-known "Peter Grimes," depicted with realistic detail and insightful characterization the lives of people in a country town. His stories often revealed a grim sense of humor, and Byron rated him highly as a poet, calling him in *English Bards and Scotch Reviewers* "nature's sternest painter, yet the best."

Dallas, Robert Charles (1754–1824), a writer and distant relation of Byron's through his sister's marriage, Dallas befriended Byron in 1808. He became Byron's literary agent, arranging for the publication of *English Bards and Scotch Reviewers* by Cawthorne and of the first two cantos of *Childe Harold's Pilgrimage* by John Murray, thus beginning Byron's long association with the prominent publisher.

Davies, Scrope Berdmore (1783–1852), a friend of Hobhouse and Byron, was a fashionable man about town who enjoyed gambling for large sums. Byron liked his sophistication and considered him "one of the cleverest men I ever knew in Conversation" (*BLJ* 9:21).

Fletcher, William (1773–c.1841), Byron's valet at Newstead Abbey. He accompanied Byron on his first tour of the continent, but Byron was constantly incensed by what he considered his inappropriate behavior and finally sent "that timberhead Fletcher" home a few months before his own return to England.

Galt, John (1779–1839), Scottish novelist, present with Hobhouse and Fletcher for part of Byron's first voyage to the continent. Galt wrote the poet's first biography, *The Life of Byron* (1830).

Gamba Ghiselli, Pietro, Count (d. 1827), Scottish novelist and the younger brother of Teresa Guiccioli. At Ravenna Byron joined with Pietro in the failed 1821 uprisings of the secret revolutionary society Carbonari against Austria. When Pietro and his father were exiled from the Romagna region for these activities and eventually, with Teresa, settled in Pisa, Byron joined the Gamba family there, and he and Pietro became close companions. Pietro greatly admired Byron. He encouraged Byron to go to Greece and eagerly accompanied him there, becoming his lieutenant at Missolonghi. Deeply saddened by Byron's death, he came to England to attend the funeral and wrote *Narrative of Lord Byron's Last Journey to Greece* (1825). He returned to the fight for freedom in Greece and, like his hero, died there of a fever.

Gamba Ghiselli, Ruggero, Count (1770–1846), Teresa Guiccioli's father. He was allied with Italy's aristocratic revolutionary parties, and though Byron's relationship with his daughter initially troubled him, he came to appreciate the courageous and politically engaged poet.

Gifford, William (1756–1826), writer of the verse satires *Baviad* and *Maeviad*, which were a model for *English Bards and Scotch Reviewers*. An important critic, Gifford worked closely with Byron's publisher, John Murray, both as editor of the *Quarterly Review* and of Byron's poems. Gifford had the greatest appreciation for Byron's works, and it was he who first recommended to Murray that he publish *Childe Harold*. Byron relied upon Gifford's good judgment as an editor in matters ranging from content to punctuation. The areas of mutual respect the two men shared for one another is the more remarkable considering Gifford's literary traditionalism and political conservatism, which sometimes influenced his editorial decisions and advice.

Goethe, Johann Wolfgang von (1749–1832), one of the most important and influential German writers; Goethe is chiefly known for his two-part dramatic poem, *Faust* (1808; 1832), and his sentimental epistolary novel

The Sorrows of Young Werther (1774) caused a sensation throughout Europe. Though the conception of *Manfred* was partly inspired by "Monk" Lewis's translating passages of *Faust* to Byron, both Byron and Goethe understood the similarities between the two works to be limited and superficial and the differences significant. Known for his dismissive remark about Byron's capacity for philosophical understanding, "The moment he reflects, he is a child," Goethe nonetheless appreciated the merits of Byron's poetry and praised it highly in reviews. In Part Two of *Faust*, the symbolic character Euphorion, poet-offspring of Faust and Helen, is based on Byron. Byron greatly valued Goethe's praise of his work and dedicated *Marino Faliero* (1820), *Sardanapalus* (1821), and *Werner* (1822) to him.

Guiccioli, Countess Teresa (1798–1873), born Teresa Gamba Ghiselli, Byron's "last attachment" was from an old aristocratic family of Ravenna. When she was eighteen years old and just out of convent school, her father married her to a wealthy, twice-widowed count nearly forty years her senior. Teresa and Byron first met at one of the *conversazioni* in Venice, and when they met again the following year (April 1819), just after Teresa's first year of marriage, they became lovers. Byron was deeply attached to Teresa for the rest of his life. He followed her to Ravenna and then to other places in Italy where she settled with her husband or family. Their relationship gradually became known and accepted, though Byron alternately jested about or resisted the shawl-carrying role of *cavalier servente*. He eventually resided in an apartment at the Palazzo Guiccioli in Ravenna, but after the Count became jealous and less accepting, Teresa's father obtained a separation decree from the Pope for his daughter. Despite feeling called to significant action in Greece, Byron remained devoted to Teresa, and she to him. After his death she returned to her husband for a while, but she left him again, living mostly in Paris and becoming romantically linked to men who were connected to Byron in some way or who shared her admiration for him, such as the poet Alphonse de Lamartine (1790–1869) or the Marquis de Boissy, whom Teresa married when she was forty-seven years of age and who used to introduce her as "Ma femme, ancienne maîtresse de Byron." She wrote two biographies of Byron including *Vie de Lord Byron en Italie* (1879, first published in an English translation in 2005).

Hanson, John (d. 1841), Byron's friend, lawyer, and business agent, dating from 1798 when Byron became the sixth baron. Hanson managed the Newstead and Rochdale estates, arranged for Byron's education, and generally looked out for his welfare. In later years, Byron grew impatient with his handling of the sale of Newstead and litigation over Rochdale, and he turned to Douglas Kinnaird for help with his business affairs.

Hobhouse, John Cam (1786–1869), the close lifelong friend of Byron since they met at Cambridge in 1807. The son of a Whig Member of Parliament and eventually elected to Parliament himself, Hobhouse was part of the liberal Whig coterie with whose political views Byron sympathized. Hobhouse accompanied Byron on his first pilgrimage, publishing *Journey through Albania* in 1813. He joined Byron in Geneva in the summer of 1816 and afterward in Italy, where he wrote the historical notes for the fourth canto of *Childe Harold*. Both in their travels and in London during Byron's years of fame, marriage, and separation, Hobhouse remained a loyal friend, one on whose good judgment Byron relied. After Byron's death, out of devotion to Byron and concern for his posthumous reputation, Hobhouse was largely responsible for the burning of Byron's Memoirs, which the poet had expected to be published.

Hodgson, Francis (b. 1781), though seven years his senior, a close friend of Byron's since 1807, when Byron was a student and Hodgson a tutor at Cambridge. Hodgson was writing satiric poetry at the time that they met, when Byron was beginning his satire *British Bards*, and both men had the common bond of having had their works attacked in the *Edinburgh Review*. Though Hodgson was ordained in 1812, Byron wrote frankly to him about his religious skepticism. Through generous gifts, Byron helped Hodgson and his father out of financial difficulties.

Hogg, James (1770–1835), born in Ettrick Forest, Scotland, and known as the "Ettrick Shepherd" due to his early occupation; Hogg's poetry was first recognized by Walter Scott. In Edinburgh, he made the acquaintance of Wordsworth, Southey, and Byron, who recommended him to John Murray. He became known especially for *The Queen's Wake* (1813), a collection of verse tales, and he wrote a number of prose works, including a biography of Scott.

Holland, Henry Richard Vassall Fox, Lord (1773–1840), leader of the moderate Whigs in the House of Lords; Holland welcomed Byron as a new member of the Opposition and advised him in the writing of his maiden speech. Lord and Lady Holland entertained some of the most select Whig society at Holland House, Kensington, and Byron was always a welcome guest. Byron esteemed the Hollands; in fact, it was partly to please Lord Holland that Byron in 1816 suppressed the fifth edition of *English Bards and Scotch Reviewers*, which contained insults to some of Holland's circle.

Hoppner, Richard Belgrave (1786–1872), a cultured and literary man, was British Consul in Venice, whom Byron befriended in 1817. Hoppner tended to Byron's affairs in Venice when Byron followed Countess Guiccioli to Ravenna in late 1819, and he and his wife took care of Allegra for a time.

Hunt, John (1775–1848), brother of Leigh Hunt, published Byron's poetry after the poet finally broke with the conservative John Murray largely over Murray's increasing hesitance to publish Byron's morally and politically controversial works, especially *Don Juan* (though Murray had published the first five cantos) and The *Vision of Judgment*. The *Vision of Judgment* was printed in the first number of the *Liberal* (October 15, 1822), the journal planned in Pisa by Byron, Shelley, and L. Hunt and published by J. Hunt. The poem (published anonymously but known to be Byron's) caused a public outcry, and Hunt was prosecuted and convicted on charges of defaming and insulting the King. Byron paid the legal fees, and his estate covered the fine, which was handed down after Byron's death. Hunt published cantos six through sixteen of *Don Juan*, along with other important works that Byron wrote in Italy in 1821 and 1822.

Hunt, Leigh (1784–1859), poet and essayist, who edited the politically liberal journal the *Examiner*, in which he expressed critical views of the Prince Regent that resulted in a fine and two years' imprisonment. His most well-known poetical works are "The Story of Rimini" (based on the

Paolo and Francesca episode in Dante's *Inferno*) and the lyric "Jenny Kissed Me." He later founded the *Liberal*, with the involvement of Byron and Shelley, with whom he was friendly at Pisa in 1822. He became chiefly known for his prose works and his important role in the development of the essay, as well as for his recognition of the genius of Keats and Shelley.

Keats, John (1795–1821),whose poetry elicited various cutting remarks from Byron, who had little appreciation for its beauty and found it puerile and self-indulgent. Byron could not repress his facetious reaction to the view, expounded by Shelley, that Keats was "kill'd off by one critique" (*Don Juan* XI.473). Keats, while appreciative of Byron's genius (as seen in his sonnet "To Byron"), was critical (and understandably envious) of the famous, worldly poet—as illustrated in his remarks to George and Georgiana Keats: "Lord Byron cuts a figure—but he is not figurative"; "He describes what he sees—I describe what I imagine—Mine is the hardest task" (letters of February 18 and September 17–27 1819).

Kinnaird, Douglas (b. 1788), met Byron at Cambridge, but their close friendship began in London in 1814, where they spent enjoyable bachelor evenings dining and drinking together. Kinnaird introduced Byron to Isaac Nathan and encouraged him to collaborate with Nathan on *Hebrew Melodies*. It was also Kinnaird who invited Byron to join, with him, the management committee of Drury Lane Theatre. Kinnaird joined a banking firm and became Byron's banker after Byron left England in 1816.

Lamb, Lady Caroline Ponsonby (1785–1828), daughter of the Earl of Bessborough and his wife, Lady Henrietta Spencer, and wife of William Lamb (son of Lord and Lady Melbourne and, later, Prime Minister under Queen Victoria). Caroline Lamb had a tempestuous affair with Byron for about three months in 1812 and a lifelong obsession with him. Clever, charming, passionate, and eccentric, she was also volatile and indiscreet (famously invading Byron's rooms disguised as a page), and she became an annoyance and embarrassment to Byron after their affair, from his point of view, had ended. Having coined the oft-quoted description of Byron as "mad, bad and dangerous to know," she further vented her vexed emotions in the roman-à-clef *Glenarvon* (1816).

Leigh, Augusta (1783–1851), Byron's half-sister through his father's previous marriage to Amelia d'Arcy, Lady Carmarthen. She and Byron did not meet until after he went to Harrow, but their similarities drew them to one another, and she quickly became, and would remain throughout Byron's life, a sympathetic confidante. In 1807 she married her first cousin, Colonel George Leigh, but during the summer of 1813 she came to London, and she and Byron became lovers. On April 15, 1814, Augusta bore a daughter, Medora Leigh, conjectured to be Byron's child, and despite Byron's marriage in January 1815 to Annabella Milbanke, whom Augusta befriended, rumors of incest persisted. Byron's letters to Augusta, the poems "Stanzas to Augusta" and "Epistle to Augusta," and the Alpine journal he kept for her in September 1816 are part of the record of his intense love for her and of their friendship on which he depended throughout his life.

Lewis, Matthew ("Monk") (1775–1818), a friend of Byron's and author of *The Monk* (1796), a Gothic novel of horror and depravity. When Lewis visited Byron at the Villa Diodati in the summer of 1816, he translated parts of Goethe's *Faust* for him, which is considered to have inspired or influenced some passages of *Manfred*.

Matthews, Charles Skinner (d. 1811), Hobhouse's closest friend, met Byron at Cambridge in 1807. He was one of Byron's circle of male friends both at Cambridge and London, and Byron admired him as both a brilliant scholar and irreverent wit. Letters he exchanged with Byron confirm the homoerotic dimension of Byron's Cambridge circle and Byron's familiarity with its code language, which recent critics have related to an aspect of Byron's poetic style (Matthews' revealing letter on this subject was published for the first time in Crompton's *Byron and Greek Love* [1985]). When Matthews drowned in the Cam river shortly after Byron returned from his trip to the Levant in August 1811, Byron was deeply saddened by his death.

Mavrocordatos, Prince Alexander (1791–1865), exiled from Greece by the Turks for resistance activities, he settled in Pisa. He was educated in eastern and European languages, and in Pisa he became acquainted first with the Shelleys and then with Byron when arrived there in the fall of 1821. He returned to Greece during the revolution and was elected President of the provisional government. After he was ousted by military factions, Byron supported him as governor of Western Greece and enabled a fleet to bring him to Missolonghi, where Byron arrived in January, 1824.

Mayer, Mr., the English Consul in Prevesa, Greece, during Byron's time there.

Medwin, Thomas (1788–1869), one of the circle of friends of Shelley (his second cousin), Trelawny, and Byron at Pisa during the period 1820–22. Medwin led a somewhat extravagant existence, had literary ambitions, and soon after meeting Byron set about drawing him out in conversations with a view to publishing them. *Journal of Conversations with Lord Byron* (1824) contains many of Byron's frank and revealing observations, along with numerous factual errors by Medwin.

Melbourne, Elizabeth Milbanke Lamb, Lady (1751–1818), one of Byron's most valued friends, was past sixty in 1812 when Byron met her. During the turbulent period of his love affair with Lady Caroline Lamb, who was married to one of her sons (a future prime minister), she became Byron's trusted confidante. She tried to warn Byron about potential trouble from his various romantic entanglements and relayed his proposal of marriage to her niece, Annabella Milbanke. After her death, Byron described her as "the best & kindest & ablest female I ever knew, old or young" (*BLJ* 6:34) and once commented that "with a littler more Youth, Lady M. might have turned my head" (Blessington, *Journal*, 132).

Milbanke, Annabella (1792–1860), Anne Isabella, the only daughter of Sir Ralph and Lady Milbanke, was an intelligent, well-read, and mathematically gifted young woman when Byron met her in London in 1812. His wish to escape the turbulent involvement with Caroline Lamb, fears over the dangerous liaison with his half-sister, Augusta Leigh, and financial difficulties provided the backdrop to his decision to propose to this impressive, morally high-minded young heiress who, unlike most of the other women who fawned over Byron, piqued his interest by her reserve.

After rejecting his first marriage proposal, she later agreed to marry Byron with a view to reforming him, which apparently was his view as well—prior to the marriage. They wed on January 2, 1815; on December 10 Lady Byron gave birth to a daughter, Augusta Ada; on January 15, 1816, she left Byron. After several attempts to persuade his wife to return to him, Byron signed the final deed of separation on April 21. Lady Byron's various confidences about their marriage became the source of rumors about his questionable sanity, his verbal and sexual abuse of his wife, and his intimacy with Augusta.

Moore, Thomas (1779–1852), the son of a Dublin grocer and a musician as well as poet, became Ireland's national lyric poet with the publication of *Irish Melodies* (1807–35) and gained a European reputation with *Lalla Rookh* (1817), a series of oriental verse tales. Byron admired Moore's poems, published pseudonymously under the name Thomas Little, the name by which Byron refers to Moore in *English Bards and Scotch Reviewers*. After threatening a duel because of a reference to him in *English Bards*, Moore met Byron at the home of a friend and fellow poet, Samuel Rogers, and he and Byron became close friends from that point on. Some of the frankest, liveliest letters that Byron wrote while he was living in Italy were to Moore, and when Moore came to Venice in 1819, Byron gave him his Memoirs. Moore sold the Memoirs, with Byron's approval, to John Murray for posthumous publication, and when they were burned after Byron's death, it was over Moore's protest. His *Letters and Journals of Lord Byron: with notices of his life*, 2 vols., was published in 1830.

Murray, John, II (1778–1843), the son of the first John Murray (1745–1793), for whom the important English publishing house was named; he became Byron's publisher in 1812, with the first two cantos of *Childe Harold's Pilgrimage*, and remained his publisher throughout most of Byron's lifetime. A political conservative, Murray founded the powerful Tory journal the *Quarterly Review*. He moved the publishing firm to 50 Albemarle Street, London, where it remained until 2002 when it was bought by the publishing conglomerate Hodder Headline. Murray and Byron frequently argued over the outspokenness of Byron's satire, until tensions mounted between the brazen author and cautious publisher during and after the printing of the first five cantos of *Don Juan*. At one point warning "you sha'n't make *Canticles* of my Cantos" (*BLJ* 6:105), Byron eventually broke with Murray and gave his manuscripts to the radical publisher John Hunt. Still, Byron's appreciation of and regard for Murray are revealed in the numerous letters that he wrote to him after leaving England.

Napoleon, see Bonaparte.

Nathan, Isaac (c.1792–1864), Jewish composer living in London, was introduced to Byron by Douglas Kinnaird, who encouraged their collaboration on *Hebrew Melodies* (1815).

Oxford, Jane Elizabeth Scott, Countess of (b. 1772), married to Edward Harley, fifth Earl of Oxford and Mortimer; Lady Oxford was liberal in politics and in her attitudes towards love, and was known to have had several lovers before Byron met her. She was forty years old then, and her "autumnal charms" attracted the twenty-four-year-old poet, on the rebound from his affair with Caroline Lamb. Byron spent a relatively happy period at Eywood, her country home, and she encouraged his participation in the House of Lords, before departing to the continent with her husband in 1813.

Peacock, Thomas Love (1785–1866), satirist and close friend of Shelley's. In his satirical romance *Nightmare Abbey* (1818), Peacock parodied Byron as Mr. Cypress, who at one point says: "Sir, I have quarreled with my wife; and a man who has quarreled with his wife is absolved of all duty to his country. I have written an ode to tell the people as much, and they may take it as they list." Byron read the caricature with good humor, acknowledging it by sending Peacock a single rose.

Pigot, Elizabeth Bridget (b. 1783), neighbor and friend of Byron's during his Harrow School and Cambridge years, when his mother had leased a house (Burgage Manor) at Southwell in Nottingham, not far from the Byron estate at Newstead Abbey. Byron would visit her during vacations, and Elizabeth and her brother John were his closest friends there. Elizabeth prepared the fair copies of some of his earliest published poems.

Polidori, Dr. John William (1796?–1821), the Italian-born physician who accompanied Byron to Switzerland in April 1816, where he was part of the social circle at the Villa Diodati that included Mary Godwin and Percy Shelley. He was a conceited young man with literary ambitions, whom Byron dismissed in September shortly before leaving for Italy, though he remained on friendly terms with him. When Polidori returned to England, he completed the ghost story Byron had begun in Switzerland and published it as *The Vampyre*. Eventually disappointed in his literary ambitions, Polidori killed himself. In 1911 William Michael Rossetti (of whom, along with Dante Gabriel and Christina Rossetti, Polidori was the uncle) published Polidori's informative though not wholly reliable diary of his summer with Byron.

Pope, Alexander (1688–1744), considered the greatest poet of the eighteenth century, known especially for satires written in heroic couplets. While most of the Romantic poets rejected the formal artificialities of eighteenth-century poetics, Byron greatly admired Pope and emulated his poetic style, especially in the early satiric works *English Bards and Scotch Reviewers* and *Hints from Horace*. Byron also repeatedly defended Pope against attacks on eighteenth-century, or Augustan, poetry, by his Romantic contemporaries, who were, in his view, "all on the wrong tack," and he became an active participant in what came to be known as the Pope-Bowles controversy, set off by a critical attack on Pope by William Lisle Bowles, a poet and editor of Pope's poetry.

Ridge, John (c. 1788–c. 1828), Nottinghamshire bookseller who printed Byron's earliest poems, including the first publically issued volume, *Hours of Idleness* (1807).

Rogers, Samuel (1763–1855), who retired from business when he was thirty years old to devote himself to poetry, became known for "The Pleasures of Memory" (1792). Byron admired his poetry, which was influenced by Pope, and praise him highly in *English Bards and Scotch Reviewers*. They were friends during Byron's years of fame in London, and *Lara* was published together with Rogers's *Jacqueline* (1814).

Rose, William Stuart (1775–1834), British poet and translator; it was Rose who, with Kinnaird in Venice in September 1817, introduced

Byron to Frere's *The Monks and the Giants*, the most immediate model for Byron's *ottava rima* poems.

Rousseau, Jean-Jacques (1712–1778), tremendously influential philosopher and political theorist from Geneva, Switzerland. His ideas about the innate goodness of human beings (who become corrupted by civilization and its institutions), about freedom and social equality as essential rights, and about the goal of government to assure freedom and equality inspired both the American and French revolutions and the Romantic movement. His chief works are *The Social Contract* (1762), *La Nouvelle Héloïse* (1761), *Emile* (1762), and the *Confessions* (1782–89). Byron admired him both for his ideas and for the personal passions he endured, and in *Childe Harold III*, Rousseau serves, with Napoleon, as a touchstone for Byron's personal preoccupations and self-projections.

Rushton, Robert (1793–1833), the handsome son of one of Byron's tenants at Newstead Abbey. Byron became attached to him, made him his page, and took him along on his first voyage to the continent. Byron sent him home, however, when they arrived at Malta, explaining to his mother, "you *know boys* are not *safe* amongst the Turks" (*BLJ* 1:222). Byron then made provisions for Rushton's education.

Scott, Sir Walter (1771–1832), already famous as a writer of verse tales (e.g., *The Lay of the Last Minstrel, The Lady of the Lake, Marmion*) by the time Byron met him in 1815, Scott went on to achieve literary fame through a series of historical novels, such as *Waverley* (1814) and *Ivanhoe* (1819). Given Scott's personal conservatism and Tory politics, the friendship and mutual admiration between these two writers is surprising. Scott, however, appreciated the deep feeling of Byron's poetry, and Byron, regretting his criticism of Scott in *English Bards and Scotch Reviewers*, placed him at the pinnacle of his 1813 ranking of living writers (see p. 181) and became a lifelong admirer, claiming that he re-read Scott's novels many times. Though they had met only a few times, Byron and Scott corresponded, and in 1821 Byron dedicated *Cain* to him.

Shelley, Mary (1797–1851), daughter of Enlightenment philosopher William Godwin and feminist Mary Wollstonecraft. She and Byron became well acquainted during the summer of 1816 on Lake Geneva, when she, Percy Shelley (with whom she had eloped though he was married), and Claire Clairmont (Mary's stepsister) frequently visited Byron and Dr. Polidori at the Villa Diodati, where she wrote the first draft of *Frankenstein*. By the time the Shelleys visited Byron in Venice, they had (after the suicide of Shelley's first wife) married, and after Shelley's death, Byron assisted Mary in practical and financial matters, giving her work copying his manuscripts.

Shelley, Percy Bysshe (1792–1822), of all the other contemporary poets with the exception of Moore, was the one with whom Byron was closest and whom he most admired personally. They spent the summer of 1816 in Switzerland in nearly daily company either at Byron's Villa Diodati on Lake Geneva or on walking tours in the region, such as the one they took together to the castle of Chillon. They shared stimulating conversations, with Shelley persuading Byron to read Wordsworth with more sympathy than he ever had before or since (as seen in Canto III of *Childe Harold*) and with Byron influencing Shelley's poem based on their relationship, *Julian and Maddalo*. Shelley visited Byron in Italy, and after they both moved to

Pisa, they saw each other regularly there. They shared fundamental liberal ideals, yet they were strikingly different in their personalities and manner of living. Shelley admired *Don Juan* immensely but was often critical of his friend's behavior, such as his debauchery in Venice or neglect of Claire Claremont (whose child with Byron, Allegra, Shelley helped raise for a time). On his part, Byron remained equivocal on the matter of Shelley's poetry, but considered Shelley "the *best* and least selfish man I ever knew. I never knew one who was not a beast in comparison." He wrote these words to John Murray in a letter of August 3, 1822, soon after receiving the devastating news of Shelley's drowning in the Bay of Spezia, where Shelley and his friend Edward Williams had taken a ride in Shelley's sailboat, the *Don Juan.*

Smith, Mrs. Constance Spencer (b. 1785), the subject of the "Sweet Florence" stanzas in *Childe Harold II* (stanzas 30–35). She was the daughter of the Austrian ambassador and wife of an English official at Malta, where Byron met her in September 1809 and for the brief time of their affair "was seized with an *everlasting* passion" (*BLJ* 2:198).

Southey, Robert (1774–1843), in his early years, a close friend of Coleridge, with whom he idealistically envisioned an agrarian communal society called "Pantisocracy." Though the work by which he is probably most widely known today is "The Story of the Three Bears" (the Goldilocks story), Southey's popular oriental tales, such as *Thalaba* (1801) and *The Curse of Kehama* (1810), influenced Byron's immensely successful oriental tales. However, Byron came to detest Southey personally and as a poet, and the feeling was mutual. Byron's bitterly contemptuous references to Southey in his letters and poetry—especially in the mock "Dedication" to Southey *in Don Juan* and in *The Vision of Judgment* (a parody of Southey's *A Vision of Judgement*)—focused especially on what Byron regarded as Southey's turncoat politics: his becoming a Tory conservative, a shift of political allegiance that Byron related to Southey's appointment as Poet Laureate in 1813. Byron's ire was further fueled by Southey's references to the Byron-Shelley circle as a "league of incest" and "the Satanic School"; the second charge, printed in Southey's letter to *The Courier* of January 5, 1822, provoked Byron, living in Pisa, to challenge Southey to a duel via a letter Byron asked Douglas Kinnaird to deliver—which Kinnaird wisely neglected to do.

Staël, Madame de (1766–1817), one of the most impressive women and intellectuals of the nineteenth century. Germaine de Staël-Holstein was the daughter of the French statesman Jacques Necker; she married a Swedish diplomat, who died in 1802, and her subsequent romantic life was as interesting and unconventional as her political thinking. As a consequence of her opposition to Napoleon in 1803, she left France and settled at Coppet, her father's estate on Lake Geneva. She became admired for her literary work, especially *De l'Allemagne* (1810), as well as for her coterie of artists and intellectuals. Byron, who first met her at social gatherings in London, was at times put off by her intellectual assertiveness ("her tongue is 'the perpetual motion,'" he wrote to Annabella Milbanke [*BLJ* 3:160]), though on the whole he came to respect her and to appreciate her kindness to him at Coppet, situated across Lake Geneva from the Villa Diodati, where Byron resided during the summer of 1816.

Stendhal, see Beyle.

Trelawny, Edward John (1792–1881), Shelley's friend and one of Byron's circle of acquaintances at Pisa, which included Edward Williams and Leigh Hunt; he was present at Leghorn when Shelley drowned. He admired Byron, was romantic, adventurous and courageous, emulating the Byronic heroes of the tales and accompanying Byron to Greece to assist in the Greek war of independence. He wrote *Records of Shelley, Byron, and the Author* (1858), in which he describes his retrieving from Shelley's funeral pyre the poet's heart, which would not burn.

Webster, James Wedderburn (b. 1789), who may have met Byron at Cambridge and whom Byron (though he liked Webster) considered to be a bit of a buffoon. Invited in the fall of 1813 by the recently married Webster to spend a few days with him and his wife at Aston Hall, Byron observed Webster's lack of attentiveness to Lady Frances and proceeded to engage in a rather intense flirtation with her, though on the verge of an affair "spared her" (*BLJ* 3:146). A few years later, upon hearing of Lady Frances's affair with the Duke of Wellington, Byron wrote "When We Two Parted."

Wellington, Arthur Wellesley, Duke of (1769–1852), distinguished soldier and commander of the British army, commanded the British, Portuguese, and Spanish forces in the Peninsular War, weakening the position of the French. His most famous victory was the defeat of Napoleon's army at the Battle of Waterloo in Belgium (June 1815). In Paris, while he was in charge of the occupation of France, two of Byron's ex-lovers, Lady Caroline Lamb and Lady Frances Webster, were rumored to be romantically involved with him. Byron, however, disliked him. After Wellington returned to England he lent prestige to the Tories and in 1829 was made prime minister.

Wordsworth, William (1770–1850), published *Lyrical Ballads* when Byron was ten years old and was an acclaimed poet when, in 1812, the young, charismatic Lord Byron became famous overnight—an upstaging of the senior poet that must have been particularly galling to him in view of his moral disapproval of Byron (the man and his poetry). Indeed, with the exception of their both being great contemporary English poets, these two men (and their poetry) could not be more unlike. In the ways Byron was traditional, in admiring Augustan poetry and classical verse forms, Wordsworth was progressive; in the ways Byron was progressive—i.e., politically—Wordsworth, who had started out a revolutionary, was conservative. Byron was sharply critical of Wordsworth's political affiliations, mocking his position as distributor of stamps for Westmorland county (for which Wordsworth was paid £400 per year). Byron also attacked Wordsworth's "Lake school" of poetry, with its focus on the sublime and ideal, at the sacrifice of the world and its facts, and with its sentimental idealization of the rustic. Yet, while Byron satirically derided Wordsworth in his poetry, it is not usually with the same *ad hominem* contempt with which he consistently abused Southey, and, in fact, after meeting Wordsworth for the first and only time in 1815, Byron told his wife, "I had but one feeling from the beginning of the visit to the end—*reverence*" (Lovell, *His Very Self and Voice*, 129).

Yusuff Pasha (fl.c.1800–1830), Turkish commander at Patras, Greece, with whom Byron negotiated for the humane treatment of Greek prisoners.

Byron: A Chronology

1788	George Gordon Byron born, January 22, in London, to Captain John ("Mad Jack") Byron and Catherine Gordon Byron (born Catherine Gordon of Gight). Byron is born with a deformed foot. After spending his wife's fortune, John Byron goes to France to escape creditors.
1789	French revolution begins (July). Byron and his mother move to Aberdeen, Scotland. Always in need of money, Byron's father makes short visits to Aberdeen.
1791	Byron's father dies in France at the age of thirty-six.
1793	France declares war on England.
1794–98	Attends Aberdeen Grammar School. Tended by nurse May Gray, who introduces Byron to Calvinism, the Bible, and sex.
1796	Forms earliest passionate attachment to distant cousin, eight-year-old Mary Duff.
1798	Inherits title, upon death of granduncle ("the wicked Lord"); becomes sixth Baron Byron of Rochdale. Moves with mother to Newstead Abbey, debt-encumbered, ancestral estate in Nottinghamshire, England. Wordsworth and Coleridge's *Lyrical Ballads* published.
1799–1801	Napoleon becomes First Consul (1799). Byron attends boarding school at Dulwich, near London. Falls in love with his first cousin, Margaret Parker (d. 1802). Doctors prescribe brace for Byron's foot.
1801–05	Attends Harrow.
1802	Treaty with France (Peace of Amiens).
1803	Newstead leased to Lord Grey de Ruthyn. Mrs. Byron leases Burgage Manor at Southwell (Nottinghamshire), where Byron stays on school vacations. At age sixteen, Byron falls in love with eighteen-year-old cousin Mary Chaworth.
1804	Napoleon made Emperor. Beginning of Byron's correspondence and friendship with his half-sister, Augusta (b. 1783 to John Byron and Lady Carmarthen, Baroness Conyers [d. 1784]).
1805	Mary Chaworth marries John Musters. Byron enters Trinity College, Cambridge (October); meets the fifteen-year-old chorister John Edleston. Nelson's victory at Trafalgar: England defeats French and Spanish fleet (October 21).
1806	*Fugitive Pieces*, first volume of poems, privately printed.
1807	*Poems on Various Occasions*, privately printed (January). *Hours of Idleness* published (June). Friendship with John Cam Hobhouse begins at Cambridge (June); Byron leaves

Cambridge for good at Christmas holiday. Augusta married to Colonel George Leigh.

1808   Residence in London or at Newstead. *Hours of Idleness* ridiculed in *Edinburgh Review* (February). *Poems Original and Translated* published (March). Peninsular War begins: England sides with Spain and Portugal against France.

1809   Byron takes seat in the House of Lords. *English Bards and Scotch Reviewers* published (March). Byron departs with Hobhouse (July 2) for travels in Portugal, Spain, and Gibraltar; sails to Malta (August); sails to Albania, where he visits Ali Pasha (October); sails to Greece (arriving in November). Begins *Childe Harold's Pilgrimage* at Janina, Greece, and completes the first canto (December).

1810   Travels through Greece and Turkey; writes the second canto of *Childe Harold* (March). Swims Hellespont (May 3).

1811   Prince of Wales made Regent due to the insanity of King George III (February). Byron writes *Hints from Horace* and *The Curse of Minerva*. Arrives in England (July) and resides in London and at Newstead. Deaths of his mother, school friends John Skinner Matthews and John Wingfield, and beloved chorister John Edleston. Writes "Thyrza" poems. Begins friendship with Thomas Moore (November).

1812   Delivers maiden speech in the House of Lords, opposing Tory bill to make frame-breaking (factory riots) a capital offense; "Ode to the Framers of the Frame Bill" appears in *Morning Chronicle* (March 2). *Childe Harold's Pilgrimage, A Romaunt* (Cantos I–II) published (March 10), bringing Byron immediate fame. Delivers second parliamentary speech, on Catholic emancipation. Begins affair with Caroline Lamb (April); proposes to Annabella Milbanke and is rejected (October); affair with Lady Oxford begins.

1813   Affair with Augusta begins (June). *The Giaour* published (June); *The Bride of Abydos* published (December). Robert Southey named Poet Laureate.

1814   *The Corsair* published (February 1), 10,000 copies sold that day. Medora Leigh, Augusta's and presumably Byron's daughter born (April). Allies invade France; Napoleon exiled to Elba; Bourbon monarchies restored. Byron writes "Ode to Napoleon Buonaparte" and *Lara*. Engagement to Annabella Milbanke (September).

1815   Weds Annabella Milbanke (January 2) at her parents' home at Seaham; Byron and Annabella live in London. *Hebrew Melodies* published with music by Isaac Nathan. Joins Management Committee of Drury Lane Theatre (May). Napoleon escapes from Elba, restored for the "hundred days," and is defeated at Waterloo (June 18). Daughter Ada born (December 10).

1816   Byron's wife leaves him (January 15). *The Siege of Corinth* and *Parisina* published together (February). Claire Clairmont initiates relationship with Byron (March). Marital separation is formalized (April 21). Byron sails for Switzerland, leaving England forever (April 25). Travels in Belgium, the Rhine valley, and Switzerland. Leases Villa Diodati on Lake Geneva; is visited by Claire, Mary Godwin, and Percy Shelley (Mary writes the first draft of *Franken-*

stein [June]). Tours Lake Geneva with Shelley. Writes *Childe Harold* III (published November) and *The Prisoner of Chillon* (published December). Tours Alps with Hobhouse and keeps Alpine Journal for Augusta (September). Writes the first two acts of *Manfred*. Leaves with Hobhouse for Italy (October 5); arrives in Milan, then Venice (October–November). Affair with landlord's wife, Marianna Segati; studies Armenian at monastery on San Lazzaro island.

1817   Allegra, Byron's daughter with Claire Clairmont, born (January 12). Venetian Carnival festivities (January–February). Completes *Manfred*; revises Act 3 at Rome in May; *Manfred* published (June); works on *Childe Harold* IV. Begins affair with Margarita Cogni. Writes *Beppo* (October). Newstead Abbey sold (December).

1818   Carnival dissipations (January–February). Meets Countess Teresa Guiccioli briefly for first time. Affair with Margarita Cogni. *Beppo* published (February); *Childe Harold IV* published (April). Keats's *Endymion* published. Moves to Palazzo Mocenigo on the Grand Canal. Claire and Shelley in Venice; Shelley writes *Julian and Maddalo,* based on his relationship with Byron. Byron begins *Don Juan* (July).

1819   Carnival dissipations (January–February). Affair with Countess Guiccioli begins (April). *Mazeppa* published (June); *Don Juan* I–II published (July). Peterloo Massacre (August). With Teresa at La Mira and Ravenna (September–December). Byron gives Memoirs to Thomas Moore (October). Drafts *Don Juan* III–IV.

1820   Death of George III; accession of George IV (January). Byron lives at Palazzo Guiccioli (Ravenna). Through relationship with Pietro and Ruggero Gamba (Teresa's brother and father), Byron becomes involved in Carbonari revolutionary activity. Translates "Francesca of Rimini" from Dante's *Inferno,* Canto 5. Shelley's *Prometheus Unbound* published (August). Writes fifth canto of *Don Juan* (October–December).

1821   Death of Keats (February 23). Byron insists on placing Allegra in a convent to be raised (March). Greek revolution begins (March). *Marino Faliero* and *The Prophecy of Dante* published (April). Death of Napoleon (May). Promises Teresa not to continue *Don Juan* (July). Gambas banished from Romagna region, move to Pisa (July). *Don Juan* III–V published (August). Writes *The Vision of Judgment* (September–October). Joins Gambas and Shelley in Pisa (November). *Sardanapalus, The Two Foscari, Cain* published together (December).

1822   Byron resumes work on *Don Juan* (January); by December completes cantos VI–XII. Death of Allegra (April). Leigh Hunt and his family arrive, and Byron, Shelley, and Hunt plan the magazine *The Liberal.* Shelley and Edward Williams drown in Bay of Spezia (July 8). Byron and the Hunts move to Genoa (September). *The Vision of Judgment* published in first number of the *Liberal* (October); *Werner* published (November).

1823   *Heaven and Earth* published (January); *The Age of Bronze* published (April). Byron befriends Lord and Lady Blessington. Finishes *Don Juan* XVI and begins canto XVII (May). Increasing interest in the Greek War of Independence; asked to join the London Greek Committee (April–May); sets sail for Greece (July 15) with Pietro Gamba and Trelawny, arriving at Cephalonia on August 3. Publishes *The Island* (June), *Don Juan* VI–VIII (July), IX–XI (August), XII–XIV (December). Byron becomes attached to Loukas Chalandritsanos in the fall. Agrees to lend Greek provisional government £4,000; embarks for Missolonghi (December 29) with Loukas, Dr. Bruno, Fletcher, and P. Gamba.

1824   Commands corps of Suliotes, personally providing for five hundred soldiers. Writes "On This Day I Complete My Thirty-Sixth Year" (January 22). *The Deformed Transformed* published (February). Suffers convulsions (February). *Don Juan* XV–XVI published (March). Final illness and death (April 9–19). On July 16, Byron is buried in the churchyard of Hucknall Torkard, near Newstead.

Selected Bibliography

EDITIONS

Poetry

Byron: Poetical Works. Ed. Frederick Page, corrected by John Jump. Oxford: Oxford University Press, 1970.

Byron's Don Juan, A Variorum Edition. Ed. T. G. Steffan, E. Steffan, and W. W. Pratt. Austin: University of Texas Press, 1957; rev. ed., 1971. Penguin Classics edition, with Introduction and Further Reading by Susan J. Wolfson and Peter J. Manning, 2004.

The Complete Poetical Works of Lord Byron. Ed. Paul Elmer More. Boston: Riverside Press, Houghton Mifflin, 1905; rev. ed. by Robert Gleckner, 1975.

Lord Byron. The Complete Poetical Works. Ed. Jerome J. McGann. 7 vols. Oxford: Clarendon Press, 1980–93.

Lord Byron: Selected Poems. Ed. Susan J. Wolfson and Peter J. Manning. Harmondsworth: Penguin, 1996.

Lord Byron's Cain: Twelve Essays and a Text with Variants and Annotations. Ed. Truman Guy Steffan. Austin: University of Texas Press, 1968.

The Manuscripts of the Younger Romantics. Byron. Gen. ed. Donald H. Reiman. 13 vols. New York and London: Garland Publishing, 1986–95.

A Selection of Hebrew Melodies, Ancient and Modern, by Isaac Nathan and Lord Byron. Ed. Frederick Burwick and Paul Douglass. Tuscaloosa and London: University of Alabama Press, 1988.

The Works of Lord Byron. Poetry. Ed. Ernest Hartley Coleridge. 7 vols. London: John Murray, 1898–1904.

The Works of Lord Byron: With His Letters and Journals and His Life, by Thomas Moore, Esq. Ed. John Wright. 17 vols. London: John Murray, 1832–33. (Poetry, vols. 7–17.)

Letters, Journals, and Other Prose

Byron's Letters and Journals. Ed. Leslie A. Marchand. 12 vols. London: John Murray, and Cambridge, MA: Belknap Press, Harvard University Press, 1975–82. Supplementary volume: *What Comes Uppermost: Byron's Letters and Journals.* Newark, DE: University of Delaware Press, 1994.

Lord Byron: The Complete Miscellaneous Prose. Ed. Andrew Nicholson. Oxford: Oxford University Press, 1991.

Lord Byron: Selected Letters and Journals. Ed. Leslie A. Marchand. Cambridge, MA: Belknap Press, Harvard University Press, 1982.

The Works of Lord Byron. Letters and Journals. Ed. Rowland E. Prothero. 6 vols. London: John Murray, 1898–1901.

The Works of Lord Byron: With His Letters and Journals, and His Life, by Thomas Moore, Esq. Ed. John Wright. 17 vols. London: John Murray, 1832–33. (*Letters and Journals of Lord Byron: With Notices of His Life,* vols. 1–6, first published 1830.)

Selected Poetry and Letters

Lord Byron: The Major Works. Ed. Jerome J. McGann. Oxford World's Classics. Oxford: Oxford University Press, 1986, 2000.

Byron's Selected Poetry and Prose. Ed. W. H. Auden. New York: New American Library, 1966.

BIBLIOGRAPHIES, REFERENCE, JOURNALS, WEBSITES

Clubbe, John. "Byron." In *The English Romantic Poets: A Review of Research and Criticism.* Ed. Frank Jordan. 4th ed. New York: Modern Language Association of America, 1985.

Coleridge, Ernest Hartley. "A Bibliography of the Successive Editions and Translations of Lord Byron's Poetical Works." *The Works of Lord Byron: Poetry,* vol. 7. London: John Murray, 1904.

Gooch, Bryan N. S., and David S. Thatcher. *Musical Settings of British Romantic Literature.* 2 vols. New York and London: Garland Publishing, 1982.

Hagelman, C. W., Jr., and R. J. Barnes, eds. *A Concordance to Byron's "Don Juan."* Ithaca, NY: Cornell University Press, 1967.

Hartley, Robert A., ed. *Keats, Shelley, Byron, Hunt and Their Circles. A Bibliography, July 1, 1962–December 31, 1974.* Lincoln: University of Nebraska Press, 1978.

Looper, Travis. *Byron and the Bible: A Compendium of Biblical Usage in the Poetry of Lord Byron.* Metuchen, NJ: Scarecrow Press, 1978.

Nicholson, Andrew. "Lord Byron." In *Literature of the Romantic Period: A Bibliographical Guide.* Ed. Michael O'Neill. Oxford: Clarendon Press, 1998.

Santucho, Oscar José, and Clement Tyson Goode, Jr. *George Gordon, Lord Byron: A Comprehensive Bibliography of Secondary Materials in English, 1807–1974, with a Critical Review of Research.* Metuchen, NJ: Scarecrow Press, 1977. Updated edition, 1997.

Wise, Thomas James. *A Bibliography of the Writings in Verse and Prose of George Gordon Noel, Baron Byron.* 2 vols. London [printed for private circulation], 1932–33.

Young, Ione Dodson. *A Concordance to the Poetry of Byron.* 4 vols. Austin, TX: Pemberton Press, 1965.

The Byron Journal

Keats-Shelley Journal

Websites

Byron Society of America: www.byronsociety.org/.

The Byron Chronology, ed. Anne R. Hawkins: www.rc.umd.edu/reference/chronologies/byronchronology/.

Byronic Images: Portraits of the Poets, His Family, and Friends: www.englishhistory.net/byron/images.html.

The International Byron Society: www. internationalbyronsoicety.org/.

The Life and Work of Lord Byron: www.englishhistory.net/byron.html.

The Literature Network: Lord Byron: www.online-literature.com/byron/.

BIOGRAPHICAL WORKS

Dallas, Robert Charles. *Recollections of the Life of Lord Byron.* London: Charles Knight, 1824.

Elwin, Malcolm. *Lord Byron's Family: Annabella, Ada, and Augusta, 1816–1824.* Ed. Peter Thomson. London: John Murray, 1975.

Franklin, Caroline. *Byron: A Literary Life.* Literary Lives. Basingstoke (U.K.) and New York: Palgrave, St. Martin's Press, 2000.

Galt, John. *The Life of Byron.* London: Colburn & Bentley, 1830.

Graham, Peter W., ed. *Byron's Bulldog: The Letters of John Cam Hobhouse to Lord Byron.* Columbus, OH: Ohio State University Press, 1984.

Gross, Jonathan David. *Byron's "Corbeau Blanc": The Life and Letters of Lady Melbourne.* Austin: Texas A&M University Press, 1997.

Guiccioli, Teresa. *Lord Byron's Life in Italy.* Trans. Michael Rees. Ed. Peter Cochran. Newark, DE: University of Delaware Press, 2005.

Jamison, Kay Redfield. "The Mind's Canker in Its Savage Mood: George Gordon, Lord Byron." In *Touched With Fire: Manic-Depressive Illness and the Artistic Temperament.* New York: The Free Press, Macmillan, 1993.

Lovelace, Ralph Milbank, Earl of. *Astarte: A Fragment of Truth Concerning George Gordon, Lord Byron, Sixth Lord Byron.* New York: Scribners, 1921.

Lovell, Ernest J., Jr., ed. *His Very Self and Voice. Collected Conversations of Lord Byron.* New York: Macmillan, 1954.

———. *Lady Blessington's Conversations of Lord Byron.* Princeton: Princeton University Press, 1969.

———. *Medwin's Conversations of Lord Byron.* Princeton: Princeton University Press, 1966.

MacCarthy, Fiona. *Byron: Life and Legend.* New York: Farrar, Straus and Giroux, 2002.

Marchand, Leslie A. *Byron: A Biography.* 3 vols. New York: Alfred A. Knopf, 1957.

———. *Byron: A Portrait.* New York: Alfred A. Knopf, 1970.

Maurois. André. *Byron.* New York: D. Appleton and Co., 1930.

Mayne, Ethel Colburn. *The Life and Letters of Anne Isabella, Lady Noel Byron.* London; New York: C. Scribner's Sons, 1929.

Minta, Stephen. *On a Voiceless Shore: Byron in Greece.* New York: Henry Holt, 1998.

Moore, Doris Langley. *The Late Lord Byron: Posthumous Dramas.* Philadelphia: Lippincott, 1961.

———. *Lord Byron: Accounts Rendered.* New York: Harper & Row, 1974.

Moore, Thomas. *Letters and Journals of Lord Byron, with Notices of his Life.* London: John Murray, 1830.

Nicholson, Andrew, ed. *The Letters of John Murray to Lord Byron.* Liverpool: Liverpool University Press, 2007.

Nicolson, Harold. *Byron: The Last Journey.* London: Constable & Co.; Boston: Houghton Mifflin, 1924; new ed., 1940.

Origo, Iris. *The Last Attachment: The Story of Byron and Teresa Guiccioli.* London: Cape and Murray, 1949.

Page, Norman, ed. *Byron: Interviews and Recollections.* New York: Humanities Press, 1985.

Quennell, Peter. *Byron: The Years of Fame.* New York: Viking Press, 1935.

———. *Byron in Italy.* New York: Viking Press, 1941.

Smiles, Samuel. *A Publisher and His Friends: Memoir and Correspondence of the Late John Murray.* 2 vols. 1891.

Soderholm, James. *Fantasy, Forgery, and the Byron Legend.* Lexington: University of Kentucky Press, 1996.

Trelawny, Edward John. *Recollections of the Last Days of Shelley and Byron.* Boston: Ticknor & Fields, 1858. Rev. as *Records of Shelley and Byron, and the Author.* 2 vols. London: B. M. Pickering, 1878.

CONTEMPORARY REVIEWS AND NINETEENTH-CENTURY CRITICISM

Arnold, Matthew. Preface to *Poetry of Byron.* Ed. Arnold. London: Macmillan, 1881. Rpt. in *Essays and Criticism,* second series. London: Macmillan, 1888. Pp. 163–204.

Chew, Samuel C. *Byron in England: His Fame and After-Fame.* London: John Murray, 1924.

Hayden, John O. *Romantic Bards and British Reviewers: A Selected Edition of the Contemporary Reviews of Wordsworth, Coleridge, Byron, Keats, and Shelley.* London, Lincoln: University of Nebraska Press, 1971.

Hazlitt, William. "Lord Byron" in *The Spirit of the Age* (1825); rpt. in *The Complete Works of William Hazlitt.* Ed. P. P. Howe. 21 vols. London: J. M. Dent, 1930–34. Vol. 11, pp. 69–78.

Hunt, Leigh. *Lord Byron and Some of His Contemporaries.* 2nd ed. 2 vols. London: 1828.

Redpath, Theodore, ed. *The Young Romantics and Critical Opinion, 1807–1824: Poetry of Byron, Shelley, and Keats, as Seen by Their Contemporary Critics.* London: George G. Harrap & Co., 1973.

Reiman, Donald H. *The Romantics Reviewed: Contemporary Reviews of British Romantic Writers. Part B: Byron and Regency Society Poets.* 5 vols. New York and London: Garland Publishing, 1972.

Rutherford, Andrew, ed. *Byron: The Critical Heritage.* New York: Barnes & Noble, 1970.

Stendhal [Marie Henri Beyle]. "Lord Byron en Italie." *Racine et Shakespeare.* Paris, 1854.

Swinburne, Charles Algernon. Preface to *Selection from the Works of Lords Byron.* London: Moxon & Co., 1866. Rpt. in *Essays and Studies.* London: Chatto and Windus, 1875.

———. "Wordsworth and Byron." In *Nineteenth Century* (April and May, 1884). Rpt. in *Miscellanies.* New York: Worthington, 1886.

Taine, Hippolyte. "Lord Byron." In *A History of English Literature.* Paris, 1866. Trans. H. Van Laun. 2 vols. New York: Holt & Williams, 1871.

MODERN CRITICISM

Collections of Essays

Beatty, Bernard, and Vincent Newey, eds. *Byron and the Limits of Fiction.* Totowa, NJ: Barnes & Noble Books, 1988.

Bloom, Harold, ed. *George Gordon, Lord Byron: Modern Critical Views.* New York: Chelsea House Publishers, 1986.

———. *Lord Byron's Don Juan.* Modern Critical Interpretations. New York: Chelsea House Publishers, 1987.

Bone, J. Drummond, ed. *The Cambridge Companion to Byron.* Cambridge: Cambridge University Press, 2004.

Bostetter, Edward E. *Don Juan: A Collection of Critical Essays.* Twentieth Century Views. Englewood Cliffs, NJ: Prentice Hall, 1969.

Brewer, William D., ed. *Contemporary Studies on Lord Byron.* Lewiston, NY: Mellen Press, 2001.

Gleckner, Robert F., ed. *Critical Essays on Lord Byron.* New York: G. K. Hall, 1991.

Gleckner, Robert F. and Bernard Beatty, eds. *The Plays of Lord Byron: Critical Essays.* Liverpool: Liverpool University Press, 1998.

Hirst, Wolf Z., ed. *Byron, the Bible and Religion: Essays from the Twelfth International Byron Seminar.* Newark, DE: University of Delaware Press; London and Toronto: Associated University Presses, 1991.

Jump, John D., ed. *Byron: A Symposium.* London: Macmillan Press; New York: Barnes & Noble, 1975.

Levine, Alice, and Robert N. Keane, eds. *Rereading Byron: Essays Selected From Hofstra University's Byron Bicentennial Conference.* New York and London: Garland Publishing, 1993.

Robinson, Charles E., ed. *Lord Byron and His Contemporaries. Essays from the Sixth International Byron Seminar.* Newark, DE: University of Delaware Press; London and Toronto: Associated University Presses, 1982.

Rutherford, Andrew, ed. *Byron: Augustan and Romantic.* London: Macmillan Press, 1990.

Stabler, Jane, ed. *Byron.* Longman Critical Readers Series. London and New York: Longman, 1998.

Trueblood, Paul Graham, ed. *Byron's Political and Cultural Influence in Nineteenth-Century Europe: A Symposium.* London: Macmillan Press, 1981.

West, Paul W., ed. *Byron: A Collection of Critical Essays.* Twentieth-Century Views. Englewood Cliffs, NJ: Prentice Hall, 1963.

Wilson, Cheryl A. *Byron: Heritage and Legacy.* New York: Palgrave Macmillan, 2008.

Books and Essays

Essays published in any of the collections listed above are indicated by the editor's name.
• Indicates works included or excerpted in this Norton Critical Edition.
•• Indicates works included or excerpted in *Byron's Poetry* (Norton Critical Edition, 1978), edited by Frank D. McConnell.

Almeida, Hermione de. *Byron and Joyce through Homer: "Don Juan" and "Ulysses."* New York: Columbia University Press, 1981.
Ashton, Thomas L. *Byron's Hebrew Melodies.* London: Routledge & Kegan Paul, 1972.
Auden, W. H. "Byron." In *The Dyer's Hand and Other Essays.* New York: Random House, 1962.
————. "Introduction." *The Selected Poetry and Prose of Byron.* New York: New American Library, 1966.
Barton, Anne. "Byron and Shakespeare." In Bone (2004).
• ————. *Byron and the Mythology of Fact.* University of Nottingham Byron Lecture, 1968.
————. *Byron: Don Juan.* Cambridge: Cambridge University Press, 1992.
————. "*Don Juan* Reconsidered: The Haidée Episode." *Byron Journal* 15 (1987): 11–20. Rpt. in Stabler (1998).
Bainbridge, Simon. "Staging History: Byron and Napoleon, 1813–1814," in *Napoleon and English Romanticism.* Cambridge Studies in Romanticism. Cambridge: Cambridge University Press, 1995.
Bate, Jonathan. *Shakespeare and the English Romantic Imagination.* Oxford: Clarendon Press, 1986.
Beatty, Bernard. *Byron: Don Juan and Other Poems. A Critical Study.* Harmondsworth: Penguin, 1987.
————. *Byron's Don Juan.* London: Croom Helm; New York: Barnes and Noble, 1985.
————. "Fiction's Limit and Eden's Door." In Beatty and Newey (1988) and Gleckner (1991).
Beaty, Frederick L. "Byron and the Story of Francesca da Rimini." *PMLA* 75 (Sept. 1960): 395–401.
————. *Byron the Satirist.* De Kalb, IL: Northern Illinois University Press, 1985.
Beevers, Robert. *The Byronic Image: The Poet Portrayed.* Abingdon (Eng.): Olivia Press, 2005.
•• Berry, Francis. "The Poet of *Childe Harold.*" In Jump (1975).
Blackstone, Bernard. *Byron: A Survey.* London: Longman, 1975.
Bloom, Harold. "George Gordon, Lord Byron." In *The Visionary Company.* Ithaca, NY: Cornell University Press, 1961, rev. ed. 1971.
Bone, J. Drummond. "The Art of *Don Juan*: Byron's Metrics." *Wordsworth Circle* 26 (1995): 97–103. Rpt. in Stabler (1998).
————. "*Beppo*: The Liberation of Fiction." In Beatty and Newey (1988).
————. "On 'Influence,' and on Byron's and Shelley's Use of *Terza Rima* in 1819." *Keats-Shelley Memorial Bulletin* 22 (1981b): 38–48.
Borst, William A. *Lord Byron's First Pilgrimage.* New Haven: Yale University Press, 1998.
Bostetter, Edward E. "Byron," in *The Romantic Ventriloquists* (1963); rev. ed. Seattle: University of Washington Press, 1975.
————. "Byron and the Politics of Paradise." *PMLA* 75 (Dec. 1960): 571–76.
Boyd, Elizabeth French. *Byron's "Don Juan: A Critical Study."* New Brunswick, NJ: Rutgers University Press, 1945.
Brewer, William D. *The Shelley-Byron Conversation.* Gainesville: University Press of Florida, 1994.
Butler, E. M. *Byron and Goethe: Analysis of a Passion.* London: Bowes & Bowes, 1956.
• Butler, Marilyn. "The Orientalism of Byron's *Giaour.*" In Beatty and Newey (1988).
————. "Byron and the Empire of the East." In Rutherford (1990).
Calvert, William J. *Byron: Romantic Paradox.* Chapel Hill: University of North Carolina Press, 1935.
Chalk, Aiden. "*Childe Harold's Pilgrimage: a Romaunt* and the Influence of Local Attachment." *Texas Studies in Literature and Language* 40.1 (Spring 1998): 48–77.
Chancellor, Paul. "British Bards and Continental Composers." *Musical Quarterly* 46 (Jan. 1960): 1–11.
• Chandler, James. "'Man fell with apples': The Moral Mechanics of *Don* Juan." In Levine and Keane (1993).
Cheeke, Stephen. *Byron and Place: History, Translation, Nostalgia.* Basingstoke, Hampshire and New York: Palgrave Macmillan, 2003.
Chew, Samuel C., Jr. *The Dramas of Lord Byron: A Critical Study.* Göttingen: Vandenhoed & Ruprecht, 1915.
• Christensen, Jerome. *Lord Byron's Strength: Romantic Writing and Commercial Society.* Baltimore: Johns Hopkins University Press, 1993.
Claridge, Laura. *Romantic Potency: The Paradox of Desire.* New York: Cornell University Press, 1992.
Clearman, Mary. "A Blueprint for *English Bards and Scotch Reviewers*: The First Satire of Juvenal." *Keats-Shelley Journal* 19 (1970): 87–99.
Clubbe, John. *Byron, Sully, and the Power of Portraiture.* Aldershot (Eng.) and Burlington, VT: Ashgate Publishing, 2005.

———. "'The New Prometheus of New Men': Byron's 1816 *Poems* and *Manfred.*" In *Nineteenth-Century Literary Perspectives. Essays in Honor of Lionel Stevenson.* Ed. Clyde de L. Ryals, et al. Durham, NC: Duke University Press, 1974. Pp. 17–47.

Cochran, Peter. "Byron's Influence on European Romanticism." In *A Companion to European Romanticism.* Ed. Michael Ferber. London: Blackwell, 2005.

•• Cooke, Michael G. *The Blind Man Traces the Circle: On the Patterns and Philosophy of Byron's Poetry.* Princeton: Princeton University Press, 1969.

Cooper, Andrew M. "Chains, Pains, and Tentative Gains: 'The Byronic Prometheus in the Summer of 1816." *Studies in Romanticism* 27 (Winter 1988): 529–50.

Corbett, Martyn. *Byron and Tragedy.* New York: St. Martin's Press, 1988.

Crompton, Louis. *Byron and Greek Love: Homophobia in 19th-Century England.* Berkeley and Los Angeles: University of California Press, 1985.

Cronin, Richard. "Mapping *Childe Harold* I and II." *Byron Journal* 22 (1994): 63–69.

Curran, Stuart. *Poetic Form and British Romanticism.* New York: Oxford University Press, 1986.

Daffron, Eric. "Disorienting the Self: The Figure of the White European Man in Byron's *Oriental Tales* and Travels." In *Mapping Male Sexuality: Nineteenth-Century England.* Ed. Jay Losey and William D. Brewer. Madison: Fairleigh Dickinson University Press; London: Associated University Presses, 2000.

Dennis, Ian. "'Making Death a Victory': Victimhood and Power in Byron's 'Prometheus' and 'The Prisoner of Chillon.'" *Keats-Shelley Journal* 50 (2001): 144–61.

Dingley, R. J. "'I had a dream . . .': Byron's 'Darkness'." *Byron Journal* 9 (1981): 20–33.

Donelan, Charles. *Romanticism and Male Fantasy in Byron's "Don Juan": A Marketable Vice.* Romanticism in Perspective. Houndmills: Palgrave Macmillan, 1999.

DuBos, Charles. *Byron and the Need of Fatality.* Paris, 1928. Trans. Ethel Colburn Mayne. New York: Haskell House Publishers, 1970.

Dyer, Gary. "Thieves, Boxers, Sodomites: Being Flash to *Don Juan.*" *PMLA* 116 (2001): 562–78.

Elfenbein, Andrew. *Byron and the Victorians.* Cambridge Studies in Nineteenth-Century Literature and Culture. Cambridge: Cambridge University Press, 1995.

———. "Byron, Gender and Sexuality." In Bone (2004).

Eliot, T. S. "Byron." In *From Anne to Victoria.* Ed. Bonamy Dobrée. London: C. Scribner's Sons, 1937. Rpt. in *On Poets and Poetry.* New York: Farrar, Straus & Cudahy, 1957.

Elledge, Paul W. *Byron and the Dynamics of Metaphor.* Nashville: Vanderbilt University Press, 1968.

———. "Chasms in Connections: Byron Ending (in) *Childe Harold's Pilgrimage* 1 and 2." *English Literary History* 62 (1995): 131–44. Rpt. in Stabler (1998).

———. *Lord Byron at Harrow School: Speaking Out, Talking Back, Acting Up, Bowing Out.* Baltimore and London: The Johns Hopkins University Press, 2000.

———. "Talented Equivocation: Byron's 'Fare thee well!'" *Keats-Shelley Journal* 35 (1986): 42–61.

Emerson, Sheila. "Byron's 'one word': The Language of Self-Expression in *Childe Harold III.*" *Studies in Romanticism* 20 (1981): 363–82.

England, A. B. *Byron's Don Juan and Eighteenth-Century Literature.* Lewisburg, PA: Bucknell University Press, 1975.

Erdman, David. "Byron's Stage Fright: The History of His Ambition and Fear of Writing for the Stage." *ELH* 6 (Sept. 1939): 219–43.

———. "'Fare thee well!'—Byron's Last Days in England." In *Shelley and His Circle, 1773–1822.* Ed. Kenneth Neill Cameron. Vol. 4. Cambridge, MA: Harvard University Press, 1961. Pp. 638–53.

Estève, Edmond. *Byron et le romantisme français.* Paris: Librairie Hachette et Cie., 1907.

•• Evans, Bergan. "Lord Byron's Pilgrimage" (1978). In *Byron's Poetry.* Ed. Frank D. McConnell. A Norton Critical Edition. New York: Norton 1978.

Escarpit, Robert. "Byron and France: Byron as a Political Figure." In Trueblood (1981).

Foot, Michael. *The Politics of Paradise: A Vindication of Byron.* London: Harper Collins, 1988.

Franklin, Caroline. *Byron: A Literary Life.* Literary Lives. Basingstoke (Eng.): Macmillan Press; New York: St. Martin's Press, 2000.

• ———. *Byron's Heroines.* Oxford: Oxford University Press, 1992.

———. *Byron and Women Novelists.* Nottingham: University of Nottingham, 2001.

Fuess, Claude M. *Byron as a Satirist in Verse.* New York: Columbia University Press, 1912.

Galperin, William H. "The Postmodernism of *Childe Harold.*" In *The Return of the Visible in British Romanticism.* Baltimore: Johns Hopkins University Press, 1993. Rpt. in Stabler (1998).

Garber, Frederick. *Self, Text, and Romantic Irony: The Example of Byron.* Princeton: Princeton University Press, 1988.

Gilmour, Ian. *The Making of the Poets: Byron and Shelley in Their Time.* London: Chatto & Windus, 2002.

• Giuliano, Cheryl Fallon. "Marginal Discourse: The Authority of Gossip in *Beppo.*" In Levine and Keane (1993).

•• Gleckner, Robert F. *Byron and the Ruins of Paradise.* Baltimore: Johns Hopkins University Press, 1967.

———. "From Selfish Spleen to Equanimity: Byron's Satires." In Gleckner (1991).

Graham, Peter. *Lord Byron.* Twayne's English Authors Series. New York: Twayne Publishers, 1998.

• ———. *Don Juan and Regency England.* Charlottesville: University of Virginia Press, 1990.

Gross, Jonathan David. *Byron: The Erotic Liberal.* Lanham, MD: Rowman & Littlefield, 2001.

———. "One Half What I should Say": Byron's Gay Narrator in *Don Juan.*" In *Mapping Male Sexuality: Nineteenth-Century England.* Ed. Jay Losey and William D. Brewer. Madison: Fairleigh Dickinson University Press; London: Associated University Presses, 2000.

Haslett. Moyra. *Byron's "Don Juan" and the Don Juan Legend.* Oxford: Clarendon Press, 1997.

Heinzelman, Kurt. "Politics, Memory, and the Lyric: Collaboration as Style in Byron's *Hebrew Melodies. Studies in Romanticism* 27.4 (Winter 1988): 515–28.

•• Hirsch, E. D., Jr. "Byron and the Terrestrial Paradise." In *From Sensibility to Romanticism: Essays Presented to Frederick A. Pottle.* Ed. Frederick W. Hilles and Harold Bloom. Oxford: Oxford University Press, 1965.

Hoagwood, Terence Allan. *Byron's Dialectic: Skepticism and the Critique of Culture.* London and Toronto: Associated University Presses, 1993.

Hodgson, John A. "The Structures of *Childe Harold III.*" *Studies in Romanticism* 18 (1979): 363–82.

Hofkosh, Sonia. "The Writer's Ravishment: Woman and the Romantic Author—The Example of Byron." *Romanticism and Feminism.* Ed. Anne K. Mellor. Bloomington, IN: Indiana University Press, 1988.

Jones, Emrys. "Byron's Visions of Judgement." *Modern Language Review* 76 (1981): 1–19.

Jones, Steven E. "Intertextual Influences in Byron's Juvenalian Satire." *Studies in English Literature* 33 (1993): 771–83.

———. "Turning What Was Once Burlesque into Romantic: Byron's Pantomimic Satire," in *Satire and Romanticism.* New York: St. Martin's Press, 2000.

Joseph, M. K. *Byron the Poet.* London: Gollancz, 1964.

•• Jump, John D. *Byron.* Routledge Author Guides. London and Boston: Routledge & Kegan Paul, 1972.

Keach, William. "Political Inflection in Byron's Ottava Rima." *Studies in Romanticism* 27 (Winter 1988): 551–62.

———. "'Words Are Things': Romantic Ideology and the Matter of Poetic Language." In *Aesthetics and Ideology.* Ed. George Levine. New Brunswick, NJ: Rutgers University Press, 1994. Pp. 219–39.

Kelsall, Malcolm. *Byron's Politics.* Sussex: Harvester Press, 1987.

• ———. "Byron's Politics." In Bone (2004).

Kernberger, Katherine. "Power and Sex: The Implication of Role Reversal in Catherine's Russia." *Byron Journal* 8 (1980): 42–49.

Knight, G. Wilson. *Byron and Shakespeare.* New York: Barnes & Noble, 1966.

• ———. *Lord Byron: Christian Virtues.* New York: Barnes & Noble, 1953; reissued 1967.

———. "The Two Eternities." In West (1963).

Kroeber, Karl. *Romantic Narrative Art.* Madison: University of Wisconsin Press, 1960.

• Lang, Cecil Y. "Narcissus Jilted: Byron, *Don Juan,* and the Biographical Imperative." In *Historical Studies and Literary Criticism.* Ed. Jerome J. McGann. Madison: University of Wisconsin Press, 1985.

Lansdown, Richard. *Byron's Historical Dramas.* Oxford: Clarendon Press, 1992.

Leask, Nigel. "Byron and the Eastern Mediterranean: *Childe Harold* II and the "Polemic of Ottoman Greece." In Bone (2004).

Leavis, F. R. "Byron's Satire." In *Revaluation: Tradition & Development in English Poetry.* London: Chatto & Windus, 1936; rpt. 1962.

Levine, Alice. *"Byron and the Romantic Composer."* In Robinson (1982).

———. "Byronic Annotations." *The Byron Journal* 35.1 (2007): 125–36.

———. "T. S. Eliot and Byron." *ELH* 34.3 (Fall 1978): 522–41.

Levinson, Marjorie. *The Romantic Fragment Poem: A Critique of a Form.* Chapel Hill: University of North Carolina Press, 1986.

Lovell, Ernest J., Jr. *Byron: The Record of a Quest. Studies in a Poet's Concept and Treatment of Nature.* Austin: University of Texas Press, 1949.

Macovski, Michael. "Byron, Bakhtin, and the Translation of History." In Levine and Keane (1993).

• Manning, Peter J. *Byron and His Fictions.* Detroit: Wayne State University Press, 1978.

———. *"Don Juan* and Byron's Imperceptiveness to the English Word." *Studies in Romanticism* 18 (1979): 207–33. Rpt. in Gleckner (1991) and Stabler (1998).

Marshall, William H. *The Structure of Byron's Major Poems.* Philadelphia: University of Pennsylvania Press, 1962.

•• Marchand, Leslie A. *Byron's Poetry: A Critical Introduction.* Boston: Houghton Mifflin, 1965.

———. *Byron: A Poet Before His Public.* 1982.

Martin, Philip W. "Heroism and History: *Childe Harold* I and II and the Tales." In Bone (2004).

•• McConnell, Frank D. "Byron as Antipoet" (1978).

• McGann, Jerome J. "The Book of Byron and the Book of a World." In *The Beauty of Inflections: Literary Investigations in Historical Method and Theory.* Oxford: Clarendon Press, 1985.

———. "Byron and the Anonymous Lyric." In *Romanticism: A Critical Reader.* Ed. Duncan Wu. Oxford (UK) and Cambridge (MA): Basil Blackwell, 1995. Rpt. in *Byron and Romanticism,* 2002.

———. *Byron and Romanticism.* Ed. James Soderholm. Cambridge Studies in Romanticism. Cambridge: Cambridge University Press, 2002.

———. *Byron and Wordsworth. The Annual Byron Lecture, Given in the University of Nottingham on 27 May 1998.* Nottingham: University of Nottingham, 1999.

———. *Don Juan in Context.* Chicago and London: University of Chicago Press, 1976.

———. *Fiery Dust: Byron's Poetic Development.* Chicago and London: University of Chicago Press, 1968.

———. "Lord Byron and the Truth in Masquerade." In Levine and Keane (1993).

———. "Lord Byron's Twin Opposites of Truth." In *Towards a Literature of Knowledge.* Oxford: Clarendon Press, 1989.

———. "My Brain is Feminine: Byron and the Poetry of Deception." In Rutherford (1990).

———. *The Romantic Ideology: A Critical Investigation.* Chicago and London: University of Chicago Press, 1983.

Mellor, Anne Kostelanetz. *English Romantic Irony*. Cambridge, MA: Harvard University Press, 1980.

———. *Romanticism and Gender*. New York and London: Routledge, 1993.

Mole, Tom. "Byron's 'Ode to the Framers of the Frame Bill': The Embarrassment of Industrial Culture." *Keats-Shelley Journal* 52 (2003): 111–29.

Newlyn, Lucy. *Paradise Lost and the Romantic Reader*. Oxford: Clarendon Press, 1993.

Newey, Vincent. "Authoring the Self: *Childe Harold* III and IV." In Beatty and Newey (1988).

Nicholson, Andrew. "Byron's Prose." In Bone (2004).

O'Neill, Michael. *Romanticism and the Self-Conscious Poem*. Oxford: Clarendon Press, 1997.

• Peterfreund, Stuart. "The Politics of 'Neutral Space' in Byron's *Vision of Judgment*." *MLQ* 40 (1979): 275–91.

Pratt, Willis W. *Byron at Southwell: The Making of a Poet*. Austin: University of Texas Press, 1948.

Praz, Mario. *The Romantic Agony*. 1930. 2nd ed. Trans. Angus Davidson, 1933. Rpt. Oxford: Oxford University Press, 1970.

Rawes, Alan. "1816–17: *Childe Harold* III and *Manfred*." In Bone (2004).

———. *Byron's Poetic Experimentation: Childe Harold, the Tales and the Quest for Comedy*. Aldershot: Ashgate, 2000.

• Reiman, Donald H. "Byron and the Other," in *Intervals of Inspiration: The Skeptical Tradition and the Psychology of Romanticism*. Greenwood, FL: Penkevill Publishing, 1988.

———. "Byron in Italy: The Return of Augustus." In Rutherford (1990).

———. "*Don Juan* in Epic Context." In *Romantic Texts and Contexts*. Columbia: University of Missouri Press, 1987.

• Richardson, Alan. "Byron and the Theatre." In Bone (2004).

———. "Escape from the Seraglio: Cultural Transvestism in *Don Juan*." In Levine and Keane (1993).

———. *A Mental Theater: Poetic Drama and Consciousness in the Romantic Age*. University Park, PA: Pennsylvania State University Press, 1988.

Ricks, Christopher. "Byron." In *Allusion to the Poets*. Oxford and New York: Oxford University Press, 2002.

Ridenour, George M. *The Style of Don Juan*. New Haven: Yale University Press, 1960.

Robinson, Charles E. *Shelley and Byron: The Snake and Eagle Wreathed in Fight*. Baltimore: Johns Hopkins University Press, 1976.

Ross, Marlon. "Scott's Chivalric Pose: The Function of Metrical Romance in the Romantic Period." *Genre* 18 (1986): 267–97.

Russell, Bertrand. "Lord Byron," in *A History of Western Philosophy*. New York: Simon and Schuster, 1945. Chapter 24.

Rutherford, Andrew J. *Byron: A Critical Study*. Stanford: Stanford University Press, 1961.

Sharafuddin, Mohammed. *Islam and Romantic Orientalism: Literary Encounters with the Orient*. London and New York: I. B. Tauris Publishers, 1994.

Shilstone, Frederick W. *Byron and the Myth of Tradition*. Lincoln: University of Nebraska Press, 1988.

St. Clair, William. "The Impact of Byron's Writings: An Evaluative Approach." In Rutherford (1990).

———. *Lord Elgin and the Marbles*. London: Oxford University Press, 1967. •

———. *That Greece Might Still Be Free: The Philhellenes in the War of Independence*. London and New York: Oxford University Press, 1972.

Stabler, Jane. *Byron, Poetics and History*. Cambridge Studies in Romanticism. Cambridge: Cambridge University Press, 2002.

• ———. "Byron, Postmodernism, and Intertextuality." In Bone (2004).

Stafford, Fiona J. *The Last of the Race: The Growth of a Myth from Milton to Darwin*. Oxford: Clarendon Press, 1994.

Stauffer, Andrew M. "The Career of Byron's 'To the Po.'" *Keats-Shelley Journal* 57 (2008): 108–27.

Steffan, T. G. "The Devil a Bit of Our *Beppo*." *Philological Quarterly* 32 (1953): 154–71.

Stein, Atara. *The Byronic Hero in Film, Fiction and Television*. Carbondale, IL: Southern Illinois University Press, 2004.

Storey, Mark. *Byron and the Eye of Appetite*. Basingtoke and London: Macmillan Press, 1986.

Sundell, Michael G. "The Development of *The Giaour*." *Studies in English Literature* 9 (1969): 587–99.

Taborski, Boleslaw. *Byron and the Theatre*. Salzburg: University of Salzburg, 1972.

Thomas, Gordon Kent. *Lord Byron's Iberian Pilgrimage*. Provo, UT: Brigham Young University Press, 1983.

•• Thompson, James R. "Byron's Plays and *Don Juan*." *Bucknell Review* 15.3 (1967).

Thorslev, Peter L., Jr. *The Byronic Hero: Types and Prototypes*. Minneapolis: University of Minnesota Press, 1962.

Trueblood, Paul Graham. *The Flowering of Byron's Genius: Studies in Don Juan*. Stanford: Stanford University Press, 1945.

Vail, Jeffrey. *The Literary Relationship of Lord Byron & Thomas Moore*. Baltimore and London: The Johns Hopkins University Press, 2001.

Vassallo, Peter. *Byron: The Italian Literary Influence*. New York: St. Martin's Press, 1984.

Watkins, Daniel P. "The Dramas of Lord Byron: *Manfred* and *Marino Faliero*. In *A Materialist Critique of English Romantic Drama*. Gainesville: University Press of Florida, 1993.

———. *Social Relations in Byron's Eastern Tales*. London and Toronto: Associated University Presses, 1987.

West, Paul. *Byron and the Spoiler's Art*. New York: St. Martin's Press, 1960.

Wilson, Frances, ed. *Byromania: Portraits of the Artist in Nineteenth- and Twentieth-Century Culture*. Houndmills: Macmillan Press; New York: St. Martin's Press, 1999.

Wolfson, Susan. "Couplets, Self, and *The Corsair*." *Studies in Romanticism* 27 (Winter 1988): 491–513.

———. "Gender as Cross-Dressing in *Don Juan*: Men & Women / Male & Female / Masculine & Feminine." In *Borderlines: The Shiftings of Gender in British Romanticism*. Stanford: Stanford University Press, 2006.

• ———. "'Their She Condition': Cross-Dressing and the Politics of Gender in *Don Juan*." *ELH* 54 (1987): 585–617.

———. "*The Vision of Judgment* and the Visions of 'Author.'" In Bone (2004).

Woodring, Carl. "Byron." In *Politics in English Romantic Poetry*. Cambridge, MA: Harvard University Press, 1970.

Index of Titles and First Lines